THE OXFORD HANDBOOK OF

PHILOSOPHY AND RACE

THE OXFORD HANDBOOK OF

PHILOSOPHY AND RACE

Edited by

NAOMI ZACK

OXFORD

UNIVERSITY PRESS

OXFORD
UNIVERSITY PRESS

Oxford University Press is a department of the University of Oxford. It furthers
the University's objective of excellence in research, scholarship, and education
by publishing worldwide. Oxford is a registered trade mark of Oxford University
Press in the UK and certain other countries.

Published in the United States of America by Oxford University Press
198 Madison Avenue, New York, NY 10016, United States of America.

© Oxford University Press 2017

First issued as an Oxford University Press paperback, 2019

Library of Congress Cataloging-in-Publication Data
Names: Zack, Naomi, 1944- editor.
Title: The Oxford handbook of philosophy and race / edited by Naomi Zack.
Description: New York : Oxford University Press, 2017. | Includes index.
Identifiers: LCCN 2016012174 (print) | LCCN 2016039717 (ebook) |
ISBN 9780190236953 (hardcover : alk. paper) | ISBN 9780190236960 (updf) |
ISBN 9780190933395 (paperback : alk. paper) | Subjects: LCSH: Race—Philosophy.
Classification: LCC HT1521 .O94 2017 (print) | LCC HT1521 (ebook) |
DDC 305.8001—dc23
LC record available at https://lccn.loc.gov/2016012174

Contents

PART III METAPHYSICS AND PHILOSOPHY OF SCIENCE

PART IV AMERICAN PHILOSOPHY AND IDEAS OF RACE

PART V CONTINENTAL PHILOSOPHY AND RACE

PART VI RACISMS AND NEO-RACISMS

PART VII SOCIAL CONSTRUCTION AND RACIAL IDENTITIES

PART VIII CONTEMPORARY SOCIAL ISSUES: EDUCATION, HEALTH, MEDICINE, AND SPORTS

PART IX PUBLIC POLICY, POLITICAL PHILOSOPHY, AND LAW

PART X FEMINISM, GENDER, AND RACE

List of Contributors

Mark Alfano is Associate Professor of Philosophy at Delft University of Technology. He received a doctorate from the Philosophy Program of the City University of New York Graduate Center (CUNY GC) in 2011, and he has been a postdoctoral fellow at the Notre Dame Institute for Advanced Study and the Princeton University Center for Human Values, as well as assistant professor of philosophy at the University of Oregon. He is the author of *Character as Moral Fiction* (Cambridge University Press, 2013) and *The Moral Psychology of the Emotions* (Rowman and Littlefield, 2016), as well as numerous articles in moral philosophy and philosophy and psychology.

Albert Atkin is a Senior Lecturer at Macquarie University in Sydney. He is interested in the philosophy of race and racism, pragmatism, language, and epistemology. He is the author of two books: *The Philosophy of Race* (Routledge, 2012) and *Peirce* (Routledge, 2015).

Robert Bernasconi is Edwin Erle Sparks Professor of Philosophy and African American Studies at Pennsylvania State University. He is a founding editor of the journal *Critical Philosophy of Race* and the editor of a number of collections on race. He is the author of two books on Heidegger, a book on Sartre, and numerous articles in critical philosophy of race and continental philosophy.

Lawrence Blum is Professor of Philosophy and Distinguished Professor of Liberal Arts and Education at the University of Massachusetts, Boston. He specializes in race studies, philosophy of education, and moral philosophy. He is the author of *I'm Not a Racist, But . . .: The Moral Quandary of Race* (Cornell University Press, 2002). His *High Schools, Race, and America's Future: What Students Can Teach Us About Morality, Diversity, and Community*, cowritten with Gloria Ladson-Billings (Harvard Education Press, 2012), is based on a high school course Blum taught for several years to a racially and ethnically diverse group of students.

Tina Fernandes Botts received a PhD in philosophy from the University of Memphis, a JD from Rutgers University Law School, Camden, and a BA in philosophy from the University of Maryland, College Park. She is Assistant Professor of Philosophy at California State University, Fresno and was Visiting Assistant Professor of Philosophy at Oberlin College in 2015–2016. In 2014–2015, she was Fellow in Law and Philosophy at the University of Michigan, Ann Arbor. She is the editor of *Philosophy and the Mixed Race Experience* (Lexington Books, 2016).

Bernard Boxill is distinguished professor of philosophy emeritus at the University of North Carolina at Chapel Hill. Since 1972 he has published widely on philosophical issues in race, affirmative action, black reparations, and the history of African American political thought.

Jacoby Adeshei Carter is Associate Professor of Philosophy at CUNY, John Jay College. He is executive director of the Alain L. Locke Society, coeditor with Leonard Harris of the *African American Philosophy and the African Diaspora* book series by Palgrave, and coeditor of *Philosophic Values and World Citizenship: Locke to Obama and Beyond* (Lexington Books, 2010). His recent contributions to pragmatism, African American philosophy, and philosophy of race include "The Insurrectionist Challenge to Pragmatism and Maria W. Stewart's Feminist Insurrectionist Ethics" (*Transactions of the Charles S. Peirce Society* 49 (1), Winter 2013) and "Does Race Have a Future or Should the Future Have Races? Reconstruction or Eliminativism in a Pragmatist Philosophy of Race" (*Transactions of the Charles S. Peirce Society* 50 (1): 29–47, 2014).

Myisha Cherry is interested in issues at the intersection of moral psychology and political philosophy. A former educator at the Fortune Society and Faculty Associate at John Jay College's Institute for Criminal Justice Ethics, she is also passionate about the relations between character, forgiveness, race, and the criminal justice system. Myisha is also the host and producer of the UnMute Podcast (http://www.myishacherry.org/the-unmute-podcast/) and is currently a PhD candidate in philosophy at the University of Illinois, Chicago. In 2016–2017, Cherry is a Visiting Edmond J. Safra Graduate Fellow in Ethics and a Santayana Fellow in the Harvard Department of Philosophy.

Andrew Conway is a Professor at Claremont Graduate University. Prior to Claremont he worked at Princeton University for eleven years and before that the University of Illinois at Chicago for eight years. He earned a BS in computer science and psychology from Union College and a PhD in experimental psychology from the University of South Carolina. His research investigates individual differences in cognitive ability, specifically the relationship between general intelligence, memory, and attention.

Tommy J. Curry is Associate Professor of Philosophy and Africana Studies at Texas A&M University, where he holds the Ray A. Rothrock Fellowship. Curry is the current president of Philosophy Born of Struggle and author of over fifty articles and book chapters on racism, critical race theory, hip-hop, nineteenth-century intellectual history, and black male vulnerability. Curry's work argues that ethnology is central to our understanding of race and gender in the nineteenth century, and their legacies.

Stephen C. Ferguson II is Associate Professor in Liberal Studies at the North Carolina A & T State University. He coauthored *Beyond the White Shadow: Philosophy, Sports and the African American Experience* with John H. McClendon III (Kendal Hunt, 2012). He recently authored *Philosophy of African American Studies: Nothing Left of Blackness* (Palgrave, 2015).

Aaron Garrett is Associate Professor of Philosophy at Boston University. He has written widely on the history of modern philosophy, including monographs on Spinoza and Berkeley, and edited many primary texts and collected volumes, including the *Routledge Companion to Eighteenth Century Philosophy* (2014), *Scottish Philosophy in the Eighteenth Century* (with James Harris, Oxford Press Scholarship Online, 2015), and the forthcoming *Oxford Handbook of the Philosophy of the Enlightenment* (with James Schmidt).

Joshua Glasgow is Assistant Professor of Philosophy and Director of the Center for Ethics, Law, and Society at Sonoma State University. He has published widely in moral, political, and legal philosophy, including numerous works on race, including *A Theory of Race* (Routledge, 2009).

Robert Gooding-Williams (PhD, Yale University) is the M. Moran Weston/Black Alumni Council Professor of African-American Studies and Professor of Philosophy at Columbia University. His areas of research and teaching interest include social and political philosophy, the history of African American political thought, nineteenth-century European philosophy, existentialism, and aesthetics. He is the author of several books, including the award-winning (2010 Best Book Award on Racial and Ethnic Political Identities, Ideologies, & Theories, Race, Ethnicity, and Politics Section of the American Political Science Association) *In the Shadow of Du Bois* (Harvard University Press, 2009).

Lewis R. Gordon holds the positions of Professor of Philosophy and Africana Studies at UCONN-Storrs; Writer-in-Residence at Birkbeck School of Law; Visiting Professor of Philosophy at the University of the West Indies at Mona, Jamaica; and Distinguished Visiting Professor at the Unit of the Humanities at Rhodes University (UHURU), South Africa. His books include *What Fanon Said: A Philosophical Introduction to His Life and Thought* (Fordham University Press; Hurst Publishers; Wits University Press, 2015) and *Bad Faith and Antiblack Racism* (Humanities Books, 1995), as well as anthologies and numerous articles. His website is http://lewisrgordon.com

Jorge J. E. Gracia is a SUNY Distinguished Professor at the University at Buffalo, has authored twenty books and more than two hundred and fifty articles, and edited twenty-six volumes. His areas of research include metaphysics, hermeneutics, historiography, ethnicity, race, medieval philosophy, and Hispanic/Latino/Latin American philosophy. He has received an National Endowment for the Humanities Fellowship and directed an NEH Summer Institute and a Seminar. He was awarded the American Catholic Philosophical Association Aquinas medal in 2011, and his book *Individuality: An Essay on the Foundations of Metaphysics* (SUNY Press, 1988) was awarded the Findlay Prize in 1992.

Michael O. Hardimon is Associate Professor of Philosophy at the University of California at San Diego. His publications include *Hegel's Social Philosophy* (Cambridge University Press, 1994), "The Ordinary Concept of Race" (*Journal of Philosophy*, 2003), "On the Idea of a Scientific Concept of Race" (*Journal of Philosophical Research*, 2012), "Race Concepts in Medicine" (*Journal of Medicine and Philosophy*, 2013), and "On the Concept of Social Race" (*Philosophy and Social Criticism*, 2014). He is the author of *Rethinking Race: The Project of Deflationary Realism* (forthcoming).

Leonard Harris is Professor of Philosophy and Director of the Philosophy and Literature Programs at Perdue University. He is coeditor with Jacoby A. Carter, of the African American and African Philosophy Book Series, (Palgrave, 2015) and of *Philosophical Values and World Citizenship* (Routledge/Lexington Books, 2010). Harris is coauthor with Charles Molesworth of *Alain L. Locke: Biography of a Philosopher* (University of Chicago Press, 2008). He is editor of *The Philosophy of Alain Locke: Harlem Renaissance and Beyond* (Temple University Press, 1989) and *Philosophy Born of Struggle: Afro-American Philosophy from 1917* (Kendall Hunt, 1984). Harris is also author of "Walker: Naturalism and Liberation," Symposium on Insurrectionist Ethics (Harrisonian Approach), *Transactions of the C. S. Peirce Society* 49 (1), Winter 2013, 93–111.

Jason D. Hill is Professor of Philosophy at De Paul University and Honors Distinguished Faculty. He specializes in moral and political philosophy. He is the author of three books: *Becoming a Cosmopolitan: What It Means to Be a Human Being in the New*

Millennium (Rowman and Littlefield, 2nd ed. 2011); *Beyond Blood Identities: Post-Humanity in the Twenty-First Century* (Lexington Books, 2009); *Civil Disobedience and the Politics of Identity: When We Should Not Get Along* (Palgrave Macmillan, 2013).

LaTasha Holden is a PhD candidate at Princeton University, working with Andrew Conway and Stacey Sinclair. Tasha received dual degrees in psychology (disciplinary honors) and art history from UNC Greensboro, working with Peter Delaney and Michael Kane. Awarded as 2012's "Distinguished Graduate," she earned an MA in experimental psychology from Towson University, working with Kerri Goodwin. Her current research explores mechanisms underlying stereotype threat aimed at mitigating the effect based on cognitive and social interventions.

Joy James is the F.C. Oakley Third Century Professor at Williams College. She is a board member of CONNECT (a Harlem-based nonprofit); and the curator of the Harriet Tubman Literary Circle digital repository at UT-Austin. James is the author of: *Seeking the Beloved Community: A Feminist Race Reader* (SUNY Press, 2013); *Resisting State Violence: Radicalism, Gender, and Race in US Culture* (University of Minnesota Press, 1996); *Transcending the Talented Tenth: Black Leaders and American Intellectuals* (Psychology Press, 1997); *Shadowboxing: Representations of Black Women's Politics* (St. Martin's Press, 1999); and editor of *The New Abolitionists; Imprisoned Intellectuals; Warfare in the American Home*; and the *Angela Y. Davis Reader*.

Chike Jeffers is Associate Professor of Philosophy at Dalhousie University in Halifax, Nova Scotia. He specializes in Africana philosophy and philosophy of race, with broad interests in social and political philosophy. He has published in journals such as *Ethics*, the *British Journal for the History of Philosophy, The Southern Journal of Philosophy*, and *The Journal of Value Inquiry*. He is the editor of *Listening to Ourselves: A Multilingual Anthology of African Philosophy* (SUNY, 2013). He is currently working on a book on W. E. B. Du Bois.

Clarence Sholé Johnson is Professor of Philosophy at Middle Tennessee State University in Murfreesboro, Tennessee. He is the author of *Cornel West and Philosophy* (Routledge, 2002) and has published articles in major scholarly journals such as *The Journal of Social Philosophy, Social Philosophy Today, The Journal of Philosophical Research, DIALOGUE: Canadian Philosophical Review, Metaphilosophy*, and *The Southern Journal of Philosophy*. He has also contributed chapters to a number of books and entries in encyclopedias.

Janine Jones is Associate Professor of Philosophy at the University of North Carolina, Greensboro. Her work includes: "The Impairment of Empathy in Goodwill Whites" in George Yancy, ed., *What White Looks Like: African-American Philosophers on the Whiteness Question* (Routledge, 2004); "Caster Semenya: Reasoning Up Front with Race" in *Why Race and Gender Still Matter: An Intersectional Approach*, Namita Goswami, Maeve M. O'Donovan, and Lisa Yount, eds. (Pickering and Chatto, 2014); and "Finding Bigger in Something Bigger" in *Knowledge Cultures* (Addleton, 2015). She is coeditor of *Pursuing Trayvon Martin: Historical Contexts and Contemporary Manifestations of Racial Dynamics* (Lexington Books, 2012), in which her piece, "Can We Imagine *This* Happening to a White Boy?" appears.

Jonathan Judaken is the Spence L. Wilson Chair in the Humanities at Rhodes College. In addition to dozens of academic articles, he has published *Jean-Paul Sartre and the*

Jewish Question: Anti-antisemitism and the Politics of the French Intellectual (Nebraska University Press, 2006) and edited *Race after Sartre: Antiracism, Africana Existentialism, Postcolonialism* (SUNY, 2008) and *Naming Race, Naming Racisms* (Routledge, 2009), and coedited *Situating Existentialism: Key Texts in Context* (Columbia University Press, 2012).

Yen Le Espiritu is Professor and former Chair of the Department of Ethnic Studies at the University of California, San Diego. An award-winning author, she has published widely on Asian American panethnicity, gender, and migration, and US colonialism and wars in Asia. Her most recent book is *Body Counts: The Vietnam War and Militarized Refuge(es)* (University of California Press, 2014).

Annabelle Lever is Associate Professor of Normative Political Theory at the University of Geneva. She specializes in contemporary political theory and ethics and public policy. She is the editor of *New Frontiers in the Philosophy of Intellectual Property* (Cambridge University Press, 2014) and the author of *On Privacy (Thinking in Action)* (Routledge, 2011) and *A Democratic Conception of Privacy* (Author House, 2014), as well as numerous scholarly articles on racial equality, privacy and security, freedom of conscience, and democratic theory and the ethics of voting.

David Lyons works on moral, political, and legal theory and political history. After teaching at Cornell University for three decades, he joined Boston University in 1995. His books include: *Forms and Limits of Utilitarianism* (Oxford University Press, 1965); *In the Interest of the Governed* (Oxford University Press, 1971); *Ethics and the Rule of Law* (Cambridge University Press, 1984); *Rights, Welfare, and Mill's Moral Theory* (Oxford University Press, 1994); *Moral Aspects of Legal Theory* (Cambridge University Press, 1993); and *Confronting Injustice* (Oxford University Press, 2013).

Ron Mallon is Associate Professor of Philosophy and Director of the Philosophy-Neuroscience-Psychology Program at Washington University in St. Louis. His research is at the intersection of the philosophy of psychology and social theory, and it focuses especially upon moral psychology, social construction, and the philosophy of race. He has twice codirected an NEH Institute on Experimental Philosophy, and he is the author of numerous articles and book chapters on the social construction of human kinds and coeditor of *An Introduction to Philosophy: Traditional and Experimental* (Oxford University Press. 2012).

Lee A. McBride III is Associate Professor of Philosophy at The College of Wooster (Wooster, Ohio). McBride specializes in American philosophy, ethics, and political philosophy. His publications include "Racial Imperialism and Food Traditions" (in *Oxford Handbook of Food Ethics*, forthcoming) and "Insurrectionist Ethics and Thoreau" (*Transactions of the Charles S. Peirce Society* 49, Winter 2013). He was guest editor for the Symposium on Insurrectionist Ethics (*Transactions of the Charles S. Peirce Society* 49, Winter 2013).

John H. McClendon III is a professor in the Department of Philosophy at Michigan State University. His areas of interests include: African American philosophers and philosophical traditions; African philosophy, Marxism, philosophy of sports and the African American experience, and philosophy of religion and African Americans. He is the author of *C. L. R. James's Notes on Dialectics: Left-Hegelianism or Marxism-Leninism* (Lexington Books, 2005) and *Beyond the White Shadow: Philosophy, Sports, and the African-American Experience*, which he coauthored with Dr. Stephen C. Ferguson II (Kendall Hunt, 2012).

Lionel K. McPherson is Associate Professor of Philosophy at Tufts University. He received his PhD in philosophy from Harvard and his AB from Princeton. His articles have appeared in *Ethics, Journal of Philosophy*, and *Philosophy & Public Affairs*, among other places. He is finishing a book, *The Afterlife of Race*, which develops the idea of socioancestry in place of "race," the case for nonexclusionary black solidarity, and proposals for black socioeconomic progress in an officially postracial era.

Ladelle McWhorter is the author of *Bodies and Pleasures: Foucault and the Politics of Sexual Normalization* (Indiana University Press, 1999), *Racism and Sexual Oppression in Anglo-America: A Genealogy* (Indiana University Press, 2009), and articles on Foucault and race theory. She coedited an expanded edition of her 1992 anthology *Heidegger and the Earth: Essays in Environmental Philosophy* for Toronto University Press (2009). She holds the Stephanie Bennett Smith Chair in Women, Gender, and Sexuality Studies and is also Professor of Environmental Studies at the University of Richmond (Richmond, Virginia). She is working on a book tentatively entitled *The End of Personhood on a Postmodern Planet*.

Charles W. Mills has been John Evans Professor of Moral and Intellectual Philosophy at Northwestern University and he joined the CUNY Graduate Center as Professor of Philosophy in 2016. He works in the general area of oppositional political theory, and he is the author of six books: *The Racial Contract* (Cornell University Press, 1997); *Blackness Visible: Essays on Philosophy and Race* (Cornell University Press, 1998); *From Class to Race: Essays in White Marxism and Black Radicalism* (2003); *Contract and Domination* (with Carole Pateman, Polity Press 2007); *Radical Theory, Caribbean Reality* (University of West Indies Press, 2010); and *Black Rights/White Wrongs: The Critique of Racial Liberalism* (forthcoming 2016).

Albert Mosley is Professor of Philosophy at Smith College in Northampton, Massachusetts. He was born in Dyersburg, Tennessee, received a BS in mathematics and a PhD in philosophy from The University of Wisconsin-Madison, and studied the history and philosophy of science at Oxford University. He has published on topics in logic, the philosophy of science and technology, African philosophy, and African American philosophy.

Susana Nuccetelli is Professor of Philosophy at St. Cloud State University. Her essays have appeared in journals such as *Analysis, The American Philosophical Quarterly, Metaphilosophy*, and *Inquiry*. Her books in Latin American philosophy include a monograph, *Latin American Thought: Philosophical Problems and Arguments* (Westview Press, 2002), an edited volume, *The Blackwell Companion to Latin American Philosophy* (Blackwell, 2009), and an anthology, *Latin American Philosophy* (Prentice Hall, 2004).

John H. Relethford (PhD, State University of New York at Albany, 1980) is Distinguished Teaching Professor at the Department of Anthropology at the State University of New York College at Oneonta. He is a biological anthropologist focusing on human variation, population genetics, and the evolution of modern humans. He is a former vice-president and president of the American Association of Physical Anthropologists, and is a fellow of the American Association for the Advancement of Science. John Relethford is also the author of *The Human Species: An Introduction to Biological Anthropology* (McGraw Hill, Higher Education, 9th ed., 2012).

Rodney C. Roberts's ancestors were among the eighty Africans enslaved aboard the brig Camden and brought to Edenton, North Carolina, in 1786 to build and labor upon the Somerset Place Plantation in Creswell, North Carolina. Raised in the Bronx, New York, he served for a decade in the US Navy. Roberts received his PhD in social and political philosophy from the University of Wisconsin-Madison, and he is currently Associate Professor of Philosophy in the Department of Philosophy and Religious Studies, East Carolina University. He is the editor of *Injustice and Rectification* (Peter Lang, 2002 and 2005), in which his essay, "Justice and Rectification: A Taxonomy of Justice" appears.

Michael Root is Professor Emeritus of Philosophy at the University of Minnesota. His current interest is the use of race in the biomedical and social sciences to describe or explain differences within a population in health or socioeconomic outcomes. He has published many papers on issues of race in science and public policy and presented papers on race at many conferences and meetings, including at the American Public Health Association and Society for Epidemiologic Research.

Jacqueline Scott is Associate Professor of Philosophy at Loyola University. She is the coeditor, with A. Todd Franklin, of *Critical Affinities: Nietzsche and African American Thought* (SUNY Press, 2006) Additionally, she has published articles in Nietzsche studies and philosophy of race.

Silvia Sebastiani is Associate Professor at the L'École des Hautes Études en Sciences Sociales in Paris, where she teaches seminars on Enlightenment historiographies and on ideology of race in the early modern period. She has written extensively on the Scottish Enlightenment and on the questions of race, gender, and history writing. She is the author of *The Scottish Enlightenment: Race, Gender, and the Limits of Progress* (Palgrave Macmillan, 2013), and she has recently coedited the *Modern Intellectual History* "Forum" on "Closeness and Distance in the Age of Enlightenment" (*Modern Intellectual History*, 2014) and *Simianization: Apes, Gender, Class, and Race* (LIT Verlag, 2015).

T. Denean Sharpley-Whiting is the Gertrude Conaway Vanderbilt Distinguished Professor of French and African American and Diaspora Studies at Vanderbilt University, where she also chairs African American and Diaspora Studies and directs the Callie House Center for the Study of Global Black Cultures and Politics. She is the editor or coeditor of six anthologies and the author of a number of books, including: *Frantz Fanon Conflicts and Feminisms* (Rowman & Littlefield, 1998); *Black Venus: Sexualized Savages, Primal Fears, and Primitive Narratives in French* (Duke University Press, 1999); *Negritude Women* (University of Minnesota Press, 2002); *Pimps Up, Ho's Down: Hip Hop's Hold on Young Black Women* (New York University Press, 2007).

Falguni A. Sheth is Associate Professor in Women's, Gender, and Sexuality Studies at Emory University. She received her PhD in philosophy from the New School for Social Research. Her research is in the areas of continental and political philosophy, legal and critical race theory, philosophy of race, postcolonial theory, and subaltern and gender studies. She has published numerous articles and two books, *Race, Liberalism, and Economics* (coedited, University of Michigan Press, 2004) and *Toward a Political Philosophy of Race* (SUNY Press, 2009). She is a columnist at Salon.com and an associate editor at *Hypatia*.

Laurie Shrage is Professor of Philosophy at Florida International University in Miami. Her books include: *Abortion and Social Responsibility* (Oxford University Press, 2003), *Moral Dilemmas of Feminism* (Routledge, 1994), an edited collection, *You've Changed: Sex Reassignment and Personal Identity* (Oxford University Press, 2009), and the coauthored textbook *Philosophizing about Sex* (Broadview, 2015). She served as coeditor of *Hypatia* from 1998 to 2003. She has contributed several pieces to "The Stone," in *The New York Times* (http://opinionator.blogs.nytimes.com/author/laurie-shrage/).

James P. Sterba, Professor of Philosophy at the University of Notre Dame, has published thirty-two books, including: the award-winning (Book of the Year Award of the North American Society for Social Philosophy 1998) *Justice for Here and Now* (Cambridge University Press, 1998), *Does Feminism Discriminate Against Men?* with Warren Farrell (Oxford University Press, 2008), *Affirmative Action for the Future* (Cornell University Press, 2009), and *From Rationality to Equality* (Oxford University Press, 2015). He is past president of the American Section of International Society for Social and Legal Philosophy, Concerned Philosophers for Peace, the North American Society for Social Philosophy, and the Central Division of the American Philosophical Association.

Shannon Sullivan is Professor of Philosophy and Health Psychology and Chair of Philosophy at University of North Carolina, Charlotte. She works in the intersections of continental philosophy, feminist philosophy, critical philosophy of race, and American pragmatism. Her most recent publications include *Good White People: The Problem with Middle-Class White Anti-Racism* (SUNY Press, 2014) and *The Physiology of Sexist and Racist Oppression* (Oxford University Press, 2015).

William Uzgalis is Emeritus Professor at Oregon State University, where he taught in the Philosophy Department and the School of History, Philosophy and Religion, for thirty-three years. He still lives in Corvallis, Oregon. His research interests include the history of modern philosophy with a particular focus on John Locke and Anthony Collins, as well as computers and philosophy, and philosophy of mind.

Kyle Powys Whyte is Associate Professor of Philosophy and Timnick Chair in the Humanities at Michigan State University and serves as a faculty member for the Environmental Science & Policy and American Indian Studies programs. His primary research addresses moral and political issues concerning climate policy and Indigenous peoples and the ethics of cooperative relationships between Indigenous peoples and climate science organizations. He is an enrolled member of the Citizen Potawatomi Nation.

Cynthia Willett is Professor of Philosophy at Emory University. Her authored books include: *Interspecies Ethics* (Columbia University Press, 2014); *Irony in the Age of Empire: Comic Perspectives on Freedom and Democracy* (Indiana University Press, 2008); *The Soul of Justice: Social Bonds and Racial Hubris* (Cornell University Press, 2001); and *Maternal Ethics and Other Slave Moralities* (Routledge, 1995). She has edited *Theorizing Multiculturalism* (1998) and is a coeditor for the *Symposia on Race, Gender, and Philosophy*. She is currently working on the ethics of music and comedy.

George Yancy is Professor of Philosophy at Emory University. He specializes in critical philosophy of race, critical whiteness studies, African American philosophy, and explores the lived dimensions of racial embodiment. He is the author, editor, and coeditor of over seventeen books. He is known for his provocative articles and his series of interviews of prominent philosophers on race within *The Stone, New York Times*. He is also Philosophy of Race Book Series Editor at Lexington Books.

Naomi Zack received her PhD in Philosophy from Columbia University and is Professor of Philosophy at the University of Oregon. Her latest book is *Applicative Justice: An Empirical Pragmatic Approach to Correcting Racial Injustice* (Rowman & Littlefield, 2016), Zack's recent books are *White Privilege and Black Rights: The Injustice of US Police Racial Profiling and Homicide* (Rowman & Littlefield, 2015), and *The Ethics and Mores of Race: Equality after the History of Philosophy* (Rowman and Littlefield, 2011, 2015). Earlier books include: *Race and Mixed Race* (Temple University Press 1993), *Bachelors of Science: Seventeenth-Century Identity Then and Now* (Temple University Press, 2006), *Philosophy of Science and Race* (Routledge, 2002), *Inclusive Feminism: A Third Wave Theory of Women's Commonality* (Rowman & Littlefield, 2005), and *Ethics for Disaster* (Rowman & Littlefield, 2009 and 2011). Zack has also produced reference books, numerous articles, and four edited anthologies.

Rocío Zambrana is Assistant Professor of Philosophy at the University of Oregon. Her work examines conceptions of critique in Kant and German idealism (especially Hegel), Marx and Frankfurt School critical theory, and decolonial thought. She is the author of *Hegel's Theory of Intelligibility* (University of Chicago Press, 2015), as well as articles on Hegel, Kant, and critical theory.

INTRODUCTION

NAOMI ZACK

It is in the nature of philosophy as critical inquiry to develop new subfields when new directions in the quest for knowledge, or in any other area of human activity, raise new intellectual problems.

American Philosophical Association, 2015

TOPICS pertaining to human races and racial difference are relatively new in academic philosophy. Before introducing the specifics of this book, it is important to situate the subfield of philosophy of race in terms of subject matter, methodologies, and more established aspects of the discipline. While philosophy of race has at times sparked controversy and a number of philosophers of race have complained about the marginalization of their work, philosophy of race has received official professional recognition.

The American Philosophical Association (APA) is the largest professional organization of academic philosophers and is generally regarded as the institutional representative of contemporary ethics and standards in the profession. The APA publishes newsletters that reflect current philosophical interest in topics of race and ethnicity: *Asian and Asian-American Philosophers and Philosophies*, *Indigenous Philosophy*, *Hispanic/Latino Issues in Philosophy*, and *Philosophy and the Black Experience*. The APA also maintains diversity committees corresponding to the foregoing newsletters, and others. There is an APA Ombudsperson on Nondiscrimination, a Committee on Inclusiveness in the Profession, and a Task Force on Diversity and Inclusiveness. In addition, the APA conducts studies of diversity and issues statements and reports about diversity in the profession. In a 2013–2014 APA demographic survey, out of about 9,100 total members, 3,800 responded to the question about race and ethnic identity. Of that 3,800, the total of those identifying as nonwhite was about 700: 244 as Asian, 101 as black/African American, 193 as Hispanic/Latino, 47 as American Indian/Alaskan Native and Pacific Islander, and 104 as "something else."

Diversity, or the inclusion of nontraditional people in the profession of philosophy, encompasses philosophers who are women, LBGTQ, and disabled, as well as people of color (APA 2015). Also, a number of members of each of these groups belong to more than one group. As in the US Census, ethnic diversity is limited to Hispanic/Latino or not (Zack 2001). All told, this is important recognition. Still, some consider it an urgent matter to increase racial and ethnic diversity among academic philosophers, at this time—not only for the sake of demographic variety but because underrepresented groups in philosophy have a long history of social disadvantage in society, from black slavery, to social oppression and intergenerational poverty. Increasing diverse presence in philosophy would acknowledge that history and provide some justice for past exclusion. Furthermore, although many philosophers continue to believe that practitioners of their profession have no race, as well as no sex (and no bodies?), many others believe that knowers, including philosophers, cannot divest themselves of race and sex. Moreover, nonwhite and nonmale philosophers have different life experience from white male philosophers, and the wealth of human experience brought into the discipline with them enriches all practitioners. However, there is not yet a consensus about the nature of the underrepresentation problem in the field of philosophy, its causes, and viable solutions. The contents of this volume, although not designed or executed to specifically address this issue in the profession, can nonetheless be read as a scholarly companion to the consideration of it.

The relatively small percentage of nonwhite and Hispanic/Latino philosophers, about 15 percent of the profession, compares to 37 percent of the total US population (US Census Bureau 2015). The teaching and research of these philosophers is more likely than that of white, non-Hispanic/Latino philosophers to focus on issues of race and ethnicity. This may in part reflect the newness of philosophy of race—a term that now includes issues of ethnicity—as a recognized subfield in philosophy. Those from groups demographically new to the academy sometimes feel it is important for them to work in new subjects associated with their identities, even though they are, of course, neither required to make that choice nor always encouraged to do so.

Both the presence of nonwhites (who under the term "people of color" usually include Hispanic/Latinos) in academic philosophy and philosophical subject matter about race and ethnicity have been met with some controversy. It is therefore important to develop understanding of the following aspects of philosophy of race, as a subfield: the history of the idea of race in philosophy; progress in social justice outside of the academy; how contemporary philosophy of race arrived in philosophy (and the tensions between mainstream philosophy and philosophy of race); the distinctive disciplinary aspects of philosophy of race; what philosophy of race contributes to philosophy; and what philosophy contributes to philosophy of race.

HISTORY OF THE IDEA OF RACE IN PHILOSOPHY

For philosophers, the study of history is mainly the study of the history of philosophy. During the European Enlightenment, three of philosophy's most revered canonical figures—David Hume, Immanuel Kant, and Georg Wilhelm Friedrich Hegel—forged foundational ideas about the existence of human races and their differences. They all assumed that human races exist and that they form a normative hierarchy, with whites, as the best, at the top. The superiority of whites to nonwhites was taken for granted throughout the American academy during the nineteenth and early twentieth centuries, as throughout the rest of society. Each race was believed to have an inherited, unchangeable *essence* that determined the physical, mental, and moral nature of its members. These past essentialist notions of nonwhites, in comparison to white Europeans, which were based on now falsified speculative biology, would be considered racist today (Zack 2002, 9–41). But the influence of the now-racist ideas about race created by Hume, Kant, Hegel, and also Nietzsche grew and spread with the emerging nineteenth-century sciences of biology and anthropology.

Essentialist and hierarchical systemic thinking about human races quietly dropped out of philosophy after the mid-1950s, along with a shift to positive concern about social justice issues that focused on race or included race. In considering that shift, a number of historical events and reactions became part of a context that is important to consider as a social, political, and ideological whole, in retrospect: the shock of Nazi antisemitic racism during World War II; President Truman's desegregation of the US military in 1948; an international focus on racial equality by the United Nations that resulted in four declarations on "The Race Question" by UNESCO, beginning in 1950 (UNESCO 1969); the official, legal end of US segregation in *Brown v. Board of Education*, in 1954 (Warren 1954; USHistoryAtlas.com 2015); and the civil rights movement that concluded with the Civil Rights Act of 1964 and the Voting Rights Act of 1965 (US Government Publications 1964, 241–258). All of these legal changes and related documents were based on the premise that all human beings are morally equal and that human capabilities are evenly distributed across racial groups. A consensus developed in the educational and international legal communities that differences in the achievements of racial groups were the result of cultural norms and structures and historical events, and not expressions of racial essences or anything else determined by biology (Lévi-Strauss 1952). Along with that shift in understanding, studies of human race eventually became subjects for history and the social sciences, rather than anthropology, biology, or speculative metaphysics.

IDEAS OF RACE IN TWENTIETH-CENTURY PHILOSOPHY

It took some time for empirically based and egalitarian work on race to enter American academic philosophy, and it was neither recognized nor prominent in the field over most of the twentieth century. Until about 1970, the dominant mainstream of academic philosophy emulated what it believed to be the rigors of science and was self-consciously aware of itself as a critical discipline with a strong emphasis on epistemology, metaphysics, and philosophy of science. During the last third of the century there was a "turn" in mainstream philosophy to philosophy of language, and a shift in philosophy of mind toward cognitive science. Over the same time period, so-called continental philosophers working in phenomenology, existentialism, and poststructuralism developed some (contested) presence in the Anglo-American academy. Also, American philosophy, or pragmatism, which had a heyday from the 1890s to 1930, waned in disciplinary prominence. John Rawls's ideal theory of justice was acclaimed as a revival of political philosophy, but attention to practical social issues was neither a priority nor even a weak duty. In addition, philosophers, like most others in the academy, were mostly white, middle- and upper-class men, whose life experience did not impel them to focus on race (Bordo 1988). Overall, the subject of race was generally overlooked, and with that, empirically based egalitarian attention to racial difference was lacking.

However, while race was neglected in mainstream philosophy, empirically based, egalitarian attention to race was provided by African American scholars throughout the humanities: philosophers in historically black colleges, such as Alain Locke at Howard University (Harris and Molesworth 2008); sociologists and historians, such as W. E. B. DuBois at Atlanta University (W.E.B. Du Bois Legacy Project 2015) and E. Franklin Frazer at Howard University (Fraser Center 2015). The first African American philosopher in an Ivy League department, William Fontaine at the University of Pennsylvania, attended to race as both a national and international subject, from the perspective of ethical relativism (Kuklick 2008).

THE US SUPREME COURT ON SOCIAL JUSTICE ISSUES IN HIGHER EDUCATION

In the United States, education has traditionally constituted primary access for socioeconomic and political advancement for minorities. It has been widely believed that college degrees provide and protect full citizenship rights and their enjoyment. While that expectation was fulfilled for early twentieth-century European immigrants who became "white ethnics," it has been more difficult to fulfill for subsequent waves of immigrants from Latin America and Asia, as well as African Americans and Native Americans. Still, after the legal gains for racial minorities in the antidiscrimination clause of the 1964 Civil Rights Act, people of color began entering the US academy in visible numbers, as students and faculty. Many of these new entrants brought different perspectives to their academic work and helped inspire institutional *missions* of integration and affirmation in higher education. Affirmative action was partly based on the principle that the academy should be more representative of the populations outside its walls. Affirming disadvantaged social identities was supposed to serve as compensation for histories of racial and ethnic exclusion and provide a way to "level the playing field" in the present (Sterba and Cohen 2003).

Thus, there were higher rates of admission and employment in US higher education for those of minority race and other forms of disadvantaged social status—but only for a while, and not without "backlash." Educational resources are limited entitlements and if nonwhites got in, to many that meant that whites did not or would not get in. There were also strong social, political, and legal objections to the idea that whites in the present should be held responsible for past racial discrimination. The principle that disadvantaged racial identities should be "affirmed," in place of merit, was dramatized as a threat to core American values.

Beginning with *Bakke* in 1978 (*Regents of the University of California v. Bakke* 1978), affirmative action policies were whittled down according to the US Supreme Court policy of *strict scrutiny*. The Court insisted that any consideration of race in admissions or employment be examined for whether a law or policy has been passed and applied to further a compelling government interest and is *narrowly tailored* to serve only that interest. The Court has recognized a compelling government interest in a diverse student body in higher education, but its insistence that policies be narrowly tailored has limited the recruitment and employment of minorities. The Court has ruled that the Civil Rights Act and Fourteenth Amendment (providing for equal protection under the law) of the Constitution do not allow "race" to be a positive factor for securing entitlements. Where affirmative action favors nonwhites who might otherwise experience covert discrimination or who belong to groups still burdened by legacies of past discrimination, the Court has looked at "race" only as a property of individuals in the time-slice of their application for admission or employment, and has thereby ruled that nonwhite race, alone, is not admissible as a qualification (Winkler 2006). The US Supreme Court's perspective on affirmative action was made explicit in two 2003 cases.

In *Graz v. Bollinger*, the practice of the University of Michigan to automatically give points for nonwhite racial identity in its undergraduate admissions process did not pass strict scrutiny (*Gratz v. Bollinger* 2003). However, in *Grutter v. Bollinger*, the Court found it constitutionally permissible for the race of applicants to be considered "holistically," as the University of Michigan School of Law application process provided. The admission process in the Michigan School of Law preferred a nonwhite over a white applicant only if their qualifications were equal. But there was a caveat in the Court's approval of that process, because Chief Justice Sandra Day O'Connor speculated that even such holistic policies would be unnecessary in twenty-five years (*Grutter v. Bollinger* 2003). That is, O'Connor apparently believed that after one generation of affirmation by race of otherwise qualified freshmen or those seeking advanced degrees, it would no longer be necessary, either for de facto social equality or a recognized desideratum of racial diversity on college campuses, to affirm nonwhite race in the higher education admissions process. It seems unlikely that O'Connor's timeline will prove realistic, but the Court has not changed its course as 2028 gets closer (*Fisher v. University of Texas at Austin* 2013). With the loss of legal support for protected classes of nonwhites as candidates for affirmative action programs, there has been a shift toward building demographic diversity within higher education. Diversity pertains to the composition of an entire student body, and it is not always clear where or how America's most historically troubled racial identities, such as blacks and Native Americans, fit into this new picture (Cherwitz 2013).

New Problems of Race in US Society

It is important to distinguish between social progress resulting from greater racial diversity in higher education and social progress throughout society. This may be a matter of how long it takes for diversity in higher education to "trickle down" toward an egalitarian society, or of recognizing the difference between barriers experienced by the nonwhite upwardly mobile middle class and the existential conditions of the nonwhite poor. Recent cases of racial profiling by US police officers, which have resulted in the killing of unarmed young black men, without indictments and convictions of the officers responsible, have made the subject of US race relations newly urgent (Zack 2015). Many observers believe that these homicides are symptomatic of systemic racial distortions that include the following: disproportionate numbers of racial minorities in a criminal justice system that has expended ten-fold in recent decades; historically high rates of racial residential segregation; and intergenerational race-associated poverty mediating both the incarceration and housing ills (Alexander 2011).

How is it that in a post–civil rights age of racial equality, people of color are disproportionately undereducated, poor, incarcerated, and more likely to be treated violently by police? The contradiction between equality as stated in law and humanitarian and scientific consensus versus the reality of social inequality and injustice cannot be adequately addressed as a psychological or ethical issue, on the level of individuals. Deeper cultural, political, and economic analyses are required to explain why and how people behave in ways that appear to violate their highest and most general legal and moral principles; that is, underlying interests and historical trends must be exposed and clearly described. Such analyses have been integral to the new scholarship emerging after racial integration became at once an ideal and precarious reality in American higher education.

THE NEW SUBJECT OF RACE IN THE ACADEMY AND PHILOSOPHY

The new scholarship about race has not always been welcomed in academic departments. The subject of race first appeared as part of "multiculturalism," an intellectual and pedagogical project seeking to rediscover the histories and voices of those oppressed or previously excluded. Few academic philosophers actively engaged in the multiculturalism debates or even bothered to explicitly reject multiculturalism as a threat to logic, critical thinking, and the established canon of their field (Webster 1997). But subjects associated with multiculturalism were not readily accepted as philosophical subjects and academic philosophers have always preserved their power to rule on what will count as philosophy, which they can do simply by omitting certain subjects and authors from individual research agenda, departmental curricula, or course syllabi. During the 1970s and 1980s, there was little interest among philosophers in subjects of race, including (or excluding) social or biological theories of race, African American thought and letters, analyses of racial divisions and racism in society, or debates about affirmative action. Also, although most philosophers, like other "left-leaning" intellectuals, abhor bigotry, they have not generally recognized a professional obligation to integrate their field demographically. And as noted, the traditional self-image of the discipline has been that philosophy itself is without race (as well as without sex).

Contrary to entrenched attitude and self-image, in the 1970s, in continuance of earlier work by Du Bois, Locke, Fontaine, and others, a small number of philosophers began to create a new subfield within academic philosophy departments. The subject was known as African American philosophy, Afro-American Philosophy, or Africana philosophy, but its content was more broadly philosophy of race. The shared aims were to reflect and advance emancipatory and critical research and thought about race, with a focus on philosophical questions and problems (Corlett 2011).

From the beginning, philosophers of race have had to demonstrate that their concerns and work remain philosophical. Although that might appear to be an unfair burden imposed on marginal members of an elitist field, it should also be noted that African American philosophy and philosophy of race are a unique presence in an abstract field. Other fields in the humanities have specializations stemming from geographical area studies. Approaches to subject matter that are inflected by the racial or ethnic identities of authors are not unusual. But no other established subfield in philosophy is explicitly focused on the problems of a specific national racial minority, primarily as understood by members of that group. These circumstances bestow an intellectual distinction on African American philosophers of race. The historical racist speculations about black intellectual inferiority are partly avenged.

Moreover, the descendants of slaves to whom literacy was forbidden do garner a modicum of respect in plying the craft of contemporary academic philosophy, not necessarily as black philosophers (which not all would desire), but as philosophers.

By the 1990s, multiculturalism in general had become less ideological and more scholarly, evolving into an apparently permanent dynamic and contested presence in US higher education. The terms for what "multiculturalism" originally represented have been replaced throughout the academy by "diversity," which refers to persistent injustice and unfairness and what should be done about it. However, the subject of race is more descriptive and less normative than the subject(s) of diversity. As a general subject for research and teaching, "race" is now comprehensive and multidisciplinary, including research and influence in the biological sciences, humanities, social sciences, law, ethnic studies, gender studies, communication, American studies, African American studies, and various fields of literature, including "English" (the name of the largest and most intellectually adventurous departments on US college campuses), as well as area-studies programs and departments, such as Native American, Asian, and Hispanic/Latino studies, and of course, geography, and cultural anthropology.

From a somewhat blurry multidisciplinary perspective, many issues of race that are live for contemporary theorists across disciplines fall under a number of established philosophical subfields: philosophy of science and metaphysics; social and political philosophy; American philosophy and pragmatism; political philosophy; philosophy of law; existentialism and phenomenology; feminism and gender studies. That is, at first sight, philosophy of race seems to line up with philosophy. But many specialists in other subfields of philosophy remain skeptical that race really is a philosophical subject. And speaking for themselves about their academic projects, many philosophers of race would be reluctant to categorize their work as applications or mere extensions of established philosophical subfields. They would argue that the established philosophical subfields neither do full justice to the intellectual innovations and immediate social relevance of their subject nor accommodate ideals of social criticism that have been developed in "race" as a multidisciplinary field that reflects a complex dimension of human existence. Resisting a narrow and overly abstract conception of philosophy, many philosophers of race would insist that their subfield is properly philosophical, in method, as well as subject matter, but that their subject matter is more fluid and dynamic than other subjects in philosophy. They may insist that philosophical methods should allow for changing content and that it is possible and sometimes morally obligatory to philosophize about social reality.

Unlike many philosophers who work in traditional subfields, philosophers of race are not overly specialized within their own subsubfield boundaries. It is rare for practitioners to restrict their expertise to just one topic, and there is a certain amount of disagreement and indeterminacy about where specific topics should be categorized. Distinctive terms may be used for topics that already have names in other philosophical traditions. For example, because racism is unethical, it could be part of ethics within considerations of the obligations people have, as related to differences in power and status. Or racism as an issue of social justice could be part of political philosophy. However, as a philosophical subject, racism is usually relegated to African American philosophy or philosophy of race. To consider another subject, issues of racial identity, including questions about its importance and taxonomy could be part of the subject of personal identity within philosophy of mind, metaphysics, or cognitive science. Instead, racial identity retains its name as a subject in philosophy of race. That subjects initiated by philosophers of race remain distinct under the names associated with that subfield could express the exclusion of race as a subject from established philosophical subfields. Or it may be that the layout of philosophy as a field, like streets in old cities, does not correspond to a rational grid. But it might be more optimistic to view topics developed by philosophers of race as new philosophical subjects that have been created with the use of both traditional and new philosophical tools or methods.

THE NATURE OF THE SUBFIELDS
OF PHILOSOPHY OF RACE

The subfields of philosophy of race are both independent of, and overlap with, the established subfields of philosophy. They reflect the multidisciplinary aspects of race as a subject and preserve and extend distinctively philosophical methods and concerns to it. The result is that some of the topics (or sub-subfields) in philosophy of race are readily recognized by other philosophers, for example, philosophy of science and philosophy of law, whereas others are not, for example, racial identity and white privilege. But insofar as most academic philosophers are increasingly unfamiliar with the specializations of many of their colleagues and could not say what the main issues in those foreign [to them] specializations are, this lack of recognition is not an unusual problem.

Although philosophy has a long history of giving birth to new fields of study, this is unlikely to occur with the subject of race, because ethnic studies and Africana and African American, as well as Hispanic/Latino studies programs and departments already exist, theoretical work on race in other fields is robust, and the philosophical aspects of philosophy of race are already quite distinct. In other words, contested or accepted, philosophy of race now has a stable presence as a subfield of academic philosophy. Moreover, philosophers of race are as adept as other philosophers in debating whether certain work is or is not philosophical.

Philosophy of race is not impervious to wider disciplinary themes and tensions. The ongoing tensions in philosophy between "analytic" and "continental" approaches have to an extent been carried over into philosophy of race, with perhaps expected incommensurable perspectives. For example, those who believe that physical science should have the last word in analyses of ideas about physical racial differences and those who prefer to rely on phenomenological accounts of human physicality within society(ies) may find it difficult to engage. But the broader analytic–continental divide throughout the profession is not as divisive among philosophers of race, because overall, solidarity and intellectual cohesion are based on shared emancipatory or progressive anti-oppressive ideals, as well as the usual disciplinary commitment to philosophical or theoretical methods. (These shared goals are evident in contributions throughout this volume and will be discussed in the Part introductions.)

CONTRIBUTIONS OF PHILOSOPHY OF RACE
TO PHILOSOPHY

For philosophers, the most important qualification for a new subject is whether it can be treated philosophically. Philosophy of race is not philosophical in primarily focusing on canonical philosophical authors or traditional philosophical questions. Philosophers of race draw on work in the history of philosophy, broadly understood, to include thinkers not recognized as philosophers in their time. Many of the problems taken up are more realistically relevant versions of traditional philosophical problems that have included the following: criteria for knowledge; the relation of generic "man" to Being or to the physical and social world; and the mind–body problem. For instance, criteria for knowledge in philosophy of race may focus on the social epistemology of ignorance; the human subject may be addressed as already "raced" in society; the mind–body problem might be treated as how bodily identification as nonwhite leads to distinctive subjective experiences in a racist society. Nevertheless, the methods are familiar—conceptual analysis and argument, with the usual scholarly apparatus of footnotes or endnotes.

The distinctive contribution to academic philosophy of studies of race is that it keeps the discipline relevant to outside social, political, scientific, and economic realities. In addition, philosophical work on race is often of theoretical interest to academics in other fields that include this subject, because philosophical work on many subjects is very similar in methodology to theoretical work in other fields. The inclusion of philosophy of race also democratically moves higher education and scholarship closer to reflecting existing human demographics and subjects of broad popular concern. Philosophy of race makes philosophy itself more humanistic by providing an opportunity for those who view their progressive and liberatory writing and teaching about race as part of a progressive vocation or calling. Traditional philosophical practice, before the historical development of philosophy of race, has also been viewed as a calling. In addition to being drawn to and having commitments to issues and problems of race, philosophers of race are drawn to and have commitments to philosophy. This raises the question of what philosophy can contribute to philosophy of race and to studies of race in other fields.

Contributions of Philosophy to Philosophy of Race

At their best, philosophers speak and write clearly, communicating what they intend to communicate to listeners and readers who understand what they hear and read, as the speaker or writer intended. Academic philosophers can and do address racial problems, in keeping with the multidisciplinary nature of the subject, by clearly explaining what these problems are, clearly explaining the history and causes of those problems, and clearly proposing solutions that accord with existing legal principles, broadly accepted moral principles, and reasonable human aspirations. Clear prose signals the intention to communicate with an audience that includes undergraduates, academics in other fields, and the public, as well as other professional philosophers. If those outside of the field, or even within the field, who are not interested in the subject of race, are not an actual audience, clarity in communication conveys an intention to include them. Some may assume that this kind of clarity is associated with an "analytic" style, but that would be mistaken, because common sense, existentialist, Americanist, and phenomenological philosophers, much like their analytic counterparts, can be clear or opaque, to different degrees.

Clear communication is a professional requirement for highly theoretical and technical work that is intended for other academics. But it can also signal accessibility to a more general audience and give authors the opportunity to courageously face up to controversy, hostility, and racism. Indeed, clear prose about the subject of race is more likely to evoke negative reactions than prose encumbered by academic jargon or obscured by specialized methodologies (Yancy 2016). The audience cannot respond to what it does not understand or what is presented in ways too technical and boring to hold its attention.

Consider, in this regard, antiblack racism (Gordon 1995), which many believe remains America's most pressing racial problem. Since the legal success of the civil rights movements of the 1960s, antiblack racism has been kept in the background of what is said in public or how people behave toward one another at work. Philosophers of race may analyze antiblack racism, show how it persists "hidden in plain sight," and explain why it is morally wrong and unjust. This is a cognitive task, using empirical information, reasoning, and calm persuasion. For example, many Americans believe that equal opportunity for wealth and other goods of life is a valuable aspect of democratic life, and they also believe that blacks have the same opportunities to achieve or acquire such goods, as do whites. When blacks do not have these goods, many white Americans blame them as individuals, applying stereotypes that they are lazy, bad, and unable to sustain standard family structures (Moynihan 1965). Philosophers of race might accept the challenge of showing how blacks do not have the same opportunities to attain these goods of life that whites do and explain how the obstacles blacks face are the result of history and present economic and social circumstances. But to speak of "a philosopher's challenge" in terms of contemporary events analyzed for a general audience is only to refer to how some philosophers of race work. Other philosophers of race would object to attention to the world in the name of philosophy, preferring this be left to theorists in sociology or anthropology, or to preachers, media pundits, or avowed public intellectuals. That is, like many philosophers in other subfields, they would prefer to restrict their discourse and argument to an audience of academic peers.

For those interested in applying philosophical insights or conclusions to the world, "ought" implies "can." Philosophers tend to deal with cognitions, ideas, and beliefs. For them to choose whether or not to address real-life issues of race or racism, they must be qualified or appropriately trained to do that—they must be able to do it. A psychologist or philosopher of psychology might object to the philosophical approach to race on the grounds that beliefs about race and racial difference are more emotional than cognitive. Such emotional beliefs are more readily evoked by "frames" that call up whole conceptual and emotional complexes, or "schema," which cannot be dislodged or dissolved by informed rational argument (Gross and D'Ambrosio 2004; Feagan 2013). However, the cognitive approach by philosophers of race is not so easily dismissed. The philosophical challenge would be to offer analyses and explanations of such frames, using the tools of philosophy to consider findings from the social sciences and other fields in the humanities. Attention may be paid to showing exactly why some beliefs are false. Indeed, false beliefs, including myths, about race are rarely cognitive errors but usually highly charged narratives that have been used to justify great social evils and the harm and death of individuals, for example, the myth of the black rapist as used to justify and motivate lynching (Somerville 2004).

Unraveling false emotionally laden beliefs is a cognitive task that philosophers can undertake. Philosophers of race may write and speak on the basis of historical knowledge that includes the following: racist components of the thought of canonical philosophical figures such as Hume, Kant, and Hegel; ideas of race from ancient through modern history; US slavery; Jim Crow laws and customs (including lynching); legal history and court decisions; the US civil rights movements; race relations in other nations; different cultural ideas of race in the past and present; and the history of affirmative action. Included in sources may be information about current events, what is reported in public and academic news and television entertainment and film, literature, and social media.

As such a constantly unfolding subject, race in the present often cries out for philosophical analysis, despite or because of its highly charged elements. Direct philosophizing about the social world is a new practice for academic philosophy that many within and without the discipline find jarring and even outrageous. But insofar as journalists and historians are rarely as critical or theoretically abstract as philosophers, who can say that philosophers are not here providing something that only they can contribute? Both freedom of speech and academic freedom permit such disciplinary transgression, and the lives and human well-being at stake in the subject matter are of greater value than disciplinary purity.

DIVERSITY AND THE STRUCTURE OF THIS VOLUME

Most contemporary philosophers who specialize in race would not claim that their intellectual work is wholly motivated by their own social identities, but few would say that such motivation is nonexistent. Since the 1970s, a general consensus has emerged in humanistic studies and among administrators in higher education that diversity in faculty demographics will lead to more diverse subject matter and that diverse subject matter will reflect diversity in authorship. The educated community no longer believes that biological race determines intellectual capacity or mental content, but many in higher education continue to believe that the differences in lived experience associated with racial difference result in generally different "perspectives." It would therefore be odd if a volume such as this were to be wholly or mainly composed by white authors. It would also be odd if there were no white authors. But, of course, racial "diversity" as an intellectual matter is more complex than a white/nonwhite distinction in identities might indicate.

In the United States, most of the scholarship in philosophy of race has concentrated on African American issues, because the US history of black chattel slavery has had a well-established influence on the intellectual life of the nation, as well as collective emotionality. Also, as mentioned earlier, African American philosophers founded African American philosophy as a subfield in the discipline in the early 1970s. Additional racial diversity came later to academic philosophy. Work on Asian American, indigenous American, Hispanic/Latino American, and Islamic American issues is not well represented in philosophy of race at this time. International issues and cultural and historical differences regarding race are also underrepresented in philosophy of race, as is robust scholarship in feminism and gender. This volume inevitably reflects those limitations, although inclusive efforts are also evident in the contents.

The volume has ten parts or subject parts, which altogether highlight contemporary scholarship on race that reflects both historical and present interests. There is a diversity of opinion and perspective within each part, as the result of pluralities of philosophical concern and method. Contributors were encouraged to present original ideas and criticize other scholarship as they independently saw fit. With fifty-one essays in ten parts, the results are comprehensive, but as a compendium rather than a textbook.

The sequence of the parts is organized both chronologically for intellectual history and logically in how the different parts are conceptually related to one another. According to philosophical tradition, it is appropriate to begin a subject with reference to canonical figures from the history of philosophy. Therefore, the essays in Part I are about ideas of race in the writings of Locke, Hume, Kant, and Nietzsche (Hegel is reserved for Part V, for his positive potential influence in contemporary continental philosophical method). This canonical representation contains much that is racist—even by the standards of their times. It therefore is immediately reasonable to ask who has been left out. In Part II, contributors discuss alternative thought about race in the modern period: eighteenth- and nineteenth-century black intellectuals writing about race in England and the United States; the anti-indigenous ideology of US settlers; ideas of rights and identity in Latin America; Asian America from a transnational perspective; and the exclusion and literal neglect of Alain Locke. By now it makes sense to ask exactly what everyone is talking about—What is race? That is the metaphysical question of Part III, which is straightforwardly answered by reference to why contemporary biological science has discredited earlier claims about the reality of human races. If race is unreal as a biological taxonomy, then should racial categories be eliminated in society? The "eliminativist" view of race is complicated by the analyses of philosophers who do not think that physical science should have the last word on human ontology. Reductions of race to ethnicity are considered as a solution to the ontological problem, and the connection between philosophy of language and philosophy of race is also examined in accord with the overwhelming importance of race in social reality.

Part IV turns to twentieth-century American philosophy or pragmatism, because one would expect that America's distinct contribution to philosophical method would be relevant to distinctly American concerns of philosophy of race. Although race was not an important subject for James, Pierce, or Dewey, Du Bois was a student of American thinkers at Harvard University, as well as of social theorists at the University of Berlin. Alain Locke, Cornel West, and Lucius Outlaw are part of the same Americanist tradition. Section V attends to a philosophical perspective on race that is inflected by continental methodology as characterized by phenomenology, existentialism, poststructuralism, Marxist critical theory, and antiracist critical theory. Hegel, Norman Mailer, Albert Memmi, Foucault, and additional non-European phenomenologists are engaged.

The philosophical approaches to race in Parts I–V all share awareness of a problem in how nonwhites, especially blacks, compared to whites, have been viewed and treated. Time and again, the reader has been presented with analyses of how whites have conceptualized nonwhites in derogatory ways that accompanied treatment of them as stupid/ugly/dangerous inferiors. *Racism* is the correct term for such conceptualization, and the prejudice, discrimination, and ways of life that have accompanied it. Part VI offers analyses of racism, as both historical and contemporary: nineteenth-century racism as terror; new social constructions of blackness as excess; white privilege that crushes nonwhites without explicit mention of race; the racialization of Muslims in post-9/11 America; and strategies of resistance.

Racism is not only a matter of individual attitudes or abstract assessment of human behavior, but daily habits and institutional practices that assign people to certain social roles, which may construct their racial identities, without even mention of their race. Human identities are created by regular and regulated social behavior. Part VII examines aspects of the social construction of race and racial identity: the blackness of black identity; how mixed race fails to be constructed; the relation of racial norms to racial identity; the morality of any racial identity; and living with racism and sexism as permanent conditions. The social constructions and identities discussed in this part, together with racism(s) as considered in Part VI, give rise to practical problems that are evident in ordinary life. Part VIII examines race in terms of injustice and police racial profiling; inequalities in education, medicine, public health, and disease; and the importance of sports in US life.

Thus far through the parts, discussion has proceeded as though ideas about race and actions following them are somewhat optional and voluntary, although based on habits and social convention. Law, in the form of legislation and court decisions, official public policy, and influential concepts and principles from political philosophy, has provided obligations, interventions, and restrictions regarding race. Part IX is about law and race: reparations for past injustice; rectification and apology; the principle of equal protection under the law; the future of affirmative action; and considerations of ideal and nonideal justice theory in terms of real life injustice. Part X concludes the volume with the topic of gender—how gender influences and shapes race and how race influences and shapes gender. Discussion of the following topics are included: ethnological theories of race and sex in nineteenth-century black writing; historical representations of black female gender from Jefferson to hip-hop culture; violent constructions of black male gender as dangerous and criminal; black feminism as critical theory; and the dimension of insult and shame in racism and sexism.

Standard use of this volume would be assignment of all ten parts in order, to a class over a semester or academic year. But fewer parts could be used or selections from parts, alone or in combination with other specialized material. As a whole or in part, these essays can serve as a path to more comprehensive research.

References

Alexander, Michelle. (2011). *The New Jim Crow: Mass Incarceration in the Age of Colorblindness.* New York: The New Press.

American Philosophical Association. (2015). "Committee: Inclusiveness in the Profession." Accessed May 16, 2016. http://www.apaonline.org/group/inclusiveness.

Bordo, Susan. (1988). "Feminist Skepticism and the 'Maleness' of Philosophy." *Journal of Philosophy* 85 (11): 619–629.

Cherwitz, Richard A. (2013). "Increasing Diversity in the Post-Fisher Era." *Diverse Issues in Higher Education*, July 10. Accessed May 16, 2016. http://diverseeducation.com/article/54561/.

Corlett, Angelo. (2011). "Race." *Oxford Bibliographies.* Accessed May 16, 2016. http://www.oxfordbibliographies.com/view/document/obo-9780195396577/obo-9780195396577-0097.xml.

Feagin, Joe R. (2013). *The White Racial Frame Centuries of Racial Framing and Counter-Framing: Centuries of Racial Framing and Counter-Framing.* New York: Routledge.

Fisher v. University of Texas at Austin, 133 S. Ct. 2411, 570 US, 186 L. Ed. 2d 474—Supreme Court (2013).

Gordon, Lewis R. (1995). *Bad Faith and Antiblack Racism*, Atlantic Highlands, NJ: Humanities Press.

Gratz v. Bollinger, 539 U.S. 244 (2003).

Gross, Kimberly, and Lisa D'Ambrosio. (2004). "Framing Emotional Response." *Political Psychology* 25 (1): 1–29.

Grutter v. Bollinger et al., 539 U.S. 306 (2003).

Harris, Leonard, and Charles Molesworth (2008). *Alain L. Locke: The Biography of a Philosopher.* Chicago: University of Chicago Press.

History.com. (2015). "Black History, Civil Rights Act; Voting Rights Act." Accessed May 16, 2016. http://www.history.com/topics/black-history/civil-rights-act.

Frazier Center, School of Social Work, Howard University. (2015). Accessed May 16, 2016. http://www.howard.edu/schoolsocialwork/centers/fraziercenter.htm.

Kuklick, Bruce. (2008). *Black Philosopher, White Academy: The Career of William Fontaine.* Philadelphia: University of Pennsylvania Press.

Lévi-Strauss, Claude. (1952). *Race and History.* Paris: UNESCO. Accessed May 16, 2016. https://archive.org/details/racehistory00levi.

Moynihan, Patrick. "Interviews with Daniel Patrick Moynihan over His Career, with a Focus on the Moynihan Report." *New York's Moynihan, Part 1.* New York: Local Projects for the Museum of the City of New York. Accessed May 16, 2016. http://www.youtube.com/watch?v=hPxkJZsz4Kc.

Regents of the University of California v. Bakke, 438 U.S. 265, (1978).

Sommerville, Diane Miller. (2004). *Rape and Race in the Nineteenth-Century South.* Chapel Hill and London: University of North Carolina Press.

Sterba, James P., and Carl Cohen. (2003). *Affirmative Action and Racial Preference: A Debate.* New York: Oxford University Press.

UNESCO. (1969). "Four Statements on the Race Question, 1950, 1951, 1964 and 1967." Paris: United Nations Educational, Scientific and Cultural Organization. Accessed May 16, 2016. http://unesdoc.unesco.org/images/0012/001229/122962eo.pdf.

United States Government Publishing Office. "PUBLIC LAW 88-352-JULY 2, 1964." Accessed June 16, 2016. https://www.gpo.gov/fdsys/pkg/STATUTE-78/pdf/STATUTE-78-Pg241.pdf.

US Census Bureau. (2015). "State and County Quick Facts, 2015." Accessed May 16, 2016. http://quickfacts.census.gov/qfd/states/00000.html.

Warren, Chief Justice Earl. (1954). "Brown v. Board of Education." *United States Reports* 347 (1954): 483.

W.E.B. Du Bois Legacy Project, Clark Atlanta University. (2015). Accessed May 16, 2016. http://cauduboislegacy.net/.

Webster, Yehudi O. (1997). *Against the Multicultural Agenda: A Critical Thinking Alternative.* Westport, CT: Praeger.

Winkler, Adam. (2006). "Fatal in Theory and Strict in Fact: An Empirical Analysis of Strict Scrutiny in the Federal Courts." *Vanderbilt Law Review* 59 (3): 793–869.

Yancy, George. (2015). "Philosophers on Race. Opionator: The Stone." *The New York Times.* Accessed May 16, 2016. http://opinionator.blogs.nytimes.com/tag/philosophers-on-race/.

Zack, Naomi. (2001). "American Mixed Race: Theoretical and Legal Issues." *Harvard BlackLetter Law Journal* 17(Spring): 33–46.

Zack, Naomi. (2002). *Philosophy of Science and Race.* New York: Routledge.

Zack, Naomi. (2015). *White Privilege and Black Rights: The Injustice of US Police Racial Profiling and Homicide.* Lanham, MD: Rowman and Littlefield.

PART I

....

IDEAS OF RACE
IN THE HISTORY
OF MODERN
PHILOSOPHY

....

RACE is one kind of difference within our species. Western ideas of races can be traced to relational and genealogical notions of tribes, clans, and lines of descent. In addition, practices such as slavery that are associated with later ideas of human difference occurred in ancient Greece and Rome. However, the idea of race as a taxonomy or demarcated system of human group differences with biological, moral, geographical, and historical foundations was new to the modern period.

The modern idea of race was developed by leading intellectuals, as well as social, political, and economic leaders. Two powerful factors contributed to this new notion. First, new practices of conquest, domination, and resource extraction by Europeans over other parts of the world during the Age of Discovery and the Industrial Revolution involved intense, systematic contact with people in Africa, Asia, and the Americas. Where earlier explorers had first visited and reported novelty, there now came to be structured settling, development, export, and exploitation. Second, the creation and development of the natural physical science of biology and the social science of anthropology over the nineteenth century afforded new conceptual tools for describing and analyzing human differences, especially differences between Europeans and those in parts of the world that became subordinate to Europe.

Philosophers have rarely had direct political power, but famous philosophers have had cultural influence over the imagination and factual beliefs of succeeding generations. For a long time, it was assumed that what canonical philosophers had to say about race was either incidental to their main intellectual work—if it had any philosophical content—or that it was in the realm of mere human opinion, if it was informally expressed. In recent decades, this assumption has shifted to more concerned enquiry about whether the ideas about human racial difference held by canonical philosophers in the modern period were an integral part of their philosophies. Contemporary philosophers of race are less likely than previous genera-tions of scholars in the history of ideas or the history of philosophy to assume good will or otherwise overlook racism or bigotry by the likes of Locke, Hume, Kant, Hegel, and Nietzsche. This is because analyses of racism and racist perspectives continue to become more subtle and penetrating, and progressives are now quite bold in discussing the racism of icons.

However, assessing the racism of revered philosophers is neither a simple matter of dis-missing "dead white men" nor retaining them as humans with foibles. Philosophical assess-ment should be balanced and fair and also without familial sentimentality. In a discipline that places a high intellectual value on knowledge of its own past, it is important to be able to accurately identify past racism without anachronism and determine how far responsi-bility extends over consequences that may not have been intended. This is not so much a question of whether our canonical ancestors were good people, but of how their philoso-phies were or were not distorted by chauvinism, arrogance, egotism, entitlement, or other disruptive forms of selfishness. This balanced and fair approach motivates the inquiries and assessments in this part. The examinations of philosophical content pertaining to race in the writings of John Locke, Immanuel Kant, David Hume, and Friedrich Nietzsche are judicious but unrestrained. The result is that the last contributor's inference of a broad racist consensus among modern political philosophers seems well supported.

John Locke was not fully part of the modern period—he is usually classified as "Early Modern"—but his England and wider world were in sufficient agitation toward future Enlightenment changes in colonialism, nationalism, science, and industry, for us to ask whether some of his thought about non-Europeans was racist. Common sense would seem to tell us that in order to be a racist, Locke would first require an idea of race or a belief that human beings are divided into races. The modern idea of race did not develop until after the late 1600s, when Locke produced his major work. But there is intellectual and humanist con-sensus that the ill will and contempt associated with modern racism has historical anteced-ents in clusters of ideas and attitudes that preceded modern ideas of race and were directed toward politically subordinated groups or those whose religions were suppressed. William Uzgalis examines Locke from within that consensus.

Uzgalis accepts Locke's practical involvement with oppressive colonial practices as a stock owner of slave trading companies and Secretary of the Lords Proprietors of the Carolinas, where slavery was constitutionally permitted. However, after a close examination of Locke's two notions of slavery, one legitimate and one illegitimate, Uzgalis finds no justification for either slavery or the oppression of Amerindians in Locke's political philosophy. Legitimate slavery for Locke was a form of captivity with forced labor imposed by the just and win-ning side of a war against the defeated; illegitimate slavery was an authoritarian deprivation of natural rights that Locke proposed representative government as a means to correct or avoid. Uzgalis reasons that Locke would have known that colonial slavery was a violation of the God-given natural rights that he otherwise explicated and upheld; he finds no textual evidence that Locke thought either Africans or Amerindians should be deprived of those rights or have illegitimate forms of slavery imposed on them. Uzgalis also shows how Locke could have defended colonial slavery by building on popular ideas of his colleagues and pre-decessors, but simply avoided that. Uzgalis thereby presents Locke as a political philosopher who rejected the doctrine of *might makes right*, but nonetheless lived out a contradiction between his political ideals and his economic and political actions.

Aaron Garrett and Silvia Sebastiani begin with textual evidence that David Hume thought there were human races and that nonwhites were inferior to whites. They note how the first two lines of an infamous footnote in Hume's "Of National Characters" from his *Essays, Moral, Political and Literary* explicitly make those points:

> I am apt to suspect the negroes to be naturally inferior to the whites. There scarcely ever was a civilized nation of that complexion, nor even any individual eminent either in action or speculation.

Garrett and Sebastiani note that Hume consistently insisted on a *natural* inferiority of blacks that set them apart from other races. He also believed that the difference between Europeans and Amerindians was as great as the difference between human beings and animals (and males and females, although that raises a host of other issues). A *polygenicist* who insisted on different origins for human races, Hume nevertheless refused to accept that geographical or climactic differences were the cause of cultural differences among human groups. This position, together with his rejection of slavery, rendered his ideology of white supremacy somewhat enigmatic, because he did not provide a convincing causal account of what he took to be racial difference.

Locke's actions and political philosophy were contradictory, and Hume was curiously silent about explaining what he thought were self-evident racial differences. In contrast to this gap and lack, Kant presents a more complicated plenum in relation to his ideas about race. Kant constructed a well-developed theory of racial difference, explicitly expressed contempt for nonwhites, and became famous for a moral theory that posited the intrinsic worth of every human being. Bernard Boxill seeks to resolve Kant's explicit racial contempt with his idea of universal intrinsic individual human worth.

Although Kant followed Hume in positing the existence of human races, unlike Hume, he was a *monogenicist*, believing that all members of the human species had common ancestral origins. Races for Kant were distinguished by traits that remained hereditary over generations. Kant studied the past of white European groups via the science of anthropology, but he reserved the study of nonwhites for geography. Although Kant achieved lasting fame for his work on ethics, metaphysics, and epistemology, most of his academic employment was based on his courses about race. Indeed, Kant is credited with having founded the science of anthropology that came to be the locus for studying non-European and nonwhite races (Eze 1997). At any rate, Kant believed that the influence of geography on members of the original human species who later dispersed resulted in irreversible racial traits. Boxill exhibits two characteristic passages from Kant's "Of the Different Races of Human Beings."

> [The] natural disposition of the Americans, betrays a half extinguished life power, [so that] one makes use of red slaves (Americans) in Surinam only for labors in the house because they are too weak for field labor, for which one needs Negroes. (Kant 2:438)
> The Negro, who is well suited to his climate, [is] strong, fleshy, supple, but who given the abundant provisions of his mother land, is lazy, soft and trifling. (Kant 2:438)

Boxill observes that these passages and a number like them, as well as Kant's acceptance of the possibility of white genocide of nonwhite peoples, are very disturbing for Kantians. He suggests that they can be reconciled with Kant's broader moral philosophy and the aim of eventual peace in his political science, by taking his use of teleology into account. According to Boxill, Kant's racial theory followed from his idea that human affairs were governed by an *unsociable sociality*—humans are drawn into mutual association but, once related, they contend to get their own ways. The result is that in the even broader vision of the common intergenerational human good, not all groups are likely to survive and the hierarchical view of race explains why some groups are less equipped for, and less worthy of, long-term survival.

Kant's view of race as Boxill interprets him resembles social Darwinism—the idea that survival and success in society depend on group talents and strengths. Nietzsche, by contrast, rejected evolutionary thought and developed a more normative notion of breeding, toward the goal of a European master race. Robert Bernasconi emphasizes the neglected contrast between Nietzsche's favorable attitude toward Jews and his antiblack racism, which included endorsement of slavery at a time when the majority in the educated European community were already abolitionists. Bernasconi notes that although Nietzsche did not often use the term "race" or rely on biology for racial differences, his reliance on spiritual and historical ideas of race was pernicious because of his Lamarkian belief that customs were physically hereditary. That is, in his insistence that "it is not in the least possible that a human being might *not* have the qualities and preferences of his parents and ancestors in his body," Nietzsche posited physical or biological mechanisms as media for cultural racial transmission. He could speak of the Germans as "the most monstrous mixing and blending of races," on the grounds of their mixed cultural heritage, but at the same time view them as the future of European excellence based on human breeding (*Zucht*) and the extinction of "bad races" (*Austerben*).

Building on his earlier work, Charles Mills presents a critical theory about white European oblivion of the human worth of nonwhites from Africa, Asia, and the Americas. It is a critical theory because it coherently explains both a history of actions of exploitation and destruction and its accompanying thought, in ways that would have been denied by actors and thinkers at that time. Mills has shown how the treatment of nonwhite Europeans and ideas about them implicitly constituted an agreement for the material benefit and elevated status of white European men. White European men implicitly subscribed to a racial contract among themselves, while explicitly subscribing to a social contract that presumed consent to government by those governed, presumably all humans. In his alternative social contract theory, Mills shows how the official social contract obscured both the domination of poor by rich among whites and the treatment of nonwhites as subhuman by whites.

Mills's insights, together with the essays here about Locke, Hume, Kant, and Nietzsche, afford us a better understanding of the coexistence of egalitarian humanism with hierarchical racism: egalitarian humanism was only for white male Europeans, so that all others, including white women, in failing to be eligible for such principles, were by implication rendered subhuman. It could be countered, however, that it was not the intention of egalitarian humanists to regard or treat nonwhite men and all women as subhuman, but that they simply did not care sufficiently about all human beings in any universal sense. However, the Enlightenment was not lacking in alternative voices on these issues, as we shall see in Part II regarding ideas about race from people of color, and in Part X about race and gender.

FURTHER READING

Bernasconi, Robert. (2014). "Silencing the Hottentots: Kolb's Pre-Racial Encounter with the Hottentots and Its Impact on Buffon, Kant, and Rousseau." *Graduate Faculty Philosophy Journal* 35 (1-2): 100–124.

Eze, Emmanuel Chukwude. (1997a). "The Color of Reason: The Idea of 'Race' in Kant's Antropology." In *Postcolonial African Philosophy: A Critical Reader*, edited by Emmanuel Chukwude Eze, 103–140. Cambridge, MA: Blackwell.

Eze, Emmanuel Chukwude, ed. (1997b). *Race and the Enlightenment: A Reader*. Cambridge, MA: Blackwell.

Popkin, Richard. (1977). "Hume's Racism." *Philosophical Forum* 9 (2-3): 211–226.

Schaub, Jean-Frédéric, and Silvia Sebastiani. (2014). "Between Genealogy and Physicality: A Historiographical Perspective on Race in the *Ancien Regime*." *Graduate Faculty Philosophy Journal* 35 (1-2): 23–52.

Zack, Naomi. (1996). *Bachelors of Science: Seventeenth Century Identity, Then and Now*, Philadelphia: Temple University Press.

Zack, Naomi. (2001). *Philosophy of Science and Race*. New York: Routledge.

CHAPTER 1

....

JOHN LOCKE, RACISM, SLAVERY, AND INDIAN LANDS

....

WILLIAM UZGALIS

ACCORDING to John Locke's most recent biographer, there is no consensus in the field about Locke's attitude toward colonial slavery (Woolhouse 2007, 101 and 187). On the one hand, Locke was involved in a variety of ways with slavery and the slave trade. Because of his involvement, he knew a great deal about these topics, probably as much as or more than any man in England. This strongly suggests to some that John Locke was a racist and his philosophical writings, particularly the *Second Treatise of Government*, where he sets forth an account of slavery, must have been intended to justify the slave trade and the institutions and practice of African American slavery and the seizure of Indian lands (Bernasconi and Mann 2005, 91; Farr 2008).

On the other hand, attempts to show that Locke is in fact trying to justify these things are open to serious criticism. The most serious of these objections is that the positions he takes about natural rights, natural law, just war, and slavery seem designed for a different purpose than justifying colonial slavery and slave trading and the seizure of Indian lands. It is widely recognized that one of Locke's explicit purposes in *Two Treatises of Government* was to refute the doctrine of Sir Robert Filmer's book *Patriarcha* concerning the divine right of kings and their right to rule by arbitrary absolute power. Filmer and his followers were apologists for the Stuart monarchs, Charles II and James II. In the *Second Treatise of Government*, Locke proposes to give a different account of the origin of government and political power in which might does not make right. It is this explicit aim that makes it difficult or impossible for him to effectively justify the institutions and practices of colonial slave trading, slavery, and the seizure of Indian lands because what makes these colonial crimes so morally abhorrent is precisely that they involve injustice and the use of force.

It has been admitted that Locke's account of slavery is a poor way to justify colonial practices, but that since Locke was a racist, that was the best he could do. I will point out that in the natural rights tradition of his day, he had the materials at hand to do a fine job of justifying these practices, but instead he gave arguments for rejecting all of them. I will also point out that Locke actually had two theories of slavery—a theory of legitimate slavery and its dark mirror image, a theory of illegitimate slavery. Recognizing that this second theory exists makes it even more difficult to interpret the *Second Treatise* account of slavery as justifying the practices of colonial conquest and slavery, for colonial slave trading and so forth required the use of force unjustly—which is the hallmark of illegitimate slavery for Locke. I will begin with the two theories because this makes it plain that Locke did intend to show that the Stuarts were attempting illegitimately to enslave the English people. Next, I will discuss the natural rights tradition and the materials that Locke could have used to justify slavery and the seizure of Indian lands. Finally, I will discuss the principal way in which it is claimed that Locke sought to evade applying his theories to Africans and Amerindians and offer a different account of how he was thinking about America.

Locke's Two Theories of Slavery in the *Second Treatise*

As noted, one important consideration that has largely gone unnoticed in the discussion of Locke and slavery is that Locke has two theories of slavery in the *Second Treatise of Government*. One is the theory of legitimate slavery expounded in Chapters 4 and 16 of the *Second Treatise*. The other is a theory of illegitimate slavery. Presumably, the theory of illegitimate slavery has largely been ignored in the debate over whether Locke is seeking to justify the institutions and practices of colonial slavery, because it is the legitimate theory that ought to do the justifying. But recognizing that Locke had a theory of illegitimate slavery tells us some important things about his intentions in writing about slavery at all, and so what shape the legitimate account took, and the constraints it put upon that account.

Locke begins Book II, Chapter 1 of the *Second Treatise of Government* by summarizing the points he made in the First Treatise against Sir Robert Filmer's arguments. These premises having been made out, the result, he says, is that "it is impossible for the rulers now on earth should make any benefit or derive any the least authority from that which is held to be the fountain of all power: *Adam's private dominion and paternal jurisdiction . . .* " (Locke 1690/1980, 6). What follows from this rejection of the divine right of kings is that

> He that will not give just occasion to think that all government in the world is the product only of force and violence, and that men live together by no other rules but that of beasts, where the strongest carries it, and so lay a foundation for that perpetual disorder and mischief, tumult, sedition and rebellion (things that the followers of that hypothesis [the divine right of kings] so loudly cry out against) must of necessity find another rise of government, another original of political power, and another way of designing and knowing the persons that have it, than what Sir Robert Filmer hath taught us. (Locke 1690/1980, 6)

In other words, Locke proposes to give an account of government in which might does not make right. He does this using his account of the state of nature, natural law, natural rights, and the state of war. One has the rights to one's own life, liberty, health, and property as means to pursue one's preservation and flourishing. The natural equality in which people find themselves in the state of nature leads to the law of nature: just as I would not have my rights to life, liberty, health, and property violated by others, so I will not violate theirs. To fail to abide by this law is to reduce oneself from the level of a rational human being to that of a beast—a creature that lives by the rule that the strongest carries it. Such a creature may be destroyed just as a wolf or a lion may. Both Locke's theories of slavery (legitimate and illegitimate) are not free standing, but are woven out of the materials of the first three chapters of the *Second Treatise*—those materials that are foundational to Locke's claim that he is producing a new rise of government, another original of political power and another way of designing and knowing the persons that have it.

The Lockean concept of war makes the connection between natural rights and natural law and slavery. One who has a steady intent on the life of an innocent victim puts himself in a state of war with that innocent victim and in doing so violates the law of nature. On Locke's account, such an aggressor ceases to be a rational human being or a person and so reduces himself to the level of a beast and can legitimately be killed or enslaved. It is not the color of his skin that makes him a subject of just punishment, but the nature of his actions. Hence, Locke's new design of persons makes being just and following the law of nature a condition for having the rights of a person. Locke makes it plain in Chapter 4, "Of Slavery" that engaging in an unjust war against an innocent victim and losing is the only way in which one can become a legitimate slave. The innocent victim, now the victor in the war, has the right to kill the unjust aggressor or to make use of him by enslaving him. Locke characterizes legitimate slavery as a continuation of the war between the just victor and the unjust aggressor (Locke 1690/1980).

For Locke, slavery (whether legitimate of illegitimate) requires the exercise of absolute, arbitrary power of the master over a slave. This means that the master may at his discretion kill the victim or engage in many kinds of arbitrary actions toward the slave. Locke's account of the limited nature of those to whom absolute power legitimately applies is in stark contrast with that of Sir Robert Filmer in *Patriarcha*, who sees the king as holding absolute power over a slave population.

As for the ending of legitimate slavery, while there is a complete ban on suicide, the unjust aggressor, now a slave, may bring about his own death at the hands of the victor should he find the conditions of his life intolerable. Slavery may also be ended by a contract for obedience by the slave and limitations on the harms the master may inflict on the slave. Thus, slavery ends at the same time as the exercise of absolute power. The conditions for becoming a legitimate slave are very narrow indeed. It is their very narrowness that makes it difficult or impossible for anyone to say that on Locke's account, the Stuart kings could legitimately enslave the population of England.

In Chapter 16, "Of Conquest" Locke sets constraints on what a just conqueror can do with respect to the unjust aggressors and their families and the other people who did not participate in the war. The only people who can be enslaved are the direct participants in the unjust war. The families and particularly the children of slaves are free and innocent and so cannot be enslaved. Nor can slaves be inherited. (James Farr [2008, 519, note 41] points out the implications of this for the purchase of slaves—that a purchaser would be in an even more remote relation to the "crime that deserves death" that one of the victor's relatives. So, if it is illegitimate for the one to inherit a slave, it is even more illegitimate to buy one.)

Furthermore, the just victor can only take as much property that belongs to the slave as is required for reparations for damage done during the war. And even this can be trumped by the needs of the aggressor's innocent family for survival. It is clear that many of these conditions mean that the institutions and practices of slave trading, slavery, and the seizure of Indian lands simply do not fit Locke's account of just conquest and legitimate slavery. What then is illegitimate slavery?

We may begin with remarks that Locke makes in the Preface to the *Second Treatise*. Twice he mentions slavery. At first he says that what remains of what he has written (the middle part of the *Second Treatise* having been lost) "are sufficient to establish the throne of our great restorer, our present King William; to make good his title, in the consent of the people . . . and to justify to the world the people of England, whose love of their just and natural rights, with their resolution to preserve them, saved the nation when it was on the very brink of slavery and ruin" (Locke 1690/1980, 5).

What this implies through its historical reference is that the Stuarts and James II, in particular, intended to enslave the nation and that James very nearly succeeded. Locke's remark about saving the country when it was on the brink of slavery and ruin clearly does not count as a case of forestalling legitimate enslaving. Locke's point is that kings who claim absolute power over their subjects are making the illegitimate claim to have the right to enslave their people—that is to take away all of their rights.

Locke's second remark about slavery in the Preface is equally negative about slavery. Speaking of Sir Robert Filmer's *Patriarcha*, Locke says: "The king and the body of the nation have so thoroughly confuted his Hypothesis that I suppose no body hereafter will have either the confidence to appear against our common safety, and be again an advocate for slavery; or the weakness to be deceived with contradictions dressed up in popular stile" (Locke 1690/ 1980, 5). We need to consider that Locke wrote the *First Treatise of Government* explicitly to counter the claims in Sir Robert Filmer's *Patriarcha* that kings have absolute power. In Locke's view not only were the Stuart monarchs attempting to enslave the nation, but their partisans were arguing that Kings by divine right have absolute power over their subjects and thus may legitimately violate the rights of their subjects to life, liberty, health, and property. Thus, according to Locke, the Stuarts were attempting to enslave the nation illegitimately, and their partisans were attempting to justify this. This is enough to show that Locke had a concept of illegitimate slavery and that he took the Stuarts to be attempting to enslave the nation illegitimately in this sense. What then is illegitimate slavery?

Illegitimate slavery is the dark mirror image of legitimate slavery. Suppose that the unjust aggressor wins the unjust war and now by force has the innocent victim in his power. The unjust aggressor is thereby in a position to violate all the natural rights of his innocent victims, but this is on the basis of force without justice. Because Locke's aim is to give a new rise to government and the people in it—in which might does not make right—it is plain that the fundamental difference between legitimate and illegitimate slavery is that in the one case absolute power over another person is a matter not just of superior force but of justice and the triumph of the innocent; while in the other case it is simply a result of superior force overcoming the innocent and just. Robert Bernasconi and Anika Mann suggest that arguments involving prisoners taken in just wars was a widely used tactic in the seventeenth and eighteenth centuries to justify chattel slavery. Did Locke, they ask, like many of his contemporaries, extend the argument beyond its limits? Or did he think that slavery did not need to be justified (Bernasconi and Mann 2005, 101)?

Once one has grasped that one of Locke's chief aims in the *Second Treatise* is to deny that the claims to absolute power on the part of rulers are legitimate, and that in fact they were attempting to use force to enslave the nation illegitimately, it becomes clear that the constraints that this puts on Locke's account of legitimate slavery make it extremely difficult, if not impossible, to use such a theory to justify the transatlantic slave trade and the institutions and practices of slavery in the colonies both at the time and later. It also becomes clear, if one knows the facts about the transatlantic slave trade and the institution and practices of colonial slavery, that they fit Locke's account of illegitimate slavery in the fundamental sense that they are the results of the unjust use of power to deprive people of their rights. Abraham Lincoln in his last debate with Stephen Douglas remarked: "No matter in what shape it comes, whether from the mouth of a king who seeks to bestride the people of his own nation and live by the fruit of their labor or as an apology from one race of men for enslaving another race, it is the same tyrannical principle." Thus, in holding that kings have no right to enslave their people, any attempt Locke made to loosen those constraints on legitimate slavery in the interest of justifying the institutions and practices of colonial slavery would have weakened his argument against the Stuarts. Still, Mann and Bernasconi remark that Locke was a racist and they add, "Racists often give bad arguments, it is the only kind they have" (Bernasconi and Mann 2005, 101). It is interesting therefore that we have some insight into the materials Locke had available for constructing his theories of slavery.

LOCKE AND THE NATURAL RIGHTS TRADITION ON SLAVERY

James Farr in his paper "Locke, Natural Law and New World Slavery" has pointed out that all the materials needed to justify the institutions and practices of the colonial slavery and the seizure of Indian lands were available to Locke in the natural rights and natural law tradition. Following Richard Tuck, Farr notes a whole series of authors who began with "states of natural freedom or premises about natural rights and duty (often) ended up justifying absolute power or just enslavement" (Farr 2008, 501). Many of these accounts would have served Locke had he wished to justify colonial slavery because many of them were crafted in part to do just that. Luis de Molina, for example, coming from a country deeply involved in the slave trade, applied the notion of voluntary slavery to blacks in the sixteenth century (Tuck 1981, 54). Farr notes that while Filmer is the one opponent Locke cited by name in Chapter 4, "Of Slavery," "Filmer, Grotius and his followers form a complex web for Locke" (Farr 2008, 501). Filmer held that people were naturally slaves, not naturally free—a view that Locke indignantly rejected. Farr focuses on the theory of Hugo Grotius, citing Richard Tuck's conclusion that "the most faithful Grotian theory available from the presses in the late seventeenth century was that of Locke" (Tuck 1981, 173). Hugo Grotius, perhaps the most influential writer on natural law and rights in the seventeenth century, was sufficiently ambiguous to lead the next generation of his followers to produce competing theories, one of which endorsed "slavery and absolutism and the other a defense of resistance and common property in extremis" (Tuck 1981, 80). Thus, as Farr remarks, had Locke wanted to justify the institutions and practices of colonial slavery:

> A simple endorsement of Grotius would have left in place the enslavement of non-combatants, women and children, the seizure of land, and especially the intergenerational institution of hereditary bondage. But again, Locke placed restrictions on all of these, the effect of which was to make new world slavery a glaring exception to his theory. (Farr 2008, 501)

One would come to the same conclusion Farr reached about Locke and Grotius by examining other authors in the natural law/natural rights tradition that he was familiar with. There were a whole series of writers who came before Grotius who held that one could voluntarily enslave oneself, including Gerson, Molina, and Suarez. Tuck notes about Suarez that he held that man has dominion over his own liberty and so drew the conclusion: "If voluntary slavery was possible for an individual, so it was for a whole people" (Tuck 1981, 56). After Grotius, Hobbes and Puffendorf also endorsed slavery. Whereas Locke rejected Hobbes, he knew and recommended Samuel Puffendorf's books, but not his account of slavery. Puffendorf held that there were degrees of slavery and so would not have assented to Locke's claim that, in effect, holding absolute power over someone is a necessary condition for slavery.

All this makes it plain that had Locke intended to justify slave trading and colonial slavery, he had a superabundance of materials at hand with which to do a fine job of it. Instead, he rejected them—all of them. If at this point one concedes that Locke's project was to give a new origin of government in which might does not make right, and that in particular this was aimed at giving an alternative to the doctrine of the divine right of kings, one may wonder whether this doctrine was intended to apply to America and Africa at all.

Given what we have discovered so far about what Locke aimed to do in the *Two Treatises of Government*, it might be doubted whether that account of a new rise of government and political power would apply to the effort to justify the institutions and practices of the slave trade, colonial slavery, and the seizure of Indian lands. Yet those who wish to maintain that Locke was trying to justify the institutions and practices of slavery and the seizure of Indian lands in the Americas (and Africa) point to numerous references to America that make it plain that Locke was thinking about America (Armitage 2004, 603–605; Arneil 1996, 2; Bernasconi and Mann 2005, 96, among others). They are certainly right about this. These critics, however, usually make an assumption that in thinking about America, Locke must have been thinking about justifying colonial slave practices, the seizure of Indian lands, and so forth (Armitage 2004, 603; Arneil 1996, 2; Bernasconi and Mann 2005, 95). For reasons noted earlier, this would have been extremely difficult. But there is another possibility. In thinking about America, Locke may have been thinking about the ways in which it illustrated some of the features of his account of the *state of nature*, which was the condition of mankind before the rise of government with genuine political power, without any intention of justifying colonial practices at all.

In Chapter 5, "Of Property" Locke makes it plain that Indians do have a right to the property of their labor when they gather berries and kill deer (Locke 1690/1980, 20). This strongly suggests that Indians had all the natural rights that Locke accorded to the rest of mankind. In *A Letter Concerning Toleration*, Locke engages in a thought experiment to illustrate the general claim that no persons ought to be deprived of their lands and lives because of their religion. This thought experiment involves Christians seeking to deprive Amerindians of their lands and killing them if they resist. In this thought experiment he makes it plain that Indians have a full compliment of natural and civil rights as long as they obey the law of nature, that is, as long as they do not violate the natural rights of others. Thus, their lands cannot be taken from them because they are not Christians (Locke 1991, 37–38). There is in this thought experiment a clear analogy between dissenters in England and the Amerindians. Thus, it is plain that Locke intended various aspects of his theories of natural rights and natural law to apply to Amerindians, and hence to human beings around the world. Here we might turn to the argument most persistently given to show that Locke did not hold that Indians had a right to their land so that it could be legitimately taken from them. Let us turn to the principal way in which scholars have argued that Locke proposed to evade the implications of his theories of natural law and natural rights so that Indian lands could be taken by European colonists. I call this argument, the argument from agricultural inefficiency.

FORFEITURE OF AMERINDIAN LAND BY THE ARGUMENT FROM AGRICULTURAL INEFFICIENCY

There are two versions of the argument from agricultural inefficiency and a corollary to both. The first is the natural law version and the second the wasteland version. David Armitage has pointed out that one can find this argument in the works of Sir Thomas More, published in *Utopia* in 1517 (Armitage 2004, 618–619). So it had certainly been deployed before Locke, and Armitage, like many others, thinks that Locke was giving this argument.

The natural law version of the argument from agricultural inefficiency claims that according to Locke's account of natural law, everyone is obliged to help the rest of mankind to survive, and that the Amerindians, being inefficient agriculturalists, failed to perform this obligation of natural law and so lost their right to their land. The corollary to that argument is that by opposing the Europeans who rightfully were taking their land, they committed a crime punishable by death or legitimate enslavement. This version of the argument is quite unconvincing once one examines the text. The only place in the *Second Treatise* where Locke talks about a natural law obligation to help the rest of mankind to survive and flourish is at the end of Section 2.6. Locke writes:

> Every one as he is *bound to preserve himself*, and not to quit his station willfully, so by the like reason when his own survival comes not in competition, ought he, as much as he can, *to preserve the rest of mankind*, and may not, unless to do justice on an offender, take away or impair the life, the liberty, health, limb, or goods of another. (Locke 1690/1980, 9)

Locke here makes it plain that one only has such an obligation to help the rest of mankind if one's own survival is not in question. Presumably this means one acquires such an obligation, only when one has the means to fulfill it. But the assumption made in the natural law version of the argument from agricultural inefficiency is that being subsistence farmers, the Indians could not help the rest of mankind, yet still had the obligation to do so. This being the case, they violated that obligation of natural law. But what the passage shows is that if they were subsistence farmers, then according to Locke they had no such obligation—and so could not be violators of the law of nature nor lose their rights to their land as a consequence.

I call the second version of the argument from agricultural inefficiency the *wasteland version*. In this version the Amerindians have lost the right to their agricultural land because they have farmed it less efficiently than Europeans would have farmed it. Thus, and this is the crucial step, it really is not agricultural land; it is wasteland and so can be legitimately taken by Europeans. Once again the corollary follows that if the Amerindians oppose Englishmen or other Europeans taking their land, they are committing a crime deserving of death and so can be legitimately killed or enslaved.

The crucial assumption in this version of the argument is that inefficiently used agricultural land is wasteland. But what Locke means by "wasteland" is land that no one is using (Locke 1690/1980, 26). It is true that agricultural land that has ceased to be used returns to being wasteland. But there is nowhere in Chapter 5, "Of Property" or elsewhere, so far as I know, any passage where Locke explicitly says that inefficiently used agricultural land is wasteland.

Note that this argument does not imply that Locke thought that there was no wasteland in America or land that no one was using. He was quite sure that there were vast tracks of wasteland. In this he was largely mistaken, and the mistake was consequential. He regarded the forest that stretched from the eastern seaboard to the Ohio valley as a commons (like the oceans) and did not recognize that the Amerindians regarded these regions as hunting grounds or that they labored to maintain these forests by, for example, burning underbrush. But his view was that there was enough and as good for both Amerindians and colonists. I dare say that no one at the time that Locke was writing, either colonial administrator, colonist, or Amerindian, would have conceived that a hundred and twenty years later, white Americans would be pouring over the mountains on their way to take the entire continent from the Amerindians.

Scholars have attempted to show that Locke held that land in America belonged to Englishmen or Europeans on the basis of a passage in Section 34 of Chapter 5, "Of Property," where Locke notes that God gave the earth to mankind in common but he did not intend it to remain that way for long. Rather, he intended to give it to "the industrious and rational (and labour was to be his title to it); not to the fancy of the quarrelsome and contentious" (Locke 1690/1980, 21). Some commentators have assumed that Locke meant that Europeans were "the industrious and rational" while the Amerindians were the "quarrelsome and contentious" and so have taken this passage to support the argument from agricultural inefficiency. Barbara Arneil argues that Locke took the Amerindians to be neither rational nor industrious (Arneil 1996, 149). But there are a number of passages in *An Essay Concerning Human Understanding* where Locke talks of the Indians he has met as rational and intelligent and writes both of ways in which European culture is superior to that of the Amerindians and vice versa (Locke 1690/1972, II, xiii, 20; II. xvi, 6; IV, xvii, 6). As for being industrious, the passage about the rational and industrious continues in such a way as to lead to the opposite conclusion from the one Arneil draws. Locke goes on from the sentence quoted earlier: "He that has as good left for his improvement, as was already taken up, need not complain, ought not to meddle with what was already improved by another's labour; if he did it is plain he desired the benefits of another's pains, which he had no right to . . . " (Locke 1690/1980, 22). The argument from agricultural inefficiency is clearly intended to justify the taking of Amerindian agricultural land by Europeans, not the taking of colonists' land by Indians. So it is plain from this passage that Locke holds that there is room enough in America for both Amerindians and English colonists, and insofar as the colonists wanted to take Indian lands under cultivation, they wanted to take what had already been improved by the cultivation of the Amerindians—something they had no right to. Thus, the passage, in fact, is a rejection of the wasteland version of the argument from agricultural inefficiency. If this were taken as an argument for taking wasteland simpliciter from the Amerindians, it would be pointless. For on Locke's view, wasteland belongs to no one and so was always available for appropriation.

Locke was most certainly a partisan of English agriculture practices, and he clearly thinks these vastly more efficient than the way in which the Amerindians use their land. Thus, he held that the same amount of industry produced vastly better results in England than in America. I would suggest that Locke's point about efficient land use is that it represents a later stage in the evolution of the state of nature, where money and commerce allow for larger landholding and a commercial agriculture and bring about the conflicts that make a civil government the best solution to those problems. Thus, Indian hunting and gathering and subsistence agriculture are part of a stage in the evolution of the state of nature that is perfectly reasonable under the conditions in which the Amerindians find themselves but cannot provide the kind of flourishing that comes with the advent of money and commerce. Still, there is no hint that Locke saw this difference as the basis for legitimately taking the agricultural lands of the Indians. There was no need to do so. There was, on his view, plenty of land for both.

CONCLUSION

Locke's extraordinary involvement with the slave trade, slavery, and Indian lands, as an owner of stocks in slave trading companies, as the valued Secretary of the Lords Proprietors of the Carolinas (who clearly had no problem with slavery), and as a government official and a colonial administrator, surely tarnishes his reputation as a great defender of liberty (Farr 2008, 497–499, for a list of Locke's posts and involvement with slavery). Indeed, given that he knew so much and was so deeply involved in these things, there is some reason to call him a racist. (For the claim that Locke was a racist, see Bernasconi and Mann 2004, 101–103). Naomi Zack, on the other hand, has made the point that the absence in the seventeenth century of the concept of race as it later came to be conceptualized might lead "us to a deeper understanding of the causes of African slavery at the time, namely religious narrowness, a strong desire for monetary gain, nationalism, and of course, the material ability to impose slavery on others" (Zack 1996, 179). Some of these motivations are ones that Locke plainly did not have. Others he may well have. The facts about his involvement with the slave trade and colonial government have led many scholars to conclude that in thinking about America, Locke must have intended to justify the institutions and practices that he knew about in more detail than probably anyone in England. Those who seek to find in his works a justification for those horrific colonial crimes are seeking to make him a consistent racist or Eurocentrist. But given the nature of the work, it cannot be done. Locke's explicit philosophical claims make the *Second Treatise of Government* a work of liberation and not a defense of colonial criminality. Those who want to speculate that Locke went beyond what he had written to somehow see it as a justification for those crimes can speculate as they will, but their claims are simply that—speculation. Locke was not involved in any contradiction between theory and practice in regard to the Amerindians. What he said and what he did fit well together. It is only in respect to slavery where there is a clear contradiction between the Lockean defense of rights and liberties and his involvement with slave trading and slavery. The contradiction is there and Locke was certainly not alone in being caught in that contradiction. But while we may want to call Locke a racist for his involvement with slavery to express our disgust at his actions, his philosophy is not racist—quite the contrary.

REFERENCES

Armitage, David. (2004). "John Locke, Carolina, and the Two Treatises of Government." *Political Theory* 32, 602–627.

Arneil, Barbara. (1996). *John Locke and Americas*. Oxford: Clarendon Press.

Bernasconi, Robert, and Anika Mann. (2005). "The Contradictions of Racism, Locke Slavery and the Two Treatises." In *Race and Racism in Modern Philosophy*, edited by Andrew Valls, 89–107. Ithaca, NY: Cornell University Press.

Farr, James. (2008). "Locke, Natural Law and New World Slavery." *Political Theory* 36 (4): 495–522.

Locke, John. (1972). *An Essay Concerning Human Understanding*, edited by Peter Nidditch. Oxford: Clarendon Press.

Locke, John. (1980). *Second Treatise of Government*, edited by C. B. Macpherson. Indianapolis: Hackett.

Locke, John. (1991). *A Letter Concerning Toleration in Focus*, edited by John Horton and Susan Mendus. London: Routledge.

Tuck, Richard. (1981). *Natural Rights Theories: Their Origin and Development*. Cambridge: Cambridge University Press.

Woolhouse, Roger. (2007). *Locke: A Biography*. Cambridge: Cambridge University Press.

Zack, Naomi. (1996). *Bachelors of Science: Seventeenth Century Identity Then and Now*. Philadelphia: Temple University Press.

CHAPTER 2

....

DAVID HUME ON RACE

....

AARON GARRETT AND SILVIA SEBASTIANI

In 1753, David Hume attached a note to his essay "Of National Characters," which had first appeared five years prior:

> I am apt to suspect the negroes, and in general all the other species of men (for there are four or five different kinds) to be naturally inferior to the whites. There never was a civilized nation of any other complexion than white, nor even any individual eminent either in action or speculation. No ingenious manufactures amongst them, no arts, no sciences. On the other hand, the most rude and barbarous of the whites, such as the ancient GERMAN the present TARTARS have still something eminent about them, in their valour, form of government, or some other particular. Such a uniform and constant difference could not happen, in so many countries and ages, if nature had not made an original distinction betwixt these breeds of men. Not to mention our colonies, there are NEGROE slaves dispersed all over EUROPE, of which none ever discovered any symptom of ingenuity; tho' low people, without education, will start up amongst us, and distinguish themselves in every profession. In JAMAICA, indeed, they talk of one negroe as a man of parts and learning; but 'tis likely he is admired for very slender accomplishments, like a parrot, who speaks a few words plainly. (Hume 1985, 629. All references to Hume to www.davidhume.org, except when noted; editorial abbreviations for Hume's works herein are at http://www.davidhume.org/texts/editorial.html#abbreviations)

The note remained in all editions of Hume's *Essays, Moral, Political and Literary* until the posthumous edition of 1777, where the first two lines were rewritten to restrict the inferior breeds of men to just those of African descent:

> I am apt to suspect the negroes to be naturally inferior to the whites. There scarcely ever was a civilized nation of that complexion, nor even any individual eminent either in action or speculation. (NC [M])

It is a very brief, but carefully worded, synoptic, and disquieting statement of Hume's views on race from the time that he wrote and published the *Enquiry Concerning the Principles of Morals* to his death. It is disturbing, both in its content and in the fact that it was the persistent, and one assumes considered, view of a philosopher who was and is an avatar of Enlightenment and who is often looked upon as a secular saint and a model of character. Still, should we care any more about what David Hume wrote and thought about race than about his views on many other subjects that are not central to what we understand as his importance as a philosopher? And if we do indeed care about Hume's thought about race, should we care about what Hume thought on these issues any more than we do about other philosophers? In this essay we will answer "Yes" to both these questions. We will attempt to contextualize Hume's views both in terms of Hume's oeuvre and also Scottish and European views on race and human differences.

UNIFORMITY AND VARIATION IN THE SCIENCES OF MAN

The note added to the "National Characters" has been the subject of a protracted and heated historiographic *querelle* ever since Richard Popkin commented on Hume's "shocking racism" in 1973 (Popkin 1973). He argued that the Enlightenment's "paradox," the "innocence" of which he aimed to unmask, was that from the very heart of the Enlightenment's universalistic conception of man sprang the nucleus of Western racist ideology. Even if Hume's note might be considered as a "casual addition," which held and expressed "the prejudices of the time," as Popkin stated a few years later, its legacy as "the rallying point of the polygenetic racists" was profound (Popkin 1977–1978, 1992). Since Popkin, there have been a growing number of discussions of Hume's views on race as well as the racial theories of Scottish philosophers, and of philosophers more generally (examples, from a rapidly increasing literature, include Gates 1985, 10–11; Immerwahr 1992; Gliozzi 1993; Palter 1995; Eze 2000, 2001; Garrett 2000, 2004; Zack 2002; Mankin 2009; Sebastiani 2013). There are a number of questions that arise in relation to this subliterature. How unique was Hume's view compared with the views of other British and Continental philosophers? And how connected was his brief discussion of race with his other, more extensively argued-for philosophical commitments?

It is unsurprising that Scottish philosophers of the eighteenth century were interested in race. Many of the best-known Scottish philosophers—Hume, Adam Smith, Adam Ferguson, Lord Kames, and so on—viewed themselves as putting philosophy and more particularly the moral sciences on a new and better footing by centering them on the sciences of man. As Hume noted in *A Treatise of Human, Nature*, these reforms of the moral sciences (which included most areas of philosophy other than natural philosophy, including epistemology, mind, moral philosophy proper, political philosophy, and aesthetics) paralleled Lord Bacon's reforms of natural philosophy (T Intro.7; SBN xvi–xvii). Bacon envisioned that the collection, comparison, and analysis of natural history and experiment would provide a proper footing for a new natural science (Bacon 2000, 222–232). The transformation of natural philosophy, the expansion of its scope and power, and the growth of its efficacy for human happiness all made good on this promissory note. In the "Introduction" to *A Treatise*, Hume claimed his own reform of the moral sciences would have if anything even greater results (T Intro.7; SBN xvi–xvii), and Hume and other Scottish philosophers sought to transform the moral sciences accordingly. Where Bacon drew on natural experiments and observations, the Scottish philosophers who were invested in the sciences of man (and who had different conceptions of it from Hume despite broad shared goals) were interested in a broad swath of observations of human experience, including travelers' reports and histories (Carey 2006). These could provide comparative "experiments" once suitably criticized and compared for discerning what were the stable and persistent features of human nature. Hume's discourse on equality and difference was based on the relationship between the "general" and the "local" uniformities of human nature—as Duncan Forbes has suggested (Forbes 1975, 116–117). His reflection on national characters was incorporated within the broader theory of the necessary connection between motives and human actions. As Hume announced in "A Dialogue," which was appended to the *Enquiry Concerning the Principles of Morals* and which appeared in the same year as the footnote in 1753 (Falkenstein and McArthur 2013):

> By tracing matters, replied I, a little higher, and examining the first principles, which each nation establishes, of blame or censure. The Rhine flows north, the Rhone south; yet both spring from the *same* mountain, and are also actuated, in their opposite directions, by the *same* principle of gravity. The different inclinations of the ground, on which they run, cause all the difference in their courses. (M Dial 26)

If the relationship between uniformity and diversity could be comparable to the opposite course of two rivers, the problem was then to discover what was mountain, what was gravity, and what was due to the differing inclinations of the ground. This could only be discerned through a wide-reaching cross-cultural and cross-historical comparison. Within this framework, diversity became, first of all, the product of history: over time, the characters of nations varied, together with the manners and virtues of individuals. Hume's diachronic approach reshaped the difference in culture and society as a historical distance. Given the uniformity of the principles of human nature, sympathy and imitation were the constant, universal causes that explained the variety of national characters together with accidental and historic factors.

Many Scottish philosophers such as Adam Smith, Adam Ferguson, and Lord Kames subscribed to a similar framework, although they put different weight on different causes. Even outliers like the Platonist Lord Monboddo, who held strong innatist and antiempiricist positions about mind and metaphysics, also utilized comparative analyses of "experiments" in some areas of philosophy. A problem for all was how to distinguish gravity from the peculiarities of the ground, how to distinguish ubiquitous properties of human nature from idiosyncratic customs or deformations of human nature. Hume's "A Dialogue" highlights this problem and points to a means for dealing with it. The work begins with a Swiftian fantasy where Hume's narrator describes a land called Fourli "whose inhabitants have ways of thinking, in many things, particularly in morals, diametrically opposite to ours" (M Dial 2; SBN 324). Hume then reveals that this "land" is in fact just a report of well-known historical actions in Ancient Greece and Rome. We fail to see how different their moral practices are from our own because of the lustre we add to their actions due to our admirations for Ancient Greeks and Romans. But the example points to the enormous diversity of human moral conventions and practices. But Hume argues, the differences are not as large as might be at first:

> The principles upon which men reason in morals are always the same; though the conclusions which they draw are often very different. That they all reason aright with regard to this subject, more than with regard to any other, it is not incumbent on any moralist to show. It is sufficient, that the original principles of censure or blame are uniform, and that erroneous conclusions can be corrected by sounder reasoning and a larger experience. (M Dial 36; SBN 335–336)

These principles are useful and agreeableness to self and others. Conventions for and against suicide, for example, may differ drastically, but the reasons for them are ultimately couched and justified in terms of this set of shared principles. "Particular accidents may, at one time, make any one of them flow with greater abundance than at another" (M Dial 42; SBN 337–338), so the free commerce of men and women which is agreeable may result in giving up some utility, presumably of knowing whose children are whose.

There are many causes of variations in customs, including geography, government, and the persistence of contingent customs. This last can give rise to what Hume calls an artificial life, when superstitious religious principles or (more rarely) extreme philosophical principles give rise to rigid rules of behavior that countervene or undermine natural sociability and agreeable and useful qualities. This is Hume's attempt to criticize some of the ways that we respond to, or fail to respond to, our shared moral principles in our ways of living. To extend Hume's analogy, artificial lives dam the flow of the Rhine and the Rhone, as opposed to letting them flow, to the detriment of both happiness and morality.

However, this analysis assumes that all of the peoples have roughly equal access to what is agreeable and useful. We would like to suggest that a puzzle for Hume was how to deal with peoples for whom the experimental report of their practices seems to have little evidence of either utility or agreeableness. One answer, suggested by the discussion of artificial lives, was that the persistent disutility and disagreeableness was due to the effect of rigid customs—for example, religious rules—that dammed up natural sociability and with it the natural affections that gave rise to and allowed recognition of the useful and agreeable. But what if there were social differences that were not amenable to this sort of explanation? This brings us to race. The word "race" had many meanings in eighteenth-century philosophy. It was often used interchangeably with "species" or "tribe," associated with "nation," while being still akin to "lineage" or "stock," and was central to natural historical discussions of animals and plants. Hume, and others, drew on the field of natural history when using the term to discuss human populations, although, like many others as well, he used the term in different senses in his works. We will focus on the natural historical sense as applied to human populations.

Natural Causes, Moral Causes, and Racial Differences

Hume originally published "Of National Characters" in 1748, five years before he added the footnote. The essay considers the source and nature of the stereotypes and generalizations about character that we ascribe to different national types as well as to the sexes, ages, and professions (soldier, priest): to employ again Forbes's apt definition, these were "local uniformities" into which the uniformity of human nature was split. There was a long tradition, which persisted through Montesquieu, Buffon, and beyond, that viewed human diversity as the consequence of the climatic difference. But Hume sought in "Of National Characters" to explain human difference solely in terms of what he termed *moral* causes:

> By *moral* causes, I mean all circumstances, which are fitted to work on the mind as motives or reasons, and which render a peculiar set of manners habitual to us. Of this kind are, the nature of the government, the revolutions of public affairs, the plenty or penury in which the people live, the situation of the nation with regard to its neighbours, and such like circumstances. By *physical* causes I mean those qualities of the air and climate, which are supposed to work

insensibly on the temper, by altering the tone and habit of the body, and giving a particular complexion, which, though reflection and reason may sometimes overcome it, will yet prevail among the generality of mankind, and have an influence on their manners. (NC 2)

For Hume both moral and physical causes can be natural causes, that is not supernatural, not artificial, and ubiquitous (T 3.1.2.7–10; SBN 473–475; EPM Note QQ; SBN 307). Many of the moral causes he was most interested in were artificial but not supernatural, ubiquitous in operation, but not in consequences (hence diversity). The distinction between moral and physical causes is both a distinction between the nature of the causes and between the consequences of the causes. Moral causes are human *circumstances*, whereas physical causes are physical *qualities* that act on humans but exist and act independently of them (air and climate). Hume placed "plenty or penury" among the moral causes, although it seems on the border between moral and physical causes (we will discuss "plenty or penury" further later on). The habits that moral causes give rise to are *changeable* and *local* (but the needs to which the habits minister are often universal), whereas physical causes give rise to *relatively permanent* and *universal* features of human populations.

Hume tried to show that moral causes were sufficient to explain the diversity of characters (NC 7) and to defuse counterexamples that seemed to need recourse to physical causes for explanation. Peoples who lived near the Arctic (e.g., the Lapps) and near the Equator (e.g., Africans) seemed to pose problems for the theory. The passage to which the footnote with which we began this essay is appended asserts that:

> If the characters of men depended on the air and climate, the degrees of heat and cold should naturally be expected to have a mighty influence; since nothing has a greater effect on all plants and irrational animals. And indeed there is some reason to think, that all the nations, which live beyond the polar circles or between the tropics, are inferior to the rest of the species, and are incapable of all the higher attainments of the human mind. The poverty and misery of the northern inhabitants of the globe, and the indolence of the southern, from their few necessities, may, perhaps, account for this remarkable difference, without our having recourse to *physical* causes. This however is certain, that the characters of nations are very promiscuous [i.e., disordered or random—AG & SS] in the temperate climates, and that almost all the general observations, which have been formed of the more southern or more northern people in these climates, are found to be uncertain and fallacious. (NC 20)

This passage corresponded almost word for word to the end of the essay "Of Commerce," published in *Political Discourses* in 1752, which rhetorically asked why none of the peoples in the tropics were capable of any art, of achieving public order in government, or of military discipline (Co 21). One reason given in both essays was indolence, linked to the fewer needs and the abundance of natural products in the tropical countries. In "Of National Characters," Hume attempted to show that widely held beliefs about the effects of physical causes on characters in extreme climes are fallacious, namely that "the northern regions have a greater inclination to strong liquors, and those in the southern to love and women." Southern peoples have equal inclinations to strong liquors, and "when ALEXANDER led the GREEKS into PERSIA, a still more southern climate, they multiplied their debauches of this kind, in imitation of the PERSIAN manners" (NC 32). Hume then goes on to add:

> But supposing the fact true, that nature, by physical principles, has regularly distributed these two passions, the one to the northern, the other to the southern regions; we can only infer, that

the climate may affect the grosser and more bodily organs of our frame; not that it can work upon those finer organs, on which the operations of the mind and understanding depend. (NC 34)

In other words, the climate affects the senses but not human minds and understanding, and it is the latter that is identified with whatever are the distinctive and uniting properties of human nature. But, given Hume's strict empiricism, we have a problem. Hume holds that ideas are derivative of the sense impressions and the passions (i.e., secondary impressions). How can we distinguish between a group of people that has permanently diminished operations of the mind and understanding due to the qualitative actions of climate and those who have consistently diminished content on which the mind and understanding operate due to moral causes?

Hume concludes the passage cited earlier with a suggestion of how to distinguish between these two possibilities: "The races of animals never degenerate when carefully tended; and horses, in particular, always show their blood in their shape, spirit, and swiftness: But a coxcomb may beget a philosopher; as a man of virtue may leave a worthless progeny" (NC 34). Physical causes (blood) give rise to characteristics of races ("shape, spirit, and swiftness"). Race characteristics remain present under good conditions; that is, the penury of circumstances cannot be a plausible explanation of mental or physical impairment. The problem remains though that it is difficult to make a judgment as to what is a race characteristic and what is an impermanent consequence of circumstances from observing peoples in impoverished climates because there is no recourse to good conditions.

Hume offers another consideration. If a quality does not persist through generations, then it is not a race characteristic. In the footnote Hume suggests further evidence as well as a test to show that some of the characteristics of peoples who live far north or south of Britain are racial. First, there is evidence that there is "no ingenious manufactures amongst them, no arts, no sciences." If we were dealing with a moral cause, we might expect that it could be overcome gradually when a coxcomb occasionally begets a philosopher. But this does not happen in the antipodes, whereas it has in other rude nations.

This evidence is unconvincing because it is evidence of the *lack* of a quality. Consistent and extreme action of the climate resulting in extreme penury might still stop even occasional progress in the arts and sciences from arising, but the lack of progress is fully explained by climate. Consequently Hume offers a second transplantation test:

> NEGROE slaves dispersed all over EUROPE, of which none ever discovered any symptom of ingenuity; tho' low people, without education, will start up amongst us, and distinguish themselves in every profession. In JAMAICA, indeed, they talk of one negroe as a man of parts and learning; but 'tis likely he is admired for very slender accomplishments, like a parrot, who speaks a few words plainly. (NC [M].1)

Hume is here contrasting a class distinction with a racial distinction. The distinction between low and high people is due to moral causes because low people will progress. But no "NEGROE slaves" will progress even when their circumstances are shifted and the impairments of climate (Africa or the Caribbean to Europe) and circumstances (slave to nonslave) are offset. Hume concludes that the characteristics that make for differences between whites and all the other species of men, and then just whites and blacks, are racial and not due to moral causes.

A question remains open: who are, aside from the Africans, the "four or five different kinds" or "species" that he mentioned in 1753–1754? In a passage of *An Enquiry Concerning the Principles of Morals,* Hume directly referred to the red-skinned (in Linnaeus's classification) Amerindians—isolated as a separate species in the course of over a century of polygenetic discourse (Gliozzi 1977; Popkin, 1987). Developing a reasoning ad absurdum intended to demonstrate that justice was an artificial, conventional, and social virtue relating to public utility, and not to any transcendental principle, Hume imagined the existence of a "species of creatures intermingled with men, which, though rational, were possessed of such inferior strength, both of body and mind, that they were incapable of all resistance, and could never, upon the highest provocation, make us feel the effects of their resentment" (SBN 190–191). Hume argued that their servile obedience and inability to resist meant that it would be impossible for such creatures to achieve the degree of equality required to establish a society. Men were tied to this different "rational species" by the capacity for compassion—the laws of humanity together with sympathy for natural virtues such as kindness—but not, strictly speaking, by any bond of justice (Moore 1976; Levy and Peart 2004). Due to such an unequal relationship, firmly established in nature, these beings would not possess any right or property.

The thought experiment from the *Enquiry* is extremely difficult to interpret, but it is clear that Hume sought to interrelate the matchless disparity that separated men from animals, males from females, and civilized Europeans from Amerindian savages (see Sebastiani 2013, 36–38, 120–123, 149–150). As a result, the immense historic superiority of the Europeans over the Amerindians, placed between the natural difference of humans to animals and men to women, was made into a natural distinction, and the American species was identified as the "other rational species."

CONTEXTS FOR HUME'S FOOTNOTE

The historical situation that Hume described was the reality of the colonies. But Hume's discourse on national characters had become intertwined with theoretical issues of the universal and particular rules of human nature: moral factors of differentiation, such as time, experience, and education, acted upon differential intellectual capacities and varied dominant passions from the outset. Prior to the sociological causes lay a natural difference between separate segments of humanity, seen as "local uniformities," which the note added in 1753–1754 to "Of National Characters" sought to make explicit. In this sense, we agree with Emmanuel Eze that Hume's footnote was "rooted both in Hume's epistemology and in his political thought" (Eze 2000, 53). How should we understand Hume's discussions of race in the context both of Scottish discussions of race and human diversity and those on the continent? What can this context tell us about Hume's decision, five years after the initial publication, to add this footnote and to make a point explicit that everywhere else remained implicit? And why did he decide to change his note and limit the target to the opposition between blacks and whites?

We will attempt to answer these questions by placing the note within the framework of the ongoing Enlightenment debates about national characters, political economy, and the natural history of humankind. Two contexts are particularly important. First, the references to blacks and to Amerindians appeared at roughly the same time, in the years immediately following the publication of the *Esprit des lois* and the beginning of Hume's correspondence with Montesquieu (Montesquieu 1950–1955, Vol. 3, 1230–1231, 1217–1222, 1255. See Mazza 2002, 27–32). Montesquieu argued very influentially that climatic differences were sufficient to explain the diversity of peoples, why some peoples tended naturally to servitude and indolence and others to liberty and progress (Montesquieu, 1950). Second, Buffon's *Histoire Naturelle* began to appear in 1749 as a scientific alternative to Linnaeus' *Systema Naturae*, providing a precise definition of "race" and "species."

The essay on "National Characters" and the first *Enquiry* both appeared in 1748, like the *Esprit des lois*. The second *Enquiry* came out in 1751: it contained both the reasoning on the different rational species and "A Dialogue," which, added in the second 1753 edition, was construed as a deliberate echo of Montesquieu's *Lettres persanes*, also including Usbeck as one of its characters(Montesquieu 1950–1955). The note on race was added in the second edition of "National Characters," published in 1753–1754 in the *Essays and Treatises on Several Subjects*. The query that Hume raised at the Select Society of Edinburgh in December 1754, "Whether the Difference of national characters be chiefly owing to the Nature of different Climates, or to moral and political causes" (Mossner 1980, 281–282), indicates his continuing engagement in a critical dialogue with Montesquieu.

In the meantime, Hume quarreled with Robert Wallace about population, which Wallace, reaffirming the current orthodoxy also supported by Montesquieu, believed to have been greater in the ancient nations (Wallace 1753). A strong point of Hume's argument, which he developed in the essay "Of the Populousness of Ancient Nations," published in *Political Discourses* in 1752, dealt with slavery; Hume viewed slavery as the greatest divide between ancients and modern economies, and the most consistent proof of the advantage of modernity. The civil development of Europe had created a humanity that could no longer accept the treatment of other peoples like animals, insofar as it accepted progressive mores emphasizing benevolence and sympathy. This did not alter, in Hume's reasoning on justice in the *Enquiry*, the natural inferiority of nonwhites based on moral difference, which explained the Europeans' exploitation of them. And contra Montesquieu, Hume's discussion of moral causes had shown not only how liberty changed from one climate to another, and from one age to another, but also how it had developed in a world of men historically and naturally separated by hierarchical divisions. The reform of the slave system in the free labor market, that would emerge fully in the final revision of his essay on "Populousness" in 1777, favored liberty and humanity, but it did not impinge upon the natural hierarchy of peoples.

Consequently, Hume rejected the prison of climate where Montesquieu had confined some peoples, but he evoked an undercurrent of natural diversity, which logically preceded any cultural or sociological explanation. This sided Hume with the supporters of polygenesis and brought him very close to Voltaire, who, while maintaining the primacy of moral causes, was the most active Enlightenment supporter of separate original creations for different races, which he positioned within the context of a larger historic analysis (Duchet 1971; Gliozzi 1979). The choice to use the terms "species," "kinds," "breeds," and "races" as synonyms also suggests proximity to Voltaire, and a rejection of Buffon's new definition of species as a "constant succession of individuals endowed with the power of reproduction," which unified humankind and took racial differentiations as mere exterior marks, impressed by the climate on the body (Buffon 1749–1789, Vol. 14, 311–312; Vol. 2, 10–11; Vol. 3, 530; Vol. 4, 385–386. See Sebastiani 2013). It was to respond to both Montesquieu and Buffon that Hume made an idea explicit that had been lurking in the 1748 edition of his essay. Hume had stated that though "temper and understanding" were to be considered as common ingredients of the whole humankind, "nature" had distributed them in different portions, conferring a specific "tincture to the national character" (NC 9; see Forbes 1975, 111). The addition of the footnote not only confirmed that physical causes, general or particular, had no impact in human affairs, but it specified the intervention of a moral cause of natural origin: the difference *ab origine* of rational capacities between the human races. As a result, the analysis of national characters as the consequence of culture and thereby changeable was limited to European peoples alone, stressed by reference to original polygenetic distinctions made by nature. It remains unclear, however, as Naomi Zack has pointed out, whether Hume used "species" meaning "races," or considered the nonwhite "breeds of men" so different from the white breed as to need different principles in order to account for their cultural development (Zack 2002, 13–18). In either case, Hume did not give empirical ground to his claim. Furthermore, his racial views seemed to contradict the assertion, put at the outset in "Of Populousness of Ancient Nations," that "there is no universal difference discernible in the human species" (PA 1).

"Learn, Mr. Hume . . . ": The Response by Contemporaries

How was the note taken up by Hume's contemporaries? And to what extent did Hume take these reactions into consideration? Because it is impossible to retrace the huge debate on this issue here, developing in Britain, across the Atlantic, and on the European continent—of which Kant's comment is just one well-known example (Zack 2002, 9–24)—we will discuss a few select responses that Hume directly engaged in the final years of his life. Hume's contemporary Lord Kames's massive and rambling *Sketches of the History of Man* (1774, expanded in 1778) can be read as a comprehensive commentary on Hume's note. Kames claimed, even more than Hume, that the internal disposition and nature of peoples were not explicable merely in terms of climate, culture, or education, but depended on a "constant and invariable," that is natural, "cause." Just as (contra Buffon) the phenotypically diverse breeds of dogs could not conceivably derive from a single shepherd-dog, so, too, there were men of different "species" or "kinds"—terms that, following Hume and Voltaire, Kames used synonymously. Within "each kind," individuals displayed a remarkable uniformity but also differed "no less remarkably from the individuals of every other kind." Echoing the terms of Hume's footnote, Kames concluded that "uniformity without variation is the offspring of nature, never of chance" (Kames 1778, Vol. 1, 74). Kames, like Hume, opposed slavery, but, notably and unlike Hume, his fragmentation of humanity did not necessarily imply the superiority of one species.

The publication, also in 1774, of the *History of Jamaica* by the planter Edward Long showed another possible political implication of Hume's racial footnote. Long quoted Hume in order to claim the inferiority of Africans and to defend slavery. Paraphrasing Hume, Long depicted blacks as the exemplification of a species "almost incapable of making any progress in civility or science" (Long 1774, Vol. 2, 353). Philanthropism, against which the planter Long reacted in the name of the prosperity of the British Empire, had found early expression in James Beattie's *An Essay on the Nature and Immutability of Truth*, published in 1770. Beattie considered "the superiority of white men over black" as an expression of Hume's skepticism, which he strongly refuted. Following a line of discussion developed at the Philosophical Society or Wise Club of Aberdeen, of which he was member, Beattie defended a uniform and universalist history of humankind. The Society, which met regularly between 1757 and 1773, consisted of Aberdeen university professors, including Thomas Reid, John Gregory, George Campbell, Alexander Gerard, and James Dunbar, who engaged in a heated debate about Hume's philosophy (see Ulman 1990; Conrad 1987). Hume was also brought to the bar by the Wise Club for his footnote. The key question (n. 96), posed by Beattie on March 22 and May 10, 1768, concerned the problem of the supposed European superiority over the rest of the world, which prompted the idea that Europe was populated by a distinct species. Question 96 read "Whether that superiority of understanding, by which the inhabitants of Europe and of the nations immediately adjoining imagine themselves to be distinguished, may not easily be accounted for, without supposing the rest of mankind of an inferior species?" As the manuscript shows, the crucial concern for the members of the Wise Club was to unmask the social and cultural dangers of polygenist hypotheses. The answer they provided was a full condemnation of Hume: "Learn, Mr. Hume, to prize the blessings of Liberty and Education, for I will venture to assure you that had you been born and bred a slave, your Genius, whatever you may think of it, would never have been heard of" (AUL, Ms 540, item no. 20, fol. 14r. See Sebastiani 2013, ch. 4). Such a criticism, which contributed to the formation of an antislavery movement in Aberdeen, led to the defense of the unity of humankind on the basis of a strong emphasis on environmental and social circumstances.

Parallel to this Scottish controversy, in continental Europe a general shift took place toward the study of physical man in natural history in the 1770s (Moravia 1970). This deep reconfiguration of the debate pushed Hume to modify his assertion about the existence of four or five different species in the note. The substitution of "never" with "scarcely ever" was perhaps a sign that Hume was willing to acknowledge the possibility that there had existed forms of civilization even among blacks (Palter 1995). This has sometimes been interpreted as a concession to Beattie and the members of the Wise Club, as John Immerwahr does (Immerwahr 1992, but see Garrett 2000). Hume, though, continued to insist on, and even reinforced, the natural inferiority of blacks. His revision of the note converged with the clear separation of the fate of blacks from that of other "species," especially the Amerindians, which Beattie, by contrast, had put together in order to demonstrate their equal and universal potential for civil development (Beattie 1770, 479–482).

Once the reference to other species was dropped, blacks remained isolated in their lack of spiritual and material development. The highly disparaging passage comparing the cases of educated persons of African descent, such as Francis Williams or Philip Quaque, to parrots, also remained unchanged, whereas Beattie had referred to them as proof of the intellectual capacity of blacks. If, then, in 1777 Hume abstained from enumerating the different humanities, in the overall economy of the note, the response to Beattie's criticisms was essentially negative. Maintaining the thesis of an original and natural distinction between diverse "breeds of men," the polygenetic inclination of Hume's reasoning remained implicit, in line with the criticism of climate theories in the whole essay on "National Characters."

However, polygenesis and the ideology of slavery were not necessarily related, as Beattie had made them appear. But the criticism of slavery by a polygenist like Hume followed another line. Rather than being based on the notion of the original equality of humankind, as attested by the Christian paradigm, it presumed the existence of a natural hierarchy of capacities among peoples. Moving beyond slavery was the direct result of the refinement of European morality, and therefore of a historical process, not the voluntary affirmation of an established and eternally valid principle.

CONCLUSION

From this excursus, two points emerge as crucial. First, the note to "Of National Characters" cannot be considered philosophically insignificant insofar as it is connected with Hume's central ideas about moral and natural causes. In addition to drawing on an already existing essay, Hume's maintenance of the note through all of the lifetime editions of his *Essays*, and careful revisions—despite convincing criticisms—strongly suggest that the ideas it expressed mattered to Hume. Second, it is not possible to isolate Hume's racial observations from the ongoing debate about national characters, the natural history of humankind, and political economy, which was at the heart of the European Enlightenment. One thing this debate shows us is that Hume's ideas about race were not shared by many of his less philosophically notable contemporaries.

There is a tendency when dealing with important philosophers to ignore or sideline their beliefs when we find them repellent and to trumpet them when they correspond to beliefs that we hold to be correct. In the former case we hold them to be unphilosophical additions and in the latter philosophical consequences of well-formed views. This makes for bad apologist history and bad philosophy. For this reason alone, it is important to highlight the cases when undeniably great philosophers held considered beliefs that we hold to be morally repugnant and which they thought followed from what we hold to be some of their important philosophical achievements. Hume's case is by no means unique. It is also important to recognize that these positions often have an afterlife due to the esteem in which these figures are rightly held.

REFERENCES

Bacon, Francis. (2000). *The New Organon*. Eds. Lisa Jardine and Michael Silverthorne. Cambridge: Cambridge University Press.

Beattie, James. (1770). *An Essay on the Nature and Immutability of Truth; In Opposition to Sophistry and Skepticism*. Edinburgh: Kincaid and Bell.

Buffon, Georges-Louis L. (1749–1789). *Histoire naturelle générale et particulière*. 36 vols. Paris: Imprimerie Royale.

Carey, Daniel. (2006). *Locke, Shaftesbury, and Hutcheson: Contesting Diversity in the Enlightenment and Beyond*. Cambridge: Cambridge University Press.

Conrad, Stephen A. (1987). *Citizenship and Common Sense: The Problem of Authority in the Social Background and Social Philosophy of the Wise Club of Aberdeen*. New York: Garland Publishing.

Duchet, Michelle. [1971] (1995). *Anthropologie et histoire au siècle des Lumières*. Paris: Albin Michel.

Eze, Emmanuel C. (2000). "Hume, Race, and Human Nature." *Journal of the History of Ideas* 61: 691–698.

Eze, Emmanuel C. (2001). "Hume, Race, and Reason." In *Achieving Our Humanity: The Idea of the Postracial Future*, 51–76. New York and London: Routledge.

Hume, David. (1758/2013). "Introduction." In *Essays and Treatises on Philosophical Subjects*, edited by Falkenstein, Lorne, and Neil McArthur, 15–40. Calgary: Broadview.

Forbes, Duncan. (1975). *Hume's Philosophical Politics*. Cambridge: Cambridge University Press.

Garrett, Aaron. (2000). "Hume's Revised Racism Revisited." *Hume Studies* 26: 171–177.

Garrett, Aaron. (2004). "Hume's 'Original Difference': Race, National Character and the Human Sciences." *Eighteenth-Century Thought* 2: 127–152.

Gates, Henry Louis. (1985). "Writing 'Race' and the Difference It Makes." In *Race, Writing, and Difference*, edited by Henry Louis Gates and Kwame Anthony Appiah, 1–20. Chicago: University of Chicago Press.

Gliozzi, Giuliano. (1977). *Adamo e il Nuovo Mondo. La nascita dell'antropologia come ideologia coloniale: dalle genealogie alle teorie razziali 1500–1700*. Florence: Sansoni.

Gliozzi, Giuliano. (1979). "Poligenismo e razzismo agli albori del secolo dei lumi." *Rivista di Filosofia* 70: 1–31.

Gliozzi, Giuliano. (1993). "L'insormontabile natura: clima, razza, progresso." In *Differenze e uguaglianza nella cultura europea moderna: Scritti (1966–1991)*, edited by Anna Strumia, 307–340. Naples: Vivarium.

Hume, David. [1742/1777] (1985). *Essays, Moral, Political and Literary*. Edited by Eugene Miller. Indianapolis: Liberty Fund.

Immerwahr, John. (1992). "Hume's Revised Racism." *Journal of the History of Ideas* 53: 481–486.

Kames, Lord (Henry Home). (1778). *Sketches of the History of Man*. 4 vols. 2nd ed. Edinburgh: W. Creech; London: W. Strahan, T. Cadell.

Levy, David M. and Sandra J. Peart. (2004). "Sympathy and Approbation in Hume and Smith: A Solution to the Other Rational Species Problem." *Economics and Philosophy* 20: 331–349.

Long, Edward. (1774). *The History of Jamaica, or, General Survey of the Ancient and Modern State of That Island. With Reflections on Its Situation, Settlements, Inhabitants, Climate, Products, Commerce, Laws, and Government*. 3 vols. London: T. Lowndes.

Mankin, Robert. (2009). "Hume et les races humaines." *Corpus, revue de philosophie* 57: 75–99.

Mazza, Emilio. (2002). *Falsi e cortesi. Pregiudizi, stereotipi e caratteri nazionali in Montesquieu, Hume e Algarotti*. Milan: Hoepli.

Montesquieu, Charles–Louis de Secondat. (1950). "De l'esprit des lois (1748)." In *Œuvres Complètes de Montesquieu*, edited by André Masson, Vol. 1. Paris: Nagel. Also available as edited by Paul Janet, at Project Gutenberg, Release Date: December 20, 2008 [EBook #27573] http://www.gutenberg.org/cache/epub/27573/pg27573.txt.

Montesquieu, Charles–Louis de Secondat. (1950–1955). "Correspondence." In *Œuvres Complètes de Montesquieu*, edited by André Masson. 3 vols. Paris: Nagel. Also available as: Lettres Persanes Par Montesquieu, Tome I, edited by André Lefèvre, Release Date: October 16, 2009 [EBook #30268], https://www.gutenberg.org/files/30268/30268-h/30268-h.htm; and Lettres Persanes Par Montesquieu, Tome II, Release Date: October 12, 2010 [EBook #33856], https://www.gutenberg.org/files/33856/33856-h/33856-h.htm.

Moore, James. (1976). "Hume's Theory of Justice and Property." *Political Studies* 24: 103–119.

Mossner, Ernest C. (1980). *The Life of David Hume*. 2nd ed. Oxford: Clarendon Press.

Moravia, Sergio. (1970) *La scienza dell'uomo nel '700*. Bari, Italy: Laterza.

Palter, Robert. (1995). "Hume and Prejudice." *Hume Studies* 21: 3–23.

Popkin, Richard H. (1973). "The Philosophical Basis of Modern Racism." In *Racism in the Eighteenth Century*, edited by Harold E. Pagliaro, 245–262. Cleveland, OH: Case Western Reserve University Press.

Popkin, Richard H. (1977–1978). "Hume's Racism." *Philosophical Forum* 9 (2–3): 211–226 (also published in *The High Road to Pyrrhonism*, edited by Richard A. Watson and James E. Force, 251–266. San Diego: Austin Hill Press.).

Popkin, Richard H. (1987). *Isaac La Peyrère (1596–1676). His Life, Work and Influence*. Leiden–New York: E. J. Brill.

Popkin, Richard H. (1992). "Hume's Racism Reconsidered." In *The Third Force in Seventeenth-Century Thought*, 64–75. Leiden–New York: E. J. Brill.

Sebastiani, Silvia. (2013). *The Scottish Enlightenment. Race, Gender and the Limits of Progress*. New York: Palgrave-Macmillan.

Ulman, H. Lewis. (1990). *The Minutes of the Aberdeen Philosophical Society 1758–1773*. Aberdeen, Scotland: Aberdeen University Press.

Wallace, Robert. (1753). *A Dissertation on the Numbers of the Mankind in Ancient and Modern Times: In Which the Superior Popolousness of Antiquity is Maintained. With an Appendix Containing Additional Observations on the Same Subject and Some Remarks on Mr. Hume's Political Discourse, Of the Popolousness of Ancient Nations*. Edinburgh: G. Hamilton and J. Balfour.

Zack, Naomi. (2002). *Philosophy of Science and Race*. New York: Routledge.

CHAPTER 3

....

KANTIAN RACISM AND KANTIAN TELEOLOGY

....

BERNARD BOXILL

IMMANUEL Kant played a leading role in the construction of a scientific concept of race, argued that the white race was superior to the other races, and was contemptuous of the black and Native American races and indifferent to their mistreatment. These views are especially troubling because they appear to contradict his famous principle of universal morality, that every human being "exists as an end in itself and not merely as a means to be arbitrarily used by this or that will" (Kant 1785, 4:428).

Most Kantians ignore Kant's racial views or claim that they have nothing to do with his philosophy; and a few critics argue that they showed that he never meant his moral principles to apply to nonwhites. In 2007 Pauline Kleingeld added an interesting twist to the debate in her essay "Kant's Second Thoughts on Race." She conceded Kant's views on race were "appalling" and contradicted his universalist moral principles, but she argued that he had "changed and improved" these views sometime during the mid-1790s when he began for the first time to condemn colonialism and slavery (Kleingeld 2007, 575, 584, 585.) I am unconvinced by her argument and contend that Kant's racial views were an inference from his teleological theory of history and have little to do with colonialism and slavery. I proceed as follows: In the first section I summarize Kant's contributions to the subject of race, his negative views of the nonwhite races, and his callous indifference to their mistreatment. In the second section I rebut Kleingeld's arguments that Kant changed his views about the races in the mid-1790s. In the third section I present my argument that his teleological philosophy of history led him to his racial views, concluding that these views are an integral part of his larger philosophy.

KANT ON RACE

....

Kant's three articles on race: "Of the Different Races of Human Beings," "Determination of the Concept of a Human Race," and "On the Use of Teleological Principles in Philosophy" were published respectively in 1775, 1785, and 1788. Also relevant are his *Review of J. G. Herder's Ideas for the Philosophy of the History of Humanity* and his writings on anthropology and geography.

Kant defended the monogenetic theory that the races are all descended from an original "stem species," which began in one part of the world. The different races appeared when members of that original stem species migrated to different parts of the world with different climates, which triggered their predispositions to produce the physical features they needed to survive in their new environments. In this way human beings came to have often strikingly different physical features. For Kant the most important of these differences was skin color. There are four races, white, black, red, and yellow (Kant 1775, 2:432).

On Kant's account, once climate and environment trigger human predispositions to produce the different racial features of the races the process cannot be reversed. This view explained why the physical characteristics of a race, skin color, for example, do not change when a race moves to a new environment. Thus, Africans' black skin is fixed and inevitably inherited. They are members of the same species as whites and can therefore interbreed and have fertile offspring with them, but the brown skin of the offspring shows that the racial characteristics of each parent are infallibly inherited.

Kant described the races in terms of their physical differences, but he usually went on to add that they were also distinguished by their unequal mental and moral characteristics with whites having the best such characteristics and the black and red or American races the worst. Here is a sampling of his comments: From "Observations on the Feeling of the Beautiful and Sublime":

> The Negroes of Africa have by nature no feeling that rises above the ridiculous. Mr. Hume challenges anyone to adduce a single example where a Negro has demonstrated talents, ... the "differences between" the white and black races "seems to be just as great with regard to the capacities of mind as it is with respect to color. (Kant 2:253)

From "Of the Different Races of Human Beings":

> [The] "natural disposition of the Americans, ... betrays a half extinguished life power, [so that] one makes use of red slaves (Americans) in Surinam only for labors in the house because they are too weak for field labor, for which one needs Negroes." (Kant 2:438)

And:

> The Negro, who is well suited to his climate, [is] strong, fleshy, supple, but who given the abundant provisions of his mother land, is lazy, soft and trifling." (Kant 2:438)

From "On the Use of Teleological Principles in Philosophy":

> [This race, the Native Americans], is too weak for hard labor, too indifferent for industry and incapable of any culture—although there is enough of it as example and encouragement nearby—ranks still far below even the Negro, who stands on the lowest of all the other steps that we have named as differences of the races. (Kant: 8:176)

From "Physical Geography":

> The Moors like all inhabitants of the hot zones have a thick skin; when one disciplines them one cannot hit them with sticks but rather whip with split canes, so that the blood finds a way out and does not suppurate under the skin. Humanity is at its greatest perfection in the race of the whites. The yellow Indians do have a meager talent. The Negroes are far below them and at the lowest point are a part of the American peoples." (Eze 1995, 61, 63)

KANT'S ALLEGED SECOND THOUGHTS ON RACE

Kleingeld objected to Charles Mills's contention, that Kant's racial views show that he made "whiteness a prerequisite for full personhood," and that his great egalitarian principle requiring equal respect for all persons was meant to apply to whites only (Mills 2005, 169). She insisted that Kant's racial views allowed that nonwhites were fully human, but she conceded that there was a "genuine contradiction" between Kant's universalist moral principles and his views about nonwhites, though he changed these views after the mid-1790s (Kleingeld 2008). I take her to mean that before the mid-1790s Kant denied that his egalitarian principles applied to the red and black races and consequently believed that their enslavement was permissible. And that after the mid-1790s when he started strongly and famously condemning colonialism and slavery that he must have come to believe that the red and black races were qualified for receiving the protection of his egalitarian moral principles.

This argument is inconclusive. Kant started condemning colonialism and slavery only after the mid-1790s, but his racial views might have required him to do so before that date. Kleingeld provides no evidence that before the mid-1790s Kant ever said or implied that colonialism and black slavery were permissible. He failed to condemn them before that date, and she provides many examples of his callousness in speaking about slavery, for example, his claim that in the tropics blacks make better slaves for outdoor work than reds, but it does not follow that he believed that enslaving blacks was permissible. The claim in question states a fact, that enslaving blacks is more profitable than enslaving reds, but does not imply that enslaving either of them is permissible. Similarly, Kant's claim that "The Mandinka are the most desirable among all Negroes because they are the most hardworking ones. They are the ones that one prefers to seek for slaves, because these can tolerate labour in the greatest heat that no human being can endure," is only a statement of fact about which black people are most profitably enslaved and not a claim that they are rightfully enslaved (Kleingeld 2014, 47). Indeed, Kleingeld's comment that Kant discusses slavery in a "very matter of fact way, making no hint" of criticizing it, practically concedes that the passages she cites do not show that Kant thought that black slavery was permissible. Kant *should* have condemned colonialism and black slavery before 1795 as loudly and strongly as he condemned it after 1795, and his failure to do so was a grievous failing, but it does not follow that before 1795 he believed that enslaving black people was permissible.

Notice next that Kleingeld like many others involved in the debate over Kant's views on race casually and repeatedly refers to Kant's "racial hierarchy" (Kleingeld 2012). If they are justified in doing so, then conceivably Kant believed that colonialism and black slavery were permissible; in a hierarchy those highly ranked have authority over those ranked lower. But as far as I can tell, Kleingeld never cites a passage in which Kant uses the term "racial hierarchy." He did rank the races, claiming that the white race ranked over the nonwhite races in intelligence, inventiveness, resourcefulness, and talent, but a ranking is not necessarily a hierarchy, and being more intelligent than another does not mean that one has any authority over him. The founders of egalitarian theory insisted on this. It is absolutely clear in Locke, and even more so in Thomas Jefferson. Although Jefferson certainly said that Negroes were less intelligent than whites, he expressly denied that this justified their enslavement, scoffing at the very idea that it did, on the ground that it implied absurdly that Sir Isaac Newton could justifiably enslave the rest of us (Jefferson 2010, 314).

If these comments are sound, then although Kant's racial views before the 1790s are offensive and false, we cannot say that he meant them to justify colonialism and black slavery or that he had to change them after the mid-1790s when he started to condemn colonialism and slavery. Why then did Kant make his offensive and ill-considered claims about the red and the black races before the mid-1790s? In the next section I argue that he was led to make them because of his teleological theory of history.

KANTIAN TELEOLOGY IN HISTORY

As far as I can tell, philosophers have not tried to explain how or why Kant arrived at his racial views. It was not as if everyone said that black and red people were stupid and lazy. Many people said the opposite. Scientific curiosity might have motivated Kant's interest in race, but it cannot account for his views about the stupidity of the red and black races unless it led him to facts that infallibly led to those views. But there were no such facts. Some of the travel literature and the books on black slavery painted a dismal picture of blacks and Native Americans, and Kant is reported to have been an avid reader of that literature. But the travelogues of Kant's day were like today's tabloids. No reasonable person took them seriously. Rousseau, who Kant is said to have read carefully, had pointed out the many reasons for being skeptical of them (Rousseau 1990, 128). And the reasons for being skeptical of what the advocates of slavery said about slavery are obvious. Moreover, Kant's principle of respect for human beings should have induced him to closely examine the evidence for blacks and red stupidity, in order to see how it might have been misinterpreted and showed normal human intelligence rather than stupidity. But even Jefferson showed a greater respect for black humanity than Kant did, making at least a show of recoiling from a confident claim that blacks were congenitally stupid (Jefferson 1982, 142). But Kant never hesitated, plunging ahead hand in hand with the rabid racists, and repeating and even adding to the lies they were spreading. What could have driven the great philosopher to such madness?

The usual explanations of how people become racists do not work for Kant. Sometimes racists hold their views in order to try to justify the unjust advantages they enjoy at the expense of blacks, but Kant did not appear to profit from slavery, and in any case, as we have seen, his racial views did not justify black slavery. The only thing that could have induced Kant to hold his appalling racial views—against every reasonable and decent principle or feeling—was one of his own philosophical theories, something that he had invented, labored on, was proud of, and was convinced was true. I argue that his teleological theory of history was that theory.

Let us begin with a brief summary of the essentials of Kant's philosophy of history. The main relevant text is his *Idea for a Universal History with a Cosmopolitan Aim*, 1784; supplemented by *Toward Perpetual Peace*, 1795; *Conjectural Beginnings of Human History*, 1786; *Theory and Practice*, 1793; and *The Critique of Judgement*, 1790. Kant begins *Idea for a Universal History with a Cosmopolitan Aim* with the claim that although human history cannot proceed by appealing to the causes of human actions since these causes are too "deeply concealed," it can nevertheless, if it "considers" human actions "in the large," allow us to "hope" that the "whole species can be recognized as a steadily progressing though slow development of its original predispositions" (Kant 1784, 8:17). And by the eighth of the nine proposition of the essay that claim had been expanded to say that we "can regard the history of the human species in the large as the completion of a hidden plan of nature to bring about an inwardly and to this end, also an externally perfect state constitution, as the only condition to which it can fully develop all its predispositions in humanity" (Kant 1784, 8:27).

When Kant was composing his theories about race, the white race had already conquered many of the nonwhite races and driven one of them to near extinction. Millions of Amerindians lived in the West Indies when the Spanish arrived there in 1492; three centuries later they had disappeared. Kant reports that a few continued to exist in only one small island, St. Vincent (Kleingeld 2014, 51). And it was already predictable that the genocide of the Amerindians in North America, already well under way, would be completed in a century or two. Significantly, Kant ranked Amerindians lower than any other race.

Africans, the race Kant ranked just above Amerindians, appeared likely to last longer than the Amerindians, perhaps because they were useful as slaves. Kant reported that in St. Domingo (now Haiti) there were 350,000 negroes and in Jamaica 200,000, with varying numbers in the other islands (Kleingeld 2014, 51). But the planters always wanted more because they found it more profitable to work the slaves to death and get new batches of slaves from Africa than to keep the slaves they already had alive. In *Physical Geography* Kant estimated that "Europeans carry away each year between 60,000 and 80,000 Negroes to America" (Eze 1997, 59).

If the slaughter continued and ended in genocide, two of the nonwhite races, the red and the black, the very ones Kant put at the bottom of his ranking of the races, would go extinct while the white race continued to thrive. Then, if nature's plan was not already completed, it would have to be completed by the white race. Consequently, the red and black races could not have been necessary for the full and complete development of all human predispositions. Assuming Kant drew that obvious inference, and reasonably supposed that races unnecessary for the full and complete development of all human predispositions had to be lazy and stupid, he would also reasonably conclude that the red and black races were lazy and stupid. In other words, his teleological theory and the looming extinction of the red and black races led him to his racial theory.

It may be objected that even if Kant allowed that the red and black races had to die for the sake of nature's plan while the white race survived to complete it, that it does not follow that he thought the red and black races inferior to the white race, for he allowed that older generations die for the sake of the rational improvement of later generations but did not think that they were inferior to later generations. But when a white generation dies, the characteristics that their environment triggered their predispositions to give them live on in their offspring and in the ensuing generations. Consequently, their deaths are consistent with the necessity of their racial characteristics for the continuing development of human predispositions. But when a race goes extinct, the racial characteristics that their environment triggered their predispositions to give them cease to exist. Consequently, these characteristics cannot have been necessary for the continuing development of all human predispositions.

Kleingeld cites Kant's claims that rationality belongs essentially to the human species and that "Properties that belong essentially to the species itself, and thus are common to all human beings, as such, are indeed unfailingly hereditary "to argue that all human races are equally rational" (Kant, "Determination" 8:99). To handle the difficulty that Kant says that rationality improves from generation to generation, she argues that the improvement is the result of a "learning process," so that the rational faculties remain the same in every generation (Kleingeld 1999, 66, 65). Assuming that a capacity for moral and mental development depends on the capacity for rational development, every race would then have an equal capacity to contribute to the development of human predispositions. But this attempt to exonerate Kant fails. In Kant's day it was widely believed that people who lived in hot climates were lazy, and that this laziness was learned, something that every generation of people living in hot places acquired for themselves, and consequently might not retain if they moved to in a cold climate. But Kant was adamant that the laziness of the red and black races was innate and inherited precisely like their physical racial features. In his view the hot climate had triggered their human predispositions to adapt them to life in a hot climate, thus making them forever lazy, claiming that they had "an already adapted natural character" that would not change and allow them to be well adapted to the cold climate. He illustrated his claim with the observation that "Indians" and "Negroes" who have been driven into "northern regions" have "never been able to bring about in their progeny (such as the Creole Negroes, or the Indians under the name of gypsies) a sort that would be fit for farmers or manual laborers" (Kant TPP: 8:174). And in a footnote he dilates on this point: "in addition to the faculty to work, there is also an immediate drive to activity (especially to the sustained activity one calls industry), which is independent of all enticement and which is especially interwoven with certain natural predispositions, and that Indians as well as Negroes do not bring any more of this impetus into other climates and pass it on to their offspring than was needed for their preservation in their old mother-land and had been received from nature; and that this inner predisposition extinguishes just as little as the externally visible one." The clear implication is that the red and black races have an innate, inherited, and unalterable laziness that would inevitably frustrate the development of their rational faculties even if they had such faculties.

It may be objected that Kantian teleology in history is an idea of reason, merely regulative not constitutive, and consequently that I wrongly assume that it led him to believe that the slaughter of the black and red races admittedly proceeding apace in his day would continue until these races were extinct. But I do not assume this.

In "Idea for a Universal History," Kant prepares us for his application of teleology to the study of history by claiming that teleology is necessary for the study of biology. He claims that if we are to understand living things, we must assume that all their natural predispositions are "determined sometime to develop themselves completely and purposively" (8:18); and then on the ground that human beings have rational predispositions that cannot ever develop completely in the life time of a single individual, but need an "immense series of generations to develop, each of which transmits its enlightenment to the next," he infers that to understand human history, we must think of it as an immense series of generations developing slowly and steadily to the full and complete development of all human predispositions (Kant 1784, 8:20). Finally, given the assumption that "an externally perfect state constitution" is a necessary condition for the complete development of our predispositions, he draws the conclusion that we cited earlier, namely that we can regard the history of the human species in the large as the completion of a hidden plan of nature to fully develop all human predispositions, and as the necessary means to that end, an externally perfect state constitution (Kant 1784, 8:27).

Since Darwin, we know that Kant's claims about the necessity of teleology for the study of history are wrong. But Allen Wood argues that "Kantian purposiveness is still well suited to the study of history" because history is "a domain characterized by contingency," and "our reason" requires that we seek for some lawful order even in such domains (Wood 1999, 224–225). Whether or not Kantian teleology in history helps in the discovery of social scientific laws, Kant did not propose it for that reason. This is clear from a series of claims throughout his writings on history. In *Idea for a Universal History*, for example, he says that his teleological idea in history reveals a "guiding thread" that "can serve not merely for the explanation of such a confused play of things human," but rather will open a "consoling prospect into the future (which without a plan of nature one cannot hope for with any ground), in which the human species" is "represented" as finally fulfilling its "vocation here on earth." Such a justification of nature—or better of providence—is no unimportant motive for choosing a particular view point for considering the world" (Kant 1784, 8:30). The word "merely" in the earlier comment makes it clear that in Kant's view the really important reason for his teleological idea in history is that it provides us with a "consoling," and hopeful, view of the future of humanity.

How can Kant's teleological idea in history console us and give us hope for the future of humanity? It cannot do this by authoritatively predicting that humanity will fulfill its vocation here on earth; Kantians' constant reminder that Kant's teleological idea is regulative, not constitutive, rules out this possibility. Common sense rules it out, too. An authoritative prediction that humanity was going to fulfill its vocation here on earth would not merely console us and make us hopeful; it would fill us with joy! But the decent *possibility* of humanity fulfilling its vocation here on earth would be consoling and would help to make us hopeful. The point is not only that most of us probably would be cheered by the possibility. It is that Kant believed that we have a duty to strive that humanity fulfill its vocation here on earth and were that end impossible then morality would require us to do the impossible, which would make morality silly. With morality itself at stake, most of us would be consoled to learn from Kant's history that the fulfillment of humanity's vocation is at least possible. There was also a practical side to the issue. If it were possible to reasonably doubt that the ends of morality were possible, despair could seduce us into failing to do our duty to strive for them, thus further depressing the likelihood of achieving them. Kant put the converse point as follows: "A philosophical attempt to work out universal world history according to a plan of nature that aims at the perfect civil union of human species, must be regarded as . . . furthering this aim of nature" (Kant 1784, 8:29). I take it then that Kantian teleology in history was designed to demonstrate that humanity fulfilling its vocation was possible or at least not impossible.

This conclusion lays down strong requirements on Kantian teleological history. Such a history can make no *predictions,* of eventual success, but it also cannot offer us fairy tales of eventual success. It must convince us that success is at least possibly achievable by a series of events that is consistent with the facts and natural laws. Kant tried to satisfy this condition. For example, he picks out unsociable sociability, an inclination both to "enter into society" and then once in society to "direct everything" so as to get our own way, as the means nature employs to bring about the development of all human predispositions. The virtue of his choice is that unsociable sociability is an unmistakable and undeniable human predisposition and further that its assumption begs no question and abstains from assuming us to have already developed our predispositions. Kant readily showed that unsociable sociability is necessary for the development of our predispositions. Given our natural "propensity to indolence," all our "talents would, in an arcadian life of perfect pastoral contentment and mutual love, remain eternally hidden in their germs; human beings as good natured as the

sheep they tended, would give their existence hardly any greater worth than their domesticated beasts." But unsociable sociability arouses us to resist each other attempts to push
us around and this "awakens" our "powers" and, drives us to "tyranny," "greed," and desire
for a "rank" among their "fellows" (Kant 1784, 8:21). Kant rejoices in the result: "Thanks be
to nature, therefore, for the incompatibility, for the spiteful competitive vanity, for the insa-
tiable desire to possess or even to dominate!" (Kant 1784, 8:21).

Unsociable sociability plausibly gets us to develop our talents. It gets us into conflicts with
others, we want to win such conflicts, and that those with developed talents tend to win conflicts. But now things get more difficult. Although Kant says that unsociable sociability also
brings about a "lawful order," he seems reticent to show us exactly how it does this. It may
be said that antagonism is a condition for a lawful order because there would be no point in
having a lawful order unless there was antagonism. But this observation does not tell us how
antagonism brings about a lawful order. And we cannot just say that it does because nature
needs a lawful order to reach its aim. That would be a fairy tale, and fairy tales will not console us or help us to hope that humanity will achieve its end.

Kantians underestimate the difficulties that Kant got himself into when he claimed that
unsociable sociability will bring about a lawful order. For example, Wood argues that as
"culture grows, the degree of peace and order required for further progress also tends to
increase, for these capacities themselves involve increasing interdependence and cooperation, and they are increasingly vulnerable to destruction by violent human conflict. This
means that as culture progresses human reason is challenged to devise ways of creating a
well ordered society in which people's antagonistic tendencies can be held in check" (Wood
1999, 213). But this argument makes it seem as if human beings suspend conflict because
they desire to keep culture progressing, while Kant tells us that human beings have a "propensity to indolence" and that it is unsociable sociability that compels them to keep culture
progressing. It may be objected that unsociable sociability makes human beings desire to
compete and outdo others and since they can do so without fighting, indeed they can do
so better when they are not fighting, for fighting lessens the resources that can be used to
win competitions, it will move them to establish a lawful order so that they can compete.
But Kant is clear that unsociable sociability moves each of us to "direct everything to get his
own way," which is the desire to dominate, not to compete, although it may often drive us to
compete. Further, to give up conflict in order to compete would be self-defeating because
it would mean ending up being dominated, and the dominated do not compete with their
dominators.

In the seventh proposition, after assuming without argument that unsociable sociability moves individuals to set up a lawful order among themselves, Kant tries to explain how
unsociable sociability leads to a lawful order among states. According to that argument,
"Nature" uses unsociable sociability to drive states into "wars"; these wars and the "never
ceasing process of armament for them," create scarcity and fear; and after "much sad experience" of these conditions states are finally driven to "enter into a federation of states" (Kant
1784, 8:24, 8:25). Plainly, Kant is suggesting that a balance of power among states has consequences which if experienced over and over again finally drives states to establish a lawful
order. Kant does not use the same means to explain a lawful order among individual human
beings because he saw that, although individual human beings may be equal in the sense that
they can kill each other, they lack the resilience (among other things) to attacks from other
human beings to make the idea of a balance of power among them plausible. His famous

comment in *Toward Perpetual Peace* that even a race of devils, if they have understanding, can establish a lawful order among antagonists makes this point. Devils not being human may have the resilience to attack from each other that humans lack and so can establish a balance of power among themselves; and not being human they do not need the long and repeated experience of the futility of a balance of power to see that they must establish a lawful order among themselves.

It may be objected that Kant mocked the idea that the "so-called balance of power in Europe" could bring about an "enduring universal peace" as a "mere figment of imagination" (Kant 1793, 8:313). But Kant's attitude in that comment is perfectly consistent with my interpretation of his argument in the seventh proposition, namely that a mere balance of power does not bring about peace; *repeated experience* of the failure of a balance of power to bring about peace eventually brings about peace and a lawful order.

It remains, however, that there must be a balance of power among states before a lawful order and an enduring peace can be established among them. Otherwise some of the states will not have the sad experience of scarcity, fear, and exhaustion, which Kant claims they must experience in order to be persuaded to establish peace. Thus, Kant could not solve the problem of establishing a lawful order by relying only on unsociable sociability. He had to appeal also to the ability of the adversaries to impose costs on each other sufficient to bring about repeated expensive and exhausting stalemates sufficient to persuade adversaries to finally seek peace. Because Kant did not argue that unsociable sociability somehow guarantees such stalemates, he seems to have had no particular reason to suppose that the stronger side in a conflict will not continue to prosecute the hostilities until the weaker side is driven to extinction. Now consider how the consequences of this result forced on Kant by his attempt to use the minimal assumption of unsociable sociability to show how a lawful order and the development of human predispositions is at least possible would affect his thinking as he surveyed the conflicts in the eighteenth century between whites on the one hand and the black and red races on the other. There were no exhausting balances of power or stalemates between these antagonists. Whites were vastly superior to their opponents in military might and economic resources and were killing them almost at will; nor did they appear exhausted by the victories of their one-sided wars. Consequently, on Kant's account of the way unsociable sociability finally forces people to make peace and establish a lawful order, whites would continue killing the red and black races until they had wiped them out. And Kant's comment "All races will be wiped out except for the white" actually predicted this result (cited in Larrimore 1999, 114). His teleology being only regulative would not have justified that prediction, but it certainly did present him with the distinct possibility that peace, order, and the development of human dispositions would be achieved through the genocide of the red and black races. Naturally, he did not applaud those looming genocides. In his words, "When I say of nature that it wills this or that to happen, this does not mean, it lays upon us a duty to do it (for only practical reason, without coercion, can do that) but rather that nature itself does it whether we will it or not" (Kant 1795, 8:365). But he was consoled by the possibility they presented as his comments in the ninth proposition predicted he would be. Calmly, he set about devising the racial theory that had to follow from the slaughter if his teleological theory was to make sense. Consequently, the conclusion I drew earlier stands. Kant's racial theory followed from his teleological theory of history.

REFERENCES

Eze, Emmanuel Chukwudi. (1997). *Race and Enlightenment: A Reader*. Oxford: Blackwell.

Jefferson, Thomas. [1787] (1982). *Notes on the State of Virginia*. Edited by William Peden. Chapel Hill: University of North Carolina Press.

Jefferson, Thomas. (2010). "To Henri Gregoire [1809]." In *The Works of Thomas Jefferson*, Vol. 9, 246–247. New York: G. P. Putnam's Sons, 1904–1905.

Kant, Immanuel. (1775/2007). "Of the Different Races of Human Beings." In *Anthropology, History, and Education*, edited by Robert Louden, trans. by Günter Zoller and Robert B. Louden, 82–97. Cambridge: Cambridge University Press.

Kant, Immanuel. (1784/1999). "An Answer to the Question: What Is Enlightenment?" In *Practical Philosophy*, edited by Mary J. Gregor, 11–22. Cambridge: Cambridge University Press.

Kant, Immanuel. (1785/2014). "Determination of the Concept of a Human Race." In *Anthropology, History, and Education, in Romanticism, Origins, and the History of Heredity*, edited by Christine Lehleiter, 143–159. London: Bucknell University Press.

Kant, Immanuel. (1793/1999). "On the Common Saying that May Be Correct in Theory but It Is of No Use in Practice." In *Practical Philosophy*, edited by Mary J. Gregor, 273–310. Cambridge: Cambridge University Press.

Kant, Immanuel. (1795/1999). "Toward Perpetual Peace." In *Practical Philosophy*, edited by Mary J. Gregor, 311–352. Cambridge: Cambridge University Press.

Kleingeld, Pauline. (1999). "Kant, History, and the Idea of Moral Development." *History of Philosophy Quarterly* 16 (1): 59–78.

Kleingeld, Pauline. (2007). "Kant's Second Thoughts on Race." *The Philosophical Quarterly* 37: 573–592.

Kleingeld, Pauline. (2008). "Kant on Historiography and the Use of Regulative Ideas." *Studies in History and Philosophy of Science* 39: 523–528.

Kleingeld, Pauline. (2012). *Kant and Cosmopolitanism*. Cambridge:. Cambridge University Press.

Kleingeld, Pauline. (2014). "Kant's Second Thoughts on Colonialism." In *Kant and Colonialism: Historical and Critical Perspectives*, edited by K. Flikschuh, and L. Ypi, 43–67. Oxford: Oxford University Press.

Larrimore, Mark. (1999). "Sublime Waste: Kant on the Destiny of the Races." *Civilization and Oppression. Canadian Journal of Philosophy* 25 (Suppl.).

Mills, Charles W. (2005). "Ideal Theory as Ideology." *Hypatia* 20 (3): 165–183.

Rousseau, Jean Jacques. (1990). *The First and Second Discourses*. Edited by Victor Gourevitch. New York: Harper Torchbooks.

Wood, A. (1999). *Kant's Ethical Thought*. Cambridge: Cambridge University Press.

CHAPTER 4

....

NIETZSCHE AS A PHILOSOPHER OF RACIALIZED BREEDING

....

ROBERT BERNASCONI

AFTER World War II, a new reading of Friedrich Nietzsche was introduced that did not try to exonerate him of racism entirely but which nevertheless sought to marginalize his discussions of race and eugenics. Commentators claimed that what he said about race was designed to disturb the dominant consensus of his contemporaries rather than to establish his own view. By drawing on his sources and building on the work of historians of science, I challenge some of these attempts. It is true that Nietzsche was, when compared with many of his contemporaries, largely favorable to the Jews, but his antiblack racism, including his defense of colonialism and slavery, has not been given the attention it merits.

Friedrich Nietzsche was a significant race theorist, even if he was not one in the same vein as either Immanuel Kant or Arthur de Gobineau. Unlike Kant, he did not present a new definition of race and, unlike Gobineau, his remarks on race do not constitute a comprehensive philosophy of history. Nevertheless, Nietzsche's importance as a philosopher of eugenics was widely understood in the first half of the twentieth century, and during that time there was an intellectual fight over who could lay claim to his legacy. Before World War I, he was widely admired by left-wing intellectuals in spite of his attacks on socialism (Stone 2002), and, as is well known, some Nazis appealed to him for authorization of their racial views (Aschheim 1992; Galindo 1995). In 1933 the word "racism" was not yet established in the English language, but it was accepted in French and already the charge was being issued that Nietzsche's thought "furnished racism with a fundamentally original ideology" (Missac 1933, 43). The defense of Nietzsche has tended to take the form of establishing his distance only from Nazi ideas of racism, a strategy employed by Georges Bataille already in 1937 (Bataille 1992, 171). In this essay I take a broader view and conclude that, although—for better or worse—Nietzsche's racial views were not as original as has sometimes been maintained, his work is significantly compromised by a deep-seated racism that many philosophers who promote the study of Nietzsche have chosen to ignore or to dismiss as unimportant. Walter Kaufmann, who in the aftermath of World War II spearheaded the Nietzsche renaissance in the Anglophone world and who did as much as anyone to liberate his writings from the distortions they had suffered from Nazi scholars, still understood that "this whole issue is of great importance" (Kaufmann 1950, 249) in a way many more recent commentators refuse to do. I will focus first on Nietzsche's concept of race and then turn to his account of breeding or eugenics in his mature thought, which I believe is where the major problem lies. I will close by turning to his deeply troubling remarks on slavery.

NIETZSCHE'S CONCEPT OF RACE

Lack of familiarity with the history of racial thought undercuts many of the interventions by philosophers into the history of racism, but this failing is especially prevalent among defenders of Nietzsche. The suggestion that "Nietzsche's prescriptive use of the term 'race' boldly reverses the popular wisdom of the day" (Conway 2002, 169), like the assertion that his descriptions "fly in the face of prevailing wisdom" (Winchester 2005, 255) needs to be modified in the light of a more thorough acquaintance with the wide variety of nineteenth-century racial ideas. Sarah Kofman dismisses the topic with astonishing speed: "Although Nietzsche several times uses the term 'race' (semitic race, Indo-European race, 'racial' limitation), he does not do so in a 'racist' sense. Nietzsche's emphasis would be impossible if 'race' carried a biological meaning for him" (Kofman 20007–2008, 29). This suggestion that a strictly biological conception of race is a prerequisite for racism fails to recognize that racism in the form of prejudice against a group of people because of characteristics attributed to them is also equally possible on the basis of a "spiritual" conception of race of the kind that some commentators attribute to Nietzsche, mistakenly thinking that this is obviously preferable. Indeed, the primary meaning of "race" in the nineteenth century was historical and so less prone to the kind of racial essentialism that arose with the rise of biological reductionism (Bernasconi 2010, 517). Nevertheless, this historical understanding of race was both widespread and pernicious and one should beware of supposing that simply because Nietzsche avoided a biologically essentialist account of race that he had broken with his contemporaries (Schotten 2009, 53).

It is true that the dominant understanding of race found in Nazi Germany in the late 1930s was very different from Nietzsche's account formulated over fifty years earlier, but the assessment of his racism has been further confused by attempts to see his discussion through the lens of the 1950 UNESCO Statement on Race, especially its reliance on a distinction between nature and culture, where race was assigned exclusively to nature (UNESCO 1971, 30–35). The suggestion was that if one abandoned the exclusively biological sense of the term "race," then one would be free from racism. It was an approach designed to build on the consensus against the Nazis, while leaving largely untouched other forms of racism, including cultural racism, segregation, and various forms of colonialism. Nietzsche's commentators have sometimes adopted a similar approach. By examining the more than 200 uses of the word "race" in Nietzsche's published and unpublished works, Gerd Schank argued with some justification that Nietzsche almost never used the term in what Schank called somewhat vaguely its "modern" sense (Schank 2000, 29, 426). Drawing on Shank's research, Paul van Tongeren claimed similarly that, because Nietzsche almost never used the words "race" and "breeding" "in their 'modern' meaning which is related to a reprehensible racism," he could not be accused of adopting "racist positions" (Van Tongeren 2003, 207). But the fact that Nietzsche's writings on race do not conform to the model of Nazi racism does not establish that they are free from other forms of racism: there are many different forms of racism, even within National Socialism, but the model of racism employed by scholars who are attempting to exonerate Nietzsche tends to be especially narrow and in fact could also be employed to exonerate some Nazis, including Heidegger.

One cannot attach any special significance to the fact that Nietzsche does not use the term "race" in a single, clearly defined sense. Not doing so was quite common at that time. Nevertheless, one can say that race was for him fundamentally about heredity (*Vererbung*) (Nietzsche 2014, 179), even though he gave a role to environment (*Umgebung*) in the formation of racial character (Nietzsche 1980, Vol. 11, 136). This was in keeping with the Lamarkian belief in the inheritance of acquired characteristics (Lamarck 1984, 113) widespread among his contemporaries, and in a Lamarkian vein he insisted that "no reflection is as important as that concerning the inheritance of characteristics" (Nietzsche 1980, Vol. 8, 301). Here, characteristics were understood not only as physical but also embracing valuations, which had a physiological dimension for him. Not only bodily characteristics but also customs and values are inherited (Nietzsche 2011, 180). Although Nietzsche conceded that education and upbringing can succeed in creating a deception around our descent, he located the problem of race in the fact that "it is not in the least possible that a human being might *not* have the qualities and preferences of his parents and ancestors in his body" (Nietzsche 2014, 179). In late 1885 or early 1886, he reaffirmed: "*Valuations are innate [angeboren] despite Locke!,* inherited [*angeerbt*]" (Nietzsche 1980, Vol. 12, 15).

A good measure of Nietzsche's selective interest in the racial science of the period is indicated by a frequently cited passage from *On the Genealogy of Morality*, where Nietzsche differentiated a blond race of Germans from the short-skulled, dark-skinned, brunet Germans (Nietzsche 2014, 222–223; Schank 2004). Although the critical edition of Nietzsche's works under the editorship of Giorgio Colli and Mazzino Montinari is unable to identify the source (Nietzsche 1980, Vol. 14, 378), he was clearly referring to Rudolf Virchow's *Gesamtbericht über die von der deutschen anthropologischen Gesellschaft veranlassten Erhebungen über die Farne der Haut, der Haare un der Augen der Schulkinder in Deutschland* (Virchow 2009, 276–475). This survey of the skin, hair, and eye color of over 6 million German schoolchildren, with accompanying maps, was an attempt to identify the various racial types that could be found among the German people, albeit exactly what the data collected shows and how Virchow himself interpreted it is still debated today (Zimmerman 2001, 135–146). Nietzsche was following the terms of the survey in broad strokes.

Nietzsche was rightly criticized by a contemporary, the German anthropologist Otto Ammon, for misusing Virchow's data in order to identify a master race and a subjugated race. Nevertheless, Ammon praised Nietzsche for recognizing the significance of race for culture, a term that was beginning to gain ever greater prominence within anthropological studies, but at the same time he believed that Nietzsche was hampered by his reliance on philology at the expense of anthropology (Ammon 1895, 173–174). So Ammon saw Nietzsche's discussion as an indication of his failure to appreciate the intricacies of the science of anthropology, especially in his subordination of that literature to his purpose of establishing a new hierarchy, but at the same time he appreciated the fact that Nietzsche grasped the fundamental point which tied cultures to races.

Nietzsche did not share the modern dogma of a dichotomy between nature and culture, with race on the side of nature. That framework was not yet in place. He believed that races were not given but made, and that nations in Europe were more a *res facta* than a *res nata* (Nietzsche 2014, 157). It is only in this sense that Schank could claim that Nietzsche understood race as "a cultural product" (Schank 2000, 86), but it would not be in a sense of "culture" divorced from "nature." Already at the beginning of the nineteenth century, Jean-Baptiste Lamarck argued that hybridization across species led over time to the formation of new races and he did not exempt humanity from this process (Lamarck 1984, 39, 169–171). So when Houston Stewart Chamberlain explained that "race is not an originary phenomenon, it is produced," he was merely summarizing a widespread nineteenth-century belief that is also in evidence in Gobineau's historical account of the operation of race mixing to create new races (Chamberlain 1899, 343; Gobineau 1983, 260). The idea was that races were also shaped by culture insofar as they arose in conjunction with natural forces, including the environment, as a result of conquests, migrations, and societal practices and taboos.

NIETZSCHE'S ACCOUNT OF BREEDING OR EUGENICS

Nietzsche was not committed to the kind of racial *biopolitics* that led some of his contemporaries to want to outlaw certain forms of race mixing altogether, but he was committed to a form of biopolitics in the sense of calling for the control of breeding practices for the sake of society as a whole. He believed that the democratic mingling of races and classes accounted for Europe's fall into a state of semibarbarism (Nietzsche 2014, 126). Similarly, he believed that if the crossed races were too dissimilar, the result would be "a physiological feeling of inhibition" (Nietzsche 2014, 319). The same prejudice was on display when he repeated the widespread view that, when races that had long been separate mixed, the resulting hybrids were not only physiologically weak but also psychologically at war with themselves (Nietzsche 2014, 94). His portrayal of the Germans as consisting of "the most monstrous mixing and blending of races" (Nietzsche 2014, 149) was simply a commentary on what he had read in Virchow. As a recent study noted, "racial diversity and the progressive integration of diverse peoples were often presented as characteristics of nineteenth-century nations, not just as problems or curiosities for racialist scholars" (Manias 2009, 737).

To our ears, Nietzsche's idea that "there is in all likelihood no such thing as pure races but only races that have become pure" (Nietzsche 2011, 180) might sound transgressive, but it was not. His hope for a "pure European race and culture" was founded on the model of the Greeks as "a race and culture that had become pure" after being formed from a number of different sources (Nietzsche 2011: 181). Nietzsche adopted this view only after consulting a number of contemporary authorities (Cancik 1997, 55–58). The same idea lay behind Nietzsche's hopes that Europeans would eventually constitute a super-race, an over-race (*Über-Rasse*) (Nietzsche 1980, Vol. 11, 136), albeit "the dull, sluggish races" of Europe represented an obstacle to this vision (Nietzsche 2014, 145). Nevertheless, the fact that new races were formed by race mixing did not contradict the value he placed on racial purity. This, too, was a widespread view at that time. When Nietzsche suggested that the European nations were not yet races in the sense that the Jews were a race, that is, "the strongest, most tenacious and purest race" (Nietzsche 2014, 156–157), he was rehearsing a view repeatedly expressed, for example, by Benjamin Disraeli, the British Prime Minister—although for Disraeli the Jews were still a branch of the Caucasian race.

Nietzsche was certainly capable of vulgar antisemitism, as when he complained that Polish Jews did not smell good (Nietzsche 2005, 44). Nevertheless, he was against treating Jews as "scapegoats for every possible public and personal misfortune," arguing that "as soon as it is no longer a matter of conserving nations, but instead of engendering the strongest possible European racial mixture, the Jew is just as usable and desirable an ingredient as the remains of any other nation" (Nietzsche 1995, 258). It is in this context, the context of his commitment to breeding a new race of Europeans, that his rejection of the growing biopolitical antisemitism of some of his contemporaries is clearest. It set him in clear opposition to Theodor Fritsch (Thomas Frey), who in later editions of his *Antisemiten-Katechismus* included "Ten German Commandments of Lawful Self-Defense," the third of which was: "You shall keep your blood pure. Consider it a crime to soil the noble Aryan breed of your people by mixing it with the Jewish breed. For you must know that the Jewish blood is everlasting, putting the Jewish stamp on body and soul to the furthest generations" (Fritsch 1892, 247). Nietzsche clearly separated himself from Fritsch (Zumbini 2003, 449–462), but the fact that he proposed selective breeding between Jews and Prussian officers of noble rank, whom he deemed "firmly defined types of the new Germanity" (Nietzsche 2014, 157), is not simply, as one commentator claims, an example of him holding views "contrary to the views of his contemporaries" (Scott 2003, 68). Rather, he seems to have been referring to Bismark's remark that one should bring together "Christian stallions of German breeding (*Zucht*) with Jewish mares" (Busch 1878, II 218).

Nietzsche did not ask the obvious question about what Jewish women might think of being paired with Prussian officers. He thought of himself as an "anti-anti-Semite" (Yovel 1998, 119–138), but even when attacking the demonization of the Jews, his argument cut both ways. He wrote: "That the Jews if they wanted—or if they were forced, as the anti-Semites seem to want—even now *could* have the upper hand, indeed quite literally mastery over Europe, is certain: that they are *not* working toward it and planning for it is likewise certain" (Nietzsche 2014, 157). It seems here that the failure of the Jews to use their strength was also a negative judgment upon them when viewed on his terms.

The fact that Nietzsche seems at times to promote race mixing and at other times to discourage it is less surprising when viewed in the historical context, especially if one recalls the way Joseph-Arthur Comte de Gobineau in his *Essai sur l'inégalité des races humaines* saw race mixing as both a precondition for civilization and the cause of its eventual decline (Gobineau 1983, 151, 227). To be sure, however, in spite of the insistence of some of Nietzsche's early readers (Richter 1911, 220), there is no clear evidence that Nietzsche studied Gobineau or repeated his positions in any detail (Schank 2000, 426–441). Nietzsche saw a role for racial mixing within Europe, and he promoted it in the name of selective breeding. Nietzsche's inspiration here was not Gobineau, but Francis Galton who, in his *Inquiries into Human Faculty and Its Development*, promoted mixing as the only way to secure improvement within a race (Galton 1883, 305–307). Nietzsche was so intrigued by Galton's book that, having been given a copy in the fall of 1883 by Josef Paneth, a Viennese scientist (Krummel 1988, 489), he found an elderly American pastor's wife who over a three-year period would translate it for him for two hours a day (Haase 1989, 634). He also knew Henry Holland's review of Galton's book that highlights its application to relations between the races (Holland 1883, 450–451). Nietzsche would not have been able to read for himself Galton's essay "Hereditary Talent and Character," but perhaps Paneth told him about the selection process of the English nobility found there (Galton 1865, 165). A trace of Galton's discussion can be heard in Nietzsche's "Skirmishes of an Untimely Man" in *Twilight of the Idols*: "Even the beauty of a race or family, the grace and goodness in all its gestures, have been worked on: beauty, like genius, is the final result of the accumulated labour of generations" (Nietzsche 2005, 220).

It was not Nietzsche's rejection of Darwin that separated him from the racial theories of the anti-Semites, as one commentator suggests (Johnson 2010, 118). It is more true to say that it was after Nietzsche rejected Darwin's evolutionary theory that he committed himself increasingly openly to eugenics (Gayon 1999, 173). To be sure, Nietzsche was interested in the issue of breeding before he became familiar with Galton. In 1876 he anticipated—albeit without advocating—that in some distant future one would see the "extinction (*Aussterben*) of bad races" and the breeding of better races (Nietzsche 1980, Vol. 8, 349). A year later he was arguing for an expansion of the concept of "misbirth" in order to prevent the propagation of deformities (Nietzsche 1980, Vol. 8, 424), an attitude reflected in 1882 in *The Gay Science*, where he appeared to advocate the killing of misshapen babies (Nietzsche 2001, 76; see also Nietzsche 1980, Vol. 13, 549–600). In a note from 1880 he wrote in the context of a discussion of "the improvement of the race" that "The *extinction* of many kinds (*Arten*) of human beings is as *desirable* as any reproduction" (Nietzsche 1980, Vol. 9, 189).

Such remarks from Nietzsche's notebooks have to be read with care, but they show to even the most generous and sympathetic reader that he had a long-standing interest in human breeding programs, was fully aware of their dangers, and saw no basis on which to speak out against them (Stiegler 2001, 114–122; for an alternative view, see Miyasaki 2015). The question of whether modern civilization was inhibiting the work of natural selection and allowing the so-called unfit to live and reproduce, so that one had to have recourse to artificial selection, was widely discussed at this time. So, for example, in later editions to his *History of Creation*, first published in 1868, Ernst Haeckel argued for the death sentence for all incorrigible criminals as a benefit to the greater part of humanity. This would set in motion an artificial process of selection, precluding these degenerate outcasts from the possibility of transmitting their injurious qualities through heredity. Haeckel called this "medical selection" or "medical breeding" (*medicinischen Züchtung*) (Haeckel 1870, 155). Familiarity with the ongoing debates conducted by Nietzsche's contemporaries make it impossible to explain away his own comments on such topics simply as "careless rhetoric" (Conway 2002, 168).

Conway correctly warns against using the term *Züchtung* (breeding) as "a careless synonym for 'cultivation' or 'acculturation'" (Conway 2002, 180; also Gayon 199, 173–174). Nietzsche frequently used the word to describe breeding in the sense of artificial selection. Nevertheless, in the most recent translation of *Beyond Good and Evil*, this word and its cognates are most frequently translated as "cultivation" (Nietzsche 2014, 7, 59, 61, 84, 99, 118, 148), in spite of the fact that Nietzsche had the word *Cultivierung* at his fingertips when he needed it (Nietzsche 2014, 142–143). It is true that the term is notoriously ambiguous (Moore 2002, 162), but the attempt on the part of Nietzsche's apologists to translate his remarks on race and on breeding into one on culture and cultivation are misguided. This strategy succeeds in concealing what from the perspective of the twenty-first century we might call the racial component of Nietzsche's theorizing and neglects the fact that what made racism so pervasive in the nineteenth century was the intertwining of the natural and the moral.

What "eugenics" offered the nineteenth century was the idea that domestic breeding could work for humans as animal husbandry had done for domestic animals. As Galton explained: "the influence of man upon the nature of his own race has already been very large, but it has not been intelligently directed" (Galton 1883, 200). Nietzsche shared these views and echoed them in a note written sometime between April and June 1885. While commenting on the way morals and religions are the chief means by which one can shape human beings to be what one wants them to be, Nietzsche wrote that "nothing seems to be more essential to me than to study the *laws of breeding* (*Züchtung*) so as not to lose again greater amount of force through disfunctional (*unzweckmässig*) unions and ways of life" (Nietzsche 1980, Vol. 11, 480). The centrality of breeding to Nietzsche's philosophy is in evidence in *The Anti-Christ* in 1888: "The problem I am posing is not what should replace humanity in the order of being (—the human is an *endpoint*—): but instead what type of human should be *bred*, should be *willed* as having greater value, as being more deserving of life, as being more certain of a future" (Nietzsche 2005, 4). Nietzsche's answer to this question, which was directed against the reigning morality of breeding, according to which "all variation is to be prevented" (Nietzsche 2003, 19), was to promote "the breeding of a *stronger race*, a race whose surplus would lie precisely in those areas where the diminished species was becoming weak and weaker (will, responsibility, self-assurance, the capacity to set itself goals)" (Nietzsche 2003, 166). In this vein, Nietzsche declared that his concern was "the problem of the order of rank between human types which have always existed and always will exist" (Nietzsche 1980, Vol. 13, 481). The means for addressing this problem was the regulation of marriage (for example, Nietzsche 2006, 51–55; 2011, 116).

Nietzsche insisted that marriage was not about love but about "the breeding of a race" (Nietzsche 2003, 102). Although a bachelor himself, he proposed that bachelors should be penalized by having to perform additional military service, whereas fathers who have multiple male children should be rewarded by being equipped with multiple votes. This was because marriage is "a matter of concern to the community" (Nietzsche 1980, Vol. 13, 495).

NIETZSCHE'S REMARKS ON COLONIALISM AND SLAVERY

I turn finally to Nietzsche's remarks, which with relatively few exceptions have not been a main focus of the secondary literature, first about Africans (Preston 1997; Gooding-Williams 2006) and then concerning his support for a predatory colonialism on the part of Europeans (Holub 1998, 42–43; Bamford 2014). In *On the Genealogy of Morality*, he presented Africans as primitive and less susceptible to pain (Nietzsche 2014, 256). Around the same time, 1887, Nietzsche showed that far from questioning the presence of Europeans in Africa, he supported the use of cruelty as a way to maintain mastery over them. He wrote in one of his notebooks: "It becomes quite obvious in practice what means one has to employ with savage peoples, and that 'barbarous' means are not optional and arbitrary, if one, with all one's European pampering, is transplanted into the Congo or elsewhere and needs to stay the master over barbarians" (Nietzsche 1980, Vol. 12, 471). The specificity of the reference to the Congo excludes most of the strategies that Nietzsche's apologists frequently deploy to take the sting from his comments. This statement comes too early to be seen as an endorsement of the "slave state" (Morel 1903) that the Congo was to become under Léopold's violent rule, but it is a clear reference to the assignment to Léopold of a large portion of the Congo in 1885 at the Berlin or Congo Conference.

The enslavement of Africans was still a prominent issue when Nietzsche was writing. For example, it was debated by the European powers at the Berlin Conference of 1884–1885 (Gavin and Betley 1973, 292). Although he sometimes used the word "slavery" very broadly, there are other occasions when his remarks on the topic cannot be dismissed as simply metaphorical (Brennan 2011; Losurdo 2012, 380–394). In the fall of 1887, in the year before Brazil abolished slavery, Nietzsche wrote in his Notebooks under the heading "Morality in the Valuation of Races and Classes": " 'Abolition of slavery'—allegedly a tribute to 'human dignity', in fact the *annihilation* of a fundamentally different species (of the undermining of its values and its happiness—)" (Nietzsche 2003, 170). The reference to a different species does not seem to have anything to do with polygenesis, but it shows that Nietzsche saw the abolition of racialized slavery, not as a gain, but in terms of the loss of a people who had been treated and exploited so badly that they formed a class apart. Although he also used the phrase "*Aufhebung der Sklaverei*" elsewhere (Nietzsche 1995, 246) instead of "*Abschaffung der Sklaverei*," which was an equivalent but more common way of referring to the abolition of slavery in German, his use of it here suggests that he may have had in mind Adolf Röttscher's pamphlet *Die Aufhebung der Sklaverei durch das Christentum*, which had only just appeared (Röttscher 1887). But one does not need this reference to make that point.

In the spring of 1884 in one of his polemics against Christianity and the French Revolution, Nietzsche included a dismissive reference to Harriet Beecher Stowe's *Uncle Tom's Cabin*, one of the abolitionist texts best known in Germany, which appeared in translation in 1853, only one year after its publication in the United States. Furthermore, already in 1871, only a brief time after the end of the American Civil War, Nietzsche suggested that "we moderns" will "perish through the lack of slavery" (Nietzsche 2008, 41). Slavery was central to Nietzsche: "in the cruder and finer sense of the word" slavery is "an indispensable means of spiritual discipline (*Zucht*) and breeding (*Züchtung*)" (Nietzsche 2014, 84. Translation modified). In this way Nietzsche succeeded in integrating his defense of slavery and his antiblack racism into his larger discussion of breeding, which, as I have shown, was one of his abiding philosophical interests.

CONCLUSION

The dominant reading of Nietzsche today attempts to marginalize the racist aspects of his philosophy highlighted here. This is not as egregious a distortion of his thinking as that found among the Nazis, but silence about Nietzsche's racist statements and his obsession with racialized breeding falsifies his thought. Even Kaufmann still recognized that no philosopher since Plato had been so concerned with breeding "though Nietzsche was perhaps rather more explicit in emphasizing the function of the spirit in heredity for which he cited Lamarck" (Kaufmann 1950, 268). For all its failings, which are in part a consequence of the fact that Kaufmann did not have an adequate critical edition of Nietzsche available to him, his interpretation did not go as far as contemporary Nietzscheans have done to minimize Nietzsche's "strange concern for breeding" (Kaufmann 1950, 268). In fact, more strange than Nietzsche's interest in human breeding, which arose from his interest in contemporary biology and philology, is the lack of concern among contemporary Nietzsche scholars with this aspect of his philosophy. I have shown here that some of the strategies deployed by philosophers to dismiss worries about this aspect of his thought cannot be sustained. That a canonical philosopher promoted the enslavement of Africans long after most civilized people had rejected the idea should not go unnoticed when it can be tied to a central theme of his philosophy. There is clearly more work to be done in this area, but when doing it, philosophers promoting Nietzsche's philosophical importance should try to avoid the temptation to engage in wishful thinking where a knowledge of the history of racism is what is called for.

References

Ammon, O. (1895). *Die Gesellschaftsordnung und ihre natürlichen Grundlagen*. Jena, Germany: Gustav Fischer.

Aschheim, S. (1992). *The Nietzsche Legacy in Germany 1890–1990*. Berkeley: University of California Press.

Bamford, R. (2014). "The Liberatory Limits of Nietzsche's Colonial Imagination in *Dawn*." In *Nietzsche as Political Philosopher*, edited by M. Knoll and B. Stocker, 59–76. Berlin: Walter de Gruyter.

Bataille, G. (1992). *On Nietzsche*. New York: Paragon.

Bernasconi, R. (2010). "The Philosophy of Race in the Nineteenth Century." In *The Routledge Companion to Nineteenth Century Philosophy*, edited by Dean Moyar, 498–521. London: Routledge.

Brennan, T. (2011). "Borrowed Light: Nietzsche and the Colonies." In *German Colonialism*, 3–28. New York: Columbia University Press.

Busch, M. (1878). *Graf Bismark und seine Leute*. 2 vols. Leipzig: Grunow.

Cancik, H. (1997). "Mongols, Semites, and the Pure-Bred Greeks." In *Nietzsche and Jewish Culture*, edited by J. Golomb, 55–75. London: Routledge.

Chamberlain, H. S. (1899). *Die Grundlagen des neunzehnten Jahrunderts*. Munich: F. Bruckmann.

Conway, D. (2002). "'The Great Play and Fight of Forces': Nietzsche on Race." In *Philosophers on Race*, edited by J. Ward and T. Lott, 167–194. Oxford: Blackwell.

Fritsch, T. (1892). *Antisemiten-Katechismus. Eine Zusammenstellung des wichtigsten Materials zum Verständniss der Judenfrage, siebzehnte vermehrte Auflage*. Leipzig: Theodor Fritsch.

Galindo, M. Z. (1995). *Triumph des Willens zur Macht*. Hamburg: Argument.

Galton, F. (1865). "Hereditary Talent and Character." *Macmillan's Magazine* 12: 157–166, 318–327.

Galton, F. (1883). *Inquiries into Human Faculty and Its Development*. London: Macmillan.

Gavin, R. J., and J. A. Betley. (1973). *The Scramble for Africa. Documents on the Berlin West African Conference and Related Subjects, 1884/1885*. Nigeria: Ibadan University.

Gayon, J. (1999). "Nietzsche and Darwin." In *Biology and the Foundation of Ethics*, edited by Jane Maienschein and Michael Ruse, 154–197. Cambridge: Cambridge University Press.

Gobineau, Joseph-Arthur Comte de. (1983). "Essai sur l'inégalité des races humaines." In *Oeuvres*, Vol. 1, 133–1166. Paris: Gallimard.

Gooding-Williams, R. (2006). "Supposing Nietzsche to be Black—What Then?" In *Look, A Negro!*, 129–137. New York: Routledge.

Haase, M-L. (1989). "Friedrich Nietzsche liest Francis Galton." *Nietzsche-Studien* 18: 633–658.

Haeckel, E. (1870). *Natürliche Schöpfungsgeschichte*. Berlin: Georg Reimer.

Holland, H. W. (1883). "Heredity." *The Atlantic Monthly* 447–453.

Holub, R. (1998). "Nietzsche's Colonialist Imagination." In *The Imperialist Imagination*, edited by S. Friedrichsmeyer, S. Lennox, and S. Zantorp, 33–49. Ann Arbor: University of Michigan Press.

Johnson, D. (2010). *Nietzsche's Anti-Darwinism*. Cambridge: Cambridge University Press.

Kaufmann, W. (1950). *Nietzsche*. Princeton, NJ: Princeton University Press.

Kofman, S. (2007–2008). "Contempt of/for the Jews." Translated by T. Strong. *New Nietzsche Studies* 7 (3–4): 7–39.

Krummel, R. F. (1988). "Josef Paneth über seine Begegnung mit Nietzsche in der Zarathustra-Zeit." *Nietzsche Studien* 17: 478–495.

Lamarck, J-B. (1984). *Zoological Philosophy*. Translated by H. Elliot. Chicago: University of Chicago Press.

Losurdo, D. (2012). *Nietzsche der aristokratische Rebell*. Hamburg: Argument.

Manias, C. (2009). "The *Race prussienne* Controversy. Scientific Internationalism and the Nation." *Isis* 100: 733–757.

Misssac, P. (1933). "Nietzsche et le Racisme." *La Grande Revue* 37 (3): 31–39.

Miyasaki, D. (2015). "Nietzsche's Naturalist Morality of Breeding." In *Nietzsche and the Becoming of Life*, edited by V. Lemm, 194–213. New York: Fordham University Press.

Moore, G. (2002). *Nietzsche, Biology and Metaphor*. Cambridge: Cambridge University Press.

Morel, E. (1903). *The Congo Slave State*. Liverpool: John Richardson.

Nietzsche, F. (1980). *Sämtliche Werke. Kritische Studienausgabe*. 15 vols. Edited by G. Colli and M. Montinari. Berlin: Walter de Gruyter.

Nietzsche, F. (1995). *Human, All Too Human I*. Translated by G. Handwerk. Stanford, CA: Stanford University Press.

Nietzsche, F. (2001). *The Gay Science*. Translated by J. Nauckhoff. Cambridge: Cambridge University Press.

Nietzsche, F. (2003). *Writings from the Late Notebooks*. Translated by K. Sturge. Cambridge: Cambridge University Press.

Nietzsche, F. (2005). *The Anti-Christ, Ecce Homo, the Twilight of the Idols: and Other Writings*. Translated by Aaron Ridley. Cambridge: Cambridge University Press.

Nietzsche, F. (2006). *Thus Spoke Zarathustra*. Translated by Adrian del Caro. Cambridge: Cambridge University Press.

Nietzsche, F. (2008). *Political Writings of Friedrich Nietzsche*. Edited by F. Cameron and D. Dombosky. New York: Palgrave Macmillan.

Nietzsche, F. (2011). *Dawn. Thoughts on the Presumption of Morality*. Translated by Brittain Smith. Stanford, CA: Stanford University Press.

Nietzsche, F. (2014). *Beyond Good and Evil/ On the Genealogy of Morality*. Translated by A. Del Caro. Stanford, CA: Stanford University Press.

Preston, W. (1997). "Nietzsche on Blacks." In *Existence in Black*, edited by L. Gordon, 165–172. London: Routledge.

Richter, C. (1911). *Nietzsche et les theories biologiques contemporaines*. Paris: Mercure de France.

Röttscher, A. (1887). *Die Aufhebung der Sklaverei durch das Christentum im ost- und weströmischen Reiche*. Frankfürter zeitgem. Broschüren, N. F. VIII, 10.

Schank. G. (2000). *"Rasse" und Züchtung" bei Nietzsche*. Berlin: Walter de Gruyter.

Schank, G. (2004) "Nietzsche's 'Blond Beast.' On the Recuperation of a Nietzschean Metaphor." In *A Nietzschean Bestiary*, edited by C. and R. Acampara, 140–155. Lanham, MD: Lexington Books.

Scott, J. (2003). "On the Use and Abuse of Race in Philosophy." In *Race and Racism in Continental Philosophy*, edited by R. Bernasconi, 53–73. Bloomington: Indiana University Press.

Stiegler, B. (2001). *Nietzsche et la biologie*. Paris: Presses Universitaires de France.

Stone, D. (2002). *Breeding Superman*. Liverpool: University of Liverpool Press.

UNESCO. (1971). *Four Statements on Race*. Paris: UNESCO.

Van Tongeren, P. J. M. (2003). "Nietzsche's Naturalism." In *Nietzsche and the German Tradition*, edited by Nicholas Martin, 207–214. Bern, Switzerland: Peter Lang.

Virchow, R. (2009). *Sämtliche Werke, 45, III. Anthropologie, Ethnologie, und Urgeschichte*. Hildesheim, Germany: Georg Olms.

Winchester, J. (2005). "Nietzsche's Racial Profiling." In *Race and Racism in Modern Philosophy*. Ithaca, NY: Cornell University Press.

Yovel, Y. (1998). *Dark Riddle: Hegel, Nietzsche and the Jews*. University Park: Pennsylvania State University Press.

Zimmerman, A. (2001). *Anthropology and Antihumanism in Imperial Germany*. Chicago: University of Chicago Press.

Zumbini, M. (2003). *Die Wurzeln des Bösen*. Frankfurt: Klostermann.

CHAPTER 5

PHILOSOPHY AND THE RACIAL CONTRACT

CHARLES W. MILLS

I wrote *The Racial Contract* (Mills 1997) twenty years ago in an attempt to demonstrate that race and white racial domination should be taken seriously as legitimate topics of political philosophy. At that time, the top-ranked philosophy journals and university presses had very little interest in these issues. Seeking a respectable mainstream philosophy framework into which they could be "translated," I hit on social contract theory. Carole Pateman's *The Sexual Contract* (1988) had been an eye-opener for me, showing how gender could be theorized within a modified contractarian framework. So, inspired by Pateman, I was trying to follow suit for race.

I will begin by sketching the essentials of contract theory, and how Pateman's and my "contracts" modify the mainstream versions. (I will use quotation marks—"the racial contract"— to indicate the critical antiracist use of the contract idea, and the disquotational phrase—the racial contract—to indicate the racist reality itself.) I will then outline three possible areas of application of the "contract": white political philosophers' views; the formation of modern white-dominated racial polities; and the theorization of corrective racial justice. Finally, I will discuss the book's reception since its publication.

BACKGROUND: SOCIAL CONTRACT THEORY, MAINSTREAM AND "RADICAL"

The Mainstream Contract: Society as Genuinely Consensual and Egalitarian

The idea of the social contract has classical and medieval roots in the Western philosophical tradition, but it really only comes into its own with modernity. The key concepts inherited from the classical tradition are the *nomos/physis* distinction, Plato and Aristotle's commitment to the objectivity of ethics, and the Stoics' invocation of natural law. The thinkers of medieval Christendom (most famously Thomas Aquinas) Christianize natural law theory, and natural rights begin to emerge as part of the apparatus. The "golden age" of social contract theory is the century and a half from 1650 to 1800, which covers Thomas Hobbes's *Leviathan* (1651), John Locke's *Two Treatises of Government* (1689), Jean-Jacques Rousseau's *Social Contract* (1762), and Immanuel Kant's *Metaphysics of Morals* (1797). After this the contract tradition goes into a decline, subject to historicist critiques by Hegel and Hegelians for its asociality and ahistoricality and by utilitarians for its commitment to natural rights independent of a social welfare foundation. ("Nonsense upon stilts!" was Jeremy Bentham's notorious dismissive judgment.) But having been deemed dead over the next 150 years, part of the museum of antiquities rather than the living tradition of Western political theory, it was, of course, spectacularly revived by John Rawls's 1971 *A Theory of Justice* (Rawls 1999) and has been thriving ever since (Boucher and Kelly 1994a).

The basic conceit of social contract theory is that we should think of society and the polity (sociopolitical structures and institutions) as consensually brought into existence by equal human beings in a presocial and prepolitical stage, usually referred to as the "state of nature." More than one commentator has suggested that it is the very simplicity and evocative power of this image that explains contract theory's longevity, despite its obvious literal falsity as historical anthropology. However, even within this seemingly straightforward figure, tremendous variation can still be found in how all of these components are conceived of. Is the contract supposed to be actual, even in an attenuated sense (a conjectural history), or is it purely hypothetical, like a thought experiment? Is the state of nature (or would the state of nature be) peaceful or warlike? Are people in the state of nature single individuals or heterosexual nuclear families? Is the human equality of the state of nature moral or physical/mental? Relatedly, is the state of nature governed by moral rules, or is it amoral? Does the moral code established in the sociopolitical order create morality or merely ratify an already-existent objective normative order? And so on.

As can be appreciated, then, the mere idea of society's having been founded on an egalitarian contract does not at all determine in any specific detail the appropriate structuring of society and the state. Accordingly, various commentators, like Will Kymlicka (1991), and David Boucher and Paul Kelly (1994b), suggest that the contract is best thought of as a device that can be put to multiple uses, rather than as an apparatus that prescribes a particular sociopolitical template. The ideal Hobbesian polity is going to be very different from the Lockean polity, and both will be very different again from the Rousseauean and Kantian polities. Nonetheless, it is at least agreed, at a minimum, that the contract idea captures two key claims, one descriptive, one normative: that the sociopolitical realm is a human creation (not an organic growth or the work of God) and that the equality of human beings in the state of nature should translate in one way or another into an equality in the societies they create and in their treatment by the governments they establish. The contract metaphor's enduring appeal inheres in its vivid epitomization and representation of these two basic truths. In Rawls (1999), of course, and the vast Rawlsian secondary literature, it is the normative aspect that is predominant.

The "Domination Contract": Society as Actually Oppressive and Hierarchical

However, I suggest that another variation exists that is not usually flagged in the secondary literature but which is crucial to the "racial contract" s argument: the idea of a "domination contract" (Mills 2007a, 2015a, 2015b). Although, as noted at the start, my immediate inspiration was Pateman's (1988) "sexual contract," a case can be made that the conceptual filiation of this idea can be traced back to Rousseau's *Discourse on the Origin of Inequality* (Rousseau 1997). In this book, published seven years before *The Social Contract*, and not generally included in the contractarian conversation, Rousseau develops the radical perspective that official contract theory is essentially a scam. The contract is really a stratagem by the rich to entrench their power and privilege behind a façade of consent and democracy. Hence, it could be regarded as a class contract among the wealthy to disenfranchise the rest of the population, who give a "consent" that is actually uninformed and manipulated.

So by this linkage, the "big three"—gender, class, and race—are all brought together in what can then be argued to be an unrecognized and undeveloped strain of the contract tradition. Pateman's (1988) "sexual contract" suggests that we theorize male gender domination in terms of a contract among men to subordinate women, while I in turn proposed (Mills 1997) that we theorize white racial domination in terms of a contract among whites to subordinate people of color. So in all three cases (class, gender, race) the contract is limited to the privileged group, entrenching their group privilege, rather than being genuinely universalist. (For a further development of the idea, and also a critique of Pateman and myself for our neglect of disability, see Stacy Simplican's recent *The Capacity Contract* [2015].) The "domination contract" is no more literal than the mainstream contract. But as a figure/metaphor/iconography of the origins of the sociopolitical realm, it obviously comes much closer to capturing the dynamics of actual human societies after the hunting and gathering stage, since all such societies from then to now have been characterized by oppressions of various kinds. So the descriptive side of the contract concept is far better represented by the "domination contract." Society is "created" (in an ongoing sense) by groups (men, the privileged classes, whites) acting in coordination to secure unfair group advantage for themselves, and not by all individuals acting on their own.

In the modern period, when most commentators claim race emerges, equal rights are gradually extended to all white men (although white workers still suffer material class disadvantages) but withheld from white women (Pateman 1988) and the new category of non-European people of color (Mills 1997). Members of the new racial category are seen as subpersons rather than full persons. Thus, the modern state and legal system generally protect group privilege—the bourgeois state, the patriarchal state, the racial state—rather than the interests of the population as a whole. The contract is exclusionary rather than genuinely inclusive. (In Pateman and Mills [2007] we try in separate chapters to work out the "intersectional" implications of these overlapping oppressions for the contract.) Correspondingly, exploitation of one kind or another (class, sex, race) is the norm rather than society's genuinely being, in Rawls's formulation, "a cooperative venture for mutual advantage" (1999, 4). And since exploitation and domination will generally not be acknowledged to be such, it means that the supposedly liberal democratic societies of modernity, rather than realizing the liberal ideal of governmental "transparency," will in fact be characterized by obfuscatory ideologies of various kinds—social manifestations of what I call in *The Racial Contract* (Mills 1997, 17–19) an "epistemology of ignorance." In this specific case of race, which is our focus here, a social-structural "white ignorance" can be regarded as pervading the sociopolitical order (Mills 2007b).

My claim is, then, that through this conceptual modification, social oppression can now be theorized within a contractarian framework. This variant of the contract idea—"radical" or "alternative" contract theory—arguably has the resources to answer many of the criticisms standardly made by progressives of mainstream contractarianism: its asociality, ahistoricity, descriptive individualism, and (particularly in the modern Rawlsian version) ideal-theory remoteness from the problems of actual societies. Rawls suggests that we think of his contract as a "device of representation" for ideal theory, which is the normative theory appropriate for a perfectly just society. The "domination contract" can correspondingly be thought of as a "device of representation" for nonideal theory, that is, the normative theory appropriate for unjust societies, because it models the oppressive sociopolitical "basic structure" (Rawls 1999, 6–7) that needs to be reformed. If liberalism, the most important political ideology of modernity, has been illiberal for the majority of the population (Losurdo 2011), then we need a normative theory sensitized to this actual oppressive history. I will come back to this issue in the section on corrective justice.

The Racial Contract and White Political Philosophy

The first possible area of application of the "racial contract" is to the theorizing of white political philosophers. With the rebirth of Western feminism in the 1960s, in what came to be called the "second wave," a major project soon became the exposure of the sexism of virtually all the male political philosophers in the Western canon. Pateman (1988) argues that we can find this sexism at work in the ways in which the main contract theorists of the classical period—Hobbes, Locke, Rousseau, and Kant—represent women and their relation to the state of nature and the public sphere/private sphere demarcation. Women are depicted as intrinsically closer to nature because of their ability to give birth. So even when they are brought into civil society, it is not as full members, but as part of a domestic sphere (the family) conceived of in "natural" apolitical terms (Nicholson 1988). Thus, rather than a gender-neutral social contract that includes everybody as equals, these male contractarians are in effect arguing for an intramale sexual contract that subordinates women to men.

I have argued that a parallel historical exercise can be carried out for race. Insofar as the leading white theorists of Western modernity generally endorsed European expansionism into, and/or colonial rule over, the nations of non-Europeans who were seen as morally inferior on racial grounds—"savages," "barbarians," "natives"—my claim is that they can likewise be thought of as tacitly, or even explicitly, endorsing a racial contract. This contract may take different forms—"the expropriation contract," "the slavery contract," or " the colonial contract" (Mills 1997, 24–26)—but its common element is the privileging of whites at the expense of people of color. (For a detailed reconstruction of the settler contract in North America and Australia, see Pateman, chapter 2, in Pateman and Mills [2007].) Rather than being viewed as equal persons with equal rights and entitlements, people of color were for the most part viewed as subpersons who could justly be subordinated.

However, a crucial difference between sexism/patriarchy and racism/white domination is that the former long predates modernity, while most scholars see racism as distinctively modern. And even for the modern period, it is not always clear—whether because of competing definitions of the terms or ambiguous historical evidence—when European conquest and rule took on a specifically "racial" character. Therefore, in general it needs to be recognized that, especially in early modernity, racism was not as solidly, unanimously, or unequivocally established, as sexism. Jennifer Pitts (2005), for example, in her study of British and French liberalism, contends that only after the beginnings of the nineteenth century does liberalism become consistently proimperialist, and that in the earlier period one can find liberal voices that are both antiimperialist and antiracist.

For those philosophers who *can* be characterized as espousing clearly racist views, however, or whose actual practices and/or silence on crucial issues (colonialism, slavery) makes their having an implicitly racist outlook the inference to the best explanation, they can be illuminatingly thought of as endorsing the racial contract (Mills 1997; Pateman and Mills 2007, ch. 8). And this assessment applies to all four major contract theorists themselves: Hobbes, Locke, Rousseau, and Kant. The crucial pieces of textual evidence and/or actual practice are Hobbes's depictions of Native Americans as "savages" still in the (apparently real for them) state of nature; Locke's investments in the slave-trading Royal Africa Company, his role in writing the Carolina Constitution, and his representation of Native Americans as incompetent appropriators; Rousseau's limiting of contemporaneous "savagery" to people of color and his noncondemnation of African slavery; and (the easiest case) Kant's racial hierarchies. But endorsement of the racial contract is not limited to contractarian theorists; it can also be found, for example, in Hume's denial of nonwhite civilization, Hegel's Eurocentric characterization of the path of the World-Spirit, and Mill's procolonial writings (Ashcraft 1972; Arneil 1996; Mehta 1999; Ward and Lott 2002; Pitts 2005; Valls 2005; Sala-Molins 2006; Elden and Mendieta 2011; Tibebu 2011; Smith 2015). The key point is not merely the racism of these philosophers, as people, but the penetration of this racism *into* their theoretical claims, both descriptive and normative. And while contemporary mainstream political philosophy is not characterized by this kind of racism, I would contend that its overwhelming silence (e.g., from Rawls and within the vast Rawls industry) on the historic realities of national and global white domination, and the corresponding need for racial justice, testifies to its complicity with the legacy and ongoing realities of these racialized systems (Mills 2009).

THE RACIAL CONTRACT AND MODERN POLITICAL SOCIETY

The "racial contract" can also serve, as I have claimed (Mills 1997, 2003, ch. 9, 2015a, 2015b), as a more accurate characterization of modern political society. At first glance, of course, such a declaration will seem like a category mistake, a blatant failure to understand that the contemporary post-Rawlsian reincarnation of the contract has long since given up any real-world pretensions. The Rawlsian contract, we will be told, is a thought experiment with its origins in Kant's stipulation that the contract is merely an "idea of reason" and not an attempted description of actual societies. But my response would be—drawing both on the classic characterization earlier cited of the contract as having *both* descriptive and normative aspects, and on Jean Hampton's (2007) self-conscious attempt to resurrect the former—that as a metaphor, the "contract" does still unavoidably provide a picture of the sociopolitical, even if a very abstract one.

As emphasized in the opening section, the classic contract represents society as a consensual creation of equal human beings, and the legacy of this representation is undeniably clear in Rawls's depiction of society as a "cooperative venture for mutual advantage" (Rawls 1999, 4). Even if this depiction was originally supposed to be idealized rather than actual, in the absence of any explicit complementary depiction by Rawls and Rawlsians of *non*ideal societies, it has in effect become—through a kind of conceptual slippage in the literature—*the tacit representation of the actual*. Discussions of the United States, for example, proceed as if white supremacy had not been central to its basic structure, with the help of an epistemology that takes the ideal form of institutions as representative rather than their actual racialized incarnations. And, as such, it is radically false and misleading. The mainstream contract is saying that society (or maybe modern Western liberal society) is basically consensual, with social oppression being the anomaly. The "domination contract" is saying that society is basically coercive, with injustices and social oppression being the norm. Obviously, these are two very different versions of the way the world actually is, and we would expect very different normative methodologies to follow from them. And this is indeed the case: mainstream contractarianism largely ignores social oppression and corrective justice, whereas radical contractarianism makes them its primary focus.

In general, then, I would claim that the "domination contract" provides for us a superior starting point for both descriptive and normative political theory, alerting us that even in self-conceivedly liberal democracies like the United States, we can expect to find oppression. But the "racial contract" version of the "domination contract" has a *particularly* important role to play because of the historical and contemporary paucity within political philosophy of critical theory on race. Marxism had its heyday in the 1970s radical academy before the rise of poststructuralism; feminism is currently thriving, even if women are still underrepresented in the profession. But critical race theory had very little presence and remains marginalized to this day (although this publication represents progress because it would have been unthinkable two decades ago).

The radicalism of the "racial contract's" challenge to mainstream theory is thus to assert that *white supremacy* is central to modernity and that it should be conceptualized as political and as founded on a "contract." *Racism* as a subject falls under ethics; a *racialized sociopolitical structure* is appropriately investigated by political philosophy. Obviously, in terms of an overall characterization of the United States, it is very different to say that the United States has historically been a racially flawed liberal democracy and that the United States has historically been a white supremacist polity. Both characterizations admit race, but in the first it is framed as marginal, while in the second it is made central and presented as structural. That is, illicit white advantage was integral to the economy, patterns of public policy, the legal system, the opportunity structure, the workings of the criminal justice system, and dominant social mores. If the latter perspective is correct, then framings of the first kind are fundamentally deceptive. They are the equivalent in political philosophy of what Rogers Smith (1997) describes for political science as the "anomaly" view of racism in US political culture. Amerindian expropriation and genocide, African slavery and subsequent Jim Crow, Mexican annexation, Chinese exclusion, and Japanese internment are represented as "deviations" from a polity nonetheless conceptualized as still somehow basically egalitarian and inclusive. The raceless social contract thus cannot deny that it is descriptively committed. Insofar as "race" as a social category and a social reality makes no appearance in the world of discourse it generates, it *is* giving us a picture of the sociopolitical world, and a picture that is fundamentally wrong.

Moreover, the intended scope of my claims in *The Racial Contract* was global, that is, not limited to the United States. In keeping with the black radical tradition, most famously W. E. B. Du Bois's (1996, 13) judgments about a global "color-line . . . the relation of the darker to the lighter races of men in Asia and Africa, in America and the islands of the sea," I contend that we need to see European expansionism in modernity as bringing into existence a white-dominated world, so that by the time of the 1884–1885 Berlin Conference's partitioning of Africa, one can legitimately speak of a white supremacy that is planetary (Pakenham 1992).

The racial contract is thus international. In the years since *The Racial Contract* was published, a growing body of literature across different disciplines has emerged to vindicate this claim about the global scope of white supremacy, a claim that can be found in the internationalist black radical tradition as far back as the nineteenth century. For example, consider the "new" imperial history (Lake and Reynolds 2008); the "imperial turn" in political theory, which makes the connections between liberalism's domestic (European) and imperial role (Mehta 1999; Pitts 2005; Losurdo 2011); and "critical" IR (international relations theory), such as Alexander Anievas et al.'s (2015) collection *Race and Racism in International Relations*, which looks at people of color "confronting the global colour line," and Robert Vitalis's (2015) *White World Order, Black Power Politics*, which brings back to historical memory the pioneering role of Howard University's black IR theorists in challenging the racism of mainstream IR.

In sum, the "racial contract" contests both the Rawlsian domestic picture of society as a "cooperative venture" and the Rawlsian international picture of equal raceless Westphalian states. (The 1648 Peace of Westphalia, which ended the Thirty Years' War and the Eighty Years' War, is generally viewed as establishing the international principles for peacefully regulating the relations of sovereign states, first in Europe and then in the rest of the world: see Wikipedia, "Peace of Westphalia.") Colonialism was global, colonialism was coercive, and colonialism was racial: a system of white domination. And even if we are in a nominally postcolonial epoch today, we are still living within the structures of illicit planetary advantage and disadvantage established by this system. In the Anglo settler states (the United States, Canada, South Africa, Australia, New Zealand) and in the Iberian settler states (the Latin American world) it is still the case that whites are generally privileged over indigenous and black populations, while now-independent nations of color are still grappling with the institutions of a Euro-dominated world. Thus, I claim the "racial contract" continues to be theoretically relevant not merely in countries like the United States, but globally.

THE "RACIAL CONTRACT" AND CORRECTIVE JUSTICE

Let me turn now to corrective justice. Originally, the main theme of Western liberal political philosophy was political obligation, but Rawls's revival of the field was also a reorientation of its concerns. Social justice was now to be the central focus, specifically the justice of what Rawls called society's "basic structure" that included the Constitution, basic rights and freedoms, property arrangements, the market, and the family. The success of Rawls's book led to a vast secondary literature, both pro and con Rawls, thereby dramatically resurrecting

Anglo-American political philosophy. But a striking feature of this work was, and still is, its almost complete exclusion of racial justice as a theme, despite the fact that racial *injustice* has obviously been central to the founding and development of the United States and indeed all the other Anglo white settler societies. The overwhelming demographic whiteness of the philosophical profession was one obvious "externalist" cause for this neglect. As the beneficiaries of racial domination, whites have no material group interest in seeking its elimination. But a key "internalist" cause was Rawls's decision to limit himself to what he called "ideal theory," the normative theory appropriate for a perfectly just, "well-ordered" society, a "cooperative venture for mutual advantage" in which the rules were designed for reciprocal benefit and people generally followed the rules (Rawls 1999, 4, 6–10).

At least according to Rawls's explicit declaration, ideal theory was only supposed to be the prolegomenon for eventually moving on to nonideal theory, which included the crucial topic of "compensatory [presumably corrective] justice." But this transition never took place in his own work—his brief excursions into nonideal theory were centered domestically on civil disobedience and conscientious objection, and internationally on burdened societies and outlaw states—nor in that of his disciples and expositors. Racial justice, falling as it does under compensatory/corrective justice, is thereby thematically excluded.

The philosophical enterprise on which I am currently engaged is the attempt to develop a contractarian theorization of corrective racial justice that uses the "racial contract" as a "device of representation" for nonideal theory. Rawls's own thought experiment stipulates that we imagine ourselves behind a veil of ignorance choosing principles of justice on prudential rather than moral grounds, and bracketing out issues of historical injustice. The context of choice is an *ideal* society, not in the sense of an "ideal" social order self-consciously correcting for past injustices but an "ideal" society *without* any such history. With the two principles of justice chosen, we are then supposed to seek to derive other principles, such as principles of corrective justice, by a four-stage sequence in which the veil (i.e., deliberators' ignorance about their own identities and societal interests) is gradually lifted (Rawls 1999, §31). But Rawls gives no details on what happens if, when the veil lifts, you turn out to be (as you will turn out to be) in an ill-ordered society, for which the dismantling of an oppressive basic structure is the imperative.

I suggest that we need a different thought experiment custom-designed for nonideal theory (Pateman and Mills 2007, chs. 3 and 4). We imagine ourselves behind a veil, choosing—again on prudential grounds—among different principles of justice, mindful of the possibility that when the veil lifts, we will be a person of color in a white supremacist state. Say, a black woman in South Side Chicago, or a Native American on the reservation, or a Latina in the Southwest. An ideal society with no history of racial or any other kind of injustice is not a choice option; the question is what measures of corrective justice we would want to see put in place to correct for this history of white supremacy. In more recent work (Mills, *Black Rights/White Wrongs*, 2017), I suggest that we would choose principles of corrective justice in three main spheres of "primary goods" that correspond to the ones Rawls demarcates: the ending of second-class citizenship (both in terms of electoral questions—e.g., the problem of white majoritarianism—and other areas like police brutality and the general biases of the criminal justice system); the ending of racial exploitation (not just ongoing practices of discrimination but also the legacy of past practices in the form of the huge wealth gap between white and black and Latino households); and the ending of racial disrespect in its multiple dimensions (e.g., routine pejorative media representations of blacks, the Confederate flag issue, the symbolism of Civil War monuments, the use of Native Americans as sports mascots, Eurocentric school textbooks, and so forth). Obviously, all kinds of political and juridical complexities will be involved here, for example, existing white property rights, and what they supposedly rule out, and First Amendment guarantees. But the point is that we would then be able to discuss these matters in a nonideal theory contract framework that made white racial domination central rather than marginal.

However, there has been little engagement in the profession with the work in which I set out this agenda in greatest detail (Pateman and Mills 2007; Mills 2015a). Therefore, at this stage it is an open question whether this use of the "racial contract" will be found worthy of further exploration. It could be that *The Racial Contract* will continue to be adopted as a text that summarizes in a straightforward and accessible narrative the history of white supremacy, namely the descriptive side of the contract, but that my attempts to develop it as a normative device of representation as well will not gain support.

RESPONSES TO *THE RACIAL CONTRACT*

Finally, let me turn to the responses to the book in the two decades since its publication. Depending on the criteria one chooses to invoke, the book is either a success or a failure. It is an academic bestseller, a favorite for course adoptions across a wide number of disciplines, and it has been very broadly cited (see Google Scholar). But—to return to my opening paragraph and the goals articulated there—it has had no impact at all on how mainstream "white" political philosophy in general, or "white" social contract theory and Rawlsianism in particular, are done. For proof, one need only consult the recent massive Blackwell *Companion to Rawls* (Mandle and Reidy 2014). Weighing in at nearly 600 pages, it has a grand total of one and a half pages on race, and certainly no mention of Charles Mills or *The Racial Contract*. Therefore, multidisciplinary success has not translated into success in my home discipline, at least within these circles. Lewis Gordon (Gordon 2006, 111–117) has argued that it was a mistake on my part to expect any response from mainstream white political philosophers. The problem is not the lack of a translation device for the political agenda of people of color, which can be solved through the device of a modified contractarianism. The problem is an antipathy to engaging with these issues (the legacies of colonialism and imperialism, of slavery and Jim Crow) *at all*. So if Gordon is correct, that goal of mine was completely naïve from the start. My hope is that even if he is right about the old white guard, a new generation of younger white philosophers might be more open, especially as the United States approaches the tipping point of its transition to a nonwhite majority, with manifestly unfinished business of racial injustice in multiple social spheres.

In progressive/"radical" circles, of course, the book has received much more attention. There have been three symposia on it (Nagel et al. 2003; Gordon et al. 1998/2010; Jagmohan et al. 2015), including a recent retrospective symposium. (It is still noteworthy, though, that none of them appeared in a philosophy journal or book.) There is one article-length critique, by Jorge Garcia (2001); a philosophy dissertation exposition and critique by Stephen Ferguson, II (2004); a political science dissertation by Maziki Thame (2009) that seeks to apply the concept in a modified way to the comparison of the class/color hierarchies of Jamaica and Barbados; and a political theory adaptation of the idea to postcolonial India

(Keating 2011). *The Racial Contract* was widely reviewed at the time of its publication, and interesting discussions and critiques can be found in these reviews, as well as in various books with sections that engage with it. I have replies in all three symposia, as well as separate article-length responses to Garcia (Mills 2003, ch. 9) and to Anthony Bogues (Mills 2015b). The final chapter of my book with Pateman (Pateman and Mills 2007, ch. 8) was a reply to many of these critics, including Ferguson. I recommend to any interested readers that they start by consulting the bibliography of this chapter, which has the most comprehensive listing of criticisms up to that date, and also look at the 2015 retrospective symposium (Jagmohan et al. 2015).

Let me conclude by listing the main lines of criticism of the book. Because they come from different theoretical directions, they are often conflicting: (i) the descriptive/explanatory pretensions of the "racial contract" are unachieved, whether because the "contract" is too coarse a device or because contractarianism is in principle unable to do this kind of work; (ii) social contract theory is a necessarily bourgeois apparatus that cannot be retrieved for a radical emancipatory class politics; (iii) social contract theory and/or liberalism more generally are part of the colonial "master's tools," and so cannot advance a postcolonial/decolonial antiracist agenda; (iv) the "racial contract" works as a demystificatory descriptive device, but not a normative one, because corrective racial justice cannot be handled within a contract apparatus; (v) the innovation of a "racial" or, more generally, "domination" contract is unnecessary, since Rawlsian theory as is can indeed be developed to handle corrective racial justice; (vi) relatedly, my criticisms of Rawls and Rawlsianism for their putative "whiteness" are unfair; (vii) the "racial contract" is insensitive to gender/class/sexual orientation/disability.

My brief responses would be as follows: (i) the "contract" device *is* able to capture the idea of people actively creating, or going along with the creation and perpetuation of, sociopolitical systems that are inclusive (the mainstream contract) or exclusionary (the domination contract), and so is, I would claim, descriptive/explanatory at this high level of abstraction; (ii) some Marxists *have* used a radicalized social contract theory to critique Rawls, but in any case racial justice, the focus of the book, is conceptually distinct from class justice; (iii) some of the master's tools, like racism, are intrinsically oppressive and morally tainted, but others, like contractarianism and liberalism, are not problematic in themselves but only contingently racialized, and are flexible enough to be adapted to different and progressive usages; (iv) by modifying the thought experiment so our choices are limited to different principles for dismantling a racialized basic structure, veiled prudential choice under nonideal circumstances can be used to generate principles of corrective justice; (v) Rawlsian ideal-theory assumptions about the nature of society (a cooperative venture for mutual advantage) are incompatible with the realities of white-supremacist societies, so to model these realities we need a significantly altered theoretical apparatus; (vi) more than forty years after the publication of *A Theory of Justice* (Rawls 1999), racial justice has yet to be tackled by the secondary literature on Rawls (see, again, Mandle and Reidy [2014]), despite the centrality of racial injustice to the making of the United States and, more generally, the modern world, which seems like pretty good prima facie evidence for its "whiteness"; (vii) the "racial contract" was just focusing on one dimension of social oppression, but the more general idea of a "domination contract" can, I believe, be extended to theorize these other dimensions also.

References

Anievas, A., N. Manchanda, and R. Shilliam, eds. (2015). *Race and Racism in International Relations: Confronting the Global Colour Line*. New York: Routledge.

Arneil, B. (1996). *John Locke and America: The Defence of English Colonialism*. Oxford: Clarendon Press.

Ashcraft, R. (1972). "Leviathan Triumphant: Thomas Hobbes and the Politics of Wild Men." In *The Wild Man Within: An Image in Western Thought from the Renaissance to Romanticism*, edited by E. Dudley and M. E. Novak, 141–181. Pittsburgh: University of Pittsburgh Press.

Boucher, D., and P. Kelly, eds. (1994a). *The Social Contract from Hobbes to Rawls*. New York: Routledge.

Boucher, D., and P. Kelly. (1994b). "The Social Contract and Its Critics." In *The Social Contract from Hobbes to Rawls*, edited by D. Boucher and P. Kelly, 1–34. New York: Routledge.

Du Bois, W. E. B. [1903] (1996). *The Souls of Black Folk*. New York: Penguin.

Elden, S., and E. Mendieta, eds. (2011). *Reading Kant's Geography*. Albany: State University of New York Press.

Ferguson, S. C., II. (2004). *Racial Contract Theory: A Critical Introduction*. Ph.D. diss. University of Kansas.

Garcia, J. (2001). "The Racial Contract Hypothesis." *Philosophia Africana* 4 (1): 27–42.

Gordon, L. R. (2006). *Disciplinary Decadence: Living Thought in Trying Times*. Boulder, CO: Paradigm.

Gordon, L. R., A. Bogues, C. Hutton, and C. W. Mills. [1998] (2010). "Symposium on *The Racial Contract*." In C. W. Mills, *Radical Theory, Caribbean Reality: Race, Class and Social Domination* (2010), ch. 8, 249–269. Kingston, Jamaica: University of the West Indies Press.

Hampton, J. (2007). "Contract and Consent." In *A Companion to Contemporary Political Philosophy*, edited by R. E. Goodin, P. Pettit, and T. Pogge. 2nd ed. Vol. 2, 379–393. Malden, MA: Blackwell.

Jagmohan, D., J. Turner, A. M. Smith, K. Lindsay, and C. W. Mills. (2015). "Dialogue: *The Racial Contract* Today." *Politics, Groups, and Identities* 3 (3): 469–557.

Keating, C. (2011). *Decolonizing Democracy: Transforming the Social Contract in India*. University Park: Pennsylvania State University Press.

Kymlicka, W. (1991). "The Social Contract Tradition." In *A Companion to Ethics*, edited by P. Singer, 186–196. Cambridge, MA: Blackwell Reference.

Lake, M., and H. Reynolds. (2008). *Drawing the Global Colour Line: White Men's Countries and the International Challenge of Racial Equality*. New York: Cambridge University Press.

Losurdo, D. (2011). *Liberalism: A Counter-History*. Translated by G. Elliott. New York: Verso.

Mandle, J., and D. A. Reidy, eds. (2014). *A Companion to Rawls*. Malden, MA: Wiley Blackwell.

Mehta, U. S. (1999). *Liberalism and Empire: A Study in Nineteenth-Century British Liberal Thought*. Chicago: University of Chicago Press.

Mills, C. W. (1997). *The Racial Contract*. Ithaca, NY: Cornell University Press.

Mills, C. W. (2003). *From Class to Race: Essays in White Marxism and Black Radicalism*. Lanham, MD: Rowman & Littlefield.

Mills, C. W. (2007a). "The Domination Contract." In C. Pateman and C. W. Mills, *Contract and Domination*, 79–105. Malden, MA: Polity.

Mills, C. W. (2007b). "White Ignorance." In *Race and Epistemologies of Ignorance*, edited by S. Sullivan and N. Tuana, 11–38. Albany, NY: State University of New York Press.

Mills, C. W. (2009). "Rawls on Race/Race in Rawls." *Southern Journal of Philosophy* 47 (Supplement): 161–184.

Mills, C. W. (2010). *Radical Theory, Caribbean Reality: Race, Class and Social Domination.* Kingston, Jamaica: University of the West Indies Press.

Mills, C. W. (2015a). "*The Racial Contract* Revisited: Still Unbroken after All These Years." *Politics, Groups, and Identities* 3 (3): 541–557.

Mills, C. W. [2009] (2015b). "Rousseau, the Master's Tools, and Anti-Contractarian Contractarianism." In *Creolizing Rousseau*, edited by J. A. Gordon and N. Roberts, 171–192. New York: Rowman & Littlefield International.

Mills. C. W. (2017). *Black Rights/White Wrongs: The Critique of Racial Liberalism.* New York: Oxford University Press.

Nagel, M. E., R. Schmitt, N. Zack, and C. W. Mills. (2003). "Symposium on Charles Mills's *The Racial Contract.*" In *Racial Liberalism and the Politics of Urban America*, edited by C. Stokes and T. Meléndez, 11–50. East Lansing: Michigan State University Press.

Nicholson, L. (1988). *Gender and History: The Limits of Social Theory in the Age of the Family.* New York: Columbia University Press.

Pakenham, T. (1992). *The Scramble for Africa: White Man's Conquest of the Dark Continent from 1876 to 1912.* New York: Avon Books.

Pateman, C. (1988). *The Sexual Contract.* Stanford, CA: Stanford University Press.

Pateman, C., and C. W. Mills. (2007). *Contract and Domination.* Malden, MA: Polity.

Pitts, J. (2005). *A Turn to Empire: The Rise of Imperial Liberalism in Britain and France.* Princeton, NJ: Princeton University Press.

Rawls, J. [1971] (1999). *A Theory of Justice.* Rev. ed. Cambridge, MA: Harvard University Press.

Rousseau, J-J. (1997). "Discourse on the Origin and the Foundations of Inequality among Men, or Second Discourse." In *The "Discourses" and Other Early Political Writings*, edited and translated by V. Gourevitch, 111–222. New York: Cambridge University Press.

Sala-Molins, L. (2006). *Dark Side of the Light: Slavery and the French Enlightenment.* Translated by J. Conteh-Morgan. Minneapolis: University of Minnesota Press.

Simplican, S. C. (2015). *The Capacity Contract: Intellectual Disability and the Question of Citizenship.* Minneapolis: University of Minnesota Press.

Smith, J. E. H. (2015). *Nature, Human Nature, & Human Difference: Race in Early Modern Philosophy.* Princeton, NJ: Princeton University Press.

Smith, R. M. (1997). *Civic Ideals: Conflicting Visions of Citizenship in U.S. History.* New Haven, CT: Yale University Press.

Thame, M. W. (2009). *Caribbean Racial Contracts?: Race, Power and Identity in Barbados and Jamaica.* Ph.D. diss. University of the West Indies (Mona).

Tibebu, T. (2011). *Hegel and the Third World: The Making of Eurocentrism in World History.* Syracuse, NY: Syracuse University Press.

Valls, A., ed. (2005). *Race and Racism in Modern Philosophy.* Ithaca, NY: Cornell University Press.

Vitalis, R. (2015). *White World Order, Black Power Politics: The Birth of American International Relations.* Ithaca, NY: Cornell University Press.

Ward, J. K., and T. L. Lott, eds. (2002). *Philosophers on Race: Critical Essays.* Malden, MA: Blackwell.

PART II

PLURALISTIC IDEAS OF RACE

MOST progressive thinkers would now consider the modern ideas of race that were first developed by European philosophers to be inadequate or oppressive. It is therefore important to realize that these were not the only ideas about race in circulation during the time they were put forth and over the period of their dominant influence. Moreover, egalitarian progress in reality and intellectual history now permit more pluralistic considerations of ideas of human racial difference, especially pertaining to hierarchical taxonomies that have excessively valorized and privileged white Europeans at the expense of other groups.

It would require many volumes to attempt to do justice to pluralistic accounts of human races and ideas about race. The project would have to attend to what different societies meant by the word "race" and the many, many variations of this concept. But that is a matter of cultural anthropology. We will see in Part III that there is now good reason for skepticism about any objective taxonomy of human races that could be invariant over societies or cultures. If race does not exist, then this or that idea of racial difference cannot claim to be the right, or best, or most accurate one. Still, posits of human races and ideas about their differences have worked as ideologies radiating out from beliefs advantaging the most powerful (so-called) racial groups. Subordinate racial groups could, and have, generated their own ideas about racial differences. But even the most resistant among the oppressed have tended to think within the framework of racial posits and comparisons put forth by those with the greatest power and status within their own self-generated racial systems. Part of the reason for this has been that physical force and economic might have been used to back up the ideas of dominant groups, and part has been a matter of the lasting psychic impact of racist ideas and posits of race.

Ideas of race developed by nonwhite intellectuals, both in Euro-America and on other continents, have provided resistance to ideas of white superiority as developed by

Euro-Americans and this resistance has been sufficiently critical and interesting for the notion of "pluralistic ideas of race" to make sense, philosophically. We therefore now turn to several of these counterperspectives, as a contrast to the hegemonic paradigm and also for informative intellectual diversity in the subject, as a value in its own right.

Albert Mosley introduces ideas of race from the discourse of Africans living in the shadow of the dominant colonialist racial theory(ies). From eighteenth-century England, Mosley considers Ignatius Sancho, Olaudah Equiano, and Quobna Cugoano; and from nineteenth-century America, David Walker, Martin Delaney, Alexander Crummell, Edward Blyden, and Frederich Douglass. African slaves were emancipated in England in 1772 but the slave trade continued. The large population of Africans in England were active in abolitionist causes. Their discussion of a well-publicized incident, in which a British captain callously threw 132 slaves overboard to collect insurance, led to the abolition of the British slave trade in 1807.

African American abolitionists contested the use of both religious and scientific principles to justify slavery. For instance, Walker, who was born a freedman, argued against the biblical justification of slavery based on the claim that Africans were the descendants of Canaan, the cursed son of Ham. Delaney, who was trained as a doctor by white abolitionists, became an early advocate of African American return to Africa. Crummell was also a nationalist, as was Blyden, who argued systematically against negro inferiority, as well as slavery. Douglass rhetorically "flipped" the definition of the "The Race Problem" from what to do with an "innately inferior race cursed by God" to what to do with a curse of greed and prejudice on whites that enabled their unrestrained exploitation of Africans. Douglass also argued for the existence of only one human race. His arguments against slavery were comprehensive and abstract enough to be extended to opposition to the exploitation of Asian workers in the "coolie" trade.

There is a difference between being violently brought to a new place and having invaders take one's place—the physical persons of Africans and their labor were valued, whereas it was the lands and places of indigenous peoples that were valued. The resistant perspectives of Native Americans have been distinct in that they were driven from their ancestral homelands, although their descendants reside on the same continent. Kyle Powys Whyte demonstrates and explains that displacement of the settler–indigenous contact, from an indigenous perspective. His analysis is striking in showing how US government criteria for entitlements, or partial recovery of what had been taken, has required proof of ancestry in ways that have been alien to actual Tribal membership. On a broad physical sweep, the erasure of indigenous culture is evident in aerial views of great swaths of land in the middle of the US continent, which are divided into "patchwork" patterns. These stable "quilts" bear little resemblance to the appearance from the air of something like the "seasonal round" of Anishinaabe, who progressed from hunting, to harvesting, to fishing, over the seasons of a year, but returned to the same places over the years. And, of course, the erasure of indigenous identity extends beyond the physical landscape into culture, as evident in the paucity of educational material about Native Americans in the US school system and past removal of indigenous children to boarding schools, where they were deprived of their languages and culture.

Africans were physically removed from homelands, and homelands were removed from Native Americans, but throughout US history, Asian Americans were seen as perpetually foreign and unassimilable in contrast to European immigrants. However, Yen Le Espiritu suggests that the identities and status of Asian Americans cannot be understood via an internal national perspective that stops at US borders. Rather, "Asian American 'alien citizenship' flowed directly from the histories of conquest, colonialism, and semicolonialism that constituted US interactions in Asia." Espiritu suggests that ideas of immigration often fail to take processes of othering and racialization into account. Nation states with large numbers of US immigrants—Mexico, China (including Taiwan and Hong Kong), the Philippines, El Salvador, the Dominican Republic, South Korea, Guatemala, Vietnam, Laos, and Cambodia—have all had intense social, political, military, and economic relations with dominant interest groups in the United States. Along with coerced contributions to empire, through globalization, colonialism, and militarism, subaltern identities have been imposed on citizens and migrants from these nation states.

The foreign policy and international relations aspect of racial identities introduced by Espiritu in regard to Asian Americans has had a longer history in Latin America, where philosophers and political theorists within and without the academy have struggled with ideas of rights and identity, especially through literary creation and criticism, as well as philosophy. Susana Nuccetelli locates the origins of this discourse in the Iberian conquest during the fifteenth and sixteenth centuries and notes its continuance into contemporary concerns related to globalism. Nuccetelli tracks the following contributions from Latin American thought to discussions of race and rights in the United States: a Thomistic absolutist theory of natural rights that influenced secular modern *natural rights* theories; a philosophy of international law; a pioneering polemic about the moral backwardness of the treatment of Amerindians and the African slave trade; and a doctrine of *compensatory justice* claiming duties of reparation for past injustices. In addition, the question of *mestajahe* or mixed race has been part of Latin American political discussions about preferred forms of government, as well as identity, since the early nineteenth century.

In the last essay in this part, "Looking for Alain Locke," Leonard Harris provides a poignant account of his search for a philosophical home for Locke's work. Locke was the first African American to receive a PhD in philosophy, from Harvard in 1918. He was best known for his support of black writers, artists, and poets during the Harlem Renaissance. He was chair of the Howard University Department of Philosophy during a career lasting over thirty years and wrote extensively in value theory about culture and cultural relativity, as well as racial theory, in the tradition of pragmatism. Locke's 1942 anthology coedited with Bernard Stern, *When Peoples Meet: Race and Culture Contact*, exhibits the relation of cultural pluralism to democracy. But Locke's philosophical contributions did not enter academic philosophy until Harris rediscovered them in 1983.

Harris recounts that it took five years to find a publisher, the University of Chicago Press, for *Alain L. Locke: Biography of a Philosopher* (2008), which he wrote with Charles Molesworth. Locke was an only child and a lifelong bachelor who left no record of the suffering attending his homosexuality. He mentored and counseled many black intellectuals and artists but displayed little drama in his own trajectory from a middle-class home, to scholarship, to cultural criticism, to more scholarship. Harris presents that quiet background as a recipe for obscurity given dispositions to devalue black thinkers and exclude their contributions. As Harris develops his account of Locke's absence from American philosophy, he interweaves a disturbing narrative about Locke's ashes, which were kept in a paper bag, until finally removed from Howard's Department of Anthropology to repose in an urn beneath a headstone in the Congressional Cemetery, in 2014, sixty years after his death.

Harris's apprehension of the double absence of Alain Locke, first philosophically, and second, literally, outlines an African American perspective or view of race and racial taxonomy as tragic loss. The deep humanity of that perspective should be considered and accepted as an alternative approach to facile taxonomies that were imagined in order to posit the superiority of one racial group—as though the worldviews and life experiences of other groups were of no importance or did not even exist. Both the original posit and its effects have occurred on the premise that human races are real biological divisions. Part III provides consideration of whether there are at present good reasons to accept that.

FURTHER READING

Harris, Leonard, ed. (1983). *Philosophy Born of Struggle: Afro-American Philosophy from 1917.* Dubuque, IA: Kendall/Hunt.

Locke, Alain. [1925] (2007). "The New Negro, 1925." In *Readings on Race, Representation, and African American Culture, 1892–1938*, edited by Henry Louis Gates and Gene Andrew Jarrett, 112–118. Princeton, NJ: Princeton University Press.

Reynolds, Glenn C. (2007). "A Native American Land Ethic." *Natural Resources and Environment* 21 (3): 16–20.

Schlund-Vials, Cathy J., K. Scott Wong, and Linda Trinh Võ, eds. (2015). *Keywords for Asian American Studies.* New York: New York University Press.

Serequeberhan, Tsenay, ed. (1991). *African Philosophy: The Essential Readings*, Harrisburg, PA: Continuum International Pub Group Book.

CHAPTER 6

"RACE" IN EIGHTEENTH- AND NINETEENTH-CENTURY DISCOURSE BY AFRICANS IN THE DIASPORA

ALBERT MOSLEY

CONTEMPORARY studies of Anglo-American intellectual history about race tend to neglect discourse on race by prominent intellectuals of African ancestry. And yet there is much to learn and reflect upon in the ideas and scholarship of eighteenth- and nineteenth-century thinkers such as Ignatius Sancho (1729–1782), Olaudah Equiano (1745–1797), and Quobna Cugoano (1757–1791) in eighteenth-century England; and David Walker (1796–1830), Martin Delaney (1812–1885), Frederick Douglass (1817–1895), Alexander Crummell (1819–1898), and Edward Blyden (1832–1912) in the nineteenth-century United States.

RACE IN THE DISCOURSE OF EIGHTEENTH-CENTURY AFRICANS IN ENGLAND

In the eighteenth century, London had more Africans than all the rest of Europe combined. Ignatius Sancho, Olaudah Equaino, and Quobna Cuguano were leaders of a group of emancipated slaves called "Sons of Africa" formed in 1787 (Northrup 2013, chap. 5). They wrote to newspapers and members of Parliament exposing the cruelties of the African slave trade. And they actively cooperated with abolitionist groups that opposed slavery. Their intellectual work was fully engaged with their experience of living in a society in which the enslavement of Africans was accepted.

Slave owners visiting England from the West Indies and Americas were often accompanied by their slave-valets. However, in 1772, Lord Mansfield ruled that enslavement of one person by another person was not a recognized legal relationship in English Common Law. This ruling effectively emancipated all African slaves in England. But it did not apply outside England, to the English colonies or to ships carrying slaves from Africa to the colonies. The issue of whether African slaves were human or mere merchandise was encapsulated in the Zong massacre of 1783. Luke Collingwood, the captain of the Zong, sailed from Africa to Jamaica with some 440 slaves. Because of his inexperience with navigation, Collingwood overshot his destination, causing a lengthened journey. After three months of sailing, 60 of the slaves were already dead and were a loss to the sponsors of the voyage. A captain was allowed to jettison part of a cargo if this was necessary to save the rest and the part jettisoned was insured. But cargo lost because of negligence of the captain was not covered by insurance. The captain jettisoned 132 Africans on the pretext that this was necessary to save the ship. The courts decided that the action of the captain and the owners was covered by insurance, even when it was shown that there was enough water and provisions for all to make port. None were charged with murder. It was no more than if horses had been jettisoned. Africans, treated as beasts of burden and deprived of hope, were transformed into beasts by West Indian and American slavery. Equaino, Cuguano, Sancho, and other prominent English abolitionists (Thomas Clarkson, Granville Sharp, etc.) used the Zong incident as a rallying call for opposing the African slave trade. The British slave trade was abolished in 1807, twenty years after the controversy sparked by the Zong incident (Northrup 2013).

Ignatius Sancho (1729–1780) was one of the most prominent free Africans of eighteenth-century England. Sancho was born on a slave ship in 1729, raised and educated with the children of the Duke of Montagu, and was provided an annuity at the Duke's death. He became a grocer in London, and his store was a meeting place for those who opposed slavery. Sancho was well educated in classical and contemporary languages. He wrote in the style of belle letters, in which he addressed current affairs in conversation with learned acquaintances, such as playwright Laurence Sterne. His collection of letters was published posthumously in 1782 (Sancho and Carretta 1998). Sancho was also well respected as a musician and had a number of his compositions performed in local concerts. He wrote a treatise on *The Theory of Music* (manuscript lost) (Sancho and Wright 1981). He was well acquainted with the literary, artistic, and political elite of his time, providing living proof that Africans were as capable of civilized pursuits as Europeans. At best, slavery made possible the benefits of literacy to the illiterate (Sancho 1782).

Olaudah Equiano (1745–1797) was kidnapped in 1756 by other Africans in what is now southeast Nigeria. He became a slave in Barbados and then Virginia, where he was sold as a cabin boy to a British naval officer, Michael Pascal, in 1754. As Pascal's assistant, Equiano learned marine technology, navigation, sail rigging, Christianity, and antislavery literacy. Robert King, a West Indian merchant, bought him from Pascal in 1763. King used Equanio's seamanship to ferry up-river to plantations in the interior, and King valued Equanio's literacy for accurate record keeping. Equiano was a very good trader and accumulated enough money ($6,000) to buy his freedom from King in 1766. He served on numerous other voyages with the British Navy, including to the Arctic. Equiano immigrated to London, worked as a servant to Dr. Charles Irving, studied the Bible, and became adept at playing the French horn. He was baptized and championed the importance of literacy and Christianity for Africa (Equiano 1782). Sancho and Equaino's views on race are best expressed in the work of their friend and comrade, Cuguano.

Quobna Cugoano (1757–1791) was born in a Fante village on the Gold Coast of what is now Ghana. He was kidnapped when thirteen years old and enslaved in the West Indies (Grenada) and the United States (Virginia). He was then bought by an English merchant, taken to England, and educated. He was baptized "John Stuart" and freed by Mansfield's

Somerset ruling that denied legal standing to enslavement on English soil. Cugoano's treatise (Cugoano 1787) was a comprehensive review of the relationship between race and slavery. He, like Equaino, argued that the modern enslavement of Africans was different in kind from traditional forms of slavery in Africa. The poverty and misery of modern slaves in the West Indies far exceeded that of traditional African slaves. Raids, kidnapping, sham convictions, and other evil practices were used to rob Africans of their freedom.

But Cugoano did not blame only whites. He recounts his own capture and betrayal by Africans. "I was first kidnapped and betrayed by some of my own complexion." And, he concludes: [I]f a man is bad, it makes no difference whether he be a black or a white devil." Whether a person is innocent or guilty of a crime is independent of the person's race. At best, modern slavery was an imperfect means by which the African could be brought to Christianity (Cugoano 1787, 12–17). In Cugoano's telling of Noah's curse on Ham, the curse was only on Canaan and his descendants. The other sons of Ham were not cursed, including Cush and the Ethiopians (Cugoano 1787, 33). Canaanites were cursed as wicked people who deserved enslavement. But Canaanites were not marked by any feature that distinguished them from the people around them.

Cugoano maintained that traditional slavery was more humane than modern slavery (Cugoano 1787, 35). The ancient slave was often a steward, apprentice, concubine, and could not be traded like chattels and goods. But there is no natural or scriptural justification for the modern enslavement of Africans (Cugoano 1787, 38). The black complexion of the African was as innocent and natural as the spots of the leopard and the red color of roses. God delights in such variety and so should human beings. Africans differ from other races only by color, not virtue or vice (Cugoano 1787, 40). Modern African slavery originates from kidnappings and enslavement by merchants and pirates. Wicked men, emboldened by greed and power, have been allowed to transgress the freedom of others for their own benefit. Such merchandisers in human beings, be they black or white, are the true progeny of Canaan and ought to be punished (Cugoano 1787, 54). Thus, Cugoano does not oppose all forms of enslavement. Traditional justice requires that those who are unjust should have their freedom constrained. Someone legally condemned to death might instead be held as a slave. And for a debt, someone might be held as a slave until the debt is paid off. "[E]very free community might keep slaves, or criminal prisoners in bondage" (Cugoano 1787, 59). But in modern African slavery, "[E]very man who keeps a slave is a robber, whenever he compels him to his service without giving him a just reward" (Cugoano 1787, 35). African slaves sent to European colonies in the West Indies and Brazil had a life of brutal labor and usually survived less than seven years. They received all the costs and none of the benefits from their labor. Cugoano argued that the slave labor of the West Indies should be replaced using free labor on the African continent to produce agricultural commodities for European markets.

RACE IN THE DISCOURSE OF NINETEENTH-CENTURY AFRICANS IN THE UNITED STATES

Although slavery was outlawed in England by Mansfield's ruling of 1772, it remained a legally recognized relationship in the English colonies. American intellectuals of African descent used religion and science to argue against American slavery. David Walker (1796–1830) was born in North Carolina as a freedman. He affiliated with the African Methodist Episcopal (AME) church and ran a clothing business in Boston (1827). Walker's book (Walker 1829) was a radical call for black Americans to rise up and oppose the oppression of slavery and racism. He often referred to whites as the natural enemies of black people. He explains this by reference to the biblical account of the genesis of races. After the flood, Noah and his three sons (Shem, Japheth, and Ham) were the only men on earth and were the progenitors of the current races. But Walker denies that contemporary Africans are the descendants of Canaan, the cursed son of Ham. Nowhere in the Bible, he asserts, are the descendants of Canaan identified as being of a black complexion. Whites who are serious students of the Bible know this, but they distort the texts to make it seem as if Africans were cursed by God. To continue their exploitation, these whites refuse to acknowledge the lie upon which slavery is justified. They fear that if their hypocrisy is exposed, Blacks will seek vengeance and reparations. Those who engage in this distortion of truth and justice make themselves into the natural enemies of those they are oppressing. Blacks who continue to serve whites as if it were their duty are equally oppressors of the black race. Walker admonished former slaves to throw off the slave habits inculcated by their white exploiters (Walker 1829, 883–84).

Martin Delaney (1812–1885) was born in West Virginia. His grandparents were of direct African origin and maintained a vision of their former life in Africa. Delaney's father was a slave but his mother was free, and he was born with free status in Charlestown, West Virginia. He was accepted at Harvard Medical School, but his admission was opposed by white students. He acquired medical training by working as an assistant to abolitionist doctors, but he believed that most whites would always oppose black achievements. He became one of first black nationalists, advocating that African Americans should return to Africa.

Delaney gives the following explanation of the origin of races: Before the flood, all people were a dark rouge complexion. However, after the flood, the three sons of Noah (Shem, Japheth, and Ham) developed different complexions. Delaney assures us that Shem was of the dark rouge complexion of Noah, that Japheth was light complexioned, and Ham was of dark complexion. These are "facts" that Delaney claims are generally conceded. It is presumed that Shem migrated to Asia, Japheth to Europe, and Ham to Africa. They were not separate creations of God, but became separate and different after God's creation, due to environmental influences on the skin (Delaney 1880).

Alexander Crummell (1819–1898) was born in New York City. His mother was a free woman and his father a former slave of African origin. Both parents were ardent abolitionists and advocated migration back to Africa. He was ordained as an Episcopal priest in 1842. Crummell studied at Queens College, Cambridge, from 1849 to 1853 and was Cambridge's first black graduate. He believed that only after Africans united would they be able to succeed, and in 1853 he moved to Liberia to help bring civilization and Christianity to Africa. But he returned to the United States in 1873, fleeing the Liberian mulatto aristocracy. In 1897, he founded the American Negro Academy.

Crummell accepted the biblical account of human creation, in which all races were formed after the flood from the various sons of Noah: Shem, Japheth, and Ham. Crummell also accepted the view that Shem and his family migrated to Asia; Japheth and his family migrated to Europe; and Ham and his family migrated to Africa. In the most common telling of the Genesis story, Noah becomes drunk and is observed naked by Ham. Noah then curses Ham, declaring that his son Canaan would be a servant of servants. Because Ham is the one guilty of the offense against Noah, many have been inclined to believe that his curse was against Ham. Crummell does a careful exegesis of Genesis to show that this view is incorrect, and that Noah's curse was not against Ham, nor against all the progeny of Ham, but only against Canaan (Crummell 1863).

Ham had four sons: Cush, and Mizraim, and Phut, and Canaan (Gen. 10:6). Canaan was the youngest and Cush the oldest. But Noah is explicit in placing the curse on Canaan, and he does not extend the curse to Cush, Mizraim, or Phut. Cush, the eldest of the sons of Ham, is viewed by Crummell as the progenitor of the Negro race, including Egypt and Ethiopia. The Canaanites did not enter Africa, Crummel argues, but instead spread to Judea, Phoenicia, and then into Europe. He concludes: "the blood of the Canaanites was more mingled with that of Europeans than with Africans; for they formed more colonies in Europe than in Africa, and their influence was stronger in Europe than in Africa" (Blyden 1862, 332–340). The descendants of Canaan in Palestine, Phoenicia, Carthage, and in their various colonies, were not black, Crummell asserts. They were not Negroes, either in lineage or color. Shut in by desert to the north and oceans to the east and west, the descendants of Cush were isolated from Europe and Asia until the fifteenth-century sea explorations. The slave trade brought Africa, and the progeny of Cush, into dynamic relationship with Europe and the progeny of Japheth. But it was not the progeny of Cush that was cursed by Noah.

Crummell does not seek some ultimate explanation of the modern enslavement of the descendants of Cush. Instead, he points out that many "races" have been enslaved, not just Africans: the Jews, the Irish, the Saxons, and so forth: "A few centuries ago, Saxons were bought and sold in Ireland and Rome. At one time slaves and cattle were a kind of currency in the land; and down to the period of the Reformation, human beings were "marketable commodities" (Crummell 1888). Slavery has existed within many diverse races. But modern African slavery is of a totally different type than traditional slavery. In ancient times, slaves sometimes rose to positions of great prominence. In modern slavery, this possibility was denied for African slaves. Modern slavery not only denied Africans their freedom, it denied that Africans had the capacity to exercise freedom responsibly. Crummell explicitly claims to have shown that the Negro was not enslaved because his race had been cursed by God (many nonnegro races have been enslaved); and that a black complexion was not a mark of God's curse (no mention is made in Genesis that the progeny of Cush had been cursed).

For Crummell, a race is an extended family, created by God and endowed with an affinity for others of that race. Because of this affinity, members of a race tend to perpetuate certain characteristic features. They are attracted to others like themselves. The contemporary mixture between blacks and whites has not been the result of mutual attractions, but the result of the rape of black women by white men. This, Crummell speculates, disadvantaged the mixed race progeny of such unions (Crummell 1995, 166–168).

Edward Blyden (1832–1912) was born in the Danish West Indies (now the Virgin Islands). He was mentored by a Dutch Reformed minister (John Knox) who encouraged Blyden to study in the United States. After Blyden was refused admission by three theological seminaries, Knox encouraged him to immigrate to Liberia. He became a professor of Greek, Latin, and West African languages at Liberia College and served as its president from 1880 to 1884. He was an advocate of Africans returning to Africa to develop Africa's special gifts and aptitudes.

Because the Negro is distinctive in complexion, hair, nose, and lips; and because the Negro is a servant of all the other races, Blyden acknowledges how easy it is to assume there is a causal relationship between these facts (Blyden 1857, 32). One of the most common explanations was that the Negro's complexion was a mark of God's curse, through Noah, on the children of Ham. And even though the curse clearly designates Canaan, it is interpreted as applying to all the descendants of Ham. This made it possible to extend the curse to all African people, and it provided a convenient justification for modern African slavery. Defenders of slavery contended that it was fruitless to endeavor to elevate the African, for he was doomed to perpetual servitude, and was, therefore, fitted for no other condition (Blyden 1857, 34). In this way, many devout Christians absolved themselves of the wrongful treatment of Africans, reasoning that since Africans had already been cursed by God, those who profited from slavery were simply fulfilling God's curse. Blyden emphasized how, even though the curse was explicitly against Canaan, it was convenient for slave owners to interpret it as if the curse were against Ham and all his descendants.

Some students of the Bible were bothered that Canaan was forced to bear the punishment when Ham was the transgressor. But Blyden gives many examples of God's curse being against both the transgressor and the transgressor's descendants. Slavery was the instrument God used to punish the Canaanites. The Israelites, having been slaves to the Egyptians, now made the Canaanites their slaves. The Canaanites became servants of servants. But, Blyden reiterates, "it was not the intention of the malediction that either Mizraim or Cush (the other sons of Ham), whose descendants peopled Africa, should be a servant of servants to Shem; but it did intend that the descendants of Canaan, whom it distinctly mentions, should be so related to Shem" (Blyden 1862, 45).

For Blyden, African slavery was the effect of sin, but not Noah's curse. He explains that Africans had knowledge of the true God in the past, but they lost it and descended into heathenism. Slavery was Africa's punishment for the sin of abandoning God. As Africans accept the true God of Christianity, they would cease to be slaves. It is the blessings promised by redemption in Christianity that make the afflictions of slavery bearable (Blyden 1862, 47). Carried away from their indigenous homes, Africans have maintained their distinctness. Like the Israelites, "The more they were afflicted the more they multiplied and grew" (Exod.1:2).

Blyden directly confronts the belief that Africans are less intelligent than Europeans. He cites an array of African intellectuals, artists, and poets to prove that Africans were as capable of European achievements as Europeans. "Arguments in our favor that would be regarded as conclusive in regard to any other race are unceremoniously discarded. Instead, the most unfavorable isolated cases are taken as fair specimens of the character of the whole race" (Blyden 1862, 52). Only when Africans are given the same opportunities as Europeans will it be possible to say if one or the other is superior (Blyden 1862, 54). Until equal conditions prevail, it is impossible to say that Africans have less or more potential than Europeans. Blyden concludes: "Give Africans the same amount of culture, from generation to generation, that Europeans have enjoyed, and their features [and thoughts] will assume the same proportion and symmetry" (Blyden 1862, 57).

Blyden believed that Africa (and Liberia in particular) could not succeed unless the slave trade was abolished and talented Africans educated under slavery returned to Africa to lead and teach. Africans could not depend on having Europeans as their primary teachers because Europeans in Africa typically suffered disease and discomfort, and projected their infirmities onto their view of African people. Africans from America would adapt better to African conditions than Europeans, and they would not be so ill fitted to their tasks. "Only the Negro would be able to explain the Negro to the rest of mankind" (Blyden 1887, 263).

Blyden considered most of those sold into slavery to have been the lower classes of Africa: slaves in Africa, or convicted criminals, or prisoners of war. Yet they have been conflated with African noblemen and scholars, as if there were no differences among Africans. Blyden emphasizes that there are many "races" in Africa, groups that have maintained their distinctiveness, such as the Fulanese, Mandingoes, Hausa, Bornous, Yoruba, and Igbo. "No short definition is adequate to include all these groups. Yet whites like to give general definitions about the nature of the African based on their experience of slaves (Blyden 1887, 273).

Blyden denies that "the Negro is the European in embryo," still underdeveloped (Blyden 1887, 276). Rather, he declares that Africans have a distinct role to play in the advance of civilization, and this role is specific to the race. Africans and Europeans "are not identical but unequal; they are distinct but equal." The African "has capacities and aptitudes which the world needs, but which it will never enjoy until the African is fairly and normally trained" (Blyden 1887, 281). "When the African shall come forward with his peculiar gifts, he will fill a place never before occupied" (Blyden 1887, 278). To fulfill this destiny, Blyden opposed racial amalgamation:

> "Let us do away with the sentiment of Race. Let us do away with out African personality and be lost, if possible, in another Race." This is as wise or as philosophical as to say, let us do away with gravitation, with heat and cold and sunshine and rain. Of course, the Race in which these persons would be absorbed is the dominant race, before which, in cringing self-surrender and ignoble self-suppression they lie in prostrate admiration. (Blyden 1893/Estebe 1994, 28.)

Frederick Douglass (1818–1895) was born Frederick Bailey, a slave in Talbot County, Maryland. After a famous fight with his overseer Covey, he escaped from slavery and changed his name to Douglass. During his early years working as an abolitionist, he was a fugitive slave and had to avoid being arrested by bounty hunters. In 1838 he married Anna Murray, a free black woman, and he was licensed to preach in 1839. He worked with William Garrison at *The Liberator* until he founded *The North Star* newspaper, whose motto was: "Right is of no sex—Truth is of no color—God is the Father of us all, and we are brethren." He traveled to Ireland in 1845, at the beginning of the potato famine, and remained in Europe for two years. During this visit, British abolitionists raised enough money to buy his freedom from his former master. At age twenty-eight, he was no longer a fugitive.

In mid-nineteenth-century America, "The Race Problem" was typically portrayed as the problem of what to do with an innately inferior race cursed by God. But for Douglass, it was a problem of what to do with a society cursed by a greed and prejudice that made possible the unrestrained exploitation of Africans. Douglass held that there was only one race, which was the human race. Many subgroups of the human race have been formed around different factors, such as sex, skin color, and religion. But humans, no matter how they are grouped, are all similar because they can feel, they can reason, and they can dream, and they therefore should not be oppressed. For Douglass, the question of what to do with slaves and former slaves "is an American problem and not a Negro problem" (Douglass 1889/2013, 724).

Douglass denied that Negroes would become extinct, as had happened to many Native American groups. And he opposed the colonization and deportation of American Negroes to Africa or South America: "If the American people could endure the Negro's presence while a slave, they certainly can and ought to endure his presence as a free man" (Douglass 1884, 411). Douglass also opposed the racial separation of Jim Crow. He rejected the notion that American Negroes could form a separate nation within America, with separate institutions and facilities.

"When we isolate ourselves we lose, in a large measure, the common benefit of association with those whose advantages have been superior to ours" (Douglass 1884, 411). Douglass believed that by living among whites, blacks could profit from the benefits whites had accumulated.

Douglass admitted that the Negro might suffer other forms of oppression by whites in the future. But he did not consider the situation of American Negroes to be any different from that of many other persecuted groups in history: "The Hebrews in Egypt, the Moors in Spain, the Caribs in the West Indies, the Picots in Scotland, the Indians in our own country, show what may happen to the negro" (Douglass 1884, 412). Instead, he asserted that the religion and civilization of the American Negro was in such close harmony with that of American whites, that to destroy the Negro would do violence to many American whites as well, and to America's own precepts. "Drive out the Negro and you drive out Christ, the Bible, and American liberty with him" (Douglass 1884, 412). Douglass cautioned that American blacks must act, not exclusively, but inclusively; not separately but together with other races and other groups to oppose oppression in all forms.

Douglass took the existence of millions of mixed-race Negroes as concrete proof that there was not natural antipathy between the black and white races. And he speculated that Americans of mixed race would become more, rather than less, numerous. "The tendency of the age is toward unification, not isolation; not to clans and classes (and complexions), but to human brotherhood" (Douglass 1884, 412). It was once degrading for a Norman to associate with a Saxon, or for a Christian to associate with a Jew, but now they are both Englishmen. In the past (and present), it may have been degrading for white Americans to associate with black Americans, but in the future they will both be only Americans. In such circumstances, intermarriage between whites and blacks will be no more problematic than intermarriage between Protestant and Catholic, Christian and Jew, English and Irish (Douglass 1884, 413). The Negro "will not be expatriated nor annihilated, nor will he forever remain a separate and distinct race from the people around him, but . . . he will be absorbed, assimilated, and will only appear finally . . . in the features of a blended race." Douglass is careful to deny that he is advocating black/white intermarriage, but only predicting this outcome: "While I would not be understood as advocating the desirability of such a result, I would not be understood as deprecating it" (Douglass 1866/2000, 590–591).

Douglass felt that American Negroes needed to be as critical of themselves as they were of American whites. He spoke against Negroes taking excess pride in the achievements of members of their own race. Instead, Douglass argued that being of a particular race was nothing to be proud (or ashamed) of. An individual can only be proud of achievements that are the result of that individual's effort and ingenuity. "Our color is a gift of the Almighty. We should be neither proud of it nor ashamed of it. But we may well enough be proud or ashamed when we have ourselves achieved success or have, by our faults, failed of success" (Douglass 1889/2013, 790). Moreover, if it is legitimate for the Negro to appeal to race pride, then it is an equally legitimate appeal for whites to be proud of their domination of blacks. "If we are proud let it be because we have had some agency in producing what we are proud of. Do not let us be proud of what we can neither help nor hinder" (Douglass 1889/2013, 790).

For Douglass, the problem was not in color, sex, religion, or ancestral origin. The problem was when such factors were used to justify oppressing others. Thus, Douglass was as much opposed to the Asian "cheap labor," or "coolie" trade, as he was to the African slave trade. After the abolishment of slavery, people from India and Asia were hired and transported to plantations in Asia and the West Indies to do the work Africans could no longer be forced to do. As coolies, these workers were viewed, not as human beings, but as sources of cheap labor and forced to work much as Africans had been under slavery. Thus, Douglass wrote: "The rights of a Coolie in California, in Peru, in Jamaica, in Trinidad, and on board the vessels bearing them to these countries, are scarcely more than those of Negro slaves brought to our shores a century ago. The suffering of these people while in transit are almost as heart rending as any that attended the African slave trade" (Douglass 1871/1955, 262). In 1871, the ship "Dolores Ugarte" sank while carrying over 500 Asian laborers to work on plantations in Asia and America. They were locked below deck, and when the ship caught fire, they were burned to death (Douglass 1871/1955, 262). This far exceeded the loss of lives in 1783 when 132 Africans were thrown overboard from the ship *Zong* in order to collect insurance.

Douglass wrote: "My sentiments . . . originate not in my color, but in a sense of justice common to all right minded men. It is not because I am a Negro, but because I am a man. It is that which gives the sympathy of the crowd to the underdog, no matter what may be his color" (Douglass 1871/1955, 262). He believed that the "sense of justice common to all right minded men" should also apply to all right-minded women and Douglass was an early supporter of women's rights (Douglass 1870, 448). Throughout his life, Douglass actively opposed the oppression of humans on the basis of race, sex, religion, and ethnic origin.

CONCLUSION

Prominent Anglo-American intellectuals of African descent during the eighteenth and nineteenth centuries used European religion, science, and philosophy to argue that Africans were not cursed by God, were not an inherently inferior people, and were not a race of "natural slaves." They accepted Christianity as the source of revealed truth, and they accepted the biblical account of the sons of Noah (Shem, Japheth, Ham) as the progenitors of the present races. But they make clear that Noah's curse on Canaan had invalidly been taken to be a curse on all the children of Ham. The curse was on Canaan and his descendants, and Africans were descendants of Cush, not of Canaan.

Anglo-American intellectuals of African descent also accepted the importance of logic and scientific reasoning. They critically engaged scientific accounts that justified the enslavement of Africans, and they offered alternative scientific accounts that gave Africans a human potential equal to that of Europeans. Nineteenth-century African American intellectuals emphasized a new concern, not just with the past origin of races, but with the future evolution of the races: Should the races be separate and distinct, or should they amalgamate and become mixed? Such questions about race and mixed race continue to bedevil the modern world. It is important to see how such questions were treated by eighteenth- and nineteenth-century intellectuals of African descent.

REFERENCES

Blyden, Edward Wilmot. (1862). *Liberia's Offering: Being Addresses, Sermons, Etc.* New York: J. A. Gray.

Blyden, Edward Wilmot. (1857). *A Vindication of the African Race Being a Brief Examination of the Arguments in Favor of African Inferiority; or Noah's Malediction.* Monrovia, Liberia: Printed by G. Killian.

Blyden, Edward Wilmot. (1887). "Africa and the African." In *Christianity, Islam, and the Negro Race*. London: W. B. Whittingham & Co., 1887; 2nd ed. 1888; 3rd ed., University of Edinburgh Press, 1967; reprint of 1888 edition, Baltimore, MD: Black Classic Press, 1994 (edition on Googlebooks), 298–324.

Blyden, Edward Wilmot. (1893). "Towards a West African Community," *Sierra Leone Weekly News*, May 27. Reprinted in Edward Wilmot Blyden, *Pan-Negro Patriot 1832–1912*, edited by Hollis Ralph Lynch, 1967, 215. Liberia: Oxford University Press.

Crummell, Alexander. (1863). *The Negro Race Not Under a Curse. An Examination of Genesis IX. 25. Reprinted, with Corrections and Additions, from the London "Christian Observer."* London, UK: British Museum Catalogue of Printed Books, 49.

Crummell, Alexander. (1888). *The Race-Problem in America*. Paper read at The Church Congress (Protestant-Episcopal Church). Buffalo, NY, November 20,. Library of Congress.

Crummell, Alexander. (1995). *Civilization and Black Progress: Selected Writings of Alexander Crummell on the South*. Edited by John Oldfield Charlottesville: University Press of Virginia,.

Cugoano, Ottobouh. [1791] (1999). *Thoughts and Sentiments on the Evil of Slavery*. New York: Penguin Classics.

Delany, Martin Robison. (1880). *Principia of Ethnology: The Origin of Races and Color: with an Archaeological Compendium of Ethiopian and Egyptian Civilization from Years of Careful Examination and Injury*. Kindle edition. Philadelphia: Harper.

Douglass, Frederick. (1866/2000). "The Future of the Colored Race. [The Future of the Negro Race]." *North American Review*, May 1866. In *Frederick Douglass: Selected Speeches and Writing*, edited by Philip Foner and Yuval Taylor, 590–591. Chicago, IL: Lawrence Hill Books.

Douglass, Frederick. (1870/2000). "The Women's Suffrage Movement." In *Frederick Douglass: Selected Speeches and Writing*, edited by Philip Foner and Yuval Taylor, 706–710. Chicago, IL: Lawrence Hill Books.

Douglass, Frederick. [1871] (1955). "Cheap Labor." In *The Life and Writings of Frederick Douglass*, edited by Philip Foner. Vol. 4, *The New National Era*, 264–266. New York: International Publishers.

Douglass, Frederick. [1889] (2013). "The Race Problem: A Speech Delivered by Hon. Frederick Douglass, before the Bethel Literary and Historical Society in Washington, D.C., April 16, 1889." In *Great Speeches by Frederick Douglas*, edited by James Daley, 88–104. New York: Dover

Equiano, Olaudah. [1782] (2003). *The Interesting Narrative of the Life of Olaudah Equaino, or Gustavus Vassa, the African*. New York: Penguin Classic.

Esedebe, Peter Olisanwuche. (1994). *Pan-Africanism: The Idea and Movement, 1776–1991*. Washington, DC: Howard University.

Northrup, David. (2013). *Africa's Discovery of Europe*. New York: Oxford University Press.

Sancho, Ignatius. (1782). *Letters of the Late Ignatius Sancho, An African. In Two Volumes. To Which Are Prefixed, Memoirs of His Life*, Vol. I. London: J. Nichols.

Sancho, Ignatius, and Vincent Carretta. (1998). *Letters of the Late Ignatius Sancho, an African*. New York, N.Y.: Penguin Books.

Sancho, Ignatius, and Josephine R. B. Wright. (1981). *Ignatius Sancho (1729–1780): Aan Early African Composer in England: The Collected Editions of His Music in Facsimile*. New York: Garland Publishers.

Walker, David. [1829] (2011). *Walker's Appeal, in Four Articles Together with a Preamble, to the Coloured Citizens of the World, but in Particular, and Very Expressly, to Those of the United States of America, Written in Boston, Massachusetts, September 28, 1829*. Chapel Hill: University of North Carolina at Chapel Hill Library.

CHAPTER 7

INDIGENEITY AND US SETTLER COLONIALISM

KYLE POWYS WHYTE

As a Neshnabé (Potawatomi), living in the United States context, indigenous persons from elsewhere often ask me: "We hear this crazy idea that whether one is Indigenous where you're from is measured by blood." Here, "blood" refers to a racial criterion that the US federal government and some US-recognized indigenous political entities use for the purpose of enrollment. Many persons find the use of blood surprising because it seems to defy indigenous cultural and political self-determination. Indeed, many of the indigenous peoples in North America have rich systems of membership based on family, clan, or other kinship identities; culturally specific processes for being recognized as a community member; and processes appropriate for the ongoing reality that there has been constant intermingling across different peoples and communities (TallBear 2007). Thus, blood seems like so much US colonial baggage.

In the US context, indigenous identity presents many difficulties in addition to blood, ranging from peculiar census definitions to accusations of identity fraud. I will discuss in this chapter a brief outline of my view that these difficulties are oppressive dilemmas and disappearances that are built into those structures of US settler colonialism that seek to erase us in our own homelands. Looking forward, I will appeal to Kim TallBear's work, which I will interpret in relation to my own work on environmental justice, to suggest at least one possible alternative for addressing issues associated with indigeneity and settler erasure.

DIFFICULTIES WITH IMPOSED INDIGENOUS IDENTITIES

The issue of whether someone is indigenous produces many difficulties. Here I will merely gloss a wide range of difficulties in very broad strokes, which means readers should take these examples as merely illustrative and by no means adequate in relation to all the facts, intricacies, interpretations, and literatures on the topic. To begin with, when people refer to "degree of Indian blood," they are usually referring to qualifications needed to enroll in a US federal program or in an indigenous political entity that are based on someone's being of the "Indian" or "Native American" race. Yet recognition by an indigenous political entity, such as a US federally recognized Tribe (e.g., Citizen Potawatomi Nation or Navajo Nation), or by a US federal program is not necessarily the same as belonging to an indigenous people. For example, someone could be Potawatomi genetically, self-reportedly, or as identified by a community, but not qualify for enrollment in a Tribe or federal program. One reason why this can be the case is that many federally recognized Tribal governments stem from US policies in particular time periods, such as the 1930s, when the US pressured Tribes to adopt certain governmental structures and membership criteria. The US policies in the 1930s meant to facilitate the leasing of indigenous homelands to extractive industries, such as oil. Hence, they cannot be considered as attempting to honor the family, cultural, or political systems of membership created outside the context of colonialism (Taylor 1980; Rusco 2000; Spruhan 2006). Moreover, methods of documenting someone's being partly or wholly of the Indian race are often ridiculous, such as historic cases where settlers used visual cues (Spruhan 2006).

Many Tribes since the 1970s are contesting Indian blood criteria and favoring more genealogical forms of "Tribal" blood or lineal descent that rely on a person's being able to trace his or her ancestry to records that are used for determining whether someone is a member of a very particular indigenous political entity, such as the Citizen Potawatomi Nation or Hannahville Indian Community (Gover 2008). Again, these genealogical forms of indigeneity can be problematic, given the ultimate origins of some of these political entities as business enterprises. Indigenous political entities can view membership through the lens of business interests and economic development strategies tied to US colonialism. Today, some Tribes have changed their membership criteria to reduce total members so as to preserve a larger share of economic revenues, hence disenrolling some persons who had been members since birth. But there is also another side of the story. Some Tribes have elected to increase their total membership to take advantage of political, cultural, and economic opportunities associated with having larger official citizenries, sometimes seeing the expansion of membership as better honoring traditional or simply more favorable kinship systems (Doerfler 2013). Owing to changes in membership criteria, someone who has always been indigenous may be enrolled, unenrolled, and disenrolled at various times during his or her life.

Indian blood and membership in a Tribal political entity are both used in a variety of contexts today. Some federal programs, such as Haskell Indian Nations University, require all candidates to be an "enrolled or official member of a Federally recognized tribe eligible for education benefits from the Bureau of Indian Affairs or at least one-fourth total degree Indian blood direct descendant of an enrolled member of a tribe eligible for BIA education benefits." State programs, such as the Michigan Indian tuition waiver, require Tribes to send letters that "certify that the above named applicant is ¼ (one quarter) or more degree of Indian blood quantum according to the available Tribal and/or Federal records. AND . . . certify that the above named applicant is an enrolled member of this Tribe, which is US Federally Recognized." In all the forms of membership just described, indigeneity is related in some way to the structure of US federal or state programs or indigenous political entities whose systems of governance are deeply influenced by the US. Controversies often ensue when Tribal membership criteria are systematically harmful to certain populations, such as when the children of women who marry outside of the Tribe cannot enroll, whereas those of outside-marrying men can enroll, or in the case of Tribes who seek to disenroll descendants of people whom the US enslaved and who became Tribal members in the nineteenth century.

There are many understandings of what indigeneity could mean that cannot be systematized because they correspond to understandings of Tribal identity that are not tied to US colonial criteria or to that of a specific indigenous political entity. Consider some examples. Being indigenous could have to do with being from a particular parentage that identifies with a particular Tribal band, clan, or set of families. These bands, clans, or families are not constitutive of any political entity and the individuals in them are not formally enrolled. Being indigenous could stem from being part of an urban community in which one was identified as Native American by both outsiders based on visual interpretation and/or by others who identify as Native American in relation to their involvement in an urban Indian center. People sometimes use the expression "phenotypically white" or "phenotypically black," and so on, to describe persons who are indigenous but who strangers interpret visually as belonging to another group.

Being indigenous could also be based on knowing that one was adopted but not knowing from what Tribe, and hence being unable to enroll in any particular indigenous political entity. Or, one's family could have practiced certain customs in a particular area for some time, but no family members are enrolled. Persons may not have any customary knowledge of their specific indigenous groups, although they grew up in a reservation area with many American Indians. There are ways that indigenous people relate to each other that are understood as indigenous but that are not historically customary, such as a certain sense of humor and way of speaking, Pan-Indian powwow culture, or a more recently adopted religion such as the Native American Church or Big Drum. Or individuals may base their Indian identity on having been identified visually by others as indigenous their entire lives, whether they grew up on reservations, were adopted, or were raised in areas with few indigenous persons or communities. Some people simply identify as belonging to their particular community or nation (e.g., Potawatomi), instead of as "American Indian" or "indigenous," which often pays respect to the colonial idea that so many different peoples are constantly lumped into one. Yet for others, "indigenous" is empowering because it denotes shared experiences of a common form of oppression.

At the United Nations, since the 1970s indigenous peoples have established a Permanent Forum on Indigenous Issues, an Expert Mechanism on the Rights of Indigenous Peoples, a Special Rapporteur on the Rights of Indigenous Peoples, and numerous caucuses, reports, and declarations. These institutions and discourses have established definitions of "indigenous" that are voluntary and refer to a particular social situation that many groups in the world face. Indigenous peoples are typically defined as societies whose self-governance precedes a period of invasion, colonialization, or settlement by other groups and who now live in territories—now controlled by nation states—in which they are the nondominant societies. Indigenous peoples often seek to continue to exercise self-determination, both culturally and politically, in the midst of the power wielded by such nation states.

There are further distinctions in the US regarding indigenous political entities. A person can have membership, based on some criterion, in a state-recognized Tribal government or an unrecognized Tribal government that seeks to be recognized by the US federal government or a US state. Unrecognized and state-recognized Tribes may fail to have the documentation needed to qualify for US federal recognition simply because they were historically trying to remain underneath the radar of settler populations or did not interact through treaties or in other ways with the US settler state. Switching to transnational issues, a person might identify as Potawatomi, for example, but live on the Canadian side of the international border, on Bkejwanong Territory (Walpole Island First Nation). The Potawatomi do not respect the significance of the US/Canadian border because they did not consent to that border as a divider between Potawatomi peoples. Yet I am aware of cases I at least find deeply disturbing, such as one in which a federally recognized Tribe sought to reduce membership by excluding "blood from Canada."

Native Hawaiians are indigenous peoples who do not share the same US government status as "mainland" federally recognized Tribes, and there is an active discussion among Native Hawaiians regarding the best way to interact with the US settler state (Van Dyke 1998). There are also differences with wide-ranging ramifications between Native Americans and Alaska Natives that are due, again, to US policies. Hispano acequia communities in the Southwest US have water use rights (e.g., the state of Colorado's Acequia Recognition Law of 2009) through the acequia system (irrigation for agriculture), which raises comparable issues to American Indian rights that preexist the formation of the US or statehood in those regions (Hicks and Peña 2003). Such political distinctions go on ad infinitum. These political distinctions, from federally recognized Tribes to Native Hawaiians, make it difficult for certain kinds of indigenous political solidarity to form since the different indigenous political entities negotiate different US structures and institutions.

Fraudulent claims to indigeneity is another long-standing issue affecting many Native communities. For example, in the late nineteenth century in Indian Territory (now the US state of Oklahoma and home to thirty-nine Tribes), many settler Americans identified as members of particular Tribes so that that they could live in areas that were designated mainly for Indians (Debo 1972). There are also historical trends of settler populations "playing Indian," or taking on Indian identities that were otherwise uncommon in their everyday lives (Deloria 1998). These "imposters" have, in some cases, been able to purchase and control traditional lands, with ensuing bad relations with nearby Tribes who have rejected their claims to indigeneity.

There are recent controversies about pointing out that people, especially scholars, activists, and politicians, who have identified as Native American, have no claim to indigenous identity in *any* of the senses described earlier. Here I choose not to name any particular people or cases out of respect for the complexity of these cases. Suffice it to say that in many cases, people have claimed to be enrolled in Tribes in which they were not enrolled. Or they have claimed to be Native American in the other senses described earlier, but friends and colleagues remember a time when they identified as white, black, or another racial identity. Or some people have parents, grandparents, and siblings who identify as something else, such as Latino or white, but one person identifies as Indian publically. Ethically thorny issues arise when people who identify fraudulently often have no connections with the communities that they claim to represent and are often considered to be taking opportunities for representation from others with social connections to particular communities or who have been chosen legitimately by those communities as representatives.

There are, in addition, widespread problems with how census surveyors and scientists identify indigenous persons. In the US Census, there is complexity relating to whether people who check boxes really count as indigenous, if they are doing so only because they have a tenuous family story of American Indian heritage. Reviewing the 2010 US Census, philosopher Sean Valles argues that indigenous identity is classified in the US Census by using inconsistent and burdensome standards. The federal demographic standards for who qualifies as "American Indian" are different from all other racial categories. Whereas every racial category is based on one's "origins" in certain "peoples" (e.g., white is defined by "having origins in any of the original peoples of Europe, the Middle East, or North Africa"), only "American Indian or Alaska Native" has the additional requirement that one also "maintains tribal affiliation or community attachment," a social component more appropriate for an ethnicity classification than a race classification. This two-factor standard can conflict with Indian or Tribal blood standards used to determine indigenous identity in many Tribal or federal contexts. It also has troubling implications for those it excludes; for example, a person born of two American Indian parents, but raised without any social or psychological connections to American Indian communities, does not qualify for *any* of the federal census race classifications (aside from "Other"). Meanwhile, Native Hawaiians are put into a separate racial grouping, splitting the indigenous US population (for a partial discussion of this view, see Valles, Bhopal, and Aspinall 2015; Humes, Jones, and Ramirez 2011).

Scientists have often defined indigenous groups as historic societies that are no longer in existence and whose genetic diversity is dying out. There can be political controversy based on how various scientific definitions can serve to sever contemporary indigenous peoples from their lands and ancestors. Much is at stake if indigenous peoples cannot exercise rights to territories, resources, human remains, burial locations, archeological sites, cultural artifacts, and so on, that are still connected to their contemporary cultural expressions, projects of cultural reconstruction, and political sovereignty (TallBear 2013).

INDIGENEITY AND SETTLER ERASURE

The difficulties described earlier can be understood as so many dilemmas and disappearances that indigenous persons face when we attempt to define ourselves in relation to US colonialism. I will define "dilemma" and "disappearance" later in this section as forms of erasure tied to settler colonialism. I will suggest that we can begin to solve these problems once we recognize that some of the most vicious conflicts are products of settler colonialism as a structure of oppression against indigenous peoples (Lefevre 2015). That is, these dilemmas and disappearances are not primarily philosophically puzzling; more significantly, their continued existence serves to advance settler colonial oppression.

I will use the term *industrial settler colonialism* to refer to one of the forms of oppression indigenous peoples face in the US sphere. To understand this form of oppression, I will need to start with a few claims about the history of indigenous self-governance in North America. Indigenous peoples practiced a wide range of governance systems and adapted to many changes over the course of many hundreds of years in North America. Indigenous self-governance differed greatly from European political traditions. For example, Anishinaabe peoples (including Ojibwe, Ottawa, and Potawatomi societies) practiced a seasonal round system of self-governance, in which structures of political authority changed throughout the year depending on what people believed to be the best way to steward ecosystems for optimal harvesting of plants and animals, with multispecies forms of responsibility connected to clan and family systems (Benton-Benai 1988; Davidson-Hunt and Berkes 2003). These systems of government were part of what made North America a homeland for many indigenous peoples. Europeans who came to North America did not intend *only* to extract resources to their metropoles and then leave. Rather, many of the Europeans intended to stay and to make

North America their homeland. For this reason, the term "settler colonialism" applies to a significant part of what happens here in the US sphere (Goldstein 2014). Indigenous peoples not only negotiate the struggle to control "natural resources." Rather, they have to negotiate the struggle of another people coming to make a homeland for themselves within indigenous homelands.

One should not underestimate the physicality and scale of the US settler homeland creation process. Europeans, and eventually US Americans, had to physically shape the lands and waters to reflect their future aspirations and fears, economic systems, cultures, ways of life, and heritages. They literally had to carve out, or inscribe, a homeland for themselves, within a territory whose ecosystems were already coupled with the social, political, and cultural institutions of different populations (e.g., the Anishinaabe seasonal round system). Moreover, for many people who want a territory to be a homeland for themselves, they have to be able to claim it as a place. That is, they have to make themselves believe that they are the "indigenous" inhabitants of that region. So the homeland process involves the creation or adaptation of stories, customs, histories, and so on, that justify settlers' own desires to have the right to live there and to make their occupation an inevitable part of their heritage and future trajectory.

The "industrial" aspect of this process has involved and continues to involve the ways that capitalism and other economic forms exploit natural and human resources as part of the support system for settler homeland inscription, maintenance, and development. Lacking long-term knowledge of the ecosystem and applying their own understandings from elsewhere to the land, they established large-scale industrial agriculture, factories, transportation systems, and hydro-technologies such as dams. These technological systems replaced indigenous technological systems, altering the ecosystems through clearing land, pollution, and the construction of barriers and arteries (e.g., roads, pipelines and dams). At the same time, industrial processes gradually distanced many settlers from an awareness of how their societies were based on these forms of natural, animal, and human resource exploitation. Indeed, many industrial processes take place on lands where the predominate populations are indigenous or people of color, or the labor required for certain industries, such as large agriculture, stems from migrant populations. Industrial settler colonialism, hence, obscures its own support systems.

In this sense, settler colonialism is not fundamentally a discursive construct or mental state (Tuck and Yang 2012). Rather, industrial settler colonialism is a physical, material, and ecological excavation that can ground and provide evidence for the discursive constructs and mental states of settlers. For example, discourses such as US agrarian myths, with obligations to till the land, find their value when one clears the land for agriculture from another's land that has not been used that way. When we fly over large parts of the US, the land is visible as the ongoing quest to fulfill a specific agricultural vision. The patchwork of fields, farms, and small towns is often considered to be "beautiful" by many settlers or emblematic of something else of value, such as "feeding the world" or "growth." Someone once told me that the only way to see "real America" was to take back highways through small towns in the "breadbasket" of the US and "New England." We can compare, at least using our imagination, how the "patchwork" sections of North America would have looked like from an airplane angle when they were under indigenous systems of self-government—for example, in an Anishinaabe seasonal round system of self-governance.

The form of oppression, then, associated with industrial settler colonialism is that settler societies seek to *erase* indigenous peoples, and in a number of ways: physically, "ecosystemicly," discursively, culturally, and so forth. When one views the land today, one no longer sees very many signs of indigenous peoples. Instead, one sees the physical manifestations of US settler society, whether that includes miles and miles of industrial agriculture in the Midwest or urban neighborhoods dotted with coffee shops and restaurants or massive military industrial or petrochemical complexes that stretch out over miles in order to manufacture weapons or produce fuel. Settler colonialism is not confined to the first generation of settlers; rather, it is the people today, too—and of nearly all political leanings—who continue to shape the physical landscape to make the land their homeland—and in the process erase indigenous peoples.

One of the key structural features of industrial settler colonialism is to facilitate erasure through the establishment of dilemmas and disappearances. Disappearances are direct productions of ignorance that render indigenous peoples invisible in their own homelands. One can locate these disappearances in technologies of disappearing themselves. For example, the US public school curriculum typically does not feature any material on indigenous peoples. In cases where it does, they are often discriminatory, such as the California "missions" assignment that students in California often do in fourth grade that involves visiting a Spanish mission. In this assignment, they become acquainted with religious and philanthropic efforts to "develop" the region for settlement. This notion of "development" is a technology of disappearing that disappears the already existing and thriving indigenous peoples in the land and the implication of some of the missions in genocide for the sake of centering settler discourses.

Boarding schools, which in the US functioned in the nineteenth and twentieth centuries, and forced relocation, such as US-sponsored Indian removal in the nineteenth century and urban relocation in the twentieth century, are another such technology. They sought to strip indigenous peoples of their languages, cultures, and ways of life. The failure of many settlers to see Tribes as sovereigns with legitimate Tribal police and courts having jurisdiction over their actions is another technology. For example, this issue has put Native women at great risk of being raped with impunity by non-Tribal members (Deer 2004). All of these things, and many more besides, are technologies of disappearance that feed into settler erasure of indigenous persons.

Dilemmas involve impositions of choices on indigenous peoples in which each decision option will produce erasure. Consider what some call the cultural dilemma in Tribal environmental governance. Since the mid-1970s, the US created a policy establishing that the US will respect Tribal governments' environmental regulation of their lands in the same way that US states do, by developing regulatory agencies that take over federal programs, such as clean air or clean water. For Tribes who have struggled to protect their lands in ways that are appropriate to their communities, this policy provides an opportunity to advance political self-determination in ways that are enforceable. Yet Tribes must qualify for certain standards set by states in order to achieve the status of being able to have their own agencies. This creates a choice for many Tribes between doing things their own ways, but not having any enforceable regulatory authority, or having enforceable regulatory authority but following the standards of the US. Either way represents problems that lead to the erasure of indigenous peoples, whether they retain distinct forms of government or adapt to governments the US recognizes. Resistance can spell great hardship for governments the US subsequently fails to recognize; conformity destroys distinct indigenous forms of government, homogenizing them with Western bureaucratic structures that may not be best for addressing key social, health, cultural, environmental, and other issues that indigenous peoples face uniquely (Ranco et al. 2011).

Although I cannot go into detail at all, it should at least be apparent that the difficulties with indigenous identity can be looked at as disappearances and dilemmas too that contribute to settler erasure. Consider the topic of racial definitions of indigeneity taken up earlier. These definitions of Indian blood disappear the social, cultural, and political (sovereign) aspects of indigenous peoples, thereby erasing indigenous collective life and self-governance in the US. Historically, degree of Indian blood was used to exclude indigenous peoples from having civil rights during the 1700s. The federal government privileged Indians with more white blood with rights, such as having "wardship" restrictions removed or being able to sell property (Spruhan 2006). One can imagine the dilemma this put people in regarding the consequences of how they sought to identify themselves. In other cases, census and scientific definitions of indigeneity disappear connections between Native Americans and Native Hawaiians or exclude indigenous histories of their connections to their own ancestors. Due to technologies of disappearing, people who misrepresent their indigenous identity are often able to succeed in doing so because academic, political, and other institutions are not accountable to indigenous peoples.

Many indigenous political identities, such as US federally recognized Tribal governments, are torn over the dilemma of whether to establish membership eligibility at one-quarter Tribal blood or lineal descent Tribal blood (descent from a single ancestor on a base roll often going as far back as 80–100 years). As Tribes must abide by the US-imposed rule that one cannot be a member of more than one federally recognized Tribe, eligibility at one-quarter Tribal blood threatens to reduce the Tribe to few members; yet lineal descent could authorize people as bona fide and voting Tribal members who never identified as indigenous their entire lives. At the same time, some indigenous peoples may find it not worth making certain tradeoffs or simply impractical to reestablish traditional forms of community and political membership. For these forms may not be respected politically by the US (which, suffice to say here for readers unfamiliar with this issue, can have multiple harmful cultural, political, and economic consequences), and the cultural and environmental conditions needed for their performance may be compromised through settler tactics such as assimilation through boarding schools and forced relocation.

Indigeneity

The debates, conflicts, and misuses of concepts of indigeneity described earlier serve to erase us as indigenous peoples in our own homelands, but there are alternatives, one of which I will sketch here in the concluding section, that is inspired by Kim TallBear's work. Although I cannot explore all of the philosophical issues of this way of thinking about indigeneity, I do want to provide some general gestures showing why this is a potential alternative.

Kim TallBear writes that "indigenous peoples themselves also privilege biological connection to ancestors (alongside connection to land), but they have evolved a more multifaceted definition of 'indigenous' that entangles political self-determination and mutual networking for survival in a global world" (TallBear 2013, 2). For TallBear, indigeneity is a complex project geared toward responding to the situations that particular groups face in exercising self-governance in a settler landscape—though biology is not excluded as a significant criterion. She goes on to state that "in many countries . . . greater numbers claim that identity category because it captures their social relationships to place, to settler or more powerful states, and to one another." Land, or the environment, is particularly important in TallBear's analysis: "For indigenous peoples, location is not simply an aid to tracking the movements of human bodies and relationships of markers. Rather, indigenous peoples understand themselves to have emerged as coherent groups and cultures in intimate relationship with particular places, especially living and sacred landscapes" (TallBear 2013, 2).

For me, as an environmental justice scholar, a key idea in TallBear's theory is that our discussions of indigenous identity should start with indigenous self-governance and land. The self-governance aspect involves the idea that indigeneity is about the collective actions of groups of people to address the problems of industrial settler colonialism, instead of a matter of determining whether a particular individual qualifies as "Indian" based on the criteria valued by, for example, some program. Starting from the environment is important, because industrial settler colonialism physically carves up the land so that it no longer resembles the homelands of people beyond the settler populations. That is, indigeneity has to be taken up as a project that seeks, in a variety of ways, to challenge the ecological aspects of colonialism and their impact on indigenous self-determination. Given that industrial settler colonialism is, in a large part, ecological, this way of thinking about indigenous identity suggests that at least some of the solutions have to be ecological, too. For unsettling industrial settler colonialism must change the relationships between humans, plants and animals, physical features of the land, and ecosystems.

Yet as an ecological phenomenon, there is also an obstinacy to some forms of industrial-settler colonialism that cannot be simply reversed in the short term or at all. That is, it will be impossible to select some time slice of indigenous society and reinstantiate that temporal period in the future. This understanding of land-based projects does not exclude the variety of indigenous persons, from those living on or around reservations, to urban Indians, to LGBTQ communities. All indigenous persons struggle with issues of space and geography as a product of industrial settler colonialism. So collective actions involving land-based practices that address industrial settler colonialism are not limited to certain types of peoples or communities.

In my own work, for example, I frequently write about cases in which indigenous peoples seek to define indigeneity through collective actions that promote self-governance and land-based practices that aim at restoring genealogical moral connections among people, non-humans, and places. Consider one example briefly. The Little River Band of Odawa Indians (LRBOI) near what is now referred to by most as the US state of Michigan sought to restore the sturgeon population in its watershed because the fish is a substantial source of food, an indicator species for monitoring the environment, a symbol of clan identity, and an integral part of ceremonies. Sturgeon required restoration because industrial settler colonialism, through overharvesting, dams, stocking rivers with nonnative fish species for sport fishing, and land-use change, destroyed the population. The destruction led both to the decline of their own community members living in the region and created long-term conflicts with the settler population (Holtgren, Auer, and Dempsey 2013; Mitchell, Auer, and Dempsey 2013).

Over a decade ago, LRBOI's Natural Resources Department sought to address settler erasure through designing a restoration project that connects Ottawa traditions of sturgeon, scientific research controlled by the Tribe, the reassertion of Ottawa self-governance over conservation in the watershed, and education of settler populations. For example, annually in September, a collective action in the form of a public ceremony occurs for releasing sturgeon back to the river that involves a pipe ceremony and feast. Each attendee returns young sturgeon in a bucket into the river. Today, this event can attract hundreds of attendees from all over the watershed. The participants, including many children, begin to feel a sense of responsibility for sturgeon restoration and conservation and an appreciation for Ottawa culture and self-governance. This is especially significant in a watershed involving human conflict and where indigenous persons were beginning to return to live. Winona LaDuke, speaking of sturgeon restoration for her Tribe (White Earth Ojibwe), writes, "Maybe the fish will help a diverse set of people work together to make something right. . ... The fish help us remember all of those relations, and in their own way, help us recover ourselves" (LaDuke 1999, 41–42).

The understanding of indigeneity in this example goes beyond issues of the ascription of indigeneity to individual persons and instead engages concepts of indigeneity through land-based collective actions. Although it is true that for many of these indigenous peoples biological ancestry and other criteria that were discussed earlier will figure in determinations of membership and identity, it is also true that these projects are invested in more expansive objectives of indigeneity that seek to undermine structures of industrial settler colonialism. Indigenous or other persons who are not members of the particular Tribes mentioned, or members of settler populations, can and are expected to learn from and contribute to these projects—though they do not, of course, somehow become members of the particular Tribes by doing so. This way of thinking about indigenous identity focuses our attention on addressing the problems of industrial settler colonialism, as opposed to debating who is or is not indigenous and hence playing into the disappearances and dilemmas of settler erasure. Although so much more can be written at this point, I hope to have established in brief that there is at least one good alternative—among possibly many others—to thinking about indigeneity that can contribute to indigenous self-determination.

REFERENCES

Benton-Benai, E. (1988). *The Mishomis Book: The Voice of the Ojibway*. Hayward, WI: Indian Country Communications.

Davidson-Hunt, Iain, and Fikret Berkes. (2003). "Learning as You Journey: Anishinaabe Perception of Social-Ecological Environments and Adaptive Learning." *Ecology and Society* 8 (1): 5.

Debo, Angie. (1972). *And Still the Waters Run: The Betrayal of the Five Civilized Tribes*. Vol. 287. Princeton, NJ: Princeton University Press.

Deer, Sarah. (2004). "Sovereignty of the Soul: Exploring the Intersection of Rape Law Reform and Federal Indian Law." *Suffolk University Law Review* 38: 455.

Deloria, Philip Joseph. (1998). *Playing Indian*. New Haven, CT: Yale University Press.

Doerfler, Jill. (2013). "'No Easy Answer': Citizenship Requirements." In *Tribal Constitutions Seminar, Native Nations Institute for Leadership, Management, and Policy*. University of Arizona, Tucson.

Goldstein, Aloysha, ed. (2014). *Formations of United States Colonialism*. Durham, NC: Duke University Press.

Gover, Kirsty. (2008). "Genealogy as Continuity: Explaining the Growing Tribal Preference for Descent Rules in Membership Governance in the United States." *American Indian Law Review* 33 (1): 243–309.

Hicks, Gregory Alan, and Devon G. Peña. (2003). "Community Acequias in Colorado's Rio Culebra Watershed: A Customary Commons in the Domain of Prior Appropriation." *University of Colorado Law Review* 74 (2): 387–486.

Holtgren, M., N. Auer, and D. Dempsey. (2013). "Bringing Us Back to the River." *The Great Lake Sturgeon*. East Lansing: Michigan State University Press, 133–147.

Humes, Karen, Nicholas A. Jones, and Roberto R. Ramirez. (2011). *Overview of Race and Hispanic Origin, 2010*. Washington, DC: US Department of Commerce, Economics and Statistics Administration, US Census Bureau.

LaDuke, Winona. (1999). "Return of the Sturgeon: Namewag Bi-Azhegiiwewaad." *News from Indian Country*, August 31, 1999 reprinted in *The Winona LaDuke Reader: A Collection of Essential Writings*. Minneapolis, MN: Voyageur Press, 2002, 35–43.

Lefevre, Tate A. (2015). "Settler Colonialism." In *Oxford Bibliographies in Anthropology*, edited by J. Jackson. Oxford: Oxford University Press, http://oxfordindex.oup.com/view/10.1093/obo/9780199766567.016.0125.

Mitchell, J., N. Auer, and D. Dempsey. (2013). "N'me." *The Great Lake Sturgeon*. East Lansing: Michigan State University Press, 21–26.

Ranco, Darren, Catherine A. O'Neill, Jamie Donatuto, and Barbara L. Harper. (2011). "Environmental Justice, American Indians and the Cultural Dilemma: Developing Environmental Management for Tribal Health and Well-Being." *Environmental Justice* 4 (4): 221–230.

Rusco, Elmer R. (2000). *A Fateful Time: The Background and Legislative History of the Indian Reorganization Act*. Las Vegas: University of Nevada Press.

Spruhan, Paul. (2006). "Legal History of Blood Quantum in Federal Indian Law to 1935, A." *South Dakota Law Review* 51: 1–50.

TallBear, Kim. (2007). "Narratives of Race and Indigeneity in the Genographic Project." *Journal of Law, Medicine & Ethics* 35: 412.

TallBear, Kim. (2013). "Genomic Articulations of Indigeneity." *Social Studies of Science* 0306312713483893.

Taylor, Graham D. (1980). *The New Deal and American Indian Tribalism: The Administration of the Indian Reorganization Act, 1934–45*. Lincoln: University of Nebraska Press.

Tuck, Eve, and K. Wayne Yang. (2012). "Decolonization Is Not a Metaphor." *Decolonization: Indigeneity, Education & Society* 1 (1): 1–40.

Valles, S. A., R. S. Bhopal, and P. J. Aspinall. (2015). "Census Categories for Mixed Race and Mixed Ethnicity: Impacts on Data Collection and Analysis in the US, UK and NZ." *Public Health* 129 (3): 266–270.

Van Dyke, Jon M. (1998). "The Political Status of the Native Hawaiian People." *Yale Law & Policy Review* 17 (1): 95–147. Article 3. http://digitalcommons.law.yale.edu/ylpr/vol17/iss1/3.

CHAPTER 8

A CRITICAL TRANSNATIONAL PERSPECTIVE TO ASIAN AMERICA

YEN LE ESPIRITU

SINCE its inception, Asian American studies has had to grapple with the theoretical shortcomings of rights-based frameworks that naturalize or reproduce liberal narratives of the nation. As the experiences of Asians in the United States have been historically dominated by legal, social, and cultural exclusion, Asian American scholars and activists have focused on inclusion, civil rights, and representational politics, proclaiming their "American" roots and demanding full citizenship in the nation (Chuh 2003; Jung 2015). Although this US-centric approach challenges exclusionary practices that have racialized Asian Americans as ineffably foreign and unassimilable, it conceptualizes their racial formation primarily within the frame of the US nation, which ends up affirming the status of the nation state as the ultimate protector and provider of human welfare. In the last two decades, Asian American studies scholars have moved beyond the nation- and rights-based frameworks, insisting that processes of Asian American racial formation need to be understood in relation to international histories and locations—or, more specifically, to US colonialism, imperialism, and militarism in Asia (Lowe 1996; Chuh 2003; Espiritu 2003). In other words, an examination of Asian Americans and race needs to do more than critique the history of exclusion, exploitation, and misrepresentation; it also needs to account for how Asian American "alien citizenship" flowed directly from the histories of conquest, colonialism, and semicolonialism that constituted the US interactions in Asia (Ngai 2004).

THE NATION-BASED FRAMEWORK: EXCLUSION, RIGHTS, AND CITIZENSHIP

In the American imaginary, Asians are deemed immigrants; and immigrants are rarely discussed in terms of race. According to Moon-Ho Jung (2015), the problem lies in part in the liberal genesis of sociological research and writing on Asian Americans, which strove to address the "Oriental problem" at the turn of the twentieth century, by demonstrating the inevitability and universality of immigration and assimilation. For the eminent sociologist Robert Erza Park and his students, Asian migrations and anti-Asian racism along the Pacific Coast in the 1910s and 1920s were emblematic of a universal *race relations cycle* of "contact, competition, accommodation, and assimilation" (Park 1950, 138). Park's race relations cycle, which shaped the dominant theoretical and methodological assumptions about race for the greater part of the twentieth century, was grounded in the liberal belief that modern American society was open to the full participation of all who were willing to participate. This framework conceptualizes the United States as a benign "nation of immigrants" and Asian immigrants as "liberal citizen-subjects in the making" (Jung 2015, 70). At the same time, influenced by Park's *marginal man thesis* that posits that individuals suspended between two cultures would always struggle with their dual identities, social scientists also expected that the transition of Asian immigrants to assimilated Americans would be prolonged and difficult, due to the immigrants' inability or unwillingness to fully discard their traditional culture and the host society's sustained prejudice against "strangers" (Park 1928, 892). As such, the continued exclusion of Asian Americans from the US national community, while acknowledged, was conceptualized not as a problem of race but of *culture*—the presumed result of the (naturalized) cultural divide separating the immigrants and their American counterparts (Leong 2015, 99).

Calling attention to the conditions of racial inequality beneath the promise of assimilation, the minority power movements of the late 1960s and early 1970s rebuked the "cultural divide" thesis for abstracting culture from the "material histories of racialization, segregation, and economic violence" (Lowe 1996, 29–30). Since then, Asian American scholars and activists have consistently pointed out that "exclusion"—in the form of "immigration restriction, detention, mass confinement, and citizenship denial"—has defined the collective experiences of Asians in the United States, thereby exposing the falsity of the liberal promise of inclusion and equal participation and representation for all (Robinson 2015, 82). Citing Asian American experiences with exclusion, Asian Americanists have insisted that we need to study immigration not only for what it tells us about the assimilability of the immigrants, but more so for what it says about the racialized foundations of the United States (Espiritu 1992; Lowe 1996). In other words, we need to study immigration as a *technology of racialization*, that is, a systematic series of mechanisms for assigning subordinate racial status to nonwhite immigrants. Although Park's race relations cycle thesis may have applied to most European immigrant groups, it did not apply to immigrants who were categorized as "Asians," among others.

In the United States, restrictive immigration laws have not only curtailed some new arrivals but have also *produced* new racial categories such as the "excludable," the "alien," and the "illegal"—categories that have outlasted the eventual repeal of these discriminatory laws.

Cumulatively, these race-based policies have put European and non-European immigrant groups on different trajectories of racial formation with different prospects for full membership in the United States. A primary site for the articulation of Americans' understanding of national membership and citizenship, US immigration laws, by drawing lines of inclusion and exclusion that demarcate the social and physical borders of the nation, produce new categories of racial difference that *normalize*—or make seem natural and customary—the resultant racial hierarchies. Most notably, the US Naturalization Act of 1790 limited naturalized citizenship to "free white persons," thus conjoining whiteness and citizenship at the very outset of the new nation. On the other hand, the 1924 Johnson-Reed Act, which excluded Asians from immigration on grounds that they were racially ineligible for citizenship, cast Asians as permanently foreign and unassimilable to the nation (Park 2004). It is partly through these restrictive policies—buttressed by popular culture in news reports, fiction, advertising, film, and television—that whites have been made into ideal citizens and Asian immigrants into a race of "aliens," the distinction that lingered long after the repeal of the discriminatory laws. In other words, citizenship, as a social and cultural institution created by the nation state, is designed to keep intact the power relations between ideal white citizens who have economic, political, and social rights, and "alien citizens" (Ngai 2004) who are routinely deprived of these rights.

Asian immigration to the United States began in the mid-nineteenth century with the developing US economy's demand for cheap and tractable labor. As Lisa Lowe (1996) has explained, in the period from 1850 to World War II, Asian immigration was a site for the eruptions and resolutions of contradictions between the nation's economic need for cheap labor and the political need to constitute a racially homogeneous nation. This contradiction was "resolved" through a series of legal exclusions—against the Chinese in 1882, South Asians in 1917, Japanese and Koreans in 1924, and Filipinos in 1934—that simultaneously consolidated immigrants from Asia as "nonwhites" and immigrants from Europe as "white" (Park 2004).

The racial exclusion of Asians from immigration, and also from naturalized citizenship, situates the Asian American political subject in critical opposition to the category of the citizen and outside of the normative teleology of immigration of legal admission, permanent-resident status, and citizenship. That is, for European immigrants, the end cause of immigration is citizenship, but not for Asian Americans. This legislative history of exclusion produced Asian Americans as "alien citizens"—persons who are presumed to be forever foreign and unassimilable (Ngai 2004, 2). And this condition of "alien citizenship" indelibly stamped the social experiences and subordination of Asians through racism against them and also underwrote major legal race policies against them, most notably the internment of 120,000 persons of Japanese ancestry during World War II, two-thirds of whom were US-born citizens (Ngai 2004, 8). The racial logic of perpetual foreigner, yellow peril, and enemy aliens is thus part of a genealogy of racialization processes that represent Asian Americans as "potential threats to the American way of life" (Rana 2015, 202).

During the post–World War II period, the racialization of Asians shifted from the threatening "yellow peril" to the domesticated "model minority" (Lee 2009). In the midst of the civil rights movement and race rebellions in cities across the United States, the popular press and social scientists began to publicize the alleged economic success of Asian Americans, in part to delegitimize black and brown demands for economic equity and formal political claims (Chan 1991, 167). In the late 1980s, social scientists, along with the media and policymakers, imposed the *model minority* moniker on recently arrived Vietnamese refugees, thereby reducing the specificities of their flight to a conventional story of ethnic assimilation (Caplan et al. 1989). Stressing the inevitability and desirability of improvement through assimilation, the *model minority myth* is grounded in the belief that modern American society is an egalitarian and "colorblind" society that offers the promise of success through individual effort, cultural adaptation, and political accommodation (Dunning 1989). At its core, the model minority myth promotes *cultural essentialism*, the idea that individuals are bearers of a bounded and unchanging culture: Asian American achievement is said to be rooted in their culture of strong work ethic, high regard for education, and family values (Lee2009).

As such, it reflected the triumph of a discourse of race in which *cultural difference*, defined as innate, and abstracted from unresolved histories of racial inequality, replaced biological traits as the new determinant of social outcomes.

Focused on exclusion, discrimination, and misrepresentation, the scholarship on "alien citizenship" dominated the field of Asian American studies for more than three decades. Although guided by an analysis and critique of power and domination in American society, this literature nevertheless oriented itself around the primary importance of the American nation and national identity. Much of the early scholarship in the field sought to establish that Asian Americans have been crucial to the making of the US nation and thus deserve full inclusion into its polity (Leong 2015). Viet Thanh Nguyen and Tina Chen (2000) have argued that this need to "claim America" was most integral to the self-representation of Chinese and Japanese Americans, the Asian American populations that have been in the United States the longest. The heavy US national focus in this scholarship promotes an Asian American subject that is narrated by modern civil rights discourse, which ultimately, even if inadvertently, bolsters the liberal narratives of the nation. However, Asian American racial formation has not been historically determined only by the social, economic, and political forces in the United States but also by US colonialism, imperialism, and wars in Asia.

"Imperialist Racial Formation": Critical Transnational Perspective to Asian America

In the United States, public discussion of immigration is fundamentally about people who cross borders. The media, elected officials, and the general public often represent border crossers as desperate individuals from the Global South migrating to the Global North in search of the "land of opportunity." This representation makes invisible border crossers from the Global North, in the form of colonizers, military troops, and corporations, who forcefully invade countries in the Global South and deplete their economic, ecological, and cultural resources. Indeed, all of the nation states from which the largest number of US immigrants originate—Mexico, China (including Taiwan and Hong Kong), the Philippines, El Salvador, the Dominican Republic, South Korea, Guatemala, Vietnam, Laos, and Cambodia—have had sustained, and sometimes very close, social, political, military, and economic relations with the United States. A critical transnational approach that stresses the historical formations and ongoing renewal of US empire is critical for understanding and confronting the histories and concerns of the newer groups of immigrants emerging out of US (neo)colonialism and wars in Asia: Filipinos, Koreans, South Asians, and Southeast Asians. Reflecting these immigration patterns, in 2010 the Japanese American share of the Asian American population fell to only 5 percent, and the five largest Asian American groups were Chinese and Taiwanese (23 percent), Asian Indian (19 percent), Filipino (17 percent), Vietnamese (11 percent), and Korean (10 percent) (Hoeffel et al. 2012, 15–16).

Critical race studies scholarship tells us that race is a concept of the modern *episteme* or knowledge, drawing its lineage from a history mired in systems of imperialism, colonization, capitalism, in campaigns of conquest and war, and in the social structure that emerged out of the European Enlightenment (Silva 2005; Rana 2015, 203). In a sweeping examination of European expansionism and racism in the last five hundred years, Charles Mills argues that what is needed is a recognition that global white supremacy "is itself a political system, a particular power structure of formal or informal rule, socioeconomic privilege, and norms for the differential distribution of material wealth and opportunities, benefits and burdens, rights and duties" (Mills 1997, 3). Junaid Rana explains how scientific racism, systematized into taxonomies of inferiority and superiority, works in tandem with histories of violent domination and exploitation: "If war is the means of achieving imperial interests, race is the historical category from which to justify and achieve colonial conquest" (Rana 2015, 207). This emphasis on "imperialist racial formation" (Kim 2008, 3) complicates voluntary migration and assimilation as a dominant trope in Asian American studies.

Moving away from the preoccupation with immigration and assimilation, an interdisciplinary group of Marxists and self-trained Asian American studies scholars charted a new direction for the field in the 1980s. In their groundbreaking book, *Labor Immigration under Capitalism: Asian Workers in the United States before World War II*, Lucie Cheng and Edna Bonacich and their colleagues (1994) argued that the pre–World War II immigration of Asians to the United States has to be understood within the context of the development of capitalism in Europe and the United States and the emergence of imperialism, especially in relation to Asia. During the late nineteenth and early twentieth centuries, the United States pursued an aggressive policy of expansionism, extending its political, economic, and cultural influence around the globe. Economic interest pushed the United States to cross the Pacific. By the first decades of the twentieth century, with burgeoning trade and investments in Asia (and Latin America), the United States emerged as the leading imperialist power in competition with western European countries and Japan. US expansion of foreign trade and investments in Asia eventually led to military takeovers and active intervention in the affairs of countries and territories in the Asia-Pacific region. American sugar plantation owners in Hawaii, with the support of US political and military powers, overthrew the Hawaiian monarchy in 1893, marking the beginning of US imperialism in that area (Trask 1993).

In 1898, as President McKinley envisioned a world that would be opened for American commercial activity, the United States fought the Spanish-American War and became a major colonizer, wrestling Guam and the Philippines (and also Cuba and Puerto Rico) from the Spaniards. The war with Spain, and especially the conquest of the Philippines, opened a new economic frontier, a new westward movement toward the hotly contested and potentially lucrative markets of China and Japan (Ickstadt 1990). Once the United States had established itself in Hawaii, Guam, and the Philippines, it transformed these islands, along with eastern Samoa and Wake Island, into strategic sites for advancing American economic and military interests (Lafeber 1998).

After World War II, globalization, colonialism, and militarism converged in the Asia-Pacific region, as the United States waged wars in Korea, Vietnam, Cambodia, and Laos, in an attempt to halt the alleged spread of Communism (Kim and Lowe 1997, vi). This expansion violently displaced residents from those nations, materializing in their eventual "return" to the US imperial center. The resulting "porosity" between the United States and Asia means that, as Lowe puts it, "there has been an important continuity between the considerate distortion of social relations in Asian countries affected by US imperialist war and occupation and the emigration of Asian labor to the United States" (Lowe 1996, 7). This history of US imperialism in Asia suggests that Asian American racial formation has never been exclusively shaped by events in the United States but has also been influenced by US colonialism, neocolonialism, and militarism in Asia.

However, the process of Asian American racial formation has been neither singular nor unified. Owing to the multiple contexts of colonialism and its various extensions within the development of global capitalism, Asians in the United Sates have experienced different processes of racialization specific to each group's historical and material conditions. The experiences of Filipino immigrants and Vietnamese refugees, two of the largest Asian American groups illustrate the importance of a critical international framework in theorizing Asian American imperialist racial formation.

Filipinos: Colonized Immigrants

Although imperialism is most often treated as a matter of economics and diplomacy, it has an embodied presence in the lives of people from colonized nations. The *situated knowledges* of Filipinos—arising from their situations as colonized nationals, immigrants, and workers—illustrate the global dimension of racism: Filipino American lives have been shaped not only by the historical racialization of Filipinos in the United States but also by the status of the Philippines in the global economy. As postcolonial theorists have pointed out, neither imperialism nor colonialism is a simple act of economic accumulation and acquisition. Both are also subject-constituting projects, supported and impelled by impressive ideological formations that designate certain countries and people as requiring and even beseeching domination from the more "civilized" ones (Said 1993). The US imperialist drive into the Philippines unleashed a consistent, disruptive, and well-articulated ideology depicting foreign rule over the Philippines as a blessing—a means to a higher form of civilization that would bring progress, well-being, and salvation to a racially, culturally, and even morally inferior country and people incapable of self-rule (Espiritu 1993, 50). That colonial ideology formally justified and codified the subordinate status of Filipinos as wards of the state, creating a juridical and cultural space for Filipinos as a separate category of beings (Mills 1997, 26). This, in turn, simultaneously helped rationalize and buttress the power of "civilized" white men, who shouldered the "white man's burden" of protecting the weak and dispensing justices (Hoganson 1998, 134–135).

For Filipinos to be depicted as incapable of self-rule, they had to be infantilized, their intellectual and emotional development impugned. The characterization of Filipinos as "children" contained the seed of condescension and arrogance from which popular justification for colonization would grow (Vaughan 1995). US image makers depicted Filipinos not only as incapable but also as unworthy of self-government. Both official and popular discourse racialized Filipinos as less than human, portraying them as savages, rapists, uncivilized beings, and even as dogs and monkeys. Viewing the annexation of the Philippines as a "divine mission," Theodore Roosevelt in 1901 characterized Filipinos as brute savages, uncivilized barbarians, and the heathen in the hands of satanic forces. President William McKinley suggested the same when he defined his future course of "benevolent assimilation" toward the Filipinos: Americans would have to take them, "educate" them, and "uplift and civilize and Christianize them" (Horlacher 1990, 43–44).

Gender beliefs, often working in tandem with and through racial beliefs, also affected the content and scope of the US imperialist project. The prominent stereotypes of the Filipinos—as uncivilized, savages, rapists, or children—all presented the Filipinos as lacking the *manly* character seen as necessary for self-government (Hoganson 1998). According to Vicente Rafael, the claim of benevolent assimilation "effaces the violence of conquest by construing colonial rule as the most precious gift that 'the most civilized people' can render to those still caught in a state of barbarous disorder" (Rafael 2000, 21).

Filipino bodies were also racialized as medically defective. In a nuanced analysis of the role of colonial medicine in the formation of colonial hegemony, Warwick Anderson delineates how the language of American medical science in the Philippines fabricated and rationalized images of the bodies of the American colonizer and the Filipinos, biologizing the social and historical context of US imperialism. The scientific papers produced by the colonial laboratory during the early 1900s, racialized Filipino bodies as dangerous carriers of foreign antibodies and germs that were threatening to white bodies and white American bodies as vulnerable but resilient and capable of guarding against the invisible foreign parasites lodged in native bodies. As such, American medical discourse, as a privileged site for producing the "truth" about the "tropics," served to consolidate racial hierarchies, naturalizing the power and legitimacy of American foreign bodies to appropriate, command, and contain the Philippines and its people (Anderson 1995).

The popular and official discourse on the Philippines from 1898 to 1902 established images—of inferiority, immorality, and incapacity—that traveled with Filipinos to the United States and prescribed their racialization, after they arrived. Filipinos, whether in the Philippines or in the United States, were presumed to be inherently incapable of assimilation and thus biologically unfit for the privilege of US citizenship.

Having stripped the people of the Philippines of their right to self-sovereignty, the United States had the sole power through its Congress to determine their colonial status. According to Jose Cabranes (1979), the record of the congressional debates over the status of the Filipinos from 1900 to 1916 reveals a widespread concern regarding the danger of placing the "Orientals" on an equal constitutional footing with the Americans. These congressional debates culminated in the 1916 Jones Act, which promised eventual independence to the Philippines. By promising *eventual* independence, however, the 1916 Jones Act in effect granted the Filipino natives "ward" status without citizenship rights (Cabranes 1979).

The relegation of Filipinos—as colonized subjects—to the status of second-class citizens underscores the fact that citizenship serves as an index of the historical and persistent racial, class, and gender inequalities of American society. As US nationals, but not citizens, Filipinos were prevented from voting, establishing a business, holding private and public office, and owning land and other property in the United States. They also had virtually no protection from race-based labor exploitation. Whereas other nationalities theoretically could appeal to their government representatives for assistance, the Filipinos, as colonial subjects, had no representation either in the Philippines or in the United States (Sharma 1984, 604–609). "The situation of US Filipinos thus foregrounds the way in which Asians emigrating from previously colonized sites are not exclusively formed as racialized minorities within the United States but are simultaneously determined by colonialism and capital investment in Asia" (Kim and Lowe 1997, 8).

Vietnamese: War Refugees

American imperialists bolstered their drive into Vietnam, and also Cambodia and Laos, with technologies of racialization that depicted US military intervention as a blessing—one that would bring progress, well-being, and salvation to a racially, culturally, and even morally

inferior country and people. These technologies of racialization formally justified and codified the subordinate status of the Vietnamese, creating a juridical and cultural space for them
as a separate category of beings. They simultaneously helped rationalize and buttress the
power of "civilized" white men, who shouldered the "white man's burden" of protecting the
weak and dispensing justice. During the period between the two world wars, American
observers frequently described the Vietnamese as "primitive," "lazy," "cowardly," "vain," "dis-
honest," "unclean," and "somnolent" (Bradley 2000, 46). With limited knowledge of Vietnam
and its people, US image makers relied almost exclusively on French Orientalist scholarship
to account for what they perceived to be "deficiencies" in Vietnamese society. As an example,
American racialization of Vietnamese men drew upon a substantial body of French writing
that characterized Vietnamese men as effeminate "boys" who were indistinguishable from
women (Bradley 2000, 55). These deprecating French assessments of Vietnamese society
were part of a broader Orientalist discourse that buttressed Western superiority by contrasting a purportedly dynamic and progressive West against the inertia ascribed to all Oriental
civilizations (Bradley 2000, 56). American adoption of French colonial ideologies points to
the intimate connection between colonialism and militarism, because US military intervention in Vietnam relied upon and benefited from past effects of French colonialization of
Vietnam (Bradley 2000).

During the period between the two world wars, American images of Vietnamese incapac-
ities also reflected a fundamental belief in racialized cultural hierarchies that had underlain
American encounters with people of color at home and abroad since the mid-nineteenth
century. These images resonated closely with the characteristics often ascribed to African
Americans and Native Americans and to southern European, Chinese, and Mexican immigrants; and as the United States became an imperial nation, to the peoples of the Caribbean,
Latin America, East Asia, and the Philippines (Bradley 2000, ch. 2). Indeed, much of what
American officials believed to be their right and even obligation to intervene in Vietnam's
civil war, rested on the widespread claim of the unique success of the American colonial
project in the Philippines to reshape backward people. But, against the racializing narratives
of the Philippines, Filipino nationalists have created alternative versions of their history that
question US pronouncements of benevolent assimilation and claims about the appropriateness of its global interventions. Writing during the height of the US war in Vietnam, Filipino
nationalist Luzviminda Francisco referred to the Philippine-American War as the "First
Vietnam" in an effort to show that the Vietnam War was not an "aberration" but representative of US imperialist foreign policy dating back to at least 1899 (Francicso 1973).

Critics of US military interventions have theorized that certain lives fall outside of
Western conceptions of who is normatively human, and thus violence against them "leaves
a mark that is no mark" (Butler 2004, 46). In her critique of US military retribution against
Arab peoples, Butler provocatively asks: "If someone is lost, and that person is not someone,
then what and where is the loss, and how does mourning take place?" (Butler 2004, 32). In
other words, if there had been no lives, there would have been no losses and therefore no
public act of grieving (Butler 2006, 36). For Butler, this is not simply a matter of "humans
not regarded as humans." Rather, certain lives fit no Western frame for the human (Butler
2006, 33). As Denise Ferreira da Silva explains, to be from a non-European point of origin
was to have a body and consciousness that could never fit the prerequisites for modern subjectivity and political agency. In the case of military conflicts, Silva contends that the United
States distinguishes between its "true friends," those of Europe and European descent, and its

"new friends" of freedom, such as the South Vietnamese, who may be rhetorically included in the territory of freedom for geopolitical necessities, but can remain here only with US military and economic aid. She argues that this distinction is sustained by a racial lexicon that defines freedom as the sole property of the West and the "new friends" as "always already constitut[ing] potential enemies of freedom" (Silva 2005, 124).

As the product of the heavily televised Vietnam War and its aftermath, Vietnamese refugees in the United States are often associated with highly charged images of Third World poverty, foreignness, and statelessness. These associations reflect the transnationally circulated representations of refugees as incapacitated objects of rescue, fleeing impoverished, war-torn, or corrupt states—an unwanted problem for asylum and resettlement countries. In May 1975, a Harris poll revealed that the majority of Americans did not welcome the refugees: more than 50 percent of those polled felt that Southeast Asian refugees should be excluded; only 26 percent favored their entry (Espiritu 2014). And yet, by the late 1980s, scholars, along with the mass media and policy makers, had begun to depict the Vietnamese as the newest Asian American "model minority" (Caplan et al. 1989), thereby dispensing with questions about US power structures that continue to consign a significant number of Vietnamese Americans to unstable, minimum-wage employment, welfare dependency, and participation in the informal economy, for years after their arrival (Ong and Umemoto 1994). Indeed, the racialization of Vietnamese refugees as the desperate-turned-successful makes the case for the appropriateness of the US war in Vietnam, bolstering the narrative of America(ns) rescuing and caring for Vietnam's "runaways," and erasing the role played by US interventionist foreign policy and war in inducing this forced migration. In other words, Vietnamese refugees, whose war sufferings remain unmentionable and unmourned in most US public discussions of the Vietnam War, have ironically become the featured evidence of the appropriateness of US actions in Vietnam: The Vietnam War, no matter the cost, was ultimately necessary, just, and successful (Espiritu 2014).

DIFFERENTIAL INCLUSION

Asians in the United States have been excluded economically, politically, and culturally from what is "national" or "American." Given this record of violence, it would be easy to read the history of Asians in the United States as one of exclusion. But this reading, although appropriate, is incomplete. Although it is true that Asians have been kept apart from "America," it is also true, or more true, that they have been at times forcibly included in it through colonialism, labor recruitment, and imperialism. Because Asians have been forced to be not only outside, but also inside, the nation, it is more accurate to characterize their encounter with the United States as one of *differential inclusion*, rather than of outright exclusion (Espiritu 2003). Differential inclusion is the process whereby a group of people becomes integral to the nation's economy, culture, identity, and power—but integral only or precisely because of their designated subordinate standing. Thus, the inclusion of Asians has been possible, even desirable, only when it is coupled with the exploitation of their bodies, land, and resources, the denial of equal opportunities to them, and the categorization of them as subpersons of a different and inferior moral status, marginalized and marked as "foreign" and "outside" the national polity.

The term 'differential inclusion' counters the myth of voluntary immigration and makes visible the deliberate and violent peopling of the United States—through conquest, slavery, annexation, and the importation of foreign labor. The idea of differential inclusion challenges the "push-pull" model that fuels the narrative of the teeming masses invading the "land of opportunity" (pushed from their place of origin and pulled to the United States) and focuses on how Asian immigrants have been coercively and differentially made to be part of the nation. This confrontation with the narrative of inclusion—of a welcoming America extending the promise of homes and citizenship to the world's poor and persecuted—emphasizes how inclusion for some racialized groups simultaneously means legal subordination, economic exploitation, and cultural degradation. Finally, the term 'differential inclusion' reminds us that we cannot examine Asian American racial formation solely in terms of racial politics within the framework of the US nation state. While important, this framework narrowly focuses on identity and representational politics within Asian America, overlooking the global politics and power that produced massive displacements and migrations of Asians in the first place. Dispelling the myth of the "land of immigrants" and calling attention to the US role in precipitating global migration in the first place, would be an important initial step toward having an honest discussion about race and racialized immigrant communities in the United States.

References

Anderson, Warwick. (1995). "Excremental Colonialism: Public Health and the Poetics of Pollution." *Critical Inquiry* 21 (3): 640–669.

Bradley, M. P. (2000). *Imagining Vietnam & America: The Making of Postcolonial Vietnam, 1919–1950.* Durham, NC: The University of Carolina Press.

Butler, J. (2004). *Precarious Life: The Power of Mourning and Violence.* London: Verson.

Cabranes, J. (1979). *Citizenship and the American Empire.* New Haven, CT and London: Yale University Press.

Caplan, N., J. K. Whitmore, and Q. L. Bui. (1989). *The Boat People and Achievement in America: A Study of Family Life, Hard Work, and Cultural Values.* Ann Arbor: University of Michigan Press.

Chan, S. (1991). *Asian Americans: An Interpretive History.* Boston: Twayne.

Cheng, L., and E. Bonacich, eds. (1994). *Labor Immigration under Capitalism: Asian Workers in the United States before World War II.* Berkeley: University of California Press.

Chuh, K. (2003). *Imagine Otherwise: On Asian Americanist Critique.* Durham, NC: Duke University Press.

Dunning, B. (1989). "Vietnamese in America: The Adaptation of the 1975–1979 Arrivals." In *Refugees as Immigrants: Cambodians, Laotians, and Vietnamese in America,* edited by D. W. Haines, 55–85. Totowa, NJ: Rowman and Littlefield.

Espiritu, Y. L. (1992). *Asian American Pan Ethnicity: Bridging Institutions and Identities,* Philadelphia, PA: Temple University Press.

Espiritu, Y. L. (2003). *Home Bound: Filipino American Lives Across Cultures, Communities, and Countries.* Berkeley: University of California Press.

Espiritu, Y. L. (2014). *Body Counts: The Vietnam War and Militarized Refuge(es).* Berkeley: University of California Press.

Francisco, L. (1973). "The First Vietnam: The Philippine-American War, 1899–1902." *Bulletin of Concerned Asian Scholars* 5 (4): 1–16.

Hoeffel, E. M., S. Rastogi, M. O. Kim, and H. Shahid. (2012). *The Asian Population: 2010.* Washington, DC: US Department of Commerce.

Hoganson, K. (1998). *Fighting for American Manhood: How Gender Politics Provoked the Spanish-American and Philippine-American Wars.* New Haven, CT and London: Yale University Press.

Horlacher, F. W. (1990). "The Language of Late Nineteenth-Century American Expansionism." In *An American Empire: Expansionist Cultures and Policies, 1881–1917,* edited by S. Ricard, 9–30. Aix-en Provence, France: Universite de Provence Service des Publications.

Ickstadt, H. (1990). "The Rhetoric of Expansionism in Painting and Fiction (1880–1910)." In *An American Empire: Expansionist Cultures and Policies, 1881–1917,* edited by S. Ricard, 9–29. Aix-en Provence, France: Universite de Provence Service des Publications.

Jung, M-H. (2015). "Empire." In *Keywords for Asian American Studies,* edited by C. J. Schlund-Vials, L. T. Vo, and K. S. Wong, 67–70. New York: New York University Press.

Kim, N. (2008). *Imperial Citizens: Koreans and Race from Seoul to LA.* Stanford, CA: Stanford University Press.

Kim, Elaine H., and Lisa Lowe. (1997). *New Formations, New Questions, Asian American Studies.* Durham, NC: Duke University Press.

Lafeber, W. (1998). *The New Empire: An Interpretation of American Expansion, 1860–1898.* Ithaca, NY: Cornell University Press.

Lee, S. (2009). *Unraveling the "Model Minority" Stereotype: Listening to Asian American Youth.* New York, NY: Columbia University Teachers College Press.

Leong, Karen. (2015). "Foreign." In *Keywords for Asian American Studies,* edited by C. J. Schlund-Vials, L. T. Vo, and K. S. Wong, 98–100. New York: New York University Press.

Lowe, L. (1996). *Immigrant Acts: On Asian American Cultural Politics.* Durham, NC: Duke University Press.

Mills, C. (1997). *The Racial Contract.* Ithaca, NY: Cornell University Press.

Ngai, Mae M. (2004). *Impossible Subjects: Illegal Aliens and the Making of Modern America.* Princeton, NJ: Princeton University Press.

Nguyen, Viet Thanh, and Tina Chen. (2000). "Editors' Introduction." *Jouvert,* 4 (1), 1–7.

Ong, P., and K. Umemoto. (1994). "Life and Work in the Inner-City." In *The State of Asian Pacific America: Economic Diversity, Issues, and Policies,* edited by P. Ong, 87–111. Los Angeles: LEAP Asian Pacific American Public Policy Institute and University of California at Los Angeles, Asian American Studies.

Park, R. E. (1928). "Human Migration and the Marginal Man." *American Journal of Sociology* 33 (6): 881–893.

Park, R.E. (1950). *Race and Culture.* Glencoe, IL: Free Press.

Park, J. S. W. (2004). *Elusive Citizenship: Immigration, Asian Americans, and the Paradox of Civil Rights.* New York and London: New York University Press.

Rafael, V. L. (2000). *White Love and Other Events in Filipino History.* Durham, NC and London: Duke University Press.

Rana, J. (2015). "Race." In *Keywords for Asian American Studies,* edited by C. J. Schlund-Vials, L. T. Vo, and K. S. Wong, 202–207. New York: New York University Press.

Robinson, G. (2015). "Exclusion." In *Keywords for Asian American Studies,* edited by C. J. Schlund-Vials, L. T. Vo, and K. S. Wong, 82–86. New York: New York University Press.

Said, Edward W. (1993). *Culture and imperialism.* New York: Vintage.

Sharma, M. (1984). "Labor Migration and Class Formation Among the Filipinos in Hawaii, 1906–1946." In *Labor Immigration Under Capitalism: Asian Workers in the United States Before World War II*, edited by L. Cheng and E. Bonacich, 579–616. Berkeley and Los Angeles: University of California Press.

Silva, D. F. (2005). "A Tale of Two Cities: Saigon, Fallujah and the Ethical Boundaries of Empire." *Amerasia Journal* 31: 121–134.

Trask, H. K. (1993). *From a Native Daughter: Colonialism and Sovereignty in Hawaii.* Honolulu: University of Hawaii Press.

Vaughan, C. A. (1995). "The 'Discovery' of the Philippines by the U.S. Press, 1898, 1902." *The Historian* 57 (2): 303–314.

CHAPTER 9

....

RIGHTS AND IDENTITY IN LATIN AMERICAN PHILOSOPHY

....

SUSANA NUCCETELLI

It is not uncommon for philosophers in Latin America to be skeptics about whether their own theorizing is somehow distinctive of this region of the world. Contra such skepticism, there is already a substantial corpus of philosophical works about human rights and collective identity that is distinctively related to Latin America's history and culture. Until the mid-twentieth century, this corpus consisted mostly of works by nonacademic philosophers, or philosophical thinkers who expressed their views in the hybrid genre of the literary essay. Scientists and literary figures who were interested in the intersection of philosophy with literature and politics then cultivated it. Later that century, academic philosophers offered their own take on these issues. Both academic and nonacademic thinkers thus provided sufficient evidence to debunk any skeptical worries about the existence of distinctive theorizing in Latin American political philosophy. The expansion of Iberians into what they perceived as a "New World" ignited a discussion among Spanish thinkers that had an impact on early modern European philosophers. It concerned human rights and ethnic identity, since for those thinkers *who* had *what* human rights depended on the identity of the peoples who met in the "New World," including Amerindians, Blacks, Iberians and their descendants in Latin America, and *mestizos* (peoples of mixed race). Some of the views developed in this discussion provided grounds for questioning the justification of colonial policies throughout modernity. The phenomenon of current globalization reignited significant aspects of that early debate.

IDEAS OF HUMAN RIGHTS DURING THE FIRST WESTERN EXPANSION

....

Two Western expansions, the so-called Iberian Conquest in the fifteenth and sixteenth centuries and the current phenomenon of globalization, have raised ethical questions about human rights in Latin America. The Iberian colonialist expansion (hereafter, simply "the Conquest") ignited a controversy in Spain about the nature of fundamental moral rights of colonized (the indigenous peoples of the Americas) and colonizers (the Spaniards). Scholastic thinkers on both sides of the Atlantic, encouraged by the Spanish Crown itself, took part in a heated controversy about this question framed within Thomist *natural law theory*. According to this theory, the deontic status of an action depends on whether it promotes or hinders values that are conducive to human flourishing—understood as a life lived in accord with what is in humans' rational nature. For nonhuman animals, although they also flourish when their natural development fulfills what is in their nature according to their species, on this theory, they lack a rational soul and therefore have no natural rights. That is, at stake for Amerindians was nothing less than their humanity. Only if they were judged "rational," would they have human or "natural" rights such as the rights to life, liberty, and property (where "liberty" also included their right to religious freedom). At stake for Spaniards were their social rights to wage war, trade, travel, and preach their religion abroad, in what they perceived as a "New World."

The controversy's principal contributions to European and Anglo-American philosophical literature were substantial: an absolutist theory of natural rights that was influential in the development of secular versions of modern *natural rights* theories; an original outline of a philosophy of international law; a pioneering polemic about the moral backwardness of the Amerindian and African slave trade; and an early doctrine of *compensatory justice* claiming duties of reparation for past injustices.

The controversy took place within a framework where all parties accepted natural law theory's theses that (1) standards for evaluative judgments are built into the order of nature itself; (2) to act rightly is to act in accordance with the true nature of things as we find them in the world; (3) people are treated justly when they are treated as they deserve in accordance with their nature; and (4) humans are by nature rational beings with inalienable natural rights to life and freedom from gratuitous harm. But soon there were two opposite sides. Philosopher and theologian Juan Ginés Sepúlveda (1951) led the conservative natural law theorists with an appeal to Aristotle's doctrine of natural slaves. Sepúlveda assumed (5), that the Amerindians were natural slaves, and concluded that they could therefore neither govern themselves nor have other liberty or property rights. In support of his premise, Sepúlveda offered as "evidence" the Amerindian practice of idolatry, cannibalism, and human sacrifice, which he thought betokened insufficient rationality. "It is demonstrated by those who have returned from the New World," writes Sepúlveda, "that those men [the Amerindians] have little mental capacity and fearful customs" (1551/2004, 40).

On the liberal side, Spanish Dominican thinkers Bartolomé de las Casas (1474–1566) and Francisco de Vitoria (1486–1546) offered more plausible and influential arguments in support of the human rights of Amerindians and other "unbelievers" (Vitoria's term). Unlike Sepúlveda, who never visited the Americas, las Casas lived most of his life in Latin America, where he was passionately devoted to seeking reforms of Spain's policies on behalf of Amerindians, for instance, in his *Memorial of Remedies for the Indies*. His firsthand experience of native peoples gave him abundant evidence to support his rejection of (5), the contention that Amerindians were "natural slaves." With the full rationality of Amerindians vindicated, las Casas appealed to his own evidence, together with natural law theorists' thesis (3) that people are treated justly when they are treated as they deserve, in accordance with their nature, to argue that the Amerindians were treated unjustly. On the same basis, he appealed to (4) that humans are rational with inalienable rights, to argue that Amerindians had natural rights. So effective were his arguments that even Emperor Charles V was persuaded, and he granted many of the reforms proposed by las Casas. The "New Laws" issued in 1542 eliminated, for example, Spain's hereditary grants of Amerindians to settlers, thus limiting the *encomienda* system used to enslave the natives. Amerindians granted in encomiendas to settlers by the local authorities were taken to "belong" to the Crown, not the settlers (Himelblau 1994).

Las Casas left abundant textual evidence of his own moral evolution that was marked by two major changes of mind. The first came after witnessing the suffering and indignities endured by Amerindians in the abuse of their human rights, the second after learning of the unspeakable toll in human suffering endured by Africans as result of the Atlantic slave trade. Reflecting on his own complicity in these abhorrent institutions, he realized that his own status as a slaveholder in Cuba was morally untenable, leading him to return his "lease" on Amerindian slaves inherited from his father to local authorities.

Later, he wrote an apology where he withdraws his previous endorsement of a petition in support of the transportation of African slaves to Latin America, thus publically renouncing the earlier position as a grave moral error (las Casas 1992b). This piece, together with other writings, shows las Casas's moral evolution. As a result of what some regard as an example in the use of reflective equilibrium (Talbot 2005), his conscience has evolved, manifesting his commitment to finding a rational way through a moral minefield but always open to challenging received principles, where necessary, to accommodate the revised moral judgments he was inclined to make in light of new evidence.

An important outcome of las Casas's writings on these issues was "Lascasianism," a doctrine, quite radical at the time, that vindicates Amerindians as fully rational beings, bearers of natural rights to life, liberty, and property, which were construed in the way of late Renaissance Thomism as intrinsic (i.e., valuable for their own sake), absolute (i.e., holding without exception), indefeasible (i.e., undermined by neither reason nor authority), and self-evident (i.e., known to be valuable just by thinking). Correlative with the natives' rights were the Spaniards' duties of reparation for past injustices. And these for las Casas required the immediate manumission of enslaved Indians, restoration of their property, and Spain's withdrawal from tribal lands (las Casas 1993, 159–167, 169–173).

In arguing for this doctrine, las Casas often departed from traditional Scholastic strategies. Against those who took the practice of human sacrifice by some Amerindians to undermine their status as rational beings, he argued (conflating explanation with moral justification) that the practice was a natural result of their intense religiosity, which led them to offer to their gods the best that they had (las Casas 1993, 162–167). Against the argument from idolatry, he proposed a "doctrine of probable error," according to which the Amerindians, though *in error* because they held "idolatrous" beliefs that were false, were nevertheless *justified*, because they held those beliefs on the advice of their own wise people, who were wise precisely because they *usually* had true beliefs and gave the right advice. Clearly, this argument might confer some degree of epistemic justification on the practices of ritual human sacrifice by some Amerindians, even if in the end it falls short of morally justifying them. But it does the work las Casas needed to rebut Sepúlveda's charge, since it shows such practices rational.

In las Casas's realist conception of natural rights, humans have them by virtue of being rational, independently of positive law or authority. Vitoria also had a realist conception of natural rights, which he presented in a series of lectures at the University of Salamanca. "On the American Indians" (1991, 231–292), an essay written by his students based on notes from his lectures, argues that although the Spaniards had "legitimate jurisdiction" in America, they had no right to wage war against Amerindians or to enslave them and take their lands and other property. The principal reasons available at the time that appeared to support the Spaniards' claim to such rights were carefully evaluated by Vitoria, who offered counterarguments to each, mostly by appeal to canon law and definition. For Vitoria, like las Casas, the question of whether Amerindians had natural rights turned largely on the facts about their rationality. Reflecting the prevalent ethnocentrism of his time, he regarded the Amerindians as somewhat "dull" and in need of tutelage, but in this he saw no reason to judge them *irrational.*

For Vitoria, however, their rejection of Christianity did not give the Spaniards a reason to size their lands or wage war against them. In "On the Law of War" (1991, 293–327), he contended that, provided the Amerindians were "innocent," since slaughter of the innocent is contrary to natural law, the Spaniards had no grounds to wage war against them. In the absence of provocation—and lacking good moral reasons—war against other nations is morally wrong. From these principles he concluded that there could not be a just war against the Amerindians, for no wrong had previously been done to Spain by these peoples. Spaniards therefore had the duty to abstain from causing harm to them. Vitoria argued that there may be legitimate reasons for waging war against some local peoples when they violate some of the sociability rights of citizens of a foreign nation, which included rights to travel freely in the local people's land, acquire citizenship, and practice their own religion. Other legitimate reasons for war included being attacked by another nation (in which case the war is always defensive and should end with the aggressor's withdrawal), and where there is a need to interfere with customs such as cannibalism and human sacrifice. But, according to Vitoria's just war theory, that Amerindians rejected the Gospel, which was a common reason invoked at the time to justify war against them, was not a sufficient reason. Vitoria's views on just war and human rights is often credited (Marks 1993; Keal 2003) with having influenced contemporary international law. Historians of international law have traced different interpretations of Vitoria's views, ranging from the standard association with the UN charter on human rights to links with postcolonial theory and the critical legal studies movement. De la Rasilla del Moral (2013, 289) finds them especially influential with "the authors of the so-called Third World Approaches to International Law (or TWAIL). The appeal of Vitoria to Third World international critical scholars is consonant with the post-colonial proclamation that TWAIL offers a 'foundational critique of the history of international law' by situating the 'colonial project at the very heart of international law.'"

By contrast, Lascasianism has been an ongoing populist phenomenon that continues to be a moral force behind movements for political and economic reform in Latin America. Among Lascasian thinkers is Gustavo Guttiérrez (Peruvian, b. 1928), the founder of the influential movement within Latin American Catholicism known as "liberation theology." Guttiérrez's (2008) version of Roman Catholic ethics is a kind of perfectionism holding that some ways of life should be promoted since they lead to human flourishing, while other, less worthy ways of life should be avoided. Ways of life that promote discrimination on the basis of race or ethnicity make people *less human.* The sense of "human" at work here is the same one invoked by las Casas in his vindication of the *humanity* of Amerindians—something we would refer to as their *personhood,* which for las Casas resided in their rational nature. Sensitive to the familiar Marxist criticism of religion as focused solely on the afterlife,

Guttiérrez argues that a crucial value Christians must seek is sympathy to the needs of the poor, discriminated, or marginalized. In Latin America, this entails a struggle for actual liberation from political and economic oppression. Such ways of life dehumanize those who suffer them. Guttiérrez thus urges an actual, "this-world" liberation. The imperative for Christians is to devote themselves now to the elimination of injustice and poverty in the world. For Guttiérrez (1968/2008, 104), "one cannot be a Christian in these times without a commitment to liberation. To be a Christian in our epoch, it is necessary to commit oneself in one way or other in the process of human emancipation."

For all their influence on the progressive ideology of the Latin American Left, however, Lascasian arguments about the morality of the Conquest are often qualified by thinkers from the same end of the political spectrum. For example, the Cuban Marxist Roberto Fernández Retamar (b. 1930) warns against the folly of complicity with the "Black Legend," which he considers a spurious sixteenth-century account of abuses in the Conquest actually made up by Spain's European rivals, especially the English, to smear Spain while disguising their own imperialist motives. On his view, Latin Americans should embrace their Spanish roots, since Spain brought to Latin America something often overlooked by critics: a valuable mix of races, cultures, and religions. Berbers, Moors, Muslims, and Jews all contributed to the enrichment of traditional Spanish culture in the Middle Ages—and, together with Catholic Christians, left their imprint in the Hispanic New World. Furthermore, no other power in the sixteenth century showed Spain's openness and moral honesty in permitting public debate over the moral permissibility of the European expansion. Arguably, however, neither the blessing of that mixed racial and cultural heritage, nor the alleged sinister motives of proponents of a "Black Legend," provide rational grounds to undermine widespread belief in the moral backwardness of the Conquest.

HUMAN RIGHTS IN THE CONTEXT OF GLOBALIZATION

The current phenomenon of globalization has reignited the debate about the nature of human rights in social and political Latin American philosophy. Among those contributing to the debate was the Argentine Eduardo Rabossi (1930–2005). On his pragmatist account, it makes no sense now to approach that debate with "foundationalist" questions such as whether there are human rights or how to analyze and classify them. For Rabossi (2004), the creation of the United Nations and its sanctioning of the Universal Declaration of Human Rights settled the issue about their existence, as shown by the resulting international and regional consensus. The failure of the United States and Britain to persuade the United Nations to sanction war on Iraq in 2003 suggests precisely that "the phenomenon of human rights . . . is taking its place in the culture of humanity" (Rabossi 2004, 148). Given this reality, only issues of adjudication (i.e., determining *who* has *what* rights) and enforcement (i.e., securing that rights are honored) can be topics for fruitful philosophical theorizing.

Thus, Rabossi questions the legitimacy of contemporary debate on foundational questions concerning human rights. But his "ban" on such philosophical theorizing needs to avoid dogmatism, for which it needs more than an appeal to the international political and legal status of those rights. Furthermore, since Rabossi himself indulges in some foundational theorizing while accounting for the relation of human rights to globalization and violence, this inconsistency suggests that his antifoundationalism may be simply untenable.

In any case, let's now consider Rabossi's positive account of the relation between human rights and globalization and violence. Globalization has been occurring since the expansion of the West in the late Renaissance. One of the virtuous consequences of the type of globalization that arose after World War II is that it has enabled a *global* civil society to be created—one rooted in political values acknowledged by organizations such as the United Nations and the Organization of American States. Moreover, the fundamental rights underwritten by these basic political values are now generally accepted (at least as worthy goals) even when they limit state sovereignty (Rabossi 2004, 147).

Yet that postwar globalization involved also violence and poverty. Although the supranational legality of our current "global civil society" provides a means to exert some control over violence as standardly construed, it has, Rabossi maintains, so far failed to control another, more subtle form of violence, namely "indirect violence," the prevalence of poverty and malnutrition. Expressing a view not uncommon among Latin American theorists, he holds that the global society has the moral duty to control indirect violence. For Rabossi, this duty is as important as protecting individual freedom, which is a fundamental human right in liberal democracy. Simply put, the objection to liberal democracy is "What good is liberty if I'm dying from starvation?" (Rabossi 2004, 150). Although the implied claim is plausible, it needs a supporting argument. After all, many question that there is a human right to health or nutrition, which unlike individual freedom, is a positive right. (Here the standard distinction is between a negative right or right not to be interfered with, and a positive right or right to be provided with something.) If Rabossi is consistent with his own appeal to international consensus against foundationalism, he would have to reject such positive rights. After all, neither health nor nutrition is a right fully acknowledged by the international community. So it seems that Rabossi needs to engage in philosophical theorizing about human rights, of the foundational sort that he rejects. In any case, answers to questions about who had what rights during the expansion of Europe and the United States in Latin America are closely related to views about the racial and ethnic identity of the people of this region, a topic to be considered next.

WHO ARE LATIN AMERICANS AND THEIR DESCENDANTS ABROAD?

Latin Americans have been concerned with establishing *who they are as a people* ethnically or racially and *what they should be*, at least since the nineteenth-century Wars of Independence. Similar questions about collective identity have concerned their descendants abroad and continue to do so. They began to be pressing during the Wars of Independence and the period of national reorganization that followed.

The Venezuelan thinker Simón Bolívar (1783–1830), called *el Libertador* for his military leadership in defeating Spanish royalist forces in the northern and western regions of South America, seems to have realized that Latin Americans, as they struggled to free themselves from their colonial masters, needed to reflect about their own ethnic and racial identity. In his "Jamaica Letter" (1815/1951) and other writings he presents the theory that Latin Americans are not exclusively European, or Amerindian, or black. Rather, they are a people somewhere between these three identities, many of whom have a "mestizo" (mixed) cultural, ethnic, and racial heritage. Bolívar thus offered the first version of the so-called *mestizaje* view that was to become popular later during the twentieth century. According to this view, Hispanics are a new ethnic group made up of ethnic, racial, and cultural traits of Europeans, Amerindians, and Africans.

Bolívar further contended that Latin Americans should devise political institutions suited to their own identity, which determine specific cultural and national characters. Thus, they should not necessarily follow the North American institutional model that others were at the time ready to emulate. Liberal democracy, he believed, might deserve praise for its success in the English-speaking world, but it was not self-evidently best for Latin American societies. This idea is part of "Bolívarism," a larger doctrine that is perhaps Bolívar's most distinctive contribution to political theory. Bolívarism is a form of social and geographical determinism, since it holds that a people's history, culture, and environmental conditions affect their national character. Its main thesis is that there is no single universally valid polity for all peoples; rather, each nation must take into account the distinctive characteristics of its own people, as well as their unique historical circumstances and the physical geography of their country, to find the form of political arrangement that works best for those peoples. Thus, Bolívarism leaves open the possibility that autocratic governments might sometimes be morally justified. That would be so whenever such a government provides stability for a nation and enables its people to flourish. Given Bolívarism, the widely held thesis that liberal democracy is the best form of government for all nations seems false. Bolívar himself appears to have admired representative democracies with elected heads of state who would have clearly limited terms of office. But he served for a time as dictator of Venezuela and advised similar authoritarian regimes for a few other Latin American nations (Bolívar 1951).

The generation that followed after Bolívar's also struggled with the problem of Hispanic identity, but it did so in the process of laying down the philosophical foundation for national unity (roughly, 1840–1880). Prominent among them are two Argentine thinkers, the liberal statesman and educator Domingo Sarmiento (1811–1888) and the political philosopher and diplomat Juan Bautista Alberdi (1810–1884). Rivals in public life, Sarmiento (1998) and Alberdi (2004), nevertheless agreed in their rejection of the mestizo view of identity and Bolívarism. Contra the mestizo view, they held that the collective identity of Latin Americans has nothing to do with racially mixed heritage, but rather with being a European transplanted in the New World. Their proper ethnic category was "criollo," meaning *Latin-American-born white descendants of Spaniards*. Contra Bolívarism, they maintained that Liberal democracy is a paramount value; thus, dictatorships are to be resisted as a form of government in Latin America.

Not only had the actual identity of Latin Americans interested Sarmiento and Alberdi, but it also influenced what they should be. According to Sarmiento, the emerging nations faced a choice between civilization and barbarism, and national development could be steered toward either the one or the other. "Civilization," he thought, would promote the interests of the criollos, while "barbarism" the interests of Amerindians and mestizos. The latter category includes individual of mixed Amerindian-Spanish descent such as the *gauchos* of Argentina, the *rotos* of Chile, and the *llaneros* of Venezuela. It is unclear where Latin

American blacks fit in Sarmiento's simple-minded picture, though it follows from his ethnic stereotypes that they were closer to "civilization" than to "barbarism" because they lived in urban areas. On the other hand, the Amerindians and the nomadic gauchos inhabited the vast Pampas, which invariably determined a "barbarian" way of life. "This constant insecurity of life outside towns," writes Sarmiento, " . . . stamps upon [them] a certain stoical resignation to death by violence . . . . Perhaps this is the reason why they inflict death or submit to it with so much indifference, and why such events make no deep or lasting impression upon the survivors" (1847/1998, 10).

Like other liberals at the time, Sarmiento regarded the civilized way of life as best and campaigned for eradicating "barbarism." His view of Latin American identity was shortly to serve as the ideological foundation for late-nineteenth-century genocide campaigns against Amerindians. About the prospects of mestizos in civil society, however, Sarmiento was ambiguous. Given his social and geographical determinism, he seems committed to holding that this group could be integrated through relocation and the fostering of "enlightened urban habits" by education. Later political thinkers, in any case, took mestizos to qualify for integration, but only if they could provide the needed labor force. Harsh, discriminatory laws were adopted for the purpose—for instance, requiring full employment for being able to refuse compulsory border-control service.

Alberdi agreed, especially with Sarmiento's claim that Amerindians were too unruly for civil society, and therefore candidates for elimination. But he disagreed with Sarmiento's proposal that education of the masses was crucial to nation building. On his view, a type of "racial cleansing" was more important, one that required promotion of European and North American immigration. In fact, he held that the nations of "South America are the product and living testimony of the actions of Europe in America. What we call 'independent America' is nothing more than Europe established in America . . . Everything in the civilization of our land is European" (1886–1887/2004, 133).

Both views were later assimilated to the autochthonous positivism of the late nineteenth century, which contributed its own pseudo-scientific basis to spread racist ideologies in Latin America. As the new nations of Latin America became more stable politically, many positivist thinkers began to reflect once again on the question of the region's ethnic and racial identity. They saw a causal connection between the region's underdevelopment and the legacy of Iberian culture, contending that this legacy was responsible for cultural and economic stagnation. On their view a radical change of values, conducted through education, was critical for flourishing. No longer content to ask simply "Who are we?" they began to pose the larger question, "Who should we be?" Their answer was heavily influenced by both British and French positivism, together with social Darwinism. The most influential positivists in Latin America were Auguste Comte (French, 1798–1857) and John Stuart Mill (English, 1806–1873). They both rejected speculative ways of doing philosophy prevalent in the nineteenth century and favored scientific accounts of the natural world based on natural causes. Among them, social Darwinist Herbert Spencer (English, 1820–1903) was most influential with his notion that societies evolve according to laws parallel to the evolution of species.

The resulting autochthonous positivism can be characterized as communitarian and perfectionist. It was communitarian in that it rejected the presumptive primacy that individual freedom has within liberalism. In Latin America, they argued, individual freedom conflicted with progress, which was the highest value for the purpose of nation building.

And it was also perfectionist, because it held that ways of life conducive to prosperity and social progress should be promoted, while those conducive to stagnation should ultimately be eradicated. But promoting such progress required a drastic change in the collective identity of Latin Americans, who should be induced to adopt the values of the French and the "Anglo-Saxons." These peoples' ways of life were believed to be responsible, at least in part, for the achievements of their nations in commerce, politics, and technology. On the other hand, among the values to be discouraged were those stemming from religious worldviews, especially Catholicism, and those inherent to Spain's and Portugal's ways of life. Accordingly, political leaders sought to transform Latin American societies by making large-scale reforms aimed at remolding peoples' minds, as well as political and social institutions. Prominent among those reforms were the secularization of public education in nearly all countries and the separation of church and state, both mostly in place by 1900 (Ardao 1963). Together with their anticlericalism, positivists offered a very unorthodox take on liberal democracy. Like the French positivists, they advocated governments led by the most learned in the positive sciences, where a strong leader might serve as executive with the counsel of experts. But unlike their European peers, they favored military dictatorships under the advice of the learned—thus initiating a tradition favorable to such regimes that marks Latin America's contemporary history.

Mexico illustrates the paradigm of failure for this positivist model of government in the early twentieth century. Although first influenced by Auguste Comte, Mexican positivists later followed J. S. Mill, whose libertarian individualism seemed congenial to capitalism, and Herbert Spencer, whose attempt to graft a pseudo-Darwinian theory onto social philosophy served as a framework for the Mexican positivists' attempt to direct the "evolution" of the Mexican people. From the highest positions in the Mexican government as well as popular publications such as the magazine *La Libertad*, Mexican positivists extolled the benefits of free-market capitalism as the true expression of "positive liberty" while supporting General Porfirio Díaz's iron-fisted rule to keep order in society. They saw in Díaz a possibility to foster progress in the long term by first establishing civil order. They regarded the values of progress and order as more important than individual liberty (Zea 1974). On their view, the masses would have to be educated before they could be trusted with democracy. Later recast as the thesis that Latin Americans are "not ready for democracy," this has become a persistent stereotype used to "justify" totalitarian regimes. In the mid-twentieth century, Peruvian political thinker Victor Haya de la Torre lamented that there were still some who thought, of Latin Americas, "Still backward people, not prepared for democracy, a function of cultured people. If it is possible to impose on them a dictatorship, they deserve it!" (1943/2004, 138).

But by the early 1900s, Latin American positivism lost appeal among the region's intellectuals who were beginning to reassess the alleged backwardness of Iberian values. They also suspected positivism's single-minded vindication of progress as the preeminent social value. The mestizaje view of Hispanic identity, first articulated by Bolívar in the early nineteenth century, was soon to be revisited and developed in new directions. Among the various mestizaje views now available, one of the more debated has been put forward by Jorge Gracia (2000). In his "family-resemblance" view of the identity of Latin Americans and their descendants abroad, the Iberian legacy is included. Like Fernández Retamar (1989), Gracia notes that in 1492 Iberians were of mixed heritage (as were the Amerindians, and the mestizo people that resulted from their encounter). Such mestizaje, he thinks, is to be valued, for having a mestizo identity may provide protection against some forms of cultural, ethnic, and racial discrimination. At the same time, there is also instrumental value for Hispanics in establishing their collective identity and giving it a name, because that can empower them as a group and be a source of pride and liberation from relations of dependence. Nevertheless, it remains to be shown that Latin Americans and Iberians are one and the same ethnic group. Given the historical circumstances outlined here, particularly with regard to conquest and colonization, together with some arguments I have presented elsewhere about the role of history in shaping Latin American identity (2007, 2009), Gracia and Fernández Retamar seem to underestimate the ethnic divide imposed by those circumstances.

REFERENCES

Alberdi, J. B. [1886–1887] (2004). "Bases and Starting Points for the Political Organization of the Argentine Republic." In *Latin American Philosophy: An Introduction with Readings*, edited by S. Nuccetelli and G. Seay, 132–137. Upper Saddle Brook, NJ: Prentice Hall.

Ardao, A. (1963). "Assimilation and Transformation of Positivism in Latin America." *Journal of the History of Ideas* 24: 515–522.

Bolívar, Simón. [1815] (1951). "The Jamaica Letter." In *Selected Writings of Bolivar*, edited by H. A. Bierck, 103–122. New York: The Colonial Press.

de la Rasilla del Moral, I. (2013). " Francisco de Vitoria's Unexpected Transformations and Reinterpretations for International Law." *International Community Law Review* 15 (3): 287–318.

Fernández Retamar, R. (1989). *Caliban and Other Essays*. Minneapolis: University of Minnesota Press.

Gracia, J. J. E. (2000). *Hispanic-Latino Identity: A Philosophical Perspective*. Oxford: Blackwell.

Guttiérrez, G. [1968] (2008). "Toward a Theology of Liberation." In *Contemporary Latin American Social and Political Thought: An Anthology*, edited by I. Márquez, 93–106. Lanham, MD: Rowman & Littlefield.

Haya de la Torre, V. R. [1943] (2004). "Is Latin America Ready for Democracy?" In *Latin American Philosophy: An Introduction with Readings*, edited by A. Nuccetelli and G. Seay, 138–142.

Himelblau, J. J. (1994). *The Indian in Spanish America: Centuries of Removal, Survival, and Integration*. Lancaster, CA: Labyrintho.

Keal, P. (2003). *European Conquest and the Rights of Indigenous Peoples: The Moral Backwardness of the Conquest*. Cambridge: Cambridge University Press.

las Casas, Bartolome de. (1992a). *Bartolome de las Casas: The Only Way*, edited by H. R. Parish. Mahwah, NJ: Paulist Press.

las Casas, Bartolome de. (1992b). *Memorial of Remedies for the Indies*, edited by V. N. Baptiste. Culver City, CA: Labyrinthos.

las Casas, Bartolome de. (1993). *Witness: Writings of Bartolomé de las Casas*, edited by G. Sanderlin. Maryknoll, NY: Orbis Books.

Marks, G. C. (1993). "Indigenous Peoples in International Law: The Significance of Francisco de Vitoria and Bartolomé de las Casas." *The Australian Yearbook of International Law* 13: 1–51.

Nuccetelli, S. (2007). "What Is an Ethnic Group?" In *Race or Ethnicity? On Black and Latino Identity*, edited by J. Gracia, 137–151. Ithaca, NY: Cornell University Press.

Nuccetelli, S. (2009). "Latin American Philosophy." In *The Blackwell Companion to Latin American Philosophy*, edited by S. Nuccetelli, S. Schutte, and O. Bueno, 343–356. Oxford: Wiley-Blackwell.

Rabossi, E. (2004). "Notes on Globalization, Human Rights, and Violence." In *The Impact of Globalized Neoliberalism in Latin America: Philosophical Perspectives*, edited by R. J. Gómez, 139–155. Newbury Park, CA: Hansen House.

Sarmiento, D. F. [1847] (1998). *Facundo or, Civilization and Barbarism*. New York: Penguin.

Sepúlveda, J. G. de. [1551] (2004). "Proloque to the Members of the Congregation." In *Latin American Philosophy: An Introduction with Readings*, edited by S. Nuccetelli and G. Seay, 39–41. Upper Saddle Brook, NJ: Prentice Hall.

Talbot, W. (2005). *Which Rights Should Be Universal?* Oxford: Oxford University Press.

Vitoria, F. de. (1991). *Vitoria: Political Writings*. Cambridge: Cambridge University Press.

Zea, L. (1974). *Positivism in Mexico*. Austin: University of Texas Press.

CHAPTER 10

··

LOOKING FOR ALAIN LOCKE

··

LEONARD HARRIS

IN 1983, I started a quest to find Locke. One day I would look in the Alain Locke Archives at Howard University, another at Beinecke Library, Yale, and yet another in the South Side Community Art Center in Chicago (on its yellowing walls there is a faded newspaper article picture of Locke and Eleanor Roosevelt dedicating the Center, May 7, 1941). No one was willing to help pay for this search. Not a dime. Why would anyone want to find Locke? Everyone knew where he was—in Harlem Renaissance discussions and his anthologies of poetry, music, and art. In 1907, he was the first African American Rhodes Scholar, and in 1918 the first African American to receive a doctorate degree in philosophy from Harvard. An only child and lifelong bachelor, I knew that he died in Manhattan in 1954, leaving no relatives, and was cremated on Long Island, New York. Why look for his philosophy?

Philosophers proclaim. Proclaiming makes the world. It tells us what exists and what to imagine. Is art good for its own sake? Is beautiful art linked mysteriously to a transcendental realm that creates its beauty? Is art a tool, like a hammer or screwdriver, which teaches virtue lessons to the unwise? These questions have worried philosophers for generations. Locke rejected metaphysical answers. According to Locke's philosophy, there is no objective nature of art for us to discover. No link to a transcendental realm or hidden metaphysical nature. Our self-expressions are all we have; we make beauty for our own sake.

Maybe this is why Locke has been so hard to find. Locke has been seen only as a cultural critic, promoter of the Harlem Renaissance, a scholar of Negro art, savant and polyglot well versed in classical literature and music. Never a philosopher. The obvious could not be seen. Unlike the lead character who was always ignored in Ralph Ellison's *Invisible Man* (1959), Locke could not be invisible. He could not exist. His kind could not be authors of original ideas. Therefore, by subsumption, Locke was a categorically impossible being—Negro and philosopher.

The concept of "cultural pluralism" was authored and promoted by several noted scholars. Locke's technical terms were intercultural "reciprocity" and "cultural convertibility." Horace Kallen, however, is usually credited with its authorship along with William James, John Dewey, and Randolph Bourne. On more than one occasion, Kallen made it clear that its source for him was Locke:

> I had a Negro student named Alain Locke, a very remarkable young man—very sensitive, very easily hurt—who insisted that he was a human being and that his color ought not to make any difference. Two years later when I went to Oxford on a fellowship he was there as a Rhodes

Scholar, and we had a race problem because the Rhodes scholars from the South were bastards. So they had a Thanksgiving dinner which I refused to attend because they refused to have Locke. [He told fellow white students that he did not want to dine with a Negro, but Locke was a Harvard man.] And he (Locke) said, "I am a human being," just as I had said it earlier. What difference does the difference make? We are all alike Americans. And we had to argue out the question of how the differences made differences, and in arguing out those questions the formulae, then phrases, developed—"cultural pluralism," "the right to be different." (Sollers 1986, 269)

Kallen, once described by Locke in notes to himself, as "a brilliant Boston Ghetto Jew," increasingly became comfortable with his Jewish heritage; they remained lifelong associates, and Kallen continued to credit Locke, even during his last interview before passing (Zoeller 2007). But Locke's name almost never appears as an author or major force promoting cultural pluralism.

Maybe Locke has been hard to find because giving Locke credit takes away from the illusion that individuals of his kind could not create concepts; some "other" has to be their source.

To be prescient is to have a true vision of the future. According to W. E. B. Du Bois's 1903 classic, *Souls of Black Folk*, "The Negro is a sort of seventh son, born with a veil, and gifted with second-sight in this American world" (Du Bois 1903, 2). "Second-sight" has two features: the ability to see into the meaning of existing life and the ability to envision the future. We cannot, however, really see the future; we see what we want or imagine to be the future. Proclaiming is an effort to create a future.

Locke's first book, *The New Negro* (1925), was a cornucopia anthology of art, literature, and historical articles. It included the German artist Winold Reiss's realistic color portraits of African American women and men and vignettes by novelists, poets, artists, university presidents, historians, and civil rights leaders. There are African motifs by Aaron Douglas, cartoons, a book cover by eighteenth-century philosopher on slavery Jacobus Elisa Joannes Capitein entitled *Dissertatio Politico-Theologica de Servitute, Libertati Christianae Non Contraria*, spirituals, short stories, and poetry. The authors ranged from the homosexual Bruce Nugent; to a revolutionary woman, Angelina Grimke; to John Dewey's close associate, Albert C. Barnes; to previously unpublished authors.

No one believed in 1925 that twenty-three-year-old Langston Hughes; Zora N. Hurston, who claimed to be in her twenties but was thirty-four; twenty-two-year-old Countée Cullen; or the twenty-six-year-old Aaron Douglas would become authors of masterpieces. Locke did. He was a forty-year-old teacher forcibly released from his position at Howard University between 1924 and 1925. He was released by Howard's white President to save costs, while whites with lesser qualifications were retained. Locke defined what was important about Harlem—its culture was the source of universal values such as balance, rhythm, and pose; the arts showed the diversity, and thereby the humanity, of African people.

The New Negro would be prized from the home of the artist Edward L. Pyrce (father of a curator at the Alain Locke Archives) in Tuskegee, Alabama, to the Bantu Men's Social Centre in downtown Johannesburg, South Africa. (I did not find any letters from Locke to his friend, Pikley ka Isaka Seme, one of three founders of the African National Congress, at the University of Johannesburg's library, but I did see a revered copy of *The New Negro* displayed in a glass case.) *The New Negro* was a source of inspiration, a model of what it is to be "somebody," and evidence that African people have cultural acumen.

Not a single person—black or white, communist or capitalist, Christian, Jewish, Muslim, or atheist—had produced a book the size of *The New Negro* (446 pp.) showing black people as dignified, elegant, studious, humorous, coy, and sanguine—pages adorned with African motifs as "classic" symbols.

By placing Reiss's portrait, the "black Madonna"—a black woman in plain clothes holding a peaceful child, posed, sedate, steely, dignified—on the first page of the book, Locke defined the nature of the beautiful. The "New Negro" has "renewed self-respect and self-dependency" because the days of demeaning stereotypes—"aunties," "uncles," and "mammies" . . . Uncle Tom and Sambo . . . "Colonel" and "George"—are over. The "Old Negro" was always more myth than real. He created a future by proclaiming its arrival.

I gave up the search between 1991 and 1994. I was just tired. Then I started to create. I made up a society called "The Alain Locke Society." At the American Philosophical Association meeting in Boston, December of 1994, I passed around a sign-in sheet that announced the establishment of the society. Signers became *ipso facto* founders. I used a copy of a standard organization constitution and by-laws from the Internet and registered the society with the government to acquire a nonprofit federal tax identification number. Federal identification numbers, like birth certificates from a hospital, prove existence. Without a dime anywhere, I hosted lecture sessions at philosophy conferences by recruiting scholars to present papers and getting the Locke Society listed as an affiliate of whatever established society would provide free lecture space. I published the *Philosophy of Alain Locke* (1989) and the *Critical Pragmatism of Alain Locke* (1999) by convincing Temple University Press that I had guaranteed buyers. This was a little fabrication on my part. No major publisher of philosophy had ever published a book about an African American philosopher, save renowned ministers or politicians. None. My books on Locke were listed under African American Studies as African American history, culture, and philosophy. They then could be listed under philosophy as well.

They were snookered in.

Maybe Locke has been hard to find because all persons of color in philosophy have been hard to find. Not a single book on the history of American philosophy by a white author, male or female, prior to 2000 included a single African American. Elizabeth Flower and Murray G. Murphey authored *A History of Philosophy in America* (1977). Hired in the same year as William T. Fontaine, an African American philosopher from Chester, Pennsylvania, Flower served under him when he was acting chairman. Flower and her coauthor never mentioned a single person of color. I interviewed her in 1976. She was very helpful and felt kindly about Fontaine, but she saw no reason to think about Fontaine as a productive philosopher. Fontaine authored several articles and two books that promoted the sociology of knowledge by blending the pragmatism of George H. Mead and the sociology of Karl Mannheim; attended the First International Congress of Negro Writers and Artists, in 1956 in Paris, helping draft its mandate; and presented at the Second International Congress in 1959. *A History of Philosophy in America, 1720–2000* by Bruce Kuklick did not include a single African American philosopher of note (Kuklick 2002). He never wrote about the almost ubiquitous presence of racism in American philosophy departments or about a black person in philosophy until his last book, a biography of Fontaine, *Black Philosopher, White Academy* (2008). His last major project at the University of Pennsylvania involved promoting appreciation of Fontaine at the University of Pennsylvania. I went to his home in Philadelphia to discuss the relationship between Locke and Fontaine and to share with him the years of research I had conducted on Fontaine a year before he published the biography. Sitting at his kitchen table, he had no answer for why black people or the reality of antiblack racism as standard practice in American philosophy departments never found a place in his earlier works. Kuklick worked most of his professional life at the same university as Fontaine. Kuklick and Flower are among the most liberal historians of American philosophy. They never saw the obvious.

My quest began in 1983 because I discovered features of Locke's philosophy, accidently, in the course of research for the anthology *Philosophy Born of Struggle: Anthology of African American Philosophy from 1917* (1983), the first anthology that focused on the works of African American philosophers. It was clear by reading nearly any of his commentaries on literature, art, or music in magazines or anthologies that he was a philosopher. The only persons that use terms like "relativism," "absolutism," "transvaluation," or "universality" are philosophers defining controversial concepts of reality. It was obvious.

Maybe he has been so hard to find because I too often relied on authors before me to tell me about Locke. And sadly, they were looking for, and found, a Negro type.

Generations of books on the Harlem Renaissance have claimed that Locke was misguided because he was moved by the false consciousness of his social class. This helped make Locke hard to find. Albert C. Barnes lectured to his Negro employees, as a part of his effort to help educate them, that Locke was a Philadelphia Negro from a poor family but worked hard to achieve. He wrote Locke to inform him that knowingly lying about Locke's heritage was good for his employees because the "poor Negro to Harvard" story is the one they needed to hear. He knew Locke's family was middle class—mother, a teacher; father, a senior civil servant; maternal grandmother, a teacher; paternal grandparents, learned, internationally traveled, free Negroes. John Dewey, an author of classical pragmatism, was Barnes's coassociate on several publications and considered by Barnes a great philosopher; Locke, a Negro.

Locke cannot win.

I found yellowed notes and cards in the basement library of the Bahá'í House of Worship, Chicago, recording his attendance at Firesides and as an active member of the Committee on Racial Amity; pictures of Locke at the Schomburg Center for Research in Black Culture, New York, and at Central High School, Philadelphia; and reference to a poem he wrote while a student. No scandalous erotica.

If the arguably pederast Socrates, the most famous Western philosopher, and arguably the most famous feminist philosopher, the polyamorist bisexual existentialist Simon de Beauvoir, can be heroes, I knew Locke could be championed as a hero by the gay intellectual community. What is it about his being that would exclude him from being considered a hero?

Maybe this is why not one paper on Locke, besides mine, was presented at any of the seven queer theory conferences I attended between 2000, at the graduate Center of the City of New York, to 2007 at UCLA: he had no story of being uncomfortable with his homosexuality and no drawer of pictures at the New York Public Library full of nude black males with particular attention to their penises like Carl van Vechten. Besides a few stories of flirtation, his story was not a source of inspiration. Without a story like James Baldwin's, author of *Giovanni's Room* (1953), who was alienated from his American homeland and lived openly abroad, Locke was boring. He was not an alienated wounded being that overcame or openly advocated; and nothing titillating. Locke critiqued what he termed "proprietorship" as a source of heterosexual prejudice—ownership of mates—and an array of prejudices against difference. His normality, self-confidence, counseling of gays from Bruce Nugent to Countée

Cullen, wonderful relationship with his mother, and his steadfast effort to infuse a respect for difference simply made him unfit as a hero.

Locke has been buried beneath a mountain of books that needed a Negro type to talk about—bourgeois, uncle-tom, white lackey, gentile, closeted gay, professional, middle-class, nonthreatening, or just "niggeratti." He is usually described as a genteel scholar that used verbose language. Yet, whether Harold Cruse's *Crisis of the Negro Intellectual* (1967), where he is pictured as the white man's lackey and delusional romantic; Anna Pochmara's *The Making of the New Negro* (2011), where he is pictured as a paternal patronizing gay homophobe; or Barbara Foley's *Spectres of 1919* (2008), where he is pictured as a ruling-class puppet, Locke is pictured as an agent for an agenda not of his making.

Locke is never an agent.

The character types used to picture Locke leave intact the following: white philosophers are just philosophers; black philosophers are just black because they say only what their racial (and class) being causes them to say. That is why "Whenever a Negro walks into a room, reason walks out" (Franz Fanon). A being purely determined by his racial, class, and gender nature just walked in.

It took five years for the well-published biographer Charles Molesworth and I to find a publisher, the University of Chicago Press, for *Alain L. Locke: Biography of a Philosopher* (2008). We used our considerable networks and publishing track records as well as a Manhattan literary agent for four years to search for a commercial publisher—she failed and we failed. The failure had nothing to do with the quality of the manuscript. Everyone considered the sample manuscript chapters we submitted well written and researched. Who needs a biography of a Negro philosopher? Such a being is just not believable. Categorically impossible.

I was asked by a Washington, DC, literary agent at her posh Georgetown home enjoying h'orderves with other potential authors to write a book on Jesse Jackson instead of Locke because I could surely find something scandalous about him that would boost sales. Besides, Locke was not a good choice for a biography. He was not a Christian, revealing his personal life would upset the proper Negro establishment, and he simply had no natural intellectual community—neither a novelist nor a political leader, neither a black feminist nor a sports hero, neither a self-effacing homosexual who discovers his true self to become openly happy, nor a poor Negro who lifts himself up by his bootstraps to join the ranks of the middle class; just self-confident, black, from a loving family, with a degree. After "Rhodes Scholar" and promoter of the Harlem Renaissance, Locke disappears from popular media. His role as cultural pluralist leader has long died as a role in African American culture, replaced by professional Christian academician public intellectuals, spirituals, hip-hop, BET, and sitcoms. A biography of Jesse Jackson would surely fit the bill.

All I could think of at the time was that the diversity Locke promoted and pictured as African American culture has arguably lost to a simple commercial picture—African American culture defined as the singing of spirituals, hip-hop, predictable political critiques, and sitcoms. The agent was right: Locke was just antithetical to prevailing categories defining life and marketable stereotypes about a person of African American heritage. He just did not fit.

I just went home. Weary.

The University of Chicago Press was convinced in 2007 that there just might be a market for a biography of the second most influential African American intellectual after Du

Bois. They either had not heard the rumor or failed to take it seriously. It was rumored that Jeffrey Stewart was working on a biography of Locke, and he had important ties to Harvard. Stewart, and many others, have published admirable work on Locke. The W. E. B. Du Bois Institute for African and African American Research at Harvard has raised funds, named rooms, and annually hosts a conference in Locke's honor; the Department of Philosophy has almost a complete blank record. No such biography existed then, and none exists now. The rumor was enough of an excuse to deter some publishers from seriously considering our Locke biography. The market would surely be flooded if two biographies existed!

What could possibly exclude Locke from being considered a sojourned creator of American pragmatism? One of his advisors at Oxford was F. C. S Schiller and Locke was an organizer of an audience for William James's lectures at Oxford. H. Münsterberg was his instructor at Harvard and he was with Münsterberg and G. Simmel, a founder of modern sociology, in Berlin. R. B. Perry, James's biographer, was Locke's dissertation advisor. His dissertation distinguished his version of value theory from others, but apart from several anthologies contrasting his philosophy to that of Aristotle, James, Marcuse, Nietzsche, Kallen, and Du Bois, he is nowhere considered as a sojourned creator. How could the intellectual architect of the Harlem Renaissance not count as a pragmatist and the Harlem Renaissance not count as an American Renaissance?

It was rumored, while I was at Harvard searching for Locke in 2001–2002, that the University of Pennsylvania, the City University of New York, and Harvard University were considering creating an Alain Locke Endowed chair in philosophy. I helped maintain one of the rumors. I walked into the office of the Harvard Philosophy Department's Chair, Christine M. Korsgaard, and told her about Locke, suggested that the department pursue an endowed Locke chair, and asked if I could be a nonresident fellow (an unpaid researcher) in her department. I know she researched Locke and never failed to mention in passing conversations that I hoped Harvard would fund a Locke chair. She recommended that I best fit as a nonresident fellow in African American Studies. It was rumored that a Locke endowed chair would be best housed under the auspices of the Office of Diversity or African American Studies because, just as Barnes thought, Locke's story—with proper revisions and omissions—is the kind of story that the wounded need to hear. Endowed chairs in philosophy are intended to honor, and be held by, real philosophers. As it turns out, no Alain Locke Endowed chair exists, anywhere. So much for the power of rumors.

Locke (his taken middle name LeRoy is the anglophile form of the French Le Roi, "king") authored the philosophy of critical pragmatism. He helped create pragmatism as a school of philosophy. His version emphasized value relativism—that values are created by humans and are always in transition. Locke fought against dogmatism and "universal uniformitarianism"—the idea that one cultural type was the teleological terminus for the good; that a single culture embodied appealing values. Locke's concept of renaissance humanity pictured a culturally plural world, not uniformity.

Rejecting race as a biological kind that caused cultural behavior, Locke promoted African American culture as a source of universal aesthetic values. Locke found common cause with Bahá'u'lláh's Bahá'í faith and its avid stance favoring color-blindness, while William James, John Dewey, and Jane Addams were entrapped in the religiously narrow racist Christian American worldview that defined reality in terms of the black/white binary and promoted a Christianity that historically gave credence to slavery. Locke's 825-page edited anthology with Bernard Stern, *When Peoples Meet: Race and Culture Contact* (1942), embodies the sort of cultural pluralism Locke considered crucial for a viable democracy.

Universal cultural traits are always born of local, albeit, ethnic, racial, national, or gendered realities, not colorless abstractions. The beautiful evinces universal forms and traits such as balance, symmetry, and structure—the type we see in Langston Hughes's poetry, Duke Ellington's rifts, William Grant Still's symphonies, or the poetry of Robert Frost and sonatas of Frédéric Chopin. Herein lies the key: seeing African American diversity is one bulwark against demeaning stereotypes. The diversity simultaneously bespeaks the common human experience. Around the corner from Busboys and Poets, a restaurant in the Langston (Hughes) Lofts in Washington, DC, on V Street is Locke's old house on R Street. It sits in quiet dignity. Not too far away is Georgia Douglas Johnson's house on S Street. It sits as if towering over the neighborhood, powerful, stately. The Ralph J. Bunche International Affairs Center sits on Sixth Street. Locke's steadfast promoting of integration and democracy has an embodied presence in his old friend's honored center. Maybe this is why we cannot find Locke—he has been overshadowed by a world that he helped create and in so doing forgets its past to live in the present moment.

Marcus Garvey, leader of the then largest civil African American organization, the Universal Negro Improvement Association, promoted the idea of the "New Negro" as pursuing a racial nation of proud Africans; Hubert H. Harrison, the revolutionary socialist, defined the "New Negro" as a worker interested in overthrowing capitalism, but Locke pictured the "New Negro" as a self-confident Afro-American—the sort of person that inhabits contemporary Harlem.

The Benta Funeral Home, West 132nd Street, is in Harlem where luminaries such as W. E. B Du Bois, Arthur H. Fauset, Ralph Bunche, Walter White, Mordecai Johnson, and representatives of the Bahá'í faith came to pay their respects at his memorial ceremony in 1954. It is around the corner from the Harlem YMCA, where numerous young artists lived; the Schomburg Collection of Negro Literature and Art (Harlem Branch) at 135th Street, where Arthur Schomburg religiously maintained manuscripts including slave narratives (Langston Hughes' remains are now buried at the Schomburg); the Harlem Museum of African Art; and seven blocks from the soapbox speakers at 125th and Lenox Avenue. This community is where Locke discovered the conjunction of African American self-expression, controlled style, and a group sense of cultural identity embodied by a new generation.

The world has been looking for Locke. There has not been a place to find him. The annual September 13 celebration of Locke's birthday at PS 208 Alain Locke Elementary School, New York, and the Alain L. Locke College Preparatory Academy, Los Angeles, California, annual class reunions are sites of education. The annual Alain Locke Day is held on April 16 by the city of Philadelphia, Pennsylvania, to recognize Locke's civic agency. Similarly, the Alain Locke Charter School in Chicago celebrates the first day of school as a day to encourage civic agency and education. Sites of intellectual discourse have included the 2007 symposium sponsored by the Association of American Rhodes Scholars at Howard University and the invited lectures at the 2013 World Congress of Philosophy, Athens, Greece, by the Alain Locke Society. These sites are not places solely for commemoration. There has not been a place solely dedicated to commemorate Locke. In a strange twist of fate, one of the geniuses that Locke supported and later became distant from, Zora N. Hurston, was buried in St. Lucie County, Georgia, without a headstone in 1960. Alice Walker, author of "Looking for Zora," provided a headstone that reads "Genius of the South" in 1973. Walker found Zora and made us see Zora.

One way to picture Locke's philosophy is the following: his cosmopolitanism is contrary to all forms of racial nationalism, his value relativism is contrary to all forms of value absolutism, including Marx's labor theory of value and Kant's transcendentalism; race for Locke is a social construction and racialism of temporary succor. Locke's aesthetic pluralism is contrary to Du Bois's aesthetic realism (the view that there are principles of beauty and its content that exist in the universe), and his cultural pluralism is contrary to all ideals of cultural uniformity. Genius.

In 2007, I learned that Locke's remains had been stored above ground: first came cremation in Long Island, New York, then to the Harlem memorial ceremony at Benta's Funeral Home, then on to Philadelphia, Pennsylvania, under the care of the executor of his estate and friend, Arthur H. Faucet. Faucet was the author of *Black Gods of the Metropolis* (1944), which first prominently revealed black religious institutions as places where business opportunities, politics, racial issues, and connections to African images are all involved. He kept Locke's ashes sacred because it was not clear who owned the remains, given no directions in Locke's will. Next Faucet's father's church, the African Episcopal Church of St. Thomas, Philadelphia, Pennsylvania, by way of Faucet's niece, Conchita Porter Morison, and Saddie Mitchell after Faucet died in 1983, and then Mitchell gave it to J. Weldon Norris, Department of English, Howard University, when she was visiting Philadelphia; then to W. Mortague Cobb Research Laboratory and Mark Mach, its director, placed his remains in an urn; then to the Alain Locke archive vault. Howard University, with no one paying, kept the relic sacred, as did all members of the caravan before, for two centuries as delivered, in a can, in a brown paper bag. Waiting. This was his family.

He was here all along.

The African Americans of the Association of American Scholars, under the leadership of George Keys, Jr., ended the wait: purchased a burial plot and headstone at the Congressional Cemetery, Washington DC. The Congressional Cemetery is the burial site of military and political luminaries such as Alexander Macomb, J. Edgar Hoover, and Belva Ann Lockwood as well as maids and slaves. Pére Lachaise Cemetery, Paris, is noted for intellectuals and musicians such as Marcel Proust, Oscar Wilde, Frédéric Chopin, and Jim Morrison. Locke', a national intellectual treasure, on September 13, 2014, was placed sixty years after his death in an urn beneath a headstone at the Congressional Cemetery, hopefully signaling a new humanist renaissance.

Du Bois's prescient vision in 1903 captured Locke's and arguably African Americans strivings: "This, then, is the end of his striving: to be a co-worker in the kingdom of culture, to escape both death and isolation, to husband and use his best powers and his latent genius."

There is now be a place where all and sundry can visit, quietly, peacefully, and meditate, recall, and commemorate, whether Bahá'í, atheist, Christian, pragmatist, and otherwise to find Locke.

Locke is categorically possible (Harris and Carter 2010; McBride 2013).

References

Du Bois, W. E. B. [1903] (2014). *The Souls of Black Folks*. Oxford: Oxford University.

Harris, Leonard, ed. (1989). *The Philosophy of Alain Locke, Harlem Renaissance and Beyond*. Philadelphia: Temple University Press.

Harris, Leonard, ed. (1999). *The Critical Pragmatism of Alain Locke*. Philadelphia: Rowman & Littlefield.

Harris, Leonard, and Jacoby A. Carter. (2010). *Philosophic Values and World Citizenship: Locke to Obama and Beyond*. Lanham, MD: Rowman & Littlefied Publishers.

Kuklick, Bruce. (2002). *A History of Philosophy in America 1720–2000*. Oxford: Oxford University Press.

Kuklick, Bruce. (2008). *Black Philosopher, White Academy*. Philadelphia: University of Pennsylvania Press.

Locke, Alain L. (1983). *The Critical Temper of Alain Locke*. Edited by Jeffrey Stewart. New York: Garland.

Locke, Alain L., ed. [1925] (1992). *The New Negro*. New York: Atheneum.

Locke, Alain, and Bernhard J. Stern, eds. (1942). *When Peoples Meet: A Study of Race and Culture Contacts*. New York: Committee on Workshops, Progressive Education Association.

McBride, Lee, ed. (2013). Special edition on Harrisonian "Insurrectionist Ethics," *Transactions of the Charles S. Peirce Society: A Quarterly Journal in American Philosophy* 49: 1.

Molesworth, Charles, and Leonard Harris. (2008). *Alain L. Locke: Biography of a Philosopher*. Chicago: University of Chicago Press.

Sollors, Werner. (1986). "A Critique of Pure Pluralism." In *Reconstructing American Literary History*, edited by Sacvan Bercovitch, 250–279. Cambridge, MA: Cambridge University Press.

Zoeller, Jack C. (2007). "Alain Locke at Oxford: Race and the Rhodes Scholarships." *The American Oxonian* 94 (2): 183–224.

PART III

METAPHYSICS AND PHILOSOPHY OF SCIENCE

In 1990, Anthony Appiah published "But would that still be me? Notes on Gender, 'Race,' Ethnicity as Sources of Identity" in the *Journal of Philosophy*. While interrogating different foundations for personal identity, Appiah, in an almost offhand way, mentioned that the biological sciences offered no support for the idea of human races. There then insued a discussion in academic philosophy of race known as "the race debates." Several questions were examined from different perspectives, discussion was sometimes at cross purposes, and not everyone participating or observing has been satisfied that these issues have been resolved: Is race real? Does race have a foundation in biology? Should race be eliminated?

It is not difficult to answer the foregoing questions if beginning terms are clarified, although that is not to say such answers will be satisfactory to all involved or invested in the debate. *Is race real?* This question depends on what is meant by "real." Obviously "race" is a real form of social division and to name a person's race is to say something factual and meaningful about her. However, the question of whether race is real is usually intended to cut deeper in a metaphysical sense so that it becomes: *Are social racial divisions and individual racial identities based on objective facts or truths about the natural world as many have claimed and believed?* The answer to this question in terms of the modern idea of race invokes human physical reality as first studied by biologists and anthropologists, who were joined over the twentieth century by human geneticists, evolutionary biologists, epidemiologists, and population scientists (to name just a few specialists). The consensus about human physical reality is that the idea of human races is neither supported by reliable data concerning human differences, nor does it add any meaningful information to such data. And so the answer to the next question, *Does race have a foundation in human biology?* is No.

Notice that the lack of a foundation for race in human biology undermines the reality of race only to the extent that ideas about human racial divisions and identity depend on the existence of such a scientific foundation. If racial divisions and identities were to be regarded as only spiritual, superstitious, mythical, or ideological, then the lack of the scientific biological foundation would have little effect on how people regard race and neither would it change their attitudes or behavior. But, insofar as the idea of human races as developed in the modern period has been welded to physical science, without that foundation, somewhat panicky questions about what should be done have cropped up: *Should race be eliminated?* First and foremost, eliminating race would be a conceptual project that could not be enforced in democratic societies with strong free speech rights. Such societies have no legal mechanisms for changing or eliminating spiritual, superstitious, mythical, or ideological ideas and beliefs. The only way race could be eliminated would be through education, and the only thing that would be eliminated pertaining to race would be the idea that it has a scientific foundation as a form of human social division and identity. We do not know whether "eliminating" false ideas of biological race, that is, removing them from educated discourse, would ameliorate or extinguish racism. It is possible that such elimination through education would dilute strong notions of human difference, but it is also possible that prejudice and discrimination based on ideas of racial difference would shift to nonbiological traits such as religion, culture, and perceived political opposition.

Albert Atkin approaches the question of whether there is scientific support for ideas of race by focusing on what is meant by "race," in both ordinary usage and science. Concerning ordinary usage, Atkin distinguishes among: meanings deriving from the meaning of race in the origin of race discourse during the modern colonial period; common folk beliefs and practices concerning race at the present time; and the philosophical "method of cases" relying on professional intuition. However, these sources are inconclusive because there is variety in originating content and a number of folk authorities conflict, as do a number of philosophers. Defining race scientifically requires a *scientific race concept* that needs to be well motivated or recognized, applicable to human populations, and able to approximate ordinary usage. Atkin next examines *subspecies* and *population clusters* as candidates for a scientific race concept and concludes that neither meets all three criteria.

The reality of race can also be addressed more directly than through an analysis of the meaning of "race." Michael Hardimon offers a minimal meaning of race based on population genetics, and John Relethford considers the reality of race in terms of recent DNA studies related to geography that suggest an altogether different model of racial groups than the classic Enlightenment taxonomy.

Hardimon draws on contemporary studies in population genetics to *philosophically* construct support for ordinary ideas of racial groups and racial difference. His aim is to develop a minimalist concept of *a* human race with these conceptually bare characteristics: patterns of visible physical features that are distinct to that group; common ancestry linking members; and origination in the same distinctive geographical location. Hardimon's proposal for race is meant to apply on a group level and does not require that all individuals in a group have the same features. He suggests that five geographically associated patterns of human genetic (hereditary) differences support a taxonomy of five races or do not preclude such a taxonomy. However, Hardimon is also aware that the contemporary population geneticists who have generated this geographical data do not themselves offer it as support for, or a definition of, a scientific race concept.

Relethford shows how contemporary genetic studies fail to provide a scientific foundation for traditional social racial taxonomy. It no longer makes sense to consider "race" as a system of human groups with internal homogeneity. He thus concludes:

> In the past, considerable attention has been given to the question of whether human races exist in a biological sense. Our current understanding of human genetic variation is at odds with traditional views of race. The past use of race as a unit of evolutionary change has been rejected. What remains today is the use of "geographic race" as a *rough* description of global genetic variation.

In "A Metatheory of Race," Joshua Glasgow seeks to determine whether "the race debate" is on firm ground. He notes that disagreement about the reality of race often involves arguments from reference: "They say what 'race' is supposed to refer to, and then they argue that there is or is not such a thing in the world." Glasgow considers whether *classificatory constructivism*, the view that race is real because we classify each other racially, could be correct. He rejects it in favor of a referential meaning of race as "*a relatively large group of people that is distinguished from other groups by having certain visible traits to a disproportional extent.*" That is, Glasgow argues that the mode of reference relevant to race is descriptive and that there is no privileged nondescriptive mode of reference that is (can be) relevant to the race debates.

In discussing race, ethnicity is often left out, and yet the two ideas have been closely related in the twentieth century. An old distinction was that racial differences are physical, whereas ethnic differences are cultural. But to see the limits of that distinction one has only to consider the notion of black culture and the fact that Hispanics and Latinos experience discrimination in the United States that is related to skin color. The final essay in this part, Jorge Gracia's "Race and Ethnicity," reintroduces "race" as metaphysically real or ontologically stable, in the wake of skeptical discussion such as the foregoing contributions to the race debates. Gracia here defends his thesis that "the concepts of race and ethnicity, and the distinction between them, can be preserved through their proper understanding." Gracia advises a *Genetic Common-Bundle View of Race* and the *Historical-Familial View of Ethnicity*. For race, some inherited features must be selected, but what they are is a matter of culture. And for ethnicity, family relation and shared history are the main requirements for identity. Gracia also explains how both race and ethnicity are relational properties that connect individuals with groups.

FURTHER READING

Appiah, Anthony. (1990). "But Would That Still Be Me? Notes on Gender, 'Race,' Ethnicity as Sources of Identity." *Journal of Philosophy* 87 (10): 493–499.

Jablonski, Nina G. (2012). *Living Color: The Biological and Social Meaning of Skin Color*. Berkeley: University of California Press.

Ruse, Michael, ed. (2008). *The Oxford Handbook of Philosophy of Biology*. New York: Oxford University Press.

Sollers, Werner, ed. (1989). *The Invention of Ethnicity*. Oxford: Oxford University Press.

Sussman, Robert Wald. (2014). *The Myth of Race: The Troubling Persistence of an Unscientific Idea*. Cambridge, MA: Harvard University Press.

CHAPTER 11

RACE, DEFINITION, AND SCIENCE

ALBERT ATKIN

DEBATES over the reality of race often rely on arguments about the connection between race and science—those who *deny* that race is real argue that there is no significant support from science for our ordinary race concepts; those who *affirm* that race is real argue that our ordinary race concepts are supported by scientific findings. However, there is arguably a more fundamental concern here: How should we define race concepts in the first place? The reason I claim that this definitional question is more fundamental is that our handling of the underlying definitional problem often determines the scientific support our ordinary race concepts need, and importantly the likelihood of finding such support. In short, the definitional question, "How do we define race?" often undercuts the question of whether race is scientifically meaningful.

In what follows, then, we shall address the definitional question by dividing the terrain into two parts. First, we shall examine the definition of race in ordinary nonscientific contexts. After all, if debates about the reality of race concern the reduction of ordinary concepts to counterparts in biological science, we had better be clear about what our ordinary concepts are, where they come from, and whether it makes sense to ask about the prospects of *naturalizing* them, that is, of turning their study over to the empirical sciences. Second, we shall examine the definition of race from the viewpoint of science itself. After all, we need to know which putative race concepts are available within current biological science, whether they form viable scientific race concepts, and whether they represent convincing candidates for naturalizing our ordinary race talk. Throughout, we shall see that by addressing definitional issues first, we can make progress on questions about the support our ordinary race concepts might receive from biological science, and do so without becoming swamped by complex specialist argument about the interpretation of cutting-edge science, which is a virtue of starting with definitional questions.

ORDINARY DEFINITIONS OF RACE

The first area we shall examine is the definition of our ordinary race concepts and racial categories. In particular, we shall look at three common suggestions for recovering ordinary definitions—from origins, from "the folk," and from the armchair—before identifying issues with each of these methods. Finally, we shall look at just what the broader implications of this are for any attempt to assess whether or not race is scientifically meaningful.

Definition from Origins

A common method of defining ordinary race concepts in philosophy is to identify the origin of present race talk (Appiah 1996). The standard view is that race concepts first emerged during the age of colonial expansion and were cemented by the endorsement of Enlightenment science (Zack 2002, 2–3). So, for instance, the need to justify slavery and the colonization of the "New World" led to claims that different groups are divided by essential differences in character, appearance, intelligence, and morality. At the same time, a set of supporting racial definitions emerged in the work of such taxonomists as Linnaeus (1758/1997). Of course, we now find these Enlightenment racial taxonomies to be scientifically baseless, but the definitional claim here is that current ordinary assertion about race is derived from and related to the assumptions and assertions of the originating period. What this means, then, is that if we want to define our ordinary concept of race and racial categories, then we need do no more than acknowledge the authoritative role that this origin plays and proceed to recover ordinary concepts by looking to expert opinion of the past.

Definition from "the Folk"

A second method is to look at the assertions and assumptions of ordinary language users more directly. Put simply, if we want to define ordinary race concepts, then we ought to examine ordinary assertion and practice. Although it is unlikely that ordinary speakers could deliver fully fledged definitions of what they mean by "race," because we behave and speak in ways that characterize and categorize people racially, we have a ready source of useable material from which to recover ordinary race concepts. For example, governments frequently use census taking to obtain statistics about their citizens, and the collected data often include information about race and ethnicity. This gives a partial guide to ordinary thought about racial categories within any given country. Additionally, we can discover common beliefs about race among "ordinary folk" by simply asking questions and conducting social research (Morning 2009). This means that we can examine ordinary thought and practice directly, and if we want to define an ordinary race concept, then we need do no more than to talk to ordinary people about race.

Definition from the Armchair

A third method for defining ordinary race concepts uses the tools of philosophical analysis. In broad terms, this project uses the familiar "armchair" method, whereby we derive definitions of interesting concepts from our philosophical intuitions, and then test and amend those definitions in light of *problem cases* derived from thought experiments. This method, commonly known as the *Method of Cases*, is a frequently used philosophical tool—the definition of knowledge as *justified true belief*, and the many suggested counterexamples (known

as Gettier cases) that seemed to undermine this definition is a particularly instructive example of how the Method of Cases works. Importantly, though, it would seem that this method
should be as applicable to the analysis of race as to any other philosophically interesting concept (Hardimon 2003, 441). What this means is that if we want to define an ordinary concept
of race, then we need do no more than look to the results of our best philosophical intuitions.

These three methods are not the only means of defining our ordinary race concept, since a
hybrid of folk and armchair views has also been proposed (Glasgow 2009), but they do represent the main methods used in the philosophy of race. More important, there are problems
with these methods that have ramifications for how we assess whether race is scientifically
meaningful. In what follows, we shall look at three related problems for these methods of
answering the definitional question, before drawing out how this impacts on our answers to
questions about the scientific reality of race: the range of origins, selection of folk authorities,
and the authority of armchair philosophy.

Range of Origins

The problem with definitions derived from origins is that there are a range of possible origins for our ordinary race concepts. On a rather standard picture, where "contemporary talk
about 'race' [is] the pale reflection of a more full-blooded race discourse that flourished in the
last century" (Appiah 1996, 38), the presumed experts are figures such as Carl Linnaeus (1758/
1997) or Immanuel Kant (1777). The scientific emptiness of these expert race concepts—for
instance, Linnaeus erroneously thought characteristics such as greed and shame were due to
race, whereas Kant thought that race was fixed unalterably by climate—is enough to mean
that ordinary race concepts derived from them are similarly empty. However, we can see
that this argument rests heavily on which historical figures are claimed as the originating
source. Why think that the pseudo-scientific concepts of Linnaeus give the origins of current
ordinary concepts? Why not figures such as W. E. B. Du Bois or Frederick Douglass (Taylor
2000)? Indeed, why not prominent recent thinkers and figures who have said much in the
public arena about race? The concern here is simply that if historical expertise is supposed
to give us our current ordinary concepts of race, the definition will depend very much on
which figures and which origins are taken to be relevant, because a Kantian origin for race
thinking will give a very different ordinary definition from a Du Boisian one. As a means for
recovering an ordinary definition, then, things are less clear than they might initially seem.

Selection of Folk Authorities

The problem with definitions derived from "the folk" is that the definition we obtain will
largely depend on who we talk to. That is, how do we identify which "folk" count? It is well
documented that different countries have different histories of racial formation. For example, the racial history of the United States suggests that ordinary race talk, focusing on skin
color and ancestry, identifies four or five racial groupings (Omi and Winant 1986). By contrast, the racial history of Brazil, focusing on a wider class of skin colors and much less on
ancestry, identifies as many as twenty-eight racial groupings (Telles 2004). Such sociological
evidence of variation in race concepts across different groups makes it clear that what we ask
of any scientific naturalization of such concepts would need to vary quite starkly. Biological

evidence needed to support a folk definition derived from the United States would look very different to that needed to support a folk definition derived from Brazil.

The Authority of Armchair Philosophy

The problem with definitions derived from "the armchair" is that it is unclear why we should think that these philosophical intuitions, these methods, or these philosophers are the ones that should define our ordinary concept of race. Part of the worry here stems from recent work in experimental philosophy, which shows that philosophical intuitions are not the stable and objective guide that many take them to be (Machery et al. 2004). In addition, two related worries are quite specific to applying this method to questions of race.

First, modern analytic tools and methodology were developed as a means of producing general accounts and definitions by abstracting away extraneous detail. Problematically, race (along with class and gender) has traditionally been treated as one of these extraneous details. Consequently, it becomes hard to see how a methodology that excludes such features can then be used as a stable source for recovering the ordinary definitions of those concepts. Second, it is not clear that standard analytic methods are well suited to defining our ordinary race concepts, because using politically significant terms such as "race" in the *Method of Cases* seems to render intuitions unstable. An account of how standard intuitions about meaning give way when dealing with gendered terms can be found in Saul (2012). It would be unsurprising to find that similar things hold for racial terms.

It therefore seems that there are problems with all three definitional methods of origin, folk, and armchair philosophy due primarily to the variety of experts, folks, and intuitions that are available for defining ordinary race concepts. But what is the significance of this general difficulty for questions about the scientific reality of race? Given the range of methods, our ordinary definitions will depend on which method we choose, and they will then further depend on which experts we think matter, or which folk we talk to, or which intuitions and thought experiments we think are important. There is no reason to think the definitions recovered from these various methods will deliver anything like a stable or uniform account of race and racial categories, but ultimately, this is what makes the definitional problem so crucial to issues about the scientific reality of race. On the one hand, it is unclear at a first pass which ordinary race concept we are (or should be) asking biological science to naturalize. On the other hand, even if it turns out that we can offer an answer to the question of whether or not some particular ordinary race concept is scientifically meaningful, it is not obvious that this marks a very significant advance. Does showing that we cannot naturalize an ordinary race concept derived from a Kantian origin show that race *is not* scientifically meaningful? Similarly, does showing that the ordinary Haitian folk concept of race *is* scientifically meaningful thereby prove the scientific reality of race in an appropriately robust sense? I suspect the answer to each of these questions is "no."

THE SCIENTIFIC DEFINITION OF RACE

Turning now to the second way of approaching the definitional concern, how might we go about trying to define race by starting with the available science? After all, it is not an incontestable fact that when we are trying to address whether race is scientifically meaning-ful that we *must* begin with our ordinary concept of race, or even think that our ordinary use *must* be the primary driver in any reductive project. However, defining race scientifically is not so straightforward as with the ordinary race concept, and this is because (except in certain very specific arenas) "race" is not a concept much used in science. What this means is that we are instead looking for an appropriate counterpart concept in the biological sciences that can be defined as a *scientific race concept*. To judge whether our putative scientific race concepts are good definitions, however, it seems reasonable to use the following three criteria:

> First, any putative scientific race concept needs to be *well motivated*. What this means is that: first, the concept should be a well-recognized and widely acknowledged scientific concept—*oxidation* and *chemical reaction* would be well-recognized explanations for cell energy; *orgone* or *odic force* would not. And, second, the concept needs to have broad application across the biological sciences and include nonhuman populations.
> Second, any putative scientific race concept needs to be *applicable to human populations*. So, for example, "strain" is a *well-motivated* taxonomic concept—it is recognized and used to describe various microorganisms, and, in laboratory circumstance, rats and mice. However, it does not apply to human populations—there are different strains of influenza virus, but there are not different strains of humans.
> Third, any putative scientific race concept needs to *approximate ordinary use* well enough to either map on to that usage or to provide good reasons for changing ordinary usage. To be clear, there is often variation between the way ordinary speakers and scientists think of the same concept. However, this need not be an automatic barrier to using scientific definitions to underpin ordinary usage, and it is seldom the case that divergence between scientific and ordinary use leads us to conclude that the science is empty. In definitional terms, then, this means that small or negligible differences between a scientific race concept and ordinary use should not be treated as automatically terminal—in this approach, scientific definitions are leading the way, and ordinary use can certainly be informed by scientific fact and discovery.

With these three criteria in place, then, we can now look at some possible scientific race concepts from the biological sciences. Although there are various concepts we might examine here, we shall only look at the two most common suggestions for defining a scientific race concept—*subspecies* and *population clusters*. In what follows, we shall outline the details of these concepts in turn, judge them by the three criteria we have introduced here, and assess the impact of these definitional issues on the question of whether or not race is scientifically meaningful.

Subspecies

The most common suggestion for defining a scientific race concept is "subspecies." However, Richard Lewontin (1972) famously argues that ordinary race talk is biologically meaning-less by using "subspecies" as a scientific race concept. Subspecies are commonly defined as isolated breeding populations within a species whose members could still breed with the members of the larger species population and produce fertile offspring. In terms of our three criteria for defining a viable scientific race concept, it is clear that "subspecies" is *well motivated*, because it is a widely recognized scientific concept in the biological sciences, and it is used as a natural division across nonhuman populations. However, once we begin to look at the second criteria, *applicability to human populations*, the viability of defining a scientific race concept in terms of "subspecies" begins to look problematic.

The problem is rather simple: human populations are not dividable into subspecies. To see why, we need to understand that a more precise definition of "subspecies" uses a well-recognized standard for marking genetic variation between subspecies. To keep matters reasonably simple, consider that individual members of any species will be highly genetically similar, but that there will nonetheless be some genetic variation among them. In humans, for instance, although we are over 99 percent genetically similar, we can still find small amounts of genetic difference between two individuals. In terms of defining subspecies, however, we need to know how much of this genetic variation is due to the normal differences we find between individuals from the *same* breeding population, as opposed to variation we find between individuals from *different* breeding populations. The greater the amount of variation attributable to *cross-group* differences, as opposed to *in-group* differences, the more likely it is that we are dealing with individuals from different subspecies. Importantly, though, in the biological sciences the standard threshold for marking the difference between two subspecies is where at least 25 percent of variation between two individuals from different breeding groups is attributable to *cross-group* rather than *in-group* difference (Smith et al. 1997).

To give a slightly extended illustration of the importance of the subspecies concept in the biological sciences, and the use of this 25 percent threshold in determining the existence of subspecies, we can look at some recent work on genetic variation in Common Chimpanzee breeding groups. It is widely recognized that there are five distinct breeding populations of the Common Chimpanzee species: *pan troglodytes versus* (found in Upper Guinea); *pan troglodytes ellioti* (found in West Cameroon); *pan troglodytes troglodytes* (found in Central Equatorial Africa); *pan troglodytes schweinfurthii* (found in Western Equatorial Africa); and *pan troglodytes marungensis* (found in Eastern Equatorial Africa). However, these five breeding groups are taken to constitute only three subspecies—*pan troglodytes versus; pan troglodytes ellioti*; and *pan troglodytes troglodytes*—because the genetic variation between the three Equatorial African breeding groups attributable to cross-group difference *is less than* the 25 percent threshold for subspecies difference. Consequently, all three of the Equatorial breeding populations are treated as the same subspecies—*pan troglodytes troglodytes*. By contrast, the genetic variation between the three recognized subspecies attributable to cross-group difference is around 30 percent—clearly above the 25 percent threshold for subspecies differentiation (Kaessmann et al. 1999; Gonder et al. 2011).

Although the use of genetic variation in Common Chimpanzee breeding groups to determine subspecies is instructive, more interesting is that by comparison, cross-group genetic variation between humans populations falls a long way short of the 25 percent threshold for subspecies differentiation. For example, Lewontin (1972) suggests that while any two human beings are 99.8 percent genetically similar, only 7 percent of the 0.2 percent genetic difference between them is attributable to cross-group variation. Indeed, more recent estimates of genetic variation in humans derived from 2002 research (Rosenberg et al. 2002) and used for comparison in Common Chimpanzee studies (Gonder et al. 2011) suggests that as little as 4 percent of variation in humans is attributable to cross-group variation. So what does this mean? Well, it means that cross-group genetic variation in humans falls well below the 25 percent threshold needed to mark subspecies. As a result, if subspecies fails to be applicable to human populations, then subspecies is not a viable scientific race concept. In terms of the scientific reality of race here, we can see that addressing our definitional question has given us one answer: "subspecies" is not a viable definition for a scientific race concept—it is a *well-motivated* definition, but it is not *applicable to human populations*. Therefore, any attempt to naturalize our ordinary race concept using "subspecies" looks wrong-headed from the start.

Population Clusters

Although it is widely acknowledged that "subspecies" is not a viable definition for a scientific race concept, there are alternative ways of dividing populations in the biological sciences that neither rely on subspecies concepts nor the related standards for counting in-group and cross-group variation. Most prominently, recent techniques used in population genetics to identify the structure and ancestral hierarchy of a given population have led to claims that *population clusters* are a viable candidate for defining a scientific race concept (Spencer 2015). So, what are population clusters, how viable are they for defining a scientific race concept, and how might they be used to argue for the reality of race?

Population geneticists identify and genetically profile various local populations or breeding groups, by adding progressively more and more local groups to their picture, to build a genetic profile of larger population groups, up to the level of recognized subspecies and species. With this genetic profile at hand, geneticists can use computer analysis to detect where genetic material and differences cluster (to however small a degree) across the larger population, and that gives them a picture of the structure and hierarchy of the larger population. For example, using population clustering analyses on the five breeding population groups of Common Chimpanzee mentioned earlier, population clustering techniques support arguments for there being only three subspecies and they are also able to identify genetic clusters that suggest the following: the *pan troglodytes versus* subspecies from Upper Guinea has been a separate breeding population for fifty-four thousand years; *pan troglodytes ellioti* from West Cameroon has been a separate breeding population for the last three hundred thousand years; the three breeding groups making up the *pan troglodytes troglodytes* subspecies in Equatorial Africa only formed separate breeding populations in the last one hundred thousand years or so (Gonder et al. 2011). These observations about how the larger population forms genetic clusters, what the larger ancestral structures are, the age at which different breeding groups form, and the genetic distance between them are interesting and useful, and they have been applied by population geneticists to many different species. Recently, this population clustering analysis was applied to humans, and the results of the 2002 study by Noah Rosenberg and colleagues (Rosenberg et. al. 2002) have proved to be of particular interest.

The Rosenberg study used population clustering techniques on more than one thousand individuals who, by self-identified race and ethnicity, came from over fifty ethnic groups. With the larger genetic profile at hand, the Rosenberg study used computer analyses to partition the larger population into various clusters, ranging from two to six. The results that reignited the question of whether or not race is biologically meaningful arose when the larger genetic group was partitioned into five clusters. The five clusters identified by computer analysis seemed to group individuals in the study into a set of populations that mirrored the racial groups suggested by participants' self-identified races. More specifically, the underlying genetic clustering grouped individuals into one of a sub-Saharan African group, readily identified as an African race; a North African and West Eurasian group, readily identified as a Eurasian race; an East Eurasian group, readily identified as an Asian race; a North and South American group, readily identified as a native American race; and finally an Oceanic group, readily identified as a Pacific Islander race. The important question that this work presents is, "Could population clustering give us a viable scientific race concept capable of supporting or naturalizing our ordinary race concepts and racial categories?"

Some have attempted to address the scientific results and claims made for the Rosenberg study directly. For example, similar cluster studies (Behar et al. 2010) seem to suggest that the sample used in the Rosenberg study is not fine-grained enough; that is, the number of participants was too small and from too narrow a geographical location (all participants were American). Our aim here, however, is not to question the science directly but to address the underlying definitional question in terms of the three criteria that we identified earlier: Is population clustering *well motivated, applicable to human populations*, and does it *approximate ordinary usage* closely enough, to either map onto current use, or provide good reasons to change ordinary use? If the answer to these three questions is "Yes," then "population clusters" seems to offer a good definition of scientific race.

It seems clear that "population clusters" meets the first two conditions. It is *well motivated* in virtue of being both widely acknowledged and applied to many nonhuman populations; and we can see from the Rosenberg study that it is *applicable to human populations*. For "population clusters" to be a viable definition for a scientific race concept then, it simply needs to *approximate ordinary use*, by either mapping or offering good reason to change ordinary usage. Arguably, though, things are not so clear cut here, and at least two issues seem to present themselves.

First, ordinary use and "population clusters" seem to make different assumptions about how neatly human populations are divided. Population clusters do not give us neat divisions between groups, and they allow for admixture or interbreeding between different populations. This means that individual membership in a population cluster will be a matter of degree, rather than an all-or-nothing affair. Our ordinary race talk, however, does not seem to allow for partial membership in a racial group. Races seem to be treated as entirely separate entities with membership in one group excluding membership in another. This looks like an important gap between "population clusters" and ordinary thought and talk about race. That need not be the end of the matter, of course, so long as treating "population clusters" as a scientific race concept suggests good reasons for changing ordinary use. However, again, it is not immediately obvious that there are good reasons.

One clear problem is that, although it has been suggested (Spencer 2015, 49) that our recognition of "mixed-race" status suggests that ordinary commitment to the exclusionary nature of racial groups is already changing in favor of the partial membership suggested by population clustering, it is not entirely obvious that this true. Identities of mixed race just as easily prove the strength of our ordinary commitment to the exclusionary nature of racial groups, especially given social and philosophical research (see Zack 1993) suggesting that mixed-race individuals are not clearly identified as members of two (or more) races, and are instead seen as either forming another separate racial group, or in the case of a black-and-white mixture in the United States, as wholly a member of one race (i.e., black).

The second issue that tells against "population clusters" approximating ordinary use is that it is not clear, despite claims made, that the five Rosenberg study clusters do map onto ordinary racial categories in a compelling way. To begin with, as we have already noted, the nature and number of racial categories vary across different social and national racial contexts. As a result, the *best* that we can say about the apparent mapping of the five Rosenberg study clusters to five ordinary racial categories is that this mirrors ordinary usage *in the United States*. Indeed, some advocates of reducing our ordinary race concepts to "population clusters" endorse the view that we should think of these issues in terms of the reality of US racial groups (see Spencer 2015, 46–47). However, this move looks problematic for two reasons. On the one hand, by conceding that ordinary race concepts are locally and socially constructed, it makes the claimed discovery that partitioning populations mirrors ordinary usage in *one* of these local contexts, looks accidental at best and suspicious at worst. On the other hand, it looks as though ordinary users of race in the United States would have to accept that their concept of race is not universal and their usage should be amended. It is difficult to see how arguments about population clustering could be used to do that.

Restricting scientific support to *US race* is not the only problem with the mapping claims. On closer inspection, the five population clusters and the five racial groups of ordinary usage do not seem to mirror each other all that neatly. In terms of ordinary US racial categories, the Eurasian group would need to map to the "white" racial category. However, many individual members of the North African/Eurasian population cluster of the Rosenberg study are unlikely to be identified as "white" in ordinary use. Ordinary American usage is unlikely to assent to any claim that a Northern European, a North African, and a Persian Tajik are all of the same race, because only the Northern European would be called "white." There may be five population clusters in the putative scientific concept, and five racial groups according to ordinary usage, but it is far from clear that they mirror each other closely enough, or that they would not require quite drastic changes in ordinary usage.

With all this said, then, it looks as though "population cluster" is not a viable definition for a scientific race concept. It is *well motivated* and it *applies* to human populations, but it does not *approximate ordinary use* nearly so well as initial claims suggested. In particular, it requires a drastic change in the way that ordinary language users think of the separation of racial groups, and it needs to concede that it captures only one among many ordinary social practices for defining race—a rather counterintuitive result for most ordinary users.

CONCLUSION

What we have seen here, then, is that questions about the scientific reality of race can be approached by looking at the more fundamental issue of how we define race in the first place. Importantly, the variety of means by which we can and could define our ordinary race concept makes the question of potential scientific support look intractable. Similarly, if we set about solving the definitional question by finding putative concepts from biological science to serve as scientific race concepts, we do not seem to have any viable candidates. Neither "subspecies" nor "population cluster" meet all three of the criteria needed to define a viable scientific race concept: "subspecies" is *well motivated*, but not *applicable*; "population cluster" is *well motivated* and *applicable*, but does not *approximate ordinary usage*. It may be that in the long run we can find ways to recover our ordinary definitions in a manner that makes the question of scientific support tractable. Or we may find viable scientific race concepts from the biological sciences. At any rate, by attending to definitional matters, as we have here, we will arrive at a clearer sense of where we really stand on whether or not race is really real.

REFERENCES

Appiah, K. A. (1996). "Race, Culture, Identity: Misunderstood Connections." In *Color Conscious: The Political Morality of Race*, edited by K. A. Appiah and A. Guttmann, 30–105. Princeton, NJ: Princeton University Press.

Behar, Doron, M. Metspalu, Y. Baran, N. M. Kopelman, B. Yunusbayev, A. Gladstein, S. Tzur, et al. (2010). "The Genome-Wide Structure of the Jewish People." *Nature* 466 (7303): 238–242.

Glasgow, Joshua. (2009). *The Theory of Race*. New York: Routledge.

Gonder, M. K., S. Locatelli, L. Ghobrial, M. W. Mitchell, J. T. Kujawski, F. J. Lankester, C. B. Stewart, and S. A. Tishkoff. (2011). "Evidence from Cameroon Reveals Differences in the Genetic Structure and Histories of Chimpanzee Population." *Proceedings of the National Academy of Sciences* 108 (12): 4766–4771.

Hardimon, Michael. (2003). "The Ordinary Concept of Race." *Journal of Philosophy* 100 (9): 437–455.

Kaessmann, H. V., V. Wiebe, and S. Pääbo. (1999). "Extensive Nuclear DNA Sequence Diversity among Chimpanzees." *Science* 286 (5442): 1159–1162.

Kant, Immanuel. (1777). "Von der verschnieden Rassen der Menschen." In *Der Philosoph für die Welt*, edited by J. J. Engel, 125–164. Leipzig: book facsimile at https://archive.org/details/derphilosophfro1enge.

Linnaeus, Carl. [1758] (1997). "The God-Given Order of Nature." In *Race and The Enlightenment*, edited by Emmanuel Chukwudi Eze, 10–14. Malden, MA: Blackwell.

Lewontin, Richard. (1972). "The Apportionment of Human Diversity." *Evolutionary Biology* 6: 381–398.

Machery, Edouard, Ron Mallon, Shaun Nichols, and Stephen Stich. (2004). "Semantics, Cross-cultural Style." *Cognition* 92 (3): 1–12.

Morning, Ann. (2009). "Towards a Sociology of Racial Conceptualisation for the 21st Century." *Social Forces* 87 (3): 1167–1192.

Omi, Michael, and Howard Winant. (1986). *Racial Formation in the United States*. New York: Routledge.

Rosenberg, Noah, J. K. Pritchard, J. L. Weber, H. M. Cann, K. K. Kidd, L. A. Zhivotovsky, and M. W. Feldman. (2002). "Genetic Structure of Human Populations." *Science* 298 (5602): 2381–2385.

Saul, Jennifer. (2012). "Politically Significant Terms and Philosophy of Language: Methodological Issues." In *Out from the Shadows: Analytic Feminist Contributions to Traditional Philosophy*, edited by Anita Superson and Sharon Crasnow, 195–216. Oxford: Oxford University Press.

Smith, H. M., Chiszar, D., and Montanucci, R. (1997). "Subspecies and Classification." *Herpetological Review* 28: 13–16.

Spencer, Quayshawn. (2015). "Philosophy of Race Meets Populations Genetics." *Studies in History and Philosophy of Biological and Biomedical Sciences* 52: 46–55.

Taylor, Paul. (2000). "Appiah's Uncompleted Argument: W.E.B. Du Bois and the Reality of Race." *Social Theory and Practice* 26: 103–128.

Telles, Edward E. (2004). *Race in Another America: The Significance of Skin Color in Brazil.* Princeton, NJ: Princeton University Press.

Zack, Naomi. (1993). *Race and Mixed Race.* Philadelphia, PA: Temple University Press.

Zack, Naomi. (2002). *The Philosophy of Science and Race.* New York: Routledge.

CHAPTER 12

MINIMALIST BIOLOGICAL RACE

MICHAEL O. HARDIMON

THE *minimalist concept of race* represents the barest, most stripped-down characterization of the ordinary concept of RACE possible. It can be arrived at by starting with the ordinary concept of race—the concept expressed in ordinary uses of the English word *race* and its cognates—and attempting to make the best possible sense of it (e.g., in terms of coherence and empirical plausibility). The minimalist concept of race represents the "logical core" of the ordinary concept. It captures what is "rational" in that concept.

The minimalist race concept can be specified as follows:
A (minimalist) race is group of human beings

(1) which, as a group, is distinguished from other groups of human beings by *patterns of visible physical features*,
(2) whose members are linked by a *common ancestry* peculiar to members of the group, and which
(3) originates from a *distinctive geographic location*.

The minimalist concept of race is a group-level concept. It does not require or allow for a "constituent definition" in Elliot Sober's sense of the term: a definition fixed by a specification of what it is for an individual to be a member of race (1994). What it is for an individual to be a member of a race is specified in terms of what it is for a group to be a race. *Race*, in the first instance, is a predicate of groups rather than individuals.

Condition (1) represents an intuitively plausible partial characterization of RACE. It captures the basic intuition that *people who belong to different races generally look different from one another.* "Generally" does not mean "always." The concept does not say that each member of race R1 looks different from every member of race R2. A given member of R may not exhibit a visible physical character typical of Rs.

The visible physical features figuring in the characterization of the concept consist of phenotypic traits such as skin color, lip form, hair type, and eye shape. Races are generally distinguished from one another by a *number* of visible features. The common objection that there is no objective reason to choose one visible physical feature over another to define "race" misses the point that "race" is not defined in terms of any *one* visible physical feature.

To count as racial, a feature must be innate. The visible physical features of race are passed down biologically to offspring from their parents. Because of this, the skin color, lip form, and eye shape of children of Rs tend to resemble the skin color, lip form, and eye shape of their parents.

The visible physical features characteristic of race form *patterns: this* skin color going with *this* eye shape and *this* hair form. It is in terms of these patterns that RACE is defined. How precisely the pattern of a given minimalist race is to be specified is a matter of some delicacy, requiring the competence of a physical anthropologist. Nonetheless, we can say that, for any given race R, there is an in-principle answer to the question, What pattern of visible physical characters does it exhibit?—an answer we can get *wrong*. This is one respect in which race-hood is objective.

The patterns of visible physical differences that count as "racial" correspond to differences of geographical ancestry. Being instances of *order in nature*, they are not gerrymandered. The concept's focus on these patterns is not arbitrary. Doing so is the concept's job. If it did not focus on them, it would not be the concept it is. *Minimalist race is inter alia a matter of color and shape.*

The minimalist concept of race does not require that the patterns of visible physical features constitutive of a minimalist races be sharply distinguished. Nor does it require a sharp distinction between the visible physical features that figure in these patterns. It allows that the lines separating races may be blurry.

Like condition (1), condition (2) represents an intuitively plausible partial characterization of RACE. It specifies that ancestry is essential to race, making it explicit that "race" is not defined in terms of physical characters alone. Hermeneutic evidence of a discursive link between RACE and ANCESTRY can be found in the etymology of the English word *race*, which, the dictionaries tell us, derives from the Italian term *razza* (meaning "race" and "lineage"). Philology suggests that the concept RACE is best understood as a modification of the concept ANCESTRY. Etymology is not always a reliable indicator of discursive content, but in the case of RACE it is. *Minimalist race is morphologically marked ancestry.* The minimalist concept does not require that the lines distinguishing the lineages of different races be sharp.

Condition (3) represents another intuitively plausible partial characterization of RACE. It makes it explicit that the ancestry that plays a role in RACE is *geographical* ancestry. Different races originate from different geographical locations. Minimalist race is morphologically marked *geographical* ancestry. The minimalist concept of race does not require sharp divisions between the geographical regions from which different minimalist races originate. It does not require that minimalist races be "discrete units."

The minimalist concept of race must be distinguished from the infamous *racialist* concept of race. The latter is the empirically refuted, traditional, pernicious, essentialist, and hierarchical race concept often mistakenly identified as *the* race concept. It maintains that races are "discrete units" that have biological essences (nonrelational features possessed by all and only members of the race) that fix normatively important features of their members such as intelligence and moral character and that races can be objectively ranked as superior and inferior on the basis of these features. It is evident that the minimalist concept of race is distinct from this concept. It is not *racialist* because it makes no reference to biological essences, and it is not *racist* because it does not associate race with normatively important features.

The rule for determination of membership in a minimalist race is that *the offspring of two members of race R is an R.* The fact that someone is a member of a minimalist race tells you *very little* about the individual. It tells you that she is likely to have skin of a certain color, lips of a certain shape, hair of a certain form, and so forth. And it tells you where her ancestors resided in 1492. It tells you nothing about her normatively important features.

The minimalist concept of race is biological because it characterizes the objects to which it purports to refer in biological terms. The visible physical features in terms of which races are defined such as skin color, lip form, hair type, and eye shape are biological properties. Differences of geographical ancestry are biogeographical. Minimalist races, if such there are, are denizens of the biological world.

The minimalist concept of race is *deflationary*. It is designed to let the racialist air out of the racialist concept of race. It is supposed to provide a *minimal* characterization of what race is. It makes it possible to represent biological race as a nonracialist and nonracist relatively modest biological kind.

THE MINIMALIST PHENOMENON OF RACE

The idea of the *minimalist biological phenomenon of race* is the idea of a correspondence in human beings between differences in the patterns of visible physical features and differences in geographical ancestry. The phenomenon is exemplified by such correlations as the one that obtains between the pattern of brown skin–kinky hair–full lips and sub-Saharan African ancestry and the correlation that obtains between the pattern of white skin–wavy hair–narrow lips and European ancestry.

The phenomenon deserves the appellation "minimalist" because it is fully specified by reference to the correspondence between differences in patterns of visible physical features and differences in geographical ancestry. No reference is made to humanly important features such as intelligence, sexuality, or morality. No reference is made to essences. The idea of sharp boundaries between patterns of visible physical features or corresponding geographical regions is not invoked. Nor again is reference made to the idea of significant genetic differences.

The characterization of the phenomenon as "biological" is warranted because, as we have noted, its constitutive features—patterns of physical features (skin color, nose shape, hair form and so forth) are biological and differences of geographical ancestry are biogeographical. The phenomenon also counts as biological in virtue of the fact that it has a biological origin in the prehistoric movements and partial isolation of human populations.

Does the minimalist biological *phenomenon* of race exist? It seems plausible to suppose that it does. There appears to be a correspondence in human beings between differences in the patterns of visible physical features and differences in geographical ancestry. Many eliminativists, who deny that races exist, accept that such a correlation exists.

The Existence of Minimalist Races

Do minimalist *races* exist? Before addressing this question, it is essential to make clear that *racialist* races do not exist. There are no racialist races. No human group is a racialist race. No human being "has" a racialist race. The existence of racialist races is precluded by population genetics: the percentage of overall human genetic variation found between human populations is small, smaller than the percentage of overall human genetic variation found within human populations, which is large (Lewontin 1972; Rosenberg et al. 2002).

Now, should it turn out that population genetics precludes the possibility of minimalist races, then, obviously, minimalist races do not exist. Our first task, then, is to determine whether population genetics precludes their existence. The answer is no. This can be seen by looking to the minimalist concept of race's "genetic profile," a specification of what must be true of human genetic variation in order for minimalist races to exist.

The minimalist concept of race's genetic profile is remarkably nondemanding. It does not require that the fraction of human genetic diversity between minimalist races exceed the fraction of diversity within them. It is compatible with within-race diversity being large and between-race diversity being small. It does not require that most genes be highly differentiated along racial lines. It does not require the existence of a substantial genetic difference between races apart from the genetic differences that underlie the obvious phenotypic differences between them. Nor does it require that the underlying variation in the genes for these differences be typical of the variation in the genome in general. Moreover, it is compatible with there being few genetic differences between races apart from the genetic differences that underlie the obvious phenotypic differences and with the genetic difference underlying the obvious phenotypic differences being atypical of the genome in general. It does not require that racial categories have great predictive power for yet unstudied characters. Nor again does it require that there be any genetic differences between races other than those found in the genes that underlie the pattern of visible physical differences that distinguish races. The demands made by the minimalist concept's genetic profile are minimal.

Because the existence of minimalist races is compatible with the findings of population genetics, it makes sense to ask: Do minimalist races exist? The answer comes down to whether there are existing human groups that satisfy the minimalist concept of race. If there are such human groups, minimalist races exist. If there are not, minimalist races do not exist.

The contention that minimalist races exist is controversial. Eliminativists about race deny that biological races of any sort exist. To support the contention that minimalist races exist, I will enlist the implicit support of the arch-eliminativist philosopher of race K. Anthony Appiah. Interestingly, Appiah, who denies that races exist, explicitly allows the existence of "groups defined by skin color, hair, and gross morphology corresponding to the dominant pattern for these characteristics in the major subcontinental regions: Europe, Africa, East and South Asia, Australasia, the Americas, and perhaps the Pacific Islands" (1996). Now it is obvious that these groups (a) exist and (b) satisfy the conditions of the minimalist concept of race. It follows that minimalist races exist, given the definition of "minimalist race."

But a skeptic might question this, allowing that there is a *loose* sense in which groups satisfying the conditions of the concept of minimalist race can be said to "exist," but insisting that the real question is whether these groups are biologically (i.e., genetically) distinct. The reasons for thinking that they are include the well-established fact that the variation between human populations is mostly "clinal" (gradual rather than sharp) (Livingston 1962). At the level of phenotype, there are no sharp lines distinguishing subcontinental populations. And most genetic variation occurs within rather than between quasi-continental populations (Lewontin 1972; Rosenberg et al. 2002).

Three replies. First, nothing in the content of the concept of minimalist race requires that minimalist races be sharply distinguished. The lines distinguishing the patterns of visible physical features that distinguish minimalist races (and the lines distinguishing individual visible physical features that figure in these patterns) may be blurry. The same is true for the lines distinguishing their genetics. Nor again is it the case that lines distinguishing the ancestry of minimalist races must be sharp. Minimalist races need not be "discrete units." They can be clines. Second, "population thinking," the general pattern of biological thought associated with the synthesis of Darwin's theory of evolution with Mendelian genetics, dispenses with the idea that biological reality requires the possibility of drawing sharp lines between groups on the basis of the individual group members' intrinsic properties. Population thinking brings with it a conception of biological existence that tolerates ontological blurriness. Third, as Elliot Sober notes, "the fact that species evolve gradually entails that the boundaries between species are vague" (1994, 206). Evolution tells us that nature constructs species in such a way that it may be impossible to draw sharp lines between races. Together these considerations provide a powerful reason for thinking that the impossibility of drawing sharp lines between minimalist races would be *not* be a good reason for doubting their existence. The idea that biological groups must be genetically distinct to be said to exist rests on an obsolete understanding of biological existence.

The Genomics of Minimalist Race

Recent advances in population genetics suggest that it may be possible to draw sharp genetic lines between minimalist races, after all. In their celebrated 2002 article, Rosenberg and colleagues deployed the computer implemented algorithm *structure* to assign 1,056 individuals from 52 populations represented in the CEPH-HGDP panel to genetic "clusters" based on measures of overall genetic similarity. The article shows that it is possible to use genetic information to assign individuals into clusters corresponding with the "major geographic areas" of Africa, Eurasia (Europe, the Middle East, Central/South Asia) and East Asia, Oceania, and America.

This result is illustrated most notably by the graph labeled "K = 5" in Figure 1 in Rosenberg et al. (2002). In this graph, the genetic clusters corresponding to five major geographic areas form a single horizontal band, consisting of five clearly demarcated segments, to which different colors are assigned. The cluster corresponding to Africa forms a segment that is mostly orange. The cluster corresponding to Eurasia forms the mostly blue segment. The cluster corresponding to East Asia forms the mostly pink segment. The cluster corresponding to Oceania forms the mostly green segment. The segment formed by the cluster corresponding to America is mostly purple. Each cluster is separated from its neighbor by a line marking a relatively sharp allele frequency break.

The article is not about race. It does not identify the populations corresponding to the five major geographic regions as races. Nor does the word "race" appear in its pages. In a follow-up paper (2005), Rosenberg and colleagues state that the result of the earlier study should not be taken as support for any particular concept of race.

Nonetheless, it is possible to bring the 2002 article to bear on the question concerning the genetic distinctness of races. For this to happen, an exogenous race concept must be introduced. The minimalist concept of race is well suited to serve this purpose. Its introduction makes it possible to address this question.

Now, as it happens, the populations corresponding to the five major geographic areas coincide at least roughly with the groups Johann Friedrich Blumenbach identified as the principal "varieties" (races) of mankind: Ethiopian, Caucasian, Mongolian, Malay, and American (1795/2000). And, as it happens, these populations are apt candidates for the application of the minimalist concept of race. They can each be plausibly regarded as a minimalist race. This is because they appear to be distinguished by patterns of visible physical features corresponding to geographical ancestry.

So let us assume that the five populations are minimalist races. What does the Rosenberg article show about the genetic distinctness of minimalist races modulo (i.e., if we make) this assumption? It shows modulo this assumption that it is possible to assign individuals to minimalist races—more specifically *continental-level* minimalist races—on the basis of genetic information alone.

It is clear why this is so. *If* the populations of the five major areas are continental-level minimalist races, to assign individuals to clusters corresponding to the five major areas *is* to assign them to clusters corresponding to continental-level minimalist races. When *structure* assigns an individual I to one of the clusters corresponding to the five major areas, it eo ipso assigns I to a continental-level minimalist race. The assumption that the five populations are continental-level minimalist races entitles us to interpret *structure* as having the capacity to assign individuals to continental-level minimalist races on the basis of markers that track ancestry.

In constructing clusters corresponding to the five continental-level minimalist races on the basis of objective, race-neutral genetic markers, *structure* "reconstructs" those races on the basis of a race-blind procedure. Modulo our assumption, the article shows the possibility of assigning individuals to such races *without knowing anything about the race* of the individuals from whose genotypes the microsatellites are drawn.

The populations studied were "defined by geography, language, and culture" (King and Motulsky 2002), not skin color or "race."

Now, as critics have pointed out, the number of cluster *structure* forms is researcher predetermined. Set K (the number of clusters) at 4 and you get four clusters. Set K at 5 and you get five clusters (Kitcher 2007). So the fact that *structure* generated 5 clusters at K = 5 in the 2002 article is not surprising. What is surprising, however, is that the clusters constitute well-formed, clearly demarcated segments that show that the populations represented are genetically "structured," which is to say, meaningfully demarcated on the basis of genetic markers. This result was in no way guaranteed by setting K at 5. Using language introduced in the 2005 paper, we can say that the K = 5 graph exhibits "high clusteredness," which is to say that the extent to which each individual was placed fully in a cluster by the K = 5 run of *structure* is high. High-clusteredness is not guaranteed by the choice of K but instead reflects the specific genetic structuredness of the populations.

Now when K was set at 6, a sixth cluster emerged consisting of members of the Kalash, an isolated group, who speak an Indo-European language and live in northwest Pakistan. Not being a continental-level population, the Kalash are not a continental-level race. But this fact in no way undercuts the idea that the inhabitants of the five major geographic areas are continental-level races.

Structure does not track race as such but rather the genetic distinctiveness of populations. The fact that *structure* represents a population as genetically distinct does not mean that the population is a race. The K = 5 graph shows that modulo our assumption, continental-level races are genetically structured. The K = 6 graph shows the same result in that it preserves the genetic boundaries between the five populations. It also shows, surprisingly, that the Kalash can be distinguished genetically from the five populations corresponding to the major geographic areas. Do the Kalash constitute a minimalist race? That depends on whether they exhibit a distinctive pattern of visible physical features corresponding to a distinctive geographical ancestry—a question on which I take no stand.

The fact that there is a race-blind "mechanical" procedure (a statistical algorithm) to assign individuals to what I have identified as continental-level minimalist races solely on the basis of genetic markers means that there is a method for assigning individuals to continental races that is utterly independent of "easily observed morphological traits" (Templeton 1999). The method is *not* "subjective" in the sense in which morphologically based race assignments are. It is not limited by or dependent on "the sensory constraints of our own species" (Templeton 1998). The method is not "purely objective" (free of any pragmatic elements), since the choice of the number of clusters to which individuals are to be assigned is researcher determined. But inasmuch (a) as the procedure is based on something "objective" (microsatellites)—and (b) is itself "mechanical," it has a fair claim to be called "objective."

Modulo our assumption, the clusters in the K = 5 graph can be taken to correspond to continental-level minimalist races: the cluster forming the mostly orange segment corresponds to the sub-Saharan African minimalist race, which is clearly demarcated from the cluster forming the mostly blue segment that corresponds to the Eurasian minimalist race, which is clearly demarcated from the cluster forming the mostly pink segment that corresponds to the East Asian minimalist race, which is clearly demarcated from the cluster forming the mostly green segment corresponding to Oceanian minimalist race, which is clearly demarcated from the cluster forming a mostly purple segment that corresponds to the American minimalist race. Modulo our assumption, the graph represents the five continental-level minimalist races as being separated by lines marking relatively sharp allele frequency breaks. Modulo this assumption, it shows that continental-level minimalist races are "genetically discrete units" in the sense of being distinguishable on the basis of genetic information alone.

Some caveats are in order. One is that the genetic differences that Rosenberg and his colleagues found between continental-level minimalist races are very small.

Within-population differences were found to account for a whopping 93 to 95 percent of genetic variation, and differences among major groups were found to constitute a mere 3 to 5 percent. The article does not suggest that there are many genetic differences between continental-level minimalist races. In fact, it indicates the opposite. Continental-level minimalist races are genetically very similar. A second caveat is that it takes lots and lots of genetic markers to draw lines between continental-level minimalist races. The clusters are constructed "on the basis of accumulated small differences in allele frequencies across many markers and many people" (King and Motulsky 2002, 2342). Moreover, the clusters cannot be constructed without the assistance of a computer-implemented algorithm. A third caveat is that the genetic markers used to draw the lines between the populations are not biologically significant in themselves. They are microsatellites, short tandem repeat sequences that do not encode any expressed genes, and are selectively neutral (King and Motulsky 2002).

"A microsatellite is any of numerous short segments of DNA that are distributed throughout the genome, that consist of repeated sequences of usually two to five nucleotides, and that tend to vary from one individual to another" (Feldman and Lewontin 2008, 99).

Nonetheless, the study shows that if the five populations are continental-level minimalist races, it is possible to draw genetic lines between continental-level minimalist races. This, in turn, is a powerful reason for thinking that continental-level minimalist races are biologically (genetically) distinct. If the five populations are continental-level minimalist races, then not only do they "exist" in some loose sense; they also *exist* in the very demanding sense that makes genetic distinctness a condition of biological existence.

To clarify, Rosenberg et al. (2002) do not provide direct support for the contention that minimalist races exist. To bring the article to bear on the question concerning the biological distinctness of minimalist races, we had to import an exogenous race concept and suppose that the populations corresponding to the five "major geographical areas" satisfy this concept. The appeal to Rosenberg's findings was not meant to *establish* the existence of minimalist races but to *rebut* the objection that minimalist races do not exist (in a strict biological sense) because they are not genetically distinct. This rebuttal does, however, provide indirect support for the existence of minimalist races. The fact that the five populations are genetically distinct provides *a* reason for thinking that minimalist races exist.

THE BIOLOGICAL REALITY OF *MINIMALIST RACE*

Is minimalist race biologically real? If the concepts of existence and reality are understood in such a way that, if something biological exists, it is eo ipso biologically real, then, in making the case for the existence of minimalist races, we have already made the case for the biological reality of minimalist race. But "biological reality" is sometimes understood in a more exiguous sense such that minimalist race is "biologically real" if and only if it is a *biologically significant kind*. Biological reality is existence *plus*, where the "plus" consists of biological significance. A philosopher of science might grant the existence of minimalist races, but nonetheless deny that the *kind* minimalist race is biologically real.

The notion of biological significance brings us to an interpretative fork. There is the standard way of interpreting it in connection to race and then there is an alternative way. On the standard view, minimalist race would have to have the sort of significance that racialist race was supposed to enjoy to be counted as biologically significant.

If racialist races existed, race would be biologically significant in the following respects: The percentage of between-race genetic variation would exceed within racial genetic variation. Between-race genetic diversity would be large and among-race genetic diversity would be small. Most genes would be highly differentiated along racial lines. There would be a large number of genetic differences between races apart from the genetic differences that underlie the obvious phenotypic differences. The genetic difference underlying the obvious phenotypic differences would be *typical* of the genome in general. Minimalist races, if they exist, do not enjoy biological significance of this sort. And for this reason minimalist races are sometimes said to lack biological significance altogether.

But in thinking about the question concerning the reality of biological race, it is essential that we get past the idea of racialist race. This, in turn, requires getting past the idea of biological significance that was associated with racialist race. We need to consider the possibility that minimalist race might count as biologically real in virtue of exhibiting a kind of biological significance that is rather more modest than that associated with racialist race.

This brings us to the alternative way of thinking about the notion of biological significance. On a more modest construal, minimalist race counts as biologically significant because a number of its visible physical features such as skin color are almost certainly evolutionary adaptations to the climate of the aboriginal home of the minimalist races. As Pigliucci and Kaplan have noted, skin color is an ecologically important trait (2003). Being an ecologically important trait, skin color is not biologically arbitrary. The same point likely holds for many other race-related visible physical features. If some racial traits are adaptive, minimalist race can be said to be adaptive. If minimalist race is adaptive, it is not a biological nullity, but instead biologically significant.

Consider biological raciation. It is the process through which human populations came to be adapted to their specific ecological circumstances as they moved throughout Eurasia and Oceania and came to people the Americas. Explaining how human beings were able to survive as they settled in new geographical regions is one aim of biology. Appeal to biological raciation and thus to minimalist race is needed for a full explanation of this *explanandum*. Because minimalist race is relevant to an explanatory aim of biology, it counts as a *relevant kind* (in Nelson Goodman's sense). And inasmuch as it is relevant to *biology*, it counts as a *biological* kind as well.

Moreover, *minimalist race* is biologically interesting in its own right. It enjoys this status because it represents a salient, distinctive, systematic dimension of human biological diversity and in this respect stands alongside *sex* and *age*. No one would think of denying their biological reality. No one should think of denying the biological reality of minimalist race.

It is just a mistake to think that a kind must exhibit the sort of robustness that racialist race claimed to be a legitimate biological kind. There is room in biology for modest, low-power biological kinds. Biology needs such kinds in order to be able to accommodate the minimalist biological phenomenon of race and the kind of kind minimalist race is. My proposal, then, is that minimalist race be recognized as biologically real in virtue of being a relatively superficial but biologically significant kind.

The general outlook I am recommending can be called *deflationary biological realism*. Deflationary biological realism is *deflationary* in that it repudiates the idea that *racialist* race is biologically real and the idea that race is a fundamental biological reality or robust biological kind. It is *realist* in that it acknowledges the limited biological significance of minimalist race.

I have tried to make a *minimalist* case for the biological reality of minimalist race—one that rests on a minimal set of non-controversial assumptions. My claim is that minimalist race can be seen to be biologically real even apart from consideration of its possible medical significance with respect, for example, to disease susceptibility and outcomes, responsiveness to drugs, and histocompatibility. The characterization I have given is not intended to preclude the possibility that minimalist race is a medically significant category. But it reflects a conjecture that, even if minimalist race should turn out to be medically significant, the force of this point will not be such as to make minimalist race a very important biological kind.

CONCLUSION

Current political realities (police killings of black men, the recent mass shooting at a black church) make prospects for removing the word *race* from our discourse dim. If we must retrain the word *race*, the question arises concerning the concept it should be used to express. The minimalist concept of race provides a nonmalific alternative to the racialist concept of race that is compatible with the findings of contemporary biology. The availability of the minimalist concept does not make it possible to use the word *race* without circumspection. When using the word *race*, it is essential to be careful. One must guard against the possibility of being taken to express the racialist concept of race or unwittingly using the word to express the racialist concept. But the specification of the minimalist concept of race makes possible to use the word *race* in a biological sense without thinking racialist or racist thoughts. This makes it a useful concept.

REFERENCES

Appiah, K. Anthony. (1996). "Race, Culture, Identity: Misunderstood Connections." In K. A. Appiah and A. Gutmann, *Color Conscious: The Political Morality of Race*, 30–105. Princeton, NJ: Princeton University Press.

Blumenbach, J. [1795] (2000). *On the Natural Variety of Mankind* in *The Idea of Race*, edited by Ed. Robert Bernasconi and Tommy L. Lott, 27–37. Indianapolis, IN: Hackett.

Feldman, M., and Lewontin, Richard. (2008). "Race, Ancestry, and Medicine." In *Revisiting Race in a Genomic Age*, edited by B. Koenig, S. Lee, and S. Richardson, 89–101. New Brunswick, NJ: Rutgers.

King, M., and A. Motulsky. (2002). "Mapping Human History." *Science* 298 (5602): 2342–2343.

Kitcher, P. (2007). "Does 'Race' Have a Future?" *Philosophy and Public Affairs* Fall 35 (4): 293–317.

Lewontin, Richard. (1972). "The Apportionment of Human Diversity." *Evolutionary Biology* 6: 381–398.

Livingstone, Richard. (1962) "On the Non-Existence of Races." *Current Anthropology* 3 (3): 279–281.

Pigliucci, M., and J. Kaplan. (2003). "On the Concept of Biological Race and Its Applicability to Humans" *Philosophy of Science* 70 (5): 1161–1172.

Rosenberg, N., J. Pritchard, J. Weber, H. Cann, K. Kidd, and M. Feldman. (2002). "Genetic Structure of Human Populations." *Science* 298 (5602): 2381–2385. doi: 10.1126/science.1078311.

Rosenberg, N., S. Mahajan, S. Ramachandran, C. Zhao, J. Pritchard, and M. Feldman. (2005). "Clines, Clusters, and the Effect of Study Design on the Inference of Human Population Structure." *PLOS Genetics*. doi: 10.1371/journal.pgen.0010070.

Sober, E. (1994) "Evolution, Population Thinking, Essentialism." In *From a Biological Point of View*, 201–232. New York: Cambridge University Press.

Templeton, A. (1999). "Human Races: A Genetic and Evolutionary Perspective." *American Anthropologist* 100 (3): 632–650.

CHAPTER 13

BIOLOGICAL ANTHROPOLOGY, POPULATION GENETICS, AND RACE

JOHN H. RELETHFORD

As a biocultural science, anthropology recognizes the multiple cultural and biological definitions of race. Biological anthropology (also known as physical anthropology) is the subfield of anthropology concerning human biological origins, evolution, and variation. Consequently, this field considers *biological* concepts of race, particularly the use of race as an evolutionary unit of analysis and as a label for geographically structured genetic variation. Thus, the focus in biological anthropology is most often on *genetic ancestry* rather than *cultural identity*, allowing that sometimes the biological and cultural aspects of race do not map exactly onto each other (Marks 1994). For example, a genome-wide study of 365 individuals who self-identified as African American (cultural identity) showed a wide range in estimated genetic ancestry, ranging from almost complete African ancestry to very little African ancestry (Bryc et al. 2010). From a biological perspective, the socially defined category of race does not fully represent the range of genetic ancestry.

There have been numerous approaches to race in physical/biological anthropology. In the early twentieth century, the primary approach to race in physical anthropology was typological and descriptive, where populations were placed into discrete clusters based on a handful of physical traits, such as skin color. (See Little and Kennedy 2010, for an extensive review of the history of the race concept in biological anthropology.) Much of the direction of the field began to change in the 1950s and 1960s, as researchers began to abandon the race concept as a way of describing and analyzing human biological variation. Part of this shift was the influence of the "evolutionary synthesis" in biology, where the emerging field of population genetics provided a way to link Mendelian genetics with the process of evolution in local populations.

In biological anthropology, the study of biological variation changed from pure description to analysis of the process of evolution, and the unit of analysis shifted from the nebulous idea of races to the study of local populations. However, these changes did not cause the biological race concept to vanish from the field. Some researchers tried to redefine race in terms of the new paradigm that tied evolutionary change to population genetics. Instead of an older typological construct, race became for some a unit of analysis consisting of clusters of local populations in regional aggregates that share similar frequencies of genetic variants. Others dismissed the race concept all together, noting that it did not adequately describe human variation, offered no insights into evolutionary process, and perpetuated outdated concepts on human difference.

We now have a much better view of human variation that has emerged from an ever-increasing body of evidence from molecular genetics and genomics and the application of the models and methods of population genetics. To assess the utility (or lack thereof) of biological definitions of race and studies of racial classification, global patterns of human genetic variation must be examined within the context of the basic principles of population genetics and the genetic history of the human species.

POPULATION GENETICS

The field of population genetics looks at genetic change within and between local populations (often defined geographically in humans, such as a town, village, or region, depending on resolution of the data). Variants of genes and DNA sequences are known as *alleles*. Evolution is defined in population genetics as a change in allele frequencies over time. Four mechanisms, known as the *evolutionary forces*, can cause a change in allele frequencies: (1) mutation, (2) genetic drift, (3) gene flow, and (4) natural selection. *Mutation* is a random change in the genetic code (DNA), and those changes that occur in a sex cell (egg in females, sperm in males) can be passed on to the next generation. Though typically low in initial frequency, mutations provide the ultimate source of all genetic variation. The other three evolutionary forces can increase or decrease the frequency of a mutant allele. *Genetic drift* is the random fluctuation in allele frequencies over time due to sampling variation. By chance, the allele frequency in an offspring generation is unlikely to be the same as in the parental population. Genetic drift can also occur when a small population splits from a parental population (*founder effect*), as the new population is unlikely to show the same allele frequencies as in the parental population because of chance. Further, because drift tends to remove or fix alleles over time, small founding populations will show less genetic variation than in the larger parental population. *Gene flow* refers to the movement of genes through migration between populations, a process that reduces genetic differences between populations. *Natural selection* leads to allele frequency change through the differential survival and reproduction of an individual's genotype (his or her genetic makeup). In general, selection can increase the frequency of an allele that provides an evolutionary advantage and decrease the frequency of an allele that is harmful, although the process can be more complicated (as when having one copy of an allele results in higher fitness than zero or two copies).

All of the evolutionary forces operate simultaneously, and they can interact in numerous and complex ways. One of the goals of population-genetic research is to determine the relative influence of the evolutionary forces in explaining patterns of genetic variation within and between populations. Many studies of population history focus on *neutral* traits, those that are not affected by natural selection, such as many blood types, short repeated sections of DNA sequences, and other genetic markers. Mathematically, we expect neutral traits to show the same underlying pattern of evolutionary history due to the effects of mutation, drift, and gene flow. Analysis of many neutral traits can provide us with a clear picture of the history of evolutionary relationships between populations, such as common ancestry, migration, and demographic changes. On the other hand, the analysis of adaptive traits focuses on the specific evolutionary history of a given trait, such as human skin color or lactase persistence, which reflects the past action of natural selection operating on past variation. The history of a specific trait may not provide any insight into the evolutionary history of populations because past historical connections can be obscured by the action of natural selection. A classic example for humans is skin color, where very dark-skinned populations are found in parts of sub-Saharan Africa and Australasia. This physical similarity reflects similar adaptation to an equatorial location with high levels of ultraviolet radiation, and not common ancestry (i.e., indigenous populations of Australia and New Guinea are not African just because they have dark skin).

GLOBAL GENETIC VARIATION AND THE HISTORY OF THE HUMAN SPECIES

The application of population-genetic methods to the study of human genetic variation has provided us with a rich body of genetic data that has been used to reconstruct the evolutionary history of the human species. This history is incompatible with traditional models of race and racial classification.

We now have the broad outlines of the history of the human species based on data from the fossil record, genetic variation in present-day populations, and variation in ancient DNA that has been recovered from our ancestors and relatives. The species *Homo erectus*, characterized by an increase in brain size and a reduction in the size of the face and teeth relative to earlier human ancestors, arose first in Africa and then began to disperse into parts of Eurasia about 1.8 million years ago. Over time, further evolutionary change took place throughout the Old World in what are sometimes referred to as "archaic" humans, including the species *Homo heidelbergensis* and the enigmatic Neandertals. Anatomically modern humans, *Homo sapiens*, appeared first in the fossil record in Africa 200,000 years ago and began dispersing into the rest of the world about 70,000 to 100,000 years ago. The African origin and subsequent dispersion of modern humans has shaped the evolutionary history of neutral traits for the human species, and it provides a basis for understanding several global patterns of variation.

There are several striking features of genetic variation that have emerged with the development of new types of genetic markers based on the analysis of DNA sequences. Two types of markers that are used extensively in global analyses of variation are *short tandem repeats (STRs)*, which are variations in the number of repeated small sections of DNA, and *single nucleotide polymorphisms (SNPs)*, which are differences in individual base pairs of DNA. Genetic variation is typically measured by the number of different alleles and their relative frequencies. Studies of DNA markers show three patterns of genetic variation *within* populations that are best explained by our species' African origin. First, the level of genetic variation is higher in sub-Saharan African populations than elsewhere in the world. Second, examination of the different alleles shows that genetic variation outside of Africa is often a subset of variation within Africa (Campbell and Tishkoff 2008). Third, the level of genetic variation outside of Africa is dependent on the distance from East Africa; those populations farther away, in terms of the geographic distance likely travelled by early humans leaving Africa, show sequential reductions in genetic variation (e.g., Li et al. 2008).

All of these observations of global diversity can be explained through mutation and genetic drift. Over time, mutations act to increase genetic variation in a population. When a founding population splits from a parental group, it is typically small and loses variation because of genetic drift (founder effect). Modern humans lived in sub-Saharan Africa perhaps 100,000 years or more before expanding out, allowing time for mutational diversity to build up in Africa. This diversity would have been reduced in a new founding population leaving Africa, resulting in a subset of alleles in the parental population and a lower level of genetic variation outside of Africa. The *serial founding model* extends this idea to dispersion of modern humans across the world, where each new founding population gave rise to another founding population over time, resulting in a sequence of founding populations dispersed geographically and a decline in genetic diversity with increasing geographic distance from East Africa (Ramachandran et al. 2005).

Another striking pattern of neutral genetic variation is the close relationship between *genetic distance* (a measure of genetic dissimilarity between pairs of populations) and geographic distance. This relationship is particularly clear when the geographic distance between pairs of populations around the world is measured in terms of likely travel routes rather than straight-line distance. For example, the geographic distance between Old World and New World populations is measured along a route that crosses over from Asia to North America in Siberia, marking the known travel of the first Native Americans, rather than a straight-line distance across the Pacific Ocean. Numerous studies have shown a positive relationship between geographic distance and genetic distance across the world; the genetic distance between pairs of populations increases as the geographic distance between them increases. Human populations tend to be more similar genetically to neighboring populations than to those farther away. The congruence between geographic and genetic distance is in part a reflection of the dispersal of modern humans out of Africa. Under the serial founding model, populations are most closely related to both parental populations and subsequent founding populations, which are both likely to be geographically proximate. In addition, a majority of gene flow between populations typically occurs at shorter distances, making neighboring populations more genetically similar over time, a pattern known as *isolation by distance*. The combined effects of serial founding and isolation by distance have led to the geographic structure seen in neutral genetic variation between human populations (Relethford 2004; Jobling et al. 2014), with serial founding having a greater impact (Hunley, Healey, and Long 2009).

Human genetic variation has also been affected by admixture with "archaic" human populations such as the Neandertals. As modern humans expanded out of Africa, they moved into lands that were already occupied by earlier humans. A long-standing question in paleoanthropology has been whether the first modern humans interbred with these archaic populations. The answer has come in recent times from the analysis of ancient DNA, including sequencing of the Neandertal genome, which has shown that between 1 and 4 percent of the ancestry of present-day people of Eurasian descent is derived from Neandertals. (Because of the history of human dispersion, Eurasian descent includes founding populations in the

Pacific and the New World as well as all of those in Europe and Asia; that is, all non-African populations.)

Ancient DNA analysis has also shown that some human populations also have a small amount of ancestry from a prehistoric Asian population known as the Denisovans (Pääbo 2014). Some present-day human populations have ancestry from both Neandertals and Denisovans, some have ancestry only from Neandertals, and some lack ancestry from either group. A picture is beginning to emerge where the vast majority of ancestry of present-day humans traces to the dispersion out of Africa by early modern humans, combined with varying low levels of interbreeding with a number of archaic human populations.

GLOBAL GENETIC VARIATION AND RACE

Do the global patterns of human genetic variation support a biological model of race? As noted by Long and Kittles (2003), this is sometimes a difficult question to answer because of the variety of different definitions of race. At one extreme, some lay views on race perpetuate the classic typological model of previous centuries, where a handful of physical traits (such as skin color) are used to identify discrete groupings of humanity within which there is little variation. Such views are clearly incompatible with the fact that genetic variation is extensive within populations (Keita and Kittles 1997; Long and Kittles 2003). Another use of the term "race," often used by evolutionary biologists, is that race is synonymous with subspecies, a division within a species that represents partially isolated groupings that are genetically divergent and, given enough time, could form new species. Human populations do not exhibit the levels of geographic isolation or genetic divergence to fit the subspecies model of race. For example, genetic divergence between human populations around the world is less than found between populations of African apes, even though humans are spread out over a much larger area of the world (Barbujani and Colonna 2010).

A more common use of the race concept today is a broad view of *geographic race*, the idea that basic divisions of humanity can be identified from clustering of genetic variation that corresponds to major geographic regions, such as sub-Saharan Africa, East Asia, and so forth. The use of geographic race as a label for genetic clusters is appealing to some, given the observed correspondence between genetic distance and geographic distance. Although there *is* genetic variation between human populations across the world, and this variation *is* geographically structured, many biological anthropologists argue that race and racial classifications are not the best way to describe or analyze this geographic structure.

One immediate problem with classification of geographic races is that much of the spatial distribution of human genetic variation is continuous in nature, making the task of partitioning the species into discrete groups arbitrary. Although global variation and population differences in genetics and morphology have long been apparent, there has never been substantive agreement on the number of races that can be used to describe this variation. The problem of dividing a continuous range of variation into a set number of discrete categories is illustrated by the simple example of the distribution of height in any large sample (Relethford 2009). Height varies continuously, but it is sometimes classified for convenience into groups of "short," "medium," and "tall" people. Here, categories of height are constructed that overlay the biological reality of the distribution of height. No one would argue that only three types of people exist—short, medium, and tall—with no intermediate heights. In addition, there is nothing inherent in the distribution of height that leads to a definite set of three groups. We could just as easily derive four, five, or more groups that describe variation in height. Compounding the problem is the issue of where to draw the line between groups; for example, what specific value of height separates people of "short" and "medium" stature?

The division of humanity into separate geographic races is often considered in the same light. If we consider that most human genetic diversity is *clinal* (that is, showing a gradient over space), then any construction of race will be necessarily arbitrary. However, this conclusion is moderated somewhat by genetic evidence that human populations sometimes form readily distinguishable *clusters*. Many genetic analyses use a clustering program known as STRUCTURE to determine if the genetic variation between individuals forms discrete geographic clusters. These studies reveal clusters of populations that largely coincide with geographic regions. For example, Rosenberg et al. (2002) analyzed hundreds of STR markers of individuals from fifty-two populations around the world and were able to identify six major genetic clusters. Five of these clusters corresponded to broad geographic regions (sub-Saharan Africa, the western and southern parts of Eurasia, East Asia, Oceania, and the Americas), and the sixth consisted mostly of people from the Kalash, an isolated population in Pakistan. However, others note that there is not sufficient evidence to choose six clusters as the best number (e.g., Bolnick 2008), showing again that choosing a set finite number of geographic clusters is not easy.

Even so, the ability of the STRUCTURE program to place individuals into different clusters that correspond largely to broad geographic groupings may be taken by some to support the notion of geographic race. However, this apparent clustering seems to contradict the evidence of a large amount of clinal variation in the underlying allele frequencies. Rosenberg et al. (2005) argued that the two findings are compatible by demonstrating that human global genetic variation consists of *both* clines and clusters. Their analyses showed that the vast majority of genetic variation between human populations was due to geographic distance, corresponding to the general clines in allele frequencies. They also investigated the genetic effect of several topographic barriers to dispersal and gene flow: the Sahara Desert, the Himalayan Mountains, and the Pacific Ocean. These natural barriers resulted in slightly higher genetic distances between populations than expected solely from geographic distance. Although the actual impact of these barriers on genetic distance is small, these slight discontinuities in the clinal structure are sufficient for the STRUCTURE program to be able to identify geographic clusters. However, a predominately clinal pattern resulting from serial founding and isolation by distance with small discontinuities due to topographic barriers does not correspond to any classic views on geographic race.

Another problem with reconciling global genetic variation with geographic races is the *nested* nature of diversity within human populations. For example, Long et al. (2009) investigated this nested structure using two global data sets, one consisting of base-pair comparisons of DNA sequences and the other using STRs. They found a nested hierarchy of genetic diversity, such that non-African diversity clustered as a subset of populations *within* the broader grouping of sub-Saharan African populations. Long et al. conclude that this nested pattern does not fit classic models of race that focus on a traditional hierarchical model, where all races or geographic clusters are at the same level of classification. That is, the classic model assumes that the species is partitioned into a set of broad geographic races that are in turn partitioned into local populations. In Long et al.'s analysis, the most exclusive grouping that included all of the sub-Saharan African populations also included all non-African populations as well, making identification of sub-Saharan Africans as a separate race an inaccurate description of genetic variation. Further, they note that because all of the populations outside of Africa cluster together, this would necessitate placing *all* populations in Europe and Asia in a single race, and placing Europeans and Asians as "subraces" within a broader Eurasian race, something not compatible with most models of racial classification. Classic racial classification schemes do not typically consider a "Eurasian race" as a subset of an African race, or Europeans and Asians to be "subraces" (see also Hunley, Healey, and Long 2009). As Long et al. note, "Several sub-sub-races would be necessary to account for the population groups throughout the world" (2009, 32–33). A strict view of race, with humanity divided into a set number of mutually exclusive geographic races, does not fit what we know about global genetic variation.

CLASSIFICATION ACCURACY AND RACE

One argument for the use of geographic races has been the high level of accuracy when classifying individuals into geographic races based on genetic traits. It is apparent from many studies that ancestral origin can be determined very accurately in some cases. For example, Xing et al. (2009) were able to classify all individuals in their study into four continental groups (sub-Saharan Africa, Europe, South Asia, and East/Southeast Asia) using data on over 240,000 SNPs. An example using physical traits is Relethford's (2009) study of fifty-seven cranial measures from six geographic regions (sub-Saharan Africa, Europe, East Asia, Australasia, Polynesia, and the Americas), where 97 percent of the individual crania could be accurately assigned to regions using discriminant analysis (a statistical method that finds the weighted combination of all traits that maximizes predictive accuracy). These and other examples suggest to some the utility of geographic races, else why would the classification accuracy be so high?

The explanation of this high level of classification accuracy is the global correlation of genetic distance and geographic distance. Studies such as those cited earlier typically sample groups of populations across large ranges of geographic distance, as when comparing a set of populations from East and South Africa with a set of populations from Northern Europe with no geographically intermediate populations. When samples are collected using local populations that are clustered geographically, they will also cluster genetically. The ability to assign an individual to a specific group is just another way of describing the strong correlation of geography and genetics. As long as there are large geographic distances between regional populations, there will be large genetic distances between the regional populations, making classification into groups easier to do (Relethford 2009). This accuracy does not mean that the groups used in the analysis are distinct races. As an analogy, consider taking samples of "short" and "tall" people. Individuals from each group can be classified 100 percent of the time based on height, but this does not mean that there are only two separate groups of people.

Equating high classification accuracy with support for biological race also runs into trouble when considering variation *within* continental regions. For example, Novembre et al. (2008) examined the relationship between geographic and genetic distance for 3,000

Europeans based on over half a million SNPs. They found a strong congruence of genetics and geography that allowed them to predict accurately a person's origin within a few hundred kilometers in many cases. The geographic structure within the European "geographic race" runs counter to a classic view of relative homogeneity within races. Similar results have been seen with physical traits and classification. For example, Ousley et al.'s (2009) analysis of craniometric variation showed that high classification accuracy is obtained between populations within geographic regions, including 89 percent accuracy when considering only eighteen measurements for individuals from North versus South Japan. If we use high predictive accuracy as an indication of racial status, then we would be forced into the ludicrous view of considering North and South Japan as separate races. If we attempt to model the structure of the aforementioned examples in terms of "subraces," we could easily either wind up with a situation where each local population on the planet is labeled as a separate race or subrace.

This issue of classification relates to the field of forensic anthropology, where practitioners must often identify personal characteristics from an individual's skeletal or dental remains, including identification of sex, age, and ancestry. Many forensic anthropologists argue against the race concept, a stance that may seem unusual given the ability of forensic anthropologists to determine ancestry. This seeming contradiction is best expressed by the title of two papers by forensic anthropologists, one by Sauer (1992) entitled "Forensic anthropology and the concept of race: If races don't exist, why are forensic anthropologists so good at identifying them?" and the second by Kennedy (1995) entitled "But professor, why teach race identification if races don't exist?"

It turns out that forensic anthropologists are quite adept at inferring ancestry, at least in a broad sense. The ability to do so is a consequence of the geographically structured variation present in the human species. Knowledge and use of this structure do not mean this structure is best represented by racial categories. If one is determining if a particular skull represents someone of European or African ancestry, then the skull is being compared to potential ancestral populations that are geographically far apart, increasing the chances of detecting sufficient difference to allow identification. Nothing in this process requires that this geographically structured variation be made up of discrete groups (races). As Sauer (1992:110) points out, " . . . to identify a person as having ancestors from, say, Northern Europe does not identify a biological race of Northern Europeans."

Conclusion: How Is the Biological Race Concept Useful?

In past centuries, race has had a biological definition typically consisting of a small number of physical traits (especially skin color) that have been used for racial classification. This approach has been replaced with an evolutionary view and a wealth of information on DNA variants. We now have an understanding of the structure of genetic variation in our species that traditional categories of race can only approximate in a very rough sense. Instead of a view of a species divided into a number of discrete groups characterized by within-group homogeneity, we see a picture of clinal genetic variation structured by geographic distance with secondary effects resulting from topographic barriers. Instead of a view where races exist as more or less independent evolutionary units, we see a nested pattern of genetic variation explicable in terms of our species' African origin and subsequent dispersion.

In the past, considerable attention has been given to the question of whether human races exist in a biological sense. Our current understanding of human genetic variation is at odds with traditional views of race. The past use of race as a unit of evolutionary change has been rejected. What remains today is the use of "geographic race" as a *rough* description of global genetic variation. Although arbitrary in terms of number and cutoff points, one can reduce global genetic variation into a smaller number of categories, although this data reduction provides, at best, " . . . a crude first-order approximation to human biological variation . . . " (Relethford 2009, 21). The real question is whether anything is gained by applying the biological race concept to the analysis of human biological variation and evolution. Although mapping continuous variation onto a small number of categories is often used as for rough description (e.g., discrete categories to describe socioeconomic class or political orientation), information on the range of variation is lost in the process. For example, if we were to analyze allele frequencies using only geographic race as the unit of analysis, we would not see many of the underlying patterns of clinal change and nested variation. Although it is sometimes useful to take regional aggregates of local populations to illustrate some general patterns (e.g., Relethford 1994), care must be taken not to confuse a statistical and geographic aggregate with a unit of evolutionary change. Application of much of population genetics works best when considering variation between local populations and not between aggregates. The fine detail of our species' evolutionary history and its impact on patterns of genetic variation are lost when trying to categorize and classify into races. The proper study of human biological variation needs to be rooted in evolutionary theory and population genetics.

REFERENCES

Barbujani, G., and V. Colonna. (2010). "Human Genetic Diversity: Frequently Asked Questions." *Trends in Genetics* 26: 285–295.

Bolnick, D. A. (2008). "Individual Ancestry Inference and the Reification of Race as a Biological Phenomenon." In *Revisiting Race in a Genomic Age*, edited by B. A. A. Koenig, S. S-J. Lee, and S. S. Richardson, 70–85. New Brunswick, NJ: Rutgers University Press.

Bryc, K., A. Auton, M. R. Nelson, J. R. Oksenberg, S. L. Hauser, S. Williams, A. Froment, J-M. Bodo, et al. (2010). "Genome-Wide Patterns of Population Structure and Admixture in West Africans and African Americans." *Proceedings of the National Academy of Sciences* 107: 786–791.

Campbell, M. C., and S. A. Tishkoff. (2008). "African Genetic Diversity: Implications for Human Demographic History, Modern Human Origins, and Complex Disease Mapping." *Annual Review of Genomics and Human Genetics* 9: 403–433.

Hunley, K. L., M. E. Healy, and J. C. Long. (2009). "The Global Pattern of Gene Identity Variation Reveals a History of Long-Range Migrations, Bottlenecks, and Local Mate Exchange: Implications for Biological Race." *American Journal of Physical Anthropology* 139: 35–46.

Jobling, M., E. Hollox, M. Hurles, T. Kivisild, and C. Tyler-Smith. (2014). *Human Evolutionary Genetics*. 2nd ed. New York: Garland Science.

Keita, S. O. Y., and R. A. Kittles. (1997). "The Persistence of Racial Thinking and the Myth of Racial Divergence." *American Anthropologist* 99: 534–544.

Kennedy, K. A. R. (1995). "But Professor, Why Teach Race Identification If Races Don't Exist?" *Journal of Forensic Sciences* 40: 797–800.

Li, J. Z., D. M. Absher, H. Tang, A. M. Southwick, A. M. Casto, S. Ramachandran, H. M. Cann, et al. (2008). "Worldwide Human Relationships Inferred From Genome-Wide Patterns of Variation." *Science* 319: 1100–1104.

Little, M. A., and K. A. R. Kennedy, eds. (2010). *Histories of American Physical Anthropology in the Twentieth Century*. Lanham, MD: Lexington Books.

Long, J. C., and R. A. Kittles. (2003). "Human Genetic Diversity and the Nonexistence Of Biological Races." *Human Biology* 75: 449–471.

Long, J. C., J. Li, and M. E. Healy. (2009). "Human DNA Sequences: More Variation and Less Race." *American Journal of Physical Anthropology* 139: 23–34.

Marks, J. (1994) "Black, White, Other." *Natural History* 103 (12): 32–35.

Novembre, J., T. Johnson, K. Bryc, Z. Kutalik, A. Auton, A, Indap, K. S. King, S. Bergmann, M. R. Nelson, M. Stephens, and C. D. Bustamante. (2008). "Genes Mirror Geography within Europe." *Nature* 456: 98–101.

Ousley, S., R. Jantz, and D. Freid. (2009). "Understanding Race And Human Variation: Why Forensic Anthropologists are So Good at Identifying Race." *American Journal of Physical Anthropology* 139: 68–76.

Pääbo, S. (2014) *Neanderthal Man: In Search of Lost Genomes*. New York: Basic Books.

Ramachandran, S., O. Deshpande, C. C. Roseman, N. A. Rosenberg, M. W. Feldman, and L. L. Cavalli-Sfroza. (2005). "Support from the Relationship of Genetic and Geographic Distance for a Serial Founder Effect Originating in Africa." *Proceedings of the National Academy of Sciences* 102: 15942–15947.

Relethford, J. H. (1994). "Craniometric Variation among Modern Human Populations." *American Journal of Physical Anthropology* 95: 53–62.

Relethford, J. H. (2004). "Global Patterns of Isolation by Distance Based On Genetic and Morphological Data." *Human Biology* 76: 499–513.

Relethford, J. H. (2009). "Race and Global Patterns of Phenotypic Variation." *American Journal of Physical Anthropology* 139: 16–22.

Rosenberg, N. A., S. Mahajan, S. Ramachandran, C. Zhao, J. K. Pritchard, and M. W. Feldman. (2005). "Clines, Clusters, and the Effect of Study Design on the Inference of Human Population Structure." *PLoS Genetics* 1 (6): e70.

Rosenberg, N. A., J. K. Pritchard, J. L. Weber, H. M. Cann, K. K. Kidd, L. A. Zhivotovsky, and M. W. Feldman. (2002). "Genetic Structure of Human Populations." *Science* 298: 2381–2385.

Sauer, N. J. (1992). "Forensic Anthropology and the Concept of Race: If Races Don't Exist, Why are Forensic Anthropologists So Good at Identifying Them?" *Social Science and Medicine* 34: 107–111.

Xing, J., W. S. Watkins, D. J. Witherspoon, Y. Zhang, S. L. Guthery, R. Thara, B. J. Mowry, K. Bulayeva, R. B. Weiss, and L. B. Jorde. (2009). "Fine-Scaled Human Genetic Structure Revealed by SNP Microarrays." *Genome Research* 19: 815–825.

CHAPTER 14

···

A METATHEORY OF RACE

···

JOSHUA GLASGOW

WHEN we debate what race is and whether it exists, the standard approach is to use an *argument from reference*. These arguments combine a premise about what is or is not in the world (an *existence* premise) with a premise about what the word "race" refers to (a *reference* premise). Consider the following example:

a) Races are supposed to be large, biological groups of people distinguished by certain visible traits. (Reference.)
b) There are no objects in the world that fit that description. (Existence.)
c) Therefore, there are no races.

Arguments from reference are widely used by people who otherwise disagree about race. As in our example, they are used by people who think that race is an illusion (antirealists). They are used by people who think that race is socially real (constructivists). They are used by people who think that race is biologically real (biological realists). They are so common that it seems fair to say that *the standard approach* to the debates about the reality of race is to use arguments from reference. In fact, arguments from reference are very common in Western philosophy generally, not just in the philosophy of race (Mallon et al. 2009). And when the topic is race, arguments of this form are widely used in a variety of fields beyond philosophy, from the biomedical and social sciences to literature.

Within the standard approach, the most common tactic is to use, as one's reference premise, a *descriptive* characterization of what "race" refers to. Here are some more examples of descriptive reference premises from a variety of disciplines and sometimes opposing race theories:

> The term "race" implies the existence of some nontrivial underlying hereditary features shared by a group of people and not present in other groups. (Graves 2001, 5)

> Definition of Race: Race is a doing—a dynamic set of historically derived and institutionalized ideas and practices that . . . associates differential value, power, and privilege with these characteristics; establishes a hierarchy among the different groups; and confers opportunity accordingly. . . . (Moya and Markus 2010, 21)

> [T]he concept of race . . . requires that the majority of humans be and always have been racially pure. (Zack 1993, 17)

All of the foregoing quotes deploy a *descriptivist* version of the standard approach: what the term "race" refers to is fixed by a set of properties (or a description). For Moya and Markus

(2010), races *by definition* have to be unequal. For Graves (2001), races have to be hereditary. For Zack (1993), races have to be pure.

Although each of these theorists expands in detail on the properties they attribute to "race," none stops to justify the descriptive approach more basically. Theories of race generally are in the business of offering claims about what "race" refers to; they are not usually in the business of defending the *metasemantic* presumptions that their claims rely on. That is, these theories analyze the meanings of racial terms, but they do not worry much about the form their analyses take. In particular, they do not pause to argue that the modes of reference that they rely on are legitimate. They simply proceed on the implicit assumptions that arguments from reference are legitimate and that any standard mode of reference, including descriptive definition, is a legitimate candidate for how "race" refers. That way, they can get on with figuring out what race is. If a metatheory of race is a theory of what kind of race theory we should pursue, then this is *the normal metatheory of race* that is often implicitly assumed across the disciplines:

1. Arguments from reference are legitimate, when determining the nature and reality of race.
2. Deploying any kind of reference-fixer in an argument from reference is legitimate. What matters is whether the reference premise is true, not what *kind* of reference-fixer is adopted in that premise.
2a. Description, specifically, is one legitimate kind of reference-fixer.

As common as these two assumptions are, normal race metatheory has come in for criticism on multiple fronts, threatening the status quo. In saying this, it is worth emphasizing that these criticisms threaten a huge swath of work on race from *potentially every academic discipline*. I will argue, though, that these attacks on standard practice are unfounded: race theorists from all disciplines can safely make arguments using descriptive definitions and arguments from reference more generally. The two background assumptions are secure.

Before getting to the critics, it is worth more clearly distinguishing *the semantics of "race"* from *modes of reference*. For our purposes, let "semantics" refer to *the criteria for successful and relevant application of a term*—in ordinary jargon, what we find in *definitions*. In this sense, the semantics of "race" lay out the conditions that any use of "race" must conform to in order to count as relevant to the operative conversation. For example, imagine that you are debating whether human races exist, and I say, "Sure they do, a marathon is a race!" You can deploy the obvious semantic reply, "That doesn't count as a race in the sense relevant for this conversation."

For any given argument from reference, there is one meaning of "race" that is operational, though there may be more than one meaning of "race" out there. Even when we are talking about human races, different people might mean to refer to different things by "race." There might be multiple concepts of race used by ordinary people; there might be concepts of race used only by specialists like medical researchers, population geneticists, or social theorists; and there might be regional or other subcultural concepts of race. For our purposes, we do not need to identify every such concept (although that would be wonderful). What we need is to specify which concept of race is operational for us. Henceforth, the relevant concept here is the *ordinary* concept of race *in the United States today*, or the multiple such concepts if there is more than one. I will simplify by assuming there is just one such concept of race but this is just a simplifying device that does not bear on the arguments that follow.

With that in mind, my own view is that for something to count as a race in the relevant sense, it must be *a relatively large group of people that is distinguished from other groups by having certain visible traits to a disproportional extent*. This is another descriptive analysis of race. Maybe it is mistaken. But assume for the moment that it is right. What this means is that you use "race" in an *irrelevant* way (for this conversation) if you fail to talk about relatively large groups of people who are distinguished by having certain visible traits disproportionally. If you use "race" to refer to a marathon, you have used "race" in an *ordinary* sense, but not the *relevant* sense. Less cartoonishly, if you use "race" to talk about *small* ancient tribes of Northern Europe, you are not really having a conversation with the rest of us when we talk about race. (Again, we might operationalize different definitions in different conversations—perhaps this variation on "race" is quite relevant for a different conversation; it is just not relevant for ordinary contemporary US racial discourse about race, on our assumption.)

Whether or not that is the correct definition of "race," there are *some* correct conditions for what "race" might refer to—see the earlier quotes for some other possible conditions. Whichever conditions supply the semantics of "race," a *mode of reference* is the *form* that those conditions take. As we have seen, sometimes words refer *descriptively*. According to my definition and the earlier quotes, "race" is one of those words. I think that "race" refers in part to *groups of people*—being a group of people is a property that something must have to count as a race. Other times words appear to refer *directly*, without any mediating description: arguably, the name "the sun" refers to that object in the sky, regardless of what description is true of it. (Even if it is no longer yellow, for example, we would still call it "the sun.") In theory, "race" could refer descriptively, directly, or via some other mode.

With that background in place, recall that both elements of the standard metatheory of race have been criticized. One line of attack accepts that arguments from reference are worthwhile but insists that there is one privileged, nondescriptivist mode of reference that should be used, against (2) and (2a). The other attack is hostile to all arguments from reference; it rejects (1). I argue next that both attacks are off target.

ARE ALL MODES OF REFERENCE EQUALLY GOOD FOR "RACE"?

Sally Haslanger (2010) deviates from normal metatheory by holding that we should *first* adopt a single best mode of reference, and only *then* can we identify the referent for "race" in accordance with that privileged mode. Against assumption (2), her privileged mode excludes all other ways of deploying arguments of reference, including the descriptive approach (2a) used by Graves, Moya and Markus, Zack, and myself. So let's call this the *exclusionary* position. Haslanger's exclusionary position would effectively take down almost all race theory done to date, in every field of study, since almost all race theory done to date fails to use Haslanger's preferred mode of reference. Rejecting assumption (2) has big consequences.

Haslanger's privileged mode is found in the *rational improvisation theory of meaning*. The basic idea to this theory is that the meanings of terms are whatever meanings competent language users invent for those terms as they dialogue with one another, within certain constraints to be examined next. Thus, language users can greatly improvise as they push language in new directions. According to Haslanger, rational improvisation theory "provides better access to the process of creating meanings that critical race and gender theorists have a special interest in, than do the dominant descriptivism and neo-descriptivism" (Haslanger 2010, 176). Moreover, according to Haslanger, not only does the rational improvisation account best capture the reference of "race," it can also help vindicate the constructivist thesis that race is socially real.

Before getting into the details, let's sketch the big picture. The immediate point I want to defend is that even if "race" does refer via rational improvisation, this point does not deliver the kind of results that Haslanger hopes for; in particular, it does not favor (or disfavor) constructivism. If this is right, then exclusively privileging rational improvisation theory is dialectically inert: it just doesn't move the needle in the race debate. The bigger point will be that this dialectical inertia generalizes: all modes of reference are in principle compatible with all theories about the nature of race. If this is right, then when exploring what race is and whether it is real, you can present your preferred analysis of "race"—your reference premise—using any mode of reference. What matters is whether your reference premise adequately captures the operative racial discourse, not what your preferred mode of reference is. You can use the idiom of descriptive definition, as most do; or you can use direct reference; or like Haslanger you can use rational improvisation (if rational improvisation theory is in fact a genuine alternative to these two modes—cf. Haslanger 2014, 112). If it is true that you can use any mode of reference, then assumptions (2) and (2a) remain intact.

Let's look more closely at Haslanger's arguments. Following Laura Schroeter and colleagues (see especially Schroeter and Bigelow 2009 and Schroeter and Schroeter 2009), Haslanger argues that language users collaborate with one another to explore the same themes in an improvisational way, creating new uses for terms as they go. That said, for rational improvisation theory we cannot just improvise in whatever ways we want. Instead, we must use coordinating intentions and a shared linguistic sensibility: we intend to use language in the way that best makes sense of our social practices, and if we deviate too far from everyone else, we no longer have the coordinating intention. This is supposed to allow the kind of freedom that we see in jazz: we can improvise to extend the "song" into new directions (perhaps beyond any descriptive confines), while still succeeding in playing the same song. That is, unless the musicians lose the coordinating intention—if they depart too far from each other, then they have simply started playing different songs. Reference works the same way, according to rational improvisation theory: as long as we maintain a coordinating intention to refer to the same things by our words, we can use those words in surprising, improvisational ways. Whereas descriptivists say that a word refers via a list of properties dictated by language use, and direct reference theorists say that the word just directly refers to an object in the world, rational improvisation theory says that the word refers via language users' dispositions to collaborate with one another in certain ways.

Now the road to conversational hell is paved with shared intentions. We are all familiar with the experience of intending to communicate about something only to discover that we are using key terms differently from one another, resulting in us talking past each other rather than co-referring. Moreover, when we do not sort out early enough that we are engaged in this kind of mere semantic dispute, we can accidentally end up with wholesale reference shift, as in the "Madagascar" example (Evans 1973): Marco Polo intended to stay with existing usage when he referred to an island off of the coast of Africa as "Madagascar"; he failed, because unbeknownst to him those other speakers used "Madagascar" to refer to part of continental Africa; nonetheless, his error became entrenched in our linguistic community, and now "Madagascar" refers to an island. Polo *intended* to collaboratively use "Madagascar" to co-refer with the original users of that term, but this intention was not itself sufficient to guarantee overlapping reference. We need another ingredient to have successful co-reference.

More generally, without some anchor to ensure that we are sharing a discussion with one another, it is all babble. If one person uses "atom" to try to talk about an indivisible object, while a modern physicist does not, we can point to common linguistic commitments to explain why they are still talking about the same thing: whatever turns out to be true of atoms, the anchor is that they are both still talking about *those things*, or whatever. If a neophyte interjects, "The most atom thing is the sky at dusk," she deviates from the semantic anchor and fails to talk about the same thing as the first two interlocutors. She has left the linguistic confines that set the boundaries of the original conversation. She is talking past the other two people.

The extra items we need to generate shared reference are propositions that all interlocutors are committed to nonnegotiably. Importantly, this is consistent with rational improvisation theory. Schroeter and Schroeter say that the speaker cannot depart too radically from others in the community or else they have different conversations—they have started new songs. The way that they put it is that true interlocutors must have sufficient substantial "congruence" in what they are talking about (Schroeter and Schroeter 2009, 18). Haslanger (2010, 182) puts it inversely: "We share a meaning if and only if we are collaborating in making sense of a shared representational tradition and our understandings are not so divergent as to undermine our collaborative intentions."

This utilization of *congruence* and *divergence* is necessary to capture the common phenomena of talking past one another and changing the subject while using the same words, as in the case of the person who says, "The most atom thing is the sky at dusk." When that happens, the speakers are having two different conversations, using identical words but deploying them with different meanings. In other words, *congruence fixes reference* on this model: the only way to succeed in referring to "race" in a manner continuous with everyone else in your conversation is for you to be sufficiently congruent with everyone else in your conversation. If I say "race" refers to *marathon* (or, say, *chair*), I am not in your conversation anymore.

So far, so good. Now Haslanger adds that while descriptivism might suggest a biological analysis of "race," if instead we go with her rational improvisation approach, "we can justify the claim that the best interpretation of our ongoing collective practice using the term 'race' is compatible with races being social kinds" (2010, 181). (To say that races are social kinds is to say that they are a social kind of thing—they are real categories that are social constructs, like students or senators or bibliophiles.) This generates the key question: do different modes of reference harbor unique possibilities for what race might be? If we choose to privilege one mode of reference, will we tip the race debate one way or the other?

Call Haslanger's claim that "race" is compatible with race being a social construct the *constructivist referential claim*. You *reject* the constructivist referential claim if you do not think that the term "race" is compatible with races being social kinds. Haslanger is right that this is easy to talk about in descriptive terms. If we say, for example, that "race" refers to biological groups, then we have rejected the constructivist referential claim. But, crucially, we need not limit ourselves to descriptivism's idiom to reject Haslanger's constructivist referential claim. Indeed, we can put it in the language of Haslanger's rational improvisation model! One could say that if you are not talking about biological groups, you have *diverged from the collaborative conversation* we were having about race. This suggests what I will call the *adaptability thesis*: semantic premises about the reference of a disputed term like "race" can be adapted to fit any respectable mode of reference. Haslanger and others (e.g., Mallon et al. 2009; Spencer 2015, 8) reject the adaptability thesis. The claim being advanced here is that it is actually true.

Let's drive home the point by expanding on how adopting rational improvisation theory does not really help support the constructivist referential claim. I think that the weight of the evidence we have about our ongoing collective practice, to use the idiom of improvisation, suggests that we cannot be trying to talk about social groups when we talk about race; to talk about "race" in ways that are thoroughly social would be divergent, not congruent. To see this, we can note that when we imagine any alleged social determinant of race being removed, that does not appear to remove race itself (Glasgow 2009, Chapter 6). For instance, consider a version of constructivism that says that race exists *just because* we classify each other racially. Call this *classificatory constructivism*. This view should be rejected. After all, imagine that we all forgot to racially classify each other for ten minutes. In that case, classificatory constructivism must say that Al Gore stops being white at the start of the period of amnesia and then starts being white again, ten minutes later, even though nothing about his body, ancestry, or anything else has changed! Race, on the ordinary concept, does not work like that. Even if we forget about race for a minute, Al Gore does not thereby stop being white.

Of course, classificatory constructivism is only one kind of constructivism (and an overly simplistic kind at that), but this argument against the classificatory version of the view generalizes to all versions. The thesis that races could be social kinds requires that social facts—be they classificatory practices, inequality, discrimination, or anything else—both sustain and extinguish race. But the amnesia thought experiment suggests that our ongoing collective practice of race-talk does not allow that. Even if we forget about race, achieve racial equality, or change any other social fact about race, race would not just disappear as a consequence. So, within the idiom of rational improvisation theory, it seems sensible to say that the race conversation has converged (tacitly, without us knowing it, perhaps) on the proposition that we have our races independent of our social practices, just as our ongoing collective practice of species-talk requires that species exist even if we forget about them. In that case, what we are doing in our collaborative linguistic practice excludes social constructs from race-hood, on pain of excessive divergence from shared understanding. If we talk about races as social kinds, we become linguistic revolutionaries.

Crucially, linguistic revolution may be a good thing! In fact, I have argued that a revolution in the reference of "race," from something biological to something social, *is* a good idea (Glasgow 2009, Chapter 7). But when we separate this prescription from the description of current language, we must recognize that this *is* changing the reference of "race," according to the present argument. Using "race" in a social way puts us into a new conversation.

The point of these reflections is *not* to provide decisive evidence that the constructivist referential claim is false. Although I find that argument against constructivism compelling, the point is to say that *adopting the rational improvisation approach* is not going to decide things one way or the other. The anticonstructivist argument just now rehearsed was originally presented in descriptive form; now it is presented in rational-improvisation form. That goes to show that reference premises in arguments from reference are not substantially impacted by adopting one or another mode of reference. We can always fit arguments for or against the constructivist referential claim to the framework of the rational improvisation approach or any other respectable approach to reference. And for that matter we can, if we like, also put the constructivist referential claim in the preferred idiom of descriptivism. We would just have to say that "race" refers to social groups! The semantics of "race"—constructivist referential claims, antirealist referential claims, and biological realist referential claims alike—can be adapted to all respectable modes of reference. This is the adaptability thesis.

If the adaptability thesis is true, then adopting *any* plausible mode of reference as your first step will neither justify nor refute the constructivist (or any other) referential claim. If all respectable modes of reference are in principle compatible with all theories of what "race" refers to—if all semantic premises can be adapted to all theories of reference and all theories of reference can be adapted to all semantic premises about "race"—then we can figure out the reference of "race" without worrying about which mode of reference we use. Of course, we still have to use one mode of reference: you cannot say "Race refers to Φ" without Φ being cashed out in *some* way, be it descriptive, directly referential, or improvisational. But using one or another mode of reference is relatively innocuous, if the adaptability thesis is true. Whichever mode you use, it is compatible with saying that race is supposed to refer to something biological, something social, or something else entirely. So don't worry about *modes* of reference; standard assumption (2) holds. Just worry about the semantics of "race."

Think about adaptability this way: trying to figure out what "race" refers to by privileging one special mode of reference is like trying to learn the news by privileging print or electronic delivery: the same content can be presented in either form.

Now you might think while what any theory of what "race" refers to can be adapted to descriptive or rational improvisation models, direct reference theory is an exception to this adaptability. On the direct mode of reference, "race" just directly refers to *an object*, without any mediating description or collaborative practice. So we cannot, on direct reference theory, say that the reference of race is *a social thing* or *a biological thing* or attribute any other *properties* to it at the semantic level—that would be descriptive. But none of this means that different theories of race are not adaptable to direct reference theory. Whatever object "race" is supposed to refer to directly, it will *be* a biological object, or a social object, or some other kind of object. And we can still debate whether those objects sufficiently reflect the operative racial discourse—we can still run arguments from reference.

My argument has so far leaned on strident assertion and argument by example. There is also a principled reason for the adaptability thesis: any general theory of reference, if it is worth anything, will be compatible with a very wide range of reasonable interpretations of our discourse. Theories of reference are meant to account for a variety of practices. It is quite difficult to even find decisive counterexamples to them, in fact, because in their most basic forms they are pliable enough to handle a vast range of linguistic practice (Jackson 1998). But in that case, it is very unlikely that they will by themselves favor any one interpretation of any given term, "race" included.

If the adaptability thesis is true, then we should abandon the exclusivist approach that we must, as a matter of principle, favor any one mode of reference. And we should give up the idea that any antecedently privileged mode of reference will settle a substantive dispute about race. The best we can do when trying to determine the nature of race is to use our best evidence about how we use "race," to determine the reference of "race." We should work from the ground up, by looking at how race-related terms are used, rather than from the top down, where we would try to impose some sort of authoritative theory of reference to privilege one interpretation of "race" independently. In the end, then, if Moya and Markus or Graves or Zack couch their conclusions about their bottom-up evidence in a descriptive way, adaptability means that they are free to do so. We should keep assumptions (2) and (2a).

As a separate matter, Haslanger also claims that rational improvisation theory can nicely handle the *moral* status of certain practices. It can, she observes, explain why it is an act of exclusion and even an "epistemic put-down" to say that someone is having her own conversation rather than using our discourse competently. It can also explain hermeneutic injustice, such as where we could not even *identify* the wrong of being sexually harassed so long as the term "sexual harassment" was not in our vocabulary. The rational improvisation model can say that when we engage in rational improvisation, those who are subordinated can liberate themselves by expanding the relevant conversation to create new conceptual resources to call attention to injustices like exclusion and harassment.

Haslanger is right that this expansion is indispensable for justice, but here, too we find adaptability: every respectable mode of reference has the same resources. As long as you believe that the words in question can be used in ways that are conversationally continuous and in other ways that amount to leaving the conversation (i.e., that are *divergent*), you can call attention to how a speaker is linguistically excluded. (That said, boundary-policing is not *always* a bad thing: sometimes we make progress by explicitly mapping our conversations and clarifying what are and are not merely verbal disputes.) The descriptivist will say that the boundary of conversation is determined by a description; direct reference theorists will have a set of objects delineate the boundary; rational improvisation theorists will require congruence. All agree that there are referential boundaries; they just disagree on how to characterize those boundaries.

Moreover, since all theories of reference are consistent with the introduction of new terminology, they can all account for the ability to powerfully introduce a term like "sexual harassment." All plausible theories of reference allow for linguistic creativity, referential surprise, and reference shift. The metalinguistic question is not whether we can introduce new terms and new definitions for old terms. The question is which *form*—description, rational improvisation, ostension—those introductions take. Philosophy of language is apolitical. Normal metatheory of race is morally safe.

CAN ARGUMENTS FROM REFERENCE REALLY HELP?

The other critique of standard practice is not to disrupt popular modes of reference but to disrupt the whole strategy of arguments from reference generally. For example, Mallon (2006) argues that since debates in the philosophy of language over how terms refer to objects in the world are so entrenched, they may never be settled. And that puts all arguments with premises about the reference of "race" in jeopardy: we will never get anywhere in race theory if we try to figure out the nature of race by trying to identify a reference for "race."

But this is too quick (Glasgow 2009, 16–19). It is possible, for one thing, that rival theories of language will converge on the same semantics of race (e.g., Appiah 1996). Moreover, because of the earlier noted point that respectable theories of reference are meant to capture a very wide range of language use, we can confidently identify what almost all terms refer to without settling the debates in the philosophy of language. We can say that Barack Obama won the 2008 US election because we know who "Barack Obama" refers to—that is, we can make an argument from reference using "Barack Obama." We do not need to settle disputes in the philosophy of language to know who is president. Similarly, it is fine to use arguments from reference in race theory, if the references we rely on for "race" do accurately capture the relevant racial discourse. Though they are important in their own right, debates in the philosophy of language are background noise for most arguments from reference (excepting those, like Haslanger, who explicitly claim that their mode of reference is privileged somehow).

However, Mallon and colleagues (2009) offer another objection to arguments from reference. Their concern has two main starting points. The first is that the reference premise in an argument from reference—for example, *"race" refers to biological groups*—is usually backed up by some cases that are supposed to make the reader think that the reference premise is true: "Hmm, in light of the amnesia case, I feel compelled to say that races cannot be social groups!" This is the "method of cases." But, second, both cross-culturally and within a culture, there are widely diverging intuitions about what the key terms refer to in such cases. So, since arguments from reference depend on stable and universal intuitions about what the terms in question refer to, and since there usually are no stable and universal intuitions about reference, we should abandon arguments from reference.

It is old news, of course, that intuitions about cases concerning controversial topics are going to vary. Consider the amnesia case presented earlier: not everyone will share the intuition that Al Gore does not lose his race for those ten minutes. But intuitions about cases are just *data* about reference. There are *other* data, including not only other possible-case intuitions but also general beliefs about the terms in question, in this case racial terms (Glasgow 2009). Moreover, this means that our reactions to cases are defeasible: I might find myself with conflicting intuitions, and I need to resolve this conflict—and learning that many people have intuitions that diverge from my intuitions might compel me to reexamine them. What we want, at the end of the day, is a premise about what "race" refers to that is consistent with the widest set of data. Some people will have incorrect intuitions about cases like the amnesia case—perhaps that someone is *me* in this case (though I think not)! Finding oneself with a surprising or incorrect semantic intuition is no more troubling than my family having different recollections of what year we took that trip to Mexico or you and a friend making different estimates of how old that person on the subway was. Just because people differ does not mean that there is no fact of the matter. The reference of a term may be elusive—we thought the name, "The Earth," referred to a flat object, and, wow, were we wrong! And, as with "race," it may be contested, and justice may hang in the balance. But we can sort it out (and, for that matter, change reference) by collecting a wide variety of cases and other inputs, considering all the data, and rendering a judgment.

CONCLUSION

We have seen that debates over the nature and reality of race commonly use arguments from reference. They say what "race" is supposed to refer to, and then they argue that there is or is not such a thing in the world. Typically, these arguments deploy a descriptive definition of "race." Although this approach has been utilized by uncountable theorists from possibly every discipline that discusses race, it has been criticized. Nevertheless, it appears that these criticisms are unfounded. The normal metatheory of race is on solid ground.

REFERENCES

Appiah, K. A. (1996). "Race, Culture, Identity: Misunderstood Connections." In K. A. Appiah and A. Gutmann, *Color Conscious: The Political Morality of Race*, 30–105. Princeton, NJ: Princeton University Press.

Evans, G. (1973). "The Causal Theory of Names." *Proceedings of the Aristotelian Society* 47 (suppl.): 187–225.

Glasgow, J. (2009). *A Theory of Race*. New York: Routledge.

Graves, J. L. (2001). *The Emperor's New Clothes: Biological Theories of Race at the Millennium*. New Brunswick, NJ: Rutgers University Press, 64–71.

Haslanger, S. (2010). "Language, Politics, and 'The Folk': Looking for 'the Meaning' of 'Race.'" *The Monist* 93: 169–187.

Haslanger, S. (2014). "Race, Intersectionality, and Method: A Reply to Critics." *Philosophical Studies* 171: 109–119.

Jackson, F. (1998). "Reference and Description Revisited." *Philosophical Perspectives, Language, Mind, and Ontology* 12: 201–218.

Mallon, R. (2006). "'Race': Normative, Not Metaphysical or Semantic." *Ethics* 116: 525–551.

Mallon, R., E. Machery, S. Nichols, and S. Stich. (2009). "Against Arguments from Reference." *Philosophy and Phenomenological Research* 79: 332–356.

Moya, P. M. L., and H. R. Markus. (2010). "Doing Race: An Introduction." In *Doing Race: 21 Essays for the 21st Century*, edited by H. R. Markus and P. M. L. Moya, 1–102. New York: W.W. Norton and Company.

Schroeter, L., and J. Bigelow. (2009). "Jackson's Classical Model of Meaning." In *Minds, Ethics, and Conditionals: Themes from the Philosophy of Frank Jackson*, edited by Ian Ravenscroft, 85–109. Oxford: Clarendon Press.

Schroeter, L., and F. Schroeter. (2009). "A Third Way in Metaethics." *Noûs* 43: 1–30.

Spencer, Q. (2015). "Philosophy of Race Meets Population Genetics." *Studies in History and Philosophy of Science Part C: Studies in History and Philosophy of Biological and Biomedical Sciences* 52: 46–55.

Zack, N. (1993). *Race and Mixed Race*. Philadelphia, PA: Temple University Press.

CHAPTER 15

RACE AND ETHNICITY

JORGE J. E. GRACIA

RACE and ethnicity pose many and complex problems for both philosophers and society at large. Some of these problems are practical, such as how to deal with racial or ethnic discrimination—and others are conceptual, such as how to distinguish race from ethnicity. But both kinds of problems tend to lead into each other. What are generally considered to be ethnic factors, such as culture, tend to be more easily the subject of identification thanks to racial phenotypes such as skin color; and what are taken to be racial factors, such as bodily shape, are frequently associated with cultural phenomena, such as a preference for a certain type of music. Recently, in the context of these problems, the direction in philosophy has been either to completely separate race and ethnicity or to argue that they are necessarily tied, but in both cases the focus is often on race. This focus has obscured the relations between them and led to misunderstandings. In what follows the issues at stake are clarified through the discussion of some important proposals that have been made concerning race and ethnicity. The thesis defended is that the concepts of race and ethnicity, and the distinction between them, can be preserved through their proper understanding.

SOCIAL AND EPISTEMIC PROBLEMS

The social problems raised by race and ethnicity are particularly significant from a practical point of view and thus have received the most attention. They concern the role of racial and ethnic groups in society: Should societies accept and encourage racial and ethnic diversity, tolerate it, or try to eliminate it? How do racial and ethnic diversity affect social unity? Should important policy decisions be affected by racial and ethnic considerations?

An issue of this sort that has attracted considerable attention in the United States has been framed in terms of what is called "the politics of difference" (Miller 1995, 132). It is common to think of societies as involving racial and ethnic elements. Some societies see themselves as White or Asian, whereas others see themselves as Christian or Muslim. Under the leadership of National Socialism, for example, some Germans set out to purify German society of Jews and Gypsies, and some Latin Americans have claimed their Spanish and Christian heritage as part of their social identity, thereby excluding black and Amerindian populations. The politics of difference is an attempt to organize groups politically to oppose such moves and make room for racial and ethnic diversity within societies. However, opponents view such efforts as threatening and destabilizing factors to social unity insofar as they favor the identity of certain groups over that of others (Elhshtein 1995, 74). In the United States, for example, this has been translated into calls to make English the official language of the country and to stop immigration from non-Europeans, because languages other than English and peoples of non-European origin do not fit the racial and ethnic profile considered characteristic by the dominant Anglo-American group.

The epistemic problems posed by race and ethnicity are related to, and often aggravated by, the lack of clear and consistent criteria for distinguishing them. The case of race is perhaps most evident because the criteria used to determine it vary from individual to individual, group to group, context to context, place to place, country to country, and time to time. Differing epistemic racial criteria preclude agreement as to who qualifies as a member of a race and provide the grounds for the argument that racial categories are subjective and hinge on context.

The epistemic difficulties posed by the instability of racial criteria are not restricted to the variability of the criteria. There is also the problem of the accessibility of the conditions used to satisfy the criteria. For example, the epistemic situation with blacks in the United States is unclear because there are no definite rules concerning degrees of mixing. Consider that the One-Drop Rule often used to determine membership in the black race (one drop of "black blood" makes you black) is imprecise not only because it is not clear what "one drop" means, but also because it is not clear how this can be effectively and practically determined. Indeed, many racially mixed persons join the white population in the United States every year, because in many cases it is impossible to determine that the person had a person of color as an ancestor.

The case of ethnicity is even more unclear than that of race, for the epistemic criteria applied to ethnic groups are very often contextual. Consider the case of Latinos in the United States. What is it that can be effectively used to identify them? That they speak Spanish? Not insofar as many persons regarded as Latinos do not speak Spanish at all, or speak Spanish only as a second language. Food? Again this is ineffective insofar as there is no food that is common to all Latinos. Music? Not possible for similar reasons. Religion? Latinos belong to all sorts of faiths, from Roman Catholic to Jewish, and Islamic to Voodoo. Lineage? Not insofar as not all Latinos are tied by descent and many Latinos have no ancestors who were Latinos, being children of non-Latino immigrants to Latin America. In short, there are no criteria that can be effectively used everywhere and at all times to identify Latinos.

THE METAPHYSICS OF RACE AND ETHNICITY

Although the social and epistemic problems raised by race and ethnicity are most often treated as particularly significant, the metaphysical problem of determining their reality and relations to each other has also been subject to sharp disagreement and debate. The underlying difficulty is that racial and ethnic categories appear to be too narrow, skewed, or inaccurate to deal with the practical problems that arise when one considers them. Do they reflect anything real outside the mind, or are they conceptual creations resulting from special interests and cultural mores? And, regardless of what they are, the question of their relation remains: Are they phenomena independent of each other, or are they tied necessarily or contingently?

In the case of race, the question of its reality comes up when some argue that scientific evidence indicates that it is not a biological reality. Race appears to be a social construction and not a characteristic of anything in the world. Some authors go so far as to argue that it is a meaningless and groundless concept, a remnant of archaic science; the black and white races are fictional concepts. Racial taxonomies appear to lack objective bases and often reflect personal and social bias.

Before genetic studies became available in the last forty years, the data on which to base racial classifications were obviously too inaccurate and unstable to support any clear conclusions. Skin pigmentation, cranial configuration, and even blood profiles, among others, proved unreliable. But recent genetic studies have not fared much better. To this, some scientists and philosophers add that racial categories arbitrarily place unwarranted emphasis on certain phenotypes, providing misleading descriptions of those who are characterized by them. Why should skin color, for example, be given the important place it is given in most racial classifications? Moreover, racial categories homogenize; they make us think of all members of a race as being the same, or very similar, whereas racial groups are very diverse not just because of the differences among their individual members, but because they contain what appear to be many subgroups.

The case against race has been based on several facts: (1) genetic differences between races are insignificant if compared with what members of different races share (Lewontin 1972; Nei and Roychoudhury 1982); (2) there is no single gene that can be used to classify populations into races (Cavalli-Sforza, Menozzi, and Piazza 1994, 19); (3) no strict correlation exists between the directly observable traits, known as phenotypes, and genetic specifications inherited from parents, known as genotypes (Cavalli-Sforza, Menozzi, and Piazza 1994, 6–7); (4) particular phenotypes are caused by different gene combinations and do not adhere to stable racial boundaries (King 1981, 50–51; Zack 2002, 43); and (5) no strict boundaries between what are considered to be racial groups exist—rather these groups gradate from one to another (Cavalli-Sforza, Menozzi, and Piazza 1994, 17–19). These considerations are the bases for the controversy concerning the reality of race: If (1)–(5) are true, is race real or is it merely a social construction? Three basic responses have been given to this question. At opposite extremes are *eliminativism* and what may be dubbed a kind of *neo-realism*. The first argues that race should be eliminated from discourse, because racial categories are always cashed out in biological terms and race has no biological basis; the second argues that race can still be regarded as having some kind of reality. Between these two opposite views, several other positions have been articulated in terms of such notions as identity and ethnicity. Most of these views can be regarded as versions of *constructionism* in that, although they preserve the notion of race, they understand it not as a biological fact but as a social construction along the lines ethnicity is commonly conceived.

The attempt to resolve the issue of the reality of race in other ways than those proposed by eliminativism or neo-realism has led to the introduction of several proposals concerning its relation to ethnicity: elimination of biological and ethnic conceptions of race and for the use of the category of racial and ethnic identity (Appiah 1996); substitution of the category of race by the category of ethnicity (Corlett 2003); preservation of both the categories of race and ethnicity with their integration into one category of ethnorace (Alcoff 2000); and preservation of both categories and their conceptual distinction in spite of the difficulties involved in their separability in reality (Gracia 2005).

Among critics of these positions who also propose versions of them are García (2015), who argues against the use of the notion of identity for either race or ethnicity; Zack (2002), who focuses particularly on the elimination of race as a biological reality; Outlaw (1996, 2015), who emphasizes the social need to preserve the category of race; and Andreasen (2000), who supports some level of reality for race based on the notion of a clade.

Eliminating Race Altogether

Like Appiah and Corlett, Naomi Zack criticizes the conception of race as something real, but, unlike Appiah, she does not favor the use of the notion of ethnic identity and, unlike Corlett, she does not propose a conception of ethnicity based on ancestry. Her view may be characterized as a radical form of eliminativism with respect to race. Following the conclusions of scientists, she maintains that race is not a biological reality independent of human thought. This makes race a social construction and not a fact in the world (Zack 2002, 106 ff). From this it follows, according to Zack, that the concept of race is both meaningless and groundless, a remnant of archaic science (2001). "Black" and "white" exist only as terms that refer to fictional concepts invented by humans; in scientific terms, they belong with such mythical notions as unicorn and centaur. Racial taxonomies, Zack argues, lack an objective basis. This is the reason why they are unstable in the hands of taxonomists, often reflecting personal preferences rather than facts. As she puts it: " 'Race' means a biological taxonomy or set of physical categories that can be used consistently and informatively to describe, explain, and make predictions about groups of human beings and individual members of these groups," whereas in fact there is no such taxonomy (2002, 1).

According to Zack, "there have been four bases for ideas of physical race in common sense: geographical origins of ancestors; phenotypes or physical appearance of individuals; hereditary traits of individuals; [and] genealogy (26)." All four fail the test of science. Hence, insofar as science does not justify the reality or concept of race, we must eliminate it. In continuing to use the term "race" as if we were referring to a biological reality, we commit the fallacy of ontological obligation according to which the existence and use of a term commits us to an ontological reality to which the term refers.

Substituting Racial Identity for Race and Ethnicity

K. Anthony Appiah has made one of the best known proposals for the elimination of race in our discourse. He argues (1) against a biological conception of race based on factual evidence or conceptual analysis and (2) against an understanding of race based on culture. In place of race, he proposes that we use the concept of racial identity. As he puts it: "First, . . . American social distinctions cannot be understood in terms of the concept of race . . . . Second, replacing the notion of race with the notion of culture is not helpful . . . And third, . . . we should use instead the notion of racial identity . . . ." (Appiah 1996, 32).

Appiah develops his criticism of the notion of race in terms of two theories of meaning, the ideational and the referential, since credible claims about race must be based on a clear meaning for the term "race." The ideational account requires a uniform set of coherent beliefs about culture that justify the use of the term (35 and 36). And the referential account requires the existence of something in the world that provides an effective causal explanation of the use of the term. The history of the concept of race in the United States shows no identifiable objective phenomenon to which people respond when they talk about race that can effectively function causally, thus failing to satisfy a referential account (40 and 72). Nor is there a uniform set of coherent cultural beliefs that satisfies the ideational account (72). The latter appears to imply a rejection of ethnicity as a coherent notion and replacement for the biological conception of race. This indicates that we do not have either a proper referent of the word "race" or a proper idea of race. In short, Appiah notes, "you can't get much out of a race concept, ideationally speaking" and "you can get various possible candidates from the referential notion of meaning, but none of them will be much good for explaining social or psychological life, and none of them corresponds to the social groups we call 'races' in America" (74).

Instead of race or the concept of race, Appiah argues, we should turn to the concept of racial identity. This adheres much better to the way we speak about races, racial phenomena, and racial groups. Thus, when we speak of race, we are using

> a label R, associated with [1] *ascriptions* by most people (where ascription involves descriptive criteria for applying the label); and [2] *identifications* by those who fall under it (where identification implies a shaping role for the label in the intentional acts of the possessor, so that they sometimes act *as an R*), where there is a history of associating possessors of the label with an inherited racial essence (even if some who use the label no longer believe in racial essences). (81–82)

Accordingly, the conditions of racial identity are as follows: ascription by others, self-identification by the labeled, and a set of descriptions, used for both ascriptions and as norms for action, that have a historical association to a label involving a racial essence. It matters not for racial identity whether race has any reality, or even whether there is a consistent concept of race. What matters is that people label some other people and themselves in certain ways and that the labels include a notion of inherited racial essence. A racial essence consists of a set of conditions considered to be necessary and sufficient for a particular race, regardless of whether in fact such conditions apply or not. For Appiah, what matters is the labeling. The label comes first, and it is only after it that other features, such as cultural traits, are associated with it and used for action (89). As he puts it: "Collective identities . . . provide what we might call scripts: narratives that people can use in shaping their life plans and in telling their life stories" (97).

Appiah's position involves both the elimination of the reality of race and of its conception as either a biological reality or a cultural phenomenon, for neither offers us a justifiable concept. Instead, he proposes certain procedures of labeling, varying descriptions, and attempts by those described to tailor action to those descriptions. Unlike radical eliminativists like Zack, who reject both race and any replacements for it, or reductionists like Corlett, who seek its replacement with ethnicity, he reduces race to racial identity. This, he proposes, reflects more accurately the way humans function with respect to racial phenomena.

AGAINST RACIAL AND ETHNIC IDENTITY

Appiah's proposal has elicited considerable opposition. Among its detractors is J. L. A. García, who rejects any talk of identity, whether racial or ethnic (García 2007, 2015), including those of Appiah, Zack, Corlett, Gracia, and Alcoff. He argues against Appiah and Zack for trying to preserve the notions of racial and ethnic identities while rejecting the notion of race (2007, 46–49); against Gracia for attempting to reconcile antiessentialist views of race and ethnicity with his commitment to a historical familial view of ethnic identity (García 2015, 92); against Corlett for his comparative and scalar conception of group identity (García 2007, 54–62); and against Alcoff for presenting normative and ideological politics as epistemology and ontology (2007, 68).

García's view, however, is not completely negative. Rather than use the concept of identity, he proposes "that we should strive toward what might be called ethno-racial skepticism and a deflationary conception of race and ethnicity" (García 2007, 69). He aims for simplicity and clarity, noting that the notions of race and ethnicity are complex and difficult, posing problems for establishing their extension and content, which are made worse by introducing the notion of identity. It might work better, "to replace as much as possible such putative, ascribed affiliations with more restrained talk of ethnic (and, more problematically, racial) *background*, especially ancestry" (73).

Avoiding identity talk in the cases of racial and ethnic groups does prevent various confusions. An example is the misguided conception of anyone's self-image as involving the group rather than the self (76). Another is the view that race or ethnicity "can give 'meaning' to its participants' (members') lives," for this is too vague to be of any use (77). Instead of emphasizing racial or ethnic affiliations, García recommends that we adopt "a new interpersonalist personalism" that focuses on our status as human beings, as rational animals, or even as creatures of God.

Substituting Ethnicity for Race

Like Appiah, J. Angelo Corlett argues for the elimination and replacement of the notion of race, but unlike Appiah's notion of identity, the replacement he proposes, namely ethnicity as genetically determined, seems similar to race.

Corlett distinguishes between two analyses, one in terms of "public-policy," and another "metaphysical," which in his view do not need to coincide (Corlett 2003, 51). His primary focus is the first, but he nonetheless offers a proposal for the second. The main purpose of a public-policy analysis of ethnicity is "to accurately classify people into categories of ethnicity for purposes of justice under the law" (46). His focus is reparations for members of ethnic and racial groups who have been subjected to discrimination and other social ills resulting from their ethnicity or race. He argues that reparations of these sorts require the accurate identification of subjects along ethnic and racial lines. This does not mean that the need for accurate classificatory criteria for ethnic and racial groups is a requirement for reparations, only, because it is also necessary for the implementation of other social policies, such as affirmative action. Although Corlett applies his proposal to Latinos, specifically, he intends that they apply to all ethnic groups, including those considered races (Corlett 2003, 60).

Corlett summarizes his view by noting that "for public policy considerations, genealogy ought to be construed as both a necessary and sufficient condition of award or benefit" (Corlett 2003, 51, et passim). For reparations to be justified in the case of Latinos, a genetic tie is both necessary and sufficient for government implementation. Nonetheless, Corlett agrees, there is more to belonging to an ethnic group than genealogy. Being Latino is more than just having Latino ancestors. It is at this point that he introduces the metaphysical analysis:

> Aside from public policy consideration, however, factors that would go toward making one more or less a Latino may include the degree to which one knows and respects a Latino language or dialect thereof; possesses and respects a traditional Latino name; engages in and respects Latino culture or parts thereof; accepts and respects himself or herself as a Latino; is accepted and respected as a Latino by other Latinos; and is construed as a Latino by outgroup members . . . . each of these conditions admits of degrees . . . . [but] neither (sic) . . . is either necessary or sufficient to make one a Latino . . . (Corlett 2003, 51)

In short, Corlett's metaphysical view of an ethnic group consists of a list of conditions (Corlett does not tell us whether the list is exhaustive) each of which is subject to degree, resulting in one being more or less a member of the group. Reflecting the gradation in the metaphysical view, the public policy view also is subject to degree, although contrasting with the metaphysical view, it is proposed as a necessary and sufficient condition for the implementation of public policy.

Substituting Ethnorace for Race and Ethnicity

The search for a satisfactory understanding of race has prompted some to argue that race and ethnicity cannot be properly distinguished and it is futile to try. This position can be considered from two sides: from the side of race insofar as it is seen as including ethnic elements and therefore as fundamentally ethnic, and from the side of ethnicity insofar as this is taken to be so permeated with racial elements that it cannot be clearly separated from them. Three considerations are used to support this view.

First, historical discussions of race have always included ethnic elements and vice versa. From the very beginning racial and cultural divisions have been intertwined. Blacks have generally been described as being different from whites not only in terms of their physical and genetic characteristics but also in terms of customs, attitudes, and achievements. Second, race cannot be separated clearly from ethnicity because the physical phenotypes on which it is often based are not easily distinguishable from cultural ones. Third, every time one tries to separate the notion of race from the notion of ethnicity, race gets entangled with ethnicity.

For instance, in the change of name from "black" to "African American" in the United States, the attempt to develop an identity based on ethnicity through the change of the name reintroduces race, because "African American" has come to mean racially black. Because of this intertwinement of race and ethnicity, Alcoff argues that there are real advantages in the use of the notion of *ethnorace* for the understanding of Latinos, for: "Using only ethnicity . . .

obscures our own awareness about how ethnic identifications often do the work of race while seeming to be theoretically correct and politically advanced" (Alcoff 2000, 42).

KEEPING RACE AND ETHNICITY

In spite of the support eliminativists find in science, their view has been attacked by some reductionists and constructionists such as Alcoff (2000), Appiah (1996), Glasgow (2009), and Gracia (2005). One early, and prominent opponent of eliminativism is Lucius T. Outlaw, Jr, who argued that, even if not a biological reality, race is real insofar as it has affected and still affects society in significant ways, a reason why it cannot be eliminated from our discourse or consideration (Outlaw 1996, 135–157). Others have continued to hold that race has some biological basis. For example, several versions of *cladism*, which looks to ancestral lineage for an understanding of racial groupings, have been proposed (e.g., Andreasen 2000, Hardimon 2003, and Kitcher 1999). This in turn has generated a strong reaction among those who reiterate scientific consensus about the lack of any biological basis for racial taxonomy (e.g., Zack 2002).

Every one of the proposals examined has disadvantages. The eliminativism of Zack and the reductionism of Appiah and Corlett fail to preserve enough of the language and concept of race to understand how race has functioned and continues to function in society. The neo-realism of some cladists is too close to the old biological notions of race for comfort. The notion of ethnorace suggested by Alcoff does not tell us how race and ethnicity are paired in this composite concept. The restriction of the notion of identity to personal identity proposed by García fails to do justice to the strong sense of racial and ethnic belonging. And the effort to preserve the notion of race for social purposes proposed by Outlaw does not explain sufficiently the role of ethnicity in our social discourse about race.

Many of the problems that affect these views are rooted in a lack of a proper understanding of race and ethnicity, and racial and ethnic identities, and of their interactions and status. A successful proposal concerning the answer to the social and epistemic questions prompted by race, ethnicity, and identity raised earlier requires proper conceptions of race, ethnicity, and identity that do not fall into an old biologism of race and take into account its difference with ethnicity and identity. This is the aim of the genetic common-bundle view of race and the historical-familial view of ethnicity (Gracia 2005, 24, 82; 2000, 27–33).

A successful strategy should begin by making a threefold distinction that applies to both race, ethnicity, and racial and ethnic identity: "a race" or "an ethnos" (or ethnic group) considered as a group of people; "race" and "ethnicity" considered as a property of members of a group; and "racial identity" and "ethnic identity" understood as the possession of a racial or ethnic property. A race as a group of people consists of a subgroup of individual human beings who satisfy the following two conditions: "[1] each member of the group is linked by descent to another member of the group who is in turn also linked by descent to at least some third member of the group; and [2] each member of the group has one or more physical features that are [i] genetically transmittable, [ii] generally associated with the group, and [iii] perceptually perspicuous" (85). Race as a property consists in the set of characteristics that satisfy these conditions. And racial identity is the higher order relational property of having such a property.

Neither one of the two conditions required by a race, taken by itself, is sufficient for racial membership, unless one were to adopt the infamous One-Drop Rule, which is inconsistent and hence unacceptable (see Malcomson 2000). The One-Drop Rule is inconsistent as a racial marker because it can function effectively only if applied discriminately to some races and not others. This entails that being related by descent to a member of some race, who is in turn related by descent to at least some third member of that race, is not enough for someone to be a member of the race insofar as the person in question may not share in any of the characteristics generally associated with members of it (Gracia 2005, 85–86). This is the reason why we say that people can change races, although in fact there is no such racial change. The change amounts to the recognition that the persons in question do not satisfy the conditions sufficient for belonging to a particular race, while they meet the conditions of belonging to another race. The change is one of labeling, that is, of what we call the persons, rather than of being, that is, of what the persons are.

Similarly, having physical features associated with a particular race does not ipso facto make a person a member of the race or serve effectively to identify the person as such (Gracia 2005, 86). Some Indians, Italians, and blacks share many phenotypes, but the first two are not regarded as members of the black race insofar as they do not satisfy the descent condition.

Although the notion of family serves to understand both race and ethnicity, the latter is distinguishable from race in that it is conceived in terms of both family and history and does not require the two stated racial conditions. Consequently, ethnicity is both more flexible and contingent on historical events, even when such historical events may include descent and certain phenotypes. It is for this reason that race and ethnicity are often confused with each other, as happens in the case of Hispanics/Latinos (Gracia 2000), and why they are difficult to distinguish in fact.

The genetic common-bundle view of race and the historical-familial view of ethnicity may be characterized as constructionist to the extent that, apart from descent and the inherited and physical character of the phenotypes that make up the distinguishing racial property of a racial group, the choice of the particular features is the result of social construction and thus may vary from society to society and place to place. Ethnicity is different from race in that it is not constrained by descent or inheritable physical phenotypes, although these may in fact be part of the distinguishing ethnic property associated with a particular ethnic group. Still, both races and ethnic groups are familial groups when this metaphor is used broadly.

The advantage of the genetic common-bundle view of race and the historical familial view of ethnicity when taken together is that they preserve the notions of race and ethnicity without the objectionable commitment to their biological reality or a too rigid and inflexible understanding of them that fails to take into account the contextual and flexible aspects of these notions, thus failing to take into account the way these notions work in society and how most of us think about them.

CONCLUSION

Discussions of race are often entangled with ethnicity and vice versa. Indeed, some of the most difficult epistemic and social problems raised concerning race have relied on solutions that involve ethnicity, and some of the same kinds of problems raised concerning ethnicity have relied on solutions that involve race. Among the most significant views proposed to avoid confusion in the epistemic and social problems raised in the context of race and ethnicity are the following: eliminativism of race (race is to be eliminated altogether); constructionism of race or ethnicity (race and ethnicity are social constructions rather than realities); reductionism of race or ethnicity (reduction of race and ethnicity to racial and ethnic identity; of race to ethnicity; of race and ethnicity to ethnorace); neo-realist views of race such as cladism; and nonreductionist views that refuse to reduce race and ethnicity to each other, or to some other notions, proposing such theories as the genetic common-bundle view of race and the historical-familial view of ethnicity. None of the views that propose the elimination of race or ethnicity, their reduction to each other or something else, or that neglect the constructive and realist elements in these phenomena, provides a viable alternative that can serve as a basis for solving the critical epistemic and social problems that come up in their discussion.

REFERENCES

Alcoff, Linda Martín. (2000). "Is Latina/o Identity a Racial Identity?" In *Hispanics/Latinos in the United States: Ethnicity, Race, and Rights*, edited by Jorge J. E. Gracia and Pablo De Greiff, 23–44. New York: Routledge.

Andreasen, Robin O. (2000). "Race: Biological Reality or Social Construct." *Philosophy of Science* 67(suppl.): S653–S666.

Appiah, K. Anthony. (1996). "Race, Culture, Identity: Misunderstood Connections." In K. Anthony Appiah and Amy Gutmann. *Color Conscious: The Political Morality of Race*, 30–105. Princeton, NJ: Princeton University Press.

Cavalli-Sforza, Luigi, Paolo Menozzi, and Alberto Piazza. (1994). *The History and Geography of Human Genes*. Princeton, NJ: Princeton University Press.

Corlett, J. Angelo. (2003). *Race, Racism, and Reparations*. Ithaca, NY: Cornell University Press.

Elshtein, Jean Bethke. (1995). *Democracy on Trial*. New York: Basic.

García, J. L. A. (2007). "Racial and Ethnic Identity?" In *Race or Ethnicity? On Black and Latino Identity*, edited by Jorge J. E. Gracia, 45–77. Ithaca, NY: Cornell University Press.

García, J. L. A. (2015). "Is Being Hispanic an Identity? In *Debating Race, Ethnicity, and Latino Identity: Jorge J. E. Gracia and His Critics*, edited by Iván Jaksić, 91–105. New York: Columbia University Press.

Glasgow, Joshua. (2009). *A Theory of Race*. New York: Routledge.

Gracia, Jorge J. E. (2000). *Hispanic/Latino Identity: A Philosophical Perspective*. Oxford: Blackwell.

Gracia, Jorge J. E. (2005). *Surviving Race, Ethnicity, and Nationality: A Challenge for the Twentieth Century*. Lanham, MD: Rowman & Littlefield.

Hardimon, Michael. (2003). "The Ordinary Concept of Race." *The Journal of Philosophy* 100: 437–455.

King, James C. (1981). *The Biology of Race*. Berkeley: University of California Press.

Kitcher, Philip. (1999). "Race, Ethnicity, Biology, Culture." In *Racism*, edited by Leonard Harris, 87–119. New York, NY: Humanity Books.

Lewontin, Richard C. (1972). "The Apportionment of Human Diversity." In *Evolutionary Biology 6*, edited by T. Dobzhansky, M. K. Hecht, and W. C. Steere, 381–398. New York: Appleton-Century-Crofts.

Malcomson, Scott L. (2000). *One Drop of Blood: The American Misadventure of Race.* New York: Farrar, Straus and Giroux.

Miller, David. (1995). *On Nationality.* Oxford: Clarendon Press.

Nei, Masatoshi, and A. K. Roychoudhury. (1982). "Genetic Relationship and Evolution of Human Races." *Evolutionary Biology* 14: 1–59.

Outlaw, Lucius T., Jr. (1996). *On Race and Philosophy.* New York: Routledge.

Outlaw, Lucius T., Jr. (2015). "Writing a Check that Philosophy Can't Cash." In *Debating Race, Ethnicity, and Latino Identity: Jorge J. E. Gracia and His Critics*, edited by Iván Jaksić, 29–37. New York: Columbia University Press

Zack, Naomi. (2001). "Race and Philosophic Meaning." In *Race and Racism*, edited by Bernard Boxill, 43–57. Oxford: University Press.

Zack, Naomi. (2002). *Philosophy of Science and Race.* New York: Routledge.

PART IV

·····································

AMERICAN
PHILOSOPHY AND
IDEAS OF RACE

·····································

HUMAN chattel slavery is an institution that has been ubiquitous throughout history, and some experts believe that current sex trafficking has resulted in more slaves alive today than at any other time (over 25 million). However, the countries that legally made slavery a vital part of their economic system (at least 10 percent) have been few: ancient Greece, ancient Rome, Brazil, the Caribbean, and the US South. It cannot be surprising that the enslavement of African Americans for close to 250 years (1620–1865), together with ideologies of their racial inferiority and that of their descendants, has had deep and enduring effects on US racial identities and race relations.

Slavery has been practiced in other parts of the modern world, but its indelible connection to racial differences may be unique to the United States. Until the late twentieth century, historians described racist ideas about black people as the cause of their enslavement—"They were enslaved because they were black"—but more recent scholarship has identified ideas about race as justifications for violence and oppression undertaken for economic reasons. One current view is that race itself is a form of ideology and racial prejudice is a rationalization for racial discrimination undertaken for reasons independent of ideas about race.

The focal point of race in American history has been black race or African ancestry. Insofar as the United States has had a distinctive history of race, there has been intellectual, political, and creative attention to the subject. So in that sense, when American intellectuals, specifically black American intellectuals—although not only blacks, because there are also non-black progressive voices—analyze race, American philosophy of race occurs. In that history, certain figures loom: Thomas Jefferson, Ralph Waldo Emerson, Mark Twain, Frederick Douglass, W. E. B. Du Bois, and up through the early twenty-first century, Cornel West.

Philosophy of race is not the only distinctly American intellectual strain. American thinkers also created a distinctive tradition of academic philosophy. Pragmatism, or Americanist philosophy, or process philosophy, was extremely popular in academic letters from the late nineteenth century to just before World War II, when core writings were produced by William James, Charles E. Pierce, and John Dewey. But pragmatism has also lived on through many tendrils and revisions, in the work of Q. V. O Quine, Hilary Putnam, and Richard Rorty, as well as iterations and variations in postmodernism. It is natural given the specifically American history of race, for American pragmatist philosophy to intersect with American philosophy of race. Many contemporary academic philosophers of race find the dynamic tools of Americanist philosophy methodologically congenial for their work on race, and others claim African American thinkers such as Douglass and Du Bois as foundational for their thought about present issues. In recent decades, the link between philosophy of race as distinctly American and American pragmatism has been emphasized by Cornel West, an avowed pragmatist and public intellectual, who has influenced many contemporary philosophers of race. (Although, despite being claimed by academic philosophers and his own distinguished career at Harvard, Princeton, and Union Theological Seminary, West does not view himself as a philosopher, primarily. He writes for his website, "I'm a blues man in the life of the mind. I'm a jazz man in the world of ideas.")

We saw in Leonard Harris's essay in Part II, that Alain Locke's philosophical work had been ignored or neglected over much of the twentieth century. Locke's dissertation advisor at Harvard was Ralph B. Perry, a student of William James, who himself worked on a naturalistic theory of value. Jacoby Carter here introduces Locke as well known for his work in value theory, aesthetics, cosmopolitanism, democracy, and cultural pluralism, but still obscure in matters of race. Locke's work on race appeared mostly in lectures during 1915–1916, but was not published until 1992, so reading Locke on race is a matter of reclamation. Carter explains that Locke conceived of race in three ways: anthropologically, which took biological factors into account; politically, or as the result of power balances; and socially, which was a matter of culture. Locke rejected the idea that races were biologically distinct but at the same time did not think they could be "eliminated" from social ideas and interactions. Carter interprets Locke as holding that race is a matter of cultural distinctions, transmitted as social inheritance.

Chike Jeffers compares and contrasts three American thinkers on ideas of racial identity: W. E. B. Du Bois, [Kwame] Anthony Appiah, and Lucius Outlaw. At issue is Appiah and Outlaw's opposing interpretations of W. E. B. Du Bois's 1897 essay, "The Conservation of Races." Delivering his essay at the first meeting of the American Negro Academy, Du Bois began by noting that "The American Negro" has always taken a keen interest in the subject of race, because of imputations of black inferiority. And, Du Bois continued, "He has, consequently, been led to deprecate and minimize race distinctions, to believe intensely that out of one blood God created all nations, and to speak of human brotherhood as though it were the possibility of an already dawning tomorrow." Du Bois recognized racial identities as based on real physical and biological differences, but he took the most important part of the idea of race into the social realm. Du Bois defined a race as a cultural group, "a vast family of human beings, generally of common blood and language, always of common history, traditions and impulses, who are both voluntarily and involuntarily striving together for the accomplishment of certain more or less vividly conceived ideals of life."

Jeffers notes that Appiah disagrees with Du Bois's definition, because in order to identify the common history that constitutes a race, the group itself would have to be defined. Appiah claims that in his list of eight races, Du Bois defines races based on their geographical origins. Outlaw takes Appiah to task for picking apart Du Bois's cluster concept of race and proposes instead a political interpretation of Du Bois's definition. As a result, Outlaw, like Du Bois, posits a value in racial identities. Jeffers resolves these conflicting approaches with reference to Appiah's later interpretation of Du Bois as emphasizing the social and psychological aspects of race: If races or racial essences are not biologically real, social racial identities are, because they "shape the ways people conceive of themselves and their projects."

In the tradition of the political dimension of racial identities mentioned by Outlaw, Clarence Sholé Johnson criticizes Cornel West, as an American pragmatist and race theorist, for his relative silence about "racially-motivated extrajudicial killings of young black men" by US police officers in recent years. Johnson insists that West has not produced the criticism to fulfill his role as a public intellectual and prophetic pragmatist:

> Pragmatism, as is well known, is an action-oriented theory that considers ideas useful only insofar as those ideas can produce results in the form of action. So prophetic pragmatism, as a variant of American pragmatism, is a philosophical position which invokes critical discourse as an instrument to engage and solve problems that confront the society, especially in situations of moral urgency.

Johnson argues that West has rested on his earlier description of a nihilistic existential threat overhanging black youth. The causes of this threat are external oppression, but the threat itself is an internal psychological and spiritual "disease of the soul." Jeffers himself identifies a new threat in the form of post-Obama antiblack violence after the election of a black president in 2008. This threat is a literal resurgence of hatred and violence, most evident in extrajudicial police killings, and it is a disease of the "body politic." Jeffers calls for a forceful pragmatist response toward social justice in this case.

In "Insurrectionist Ethics and Racism," Lee McBride turns to Leonard Harris and Angela Davis for inspiration regarding "human liberation and social amelioration in the face of racism." According to Harris, racism strips a racialized population of its humanity, through degradation, terror, and humiliation. McBride, in the tradition of Frederick Douglass and Martin Luther King, Jr., as well as Leonard Harris, rejects moral suasionist methods for correcting racism. Needed are struggle and resistance—revolution. Angela Davis has supported insurrectionist ethics in relation to racial justice: opposition to racist norms and authorities; radical action on behalf of racialized populations; universal liberation through particular group advocacy; the cultivation of individual character traits of defiance and resistance.

Robert Gooding-Williams explores the relationship between antiracist critical theory and the history of African American thought, in terms of a debate between anachronists and antiquarians about the relationship between the current practice of philosophy and the study of the history of philosophy. The basic issue is the relation between present normative concerns regarding race, and intellectual and political philosophical history; the question is how to reconcile contemporary urgencies without misinterpreting or distorting past thought. Gooding-Williams works through this problematic with the examples of the social and political thought of Du Bois and Frederick Douglass. He concludes that it is necessary both to be sensitive to contextualized historical meanings and concerns and to relate the present to the past. And indeed, this process of learning from past thinkers in order to move forward from injustice in the present, is an ongoing project exemplified in all of the essays in this part.

FURTHER READING

Appiah, Kwame Anthony, and Martin Bunzl, eds. (2007). *Buying Freedom: The Ethics and Economics of Slave Redemption*. Princeton, NJ: Princeton University Press.

Douglass, Frederick. (1845). *A Narrative of the Life of Frederick Douglass*. Boston: Anti-Slavery Office.

Dubois, W. E. B. (1903). *The Souls of Black Folk*. Accessed May 16, 2016. http://www.gutenberg.org/ebooks/408.

Finley, Moses I. (1980). *Ancient Slavery and Modern Ideology*. New York: Viking Press.

Jefferson, Thomas. (n.d.). "Notes on the State of Virginia." Massachusetts Historical Society. Accessed May 16, 2016. http://www.masshist.org/thomasjeffersonpapers/notes/.

Rorty, Richard M. (1989). *Contingency, Irony, and Solidarity*. Cambridge: Cambridge University Press.

West, Cornel. (1989). *The American Evasion of Philosophy: A Genealogy of Pragmatism*. Madison: University of Wisconsin Press.

West, Cornel. (n.d.). *Official Website*. Accessed March 29, 2015. http://www.cornelwest.com/index.html#.VRjkU7lozcs.

CHAPTER 16

BETWEEN RECONSTRUCTION AND ELIMINATION

Alain Locke's Philosophy of Race

JACOBY ADESHEI CARTER

ALAIN Locke is known as a preeminent African American philosopher. Locke is perhaps best known for his work in value theory, aesthetics, cosmopolitanism, democracy, and cultural pluralism. Although it is known that he did work on the philosophy of race, and his conception of ethnic or social race has received some attention in the literature, he is not prominently featured in contemporary philosophical discussions of race. This is likely due in part to the fact that few of his published philosophical works are concerned exclusively with race, though issues of race frequently receive some attention, or are present just beneath the surface of his work. Perhaps an even better reason is that his most extensive contribution to the philosophy of race was a series of lectures he delivered in 1915 and 1916, but which were not published until 1992. In the intervening decades, race theory developed largely in ignorance of Locke's contribution to the field. As a consequence, many of his insights and arguments have not had the impact on the development of the philosophy of race as they might have had otherwise. This is perhaps an historical accident in need of correction.

Locke had a prescient understanding of race, which was thoroughly informed by the emerging fields of anthropology, social science, and a critical historical analysis of past and present societies. He foresaw a number of advances in the theory of race, and he contributed an historical, political, economic and social analysis of race that was scarcely to be found near the turn of the previous century. Unfortunately, his most significant work in the field has gone largely unrecognized because it remained unpublished for over seven decades. It is to be hoped that attention to Locke's philosophy of race in light of the present state of the field of philosophy of race will have a positive impact on the questions contemporary philosophers ask, the lines of argumentation that they run, and the concepts they invoke, in further study of such an important human phenomenon.

Locke distinguishes between three primary conceptions of race: theoretical or anthropological, political, and social. Anthropological conceptions of race seek to explain racial differentiation in terms of biological or ethnological features of human populations. On such accounts, racial difference is a matter of historical or natural deviation between human populations. Political conceptions of race are based on successful or unsuccessful interracial contacts that leave social groups in comparatively dominate or subordinate positions. On this account, racial differentiation is the result of the exercise or lack of political power. Finally, social conceptions of race account for racial differentiation in terms of uniquely characteristic cultural traits. On this account, racial differentiation is the by-product of sub-cultural inflection.

Locke's philosophy of race offers not only an analysis of the meaning of the concept of race, that is, an explication of what aspect of the world we are referring to when we use racial discourse, but additionally, a careful and critical examination of the social-psychological dimensions of race, which prefigures a number of contemporary questions and concerns. Locke separates conceptually his analysis of the underlying social, political, and economic causes of social differentiation, which produce various social groupings including races, from the socially imbedded and encoded practices, and epistemological standpoints that inform the phenomena of race contacts and interracial relations. He writes:

> The closest scrutiny of the earlier kinds of grouped differences in human society show[s] them to have been largely practical and economic in their derivation. So that even when they did run parallel to what was fundamentally a racial difference, the difference *was not apprehended* [as] racial difference but *as* a caste or class difference. So that when we see that largely the castes in India follow ethnic lines we are apt to be misled and think that they are racial in origin. As a matter of fact the castes in India have produced races rather than having arisen out of races. They started largely as economic differentiations, class differences, caste differences, but because they were enforced by a strict [social code,] by strict marriage laws, they have practically resulted in racial differences. So that in the East today a caste represents a race, practically, a difference of blood, but originally they represented a difference of occupation and a difference, as we would call it, of class. (Locke 1992, 46)

This example from Locke illustrates that the underlying causes of social differentiation can be social, religious, political, or economic, depending perhaps on one's religious sect, occupation, language, or ownership and control of resources or social goods. The example further shows the distinction between the causes of group difference and the social practices such as marriage restrictions, social codes that limit interactions with certain groups, legal segregation, and so on that racialize different groups. It also alludes to the ways in which the various standpoints of groups as dominant or inferior, in the sense of having access or control over economic resources and social goods function in accordance with our practices of social differentiation.

Various elements in Locke's philosophy of race lend themselves to different readings of how to characterize his theoretical position. For instance, he denies that races are biologically distinct populations of human beings, and he argues that putatively biological conceptions of race are social fictions. This would seem to align him with present *fictionalist*, or *antirealist* accounts of race, on the side of what is known as racial *eliminativism*. However, Locke professes to think that race is a fundamental category for understanding human social interaction, and as such he does not think that we could well do without such a concept. More than that, he is doubtful given the prominence of race in social discourse that the idea could easily be gotten rid of, if at all. This seems to reflect an *antieliminativist* position. But Locke further claims that the *only* viable meaning of race is social. This seems to align him with contemporary *constructionist* accounts of race. He argues that as race in the social sense is the only plausible meaning of the concept, it should be substituted for alternative conceptions of race. Here, it seems that Locke endorses a form of *substitutionism*. Locke is committed to the idea that our racial understanding needs to be reworked and argues that outmoded conceptions of race need to be thoroughly critiqued and our present understanding of race informed by careful historical analysis and contemporary social science. This suggests that his view might align more closely with *reconstructionist* views of race.

RACE AND ANTHROPOLOGY

According to Locke, racial differences and racial prejudices are undeniable, but invariably the historical result of economic and social causes. Social, historical, and economic processes lead to differentiations in cultures and types of civilization, and in some instances those distinctions correspond to racial differences. Locke held that racial differences parallel racial inequalities, but racial differences are not necessarily the cause of racial inequalities; the former are better explained by ethnological and social elements, and the latter are best explained in terms of political and economic factors (Locke 1992, 1–14).

Locke attributes the notion that race is a determining factor in culture to Arthur de Gobineau, though he claims its scientific justification comes primarily from the social evolutionary theory of Herbert Spencer (Locke 1992, 189). The notion of a fixed relationship between race and culture was used primarily to justify the social evolutionist belief in a series of historical stages in progressive social development. That notion of a fixed linkage between race and culture was the analogue in social theory to the concept of heredity in biology. The stock notions of *race capacity* and *racial heredity* similarly went through a process of acceptance, rejection, and revision by the time Locke wrote about culture and race (Locke 1989, 189). Several lines of argument had disproved the false notion that race and culture stand in a fixed relationship, along with the mistaken belief that they justify a "supposedly universal process of development" (Locke 1989, 189–190). If the proponents of such theories acknowledged them to be "the philosophy of a particular phase of civilization," they would be less disagreeable (Locke 1992, 3). Yet these theories go well beyond such claims and purport to have discovered anthropological and ethnological evidence of objective race distinction and hierarchy. They further claim that civilization is the result only of the activity of the dominant race group. Locke here relies on the anthropological work of Franz Boas and others to demonstrate that such conclusions are unfounded.

Locke's understanding of race is influenced by the anthropology of his time. From Frantz Boas he derives the notion that racial types are not permanent (Locke 1992, 75–76). Locke's belief that race and culture are not causally linked, that they can, and often do, vary independently of each other, stems from the work of R. H. Lowie (Locke 1989, 189–190). E. Sapir supplies him with the idea that the historical, rather than biological or inherently psychological explanation of unique cultural or ethnic traits does not undermine the existence of such traits (Locke 1989, 190). Locke develops part of his account of social race, and the understanding of racial differentiation in terms of assimilative processes, from Flinder-Petrie (Locke 1989, 191–192). Finally, he derives the view that race practices are deeply rooted in imperialism from Lord E. B. Cromer (Locke 1992, 64). Locke writes:

> The physical differences of men, those anthropological differences which are most useful in anthropology, have no meaning other than for purposes of descriptive classification . . . these anthropological factors are themselves both subject to change and perfectly unreliable as clues

to any sociological meaning of the term "race." And since that biological history is in itself on such a scale as to be incommensurate with the social history of the same group, and that there is, of course, no parallel between the anthropological factors of race and its position in social culture or adaptability for social culture, any judgement about the influence of biological factors on social culture is a false and very risky reduction. (Locke 1992, 5)

Locke argues that because the factors underlying biological diversity across human populations are themselves variable, they cannot function as a static basis for the sociological concept of race. The anthropological factors that drive human subspeciation, such as physical and social reproductive isolation, vary, and in varying, these factors can produce a variety of consequences within a given population and across populations (Locke 1989, 190–192 see also Locke 1992, 4–6). The genetic or biological history of a population need not vary conterminously with the group's social history. Moreover, the social distinctions that are drawn need not coincide with the racial distinctions that are drawn on the basis of a perceived biological similarity within a population.

RACE AND SOCIAL CULTURE

In his positive view of the relation of race to culture, Locke recognizes that there is "an open question as to the association of certain ethnic groups with definite culture-traits and culture types, under circumstances where there is evidently a greater persistence of certain strains and characteristics in their culture than of other factors" (Locke 1989, 190). The relative stability and resiliency of such factors to historical modification demarcates the distinctively ethnological dimension of race, which Locke's revised concept of ethnic or social race is meant to cover (Locke 1989, 192).

Locke acknowledges that there is at the time no anthropological explanation to be given for the seemingly stable and stock character of certain ethnic traits, but he supposes they are best interpreted as ethnically characteristic. That is, such ethnic traits are not absolute or permanent and neither is there psychological evidence sufficient to construe them as inherent. Yet they seem to be integrally connected in ways that are not sufficiently explained by historical combinations. Locke further comments that it is difficult to find common historical causes that account for the "relative constancy" of these ethnic traits (Locke 1989, 193–196).

By way of illustration of Locke's point here consider African Americans. On Locke's view they share a common culture with white Americans in terms of language, religion, aesthetic sense, and many other cultural elements. However, even in having these things in common, there are characteristic, qualitatively distinct, and phenomenologically unique forms which that common language, religion, and aesthetic sense takes among African Americans that are not characteristic of white Americans. Characteristic differences include the uniquely Negro dialect captured so masterfully by the poetry of Paul Lawrence Dunbar, the frenzied religious expression described by W. E. B. Du Bois, and the emotional depth and force of Negro spirituals.

Locke contends that we need not deny that there are characteristically racial modes of living in denying that they are hereditary, biological, or psychological traits (Locke 1992, 11–13). Locke suspects that a more tenable doctrine of the relationship of race and culture would have emerged if more attention had been paid to the ethnic, rather than anthropological characters of populations. If this had been done, race would likely have been understood to be socially inherited, and racial distinctions would be understood as "due to the selective psychological 'set' of established cultural reactions" (Locke 1989, 191). On this view, race is an importantly learned or epistemic mode of being. Persons not only acquire race through a process of enculturation or socialization, but once acquired, race conditions the way they perceive and understand the world.

"Race" according to Locke, is "primarily a matter of social heredity" (Locke 1989, 191). Moreover, he argues that race is "either favorable or unfavorable social inheritance," which is often erroneously ascribed to supposed physical inheritance (Locke 1992, 12). Cultures, on Locke's account, are often complex amalgamations of racial groups, and ethnicities are the result of particular social histories (Locke 1989, 193–194). Races, are better understood as "concrete culture-types," according to Locke, which are "composite racially [read biologically] speaking, and have only an artificial ethnic unity, of historical derivation and manufacture" (Locke 1989, 194). This notion of "artificial ethnic unity" is a curious feature of Locke's view that he is not at pains to clarify (Locke 1989, 194). It can be read, as suggested earlier, as an antirealism or factionalism about race or ethnicity. The phrase "historical derivation and manufacture" indicates that ethnicity or ethnic unity is a constructed phenomenon for Locke, but that need not make it unreal. Artifacts can, but need not be real or naturally occurring.

Locke contends that the conception of inferior or superior races emanates from "the political fortunes and political capacities of peoples" (Locke 1992, 22). Politically and economically successful groups are in a position to impose an identity on other groups. Political and economic success enables groups to impact and control contacts with other groups, thereby establishing their status as dominant. Comparatively unsuccessful groups are subject to the terms of intergroup contacts established by the dominant group. A political race, according to Locke, is a dominant racial group able to safeguard its own identity, impose a racial identity on other groups, and shape interracial contacts (Locke 1992, 22–23). Politically dominant races are able to claim sole responsibility for the creation and flourishing of a society and deny to any subordinate racial groups in the society a role in shaping that society's character or success. As Locke sees it, the political conception and practice of race is deeply rooted in imperialism (Locke 1992, 22–26). He writes: "Imperialism is . . . essentially the practical aspect of what one might call "race practice" as distinguished from race theory, and all those peoples that in political life have managed to dominate [the] political life [of other peoples] are imperialistic peoples" (Locke 1992, 24).

For Locke the perpetuation of racial idioms runs the risk of continuing racism, provincialism, oppressive race practices, and social stratification and division. In claiming this, he does not dismiss the possibility that there may be beneficial aspects of racial identification in some contexts (Locke 1992, 52–58, and 63–67). Locke formulates the problem as one of particular concern for those with cosmopolitan sensibilities and value commitments. If race has an important bearing on cultural progress and distinctiveness, are those consequences of racialism sufficient to outweigh the negative consequences of racialism in terms of prejudice, chauvinism, pernicious race creeds, and negative race practices?

By race creed, Locke means an action-guiding set of beliefs or aims concerning racial differentiation and practice held and taught by a social group, typically a dominant one. Race creeds originate, motivate, and reinforce race practices (Locke 1992, 63). Locke contends that race creeds are a modern invention, and he speculates that older forms of racialism differ from contemporary conceptions in that the former were often instinctual practices that were not informed by a "doctrine of race," whereas the latter are characterized by a malevolent and specious justification of irrational practices and beliefs (Locke 1992, 63–64).

Ethnic/Social Race

A necessary condition for the existence of a race on Locke's account is the "sense of kind, that sense of kith and kin" (Locke 1992, 11). Locke argues that the essential element in racial differentiation is this sense of kinship; that is, the realization and understanding among a group of people that "different practices [operate in] their society from those which [operate in other societies and therefore] determine their treatment of other groups" (Locke 1992, 20). Locke's claim is not that the sense of kind invariably becomes a racial sense; in fact, he argues that it is that same consciousness of kind that produces other social classes (Locke 1992, 20–22). The race sense is not in itself pernicious, according to Locke, it becomes so when it is based on invidious social practices (Locke 1992, 20).

The race sense determines the accentuated values, and the values in turn produce the persistence or resistance of certain culture-traits; that is, distinguishing qualities of the culture in terms of elements that are noticeably present or lacking (Locke 1989, 194–196). The persistence and resistance, or acceptance and rejection, of culture-traits—ways of acting, speaking, interrelating, worshipping, eating, expressing, and so on—establish a dominant pattern in a given culture. This dominant pattern consists of social norms toward which members of the group conform. With sufficient conformity around those norms, a culture-type is eventually established (Locke 1989, 194–195).

The sense of race is a functional aspect of culture. This race sense helps to emphasize and accentuate the values that become the conscious and salient symbols and tradition of the culture. These emphasized values are operational in the culture-making process and explain the persistence or resistance of cultural traits. The dominant patterns in a given culture are set by these stressed values. Moreover, these dominant patterns become social norms around which social conformation converges, and this eventually establishes what Locke calls the culture-type.

Locke argues that the biological or anthropological conception of race is an ethnic fiction (Locke 1992, 11–12). It is an ethnic fiction in two ways, one negative and one positive. On the negative side, the lack of correspondence or necessary relationship between a supposed biological and anthropological foundation for racial differentiation and the actual social groups that are distinguished points to the way in which race is an ethnic fiction. Specifically, non–biologically determined ethnic groups (or other kinds of social groups) are taken to be to be coextensive with supposedly biologically distinguished populations, when in fact they are not. In claiming that races are ethnic fictions, Locke is not claiming that races do not exist, or that they are not real. Rather, the claim is that the biological or anthropological factors—purity of blood, or purity of type—that are believed by some to differentiate races are not in fact the permanent or necessary designators of race groups. Races are the result of various interminglings and crossings of supposed biological or anthropological types. There is a fetishizing of the notion of biological purity as important to the concept of race, but that association of biology with race is merely fictitious. Locke writes: "As I pointed out, these groups, from the point of view of anthropology, are ethnic fictions. This does not mean that they do not exist, but it can be shown [that these groups do] not have as [permanent] designations those very factors upon which they pride themselves" (Locke 1992, 11).

On the positive side of Locke's view that race is an ethnic fiction, there is the fact that people self-identify as members of racial groups and forge psychologically a unity and coherence for racial groups that need not exist in reality. Such a sense can undeniably work to the benefit of a racial group. In showing that some conceptions of race are ethnic fictions, Locke does not mean to deny the practical utility of racial identification or ascription.

According to Locke, race is merely favorable or unfavorable social inheritance that masquerades as biological or anthropological inheritance; racial differences and inequalities are thus mistakenly attributed to factors that have not caused them, and hence will not determine either the duration or amelioration of inequalities and differentiations (Locke 1992, 12). The permanence of racial groups, if it is to be promoted, must be based on something other than notions of purity of blood or type. Conversely, if racial inequalities are to be eradicated, that too will likely require attention to, and control of, factors and elements of putatively racial groups other than their supposed biological or anthropological similarity.

LOCKE AND CONTEMPORARY RACE THEORY

What race amounts to for Locke is the characteristic differentiation of culture-type perpetuated through social heredity. Locke states that "[r]ace in the vital and basic sense is simply and primarily the culture-heredity, and that in its blendings and differentiations is properly analyzed on the basis of conformity to or variance from culture-type" (Locke 1989, 192). In other words, race is a matter of distinctive variations within culture, transmitted across generations. Such a view raises a whole host of questions for contemporary race theory. For one, Locke's view would mean that there are far more races on the planet than previously thought. In fact, many of the groups putatively regarded as one race will be found on this account to constitute several different races.

Although there are ways to explain it, a people will have the culture they have partly in consequence of the conditions under which they engage in cultural production. Relative lack, or ample availability, of resources is very likely to have an effect on the particular forms of expression various groups produce. Thus, on Locke's account, two distinct conceptions of race emerge: one, anthropological or biological race, the other, social or ethnic race. The latter, he claims is the more useful in explaining cultural assimilation, as the former has been thoroughly undermined as the cause of cultural variation. Moreover, the distinctions made, the very populations constituted by, anthropological race, rarely if ever coincide with those of ethnic race. The two conceptions carve up the world differently, and of the two Locke finds ethnic race the more scientifically tenable and useful. This is a matter of some debate in recent work in the philosophy of race. Also, advances in anthropology in recent decades have raised important questions about the viability and usefulness of treating genetically discernable populations of human beings as races. Locke provides us further reason to doubt the viability of such projects. Moreover, he was adept enough to envision that even in the light of such advances, it is a separate question whether or not the biological populations of anthropologist track closely the social populations putatively taken to be races.

Locke argues that the sociological conception of race which understands races as phases and stages and various groupings within social culture is the only sane understanding. It is a feature of every known civilization that it creates its own type—its own characteristic form and function. A civilization comes to know itself, and is known by others, to the extent that it recognizes itself, or is recognized as, of a certain or particular type. For Locke, civilization type is importantly related to the conception of social race—the only viable account of race on his view, after he has argued against physical and political conceptions—insofar as a social race just is "a conception of civilization type or civilization kind" (Locke 1992, 88).

The claim that race is a fact in the social or ethnic sense seems to align Locke's view with contemporary constructionist accounts of race. Moreover, the observation that social or ethnic race has been erroneously associated with physical race suggests that Locke would share with many contemporary constructionists writing about race today, the belief that races are not biologically distinct populations. Race for Locke is a social, and not a biological, reality. It is significantly related to social culture. Races are determined or differentiated by social land historical forces of the same sort that cause differences in culture-type between nations and classes. He is thus lead to a reconstructionist view of race, believing that a thorough redefinition of race is necessary. He simultaneously argues for "the independent definition of race in the ethnic or social sense, together with the independent investigation of its differences and their causes apart from the investigation of the factors and differentiae of physical race" (Locke 1924, 426).

Locke's understanding of race changes many of the dynamics of contemporary race theory and practice. Every civilization, Locke argues, in understanding its characteristic type, imposes the standards of that type on any individual or group that aims to participate in the civilization. Locke admits that the imposition of this standard is somewhat arbitrary, but not for that reason any less required for membership and participation. The standards of conformity required for participation in a particular civilization can be more or less stringent, and the degree of conformity required can vary. It is of course possible that an individual or group might decide to reject the specific standards of incorporation into a given civilization type, but such rejection will affect the level of participation an individual or group is able to attain in a civilization, or if they are able to participate at all. Social assimilation, or the assimilation of social culture, is on Locke's understanding a necessity of modern political and social organization.

One must, of course, distinguish between physical and cultural assimilation. The two are not necessarily linked, and one can occur to a greater or lesser degree without the other. Locke contends that the supposed superiority and inferiority of racial groups is rooted in the various degrees of success achieved by each group. Locke understands what was for him contemporary talk about superior and inferior races to really be talk of the success or failure of ethnic groups. This is one of the difficulties in Locke's philosophy of race. At times, it seems that for Locke races are various forms of social differentiation, such as classes, castes, ethnic groups, or subcultures, united by a sense of solidarity and conceived in a particularly racial way, both internally and externally.

Locke can be fruitfully read as a qualified or partial eliminativist. There are certainly eliminativist strands in Locke's philosophy of race. He does not want to eliminate the concept of race, but he does want to eliminate certain race practices, race creeds, and some pernicious forms of race prejudice. Others of these things he argues should be reconstructed and still others left to undergo transformation as the result of other social phenomena. In the case of race prejudices, Locke argues that they should be eradicated. Race prejudices, Locke claims, are ultimately based on cultural differences and differences in the type of civilization. Racial difference is in reality a difference in the social consciousness of groups. Race prejudice erroneously assigns that variation to biological and anthropological factors that have been shown to be unrelated to racial groups. This leaves racial prejudice in the paradoxical situation of being "an almost instinctive aberration in favor of anthropological factors erected into social distinctions" without any scientific warrant for so doing (Locke 1992, 10). Our race prejudices are rooted in certain aberrant psychological predispositions and tendencies. Often times, these habits function unconsciously, but though unconscious, Locke does not think they are beyond the purview of control and adaptation. Moreover, race creeds are for Locke distorted conceptual schemes and at the root of our notions of racial superiority and inferiority. Locke argues that both race prejudice and race creeds can and should be eliminated as features of our race practice. This is what leads me to characterize his view as a partial or qualified eliminativism. Although he is ultimately in favor of retaining the concept of race, he also strongly advocates jettisoning the more pernicious forms of our race practice.

References

Locke, A. (1924/1989). "The Concept of Race as Applied to Social Culture." In *The Philosophy of Alain Locke: Harlem Renaissance and Beyond*, edited by Leonard Harris, 424–429. Philadelphia: Temple University Press.

Locke, A. (1992). *Race Contacts and Interracial Relations: Lectures on the Theory and Practice of Race*. Edited by Jeffery C. Stewart. Washington, DC: Howard University Press.

CHAPTER 17

DU BOIS, APPIAH, AND OUTLAW ON RACIAL IDENTITY

CHIKE JEFFERS

W. E. B. Du Bois's 1897 essay, "The Conservation of Races," has been described as holding something like the significance for contemporary philosophy of race and African American philosophy that Descartes's *Meditations on First Philosophy* holds for modern epistemology and philosophy of mind. It attained this status not immediately, though, but rather in the wake of Kwame Anthony Appiah's engagement with it in his 1985 article, "The Uncompleted Argument: Du Bois and the Illusion of Race." Appiah's article helped stimulate debates about the nature and existence of race that remain central to philosophy of race today. One of the most prominent contributors to these debates is Lucius Outlaw—indeed, the "Appiah-Outlaw debate" has often been treated as the most important instance of the conflict over "Conservation" (Gooding-Williams 1996; Stubblefield 2005).

I will describe that debate and discuss what has become of it in more recent times. I will focus on the question of the value of a racial identity more than on the existence of races, but these issues are, in the context of this debate, intimately connected. My aim will be to illuminate the philosophical contributions of Du Bois, Appiah, and Outlaw as well as to show that, as a result of evolution on Appiah's part, we can observe the gradual development of a kind of consensus among the debate's two participants.

DU BOIS ON RACIAL IDENTITY

Du Bois delivered "Conservation" on March 5, 1897, to the group of men gathered for the first meeting of the American Negro Academy. One striking thing about the way the essay opens is how Du Bois describes, sympathetically explains, and yet also sharply criticizes tendencies that he ascribes in a generalizing manner to the "American Negro." He begins:

> The American Negro has always felt an intense personal interest in discussions as to the origins and destinies of races: primarily because back of most discussions of race with which he

is familiar, have lurked certain assumptions as to his natural abilities, as to his political, intellectual and moral status, which he felt were wrong. (Du Bois 1996, 38)

Familiarity with discussions of race in which black inferiority has been either implicitly assumed or explicitly proclaimed leads naturally, Du Bois suggests, to a kind of touchiness about the subject. Also natural is the proactive response to such discussions and implications that Du Bois describes:

> He has, consequently, been led to deprecate and minimize race distinctions, to believe intensely that out of one blood God created all nations, and to speak of human brotherhood as though it were the possibility of an already dawning tomorrow. (Du Bois 1996, 38)

Du Bois thus introduces us, in the first paragraph of "Conservation," to a perspective according to which the best way to think about race is to think about it as little as possible, to downplay its importance, and to uphold instead the unity of the human species both as a reality and as an ideal. He then criticizes this perspective, claiming that "in our calmer moments we must acknowledge that human beings are divided into races" (Du Bois 1996, 38–39). He implores his audience to take the reality of race seriously with this admonition: "It is necessary, therefore, in planning our movements, in guiding our future development, that at times we rise above the pressing, but smaller questions of separate schools and cars, wage-discrimination and lynch law, to survey the whole question of race in human philosophy and to lay, on a basis of broad knowledge and careful insight, those large lines of policy and higher ideals which may form our guiding lines and boundaries in the practical difficulties of everyday" (Du Bois 1996, 39).

This passage is notable, first, because it tells us more about the perspective on race that Du Bois ascribes to African Americans and which he wishes to challenge. He indicates that, from this perspective, speculative discussions of the origins and destinies of races warrant suspicion and even scorn, but discussions of race may be seen as important and worth having if they concern such practical problems as what to do about racial segregation in education and transportation, racial discrimination in employment, and racially motivated extrajudicial killings. Indeed, we can presume that the viewpoint being described here consistently holds race to be a matter of illegitimate division, whether illegitimate in the sense of being false, as in the case of beliefs about white superiority and black inferiority, or illegitimate in the sense of being morally wrong, as in the case of the social, political, and economic subjugation of African Americans under Jim Crow law in the South and systematic discrimination elsewhere. From this perspective, having a racial identity is not something to value. It is, at best, a current imposition upon one's personal identity that one ought to acknowledge as significant given the ways it is related to one's chances of safety and success in life. When envisioning the future, however, it is something that one should hope all people will eventually be able to transcend in order to become more invested in our shared humanity.

What the quoted passage also tells us, though, is that Du Bois rejects this way of thinking as narrow and hasty. It is, in his view, missing something. So what might that be? Could it be that the politically minded African American who repudiates racial difference is missing something because (sticking with the pronoun Du Bois used) his position is a kind of antiscientific wishful thinking that ought to be replaced by a sober acceptance of the natural fact that human bodies and bloodlines differ in significant ways? Du Bois considers such a possibility and thus the second perspective on race that he evaluates views racial difference as part of the natural world, to be studied by the methods of natural science. Racial identities, on such a view, whether we value them or not, will be firmly grounded in our physical and biological differences.

As it turns out, though, Du Bois does not think looking to natural science reveals clear divisions between humans, grouping them into distinct races. In his view, scientists have failed to carve up the physical variety of humankind, in a nonarbitrary way, into discrete sets of characteristics corresponding to discernibly significant groups. He thus claims that "the grosser physical differences of color, hair and bone go but a short way toward explaining the different roles which groups of men have played in human progress" (Du Bois 1996, 40). Races "transcend scientific definition." although they are nevertheless "clearly defined to the eye of the historian and sociologist" (Du Bois 1996, 40). So what, then, on his view, is a race? Du Bois answers:

> It is a vast family of human beings, generally of common blood and language, always of common history, traditions and impulses, who are both voluntarily and involuntarily striving together for the accomplishment of certain more or less vividly conceived ideals of life. (Du Bois 1996, 40)

With its talk of shared traditions and impulses, we may identify this definition as one that depicts a race as a kind of cultural group.

Here, finally, we come upon a view of race that makes it easy to understand why a person might not merely acknowledge but also value her racial identity. If racial identities are, properly understood, cultural identities, a strong sense of attachment to one's race is as normal as any kind of pride in being part of a culture. In the case of the black race, Du Bois wants to go further: it is not just normal but imperative that black people value their racial identity. To see why, note first that, given his view that races are characterized in part by the fact that they strive for various ideals, the existence of racial diversity is directly linked to human progress. Modern civilization, as Du Bois understands it, is the result of strivings leading to distinctive cultural contributions by groups he considers to be races: the English have stood for "constitutional liberty and commercial freedom," the Germans for "science and philosophy," the Romance nations for "literature and art" (Du Bois 1996, 42). According to Du Bois, "some of the great races of today—particularly the Negro race—have not as yet given to civilization the full spiritual message which they are capable of giving" (Du Bois 1996, 42). If black people fail to value their racial identity, they do a disservice not only to themselves but to the world as a whole. They rob themselves and the world of the valuable cultural gifts that their particularity enables them to develop.

We therefore have in "Conservation" an argument for seeing racial identities as valuable, with particular focus on the value that has come into the world and that can be brought into the world through black racial identity. The investment in perpetuating and strengthening black identity that Du Bois encourages is not meant to replace opposition to antiblack oppression. He exhorts his people: "as a race we must strive by race organization, by race solidarity, by race unity to the realization of that broader humanity which freely recognizes differences in men, but sternly deprecates inequality in their opportunities of development" (Du Bois 1996, 44). Racial hierarchies ought to be fought but not through seeking to transcend race. Racial diversity ought to be valued as a source of progress, and racial identities are not to be thrown off but embraced.

APPIAH AGAINST DU BOIS

Appiah's work on race leading up to and including his 1992 book, *In My Father's House: Africa in the Philosophy of Culture*, takes us in the opposite direction of "Conservation"—that is to say, toward not valuing but rather seeking to leave behind and go beyond racial identities. In "The Uncompleted Argument," later revised and included as Chapter 2 of *In My Father's House*, he famously criticizes the idea that Du Bois offers us a consistently sociohistorical account of race in "Conservation." Here is how his argument goes: Du Bois's definition of race, quoted earlier, includes references to common blood and common language, although these are qualified as being "generally" rather than "always" part of what distinguishes a race, and then references to common history, common traditions, common impulses, and common strivings toward ideals. Clearly, if Du Bois has gone beyond the scientific definition, common blood must not be of central significance. Common impulses and strivings should be set to one side because these will either be rooted in shared biological features or shared sociohistorical features, but they cannot themselves be what distinguish races. Common language is also obviously inessential, as one can see in the case of the black race, which is not unified by any one language. This leaves us to ponder the common history and common traditions components, which Appiah does not separate. He asks: "What is a family of common history?" (1985, 26; 1992, 31). Then he makes what is perhaps his most important move, arguing that to appeal to a common history to distinguish a group is circular and thus uninformative: "sharing a common group history cannot be a criterion for being members of the same group, for we would have to be able to identify the group in order to identify its history" (1985, 27; 1992, 32).

But what, then, is left? What else could be the basis for distinguishing races on Du Bois's account? Appiah finds the key in reconsidering Du Bois's idiosyncratic list of eight major races: "the Slavs of Eastern Europe, the Teutons of middle Europe, the English of Great Britain and America, the Romance nations of Southern and Western Europe, the Negroes of Africa and America, the Semitic people of Western Asia and Northern Africa, the Hindoos of Central Asia and the Mongolians of Eastern Asia" (Du Bois 1996, 40). He notices a similarity among these groups that Du Bois does not explicitly mention, namely, that they are each associated with a particular geographical region, at least ancestrally. "Du Bois' talk of common history," argues Appiah, "conceals his superaddition of a geographical criterion: group history is, in part, the history of people who have lived in the same place" (1985, 28–29; 1992, 33). Once this implicit geographical element of the definition is uncovered, Appiah perceives a relatively consistent way of distinguishing different races: "The criterion Du Bois actually uses amounts to this: people are members of the same race if they share features in virtue of being descended largely from people of the same region" (1985, 29; 1992, 33–34).

What kind of features they share, however, depends on which race is in question. As Appiah understands it, "Anglo-Americans are English" because of a shared cultural feature—that is, they speak English in virtue of being descended from settlers from the British Isles (1985, 29; 1992, 33–34). Insofar as the feature that distinguishes it as a race is cultural, I take it that Appiah can have no quarrel with this race being described as sociohistorical. On the other hand, if "Afro-Americans are Negroes," it cannot be a matter of language, as they speak the same language as Anglo-Americans and not any indigenous African language (1985, 29;

1992, 33–34). What they most clearly share with those in their land of ancestral origin is a set of physical features. But, if Appiah is right about this, then there is nothing sociohistorical about what distinguishes the black race from others. Appiah concludes that Du Bois failed to transcend the scientific definition of race and that what he opposes in "Conservation" is not so much the idea that physical difference is significant but rather the association of black physical difference with inferiority: "Du Bois elected, in effect, to admit that color was a sign of racial essence but to deny that the cultural capacities of the black-skinned, curly-haired members of humankind—the capacities determined by their essence—were inferior to those of the white-skinned, straighter-haired ones" (1992, 34).

It should already be evident that this critique has negative implications for the idea of valuing racial identity, especially black racial identity. Du Bois had seemed to suggest that once we recognize races as primarily cultural groups, we will see embracing one's racial identity as an important element of encouraging useful cultural contributions. Appiah suggests, on the other hand, that this project is hopeless, as only groups that we are unlikely to classify as races—like the English—will plausibly count as culturally delineated. The race most important to Du Bois, by contrast, may count as a paradigmatic race but that is precisely because the term "Negro" refers to a grouping of various peoples along physical lines that can only be seen as having distinctive cultural capacities if we buy into the biological essentialism that Du Bois appeared on the surface to be displacing. To embrace one's racial identity, as a result, is to misguidedly embrace the illusion that racial concepts can coherently and accurately describe reality. Freedom from such illusion, on the other hand, will involve ceasing to identify as members of different races.

A second way in which Appiah portrays investment in racial identity as problematic during this early part of his work on race is through his conception of racism. Appiah distinguishes between racialism, extrinsic racism, and intrinsic racism. Racialism is belief in the existence of races. Since Appiah at this point views talk of races as reducing ultimately to ideas of biological difference, he defines racialism as the view that "there are heritable characteristics, possessed by members of our species, which allow us to divide them into a small set of races, in such a way that all the members of these races share certain traits and tendencies with each other that they do not share with members of any other race" (1992, 13). Racialism is false but is not necessarily morally problematic, as one may believe that people of each race, despite their differences, deserve equal respect and equal treatment. Racism denies this. Extrinsic racists make distinctions in how they treat people of different races on the basis of the moral value of the characteristics they take different races to possess. They believe that "members of different races differ in respects that *warrant* the differential treatment" (Appiah 1992, 13). Intrinsic racism, by contrast, does not depend on evaluations of different racial traits. For intrinsic racists, "the bare fact of being of the same race is a reason for preferring one person to another" (Appiah 1992, 14).

Appiah sees Pan-Africanism of the kind espoused by Du Bois in "Conservation" as motivated by intrinsic racism (1992, 45). He notes that we are quicker to see extrinsic racism as wrong, because those who have used racial difference as justification for oppression have generally appealed to extrinsic racist ideas while, in response to such oppression, "the discourse of racial solidarity is usually expressed through the language of *intrinsic* racism" (1992, 17). That being said, it remains the case that, in his view, intrinsic racism is not only problematic because it depends on the false notion of racialism; it is also "a moral error" (1992, 18). This is because, "[e]ven if racialism were correct, the bare fact that someone was of another race would be no reason to treat them worse—or better—than someone of my race" (1992, 18). Valuing racial identity in the way that Du Bois encourages in "Conservation" is therefore portrayed in Appiah's work from this time as involving not only investment in the importance of something that is not actually real but also the moral wrong of racism. Appiah gives us multiple reasons to give up on racial identities, to define ourselves in ways that ignore the myth of race and affirm our shared humanity as well as the equal value of all.

Outlaw Against Appiah

The best known version of Outlaw's critique is his 1996 essay, " 'Conserve' Races? In Defense of W. E. B. Du Bois." Outlaw condemns Appiah's step-by-step strategy of analyzing and evaluating "*individually* each of the elements in Du Bois's definition" (Outlaw 1996, 23). It seems to Outlaw that what Du Bois offers us is "a *cluster* concept" in which no single element of the definition is fundamental and thus no single element could bear the weight of being evaluated as that upon which all the others depend (1996, 28). Appiah's focus on the common history component and his criticism of it as circular is an example of the kind of worthless point-scoring that Outlaw sees as resulting from this inappropriate approach.

Outlaw also charges Appiah with missing the major motivating aim behind Du Bois's account of race. "It is *not* simply—or even primarily—an effort devoted to definition and taxonomy," he writes, but rather "a decidedly *political* project" (1996, 28). Rather than focusing above all on whether Du Bois provides a *description* of race that makes it clear how to neatly fit people into distinct categories, Outlaw believes we need to acknowledge and appreciate Du Bois's effort to offer a particular *prescription* to a specific group of people experiencing certain living conditions. As he puts it, "Du Bois's project involves prescribing norms for the social reconstruction of personal and social identities and for self-appropriation by a people suffering racialized subordination, which norms were to aid in mobilizing and guiding members of the race in their efforts to realize emancipatory social transformation leading, ultimately, to a flourishing humanism" (1996, 28).

Outlaw argues for the value of racial identity in a way that builds on Du Bois. Given the ways in which intergenerational cultural transmission can benefit individuals and communities, it seems to Outlaw that it would be completely compatible with the future flourishing of humanity if racial diversity, understood as a form of cultural diversity, were to remain a feature of human life indefinitely. Thus, he writes that "for many of us the continued existence of discernible racial/ethnic communities of meaning is highly desirable, *even if, in the very next instant, racism and invidious ethnocentrism in every form and manifestation were to disappear forever*" (1996, 34). Another way to put this is that Outlaw believes in the goal of racial equality rather than and, indeed, *in opposition to* the goal of a postracial world.

Appiah's Evolution

Appiah's seminal 1996 essay, "Race, Culture, Identity: Misunderstood Connections," is divided into two parts: "Analysis: Against Races" and "Synthesis: For Racial Identities." The first part is a sophisticated new argument for the position that there are no races. Appiah intertwines philosophy of race with philosophy of language, arguing that whatever theory of meaning we adopt, the word "race" will not be plausibly understood as referring to anything real.

In the second part of the essay, however, Appiah reflects on and explains why denying the existence of races and thus decrying belief in their existence does not mean denying the existence or downplaying the importance of *racial identities*. He begins by bringing up his previous argument that Du Bois managed "not to replace a biological notion but simply to hide it from view" (Appiah 1996, 75). With admirable humility, he admits that "there are various difficulties with the way that argument proceeded" and he announces his intention to do better by trying to "reconstruct a sociohistorical view that has more merit than I previously conceded" (1996, 75). Note that there is a footnote to one of the quotations just mentioned in which he makes it clear who did the most to spur him to make this effort: "Lucius Outlaw has remonstrated with me about this in the past; these rethinkings are prompted largely by discussion with him" (1996, 75).

So what is the new sociohistorical view that Appiah presents to us? It involves first recognizing that, while racial essences are not real, the practice of applying racial labels to people—historically, on the basis of mistaken beliefs concerning racial essences—is real and has obviously had very important effects. Focusing on the United States, Appiah notes that processes such as the racialization of slavery and, later on, immigration from China and other parts of East Asia resulted eventually in the relative stability of the practice of labeling some as black, some as whites, and some as "Orientals" (we can perhaps take the fact that he leaves out others, such as people from South Asia, as a sign that he takes the practice of labeling them as a distinct race to have been comparatively less stable). Appiah writes: "The result is that there are at least three sociocultural objects in America—blacks, whites and Orientals—whose membership at any time is relatively and increasingly determinate" (1996, 77).

What interests Appiah, though, is not merely the social but rather most of all the psychological effects of the application of racial labels. These labels can "shape the ways people conceive of themselves and their projects" (1996, 78). Racial identities, as Appiah understands them, exist because people who meet the socially accepted criteria for the application of a racial label R and who are thus ascribed the identity of being an R often actually identify as an R, "where identification implies a shaping role for the label in the intentional acts of the possessors, so that they sometimes act *as an R*" (1996, 79). It is sensitivity to the meaningfulness of this psychological phenomenon that leads Appiah in this essay to acknowledge, to a certain extent and in certain ways, the value of racial identity.

First, Appiah acknowledges that the possession of a racial identity is *not* reducible to a mistaken belief that one has inherited a particular essence. He certainly thinks that identifying with a racial label causally depends upon "a history of associating possessors of the label with an inherited racial essence" (1996, 81–82). But it is possible, he grants, for the label and the associated identity to outlive belief in racial essences "provided both ascription and identification continue" (1996, 82). Second, Appiah recognizes that it makes good sense for people whose racial identities are disparaged because of their subordinate place in a traditional racial hierarchy to react to this not by giving up their racial identity but by demanding respect. He writes:

> An African-American after the Black Power movement takes the old script of self-hatred, the script in which he or she is a nigger, and works, in community with others, to construct a series

of positive black life scripts. In these life scripts, being a Negro is recoded as being black: and this requires, among other things, refusing to assimilate to white norms of speech and behavior. And if one is to be black in a society that is racist then one has constantly to deal with assaults on one's dignity. In this context, insisting on the right to live a dignified life will not be enough. It will not even be enough to require that one be treated with equal dignity despite being black: for that will require a concession that being black counts naturally or to some degree against one's dignity. And so one will end up asking to be respected *as a black*. (1996, 98)

What Appiah recognizes here shows what makes "Conservation" so powerful: Du Bois's call, way before the Black Power movement, for African Americans to demand respect not through their blackness being put aside but precisely through respect for the value of their black identity.

However, Appiah also believes that tensions naturally arise between valuing not just racial identity but any collective identity, on the one hand, and valuing individual autonomy, on the other. He argues that collective identities have a tendency to "go imperial": to become demands for authenticity that too tightly restrict the freedom of the individual to shape a life of his or her own choosing (1996, 103). This reason for ambivalence is expressed at the very beginning of the essay, when he is setting out what he hopes to accomplish in it, in a way that seems to continue to point us toward the goal of a postracial future: "I will argue for an ethical conclusion: that there is danger in making racial identities too central to our conceptions of ourselves; while there is a place for racial identities in a world shaped by racism, I shall argue, if we are to move beyond racism we shall have, in the end, to move beyond current racial identities" (1996, 32).

"Race, Culture, Identity" is thus a site of compromise and creativity but also ambivalence. After this essay, Appiah's interest in identity continued to grow, as can be seen in his 2005 book, *The Ethics of Identity*, and his 2006 book, *Cosmopolitanism: Ethics in a World of Strangers*. In *The Ethics of Identity*, Appiah treats John Stuart Mill as a useful guide to thinking about identity precisely because of how concerned he was about individual autonomy. Appiah argues that Millian individualism does not mean lacking regard for social identity—indeed, "individuality presupposes sociability" (Appiah 2005, 20). Although much of the book thus focuses on the compatibility of concerns for individual and social identity, its last chapter, "Rooted Cosmopolitanism," and his subsequent book, *Cosmopolitanism*, focus on the compatibility of concern for specific social identities with concern for our globally shared identity as human beings. It is part of Appiah's definition of cosmopolitanism that those who count as cosmopolitan "take seriously the value not just of human life but of particular human lives, which means taking an interest in the practices and beliefs that lend them significance" (Appiah 2006a, xv). What this means is that cosmopolitans necessarily locate some value in social identities, since these are among what gives value to particular human lives. I see Appiah's appreciation of the value of social identities in both of these books as usefully preparing the way for consensus with Outlaw.

Let us now look at Appiah's 2007 essay "Does Truth Matter to Identity?" Appiah argues in this essay that there are many ways in which what is true or what one can truly explain does not matter much to the ethical significance of identities. Where truth does matter to identity is in what Appiah calls the "normative grounding" of an identity, which he defines as the truths about identities that "justify the place they have in people's lives" (Appiah 2007, 40). Building on what we saw him admit in "Race, Culture, Identity," Appiah notes that, while many take the lack of distinctive biological properties distinguishing "racial groups" to mean that these cannot be normatively grounded identities, this seems to him, in 2007, unlike in the 1980s and early 1990s, "just plain wrong" (2007, 41; see also Appiah 2006b).

It is notable, though, that there are also significant contrasts with "Race, Culture, Identity." First, perhaps precisely because of the point just mentioned concerning the irrelevance of the nonexistence of racial essences, nowhere in this essay does Appiah view it as necessary to contrast his acceptance of the reality of racial identities with a denial of the existence of races. Secondly, and even more strikingly, though, is what he says in a section of the essay entitled "Abandoning Identities." A central point of the section is that social identities are so flexible that one should remain generally open-minded about reform being sufficient for overcoming ethical or epistemic inadequacies, rather than abandonment being necessary. In the case of racial identities, he reflects critically on the way an account of race like the one Michael Omi and Howard Winant famously developed, according to which we can study different "racial formations," seems to provide an argument for working toward the eventual abandonment of racial identities, because "it looks as though they keep reconfiguring themselves somehow as mechanisms of oppression" (Appiah 2007, 39). Appiah resists this thought: "But I am enough of a Pollyanna to think that it is not yet clear that this is what they must be" (2007, 39). As subtle as it may be, we have here Appiah expressing optimism about whether racial identities in the future may be justifiable sources of value rather than forever being part of a dynamic but irredeemable configuration of oppression and privilege. This is the goal of racial equality, rather than a postracial world.

The last aspect of Appiah's evolution to be mentioned is found in his 2013 book, *Lines of Descent: W.E.B. Du Bois and the Emergence of Identity*. That work combines, as the title indicates, Appiah's return to thinking about Du Bois but also his continued interest in identity. Appiah argues that Du Bois did much to originate what he describes as the presently dominant conception of social identities. When Appiah spells out what he takes this to be, he describes "the nominal, normative, subjective classifications of persons" (Appiah 2013, 152). But this is precisely Appiah's account of identity, which means that, in this most recent book, Appiah sets up Du Bois not as an unfortunate hostage of the concept of race but rather as a valued predecessor and a source of inspiration with respect to his own conception of race. The transformation is thus complete, and the Du Boisian consensus has been achieved.

It would be misleading to suggest that Appiah and Outlaw have become theoretically indistinguishable. They remain very different. What I am arguing is that, in spite of their differences, Appiah's evolution has brought it about that they can agree on an answer to the question of whether we may have good reason to value racial identity and desire its indefinite persistence. Whereas the early Appiah led us to say "no," Appiah today, like Outlaw, can explain and defend answering "yes." Furthermore, both treat Du Bois as providing grounds for such an answer. If, as I do, one finds this a welcome point of consensus, the interesting question becomes: Where do philosophers interested in racial identity go from here?

REFERENCES

Appiah, Kwame Anthony. (1985). "The Uncompleted Argument: Du Bois and the Illusion of Race." *Critical Inquiry* 12 (1): 21–37.

Appiah, Kwame Anthony. (1992). *In My Father's House: Africa in the Philosophy of Culture*. New York: Oxford University Press.

Appiah, Kwame Anthony. (1996). "Race, Culture, Identity: Misunderstood Connections." In *Color Conscious: The Political Morality of Race*, edited by K. Anthony Appiah and Amy Gutmann, 30–105. Princeton, NJ: Princeton University Press.

Appiah, Kwame Anthony. (2005). *The Ethics of Identity*. Princeton, NJ: Princeton University Press.

Appiah, Kwame Anthony. (2006a). *Cosmopolitanism: Ethics in a World of Strangers*. New York: W.W. Norton.

Appiah, Kwame Anthony. (2006b). "How to Decide If Races Exist." *Proceedings of the Aristotelian Society* 106 (1): 365–382.

Appiah, Kwame Anthony. (2007). "Does Truth Matter to Identity?" In *Race or Ethnicity? On Black and Latino Identity*, edited by Jorge J. E. Gracia, 19–44. Ithaca, NY: Cornell University Press.

Appiah, Kwame Anthony. (2013). *Lines of Descent: W. E. B. Du Bois and the Emergence of Identity*. Cambridge, MA: Harvard University Press.

Du Bois, W. E. B. (1996). "The Conservation of Races." In *The Oxford W. E. B. Du Bois Reader*, edited by Eric J. Sundquist, 38–47. New York: Oxford University Press.

Gooding-Williams, Robert. (1996). "Outlaw, Appiah, and Du Bois's "The Conservation of Races." In *W. E. B. Du Bois on Race and Culture: Philosophy, Politics, and Poetics*, edited by Bernard W. Bell, Emily R. Grosholz, and James B. Stewart, 39–56. New York: Routledge.

Outlaw, Lucius. (1996). "'Conserve' Races? In Defense of W.E.B. Du Bois." In *W. E. B. Du Bois on Race and Culture: Philosophy, Politics, and Poetics*, edited by edited by Bernard W. Bell, Emily R. Grosholz, and James B. Stewart, 15–38. New York: Routledge.

Stubblefield, Anna. (2005). *Ethics Along the Color Line*. Ithaca, NY: Cornell University Press.

CHAPTER 18

CORNEL WEST, AMERICAN PRAGMATISM, AND THE POST-OBAMA RACIAL/ SOCIAL DYNAMICS

CLARENCE SHOLÉ JOHNSON

RECENT violent racial events in the United States, sparked by a number of killings of young black men beginning in Florida with Trayvon Martin's murder by a white "crime vigilante," George Zimmerman, have provoked critical discussions about the issue of racial violence by whites against young black males in the contemporary United States (Yancy and Jones 2013; Zack 2015, 63–65 and 76–86). Trayvon Martin's killing was followed in relatively quick succession by the killing of nineteen-year-old Michael Brown by a white police officer in Ferguson, Missouri, and of twelve-year-old Tamir Rice in Cleveland, Ohio. Then, Eric Garner was asphyxiated by a group of white police officers in New York City, and after that, Freddie Gray died under suspicious circumstances while in police custody in Baltimore, Maryland. Finally, fifty-year-old Walter Scott was shot in the back while fleeing a white police officer in South Carolina (Schmidt and Apuzzo 2015). Considering that all these victims of violence were unarmed, their untimely deaths within the context of a racial encounter are all the more egregious because those deaths seem to indicate a pattern, and so highlight a very potent existential threat hovering over every young black male in the society. As a major crisis for the nation, but especially for black America, such a pattern of extrajudicial killings has motivated a public outcry against racial injustice from various quarters of the society with calls for social and racial justice.

But while such calls have been made and outrage expressed in certain news media outlets and by multiracial social activists "in the field," there seems to have been a philosophically inaudible response from Cornel West, a leading protagonist of social justice. As I show later, West does respond in some way, but his response is neither philosophical nor robust compared to the kind he offers to what he calls the nihilistic threat to black America (West 1994). West's theoretical silence is therefore cause for concern in light of his self-definition as a prophetic pragmatist and a public intellectual, a self-described intellectual freedom fighter whose role is to serve as a critical organic catalyst for change in society (hooks and West 1991, 27–30; also Osborne 1996, 137). It is West's philosophical silence on the specific issue of the extrajudicial killings of young black males that I examine in this study. In particular, I contrast West's use of his prophetic pragmatism to articulate and discuss some social issues internal to the African American community, as brought out in his bestseller *Race Matters* (West 1994), with his comparative silence on the aforementioned number of racially motivated extrajudicial killings of young black men. Of course, it does not follow from West's alleged silence on this new existential threat facing young black men that he has nothing to offer by way of addressing it. However, it would be disingenuous of scholars of West's views to ignore his relative lack of visibility (or his opacity) on this matter if they do not interrogate it, especially in the context of West's self-identification as prophetic pragmatist already noted. It is precisely such interrogation I undertake here. To begin, some contextualization of West's philosophical position is in order.

CONTEXTUALIZING PROPHETIC PRAGMATISM

Most philosophers situate themselves and their work within an intellectual tradition, and Cornel West is no exception. West's intellectual framework is eclectic, being a potpourri of American pragmatism, Marxist social thought, Kierkegaardian existentialism, and black prophetic Christianity (Johnson 2003). So it suffices to say here that West draws upon these different intellectual traditions to define his intellectual position, which he calls prophetic pragmatism. It is his prophetic pragmatist stance I want to briefly elaborate in order to engage the current racial and social issue that concerns me, viz. the new existential threat to black males.

Pragmatism, as is well known, is an action-oriented theory that considers ideas useful only insofar as those ideas can produce results in the form of action. So prophetic pragmatism, as a variant of American pragmatism, is a philosophical position that invokes critical discourse as an instrument to engage and solve problems that confront the society, especially in situations of moral urgency. And it is through the utility of critical discourse that prophetic pragmatism seeks to alter the social and political landscape of individual lived realities (Johnson 2003, 18–20).

West uses the term "prophetic" to brand his own variant of American pragmatism in order to call attention to the moral dimension of his purpose. He likens himself to the ancient biblical prophets who traveled from place to place to call out the moral and social failings in ancient Jewish society. As pragmatist, West allies himself with the pragmatist outlook of Ralph Waldo Emerson and John Dewey because both Emerson and Dewey were concerned with the prevailing social issues that confronted the society of their day, with a view to putting forward solutions to those issues (West 1989). West's prophetic pragmatist stance is amply demonstrated in his *Race Matters* (1994), where he engages various social issues in the black community in particular, but in the larger American society overall.

One such issue West takes up in *Race Matters* (1994) is what he characterizes as the existential threat that hovers over the black youth. The existential threat is a life of absolute worthlessness and utter bleakness that eventuates in social, and sometimes physical, death. West describes this threat as "nihilistic," and he defines this specific form of nihilism as a life without meaning, hope, love, and care. West identifies the source of this nihilistic threat as certain (external) factors over which the black youth have little or no control: economic forces and institutions that for the most part deprive them of gainful employment and so render them useless in the political economy; negative sociocultural forces such as a militaristic and machismo outlook that valorizes violence and uses it as a statement of affirming masculinity, an outlook that thus influences their behavior; institutional failure in the black community that is familial, religious, and secular, with the consequence that such institutions fail to provide a sense of purpose; and a paucity of quality leadership (among the elders) in the black community. As an intellectual, West identifies this threat, conceptualizes it, and traces its sources to the institutional setup and/or breakdown of values in the society at large. As a prophetic voice, similar to the biblical prophets, he calls out what/whom he considers the culprit(s) for the phenomenon in question. And as a pragmatist in the tradition of Emerson and Dewey, he proposes some solutions (in the form of ideas) to address the problem. His solution consists of an ethic of (self-) love and a politics of conversion. An ethic of love is a psychic transformation of the self by which a person would see himself or herself as intrinsically valuable, and thus would adopt a new outlook that would enable her or him to combat a hitherto bleak outlook on life. A politics of conversion is, in essence, a social practice of seeing one's humanity reflected in others and vice versa, and this would motivate each person to see himself or herself as the other's keeper.

At this point it is worth distinguishing between the originating cause of the nihilistic threat and the threat itself. According to West, the causal origin of the nihilistic threat is *external* in the sense of the politicoeconomic and sociocultural institutional forces over which the youth have no control. But the resulting nihilistic threat itself is an internal psychological effect from these external forces. More perspicuously, nihilism is an *internal long-term dispositional condition of the youth*, a psychological malady/affliction, "a disease of the soul" as West calls it, which infects the overall psyche of the youth and carries over to their outlook about life's utter *meaninglessness*. This bleak existential outlook then gets expressed in the kind of overt actions the youth perform: crime, violence, senseless killings, and the like. Of note, the victims of such crimes, as are the perpetrators for whom life has no meaning, are themselves mainly black. This is because the crimes occur mainly within black underclass neighborhoods. Since nihilism, as distinct from its cause, is a psychological condition, West's proposed remedy therefore is a *psychological transformation* in the form of an ethic of (self-) love and a politics of conversion.

No doubt, West, in distinguishing and critiquing the external causative factors that produce this psychological effect in the youth, is also *implicitly* arguing that a condition of eliminating this psychological effect is to dismantle the causative factors in the first place. However, because his explicit argument to obviate the disease of the soul is a psychic transformation *even if the external causative factors remain in place*, some therefore think that his proposed solution to the alleged nihilistic threat does not go far enough. For example, West proposes an ethic of love and a politics of conversion as solution to the nihilistic threat, and he also criticizes the political leadership in the black community. But he fails to call out economically successful blacks for failing to provide economic leadership that could possibly help alleviate the dismal economic condition in the community which is partly responsible for the nihilistic outlook (Johnson 2003). But others even doubt that the existential condition West characterizes as nihilistic actually obtains in the black community (Lott 1994). And yet still others have charged West with reducing the sociocultural factors that influence black inner-city life into an incurable pathological condition of the black residents themselves, thereby unfairly rendering them blameworthy for their plight (Headley 2001, 72–76; also Dyson 2015, 27). Except to note that these criticisms have been leveled against West, I will not pursue them further. Instead, I want to contrast the nihilistic/existential threat thus outlined, and West's examination of it, with the *new* existential threat to black men in our contemporary social set-ting, and West's apparent opacity or lack of visibility in addressing it. By this I mean that West has not employed his prophetic pragmatist theory to deal with this new threat.

I propose to call this new threat the post-Obama existentialist threat to black males in the contemporary United States. This is because, although historically black men have lived under the throes of white violence that often times have culminated in death, the 2008 elec-tion of Barack Obama to the presidency of the nation has brought about a resurgence of this historic threat with an intensity and ferocity that has shocked the post–civil rights genera-tion. I speak of resurgence because during Reconstruction extreme violence and horrifying death were visited on black men by organized militia such as the Ku Klux Klan and other white supremacist groups. Violence and murder were visited on black men, in particular, for endeavoring, among other things, to exercise the franchise subsequent to the ratification of the Fourteenth Amendment that conferred citizenship on African Americans (Painter 2007, ch. 7). In such a climate of intense antiblack violence, intimidation, and terrorism, it can rea-sonably be said that white supremacists regarded the concept of *black rights* as an oxymoron. With time, however, and specifically with the passage of the Civil Rights Bill in 1964, US soci-ety seemed to have been moving away, even if very slowly, from its shameful past. And so, in our own contemporary setting, Obama's 2008 election was taken by some to be the most visible sign of racial progress that signals the advent of a postracial society. This belief now needs to be reevaluated, however, both in light of the disrespect and sometimes downright insult leveled at the President and the surge in violence aimed at black men. The nature of this post-Obama threat therefore warrants further elaboration.

THE NATURE OF THE POST-OBAMA EXISTENTIAL THREAT

The post-Obama existential threat consists of, among other things, the extrajudicial kill-ings of black men by (mainly) white law enforcement officers and white self-appointed crime-fighting vigilantes (thrill/kill-seekers?). This phenomenon is reminiscent of the Reconstruction period mentioned previously. But it is new in the sense that it marks *a resur-gence of racial hatred whose specific impetus is the election of a black man to the highest echelon of power in the nation and (arguably) the world.* As reported in the weekend edition of *USA Today* (June 19–21, 2015), "The number of extreme-right hate groups—which include white supremacists and anti-government militias . . . have surged since 2009, said Mark Pitcavage, director of investigative research of the Anti-Defamation League. The surge is fueled by anti-government groups, which proliferated after the election of President Obama in 2008" (*USA Today* June 19–21, 2015, p. 4A).

Obama's election threatens the status quo of white power and signals the advent of a new power dynamic in the society. So self-appointed custodians of white power, some of whom act in their official capacities while others act as "lone wolves," react to and resist what they see as the challenge posed by Obama's election and, in their minds, the potential loss of white racial power and privilege. This resistance, I submit, is manifested in various ways, from the blatant disrespect shown to, and insult hurled at, President Obama to the extra-judicial racial killings of black men in particular. A few examples of such insults include the following: South Carolina Congressman Joe Wilson's breach of protocol and decorum in interrupting the President by shouting "You Lie!" as the President was delivering his 2009 State of the Union address to the Joint Houses of Congress (CNN 2009); conservative activist and musician Ted Nugent referring to President Obama as a "subhuman mongrel" (Fernandez 2014); and former Governor of New Hampshire, John Sununu, constantly using unsavory political rhetoric to describe the President (Volksy 2012).

If the President can be subjected to such vitriol as outlined here, then we should not be surprised that young black men can be manhandled and violated with impunity the way they are. Even as I compose this essay, CNN and other news media outlets are reporting about a hate crime at the historic AME Church in South Carolina in which a twenty-one-year-old white male went into the church yesterday (June 16, 2015), at about 9.00 p.m., and shot and killed nine African American parishioners during a prayer meeting (Eversely 2015). The shooter was later identified as Dyllan Roof. In a posting on June 18, 2015, entitled "Charleston Church Shooting Suspect Dylann Roof Captured in Shelby, North Carolina," *Huffington Post* journalist Andres Jauregui reported that Roof said, "I have to do it. You [black men] rape our women and you're taking over our country. And you have to go" (Jauregui 2015). Roof's victims were three men, including the church's pastor South Carolina State Senator Clementa Pinckney, and six women. It should be noted that in one of Dylan Roof's Facebook postings, which was subsequently removed after the shootings, Roof was shown holding up and waving the Confederate flag while burning the United States flag.

Given this backdrop, I submit that the post-Obama existential threat, particularly to young black men, is a form of white resistance to what may be considered the affront of black men to aspire to occupy positions of political power and authority in the polity. This explains the post-Obama resurgence of racial hatred of black men, in particular, and the violence and killings to which young black men are subject. I have therefore characterized the new phenomenon as the post-Obama existential threat to young black men. To repeat, the post-Obama existential threat to black men is a direct response to the election of Obama to the presidency of the nation. That this racial fact is not lost on the President is clear from the President's eulogy at the funeral service of South Carolina Senator Clementa Pinckney, who also was a friend of the President (CNN 2015). In his eulogy the President, besides recognizing each of Roof's other victims, commented on the pain the Confederate flag has caused African Americans since the Civil War: "For too long, we were blind to the pain that the Confederate flag stirred in too many of our citizens. It's true, a flag did not cause these murders. But as people from all walks of life, Republicans and Democrats, now acknowledge . . . as we all have to acknowledge, the flag has always represented more than just ancestral pride. For many, black and white, that flag was a reminder of systemic oppression and racial subjugation. We see that now." The President then called for the removal of the Confederate flag from the grounds of the South Carolina legislature (CNN 2015).

The Causal Origin of the Post-Obama Existential Threat

The causal origin of the post-Obama existential threat, similar to that of the nihilistic threat, is external because it comes from the institutions and structures of power in the society, namely, law enforcement, the Grand Jury system, the judiciary, and so on. Unlike the nihilistic threat, however, wherein crimes committed within the black community as a result of a cynical outlook are interrogated and their perpetrators punished, the perpetrators of anti-black crimes committed in the context of the post-Obama existential threat invariably get off scot-free. Well-documented cases of this phenomenon range from the nonindictment of police officer Darren Wilson, who shot and killed Michael Brown in Ferguson, Missouri, to Eric Garner, mentioned earlier, who was asphyxiated by a group of officers in broad daylight, followed by the Staten Island Grand Jury exonerating the police officers. (For some more examples of violence and gruesome killings of black men, see, for example, Yancy 2005, 2–5, and also Yancy 2008; see also Zack 2015, ch. 3) This point about the nonindictment or exoneration of perpetrators of crimes against young black men in particular is of the utmost importance, because it brings out the nature of the injustice black men experience in the post-Obama era. When the existing legal-institutional structures to which recourse is sought for, and on behalf of, the victims of extrajudicial killings by police and vigilante individuals consistently fail the aggrieved parties, and instead exonerate the culprits, one is but left to conclude that such violence and killings are sanctioned by the society. To summarize, the post-Obama existential threat to black men is a racialized threat from white America and is located within the institutions of power in the society whose agents then execute it. These agents include mainly law enforcement personnel, jurors, the grand jury system, and any "lone wolf" or vigilante who, empowered and enamored by the prevailing racial power dynamic that privileges whites, believes that he will be exonerated by the judicial system for violating the rights of black men.

But some are quick to defend the status quo, in particular law enforcement officers, by pointing to the phenomenon known as black-on-black crime and violence, especially among young black males. Such black-on-black crime is ritualistically reported on the local evening news channels on a daily basis. Drawing upon such news reports, and invoking statistics, defenders of the status quo contend that young black men kill each other in much greater numbers than they are killed by law enforcement; therefore, young black men pose a more severe existential threat to each other than from law enforcement. In short, police violence and killings are not as bad as they appear or as are presented in the media. Naomi Zack has noted that this (type of) argument was most recently advanced by former New York City Mayor Rudolph Giuliani in a debate with Michael Eric Dyson on "Meet the Press" of November 24, 2014 (Zack 2015, xii–xiii).

While Dyson has responded to this argument by noting that it is a red herring, a fallacious form of reasoning to deflect attention from the real issue at stake, namely police brutality against black men, Zack has responded to it by pointing to the unconstitutionality of police actions against black men. In particular, Zack contends that police conduct violates the guarantees provided by Fourth, and Fourteenth Amendments to the US Constitution. The Fourth Amendment protects all citizens against unreasonable searches and seizures, but this protection is abridged by, for example, the New York City "stop and frisk" policy whereby officers of the New York City Police Department (NYPD) randomly can stop, detain, and frisk an individual upon merely believing that the individual looks suspicious. Candidates on whom the policy has been executed the most have been young men of color, but especially black men. The Fourteenth Amendment guarantees equal protection to all citizens but, as Zack points out, this guarantee is constantly abridged by police racial profiling. Of significance, as Zack notes, law enforcement abridgement of these constitutional protections has consistently gained support as recently as 2013 from no less a body than the US Supreme Court in a ruling known as the Graham Decision. The Court ruled that a police officer's reasonable assessment while pursuing a public safety objective can supersede the Fourth Amendment protections because in those situations the police officer has to make a split-second decision (Zack 2015, 86–90). It is precisely the supplanting of the Fourth and Fourteenth Amendments protections with police "reasonable" assessment, meaning perception, that we see in police searches and seizures of many young black men, in the NYPD implementation of "stop and frisk" policies, and sometimes in the summary extrajudicial killings of young black men by law enforcement officers. In light of these considerations, as Zack rightly concludes, present policies violate these constitutional guarantees, especially "police killings that rest in impunity when grand juries do not indict and trial juries do not convict, violate, ultimate, nonnegotiable rights" (Zack 2015, xiii).

Dyson is right that the Giuliani-type argument is simply fallacious, and Zack is absolutely correct to focus on the unconstitutionality of social practices and police conduct that target men of color. But in addition to these refutations another response can be offered against the Giuliani-type argument that invokes black-on-black crime to rationalize police (and generally white) brutality of black men. Intraethnic or intraracial violence is not peculiar to blacks. Violence and crime occur within communities and groups sometimes because of the prevailing socioeconomic conditions that affect people and influence their actions. That is a fact of human nature, especially in times of scarcity, need, and desperation. However, crimes that target individuals because of their group characteristics/membership are very different in nature from crimes grounded in socioeconomic conditions alone. It is in this respect that the former crimes are more reprehensible than ordinary crimes. Jews were targeted by Nazis because of their Jewish identity. In our own contemporary setting, gays, lesbians, and transgendered persons are often targeted because of their group features and membership. The same is true of racial crimes against blacks. All such crimes against persons because of their group characteristics/membership are appropriately called hate crimes in the United States because they are motivated by and reflect the power dynamic in society. In this dynamic, members of the dominant (read powerful) group individually or collectively vilify and violate members of subordinate (read powerless) groups. Again, when the means to redress grievances of subaltern groups and/or persons exist only formally, as in the availability of access to the legal system, but the adjudication more often than not fails to bring justice to the aggrieved party, then there can be no doubt that the society tacitly sanctions such violations. This state of affairs historically has been the predicament of blacks in the United States with all-white jury acquittals of white criminals of violations, including murders, of black men. One of the most notorious cases in this connection occurred in 1955 in Mississippi, where an all-white jury acquitted the murderers of Emmett Till, a fourteen-year-old black male, for merely flirting with a white woman. We have a similar phenomenon in our own time in the litany of crimes against black men mentioned earlier that have gone unpunished or whose perpetrators have been absolved from wrongdoing. In sum, in the post-Obama United States, there has been an intensification of violence and murder of black men, and this makes the post-Obama existential threat even more insidious and pernicious than the nihilistic threat. It is more insidious and pernicious because the 2008 election of Obama was thought to have heralded a new and positive phase in race relations in the United States. The upsurge in the violence and murder of black men by law enforcement and white vigilantes has given the lie to that way of thinking.

The foregoing account of the nature and source of the post-Obama existential threat is meant to show that this threat is significantly different from the nihilistic threat of which West speaks. Whereas West characterizes nihilism as a disease of the soul, the post-Obama existential threat to black men may aptly be characterized as a disease of the body politic, for it is directly related to Obama's ascent to the presidency of the nation and is anchored within and sometimes manifested through the various institutions of power in the society. Given the institutional structures within which the post-Obama existential threat is located, therefore, it would seem to be morally obligatory for Cornel West to address it in much the same way as he addressed the nihilistic threat as a prophetic pragmatist and an advocate of social justice. What, if anything, has been West's prophetic pragmatist response to this threat? Regrettably, nothing substantive.

Prophetic Pragmatism and the Post-Obama Existential Threat

Other than joining protesters in Ferguson, Missouri, to protest the killing of Michael Brown by Police Officer Darren Wilson and to be publicly seen being handcuffed, and making television appearances decrying President Obama, West seems to have offered nothing of substance to address the existential crisis in question. And this has led some of his critics to intimate, if not explicitly deride, his Ferguson, Missouri, arrest and others as publicity stunts, performances for the cameras. Michael Eric Dyson, for example, in critiquing West's self-characterization of his intellectual engagements and activities as "prophetic," sees West's arrest in Ferguson as a "self-styled resistance to police brutality, evidenced by . . . [West's] occasional willingness to get arrested in highly staged and camera-ready gestures of civil disobedience" (Dyson 2015, 19). In some ways, the criticism is that West is guilty of the very kind of opportunistic media-courting conduct he leveled at the Rev. Jesse Jackson and Al Sharpton, saying that both political activists are "ontologically addicted to the camera" (Dyson 2015, 19). For my present purpose, however, the significance of the criticism here is that West does not offer any well-articulated programmatic solution to the post-Obama existential threat as he does to the nihilistic threat. The key question he poses at strategic points in *Race Matters* to address the nihilistic threat is "What needs to be done?" (West 1994, 11, 28, 66). And, as noted earlier, he does offer some coherent, even if problematic, solutions to this question, for better or worse. But with respect to the post-Obama threat, he neither poses a similar strategic question nor offers any proposed solution. Instead, all he offers are anti-Obama rhetorical attacks, some of which would be most welcomed by Obama's political adversaries from the conservative Right.

For example, in an interview with Thomas Frank (2014) in *Salon.com*, West alleges that Obama "posed as a progressive and turned out to be a counterfeit"; that Obama is "just another neoliberal centrist with a smile and with a nice rhetorical flair"; and that Obama is "a brown-faced Clinton. Another opportunist. Another neoliberal opportunist." In this connection, even West's response to the killing of Michael Brown is to attack President Obama by saying that Obama and his administration were "silent" on the matter, and that they only put out a statement days later after the incident. And he goes on to allege that the President "[sent] out a statement on the death of brother Robin Williams before [he] sent out a statement on brother Michael Brown" (see also Qui 2014).

We have a major crisis facing the black community. But instead of addressing it, West crassly engages in racial politics by being more concerned with the time-line of the President's response to the death of a cultural icon, who happens to be white, in comparison to his response to the death of an ordinary black man. By investing his energy on anti-Obama diatribe to the point of degenerating into name-calling in such a situation of moral urgency in African American life, West forces us to question both his own view of the relevance and value of his prophetic pragmatism and the depth of his commitment to existentialism. For, as a pragmatist of the Deweyan stripe as he claims to be, albeit a prophetic one, West ought to respond to the crisis in question using the "intellectual tool" he has adapted from American pragmatism. That is what Dewey would have done. And as an existentialist of the Kierkegaardian stripe, who purports to be concerned with (issues of) disappointment, dread, disease, and death (hooks and West 1991, 33; Osborne 1996), he ought to address the existential threat to black men—for quite literally each of these issues is implicated in their life. These imperatives seem to have been subordinated to West's anti-Obama political crusade. Perhaps an unfair but germane criticism one can level at West in this regard is to echo a variant of former Harvard president Lawrence Summers's rebuke of West when West was a faculty at Harvard: Do something constructive that is prophetically and pragmatically substantive to address the post-Obama existential threat to young black men rather than engage in political name-calling and spouting out worn-out generalized platitudes about the vicious legacy of white supremacy (Johnson 2003, 175–182). This is by no means to minimize the effect of white supremacy on the lived reality of people of color. But when the legacy of white supremacy is used merely as a rhetorical tool, without much content, then it reduces to a hackneyed phrase.

But shouldn't West's street protests count as a response? After all, West tells us in *Race Matters* that although his young age precluded him from being present in the courts and boardrooms during the civil rights discussions and deliberations in the 1960s, his young age did not stop him from being out in the streets protesting (West 1994, 95). So we should not be surprised now to find him participating in street protests to effect social change, even, or especially, if such participation will lead to him being arrested with other protesters. The point is that he believes that he has an obligation to take part in such protests, and he has done so in Ferguson.

The appropriate response to this line of reasoning, however, is that prophetic pragmatism purports to be a theory that uses the power of ideas to effect social change, not a method to fulfill an obligation of using street protests to attract media attention. Declaring "I came here to go to jail" and "not to give a speech," as West stated on being arrested (Magagnini 2014), is not what one understands as the *theory* of prophetic pragmatism. If the theory is as I have represented it, namely, a variant of American pragmatism whose methodology consists in deploying critical discourse as a means to effect social change, then there is no evidence that West has deployed the theory to address the post-Obama existential threat to young black men. Yet this threat is a situation of moral urgency that calls for just such use of the theory in a way similar to West's use of the theory in addressing the (arguably) nihilistic threat to black America. My point here, in other words, is that the present existential threat requires an equal penetrating and trenchant critique as West offers in dealing with the nihilistic threat *with comparable suggestions on how to overcome it*. There is nothing comparable from West on this score. And this prompts one to wonder aloud whether or not West's prophetic pragmatism reached its zenith in 1994 with *Race Matters*, concerning relevance and practical usefulness.

Still, it may be asked, why should West's "voice" matter in response to this new existential threat? It matters because West unquestionably has intellectual and social capital that, if channeled properly, can bring attention to this phenomenon. The lives of black men are at stake. A dead black man is a life lost. We fear for ourselves and our sons. The tremendous number of killings that have been recorded in the recent past should make anybody who professes to be an advocate of racial and social justice put aside all other political interests, whatever they may be, and privilege this existential concern. This privileging of the existential concern over other political interests is obligatory unless, of course, those political interests would be instrumental to addressing the existential concern. But it is not such prioritization of interests we get from West, and hence we do not see an effective use of his intellectual and social capital. Instead, we see West championing an anti-Obama crusade (with Tavis Smiley) at every opportunity, by haranguing the President, alleging that the President has not done much, if anything, for black America, and that the President is not liberal enough. At the risk of committing an ad hominem against West, one is compelled to pose the following question: As a professor in the academy, what has West done for Historically Black Colleges and Universities (HBCUs), other than giving occasional lectures and basking in the adulation of the students and some faculty members, while enjoying the full benefit, material and otherwise, of faculty membership in white neoliberal Ivy League institutions? True, West is no longer with the Ivy Leagues; he is now at the Union Theological Seminary in New York. However, it was in the Ivy Leagues, specifically Princeton and Harvard, that he built up his professional career as the eminent scholar he is. Apropos here is Dyson's criticism in a slightly different but relevant context: "West remains an elite academic and can hardly be said to have ever been a true outsider [of society's power structure], given his position in the academic elite and the upper reaches of the economy, but he hungers to be seen as rebellious. In truth, West is a scold, a curmudgeonly and bitter critic who has grown long in the tooth but sharp in the tongue when lashing one-time colleagues and allies" (Dyson 2015, 23). Perhaps these are unfair criticisms, but then so too is West's criticism of the President, given all the economic and political woes the President inherited from his predecessor and the political contours the President has had to navigate since taking office.

But back to the post-Obama threat. What conclusion then can we draw from all this about prophetic pragmatism, the post-Obama existential threat, and the racial/social dynamics of contemporary society? Unfortunately, the conclusion has to be negative. Despite its potential, prophetic pragmatism, as a variant of American pragmatism, has not offered much by way of providing a solution to the unsavory racial/social dynamics in the society. This is seen through Cornel West's failure to deploy it to engage the post-Obama existential threat to people of color but particularly young black men.

References

CNN. (2009). "Joe Wilson Says Outburst to Obama Speech 'Spontaneous." Accessed June 24, 2015. http://www.cnn.com/2009/POLITICS/09/10/obama.heckled.speech.

CNN. (2015). "Full Text of President Obama's Eulogy for Clementa Pinckney." Accessed July 2, 2015. http://www.cnn.com/2015/06/27/politics/obama-eulogy-clementa-pickney/.

Dyson, Michael Eric. (2015). "The Ghost of Cornel West." *The New Republic.* Accessed April 23, 2015. http://www.newrepublic.com/article/121550/cornel-wests-rise-fall.

Eversley, Melanie. (2015). "9 Dead in Shooting at Black Church in Charleston, S.C." *USA Today.* Accessed June 17, 2015. http://www.usatoday.com/story/news/nation/2015/06/17/charleston-south-carolina-shooting/28902017/.

Fernandez, Manny. (2014). "Ted Nugent Apologizes for Obama Insult." *The New York Times.* Accessed June 24, 2015. http://www.nytimes.com/2014/02/22/us/ted-nugent-apologizes-for-obama-insult.html?_r=0.

Frank, Thomas. (2014). "Exclusive: Cornel West Talks Ferguson, Hillary, MSNBC—and Unloads on the Failed Promise of Barack Obama." *Salon.* Accessed June 24, 2015. http://www.salon.com/2014/08/24/cornel_west.

Headley, Cleavis. (2001). "Cornel West on Prophecy, Pragmatism, and Philosophy: A Critical Evaluation of Prophetic Pragmatism." In *Cornel West: A Critical Reader,* edited by George Yancy, 59–82. Malden, MA: Blackwell.

hooks, bell, and Cornel West. (1991). *Breaking Bread: Insurgent Black Intellectual Life.* Boston, MA: South End Press.

Jauregui, Andres. (2015). "Charleston Church Shooting Suspect Dylann Roof Captured In Shelby, North Carolina." *The Huffington Post.* Accessed June 29, 2015. http://www.huffingtonpost.com/2015/06/18/dylann-roof-captured_n_7612986.html.

Johnson, Clarence. (2003). *Cornel West and Philosophy.* New York and London: Routledge.

Lott, E. (1994). "Cornel West in the Hour of Chaos: Culture and Politics." *Race Matters. Social Text* 40 (Fall): 39–50.

Magagnini, S. (2014). "Q & A: Sacramento Native Cornel West Discusses His Arrest in Ferguson, MO." *The Sacramento Bee.* Accessed June 29, 2015. http://www.sacbee.com/news/local/article3080739.html.

Osborne, Peter. (1996). *A Critical Sense: Interviews with Intellectuals.* London and New York: Routledge.

Painter, Nell Irvin. (2007). *Creating Black Americans.* New York and Oxford: Oxford University Press.

Qui, Linda. (2014). "Cornel West: Obama Reacted Quicker to Robin Williams' Death than Michael Brown's." *Politifact.* Accessed June 26, 2015. http://www.politifact.com/punditfact/statements/2014/aug/26/cornel-west/cornel-west-obama.

Schmidt, M. S., and M. Apuzzo. (2015). "South Carolina Officer is Charged with Murder of Walter Scott." *The New York Times.* Accessed July 1, 2015. http://www.nytimes.com/2015/04/08/us/south-carolina-officer-charged-with-murder-in-black-ma.

Volksy, Igor. (2012). "John Sununu's History of Racial Remarks about Obama." In *ThinkProgress. org.* Accessed June 24, 2015. http://www.thinkprogress.org/politics/2012/10/26/1094491/john-sununus-history.

West, Cornel. (1989). *The American Evasion of Philosophy: A Genealogy of Pragmatism.* Madison: The University of Wisconsin Press.

West, Cornel. (1994). *Race Matters.* New York: Vintage Books.

Yancy, G. (2005). *White on White/Black on Black.* Lanham, MD: Rowman and Littlefield.

Yancy, G. (2008). *Black Bodies, White Gazes.* Lanham, MD: Rowman and Littlefield.

Yancy, G., and Janine Jones, eds. (2013). *Pursuing Trayvon Martin.* Lanham, MD: Lexington Books.

Zack, Naomi. (2015). *White Privilege and Black Rights: The Injustice of US Police Racial Profiling and Homicide.* Lanham, MD: Rowman and Littlefield.

CHAPTER 19

....

INSURRECTIONIST ETHICS AND RACISM

....

LEE A. MCBRIDE III

THE subject of racism and the liberation of the racially oppressed, or those who are immiserated and stripped of honor and assets, merits an account of insurrectionist ethics. Accounts of both racism and insurrectionist ethics have been provided in the work of Leonard Harris. Needed is an outline of the types of moral intuitions, character traits (or virtues), and methods required to garner impetus for the liberation of oppressed groups. The core tenets of insurrectionist ethics can then be highlighted through the work of Angela Davis. As a result, insurrectionist ethics and its militant posture of resistance are seen to be crucial to human liberation and social amelioration in the face of racism. This impetus and advocacy are aimed toward creating social and material conditions fundamentally different from the confining and destructive conditions that constrict the freedom of racialized populations (Harris 2002b; McBride 2013a, 31).

RACISM AND LIBERATION

....

Leonard Harris describes racism as "a polymorphous agent of death, premature births, shortened lives, starving children, debilitating theft, abusive larceny, degrading insults, and insulting stereotypes forcibly imposed" (Harris 1999b, 437). Racism, on this view, names a network of interrelated forces and barriers which conspire to systematically strip a racialized population of its humanity, typically involving degradation, unspeakable terrors, and humiliation (Harris 1999b, 437). Racist practices and institutions invariably deny a racialized population ownership of, or access to, material resources, stunting that population's ability to accumulate and transfer assets across generations. Thus, racism is a polymorphous network of interrelated forces and barriers that allows one group to empower itself by not only stigmatizing and dehumanizing a targeted group but also stripping that group of its assets and material resources (Benedict 1999, 35–36, 39; Harris 2002a, 247).

I find this conception of racism compelling, for it captures more than race-based ill will or self-delusion (Garcia 1999; Gordon 1999). It does not reduce racism to a merely anthropological or economic structural phenomena (Balibar 1999; van den Berghe 1999). It links racism with material disparity and the denial of basic human dignity, explaining how stigmatized populations are stripped of honor and assets. It captures both the terror and brutality, as well as the material losses/gains of racism. It accounts for the strategic developments, the tactics, and the blood and violence that brought about the racialized groupings and material conditions recognized today (cf. Foucault 2003, 304). This notion of racism emphasizes the actual destruction of life, and thereby futures of, racialized populations (cf. Patterson 1982).

But how does one liberate himself or herself from the destructive forces of racism? I, like Frederick Douglass, Martin Luther King, Jr., and Leonard Harris, do not believe that racist practices and institutions are (or have been) sufficiently annulled or ameliorated by *moral suasionist* means. By moral suasionist means, I refer to methods confined to moral pleas, appeals, and attempts at persuading one's oppressors to abandon their racist ways and dismantle the conditions that confer upon them power, privilege, and prosperity. Moral suasionists are typically committed to approaching their oppressors with civility, courteousness, compassion, and humility. The attempt is made, through great shows of humanity and cultural achievement, to convince one's oppressor that the racialized group in question is, in fact, fully human and thereby deserving of basic human dignity, educational and economic opportunity, and freedom from racial boundaries and impediments.

Given the particularly odious nature of racist forms of oppression, I am confident that liberation will not be had without some form of resistance and compulsion. The classic articulation of this claim runs:

> If there is no struggle there is no progress. Those who profess to favor freedom and yet depreciate agitation, are men who want crops without plowing up the ground, they want rain without thunder and lightning. . ... This struggle may be a moral one, or it may be a physical one, and it may be both moral and physical, but it must be a struggle. Power concedes nothing without demand. It never did and it never will. (Douglass 1985, 204)

Here, Frederick Douglass asserts that it is unrealistic to assume that one's oppressors will concede their dominance without some form of struggle against the instantiated racist barriers and forces. This resistance can manifest in numerous ways: moral, physical, or both moral and physical. Along similar lines, Martin Luther King, Jr. asserts that it is fallacious to think that ethical appeals and persuasion alone will bring about justice. Indeed, ethical appeals will need to be made, but those appeals will need to be undergirded by "some form of constructive coercive power" (King 2010, 137). King suggests that an adequate course of action will lie neither in passively relying on moral suasion nor in actively succumbing to violent rebellion, but in a higher synthesis that reconciles the truths of these two opposing positions (King 2010, 137–138).

Leonard Harris argues that the egregious joys, the privilege, and power acquired through the profit secured by racist practices and institutions will not be negated by the mere change of beliefs (Harris 1998a, 455). Neither well-intentioned platitudes nor heartfelt lamentation will ameliorate those material conditions that have debilitating effects on racialized populations. Any genuine change of heart and mind must be accompanied by concrete changes in ownership, control, participation, and access to material reality to have any real effect (Harris 1998a, 455; 1999b, 448; 2002c, 157–158). Destroying racism will require more revolutions; it will require disturbance to the dominant paradigm; it will require insurrectionist conduct. Whether these revolutions are violent or not, racist hegemonies will concede nothing without resistance, demand, and coercion (Davis 1998, 57; Harris 1999b, 448–449).

INSURRECTIONIST ETHICS

Insurrectionist ethics is an attempt to work out the types of moral intuitions, character traits, reasoning strategies that culminate in action (*phronesis* or practical reason), and methods required to garner impetus for the liberation of oppressed groups (Harris 1999a, 2002b; McBride 2013b, 27). Numerous historical figures—including David Walker, Maria Stewart, Margaret Garner, Harriett Tubman, John Brown, and Henry David Thoreau—have prompted ethical questions about rebellious activity (Carter 2013; Harris 2013; McBride 2013b). What counts as justified protest? Do slaves have a moral duty to insurrect? How does one discern when to be overtly indignant and when to be rebellious by more surreptitious means? What character traits and modes to resistance are most conducive to liberation and the amelioration of oppressive material conditions? These are the treacherous waters that insurrectionist ethics attempts to navigate.

As I interpret it, insurrectionist ethics espouses four core tenets (Harris 2002b, 192; McBride 2013a, 32). The moral exemplar in insurrectionist ethics will hold to each of these tenets.

1. Practitioners of insurrectionist ethics exhibit a willingness to defy norms and convention when those norms sanction or perpetuate injustice or oppression (Harris 2002b, 195; McBride 2013a, 32). They are willing to challenge civic and moral authority when those authorities conspire to denigrate a population, allowing a dominant group to strip a subaltern group of its labor or its property. And, thus, the practitioner of insurrectionist ethics sees reason to disrupt relatively stable social orders, if those social orders countenance racist practices and institutions. To this end, he or she may endorse acts of resistance, which can take various forms, including satirical publications, irreverent protest, civil disobedience, subterfuge, or physical violence.
2. Insurrectionist ethicists maintain conceptions of personhood and humanity that motivate moral action against obvious injustice or brutality, justifying militancy and radical action on the behalf of persecuted peoples (Harris 1999a, 238; McBride 2013a, 32). Personhood, here, assures membership in the human family and secures those basic human dignities afforded to its members. Yet these basic entitlements are contingent upon one's ability to be recognized as a representative of the human family (Harris 1992, 202–203).

Historically, countless populations have been denied full personhood based on sex, religion, caste, ethnicity, and race. Without these entitlements, these populations are regarded as mere objects to be bought and sold, tools for material production, beasts of burden, or degenerates to be imprisoned, committed, or exterminated (Davis 1998, 104–105, 114–115). Chattel slavery in the United States is thus a prime example. People of African lineage were denied full personhood. Based on perceived race, a population was excluded from membership in the human family, rescinding that population's claim to basic human dignities (Walker 1965, 26; Harris 1999a, 229, 234–235). Given the brutality, the theft of labor and lives, the terror of torches in the night, the inhumanity of institutionalized slavery, the insurrectionist ethicist sees slavery as vile and egregiously unjust. Indignant, the insurrectionist ethicist advocates militant acts of resistance on behalf of the enslaved. The insurrectionist takes opportunities to disrupt racist practices and institutions that perpetuate slavery (Harris 1999a, 235; 2003, 82).

This commitment to humanity, to the recognition and dignity of oppressed persons, offers ardent motivation to engage in insurrectionist moral action. And resistance can be a highly risky endeavor. Insurrectionists risk reputation and livelihood, since disrupting the social order typically involves confrontation with established authority and opinion, decline in social status, disadvantages to one's family (figurative and literal) lynch mobs, and material losses (Harris 2002b, 196; McBride 2013a, 33). Nevertheless, the practitioner of insurrectionist ethics dutifully acts on behalf of oppressed populations, even when consequences are likely to be unfavorable in the immediate future (Harris 2002b, 208).

3. The practitioners of insurrectionist ethics work to achieve a broader, more universal liberation through the advocacy of particular oppressed groups (indigenous peoples of North America, black Americans, Dalits of India, etc.) (Harris 2002b, 196; McBride 2013a, 33). Insurrectionists understand that social agency is required to make substantial changes in institutional and material conditions, and that social agency is not marshaled without the concerted effort of individuals mobilizing around shared goals and identity. And these communities and coalitions of resistance rely upon representative heuristics (Harris 2002b, 207). Representative heuristics, here, is the idea that individuals or subgroups within a population represent the whole population (Harris 2002b, 197). These groupings function as heuristics in the process of building effective, social agency aimed at a localized form of struggle, demand, and compulsion.

But insurrectionists are not committed to these particular social groupings as stable categories or natural kinds (Harris 2002b, 198). These social groupings serve merely as political coalitions or communities of struggle, which are created in reaction to oppressive or unjust social contexts. It is not assumed that all members of these groups necessarily share the same essential feature, be it phenotype, culture, socioeconomic status, caste, or gender (Harris 1999b, 440–443; 2002b, 198; Mohanty 2003, 46; Lugones 2003, 159; 2006, 84). Socially constructed racialized communities, feminist coalitions, and other groups of resistance are understood as porous, evolving communities with contingent futures (Harris 1997; Mohanty 2003, 46). If the object of resistance is annulled, the bonds that hold these coalitions and communities of resistance together may dissolve or become less salient. The insurrectionist can envision a world that will overcome the bounded local identities and social categories that they represent (Harris 2002b, 198). That is, they represent social groupings that they ultimately hope their insurrectionist action will render anachronistic. As such, this position runs contrary to nationalisms and rooted identities; it opens possibilities for moderate forms of cosmopolitanism, multiplicitous subjectivities, and intercultural polyglossia (Lugones 2006, 84; Harris 2010, 70; Locke 2010, 143).

4. Insurrectionist ethicists give esteem to insurrectionist character traits (Harris 2002b, 196; McBride 2013a, 33–34). On this view, audacity, tenacity, enmity, indignation, and guile are recognized as valued character traits to exhibit when faced with debilitating networks of oppression (e.g., the degradation and brutality of racism). While some (e.g., moral suasionists) endorse more conventional character traits (such as civility, restraint, compassion, and humility) in like circumstances, the insurrectionist ethicist

holds that the valorization of such character traits in persecuted populations is counterproductive. These conventional character traits render an oppressed population self-effacing, submissive, impotent, and pliable. This, in effect, pacifies and binds these populations, squelching even the notion of resistance.

In particularly egregious settings, the practitioner of insurrectionist ethics gives approbation to those character traits that embolden a beleaguered people, that disrupt commonplace yet morally abhorrent social practices, that passionately give rise to social agency. Insurrectionist character traits help to make resistance possible; they allow for the bold, tenacious voices that demand the liberation of the oppressed (Harris 2002b, 208).

INSURRECTIONIST ETHICS AND ANGELA DAVIS

I will now revisit each of the four core tenets of insurrectionist ethics in relation to race-based oppression. Again, racism, here, is understood as a polymorphous network of interrelated forces and barriers that allows one group to dehumanize another group and strip it of its assets and material resources. For illustrative purposes, I locate the tenets of insurrectionist ethics in the life and philosophical works of Angela Davis. (The numbers in this section correspond to each of the core tenets, but in relation to Angela Davis.)

1. Davis shows a willingness to defy norms and authority when those norms and authorities perpetuate racism. It is well documented that she has had some run-ins with commonplace norms and authority. Davis, in 1969, was a brilliant assistant professor of philosophy at UCLA, an outspoken black feminist and political activist. She, at that time, was a member of the Communist Party USA and was associated with the Black Panther Party. The prospect of an audacious black woman advocating communism, feminism, and black liberation at one of California's premier universities was not received well. At the behest of the Governor, the UCLA Board of Regents removed Davis from her position in 1970, citing her radical activism and her membership in the Communist Party. Shortly thereafter, Davis was charged with "aggravated kidnapping and first degree murder." A warrant for her arrest was issued, and Davis was placed on the FBI's Ten Most Wanted Fugitives list. Davis was eventually arrested and placed on trial, spending sixteen months in prison, some of which were spent in solitary confinement. Davis recounts, "I would not let them conquer me. I transformed my frustration into raging energy for the fight" (Davis 1998, 35). Davis was acquitted of all charges. I rehearse this episode only to establish that Davis clearly stood in defiance of commonplace norms and authority figures, institutions, and organizations, which were linked to the perpetuation of racist practices and institutions: capitalism, white privilege/anti-black racism, misogyny, the UCLA Board of Regents, the Governor of California, and the Federal Bureau of Investigation (FBI).

In a number of her books, Davis documents historical figures who rise defiantly to oppose racist practices and institutions (especially slavery). Frederick Douglass, Harriet Tubman, Gabriel Prosser, Nat Turner, Sojourner Truth, and Margaret Garner are evoked and celebrated. Each, in their own way, evinces "a militant posture," "a posture of resistance," or "a revolutionary stance" (Davis 1983, 64; 1990, 14; 1998, 59, 55). This "posture" or "stance" need not manifest in a literal placement of feet, shoulders, and fists, like a boxer. Rather, this "militant posture" refers to one's disposition to resist and actively struggle against the practices and debilitating effects of racist oppression. The posture of resistance located in these historical figures emphasizes a long tradition of people dedicated to defiantly resisting racist oppression in the United States.

2. Davis maintains a conception of personhood and humanity that militates acts of resistance and radical action on behalf of racialized populations. The enslaved peoples of African descent (Negroes) were not initially granted full personhood in the United States. They were decidedly excluded from the human family, and thus denied basic human dignities. These people were stripped of their humanity and denied their freedom (Davis 1998, 55). They were bought, sold, and inherited. They were molested and raped; their children and breast milk harvested (Davis 1983, 7; 1998, 123; Dotson 2013, 82). They were reduced to "inorganic conditions of production" (Davis 1998, 114, 115). Davis argues that it is racist ideology that conditioned and justified the move to classify Negroes as subhuman. Great wealth and power were amassed in the exploitation of black bodies and black labor. Thomas Jefferson, for example, had calculated that "he was making a 4 percent profit every year on the birth of black children" (Wiencek 2012). In this blatant and egregious denial of humanity, Davis finds motivation for resistance/struggle. Those encumbered by racist forces and barriers must engage in "a dynamic, active struggle for liberation" to even have a chance at asserting the basic human dignities of their racially oppressed group (Davis 1998, 54). "Resistance, rejection, physical and mental, are fundamental moments of the journey toward freedom" (Davis 1998, 57).

Historically, resistance took many forms. Nat Turner and Denmark Vesey courageously planned and led armed slave insurrections. But the militant posture manifested in more surreptitious forms, including feigned illness, studied indolence, sabotage of production, arson, infanticide, and poison (Davis 1983, 39). In any event, the act of resistance stood as "an implicit rejection of the entire institution of slavery, its standards, its morality" (Davis 1998, 55). These insurrectionists fought to maintain or liberate groups of enslaved people at the risk of death for themselves and their loved ones.

3. Davis works to achieve a broader, more universal liberation through the advocacy of particular oppressed groups. Black Americans, particularly black women, take center stage in many of Davis's books. Davis is a black woman, an American. She situates herself in a long tradition of black women that have taken the militant posture. Davis writes: "An intricate and savage web of oppression intruded at every moment into the black woman's life during slavery. Yet a single theme appears at every juncture: the woman transcending, refusing, fighting back, asserting herself over and against terrifying obstacles" (Davis 1998, 125). Black women were "forced to leave behind the shadowy realm of female passivity" in order to assume their posts as "warriors against oppression" (Davis 1998, 125).

But Davis is not a black nationalist; her adoration and advocacy for black women do not preclude her from recognizing the contingency of particular racialized identities and provincialisms (Davis 1998, 281–282; 2012, 73). She says:

> I grew up thinking of myself as a "Negro," largely unable to articulate the extent to which social inferiority was constructed as an essential dimension of the "Negro." It is important to recognize the various forms of agency with which identities can be and are constructed, in order not to get stuck in them, in order not to assume that racialized identities have always been there. A "black" subject was created. We can also create a "women of color" subject. (Davis 1998, 300)

In fact, Davis advocates a revolutionary, multiracial women's movement that addresses the main issues affecting poor and working-class women transnationally (Davis 1990, 7). Davis argues that women of color must be willing to appeal for multiracial unity, to look beyond racial and ethnic conventions, so that shared political goals can be pursued (Davis 1990, 11, 151). She writes:

> As Afro-American women, as women of color in general, as progressive women of all racial backgrounds, let us join our sisters—and brothers—across the globe who are attempting to forge a new socialist order—an order which will reestablish socioeconomic priorities so that the quest for monetary profit will never be permitted to take precedence over the real interests of human beings. (Davis 1990, 14)

Hence, Davis envisions a broader, more universal form of human liberation, yet she works on behalf of black women and women of color to approach this form of universal human liberation.

4. Davis esteems insurrectionist character traits, especially when faced with racist practices and institutions (like slavery). She notes that particular character traits, such as, piety, compassion, obedience, patience, and humility, were inculcated among the enslaved (Davis 1998, 59). These character traits kept the enslaved population docile and acquiescent. Slave owners were known to devise unspeakable terrors for those slaves who overtly exhibited ambition, intelligence, literacy, or passionate opposition to racism and slavery (Davis 1983, 28). Slave owners did not want the masses of enslaved people to assume the militant posture of Gabriel Prosser, Harriett Tubman, or Frederick Douglass (Davis 1998, 59). It is worth noting that these three figures assume the revolutionary stance, yet in different ways. Gabriel planned an armed rebellion, set on capturing Richmond, Virginia. Tubman worked surreptitiously, spiriting slaves to freedom on the Underground Railroad. Douglass displayed his posture of resistance in memoirs, essays, newspaper editorials, and public lectures. The militant posture, so understood, does not require pitchforks and machetes. It requires defiance/resistance. This allows Davis to honor "consciously rebellious black women"; enslaved women who inspired and participated in a multitude of defiant acts; women driven to protect their children by their passionate abhorrence of slavery (Davis 1983, 29; 1998, 126; Dotson 2013, 81). There are untold numbers of black women who toiled under their master's whip, protected their families, stood militantly against slavery, and who were terrorized and raped, but never subdued. These women represent "a legacy of hard work, perseverance and self-reliance, a legacy of tenacity, resistance and insistence on sexual equality" (Davis 1983, 29). Davis, thus, gives approbation to those character traits that embolden racially oppressed populations, disrupt morally abhorrent social

practices, and passionately gives rise to social agency. As such, insurrectionist character traits help to make possible various forms of resistance as well as the authoritative
voices that demand the liberation of the oppressed (Harris 2002b, 208).

But conditions have changed; slavery was abolished in the United States in 1865.
Nevertheless, the *legacy* of white supremacy and chattel slavery still lingers in our practices
and institutions, in the forces and barriers that deride and confine those people who do not
qualify as white (Davis 2012, 174). Intentionally or not, structures and institutions persist
that systematically strip racialized populations of their humanity, including damning stereotypes, quotidian forms of degradation, and the terror of unprovoked and unwarranted
violence. Moreover, racialized populations were denied ownership of, or access to, material
resources for centuries, and this has stunted these populations' ability to compete in the market, accumulate assets, and provide excellent educational opportunities for their children.
Hence, the grave disparities in the ownership of property and assets, disparities in seats of
political and economic power, disparities in educational opportunities, disparities in social
capital, disparities in incarceration, and disparities in the confidence and civility afforded.

Davis, today, is very much concerned with combating structural racism and the abolition
of the prison industrial complex in the United States. She has also turned her attention to
the building of transnational coalitions to combat all forms of oppression. Davis prods her
readers to develop imaginative scenarios of liberation. We must challenge ourselves to imagine a world without structural racism, a world without a prison industrial complex, a world
without war, a world in which women are not assumed to be inferior to men, a world in
which binary conceptions of gender no longer govern modes of association, a world without
xenophobia, a world without antipathy toward immigrants, and a world in which violence is
eliminated from state practices as well as from our intimate lives (Davis 2012, 132–133). She
writes:

> This is just the beginning of a very long agenda for social change. If we are to fashion ourselves
> today into agents of social change, we will have to do a lot of work, a lot of work on ourselves,
> a lot of work with each other, and we have to try to make sense of what appears to be a really
> depressing world. (Davis 2012, 133)

To create social amelioration, social agency will need to be garnered. To garner social agency,
concerned people will need to get involved around a shared goal. This, in turn, relies upon
bold individuals willing to buck convention in order to expose the injustice of a particular
form of oppression. The push for social amelioration seems to require those character traits
that steel and embolden oppressed populations, disrupt morally abhorrent social practices,
and passionately give rise to social agency.

Insurrectionist ethics can play a crucial role here. Those who struggle under oppressive
conditions today can learn from this robust "tradition of supreme perseverance and heroic
resistance" (Davis 1998, 127). Insurrectionist ethics and this militant posture of resistance are
required to garner the impetus and coalitions of struggle needed to create social and material conditions fundamentally different from the confining and destructive conditions that
constrict the freedom of racialized populations (Harris 2002b; Davis 2012, 132–133; McBride
2013a, 31).

References

Balibar, Etienne. (1999). "Class Racism." In *Racism*, edited by Leonard Harris, 201–212. Amherst, NY: Humanity Books.

Benedict, Ruth. (1999). "Racism: The *ism* of the Modern World." *Racism*, edited by Leonard Harris, 31–49. Amherst, NY: Humanity Books.

Carter, Jacoby Adeshei. (2013). "The Insurrectionist Challenge to Pragmatism and Maria W. Stewart's Feminist Insurrectionist Ethics." *Transactions of the Charles S. Peirce Society* 49 (1): 54–73.

Davis, Angela Y. (1983). *Women, Race, & Class*. New York: Vintage Books.

Davis, Angela Y. (1990). *Women, Culture, & Politics*. New York: Vintage Books.

Davis, Angela Y. (1998). *The Angela Y. Davis Reader*. Edited by Joy James. Malden, MA: Blackwell.

Davis, Angela Y. (2012). *The Meaning of Freedom*. San Francisco: City Lights Books.

Dotson, Kristie. (2013). "Querying Leonard Harris' Insurrectionist Standards." *Transactions of the Charles S. Peirce Society* 49 (1): 74–92.

Douglass, Frederick. (1985). "The Significance of Emancipation in the West Indies: An Address Delivered in Canandaigua, New York, on 3 August 1857." *The Frederick Douglas Papers, Series One: Speeches, Debates, and Interviews*. Edited by John Blassingame. Vol. 3, *1855–63*, 183–208. New Haven, CT: Yale University Press.

Foucault, Michel. (2003). "Truth and Power." In *The Essential Foucault*, edited by Paul Rabinow and Nikolas Rose, 300–318. New York: The New Press.

Garcia, Jorge L. A. (1999). "The Heart of Racism." In *Racism*, edited by Leonard Harris, 398–434. Amherst, NY: Humanity Books.

Gordon, Lewis. (1999). "Antiblack Racism and Ontology." In *Racism*, edited by Leonard Harris, 347–355. Amherst, NY: Humanity Books.

Harris, Leonard. (1992). "Honor: Empowerment and Emasculation." In *Rethinking Masculinity*, edited by Larry May and Robert Strinkwerda, 191–208. New York: Rowman & Littlefield Publishers.

Harris, Leonard. (1997). "The Horror of Tradition or How to Burn Babylon and Build Benin While Reading a *Preface to a Twenty-Volume Suicide Note*." In *African-American Perspectives and Philosophical Traditions*, edited by John Pittman, 94–118. New York: Routledge.

Harris, Leonard. (1998a). "Universal Human Liberation." In *Theorizing Multiculturalism*, edited by Cynthia Willett, 449–457. Malden, MA: Blackwell Publishers.

Harris, Leonard. (1999a). "Honor and Insurrection or A Short Story about why John Brown (with David Walker's Spirit) was Right and Frederick Douglass (with Benjamin Banneker's Spirit) was Wrong." In *Frederick Douglass: A Critical Reader*, edited by Bill Lawson and Frank Kirkland, 227–242. Malden, MA: Blackwell.

Harris, Leonard. (1999b). "What, Then, is Racism?." In *Racism*, edited by Leonard Harris, 437–450. Amherst, NY: Humanity Books.

Harris, Leonard. (2002a). "Community: What Type of Entity and What Type of Moral Commitment." In *The Quest for Community and Identity*, edited by Robert Birt, 243–255. Lanham, MD: Rowman & Littlefield Publishers.

Harris, Leonard. (2002b). "Insurrectionist Ethics: Advocacy, Moral Psychology, and Pragmatism." In *Ethical Issues for a New Millennium*, edited by John Howie, 192–210. Carbondale: Southern Illinois University Press.

Harris, Leonard. (2002c). "Universal Human Liberation and Community: Pixley Kalsaka Seme and Alain Leroy Locke." In *Perspectives in African Philosophy*, edited by Claude Sumner and Samuel W. Yohannes, 150–159. Addis Ababa, Ethiopia: Addis Ababa University.

Harris, Leonard. (2003). "Tolérance, Réconciliation et Groupes." *Guerre et Réconciliation, Journée de la philosophie à l'UNESCO* 5: 59–94.

Harris, Leonard. (2010). "Conundrum of Cosmopolitanism and Race." In *Philosophic Values and World Citizenship: Locke to Obama and Beyond*, edited by Jacoby Carter and Leonard Harris, 57–73. Lanham, MD: Lexington Books.

Harris, Leonard. (2013). "Walker: Naturalism and Liberation." *Transactions of the Charles S. Peirce Society* 49 (1): 93–111.

King, Martin Luther, Jr. (2010). *Where Do We Go From Here: Chaos or Community?* Boston: Beacon Press.

Locke, Alain. (2010). "World Citizenship: Mirage or Reality?" In *Philosophic Values and World Citizenship: Locke to Obama and Beyond*, edited by J. A. Carter and Leonard Harris, 139–146. Lanham, MD: Lexington Books.

Lugones, María. (2003). *Pilgrimages/Peregrinajes: Theorizing Coalition against Multiple Oppressions*. New York: Rowman & Littlefield.

Lugones, María. (2006). "On Complex Communication," *Hypatia* 21 (3): 75–85.

McBride, Lee. (2013a). "Insurrectionist Ethics and Thoreau." *Transactions of the Charles S. Peirce Society* 49 (1): 29–45.

McBride, Lee, ed. (2013b). "Symposium on Insurrectionist Ethics." *Transactions of the Charles S. Peirce Society* 49 (1): 27–111.

Mohanty, Chandra Talpade. (2003). *Feminism without Borders*. Durham, NC: Duke University Press.

Patterson, Orlando. (1982). *Slavery and Social Death*. Cambridge, MA: Harvard University Press.

Van den Berghe, Pierre L. (1999). "Ethnicity as Kin Selection: The Biology of Nepotism." In *Racism*, edited by Leonard Harris, 50–73. Amherst, NY: Humanity Books.

Walker, David. (1965). *Appeal to the Coloured Citizens of the World, but in Particular, and Very Expressly, to Those of the United States of America*. New York: Hill and Wang.

Wiencek, Henry. (2012). "The Dark Side of Thomas Jefferson." *Smithsonian Magazine*. Accessed May 10, 2016. http://www.smithsonianmag.com/history/the-dark-side-of-thomas-jefferson-35976004/#56SAdKpPsTPoKuSE.14.

CHAPTER 20

HISTORY OF AFRICAN AMERICAN POLITICAL THOUGHT AND ANTIRACIST CRITICAL THEORY

ROBERT GOODING-WILLIAMS

How should we understand the relationship between the study of the history of African American political thought and the current practice of antiracist critical theory, a philosophical but equally interdisciplinary enterprise that aims to advance the cause of racial justice? In *In the Shadow of Du Bois* (Gooding-Williams 2009), a book that focuses on the political thought of W. E. B. Du Bois and Frederick Douglass, I argue that the history of African American political thought belongs to a broader, Afro-modern tradition of political theory, an impressively rich body of writings bound together by several thematic preoccupations, including the political organization of white supremacy, the nature and effects of racial violence, and the possibilities of black emancipation. What might we make of the relationship between the study of this history and the enterprise of antiracist critique? *Shadow* never explicitly addresses this question. As we shall see, however, its readings of Du Bois and Douglass tacitly speak to it.

Following Sally Haslanger, I use "antiracist critical theory" to describe the institutional and ideological critique of "unacceptably unjust" practices of "racial oppression in general and white supremacy in particular" (Haslanger 2012). Institutional critique highlights the features of a social practice relevant to normative evaluation and explicitly adduces normative concepts to evaluate that practice. Ideology critique exposes, analyzes, and critically examines the conceptual and narrative frameworks that organize our practices. Driven by an emancipatory interest in comprehending and remedying racial injustice, antiracist institutional and ideology critique draws inspiration from antiracist social activism, aspiring, in Karl Marx's words, to clarify at least some among "the struggles and wishes" of the age (Marx 1967).

The question as to the relation between studies of the history of African American political thought and the current practice of antiracist critical theory—including much of contemporary African American political thought—will strike many professional philosophers as at once strange and familiar. It will strike them as strange, for antiracist critical theory and inquiry into the history of African American political thought have gained but a toehold in the profession. It will strike them as familiar, for the question raised is a version of a more general yet notably commonplace question: How should we understand the relationship between inquiry into the history of philosophy and current practices of philosophy?

Reversing the trajectory of my remarks so far, I divide the remainder of the present essay into three parts. First, I sample a portion of the mainstream, philosophical literature that, during the last thirty years or so, has analyzed the relation between inquiry into the history of philosophy and current practices of philosophy. Second, and more briefly, I examine a recent discussion of that relation that references inquiry into the history of African American political thought, the normative concerns of antiracist critical theory, and study of one of Du Bois's essays. Finally, I recur to *Shadow*'s interpretations of Du Bois and Douglass, which I adduce to show how the study of the history of African American political thought can contribute to the project of antiracist critical theory.

THE HISTORY OF PHILOSOPHY AND CURRENT PRACTICES OF PHILOSOPHY

Published in 1984, *Philosophy in History* (Rorty, Schneewind, and Skinner 1984) is an anthology coedited by Richard Rorty, J. B. Schneewind, and Quentin Skinner. In the anthology's introduction, its editors frame their analysis of the relation between the ongoing practice of philosophy and the study of philosophy's history with reference to a dispute between, on one hand, intellectual historians who charge analytic philosophers writing the history of philosophy with anachronism, claiming that they read "current [philosophical] interests back into the past," and, on the other hand, analytic philosophers who charge intellectual historians with antiquarianism, accusing them of " 'not getting at the *philosophical* point.' " Responding to this dispute, the editors suggest that we forget the "bugbears" of anachronism and antiquarianism, insisting that "[i]f to be anachronistic is to link a past X to a present Y rather than studying it in isolation, then every historian is always anachronistic"—adding that "conversely, if to be antiquarian is to study X without regard to . . . [contemporary] concerns, nobody has ever succeeded in being antiquarian." Considering just this suggestion, one might very well conclude that Rorty, Schneewind, and Skinner mean to side with analytic philosophers against the intellectual historians, because, they propose, anachronism is inevitable, antiquarianism impossible. But that would be the wrong conclusion to draw, for the pivotal point of their argument is to *refocus* the intellectual historian's critique. Insisting that " '[a]nachronism' is . . . not the right charge to make," the editors of *Philosophy in History* claim that the analytic philosopher's approach to the history of philosophy goes astray, not because it is anachronistic, but because it is anachronistic in the wrong way; that is, because it approaches the history of philosophy in the spirit of a pre-Kuhnian view of the history of the hard sciences, according to which "questions do not change, but answers do." By contrast, the editors argue, the major task of a Kuhnian "historian of a scientific discipline is to understand when and why the questions changed. The principal defect of the kind of history of philosophy to which analytic philosophy has given rise is its lack of interest in the rise and fall of questions."

To throw into sharper relief the issues raised by the introduction to *Philosophy in History*, I turn to two of Daniel Garber's essays (Garber 1989, 2001, 2005). Because Garber's scholarship focuses on early modern European philosophy, it would seem to have little bearing on the study of the history of African American political thought. As we shall see, however, his persistent defense of an approach to the history of philosophy that embraces the antiquarianism of the intellectual historian has a general significance that extends well beyond his particular historical interests, and it finds a parallel in recent work on the political thought of W. E. B. Du Bois.

In his 1989 essay, entitled, "Does History Have a Future? Some Reflections on Bennett and Doing Philosophy Historically," Garber invokes Jonathan Bennett's "use" of the history of philosophy and, in particular, Bennett's study of Spinoza's *Ethics*, to motivate his account of an alternative but complementary use to which the history of philosophy can be put. Bennett recommends the history of philosophy, because studying that history can help discover philosophical truth. So conceived, Garber writes, "the history of philosophy is a kind of storehouse of positions and arguments, positions and arguments that we can use as guides and inspirations to the positions we should take, or illustrations of dead ends we should avoid" (14). But, according to Garber, Bennett's approach to the history of philosophy courts danger. First, because regarding the history of philosophy "as contributing to the discovery of philosophical truth, we are led to emphasize those portions of a philosopher's work that speak to our interests, that address our conception of where philosophical truth is to be found leaving other aspects of the work aside." And second, because our interest in philosophical truth often leads us to reconstruct an historical figure's position "in terms that make sense of it to our philosophical sensibilities, whether or not the reformulation captures anything the philosopher himself would have acknowledged." In both cases Garber worries that "the focus on philosophical *truth* distorts our *historical* understanding of the figure and his position" (16–17).

Garber insists that, while his discussion of Bennett's approach to the history of philosophy sounds like a criticism, it is not, for "if our goal is philosophical truth, then historical veracity can have only instrumental value at best; it is of value only insofar as it helps us attain our principal goal." Notwithstanding this disclaimer, it is difficult *not* to notice the affinity between Garber's description of the use of the history of philosophy that Bennett exemplifies and Rorty, Schneewind, and Skinner's *explicitly critical* description of the use of the history of philosophy that the analytic philosopher who is anachronistic in the wrong way exemplifies. For what both descriptions depict is an approach that judges the writings of philosophers past to merit serious attention only if they express insights that bear on the interest of present-day philosophers in discovering the correct answers to questions having philosophical currency.

It is also difficult not to notice the affinity between the alternative to Bennett's approach that Garber proposes and the alternative to wrongly conceived anachronism that Rorty, Schneewind, and Skinner advance. For contrasting his method—what he characterizes as "disinterested" history of philosophy—to Bennett's, Garber writes that "Bennett's history of philosophy seeks philosophical truth, *answers* to philosophical questions . . . [while] mine seeks the *questions themselves*." Declining, again, to criticize Bennett, and avoiding the adversarial attitude animating the introduction to *Philosophy in History*, Garber concludes that "[w]e cannot ignore the ways in which past thinkers are involved in projects similar to ours . . . At the same time, we cannot ignore the ways in which they differ from us . . . the way in which they ask different questions and make different assumptions. Both are important to a genuine historical understanding of the philosophical past, but just as important, we as philosophers can learn from both" (Garber 2001, 30).

In "What's Philosophical about the History of Philosophy" (Garber 2005), Garber makes a more forceful case for his approach to the history of philosophy, maintaining that "in times like these, where the analytic paradigm is in what many consider a crisis," the disinterested history of philosophy that he now calls "antiquarian history of philosophy" has a distinctive contribution to make. Here, like Rorty, Schneewind, and Skinner more than twenty years earlier, Garber himself invokes Kuhn, arguing that when the paradigm of "normal philosophy," or "the 'normal scientific' phase of philosophical research," suffers crisis, "the antiquarian . . . the most history-bound historian of philosophy . . . can provide the philosopher with fresh views of the subject. He can show the philosopher alternative ways of conceiving what philosophy is. Realizing how philosophical problems, as well as the very concept of philosophy, have changed over the years can help us free ourselves from the tyranny of the present, essentialism with respect to the notion of philosophy itself. It can also help us to see some of the philosophical problems that grip us in new ways" (Garber 2005, 145). Writing now with a more insistent and expressly more polemical tone than he had still advanced in 2001, when he republished "Does History Have a Future" as the first chapter of *Descartes Embodied*, Garber boldly proclaims in conclusion that "History of Philosophy, if viewed as a repository for more than assorted arguments and errors, could produce a decisive transformation in the image of philosophy by which we are now possessed" (Garber 2005, 146).

Garber's altered tone likely reflects the sense of crisis he expresses, but it may also involve what Robert Brandom represents as a feature of the "sociology" of American philosophy circa 2002, the year that Brandom's *Tales of the Mighty Dead* (Brandom 2002) appeared, and a year after the publication of *Descartes Embodied*. "A generation ago," Brandom writes, "the history of philosophy tended strongly toward *de re* readings"—that is, toward readings that, in contrast to de dicto interpretations, comprise ascriptions "relative to a context (from a point of view) that is *not* restricted to commitments the interpreter takes it would be acknowledged by the author of the text." By 2002, however, the profession had witnessed a sea change, "for there . . . [had] been a substantial backlash to this practice, in favor of immensely patient and textually informed *de dicto* readings" (104, 107).

Brandom's de dicto readings correspond roughly to Garber's antiquarian history of philosophy, and his de re readings to a philosophical truth-seeking approach to the history of philosophy that Brandom, like Garber, associates with Jonathan Bennett. Perhaps Garber's 1989 essay and Rorty, Schneewind, and Skinner's introduction helped to begin the shift from one approach to the other, and perhaps the new insistence with which Garber later advances his cause reflects that shift—which he himself helped to initiate.

Whereas Garber (1989, 2001) first mounts a largely epistemic argument for the disinterested history of philosophy, proposing that his approach contributes to historical understanding and philosophical learning, he later (Garber 2005) more radically implies that disinterested, antiquarian history can do two things: (1) bring to light alternative ("fresh") ways to conceptualize philosophy; and (2) effectively alienate and distance us from the contemporary practice of philosophy—what I take him to mean when he writes of freeing ourselves from the tyranny of the present. It is with an eye to the possibility that work in the history of philosophy can have effects of *these* sorts that I should now like to consider an essay by Charles Taylor.

Taylor's "Philosophy and its history" (Taylor 1984) is the lead essay in the Rorty, Schneewind, and Skinner volume, and, while Taylor never mentions Kuhn, his talk of "paradigms" and "models" suggests a broadly Kuhnian picture of the history of philosophy. Unlike the volume's coeditors, however, Taylor is less interested to point out the defects in a particular way of writing the history of philosophy than he is to establish the central importance to philosophical criticism of genetic accounts of our philosophical models.

For Taylor, the history of philosophy is, to a large extent, the history of philosophical models. What defines a model is a "cluster of assumptions," such as the cluster of assumptions that define one of Taylor's favorite examples, the "epistemological model." Taylor explains his concept of the epistemological model in many places, but in the essay in question limits himself to stating that it understands our awareness of the world "in terms of our forming representations—be they ideas in the mind, states of the brain, sentences we accept or whatever—of 'external' reality" (Taylor 1984, 18).

One critical premise of Taylor's argument is that our practices—including "our manner of doing natural science . . . our technology . . . some at least of the dominant ways in which we construe political life . . . [and] our ways of healing, regimenting, organizing people in society"—embed philosophical models (Taylor 1984, 20). Extrapolating to nonscientific practices Kuhn's idea (see Kuhn 2012) that the practice of normal science is rooted in a scientific community's common commitments, the shared constellation of assumptions, theories, techniques, and so forth that Kuhn called a "paradigm" but later a "disciplinary matrix," Taylor holds that a wide range of our practices may well embed a single model as their organizing principle. Another important premise is that we tend to accept as unquestionable and too obviously true to mention the models that our practices have come to embed, so that it becomes quite difficult "to see what an alternative would look like." From these premises Taylor argues that to liberate ourselves from the presumption that an embedded model provides a uniquely intelligible interpretation of some subject matter—with respect to the epistemological model, a uniquely intelligible interpretation of mind in the world—we require a genetic account of that model; that is, an account that retrieves the formulations through which the embedding in practice initially took place. Thus, the philosophical criticism of the epistemological model requires that one return to Descartes, for "if one wants to be able to see this model no longer just as the contour map of the way things obviously are with the mind-in-the-world, but as one option among others, then a first step is to see it as something one could come to *espouse* out of a creative description, something one could give reasons for. And this you get by retrieving the foundational formulations" (19–20).

Like Garber, Taylor thinks that the study of the history of philosophy can effectively distance and alienate us from inherited philosophical models and, as a result, help us to begin both to appreciate alternatives to these models and to take seriously the "new issue[s]" that these alternatives seem to raise. Notice, however, that Taylor reverses the causal order that Garber's remarks suggest. For Garber, antiquarian history of philosophy, precisely *because* it affords the philosopher fresh views of her or his subject matter, can help to liberate her or him from the tyranny of the present. But this emancipatory strategy is not likely to be effective, Taylor suggests, if the fresh views adduced by the antiquarian "look bizarre and inconceivable." And they *will* look bizarre and inconceivable, he argues, unless the philosopher has already taken up a distanced and critical stance toward the inherited models that "captured in the force field of a common sense," he otherwise accepts as unquestionable (Taylor 1984, 24).

I have dwelt on Charles Taylor's contribution to the Rorty, Schneewind, and Skinner volume, for, as I detail below, it corresponds to the approach to Du Bois I take in *Shadow*.

Before saying more about my study of Du Bois, however, and about my own approach to the history of African American political thought, I wish briefly to consider Paul Taylor's recent discussion of the history of African American thought and its relation to some contemporary examples of antiracist critical theory. P. Taylor's essay raises questions about that relation similar to those raised by Garber's engagement with Bennett and by Rorty, Schneewind, and Skinner's critique of the use of the history of philosophy that Bennett exemplifies. Unlike *Shadow*, however, the essay does not take up the possibility of giving a genetic account of philosophical models central to the history of African American political thought.

PAUL TAYLOR ON HISTORICISM AND PRESENTISM

P. Taylor's "Bare Ontology and Social Death" (Taylor 2013a) is groundbreaking because, as far as I know, it is the first contribution to African American political theory that considers in general terms the relation between historicist readings (Garber's antiquarian and Brandom's de dicto readings) of the received Afro-modern and, more generally, Africana canon of political thought and presentist readings (Garber's philosophical truth seeking and Brandom's de re readings) of that canon. In particular, P. Taylor's essay takes up Robert Bernasconi's and Chike Jeffers's historicist interpretations of Du Bois's "The Conservation of Races" (see Du Bois 1997; Bernasconi 2009; Jeffers 2013), arguing that Bernasconi's and Jeffers's readings of Du Bois effectively break with an entrenched scholarly tendency to treat "Conservation" first and foremost as an extended philosophical reflection on the concept of race.

On P. Taylor's account, Bernasconi's and Jeffers's articles are best appreciated against the backdrop of what he dubs "The Du Bois Debates," by which he refers (a) to K. Anthony Appiah's defense of racial eliminativism by way of an interpretation of "Conservation" in the late 1980s and early 1990s (see Appiah 1992); (b) to a number of conference papers and published essays that, thereafter, critically responded to Appiah's interpretation of "Conservation"; and (c) to Appiah's rejoinder to these criticisms, which, P. Taylor writes, "satisfied everyone, more or less," due to the distinction Appiah drew between race and racial identity. Appiah's interpretation of "Conservation" initially drew attention because it used Du Bois's essay forcefully to defend the core eliminativist thesis that we should abandon race talk for the reason that there are no races. The debates about Appiah's Du Bois interpretation waned when Appiah conceded that racial identities exist, even if races do not (Appiah 1996).

Bernasconi and Jeffers respond to the Du Bois debates, P. Taylor notes, by charging them with presentism (Bernasconi more explicitly than Jeffers)—that is, by stressing that they "overlooked the distance between Du Bois's actual preoccupations and our own," thus missing an important "part of the lasting contribution" of Du Bois's essay. For Bernasconi, bent on restoring Du Bois to his proper discursive context, this meant failing to see that "Conservation" is not at all about the concept of race, but about Du Bois's interest in seeing mixed-race and pure-race Negroes unite around the same ideals—that is, his interest in black survival. For Jeffers, it meant paying too little attention to Du Bois's interest in the future of black cultural life worlds.

P. Taylor acknowledges the importance and force of Bernaconi's and Jeffers's historicist readings of "Conservation," and he even adds fuel to their antipresentist fire by diagnosing the presentism of the interpretations they criticize—interpretations preoccupied with racial eliminativism in the manner of 1990s antiracist critical theory—as motivated by the increasing prominence of "a wider anti-anti racist politics . . . [The] slippage between eliminativist argument and anti-anti-racist politics on the ground was, for some partisans to the early Du Bois debates, precisely the issue" (Taylor 2013b, 386). For these partisans, Taylor explains, the disturbing issue raised by Appiah's reading of Du Bois was that racial eliminativism seemed to reinforce the conservative arguments for color-blindness that tended to animate anti-antiracist politics.

Ultimately, P. Taylor suggests that we should not reject presentist readings of "Conservation," or, for that matter, of any other contributions to the history of African American political thought, for presentist and historicist readings can complement one another, a position that echoes Garber's 1989 essay. "It is important to get Du Bois right, to restore him to his context," P. Taylor insists. "But is also important," he continues "to remember that he was trying to solve certain problems . . . and that if he were around today he would probably be keen to apply his prior self's hard-won insights to contemporary questions" (381). A valuable moral of P. Taylor's argument is that the interests and purposes of the interpreter typically drive the interpretations of received texts, and that the identification of those interests and purposes can help to clarify both the conflict and the complementarity of alternative interpretations.

GOODING-WILLIAMS: *IN THE SHADOW OF DU BOIS*

Returning now to *Shadow*, two broad purposes shaped the argument of that book. Focusing on Du Bois's *The Souls of Black Folk* (Du Bois 1997), *Shadow*'s primary purpose was to reconstruct *Souls*'s response to Jim Crow or, more exactly, its answer to the question: What sort of politics should African Americans conduct to counter Jim Crow, a white supremacist regime that exploited black labor, restricted black suffrage, and segregated the races in schools, housing, and the use of public facilities (Du Bois 1997)? *Souls* proposes, I argued, that a politics fit to respond to Jim Crow must satisfy two conditions.

One condition relates to Du Bois's description of African Americans as "masses"—namely, to his characterization of African Americans as an aggregate of uncultured, premodern slaves or former slaves. The other relates to his description of African Americans as a "folk"; that is, to his characterization of African Americans as a group united by a collectively shared ethos, or spirit. For Du Bois, a politics suitable to counter Jim Crow had both to uplift the backward black masses—to assimilate them to the constitutive norms of modernity—and to heed the ethos of the black folk. In other words, it had to be a politics of modernizing "self-realization" that expressed the spiritual identity of the folk—what in the book I termed a *politics of expressive self-realization*. Du Bois envisions black elites—the so-called talented tenth—as deploying the politics of expressive self-realization to rule and uplift the black masses. Elite control of black politics can be authoritative and effective, he argues, only if it expresses a collective spirit that unites black people.

In addition to reconstructing and analyzing Du Bois's arguments for a politics of expressive self-realization, *Shadow* aimed—and this was its second, broad purpose—to cast that politics in a critical light. *Shadow* uses Frederick Douglass's *My Bondage and My Freedom* (Douglass 1987) and Douglass's depiction of an antiexpressivist, antielitist picture of black politics to throw into relief several limitations and blind spots in Du Bois's understanding of black politics. It also brings its readings of Douglass and Du Bois into conversation with contemporary, often Du Bois-echoing debates about the nature of African American politics, the relevance of black identity to black politics, and the plight of the black underclass.

Back of both purposes was an appreciation for the historically extended, philosophical authority exercised by *Souls* and, more generally, by the political thought of the young Du Bois. The conceptual and normative commitments shaping Du Bois's early political thought—his elitist understanding of black politics, his expressivism, and his conception of the Negro problem—have exerted considerable influence on African American political theory and activism in the twentieth and early twenty-first centuries (Gooding-Williams 2009). In addition, Du Bois's philosophical authority had been so compelling and far reaching that it had tended to overshadow and foreclose potentially fruitful, alternative possibilities for understanding black politics. The point of reconstructing Du Bois's philosophical response to Jim Crow was explicitly to grasp the conceptual and normative commitments shaping his early thought as elements of a coherent argument. In a related vein, the point of turning to *Bondage* was to recover for post–Jim Crow African American political theory possibilities for understanding black politics that the force of Du Bois's philosophical authority has tended to obscure.

To return to C. Taylor—that is, to restate *Shadow*'s reconstructive agenda in C. Taylor's idiom—the primary purpose of my book was to advance a genetic account of the young Du Bois's political theoretical model of black politics; that is, to retrieve his foundational, creative redescription of black politics, for which he could and did give reasons. I thought it was important to retrieve that model, because it seemed to me that, over time, our practices of construing and envisioning the possibilities available to black political life—and here I meant especially to include the practice of post–Jim Crow African American political thought—had come to embed a number of unquestioned and difficult-to-question assumptions that echoed the writings of the young Du Bois.

To be sure, my point was *not* to suggest that the theoretical richness of Du Bois's oeurvre, early or late, could be reduced to these assumptions. Rather, it was to highlight their centrality, to show how and why, despite some tensions between them, they appeared to hang together, and to gain some distance from them—at least enough distance to begin to regard them as optional. Like C. Taylor, but unlike Garber, it seemed to me that, to loosen the grip of Du Bois's early response to Jim Crow on African American political thought and activism, and to begin to take seriously historical alternatives—that is, to begin to regard historical alternatives not as bizarre, but as plausible and as deserving consideration—it was initially necessary to engage Du Bois's thought on its own terms. Once engaged, it seemed reasonable critically to consider Du Bois's thought in the perspective of one of those alternatives—Douglass's *Bondage*—and to bring the thought of both thinkers to bear in evaluating contemporary contributions to African American political theory (again, this was *Shadow*'s second, broad purpose).

Here, the purpose of my argument was not, as K. Anthony Appiah (2011) suggests in a review of *Shadow*, simply to "counterpose" Du Bois's errors to Douglass's insights; rather it was to consider contemporary African American political theory in a new light—that is, in the perspective of an account of Douglass's political thought that questions several commitments that contemporary African American political theory takes over from Du Bois. Put differently, the point of my Douglass-inspired assessment of Du Bois's early political thought and its current avatars was ideology critique, understood as a feature of antiracist critical theory (again, see Haslanger 2012). For the point of that assessment was to expose, analyze, and critically revalue the conceptual framework that the young Du Bois has bequeathed to African American political theory and activism in the twentieth and twenty-first centuries. It is obvious, I hope, that I am not supposing here that the conceptual framework Du Bois bequeathed to us was racist, but simply that antiracist politics, no less than the unacceptably unjust practices it opposes, can be a target of ideology critique.

A few words, finally, as to the character of my readings of Du Bois and Douglass. Are they historicist and de dicto, or presentist and de re? Are they predicated on commitments that Du Bois and Douglass did or would acknowledge, or do they depart from those commitments?

My reconstruction of Du Bois's thought is, I believe, historicist and de dicto. In connection to this assertion, I should like to express three thoughts: first, that my reading of Du Bois can accommodate the insights for which P. Taylor rightly praises Bernasconi's and Jeffers's essays; second, and to borrow again C. Taylor's terminology, that because the point of my reconstruction of *Souls*'s political theoretical response to Jim Crow was to present it as a set of claims for which Du Bois could and did give reasons, I sought to interpret that response with reference to commitments and considerations that Du Bois did or would acknowledge; third, and finally, that I also sought to highlight the extent to which the thought of many of Du Bois's heirs still stems from commitments that Du Bois did or would acknowledge.

Regarding my reading of Douglass, many of the particulars of my argument—my interpretation of the fight with Covey (Douglass's struggle, as a slave, against the effort of Edward Covey, "the Negro breaker," to break him), as Douglass depicts it in *Bondage*, for example— were historicist and de dicto. But the larger argument, I think, is presentist and de re for a reason that I adduce in the introduction to *Shadow*: namely, that I insistently read *Bondage* with an eye to a range of questions prompted by my reading of *Souls*: What is African American politics? Should African American politics take the form of political expressivism? Is white supremacy best understood as a form of social exclusion? *Bondage* I interpret as giving answers to these questions, but I am hard put to defend the claim that, in attributing those answers to Douglass's autobiography, in the terms I use to attribute them, I consistently appeal to commitments that Douglass would acknowledge. For example, my interpretation of the plantation politics *Bondage* depicts presupposes that politics generally, and African American politics in particular, need not be understood *as rule*, as what some human beings do to others, deciding for them, or commanding them, but can usefully be conceptualized *as action-in-concert*, as what human beings do together, responding to one another's initiatives (see Gooding-Williams 2009). I doubt that Douglass would avow that presupposition. Still, I am committed to the claim that politics can be so conceptualized, and that *Bondage* depicts Douglass's plantation politics as ruler-less action-in-concert.

In sum, then, and in keeping with P. Taylor's insight that historicist and presentist readings can be productively combined—that they can complement one another—the argument and ideology critique that I advance in *Shadow* shows that readings of both sorts can fruitfully expand both the study of the history of African American political thought and our sense of the possibilities available to black politics.

CONCLUSION: HISTORY AND ANTIRACIST CRITICAL THEORY

The sweep of contemporary contributions to antiracist critical theory is extensive and includes expansive genealogical and critical historical accounts of modern racism; astute conceptual analyses of the interplay of racial and gender oppression; systematic explanations of the roles that policing, prison growth, and segregation play in perpetuating racial inequality; and nuanced appraisals of recent black politics—including the "Black Lives Matter" movement. Not all these efforts take up the history of Afro-modern or African American political thought, but many do, and when they do, they typically complicate our understanding of the relationship between the issues that engage contemporary critical theorists and the issues that engaged some of their predecessors (Shelby 2005; Sundstrom 2008; Gooding-Williams 2009; Dotson 2013). When they do not, we may well find that these efforts reflect an overly narrow range of philosophical and political imagination (Scott 2012; Taylor 2013b).

REFERENCES

Appiah, K. Anthony. (1992). *In My Father's House: Africa in the Philosophy of Culture.* New York: Oxford University Press.

Appiah, K. Anthony. (2011). "Battling with Du Bois." *New York Review of Books.* December: 81–85.

Appiah, K. Anthony, and Amy Gutmann. (1996). *Color Conscious.* Princeton, NJ: Princeton University Press.

Bernasconi, Robert. (2009). "'Our Duty to Conserve': W.E.B. Du Bois's Philosophy of History On Context." *South Atlantic Quarterly* 108 (3): 519–540.

Brandom, Robert B. (2002). *Tales of the Mighty Dead: Historical Essays in the Metaphysics of Intentionality.* Cambridge, MA: Harvard University Press.

Dotson, Kristie. (2013). "Knowing in Space: Three Lessons from Black Women's Social Theory." *Social Science Research Network.* Accessed May 11, 2016. http://ssrn.com/abstract=2270343.

Douglass, Frederick. (1987). *My Bondage and My Freedom.* Edited by Williams L. Andrews. Urbana: University of Illinois Press.

Du Bois, W. E. B. (1997). *The Souls of Black Folk.* Edited by David W. Blight and Robert Gooding-Williams. Boston: Bedford Books.

Garber, Daniel. (1989). "Does History Have a Future? Some Reflections on Bennett and Doing Philosophy Historically." In *Doing Philosophy Historically*, edited by P. Hare, 25–43. Buffalo, NY: Pergamon Press.

Garber, Daniel. (2001). *Descartes Embodies: Reading Cartesian Philosophy Through Cartesian Science.* New York: Cambridge University Press.

Garber, Daniel. (2005). "What's Philosophical about the History of Philosophy?" In *Analytic Philosophy and History of Philosophy*, edited by Tom Sorrell and G. A. J. Rogers, 129–146. Oxford: Oxford University Press.

Gooding-Williams, Robert. (2009). *In the Shadow of Du Bois: Afro Modern Political Thought in American.* Cambridge, MA: Harvard University Press.

Haslanger, Sally. (2012). *Resisting Reality: Social Construction and Social Critique*. New York: Oxford University Press.

Jeffers, Chike. (2013). "The Cultural Theory of Race." *Ethics* 123: 403–426.

Kuhn, Thomas. (2012). *The Structure of Scientific Revolutions*. 4th ed. Chicago: University of Chicago Press.

Marx, Karl. (1967). "An Exchange of Letters." In *Writings of the Young Marx on Philosophy and Society*, edited and translated by Loyd D. Easton and Kurt H. Guddat, 203–215. New York: Doubleday.

Rorty, Richard, J. B. Schneewind, and Quentin Skinner. (1984). *Philosophy in History: Essays on the Historiography of Philosophy*. Cambridge: Cambridge University Press.

Scott, David. (2012). "The Traditions of Historical Others." *Symposia on Gender, Race and Philosophy* 8 (1): 1–8.

Shelby, Tommie. (2005). *We Who Are Dark: The Philosophical Foundations of Black Solidarity*. Cambridge, MA: Harvard University Press.

Sundstrom, Ronald. (2008). *The Browning of America and the Evasion of Social Justice*. Albany: State University of New York Press.

Taylor, Charles. (1984). "Philosophy and Its History." In *Philosophy in History*, edited by J. B. Schneewind and Quentin Skinner; Charles Taylor, Ian Hacking, Wolf Lepenies, 17–30. Cambridge: Cambridge University Press.

Taylor, Paul C. (2013a). "Whose Integration, What's Imperative?" *Symposia on Gender, Race, and Philosophy* 9/2 (Fall 2013): 1–5.

Taylor, Paul C. (2013b). "Bare Ontology and Social Death." *Philosophical Papers* 42 (3): 369–389.

PART V

....

CONTINENTAL
PHILOSOPHY
AND RACE

....

As suggested in the volume introduction, the dividing line between so-called continental and analytic philosophy is not as sharp in philosophy of race as in other subfields of contemporary philosophy. Nevertheless, when race is explored through Hegel, Marx, Sartre, Fanon, and Foucault, there is a marked change in observable terrain from when the train travels through the official and alternative histories of philosophy, philosophy of science, or American philosophy.

Continental philosophical methodology in a study of any kind of human experience has the potential to yield phenomenological insights. Phenomenological insights about racial identities and interactions can reveal how human beings subjectively experience self, other, and self and other in relationship. The point here is that continental philosophical approaches to race have the potential to analyze real, concrete human situations in individual life and society, instead of approaching the subject abstractly, within a practice of strict objectivity. That is, full recognition is given to the existing human subject, who is actually or potentially the author and designer of the social and physical scientific investigations that would otherwise be a source of truth—real live human beings create science.

The continental approach to race is able to yield deep moral and existential truths about race relations and racism that might otherwise require literary brilliance that would not be as trustworthy for veracity. A couple of well-known examples by Jean-Paul Sartre and Franz Fanon, which happen to mirror one another, will help make this general point before delving into the specifics of this part. In *Anti-Semite and Jew*, despite Sartre's general claims that his philosophical perspective of existentialism cannot provide an ethics, he describes the flawed character of the French anti-Semite. The anti-Semite bases his self-worth on something he was already born with, instead of on the process and results of his own choices and actions—he objectifies himself: "His virtue depends upon the assimilation of the qualities which the work of a hundred generations has lent to the objects which surround him; it depends on property. It goes without saying this is a matter of inherited property, not property one buys" (Sartre 1948, 23). Fanon, by contrast, writes about how European whites have objectified him. In describing his reaction to the famous passage in which a little boy reacts to him with alarm—"Look, a Negro! *Maman*, a Negro!"—Fanon writes, "My body was returned to me spread-eagled, disjointed, wrapped in mourning" (Fanon 1952, 93). Today, as over half a century ago, Sartre and Fanon's readers intuitively understand that the human subject is not a thing, so that when people render themselves effortlessly superior things or render others automatically inferior things, something has gone badly wrong in human relations.

The contemporary continental focus on the living, feeling, changing, choosing, human subject has its most powerful antecedents in philosophers who based the whole world on the human mind or *spirit*. Nevertheless, as we saw regarding Kant in Part I, there is nothing inherent in philosophical idealism that predisposed thinkers to support racial egalitarianism. Indeed, Hegel, in perhaps the most intense associations of race with [the spirit of] geography in the modern period, wrote about Africans in terms that are shameful and shocking today:

> From the earliest historical times, Africa has remained cut off from all contact with the rest of the world. It is the land of gold, forever pressing in upon itself, and the land of childhood, removed from the light of self-consciousness history and wrapped in the dark mantle of night. (Hegel 1997, 31)

Apart from this view of Africa, which Hegel extended to its inhabitants, he has not generally been considered an existentialist, or even as in this case, a negative existentialist of blackness. Indeed, Søren Kierkegaard used Hegel as a bad example for his own existentialist philosophy. So, methodologically, as well as in content, Hegel does not appear to be a possible friend of antiracist continental approaches. However, as Rocío Zambrana explains, extensive use has been made of at least one of Hegel's insights that historically applies to race relations, namely the relation between history and freedom. For Hegel, freedom is an historical development requiring autonomy in the Enlightenment sense that entails recognition by "the other" (another person who is different from oneself in some important way). Freedom cannot be exempt from the laws of nature, but "modes of individual and collective self-understanding, and their institutional embodiments, are said to be free, to make possible a free life, if they are products of self-articulation, rather than products of nature." According to Hegel, slavery occurs among Africans because they do not have aptitude for culture. Mere victory in war can result in enslavement which then has the form of what Hegel considers an "absolute injustice." But, based on interpretation of his early work on the revolution in Haiti and his meaning of universalism, Zambrana argues that Hegel did not always locate Africans outside of history and thereby incapable of freedom. And she thereby calls for present Hegelians to build on that potential universalism in his thought.

Insofar as Marx is said to have applied a Hegelian analysis to material inequalities, it may seem as though Hegelian methods could be useful for considering poverty as an inequality accompanying racial hierarchy. Stephen Ferguson believes that from a Marxist perspective, the overuse of race as a primary analytic category in social explanation "may obscure the political struggles of the black working class." But Ferguson does not want to go so far as to claim that all forms of oppression are ultimately a matter of, or reduce to, economic class. He follows the black Communist Doxey A. Wilkerson in drawing a distinction between a biological fact of race and social myths of racial inequality. The biological reality or nonreality of race is not the whole story, however. Rather, "the ontological status of race can only be disclosed through the examination of the real, material relations, social institutions and social practices that give rise to the necessity for racial categories and take the form of racist ideology." Ferguson emphasizes that race is primarily a social category that cannot be abstracted from racism. But the anatomy of racism is an integral part of the economy of capitalism, so that class differences within racial groups must be recognized.

Jonathan Judaken relates race to existentialism as a mid-twentieth century world view. His analysis is anchored on Normal Mailer's "The White Negro" and Albert Memmi's *Pillar of Salt*. Judaken draws from cultural critics who did not write fiction, to show how these texts were moments in a passage from understanding racism as an individual problem or subject, to a political and economic condition. Mailer used his figure of the American hipster to associate his criticism of bland "Father Knows Best" culture with existentialism. Rejecting the prevailing idea that racial essence determined identity, Mailer slightly revised Sartre's "existence precedes essence" to "Man is then not only his character, but his context." James Baldwin criticized Mailer for his appropriation of black identity for white "hipness," because he did not go below the surface of black stereotypes as hypersexual criminals and psychopaths.

Relevant to Baldwin's critique of Mailer was the shift in Sartre's view from his treatment of anti-Semitism to antiblack racism. Whereas Sartre had criticized the anti-Semite in terms of individual vice, in considering antiblack racism, through the influence of Frantz Fanon, he took a more political approach. Sartre came to insist that the freedom of blacks required the freedom of all humankind. As part of that position, Sartre criticized Memmi's location of racism in individual psyches, as well as his refusal to recognize the connection of racism with an economic system. Although Memmi ultimately adopted a more Marxist perspective in response to Sartre, he continued to insist that racism ultimately rested on a Sartrean idea of bad faith, as well as anxiety about, and fear of, the other.

Ladelle McWhorter turns to Foucault to consider the intellectual trajectory from scientific racism to neoliberal biopolitics, and how racism survived its scientific demise toward resurrection in new forms of oppression. As a genealogist, McWhorter cautions that racism "exists only in its various historical manifestations in (usually institutionalized) practices, including the rationalizing practices that give those practices their sense, and it changes as networks of power change." Thus, McWhorter traces the history of "race" as a product of institutions. In the eighteenth century, "race" meant linear descent but by the nineteenth, it was primarily a matter of appearance, followed by differences in development. After World War II, within educated communities, racism came to be regarded as a form of ignorance. Over this period, modern societal practices of normalization through discipline were perfected, for schools, military camps, hospitals, asylums, and prisons. Also, sexuality came to be socially formed and technologized as "biopower," which through eugenics was a new powerful tool of racial discipline—before Hitler (Nazi race theory directly placed the idea of human breeding for the good of society in very bad repute). Since Foucault wrote, neoliberalism has produced explanations of inequality based on individual traits, rather than wider social, political, or economic systems. And although this new individualism may involve less discipline against whole categories of human beings, there is a customized, niche-consumption division of populations that favors those who can contribute and consume more, while at the same time disciplining and controlling subgroups who are less engaged with the mass system.

Lewis Gordon approaches the assumption that phenomenology is a product of Western "continental" thought, with considerable skepticism. Gordon focuses on Africana existentialist, but not transcendental, phenomenology. Although he does not view these two approaches as opposed, he distinguishes between them insofar far as "existential phenomenology asserts a fundamental *incompleteness* at the heart of our relationship with reality, whereas transcendental phenomenology explores the conditions by which such claims about knowledge are possible." Gordon goes on to introduce and explore several related Africana phenomenological insights, in a critique of Afro-pessimism. The Afro-pessimistic claim that blackness is social death raises the question of why the fundamental foundation of the social world should be the "attitudes and perspectives of antiblack racists." Also, Gordon claims that the posit of social death is itself a form of bad faith (mauvaise foi) because existing (standing out) as not existing (not standing out) is a conundrum. Furthermore, such ideas of nonexistence preclude that equality between members of different groups which is necessary for there to be ethics and morals. That is, if we do not share the same humanity, then we cannot impose obligations on others, morally evaluate them, or make demands for ourselves to others.

Further Reading

Fanon, Frantz. [1952] (2008). *Black Skin, White Masks.* Translated by Richard Philcox. New York: Grove Press.

Gordon, Lewis R., ed. (1996). *Existence in Black.* New York: Routledge.

Hegel, Friedrich Georg Wilhelm. (1997). "Geographical Bases of World History." In *Race and the Enlightenment: A Reader*, edited by Emmanuel Chukwudi Eze, 110–149. Cambridge, MA: Blackwell.

Sartre, Jean-Paul. (1948). *Anti-Semite and Jew: An Exploration of the Etiology of Hate.* New York: Schockten Books.

Stewart, Jon. (2003). *Kierkegaard's Relations to Hegel Reconsidered.* Cambridge: Cambridge University Press.

CHAPTER 21

....

HEGEL, HISTORY, AND RACE

....

ROCÍO ZAMBRANA

Where is the *Rhodus*
on which the political philosopher
is supposed to perform his political dance?

Henrich Paulus (quoted in Bernasconi 2000)

NOTWITHSTANDING the critical reception of Hegel's philosophy of history throughout the nineteenth and twentieth centuries, versions of his defense of modernity are alive and well. Consider, for instance, Axel Honneth's work (2014). It is a normative reconstruction of Hegel's claim that historical development is a matter of the actualization of freedom. The Hegelian notion of freedom remains tied to an Enlightenment conception of autonomy, yet it recognizes the social conditions of possibility for autonomous agency. Such conception of freedom is itself the historical achievement of Western modernity. It is articulated through struggles for recognition pursued by different social movements (Honneth 1996). Although we should interrogate the forms of exclusion and violence out of which it is born, the Enlightenment conception of freedom retains normative power on its own. An institution or practice can thus be assessed in light of its capacity to actualize freedom. A philosophy of history and its world-historical perspective is accordingly necessary not only for reconstructing this conception of social freedom but also for establishing social freedom as the correct normative framework for thinking about justice.

Honneth's work is arguably the most prominent example of a "reactualization" of Hegel's conceptions of history and right. It is exemplary of one of two approaches to Hegel's thinking of history. Honneth seeks to further develop the *form* of Hegel's arguments, dropping the offensive content—Hegel's comments on race—that would contaminate the normative power of Hegel's insights. Robert Bernasconi's work is exemplary of the second approach, which seeks to assess the form of Hegel's philosophy of history by interrogating the *content* of Hegel's *Philosophy of Spirit* and his *Lectures on the Philosophy of History*. Indeed, Bernasconi has called attention to the role that race plays in the unabashed Eurocentrism of Hegel's philosophy of history (see Bernasconi 1998, 2000, 2003, 2010). For example, he has examined Hegel's treatment of the sources on which he based his infamous treatment of Africa in order to call into question Hegel's notion of world history (Bernasconi 1998). Bernasconi has also suggested that the relation between Hegel's anthropological account of race and his philosophy of world history establishes the racial basis of the latter (Bernasconi 2000).

In what follows, I examine the entwinement of Hegel's philosophy of history and his treatment of race. I do so, however, not in order to provide an assessment of Hegel's views on race, which should simply be rejected. Rather, I aim to consider the ways in which scholars and teachers working within a Hegelian context ought to engage Hegel's understanding of history and of a philosophical thinking of history. My focus takes up Bernasconi's important challenge to contemporary philosophy. He argues that we ought to engage the ugly passages of the Western canon, yet not merely to establish the racism of historical figures such as Locke, Kant, or Hegel. Instead, we ought to reflect on the "institutional racism of a discipline that has developed subtle strategies to play down the racism of Locke, Kant and Hegel, among others, with the inevitable consequence that, for example, in the United States philosophers are disproportionately white" (Bernasconi 2003, 35). In this context, it is instructive to consider Susan Buck-Morss's *Hegel, Haiti, and Universal History*. Buck-Morss both examines the entwinement of history and race in Hegel, and she defends a reconstructed notion of universal history. Her argument hinges on an interrogation of the academic practices that repressed Hegel's knowledge of the revolution in Haiti. She thereby attempts to develop further Hegelian insights by marking the very limits of Hegel's thought and Hegel scholarship.

HEGEL ON RACE AND WORLD HISTORY

Hegel's comments on race are part of his discussion of anthropology within his account of subjective spirit, but they gain theoretical significance within his discussion of world history, which is part of his account of objective spirit. It is important to bear in mind that with the notion of spirit, *Geist*, Hegel denotes both individual mind and collective mindedness. In the *Encyclopedia of Philosophical Sciences*, comprised of a logic, a philosophy of nature, and a philosophy of spirit, Hegel gives an account of subjective spirit through an anthropology, a phenomenology, and a psychology. He gives an account of objective spirit through an assessment of right, morality, and ethical life (family, civil society, state), which includes world history. In the anthropology of the *Philosophy of Spirit*, Hegel's comments on race are an abridged version of what is explored at greater length in the *Lectures on the Philosophy of History*. To be sure, there are substantive editorial challenges that need to be kept in mind when assessing the additions to the *Philosophy of Spirit* and the *Lectures on the Philosophy of History* (see the introduction to Hegel 2011 and Walker 2014). These texts are comprised of student transcriptions and author manuscripts. Nevertheless, both discussions respond to a thorny, yet central issue in Hegel's system: the relation between nature and spirit.

Although spirit has nature as its "presupposition," Hegel argues that spirit is the "truth" of nature (Hegel 1978, 24, 25). Famously, Hegel maintains that nature "vanishes" in this truth. Key to understanding this odd claim is the conception of freedom that is at the core of Hegel's idealism. Hegel's notion of freedom transforms Kantian autonomy by understanding spontaneity relationally. In this context, we must understand freedom in light of Hegel's characterization of spirit as a "product of itself" (Hegel 1975, 51). Spirit is a form of individual and collective self-relation. It is a form of self-consciousness through practices and institutions of self-articulation (see Zambrana 2015b). A form of life articulates the truth of nature, self, and society through scientific, political, artistic, religious, and philosophical practices. Now, Robert Pippin argues that, although initially an awkward characterization, we should understand the nature–spirit relation as a form of "compatibilism" (Pippin 1999). Because (*contra* Kant) Hegel rejects all accounts of freedom that require an appeal to a realm exempt from the laws of nature, Hegel's insistence that spirit leaves nature behind must be tempered. It is not an ontological claim, but rather a claim about the type of account giving that is appropriate. We can account for social-historical phenomena appropriately by appealing to the institutional actualization of freedom, rather than appealing to determinations of nature. In other words, modes of individual and collective self-understanding, and their institutional embodiments, are said to be free, to make possible a free life, if they are products of self-articulation, rather than products of nature.

This is the framework for making sense of the metaphysics laid out in the introductions to the *Lectures on the Philosophy of History*. Moreover, it is the framework for making sense of the relation between Hegel's anthropological discussion of race and the philosophical discussion of world history. The common thread between the two discussions is Hegel's insistence on tracking racial diversity to geographical, geological, and climactic diversity. In fact, Hegel rejects the monogenesis and polygenesis debate crucial for his predecessor's accounts of race (see de Laurentiis forthcoming and Parekh 2009). In the *Philosophy of Spirit*, Hegel argues that the variability of the "soul" or "natural spirit," which is to say all "planetary life," is the result of geological transformations (Hegel 1978, §392; see de Laurentiis forthcoming). He adds that this includes humankind and its races (*Rassen*), peoples (*Völker*), and native groups (*Lokalgeister*). In the *Lectures*, Hegel argues that history is progress, since it is the development of the consciousness of freedom. It is humankind's progressive freedom from nature through becoming conscious of its capacity to be a product of itself. Freedom is here not something abstract or individual, but exhibited in the type of institutions distinctive of a people. In the *Lectures*, Hegel tracks the actualization of freedom from east to west. World history begins in China and ends in Europe. Properly speaking, world history begins in Persia, which is deemed to belong to the "Caucasian race," and hence to begin "continuous history" (Hegel 1956, 180). As we will see, Africa is outside of history. America remains indeterminate (see Hegel 1975, 170).

In the addition to section 393 of the anthropology, Hegel argues against the idea that the "mental and spiritual superiority of one race over another" could be explained by descent. "[M]an is implicitly rational," he reportedly explains, and "herein lies the possibility of equal justice for all men and the futility of a rigid distinction between races which have rights and those which have none." Nevertheless, he adds that the difference between races is a "natural difference," one that derives from geographical location. Hegel proceeds to explain the "distinctive character" of the continents, which provides the basis for his account of the classification of the races. To be sure, Hegel simply accepts Kant's division of four races and Blumenbach's five varieties (see Bernasconi 2010). However, geological, geographical, and climactic circumstances determine a race's capacity to achieve consciousness of freedom, to leave behind its natural existence. We should immediately note that Hegel's distinction between the universal rationality of humankind and the natural difference of the races follows his nature–spirit distinction. As social-historical, "man" is implicitly rational. Justice is a matter for all. As natural, different races admit of different capacities and dispositions.

In both the anthropology and the lectures on history, Africa and Africans fare the worst. Infamously, Hegel argues the following (see Hegel 1978, §393; 1975, 173ff.). North Africa "up to the boundary of the sandy desert" is not Africa proper. Its inhabitants are not Africans, "that is, Blacks [*die Neger*]," but rather European in character. Africa proper, sub-Saharan Africa, is a "landmass belonging to a compact unity." Its "fiery heat" is "a force of a too powerful nature for man to resist, or for spirit to achieve free movement and to reach a degree of richness which is necessary for it to cultivated form of actuality." Because it is cut off from sea, its inhabitants are cut off from economic and cultural commerce. Its inhabitants are therefore a "race of children that remain immersed in a state of naiveté." They are tied to sensuousness, which is reflected in their disposition and their religion (see Bernasconi 1998, 2000). They lack the "drive [*Trieb*] toward freedom." Though they can be educated (*Bildung*), they have no propensity (*Trieb*) for culture (*Kultur*). These claims inflect his assessment of slavery. Slavery is a natural relation among Africans. The slave and the master are thus "distinguished arbitrarily," by the contingency of victory in war. This contingency establishes African slavery as an "absolute injustice," by which he means outside of proper political relations. Addressing the Atlantic slave trade, Hegel concludes that slavery is best "eliminated gradually," as a part of a process of education (*Bildung*). Through slavery, Europeans had begun the process by which Africans could become conscious of their own freedom.

Africa is outside of history, it seems, given its natural determination. The nature–spirit relation that frames the intersection of race and history in Hegel's system, however, complicates matters. Indeed, it opens up interpretive space that has allowed for defenses of Hegel against the charge of racism, as we will see. Hegel states that the subject matter of a philosophy of history is the "world historical significance of peoples," not races. In section 394 of the anthropology, Hegel argues that racial diversity "expresses itself in particularities, in spirits which may be said to be localized." This expresses itself both "externally" and "internally," both in ways of life, bodily constitution, and disposition, and in the propensity and capacity of "intellectual and ethical character." In the addition, we read that Hegel argues that the history of peoples "exhibits the persistence of this type in particular nations." National difference is as "unchangeable" as the "racial variety of men." Hence, "national character" is but the "germ out of which the history of the nations develops." The historical significance of peoples is thus established by a move from a "natural history of man" to a world-historical perspective. This is to say, for Hegel, we must move from a natural to a spiritual (*geistige*) explanation of individual and collective character if we are to assess a people's capacity for freedom.

In Hegel's philosophy of history, it is not nations but rather the nation as a state, *Volk als Staat*, as he puts it in the *Philosophy of Right*, that exhibits freedom (Hegel 1991, 331). The move from race and indeed national character to the nation as a state concerns the self-consciousness of a nation. Such a nation is no longer tied to natural dispositions. It is a matter of rational institutions that embody freedom, that make possible autonomy. This is the normative core of Hegel's famous claim that world history is a court of world judgment—"Die Weltgeschichte ist das Weltgericht" (Hegel 1991, 341). World history can judge, given the "rationality" of institutions that comprise a way of life. The move from a natural to a *geistige* account of peoples is thus tantamount to a move from a crude biological notion of race to an account of culture as the basis for understanding the progress of world history. This has been the crucial point for defenders of Hegel, like Joseph Mccareny. Mccarney points out that, for Hegel, insofar as people are also nations, their principle is a natural one (see Mccarney 2000, chap. 9). Far from basing his account of world history on race, he stresses, Hegel understands world history as a matter of ethical-political institutions. World history is a matter of the "rationality" of those institutions, where rationality is defined in light of an Enlightenment conception of freedom. Given that "groups whose principle is a natural one, such as nations, tribes, castes and races, cannot as such figure as historical subjects," Mccarney writes, "[i]t follows that, for Hegel, there literally cannot be a racist interpretation of history" (Mccarney 2003, 33).

In contrast, Bernasconi argues that, while such terminological moves might map onto the nature–spirit relation such that they indicate a move away from a crude biological notion of race to a notion of cultural difference, Hegel reinscribes the hierarchy of races in his philosophy of history (Bernasconi 2000, 2003). Notwithstanding the move from a natural to a spiritual account, in the *Lectures* Hegel argues that "nations whose consciousness is obscure" are not the "object of philosophical history of the world." That is to say, peoples who have not achieved self-consciousness of their freedom, who have not left nature behind, are not "objects" of world history. They are not part of the progress of history as reconstructed by a philosophy of world history. Yet, rather than ignored, these peoples are deemed "savages." What is more, Europeans are not only deemed cultured. They are vehicles of culture. For Bernasconi, assessment of a people in light of their capacity to break with the bonds of nature clearly tracks the racial hierarchy at the center of Hegel's natural history of humankind. That the beginning of world history is linked with the "Caucasian" race, that Africa is literally outside of history, are determinations that remain tied to the naturalist account of the anthropology. Bernasconi makes clear that this does not merely expose Hegel's Eurocentrism. It expresses the *racial* politics of nineteenth-century European and American colonialism (Bernasconi 2000, 190–191). Hegel's views on race, then, should make us question the nature–spirit distinction that structures Hegel's thought. Therefore, they should make us question the conceptual structure of Hegel's philosophy of history.

Earlier I stated that Hegel's comments on race gain theoretical significance within his discussion of world history. Hegel's insistence that the truth of nature is spirit presses us to assess the relation between race and history in light of the world historical sublation (*aufhebung*) of race. This does not mean an overcoming of race, however. As Bernasconi's work has shown, the *aufhebung* in question retains the determinations of nature sketched in the anthropology within Hegel's philosophy of history. Race remains inseparable from world history, even if we argue that they are distinguishable modes of giving an account of the history of humankind. A world historical perspective, which aims to critically assess the actualization of freedom by tracking its institutional embodiment, remains tied to a conception of freedom that gains descriptive traction and normative force from opposing its non-Western, indeed non-"Caucasian" Other. Although Mccarney's defense of Hegel is theoretically acute, the entanglement of race and history in Hegel cannot be denied. The question becomes, Why should it be denied? Does recovering Hegelian concepts depend on purifying them from their problematic content? Most important, what are the consequences of this theoretical operation?

World History as Universal History

In her important essay "Reason, Power, and History," Amy Allen calls attention to the philosophies of history that frame contemporary critical theory (Allen 2014; cf. Zambrana 2015a).

The essay focuses on Jürgen Habermas's understanding of historical progress, arguing that this philosophy of history has made possible critical theory's virtual silence on colonialism and imperialism. Habermas and Honneth, among others, have failed to substantially engage the postcolonial and decolonial critiques of modernity, given the notions of historical progress that they have sought to recover from the Enlightenment tradition, albeit in a nonmetaphysical key. In attempting to carry forward the unfinished project of the Enlightenment, they have failed to fully assess modernity's violence.

The entanglement of race and history in Hegel deepens the problems that Allen identifies. Here, considering Susan Buck-Morss's *Hegel, Haiti, and Universal History* is instructive (see Buck-Morss 2009). Buck-Morss examines the entwinement of history and race in Hegel, yet she does so in order to recover, rather than reject, "modernity's universal intent" (Buck-Morss 2009, ix). Indeed, she confronts Hegel in order to radically reconstruct a Hegelian notion of universal history. Such reconstruction, however, depends on critically assessing the academic practices that repressed Hegel's knowledge of the revolution in Haiti—knowledge of a slave revolt that culminated not only in the elimination of slavery but also in the founding of a black republic, the Republic of Haiti. Buck-Morss's work, then, attempts to recover Hegelian insights by marking the limits of Hegel's thought, by articulating precisely where and how it fails. But more important, she attempts to recover Hegelian insights by marking the limits of Hegel scholarship.

In *Hegel, Haiti, and Universal History*, Buck-Morss confronts Hegel's account of Africans as outside of history and of slavery as requiring gradual dissolution with his own knowledge of the Haitian Revolution. Hegel had knowledge of the Haitian Revolution through the leading political magazine of his time, *Minerva*, which not only reported on the events in St. Domingue but also ran a series devoted to the revolution from fall 1804 to winter 1805. This year-long series included "source documents, new summaries, and eye witness accounts" (Buck-Morss 2009, 42). Hegel's early philosophical development was inspired by the events in Haiti, Buck-Morss argues, while his mature lectures on Africa are simply evidence of Hegel becoming "dumber" throughout the years (Buck-Morss 2009, 73). Indeed, Buck-Morss argues, Hegel's early conceptions of lordship and bondage and his famous master–slave dialectic in his 1807 *Phenomenology of Spirit* were inspired by the revolution in Haiti. His mature lectures on Africa express a conservative view in tension with his early work.

What is crucial for Buck-Morss is the fact that the significance of the Haitian Revolution for Hegel's early work was repressed within Hegel scholarship. Silence about Hegel's knowledge of the revolution is a product of an Enlightenment bias, which developed a notion of universal equality that underestimated the events in St. Domingue. Such notion privileged the French Revolution, which in turn led to privileging the significance of the French Revolution in Hegel's intellectual development (see Buck-Morss 2009, 48ff.). The repression, Buck-Morss argues, is also a product of a North-American ignorance, which follows from the exclusion of the Haitian Revolution from histories of the Age of Revolutions and the Enlightenment. The crucial point is that specialized scholarship that fragments the production of knowledge into fields that do not collaborate made the conjunction of Hegel and Haiti an unlikely one (see, e.g., Buck-Morss 2009, 22–23). Indeed, the division between philosophical work and historical work made possible a lack of reflection on how Hegel's most influential philosophical claims were developed from historical sources that ought to have made some of those very claims untenable.

For Buck-Morss, uncovering Hegel's knowledge of the Haitian Revolution recovers the world historical significance of the events in St. Domingue. This recovery incorporates what Hegel called "unhistorical histories" into world history, thereby subverting an Enlightenment narrative from within. It interrupts the official narrative of histories of and by the Enlightenment. But it also interrupts the very idea of world history distinctive of the Enlightenment tradition and central to Hegel's own philosophy of history. This interruption makes possible counternarratives. "What happens when," Buck-Morss writes, "in the spirit of dialectics, we turn the tables and consider Haiti not as a victim of Europe, but as an agent in Europe's construction" (Buck-Morss 2009, 80)? We would be able to construct an alternative history of modernity as a product of the colonial system. Now, for Buck-Morss, this interruptive operation rewrites, rather than rejects, modernity's universal intent. Indeed, a counternarrative remains a *universal* history, one in which "human universality emerges in the historical event at the point of rupture" (Buck-Morss 2009, 133). Marginalized events, instead of history's progress, ground a universalist perspective. A universalist perspective is necessary, if we are committed to bringing to light what Buck-Morss calls our "inhumanity in common" (Buck-Morss 2009, 138ff.). For Buck-Morss, then, the *failures* of universal emancipation must inform our conceptions of universal intent. The crucial point is that unhistorical histories and the counternarratives that they make possible "inspire action," rather than reinscribe power (Buck-Morss 2009, 110).

Buck-Morss's work helps us think through the entanglement of race and history in Hegel's work. But it does so by pushing us to think through the entanglement of race and history in our academic endeavors—repressions that are produced by conceptions of race, by conceptions of history, by disciplinary divides. Buck-Morss's book attempts to "blast open the continuum of history," to borrow Walter Benjamin's words, by rescuing the "unhistorical history" of the Haitian Revolution from oblivion, a forgetting imposed by a Hegelian understanding of world history (Benjamin 1969, thesis 15; for Buck-Morss's work on Benjamin, see, for example, 1991). In other words, the book crumbles the official narrative that a Hegelian philosophy of world history weaves, which privileges the French Revolution. Whether or not we agree that what ought to be salvaged in Hegel is the universal intent of his philosophy of history, the lesson here is that we ought to reflect on the repressions that our academic practices consciously or unconsciously preform. When we read, teach, and write on Hegel, we cannot afford to ignore this lesson. For what Buck-Morss's work achieves, what Bernasconi's work also achieves, is blasting open the continuum of Hegel scholarship.

HOW TO READ HEGEL

In his "Hegel at the Court of the Ashanti," Bernasconi turns the tables and puts Hegel on trial. He exposes Hegel's treatment of the source materials from which he based his lectures on Africa, arguing against those who excuse Hegel's Eurocentrism by blaming his scholarly resources (see Bernasconi 1998, 41ff.). Hegel, for example, embellished stories of cannibalism and human sacrifice, thereby facilitating his characterization of Africans as outside of the rational unfolding of world history (Bernasconi 1998, 48). In *Hegel, Haiti, and Universal History*, Buck-Morss discusses Bernasconi's essay and stresses one aspect of his account. She emphasizes the fact that, for Bernasconi, it is vital to turn the tables on Hegel because it presses us to reflect on ourselves. "[T]here must always be a reflexive moment," Bernasconi writes, "in which the reader of Hegel, as of the travel diaries on which Hegel based his account, must ask him- or herself about the extent that he or she remains captive to this account, not only in maintaining a certain image of Africa, but also in retaining a conceptuality about Europe and about history that is more closely tied to that image than one is aware until the question is asked" (Bernasconi 1998, 43–44). Albeit in different ways, Buck-Morss and Bernasconi interrupt Hegel's narrative in order to interrupt our own.

Reading Hegel today requires such critical interruption, whether we aim to reject Hegel's idealism or to recover aspects of Hegel's idealism that we might deem insightful. Here again the point is not merely theoretical. We must not merely read Hegel with critical acuity, developing intellectual strategies to engage the ugly passages in Hegel's corpus. It is practical. We must read Hegel by interrogating rather than suppressing those very passages that might call his theoretical armature into question. Doing so might address some of the problems in professional philosophy that Bernasconi identifies, much more so than excising Hegel from our reading lists. In closing, then, allow me to suggest what a critical-interruptive reading that responds to the challenging intersection of history and race in Hegel's corpus requires.

A critical-interruptive reading of Hegel would need to transform the two general approaches to Hegel's thinking about history that I mentioned at the beginning of this chapter. Recall that while the first seeks to develop the form of Hegel's arguments by dropping the offensive content of Hegel's thought, the second seeks to call into question the form of Hegel's idealism by interrogating the difficult content of Hegel's corpus. A critical-interruptive reading of Hegel requires acknowledging that although the form and content of Hegel's claims can be distinguished, they cannot be seen as separable. Indeed, we fail to critically examine the form *and* the content of Hegel's corpus if we ignore their entanglement. This means that engaging Hegel's thoughts on race cannot be the sole task of those who seek to crumble the structure of Hegel's idealism or of those who work on philosophy and race. It should be a task for any and every reader of Hegel. Perhaps, we might add, it should especially be a task for those who find elements of Hegel's thought insightful.

Within Hegel scholarship, there are compelling interpretive options that could be seen as methodologically critical-interruptive. We find attempts to think through the moments in Hegel's writings where he examines the forms of violence intrinsic to modernity, and to rethink Hegelian negativity as a way of rewriting the task of a philosophical thinking of history (see, e.g., Comay 2010; de Boer 2010; Nuzzo 2012; Zambrana 2015b). We also find attempts to rewrite his defense of modernity, his conception of history, or his understanding of right by focusing on what might be seen as marginal elements of Hegel's social-political thought (see, e.g., Buck-Morss 2009; Ruda 2011; Moland 2011). These interpretive options are critical-interruptive in their method, since they require reading Hegel beyond the Hegelian framework. They hinge on constructing a counternarrative about Hegel's texts by focusing on an element in Hegel's thought that calls its structure—as traditionally understood—into question. The intersection of history and race in Hegel, however, presses us to take these reading practices much further. They press us to confront Hegel's texts with the "unhistorical histories" and, indeed, the "unhistorical peoples" that were understood as "unhistorical" by his account of world history.

REFERENCES

Allen, A. (2014). "Reason, Power and History: Re-reading the Dialectic of Enlightenment." *Thesis Eleven* 120 (1): 10–25.

Benjamin, W. (1969). "Theses on the Philosophy of History." In *Illuminations*, translated by Harry Zohn, edited by Hannah Arendt, 253–264. New York: Schocken.

Bernasconi, R. (1998). "Hegel at the Court of the Ashanti." In *Hegel after Derrida*, edited by S. Barnett, 41–63. London: Routledge.

Bernasconi, R. (2000). "With What Must the Philosophy of History Begin? On the Racial Basis of Hegel's Eurocentrism." *Nineteenth Century Contexts* 22 (2): 171–201.

Bernasconi, R. (2003). "Hegel's Racism. A Reply to McCarney." London, England: Central Books, *Radical Philosophy Group*, 35–37.

Bernasconi, R. (2010). "The Philosophy of Race in the Nineteenth Century." In *The Routledge Companion to Nineteenth Century Philosophy*, edited by D. Moyar, 498–521. London: Routledge.

Buck-Morss, S. (1991). *The Dialectic of Seeing: Walter Benjamin and the Arcades Project.* Cambridge, MA: MIT Press.

Buck-Morss, S. (2009). *Hegel, Haiti, and Universal History.* Pittsburgh, PA: University of Pittsburgh Press.

Comay, R. (2010). *Mourning Sickness: Hegel and the French Revolution.* Palo Alto, CA: Stanford University Press.

De Boer, K. (2010). *On Hegel: The Sway of the Negative.* London: Palgrave.

de Laurentiis, A. (2014). "Race in Hegel: Text and Context." In *Philosophie Nach Kant: Neue Wege Zum Verständnis von Kants Transzendental- Und Moralphilosophie*, edited by Mario Egger, 591–624. Berlin: De Gruyter.

Hegel, G. W. F. (1842). *Vorlesungen über die Philosophie der Geschichte, Werke.* Edited by E. Moldenhauer and K. Michelet. Vol. 12. Frankfurt: Suhrkamp.

Hegel, G. W. F. (1956). *Lectures on History.* Translated by J. Sibree. New York: Dover.

Hegel, G. W. F. (1975). *Lectures on the Philosophy of World History.* Translated by Nisbet. Cambridge: Cambridge University Press.

Hegel, G. W. F. (1978). *Hegels Philosophie des subjektiven Geistes/*Hegel's Philosophy of Subjective Spirit. 3 vols. Edited and translated by M. Petry. Dordrecht, The Netherlands: Reidel.

Hegel, G. W. F. (1991). *Elements of the Philosophy of Right.* Translated by Nisbet. Cambridge: Cambridge University Press.

Hegel, G. W. F. (2011). *Lectures on the Philosophy of World History.* Edited and translated by R. Brown and P. Hodgson. Vol. 1, *Manuscripts of the Introduction and the Lectures of 1822–3.* Oxford: Oxford University Press.

Honneth, A. (1996). *Struggle for Recognition: The Moral Grammar of Social Conflicts.* Cambridge, MA: MIT Press.

Honneth, A. (2014). *Freedom's Right.* New York: Columbia University Press.

McCarney, J. (2000). *Hegel on History.* London: Routledge.

McCarney, J. (2003). "Hegel's Racism? A Reply to Bernasconi." *Radical Philosophy* 119: 35–37.

Moland, L. (2011). *Hegel on Political Identity: Patriotism, Nationality, Cosmopolitanism.* Evanston, IL: Northwestern University Press.

Nuzzo, A. (2012). *Memory, History, Justice in Hegel.* New York: Palgrave.

Parekh, S. (2009). "Hegel's New World. History, Freedom, and Race." In *Hegel and History*, edited by W. Dudley, 111–133. Albany: State University of New York Press.

Pippin, R. (1999). "Naturalness and Mindedness: Hegel's Compatibilism." *European Journal of Philosophy* 7: 2.

Ruda, Frank. (2011). *Hegel's Rabble: An Investigation into Hegel's Philosophy of Right*. London: Continuum.

Walker, N. (2014). "Review of G. W. F. Hegel, Lectures on the Philosophy of World History, Vol. I: Manuscripts of the Introduction and the Lectures of 1822–3." *Notre Dame Philosophical Reviews*, 2011.12.14. http://ndpr.nd.edu/news/27787-lectures-on-the-philosophy-of-world-history-vol-i-manuscripts-of-the-introduction.

Zambrana, Rocío. (2015a). "Normative Ambivalence and the Future of Critical Theory: Adorno & Horkheimer, Castro-Gómez, Quijano on Rationality, Modernity, Totality." In *Critical Theory and the Challenge of Praxis*, edited by S. Giachetti Ludovisi, 101–116. London: Ashgate.

Zambrana, Rocío. (2015b). *Hegel's Theory of Intelligibility*. Chicago, IL: Chicago University Press.

CHAPTER 22

....

EXPLORING THE MATTER OF RACE
A Materialist Philosophical Inquiry

....

STEPHEN C. FERGUSON II

THE trope of race has become one of the defining features of contemporary African American philosophy. It is often the case that philosophical investigations into blackness and whiteness and discussions about racism semantically offer us instances of redundancy. In post-Rawlsian political philosophy, "race talk" has become a surrogate for discourse about racism, racial inequality, and national oppression. From a Marxist perspective, a simplistic use of race as the key analytic category in social explanation has left the political struggles of the Black working class lost in the whirlwind of "race matters."

I do not want to rehearse the zigzag historical evolution of Marxist writings on the dialectical relationship between race, racism, national oppression, and class exploitation. It has always been the Communist position that the goal of any revolutionary movement should build a multiracial, multigendered international working-class organization or organizations. Proletarian internationalism puts the fight against racism and sexism at the center of the working-class struggle against capitalist exploitation.

Marxist work on race and racism extends beyond the ivory towers. A great deal of the work is found in political pamphlets, nonacademic journals like *Political Affairs, Freedomways, Bolshevik*, and *Forward*, in addition to organizational newspapers associated with groups like Sojourners for Truth and Justice, Communist Workers Group (ML), and the League of Revolutionary Black Workers. The Marxist perspective has its origins in the 1928 resolution of the Communist Party of the United States of America (CPUSA) (Haywood 1948; Lenin 1964). Prior to 1928, there were various socialist vis-à-vis Marxist positions on the "Negro Question" (Jones 1946; Solomon 1998; Berland 1999, 2000; Bohmer 2005; Foley 2008).

I examine the *biological fact* of race and the *social myth* of racial inequality. I offer a materialist philosophical perspective on the social ontology of race, with due consideration given to the material context of social relations of production and the State as an instrument of the ruling class. In contrast to liberal critics such as Charles Mills, I argue that a materialist analysis does not reduce all forms of oppression to class, that is, what is popularly referred to as "class reductionism." I take class reductionism to be the attempt to reduce racism to a purely economic phenomenon. In turn, the "deconstruction of class" requires some form of cultural theory, discourse theory or psychoanalysis to explain race and/or racism. Instead, a Marxist analysis renders capitalism as context and determinate ground for the explanation of racism on a materialist basis. I therefore argue that while Marxists have focused on the political economy of racism, it does not follow that racism, from a Marxist perspective, is purely economic in nature. I also argue that race should not be posited theoretically as having an independent life and force of its own. The theoretical tension between a materialist and idealist analysis of racism is evident in the developing "Black Lives Matter" movement.

BIOLOGICAL FACT OF RACE VERSUS THE SOCIAL MYTH OF "RACIAL INEQUALITY"

Philosophers such as Anthony Appiah and Naomi Zack have devoted substantial critical attention to examining the biological facts concerning race (Zack 2002, 2011). In response to the efforts to provide a biological foundation to notions of race, both Appiah and Zack argue that race is an ontological illusion. This perspective argues that the reality of race cannot be scientifically proven. Because there is no proof of its existence in *nature*, then race cannot in all *reality* exist. Because races do not exist in the natural (particularly the biological) world, then Appiah claims racial classifications are without propositional content, that is, meaningless. Hence, we have a word with no meaning; an idea or concept of race with no ontological grounding—it is simply not in the world. Appiah, for instance, would have us believe that the social world of race and racism is an illusion or phantasm that can be merely ignored just as we would dismiss creepy sounds as not having any supernatural reality (Appiah 1985, 1990).

Marxist analysis of racism and national oppression, particularly as it relates to questions of political tactics, strategy, and theory, offers a counterargument to the so-called argument from illusion. Historically, Marxism places emphasis on the relationship between racism, national oppression, class formation, and bourgeois civil society. Racism did not predate the "rosy dawn" of capitalism; the origins of racism can be directly tied to the capitalist process of primitive accumulation (Marx 1967, 703). The link that historically tied capitalism to racism was the slave trade and slavery. Slavery was crucial and central to the emergence of capitalism. The international character of the slave trade and slavery was the reflection of a world capitalist market. The initial accumulation of large sums of capital, which in turn, was invested in the exploitation of European workers, derived from the trade in slaves and the plantation staple economies in the so-called New World.

A class analysis of racism begins with the presupposition that in class societies power is not distributed equally, nor is it an effect primarily of discourse. Rather, power is always constituted at the level of production—at the level of the separation between those who own the means of production (as a class) and those who do not own these means of production and thus are forced to sell their labor power in order to survive (as a class). Power is a structural relation deployed (particularly through the mediation of the State) for the purposes of exploitation, and not a free-floating abstraction to which all people, regardless of their position in the social division of labor, have access. To posit otherwise (as in Foucauldian social theory) is to fall victim to philosophical idealism.

While all slaves were necessarily Black, not all exploited people in the United States were Black. The majority of slaves were owned by only 4 percent of the Southern white population; for fifty of the first sixty-four years of US history, the president was a slave owner. But most Euro-Americans were not slave owners. As of 1860, one-third of Southern white people had no assets of any kind, including slaves and land (Lui et al. 2006, 236).

From a materialist perspective, there is a distinction between racialist ideology and racism as a material institution and practice. Racist ideology is part of the ideological superstructure. An ideological superstructure was erected on top of the capitalist slave regime which "spun tight ideological webs of their right to domination" over the supposed inferior Black race (Wright 2008, 16).

In the early 1950s, the black Communist Doxey A. Wilkerson argued against the pseudo-scientific foundation of racist ideology. He does not suggest that we eliminate "race talk" from political and social scientific discourse. Rather, Wilkerson argues we should establish a distinction between the *biological fact* of race and the *social myth* of racial inequality. As Wilkerson explains,

> The objective physical differences which alone constitute the basis for grouping human beings into races, in and of themselves, are devoid of social significance. Race *per se* plays no role in the development of nations or other social formations. This is by no means true, however, of the *social myth of racism*, which has attached to the biological fact of race a social significance by no means inherent in the physical traits themselves. This myth has played and continues to play an important role in social and political development. (Wilkerson 1952, 20)

Since the mid-twentieth century, scientists—particularly biologists and anthropologists—have brought into disrepute the notion that there is a biological or genetic foundation of race and racial inequalities (Graves 2004). As biological justifications for social inequality have relatively declined in popularity, we find that culturalist arguments have gained more ground for politically significant ascriptive differentiation. That is to say, there are many narratives of inequality based on ascriptive status that sort populations of people—based on comparative aesthetic, moral, and intellectual claims—for the purposes of reproducing the system of social power and stratification based on capitalist labor relations.

Wilkerson does not accept the presupposition—implicit in Zack and Appiah's argument—that "all ontological descriptions and accounts are confined to and exhausted by the natural sciences" (McClendon 2004, 212). From Wilkerson's materialist perspective, while some categories, concepts, or ideas may be a distortion of reality (or false consciousness) they are nevertheless grounded in material reality. The scientific task before us is to uncover how concepts or categories are connected to material reality, how they reflect objective reality (even in a distorted manner). The reality of race and racism cannot be addressed by denying their ontological status. Better yet, the ontological status of race can only be disclosed through the examination of the real, material relations, social institutions, and social practices that give rise to the necessity for racial categories and take the form of racist ideology.

The materialist approach recognizes the ontological status of race as preeminently social. The ontological status of race derives from its existence in material reality, being "in the world," albeit of the social rather than natural world. Race, as a social category, is in the world, because it is a social category, and as such possesses ontological status. Because race is a social category that emerges from historically determinate social relations, it is an object of social *scientific* investigation. Wilkerson observes that to undertake the investigation of race on purely natural/physical scientific premises is to commit—in the words of Gilbert Ryles—a category mistake (Ryle 2002, 16–23). Linda Burham and Bob Wing, members of the Communist group Line of March, astutely note:

> But simply because the category of race does not exist in *nature* does not mean that it does not exist as a *real social relation*. In this the category race is not at all unique. Clearly, capital does not exist in nature either. And yet the capital relation is the central relation of the capitalist mode of production . . .

Furthermore,

> Race and racial oppression are real, scientific social categories. Given the pervasiveness of the social relations of racial oppression in our society, these relations appear to be inherent in the biological diversity of humankind. Science can dispose of the *idea* that race is a natural division of humanity. But it cannot dispose of the racist social relations which have been brought into being by capitalism and which can only be eliminated by the destruction of that social formation. (Burnham and Wing 1981, 41–42)

Racism as a material practice employs the social myth of racial inequality. Race in abstraction from racism does not have any causal powers. "Race matters" but only in the context of particular social relations of production; it has no instrumental value outside of bourgeois relations of production. On this account, bourgeois relations of production are antecedent to the birth of racialized individuals and define the context within which all forms of social inequality are generated. Capitalist exploitation is intimately tied to the racial and gender division of labor. People, in fact, act on the basis of their understanding of race, but the social structures of capitalism determine the form that human agency takes and the outcome of that agency. Indeed, concepts and categories held by people and acted upon by people may be incorrect. One could think of the number of people who act upon the unjustified belief that horoscopes are true.

Prima facie, race is nothing more than a phenotypic ascription, for example, skin color, hair texture, eye shape, lip formation, and so on. Race as a phenotypic ascription, in the context of racism, functions as an instrumental value. The instrumental value of any phenotypic ascription of race is to establish an empirical basis for identifying the putative superior and inferior groups. Race, therefore, is preeminently social in character. Race as a social category, like all social categories, must not be comprehended in any naturalistic manner and therefore can only be correctly seen in abstraction of nature or natural (phenotypic or genetic) ascriptions. The instrumental value of race emanates from the social relations, institutions, and practices comprising bourgeois civil society.

My point is that there is a serious danger of reification if race is abstracted from racism—a practice prevalent among philosophers and social theorists drunk on postmodernism/poststructuralist ideology. Racism in the form of material institutions and practices gives life to race as a social category. Here I am merely asserting a categorical distinction between racism and race.

Let me be clear, I am arguing that race has an ontological reality. However, I am arguing that race in and of itself is not an explanatory structural concept. Discourse about white privilege, whiteness, and Blackness have to be seen as categorically distinct from discourse about racism qua racial inequalities. To put it simply, from a Marxist perspective, fighting racism is not about being anti-white or getting white people to recognize their white privilege or "possessive investment in whiteness" (Lipsitz 1995). Race as a social category is distinct from racism as a social (material) relation or practice. Racism is one of many social relations within the US bourgeois social formation.

Racist ideology is a form of bourgeois ideology which functions to keep the working class divided against the dictatorship of capital. As Marx and Engels so famously put it, the ruling ideas of any society are those of the ruling class. Bourgeois philosophers, intellectuals, and politicians frequently seek to justify bourgeois class dominance and other social divisions within bourgeois civil society. While bourgeois ideological hegemony may take on a political or cultural form, its primary functional role is the maintenance of capital accumulation and the reproduction of capitalist exploitation. Ascriptive hierarchies—whether biological, cultural, racial, or gender in character—are key to the justification of the dictatorship of the bourgeoisie. As Adolph Reed notes, "Ascriptive hierarchies sort populations into categories of classification that are in principle set off from one another by clear, uncrossable boundaries" (Reed 2002, 271). The assignment of civil membership, worth, and rights vis-à-vis privileges is based on belonging to the appropriate or superior population or group. A cursory examination of United States history provides more than ample evidence of this fact. For instance, a number of prominent United States politicians and intellectuals, such as Thomas Jefferson, Andrew Jackson, George Fitzhugh, and John C. Calhoun, drew from Aristotle's idea of social division based on natural differences in order to justify the racialized character of capitalist slavery as a putatively natural institution. Where Aristotle differentiated between Greeks and barbarians to justify the enslavement of non-Greeks, John C. Calhoun and others argued that Africans were uncivilized and would appreciably advance in terms of culture and civilization through the institution of slavery (Calhoun 1837). This racist ideology was later codified in United States constitutional law (Simba 2010, 17–68). The whole legal, moral, and ideological superstructure of capitalism in the United States—from its formation until the end of slavery—rested on the configuration of bourgeois property relations, and the vast majority of Black people were relegated to the position of chattel, property without basic human and civil rights.

CRITIQUE OF DUAL-SYSTEMS THEORY

There has been a philosophical tendency to construct racism as autonomous from capitalism as a mode of production. It may be conceded that racism arose with capitalism, but racism subsequently took on "a life of its own." Here we have an abstract conception of structures such that racism constitutes a structure that reproduces itself independently of the "laws of motion" of capitalism. It basically functions independently from, but mysteriously in interaction with, capitalism. There is a tendency to characterize racism as the "possessive investment in whiteness" that does not necessarily vary historically in content and meaning (Mills 2004).

In opposition to "white Marxism," the Afro-Caribbean philosopher Charles Mills proposes such a dual-systems theory with racism existing relatively independent of, and distinct from, capitalist relations of production. The Racial Contract (or white supremacy)—we are led to believe by Mills—has an agency all its own (Mills 1997). Under the guise of "black radical liberalism," Mills suggests that one manner in which racial exploitation differs from class exploitation is the unequal distribution of wealth among Euro-American and African American people (Mills 2004). Here, we have the assumption that racial inequality results from the caste-like system of white supremacy. For example, it has been reported that—as of 2013—the median wealth of white households is thirteen times that of Black households—$141,900 versus $11,000 (Kochhar and Fry 2014). These statistical facts appear to need no commentary to convey their meaning. Alas, if appearance and essence coincided, there would be no need for science. As Martha Gimenez et al. observe: "Broadening the discussion of Black/white differences in wealth ownership to consider class differences within the white population would have put the information in perspective" (Gimenez, Muschert, and Fothergill 1997, 110). While income and wealth disparities between white and Black people may be an empirical indicator of the existence of racism (or as Mills would put it, white supremacy) this approach ignores the existence of class differentiation among white and Black people. This approach to racial inequality commits the fallacy of composition by assuming that what is true of some whites is true of all whites. As the socialist Oliver Cox noted—so many years ago—this approach "lumps all white people and all Negroes into two antagonistic groups struggling in the interest of a mysterious god called caste. This is very much to the liking of the exploiters of labor, since it tends to confuse them in an emotional matrix with all the people" (Cox 1959, 520). Mills's analysis ignores the fact that the top 10 percent of US households—which are multiracial and multigendered—own 70 percent of the wealth, more than is owned by the bottom 90 percent. The "race-first" discourse (1) ignores the class nature of race relations and ultimately (2) mystifies the real determinates of racism in the United States, by framing race relations in terms of a caste system. The origin and continued reproduction of racism have to be grounded in capitalist social relations of production and the dynamics of class struggle. Mills's concept of racial exploitation buries the realities of class struggle beneath the mystical veil of a Racial Contract. Rather than a Hobbesian state of nature or the Rawlsian original position, we have the equally fantastical Racial Contract abstracted from capitalist (class) exploitation.

As a philosophical trend, contemporary critical race theory focuses on the *political* and *cultural* representation of racial differences and, in turn, relegates the *economics* of difference to the margins of the theoretical universe. Under the spell of "race first" discourse, the Black working class is encouraged to become race conscious, that is, conscious of racial differences. But insofar as class consciousness is concerned, the Black working class is encouraged to speak contemptuously of "white trash" and forever love the lumpen bourgeois ideology of fictional characters like Lucious Lyon of the TV musical drama *Empire* and James "Ghost" St. Patrick of the television drama series *Power*, or the real-life rap artist turned businessman Shawn "Jay-Z" Carter.

From a materialist perspective, class differences are not reflective of differences in terms of status, lifestyle, or income. Class is one's objective relationship to the means of production. Exploitation, from the standpoint of Marxism, derives from one's objective relations to the means of production where power is attached to owning the means of production. Because the working class is not in possession of the means of production, they are subject to exploitation in the sphere of production. Because of the objective phenomenon of socialized production that is privately appropriated by the bourgeoisie, both Black and white workers are exploited under capitalism. Workers share this despite racism, differences in culture, chauvinism on the part of white workers, and so on. The struggle to overthrow capitalism and the fight against racism and chauvinism are not mutually exclusive, but integrally united. This

EXPLORING THE MATTER OF RACE   267

is not a purely academic question that can be politely ignored, given the fact that the vast majority of Black people are members of the working class.

Not all Black people are subject to exploitation in the Marxist sense. Some Black people as a result of their relationship to the means of production are exploiters and oppressors. Here we could mention Oprah Winfrey (CEO of Harpo, Inc., and OWN network), Kenneth I. Chenault (Chairman and CEO of American Express), Carl Horton (CEO of the Absolut Spirit Company Inc.), or Richard Parsons (former CEO of AOL Time Warner). Can we seriously entertain the claim that Barack Obama or Oprah Winfrey as members of the ruling class are at a disadvantage with respect to the white working class? An analysis of racism cannot be abstracted away from the class character of capitalism (McClendon 2004).

"Black Lives Matter" and the Difference That Class Makes

The dual-system view is prevalent among activists in the spontaneous campaign associated with the war cry "Black Lives Matter." Let us recall that Communists support every movement to the extent that it fights against imperialism. And still it is worth noting that every anticapitalist movement is not revolutionary in character. "Black Lives Matter" has the potential to become a revolutionary movement. Yet it must fight against forms of bourgeois ideology that are attempting to derail the revolutionary character of this campaign, regardless of the fashionable and revolutionary garb in which it may drape itself.

The frustration of working-class youth, men, and women in Ferguson, Missouri, is beginning to congeal into an actual movement. However, at the same time, we are witnessing a bundle of contradictory ideas and beliefs associated with "Black Lives Matter." One of the most prevalent beliefs emerging from this strain of antiracist politics has been a level of visceral and vitriolic anti-Marxism. In an effort to avoid the scarecrow of "class reductionism," we are presented with a whole battery of "new" arguments. (Aside from snide dismissals of Marxism, I am not aware of any direct, clearly expressed arguments against Marxism, or more specifically a class analysis of racism.) For instance, Marissa Johnson, cofounder of the Seattle "Black Lives Matter," rallied against Democratic presidential candidate Bernie Sanders for being a "class reductionist" and not recognizing that the struggle for racial democracy is separate from issues related to economic inequality (MSNBC NewsNation, August 1, 2015). As such, it could be implied that the fight for racial democracy is the antipode of socialist democracy; that is to say, addressing grievances that could be construed as specifically racial takes precedence over, and is separate from, dealing with issues of the redistribution of wealth or the elimination of capitalism. This position is rooted in the *explanatory* primacy of race. I think the political scientist Adolph Reed is on the right track to argue that the "race first" position reflects the neoclassical economic presupposition—associated with Milton Friedman, Gary Becker, and Thomas Sowell—that "the market is a just, effective, or even acceptable system for rewarding talent and virtue and punishing their opposites and that, therefore, removal of 'artificial' impediments to its functioning like race and gender will make it even more efficient and just" (Reed 2009).

If Marissa Johnson's views are representative of the "Black Lives Matter" campaign, we have a politics of identity which is obscuring the class character of political shootings and the criminal justice system. To be blunt, this "new social movement" has let capitalism off the hook by blaming injustice on racism abstracted from class dominance. As Loic Wacquant has noted: "the national obsession for the black-white duality . . . obfuscates the fact that class disproportionality inside each ethnic category is greater than the racial disproportionality between them" (Wacquant 2014, 43–44). If the vast majority of victims of police shootings—whether Euro-American, African American, Latino American or Asian American—are from working-class backgrounds, how do you separate racism from class exploitation and domination?

To be fair, it is possible to imagine "class differences" without exploitation, if we assume that class is Weberian in nature and really about status, income, occupation, or education. However, from a Marxist perspective, as Ellen Wood astutely notes, "the difference that constitutes 'class' as an 'identity' *is*, by definition, a relationship of inequality and power, in a way that sexual or cultural 'difference' need not be" (Wood 2002, 258). Moreover, capitalists can come to see that "Black Lives Matter" and still engage in the exploitation of labor without regard to race, gender, sexuality, or other differences. Rather, the point is that capitalist exploitation depends on the reduction of all workers—men and women, black, white, Latino, and Native American—to the abstract labor, "interchangeable units of labor abstracted from any particular personal or social identity" (Wood 2002, 279).

My critique should not be taken to imply that "All Lives Matter." The counterdiscourse of "All Lives Matter" is an example of false universalism. Universality without the specific content provided by particularity becomes an arid (empty) abstraction. What results when universality is separated from particularity is abstract (or false) universality. When humans are seen as devoid of particularity (particular racial identity or gender for instance), then abstract universalism is the result. It is important to make note of this fact because one's blackness or gender is a particular instantiation and constituent expression of the universal category—humanity. We should avoid all philosophies of particularity that lead us to metaphysical exclusivism. And we should avoid all philosophies of universality that are blind to particularity.

At the end of the day, this approach to racism does not have a conception of totality structured by the exploitation of wage labor, the pivot on which bourgeois civil society rests. As György Lukács insisted, the concept of totality is vital to making sense of the complexities of the historical process:

> Only in this context which sees the isolated facts of social life as aspects of the historical process and integrates them in a totality, can knowledge of the facts hope to become knowledge of reality. (Lukacs 1971, 8)

In effect, with dual-systems theory, we have a view of bourgeois civil society such that a number of discrete elements cannot be understood in terms of a single totality. Bourgeois civil society is left fragmented into pieces like Humpty-Dumpty—a fragmented mess of indeterminate pluralities or differences.

How are we to conceive of a totality which involves an "ensemble of social relations" that are not reducible to one another yet form a structural whole? Marxism does not accept the causal pluralism associated with intersectionality and its holy Trinity of race, class, and gender. Rather than see class as one of many factors affecting the lives of African Americans, a scientific, that is, materialist, approach argues that the anatomy of racism has to be sought in the political economy of capitalism. From a Marxist perspective, the "ensemble of social relations" constitutive of any social formations are grounded in social relations of production. Here I am using "ground" in the Hegelian sense of determinate foundation. This is not a form of reductionism where the social or all social relations are the same as the social relations of production, that is, class relations. Consequently, racism is not reducible to the social relations of production. But racism takes on the character that it does in virtue of its relationship to bourgeois relations of production. Although racism is not reducible to capitalist class exploitation, it cannot be abstracted from it. African American political economic realities, slavery, sharecropping, unemployment, underemployment, low wages, poverty, and disparities in income and wealth vis-à-vis whites are all empirical indicators of how capitalism is intrinsically tied to racism and racialized production relations. Racism in and of itself is not a sufficient reason for the operation of the structural whole, that is, bourgeois civil society. To put it bluntly, class counts. It has real political consequences for the lives of individuals, the functioning of the State, and bourgeois civil society.

REFERENCES

Appiah, K. A. (1985). "The Uncompleted Argument: Du Bois and the Illusion of Race." *Critical Inquiry* 12 (1): 21–37.

Appiah, K. A. (1990). "Racisms." In *Anatomy of Racism*, edited by David Theo Goldberg, 3–17. Minneapolis: University of Minnesota Press.

Berland, O. (1999). "The Emergence of the Communist Perspective on the 'Negro Question' in America: 1919–1931 (Part One)." *Science and Society* 63 (4): 411–432.

Berland, O. (2000). "The Emergence of the Communist Perspective on the 'Negro Question' in America: 1919–1931 (Part Two)." *Science and Society* 64 (2): 194–217.

Bohmer, P. (2005). "Marxist Theory of Racism and Racial Inequality." In *African Americans in the U. S. Economy*, edited by Cecilia A. Conrad, John Whitehead, Patrick Mason, and James Stewart, 94–100. Lanham, MD: Rowman & Littlefield.

Burnham, L., and B. Wing (1981). "Toward a Communist Analysis of Black Oppression and Black Liberation, Part 1, Critique of Black Nation Thesis." *Line of March* 2 (1): 21–88.

Calhoun, John C. (1837). "Slavery, A Positive Good." Accessed May 12, 2015. http://teachingamericanhistory.org/library/document/slavery-a-positive-good/.

Cox, Oliver C. (1959). *Caste, Class, & Race: A Study in Social Dynamics*. New York: Monthly Review Press.

Foley, B. (2008). *Spectres of 1919: Class and Nation in the Making of the New Negro*. Urbana: University of Illinois Press.

Gimenez, M. E., G. W. Muschert, and A. Fothergill. (1997). "Considerations on Wealth, Class and Race." *Critical Sociology* 23(2): 105–116.

Graves, J. (2004). *The Race Myth: Why We Pretend Race Exists in America*. New York: Dutton.

Haywood, H. (1948). *Negro Liberation*. New York: International Publishers.

Jones, C. (1946). "On the Right to Self-Determination for the Negro People in the Black Belt (Discussion Article)." *Political Affairs* 25 (1): 67–77.

Kochhar, R., and R. Fry. (2014). "Wealth Inequality has Widened Along Racial, Ethnic Lines since End of Great Recession." *Pew Research Center*. Accessed July 11, 2015. http://www.pewresearch.org/fact-tank/2014/12/12/racial-wealth-gaps-great-recession/.

Lenin, Vladimir I. (1964). *Critical Remarks on the National Question*. In *Collected Works*. Vol. 20, 17–51. Moscow: Progress Publishers.

Lipsitz, George. (1995). "The Possessive Investment in Whiteness: Racialized Democracy and 'White' Problem in American Studies." *American Quarterly* 47 (3): 369–387.

Lui, Meizhu, Barbara Robles, Betsy Leondar-Wright, Rose Brewer, and Rebecca Adamson, with United for a Fair Economy. (2006). *The Color of Wealth: The Story Behind the U. S. Racial Wealth Divide*. New York : New Press.

Lukacs, G. (1971). *History and Class Consciousness*. London: Merlin.

Marx, K. (1967). *Capital*. Vol. 1, *A Critique of Political Economy*. New York: International Publishers.

McClendon, J. H., III. (2004). "On the Nature of Whiteness and the Ontology of Race: Toward A Dialectical Materialist Analysis." In *What White Looks Like: African-American Philosophers on the Whiteness Question*, edited by George Yancy, 211–225. New York: Routledge.

Mills, C. W. (1997). *The Racial Contract*. Ithaca, NY: Cornell University Press.

Mills, C. W. (2004). "Racial Exploitation and the Wages of Whiteness." In *What White Looks Like: African-American Philosophers on the Whiteness Question*, edited by George Yancy, 25–54. New York: Routledge.

MSNBC NewsNation. (August 1, 2015). "Interview with Marissa Johnson." *MSNBC*. Accessed May 12, 2016. https://www.youtube.com/watch?v=-ajWs3z8rso.

Reed, Adolph. (2002). "Unraveling the Relation of Race and Class in American Politics." *Political Power and Social Theory* 15: 265–274.

Reed, Adolph. (2009). "The Limits of Anti-Racism." *Left Business Observer*. Accessed May 12, 2016. http://www.leftbusinessobserver.com/Antiracism.html

Ryle, G. (2002). *The Concept of Mind*. Chicago: University of Chicago Press.

Simba, M. (2010). *Black Marxism and American Constitutionalism: An Interpretive History from Colonial Background to the Great Depression*. Dubuque, IA: Kendall Hunt.

Solomon, M. I. (1998). *The Cry Was Unity: Communists and African Americans, 1917-36*. Jackson: University Press of Mississippi.

Wacquant, Loïc. (2014). "Class, Race and Hyperincarceration in Revanchist America." *Socialism and Democracy*, 28:3, Special Issue, *The Roots of Mass Incarceration: Locking Up Black Dissidents and Punishing the Poor*, 35–56.

Wilkerson, D. (1952). "Race, Nation and the Concept 'Negro.'" *Political Affairs* (August): 13–26.

Wright, R. (2008). *12 Million Black Voices*. New York: Basic Books.

Zack, N. (2002). *Philosophy of Science and Race*. New York: Routledge.

Zack, N. (2011). *The Ethics and Mores of Race: Equality after the History of Philosophy*. Lanham, MD: Rowman & Littlefield.

CHAPTER 23

RACE AND EXISTENTIALISM
The Dialectic from Mailer's "The White Negro" to Memmi's Racism

JONATHAN JUDAKEN

My thesis is twofold: first, race is central to the development of existentialism and its key axioms; and, second, understanding this broadens the existential map beyond Europe and its philosophical traditions. I open with some pages ripped from the Jewish American Norman Mailer, a self-styled "white Negro." This is followed by a focus on the Jewish-Tunisian-French-African Albert Memmi. Neither author is a familiar name, especially when the existentialist canon is reduced to the four titans of the continental canon: Kierkegaard, Nietzsche, Heidegger, and Sartre. But Mailer's and Memmi's role within existentialist circles in the Mediterranean orbit and across the black and Jewish Atlantic reveal how circumscribed and historically decontextualized the conventional set of figures are who stand for existentialism.

Mailer's "The White Negro" and Memmi's *The Pillar of Salt*, alongside some retorts to each, will be used to tease out some key themes and discussions at the crossroads of race and existentialism: (1) the meaning of being human or the question of subjectivity, wonderfully evoked by Fanon's immortal words, "O my body, make me a man who questions!"; (2) life as a conflict of interpretations and the structure of the gaze, indicated by James Baldwin's response to Mailer's "The White Negro"; (3) the exchange about whether race is an idea or a set of social structures between Sartre and Fanon, which preceded Mailer and Baldwin on the subject; (4) the ramifications of this discussion as they emerge in Sartre's critique of Memmi in his Preface to *The Colonizer and the Colonized*, an *auto-critique* since Memmi uses a number of Sartrean axioms to assess colonial racism; (5) Memmi's later work, simply titled *Racism*, which registered this criticism, while still focusing on the root of racism as linked to the anxiety produced by the unease, fear, and fascination with the racial Other, a product of fashioning racial subjects as what Fanon termed "phobogenic objects." *Racism* crystalizes some of the key insights of existentialist approaches to race and racism. This short illustrative intellectual history poses a challenge for what Lewis Gordon calls "disciplinary decadence" or what Gayatri Spivak calls the "disciplinary fear" of philosophy. Including these figures in discussions about race and existentialism helps to shift the geography of reason beyond the European tradition and redraws the map of the conversation in literary and sociological terms as much as philosophical categories, even as it helps us to understand some of the underlying causes of racism from an existentialist purview (Gordon 2006; Spivak 2003, 19).

MAILER'S "THE WHITE NEGRO"

Norman Mailer's, "The White Negro" is an audacious essay, and certainly one of the key statements of the American counterculture in the 1950s (Jackson and Saxe 2015). It challenges the blandness of "Father Knows Best" 1950s Americana by linking Mailer's critique of the conformity of American culture with existentialism. Mailer does this by taking on a set of stock images about the American hipster, whom he identified with the black jazz artists and cultural innovators of Greenwich Village and other American cities. For Mailer, these hipsters embody the existentialist ethos he extols. Because his essay is a literary exercise, he imagines them as a demimonde of delinquents and rule breakers who transcend the limits of American conventionality, social climbing, and the life of the parvenu.

Mailer sets his intervention in the post-Holocaust wasteland of Jim Crow America. If Mailer's location were specific, the contours of his context could be generalized for the existentialist heyday that stretched from the late 1920s to the 1960s. It was a maimed world. It was deformed by "the psychic havoc of the concentration camps and the atomic bomb" weighing "upon the unconscious mind of almost everyone alive in these years." It was a world in which instant mass death was still familiar, which posed for many "the most hideous questions about . . . [human] nature." This could not be avoided for, "The Second World War presented a mirror to the human condition that blinded anyone who looked into it" (Mailer 1998, 211). When Mailer spelled out what was reflected in that mirror about human subjectivity, it was an echo of Jean-Paul Sartre: "Man is then not only his character, but his context," he wrote (Mailer 1998, 226). This was Mailer's translation of Sartre's famous bumper sticker for existentialism: "Existence precedes essence," fired out in his celebrated manifesto, *Existentialism Is a Humanism* (Sartre 2007). What is interesting is not that Mailer reworks Sartre's earlier formulation, but that like Sartre he counterpoises this core insight of existentialism to the racist formula that racial essence defines our identity.

Like Judge Wilhelm in Kierkegaard's *Either/Or*, Mailer suggests that in post-Holocaust Jim Crow America, one had to choose between contrasts: "One is Hip or one is Square . . . one is a rebel or one conforms" (Mailer 1998, 212). According to Mailer, to choose the Hip was to side with the Negro, for Negros are "the source of Hip." This is the case because they had "been living between totalitarianism and democracy for two centuries" (Mailer 1998, 213). Cornel West updated the point in *Democracy Matters*: "Race is the crucial intersecting point where democratic energies clash with American imperial realities in the very making of the grand American experiment of democracy" (West 2014, 20, 14). To side with Negros, for Mailer, meant "Sharing a collective disbelief in the words of men who had too much money and controlled too many things" (Mailer 1998, 213). It was to choose to align with those beaten down by American racism.

American existentialists, Mailer mused, were "a new breed of adventurers who drifted out at night looking for action with a black man's code to fit their facts. The hipster had absorbed the existentialist synapses of the Negro, and for practical purposes could be considered a white Negro" (Mailer 1998, 214). This is the key quote of the whole essay, since all of Mailer's claims are distilled. He aligns with a jazz-inspired sensibility and an existentialist critique of systems of thought and conventions of discipline. Quoting Robert Lindner's *Rebel Without a Cause*, he urges his readers to opt for the code of an "agitator without a slogan, a revolutionary without a program" (Mailer 1998, 225). Mailer's focus on individual nonconformity clashes with an existential critique that avows politics, however, hollowing out his political program from his racial identification and limiting its radicalism. This was quite in contrast to the French postwar existentialists like Sartre that Mailer was assimilating into an American idiom.

As George Cotkin has demonstrated, Mailer's "The White Negro" was part of a broader trans-Atlantic conversation about existentialism. There was much in common between Sartre and Mailer, Cotkin avers: both were hypermasculine and each railed against the bourgeois culture that created them. Mailer's Negro hipster drew from Sartre's portrait of the thief, homosexual, and writer Jean Genet. As Cotkin notes, however, for Mailer, "the French had developed a philosophy of alienation that was aloof from its own assumptions, aware of absurdity but without a religious or passionate sense of purpose that would propel the individual beyond that absurdity" (Cotkin 2003, 193). Consequently Mailer's "The White Negro" sought to establish an American existentialism by contrasting it with the Paris school but also by translating Sartre's philosophical vocabulary and applying it to think through the racial organization of American society. Mailer was doing so in terms that Sartre had abandoned in his own antiracism, for precisely the reasons articulated by James Baldwin in his reply to Mailer.

BALDWIN'S "THE BLACK BOY LOOKS AT THE WHITE BOY"

The transracial and transnational nature of the conversion between existential thinkers is evident in Baldwin's critique of Mailer's White Negro essay, "The Black Boy Looks at the White Boy" (Baldwin 1985). In his reflections, Baldwin patiently, as a friend and fellow writer, seeks to explain to Mailer the shortcomings of his piece. According to Baldwin, their differing views stem from their alternate positions in American society, "a black boy from the Harlem streets" and "a middle-class Jew" (Baldwin 1985, 289). These subject positions shape how they view American racism. The responsibility of the America writer, claims Baldwin, is to "excavate the buried consciousness of this country" (Baldwin 1985, 301). Mailer fails in this, however. Rather than confront the American political unconscious, his essay marinates in conventional stereotypes about blacks as criminals, psychopaths, and hypersexual, even as it affirms them as transgressive of American cultural norms. These tropes, Baldwin notes, present "so antique a vision of the blacks" that he upbraids Mailer for failing to repudiate them.

"Our relationship," writes Baldwin, "collided, with that myth of the sexuality of Negroes which Norman, like so many others, refuses to give up" (Baldwin 1985, 292). Baldwin explicitly also calls out Jack Kerouac and other Beat writers for likewise romanticizing outcast Negroes. And Baldwin slams Mailer for his appropriation of black turns of phrase: "why should it be necessary to borrow the Depression language of deprived Negroes, which eventually evolved into jive and bop talk, in order to justify such a grim system of delusions? Why malign the sorely menaced sexuality of Negroes in order to justify the white man's own sexual panic?" (Baldwin 1985, 297). Mailer did so as a critique of the American status quo, which he understood imposed a binary opposition of racial markers (i.e., a "one drop" rule). And perhaps Mailer's Jewishness bent him in this direction, since scholars have shown how Jewishness and whiteness have a complicated and entwined history that subverts a straightforward black–white dichotomy (Gilman 1991; Brodkin 1998; Painter 2010).

But Mailer's suggestions about the malleability of identity in the title of "The White Negro," which stemmed from his existentialist insights about subjectivity, had boundaries for Baldwin. Race is intersubjective and relational, Baldwin recognizes. But it is not as volitional as Mailer suggests. Standpoint shaped how the terms of Mailer's essay were interpreted differently, because experienced differently for black and white boys like Baldwin and Mailer. By taking umbrage with the title of Mailer's piece, Baldwin highlights the point of his own title: intersubjectivity and the gaze operate within a social framework shaped by power. Mailer was avoiding this issue and thus avoiding what structured the "buried consciousness" of American culture.

SARTRE AND FANON ON RACE, 1946–1956

This exchange between Mailer and Baldwin echoed an earlier one between Jean-Paul Sartre and Frantz Fanon. To appreciate how it came about, let's go back to Sartre's original antiracist forays in the 1930s, provoked by French anti-Semitism and racist fascism (Judaken 2006, 2008). Sartre's first antiracist intervention opposed anti-Semitism in literary form in his ironic story "The Childhood of a Leader" included in his collection *The Wall* (1939/1969). "Childhood" is a *bildungsroman* of a boy who believes he finds his true identity as an anti-Semite and a member of the *Camelots du roi*, the shock troops of the Action Française, the crucible for French fascism (Soucy 1995; Sanos 2013).

Following the liberation from the jackboot of the Nazi occupation in the last months of 1944, Sartre developed the existential theory behind his short story in his *Réflexions sur la question juive* (*Anti-Semite and Jew*), which was published as a book in 1946. In this work, Sartre extended his earlier literary portrait into a full-throttled existential and phenomenological analysis of Judeophobia. His central claim is that the anti-Semite is a man of bad faith or self-deception (*mauvaise foi*): "Antisemitism, in short, is fear of the human condition" (Sartre 1948, 54). Although Sartre used the word "fear," what he clearly meant was that anti-Semites flee from the *anxiety* of defining themselves, by means of their hatred and contempt of Jews.

In making this contention, Sartre picked up on a key distinction, introduced by Heidegger in his existentialist opus *Being and Time* (1927), between fear and anxiety. Fear, Heidegger insisted, has a fixed object—we fear the mugger who assaults us, for example. Anxiety is free-floating; it is provoked by the groundlessness of our being (Heidegger 1962, 179–182). When we tune into this situation of anxiety, which Sartre termed "contingency," it manifests bodily as nausea: the sickly taste of our ontological freedom, explored by him in his novel *Nausea* (Sartre 1964a). What the fascist racist avoids, Sartre illustrated in "Childhood," was to assume responsibility for the ontological freedom to define ourselves through our choices.

In Sartre's early antiracism, fascist anti-Semitism was thus analyzed as a case of bad faith: an inauthentic response to man's situation in the world and being with others. Sartre's foundational point was that anti-Semites are deeply *anxious* about the constitutive limits of what defines us as humans—change, death, and a world we share with Others, since these others might well call into question our essence and values. Denying their ontological freedom, anti-Semites define themselves through *abjection*, asserting their values by contrasting them with typologies of the degenerate Jewish Other. As such, they flee responsibility. They escape from it by focusing their passions on "the Jew," a free-floating symbol of decadence that they deem must be eliminated to redeem the world.

"Replace the Jews with the Black, the antisemite with the supporter of slavery," Sartre later quipped, "and there would be nothing essential to be cut from my book [on the Jewish Question] (Watteau 1948, 228). Sartre's anticolonialist essays written from 1945–1960 nonetheless show how he enlarged his approach to racism as he shifted from opposing anti-Semitism to rebuking antiblack racism. In his writings on blacks in America (1945), in his play *The Respectful Prostitute* (1946), in his excursus on "The Oppression of Blacks in the United States," in *Notebooks for an Ethics* (1947–1947), in "Présence noir" (1947), "Black Orpheus," (1964b), and in most of his writings on colonialism gathered in *Situations V* (*Colonialism and Neo-Colonialism* 1964), Sartre developed a multipronged critical theory of racism that went beyond his earlier existentialist critique of fascist Judeophobia in France (Judaken 2008).

Sartre's antiracist writings in this period laced together an approach that transcended his earlier emphasis on individual existential or ontological freedom. He continued to maintain that racism depends upon the bad faith of a Medusa-like gaze, reifying others, turning them into objects as a way of defining one's own subjectivity. But he was now insisting that the freedom of individuals is dependent upon the freedom of all. Simone de Beauvoir used a quote from Dostoevsky as an epigraph to her novel *The Blood of Others* that acutely summarized Sartre's view: "Each of us is responsible for everything and to every human being" (Beauvoir 1948). This formulation encapsulates the notion of "metaphysical guilt" that the founder of German *Existenz-philosophie*, Karl Jaspers, developed in his 1947 essay *Die Schuldfrage* (*The Question of German Guilt*): "There exists a solidarity among men as human beings that makes each co-responsible for every wrong and every injustice in the world, especially for crimes committed in his presence or with his knowledge" (Jaspers 2000, 26). Sartre frequently reworked this idea in his post-Holocaust reflections on colonial racism.

Sartre also began to tease out from the work of negritude poets like Léopold Senghor and Aimé Cesaire how their writing revealed the semiotics of racism and the need to explode the stereotypes that legitimated exploitation, a project evident in his essay "Black Orpheus" that prefaced Senghor's *Anthologie de la nouvelle poésie nègre et malgache de langue française*. But Fanon's simultaneous critique of his negritude forefathers, alongside his swipes at Sartre, with both followed by the unfolding of the French-Algerian war, gave rise to Sartre's deeper appreciation of the structural and institutional forms of racism involved in colonialism.

Fanon's critique of Sartre was woven into his first published article, "The Lived Experience of the Black," which appeared in May 1951 in *Esprit*, the rival Catholic journal that vied with Sartre's *Les Temps modernes* as the prime mover of Left Bank cultural analysis in the postwar years (Bernasconi 2012). Fanon's early approach to antiblack colonial racism was akin to Sartre's *Anti-Semite and Jew* since Fanon's considerations are generated by his encounter with the racist gaze that objectified him as black. In "Lived Experience," he describes a primal scene of hearing a child utter, "Look! A Negro! . . . Mama, see the Negro! I'm fright-ened!" He came to understand from this encounter, as he reflects upon its significance, that "I am a slave not to the 'idea' others have of me but to my appearance" (Fanon 1967, 116).

Fanon consequently distanced himself from Sartre's position by suggesting that Jews could more readily assimilate into white culture, but their black bodies betrayed those who looked like Fanon. Sartre's Preface to Senghor's anthology, Fanon also suggests, was too enthusias-tic about embracing tropes of blackness that identified them with nature, timeless instincts, rhythm, and fecundity, even if these were used tactically as a moment in what Sartre dubbed the dialectic of "antiracist racism" (Sartre 1964, 18). As Abiola Irele incisively put it, "Sartre's term ["antiracist racism"] therefore meant a negro racial pride designed to destroy racial-ism itself" (Irele 1964, 9). If this was its intent, V.Y. Mudimbé nevertheless derides Sartre: "[Senghor] asked for a cloak to celebrate négritude; he was given a shroud" (Mudimbé 1988, 85). Fanon understood that Sartre was parroting Senghor in the essay, who is likewise cri-tiqued. Fanon faults not only the abstraction of the Hegelian dialectic employed by Sartre (Oliver 2003), which denies the lived experience of blackness, but also both Sartre's and Senghor's romanticized, homogenized valorization of the song and dance of African culture, and their idealized veneration of African customs, as its own form of essentializing reiter-ated tropes of blacks produced by the lens of European primitivism.

Fanon's essay was later included as the renowned fifth chapter of *Black Skin, White Masks*, a book where Fanon did for Negrophobia what Sartre had done for Judeophobia. He wanted to show how blacks, like Jews, were phobogenic objects, producing the anxiety that racists sought to contain by essentializing and objectifying them. But Fanon also began to explore the material and institutional formations that constitute racism. The impact of Fanon's cri-tique, as well as Sartre's deepening understanding of colonial racism as a result of his involve-ment in the French-Algerian war (Le Sueur 2001), was clear in his Preface to Albert Memmi's *The Colonizer and the Colonized*.

SARTRE'S CRITIQUE OF MEMMI, 1957

To appreciate Sartre's critique, let's first discuss the evolution of Memmi's oeuvre. Memmi achieved his first acclaim with the publication of the *Pillar of Salt*, his semiautobiographical novel published in 1953, which became widely read after Albert Camus prefaced it and it won the prestigious Prix Fénéon in 1955. Camus's short, but powerful endorsement zeroed in on the core theme of the novel written by a Jewish-French-Tunisian author, whose main char-acter defines himself by his refusals of how he is perceived by others. He thus embodied the authenticity that Sartre preached. "This awareness," Camus tells us, "allows him [Memmi] to remain who he is and to pay attention at the same time to the contradictions of others, whether they are French or Arab" (Camus 2011, 15–16).

Like Sartre's short story, "Childhood," Memmi's novel is a coming-of-age narrative, con-centrating on Alexandre Mordekhai Benillouche, who reaches self-consciousness in colo-nized Tunisia immediately following the Vichy occupation. He seeks to transcend the limits of his Jewish, African, and Arab past in order to achieve the ideal of success he has internal-ized from his French education. To do so, he is supposed to never look backward, like the biblical wife of Lot, an allegory that Memmi uses as the title, and also a leitmotif in the novel.

The "Prologue" launches *The Pillar of Salt* by staging the crisis that frames it. The protago-nist sits for the *agrégation*, the examination that would confer upon him the right to teach philosophy in a university, when he realizes that this is a sham: he cannot go on playing "this part that I've been acting" (Memmi 1992, ix). He continues to write for the seven hours of the exam, but it is his own story that he has begun to compose, rather than respond to the externally imposed imperatives of the examiner's questions, which he now understands are a microcosm of his colonial condition.

Each chapter describes a moment of conflict with the prescripted roles set out for him. It begins in his "blind alley," the street in Tunis where he was born and raised, the son of a saddler and a Jewish Berber. He describes his earliest childhood memories where he was enveloped in the protection of the rites and rituals of his Jewish upbringing in a poor quarter of the city. His separation from this world came about through the schooling provided by the Alliance israélite universelle, who established schools around the Jewish Mediterranean to aid their imperiled brethren. This cleavage was accelerated by his attendance at the French lycée, where he was selected for a scholarship.

In the *Pillar of Salt*, Memmi describes how Alexandre Mordekhai Benillouche constantly confronts the tensions built into his very name, which he dreads he must announce at the beginning of his classes. He was named Alexandre to signify allegiance to "the wonderful West . . . their idea of Europe," after Alexander the Great, whose legacy shaped his French and European past. His middle name was Mordekhai, taken from the great Maccabee leader who fought against the Hellenization of Alexander's inheritors—the internal tensions are already palpable. His last name was Benillouche, both Berber and Arab. But he had learned from surviving anti-Jewish riots by these groups that he did not belong in this community. Ultimately, he comes to realize that he is a Jew, whose home is in the ghetto, whose legal status is native African, who comes from "oriental background," and who is poor. "I had learned to reject these four classifications," he writes (Memmi 1992, 94). "[But] in the long run, I would always be forced to return to Alexandre Mordekhai Benillouche, a native in a colonial country, a Jew in an anti-Semitic universe, an African in a world dominated by Europe" (Memmi 1992, 96). Memmi's character thus represents the internal contradictions that are exposed when a figure outside the boundaries of belonging traverses essentialized ethnographic borders.

Memmi's next major work was his classic, *Portrait du colonisé précédé du colonisateur* (*The Colonizer and the Colonized* 1957). It was consecrated by the "Preface" Sartre wrote, originally as a review but subsequently permanently attached to Memmi's text, helping establish it as an enduring anticolonial tract. Sartre commended Memmi's inquiry since his biography—between colonizer and colonized, Jew and Arab, Occident and Orient—clearly allowed him to appreciate both the dominator and the dominated from the inside. Memmi's analysis is modeled on Sartre's intersubjective dialectic of the gaze. He translates this via two ideal types depicted as two portraits locked in a struggle: "Portrait of the Colonizer" and "Portrait of the Colonized." Drawing on the same Hegelian heritage of the master–slave dia-lectic, *Anti-Semite and Jew* remained foundational for the two portraits Memmi draws: the colonizer is a kindred soul to the phenomenology of the anti-Semite and the situation of the colonized overlaps with Sartre's portrait of "the Jew." Memmi's existential premises concern-ing freedom and authenticity in a specific situation are also derived from Sartrean precepts.

Sartre is nevertheless critical of Memmi's subtle psychological depiction of the relation-ship within colonization and how this results in the interiorization of colonial hegemony.

As Lia Brozgal points out, Sartre's critique is based on three points: "First, whereas Sartre views racism as implicit in the system of colonialism that creates benefits for the colonizer to the detriment of the colonized, for Memmi, racism is located within individuals and is mobilized by the colonizer in order to justify the colonial enterprise and his place within it" (Brozgal 2013, 142). Second, Sartre's Marxist emphasis prioritizes an economic assessment of colonialism. The third point is definitely hammered home by Sartre: "The whole difference between us arises," Sartre asserts, "because he sees a situation where I see a system" (Sartre 1965, xxv). Sartre had made this shift in his thinking by the time of his speech "Colonialism Is a System" (Sartre 1964), which reflected the subsuming of his existential-phenomenological analysis within his developing existential Marxist framework.

In his Preface to Memmi's *The Colonizer and the Colonized*, Sartre made clear that racist rationales are a function of a system of exploitation, rather than a matter of phenomenologies, as Memmi drew them: "Colonialism denies human rights to human beings whom it has subdued by violence, and keeps them by force in a state of misery and ignorance that Marx would rightly call a subhuman condition. Racism is ingrained in action, institutions, and in the nature of the colonialist methods of production and exchange" (Sartre 1965, xxiv). While racism operates psychically, conditioning how we perceive and receive the Other, serving to dehumanize colonial and racialized subjects so that human rights and equality need not be extended to them, Sartre's point now is unequivocally that racism is enmeshed in the power structure and material system of oppression itself.

Discrimination functions not only cognitively and intersubjectively, but within institutions and everyday practices and policies. Racism is not only an idea, but an ideology. The racist colonial system "is embodied in a million colonists, children and grandchildren of colonists, who have been shaped by colonialism and who think, speak and act according to the very principles of the colonial system" (Sartre 2001, 44), wrote Sartre. The racist system therefore shaped both the colonized and the colonizer, infecting all "with its racism" (Sartre 2001, 47).

Memmi's Racism

Although Sartre's analysis clearly took a Marxist turn not shared by Memmi, the influence of Sartre's critique was registered in Memmi's summa, *Racism*. This work magnified Memmi's understanding of racism, which was not really front and center in *The Colonizer and the Colonized*. Now Memmi clearly claimed, "*racism illustrates, summarizes, and symbolizes the colonial relation*" (Memmi 2000, 35). Memmi's *Racism* developed a social theory of racism that he termed a "raciology" (Memmi 2000, 191), which went beyond describing the contradictions of his own situation fictionally in *The Pillar of Salt* and analytically in *The Colonizer and the Colonized*. He now sought to both define and treat the problem that he also diagnosed.

In *Racism*, Memmi works from a definition to elaborate a theory: "Racism is the generalized and final assigning of values to real or imaginary differences, to the accuser's benefit and at his victim's expense, in order to justify the former's own privileges or aggression" (Memmi 2000, 169). In explicating this definition and explaining how it came about, Memmi begins with a historical overview of race thinking, from Aristotle through H. S. Chamberlain, that provided the rational justification for everything from slavery to genocide. The result was not only a body of concepts but also an "underlying system of emotions and convictions that structure its discourse and govern its conduct" (Memmi 2000, 22). In *Racism*, Memmi understands racial discourse as systemically produced.

These systems of thought were integrated organically into the national cultural traditions of groups from France to South Africa. These notions legitimated oppression or persecution through the assertion of the superiority of one group over another on religious or biological or cultural grounds as a result of a claim about unalterable differences. These purported differences could take many forms—biological, economic, psychological, or metaphysical. Racists focus on differing factors in different situations including, "the color of one's skin, facial features, . . . one's character, or one's cultural tradition" (Memmi 2000, 78), depending upon the national and historical context.

Racism is consequently a subset of ethnophobia, Memmi claims: the ascription of blame onto specific groups we are taught to fear. More generally it is a product of "heterophobia," which legitimates attacking those designated foreign or strange or otherwise Other who provoke or are stoked by our anxiety. This is because "difference is disquieting; it reflects the unknown, and the unknown often seems full of danger. Difference disturbs even when, at times, it seduces" (Memmi 2000, 27).

Racism consequently operates "in bad faith" (Memmi 2000, 193) and its function is "anxiety alleviation and ideological distraction" (Memmi 2000, 195). Alongside individual and psychic fears, Memmi also discusses financial exploitation and avarice, which are all sources of human aggression and domination (Memmi 2000, 196). He knits these factors together, writing that ultimately the "machinery of racism . . . produces a vast lexicon of official words, gestures, administrative texts, and political conduct" with "one undeniable goal: the legitimization and consolidation of power and privilege for the colonizers" (Memmi 2000, 38). Put otherwise, "racism subsumes and reveals all the elements of dominance and subjection, aggression and fear, injustice and the defense of privilege, the apologist of domination with its self-justifications, the disparaging myths and images of the dominated, and finally the social destruction or social nullification of the victimized people for the benefit of their persecutors and executioners" (Memmi 2000, 93). Memmi's *Racism* thus clearly consolidated an existentialist analysis of race that we have traced in the work of Mailer and Baldwin, Sartre and Fanon, and between Sartre and Memmi.

However. Memmi does not rest content with his description of racism. He proposes a three-pronged antiracist agenda. First, we must become conscious of racism, not only in others, but also in ourselves (Memmi 2000, 146). Existentialist antiracism begins with self-consciousness. This entails the "exercise of empathy . . . to understand the suffering of the other, his humiliation, his pain at being, insulted or struck" (Memmi 2000, 147). But it also demands self-examination about the relative privilege of different social groups. Second, antiracism requires continual and ongoing pedagogical approaches, sensitive to how racism morphs and changes. This begins with teaching children to enjoy differences, rather than fear them, but also demands ongoing education in schools and universities. And third, existentialist antiracism is political. It cannot be limited to individuals and intersubjective dyads; it cannot rest content to fight against prejudice: "[i.e.] attitude, affective-imaginary disposition, linked to ethnic stereotypes and coined as 'opinions' and 'belief'" (Taguieff 2001, 145). The politics of existentialist antiracism must "*struggle against all oppression*" and "*combat all forms of domination*" (Memmi 2000, 154, 157).

Conclusion

Memmi's *Racism* is a useful summa for appreciating how existentialist quarrels about raciology changed as a result of a transnational and transglobal conversation. Memmi, like Mailer, began as a fiction writer whose creative work explored the existentialist parameters of identity construction. The "White Negro" was an experimental work, stretching the idiom of the American avant-garde by associating it with the vocabulary of existentialism and the embrace of blackness as a critique of American conventionality. This was a stab at Jim Crow racism. But in doing so, as Baldwin pointed out, Mailer slid into fetishizing many images that trapped blacks in a nexus of stereotypes. Fanon had earlier suggested something similar about Sartre's "antiracist racism" in "Black Orpheus," pointing Sartre toward a more holistic assessment of the machinery of racism that linked ideas with ideology toward understanding how they were fused into everyday practices and institutional forms. Fanon's critique, alongside Sartre's deepening involvement in the Algerian conflict by 1957, had led him to move beyond understanding racism as a "bad faith" response to an individual existential situation; he now understood racism as structured by the colonial system. Memmi's later work integrated Sartre's critique, even as he developed his own wholesale theoretical understanding of racism that continued to find the root of racism in "bad faith" and the anxiety and fear of the racial Other, as had Sartre's early existentialist essays. *Racism* explains the mechanisms of racial subjectification by recounting its long conceptual history in the discourse of the West, its propagation in religious works and associations, their incorporation into science, and into political conflicts. If Memmi's analysis is triple (individual, social, and political), so is his remedy for racism: auto-critique, education, and collective mobilization aimed at overcoming all forms of oppression and heterophobia.

References

Baldwin, James. (1985). "The Black Boy Looks at the White Boy." In *The Price of the Ticket: Collected Nonfiction, 1948–1985*, 389–404. New York: St. Martin's.

Beauvoir, Simone de. *The Blood of Others*. New York: A. A. Knopf.

Bernasconi, R. (2012). "Situating Frantz Fanon's Account of Black Experience." In *Situating Existentialism: Key Texts in Context*, edited by Jonathan Judaken and Robert Bernasconi, 336–359. New York: Columbia University Press.

Brodkin, K. (1998). *How Jews Became White Folks and What That Says about Race in America*. New Brunswick, NJ: Rutgers University Press.

Brozgal, L. (2013). *Against Autobiography: Albert Memmi and the Production of Theory*. Lincoln: University of Nebraska Press.

Camus, Albert. (2011). "Preface to *The Pillar of Salt*." Translated by Scott Davidson. *Journal of French and Fancophone Philosophy—Revue de la philosophie française et de langue française* 19 (2): 15–16.

Cotkin, G. (2003). *Existential America*. Baltimore: Johns Hopkins.

Gordon, L. (2006). *Disciplinary Decadence: Living Thought in Trying Times*. Boulder, CO: Paradigm Press.

Gilman, S. (1991). *The Jew's Body*. New York: Routledge.

Heidegger, Martin. (1962). *Being and Time*. New York: Harper and Row.

Irele, A. (1964). "A Defence of Negritude: Apropos of *Black Orpheus* by Jean-Paul Sartre." *Transition* 13 (March-April): 9–11.

Jackson, J., and Saxe, R. (2015). *The Underground Reader: Sources in the Transatlantic Counterculture*. New York: Berghahn.

Jaspers, K. (2000). *The Question of German Guilt*. New York: Fordham University Press.

Judaken, J. (2006). *Jean-Paul Sartre and the Jewish Question: Anti-antisemitism and the Politics of the French Intellectual*. Nebraska: University of Nebraska Press.

Judaken, J., ed. (2008). *Race after Sartre: Antiracism, Africana Existentialism, Postcolonialism*. New York: State University of New York Press.

Le Sueur, James. (2001). *Uncivil War: Intellectuals and Identity Politics During the Decolonization of Algeria*. Philadelphia: University of Pennsylvania Press.

Mailer, N. (1998). "The White Negro." In *The Time of Our Time*, 211–230. New York: Random House.

Memmi, A. (1965). *The Colonizer and the Colonized*. New York: Orion Press.

Memmi, A. (1992). *The Pillar of Salt*. Boston: Beacon Press.

Memmi, A. (2000). *Racism*. Minnesota: University of Minnesota Press.

Mudimbé, V. Y. (1988). *Invention of Africa: Gnosis, Philosophy, and the Order of Knowledge*. Bloomington: Indiana University Press.

Oliver, K. (2003). "Alienation and Its Double; or the Secretion of Race." In *Race and Racism in Continental Philosophy*, edited by Robert Bernasconi with Sybol Cook, 176–195. Bloomington: Indiana University Press.

Painter, N. I. (2010). *The History of White People*. New York: W. W. Norton.

Sanos, S. (2013). *The Aesthetics of Hate: Far-Right Intellectuals, Antisemitism, and Gender in 1930s France*. Stanford, CA: Stanford University Press.

Sartre, Jean-Paul. (1939/1969). "The Childhood of a Leader." In *The Wall*, 84–144. New York: New Directions Books.

Sartre, Jean-Paul. (1948). *Anti-Semite and Jew*. New York: Schocken Books.

Sartre, Jean-Paul. (1964a). *Nausea*. New York: New Directions Books.

Sartre, Jean-Paul. (1964b). "Black Orpheus." *The Massachusetts Review* 6 (Autumn): 13–52.

Sartre, Jean-Paul. (2001). *Colonialism and Neo-Colonialism*. New York: Routledge.

Sartre, Jean-Paul. (2007). *Existentialism Is a Humanism*. New Haven, CT: Yale University Press.

Soucy, R. (1995). *French Fascism: The Second Wave, 1933–1939*. New Haven, CT: Yale University Press.

Spivak, G. C. (2003). *Death of a Discipline*. New York: Columbia.

Taguieff, P-A. (2001). "The Theories of Prejudice and the Meanings of Racism." In *The Force of Prejudice: On Racism and Its Doubles*, 141–179. Minneapolis: University of Minnesota Press.

Watteau, M. (1948). "Situation raciales et condition de l'homme dans l'oeuvre de Jean-Paul Sartre." *Présence africaine* 2 (January): 209–229.

West, Cornel. (2014). *Democracy Matters: Winning the Fight Against Imperialism*. New York: Penguin.

CHAPTER 24

FROM SCIENTIFIC RACISM TO NEOLIBERAL BIOPOLITICS
Using Foucault's Toolkit

LADELLE MCWHORTER

CRITICS have accused Michel Foucault of disempowering his readers by leaving them with no sense of political direction (Foucault 1994, 234). His genealogical analyses simply analyze, and his bleak depictions of interlocking and mutually reinforcing power relations provide no instructions for action and no hope for effecting change. Why, then, should social justice advocates and antiracists in particular bother to explore his work? Foucault responded to this charge:

> Critique doesn't have to be the premise of a deduction that concludes, "this, then, is what needs to be done." It should be an instrument for those who fight, those who resist and refuse what is. Its use should be in processes of conflict and confrontation, essays in refusal. It doesn't have to lay down the law for the law. It isn't a stage in a programming. It is a challenge directed to what is. (Foucault 1994, 236)

Genealogy does not pose as political motivation, let alone moral imperative. It is a tool for those already engaged in resistance—not to dictate action but to enrich ongoing processes of analyzing and strategizing. With that understanding of genealogy's role, as I have argued (McWhorter 2009) and will argue here, Foucault's method can be extremely useful for confronting racism. In particular, his concepts of normalization and biopower are crucial for understanding how racism survived the demise of the nineteenth-century science that supported it and how it persisted throughout the twentieth century despite social, political, and economic change.

FOUCAULT'S METHOD

Genealogical work emphasizes contingency and complexity, as Colin Koopman puts it (Koopman 2013, chapter 3). It assumes that whatever phenomena it problematizes were formed in the forces of history rather than given throughout time and universally (Foucault 1998, 376). Racism, a genealogist would therefore assume, exists only in its various historical manifestations in (usually institutionalized) practices, including the rationalizing practices that give those practices their sense, and it changes as networks of power change. Despite its contingency, however, racism is a remarkably persistent feature of our cultural landscape. From a genealogical perspective, then, we must wonder, What gives racism that ability to persist, its *apparent* transhistorical stability? This is the question genealogy investigates.

A genealogist of racism looks first for moments when racism's operations seem unfamiliar, for what Foucault calls "a breach of self-evidence" (1994, 226). In their modern origins, ideas of race soon became coextensive with what theorists today view as racism, so in considering such breaches, we can begin with "race." In the eighteenth century *race* named lineal descent and tradition, not appearance, and there were as many races as there were clans or tribes. Only in the nineteenth century did it become primarily a matter of physical appearance. Later, after it became an object of science, race came to mean an essentially temporal and developmental phenomenon rather than either a given morphology or a matter of familial descent. Scientific studies of race quickly became hierarchical taxonomies that privileged white Europeans and that gave rise to the eugenics movement, which was then disrupted by both political and scientific events in the 1930s. After World War II, racism began to be treated as a hallmark of ignorance and then as a deep-seated psychological trait, as opposed to a rationally communicable belief system. In this new intellectual climate, arguments could be made against (some) racist laws and practices, and civil rights movements for oppressed minorities and underclasses gained traction. Whereas racism had once been the avowed position of respected elites, it was now the pernicious fantasy of the ignorant or sick, and the way to fight it was through education, therapy, and moral suasion. If we study the transformations in power that occurred surrounding these various shifts, we may develop an understanding of racism that will inspire new and possibly more effective strategies for combatting it.

What realignments of forces—institutions, practices, theories, values, eruptive events—effected such shifts? Having identified breaches of self-evidence, historical moments when big shifts in practices seem to have occurred, the genealogist seeks the multiplicity of "connections, encounters, supports, blockages, plays of forces, strategies, and so on, that at a given moment establish what subsequently counts as being self-evident, universal, and necessary" (Foucault 1994, 226–227). The goal is to produce a description of forces surrounding these disruptions of continuity. Very likely this effort will lead outside the field in which the "object" occurs. Foucault notes, for example, that his study of imprisonment practices in *Discipline and Punish* led to analysis of schooling, military discipline, and so on (Foucault 1994, 227; 1978). Foucault's research trajectory followed practical concerns that had generated disciplinary regimes that practitioners then articulated in abstract, communicable terms. This facilitated importation of those practices and their rationalities to other domains (imprisonment practices being only one), and the overall result has been an archive for genealogists to exploit.

Genealogy is thus analytic and diagnostic. Its discoveries implicitly suggest where we might focus our attention by revealing the points at which a network of power is, despite its appearance of invulnerability, potentially unstable, thus providing clues for how to transform the practices that shape us. Genealogy is not inherently normative in the sense of advocating a set of values and a plan of action. It is a tool for those who want to formulate values and plans, to make change.

If we want to dismantle the institutions and practices that are racism today, taking up the genealogical tool means, first, looking at these moments where racism, while recognizable in some degree, is differently manifested. The rise of scientific racism is one such moment in comparison with racisms informed by the lineal concept of race that preceded it (see McWhorter 2009, 55–62). Subsequently we can identify others, such as eugenics and practices of surveillance, control, and normalization that have endured through neoliberalism.

A Genealogical Fragment: The Prehistory of Scientific "Race"

Our genealogy might begin as the eighteenth century drew to a close, with the onset of convergence among disparate practices that would, along with a series of political events, soon generate what we now call scientific racism. Among them were three: (1) the overturning of the theory of preformation and its replacement with a version of epigenesis, and subsequently, the biological theory that ontogeny recapitulates phylogeny, (2) the question of human diversity in comparative anthropology, and (3) the problematization of the slave trade and then slavery as an American institution. These three different sets of events supported a shift in the meaning of *race* from lineal descent to morphology; race became less a matter of ancestry and more a matter of visible embodiment as it was affected by environmental factors. That is, races could be classified by direct observation and their observed differences explained by ancient patterns of migration to different climates (see Kant 2000, 13ff; Smith 1965).

Not until the twentieth century was there a concept of culture as plural—as in the relatively recent concept of "multiculturalism." Instead, anthropologists spoke of civilization, a unitary phenomenon. Some racialized groups lived according to the standards of civilization, and some did not. Anthropologists used the newly prevailing concept of race—human bodies in long-term interaction with climate—to explain this observed "fact": Comfortable climates present few challenges and require little innovation for survival; consequently, sophisticated forms of technology and government never emerge in them. It just so happened that almost all dark-skinned peoples inhabited congenial climates (the brown "Laplanders" were an explicable exception), while whites inhabited harsh ones. *Voilà*, morphology and civilization converged (Jefferson 1944, 88; Kant 2000, 17).

This convergence presupposed an earlier scientific controversy between epigenesis, the view that living matter actually organizes itself into new configurations; and preformationism, the idea that, while living matter grows or declines, it cannot change its form, which was resolved by the nineteenth century in favor of epigenesis (Müller-Sievers 1997, 28, 38–41).

With the triumph of epigenesis, natural historians began to find developmental forces inherent in matter itself, allowing living matter to change in response to environmental conditions. Thus natural history gave way to the new science of biology, the science of life. Among the many ideas that appeared upon this transformation was anatomist Carl Friedrich Kielmeyer's suggestion that stages of mammalian fetal development replicate the adult morphologies of other creatures. His claim inspired Johann von Autenrieth, who held that higher mammals (e.g., humans) exhibit the morphologies of lower animals (e.g., fish) on their way to expressing their species-appropriate forms, a view later encapsulated in the phrase "ontogeny recapitulates phylogeny." In other words, lower animals are but living stages of higher animals' development in utero; higher animals thus coexist alongside the living forms they have surpassed (Gould 1977, 126).

Biologists' attention to fetal development was paralleled by a new attention to development in the emerging field of comparative anthropology. Based on a collection of "specimens" from Africa, Tasmania, and Australia in 1800, European anthropologists held that peoples in different parts of the world differ anatomically in such features as arm length relative to height, genital size, and most important, cranial capacity. Anthropologists used this new collection, in addition to Blumenbach's eighteenth-century collection, as the basis not only for typological theories but also for a developmental theory of racial difference (Gould 1977, 82–107, 122–142).

Anatomical differences between groups, already understood as the effects of environment, were now seen as indications of more and less developmental progress. In warm, fertile areas where little effort is required to feed oneself and little preparation for seasonal changes is necessary, people did not develop large brains and therefore had relatively small crania. In cold, harsh climates where lack of foresight and hard work results in death by starvation, people developed large brains and had large crania. Beyond serving as an indicator of racial difference, then, cranial capacity became a measure of both differential intellectual and social racial development. This measure also indicated that women are less developed than the men of their respective race, and it bespoke race and sex differences in the capacity to solve problems, exercise sound judgment and self-control, and in general govern one's own life and the lives of others. New anthropological theories of race suggested that the peoples of Africa and the Southern Hemisphere were simply less intellectually and morally capable than (male) peoples in Northern Europe and, hence, less civilized (Jefferson 1944; Kant 2000).

The new biology and the new anthropology reinforced each other, giving rise to a widespread belief, among educated Europeans and North Americans, that adult white males were not merely physically different from, but more and better developed than white children and females, and nonwhite peoples everywhere. When the American institution of chattel slavery came under fire in the nineteenth century, these theories were marshaled to lend it scientific defense and through repetition in public discourse gained wide currency even among less educated whites. The "lower" races had to be kept under close surveillance and supervision, so the thinking went, because they were like the children of the "higher" races in terms of their cognitive abilities and capacity to delay gratification. Freedom for them would be disastrous, because they would act on impulse, without considering consequences. They would not be able to take care of themselves. Worse still, they would pose a danger to whites, just as gangs of unsupervised adolescents tend to run amok, respecting neither property nor persons (see Fitzhugh 1960; Wish 1960; Connor 1965; Muhammad 2010, 17–20).

No one at the time called this body of work "scientific racism." That appellation was coined in the twentieth century to name something that social and biological scientists were interested in repudiating. In the nineteenth century, on the contrary, what we now call "scientific racism" was, simply, *science*—scientific study of the perceived anatomical and social differences across human groups. Its practitioners were among the most renowned scholars and experimentalists of their time such as Samuel George Morton, Josiah Nott, George Glidden, and Louis Agassiz. Among their influential works were Morton's 1839 *Crania Americana* and

1844 *Crania Aegyptiaca* and Nott and Glidden's 1854 *Types of Mankind* (see Fredrickson 1971, 77; Brace 2005, 80). Yet, by the mid-twentieth century, this body of work was the object of ridicule and condemnation. Things—power relations—had shifted dramatically. Here is another moment for genealogical analysis.

Two Concepts: Normalization and Biopower

At this point in the analysis, we do well to employ two concepts that Foucault introduced in his genealogies of modern incarceration and sexuality: normalization and biopower. "Normalization" is a set of management techniques that became ubiquitous over the course of the nineteenth and twentieth centuries. They grew out of disciplinary techniques adapted from monastic practices for pedagogy and military training. Adaptation for the military occurred, according to Foucault in *Discipline and Punish*, when authorities in Europe began to conscript soldiers from the peasantry rather than exclusively from the nobility. Warriors were no longer born but were made out of ordinary bodies. Recruits required discipline. New techniques enabled military leaders to treat bodies as sets of movable parts that could be trained through graduated exercises to interact in ways conducive to both good soldiering and strict obedience to commanders (Foucault 1978, 138). Bodies were effectively machines that could be retooled. Over time, however, trainers realized that not all bodies responded to these techniques. Some just could not manage a rifle, march in time, or follow instructions. Similarly, educators discovered that no matter how carefully they adjusted their disciplinary practices, some pupils did not conform. Some bodies were stubborn; it was as if, unlike machines, they had their own internal temporality of development—as if, as biologists soon began to say, living matter had its own inherent principles of self-organization.

The best option was not to work against these posited forces but to harness and guide them. Disciplinarians observed developmental trajectories and kept records from which they generated statistical norms. These norms could, in turn, be used to assess and evaluate individuals and devise yet more carefully calibrated disciplinary techniques for training outliers. Mechanical discipline gave way to normalizing discipline. Development was not only a phenomenon to be studied, as biologists at the time were beginning to do; it was a force to be managed and a resource to be cultivated (Foucault 1978, 168–169).

Normalizing disciplinary practices swiftly spread—from military camps and schools to hospitals and asylums—and it made possible new institutions as well, such as the modern mental institution and the prison. Sexuality, conceived not as simple reproductive activity but as developmental mentality and behavior, came into existence in this midst of this explosion of normalizing disciplinary practices, as Foucault demonstrates in *The History of Sexuality, Volume 1*. Sexuality became the engine of much of individual development and, through reproduction and family life, the engine of social and species development as well (Foucault 1980, 68–69). By the end of the nineteenth century, sexuality functioned as both guarantor of and greatest danger to each individual's developmental health, as well as the reproduction of the next generation. It became, therefore, the managerial key to a vast number of other aspects of human life; educators, psychiatrists, psychoanalysts, physicians, and criminologists (among others) set to work to determine its norms in order to control and cultivate its forces. As these techniques took hold, all sorts of governmental institutions

began to make human life "itself," that is, the vital processes that characterized their populations, the target of power—hence Foucault's term "biopower." The analytic value of these two
concepts will be evident in our next genealogical fragment.

ANOTHER GENEALOGICAL FRAGMENT: EUGENICS

These techniques, which included surveillance and data gathering, conditioned and were
conditioned by the sciences of the time. Scientific racism, rapidly assimilating Darwin's evolutionary theory, promoted the idea that Northern Europeans and their American descendants were at the forefront of human development, far superior in intellect, self-control, and
physical fitness to their "Asiatic," "Indian," "Negro," and "Mediterranean" contemporaries,
who represented stages of evolution that whites had long surpassed. Northern Europeans
had become superior because of the pressures of the environments where they had evolved.
Cold, harsh climates killed individuals who lacked the physical strength, intellectual ability, and self-restraint to work and plan ahead for winter scarcity, leaving only those who
were "fit" for that climate to survive and propagate. Warm, inviting climates produced no
such pressure, so the stupid and the impulsive could flourish and prevail. However, in the
midst of new techniques for managing individual development, science gave reasons for
concern regarding racial development, which they understood as coextensive with human
development.

Evolutionary conditions had obviously changed. First, Northern Europeans were not
confined to Northern Europe anymore, but had spread over the globe, where many inhabited warm and fertile climates. Furthermore, Europeans' and Euro-Americans' superior
technologies had made their lives much easier; steam and coal engines made production less
taxing, and medicine allowed even the weak to survive and reproduce. Their Christian morals led them to pity the less well endowed and provide for them what they could not provide
for themselves, thereby further increasing the number of those who would have perished
in former times. In short, the evolutionary pressure was off. And that "fact," coupled with
the "fact" that descendants of Northern Europeans now lived among members of the "lower
races" with whom some of them might mate (voluntarily or involuntarily as the result of the
latter's impulsive violence), inspired fear that human evolution was about to come to a grind-
ing halt. The white race was committing suicide.

This fear might have remained confined to scientifically educated elites, had it not been for
a number of other events that affected a broader swath of the population in the United States
and Western Europe. Labor leaders were interested in curbing the influx of immigrants to
keep wages up. The alleged developmental inferiority of Asians and Southern and Eastern
Europeans cemented an otherwise unlikely alliance between a professional class and labor
unions (Reilly 1991, 23–24). Capitalists feared Eastern European immigrants would bring
with them anarchism and communism and stir up trouble that would threaten their business interests. Immigration restrictions enacted in the United States, Canada, and Western
Europe through the early twentieth century accorded with several agendas, as well as science. Local governmental officials were interested in reducing the number of beggars and
drifters, scientific racism provided them with arguments for state and federal spending on
institutions to confine such people and sex-segregate them so they could not produce more

mouths to feed (Carlson 2001, 188–194). Reformers wanted to clean up tenements, rescue children from negligent parents, and minister to the mentally ill, which pitted them against slum lords, reluctant governments, and taxpayers, but the new concern with bettering the human race gave them momentum. When financial constraints clashed with goals of such "racial hygiene," resourceful reformers sought legislation to allow, instead of lifelong institutionalization, mass sterilization of the poor, the immoral, the mentally ill, and the cognitively disabled, all of whom were now seen as drags on human evolution. We see a similar alliance between race science and the birth control movement. Disparate though these movements and concerns were, they coalesced to produce new social and political practices that contributed to twentieth-century eugenics (Brunius 2006; McWhorter 2009, 203–230).

Sexuality was key to racial discipline, to the management of human evolution for the purpose of "fitness" and "betterment," just as it was to individual development and maldevelopment. Eugenicists sought to control the sexuality of "inferior individuals" to prevent inferiority from reproducing itself. The aim was to protect the white nuclear family and the future, "better" population whose birth depended upon it (Smith and Nelson 1989, 234; Kline 1997, 106ff; Carlson 2001, 204–214). At the movement's height, eugenic rhetoric infused virtually all public discourse in industrialized countries. Purging the human race of inferior "germ plasm" through managed sexuality was a progressive enterprise, the new heart of social reform. This was the first major consolidation of "biopower" (Foucault 1978, 140); the target of the exercise of power on a massive scale was human biological existence.

Then came Hitler. Eugenics opponents were quick to point out the similarities—indeed, the continuity—between domestic eugenics policies and Hitler's campaigns against the disabled and the non-"Aryan." Eugenics' progress stalled as policymakers grew reluctant to be perceived as "Hitlerite." Social and biological scientists began distancing their work from their forebears'. "New" developments in genetics (some of which were already thirty years old) were brought forward to undercut eugenicist positions and proposals (Larson 1995, 147; Carlson 2001, 285; McWhorter 2009, 231–244).

In response, the movement changed tactics. American Eugenics Society President Frederick Osborn embraced the new science, which showed that, statistically, there was actually more variation of genotypes within groups than between them. "[I]it would be unwise for eugenicists to impute superiorities or inferiorities of a biological nature to social classes, to regional groups, or to races as a whole," he wrote. "Eugenics should therefore operate on the basis of individual selection" (Osborn 1937, 106). Eugenicists still believed that, on balance, white people were superior, but they admitted that there might be some fit Negroes, Jews, and Asiatics. Policies discriminating against entire racial groups were thus counterproductive. Eugenicists turned to marriage and then genetics counseling to influence "natural" selection, meanwhile changing the names of their organizations and publications. Population management for the betterment of the human race was still their goal, but efforts would be focused on influencing individual choice rather than dictating law or policy.

However, by World War II, eugenic values were deeply embedded in popular culture in almost all industrialized nations. While the overarching goal of (human) race betterment was officially repudiated, bias toward the poor, disabled, and dark-skinned remained (Gannett 2001, 490; McWhorter 2009, 245–258). Quite apart from that, however, biopolitical techniques of population management had proven extremely useful in furthering a wide variety of governmental and financial goals. Keeping populations under surveillance and segregating them for productive efficiency and risk reduction were essential means for managing a growing industrial economy. It was necessary to renounce racial "prejudice" (officially and scientifically), so steps were taken to disavow "racism," while surveillance, data collection, and population management intensified (Kline 1997, 104).

Production, circulation, and technological progress became more important than race betterment. But ideas for achieving those ends were formed in a eugenic era, where it was assumed that productive, innovative, and law-abiding individuals matched the profile of the supposed *evolutionary avant garde*: male, "fit" (not disabled), of normal intelligence quotient, heterosexual, and of Northern European descent (Paul 1995, 125; 1998, 142). Such individuals were produced in households made up of father-headed families with clear gender and racial divisions and identities. Thus the biopolitical focus became the individual and his or her role in the nuclear family. Immigration restrictions persisted, then, and sterilizations continued into the 1970s. But the reasons given (if ever anyone asked) cited individual well-being and economic benefit.

"Racism" itself was invented in this process. The term was coined as a means of distinguishing good exercises and networks of biopower from bad. Hitler was a racist because, unlike Osborn, he assumed *all* members of the Jewish and Negro races were unfit and treated them as such, indiscriminately. According to Osborn's new dicta, he should have judged them fit or unfit as individuals. The rhetoric of individuality and the celebration of the individualizing nuclear family as the cradle of humanity's future replaced the rhetoric of racial hygiene. But institutionalized oppression went largely unchallenged.

RACISM IN A DISCIPLINARY SOCIETY

The deeply embedded assumption that the heterosexual nuclear family was requisite for normal development that would lead to success persisted in government, courts, education, and medicine. People who did not come from or form such families (and lived in single parenthood, homosexual pairing, multigenerational households, or by themselves) were deviant and likely dangerous (Goddard 1927, 101). Likewise, poverty was a clear indicator of intellectual or moral developmental failure. But some institutional innovation did occur as a retreat from early eugenic racial profiling. In the United States, a new concern for "underprivileged" children and a willingness to reconsider Jim Crow emerged in a few corners of public discourse (driven in part by the fact that Soviet propaganda used Jim Crow to illustrate the hypocrisy of liberal capitalism). Here and there a progressive white person suggested that every individual should have an opportunity to prove himself (or even herself), that equal opportunity meant that Negro children get the same schooling as whites, or that children of the poor needed a "head start" in order to take advantage of the schooling offered to them. A booming postwar economy financed programs designed to provide opportunities, and an organized civil rights movement coupled with the new technology of television generated images of respectable Negroes who asked to be judged not by the color of their skin but by the content of their characters (Johnson 2007).

As long as advocates for social justice—racial or economic (or even sexual)—stuck to the normalizing, individualist agenda, their claims could be assimilated to biopolitical networks that now permeated liberal capitalism. By contrast, structural analyses got little traction, and their advocates were labeled as Communists. Still, as doors opened for many people, racism was declared a thing of the past; only backward people were racists anymore, and society as a whole could not be held responsible for their actions or attitudes (Bonilla-Silva 2003, 173). Elites made a point of marginalizing those "backward" people and spotlighting members of formerly "inferior" racial groups who had seized opportunities and proven themselves normal people, even individuals of merit.

Race no longer signified more or less stable stages of human development; indeed, races were no longer intellectually or morally homogenous groups. Racism, as it was construed when the term was introduced, really did recede into the backwaters; psychologists declared *it* abnormal, the symptom of developmental failure and mental pathology. But the result was not racial equality. And it could not have been. The norms by which individuals were to be measured had arisen in the context of white supremacy and capitalist production and consumption. Normal human development was modeled on white, Protestant, middle-class, heterosexual development, and it was measured by white, mostly Protestant, middle- and upper-middle-class, and at least officially heterosexual, clinicians and educators. Moreover, the outcomes that proved normal development had occurred were bodied forth in the lifestyles of middle-class white married couples raising normal children. Racist beliefs were generally discredited; racist attitudes were generally condemned. But the idea that people should be subject to continual surveillance and measurement against developmental norms is still firmly in place. Not every member of previously "inferior" races is subject to racial "prejudice" at every moment and in every context, as their ancestors were. But at the first sign of "abnormality" the old mechanisms of containment and constraint will close in. We live in a normalizing society, as Foucault declared. And this fact falls especially hard on anyone who does not fit the implicitly white ideal. But that is not what a majority of people believe.

Most white people and many people of color, at least in the United States, are loath to think that white supremacy is an inherent feature of our capitalist, neoliberal society. Instead, they think racial inequalities linger because some whites still judge individuals by their racial identities rather than their personal merit. Perhaps unconsciously or secretly, twenty-first-century whites really do believe old-style scientific racist tenets. The answer, therefore, is more moral exhortation, more education, or elimination of all such people from positions of authority—more of what has been done for the last sixty years. Those strategies did combat some forms of racism and did make many people's lives much better. But their efficacy has empirically obvious limits. By revealing the power of normalization rather than veiled scientific racism at the center of many contemporary racist effects, genealogical analysis suggests a different approach. What must be dismantled is not a belief system or even individual attitudes; it is normalizing discipline and its accompanying practices of biopower. The solution is not to raise everybody to acceptable standards of normality; it is to undermine normality's power to dictate the terms of human lives.

Racism and Neoliberalism

Much has changed since Foucault's analyses of normalization and biopower in the 1970s. It would be foolish not to take genealogical account of that change, some of which, remarkably, Foucault himself anticipated. In his lecture series at the Collège de France in 1979 (Foucault 2008, 317), he discussed a phenomenon just then emerging, which, following

Milton Friedman, he termed "neoliberalism." Since 1979, neoliberalism has become the prevailing mode of governing in capitalist countries and their client states. Whatever race and racism are in the twenty-first century, they are undoubtedly deeply marked by neoliberalism, for if they were not they could not persist in this transformed political and social terrain. To understand and counter the racism we face, we must analyze this new formation of biopower.

Foucault traces neoliberalism to reactions against governments' taking on the well-being of their populations as a central function, as was supposedly done in enactment of the Beveridge Report in Great Britain, the New Deal in the United States, and during German reconstruction after World War II (Foucault 2008, chapters 5–7, 9). Neoliberals held that government's central function is to provide the national security and legal structure to insure contracts. It should not regulate prices, markets, or industries; provide consumer or environmental or worker protections; or guarantee people education, health care, or jobs. The market will take care of all those things if governments refrain from interfering. Moreover, government assets beyond those absolutely essential for functioning of security, courts, and legislatures should be privatized. In a booming economy, Keynesian economic policies remained in force, but once the postwar economy stagnated, neoliberalism got a hearing, and neoliberals were elected to office. Their policies set in motion a global movement whose new normal now pervades capitalist society discursively and, to a great extent, politically and legally as well (Mirowski and Plehwe 2009).

Neoliberalism valorizes competition and individualizes both failure and success; moral worth is equated with competitive success in material terms. To this extent, it replicates the major features of disciplinary normalization. But there are differences, two of which will suffice as illustration. For capitalism to expand beyond colonization of previously noncapitalist regions, consumers' desires must expand and diversify. A diversity of cultures fosters a diversity of desires, especially if one set of cultural consumables can be marketed to members of other cultures as a new fashion. Neoliberal individualism differs from the individualization of normalizing discipline, therefore, in that it encourages (some) divergence from norms. Gay is good if it presents a demand for specialized vacations. Black is beautiful if it sells sneakers and baggy jeans. Neoliberalism encourages departures from the norm as long as they can be construed as matters of taste and those exhibiting them are moneyed enough to function as consumers. Industrialized production required rigorous discipline on a massive scale; postindustrial consumption requires a certain (controlled) lack of discipline. A genealogy of racism in the twenty-first century would need to identify the points at which normalizing discipline retreats and those at which it remains in force, and how that happens.

A second illustrative difference concerns the fate of those who are not moneyed enough to consume—an increasingly large number as neoliberalism makes possible a striking new concentration of wealth. Industrial production absorbed enormous numbers of people as laborers. Neoliberalism does not need nearly so many of them. If they have no income streams other than that generated by labor, there is no place for them. They are not drags on evolution, but they may be drags on the economy, especially if their poverty drives them to steal or riot.

Any analysis of racial oppression in the present day must take account of these changes—of the new ways in which nonwhite populations and cultures can be and sometimes are treasured and of the ways in which both nonwhite and white populations can be simply abandoned, incarcerated, or otherwise "encouraged" to pass out of existence. This is not our foreparents' racism, which does not mean that it is not racism at all. It simply means we have genealogical work to do before we can formulate the strategies we need to dismantle the structures that oppress us.

CONCLUSION

Foucault's examination of neoliberalism stopped at 1980, but the tools he provided via concepts such as normalization and biopower and methods such as genealogy can be used to study this new racial situation. How useful they will be is an empirical question and a question of strategy. What is obvious, however, is that racism cannot be fully understood, let alone countered, if we insist that it is merely a matter of individual choices, actions, attitudes, and beliefs. "Both race and racism are profoundly historical," Angela Davis reminds us. Even if biological and essentialist racisms no longer hold sway: "It would be erroneous to assume that we can also willfully extricate ourselves from histories of race and racism. Whether we acknowledge it or not, we continue to inhabit these histories, which help constitute our social and psychic worlds" (Davis 2012, 169). That is, racism cannot be addressed without knowledge of the historical forces that brought us to this point and the biopolitical networks that currently enforce it.

REFERENCES

Bonilla-Silva, Eduardo. (2003). *Racism without Racists: Colorblind Racism and the Persistence of Racial Inequality in America*. Lanham, MD: Rowman and Littlefield.

Brace, C. Loring. (2005). *"Race" Is a Four-Letter Word; The Genesis of the Concept*. New York: Oxford University Press.

Brunius, Harry. (2006). *Better for All the World: The Secret History of Forced Sterilization and America's Quest for Racial Purity*. New York: A. A. Knopf.

Connor, Paul. (1965). "Patriarchy: Old World and New." *American Quarterly* 17 (1): 48–62.

Davis, Angela Y. (2012). *The Meaning of Freedom, and Other Difficult Dialogues*. San Francisco: City Lights Books.

Fitzhugh, George. (1960). *Cannibals All! Or Slaves Without Masters*. Edited by C. Vann Woodward. Cambridge, MA: Belknap Press of Harvard University Press.

Foucault, Michel. (1978). *Discipline and Punish: The Birth of the Prison*. Translated by Alan Sheridan. New York: Vintage Books.

Foucault, Michel. (1980). *The History of Sexuality* Translated by Robert Hurley. Vol. 1, *An Introduction*. New York: Vintage Books.

Foucault, Michel. (1994). "Questions of Method." In *Power: Essential Works of Foucault 1954–1984*. Edited by James D. Faubian. Vol. 3, 223–238. New York: The New Press.

Foucault, Michel. (1998). "Nietzsche, Genealogy, History." In *Power: Essential Works of Foucault 1954–1984*, edited by James D. Faubian, Vol. 3, pp. 369–391. New York: The New Press.

Foucault, Michel. (2008). *The Birth of Biopolitics: Lectures at the Collège de France 1978–1979*. Translated by Graham Burchell. New York: Palgrave Macmillan.

Fredrickson, George. (1971). *The Black Image in the White Mind: The Debate on Afro-American Character and Destiny, 1817–1914*. New York: Harper and Row.

Gilman, Stuart. (1983). "Degeneracy and Race in the Nineteenth Century: The Impact of Clinical Medicine." *Journal of Ethnic Studies* 10 (4): 27–50.

Goddard, Henry Herbert. (1927). *The Kallikak Family: A Study in the Heredity of Feeble-Mindedness*. New York: The Macmillan Company. This was originally published in 1912.

Gould, Stephen J. (1977). *The Mismeasure of Man*. New York: W. W. Norton.

Jefferson, Thomas. (1944). *Basic Writings of Thomas Jefferson*. Edited by Philip S. Foner. New York: Wiley.

Johnson, Davi. (2007). "Martin Luther King Jr.'s 1963 Birmingham Campaign as Image Event." *Rhetoric and Public Affairs* 10 (1): 1–25.

Kant, Immanuel. (2000). "On the Different Human Races." Translated by Jon Mark Mikkelsen. In *The Idea of Race*, edited by Robert Bernasconi and Tommy Lott, 8–22. Indianapolis, IN: Hackett.

Kline, Wendy. (1997). *Building a Better Race: Gender, Sexuality, and Eugenics from the Turn of the Century to the Baby Boom*. Berkeley: University of California Press.

Koopman, Colin. (2013). *Genealogy as Critique: Foucault and The Problems of Modernity*. Bloomington: Indiana University Press.

Larson, Edward J. (1995). *Sex, Race, and Science: Eugenics in the Deep South*. Baltimore: Johns Hopkins University Press.

McWhorter, Ladelle. (2009). *Racism and Sexual Oppression in Anglo-America: A Genealogy*. Bloomington: Indiana University Press.

Mirowski, Philip, and Dieter Plehwe. (2009). *The Road from Mont Pelerin: The Making of the Neoliberal Thought Collective*. Cambridge, MA: Harvard University Press.

Muhammad, Khalil Gibran. (2010). *The Condemnation of Blackness: Race, Crime, and the Making of Modern Urban America*. Cambridge, MA: Harvard University Press.

Müller-Sievers, Helmut. (1997). *Self-Generation: Biology, Philosophy, and Literature Around 1800*. Stanford, CA: Stanford University Press.

Nott, Josiah, and George Glidden. (1854). *Types of Mankind: or, Ethnological Researches*. London: Trübner and Co.

Osborn, Frederick. (1937). "Implications of the New Studies in Population and Psychology for the Development of Eugenic Philosophy." *Eugenical News* 22 (6): 104–107.

Paul, Diane B. (1998). *The Politics of Heredity: Essays on Eugenics, Biomedicine, and the Nature-Nurture Debate*. Albany, NY: SUNY Press.

Paul, Diane B. (1995). *Controlling Human Heredity: 1865 to the Present*. Atlantic Highlands, NJ: Humanities Press.

Reilly, Philip R. (1991). *The Surgical Solution: A History of Involuntary Sterilization in the United States*. Baltimore: Johns Hopkins University Press.

Smith, Samuel Stanhope. [1880] (1965). *An Essay on the Causes and Variety of Complexion and Figure in the Human Species*. Edited by Winthrop D. Jordon. Cambridge, MA: Harvard University Press.

Wish, Harvey. (1960). *Ante-Bellum Writings of George Fitzhugh and Hinton Rowan Helper on Slavery*. New York: Capricorn Books.

CHAPTER 25

PHENOMENOLOGY AND RACE

LEWIS R. GORDON

THE question of phenomenological approaches to the study of race requires addressing several misunderstandings that may immediately occur in the conjunction "phenomenology *and* race." The first pertains to phenomenology. There are varieties of phenomenological approaches in what is called the Western tradition that often lead to the elision of other forms mostly because of the tendency to deem as "Western" anything that is *the exemplification* of what it "really" means to do anything at all. Thus, the tendency is to treat phenomenology as if it were exclusively produced in the West, and along with that, its various modes, whether "existential" or "transcendental," as if they were the same. It is for this reason that phenomenology is often placed in the Western philosophical curriculum as a species of "Continental" philosophy, which, too, pretty much means an area of *Euro*-Continental thought. The consequence is that bringing phenomenology and race together from this perspective amounts to doing so-called "applied" Euro-Continental philosophy.

Ideas did not, however, exclusively emerge from Europe, and the telling of European intellectual history often sanitizes it of its influences *from* the rest of the world. A reflection on imperialism could easily discount the fallacies at work in that regard. It is simply impossible to conquer and then colonize peoples all across the globe without also learning from and being influenced by them. And more, it is also a fallacy to look at the history of the rest of the world exclusively through the lens of being conquered and colonized peoples. We often forget that such was also the history of the people who became part of Christendom and subsequently Europe. They, too, experienced conquest, learned from, and also influenced their conquerors and colonizers. Africana phenomenology in this context means drawing upon the Africana context to see what we tend not to see. Doing such has vast philosophical implications, but as the focus here is phenomenology and race, I encourage the reader to seek those developments elsewhere (e.g., Outlaw 1996; Gordon 2006, 2008). Here, I will consider the study of race, racism, and the power dynamics behind their manifestations.

STUDYING RACE AND RACISM

The Africana phenomenological approach here could also be called Africana *existential* phenomenology. Interpreted as opposed to transcendental phenomenology would be a mistake because the existential and the transcendental need not be the rejection of each other. Much of this depends on the commitments of thought at hand. The antagonistic approach would be such an instance. If, however, one understands that human beings are not gods capable of "complete" knowledge of all there is, the question of *human relationships* to reality comes to the fore, and this, as I have argued elsewhere (Gordon 2000, 2006, 2013a, 2013b), brings the two together in an additional aspect of human reality, namely, our potential, as linguistic and metalinguistic creatures, to generate paradoxes. To see how the problem of conjoining the two emerges, the readers should bear in mind that existential phenomenology asserts a fundamental *incompleteness* at the heart of our relationship with reality, whereas transcendental phenomenology explores the conditions by which such claims about knowledge are possible. That human reality involves evaluating itself, including the conditions of its possibility, suggests that this divide may be a false dilemma. Development of that thesis cannot be done here but could be found in other studies (Caws 1992; Gordon 2000, 2010).

In 1995, my books *Bad Faith and Antiblack Racism* and *Fanon and the Crisis of European Man: An Essay on Philosophy and the Human Sciences*, the inauguration of my addressing many of the themes I will offer here, came to print amid some controversy in the academic study of race and racism. There is a simple version of my argument: Racism requires denying the humanity of other groups of human beings through the organization of them under the category of a race and then denying the ascription of human being to them. The performative contradiction is that they would first have to be identified as human beings in order to deny their being such. It is thus a form of mauvaise foi. Because racism is a form of mauvaise foi, antiblack racism, as a species of racism, must also be a form of mauvaise foi. Simple enough. The implications, however, are where there is the proverbial philosophical and social theoretical action.

The philosophical problem is: How is this possible? We could talk about how this historically emerged, as people were not always referred to as races. We could also talk about the relational elements I mentioned, as human difference was spoken about in many ways, primarily gendered ones, before racialized ones. I have already hinted at the philosophical problem of "substance" as nonrelational versus relational. Internal to phenomenology, substance is an ontological concept that is part of what Husserl calls "the natural attitude." Phenomenological work involves bracketing, parenthesizing, or suspending that attitude in order to focus on the phenomenon under investigation. This does not involve eliminating one's relationship to reality but instead reorienting oneself to relevant acts of knowing, learning, and understanding. It is thus relational throughout, which is why nonrelational commitments lead to contradictions. The added philosophical problem is about mauvaise foi. As it involves pleasing falsehoods—lies—being believed by the liar, the problem of how one could lie to oneself emerges. And more, there is the question of whether lying to oneself is possible in models of human subjects placed outside of social reality. As space is limited, what I will here contend in terms of this last one is that there is a performative contradiction involved in the denial of social reality as the effort is done *through a social practice*—namely, communication. And more, the condition for the possibility of meaning must be rejected to support a nonrelational legitimacy of such assertions. Mauvaise foi, in other words, requires an attitude of circumventing or disarming evidence, and evidence is that which appears for others, including the self as other.

That antiblack racism is a form of mauvaise foi raises some pressing questions. Is it the same as all other forms of racism? Blackness functions, after all, in peculiar ways in societies that have produced antiblack racism. A response to the #BlackLivesMatter movement, for instance, is often that all lives matter. That is true the extent to which each group lives under conditions of equal respect for life. What advocates of #BlackLivesMatter are doing is responding to a world in which some lives matter a lot more than others, whose lives evidentially matter a lot less. The history of antiblack racism amounts to the conviction that black people are only valuable the extent to which there is use for their labor or, worse, profiting from their misfortune, as we see with the heavily racialized prison industrial complexes in the United States and similar countries (Davis 2006; Alexander 2012; Schenwar 2014). It collapses into the expectation of justified existence in a context in which the justification for whoever stands as most valued is intrinsic. Members of the dominant group could thus seek their justification—*if they wish*—*personally*, through mechanisms of love, professional recognition, athletic achievement, and so on. Moreover, that such society renders some groups as positive and others as negative leads to notions of legitimate presence (illegitimate absence) and absence (illegitimate presence).

Should the analysis remain at white and black, the world would appear more closed than it in fact is. For one, simply being born black would bar the possibility of *any* legitimate appearance. This is a position that has been taken by a growing group of theorists known as "Afro-pessimists" (Wilderson 2010; Sexton 2011). Black for them is absolute "social death." It is outside of relations. Missing from this view, however, is at least what I argued in *Bad Faith and Antiblack Racism*, which is that no human being is "really" any of these things; the claim itself is a manifestation of mauvaise foi. The project of *making people into such* is one thing. People actually becoming such is another. This is an observation Fanon also makes in his formulation of the zone of nonbeing and his critique of Self–Other discourses in *Peau noir, masques blancs* (*Black Skin, White Masks*).

Fanon distinguishes between the zone of nonbeing (nonappearance as human beings) and those of being. The latter presumes a self-justified reality, which means it does not call itself into question. The former faces the problem of illegitimate appearance (Fanon 1952, chapter 5; Gordon 1999; Alcoff 2006; Yancy 2008). Thus, even the effort "to be" is in conflict as the system in question presumes legitimate absence of certain groups. Yet, paradoxically, the human being comes to the fore through emerging *from* being in the first place. Thus, the assertion of being is also an effort to push the human being out of existence, so to speak. The racial conflict is thus changed to an existential one in which an existential ontology is posed against an ontology of being. Existential ontology pertains to human being, whereas ontological being pertains to gods. This is why Fanon concludes that racism is also an attack *against* human being, as it creates a world in which one set stands above others as gods and the rest as below human. Where, in this formulation, stand human beings? The argument itself gains some clarity with the etymology of "existence," which is from the Latin expression *ex sistere* (to stand out, to emerge—that is, to appear). Blacks thus face the paradox of existing (standing out) as nonexistence (not standing out). The system of racism renders black appearance illicit.

This conundrum of racialized existence affects ethics and morals. Ethical relations are premised on selves relating to another or others. The others must, however, appear as such, and they, too, manifest themselves as selves. Implicit in such others as other selves is the formalization of ethical relations as equal, as found in the thought of Immanuel Kant and shifted in deference to the other in that of Emmanuel Levinas. Racism, however, excludes certain groups from being others and selves (if interpreted as being of a kind similar to the presumed legitimate selves). Thus, the schema of racism is one in which the hegemonic group relates to its members as selves and others, whereas the nonhegemonic groups are neither selves nor others. They, in effect, could only be such *in relation to each other*. It is, in other words, a form of ontological segregation as a condition of ethics and morals. The fight against racism, then, does not work as a fight against *being others or The Other*. It is a fight *against being nonothers*.

Fanon's insight demands an additional clarification. Racists should be distinguished from racism. Racists are people who hold beliefs about the superiority and inferiority of certain groups of racially designated people. Racism is the system of institutions and social norms that empower individuals with such beliefs. Without that system, a racist would simply be an obnoxious, whether overtly deprecating or patronizing, individual. With that system, racist points of view affect the social world *as reality*. Without that system, racists ultimately become inconsequential and, in a word, irrelevant beyond personal concerns of saving their souls from unethical and immoral beliefs and choices. Fanon was concerned with racists in his capacity as a psychiatrist (therapy, if necessary), but he was also concerned with racism as a philosopher, social thinker, and revolutionary (Fanon 1959/1975). The latter, in other words, is a system, from an antiracism perspective, in need of eradication.

An objection to the Afro-pessimistic assertion of blackness as social death could thus be raised from a Fanonian phenomenological perspective: Why must the social world be premised on the attitudes and perspectives of antiblack racists? Why don't blacks among each other and other communities of color count as a *social* perspective? And if the question of racism is a function of power, why not offer a study of power, how it is gained and lost, instead of an assertion of its manifestations as ontological?

An additional problem with the Afro-pessimistic model is that its proponents treat "blackness" as though it could exist independent of other categories. A quick examination of double consciousness (Du Bois 1903)—a phenomenological concept if there ever were one by virtue of the focus on forms of consciousness and, better, that of which one is conscious, that is, intentionality—would reveal why this would not work. Double consciousness involves seeing oneself from the perspective of another that deems one as negative (for example, the Afro-pessimistic conception of blackness). That there is already another perspective makes the subject who lives through double consciousness relational. Added is what Paget Henry (2005) calls *potentiated double consciousness* and Nahum Chandler (2014, 60–61) calls *the redoubled gesture*, which is the realization that the condemnation of negative meaning means that one must not do what the Afro-pessimist does. Seeing that that position is false moves one dialectically forward into asking about the system that attempts to force one into such an identity. This relational matter requires *looking beyond blackness* ironically in order to understand blackness. This means moving from the conception of meaning as singular, substance-based, fixed, and semantical into the grammar of how meaning is produced. Such grammars, such as that of gender, emerge in interesting ways (Gordon 1999, 124–129; 1997, 73–74).

However, as all human beings are manifestations of different dimensions of meaning, the question of identity requires more than an intersecting model; otherwise there will simply be one (a priori) normative outcome in every moment of inquiry: whoever manifests the maximum manifestation of predetermined negative intersecting terms. That would in effect be an essence before an existence—indeed, before an actual event of harm. This observation emerges as well with the Afro-pessimist model when one thinks of *pessimism* as the guiding attitude. The existential phenomenological critique would be that optimism and pessimism are symptomatic of the same attitude: a priori assertions on reality. Human existence is contingent but not accidental, which means that the social world at hand is a manifestation of choices and relationships—in other words, human actions. Because human beings can only build the future instead of it determining us, the task at hand, as phenomenology-oriented existentialists from Beauvoir and Sartre to Fanon, William R. Jones, and this author have argued, depends on *commitment*. This concern also pertains to the initial concerns about authenticity discourses with which I began. One could only be pessimistic about an outcome, an activity. It is an act of forecasting what could only be meaningful once actually performed. Similarly, one could only be optimistic about the same. What, however, if there were no way to know either? Here we come to the *foi* element in mauvaise foi. Some actions are deontological, and if not that, they are at least reflections of our *commitments*, our *projects*. Thus, the point of some actions is not about their success or failure but whether we deem them worth doing. Taking responsibility for such actions—bringing value to them—is opposed to another manifestation of mauvaise foi: the spirit of seriousness.

The spirit of seriousness involves attributing a form of materiality to human values that elides the human role in the construction of those values. Detailed analyses of this form of mauvaise foi in Africana phenomenology emerges in the thought of George Yancy (2008) and this author (Gordon 1995, 1997, 1999, 2000). The importance of this concept pertains to the understanding of racism not only as a social phenomenon but also a *value*. It addresses what Abdul JanMohamed (2011) calls our social *investments* in such phenomena. Returning to the distinction between racists and racism, the former are what existentialists such as Sartre and Beauvoir call "serious" people and the latter is the system that supports such values as supposedly objective features of reality. In other words, the formers' values are preserved in the latter as ontological.

The turn to social reality raises an important theme of Africana phenomenology, and, indeed, all phenomenological treatments of oppression: Discussions of race and gender make no sense without a philosophical anthropology. In Africana philosophy, the answer is straightforward: Euro-modernity denied the humanity of whole groups of people, which means the question of what it is to be human was crucial. These considerations emerged not only in colonial and racist terms but also at reflective levels of method as hegemonic models of "science" began to dominate concerns for legitimacy. Many such models were premised, however, on ideological frameworks in which greater value was placed on "purity" in which mixture is supposedly "impure." The result is a philosophical anthropology in search of so-called purity as a standard of not only human value but also identity. Kimberlé Crenshaw (1991) offers a critique through her work on intersectionality in legal theory. Examples in Africana phenomenology include Michael Monahan's *The Creolizing Subject* (2011), Jane Anna Gordon's *Creolizing Political Theory* (2014), and writings by this author (Gordon 1997, 2006, 2010). The arguments they advanced reject any philosophical anthropology of converging "purities," where separate, pure "races" meet. Instead, the notion of racial purity is rejected from the outset. The authors, however, go further, as with the discussion of intersectionality, to propose questions of mixture at methodological levels. It is the appeal to methodological purity that obscures lived realities of mixture. In other words, the actual human world is not one of purity (being-in-and-by-itself) but instead relations of living negations of purity (existence, being-and-negations-of-and-for-being, and more).

Monahan and J. Gordon prefer the term *creolizing* for this reason because it is, they contend, a *radical* kind of mixture—one that in effect manifests not only new forms of being but also challenges the stasis of being. Their use of the present participle is to illustrate that mix-ing—especially of the licit and the illicit—is not a closed achievement but instead an ongo-ing activity of reality. From their argument, purity, like normativity, is an effort of imposing closure on the openness or, as Fryer contends (2008), queer dimensions of reality. Put dif-ferently, ascribing ontological status to purity and straightness does not work. It requires, in effect, denying the elements of reality that do not match up and involves attempting to force reality into a preferred or pleasing falsehood instead of a (for the purist) displeasing truth. In effect, creolizing militates against disciplinary decadence or, in other words, mauvaise foi. As the context is human reality, the conclusion of Africana phenomenology presenting an open anthropology comes to the fore. This openness raises one of the final ingredients, if we will, for this discussion: the relationships between humanity and freedom.

The freedom question is paradoxical: to be free means also to possess the ability to evade it. This is what critics of this approach, premised on a phenomenological treatment of mauvaise foi, miss. Existential phenomenology collapses into an essentialism, they protest, because of the assertion of human reality as freedom. Others also read discussions of mauvaise foi as appealing to an essential unavoidability collapsed into futility. What they fail to ask, how-ever, is what human reality would be if human beings were *incapable* of acting in mauvaise foi. Could a being incapable of attempting to evade its freedom truly be free? Would not the absence of that capability mean human beings *must* essentially act in good faith? What, then, would happen to freedom? And if there were no freedom, wouldn't human beings simply have a nature that poses none of the recognizable human problems because human behavior would already be determined? These considerations occasion what could be called an indi-rect proof: Human freedom exists by virtue of our efforts to evade it. This kind of argument is also, by the way, a form of transcendental argument as it points to a condition for the pos-sibility of what is being studied. This kind of transcendentalism, where existence and condi-tions of possibility meet, could also be called *ironic* as it is premised on what "is" by virtue of what it is not.

Peter Caws (1992), in his discussion of Sartre's structuralism in his debate with Lévi-Strauss, reminds us that the aim of bringing human responsibility to human relations is a plea for the realization of the human role in a human world. It is structure in human terms, which means it requires a philosophical anthropology premised on metaevaluation, metacritique, metatheory, and incompleteness. I regard all this as a way of saying that Euro-modernity posed challenges to what it means to be human, free, and responsible for the conditions by which any practice as such is justified. Race, gender, class, and sexuality, from this perspec-tive, can be illuminated through these three considerations, but we should remember that, as illumination, we receive only part of the story as these categories and their relationship to each other are, from this approach, still in the making. There could, in other words, be more categories to come as the relationship across the extant human identities continue to shift and disorient what it means to be human.

RACE AND RACISM FROM A PROSTHETIC GOD

At this point, I would like to offer some existential phenomenological considerations on power because race, engenderment, sexual orientation, and class make no sense without it.

The earlier distinction between racists and racism raises an additional one between choices and options. The former pertains to individuals; the latter, to the material conditions and social world. To illustrate, think of the use of the word "choice" in discussions of the legal status of abortion. If abortion were made illegal, would women still have a choice? They would only have the option of choosing an illegal abortion, should they decide to have an abortion. Their choice, so to speak, would be premised on their willingness to violate the law. The law, in other words, determines the options available to them. Their choice, however, is theirs. In effect, illegality would become a fundamental part of being a woman, even if she were never pregnant. The possibility would haunt all her heterosexual encounters. Racial segregation could be read similarly: Such systems limit the options available for racially subjugated people to make ordinary choices. They increase the probability of choices in conflict with the law as the hegemonic group's identity would be premised on a legal system *for* its members. The options available for hegemonic groups to make meaningful choices would exceed those of dominated groups. As the latter's options are fewer, they would exhaust choices pertaining to them and consequently shift to choices premised on limitations. In effect, they would become adverbial, focusing on the ways in which they could play with their limited options, and as those are exhausted, they would move ever inward to a point of implosion. The hegemonic group could thus continue making choices of acting *on the world*, of relating to available options in an ever-expanding world of possibility. The dominated groups express their agency on what is ultimately as far as they could go: themselves.

We see here the classic existential thesis on anguish, which is a confrontation with the self via the choices one makes. The options here are what are circumscribed, proscribed, and prohibited by law. As law is power emanating from legal institutions, and as the latter are creations of the social world, which in turn is created by the vast network of intersubjective relations constituting the human world, the question of choice could be summarized as one's relation to the proverbial others.

Choices, however, are also exemplifications of power, even where fairly limited. Choosing is an act, and actions are, in a nutshell, something in and of themselves we are able to make happen simply by virtue of thinking, expressing, and attempting them. A failed action is nevertheless an act. Our actions are the choices made manifest through our body. Thus, the "reach" of our choices at that level is concrete: the capacities of consciousness in the flesh—in short, our bodies. And what are our bodies? A body is simply a point of view or perspective from which reality is made manifest. A body is what makes expressions "here" and "there" possible. We *live* our bodies *here* and *there*. At this point, we are no different from most animals in that our impact on the world is the extent to which we are able physically to reach for and touch things. That touch, so to speak, could also be considered force. The emergence of language, communication, a social world, and culture transformed our reach and our abilities. That constellation enabled us to build worlds of meaning and reach, through the web of intersubjective relations, regions and things far beyond the physical one of our body. A slew of other meaningful activities and circumstances emerge in that world, the human one, such as power and norms. To use a formulation from Freud, culture is a prosthetic god. It is so because it is the manifestation of power, which at this point could be defined simply as the ability to make things happen.

Gods are beings that could make things happen such as our safety, longevity, and happiness. The first is achievable through protecting us from the elements; the second through prolonged health; and the third through regulating our interactions with others in ways that minimize misery and facilitate happiness—in short, the creation of laws. This last category could also work in the opposite way: It could regulate our interactions in ways that maximize misery. That is achievable through reducing the options available for us to live a meaningful life, for our choices, in other words, to be such. One model of power is devoted to human flourishing; another model is harnessed for the negation inward to the point of implosion.

Read through this phenomenological treatment of social reality, the distinction between racists and racism becomes one between choices and options. Eradicating racism means limiting the options by which racist choices could have an impact on the social world, in other words, the world of others. The eradication of racism does not, however, entail the same for racists. It does, however, mean achieving what is no doubt their greatest fear: their irrelevance.

SOME CONCLUDING REMARKS

Africana existential phenomenology offers a set of conceptual tools and methodological approaches that may be useful even for philosophers and related theorists who do not necessarily come to the study of philosophical problems from a phenomenological perspective. The analytical philosopher of race Charles Mills, for example, explores themes of racial embodiment and mauvaise foi as an explanatory tool in his influential work *The Racial Contract* (1997, 93, 98), and his later critique (Mills 2005) of John Rawls's notions of ideal and nonideal theory is akin to the discussions of "perfect evidence" and formalism in Africana existential phenomenology (e.g., Gordon 1995, 1999, 2000, 2011). Similarly, Rainer Spencer (1999, 2006) and Naomi Zack (1993) explored existential phenomenological conceptions of lived experience in their work on mixed race. Africana phenomenology also emerges in discussions of race and racism in critical pedagogy (Haymes 2000, 2001, 2003, 2008), decolonial thought in Latin America (see, e.g., Maldonado-Torres 2008; Mignolo 2011), literary theory (Parris 2015), and, as we have seen, political theory (Mills 1997; Monahan 2011; J. Gordon 2014) and queer theory (Ahmed 2006; Fryer 2008).

The arguments of Africana phenomenology outlined earlier raise concerns about the human being's relationship to human problems. Those problems also include the human relationship to that which is not human, including metaphysical entities. The use of "human" here reveals the importance and significance of philosophical anthropology for Africana phenomenological reflection on race and racism. The insistence of exploring how philosophical anthropology underwrites race is one among its many contributions to contemporary philosophy and social thought. A similar argument emerges in terms of other categories of philosophical investigation—for example, the philosophy of history and philosophy of science. The problem of illicit appearance raises many challenges for the philosophy of history, as the question of what is suppressed by hegemonic history comes to the fore. In terms of science, the question of what it means to do rigorous science comes forth because of critical concerns regarding imposed methodology or, more concrete, the options available for certain phenomena—such as racism—to appear in scientific terms. This may mean questioning the scope and validity of science as presently conceived. As a relational activity, Africana phenomenology is, then, one of expanding options in a world where the lack thereof leads to meaningless choices and, consequently, human suffering.

References

Ahmed, Sara. (2006). *Queer Phenomenology: Orientations, Objects, Others.* Durham, NC: Duke University Press.

Alcoff, Linda Martín. (2006). *Visible Identities: Race, Gender, and the Self.* New York: Oxford University Press.

Alexander, Michelle. (2012). *The New Jim Crow: Mass Incarceration in the Age of Colorblindness.* New York: The New Press.

Beauvoir, Simone de. (2015). *The Ethics of Ambiguity.* New York: Philosophical Library.

Caws, Peter. (1992). "Sartrean Structuralism?" In *The Cambridge Companion to Sartre,* edited by Christina Howells, 293–316. Cambridge: Cambridge University Press.

Chandler, Nahum Dimitri. (2014). *X—The Problem of the Negro as a Problem for Thought.* New York: Fordham University Press.

Crenshaw, Kimberlé. (1991). "Mapping the Margins: Intersectionality, Identity Politics, and Violence Against Women of Color." *Stanford Law Review* 43 (July): 1241–1299.

Davis, A. Y. (2006). "Racialized Punishment and Prison Abolition." In *A Companion to African-American Philosophy,* edited by T. L. Lott and J. P. Pittman, 360–372. Malden, MA: Blackwell Publishing.

Du Bois, W. E. B. (1903). *The Souls of Black Folk: Essays and Sketches.* Chicago: A.C. McClurg & Co.

Fanon, Frantz. (1952). *Peau noire, masques blancs.* Paris: Éditions du Seuil.

Fanon, Frantz. [1959] (1975). *Sociologie d'une révolution: l'an V de la révolution algérienne.* 2nd ed. Paris: François Maspero.

Fryer, David Ross. (2008). *Thinking Queerly: Race, Gender, and the Ethics of Identity.* New York: Routledge.

Gordon, Jane Anna. (2014). *Creolizing Political Theory: Reading Rousseau through Fanon.* New York: Fordham University Press.

Gordon, Lewis R. (1995). *Fanon and the Crisis of European Man: An Essay on Philosophy and the Human Sciences.* New York: Routledge.

Gordon, Lewis R. (1997). *Her Majesty's Other Children: Sketches of Racism from a Neocolonial Age.* Landham, MD: Rowman & Littlefield.

Gordon, Lewis R. (1999). *Bad Faith and Antiblack Racism.* Amherst, NY: Humanity/Prometheus Books.

Gordon, Lewis R. (2000). *Existentia Africana: Understanding Africana Existential Thought.* New York: Routledge.

Gordon, Lewis R. (2006). *Disciplinary Decadence: Living Thought in Trying Times.* New York: Routledge.

Gordon, Lewis R. (2008). *An Introduction to Africana Philosophy.* Cambridge: Cambridge University Press.

Gordon, Lewis R. (2010). "Theory in Black: Teleological Suspensions in Philosophy of Culture." *Qui Parle: Critical Humanities and Social Sciences* 18 (2): 193–214.

Gordon, Lewis R. (2012). "Essentialist Anti-Essentialism, with Considerations from Other Sides of Modernity." *Quaderna: A Multilingual and Transdisciplinary Journal* 1. Accessed May 14, 2016. http://quaderna.org/wp-content/uploads/2012/09/Gordon-essentialist-anti-essentialism.pdf.

Gordon, Lewis R. (2013a). "Race, Theodicy, and the Normative Emancipatory Challenges of Blackness." *South Atlantic Quarterly 2013* 112 (4): 725–736.

Gordon, Lewis R. (2013b). "Thoughts on Dussel's 'Anti-Cartesian Meditations.'" *Human Architecture: Journal of the Sociology of Self-Knowledge* 11 (1): Article 7. http://scholarworks. umb.edu/humanarchitecture/vol11/iss1/7.

Gordon, Lewis R. (2014). "Der Realität zuliebe: teleologische Suspensionen disziplinärer Dekadenz." In *Der Neue Realismus*, edited by Markus Gabriel, 244–267. Berlin: Suhrkamp Verlag.

Gordon, Lewis R. (2015). *What Fanon Said: A Philosophical Introduction to His Life and Thought*. New York: Fordham University Press.

Haymes, Stephen N. (2000). "Africana Philosophy of Education and the Problem of Ontology: Some Preliminary Thoughts." *Philosophical Studies in Education* 32: 87–94.

Haymes, Stephen N. (2001). "Pedagogy and the Philosophical Anthropology of African American Slave Culture." *Philosophia Africana* 4 (2): 67–93.

Haymes, Stephen N. (2003). "Race, and Paulo Freire's Philosophy of the Oppressed." *Radical Philosophy Review* 5 (1/2): 165–175.

Haymes, Stephen N. (2008). "Thoughts About the Absence of Africana Philosophy in the Philosophy of Education." *Philosophy of Education Yearbook* 153–156.

Henry, Paget. (2005). "Africana Phenomenology: Its Philosophical Implications." *The C.L.R. James Journal* 11 (1): 79–112.

JanMohamed, Abdul. (2011). "Introduction." In *Reconsidering Social Identification: Race, Gender, Class and Caste*, 1–18. New Dheli: Routledge India.

Jones, William R. (1997). *Is God a White Racist? A Preamble to Black Theology*. Boston: Beacon Press.

Mignolo, Walter. (2011). *The Darker Side of Western Modernity: Global Futures, Decolonial Options*. Durham, NC: Duke University Press.

Mills, Charles W. (1997). *The Racial Contract*. Ithaca, NY: Cornell University Press.

Mills, Charles W. (2005). "'Ideal Theory' as Ideology." *Hypatia* 20 (3): 165–184.

Maldonado-Torres, Nelson. (2008). *Against War: Views from the Underside of Modernity (Latin America Otherwise)*. Durham, NC: Duke University Press.

Monahan, Michael. (2011). *The Creolizing Subject*. New York: Fordham University Press.

Outlaw, Lucius T. (1996). *On Race and Philosophy*. New York: Routledge.

Parris, LaRose T. (2015). *Being Apart: Theoretical and Existential resistance in Africana Literature*. Charlottesville: University of Virginia Press.

Schenwar, Maya. (2014). *Locked Up, Locked Out: Why Prisons Don't Work and How We Can Do Better*. San Francisco: Berrett-Koehler.

Sexton, Jared. (2011). "The Social Life of Social Death," *InTensions Journal* (5): Accessed May 14, 2016. http://www.yorku.ca/intent/issue5/articles/pdfs/jaredsextonarticle.pdf.

Spencer, Rainer. (1999). *Spurious Issues: Race and Multiracial Identity Politics in the United States*. Boulder, CO: Westview.

Spencer, Rainer. (2006). *Challenging Multiracial Identity*. Boulder, CO: Lynne Rienner.

Wilderson, Frank. (2010). *Red, White, and Black: Cinema and the Structure of U.S. Antagonisms*. Durham, NC: Duke University Press.

Yancy, George. (2008). *Black Bodies, White Gazes: The Continuing Significance of Race*. Lanham, MD: Rowman & Littlefield.

Zack, Naomi. (1993). *Race and Mixed Race*. Philadelphia: Temple University Press.

Zack, Naomi. (1997). Naomi Zack, "Race, Life, Death, Identity, Tragedy and Good Faith." In *Existence in Black: An Anthology of Black Existential Philosophy*, edited by Lewis R. Gordon, 99–110. New York: Routledge.

PART VI

....

RACISMS AND
NEO-RACISMS

....

LOGICALLY, it would seem as though ideas about race would have to precede racism. But the subject of racism is more broad and complicated than the subject of race, for at least these two historical reasons. First, the kind of prejudice (prejudged cognitions and negative emotions) and discrimination (treating people differently on the grounds of group identities) that constitute racism have a longer history than the modern idea of race, for instance in European anti-Semitism. And second, insofar as modern ideas of race have been in the service of dominant interests in international and internal interactions, these ideas of race are ideologies that have devalued nonwhite groups. That is, ideas of race are themselves already inherently racist.

In philosophy, racism has been treated as attitudes and actions of individuals that affect nonwhites unjustly and social structures or institutions that advantage whites and disadvantage nonwhites. The first is hearts-and-minds or classic racism, for instance the use of stereotypes and harmful actions by whites against people of color, as well as negative feelings about them. The second is structural racism or institutional racism, for instance, the facts of how American blacks and Hispanics are, compared to whites, worse off on major measures of human well-being, such as education, income, family wealth, health, family stability, longevity, and rates of incarceration.

Both classic racism and institutional or structural racism result in differences in social status that are remarkably enduring despite the achievement of formal equality through the 1964 Civil Rights Act, the 1965 Voting Rights Act, and the 1965 Immigration Act, as well as *Brown v. Board of Education* in 1954. Given the enormous importance of education in upward socioeconomic mobility and social status, *Brown* alone should have begun to change social racial disparities in lasting ways. However, that has not happened.

In the early twenty-first century, the United States maintains historically high rates of residential racial segregation. The American educational system is locally financed by property taxes, with schools in poor nonwhite neighborhoods struggling with extremely disadvantaged resources compared to schools in mainly white neighborhoods. Poverty and undereducation are strongly correlated with disproportionately high rates of incarceration under what Michelle Alexander has called "the new Jim Crow," in a book by that title. Moreover, recent high-profile incidents of police homicide of unarmed young black men have resulted in the strange coincidence of a movement called "Black Lives Matter" with the second term in office of the first African American president.

What Lewis Gordon critiqued as Afro-pessimism in Part V is evident in descriptions of contemporary racism that may seem to border on despair as the price of being able to understand contemporary race relations, not only in the United States, but throughout the world. Part of such pessimism has been unflinching reflection on some of the worst aspects of past racism. In "The Quartet in the Political Persona of Ida B. Wells," Joy James examines antilynching activism and advocacy reported in Wells's writings, focusing on the 1892 pamphlet *Southern Horrors: Lynch Law in All Its Phases*. James argues that Wells's political analysis of racial-sexual violence within US democracy remains influential to the present. Wells advocated Afro-American autonomy and self-defense to counter racial terror and rape, and she was sharply critical of antirape discourse that demonized black men by pretending that white women never entered into voluntary sexual relationships with them. In relating Wells's combative stance to the present activism of members of Black Lives Matter and the Black Women's Blueprint, James emphasizes how racism continues to kill, as well as demean.

Janine Jones also views a continuity between past and present racism in the perception and treatment of black people as *waste*. Drawing on metaphysical analysis by Frank Wilderson, Jones claims that whites imagine blacks to be alienated from language and thereby degraded and rendered abject. Jones asks what it means "to be black, excess, and recyclable, as well as black, excess, and *nonrecyclable*." She understands the nonrecyclability of excess black embodiment beginning in the late twentieth century to be a situation that no longer allows black bodies to be recycled into white wealth, through their labor. Work is "invested with reason," but when investment in projects involving black work are no longer profitable, the result is *waste*. And, "black waste under these conditions is not recyclable. It must be disposed of." This is where and when Jones claims that mass incarceration and dense segregation have entered the picture. (With very bleak irony, Jones concludes with an account of how the literal excrement of poor black people has been confiscated by police in Cape Town, South Africa.)

The latest new conceptual tool for considering racism is the idea of white privilege. Whites in the United States do not have explicitly designated privileges based on race, but a number of theorists and media pundits now address the contrast in human well-being between whites and nonwhites as a condition of "white privilege." Shannon Sullivan begins her by analysis of white privilege by discussing racial disparities in wealth, health, incarceration, children as welfare clients, high school graduation, and beauty standards and preferences based on race. She observes that many of the advantages automatically enjoyed by whites are subtle, because the disadvantages experienced by nonwhites may be distributed without reference to race. For instance, when police practice racial profiling in minority neighborhoods that have high crime rates, their behavior can be justified by preexisting crime rates. Or, "zero tolerance" of "disruptive" and "insubordinate" behavior picks out black children for discipline in schools, without mention of their race. Still, white privilege is not monolithic among whites and some nonwhites are better off in economic and social measures than whites. Sullivan therefore suggests that there be a revision in terminology to *white class privilege*. She argues that while racial injustice often involves violation of human rights for non-whites, which are not violated for whites, the concept of white class privilege remains useful for understanding how racial disparities and disadvantages ensue from habitual behavior and unquestioned social norms that favor whites.

There is an assumption in arts and letters, as well as philosophy and everyday life, that racial categories and racism are stable—what counts as races does not change over time or within memory in a single life span; and racism is a fixed set of attitudes and behavior directed toward members of a race. However, we have already seen how it is plausible to view racism as logically, as well as historically, prior to race. Falguni Sheth takes this a step further and sees race itself as formed through political action, with new *racializations* accompanying new oppressive and discriminatory practices. Sheth's main example or case study is terrorist suspects after 9-11. Her insights are supported by the broad fact that members of the US public did come to think that they could phenotypically identify such suspects on sight, when the groups they belonged to did not stand out racially before 9/11. (Indeed, both Arab Americans and South Asians were officially categorized as racially white on the US Census and other forms, in the 1970s.) At the same time, the terms "water-boarding" and "extraordinary rendition" and accounts of harassment and immediate deportation entered political discourse. There were also new fears of internal terror and considerable tolerance for new inconveniences in airline travel to prevent violence in the skies.

This is not to suggest that there have not been real and continuing dangers from militarized Muslims, but Sheth's account of recent racialization of Middle Eastern men, Muslims, and South Asians reveals a technology of race that many are not aware has been an integral part of the War on Terror. Preemptive policing, backed up by panicky moral judgment, has spread from Muslim or Islamic "types," to all immigrants, and not only in the United States. Anti-immigrant sentiment has grown more intense in Europe following terrorist attacks in Paris in November 2015 and as of this writing, it has motivated the United Kingdom's exit from the European Common Market (Brexit).

In "State Racism, State Violence, and Vulnerable Solidarity," Myisha Cherry examines what sustains state racism and state violence. She suggests that law can create a "subrace" out of those who are feared and held in contempt by white majorities. In Foucaudian terms, this subrace is countered not by another race, but by a superrace and the overall result is state racism. Cherry's somewhat optimistic solution is to look toward the creation of solidarity among members of oppressed groups that extends to those who are comparatively privileged, resulting in "vulnerable solidarity." This optimism arises from the same context in which a political form of race has emerged, that is, "a government of the people, by the people, and for the people." Cherry refers to US history to support her insight of universal vulnerability: "Even members of the superrace who do not become members of the subrace can nonetheless be impacted by state violence targeted toward the subrace. Although the War on Drugs has been a war on black, brown, and poor bodies, for example, there have been some casualties within the superrace."

FURTHER READING

Alexander, Michelle. (2010). *The New Jim Crow: Mass Incarceration in the Age of Colorblindness*. New York: The New Press.

Bonilla-Silva, Eduardo. (2014). *Racism without Racists: Color-Blind Racism and the Persistence of Racial Inequality in America*. Lanham, MD: Rowman & Littlefield.

Kozol, Jonathan. (1991). *Savage Inequalities: Children in America's Schools*. New York: Crown.

Yancy, George. (2012). *Look! A White!: Black Bodies, White Gazes*. Philadelphia: Temple University Press.

Zack, Naomi. (2015). *White Privilege and Black Rights: The Injustice of US Police Racial Profiling and Homicide*. Lanham, MD: Rowman& Littlefield.

CHAPTER 26

THE QUARTET IN THE POLITICAL PERSONA OF IDA B. WELLS

JOY JAMES

Although the race was wild over the outrage [of lynching], the mockery of law and justice which disarmed men and locked them up in jails where they could be easily and safely reached by the mob—the Afro-American ministers, newspapers and leaders counselled obedience to the law which did not protect them.

Ida B. Wells, *Southern Horrors*, 1892

I am a Black revolutionary woman . . . .
accused of every alleged crime . . . .
[police] have plastered pictures alleged to be me . . . .
issued orders to shoot on sight and to shoot to kill.

Assata Shakur, "To My People," 1973

MULTIPLE aspects of praxis, from Christian to Marxian and beyond, are reduced here to a quartet of concepts in the political persona of antiterror activist Ida B. Wells. This quartet, excerpted from a letter by a black maternal political fugitive, focuses on the revolutionary black woman; criminalization of blackness (Muhammad 2011); commoditization of black icons; and repression of black resistance to racism and rape.

My exploration of antilynching crusader Ida B. Wells uses an excerpt from an open letter by former Harlem Black Panther Party (BPP) member and Black Liberation Army political prisoner Assata Shakur (Joanne Chesimard), a political fugitive living in Cuba (Shakur 1987). The increased $2 million bounty levied and the Federal Bureau of Investigation (FBI) placing Shakur on its "terrorist" list, like the rise of the mass movement Black Lives Matter against antiblack killings and rapes by police and deputized whites, appears coterminous with the anomaly of the first black president of the United States, a democracy born from slave states.

Historian John Bracey stated at a 1992 University of Massachusetts–Amherst forum that although blacks admired the courageous stance Wells took against lynching, they would likely not wish her to move next door—proximity to radicals increases vulnerabilities. Similar could be said of Shakur—better to cheer her from the safety of another country or century than incur the wrath of police and governance that criminalized her and the BPP and seek her (political) demise. Viewing "law and order" as a mandate for racial hierarchies, Wells calls for resistance; and so, like Shakur, has become the embodiment of a revolutionary persona. Despite this emphasis on radicalism, Wells is conflicted and seeks harbor within legal structures, writing in "The Remedy" of *The Red Record*:

> It is a well-established principle of law that every wrong has a remedy. Herein rests our respect for law. The Negro does not claim that all of the one thousand black men, women and children . . . hanged, shot and burned alive during the past ten years, were innocent of the charges made against them. . . . But we do insist that the punishment is not the same for both classes of criminals. (Wells 1895, 58)

"A BLACK REVOLUTIONARY WOMAN"

The Negro Women's Club movement raised funds to publish Ida B. Wells's political pamphlets *Southern Horrors: Lynch Law in All Its Phases; The Red Record*; and *Mob Rule in New Orleans* (Wells 1892, 1895, 1900). Her autobiography, *Crusade for Justice* (posthumously edited by her daughter Alfreda M. Duster [Wells 1970]), is popularized through William Greaves's documentary, *Ida B. Wells: A Passion for Justice*, which features Toni Morrison's skillful reading of Wells's works (Greaves 1989). A revolutionary persona with no male peer, Wells's pulpit candor decried the lethal manipulation of "rape" into a category of white victimization. She satirized white society for defining voluntary associations between black men and white women as "rape" while ignoring forced and violent associations between white men and black women.

Associated with the antilynching movement, although not generally recognized as the architect of small antiracist, profeminist organizations, Wells was maneuvered out of the founding leadership of the National Association for the Advancement of Colored People (NAACP) by W. E. B. Du Bois and the white philanthropist Mary White Ovington (James 1997). Her memoir records regret that she was unable to influence the civil rights organization to better address the concerns of working-class and poor blacks most vulnerable to racist atrocities and exploitation (Wells 1970).

Unlike Frederick Douglass and Du Bois, Wells publicly asserts that Afro-Americans must mobilize for protections against white society and governance that hinder black equality and safety. She focuses on "terror" rather than on "inequality" to attack the horrors and fragility of lives and kinship destabilized or destroyed by theft, torture, rape, and murder. Wells courageously confronts the taboo of her era: sexual terror as a weapon of racial subjugation. *Southern Horrors* and *The Red Record* document that despite the charges of black sexual savagery against white females, most interracial rape linked to lynching materialized when black women and children were raped prior to and during lynching, as well as lynched with black males (who were sexually assaulted during lynchings) that assisted them in resisting or avenging rape by white males. Lynching apologists obscured (for whites) the reality that interracial rape was a constant nightmare for black females yet rare for white females. Most interracial rapists of that era would be white males; a correlation between interracial sex crimes and extrajudicial executions would have rendered the majority of the lynched white. Wells illustrates how white male rapists were rarely punished:

> In Nashville . . . a white man, Pat Hanifan, . . . outraged a little Afro-American girl, and, from the physical injuries received, she has been ruined for life. He was jailed for six months, discharged, and is now a detective in that city. In the same city, last May, a white man outraged an Afro-American girl in a drug store. He was arrested, and released on bail at the trial. It was rumored that five hundred Afro-Americans had organized to lynch him. Two hundred and fifty white citizens armed themselves with Winchesters and guarded him. A cannon was placed in front of his home, and the Buchanan Rifles (State Militia) ordered to the scene for his protection. The Afro-American mob did not materialize. (Wells 1892, 8)

After deconstructing the specious rationalizations for white terror—Negro domination of whites through the vote; Negro race riots; black male sexual assaults of white females—Wells notes that the accusation of black sexual savagery became the apologia for lynching (Wells 1895). She critiques white chivalry's mythology to argue that it garners "little respect from the civilized world, when it confines itself entirely to the women who happen to be white" (Wells 1892, 3). Noting their duplicitous prosecutorial performances, Wells accuses white males of centuries of interracial rape:

> To justify their own barbarism they assume a chivalry which they do not posses. True chivalry respects all womanhood, and no one who reads the record, as it is written in the faces of the million mulattoes in the South, will for a minute conceive that the southern white man had a very chivalrous regard for the honor due the women of his own race or respect for the womanhood which circumstances placed in his power. (Wells 1892, 3)

Whites defined consensual sexual relationships between white women and black men as assaults punishable by the death of the black male lover. Wells redefines them as voluntary and represents white male sexual relationships with black females, en mass, as rape. The moral and legal prosecutors of sexual violence in Wells's era, white men were the least prosecuted and censured for sex crimes. In her August 4, 1894, post from Liverpool as a special correspondent for the anti-lynching Chicago newspaper *Inter-Ocean*, Wells writes: "The machinery of law and politics is in the hands of those who commit the lynching . . . it is only wealthy white men whom the law fails to reach" (Wells 1894, 9). In contrast to virtual immunity for elite white males, and the charges of "assault" for adulteries, she observes: "Hundreds of Negroes including women and children are lynched for trivial offenses on suspicion and in many cases when known to be guiltless of any crime . . . the law refused to punish the murderers because it is not considered a crime to kill a Negro" (Wells 1970, 157).

Locating sovereign powers—the right to decide who lives or who dies—within racial-sexual animus as the driving engine for economic and libidinal accumulation, Wells dethrones the sovereignty of white manhood, contesting its right to rule by identifying it as the rule of rapists and terrorists. She argues that the United States essentially has no binding social contract with Afro-Americans and so black Americans have no binding contract with the United States; and inverts the white nationalist script: governance so violent and pernicious has abdicated its right to rule (Wells 1970).

The rise of the Ku Klux Klan during Wells's childhood established a symbol of antiblack terror (a century later it appears as "Amerikkka" in Shakur's *Assata* [1987]), a signifier that wars against African descent people despite a civil war to preserve the union led to an undefeated confederacy, as interregional, intergenerational white bonds permitted and profited from lynching, the convict prison lease system, Jim Crow segregation, mass incarceration, police/prison rapes, and killings. *The Birth of a Nation*, D. W. Griffith's cinematic championing of white supremacy through the violence of the KKK, features southern aristocrats mourning President Abraham Lincoln's death and bonding and marrying with their northern peers who had defeated them in battle (Griffith 1915). Wells flips the script. Her etymology inverts the speech and meanings of racial sovereigns: "lynching," understood as "law-and-order" interventions, becomes "racist murders" by white rapists. The emperor's undress requires Afro-American flight through migration or fight through armed self-defense.

For Wells, lynching mystifies rape and derails prohibition and prevention. (When mob lynching gave way to legal prosecutions, black males were disproportionately imprisoned and executed for interracial rape charges on unsubstantiated charges.) Wells tramples the twin myths of white supremacy: sexually pure and racially civilized. She rejects the discourse of black deference as a form of civility, viewing the mandate to forgive atrocities as rendering Afro-Americans more vulnerable to racist aggression.

Wells's revolutionary rhetoric and strategies linked to nonelite blackness grew, as did her vulnerability to attack and misrepresentation. She endeared herself to the working class and poor who benefitted directly from her militancy. But the poor rarely author the historical record read in the mainstream, and Wells speaks with their voice and grief, and channels the outrage that although terrorized they are criminalized by their assailants.

"Accused of Every Alleged Crime"

Without the historicity of Ida B. Wells, one might lose sight of what it means to be stripped of virtue and honor, humiliated, criminalized, and hunted. One might also forget the meaning of battling for honor and risking life to gain life. With sex crimes real or fabricated, the only offense that galvanized white consensus for racial terrorism, Wells attacked the lynch rallying call of "rape!"; used in only a fraction of lynchings, it was highly effective. Sexually denigrated under white supremacy, Wells publicly exposes the duplicity of the rape trigger: interracial rapes, a fraction of actual rapes, become the signifiers for "rape"; whiteness the signifier for "virtue"; blackness the synonym for "savage." Anomaly supplants norm. The sexual predator is collectivized and fetishized as black; the sexual protector as white; the racial subjugation of a race enslaved by exploitation and violence is thus validated. Rapes, unsurprisingly, remain underprosecuted.

Accused of aiding and abetting every crime attributed to blackness, Wells foments rebellion, disturbing the equilibrium of conventional political alliances. Her legacy is often viewed as a political anachronism given the passing of lynching. However, antiblack violence endures, legitimized by both the continued criminalization of blackness and official condemnations of racist terror.

In June 2005, the US Senate passed Resolution 39, marking the official closure to lynching. The bipartisan agreement cemented lynching as a horrific historical artifact in the minds

of the public, and it was accompanied by the first government apology for the mass murder (the press used the verb "treatment") of black Americans. Lynching survivors and the
descendants of the slain viewed proceedings in the Senate gallery, lunched with Congress;
posed for photos, and spoke with the press (Thomas-Lester 2005). *The Washington Post*
quoted denunciations of lynching by Louisiana Senator Mary Landrieu, "There may be no
other injustice in American history for which the Senate so uniquely bears responsibility";
and Virginia Senator George Allen, "[lynching is] the brutal atrocity that plagued our great
nation" (Thomas-Lester 2005). Georgia Congressman and former SNCC activist John Lewis,
echoing Ida B. Wells to describe lynching as an extension of slavery, demanded an apology
for slavery.

In August, following the failures of substandard Army Corps of Engineers levies and
FEMA, Louisiana Governor Kathleen Blanco and President George W. Bush issued shoot-
to-kill edicts for "looters" racially configured as black New Orleans residents abandoned
after Katrina. That homicidal edict applied to black maternals seeking food, formula, and
diapers, but seemed to veer from whites seeking survival by "searching for" food and water.
Antilynching governance had already plastered pictures of the death of lynching with the
passage of Resolution 39; so the "treatment" of black Katrina survivors was barely perceived
by society as an accusation of crimes to incite antiblack terror.

"Plastered Pictures Alleged To Be Me"

Both *Southern Horrors* and *The Red Record* document lynching atrocities, with the preface
by abolitionist Frederick Douglass, who paints a prophetic portrait of Ida B. Wells:

> DEAR MISS WELLS:
> Let me give you thanks for your faithful paper on the lynch abomination now generally
> practiced against colored people in the South. There has been no word equal to it in convinc-
> ing power. I have spoken, but my word is feeble in comparison. You give us what you know and
> testify from actual knowledge. You have dealt with the facts with cool, painstaking fidelity, and
> left those naked and uncontradicted facts to speak for themselves.
> —Honorable Frederick Douglass (Wells 1892, 3–4)

Douglass's praise introduced Wells to a greater public and protected her from her black
detractors and perhaps fractured some white support for lynching. He praises her courage
and boldness without directly recommending her raw confrontations with white domination through rape and terror, and her advocacy for armed self-defense—all disturbing to
governance, whites, and some black elites. Contemporaries sought to dilute her radicalism.
Yet her growing popularization after her death—in ways that avoid or engage her self-defense
advocacy—suggests a political need for the political persona of Ida B. Wells. Still, misleading, dismissive portraits of Wells are produced. Wells's attempts to simultaneously denounce
rape and lynching are dismissed by feminist accusations that she is indifferent to the rapes of
white women by black men, due to an overemotional investment in the protection of black
males. Unintentionally, these accusations converge with the charges brought by white racists that she is an apologist for rape (James 1997). An antiracist protofeminist and fierce
antagonist to white rapists, Wells noted both white female complicity in lynching and the

courage of white women who "loved and lived openly with" Afro-American men (she makes no mention of same-sex interracial desire [Wells 1892]). A colleague of Susan B. Anthony, and a suffragist, as was her antilynching contemporary Mary Church Terrell, Wells's militancy is caught in the crosshairs of divergent camps. In her own preface to *Southern Horrors*, Wells clearly takes on her detractors, asserting that her writing

> is not a shield for the despoiler of virtue, nor altogether a defense for the poor blind Afro-American Sampsons who suffer themselves to be betrayed by white Delilahs. It is a contribution to truth, an array of facts, the perusal of which it is hoped will stimulate this great American Republic to demand that justice be done though the heavens fall. (Wells 1892, 4)

Wells's activism exhibits strategic passion, militancy, and specificity; it is not bound by ideology, coalitions, institutional funding, or interracial alliances with white elites. The red record of lynching is not gender specific. The numbers of murdered males outnumber the number of females; the casualty count skews male but reflects an ungendered phenomenon that embodies collective punishment. Terror and community shape Wells's political persona. Her revolutionary persona transcends gender lines, and so inaccurate portraits of her as indifferent to female victimization, counterfeminist, or a racial chauvinist, are more easily fabricated.

A post-Reconstruction, independent, and radical young woman, Wells was coolly received by the more cautious and connected. Wells's more influential peers included Du Bois, with a PhD from Harvard, and Terrell, with degrees from Oberlin. Their training and networks eluded Wells, who, orphaned at fifteen and largely self-taught as a journalist, never graduated from college. Du Bois, Terrell, and other black elites benefitted from the excitement and mass agitation that surrounded Wells's incendiary critiques—she infamously declares that she will use the pistol in her handbag to sell her life dearly to a lynch mob (Wells 1970). Her data collection on lynching was daring (she would disguise herself as a black sharecropper and visit imprisoned black men and boys facing lynch mobs to take their testimonies). Both black elites and whites sought to excise or supplant her political persona from public memory, likely due to competitive proprietary politics and a desire to ban her praxis of radical autonomy and self-defense.

The production of icons from black struggles seems inevitable. The National Park Registry landmark status of Wells's Chicago home and her 1990 US postage stamp (issued several years before the Malik El-Shabazz [Malcolm X] stamp) likely reflect the demands of black and antiracist citizens. Iconic desire, though, does not foreclose commoditization and false representations that veil the continuation of lethal repression.

"ISSUED ORDERS TO SHOOT ON SIGHT AND TO SHOOT TO KILL"

> Mr. Fleming [co-owner with Wells of the *Free Speech*] had to leave town to escape the mob, and was afterwards ordered not to return; letters and telegrams sent me in New York where I was spending my vacation advised me that bodily harm awaited my return.
>
> Ida B. Wells

Wells grieved murdered kin and sought justice by risking her life in order to pass through fear into resistance. One lynching out of thousands created a catalyst for an editor, a harbinger of rebellion. The 1892 lynching of Thomas Moss, the father of Wells's two-year-old goddaughter, Maureen, was the murder that created a crusader; grief at the destruction of her surrogate family and rage at democracy's betrayals were Wells's rite of passage into revolutionary struggle. Wells recalls that the men lynched in Memphis had focused on hard work and economic wealth as a resolution to racial repression; "eschewing politics," they built the People's Grocery, which economically threatened a local white grocer, Barrett, who in turn physically threatened the black businessmen and led armed white plainclothes officers—who later claimed they were trying to serve a warrant—at night through the back alley toward the People's Grocery. Thinking they were under attack by Barrett, the men shot at the intruders, wounding several; realizing they were police, they ceased firing. Thirty-one businessmen were jailed as "conspirators," according to Wells, and a mob removed the president, manager, and clerk of the People's Grocery from jail to offer a "lesson of subordination" by lynching them (Wells 1892).

After authorities failed to act against the lynching of "some of their best citizens," black Memphis communities organized economic boycotts and mass migration to cripple the city's economy. Familiar strategies were deployed to undermine black resistance: white city leaders called upon the *Free Speech* to urge black patronage to return to white businesses. When the editors refused, white citizens passed resolutions condemning the lynching but did not prosecute the killers. Afro-American communities were so divided that Wells—using language Malcolm X would later codify into field-house slave conflict—distinguishes between the compromises of willing "slaves" and the militancy of activists demanding self-defense.

Wells writes that when official black leadership urged blacks to remain law-abiding, their "counsel was heeded and not a hand was uplifted to resent the outrage." The *Free Speech* responded differently. Following its editorials, Memphis's Afro-American community left for Oklahoma and elsewhere in droves. The white press began a campaign of character assassination of both those killed by lynching and those protesting it. Wells denounced southern whites in their passivity or acquiescence to lynching as accomplices just as guilty as lynchers. Wells's 1892 controversial *Free Speech* editorial prompted white city leaders to meet at the Cotton Exchange Building:

> Eight negroes lynched since last issue of the *Free Speech* one at Little Rock, Ark., last Saturday morning where the citizens broke(?) into the penitentiary and got their man; three near Anniston, Ala., one near New Orleans; and three at Clarksville, Ga., the last three for killing a white man, and five on the same old racket—the new alarm about raping white women. The same programme of hanging, then shooting bullets into the lifeless bodies was carried out to the letter. Nobody in this section of the country believes the old thread-bare lie that Negro men rape white women. If Southern white men are not careful, they will overreach themselves and public sentiment will have a reaction; a conclusion will then be reached which will be very damaging to the moral reputation of their women. (Wells 1892, 1895, 3)

On May 25, Memphis's white The *Daily Commercial* quoted the last two sentences of her editorial and issued a threat: "Those negroes who are attempting to make the lynching of individuals of their race a means for arousing the worst passions of their kind are playing with a dangerous sentiment" (Wells 1892). The *Evening Scimitar* reprinted The *Commercial* editorial, adding commentary of castration of the editorial author whom they presumed to be male:

> If the negroes themselves do not apply the remedy without delay it will be the duty of those whom he has attacked to tie the wretch who utters these calumnies to a stake at the intersection of Main and Madison Sts., brand him in the forehead with a hot iron and perform upon him a surgical operation with a pair of tailor's shears. (Wells 1892, 4)

After the Cotton Exchange Center meeting, creditors took over The *Free Speech* and sold it, ending Memphis's influential organ of black radicalism. But Wells's writings had revealed the stains on white "virtue":

> The miscegenation laws of the South only operate against the legitimate union of the races; they leave the white man free to seduce all the colored girls he can, but it is death to the colored man who yields to the force and advances of a similar attraction in white women. White men lynch the offending Afro-American, not because he is a despoiler of virtue, but because he succumbs to the smiles of white women. (Wells 1892, 2)

In *Southern Horrors*, under the category "self-help," autonomy and uncompromised resistance in self-defense evolve: "the Afro-American can do for himself what no one else can do for him. The world looks on with wonder that we have conceded so much and remain law-abiding under such great outrage and provocation" (Wells 1892, 15). Advocating economic disruption, Wells argues that black labor rehabilitated the South devastated by war and calls for strikes:

> If labor is withdrawn capital will not remain. The Afro-American is thus the backbone of the South. A thorough knowledge and judicious exercise of this power in lynching localities could many times effect a bloodless revolution. The white man's dollar is his god, and to stop this will be to stop outrages in many localities. (Wells 1892, 15)

Viewing lynching as an extension of slavery, Wells's political persona bridges insurrections: antebellum slave rebellions; 200,000 black civil war combatants; southern civil rights Deacons for Defense and Justice; northern black liberation Black Panther Party. She observes:

> The only times an Afro-American who was assaulted got away has been when he had a gun and used it in self-defense. The lesson this teaches and which every Afro-American should ponder well, is that a Winchester rifle should have a place of honor in every black home, and it should be used for that protection which the law refuses to give. When the white man who is always the aggressor knows he runs as great risk of biting the dust every time his Afro-American victim does, he will have greater respect for Afro-American life. (Wells 1892, 16)

For Ida B. Wells, US democracy's subjugation of black lives is revealed in its triumvirate: sex, money, and domination through violence. Rebellions thus focus on rape, economic exploitation, and lynching or police murder.

CONCLUSION: RESURGENCE REBELLION

The heirs to Ida B. Wells's political persona include civil rights icons Ella Baker, Rosa Parks, and Mamie Till. Baker and Parks organized around the 1930s Scottsboro case of legal lynching in which black Alabama youths were falsely arrested, convicted, incarcerated, and tortured for years, for allegedly raping two white women (one testified in their defense, admitting that white young hobos having instigated and lost a fight on a train with black youths also traveling to seek work used false accusations of rape as racial revenge). With pliability lacking as middle-aged, seasoned activists, Baker and Parks as young women seemed malleable to NAACP liberal, legalistic directives. Baker worked as a field coordinator; Parks organized in Alabama in the 1940s on interracial rape cases with black women and girls who survived rape by white men (McGuire 2012). The NAACP attempted to harness Mamie Till, the grieving mother of fourteen-year-old Emmett, to its national agenda, but her rage moved her "off script." Wells, rejected by the NAACP, could not be placed into the role of organizational spokesperson or consumable icon, roles that the revolutionaries within Baker, Parks, and Till eventually rejected.

Today's mass mobilizations against antiblack terror focus on government police forces, not on rape or lynching, although citizens are asked to see police as agents against violence and lynching. With immunity from most prosecution, police and prison guards, through rape, torture, and homicide, invoke the racial sovereign of past centuries. Wells's critique of corrupt policing in 1900 New Orleans resonates today (Wells 1900; PBS Frontline 2015). In her adopted hometown, Chicago, a 1969 joint FBI-Chicago police task force predawn raid killed Black Panther Party members Fred Hampton and Mark Clark while they slept (the government later settled with survivors and families for $1.8 million [Massiah 1990]). In 2007, Chicago's Cook County paid $19.7 million to survivors falsely imprisoned through a police torture ring largely targeting black men. Police terror inspired Chicago's "We Charge Genocide" activism, an invocation of the 1951 petition to the United Nations on antiblack discrimination and lynching; and police rapes inspired the Black Women's Blueprint UN tribunal on the rape of black women and girls. Wells documents these historical phenomena. Their continued reoccurrence despite financial compensation for grief and the purchase of justice with multi-million-dollar settlements (paid from tax revenues, an additional "black tax" on pain and suffering) fosters new forms of militancy.

The political persona of Ida B. Wells embodies a nongendered, maternal resilience in which individual sacrifice enables family and community. Before marriage and children, Wells appears in a long line of maternal women who change sacrifice into a form of political activism. Such sacrifice, disproportionately expected from and borne by radical black females, leads to self-harm if the capacity of revolutionary impulse and productivity exceeds the capacity for resiliency in recovery from trauma.

Intergenerational, systemic, or structural, lynching and torture alter epigenetics. Genocide, racial capital/rape, enslavement and poverty, dishonor and disrespect as environmental conditions rewire us not just for trauma but also for rebellion. In the face of scarcity, insecurity, and threats, we inherit potential disabilities as well as resiliencies that transform political experience. Wells commingles black suffering and rebellion. Some focus on suffering; others on militancy. Her public persona embraced both. This is the source of Ida B. Wells's political power in radical agency manifesting in a quartet that spans generations.

Black Lives Matter activists don shirts emblazoned with "Assata Taught Me" and post selfies/photos online commingling their visages with that of a FBI political fugitive, a black revolutionary woman (James 2009). Wells, also a fugitive during her era, offers a template to question which teachings to follow or critique; how best to manage defiance, discipline, and fear within political lineage. Young activists never met Wells and will likely never meet Shakur, exiled in Cuba for decades. Yet they read, write, and analyze. They speak and organize. Some are arrested. Some pray. In the mix of their political personas rests the quartet of Ida B. Wells, the ancestor mother who cautions: "The gods help those who help themselves" (Wells 1892; Braxton 1989).

REFERENCES

Braxton, Joanne. (1989). *Black Women Writing Autobiography: A Tradition Within a Tradition.* Philadelphia: Temple University Press.

Greaves, William, director. (1989). *Ida B. Wells: A Passion for Justice.* Produced by San Francisco, CA: California Newsreel.

Griffith, D. W., director. (1915/2016). *The Birth of a Nation.* Produced by D. W. Griffith and Harry Aitken, Epoch Production Co.

James, Joy. (1997). "Sexual Politics: An Anti-Lynching Crusader in Revisionist Feminism." *Transcending the Talented Tenth.* New York: Routledge Press.

James, Joy. (2009). "Framing the Panther: Assata Shakur and Black Female Agency." In *Want to Start a Revolution?*, edited by Dayo Gore et al, 138–160. New York: NYU Press.

Massiah, Louis et al. director. (1990). *Eyes on the Prize Pt. II, A Nation of Law?1968–1971.* PBS https://freedocumentaries.org/documentary/pbs-eyes-on-the-prize-america-at-the-racial-crossroads-1965-1985-a-nation-of-law-1968-71-season-2-episode-6.

McGuire, Danielle. (2012). *At the Dark End of the Street: Black Women, Rape and Resistance—A New History of the Civil Rights Movement from Rosa Parks to the Rise of Black Power.* New York: Vintage Books.

Muhammad, Khalil Gibran. (2011). *The Condemnation of Blackness.* Cambridge, MA: Harvard University Press.

PBS Frontline. (2015). "Another Setback for Prosecutors in Post-Katrina Police Shootings." Accessed May 14, 2016. http://www.pbs.org/wgbh/frontline/article/another-setback-for-prosecutors-in-post-katrina-police-shootings/.

Shakur, Assata. (1973). "To My People." Accessed May 14, 2016. http://www.assatashakur.org/mypeople.htm.

Shakur, Assata. (1987). *Assata: An Autobiography.* London: Zed Press.

Thomas-Lester, Avis. (2005). "A Senate Apology for History on Lynching." *Washington Post.* Accessed May 14, 2016. http://www.washingtonpost.com/wp-dyn/content/article/2005/06/13/AR2005061301720.html.

Wells, Ida B. (1892/1993/1994). *Southern Horrors: Lynch Law in All Its Phases.* New York: New York Age. Accessed June 26, 2016. http://www.womenspeecharchive.org/files/Wells_1893_LYNCH_LAW_IN_ALL_ITS_PHA_EED47EF7FF7F2.pdf and http://www.homeworkforyou.com/static/uploadedfiles/User_3774622014TheProjectGutenbergeBookofSouthernHorrors_LynchLawInAllItsPhases,byIdaB.Wells-Barnett.pdf.

Wells, Ida B. (1895). "Against Lynching." *Chicago Inter-Ocean,* August 4, 1894, 9.

Wells, Ida B. (1895). *A Red Record: Tabulated Statistics and Alleged Causes of Lynchings in the United States, 1892–1893–1894.* Chicago: Ida B. Wells. Accessed May 14, 2016. http://www.gutenberg.org/files/14977/14977-h/14977-h.htm.

Wells, Ida B. (1900). *Mob Rule in New Orleans.* Chicago: Ida B. Wells.

Wells, Ida B. (1970). *Crusade for Justice: The Autobiography of Ida B. Wells.* Edited by Alfreda M. Duster. Chicago: University of Chicago Press.

CHAPTER 27

···

TO BE BLACK, EXCESS, AND NONRECYCLABLE

···

JANINE JONES

ONE way of understanding the white man's burden is as a waste management problem. The White West abjected Africans and people of African descent (hereafter, Africana people), thereby enacting and enabling their perception and treatment as a form of waste. When Africana people today chant "Black lives matter," they do so against the historical perception and treatment of black people as *waste*. But black waste *has* mattered to white, Western economies, having enabled and sustained economic, aesthetic, and psychological advantages for white beneficiaries of those systems. This is discernable in the metaphysics of a white imaginary of black abjection, once that metaphysics is elucidated. The elucidation reveals the structure of a humanist discourse, which (following the spirit of Frank Wilderson), imagines black bodies as alienated from language, and the degradation entailed by such alienation. *Pace* Wilderson, within this humanist discourse, violence accrues to the black body as "a result of transgressions, whether real or imagined, within the Symbolic Order" (Wilderson 2010, 54). In the current global, economic circumstances, it has become unclear how to *treat* black embodied waste, which now appears to be nonrecyclable. But there may be a response to the white man's new burden.

COUTURE AND SUTURE

···

In a discussion with D. Cooper, J. P. Faye, M-O. Faye, and M. Zecca on confinement, psychiatry, and prison, Michel Foucault cited a certain M. Léveille, a French man. According to Foucault, Léveille, in 1890, declared to the Russians:

> We Europeans, we encounter many difficulties dealing with these individuals who are criminals, but who are, first and foremost, mentally ill—criminals because they are mentally ill and mentally ill to the extent they are criminals. We don't know what to do because we do not have facilities to receive them. But you Russians, who possess vast swathes of virgin territory in Siberia, you would have no trouble handling all these people whom we make outcasts, whom we send to Guyana or to New Caledonia. You have Siberia. On the seam that joins medicine to the penal system, you could organize large work camps for these individuals. You could use

them for that and thereby develop this land of such promising wealth. (Translated by author from Foucault 1977, 335)

Foucault concluded that Léveille had defined the *gulag*—forced labor camps in the USSR. Foucault further believed that "the idea that there could be a politico-medical—politico-penal-medical or medical-political-penal system—with an economic function that enabled the creation of wealth in virgin territory" (translated by author from Foucault 1977, 335) was a novel idea. Arguably, the idea was not as novel as Foucault made it out to be. Let's frame it a little differently. When we understand the psychiatric-medical component, of which Foucault speaks, as a form of public hygiene, then we can understand that Léveille's vision had already been realized by Europeans and Euro-Americans in Africa and the Americas. Both groups had successfully joined public hygiene projects (projects for creating public order among chaotic, potentially contaminating abject(ed) "people") via penalizing/criminalizing projects. They had done so through the exploitation and alleged reparation of those peoples' bodies—a sine qua non for sewing the joint that would generate white wealth from its creation.

Léveille's vision for an economic, public hygiene-wellness/civilizing project—to be elaborated through workcamp-to-landwealth development plans—enlisted an eye-catching circular definition of criminality and mental illness. The vision itself captures the salvational, "civilizing" processes of enslavement and colonization used to abject Africana people in order to create white wealth on land perceived as virgin and empty—as lacking people. Indigenous people of the Americas and their lands were subjected to similar processes.

Where I use the term "seam" in my translation of Foucault's passage, Léveille is quoted not as using "suture," which in French connotes stitches made *on the body* in order to repair it. Foucault quotes Léveille as using "couture," connoting "seam" as understood in the world of couture, haute couture, and prêt-à-porter. Yet isn't Léveille suggesting the reparation of transgressive *bodies*—criminal/mentally insane embodiments—by working them out of their criminal, mentally insane condition (i.e., working them to death) and creating wealth in the process? I believe that is precisely what he is getting at. Nevertheless, it is important to retain Léveille's word choice, which focuses on what will be created and ready to use, rather than on the bodies that will be saved and repaired, requiring their annihilation in the process.

Like Léveille, white actors historically involved in humanist, abjecting projects may envision processes of *couture* implementing mechanisms that raised Africana people out of muck—the waste of a humanoid-type form on blackness: the waste of blackness on a humanoid-type form.

What was this abject(ed) waste from which black bodies were lifted, where, for success, the extraction process necessitated the use of abject slave boats and *slave-labor* work-to-death camps, euphonized as plantations and haciendas, thereby euthanizing their meaning? How might we describe its metaphysical structure in the white imaginary? How were abject(ed) Africana people supposedly *repaired*—made better though not equal—through tailoring processes that entailed their salvation through their own destruction? In the following, I answer these questions. My responses set up a plausible account of what it means for Africana people to be black, excess, and recyclable, as well as black, excess, and nonrecyclable, where nonrecyclability is a disquieting condition of excess black embodiment in the late twentieth century and twenty-first century, to date.

RECYCLABILITY VERSUS NONRECYCLABILITY

Nonrecyclability was not a condition of blackness at a time when Europeans and Euro-Americans participated in stitching seams to join civilizing, enslavement/colonizing processes to white wealth creation. At that time, recyclability of Africana people was the reigning state of affairs. Slavery, colonization, sharecropping, chain gangs, Jim Crow schemes, and so on—all forms of recycling—were modes by which black waste (to be explained later) was resurrected into and maintained as bodies. Concomitantly, they were means of white wealth creation. Although the resurrection and continual reparation (maintenance) of black bodies is conceptually distinct from the death and destruction of black people, it is effectively consubstantial with it on the white plan for black salvation and white wealth creation. Recyclability spells death and destruction for black people, as does nonrecyclability. But death and destruction for nonrecyclable black bodies is effected through waste *disposal* projects (e.g., pipeline to prison arrangements) rather than through resurrection and reparation *recycling* ventures. Nonrecyclability of waste emerges when recycling ends. Recycling ends when work goes south: when waste must then be wasted.

Abjection is necessary for understanding how Western logics could foresee and then effectively see the destruction of black bodies as resurrection and reparation *for* black "people," as a form of "salvagion" *for* black "people,"—as in salvation-salvaged—that is, an ongoing operation forged upon Africana people so that they might be delivered from (their) evil, and saved long enough, and well enough, to add value to white people's assets. What was the evil waste Africana bodies were mired in, from which they needed saving at the expense of their own lives? Abjection will tell us a lot about that.

Critical race theorists have viewed abjection as central to understanding the existential condition of Africana people. Frantz Fanon's work in *Black Skin, White Masks* theorizes blackening of Africana people. This is a way of talking about abjecting them. Audre Lorde's recounting of her treatment as a roach speaks to abjection (2007, 147). Hortense Spillers's theorizing about Africans and their descendants being reduced to flesh locates their construction in the abject (1987, 67). More recently, Darieck Scott, in *Extravagant Abjection*, argues that black people can find a form of empowerment through their abjection. Samuel R. Delany, discussed in Scott, wrote a fictional story, *The Mad Man: Or the Mysteries of Manhattan*, about a black, gay, graduate student in philosophy, John Marr, who *works with* his black abjection. He seeks out abject white sexual partners (white men degraded through poverty, homelessness, and educational impoverishment) for sexual pleasure, stimulated, in part, by their abjectification of his blackness through racially charged wordcraft: for example, " You gotta grow you some wool, nigger, so I can hold you by your head!" (Delany 2002/2015, loc. 8310). Marr is rich in racially charged repartee: "Letting my speech get a little blacker than it usually was, I said: 'Cum and nigger piss—that should be a real treat for you, honky' " (Delany 2002/2015, loc. 2755).

I will focus on what we can understand about the metaphysics of abjecting Africana people by bringing into conversation ideas from Julia Kristeva, in *Powers of Horror*, with some of George Bataille's ideas on sex and death. Abjection is intimately and ultimately related to sex and death. As Scott explained, one of Fanon's essential points was that "blackness functions in Western cultures as a repository for fears about sexuality and death" (Scott 2010, 4).

Centrally locating blackness in abjection, we can understand that no matter how significant science has been in constructing blackness, it does not usurp abjection's foundational, structural, imaginal role. We should not expect embodied black abjects to disappear because science *now* challenges claims about race. With abjection at the helm and science backed by the epistemic virtue of defeasibility, we should not be surprised if science seeks repeatedly to sanction ideas about abject black people. Indeed, science may develop new, allegedly objective technologies for the task. Let's begin with a brief understanding of whiteness. For it is in hierarchical, negative opposition to whiteness that the construction of blackness was required.

WHITENESS: MYTH AS WORLD MAKER

In "Who Was White? The Disappearance of Non-European White Identities and the Formation of European Whiteness," Alastair Bonnett argues that a unique concept of whiteness—" a triple conflation of White = Europe = Christian"—was necessary for consolidating European imperial, colonial power. Whiteness depended on an ideology of white European superiority as a necessary weapon for conquest, and blackness as a necessary corollary of defeat. Whiteness empirically discovered its worldly antithesis in Africa and "The New World." African people, conceptualized by Europeans as black, became worldly constituents of *perceived* blackness. Thomas Hasler (Delany's fictional, murdered Korean American philosopher, whom the fictional John Marr researches) described how we construct certain rhetorical structures—so-called Hasler structures: "We must first systematize a field of similarities against which later discernable differences can be cognized as information."

Hasler structures provide a superb description of what Europeans and Euro-Americans did, and what Bonnett, in part, argues they did. To wit, they systematized a field of similarities of whiteness around the notions of Europe, Christianity, and skin color, against which later discernable—that is, perceived differences (African, non-Christian, dark skinned) could be received as information. Through Africans a *polar* racial difference could be grounded in perceived black skin versus perceived white skin. Perceived black skin could be presented as abject to sight, sound, touch, smell, and taste in lived experience.

We find the power (attraction) of the move from conception of blackness in thought to perception of black bodies in lived experience (from representation of blackness in narratives to perception of black skin by the senses) in the role Jesus Christ plays in Christianity. This is worth mentioning, given the role that Western understandings of Christianity played in abjecting Africana people. Accounts of Christ provided Christians an excellent model for going from conceiving (representing) an idea about an entity (God) to perceiving it (presenting it) in the flesh, in order to bring about a deeper understanding *and feel* for the entity in question.

Theologians concur that Christ's embodiment incarnates the divine presence, and thereby *represents* God. But Christ is also the manifestation of the divine presence by the body through the flesh. Such manifestation requires a *presentation* of the body, of the flesh, to the senses. But being bodily, Christ is also a degenerate mode of the divine.

"Christian" from "Christos" means to witness. Presenting embodiment to sensory experience provides impeccable conditions for witnessing, testifying, and intersubjective agreement: a nexus providing prime breeding grounds for claims about objectivity grounded in the empirical. Furthermore, Christ's resurrection, and the eventual resurrection and reparation of Christians—who, if faithful, access the wealth of the kingdom of heaven through Christ's death and resurrection—required his abjection through the mortification of his flesh. Plausibly, these Christian ideas, which combine resurrection from the degenerate, reparation through resurrection, and access to wealth as reward, influenced European and Euro-American views on how to abject Africana people successfully and profitably. Perceived blackness—made possible in part by the interplay of physical features of the materiality of skin and human visual perception, but also, arguably, in greater part, by cultural processes instrumentalizing features of the materiality of the skin—ushered in white recognition of a state of disgrace dwelling throughout Africa, not incidentally, home to Ham.

Ham was white on European understandings of who he was. Banished to Africa, a black badge advertised Ham's moral turpitude. His African progeny—biological and conceptual extensions of his white body (but not his white self, which went missing)—possess black skin. The relation of Ham to his progeny mirrors what Oyèrónké Oyčwùmí argues. Namely, in the West difference expressed as degeneration "brought together two notions of difference, one scientific—a deviation from original type—and the other moral, a deviation from a norm of behavior. *But they were essentially the same notion, of a fall from grace*" (Oyewùmí 1997, 1, emphasis added). Thus, while perceived black skin is contingent to being abject, through what Oyewùmí calls body reasoning, perceived black skin is *constitutive* of abjecting Africana people. In *L'Éroticism*, Georges Bataille maintains that in the Western imaginary, blood signals violence by being a sign of the effect of being sullied through violence (Bataille 2011, 56). Arguably, the same holds for skin perceived by the Western imaginary as dark or black skin. After all, we are dealing with an imaginary that (seriously) understood the black fur of cats as a sign of the devil. Perceived black skin announces to the white imaginary the presence of an excess of violence. But an excess of violence requires greater violence to put it down for the (re)establishment of an orderly, hygienic state of affairs.

PREIDENTITY, PRESUBJECT, AND PREOBJECT: THE POWERS OF THE BLACK MATERNAL UNABJECTED

> Everything I felt by now was happening not in words but in urges and sensations and feelings.
>
> *The Mad Man*

In "Against Abjection," Imogen Tyler reminds us that Kristeva proposes a model of subjectivity whereby the infant must bodily and psychically abject maternal origins in order for an independent, speaking human to emerge—thereby making matricide "our vital necessity" (Tyler 2009, 81). Leaving aside the important warning Tyler issues to feminists who use Kristeva to theorize maternal subjects, when Kristeva's account might be as mother-free as Lacan's, let's focus on the conceptual idea that the maternal must be abjected or left behind. What is at risk for the infant that remains *in* the maternal?

Remaining in the maternal realm, the infant cannot attain the symbolic world: the world of speech and thought. The infant remains in a world of urges, sensations, and feelings (where we should distinguish feelings from emotions, whose existence require symbolic articulation). The infant, mired in the maternal, cannot emerge as an individual, for an individual is an entity transformed into a *subject* within the symbolic world. As Deborah Covino explains, Kristeva's idea of the maternal was inspired by Plato's idea of the *chora*. But for Plato the *chora* was little more than a receptacle—"a kind of non-thing with respect to being" that nourished the child. For Kristeva, the *chora*, contra Plato (and Lacan), is a realm of semiotic drives and desires, continuous with the symbolic world, and of which symbolic language is an outgrowth (Covino 2004, 17–21). What is important for our purposes is that the maternal, with its urges, drives, and sensations, *must* be left behind. Imagined (by Plato) as being discontinuous with the symbolic world, the maternal chora must be abjected by the infant. Covino writes:

> One of Kristeva's interests is the ways in which the necessary abjection of the mother—our separation from her in order to become individualized, to take objects, to enter language, to become good citizens of the family and the social world—is mistranslated into the abjection of women in general, who are reduced to the maternal function.
> The abject is [hence] . . . a more radical alterity than the semiotic: it refers to the power of the mother's body over the child, a power that is not perfectly brought *under the control of the Symbolic or the Paternal Order.*
> [Further] the semiotic mother . . . does participate in the process of imposing patterns and order on the mother because she is, as Kelly Oliver says, "pre-identity, presubject, preobject", and in that way, *utterly non-compliant with the clean and proper bodies regulated by the symbolic order.* (Covino 2004, 21–22)

Covino explains that the semiotic mother—the *chora*—participates in the process of imposing patterns and order on the mother. My view is that the movement of semiotic drives, urges, and sensations within the internal space of the mother *imprints* patterns on her body, reflecting *their* order. Such expression is thought to corroborate an order of preidentity, presubject, and preobject, which supposedly threatens the symbolic order. From the perspective of a certain understanding of the symbolic, such patterns are conceived as noncompliant and destructive of the symbolic. Thus, the mother is dangerous, wittingly or unwittingly, and so is whatever else that bears those chaotic patterns.

Some feminists speak of *the* maternal body.

Enter the *black* maternal body: the mother lode.

If the myth of the Holy Virgin—the mother of Christ—domesticated the mother, as Covina claims Kristeva has shown that it has, in "Stabat Mater" (Kristeva 1982; Covina 2004, 21), Mary, mother of God, failed to domesticate the threat posed by the black mother. Worldly female Africana constituents provided evidence to white, European observers (viewing through the lens of a white imaginary) of her intractable, devouring force. It would seem that Foucault and his friends might concur with the view I am proposing. Let's revisit another segment of their conversation on mental illness.

D. COOPER: But psychiatric definitions of the "extremely ill" are very interesting . . . Working class, first. Jewish more so than non Jewish. Black more so than non-black.
M. ZECCA: And women . . .

D. COOPER: . . . rather than men. Obviously, it's the black woman who provides the most perfect example of the mentally ill. (translated by author from Foucault 1977, 339)

Reintroducing Léveille's circular definition of mental illness (see earlier), black women
would therefore also provide the most perfect example of criminality—not black men, as is
commonly thought. Perhaps we might say that if worldly conditions have brought it about
that black men are perceived as exemplars of criminality, the white imaginary *knows* that
black femaleness is foundational to the essentiality of black crime.

What was the ultimate crime of African women? How did they make it possible for
Europeans to see only vast expanses of empty land in Africa, with no *real people* resid-
ing on it? It was the black maternal *chora's success* in devouring her offspring and hindering them from entering the symbolic realm that did the dirty deed. The white imaginary
could take "facts" about mind and materiality as evidence of her degenerate success. Note
that I say materiality and not "the body," for I will argue later that it was Europeans and
Euro-Americans who brought the black body into being from its black, *chora*-imprisoned
materiality.

Regarding mind, it simply went missing. Europeans and Euro-Americans took a look
around *their* black(ened) Africa and could see no evidence of mind, because they could
see no evidence of rationality. But there could be no rationality because Africans had failed
to enter the realm of the symbolic. Following the theory of abjection explained earlier, the
devouring black maternal had kept her children mired in urges, sensations, feelings, all
indistinguishable from each other—everything continuous, as before birth. No subjects, as
in death. Not surprisingly, this is precisely how black "people" have been described by the
white imaginary: as being all urges, impulses, emotions run wild—and sex. On another level
of representation, what is being described is a state of preidentity, presubject, preobject—a
state that offers no bodies, as such. Rather, what we have is continuous black materiality,
requiring an excess of violence to break it up into distinguishable, *discontinuous* parts. Here,
we should not mistakenly invoke the idea of making *individuals*. Individuals are subjects.

Hegel gave his version of the view that African people had not entered the symbolic in his
1830–1831 lectures on Africa:

> The peculiarly African character is difficult to comprehend, for the very reason that in refer-
> ence to it, we must quite give up the principle which naturally accompanies all *our* ideas—the
> category of Universality. In Negro life the characteristic point is the fact that consciousness
> has not yet attained to the realization of any substantial objective existence . . . in which the
> interest of man's volition is involved and in which he realizes his own being. This distinction
> between himself as an individual and universality of his essential being, the African in the
> uniform, undeveloped oneness of his existence has not yet attained. . . . We must lay aside all
> thought of reverence and morality—all that we call feeling—if we would rightly comprehend
> him. . . . At this point we leave Africa, not to mention it again. For it is no historical part of
> the World; it has no movement or development to exhibit. What we properly understand by
> Africa, is the Unhistorical, Undeveloped Spirit, still involved in the conditions of mere nature,
> and which had to be presented here only as on the threshold of the World's History. (Hegel
> 1956, 93)

French President Nicholas Sarkozy gave his twenty-first-century version of the presym-
bolic African to a public composed of students, professors, and politicians at Cheikh-Anta-
Diop University in Dakar, on July 26, 2007. Having recognized that colonization was a huge

mistake, Sarkozy stated "the colonizer took but he also gave. He constructed bridges, roads, hospitals and schools" (Hofnun 2007, my translation). Sarkozy explained to his primarily black African audience that "The African had not sufficiently entered history: for the African there is no place for the human adventure or for the idea of progress. He never propels himself into the future" (Hofnung 2007, my translation). Sarkozy's speech let it be understood that it was up to the White West to propel the African into the future if the African was to enter humanity. That project had always required an excess of violence, a fact Sarkozy failed to fully acknowledge.

The other key feature Europeans and Euro-Americans observed on people-free African, virgin land was an overabundance of untrammelled sex, particularly outrageous on the part of African females. As Jennifer Morgan writes in *Laboring Women*,

> Ideas about black sexuality and misconceptions about black female sexual behavior formed the cornerstone of Europeans' and Euro-Americans' general attitudes toward slavery.... Before they came into contact with enslaved women either in West Africa or on American plantations, slave-owners' images and beliefs about race and savagery were indelibly marked on the women's bodies. ... Images of black women's reproductive potential, as well as images of their voracious sexuality, were crucial to slave-owners faced with female laborers. The act of forcing black women to work in fields both required and resulted in work and sex becoming intrinsic to one another. (Morgan 2004, 8)

Black female sexuality was harnessed, and punished, for profit. The white father would use the requisite violence to abject her himself, in order to raise her offspring: to erect black bodies from their maternal muck, whose patterns they would continue to bear having failed to *abject themselves* from it. The forceps used by the white father for extracting black bodies was work; and following Morgan, therefore, sex as well.

FROM EXTRAVAGANT BLACK ABJECTION TO WORK-BOUND BLACK BODIES

In the primeval abject condition of blackness mired in the maternal *chora* (see earlier), blackness does not offer bodies. Bodies are discontinuous. Waste—muck, slime—and the *chora* are not. They are continuous. The universal existential condition of continuity contains the primal fears that the White West projected onto Africana people as *their* very own essential existential condition. From black continuity, the white father would extract black gold, nuggets—discontinuous entities that could count as bodies. And count those bodies he would, the value of each assessed for all its speculated worth.

It is often said that one black person functions as though representing the entire race of black people. Keeping in mind a theory of black abjection, arguably, representation is not the fundamental relation governing how one black person is related to another. A more appropriate concept would harken back to the existential condition of primeval black abjection within the devouring black *chora*. Thus, the relationship to be captured by a concept (as yet unnamed) is that between "different" boundary-less spatial-temporal areas of endless merging and demerging and remerging: hallmarks of the abject. Contra Delany's fictional philosopher Hasler, who believed "the messy is what provides the energy which holds any system within it coherent and stable" (Delany 2002/2015, loc. 4628–4638) (or we might invoke the view of the semiotic as that which enables the symbolic and makes it hold), the Western imaginary sees messiness as destructive of system and order. It requires, as Mary Foltz explains in "The Excremental Ethics of Samuel R. Delany," the construction of "hegemonic discourses of physical health, sanity, normalcy, and cleanliness" (Foltz 2008, 46). Hygienic techniques, sewn together via land development projects, must be applied to clean up black masses. In other words, abjectifying processes fashion black bodies and create wealth for the real living. Raised black bodies, which carry the patterns of their primeval situation, serve as constant reminders of it. Therefore, a black body may not *represent* other black bodies so much as it is seen and "remembered" as being in and through them, just as they are in and through it. The fabricated distinction of black bodies is only apparent. It is a *mere* surface distinction. A real distinction requires minds capable of distinguishing themselves from real Others. Lacking rationality, this mental process is not available to raised black bodies. And if Hasler is right in saying "Discourse [which is public] is the effect of materiality on language" (Delany 2002/2015, loc. 1315), then black bodies themselves cannot serve as evidence to third (white) persons that they are truly distinct from other persons. For the materiality of the black body—bearing the stamp of the chora—does not, in the white imaginary, produce discourse, because it does not speak genuine language.

BATAILLE: SEX IN THE SINGLE CELL

> Life is not a condemnation of death, but its exclusion.
>
> Bataille-inspired

Georges Bataille's rendering of how sex works in the single cell will tell us a lot about the relation between continuity and discontinuity—the relation between life and death. A single cell *a* is discontinuous. However, there is continuity, and excess, within it, as within Kristeva's *chora*.

> When *a'* and *a"* emerge from *a* through asexual reproduction, continuity is not immediately obliterated. For a moment, it is suspended. At such moment, that which is not yet *a'* is continuous with *a."* But then plethora (an excess) compromises this continuity. In fact, plethora caused the slippage that brought about the division of *a* in the first place. In the suspended moment there is not yet real separation, but ambiguity. Through plethora, *a* went from a state of rest to a state of violent agitation, which overtook the whole of its being, vitiating its continuity. Violent agitation, beginning within *a's* continuity, engendered the violence required for separation, from which discontinuity proceeded. Finally, rest was reestablished in a resulting discontinuity; that is, where *a'* and *a"* exist as distinct beings—that is, as discontinuous entities. In this state *a* no longer exists because death always annihilates individual discontinuity, which appears every time continuity is profoundly exposed. Sex in the single cell is death's first and ultimate truth. It announces the fundamental discontinuity of a being (and being) and reveals the lie of discontinuity. (Translated by author from Bataille 2011, 104–105.)

Black body extraction requires a plethora, an *excess of violence* to break up the continuity of black (female) sex that allegedly makes no invidious distinctions. Such excess violence came in the form of work, forced labor. Following the white imaginary under discussion, it makes sense that this should be so. For as Bataille wrote, "In our lives, excess manifests itself to the extent that violence wins out over reason" (translated by author from Bataille 1986, 44). The black *chora* devouring her offspring, hindering their entrance into the symbolic, describes a fundamental existential situation of violence winning out over reason. This is a major problem for public hygiene! Reason—the white man's gift and burden—must be imposed to reestablish order. And how better to do that than through work. For work entails a type of violence which, as Bataille wrote, "is never a stranger to reason" (translated by author from Bataille 1986, 47). Work presupposes:

> the recognition of the basic self-identity of the object used in work, and the difference—resulting from work—between the object used and the material that composes it. Likewise, work implies consciousness of the utility of the instrument, of the series of operations of cause and effect in which it will take part. The laws that preside over the operations mastered, from which tools are derived or for which they serve, are first and foremost laws of reason. These laws regulate changes conceived by work and effected by it. Undoubtedly a primitive could have articulated them in a language that would give him consciousness of the designated objects, but not consciousness of the designation, of language itself. (translated by author from Bataille 1986, 46–47)

The black body emerges through work not only because work materially fashions discontinuity from continuous materiality, like fat transforming into muscle from pumping iron. Work, following Bataille, is invested with reason. Though black bodies cannot access reason for themselves through work, like the discontinuous tools they use, they will be involved in endeavors possessing utility, and operations of cause and effect. They will be conscious *of* these endeavors and operations (some might say, as a mule would be), without possessing consciousness or understanding of what those endeavors and operations are. Being *conscious of* discontinuous realities is sufficient for endowing black bodies with a discontinuity of their own, but not with a mind of their own.

Against all odds, black bodies did possess real minds of their own in two types of case. First, there was disobedience to white people, recognized by the white imaginary not only as a form of conscious intent, but as a form of criminal intent. Second, we have *willful* submission—that special form of black agency or black subjectivity, elucidated by Saidiya Hartman in *Scenes of Subjection*—which made it conceptually impossible to rape black females, as they were always ever too consciously *willing* to submit sexually to white masters. As we go on to ponder the conceptual (im)possibilities of white men raping black men, we might ask how the following case would have been understood. In 1787, in Maryland, William Holland, a white man had a free black woman, Elizabeth Amwood, "Pull up her Close and Lie Down he then Called a Negrow Man Slave" "and ordered him to pull Down his Britches and gitt upon the said Amwood and to be grate with her," while another white man John Pettigrew pointed a pistol at the unnamed slave (Foster 2011, 445). Question: Would Holland's self-professed act of "putting a Mare to horse" (Foster 2011, 445) have been categorized, in the white imaginary's discourses, as willful submission on the part of the black enslaved man? Or would willful submissive aggression have better described his genuine act of consciousness? How about willful aggressive submission? From impoverished minds to consciousness through mastered minds, embodiment by way of work may have been black(ened) people's best bet.

With diminishing returns on white investment in black body extraction, frightening numbers of black people no longer have work. Black bodies risk returning to that from which they were extracted by force through work—a mass of underdeveloped blackness: waste. Black waste under these conditions is not recyclable. It must be disposed of. Warehousing blackness through mass incarceration and densely populated segregated spatial-temporal arrangements has provided some relief for white waste management. But the former is proving to be costly, and it is turning out that the ground surfaces allotted for segregation could be valuable, if blackness were cleared out. Under these conditions, black lives may not matter. With little work to keep black bodies raised up and producing white wealth for next to nothing, except their own mindless deaths, how could they possibly matter?

Un Concours de Circonstances

"As usual the police were used to taking our own feces, because it's our own feces! We didn't take anyone's feces . . . our own feces that we produce everyday . . . . But now the police are taking our feces and we don't even know where they're taking our feces to, because our feces didn't commit any crime!"

SABC Digital News 2013

But, after all, a black body *is* a terrible thing to waste. New possibilities for recycling supposedly nonrecyclable black bodies are awaiting discovery. Consider two states of affairs currently on a collision course, just now when so many black people are out of work: black people without toilets, some of whose feces have been confiscated by the police during poo protests over their toilet-less condition, and medicine's interest in fecal microbiota transplantation. Sewing the seam between medicine and shit might just put black bodies back in business: for the wages of waste.

References

Bataille, G. (2011). *L'Érotism*. Paris, France: Les Éditions de Minuit.

Bonnett, A. (1998). "Who Was White? The Disappearance of Non-European White Identities and the Formation of European Racial Whiteness." *Ethnic and Racial Studies* 21 (6): 1029–1055.

Covino, D. C. (2004). *Amending the Abject Body: Aesthetic Makeovers in Medicine and Culture*. New York: State University of New York Press.

Delany, Samuel R. (2002/2015). *The Mad Man: Or the Mysteries of Manhattan*. New York: Open Road Integrated Media.

Fanon, F. (2008). *Black Skin, White Masks*. New York: Dover Press.

Foltz, M. C. (2008). "The Excremental Ethics of Samuel R. Delany." *SubStance* 37 (2): 41–55.

Foster, Thomas A. (2011). "The Sexual Abuse of Black Men under American Slavery." *Journal of the History of Sexuality* 20 (3): 445–464.

Foucault, M. (2001). *Dits et Écrits: Tome 2: 1976–1988*. Paris: Broché.

Hartman, Saidiya V. (1997). *Scenes of Subjection: Terror, Slavery, and Self-Making in Nineteenth-Century America*. New York: Oxford University Press.

Hegel, F. (1956). *The Philosophy of History*. New York: Dover.

Hofnung, Thomas. 2007. "Le jour où Sarkozy stupéfia l'Afrique." *Liberation*. Accessed September 29, 2015. http://www.liberation.fr/politiques/2007/10/09/le-jour-ou-sarkozy-stupefia-l-afrique_12060.

Kristeva, Julia. (1982). *Powers of Horror: An Essay on Abjection*. New York: Columbia University Press.

Kristeva, Julia. (1985). "Stabat Mater." *Poetics Today* 133–152.

Lorde, A. (2007). *Sister Outsider*. Berkeley, CA: Crossing Press.

Morgan, J. (2004). *Laboring Women: Reproduction and Gender in New World Slavery*. Philadelphia: University of Pennsylvania Press.

Oyěwùmí, Oyèrónkẹ́. (1997). *The Invention of Women*. Minneapolis: University of Minnesota Press.

SABC Digital News. (2013). "Human Excrement was Confiscated from a Group of People at the Cape Town Train Station." *YouTube*. Accessed October 30, 2015. https://www.youtube.com/watch?v=dcOYzKITsyE.

Scott, D. (2010). *Extravagant Abjection: Blackness, Power, and Sexuality in African American Literary Imagination*. New York: NYU Press.

Spillers, H. (1987). "Mama's Baby, Papa's Maybe: An American Grammar Book." *Diacritics* 17 (2): 64–81.

Tyler, I. (2009). "Against Abjection." *Feminist Theory* 10 (1): 77–98.

Wilderson, F., III. (2010). *Red, White, and Black: Cinema and the Structure of U.S. Antagonisms*. Durham, NC: Duke University Press.

CHAPTER 28

WHITE PRIVILEGE

SHANNON SULLIVAN

In the wake of the de jure equality established in the United States by the Civil Rights Act of 1964 and the creation of the Equal Employment Opportunity Commission (EEOC), de facto racial inequalities that favor white people continue to exist and in many cases have increased. In 2010, for example, the median net household worth of white American families was $110,729 compared to $4,955 for black American families—a whopping 2,234 percent difference favoring white people (Lubby 2012). In 2012, African American women made 64 cents and Latinas earned 55 cents for every dollar that a non-Hispanic white man made (Kerby 2013). Racial disparities in wealth are not the only problem that lingers after the end of legalized racial segregation, however. Racial disparities in health also exist, for example in higher rates of coronary artery disease, diabetes, stroke, HIV/AIDS, and infant mortality for African Americans, Native Americans, and Pacific Islanders (Smedley et al. n.d., 1). In addition, as of 2005, African Americans were incarcerated at nearly six times the rate of white people; Hispanics were incarcerated at nearly double the rate of white people (Mauer and King 2007). Black families regularly are the targets of child welfare services that shift black children into foster homes, a process that fuels the school-to-prison pipeline since children in foster homes are significantly more likely to go to prison than children who remain with their parents/families (Roberts 2002). While the racial gap in high school graduation rates has narrowed somewhat, in 2012–2013 white students still graduated at a much higher rate (86.6 percent) than Hispanic students (75.2 percent), black students (70.7 percent), and American Indian students (69.7 percent) (Bidwell 2015). A racialized aesthetics continues to benefit white people and penalize people of color: white beauty standards are normative, especially for women, positioning dark-skinned and black women as "the beauty don'ts" in contrast to white women as "the beauty dos" (*Bossip* 2015).

The list could go on. The point of it is that even though most of these disparities are the remnants of decades of chattel slavery and centuries of legalized white supremacy, none of them are against the law today. Put another way, the civil rights movements of the 1950s and 1960s were successful in that they eliminated de jure Jim Crow. But "the new Jim Crow" is vibrantly alive and well (Alexander 2012), and one could say that it includes not just the War on Drugs and racial profiling by police analyzed by Alexander but also numerous social, educational, and aesthetic practices. Complex systems of racial disparities exist not just in the United States but also in Canada, England, France, Germany, South Africa, and other countries that have outlawed racial discrimination and forced segregation. Racial disparities continue to harm people of color and unfairly benefit white people, even though equality of opportunity is legally mandated and most white people today would say that racism is morally wrong.

What should we call the role of whiteness and the benefits to white people in this extralegal system of racial injustice? This question is not merely academic, as if linguistic accuracy were the only or primary issue at stake. More important, the question is political because how we conceive what in 1965 was called "the white problem in America" that persists half a century later (*Ebony* 1965) will impact both how we try to solve it and whether those attempts will be effective. Backing up a step, how we conceive the white problem also will impact whether it is even acknowledged in the first place. One of the main features of racial inequality after the end of de jure Jim Crow is its relative invisibility. Today white advantages often are subtle, even hidden, and they frequently are difficult to prove empirically or pinpoint with certainty. When they can be demonstrated, as in the case of institutional racial biases against people of color, they often are explained away as the result of something other than racial bias. For example, when asked to address the racial profiling of black people by predominantly white police forces, former New York City mayor Rudolph Giuliani responded that black-on-black crime was the real problem and that "white police officers wouldn't be there [in black neighborhoods] if [black people] weren't killing each other 70 percent of the time" (quoted in Zack 2015, xii). In other cases, racial inequalities benefitting white people operate without explicitly mentioning race or whiteness at all. K-12 school suspension rates, for example, tend to be extremely racially imbalanced, penalizing black students disproportionately, but they often are discussed as race-neutral matters of "zero tolerance" of "disruptive" and "insubordinate" behavior (see, for example, data from Charlotte, North Carolina's school system [Dunn 2015]). In this context, "zero tolerance," "disruptive," and "insubordinate" are examples of what could be called code words for racial matters, just as terms such as "poverty," "ghetto," and "affordable housing" tend to signal black people without naming them. Practices such as these tend to camouflage race and white advantage, making it all too easy for white (and other) people to deny that they exist and for racial inequality to hum along unchallenged (Sullivan 2006). We need to be able to name the subtle and often unspoken role that whiteness plays in systems of de facto racial injustice so that it does not become even less visible and more insidiously convoluted than it already is.

The term "white privilege" attempts to make these systems visible and to decrypt their code words. The concept marks that something different with regard to race developed in the United States and similar nations as a transformation of previous forms of white domination. (While a rich history of African American criticism of whiteness existed prior to and during the civil rights movement [see, for example, Du Bois 1999 and *Ebony* 1965], that criticism is written in the context of explicit and [then] legal forms of white advantage.) Significant problems with the concept of white privilege exist, however, and some scholars have argued that it does not capture adequately contemporary forms of racial injustice. Alternative concepts for describing de facto systems of racial injustice include (global) white supremacy and rights discourse (either human rights in general or, e.g., black rights in particular). In what follows, I will examine the advantages and disadvantages of the concept of white privilege, comparing it to various alternatives. I conclude that the concept should be modified to that of white class privilege and that, to be maximally effective, racial justice movements need the concept of white class privilege in addition to that of human rights and white supremacy.

THE INVISIBILITY OF NORMATIVE WHITENESS

Peggy McIntosh's (1989) seminal essay on white privilege describes it as an invisible knapsack of unearned advantages for white people. On McIntosh's account, white privilege is like a tool kit containing a number of handy gadgets that help one succeed in life and make it more pleasant and easier to tackle the challenges one faces along the way. For example, the white knapsack includes many privileges related to control: being able to arrange to be around people of the same race, being able to protect one's children from being around people who do not like them, and being able to choose when it is convenient or pleasant to think about one's race. Other white privileges include being able to take for granted a world that is geared toward white people; for example, white people easily can see people of their own race represented in important cultural stories, national heroes, children's magazines, and even greeting cards and the packaging of beauty and personal care items. And still other white privileges are psychological, allowing white people to be individuals who do not have to speak for their race and to shop, drive, and visit expensive restaurants without being followed, pulled over by the police, or made to feel unwelcome (McIntosh 1989, 10–11). For McIntosh, white privilege is found in the small details of quotidian life, in countless daily experiences in which white people experience advantages because of their race that other racial groups do not.

As McIntosh argues, one of the most significant features of white privilege is that it operates as if it is nonexistent. No one is supposed to see or notice it since it functions best when it is hidden and undetectable. Speaking self-reflectively, McIntosh explains that white privilege is "an invisible package of unearned assets which I can count on cashing in each day, but about which I was 'meant' to remain oblivious" (1989, 10). White people's cluelessness about their racial privilege allows them simultaneously to benefit from that privilege and to deny that systems of white dominance exist. Hand in hand with white obliviousness, then, goes white silence about race and about whiteness in particular. Not just white privilege, but whiteness itself is a "taboo subject" (McIntosh 1989, 12). Talking about whiteness would bring unfair racial practices and structures to conscious awareness, revealing how the world is set up to benefit white people.

Roughly a decade after McIntosh's knapsack essay, Patricia J. Williams further examined "the small aggressions of unconscious racism" that have multiplied after the end of de jure Jim Crow (Williams 1997, 61). Williams characterizes the power of race and the normativity of whiteness as a "public secret" in contemporary America: we all know that race exists and makes a difference in people's lives, but we are supposed to be colorblind, performing a "civil ritual that requires us to say in the face of all our differences, We are all one" (1997, 12). "I don't see race, I just see people" would be the white creed of this civic ritual, and its alleged colorblindness allows the unsaid and unconscious operations of white privilege to function undisturbed. It also allows white people to understand themselves as ignorant and innocent of any (conscious) involvement with race or white dominance. (For more on white ignorance, see Mills 2008.) White people's racial privilege often takes epistemological form through "a profoundly invested disingenuousness, an innocence that amounts to the transgressive refusal to know" (Williams 1997, 27). Their solution for the problem of racial inequality mirrors this denial, moreover, fiercely hanging onto white ignorance and white innocence. As Williams argues, white people's typical response when they do see racial inequality is to wish that people of color also did not have to understand or even notice race. Apologetically issuing to people of color an "anxious call to colorblindness: *Would that you would just not know, too*" (Williams 1997, 28), white people often implicitly insist that people of color should stop being aware of racial differences in treatment and status—which is to say, they should become more like white people.

WHITE INTENTIONS AND WHITE RESPONSIBILITY

At its core, the concept of white privilege denotes de facto racial advantages of which white people typically are not consciously aware. Those advantages and the accompanying white ignorance can be of all types, from not knowing that people of color often are tailed in boutique clothing stores, while they are not, to not knowing that the 2008 recession nearly doubled the gap in wealth between white and black Americans (Lubby 2012). In other words, white privilege can be personal and individual, or impersonal and structural, or both. The examples of white privilege provided in McIntosh's knapsack essay tend to be highly personal and individual, however, and when they involve institutional and structural privileges—such as the housing and financing market "allowing" one to buy a house where one wants to live, or K-12 educational materials that depict the race of one's child (McIntosh 1989, 10)—McIntosh presents them in terms of their personal effects on white people as individuals. Perhaps for this reason, philosophical scholarship on white privilege often focuses on the psychological dimensions of white privilege, underscoring its unintended nature. On this view, a white person can benefit from a system of white privilege without being biased or racist against people of color.

This focus has the two-pronged advantage of (1) helping white people to realize how racial advantage intimately operates in their own lives while (2) giving them a way to do this without becoming defensive and retreating from thinking about race and racism. By separating the issue of white racial advantage from white people's intentions and deliberate choices, the concept of white privilege provides a helpful response to the white claim, "I can't help it that I was born with white skin, so you can't blame me that white people are privileged!" Often the best response is "You're right, you didn't choose your race and no one is blaming you for being born white." Removing the feeling of being accused and blamed for situations that one did not choose can make it psychologically easier for white people to see how whiteness privileges them despite their intentions.

And yet this benefit is simultaneously a problem. The notion of white privilege can funnel white people's attention and energy into mere introspection and consciousness raising. White people's critical self-examination is not problematic in and of itself, and McIntosh's knapsack essay is an excellent exercise for that process. However, as some philosophers have charged, white self-examination through the concept of white privilege can become an end in itself, rather than a means toward racial justice for people of color. Instead of leading to political and other forms of action against racism, white privilege discourse often bogs down white people in anguished personal and confessional soul searching, leaving them floundering in their guilty awareness of their privileges (Kruks 2005, 183; Zack 2015, 3, 20–21). Precisely because white privilege is detached from white people's conscious intentions and choices, it can seem impossible to give up. "How, after all, could one give up a privilege that literally is in one's skin?" as Lewis Gordon (2004, 177) rhetorically demands. The concept of white privilege, then, ironically can lead to a further entrenchment of white domination by focusing attention on the distress and self-paralysis of well-intentioned white people rather than the needs and interests of people of color.

To address this concern, philosophers working with the concept of white privilege have underscored the need for white people to use white privilege against itself (Kruks 2005) and have argued that white people can and should take responsibility for their unconscious habits of white privilege (Sullivan 2006). The challenge remains, however, to ensure that the personal remains connected to the political when it comes to white people's involvement in racial justice movements. "What should white people do?" (Alcoff 1998). The answer to this question should "go beyond displaying the suffering and discomfort of [typically] women who are [racially] privileged" and to help white people "become subjects in planning and acting justly" with regard to race (Zack 2015, 23–24).

"White Privilege" Versus "White Supremacy" and "Global White Supremacy"

Even though the concept of white privilege includes institutional and structural inequalities that favor white people, perhaps because of the concept's frequent personal focus it has been criticized for "not hav[ing] the gravitas or urgency of either moral principle or social, institutional, and political action" (Zack 2015, 4). A similar charge is that the concept of white privilege does not capture the fact that race is a political system of domination. Philosophers such as Charles Mills thus prefer alternative terms such as "white supremacy" and "global white supremacy" to name ongoing systems of racial dominance and injustice. As Mills (1998, 98) explains, by "white supremacy" he means "a latitudinarian conception [of the term], one that encompasses de facto as well as de jure white privilege and refers more broadly to the European domination of the planet that has left us with the racialized distributions of economic, political, and cultural power that we have today." Mills adds, "we [also] could call it global white supremacy," and he argues for the concept because of its ability to bring out the racial dimensions of European colonialism and imperialism (1998, 98–99).

By using "white supremacy" as an umbrella term for both de jure and de facto white privilege—or, alternatively, "global white supremacy" to indicate the reach of these privileges across the world—Mills attempts to rework the term beyond its customary meaning. The term has the gravitas that "white privilege" does not, and it allows Mills to support his point that race and racism are political systems, not merely an incidental physiological feature of human life or a matter of individual bias. But the drawbacks of describing ongoing white advantages as "white supremacy" or even "global white supremacy" can outweigh its benefits. The customary meaning of "white supremacy" can interfere with the political efficacy of the term used in a latitudinarian way in a post–civil rights era.

"White supremacy" typically denotes two different, but somewhat related things. First, it means legalized white superiority: for example, the myriad laws governing race in the United States before the 1950s and 1960s civil rights movements, such as the 1857 *Dred Scott v. Sandford* US Supreme Court decision, which declared that black people had no rights to be respected, or the 1920 Mississippi state law forbidding the publishing or circulating of material in favor of social equality between white and black people (Hemingway 1921, 132). White supremacy in this sense no longer exists in the United States or in most other countries across the globe. This is not to say that white supremacy has been eradicated completely. Rather the term designates situations in which governments have formally and legally sanctioned white superiority, and those sanctions generally have been eliminated. To use "white supremacy" to designate informal systems of white advantage ("white privilege") thus is confusing at best and paves the way for dismissing the reality of white privilege at worst. As Naomi Zack (2015, 8) has argued, "present white advantages are not the result of a white supremacist system and to exaggerate the system of institutional racism or specific racist events, in those terms, is not only a conceptual error, but a political mistake." In addition to making it appear that white privilege is not real because white supremacy does not exist, calling this system "white supremacy" might actually grant it too much importance. Veering too far the other direction from "white privilege," the term "white supremacy" might make systems of white advantage seem monolithic, permanent, and thus impossible for people of color to overcome (2015, 8).

Another problem with the terms "white supremacy" and "global white supremacy" is that despite Mills's inclusion of various forms of white privilege in them, they tend to conjure up the second meaning of "white supremacy." This is the "big booted oppression" of the Ku Klux Klan and other violent white separatist groups (Williams 1997, 61). Unlike the first type of white supremacy, this form operates outside the law (although arguably the activities of the Klan and related groups were implicitly sanctioned by the US government for many decades). Despite their differences, extralegal white supremacy shares with its legalized cousin the characteristic of being explicit and visible, relatively easy to point to and identify because it identifies itself. This is the distinguishing feature of white supremacy, whatever its legal status. In contrast with the relatively subtle, unspoken, and invisible operations of white privilege, explicit, self-declared white supremacy typically is visible, sometimes even hypervisible.

Conflating the two forms of white advantage thus is a mistake, politically as well as conceptually. When twenty-first-century white privilege is equated with the white hoods, lynchings, and cross burnings of past white supremacy, it is easy for many white people to deny that white domination exists today in any kind of meaningful or prominent way. White supremacy has lost, so the thinking goes, conquered by the civil rights movement and relegated to ridicule when its members make bizarre appearances on daytime television. Those who are "complaining" about white supremacy are not working for racial justice. They are attempting to give people of color an unjust advantage over white people by means of reverse discrimination. Explicit or big-booted forms of white supremacy still exist both in the United States and across the globe, however. (On "hate music concerts" and other forms of contemporary Aryan hate in the United States, see Simi and Futrell 2015.) The term "white supremacy" is more effective for racial justice movements when it is reserved for these extremes. This creates the need for an additional concept that would acknowledge the decline of overt and legalized white domination (= white supremacy) and recognize that a great number of implicit forms of white domination continue to exist (= white privilege).

"WHITE PRIVILEGE" VERSUS WHITE CLASS DIFFERENCES

Which white people really benefit from these so-called white privileges, however? Do all white people benefit from them equally or in the same way? The answer to the latter question is no, which leads to another significant problem with the concept of white privilege. It tends to imply that all white people benefit from racial advantages to the same degree, lumping white people together into an indistinguishable, monolithic group. The term "white privilege" is not fine grained enough: it does not reflect class, ethnicity, gender, and other salient differences among white people. In particular, the concept of white privilege glosses over class differences among white people, erasing the ways in which middle- and upper-class white people serve as the normative model of whiteness. In Lewis Gordon's words, "the white-privilege argument creates an imaginary ideal whiteness as the norm for all whites. . ... Thus the larger populations of whites find themselves structured as a reality that has nothing to do with their lived experience" (2004, 176). If there are indeed informal advantages that some white people receive, they arguably do so not only because of their race (Zack 2015, 10). They do so because of their middle-to-upper-class status.

Poor, lower-class white people do not receive the same "wages of whiteness" that middle- and upper-class white people do (Du Bois 1998). Poor white people often are seen as the "white trash" of American society, denigrated and dumped on by middle- and upper-class white people for allegedly being too stupid, dirty, and uneducated to function as proper whites (Sullivan 2014). In addition, some middle- and upper-class people of color receive more societal privileges than lower-class white people do. Race and class, along with other salient axes of human life, are inextricably tangled together in systems of privilege. But this does not mean that race plays no role in awarding advantages to white people in the United States today. It also does not mean that the concept of whiteness necessarily should be abolished (as, for example, the journal *Race Traitor*, http://racetraitor.org, urges) and replaced by ethnic identities (for example, Irish, Italian, and so on) understood through the prism of class. Class differences between white people, as well as a smaller number of middle-to-upper-class people of color, often are used to buttress the racial privileges of middle-to-upper-class white people. The concept of whiteness is a useful analytic tool for understanding those complex relationships. Rather than drop the notion of white privilege, the term should be modified to *white class privilege* to better capture the stew of race and class that unevenly provides societal advantages to white people. As the concept of "white class privilege" is developed, moreover, it needs to be used as a tool of *intersectionality*. Intersectionality examines how identities and forms of oppression are interconnected and cannot be separated from each other. White class privilege is enmeshed with gendered, national, hemispheric, and other salient characteristics of human experience, and the ultimate point of understanding this tangle should be to eradicate all forms of injustice, not merely race and/or class oppression (May 2015).

"WHITE PRIVILEGE" VERSUS HUMAN RIGHTS

Finally, one of the primary criticisms of the concept of "white privilege" (and "white class privilege," by extension) is that what is in question are not privileges at all, but rights. McIntosh herself launched an early criticism of "white privilege" along these lines in her 1989 knapsack article. As McIntosh explains, the term "privilege" is not detailed or precise enough to capture the variety of advantages that unfairly accrue to white people. The instances of white privilege McIntosh provides include both "privileges" that a just society should provide everyone regardless of race, and "privileges" that effectively are a license to dominate and oppress others (1989, 11). One can think here of the difference between items in McIntosh's knapsack: for example, the privilege of being able to criticize one's government without penalty versus the privilege of remaining oblivious to the language and customs of other racial groups without penalty. The former is a "positive advantag[e] which we can work to spread" while the latter is a "negative typ[e] of advantag[e] which unless rejected will always reinforce our present hierarchies" (1989, 11). As McIntosh charges, referring to both of types of examples as "white privilege" can be misleading—for example, why would white people want to give up their ability to freely criticize the government?—and it tends to cover over systems of white dominance.

Although McIntosh does not reference human rights by name, her self-criticism approximates the charge that positive forms of white "privilege" are really rights and that *this* is why a just society would provide them to all people regardless of race. White people should not have to give up fundamental human rights in order to eliminate racial injustice. As Lewis Gordon (2004, 176) observes, criticizing positive forms of so-called white privilege "requires condemning whites for possessing, in the concrete, features of contemporary life that should be available to all, and if this is correct, how can whites be expected to give up such things?" The advantages that white people currently enjoy in comparison to most people of color are not extra perks that need to be taken away to level the racial playing field. In Zack's (2015, 4) words, a so-called white privilege actually "is a *right* that is protected for whites and not for nonwhites," and racial injustice primarily occurs because of the lack of protection of black and other people of color's human rights, not because white people have extra advantages on top of basic rights.

Consider the 2014 fatal shooting of Michael Brown in Ferguson, Missouri. An African American teenager, Brown was unarmed when he was gunned down by a white police officer, and the officer was not charged with any crime (CNN 2014). While the Fourteenth Amendment to the US Constitution ensures all citizens equal protection under the law, Brown received no such protection. His case is like that of many other African American men and boys, and the difference between how they and white men and boys are treated is unjust. In general, white men and boys can expect that their Fourteenth Amendment and other constitutional rights will not be ignored because of their race and that if law enforcement officers violate those rights, they will be prosecuted accordingly.

Is the injustice suffered by Michael Brown a product of white privilege? Is the problem that he did not get something extra that white people do? In an important respect, the answer to these questions is no. As Zack argues, surely "we have not sunk so low in American society that plain, simple, justice according to the Constitution must be regarded as a perk" (2015, xiii). The injustice of Michael Brown's death is not that white people have the "privilege" of having their constitutional rights respected. Rather it is that the same rights should be respected in all cases, including that of black people. The "crucial issue at stake is application of the forms of justice that are stated in U.S. Constitutional Amendments and the Civil Rights legislation of the 1960s, to black Americans," and the language of privilege is not particularly helpful in this respect (Zack 2015, xvi).

As this example demonstrates, the language of rights can be a powerful tool for addressing injustice. Whether one views human rights as preceding the law or instantiated by it, the discourse of rights establishes an explicit baseline for how all people should be treated and gives normative force to efforts to universally uphold that treatment. (Zack [2015, 16] argues the former, but I think the larger point is independent of that position.) Human rights discourse can be thought of as issuing a categorical imperative (Gordon 2004, 175). When a person's rights are violated, rights discourse is effective because it can clearly identify a law—be it legal or "merely" the moral law—that has been transgressed. Rights discourse functions best, in other words, when the treatment of a person alleged to be unjust is fairly easy to pick out and see, even if not everyone agrees that it was unjust.

Because rights discourse does not function as well in situations where social customs and habits create injustice, however, it cannot do all the work that social justice movements need. Something like the notion of white class privilege is still necessary to identify the extralegal advantages that middle-to-upper-class white people generally enjoy. (See also Eric Posner's [2014] argument that human rights law has failed because of its ambiguous and top-down nature.) Take the example of a middle-class white person who is pampered by a boutique clerk while a black person (even if middle class) is tailed by an undercover security person. Or consider the example of a city bus driver who waits for a white person running to catch the bus, but pulls away when a black person tries to run up and hop on. Nothing illegal has taken place in either case, but the difference in treatment nevertheless is unjust. White people, especially middle-to-upper-class ones, often are the beneficiaries of racial micro-kindnesses such as these, mirroring the racial micro-aggressions that often are inflicted on black and other people of color. Given the significant effects of chronic psychological and emotional stress on physiological health, "micro" in this context is not a synonym for "small" or "trivial." (For more on racial micro-kindnesses benefitting white people and the physiological effects of racialized stress, see Sullivan 2015, especially chapters three and four.) While it might not be as obvious or immediate as the macro-aggressions of bullets and chokeholds, racial micro-aggressions can and do kill, just as racial micro-kindnesses can and do support health and well-being.

In the case of Michael Brown, we can say both that his rights were violated and that white class privilege was in play, conditioning the perception of police officers (and others, including not just white people but potentially people of color). Middle-class white people typically are perceived as law-abiding and upstanding citizens apart from any particular action that they have taken, while black people and especially black men tend to be perceived as aggressive criminals. To understand fully the injustice of what happened in Ferguson, we need to grapple with both the black rights that were violated and the white class privilege that laid the groundwork for that violation.

And yet the question persists: Is "white class privilege" the best concept to use here? Calling middle-to-upper-class white people's extralegal racial advantages "privileges" can be misleading since the word "privilege" comes from the Latin *privus* and *lex*, meaning one's own law, or "exempt[ing] oneself from laws applied to others" (Gordon 2004, 174). When a white person is perceived as a model citizen (whether in a store, on the street, or elsewhere), she is not being exempted from a law that is being applied to others. Her relationship with the law is not the primary issue, and yet that is precisely what the term "privilege" tends to suggest. Here is where more work in the area of critical philosophy of race is needed, to develop a concept that accurately and fully captures the extralegal complexities of normative whiteness and white class advantage. In the twenty-first century, those advantages continue to combine with rights violations and, to a lesser degree, white supremacy, producing significant racial injustices for people of color.

REFERENCES

Alcoff, Linda Martín. (1998). "What Should White People Do?" *Hypatia* 13 (3): 6–26.

Alexander, Michelle. (2012). *The New Jim Crow: Mass Incarceration in the Age of Colorblindness*. New York: The New Pres.

Bidwell, Allie. (2015). "Racial Gaps in High School Graduation Rates Are Closing." March 16. *U.S. News and World Report*. Accessed June 1, 2015. http://www.usnews.com/news/blogs/data-mine/2015/03/16/federal-data-show-racial-gap-in-high-school-graduation-rates-is-closing.

Bossip. (2015). "Mainstream Media Still Pushes The White Beauty Standard, and We're Fed Up." Accessed May 26, 2015. http://bossip.com/1125218/cosmopolitan-magazine-black-models-beauty-donts-racist/.

CNN. 2014. "What Happened when Michael Brown met Officer Darren Wilson." Accessed May 30, 2015. http://www.cnn.com/interactive/2014/08/us/ferguson-brown-timeline/.

Du Bois, W. E. B. (1998). *Black Reconstruction in America: 1860–1880*. New York: The Free Press.

Du Bois, W. E. B. (1999). "The Souls of White Folk." In *Darkwater: Voices from Within the Veil*, 55–74. New York: Humanity Books.

Dunn, Andrew. (2015). "New Approach Leads to Drop in CMS Suspensions." *The Charlotte Observer*. May 31. Accessed June 1, 2015. http://www.charlotteobserver.com/news/local/education/article22631922.html.

Ebony. (1965). Special Issue on "The White Problem in America." August.

Gordon, Lewis R. (2004). "Critical Reflections on Three Popular Tropes in the Study of Whiteness." In *What White Looks Like: African-American Philosophers on the Whiteness Question*, edited by George Yancy, 173–194. New York: Routledge.

Hemingway, William. (1921). *The Annotated Mississippi Code, Supplement of 1921*. Indianapolis: The Bobbs-Merrill Company Publishers.

Kerby, Sophia. (2013). "How Pay Inequity Hurts Women of Color." *Center for American Progress*. Accessed May 26, 2015. https://www.americanprogress.org/issues/labor/report/2013/04/09/59731/how-pay-inequity-hurts-women-of-color/.

Kruks, Sonia. (2005). "Simone de Beauvoir and the Politics of Privilege." *Hypatia* 20 (1): 178–205.

Luhby, Tami. (2012). "Worsening Wealth Inequality by Race." *CNNMoney*. Accessed May 22, 2015. http://money.cnn.com/2012/06/21/news/economy/wealth-gap-race/.

Mauer, Marc, and Ryan S. King. (2007). "Uneven Justice: State Rates of Incarceration By Race and Ethnicity." *The Sentencing Project*. Accessed May 26, 2015. http://www.sentencingproject.org/doc/publications/rd_stateratesofincbyraceandethnicity.pdf.

May, Vivian. (2015). *Pursuing Intersectionality, Unsettling Dominant Imaginaries*. New York: Routledge.

McIntosh, Peggy. (1989). "White Privilege: Unpacking the Invisible Knapsack." *Peace and Freedom* July/August: 10–12.

Mills, Charles. (1998). *Blackness Visible*. Ithaca, NY: Cornell University Press.

Mills, Charles. (2008). "White Ignorance." In *Race and Epistemologies of Ignorance*, edited by Shannon Sullivan and Nancy Tuana, 13–38. Albany: State University of New York Press.

Posner, Eric. (2014). *The Twilight of Human Rights Law*. New York: Oxford University Press.

Roberts, Dorothy. (2002). *Shattered Bonds: The Color of Child Welfare*. New York: Basic Books.

Simi, Pete, and Robert Futrell. (2015). *American Swastika: Inside the White Power Movement's Hidden Spaces of Hate*. Lanham, MD: Rowman and Littlefield.

Smedley, Brian, Michael Jeffries, Larry Adelman, and Jean Cheng. (n.d.). "Briefing Paper: Race, Racial Inequality, and Health Inequalities: Separating Myth from Fact." Accessed May 22, 2015. http://www.unnaturalcauses.org/assets/uploads/file/Race_Racial_Inequality_Health.pdf.

Sullivan, Shannon. (2006). *Revealing Whiteness: The Unconscious Habits of Racial Privilege.* Bloomington: Indiana University Press.

Sullivan, Shannon. (2014). *Good White People: The Problem with Middle-Class White Anti-Racism.* Albany: State University of New York Press.

Sullivan, Shannon. (2015). *The Physiology of Sexist and Racist Oppression.* New York: Oxford University Press.

Williams, Patricia J. (1997). *Seeing a Color-blind Future: The Paradox of Race.* New York: The Noonday Press.

Zack, Naomi. (2015). *White Privilege and Black Rights: The Injustice of U.S. Police Racial Profiling and Homicide.* Lanham, MD: Rowman and Littlefield.

CHAPTER 29

··

THE RACIALIZATION OF MUSLIMS IN THE POST-9/11 UNITED STATES

··

FALGUNI A. SHETH

ALTHOUGH it is conventional to suggest that attacks on 9/11 changed the world as Americans (and others globally) understood it, I want to suggest a Copernican turn in thinking about the aftereffects of 9/11. Certainly, it is the case that the myth of American immunity from political violence, or American exceptionalism, namely that the United States was untouchable by the violence that seemed to affect the rest of the world, was shattered on September 11, 2001. However, this myth emerges in a vacuum—without an exploration of the history and context that preceded 9/11. Despite appearances to the contrary, the US government's legal and political response to 9/11 reflected the unfettering of political, law enforcement, and military constraints in order to depict the US's potential towering sheer might "against the terrorists." This display was also mirrored through the authorization of the war against Iraq (widely agreed to be an irrelevant response to 9/11).

I want to argue for a functional account of race, in which laws and public policies are used to render certain populations vulnerable, possibly criminalizing them, rendering them without legal or political protection, and creating a hostile environment in which those populations are vilified and susceptible to political, social, and cultural targeting by the larger society around them. Muslims in the post-9/11 United States have become racialized through a series of laws and public policies ostensibly designed to protect the American public. However, the US's social and political approach to law and public policy to buttress national security has created a hostile context for Muslims. Ultimately, it has been effective in rendering them not just a religious group that has been discriminated against, but it has racialized them and led to their vilification and dehumanization as a racial group.

In effect, by instituting a short-term emergency response to the September 11 attacks—one which has been renewed multiple times in the last fifteen years, the US government facilitated a new stage in the history of racial profiling that did less to intercept terrorists than it did to reconstruct a new architecture of racial hierarchy. The new policies and laws instituted in the name of conducting a War on Terror have contributed to the racialization of (mostly) men and (more recently) women of Middle Eastern, Muslim, and South Asian backgrounds. As well, the language of preemptive policing and the "War on Terror" have facilitated the ever-expanding theater for the racial profiling of other populations who are associated with controversial public policy issues related to who belongs to the nation.

TECHNOLOGIES OF LAW AND RACE

The events of 9/11, broadly agreed to be a terrorist act, engendered a new political, cultural, and legal epoch referred to as the "War on Terror." This epoch was facilitated by the nearly unanimous passage of the USA PATRIOT Act by the US Congress within six weeks of September 11, 2001 (*USA PATRIOT Act* 2001). The key framework of the PATRIOT Act was "preemptive policing," which explicitly reversed the long-rehearsed (at least rhetorically) US Constitutional admonition of "innocent until proven guilty." Preemptive policing, in effect, was a form of racial profiling for "potential terrorists." However, even though the demographics of the nineteen attackers were fairly clear and distinct (mostly Saudi and part of Al-Qaeda), the hunt for terrorists was rather generally translated into an expansive hunt for Middle Eastern/Arab/South Asian Muslims (9/11 Commission on Terrorist Attacks Upon the United States 2004).

Corresponding to the USA Patriot Act was the creation of a new governmental office: the Department of Homeland Security (DHS) in January 2002 ("Creation of the Department of Homeland Security" 2015). The DHS was inaugurated to guard the "Homeland" against foreign enemies or sabotage. As part of its new provenance, immigration enforcement and services were shifted to the DHS, with various responsibilities divided into three parts: United States Citizenship and Immigration (USCIS); Immigration and Customs Enforcement (ICE); and Customs and Border Patrol. The role of the DHS engendered a new way to think about the United States in the aftermath of the trauma of 9/11: as a homeland to be guarded at all costs against foreign enemies, rather than as a polity where all residents would be given due process.

THE WAR ON TERROR: WARRANTED OR
A TECHNOLOGY OF RACE?

How should we understand the War on Terror in relation to Muslims? Is the War on Terror merely an analytical approach to finding terrorists, while leaving a few psychic, punitive, or existential casualties? Or does it lead to a more nefarious and less productive outcome? And how do we know? A standard response to criticism of the War on Terror has been that the United States must protect itself in response to terrorist threats, and national security mandates that those who are hostile to Americans or the United States as a predominantly Christian nation be viewed with skepticism and scrutiny. If there are Muslims who are mistakenly caught up in the hunt, and mistakenly harmed, that is collateral damage, and it is a small price to pay to keep the United States safe. Such a view can ostensibly be located in a conventional utilitarian framework: Does the number of people kept safe outweigh the number of people harmed? At one level, this seems like a solid and simple calculation: Given that the United States has over 300 million residents, the benefits of keeping them safe clearly outweigh the harm of racial profiling, preemptively policing, and incarcerating thousands of Muslims without a trial.

However, through a philosophy of race approach that understands race as a technology of division and management, we might want to consider what 'harm' looks like in relation to Muslims, non-Muslims, and global peacekeeping obligations. "Harm," broadly construed, does not necessarily mean exclusively physical violence to those who are falsely targeted in the hunt for terrorists. By harm, I mean long-term deleterious effects and living conditions that affect one's ability to lead a life that is absent of the fear of being politically, culturally, or socially targeted, and not merely hurt, as Joel Feinberg makes the distinction (Feinberg 1984,45). If we think of harm as the fear and worry affecting Muslims who are not targeted, but who live with the daily threat of being falsely suspected of terrorist proclivities; or non-Muslims who might be construed as Muslims; all vulnerable residents of a polity might be affected by policies that, only explicitly, are intended to "root out" the evil, but in fact can be deployed toward other "unruly," threatening, or irritating populations (Sheth 2004). Ethnic historical narratives have illustrated this tendency repeatedly: from the targeting of slaves and free blacks in the United States, to Japanese Americans and other Asian populations through Alien Land Laws (Aoki 1998) and antimiscegenation laws (Pascoe 1996), to the targeting of lesbians, gays, and disabled populations under the German regime. There are many such instances of the ever-widening scope of targeting of unliked populations by a majority or dominant population (Sheth 2009, chap. 6).

There is another aspect to consider here: Are public policies and laws necessarily race-neutral? Most public policies assume that they will be applied to all equally; that only wrong-doers will be in violation of them, and hence that punishment and justice are equal and fair. But this premise is predicated upon the idea that most polities have a fair playing field, which as Charles Mills argues, is untrue (Mills 1997).

TECHNOLOGIES: BIOPOLITICS, RACE, AND ONTOPOLITICS

Mills argues that the Racial Contract is the counterpart and foundation of the idea of the Social Contract. As such, it facilitates a racial hierarchy between *persons* and *subpersons*, by which nonwhites are subject to a subhuman status through and at the expense of whites. Mills points to the purpose of the Racial Contract as "always the differential privileging of the whites as a group with respect to the nonwhites as a group, the exploitations of their bodies, land, and resources, and the denial of socioeconomic opportunities to them" (Mills 1997, 11). He adds that "[a]ll whites are beneficiaries of the Contract, though some whites are not *signatories* to it" (Mills 1997, 11).

The main premise of the Racial Contract is that some populations are already more politically vulnerable than others—especially those that are already racially, culturally, and socially marginalized. As such, how laws are written often has an enormous differential impact, as Dorothy Roberts illustrates so well (Roberts 1997, chap. 4). To a large extent this is because the passage of various public policies often plays to public fear and hostilities, cementing them and confirming them, rather than reflecting productive or effective strategies to deal with social problems. One critical approach to the question of the War on Terror would ask about the contents and creation of the USA PATRIOT Act, and some of its concomitant and emergent laws.

While considering the Racial Contract in the context of US history results in an emphasis on how blacks have been treated, it would be conceptually limiting to restrict our analysis to the stark systemic dynamics between whites and blacks within the domestic confines of the United States. There is a certain applicability of the Racial Contract to a range of other nonwhite populations, on both sides of the racial hierarchy. Thus, for example, we could consider the intensive war against black Americans—as conducted by both white and nonwhite police officers, the war against undocumented migrants, and, as I do here, the War on Terror, as waged against darker populations in the United States. In addition, internationally there is widescale physical and psychic degradation of suspected terrorists—as engaged "off-site" by white and nonwhite agents for the CIA and the US government to be part of the Racial Contract ("Senate Select Committee on Intelligence: Committee Study of the Central Intelligence Agency's Detention and Interrogation Program" 2014). All of these practices were initiated or continued and facilitated over the course of the last two US presidential administrations.

In these examples, the stark racial divide between whiteness and nonwhiteness does not map squarely onto the contemporary US Racial Contract. That messiness suggests that white supremacy is now less about skin color and more a matter of the dynamics of institutional and legal power. In this sense, consideration of the Racial Contract works in tandem with Michel Foucault's ideas about biopolitics, governmentality, and race (Foucault 2003; January 18 and 25 lectures). Foucault explored the ways in which disciplinary and regulatory power are exerted to manage populations. Through his painstaking illustrations of discipline and biopower, we see that the effects of laws can never be neutrally applied to any population, and that power itself is always exerted on behalf of some, and against others.

Foucault goes a step further and argues that the way that sovereign power manages populations is by managing the right of life and death—more precisely by controlling the right to kill. In contemporary times, that right is exemplified through forcing some to live and allowing others to die. It is, as Foucault suggests, a "'biopolitics' of the human race." It is, in other words, a form of racism (Foucault 2003, March 17, 1976 lecture). He defines racism as follows:

> [Racism] is primarily a way of introducing a break into the domain of life that is under power's control: the break between what must live and what must die. The appearance within the biological continuum of the human race of races, the distinction among races, the hierarchy of races, the fact that certain races are described as good and that others, in contrast, are described as inferior: all this is a way of fragmenting the field of the biological that power controls. *It is a way of separating out the groups that exist within a population.* It is, in short, a way of establishing a biological-type caesura within a populations that appears to be a biological domain. This will allow power to treat that population as a mixture of races, or to be more accurate, to treat the species, to subdivide the species it controls, into the subspecies known, precisely, as races. This is the first function of racism: to fragment, to create caesuras within the biological continuum addressed by biopower. (Foucault 2003, 254–255; emphasis mine)

Racism then is a divide that can be controlled and directed through sovereign power; moreover, it has the additional function of inducing a relationship of war that underlies society

(Foucault 2003, 255). This war need not be military in style, but rather engaged in through various regulatory mechanisms: public policies, statutes, laws, and so on. Through Foucault's framework of biopower and racism, we can see how a federal law such as the USA Patriot Act might be read as something other than a pragmatic approach to intercepting terrorists for the purposes of National Security, namely by creating the conditions by which the War on Terror is a mode of expanding state power, while leaving minority populations unprotected from the mistaken, careless (and unaccountable), or overreaching vagaries of the representatives of sovereign power: NSA policies; CIA and ICE agents; federal, state, and local law enforcement agencies; immigration and secure communities laws (Foley 2015; Khan 2015); material support statutes; and speech statutes that punish some portions of the populations and not others (Hong 2015).

Foucault's work on biopolitics and race is predicated on technologies of production and power. He defines four of them, but I want to highlight only two of them here: "technologies of production, which permit us to produce, transform, or manipulate things," and, "technologies of power, which determine the conduct of individuals and submit them to certain ends or domination, an objectivizing of the subject" (Foucault 1988, 18). As mentioned, these two operate with other technologies in which subjects themselves conform to disciplinary efforts, but I emphasize these two since they reflect the ways in which the USA Patriot Act and other policies and regulations have enabled the racialization of Muslims in the post-9/11 era. I have argued elsewhere that race is a technology of law. Technology, as I develop my understanding elsewhere, is more than merely instrumental. It has a processing function, a concealment function, and a specific public appearance, in the same way that a tractor on a farm inhales the wheat and chaff, separates them, and transforms raw material into some other, digestible form (Sheth 2004). According to Martin Heidegger, technology is also something that is not necessarily intentionally and deliberately applied in a neutral vacuum, but rather is already part and parcel of a social, political apparatus (Heidegger 1950). In this formulation, I suggest, race as a technology has three primary functions: to take up and process that which is threatening, and ultimately to conceal this function as violence within sovereign power, by proposing it as a pragmatic, neutral solution to the threat (Sheth 2009, chap. 1).

On this premise, then, the USA PATRIOT Act is a piece of legislation that upended the legal, political, and cultural framework upon which the US polity was predicated: it opened up a space, as mentioned earlier, for the preemptive policing of potential threats, by insisting that such policing was necessary for the effective anticipation and apprehension of threats. In doing so, it neglected or pushed back the prevalent rhetorical discourse of the US legal framework of producing charges or accusations and providing evidence to demonstrate the veracity of the charges prior to sentencing. Of course, as antiprison and antiblack racism scholars and activists have attested, the old framework of "innocent until proven guilty" was not generally applied to African American or other minority citizens of the United States (Davis 2003; Alexander 2010).

As well, the expansiveness of the USA Patriot act enabled other sweeping and invasive pieces of legislation to be expanded and enforced anew. Material support statutes, or those which criminalize the aiding and abetting of terrorists through dubious practices of association, such as providing a couch for a "suspected" terrorist to sleep on (perhaps because he was a sibling or an old school friend) (Rovner and Theoharis 2012), or donating money to an international charity that was post facto deemed by the State Department to be an organization that supported terrorists (Gosztola 2012), would also apprehend those in their dragnet who were considered "sympathetic" to terrorism, regardless of the demonstrability of those charges.

There were additional legal statutes that were dusted off and circumvented, such as the 1977–8 FISA (Foreign Intelligence Surveillance Act), allowing for warrantless surveillance of "suspected" terrorists outside of the United States (Risen and Lichtblau 2005). Newly instituted was a government-created database of No-Fly List passengers (Bonner 2015), the names of which were kept secret unless they visited an airport in order to travel. Even though federal judges have ruled that no-fly lists are unconstitutional, there still is no way to find out whether one's name is on the list, which makes it infinitely more difficult to challenge the government, although some have done so successfully after having been caught in that dragnet (Sullivan 2014).

There is another level of racialization that augments biopolitics. Biopolitics by itself cannot account for the ambiguity and elisions between the category of "terrorists," "Muslims," and other seemingly dangerous or "unruly" populations. In part, this is because the racial limits of the population of "suspected terrorists" seems to expand and shift directions depending upon various political controversies or fears that are highlighted at various points since 9/11. As such, I want to suggest *ontopolitics*, as a form of politics that can operate alongside biopolitics. As I have suggested elsewhere, the scope of management of ontopolitics includes:

> non-biological, indeed moral, cultural, social, ontological categories that are recalled by Foucault in *Abnormal*, among other writings. Moreover, ontopower—as a mode of inscribing racism, parallels a Foucauldian dialectic between sovereignty, (disciplinary/regulatory) power, and population. The framework of ontopolitics—like biopolitics—requires a simultaneous analysis of discourse and power, as well as juridical sovereignty (through the forms of criminal, migration, anti-terrorist laws), in addition to sequestering practices such as detention centers, public safety hearings, anti-mosque/Islam regulations or zoning, etc.,—in order to trace ontopolitical racism. (Sheth 2011, 55)

The laws adopted in the aftermath of 9/11, while ostensibly designed to police crime and apprehend criminals who were a danger to the polity, were problematic because they are based not on demonstrable evidence of criminality, but on cultural ignorance tied to moral judgment, along with ungrounded sensational stereotypes and fears of Muslim men and women, and a myopia based on a monolithic understanding of Islam. As we know, of any cultural, political, social, religious, racial, or ethnic group, there are very few, if any, commitments that all members of the group have in common. As such, to assume that most or all Muslims subscribe to principles of destruction or harm or injury, merely because some who identify as Muslim behave in this way, is to vastly and illogically overgeneralize about a group of people as complex as any other group: Christian, Hindu, Jewish. While it is understandable that such fears can beset us during times of violence and chaos, our ability to think through conflations, fears, and overdetermination can be especially useful in order to avoid waging hate and hostility against feared and unknown populations.

Through the lens of biopolitics and ontopolitics, then, we can explore the ways that the racializing of Muslims, as well as other populations such as Latinos, is already prepared through a political-legal apparatus that takes as its premise that "foreigners,"—those who are not easily assimilated as Americans, or part of white supremacy—are necessarily understood as cultural, political, existential enemies to the polity and must be surveilled, guarded, and otherwise managed, vilified, or quarantined.

THE RACIAL COMPLEXITIES OF THE HOMELAND

What does it mean to discuss the "racialization" of Muslims? Aren't Muslims a religious group? As such, isn't racism an inappropriate term for Islamophobia? It is true that if what people despised, feared, or hated was the religion of Islam, and discriminated, harassed, or persecuted based on Islamic religion, then this would be a case of religious discrimination or bigotry, rather than racism. However, it is also clear that most people, including various national governments, who engage in policies or acts of discrimination, do not know with much accuracy what the tenets of Islam are, let alone what Muslims believe. Widespread cultural and social fear and hostility of "Muslims" is not being directed against Muslims exclusively, but against the "trope" of Muslims, or against the figure of "The Muslim." That is, it is being directed against an image of what Muslims must be: darker but often nonblack populations who are interpellated as being from the Middle East. Much of this is often led through sovereign power, through the governmental management of populations, and through ontopolitics. In what follows, let me suggest an augmentation, or variation, of the Racial Contract, ontopolitics, and of additional technologies of race, as these are embedded in the notion of the Homeland.

The Homeland has become a new racial imaginary for the United States. It came into visibility in the various state-led, media-driven, and racial-cultural responses to the events of September 11, 2001. As mentioned earlier, it was officially inaugurated through the creation of the Department of Homeland Security in 2002, which was to oversee all things related to the War on Terror and immigration. There was, of course, a strong association between those two. Homeland calls to mind *Heimat*, with all of its affective associations, ethnic ties, and cultural unity, as linked with Austria and Germany during 1920s and 1930s (Blickle 2002). *Heimat*, broadly echoing the notion of Home and cultural unity, evokes a similar sense of the norms and superiority of the US Homeland; ironically, Michael Chertoff, the first director of the Department of Homeland Security purported to be unaware of the unsavory associations of Homeland (Becker 2002). The Homeland allows for the possibility of understanding the Racial Contract as it applies to persons, subpersons, and nonpersons, such as Latino migrants and peoples of Muslim/Middle Eastern/South Asian (MEMSA) descent, who are most recently among the nonsignatories. The contours of the Homeland also allows us to see a slightly different dimension of white supremacy, as it accommodates and absorbs certain nonwhites in the name of a united America.

Since its explicit invocation, the Homeland has remained strongly tangible, illustrating certain political antagonisms between populations who might otherwise be allied. These antagonisms revealed a new configuration of "white supremacy," in which the membership of populations of color has become more frequent. The associations between (seemingly) non-Muslims and whites have become part of a national imaginary of patriotic unity. In this seemingly color-blind configuration, "true Americans" are united in their support of certain jingoist agendas like the War on Terror, in which the casual genocide of Iraqi and Afghani civilians, and the droning of Pakistani and Yemeni civilians has become a by-product of

"National"/"Homeland" Security. The image of patriotic unity has shifted in terms of colors and hues; it encompasses various strata and political ranks—from Congress politicians to ordinary Democrats and Republicans, academics, feminists, and antiracist activists. The contours of support for the War on Terror ebbs and flows depending on various factors, including whether it is an election year.

As well, there has been a sustained renewal of an anti-immigrant agenda, which also calls into question the narrow racial formation of white supremacy. At the federal and state levels, we have seen not only white, but multiple black, Latino, and Asian officials, who have for six years led a charge against undocumented migrants appearing as mostly Latino (Gonzalez-Barrera and Krogstad 2014). And finally, most recently, there has been a renewed attention to white police violence as directed against young black boys, girls, men, and women, even as there have been many nonwhite police officers who are implicated in incidents of political violence. Nonwhite police officers are also targets of violence (Mueller and Baker 2014).

THE POST-9/11 LANDSCAPE: RACIALIZING MUSLIMS AND OTHER OTHERS

Due to the new post-9/11 landscape, those perceived as Muslim are being racialized, often more with a view to the expansion of state power in the name of National Security, rather than through an effective hunt for terrorists. It is also worth considering the open hostility that Syrian refugees have met, due to the illogical, but racialized, association between the November 2015 Paris bombings and the mass migration from Syria, and concomitant pleas for refuge in the United States and Europe. After the Paris bombings, the US governors of over thirty states declared that they would no longer accept Syrian refugees due to the threat of terrorism, even though there are no connections between the perpetrators of the Paris attacks and Syrian Islamic extremists (Fantz and Brumfield 2015). Prior to the Paris bombings, leaders of European and other nations, from Hungary to Austria, were either openly declaring their opposition to accepting Syrian Muslims into Christian countries or were quietly "offshoring" them to other countries (Al-Jazeera 2015; Kleinfeld 2015). It is notable that in the run up to the 2016 presidential elections, multiple presidential candidates are openly discussing the banning of Muslims from the American polity and gaining significant leads in the pre-election polls as a result (Berman 2015; Ferguson 2015).

While it would be gratuitous to speculate here about the connection between the US-led War on Terror program domestically and internationally, and the Syrian crisis, it is noteworthy that fifteen years of active racializing and discrimination against Muslims in the United States, and the broadly indiscriminate targeting of Muslims internationally, has melded seamlessly into an intense and acceptable worldwide hostility toward Muslims, regardless of their religious views, opposition to Islamic extremism, or their general comportment. As a result, Muslim hating, and race baiting against Muslims by political leaders around the world, seems to suggest that it is perfectly acceptable to wage a legal, cultural, military, and political war against Muslims, in the name of "National Security" and political profit. There seems to be ample evidence that the War on Terror, seen through the lens of philosophy and race, has been an effective way, not to fight terrorism, but to lead to the increasing vulnerability and vilification—the racialization—of Muslims around the world.

REFERENCES

9/11 Commission on Terrorist Attacks Upon the United States. (2004). "The 9/11 Commission Report." Accessed May 16, 2016. http://www.9-11commission.gov/report/911Report.pdf.

Alexander, Michelle. (2010). *The New Jim Crow: Mass Incarceration in the Age of Colorblindness*. New York and London: New Press.

Al-Jazeera. (2015). "Hungarian PM: We Don't Want More Muslims." September 4. Accessed May 16, 2016. http://www.aljazeera.com/news/2015/09/refugees-hungary-train-station-150903064140564.html.

Aoki, Keith. (1998). "No Right to Own?: The Early Twentieth-Century 'Alien Land Law' as a Prelude to Internment.'" *Boston College Law Review* 40: 37–72.

Becker, Elizabeth. (2002). "Prickly Roots of 'Homeland Security.'" *New York Times*, August 31. Accessed May 16, 2016. http://www.nytimes.com/2002/08/31/us/washington-talk-prickly-roots-of-homeland-security.html.

Berman, Russell. (2015). "Donald Trump's Call to Ban Muslim Immigrants." *The Atlantic Monthly*, December 7. Accessed May 16, 2016. http://www.theatlantic.com/politics/archive/2015/12/donald-trumps-call-to-ban-muslim-immigrants/419298/.

Blickle, Peter. (2002). *Heimat: A Critical Theory of the German Idea of Homeland*. Rochester, NY: Camden House.

Bonner, Raymond. (2015). "One Woman's Case Proves: It's Basically Impossible to Get Off the 'No-Fly List.'" *The Daily Beast*, December 15. http://www.thedailybeast.com/articles/2015/12/15/one-woman-s-case-proves-it-s-basically-impossible-to-get-off-the-no-fly-list.html.

"Creation of the Department of Homeland Security." (2015). *US Government Office*. Accessed December 14. http://www.dhs.gov/creation-department-homeland-security.

Davis, Angela. (2003). "Racialized Punishment and Prison Abolition." In *A Companion to African-American Philosophy*, edited by Tommy Lott and John P. Pittman, 360–68. Malden, MA: Blackwell.

Fantz, Ashley, and Ben Brumfield. (2015). "More than Half the Nation's Governors Say Syrian Refugees Not Welcome." *CNN.com*. Accessed May 16, 2016. http://www.cnn.com/2015/11/16/world/paris-attacks-syrian-refugees-backlash/.

Feinberg, Joel. (1984). *Harm to Others*. Vol. 1. New York: Oxford University Press.

Ferguson, David. (2015). "Ben Carson Calls Fear of Muslims 'a Gift'—Plans to Defeat ISIS with Probe of Muslim Civil Rights Group." *Raw Story*, December 15. Accessed May 16, 2016. http://www.rawstory.com/2015/12/ben-carson-calls-fear-of-muslims-a-gift-plans-to-defeat-isis-with-probe-of-muslim-civil-rights-group/.

Foley, Elise. (2015). "Obama Faces Growing Rebellion Against The Secure Communities Deportation Program." *The Huffington Post*, April 24. Accessed May 16, 2016. http://www.huffingtonpost.com/2014/04/24/secure-communities_n_5182876.html.

Foucault, Michel. (1988). "Lectures at Vermont University in October 1982." In *Technologies of the Self*, edited by Luther H. Martin, Huck Gutman, and Patrick Hutton, 16–49. Amherst: University of Massachusetts Press.

Foucault, Michel. (2003). *Society Must Be Defended: Lectures at the Collège de France 1975–76*. Translated by David Macey. New York: Picador Press.

Gonzalez-Barrera, Ana, and Jens Manuel Krogstad. (2014). "U.S. Deportations of Immigrants Reach Record High in 2013 | Pew Research Center." *Pew Research Center*. Accessed May 16, 2016. http://www.pewresearch.org/fact-tank/2014/10/02/u-s-deportations-of-immigrants-reach-record-high-in-2013/.

Gosztola, Kevin. (2012). "HSBC Bankers Get No Jail Time for Terrorist Financing While Somali Sentenced for Charity." *Shadow Proof*, December 16. Accessed May 16, 2016. https://shadowproof.com/2012/12/16/hsbc-executives-get-no-jail-time-for-terrorist-financing-while-somali-sentenced-for-giving/.

Heidegger, Martin. (1950). "Question Concerning Technology." In *Martin Heidegger: Basic Writings (1977)*. New York: Harper & Row.

Hong, Nicole. (2015). "'Material Support' Statute Is Front and Center in Antiterror Push." *The Wall Street Journal*, May 27. Accessed May 16, 2016. http://www.wsj.com/articles/material-support-statute-is-front-and-center-in-antiterror-push-1432719002.

Khan, Naureen. (2015). "Five Years after SB 1070, Arizona Immigrants Defy Climate of Intimidation." *Al Jazeera*, March 23. Accessed May 16, 2016. http://america.aljazeera.com/articles/2015/3/23/five-years-after-sb-1070-arizona-immigrants-defy-law.html.

Kleinfeld, Philip. (2015). "Austria Accused of 'Outsourcing' Syrians to Slovakia." *Aljazeera*, October 19. Accessed May 16, 2016. http://www.aljazeera.com/indepth/features/2015/10/austria-accused-outsourcing-syrians-slovakia-151012095750675.html.

Mills, Charles. (1997). *The Racial Contract*. Ithaca, NY: Cornell University Press.

Mueller, Benjamin, and Al Baker. (2014). "2 N.Y.P.D. Officers Killed in Brooklyn Ambush; Suspect Commits Suicide." *The New York Times*, December 20. Accessed May 16, 2016. http://www.nytimes.com/2014/12/21/nyregion/two-police-officers-shot-in-their-patrol-car-in-brooklyn.html.

Pascoe, Peggy. (1996). "Miscegenation Law, Court Cases and Ideologies of 'Race' in Twentieth Century America." *The Journal of American History* 83 (1): 44–69.

Risen, James, and Eric Lichtblau. (2005). "Bush Lets U.S. Spy on Callers Without Courts." *New York Times*, December 16. Accessed May 16, 2016. http://www.nytimes.com/2005/12/16/politics/bush-lets-us-spy-on-callers-without-courts.html.

Roberts, Dorothy E. (1997). *Killing the Black Body: Race, Reproduction, and the Meaning of Liberty*. New York: Vintage books.

Rovner, Laura, and Jeanne Theoharis. (2012). "Preferring Order to Justice." *American University Law Review* 61 (5): 1331–1415.

"Senate Select Committee on Intelligence: Committee Study of the Central Intelligence Agency's Detention and Interrogation Program." (2014). Declassified Executive Summary. Washington, DC: US Senate.

Sheth, Falguni A. (2004). "The Technology of Race: Enframing, Violence, and Taming the Unruly." *Radical Philosophy Review* 7 (1): 77–98.

Sheth, Falguni A. (2009). *Toward a Political Philosophy of Race*. Albany: State University of New York Press.

Sheth, Falguni. (2011). "The War on Terror and Ontopolitics: Concerns with Foucault's Account of Race, Power Sovereignty." *Foucault Studies* 12 (September): 51–76.

Sullivan, Gail. (2014). "Why the No-Fly List Was Declared Unconstitutional." *Washington Post*, June 25. Accessed May 16, 2016. https://www.washingtonpost.com/news/morning-mix/wp/2014/06/25/judge-rules-no-fly-list-unconstitutional/.

USA PATRIOT Act. (2001). *115 Stat. 272*. Accessed May 16, 2016. https://www.gpo.gov/fdsys/pkg/PLAW-107publ56/html/PLAW-107publ56.htm.

CHAPTER 30

STATE RACISM, STATE VIOLENCE, AND VULNERABLE SOLIDARITY

MYISHA CHERRY

IN 2014, #BlackLivesMatter, a popular hashtag started by three black queer women–Alicia Garza, Patrisse Cullors, and Opal Tometi—exploded all over social media. The women created the hashtag as a call to action after the death of seventeen-year-old Trayvon Martin at the hands of George Zimmerman, who at the time was not being held accountable for the crime. #BlackLivesMatter soon turned into a movement that sought to bring attention to and fight against the seemingly increasing state violence against black people. Activists on social media and in the streets, declared "# Black Lives Matter!" when Michael Brown was killed by a Ferguson Police officer; twelve-year-old Tamir Rice was killed by a Cleveland police officer; Freddie Gray was found dead in a police van; Eric Garner was killed by the NYPD; and Sandra Bland was arrested for refusing to put out her cigarette and eventually found dead in her cell. What makes this hashtag unique is the implication that it isn't only *some* black lives that matter, that is, not only the mostly commonly referenced male lives. Rather, the hashtag suggests that *all* black lives matter, including queer, trans, disabled, and female. This movement includes all those black lives who have been marginalized within the black liberation tradition, as well as in greater society. The movement highlights the ways in which black people have been traditionally deprived of dignity and human rights.

In an essay penned in "The Feminist Wire," Alicia Garza states:

> Black Lives Matter does not mean your life isn't important—it means that Black lives, which are seen as without value within White supremacy, are important to your liberation. Given the disproportionate impact state violence has on Black lives, we understand that when Black people in this county get free, the benefits will be wide reaching and transformative for society as a whole. (2014)

Despite the intention, the message fueling the Black Lives Matter movement has been co-opted, dismissed, and misunderstood by politicians, celebrities, and allies. On July 31, 2015, Officer Sean Bolton was allegedly shot and killed by Tremaine Wilbourn while conducting a traffic stop in Memphis, Tennessee. The officer was white; the suspect was black. During a press conference, Memphis's Director of Police Services, Tony Armstrong (who is also black), noted that the shooting is a reminder of how dangerous their jobs are. Noting that this was his fourth time in 2015 announcing the death of an officer, he stated: "There's a theme that 'Black Lives Matter.' And at the end of the day, we have to ask ourselves 'Do *All* Lives Matter?' Regardless of race, creed, color, economic status, what profession that person holds, 'All Lives [Do] Matter' " (Karimi and Shoichet 2015).

While "All Lives Matter" is true in theory, in practice, some lives do not matter. This makes the "All Lives Matter" rhetoric extremely problematic. In a civic democracy where belonging and acknowledgment are key, how has it come about that only some lives matter and at the same time, some accept the "All Lives Matter" rhetoric as tenable? Michel Foucault gives us some insight on how state racism creates hierarchies that determine which lives matter. Malcolm X shows how the state uses the media and statistics to perpetuate the myth of black criminality and thus justifies state violence against certain groups. Instead of adopting nihilism, Malcolm X reminds us of the power of the people to challenge and transform systems and structures whose practices have contributed to the elimination of black bodies. The exercise of this power through democratic procedures and organizing around collective vulnerabilities is what is needed to ensure that all lives can actually matter, not only in theory but also in practice.

We need to understand how it has come about that only some lives matter. Foucault offers useful tools for understanding why some lives do not matter, in his analysis of the superrace and subrace within a society. At the same time, the use of antiblack crime statistics as a self-fulfilling prophecy has justified excluding the subrace from the group of lives that matter. Malcolm X provided a parallel analysis of racial oppression in the United States, and also a path toward "more lives mattering" through democratic procedures. The idea is for the people to use their power to make all lives matter.

DO ALL LIVES MATTER?

Armstrong's comments were not unique. Some celebrities and so-called white allies responded to the hashtag "Black Lives Matter" on the Internet with the new hashtag "All Lives Matter." However, Armstrong's position as Director of Police Services made his response uniquely problematic for several reasons. Armstrong's declaration not only serves as an erasure of the current crisis of a string of homicides of black unarmed civilians at the hands of the police, but it further creates a distraction from that fact. On the nationally syndicated news network CNN, Armstrong's comments premiered immediately following a segment covering the killing of Samuel DuBose by a Cincinnati Campus police officer (http://www.cnn.com/2015/07/30/us/ohio-sam-dubose-tensing/). It is true that officers should not fear the possibility of murder while executing their jobs. It is equally true that innocent black people should not fear the possibility of being murdered at the hands of the police. These two truths are not mutually exclusive.

Another important aspect of the Bolton and Wilbourn case to consider is that this particular officer's stop in Memphis was indeed a dangerous one. The suspect was armed and allegedly engaged in illegal activity. This is very much different from the circumstances of the cases activists protested while declaring "Black Lives Matter." In those cases, the victims were not committing any felonies, the victims did not have any weapons, and neither were they attacking the officers involved. Armstrong's statement was not only a distraction from the current reality of police killings, but it served as a justification for racially biased police stops and killings. It supported the myth that police have a right to feel that their lives are threatened in all circumstances and that all citizens of color should be treated with suspicion.

Finally, Armstrong's statement was simply not true. The reason the Black Lives Matter movement is necessary is because these lives have been traditionally undervalued and mistreated as compared with other groups of people. If all lives truly mattered, a Black Lives Matter movement would not be necessary. Speaking with philosopher George Yancy in the *New York Times*, Judith Butler states that "Black Lives Matter" is obviously true but has not been historically realized. She continues:

> So what we see is that some lives matter more than others, that some lives matter so much that they need to be protected at all costs, and that other lives matter less, or not at all. And when that becomes the situation, then the lives that do not matter so much, or do not matter at all, can be killed or lost, can be exposed to conditions of destitution, and there is no concern, or even worse, that is regarded as the way it is supposed to be. The callous killing of Tamir Rice and the abandonment of his body on the street is an astonishing example of the police murdering someone considered disposable and fundamentally ungrievable. (Yancy and Butler 2015, 156)

The treatment of black bodies by the police is a direct indication of how the police on a national level perceive the value of black lives. The life of the police officer who was killed in Memphis *did* matter. Its value was shown in the way his colleagues and the media praised his life in the media, and in how quickly justice was administered in his case. This same value is not shown in the way the police encounter and handle black lives, in the way the media describes these lives after they have been taken, or in the way the justice system responds to their deaths. It has been shown, time and again over the decades, that the state not only seeks justice for the lives they believe matter, but through an intricate system of institutionalized state racism and violence, the police and justice systems of this country declare which lives matter and which ones do not.

State Racism and State Violence

The police are the enforcers of the law and they act on behalf of the state. One of the purposes of state violence, or politically sanctioned violence, is to maintain general order. The state describes this authorized violence as legitimate force. Some examples of state sanctioned violence used by the police are deadly force, police harassment and excessive force (brutality), and intimidation tactics. The police enjoy impunity with respect to their actions, while the prime targets of state violence have always been ethnic minorities and indigenous people. The police who engage in state violence also engage in state racism. State racism is a prerequisite to state violence. Michel Foucault gives us some insight on this relationship.

Foucault, in "Society Must Be Defended," writes that racism arises not by creating a polarity between two distinct races but when a single race or society is split into a [super]race and [sub]race (Foucault 2003). He calls this *state racism*. State racism fragments a society; it creates distinctions, hierarchy, and assigns good qualities to the superrace and bad qualities to the subrace. The superrace is the true race, which defines the norm, while the subrace is portrayed as the deviant from the norm and a biological threat. To normalize the population, the subrace must be excluded and segregated from the superrace. Biopower's focus is not to defend the state against the threat of another state, but to defend the state against the threat posed by the subrace. It is no longer state against state, but the state is "protector of the superiority and purity of the [super]race" (Foucault 2003, 81).

For Foucault, state racism not only fragments society but also promotes the mantra that if you want to live, you must take lives; it establishes a relationship between "my life" and "your death." Those deemed abnormal are eliminated so that the superrace can thrive. Their death makes life in general healthier. Because the subrace is a biological threat, killing is justified. State racism is the "precondition that allows the state to kill." Foucault suggests that this death is not only physical but can include political death and rejection.

The subrace can be any group the state deems abnormal, or lesser. The state promotes the idea that this abnormal group is to be feared and that society must at the very least, be suspicious of it, and in the most extreme cases, kill its members. One of the ways to promote fear is to make the subrace synonymous with criminality. As a result, the subrace is often over-criminalized and surveilled. State violence can therefore be viewed as a biopolitical project of protecting the superrace from the "now criminal" subrace (Davis 2003; Alexander 2011).

Foucault lets us know that even if we as citizens decide to be color-blind, *antiblack racism* may be eliminated but *state racism* will still be alive and well. While antiblack racism may point to cruel treatment based on the color of one's skin, state racism is cruel treatment based on whatever reason the state gives that will convince others that a particular body is a threat. John Adams once said that "the form of government which communicates ease, comfort, security, or, in one word, happiness, to the greatest number of persons, and in the greatest degree, is the best" (Adams and Peek 1954, 85). America proves its exceptionalism and its power through the protection and security it provides to its citizens. Unfortunately, this protection comes at the cost of the protection and security of those citizens erroneously depicted as an inside threat. State racism, therefore, is a strategic tool, used by the state to create and maintain overall order and power.

In the United States, society has historically been divided into the "deviant" black and brown communities, and the "innocent" others. Black and brown bodies are the subrace, and bad qualities have traditionally been ascribed to them. They have been stereotyped as lazy, ruthless, freeloaders, and dangerous, while other bodies are depicted as pure and innocent. These "innocent" others are the superrace. To protect the superrace, black and brown bodies must be eliminated. The role of the police is to protect "the others" by eliminating the subrace. They are eliminated through police brutality, stop-and-frisk polices, and even death. Police brutality and excessive force led to the physical death of Samuel Dubose and Rekiya Boyd. Disproportionate, biased arrests have led to the mass incarceration of black and brown people. Mass incarceration not only eliminates black and brown bodies from the population for the specified time of their incarceration, but it eliminates them even when they physically return back to their communities. These black bodies suffer the death of their identities as citizens, with their voting rights stripped and the denial of the right to sit on juries. They are locked out of the economic market because of their record and, until recently, did not have the ability to obtain federal education funding. They are effectively eliminated from society with these exclusions (Travis 2003). The primary reason given is the "threatening" and "deviant" quality of the subrace.

UNDERSTANDING THE CAMPAIGN OF STATE VIOLENCE ON BLACK BODIES

It seems safe to conclude that only those lives that do not threaten the lives of the superrace "matter." If the state can show that a group of people are a threat to the population, then that becomes proof that their lives do not matter and their elimination and oppression are justified. Some believe that black lives do not matter because of their perceived "bad" qualities and the threat they pose to society. But where exactly do these myths come from, and how does the state succeed in spreading them? In a June 8, 1964, interview with Mike Wallace, Malcolm X states, "the police commissioner feeds the type of statistics to the white public to make them think that Harlem is a complete criminal area where everyone is prone towards violence. This gives the police the impression that they can then go and brutalize the Negroes, or suppress the Negroes, or even frighten the Negroes (*CBS News* June 8, 1964.)." In a 1962 speech given at the memorial service of Ronald Stokes—a black man killed by the LAPD—Malcolm talked about the role of the media in this.

> The control press, the white press inflames the white public against Negroes. The police are able to use it to paint the Negro community as a criminal element. The police are able to use the press to make the white public think that 90%, or 99%, of the Negroes in the Negro community are criminals. And once the white public is convinced that most of the Negro community is a criminal element, then this automatically paves the way for the police to move into the Negro community, exercising Gestapo tactics stopping any black man who is . . . on the sidewalk, whether he is guilty or whether he is innocent. Whether he is well dressed or whether he is poorly dressed. . . . As long as he is black and a member of the Negro community the white public thinks that the white policeman is justified in going in there and trampling on that man's civil rights and on that man's human rights. (Mossberg 2012)

Malcolm X gives us three components of a successful campaign by the state, enacted by the police, that justifies their state violence against black bodies: (1) crime statistics, (2) participation of the media, and (3) the approval of the general public. Each component has a unique role, although they are interrelated. I will explain each one respectively.

The police use crime statistics to justify their presence in black communities. The news media uses crime statistics to inform the public of black criminality. Statistical evidence is seen as scientific and mathematical truth: numbers reflect the truth; they do not, cannot, lie. We all may have personal beliefs, but a look at the numbers is supposed to bring us to the truth of the matter. But is this true? In a November 2014 *Meet the Press* interview, former Mayor of New York, Rudy Guiliani, stated that 93 percent of blacks are killed by other blacks. "We're talking about the exception here," he remarked in reference to the killing of a black man by a white man in Ferguson (Paquette 2014). Given the recent killings and violence of white cops on black citizens, Giuliani's claim was made to implicitly suggest that black-on-black crime is more prevalent and attention should be more focused on it than on police brutality. He introduced crime statistics to bring us all to that truth. In 2013, 38 percent of murders were committed by blacks while 31 percent were committed by whites; from 2011 to 2013, 38.5 percent of those arrested for murder, rape, robbery, and aggravated assault were black. African Americans make up 30 percent of the US population, but they make up

60 percent of the prison population (Federal Bureau of Investigation 2013). These are the crime statistics that are used to justify black criminality and thus a police state. However, here are several reasons why we should not put all of our trust in such crime statistics that are used to justify allegations of black criminality and, thus, state violence.

First, crime statistics may be produced out of the self-interest of police departments. When crime rises, cities hire more police. To increase the size of their department and other resources, the police have a vested interest in arresting more people. In the Justice Department's report on the city of Ferguson in 2015, for example, it was revealed that unjustified arrests were made on black people to generate funding for the city (Grow 2015). If crime statistics are high, more funding enters into a police department and it funds city government. On this view, crime statistics do not point to guilt or innocence but to biased targeting, need for money, and department corruption.

Second, the phenomenon known as "black-on-black crime" is often used to explain high crime rates in black communities. The concept of "black-on-black crime" describes how violent blacks are to each other, and it assumes that this type of violence is nonexistent in other racial communities. But the label "black-on-black" crime is misleading. Crime is most frequently intraracial. Most crime is committed by friends or acquaintances of the victim, and this usually falls within racial lines. So if there really is a phenomenon known as "black-on-black" crime, there is also a phenomenon known as "white-on-white" crime. From 1980 to 2008, 84 percent of white victims were killed by white offenders because most crime happens within close communities. This fact is never used to justify the presence of police in white communities or to paint whites as a criminal element.

A third reason to be careful in using crime statistics as proof of black criminality is because of the bias in arrests and sentencing. In the United States, people of color are disproportionately arrested, sentenced, and incarcerated when compared to white people accused of similar offenses. The Center for American Progress reports that this racial disparity is not necessarily due to the fact that blacks are more criminal than whites but because of implicit bias in sentencing, lack of proper legal representation due to poverty, racial bias of juries, overpolicing of communities of color, and the disproportionate targeting of blacks as criminal suspects (Kerby 2012). They also report that students of color face harsher punishments in school than their white peers. African American students are arrested far more often than their white classmates. In "Justice on Trial: Racial Disparities in the American Criminal Justice System," national survey data show that in the federal system, black offenders receive sentences that are 10 percent longer than white offenders for the same crimes. Blacks are more likely to be sentenced to prison for the same crime than whites. One-third of people of color sentenced to prison would have received a shorter or nonincarcerated sentence if they had been treated in court the same way as white defendants facing similar charges. Blacks and Latinos are three times more likely to be searched than whites. African Americans are incarcerated at nearly six times the rate of whites (*CivilRights.org* 2005). A number may provide a picture of those who enter the criminal justice system, but it does not show the systematic bias that had a role in placing that person there.

In racial profiling, sentencing statistics are abused. Naomi Zack in *White Privilege and Black Rights* notes that conservatives make use of sentencing and conviction statistics to justify the racial profiling of certain groups (Zack 2015). For them, the fact that 1 out of 15 African American men are in prison proves the criminality of blacks. Statistics like these are supposed to prove to us who the criminally suspect are. But, Zack points out, if 1 out of 15 African American men are in prison, 14 of them are not. They are law-abiding. These statistics do not show that most African American men are criminals. It shows that the majority of African American men are not criminals. An abuse of these statistics results in racially profiling a majority of law-abiding citizens. Instead of protecting this law-abiding majority, police "arbitrarily target members of a law-abiding, numerical majority, at any given time" (Zack 2015, 56). This makes racial profiling unjust. It also shows the ways in which statistics can be used to perpetuate certain unjust practices and target certain groups. We have reasons not to be easily convinced of crime statistics that attempt to prove black criminality. But those who are not critical will be convinced by this tactic. Malcolm X argued that the police release these crime statistics to the news media. The news media, armed with the power of persuasion and sensationalism, had and still have an effect on the public. While there are members of the public who hold explicit bias toward blacks, there are also those who, as a result of the media, will hold implicit bias toward blacks. This is not surprising, given that implicit bias literature notes that the media and news programming are often verified origins of implicit bias (Oliver 2003).

Explicit bias and implicit bias of the public have real-world behavior effects. In his *New York Times* piece "Crime, Bias and Statistics," Charles Blow quotes an interesting discovery by the Sentencing Project as it relates to "how bias informs [crime] statistics and vice versa."

> Whites are more punitive than blacks and Hispanics even though they experience less crime . . . . White Americans who associate crime with blacks and Latinos are more likely to support punitive policies—including capital punishment and mandatory minimum sentencing—than whites with weaker racial associations of crime. (Blow 2014, A19)

Along the same lines, Lisa Bloom in *Suspicion Nation*, writes, "The standard assumption that criminals are black and blacks are criminals is so prevalent that in one study, 60 percent of viewers who viewed a crime story with no picture of the perpetrator falsely recalled seeing one, and of those, 70 percent believed he was African-American. When we think about crime, we 'see black,' even when it's not present at all" (Bloom 2014, 232). The power of the media's use of crime statistics and sensationalism makes it so that the general public not only approves of state violence, but through the public's implicit bias, they can play an active role in the elimination of the subrace.

Although it seems that Malcolm X's description of the campaign of state violence and all its participants is full of gloom and doom, Malcolm X also explains the importance of "the public," not only in relation to the media and the police but also as members of a democracy. There may be crime statistics, the police, and the news media, but this system will not be complete without the public thinking that the police are justified in trampling on black people's civil rights.

A democracy is "a government of the people, by the people, and for the people." The people are all citizens, not just the majority or what Malcolm X refers to as "the general public." Although there are elected officials that act on the people's behalf, these representatives are answerable to the people. There are times in which it seems that elected officials answer more to themselves or to special interest groups, but it is "the people" who vote them into office and whose opinion has some weight. The police cannot just do anything they want to do to people, without falling into public disfavor. To not upset too much of a certain group, the state must make an appeal to certain members of the people (the majority). But, as I have previously argued, the state also creates the myth of an inside threat and presents a case that they, through the police, will defend *some* of the people against such a threat. If the state's appeal is successful, the police can engage in certain practices and enact certain policies against vulnerable citizens who are viewed as threats. Malcolm X's analysis all comes together here.

To justify the overpolicing of certain communities, the police must justify their actions to the general public by using crime statistics. The news media uses these statistics to perpetuate the stereotype of black criminality. Through persuasive use of crime statistics, the police are thus able to win public opinion, mostly white. If the superrace (nonblacks) is convinced that they should be afraid of certain groups and that the police can keep them safe, there is sufficient justification of the state's need for state violence. But the police and the news media do not have the final say! For, if the police can use democracy to achieve their goals, the people can also use democracy to achieve the goal of making sure citizens are not unjustly and inhumanely eliminated by the state.

RADICAL DEMOCRACY AND VULNERABLE SOLIDARITY

Democracy is a form of government that gives power to the people. Democracy is also relational. It is about the people's relationship with the state and also about the people's relationship with each other. A democratic voice gives communities power. Politicians will only do what their constituents force them to do. Therefore, through the use of a collective voice, it can be the people that force politicians to do things. The people's voice is backed up with the vote to elect officials with certain policies. When the state abuses certain groups, it is because there is an accepted belief that they can get away with it with no consequences. The state may believe that that community is disempowered and that even if they have a voice, they have no vote or their vote doesn't make too much of a difference—or they do not vote. To continue to abuse people of color in cities that are predominately black appears to be political suicide for the people would collectively use their political power to remove officials from office, they would vote against unfair policies, and they would contest oppressive and unequal treatment of which they are the targets. But it is not suicide if the only voice and vote that rise up are from whites who may not care what happens to nonwhites. In this way, whites are no longer the minority but they become the majority. Whites become the "general public" that the state is accountable to. In doing so, "the people" are neglected.

Radical democracy takes democratic tools seriously and uses them against institutions and people that seek to use democracy as a way to promote injustice and oppression. When practicing radical democracy, the people see the value in their voice, their vote, disruption, and organizing. Voting can be a revolutionary act. If you don't believe me, consider Ella Baker, Fannie Louie Hamer, and the students who attempted to register blacks to vote during Freedom Summer in 1964. Having a voice and a vote says to the state, " You are accountable to me and you will pay for your unjust actions with my voice and my vote against you." This vote is not only a silent act, privately done in a booth. In radical democracy, the people know that their vote can be used as a threat and as leverage to draw attention to their oppression to hold the state accountable, and to eventually end unjust practices and policies. This is what makes voting a radical act. With a voice, the people can declare that if stop-and-frisk policies do not end, they will respond in disappointment and disagreement with their vote. When unjust practices are performed by an entity that is not elected by the people, such as the police, the people go after the public officials who are responsible for giving the police power, for example, the mayor. "Going after" these public officials includes creating their own public campaigns and boldly making their frustrations clear. The people can declare that if politicians do not listen to them, they will not be excluded from the political process. The people will create their own political party if they have to.

Democracy is also about the people's relationship with each other. A history of social movements in the United States not only shows the fight and organizing power of certain groups, but it also shows the diverse groups who have been oppressed in this country. There has been religious oppression, gender oppression, oppression against immigrants, Muslims, blacks, gays, the Japanese, Native Americans, and labor groups. Since the establishment of America, there has been state violence. The subrace and superrace distinction has always existed in America. This list of historically oppressed victims also lets us know that, at any time, any of us can be placed into the subrace category. Even members of the superrace who do not become members of the subrace can nonetheless be impacted by state violence targeted toward the subrace. Although the War on Drugs has been a war on black, brown, and poor bodies, for example, there have been some casualties within the superrace. White drug "criminals" have been what Michelle Alexander refers to as "collateral damage in the War on Drugs" (Alexander 2011, 205). The war that was waged on black and brown people has affected white people, and in reality, we are all vulnerable to state violence.

We *all* are hurt by the injustice of others. As Martin Luther King, Jr. proclaimed in his *Letter from a Birmingham Jail*, a "threat to justice anywhere, is a threat to justice everywhere" (King 1963). Simultaneously, we are also helped by the justice of others. This is what Alicia Garza meant when she said that once black people get free, the benefits will transform society. All citizens are vulnerable to state racism because at any time the state can reduce a particular group to the subrace category, and their delegation to that category, as well as the violence that is directed to them as a result, has a huge impact on *all* people. State violence and state racism is never really a black or a brown issue. It is an American issue. In our democracy, with a government for the people by the people, we are all affected by each other. This fact not only brings to light our own vulnerability, but it also gives us a wonderful opportunity for solidarity and activism. Vulnerable solidarity is solidarity that is formed based on the vulnerability that we all face as citizens to be targeted and/or affected by state racism and state violence.

The concept of vulnerable solidarity is beneficial when fighting against state racism and state violence because vulnerability creates a stronger motivation to fight against injustice than emotions like empathy. Research indicates that empathy is prone to in-group bias and does not extend across gender and racial lines as we might think (Prinz 2011), but it seems intuitively obvious that a sense of vulnerability is universal and much more powerful. In vulnerable solidarity, citizens understand that we are all susceptible to attack or harm by the state. Vulnerable solidarity opens up the bonds of trusts among "vulnerable" groups, which may be difficult to do with groups defined by their superrace and subrace identities. Instead of joining a cause because it has a direct impact on our social positioning now, people will join causes because they will know that all injustices have an impact on us all; if not directly, indirectly, if not now, in the future.

This is not to deny the black solidarity that Tommie Shelby describes in *We Who Are Dark* (Shelby 2007). Shelby argues that a collective identity should not be the basis of Back solidarity. Instead, black solidarity should be based on blacks' commitment to end racist practices. For Shelby, removing the collective identity condition will not only unite blacks who have various ways of identifying as black, but it will also allow for nonblacks to join in on the fight for social justice with blacks. On Shelby's account, it is blacks who are vulnerable and committed to ending racism, and it is nonblacks who are sympathetic to their plight. On my view, black solidarity can coexist with vulnerable solidarity. But vulnerable solidarity recognizes that shared commitment is not the only thing that can tie us together nor the only motivation for political resistance, but also shared vulnerability. Shelby writes that other groups' solidarity commitments have often been used to "exploit the economic and political disadvantages of African Americans as a group. And whites in power sometimes favor these other groups over blacks, creating resentment and competition between minority groups" (Shelby 2007, 241). I think this competition happens when oppressed groups see their oppression and the political response to it as separate from each other. Vulnerable solidarity sees oppression, particularly state racism and state violence, as something that affects us all and something we are all vulnerable to. This is not to say that we all experience state violence in the same way. We must listen and give credence to the testimony of others whose experiences are different than our own. Vulnerable solidarity is also not an excuse to take political organizing power away from those who may be experiencing oppression now and give organizing power to the citizen who may experience state violence in the future. This may only reinforce the superrace and subrace distinction.

How we are to organize based on vulnerable solidarity is too much to cover here. What should be noted is that vulnerable solidarity is a unique way of looking at our relationship with each other and our relationship with the state. In vulnerable solidarity, we no longer see our privilege as stable. We no longer see each other as merely suspects or victims, but as comrades. We no longer see our country as perfect, but in need of radical transformation. Overall, vulnerable solidarity would allow for collective self-defense against injustice. In this sense, we all join together and become one—"the people"—that unjust police forces and the government must answer, listen, and respond to. Vulnerable solidarity that arises from state racism widens the scope of not only potential victims but also potential participants in fighting against the injustice of state violence and state racism. It sends a loud message to the state, that the distinctions that they create will not be tolerated. *We* are the people! All of our lives should matter and we will fight together to make it so.

REFERENCES

Adams, J., and G. A. Peek, G. A. (1954). *The Political Writings of John Adams: Representative Selections*. New York: Liberal Arts Press.

Alexander, Michelle. (2011). *The New Jim Crow: Mass Incarceration in the Age of Colorblindness*. New York: New Press.

Bloom, L. (2014). *Suspicion Nation: The Inside Story of the Trayvon Martin Injustice and Why We Continue to Repeat It*. Berkeley, CA: Counterpoint.

Blow, Charles. (2014). "Crime, Bias, and Statistics." *The New York Times*, September 7. Accessed May 16, 2016. http://www.nytimes.com/2014/09/08/opinion/charles-blow-crime-bias-and-statistics.html?_r=1.

Civil Rights.Org. (2005). "How is the Criminal Justice System Racist? Accessed on June 19, 2016. http://www.publiceye.org/defendingjustice/pdfs/factsheets/10-Fact%20Sheet%20-%20System%20as%20Racist.pdf.

Davis, Angela. (2003). *Are Prisons Obsolete?* New York: Seven Stories Press.

Federal Bureau of Investigation. (2013). *Crime in the United States 2013. Uniform Crime Reports.* Accessed May 16, 2016. https://www.fbi.gov/about-us/cjis/ucr/crime-in-the-u.s/2013/crime-in-the-u.s.-2013/tables/table-43.

Foucault, Michel. (2003) *Society Must Be Defended, Lectures at the Collège de France, 1975–1976 (No.3)*. New York: Picador.

Garza, Alicia. (2014). "A HerStory of #BlackLivesMatter." *Feminist Wire*, October 7. Accessed May 16, 2016. http://www.thefeministwire.com/2014/10/blacklivesmatter-2/.

Grow, Kory. (2015). "Ferguson Police Racist, Unconstitutional, Justice Department Says." *Rolling Stone*, March 5. Accessed May 16, 2016. http://www.rollingstone.com/culture/news/ferguson-police-racist-unconstitutional-justice-department-says-20150305.

Karimi, Faith, and Shoichet, Catherine. (2015). "Memphis Shooting: Suspect in Officer's Slaying Arrested." *CNN*. Accessed May 16, 2016. http://www.cnn.com/2015/08/03/us/memphis-officer-killed-traffic-stop/.

Kerby, Sophia. (2012). "The Top 10 Most Startling Facts About People of Color and Criminal Justice in the United States." *Center for American Progress*. Accessed May 16, 2016. https://www.americanprogress.org/issues/race/news/2012/03/13/11351/the-top-10-most-startling-facts-about-people-of-color-and-criminal-justice-in-the-united-states/

King, Martin Luther Jr. (1964/1986). "Letter from the Birmingham Jail." In *Why We Can't Wait*, ed. Martin Luther King, Jr., 95–110. Boston, MA: Beacon Press.

Mossberg, Donnie. (2012). Malcolm X Speech in Los Angeles (May 5, 1962). *YouTube* Accessed May 16, 2016. https://www.youtube.com/watch?v=gpr6PK-Cz3c&list=PLnUXGZWN-riQYIt6zohNwxbhYnlE373Xg.

Oliver, M. B. (2003). "African American Men as 'Criminal and Dangerous': Implications of Media Portrayals of Crime on the 'Criminalization' of African American Men." *Journal of African American Studies* 7 (2): 3–18.

Paquette, Danielle. (2014). "Giuliani: "White Police Officers Wouldn't Be There If You Weren't Killing Each Other." *Washington Post*, November 23. Accessed May 16, 2016. http://www.washingtonpost.com/blogs/post-politics/wp/2014/11/23/giuliani-white-police-officers-wouldnt-be-there-if-you-werent-killing-each-other/.

Prinz, Jesse J. (2011). "Is Empathy Necessary for Morality." In *Empathy: Philosophical and Psychological Perspectives*, edited by Amy Coplan and Peter Goldie, 211–229. New York: Oxford University Press.

Shelby, Tommie. (2007). *We Who Are Dark: The Philosophical Foundations of Black Solidarity*. Cambridge, MA: Harvard University Press.

Travis, Jeremy. (2003). "Invisible Punishment: An Instrument of Social Exclusion." In *Invisible Punishment: The Collateral Consequences of Mass Imprisonment*, edited by M. Mauer and M. Chesney-Lind, 15–36. New York: New Press.

Yancy, George, and Judith Butler. (2015). "What's Wrong With 'All Lives Matter'?" *New York Times* 12: 156.

Zack, Naomi. (2015). *White Privilege and Black Rights: The Injustice of U.S. Police Racial Profiling and Homicide*. Lanham, MD: Rowman and Littlefiled.

PART VII

··

SOCIAL CONSTRUCTION AND RACIAL IDENTITIES

··

THE essays in Part III showed that in the contemporary biological sciences, there is no independent support for a taxonomy of human races. And, in considering racism in Part VI, it became evident that racism at this time is less a matter of thoughts and feelings in individuals and more the result of institutional structures and political practices in society. The absence of real biological races and the location of racism in the effects of institutions and politics imply that race and racism are practical and ideological, matters of what people do and of values that benefit some groups in society, rather than how people intrinsically *are*. In other words, race and racism are the result of historical events and power arrangements. Against that backdrop, it can be claimed that racial identities—what people are—are *socially constructed*.

In the early twenty-first-century, most social theorists and their readers have an intuitive understanding of the concept of *social construction*. But this does not mean it is easy to define apart from the kind of facile usage that says, "Of course racial identities are socially constructed!" After examination of such usage, we might consider "social construction" as a topic somewhat independent of race.

Speaking very roughly, the concept of social construction is in play with regard to race whenever beliefs about biological race are dissolved or beliefs about the psyches, character traits, and cultures of different races are shown to be false. That is, if racial divisions and different behavior based on perceived racial differences persist in the lack of a biological reality of race, then what is taken to be real about race must be the result of what has happened and continues to happen in society. Thus, insofar as the biological sciences have not supported ideas of human racial essences as determining the traits of this or that race, the essentialist biological idea of race is a social construction, belonging to past, and now revised, science. And, if members of a given minority "race" do not in reality have the vices or behavior ascribed to them by an oppressive majority race, then these traits and the identities resulting from them are social constructions in society. To say that an identity is socially constructed is to deny that it has the objective reality ascribed to it. Rather, that identity is the result of beliefs and practices in society or specialized segments of society and it may or may not have a factual foundation apart from those beliefs and practices.

John Searle, in *The Construction of Social Reality* (1995), offers an analysis that relates physical facts to mental facts, which explains social reality. One could account for ideas of race in society by making a distinction between human physicality as physical facts and mental facts such as attitudes and beliefs (and also patterns of behavior based on both the prior physical and mental facts) in the social world. Analyses based on that distinction could account for how the hard physical facts of health as associated with racial difference are in fact embodiments of mental facts (Gravlee 2009). Closer to the subject of race, in several, very famous, short articles, Ian Hacking introduced the idea that people are made up in the social sciences, as well as in lay society:

> How does making up people take place? Long ago, "hip" and "square" became common names in white middle-class culture. By a parody of Nietzsche, two new kinds of people came into being, the hip and the square. As is the way of slang imported from another social class, both kinds had short shelf lives. But I am concerned with the human sciences, from sociology to medicine, and they are driven by several engines of discovery, which are thought of as having to do with finding out the facts, but they are also engines for making up people. The first seven engines in the following list are designed for discovery, ordered roughly according to the times at which they became effective. The eighth is an engine of practice, the ninth of administration, and the tenth is resistance to the knowers: 1. Count! 2. Quantify! 3. Create Norms! 4. Correlate! 5. Medicalise! 6. Biologise! 7. Geneticise! 8. Normalise! 9. Bureaucratise! 10. Reclaim our identity! (Hacking 2006, 5)

Thus, Hacking refers to professional practices of focusing on a population and distinguishing it from other populations according to available scientific and political technologies. If one also considers the importance of naming, then examinations of how specific racial groups are socially reconstructed would be part of Hacking's tenth "engine," "Reclaim our identity!"

Finally, and very specifically relating to racial groups over US history, Michael Omi and Howard Winant have provided widely received accounts of how the main US social racial groups came into existence, where before their members were not regarded as races in important or problematic ways. They write: "To say that race is socially constructed is to say that it varies according to time and place" (Omi and Winant 2015, 13). The philosophical task, however, is not so much to relate how past constructions of race occurred, but to show how present and emerging constructions are not the natural or inevitable factually-based realities they are presented as being. The authors in this part examine contemporary racial identities along these lines.

In "Black American Social Identity and Its Blackness," Lionel McPherson examines two assumptions about black identity: having traceable African ancestry is necessary to be black American and having a certain amount of black ancestry is sufficient to be black American.

According to McPherson, black identity cannot be separated from having African ancestry, but this does not mean that everyone who has African ancestry is black. McPherson notes that there is no longer a legal compulsion to identify as black if one has traceable African ancestry, and that some individuals with traceable African ancestry may elect to identify as mixed race or Caribbean American. McPherson then returns to W. E. B. Du Bois, in opposition to K. Anthony Appiah's critique of him (see Chike Jeffer's "Du Bois, Appiah, and Outlaw on Racial Identity" in Part IV), to develop an insight about cultural and political solidarity for blacks generally, and black Americans in particular. McPherson accepts Du Bois's contested notion of race, not as a form of essentialism or some enigmatic metaphysical spirituality, but as the "social heritage of slavery; the discrimination and insult." For Du Bois, the social heritage of slavery "binds together not simply the children of Africa, but extends through yellow Asia and into the South Seas." McPherson interprets Du Bois to mean that the lived experience of being racially black in the United States is the basis of black American identity. And McPherson goes a step further, suggesting that black American identity is not so much racial in the sense of having African ancestry, but *socioancestral*. McPherson concludes:

> Socioancestral groups are a function of color-conscious social dynamics that reflect facts about a particular component of the continental ancestry of a group's members. These social dynamics are directly grounded in social reality, not in convictions about what races as such are. Black Americans can be more productively thought of as belonging to a larger black group—namely, a group comprising Africa-identified peoples.

Even though they change as social constructions, American racial identities have stability that can be related in historical, familial, and generational accounts of how they become constructed. In "How Mixed Race Is Not Constructed," I argue that this is not the case for the category of mixed race, particularly mixed black and white race. One obvious reason is that not everyone in a mixed-race person's family is of the same race. A variety of motives from self-interest, to lack of racial solidarity, to a sense of justice, could motivate choosing mixed-race identity. Passing for the race others think one is not and conforming or not to norms for racial identities raise ethical questions for members of mixed-race groups. Because these groups are the fastest growing racial category of US births, these questions of autonomy or freedom versus loyalty and constraint are not likely to blow over.

Ron Mallon, in "Racial Identity, Racial Ontology, and Racial Norms," observes that there are widespread or common racial norms, which prescribe or proscribe behavior based on racial identities. Examples range from dressing or speaking in certain ways that are or are not expected given racial identities, to more important actions of solidarity. Mallon takes racial identities to be membership in, or designation as, racial kinds. However, the reality of such kinds is disputable, but even if they were real, it is not clear how racial identities could necessitate racial norms. From a liberal perspective, consent to obligations to other members of one's group would be required before such obligations could be justly imposed or reciprocity demanded. A strong communal sense of racial identity could support such norms, but that kind of group cohesion is neither evident nor possible in American life, because it is not materially supported by the nature of group life. Before concluding with general skepticism about whether any racial norms can be justified, Mallon writes:

> Note first that contemporary American races and ethnicities—African American, Asian American, Italian American, Jewish American, and so on—are not geographically local

identities. They are rather *big* groups of *diverse* people distributed across the United States, and they have a range of different attitudes and alignments. It is thus implausible to regard all members as in a reciprocal cooperative community with one another. While there may be spatiotemporally local conditions in which race or ethnicity is coextensive with a cooperative community, this is not the typical case for American racial identities.

Jason D. Hill claims that it is not moral to hold a racial identity, boldly proclaiming at the outset of his essay, "The concept of race, simpliciter, is bad. The concomitant practice of holding a racial identity voluntarily and living one's life as a raciated creature is a form of biological collectivism and racial subjectivism." Hill presents strong or radical cosmopolitanism as a theory of the self, and a moral system based on rational principles. By contrast, to "hold a racial identity" involves self-deception and willed ignorance about both self and others. Seeing oneself and others in terms of the traits of racial groups is a process of "associating" individuals with groups in ways that obscure their real capabilities and characteristics. Moreover, holding a racial identity is misanthropic, because it precludes ethical interactions with other human beings on an egalitarian foundation. When racial identities are stripped of their racist values, the biological emptiness of race makes them "empty sets."

Still, Hill does recognize a political and moral need for a self-view that can enable advocating and acting on behalf of those who have been treated unjustly or oppressed, based on racial or other disadvantaged identities. For ethical motivation and political and social values, Hill claims that cosmopolitanism does a much better job than any racial identity:

> Not only is ["cosmopolitanism"] a wholesaler in the realm of the moral work it does on behalf of representing seemingly disparate groups of people who are unjustly treated, it is also a viable replacer for racial identities. Unlike holders of racial identities, the *cosmopolitan* is both the possessor of a distinct self with a unique moral psychology and the holder of an identity suffused with real attributes.

To cap a general consensus that actual moral experience is more important than fixed racial identities, based on understandings that these identities are socially constructed, this part ends with a somewhat pessimistic, but nonetheless strengthening, perspective. Jacquline Scott in "Effortful Agon" proposes a different way to think and feel about race than one optimistically based on the right identity or reassurance that everything will be alright. Scott quotes the poet Gwendolyn Brooks's "Truth-tellers are not always palatable. There is a preference for candy bars" as a description of her own advocacy of unpalatable truths about race. Drawing on Nietzsche, who spoke of meaninglessness as a chronic existential disease, Scott suggests that we view racism as a permanent part of our social condition and instead of trying to cure it, "try to fortify our bodies/immune systems and minds/psyches, so that we can better flourish despite this disease." The ultimate goal would be to "celebrate ourselves as individuals and communities and our power to struggle against seemingly impossible odds." Scott's project is to become Nietzschean philosophers or *Versuchers*—experimenters, tempters, and attempters: "We need to see the possibility of racialized discomfort as potentially being about growth, and not necessarily as a sign that something is wrong. It, therefore, requires courage."

FURTHER READING

Gilroy, Paul. (2002). *Against Race*. Cambridge, MA: Harvard University Press.

Gravlee, Clarence C. (2009). "How Race Becomes Biology: Embodiment of Social Inequality." *American Journal of Physical Anthropology* 139 (1): 47–57.

Hacking, Ian. (1999). "Making Up People." *The Science Studies Reader* 18: 590. Accessed May 16, 2016. http://www.ts-si.org/files/HackingMakingUpPeople.pdf.

Omi, Michael, and Howard Winant. (2006). *Racial Formation in the United States.* 3rd ed. New York: Routledge.

Searle, John R. (1995). *The Construction of Social Reality.* New York: Simon and Schuster.

....

CHAPTER 31

BLACK AMERICAN SOCIAL IDENTITY AND ITS BLACKNESS

....

LIONEL K. MCPHERSON

How to understand Black (or African) American social identity is confusing and often confused. There are two main sources of confusion: widespread social practice whereby Americans who have visible sub-Saharan African ancestry, and thus "look black," typically are seen as black American; and widespread belief that Black Americans are members of "the Black race." Both reasons contribute to a default presumption that the basis of black American social identity is objective in the sense that having some traceable African ancestry is necessary. There is also a stronger default presumption: that having a substantial, if undefined, quantum of African ancestry—whether indicated by looking black or by some purported biological fact—is sufficient for an American to be Black American. This stronger presumption is misguided.

Traceable African ancestry represents the blackness, as it were, of Black American social identity. There is an established understanding that persons who have no African ancestry cannot be Black American, regardless of how they look or whether they identify with Black American people, politics, or culture. Unlike gender identity, for example, which can come apart from its conventional grounding in assigned biological sex, Black American social identity does not come apart from its grounding in traceable African ancestry. This is as uncontroversial as observing that Asian Americans must have some traceable Asian ancestry, White Americans must have some traceable European ancestry, and so on. But it does not follow that every American who has traceable African ancestry must be Black American.

The "one-drop rule" of hypodescent meant, legally and socially, that having any traceable African ancestry was sufficient for subordinate racial classification as black or at least not white. There continues to be an established understanding that visible African ancestry is fundamentally at odds with whiteness. Yet the one-drop rule has socially declined enough that Americans whose African ancestry is both traceable and visible are no longer compelled to accept a Black American social identity. For instance, Louisiana repealed its 1970 law according to which "anyone having one thirty-second or less of 'Negro blood' should not be designated as black by Louisiana state officials. . . . [State Assistant Attorney General Ronald Davis] says he is pleased because the repeal of the law means that 'the state is not in the business of officially determining race'" (Marcus 1983). Some Americans who have traceable African and non-African ancestry identify instead as "mixed race" or "multiracial."

Additionally, some Americans who have traceable African ancestry might affirm not a Black American social identity but a different Africa-identified kind (e.g., Caribbean American). These cases help to illuminate why being Black American has become an elective social identity—which is not to deny the social reality of widely being presumed to identify as Black and thereby ascribed that identity.

The conceptual fact remains that having some traceable African ancestry is a necessary condition for Black American social identity. To be seen as Black American is typically to be regarded as an American descendant of slaves in the United States or an American who, if not a descendant of these slaves, belongs to the same continentally identified group (i.e., African). In other words, Black American social identity is inextricably associated with Africa and the legacy of slavery in the United States. Why an emphasis on slavery? The sociologist Orlando Patterson has argued that profound dishonor is a central feature of slavery; and in a society that practices race-based chattel slavery, the dishonor would be inherited by persons born into slavery or, more broadly, into the same racial group defined through slavery (Patterson 1982, 78, 58). Such a story seems undeniably part of the explanation for the enduring significance of black (and nonblack) color consciousness in the United States. A revisionist interpretation of Black American social identity would be called for if the association with slavery were to become marginal.

Confusion and contestation start just beyond the minimal requirement of traceable African ancestry. Belief that Black Americans are members of the black racial group often carries certain expectations about not only what they look like but also how they are distinctively inclined to think and act. Some race theorizers continue to be preoccupied with the notion that there is "an open question" as to whether blacks, to some significant degree, are by nature a race intellectually less capable or more predisposed to violence than whites; the question is supposed to be compelling for reasons usually not made explicit. By contrast, there is no longer much interest in pursuing such inquiry about differences within racialized groups, that is, within large groups treated as if they constitute natural races; whether Irish, Italians, or Poles, for instance, are intellectually inferior peoples within a white race is not a live question (see, e.g., Ignatiev 1995). The social dynamics of racial speculation can be highly variable and seemingly arbitrary—which is to say, more bluntly, that racial biases are often unequal in substance and impact. This partly explains why color-conscious social identity still matters, apart from any purportedly natural facts about racial difference.

My aim here is to set forth an account of Black American social identity. While remaining agnostic about whether human races exist somehow as part of the natural world, I will elaborate why the tendency to reduce color-conscious social identity to racial classification is a mistake. The fairly recent arrival of elective Black American social identity—given the publicly viable option to self-identify as Black, or not, rather than simply be ascribed that identity—does not represent, contrary to familiar fears, a serious threat to Black solidarity but instead strengthens solidarity among persons who could identify as Black American, as most native-born Americans who have visible African ancestry continue to do.

WHAT BLACK AMERICANS ARE NOT MERELY

"The truth is that there are no races: there is nothing in the world that can do all we ask 'race' to do for us," Anthony Appiah concludes in his influential essay "The Uncompleted

Argument: Du Bois and the Illusion of Race" (Appiah 1986, 35–36). Appiah's "truth" is provocative and powerful but overreaches. There and in subsequent work, he casts suspicion that Black American social identity depends on commitment to an essentialist idea of race (whereby distinctive racial essences yield innate cognitive differences between races). The error of this suspicion is instructive; ironically, it is an error Appiah shares with W. E. B. Du Bois. The discussion in this section is a case study of how the race idea misleads in thinking about Black American social identity.

Du Bois knew better than to accept a thick biological understanding of race. In "The Conservation of Races," he rejects scientific racialism that placed blacks at or near the bottom of a racial hierarchy, especially regarding intellectual ability and moral sensibility. He recognizes that "the grosser physical differences of color, hair and bone go but a short way toward explaining" the contributions that different racial groups, including blacks, have made to world culture (Du Bois 1897, 816). Of course, physical differences could hardly explain broad cultural developments. Du Bois does believe, though, that different racial groups are suited to make different cultural contributions.

The problem is that Du Bois seems to fall into the trap of racial essentialism. He appeals to "subtle forces [that] have generally followed the natural cleavage of common blood" and that "[a]t all times . . . have divided human beings into races, which . . . perhaps transcend scientific definition" (Du Bois 1897, 816–817). Such a stable division into races would have to depend on some unifying property that yields the respective membership of each racial group. Presumably, this property would be a heritable trait: there is nothing that Africa-identified persons have distinctively always had in common other than whatever might be inherited via traceable African ancestry. Appiah argues that Du Bois imagines there is a black people—across epochs, continents, languages, and subcultures—whose natural endowment, like that of other major races, renders them distinctive contributors to world culture as revealed through their common history.

This vision should have seemed implausible to Du Bois. As he observes, "race differences have followed mainly physical race lines, yet no mere physical distinctions would really define or explain the deeper differences—the cohesiveness and continuity of these groups" (Du Bois 1897, 818). The question, then, is what kind of heritable trait would explain racial "cohesiveness and continuity." Du Bois seems to imply by default that the different races have different natural psychological dispositions. "The deeper differences," he claims, "are spiritual, psychical, differences—undoubtedly based on the physical, but infinitely transcending them" (Du Bois 1897, 818). Their underlying source remains mysterious. Nor do they neatly correspond to ancestry: as Du Bois was aware, many Black Americans (he included) have been of mixed continental ancestry.

Our purposes here do not concern trying to better grasp how Du Bois understands the idea of race. The pertinent question for us is why he would go to such lengths to propose a variation of racial essentialism. Du Bois's main motivations evidently are twofold: to resist the theorizing and practice of racial hierarchy, which rationalized the subordination of blacks on grounds of their alleged natural (intellectual and moral) inferiority; and to articulate a solid foundation for cultural and political solidarity for blacks generally and Black Americans in particular.

In "Dusk of Dawn," Du Bois in effect gives up his earlier attraction to racial essentialism. He acknowledges that "neither my father nor my father's father ever saw Africa or knew its meaning or cared overmuch for it," while his "mother's folk were closer and yet their direct connection, in culture and race, became tenuous." What black Americans have in common, he continues, "the real essence of [their] kinship," is less "the badge of color" than the "social heritage of slavery; the discrimination and insult; and this heritage binds together not simply the children of Africa, but extends through yellow Asia and into the South Seas" (Du Bois 1940, 639–640). This type of "essence" is found in a roughly shared experience of racial subordination, not in nature. Appiah questions such an expansive approach to color-conscious solidarity: "How can something [Du Bois] shares with the whole nonwhite world bind him to only a part of it?" (Appiah 1986, 34–35).

Although Du Bois's thought in that "Dusk of Dawn" passage is compressed, the meaning seems clear enough. As a self-identified "Negro," he is expressing solidarity with other nonwhites, who in Western racialist ideology are held to be naturally inferior to whites in critical respects. More specifically, he is expressing solidarity among persons subject to Western racialist ideology on account of their African ancestry. Most specifically, he is expressing solidarity among Americans who, regardless of any non-African ancestry they have, also have traceable African ancestry that is a defining feature of lived experience under the peculiar variety of color-conscious subordination associated with slavery and its aftermath in the United States.

So Appiah misses the point when observing that "Du Bois' experience of 'discrimination and insult' in his American childhood and as an adult citizen of the industrialized world was different in character from that experienced by, say, Kwame Nkrumah in colonized West Africa" (Appiah 1986, 35). The difference highlights rather than undermines how Du Bois thinks about color-conscious solidarity: the shared theme is nonwhite inferiorization, which represents a shared "insult" and not, as Appiah surmises, merely "the *badge* of insult" (Appiah 1986, 35). This point is fully compatible with recognizing that there are diverse manifestations of nonwhite inferiorization. Du Bois, then, is well positioned to argue that while color-conscious ties might indeed be "tenuous" among Africa-identified peoples globally, there is a distinctive character to the black subordination experienced (and responded to) by Africa-identified persons in the United States. We can draw the lesson that in a descriptive sense, Africa-identified persons rooted in the United States have constituted a Black American people. No appeal to race is needed to support this descriptive claim.

Du Bois also suggests there is a Black American people in a normative sense. As long as Africa-identified persons rooted in the United States are clearly subject to color-conscious subordination, there is little practical question of most continuing to identify as black, namely, as a function of enculturation in a racialized society. But what if many Black Americans were to put their faith in the professed public ideal of a "postracial" society, for instance? This could threaten Black solidarity, leading to cultural loss and, insofar as social equality remains far from realization, tragic political miscalculations (e.g., counting on "colorblind" policy to deliver racial justice progress). Du Bois anticipates the dream of a postracial society and is having none of it in "The Conservation of Races":

> If I strive as a Negro, am I not perpetuating the very cleft that threatens and separates Black and White America? Is not my only possible practical aim the subduction of all that is Negro in me to the American? Does my black blood place upon me more obligation to assert my nationality than German, or Irish or Italian blood would?
> It is such incessant self-questioning and the hesitation that arises from it, that is making the present period a time of vacillation and contradiction for the American Negro; combined race action is stifled, race responsibility is shirked, race enterprises languish. . . .

... We are Americans, not only by birth and by citizenship, but by our political ideals, our language, our religion. Farther than that, our Americanism does not go. At that point, we are Negroes, members of a vast historic race. ... [I]t is our duty to conserve our physical powers, our intellectual endowments, our spiritual ideals; as a race we must strive by race organization, by race solidarity, by race unity to the realization of that broader humanity which freely recognizes differences in men, but sternly deprecates inequality in their opportunities of development. (Du Bois 1897, 821–822)

For Du Bois, the lived experience of racial blackness in the United States would objectively ground being Black American. A duty to conserve the cultural and political value that he supposes comes with this racial blackness would ground an obligation to identify as Black American and join in Black solidarity. Du Bois thus attempts to end "incessant self-questioning" about who Black Americans are by preempting any serious doubt about the descriptive basis of their social identity (viz., racial blackness rooted in the United States) and the normative basis of their social identity and their solidarity (viz. black racial duty). Of course, bare facts of race could not establish that members of any racial group have an obligation to join in solidarity—which is why he introduces the value claims that Black Americans have distinctive, important contributions to make to world culture and necessary contributions to make to their pursuit of social equality.

Underlying Du Bois's normative claims about a Black American people—and characteristic of Black nationalist thought generally—is a fear that too many members, especially the most talented or privileged (e.g., "The Negro Race, like all races, is going to be saved by its exceptional men" [Du Bois 1903, 842]), will not join in solidarity. Prospective nonjoiners might reject identifying as Black American, say, in the name of being multiracial; or while accepting the descriptive label of Black American, they might seek assimilation to a dominant, White culture; or though affirming a black cultural orientation, they might be indifferent to black political solidarity. There is the familiar phenomenon whereby mainstream favor is shown to "good Negroes" seemingly comfortable with second-class status in society. They can be confused with other Black Americans who pragmatically adopt a quietist approach in the spirit of Booker T. Washington's counsel: "To those of my race who depend on bettering their condition in a foreign land or who underestimate the importance of cultivating friendly relations with the Southern white man ... I would say: 'Cast down your bucket where you are' ... " (Washington 1895/2008, 92–93). The nonjoiner's road to color-conscious social equality could well be interminably slow.

While Du Bois's fear of threats to Black solidarity is not imagined, he worries too much about the prospect of defection or complacency. He overestimates the temptation to dis-identify as black American, abandon black community ties, or publicly align oneself (as an ostensible member of the group) against the group's understanding of its best interests. Africa-identified persons rooted in the United States have not often deemed the incentives to make such choices worth the trouble. More basically, Du Bois underestimates the force of lived experience that has sustained Black American social identity. Dating from slavery, there have been strong norms of solidarity among Americans whose blackness is visible (see, e.g., Davis 2014, 54–55), which is why the charge of "sellout" or "Uncle Tom" has the capacity to wound even those who might be said to defiantly fit the profile. As Tommie Shelby observes, "[B]lacks frequently call upon, even pressure, one another to become a more unified collective agent for social change" (Shelby 2005, 201).

Long-standing norms of Black solidarity are not strong enough for Du Bois, however. The reason is these norms do not foreclose room for individual choice: they have not strictly required identifying as Black American in the first place. (Consider that there is no custom of outing regular persons who "pass" as white.) This would explain Du Bois's intervention and why he speculates in search of a nonelective basis for being Black American—and that basis, at least in "Conservation," is race on an essentialist-type understanding. Some objective fact of racial blackness would ground black racial duty that normatively binds racially Black Americans to Black American social identity and Black solidarity. To this extent, Du Bois perpetuates the tendency to reduce color-conscious social identity to racial classification. Since many Black Americans are of mixed continental ancestry (and the African component is not always conspicuous), their racial blackness would somehow be a property that "transcends" the total facts of their continental ancestry.

There are no essentialist facts of race, nor any other stable, objective criteria by which all persons who have visible African ancestry must be racially black. There has been, though, an entrenched belief that Americans who have visible African ancestry must be Black American, their color-conscious social identity supposedly given by their racial blackness. Despite his emphasis on the critical role of the "social heritage of slavery" in shaping Black American social identity, Du Bois reveals a lack of conviction about the power of that heritage in sustaining commitment to the identity. To be marked as an Africa-identified person in the United States continues to give rise to a widespread sense (among the native born) of common fate, under persistent conditions of black subordination, as Black Americans. There is no need for such persons to be invested in some essentialist idea of race as the foundation for their color-conscious social identity. This is where Appiah amplifies Du Bois's error, in the service of a competing conclusion.

Many Black Americans, Appiah argues, still accept a fairly literal version of the one-drop rule; but very many persons who would be Black American by this rule do not look black, are not even aware that they have traceable African ancestry, and thus are seen by others and regard themselves as racially white. Although Appiah concedes that most Americans know the one-drop rule does not neatly sort blacks and whites, he asserts that this admission of vagueness in the application of racial criteria gets treated as "a minor anomaly that makes little practical difference." He claims, "The result is that the norm of solidarity for African-Americans entails that African-Americans very often have, in the one-drop rule, a reason for identity-based generosity to people they believe, on the basis of another part of their social conception, to be white. If they acted on the one-drop rule-based norms, their identity-based generosity would be directed more often than not toward people they regard as whites" (Appiah 2002, 284; for a critical response, see McPherson and Shelby 2004). Such "incoherence," as Appiah calls it, would undermine legitimate color-conscious policies, for instance, affirmative action.

Appiah has insisted on assuming that Black American social identity depends on commitment to essentialist, "one-drop" racial blackness. He needs this implausible assumption in order to drive his broader argument about deep incoherence (and restrictive "life scripts" [Appiah 1996, 97–99]) in that identity. But observers steeped in American racial discourse and practice have known that the notion of "one drop of black blood" long ago became figurative for visible African ancestry, as in, "looks black" because of that ancestry. Du Bois knew this as well—which is why, when not preoccupied with trying to objectively specify racial blackness, he is satisfied loosely referring to Black Americans, for example, in "We who are dark can see America in a way that white Americans cannot" (Du Bois 1926, 993).

In sum, Black American social identity cannot plausibly be interpreted merely in terms of being racially black, whatever that is taken to mean, and American. Nor are Black Americans simply native-born Americans who have some substantial quantum of African ancestry. The latter contention was not always true.

BLACK AMERICAN SOCIAL IDENTITY
VIA SOCIOANCESTRY

Black Americans must have some traceable African ancestry. We can make this conceptual observation without the idea of race, since "blackness" can be understood more plainly in terms of African ancestry: the race idea's intervention is unnecessary. Indeed, viewing Black Americans as a black race subgroup is misleading. Regardless of whether there intelligibly could be human races in some sense or other, the problem is specifying criteria that adequately match ordinary racial ascriptions. If some biological account of racial criteria is given—say, in terms of genetic markers—there often will be mismatches between how persons are racially classified and how they are seen as looking, particularly in countries (e.g., the United States, Brazil) where there has been extensive reproductive mixing of continental ancestry.

If biological criteria for blackness were to capture having any traceable African ancestry, many Americans who have had a white social identity (i.e., White Americans) would count as racially black. By contrast, if biological criteria for blackness were to capture having mainly African ancestry, many Americans who have had a black social identity (e.g., Black Americans) would count as racially nonblack. Even if racial classifications could be revised to correspond more tightly to color-conscious social identities as they generally are, the biological criteria (perhaps they could be had by discovering genetic markers for distinctively African physical features) would not represent racial facts that establish natural, objective boundaries of racial classification: the chosen biological criteria would be chasing, so to speak, ordinary racial ascriptions.

Another hurdle for biological criteria is that ordinary racial ascriptions are not globally uniform. In the United States, for example, any visible African ancestry widely translates as monoracially black; in Brazil, different shades (roughly indicating different fractions) of African ancestry widely translate as either monoracially black (i.e., "preto") or multiracially nonblack (e.g., "pardo"). Accounts of race as a social construction, the standard alternative to biological accounts, run into a similar issue: social criteria vary across societies and can be unstable within a society, even as ordinary racial ascriptions remain tied to foundational notions of natural major races (e.g., black/Negroid, white/Caucasoid, yellow/Mongoloid). What "race" talk is supposed to mean is often ambiguous and contested across and within societies.

With this background in mind, I have argued elsewhere for moving on from the race idea and racial thinking, which can be displaced by the idea of *socioancestry* (McPherson 2016). Black Americans are not a racial group; nor is it obvious how they, on the whole, are plausibly supposed to belong with native sub-Saharan Africans (i.e., those who have no non-African ancestry) to a single black race, since many Black Americans have non-African ancestry (like many other Africa-identified persons in the New World). The one-drop rule for racial blackness, while weakening, remains socially prevalent in the United States and evidently retains enough hold over ostensibly common-sense racial thinking to keep insinuating itself in accounts of race as a biological or a social kind.

Earlier I observed that descriptively, Africa-identified persons rooted in the United States have constituted a Black American people. Now I am claiming that they are not helpfully viewed as belonging to a larger black racial group. Black Americans can be more productively thought of as belonging to a larger black socioancestral group—namely, a group comprising Africa-identified peoples. Socioancestral groups are a function of color-conscious social dynamics that reflect facts about a particular component of the continental ancestry of a group's members (McPherson 2016, 14). These social dynamics are directly grounded in social reality, not in convictions about what races as such are. For the black socioancestral group, paradigmatic social dynamics track visible African ancestry, without a default presumption that socioancestral blacks have traceable African ancestry only or mainly. Under this black group, Black Americans constitute a black socioancestral subgroup and would have a socioancestrally Black social identity.

The familiar notion among philosophers, natural scientists, social scientists, and laypeople that talk of races is almost ineliminable in our discourse—without risking conceptual, biological, sociological, or common-sense denial or debilitating confusion—is a stubborn illusion. To counter this illusion, I emphasize the following point: "the notion that 'race' talk is central to the social dynamics of color seems to arise from losing sight of the fact that visible continental ancestry, not the race idea, is the root of the social reality of color consciousness" (McPherson 2016, 13). More thoroughly displacing talk of races with talk of continental descent would yield an improvement in clarity and greater distance from racialist baggage. But "socioancestry" does important work that neither "race" nor "continental descent" talk has done with transparency and stability.

The "socio" in "socioancestry" serves double duty in representing color-conscious social dynamics. For one, it makes reference to distinctive physical features that typically (subject to local variation) are seen as distinguishing continentally identified groups. This is the basis for ascribed color-conscious social identities. Secondly, it refers to self-identifying and collectively identifying as a color-conscious member (given the associated ancestry) of a particular continentally identified group. These ways of identifying can be more historical and sociological than thickly cultural, which is a reason not to equate socioancestry with ethnicity (McPherson 2016, 15). That Black Americans are a black socioancestral subgroup is plainly compatible, though, with recognizing that there is often an ethnic dimension to Black American social identity.

How are we to more concretely understand the transition from racial to socioancestral thinking for the case of black Americans? I propose this:

> Americans who formerly would be recognized as racially black have a reasonable foundation for identifying with the particular mode of socioancestral blackness constitutive of . . . a Black American social identity: namely, they have some traceable African ancestry and (a) strongly identify as descendants of slaves in the United States, or (b) when not descendants of slaves in the United States, strongly identify with them via distinctively African physical features and the social status or reception that accompanies those features. (McPherson 2016, 15)

Along these lines, Black Americans constitute a people and a black socioancestral subgroup. The idea of socioancestry lends support to a coherent, nonracial, quite straightforward sense of their color-conscious national and global Africa-identified social identity.

There is a fair question to ask about what it means to strongly identify as or with descendants of slaves in the United States. Additionally, there is a question as to the manner of identifying more broadly and tenuously (recalling Du Bois) as a member of a group comprising Africa-identified peoples. Paul Taylor's view of blackness suggests a helpful response: "social conditions assign probabilistic meaning to appearance and ancestry," such that the identifyings in question would reflect a sense, as Africa-identified persons, of common fate under conditions of bias against or subordination of blacks. More specifically, Taylor argues, racialism in practice has been determined "to link appearance and ancestry to social location and life chances" with "the effects of earlier [systemic] efforts continu[ing] to shape our life chances in ways that disproportionately disadvantage specific populations" (Taylor 2004, 86). To be clear, my rendering of Taylor's view is contraindicated by his defense of the idea of races as social constructs. But I take the spirit of arguments for the social reality of races to be generally aligned with my call for socioancestral, instead of racial, color consciousness.

BLACKNESS AND THE MULTIRACIAL CHALLENGE

I return to a claim I announced near the beginning: being Black American was not always but has become an elective color-conscious social identity. By this I mean that Americans, including individuals who fit a conventional color-conscious profile as black, are no longer bound by rigid social practice and policy to identify with the corresponding, Africa-identified, monochromatically black social identity. Largely through the efforts of advocates for mixed-race or multiracial recognition, meaningful room in public discourse has opened for individuals to self-identify through color-conscious designations of their preference (see, e.g., Zack 1993 and Sundstrom 2008).

Functionally, of course, this room is available only within conceptual limits: persons who could count as multiracial must have traceable ancestry from more than one continent. The mainstreaming of multiracial recognition was given a state boost when the US Census in 2000 started allowing multiracial self-identification. Somewhat anticlimactically, there has been a very modest increase in the percentage of persons—from .6 percent to 1.0 percent of the total US population—who self-identify as "Black or African American in combination" with another "race" as compared to persons who self-identify as "Black or African American alone" (from 12.3 to 12.9 percent) (Rastogi et al. 2011, 3). Regardless of the numbers or the influence on racial thinking, allowing the option to self-identify as multiracial addresses a type of argument made by Naomi Zack: "If people who think they are monoracial have a right to racial identities, then so ought people who are *biracial* or *multiracial* have that right. To deny mixed-race adults or children identities as mixed is to discriminate against them on racial grounds" (Zack 1998, 22). Note the slide between racial identities and racial being in this argument. Referring to President Barack Obama, for example, Zack writes, "I do not think there is any problem with a mixed-race person choosing to identify as black" (Zack 2010, 11)—as if true mixed-race being might raise a current paradox for monoracial self-identification.

We see again the tendency to reduce color-conscious social identity to racial classification. Black American social identity is not really a racial identity, despite the historically close association between color-conscious social identity and racial classification that would support specifically racial identities. Indeed, Black Americans have always realized that their racialized blackness is not at odds with having traceable African and non-African ancestry: being Black American has not generally been interpreted as representing only facts of continental ancestry. The one-drop rule, whose very purpose was to resolve racial classification in cases of mixed continental ancestry, reflects this social reality. The rule's scientific pretensions hardly masked its primary role as a color-conscious heuristic for situating persons in a society legally and socially committed to black subordination.

In short, being Black American is not a racial designation. That many Black Americans are of mixed continental ancestry has been no barrier to their racial classification as black: the blackness of their visible African ancestry, not the total facts of their ancestry, was racialized. However, the sensible response is not to claim that many Black Americans are, in fact, not black but racially mixed. Such a response runs the risk of racially essentializing color-conscious social identities, as if these identities do or were supposed to represent true racial being (at least for nonwhites). Without racialism, there is no broadly meaningful content anyway to racial identities.

Thus, I argue, having traceable African and non-African ancestry does not provide any distinctive, natural rationale for self-identifying as multiracial and disidentifying as Black American, since that rationale rests on a category mistake. But a social libertarian rationale for multiracial recognition is sensible: persons in a liberal society should be free to pursue their own, noninjurious conceptions of the good, which includes the freedom to adopt color-conscious identities of their preference. By this standard, no one is under an obligation to self-identify as Black American or black; and this is equally true for persons who fit the paradigmatic profile, namely, they have traceable sub-Saharan African ancestry only and are native-born descendants of slaves in the United States (though in this case, they would appear to have no other color-conscious social identity available to them).

Contrary to the fears of Black Americans who care about Black solidarity, there has been no mass rush to exit from Black American social identity. The push for greater mainstream recognition of multiracial identities only highlights that being Black American is no longer an overwhelmingly ascribed color-conscious social identity that native-born Americans who have visible African ancestry are virtually "stuck with," whether they like it or not. A proactively affirmative Black American social identity came to represent, dating from slavery, resistance to the dishonor and mistreatment that have attached to blackness in the United States. The option to disidentify as Black American or black only strengthens the appearance and reality of commitment to electively identifying as Black American, understood in a socioancestral sense.

References

Appiah, Anthony. (1986). "The Uncompleted Argument: Du Bois and the Illusion of Race." In "*Race,*" *Writing, and Difference,* edited by Henry Louis Gates, Jr., 21–37. Chicago: University of Chicago Press.

Appiah, Anthony K. (1996). "Race, Culture, Identity: Misunderstood Connections." In *Color Conscious: The Political Morality of Race,* edited by K. Anthony Appiah and Amy Gutmann, 30–105. Princeton, NJ: Princeton University Press.

Appiah, Kwame Anthony. (2002). "The State and the Shaping of Identity." In *The Tanner Lectures on Human Values,* edited by Grethe B. Peterson, 235–299. Salt Lake City: University of Utah Press.

Davis, David Brion. (2014). *The Problem of Slavery in the Age of Emancipation*. New York: Knopf.

Du Bois, W. E. B. (1897). "The Conservation of Races." In *Writings*, 815–826. New York: Library of America.

Du Bois, W. E. B. (1903). "The Talented Tenth." In *Writings*, 842–861. New York: Library of America.

Du Bois, W. E. B. (1926). "Criteria of Negro Art." In *Writings*, 993–1002. New York: Library of America.

Du Bois, W. E. B. (1940). *Dusk of Dawn: An Essay Toward an Autobiography of a Race Concept*. In *Writings*, 551–802. New York: Library of America.

Ignatiev, Noel. (1995). *How the Irish Became White*. New York: Routledge.

Marcus, Frances Frank. (1983). Louisiana Repeals Black Blood Law. *New York Times*, July 6. Accessed December 23, 2015. http://www.nytimes.com/1983/07/06/us/louisiana-repeals-black-blood-law.html.

McPherson, Lionel K. (2016). "Deflating 'Race.'" *Journal of the American Philosophical Association* 1 (4): 647–693.

McPherson, Lionel K., and Tommie Shelby. (2004). "Blackness and Blood: Interpreting African American Identity." *Philosophy & Public Affairs* 32 (2): 171–192.

Patterson, Orlando. (1982). *Slavery and Social Death: A Comparative Study*. Cambridge, MA: Harvard University Press.

Rastogi, Sonya, Tallese D. Johnson, Elizabeth M. Hoeffel, and Malcolm P. Drewery, Jr. (2011). "The Black Population 2010." Washington, DC: US Census Bureau. Accessed May 16, 2016. https://www.census.gov/prod/cen2010/briefs/c2010br-06.pdf.

Shelby, Tommie. (2005). *We Who Are Dark: The Philosophical Foundations of Black Political Solidarity*. Cambridge, MA: Harvard University Press.

Sundstrom, Ronald R. (2008). *The Browning of America and the Evasion of Social Justice*. Albany: State University of New York Press.

Taylor, Paul C. (2004). *Race: A Philosophical Introduction*. Cambridge: Polity Press.

Washington, Booker T. [1895] (2008). "The Atlanta Exposition Address." In *The Booker T. Washington Reader*, 92–93. Radford, VA: Wilder.

Zack, Naomi. (1993) *Race and Mixed Race*. Philadelphia: Temple University Press.

Zack, Naomi. (1998). *Thinking about Race*. Belmont, CA: Wadsworth.

Zack, Naomi. (2010). "The Fluid Symbol of Mixed Race." *Hypatia* 25 (4): 875–890.

CHAPTER 32

HOW MIXED RACE IS NOT CONSTRUCTED

US Identities and Perspectives

NAOMI ZACK

THE word "race" often means racism, and common usage rarely examines the ontology or taxonomy of human races. Let's for metaphysical purposes suppose that "race" means distinct human races in a biological sense and that biology is the science that determines whether human races exist. If experts in biological anthropology and population genetics conclude that there is no biological human racial taxonomy, then according to science, human races do not exist. However, people have believed that human races exist, in a biological sense, throughout modernity, and they have acted on their ideas about race or used those ideas to justify certain kinds of actions. If we now know that people have been mistaken about the existence of biological race, then such beliefs, ideas, and actions in the past and present must be the "social construction of race." We can evaluate the content of the constructions of each race believed to have existed and also evaluate treatments of races in social taxonomies.

Some people have parents or ancestors who are not all members of the same socially constructed race. It seems obvious, especially in the case of people who have both black and white parents or ancestors, that their social construction as mixed has not received the same attention as the social construction of those who are either black or white. The norm is that mixed black and white people (MBWs) identify themselves as black, are identified as black by others, and identify with black people. However, if MBWs identify as mixed, their identities seem less constructed, because those identities are not the norm for this population in the United States. What can it mean to have an underconstructed racial identity as an MBW in an antiblack racist society where most MBWs identify and are identified as black? Historical and cultural analysis is necessary to understand how black came to be the preferred identity for MBWs, so that claims that MBWs really are, or should be viewed as, mixed, can be examined. I begin with a brief recap of the modern idea of race in terms of philosophy and the biological sciences and then focus on some of the motives for claiming MBW identities.

THE MODERN IDEA OF RACE
IN PHILOSOPHY AND SCIENCE

The modern idea of race was first presented as a system of biological classification, based on the new nineteenth-century sciences of biology and anthropology (Count 1950; Eze 1997). These sciences have now moved on, but "common sense" holds onto earlier ideas about race that issued from experts in those sciences. Also, the history of the social world related to those ideas has a legacy in the present, and that history is ongoing, as people continue to revise and embellish what common sense is holding onto. There are no laws prohibiting false ideas about race, and those who express them are protected by free speech rights. But since so much that people have a right to say and continue to say about race is false, it remains important to understand the general public's metaphysical beliefs about race.

Individuals have physical traits that are considered racial traits in society, and those physical traits are hereditable and occur more frequently in different social racial groups. The physical contrast between different social racial groups has sometimes seemed extreme or was described as extreme when two groups that did not evolve in geographical proximity were suddenly brought together, for example, slaves from sub-Saharan Africa and American settlers from Northern Europe. The most salient racial trait of skin color or hue is, in terms of evolutionary biology, a *cline*: skin color varies continuously among original populations, in a gradient from dark to light, which is directly related to their distance from the equator, where the sun shines most intensely and dark skin was an evolutionary advantage. But even extreme apparent physical differences would not in themselves ground a scientific biological taxonomy, which would have to be independent of social divisions. The need for an independent scientific foundation is underscored by the fact that there is greater variety in phenotypical ("what you see") racial traits within any of the major races in society than between or among them. For example, some white people have darker skin than some black people (Jablonski 2012).

No independent scientific foundation for social racial divisions has been found in the biological sciences, although there is a long history of failed searches—in blood, genes, phenotypes, genotypes, and heritability within populations. As well, over the nineteenth century, the assumptions and speculations of philosophers influenced then-new sciences of anthropology and biology. During the Age of Discovery, philosophers, like many other cultivated Europeans, were dazzled by travelers' reports of human variety in parts of the world that held the promise of valuable resources for Europeans (American Anthropological Association 1998). So striking were the descriptions of human cultural and physical differences, that to accept the reality of distinct human races—if not species—seemed no more than a matter of common sense. David Hume took the existence of human races as self-evident, asserting that only whites had significant achievements (Hume 1875, 252). Immanuel Kant referred to no less an authority than the esteemed Mr. Hume as support for his belief that the existence of human races was obvious, and based on that, he could make idle remarks such as "This fellow was quite black . . . clear proof that what he said was stupid" (Kant 1775, as quoted in in Eze 1997, 38). Georg Wilhelm Hegel scarcely needed the blessings of either Hume or Kant to describe Africa as "the land of childhood . . . enveloped in the dark mantle of night," where "the Negro exhibits the natural man in his completely wild and untamed state" (Hegel 1831, as quoted in Eze 1997, 148–149).

The philosophical acceptance of racial taxonomy included the belief that *essences* for each race also existed. However, no racial human essence has ever been discovered in the biological sciences. The closest things to racial essences might have been blood types, genotypes, or DNA. But investigations of these factors have not yielded anything distinct to specific social races: There are hundreds of human blood types, and none of them line up with social race (Weiner 1950); racial traits are just like any other physical traits—no race gene or specifically racial DNA has ever been detected; DNA markers indicate the likely geographical location of an individual's ancestors, but they do not determine protein, with which physical racial traits would have been constructed. The current scientific consensus is that all modern humans originated in Africa about 100,000 years ago, and there is some doubt about what the skin color of our earliest ancestors was—if they were covered in hair, they might have had very pale skin, like chimpanzees (Jablonski and Chaplin 2000).

The scientists who mapped the human genome found no evidence of specifically racial genes. Of course, there are genes for skin color that people inherit from their parents. There were regulations about human breeding under slavery and the "antimiscegenation" laws of the Jim Crow era lasted until 1967 (*Loving v. Virginia* 1967). The results were family traditions of racial identity, with distinct intergenerational cultures associated with social race. However, family lines are genealogical and whole individuals are units of ancestry and descent. By contrast, genes, the real transmitters of hereditary traits, are parts of individuals that get passed on to future generations through discrete events of conception. For example, someone may know that her great grandmother was of X race, but there is no way to know which genes considered racial in society were inherited by a parent and then by that individual.

In popular thought, social race continues to be closely associated with ancestral origins, that is, blacks in Africa and blacks from Africa. The contemporary *out-of-Africa thesis* in biological anthropology posits an origin of all modern humans in Africa, from which there were a number of main migrations, two migrations from Africa to Asia and then from Asia to Europe, and also a third migration from Asia to the Americas. Depigmentation is hypothesized for adaptation among the early dark-skinned populations who migrated to Asia, and in some cases, further travels may have resulted in repigmentation, a process taking 20,000 or 40,000 years either way (Jablonski 2012).

The *multiregional theory* is the distant rival to the out-of-Africa thesis, holding that different racial groups originated in Europe, Africa, and Asia. But multiregionalists believe there were sufficient mixtures among these populations to make it unlikely that isolated breeding populations could have become races. Over the twentieth century, some population geneticists tried to replace the idea of race with that of populations, defined as groups whose members mostly breed among themselves over generations. However, there are hundreds of thousands of human populations, and the only way to determine which are races is by projecting antecedent social criteria for racial membership onto some populations (Zack 2002, 52–53).

Claiming Mixed Black and White Racial Identities

Although biological race is not real, many people still assume that it is. No one can wave a magic wand and dispense with or "eliminate" race from social reality. Race, as a system of social categories, remains in full force in practical life and requires constant cultural analysis and moral criticism. The tradition of MBW black identity is a practice of *hypodescent* or assigning the race of the lower status parent to offspring. US hypodescent began in slavery. By the eighteenth century, only blacks could be slaves. Inheritance was the mechanism for continuing slavery and protecting capital in slaves, and children born to slave mothers were automatically slaves, even if their fathers were free white men. Jim Crow laws continued both the low status of blacks and hypodescent.

The demographics concerning MBWs are somewhat ambiguous. The US mixed-race population has had the highest birthrate of any racial group since 1967. The 2010 US Census recorded 9 million people who checked more than one box for race, an increase of 30 percent over the 2000 Census. The 1.8 million respondents who checked black and white were about 20 percent of mixed race respondents. But this does not contradict the norm of identifying MBWs as black, instead of as mixed. The census asks people what they are and not how they themselves and others in society further classify them. So far, few philosophers have attended to mixed black and white race, as a subject outside of African American philosophy. That is, most philosophers of race follow the social norm of categorizing MBWs as black.

It is important not to exaggerate the practical importance of the social reality of MBWs who do not identify as black, but insist on identifying as mixed. For one thing, if races have no scientific biological existence, then neither do mixed races! And for another, we can only speculate and draw on autobiographical, narrative, or fictionalized accounts to answer the question, Why do some MBWs identify as mixed, instead of black? Three groups of motives suggest themselves: self-interest, false ideas about biological race, and araciality, or a desire not to engage with race. Discussion of these motives involves consideration of the construction of blackness from MBW heritage, rights of people of mixed heritage, the logic of US hypodescent, passing, and the connection of what J. S. Mill called "social tyranny" with US local government.

Self-Interest in Claiming Mixed MBW Identities

In an antiblack racist society, some mixed black and white people may claim a mixed identity to avoid a black identity with economic and social disadvantages and lower status. And in avoiding a black identity, they may wish to draw closer to a white identity. That self-serving motive takes advantage of both institutional and hearts-and-minds racism, because white identities are not innocent but part of a legacy of oppression and exploitation of blacks. Perhaps the individual has a Nietzschean-type will to power and is not overly bothered by benefitting from collective wrongs committed by others. There may also be antiblack racism in the psyche of the MBW person, since we already know that there are self-hating types who wholly or partly recognize that they have despised social identities and punish themselves for it.

Lingering Beliefs about Biological Race

If one thought that black and white races were biologically real and knew that one had ancestry from both, it might seem to be a matter of integrity to insist that one be recognized as mixed. Such insistence immediately runs into opposition from the logic of the US racial system. While this system might be described by participants as a matter of skin color, alone, in reality, it is also a matter of ancestry. The US system of black and white racial identities requires that in order to be white, a person have no known black ancestry, while to be black, any known black ancestry is sufficient. Ancestry is determined by the race of immediate kin, but the one-drop rule, which became the law of the land at about 1900, specifies that the black ancestor may be many generations back—the "one drop" refers to "one drop" of "black blood," on the mistaken theory that blood is inherited by race (Hickman 1997). Notice that this definition defines black and white as logical contradictories, so that it is assumed that people are either black or white and not some third thing, and of course, not both. On the face of it, such a disjunction is unrealistic, because in addition to blacks and whites, there are Asian and indigenous racial groups. In reality, this "logic" conceals the process by which an MBW becomes "constructed" as black, so we might now consider that, in terms of a recent high profile example.

Constructing MBWs as Black—The First Black President

The process of constructing black racial identity from mixed black and white ancestry was publicly displayed during the period of time spanning Barack Obama's presidential candidacy and inauguration. While Obama was a rising political star in the Senate and during the early days of his candidacy, many Americans thought that he could be a bridge between blacks and whites. Obama frequently offered the story of his personal heritage for public inspiration: His mother had been a white woman from Kansas, his father a black student from Kenya, and he was raised in the multiracial state of Hawaii (Obama 2008). However, after the election, the official congressional *bioguide* seamlessly omitted any reference to Obama's mixed-race ancestry, referring to him as the first African American president of the *Harvard Law Review* before his 1991 JD:

> Born in Honolulu, Hawaii, August 4, 1961; obtained early education in Jakarta, Indonesia, and Hawaii; continued education at Occidental College, Los Angeles, Calif.; received a B.A. in 1983 from Columbia University, New York City; worked as a community organizer in Chicago, Ill.; studied law at Harvard University, where he became the first African American president of the Harvard Law Review, and received J.D. in 1991; lecturer on constitutional law, University of Chicago; member, Illinois State senate 1997–2004; elected as a Democrat to the U.S. Senate in 2004, and served from January 3, 2005, to November 16, 2008, when he resigned from office, having been elected president; elected as the 44th President of the United States on November 4, 2008. (Zack 2010; US Congress 2015)

According to this account, it goes without saying that Obama was African American when elected president, because he was African American before he got his law degree. And, indeed, since his election, he has been ubiquitously referred to as "The First African American President of the United States." This is not to say that there is any evidence that Obama resisted that identification or that he should have resisted it, but merely to indicate that the progress of his identification as black was a process of social construction rather than any kind of biological, or even familial or genealogical, inevitability.

Attacking the Logic of US Black or White

Returning to exploration of a mixed MBW identity claim, based on biology, the mixed-race person who attacks the US "logic" of black and white racial identities may or may not realize that she is engaged in a second-order or metaracial project. If she believes that races are real, that error or ignorance detracts from the "meta" nature of her position. But let's assume only that she knows that other people believe two things: that there are biological races and that all who are mixed descendants of blacks and whites are black. To insist that all MBWs are not black may be to accept a belief that black and white races are biologically real. To accept the racial reality belief and reject the belief that all MBWs are black requires an understanding of how the one-drop rule or hypodescent has no factual basis. The MBW claiming mixed instead of black identity might say to those who both believe that races exist and subscribe to the one-drop rule: "It doesn't make sense to claim that all mixed black and white people are black, if blacks and whites are distinct biological races. Races are types of whole organisms, not isolated traits, and there is no evidence that black racial ancestry dominates all or any other ancestry. If you are going to base your claim on biology, then claims about the dominance of certain traits require evidence of that dominance."

Alternatively, the mixed MBW person might argue morally and say: "It is not just or fair to confer racial identities on people who are falsely thought to be racially 'pure' and withhold them from those who are racially mixed or 'impure.'" The justice the mixed MBW is imagined to be invoking has never existed in matters of racial identity. And we could ask, What would be gained as a result of that kind of justice? If some MBWs were widely and officially recognized as mixed, that would be the beginning of a new social construction of race. Given the violent and unjust actions that have attended every other social construction of race, it may not be wise to insist on such a new construction for this case. Nevertheless, it is important to understand the components of justice for mixed-race people.

Rights for People of Mixed Heritage

Psychologist Maria P. P. Root's well-known 1993 "Bill of Rights for People of Mixed Heritage" is highly relevant to the justice of MBW racial recognition. Root there asserted twelve rights:

Bill of Rights for People of Mixed Heritage

I HAVE THE RIGHT . . .
[1] Not to justify my existence in this world.
[2] Not to keep the races separate within me.
[3] Not to justify my ethnic legitimacy.
[4] Not to be responsible for people's discomfort with my physical or ethnic ambiguity.
[5] To identify myself differently than strangers expect me to identify.
[6] To identify myself differently than how my parents identify me.
[7] To identify myself differently than my brothers and sisters.
[8] To identify myself differently in different situations.
[9] To create a vocabulary to communicate about being multiracial or multiethnic.

[10] To change my identity over my lifetime—and more than once.

[11] To have loyalties and identification with more than one group of people.

[12] To freely choose whom I befriend and love. (Root 1993)

Root's Bill of Rights has been received as encouragement and support for people who claim mixed racial identities (Ortiz 2012). But Root does not tell us what is meant by a "right" and neither does she specify any particular racial mixture or distinguish among racial mixtures. Many Americans have mixed heritage, but some sites of mixture are more fraught than others, namely MBWs, because of the one-drop rule. So what kinds of rights can be asserted for MBWs? There are human rights, which are often unenforced and civil rights that are officially protected by law for African Americans but also often unenforced. Still, some US rights have been enforced, such as Root's [12], the right to freely choose "whom I befriend and love," which would include the right to marry who one chooses. (The right to marry a person of a different race was secured over all US states in 1967, when the US Supreme Court ruled that remaining antimiscegenation laws were unconstitutional [*Loving v. Virginia* 1967].) But other rights, such as the right against unreasonable searches and seizures, are violated with impunity by the actions of police officers against African Americans and those who look African American but are in reality MBWs (Zack 2015, chaps. 1–2).

It is not new or unusual to reassert humanitarian rights or existing legal rights for a particular group. The United Nations began with its Universal Declaration of Human Rights in 1948, as applicable to all subgroups of humanity. But since 1948, the United Nations has produced a plethora of rights declarations for racial minorities, women, children, and refugees, as reminders of their universal rights or calls for special policies to implement them (Zack 2011, 161–166; 2014, 353–356). Root's reference to preexisting rights could be read as a reminder, along the same lines. For instance, to be able to self-identify and to do so differently from how strangers and family members identify one [5], [6], [7], is a preexisting free expression right. Also, the creation of a vocabulary to communicate one's multiracial experience [9] falls under free speech rights. Having loyalties and identification with more than one group of people [11] falls under rights of association and affiliation, both American and international, as does [12], the right to choose who to befriend and love.

Several of Root's stated rights are not rights, but are moral and social freedoms to behave in ways that are already broadly recognized for members of monoracial groups, that is: Not to justify one's existence [1] and "ethnic legitimacy" [3] (although "ethnic legitimacy" is not defined). Not to be responsible for the discomfort of others with one's physical or ethnic ambiguity [4] is a call for civility on the part of those who are not racially mixed.

However, Root does proclaim three new rights: [2] not to keep the races separate within me; [8] to identify myself differently in different situations, and [10] to change my identity over my lifetime, more than once. Root's [2], "Not to keep the races separate within me," either supports a psychologically unified sense of self or is based on false biological notions of race. But [8] and [10], changing ones's identity in different contexts and over a lifetime, may be more radical demands for social change that will accommodate new identities. Contextual change of racial identity during the same time period could be a casual acceptance of how others identify one or a matter of deliberate or inadvertent passing as a social race one is not. A right to pass moves passing from a deceptive and morally questionable practice to a legitimate one. A right to change one's racial identity over a lifetime would be opposed to traditional categorizations of black and white racial identities in the United

States (although oddly, not in South Africa, where legal mechanisms for race change were instituted under apartheid (Carter 2012, 20–22).

New Constructions of Mixed MBW Race

The American tradition of racial identity remains sufficiently essentialist so that the recognized "right" to change one's racial identity over a lifetime—which as a right means that others have no right to disapprove or obstruct or punish one for doing so—would require a new racial construction for MBW persons. And that new construction would evoke the skepticism already noted. The construction of a race has been an intergenerational practice that supervenes on enforced human breeding; for example, people with racial traits identified as "black" have children with others with the same traits and those children carry on that practice. In a segregated society, racial groups thus formed through intergenerational social practices may live in the same neighborhoods and be subject to the same social, legal, economic, and political problems. Except for isolated sub-subcultures (Greissman 1972; Countries and Their Cultures 2015), this has not occurred with bi- or multiracial Americans, and it is difficult to imagine how it could be a positive project. Multiracial people would not be white, so they would have to deliberately and positively go about constructing a new subaltern identity, or perhaps an identity of struggle. Membership in the kind of intergenerational communities that constitute American racial groups would be voluntary in this case. Such a construction would be historically new, because previous constructions of race have been supported by oppressive laws specifically targeted against some groups (see Zack, Chapter 46, this volume). A deliberate construction of mixed MBW as a multigenerational lifestyle could be a new social movement(s).

Aracial Mixed MBW Identity

We now consider a third kind of mixed MBW claim and its motives. Here, the MBW person begins with knowledge that there is no foundation for biological race; most people think that there is a foundation for biological race; and custom has established that those with black and white ancestry, who would be racially mixed if there were a foundation for biological race, are black. Let us assume that the MBW person accepts this entire situation and does not go out of her way, as in the previous case, to argue with those who still believe that there are biological races and also believe that all of the MBWs are black. She knows that she has ancestry from more than one racial group and checks two (or more) race boxes on official forms. But she does not go out of her way to identify with either blacks or whites and does not spend a lot of energy advocating for the rights of racially mixed people. What kind of racial experience might that motivation and position generate?

We have not said what the positive motivation is in this case, because the person who identifies as mixed in this way does not seem to have anything to gain. Blacks may or may not accept her as either black or mixed, and many whites will not understand "what" she says she is. There are no special entitlements or sympathies for self-declared mixed MBWs in the United States. On the contrary, she may in the twenty-first century be called what she would have been called in colonial times—"spurious issue" (Spencer 1999). There is no stable, mixed MBW community that she can join, apart from websites and social media (Mixed Heritage Center, www.mixedheritagecenter.org; Mixed Nation, www.facebook.com/MixedNation). In effect, this person is avoiding race insofar as it pertains to her. As mixed, her personal position is aracial. She may advocate for social justice for black Americans, in her civic or professional life—but there is no inconsistency if she does not.

The aracial position might yield glimpses of how life might be for many more people if they made "race" less relevant to themselves. One wonders, how many of the 19 million US Census 2010 respondents who checked "Some Other Race," which was an increase of 4 million from the 2000 Census (US Census Bureau 2010a, 2010b), see themselves as aracial and what their experiences are like.

Passing and Social Tyranny

Because human beings are complicated psychologically, it seems safe to assume that all or most MBWs who identify as mixed do so from motives combining self-interest, advocacy, and avoidance of race. The situation is further complicated, because in considering these three motivational options for MBWs who identify as mixed, the motivations of the mixed person who actively passes or attempts to pass for white have been left out. Passing for white is only an option for those who look white. At different times in US history, the fact or possibility of passing has been the site of public hysteria and fascination on the part of whites who feared contamination, caused grief in black families over losing relatives, and resulted in loss of their families of origin to those who left them in successfully passing as white (Piper 1992; Larson 2007). Accurate numbers and first-person accounts of those who have so passed have been elusive (Conyers and Kennedy 1964). The secrecy of such passing and black fears of violent retaliation by whites or those who have passed is part of US folklore up to the present (Butler 2014).

The phenomenon of black-to-white passing reveals how thoroughly social American racial identities are. There have never been laws specifying that everyone must identify as a member of a particular race and US Census response requires voluntary identification. Moreover, US courts have refused to grant a right to individuals to change their racial classifications after they have been specified on birth certificates. The judicial reasoning has acknowledged the lack of science or objective criteria for racial identity, but supported the custom of the time and place where a person is born as a standard for racial identification (Gilroy 1982). Racial identity, in general, has been social tyranny by any relevant majority. This means that all American racial identities and especially MBW identities are the outcome of interactions and conflicts between what their subjects want them to be and what others, often more powerful, want them to be. We would do well to remember what J. S. Mill cautioned about such oppression (although it is doubtful that he would have extended his thoughts to mixed race):

> Like other tyrannies, the tyranny of the majority was at first, and is still vulgarly, held in dread, chiefly as operating through the acts of the public authorities. But reflecting persons perceived

that when society is itself the tyrant—society collectively over the separate individuals who compose it—its means of tyrannizing are not restricted to the acts which it may do by the hands of its political functionaries. Society can and does execute its own mandates; and if it issues wrong mandates instead of right, or any mandates at all in things with which it ought not to meddle, it practices a social tyranny more formidable than many kinds of political oppression, since, though not usually upheld by such extreme penalties, it leaves fewer means of escape, penetrating much more deeply into the details of life, and enslaving the soul itself. Protection, therefore, against the tyranny of the magistrate is not enough; there needs protection also against the tyranny of the prevailing opinion and feeling, against the tendency of society to impose, by other means than civil penalties, its own ideas and practices as rules of conduct on those who dissent from them; to fetter the development and, if possible, prevent the formation of any individuality not in harmony with its ways, and compel all characters to fashion themselves upon the model of its own. There is a limit to the legitimate interference of collective opinion with individual independence; and to find that limit, and maintain it against encroachment, is as indispensable to a good condition of human affairs as protection against political despotism. (Mill 2011, 7)

Mill assumes that social tyranny is distinct from government oppression. But on local levels in the United States, prevailing social mores and norms determine local government oppression. And the federal government has a consistent record of being too slow or generally reluctant to protect citizens against oppression by local government officials, even by simply applying or enforcing existing federal law. For example, although President Eisenhower did support integration by sending federal troops to Arkansas, in 1957, three years after *Brown v. Board of Education*, many K-12 schools remained racially segregated, throughout the United States over the twentieth century, and until now. And, although the Fourteenth Amendment provides for equal protection under the law, the US Supreme Court has not found it relevant to criminal justice cases where nonwhites are treated differently from whites (Zack 2015, 49, 77, 88–89).

The absence of federal government protection of individuals who have been treated unjustly by local government officials, who are in turn influenced by local beliefs and power structures, is nothing new in US matters of race and racism. It is in part what is meant by "freedom" in our federal system. Thus, what Mill refers to as "political oppression" is in the United States largely coextensive with social oppression. That is, regarding race and racism, "freedom" often means rule by oppressive custom, based on tradition. Opportunities for mixed-race racial construction—if that is a desirable goal—will continue to depend on social changes among traditionalists of all races. The mix of prejudice, dominance, fear, ignorance, and inertia makes the material to be worked with both amorphous and intransigent. But rapid reactions to demographic changes are also part of the historical process that is flypaper for us all. The 20 percent of mixed Americans who checked black and white on the 2010 census may be joined by others who claim MBW as an identity in its own right, or the "Some Other Race" category may grow. That the fastest growing live-birth category continues to consist of mixed-race individuals is raw material for real change.

References

American Anthropology Association. (1998). "AAA Statement on Race." *American Anthropologist* 100 (3): 712–713.

Butler, Meg. (2014). "Michelle Obama Still The First Black First Lady? Historical Figures You Didn't Know Were Black." *Madame Noir*, Oct. 2. Accessed May 18, 2016. http://madamenoire.com/481003/historical-figures-you-didnt-know-were-black/2/.

Carter, Prudence L. (2012). *Stubborn Roots: Race, Culture, and Inequality in U.S. and South African Schools*. New York: Oxford University Press.

Conyers, James, and T. Kennedy. (1964). "Reported Knowledge Negro and White College Students Have of Negroes Who Have Passed as Whites." *Journal of Negro Education* 33 (4): 454–459.

Count, Earl W., ed. (1950). *This Is Race: An Anthology Selected from the International Literature on the Races of Man*. New York: Schuman.

Countries and Their Cultures. (2015). "American Isolates." Accessed May 18, 2016. http://www.everyculture.com/North-America/American-Isolates.html.

Gilroy, James. (1982). "Suit on Race Recalls Lines Drawn under Slavery." *The New York Times*, Sept. 30. Accessed May 18, 2016. http://www.nytimes.com/1982/09/30/us/suit-on-race-recalls-lines-drawn-under-slavery.html.

Greissman, B. Eugene. (1972). "The American Isolates." *American Anthropologist* 74: 693–734.

Eze, Emmanuel Chukwudi, ed. (1997). *Race and the Enlightenment: A Reader*, Cambridge, MA: Blackwell.

Hickman, Christine B. (1997). "The Devil and the One Drop Rule: Racial Categories, African Americans, and the U.S. Census." *Michigan Law Review* 95 (5): 1161–1265.

Hume, David. (1875). "Of National Characters." In *Essays Moral, Political and Literary*, edited by T. H. Green and T. H. Grose, eds., essay XXI. London: Longmans, Green and Col.

Jablonski, N. G., and G. Chaplin. (2000). "The Evolution of Human Skin Coloration." *Journal of Human Evolution* 39 (1): 57–106.

Jablonski, N. G., and G. Chaplin. (2012). *Living Color: The Biological and Social Meaning of Skin Color*. Berkeley: University of California Press.

Larsen, Nella. (2007). *Passing*. New York: Modern Library.

Loving v. Virginia, U.S. Supreme Court, 1967 (395). Accessed May 18, 2016. https://www.law.cornell.edu/supremecourt/text/388/1.

Mill, John Stuart. (2011). "On Liberty." *Project Gutenberg*. Accessed May 18, 2016. https://www.gutenberg.org/files/34901/34901-h/34901-h.htm.

Obama, Barack. (2008). "We the People, in Order to Form a More Perfect Union." *Politico*, March 18. Accessed May 18, 2016. http://www.politico.com/news/stories/0308/9100.html.

Ortiz, Adam. (2012). "Revisiting Dr. Maria Root's Bill of Rights for People of Mixed Heritage." *Multiracial Network Blog*. Accessed May 18, 2016. https://multiracialnetwork.wordpress.com/2012/09/10/revisiting-roots-bill-of-rights/.

Piper, Adrian. (1992). "Passing for White, Passing for Black." *Transition* 58: 4–32.

Root, Maria P. P. (1993). "Bill of Rights for Racially Mixed People." Accessed May 18, 2016. https://multiracialnetwork.files.wordpress.com/2012/09/billofrights.png.

Spencer, Ranier. (1999). *Spurious Issues: Race and Multiracial Identity Politics in the United States*. Boulder, CO: Westview Press.

US Census Bureau. (2010a). "The Two or More Races Population, 2010." Accessed May 18, 2016. https://www.census.gov/prod/cen2010/briefs/c2010br-13.pdf.

US Census Bureau. (2010b). "Overview of Race and Hispanic Origin." Accessed May 18, 2016. http://www.census.gov/prod/cen2010/briefs/c2010br-02.pdf.

US Congress. (2015). "Obama, Barack." Accessed May 18, 2016. http://bioguide.congress.gov/scripts/biodisplay.pl?index=O000167.

Weiner, Alexander S. (1950). "Anthropological Investigations on the Blood Groups." In *This is Race: An Anthology Selected from the International Literature on the Races of Man*, edited by Earl W. Count, 679–687. New York: Henry Schuman.

Zack, Naomi. (2002). *Philosophy of Science and Race*. New York: Routledge.

Zack, Naomi. (2010). "The Fluid Symbol of Mixed Race." *Hypatia* 25 (4): 875–890.

Zack, Naomi. (2011). *The Ethics and Mores of Race*. Lanham, MD: Rowman and Littlefield.

Zack, Naomi. (2014). "Philosophical Theories of Justice, Inequality, and Racial Inequality." *Graduate Faculty Philosophy Journal* 35 (1–2): 353–368.

Zack, Naomi. (2015). *White Privilege and Black Rights: The Injustice of US Police Racial Profiling and Homicide*. Lanham, MD: Rowman and Littlefield.

CHAPTER 33

....

RACIAL IDENTITY,
RACIAL ONTOLOGY,
AND RACIAL NORMS

....

RON MALLON

IN contemporary social discourse, I am said to have a sexual identity, a gender identity, a racial identity, and a national identity. What does this sort of talk mean? As a first pass, we can say that my identity is what makes me what I am. My *personal* identity makes me the person that I am. My *kind* identities make me a member of the kinds to which I belong. Prima facie, most of these contemporary claims about *social identity* are claims about a certain sort of kind identity—claims about the sort of person one is. Here I focus upon the case of race and of racial identity. Claims about racial identity are an important feature of contemporary social life, but the character of identity itself remains unclear.

One question is raised by race itself: What does race have to be for racial identification to be possible? The importance of this question is further compounded by common appeals to racial identity in racial norms—norms that prescribe or proscribe behaviors based on racial identity. Consider some examples. People are sometimes criticized for dressing or grooming in a way that is not racially typical, such as wearing certain clothing, a hairstyle, or employing a vocabulary or way of speaking that stands out. Relatedly, a person's racial identity is often seen to confer a presumptive entitlement to certain sorts of cultural expression while others may be criticized for the same expressions, for example, white artists who adopt forms of cultural expression originating with black artists. Choices of sexual or romantic or marriage partners are sometimes criticized on the grounds that the chosen partner is not of an appropriate race. And one's political opinions may be viewed as a betrayal of one's race, as in the perceived obligation of black public figures to refrain from public criticism of black persons or culture. Such racial norms are controversial. Crucially, they seem to explicitly refer to racial identity. But it is not clear how race, understood as a kind of person, could justify such norms.

Here, I explore what racial identity is and how it might connect to racial norms. I argue that the existence of racial identity presupposes the existence of race, and that certain understandings of what racial identity amounts to presuppose much more. One such understanding, a *strong communal* account of race, could support racial norms, and so one way of understanding appeals to racial norms is that they are appeals to strong communal interpretations of race. But I also argue that contemporary American racial groups do not have this strong communal character and so appeals to shared race or racial identity do not justify racial norms. I close by considering whether any racial norms are or might be justified and, if so, how.

Racial Identity as a Collective Identity

Kwame Anthony Appiah (2005) understands racial identities to be instances of "collective identities," underlining that the sorts of kinds that we are interested in are those that shape our connections to others. Appiah's account is complex but very general; he writes that "every collective identity seems to have the following sort of structure":

> First, it requires the availability of terms in public discourse that are used to pick out the bearers of the identity by way of criteria of ascription, ... Let us call a typical label for a group "L." This consensus is usually organized around a set of stereotypes (which may be true or false) concerning Ls, beliefs about what typical Ls are like, how they behave, how they may be detected ...
>
> A second element of a social identity is the internalization of those labels as parts of the individual identities of at least some of those who bear the label. ... We can call this *identification as an L*. Identification as an L ... means thinking of yourself as an L in ways that make a difference ...
>
> The final element of a social identity is the existence of patterns of behavior toward Ls, such that Ls are sometimes *treated as Ls*. (2005, 66–67)

Consider these aspects of racial identities further.

Classification as

Appiah's account requires *classification as,* where widespread labels and descriptions are applied both in the *first person* (by oneself to oneself) and in the *third person* (by oneself to others and by others to oneself). "Classification as" essentially involves some label and concept of L. A "concept" of L is the meaning that L expresses. For example, "Jewish" expresses the property *Jewish*. "Irish" expresses the property *Irish*, and "black" expresses the property *black*.

Identification as in Two Senses: Life-Shaping and Communal Identity

By itself, "classification as" is a thin or minimal sort of identity, because one could classify as "brown-eyed" or as "taller than five feet." But Appiah is interested in identifying a stronger sense of identity, one that involves what he calls "identification as," where that involves "thinking of yourself as an L in ways that make a difference." Identification can make a difference in two distinct ways (Appiah 2005, 66–67).

The first, *life-shaping* sense of "identification as" occurs when a person allows one's ideas about Ls to shape her choices of actions, plans, and projects in ways that can be positive or negative (Appiah 1996, 78; 2005, 68). Concepts of L are generally associated with *conceptions* of L, or sets of beliefs and associations that represent features of L and its relations to the world. These include what Appiah calls a "set of stereotypes" about Ls, but they might also include beliefs such as: "The Irish are from Ireland"; "White people are usually ignorant of the social advantages that a racially white appearance bestows"; or more generally, "Members of L have L-typical features."

Like stereotypes, these beliefs can be true or false. Importantly, all this information can shape one's own actions, plans, and projects in a variety of ways: by suggesting actions, scripts, narratives, and projects for those who fall under "L." The second dimension of "identification as" is *communal* identity. Appiah explains how the label "makes a difference" in this sense:

> Perhaps thinking of yourself as an L shapes your feelings (so you respond with pride as an L when an L triumphs); perhaps it shapes your actions, so that you sometimes do something as an L (offering a helping hand to another L, perhaps, who is otherwise a stranger; or restraining your public conduct by the thought that misbehavior will reflect badly on Ls. Often, then, being an L carries ethical and moral weight . . . (2005, 68)

Communal identity has varying degrees of strength. At the weaker end, communal identity involves simple affective resonance with other members of your community. In St. Louis where I live, nearly everyone seems to affectively resonate with the performance of the Cardinals baseball team, for instance. At the stronger end, it shades into an explicitly recognized moral community toward which one has open-ended reciprocal obligations to others. Consider the behavior of a small, tight-knit religious community. Or consider the concerted cooperation of union officials, members, and their families during a successful strike. Even more cohesive cooperation might be found among members of a military unit. And we can see strong communal cooperation by a racial community if we consider, for example, the cooperation of African Americans in Alabama during the successful 1955–1956 Montgomery bus boycott. In all these cases, ongoing, open-ended cooperation by a group generates social goods for group members. These examples amount to *strong* cases of communal identity because they demand that the world be arranged in certain ways and impose personal demands upon those who participate in them. One can see oneself as a member of a racial group, even in ways that "make a difference," without thereby taking oneself to be bound into such a demanding cooperative enterprise in virtue of shared race.

It is plausible that strong communal identity could underwrite communal-specific racial norms. If members of a cooperative community consistently receive the assistance of others or of a group, but fail to cooperate in return, that may be grounds for censure, and ultimately ostracism. To fail to cooperate risks a failure to sustain such a cooperative community in the face of unchecked freeriding. If having a racial identity just is being a member of a strongly reciprocal community, it makes sense that norms required for that community would appeal to racial identity.

Because racial classification typically involves criteria that are themselves objective features of a person, one typically falls under a racial concept independent of the content of one's beliefs, choices, or decisions. But because they seem to carry "ethical and moral weight," collective identities centered on race raise the question of whether one could have a strong communal identity without having chosen it. The issues here are complex, but we can say roughly that from a liberal perspective, such collective obligation is always a product of, and derives its moral force from, individual consent to the arrangement. From this perspective, no one can have special communal obligations in virtue of a racial identity unless the person consents to membership in the collective identity (although perhaps the consent could be tacit or dispositional). In contrast, from a communitarian perspective, a communal identity can be unchosen, but still result in moral obligation. On this conception, we simply find ourselves with moral duties just as (and because) we find ourselves to be classified as members of races.

Appiah emphasizes a role for choice in both the project-shaping and communal dimensions of "identification as." "Someone who has gay identity is doing more than simply acknowledging the fact that he has homosexual desires, and someone who has an identity as a black person is doing more than simply acknowledging an African ancestry" (2005, 70). And in an earlier discussion regarding racial identity, he explains that "where my ascriptive identity is one on which almost all my fellow citizens agree, I am likely to have little sense of choice about whether the identity is mine; though I *can* choose how central my identification with it will be—choose, that is, how much I will organize my life around that identity" (1996, 80).

Classification and Identification: Conceptual Connections

All these distinctions are important because it is easy to focus upon what is perhaps an idealized case, the person who is first and third person classified as an L and who identifies as an L. But these dimensions can be pulled apart, conceptually and practically.

Both "identification as" an L and third-person "treating as" an L conceptually require "classification as" an L, and "identification as" an L involves some additional endorsement or affective alignment with label bearers that changes one's behavior. In contrast, mere "classification as" an L (in the first or third person) need not result in thinking of yourself or another as an L in (as Appiah has it) ways that "make a difference." One can self-classify as belonging to a category without being very affectively aligned with that category, for example, "brown-eyed" or "taller than five feet." This is at least a part of what Appiah has in mind when he speaks of there being "something more" to a racial identity than acknowledgment of one's biological lineage.

So we can distinguish the weaker "classification as" from the stronger "identification as" and the third-person "treating as." But classification as L, identification as L, and treating as L all employ some label "L" whose meaning seems essential to the identity. What is the meaning of "L"? That is, what is the meaning of racial or racialized terms like "Asian," "black," "Hispanic," "Jewish," "Latino," and "white"?

MUST RACE BE, FOR RACIAL IDENTITY TO BE?

Philosophical accounts of meaning are quite complex, but we can make some progress simply by noting that a common candidate for an aspect of meaning is the *referent*, or the thing in the world that the term is about. For race, there are broadly three different candidate referents and three different accounts of what race might be. On one family of accounts, race is a *biological kind*. Traditional *racialism* holds that races are characterized by the possession of endogenous features that determine race-typical properties. Nowadays, most biologically sophisticated theorists reject traditional racialism as biologically implausible though some offer more sophisticated biological interpretations (e.g., Andreasen 1998; Spencer 2014). A second, *skeptical* answer argues from the failure of a biological racialism to the conclusion that race simply does not exist (e.g., Zack 1993, 2002; Appiah 1995, 1996; Blum 2002). Racial terms pick out nothing. A third *constructionist* family of answers is that racial terms pick out some sort of real social entity or institution that is caused or constituted by our social and conceptual practices (e.g., Outlaw 1995; Mills 1998; Taylor 2013).

We just noted that classification as a member of a race L involves using a label "L" that expresses a property L. This practice assumes, and so "classification as" depends upon, a rejection of racial skepticism. If *L* does not exist, then every act of classifying oneself or another as an *L* is a mistake. A fortiori, "identification as" and "treating as" also must reject skepticism, because they presuppose successful classification as an L.

Skeptics can, of course, embrace this result, and some would take recognition of it to urge an abandonment of racial identity all together. However, as Lucius Outlaw perspicuously remarked early in the philosophical debate over the metaphysics of race: "For most of us that there are different races of people is one of the most obvious features of our social worlds" (1990, 58). It is thus tempting, even for many racial skeptics, to seek some amelioration of this consequence. What could a defender of racial identity who embraces racial skepticism say?

One possibility for the skeptic is to appeal to some sort of *substitutionism* about the referent of race used in racial identification. On this view, a racial skeptic might allow that race does not exist but insist that there is nothing to stop us from using racial terms to pick out some sort of social kind or group going forward (Glasgow 2009). However, on this view, all the ordinary, unreformed people with ordinary, unreformed views about race are still mistaken in engaging in racial "classification as," "identification as," and "treating as."

A related tack for the skeptic to ameliorate the denial of racial identity is to supplement an account of the nonexistence of race with an account of the existence of something else. Appiah (1996), for example, qualifies his racial skepticism with an account of racial identities. However, if what we have just argued is correct, on Appiah's own account, "identification as" an L requires that there be some property or kind L. Racial identification, as he articulates it, involves quantification over something that does not exist. If race does not exist, then racial identity also involves an individual or collective mistake.

A third option might be racial *contextualism*, the view that racial terms have different meanings in different contexts. In contexts of "identification as," racial terms could be used in a way that picks out something real (e.g., a social kind), while in contexts concerned with the reality of race, simpliciter, racial terms refer to nothing. While such contextualism is a possibility, it obviously opens up ground for opponents of skepticism to reply: Why not just say that "race" picks out something real all along, and not only in cases of racial identity?

A final option for the skeptic is to distinguish an *additional* sense of racial identity that I will call *identification with*. Sometimes we identify with the values that are represented in the conception of a kind of person. One might identify with a soldier's values of discipline and honor, or with the values of a particular community. "Identifying with," in this sense, involves taking the descriptions, narratives, and associations linked with a category as grounds for shaping one's projects. But, importantly, it seems possible to "identify with" things that one is not and even cannot be. My father, born in 1940 in central Kansas, identified powerfully throughout his life with the fictionalized cowboys he saw depicted in the television shows and movies of his childhood although he was not himself a cowboy or rancher (nor did he take himself to be).

"Identification with" opens the possibility that we can use even fictional categories or properties as ideals or guides, such as the fictional racial properties of a Vulcan. In her book *Thinking in Pictures: My Life with Autism*, Temple Grandin reports being a fan of *Star Trek*, writing that she "strongly identified with the logical Mr. Spock" who did not allow emotions to "overpower logical thinking" (2006, 152). Here "identification with" could involve the conception of a category shaping self-understanding and behavior in something like the project-shaping sense that Appiah describes. This suggests that the skeptic could allow that racial identity is the act of "identifying with" some values, traits, or narratives that are associated with (or represented in the conception of) a particular race, even if one's beliefs in the existence or character of the category are actually mistaken. "Identification with" in this sense can occur even if skepticism is true.

What Must Race Be Like for There To Be Racial Identification?

In contrast to racial skepticism, realist (biological and constructionist) theorists hold that race is a real kind. Thus, for realists, "classification as" is possible, as is "identification as" and "treating as." Still, racial realists get their various stripes because they disagree about the nature of the properties—biological or social or both—that constitute or ground racial kinds. Racial identification presupposes the existence of race. But does it presuppose anything further about the character of race? What must race be like to support the various aspects of racial identification?

Much has been written about the failure of biological accounts of race, and there are now sophisticated discussions of these arguments that I will not discuss further here (e.g., Appiah 1996; Zack 2002; Kitcher 2007; Templeton 2013). Instead, I will continue to focus upon racial identity. While racial identity presupposes the existence of race, it may not presuppose much about the exact character of the properties or processes that constitute, ground, or sustain it.

We find ourselves in a world not of our own making that, for many of us, is divided into races upon our arrival. The explanation of racial differences might be (for all we pretheoretically know) biological or social or some complex combination. Crucially, practices of racial identification proceed without settling this question: Once we learn the ascription conditions for the types to which we and others are said to belong, we classify ourselves and others as members of races.

A familiar thought from the philosophy of language is that the conception that we associate with the label gives our "epistemic take" on the nature of the underlying kind. Descriptivists about reference have suggested that our terms refer to whatever thing uniquely or best satisfies the conception (e.g., Lewis 1970, 1972). If nothing does (as skeptics insist in the case of race), then the label or term does not refer. Externalists about reference, however, have famously suggested that the nature of the kind itself could be very different than anything we believe about it (Kripke 1972/1980; Putnam 1975). If externalists are right, then it would be wrong to read the conception associated with a label as expressing necessary conditions for falling under the label. Given this, the best strategy might be not to ask what people with racial identity think about race, but rather what racial identification seems to presuppose about race. What would race have to be like to support racial identification?

"Identification as" in the project-shaping sense requires that we take our own conceptions of racial identity as a guide for how we behave in the world. Any robust conception of racial identity (whether it emphasizes biology, culture, or both) is likely to shape our behavior in this way. It happens because facts about the kinds that we belong to are relevant to which of our plans are likely to succeed and which to fail. If people like me normally succeed in activities like this and do not usually succeed in activities like that, perhaps I will choose this over that. (In this way, conceptions of kinds may produce "looping effects" that confirm the conceptions.) The important thing is that project-shaping "identification as" seems to rely on the existence of race, and on the presence of ideas about race, but it does not depend upon those ideas having any very specific content. Nor does it depend upon those ideas being accurate indicators of the actual character of race. Indeed, what I called "identification with" is the extreme case in which this project-shaping of racial conceptions could proceed, shorn of even the existence of an actual referent.

"Identification as" in the communal sense is more complex. At the weak end of communal identity, nearly any label that we apply to ourselves and others produces some affective realignment favoring in-group over out-group members (e.g., Tajfel et al. 1971, Dunham, Baron, and Carey 2011; Cikara and Van Bavel 2014). That is to say, *even arbitrary labels* that are *conspicuously made up* "make a difference" to people's feelings and preferences. In these minimal cases "identification as" does not presuppose anything substantive about the nature of race itself. In contrast, if we understand "identification as" in a strongly communal sense, it does seem to presuppose participation in a genuine cooperative community. This requires both the existence and ongoing cooperation of others in the community, and it also requires a system of reciprocal dispositions to cooperate extending through time and across the members of the community. Strong, communal identification thus places very substantial constraints on what L could be: it has to be a collective group, the members of which are engaged in ongoing cooperative projects. This assumption goes well beyond the mere existence of race understood either as a biological or a social kind. Even if races were purely biological kinds, they need not form such communal groups. Most biological kinds are not members of prosocial communities in this sense, and many biological human kinds are not bases of prosocial communities. Similarly, many constructionist accounts of race do not realize strong communal forms of identity. If, for example, racial identities exist because of subjection to common forms of racial classification within a system of racial labeling, this does not imply that those subject to shared racial labels do, or should, form a collective group in some stronger sense.

COMMUNAL IDENTITY AND RACIAL NORMS

Where it exists, strong communal identity does carry with it the possibility of a very substantive interpretation of Appiah's intimation of "ethical and moral weight." Communal "identification as" involves not only affective resonance with others but ongoing, robust cooperative connections that require norms to exclude those who would freeride on the goods produced by in-group cooperation. Racial norms might then be justified by appeal to their necessary role in sustaining a community that is itself good in myriad ways (Sandel 1982; Kitcher 1999, 2011). Indeed, one way to interpret common appeals to racial norms is as implicitly assuming that racial identity is strongly communal.

But communal forms of identity strong enough to sustain racial norms directed at thwarting freeriding on the goods produced by in-group cooperation make very substantial assumptions about the social organization of racial groups. Since not all social practices of labeling persons produce cooperative communities that produce collective goods and face the dangers of freeriding, even constructionist accounts of race would have to be of a very special and demanding sort.

In fact, strong communal "identification as" is a poor source for grounding the legitimacy of actual contemporary racial norms because prototypical contemporary American races are not strongly communal in this sense. Note first that contemporary American races and ethnicities—African American, Asian American, Italian American, Jewish American, and so on—are not geographically local identities. They are rather *big* groups of *diverse* people distributed across the United States, and they have a range of different attitudes and alignments. It is thus implausible to regard all members as in a reciprocal cooperative community with one another. While there may be spatio-temporally local conditions in which race or ethnicity is coextensive with a cooperative community, this is not the typical case for American racial identities.

We can add to this that it is implausible to regard contemporary racial identity as involving consent—even tacit or dispositional assent—to an ongoing, reciprocal system of cooperation with members of one's race. And suggesting that obligations to a cooperative community exist in the absence of such consent (as on a communitarian conception might) is a very strong and difficult-to-defend assumption. Without this contentious assumption, and in the absence of actual consent, it is hard to see how racial groups could ground obligations to abide by racial norms.

In short, while it is true that racial (among other) identities mediate and direct prosociality in ways that matter, they do not provide a strong communal foundation for regulating in-group and out-group members since American racial groups do not, in fact, form such racial communities and because communal obligations plausibly require consent. If these arguments are right, then racial identity does not ground racial norms.

Racial Norms, but Not From Racial Identity

Many racial norms seem like attempts to regulate behavior in ways that assume racial identities form communal groups. For example, consider the norm that members of a racial group bear a special obligation not to publically criticize the racial group (beyond any obligation borne by nonmembers). But if there are no racial collectives of the sort that could support cooperative racial norms, does that mean that there are no legitimate racial norms? Again, some would be happy to abandon all racial norms as mistaken and unjust, and surely some—perhaps many—of them are. But given their pervasiveness in contemporary social life, is a less revolutionary path available to the racial identity theorist?

I have argued against understanding racial identity as a source of racial norms, but I am not skeptical about the existence or normative force of racial norms. For instance, the following seem like norms that rightly (if defeasibly) characterize contemporary American social life: White people should not use the "n-word" to insult or degrade or harass. People should not misrepresent or lie about their race (according to commonly excepted criteria) in order to occupy a job or another valuable social position. White people who enjoy the benefits of historic injustice ought to work to, and certainly ought at least acquiesce to, attempts to rectify such injustice even at reasonable cost to themselves.

But if these are genuine norms, they must have some other grounding than in racial identity. A plausible alternative source for such racial norms is simply applications of general moral norms, norms like: do not insult, degrade, or harass people; do not lie; be fair. When these general norms are applied in a society that divides itself with racial labels, they may fall differently upon different people in different circumstances, producing norms that mention race. But they do not appeal to racial identity as the source of their justification.

Consider just one sort of example. Suppose you and a friend are walking by a lake. You, but not your friend, see that someone is struggling in the lake and may drown. This knowledge plausibly imposes a moral obligation on you to act, an obligation not shared by your friend. For instance, it would be wrong for you, but not for your friend, to continue to walk along as before. Standpoint epistemologists have urged that an individual who is treated as a member of L may thereby occupy a special epistemic position. Such a position could, for example, produce knowledge of the situation of Ls that is not usually shared by non-Ls (Alcoff 2001), and such knowledge might, in some circumstances, impose moral obligations to act in certain ways.

If racial identities result in a situation in which certain sorts of beliefs are distributed differently across different racial identities, and if possession of such beliefs produces moral obligation, a difference in racial identity could produce a difference in moral obligation. These obligations stem not from the nature of race or racial identity itself, but from the much weaker assumption that, whatever race or racial identity is, it influences one's belief set in systematic ways.

Conclusion: Ontology, Identity, Normativity

While there has been much work in recent years on the metaphysics of race, there has been less on racial identity. This is unfortunate if, as I have argued here, what we say about racial identity constrains and is constrained by what we say about race itself, and both further constrain, and are constrained by, the common application of racial norms. Racial identification seems to involve a commitment to racial classification and some sort of realism about race. Racial norms, if they are to be justified by appeal to racial identity, require strong communal accounts of what race is. But these communal forms of racial identity require demanding social arrangements among members of a racial identity that are not in place for prototypical national racial categories in the contemporary United States. It follows that racial norms cannot be justified by appeal to racial identity. If they are to be sustained, they must be justified in some other way.

References

Alcoff, L. (2001). "On Judging Epistemic Credibility: Is Social Identity Relevant?" In *Engendering Rationalities*, edited by N. Tuana and S. Morgan, 53–80. Albany: State University of New York Press.

Andreasen, R. O. (1998). "A New Perspective on the Race Debate." *British Journal of the Philosophy of Science* 49: 199–225.

Appiah, Anthony. (2005). *The Ethics of Identity*. Princeton, NJ: Princeton University Press.

Appiah, K. Anthony. (1995). "The Uncompleted Argument: Du Bois and the Illusion of Race." In *Overcoming Racism and Sexism*, edited by L. A. Bell and D. Blumenfeld, 59–77. Lanham, MD: Rowman and Littlefield.

Appiah, K. A. (1996). "Race, Culture, Identity: Misunderstood Connections." In *Color Conscious: The Political Morality of Race*, edited by K. A. Appiah and A. Guttmann, 192. Princeton, NJ: Princeton University Press.

Blum, L. (2002). "*I'm not a Racist But . . .*". Ithaca, NY: Cornell University Press.

Cikara, M., and J. J. Van Bavel. (2014). "The Neuroscience of Intergroup Relations: An Integrative Review." *Perspectives on Psychological Science* 9: 245–274.

Dunham, Y., A. S. Baron, and S. Carey. (2011). "Consequences of 'Minimal' Group Affiliations in Children." *Child Development* 82 (3): 793–811.

Glasgow, J. (2009). *A Theory of Race*. New York: Routledge.

Grandin, Temple. (2006). *Thinking in Pictures and Other Reports from My Life with Autism*. New York: Vintage Books.

Kitcher, P. (1999). "Race, Ethnicity, Biology, Culture." In *Racism*, edited by L. Harris, 87–120. New York: Humanity Books.

Kitcher, P. (2007). "Does 'Race' Have Future?" *Philosophy and Public Affairs* 35 (4): 293–317.

Kitcher, P. (2011). *The Ethical Project*. Cambridge, MA: Harvard University Press.

Kripke, Saul A. [1972] (1980). *Naming and Necessity*. Cambridge, MA: Harvard University Press.

Lewis, D. (1970). "How to Define Theoretical Terms." *Journal of Philosophy* 67: 426–446.

Lewis, D. (1972). "Psychophysical and Theoretical Identifications." *Australasian Journal of Philosophy* 50: 249–258.

Mills, C. (1998). *Blackness Visible: Essays on Philosophy and Race*. Ithaca, NY: Cornell University Press.

Outlaw, L. (1990). "Toward a Critical Theory of 'Race.'" In *Anatomy of Racism*, edited by D. T. Goldberg, 58–82. Minneapolis: University of Minnesota Press.

Outlaw, L. (1995). "On W.E.B. Du Bois's 'The Conservation of Races.'" In *Overcoming Racism and Sexism*, edited by L. A. Bell and D. Blumenfeld, 79–102. Lanham, MD: Rowman & Littlefield.

Putnam, Hilary. (1975). "The Meaning of 'Meaning.'" In *Mind, Language and Reality: Philosophical Papers*, 215–271. New York: Cambridge University Press.

Sandel, M. (1982). *Liberalism and the Limits of Justice*. New York: Cambridge University Press.

Spencer, Q. (2014). "A Radical Solution to the Race Problem." *Philosophy of Science* 81 (5): 1025–1038.

Taylor, Paul. (2013). *Race: A Philosophical Introduction*. Malden, MA: Polity Press.

Tajfel, H., M. G. Billig, R. P. Bundy, and C. Flament. (1971). "Social Categorization and Inter-Group Behavior." *European Journal of Social Psychology* 1: 149–178.

Templeton, A. R. (2013). "Biological Races in Humans." *Studies in History and Philosophy of Science Part C: Studies in History and Philosophy of Biological and Biomedical Sciences* 44: 262–271.

Zack, Naomi. (1993). *Race and Mixed Race*. Philadelphia: Temple University Press.

Zack, Naomi. (2002). *Philosophy of Science and Race*. New York: Routledge.

CHAPTER 34

IS IT MORAL TO HOLD A RACIAL IDENTITY?

A Cosmopolitan Response

JASON D. HILL

I make a controversial claim, and it is this: holding a racial identity is problematic because it turns one into a practicing racist. On the surface this should not be controversial. White supremacists of all stripes, either of the North American variety or the Nazi counterpart, have given us ample evidence of the nefarious nature of strong racial identities, especially when they are wedded to a political ideology that demonizes racial minorities, such as blacks or Jews. I am, however, going to go much further in the scope of my argument to suggest that the concept of race, simpliciter, is bad. The concomitant practice of holding a racial identity voluntarily and living one's life as a raciated creature is a form of biological collectivism and racial subjectivism. For reasons I shall make obvious, it matters not whether one is black, white, Indian, or a member of any other designated group; the principle that binds all racial identities together—*polylogism*—is identical. To self-referentially hold a racial identity is, I shall argue, to collude with a great social evil. This matters not if one is a member of a minority group (black) without the political means to institutionally discriminate on a large scale. It diminishes the scope of one's sociopolitical reach, not the fundamental nature of who one is. Thus, I shall argue that Cornel West is categorically wrong to argue, as he does, that *blackness* is an ethical identity (West 1994). Blackness, I shall prove, is conceptually vacuous— an empty set. Compared to its white counterpart—*whiteness*—the practitioners of which have sociopolitical powers to enforce institutionalized racial discrimination, blacks who are racial practitioners become "petty racists" who, like the holders of all strong racial identities, are racial codependents.

As an antidote, I shall posit the identity of the cosmopolitan as conceptually more robust given that it and its practitioners are imbued with moral traits and attributes that locate the constitutive features of the term and the identity of those who practice cosmopolitanism. Contra Anthony Appiah's rifts on cosmopolitanism which render it indistinguishable from multiculturalism and pluralism, and whose soft-core rendition of the term places it within the pantheon of mere sentiments, I will argue that strong or radical cosmopolitanism is a just moral competitor term to racial identities, which, by nature, are exclusive and arbitrarily discriminatory. Cosmopolitanism is both a theory of the self and a robust moral system replete with its own moral psychology. My goal here is to argue that, aside from functioning as a more benevolent and humane way of existing with one's fellow human beings, cosmopolitanism does the work of political advocacy in a far deeper and dignified manner than, say, any alleged ethical dimension of a racial identity. In short, cosmopolitanism as a lived philosophy, racially and ethnically cleanses the individual of the empirically untenable and largely imagined attributes one is deemed to have and, which, unfortunately, one has falsely adopted as a proper designator for who one is. Concomitantly, cosmopolitanism corrects the empirically false beliefs that race consciousness generates about the moral and ontological status of individuals *because* of their racial identities.

RACIAL IDENTITIES

Racial markers are conceptually ambitious in that they purport to convey information about persons that, if taken seriously on the conceptual level, would yield necessary and sufficient conditions that all persons falling under a racial category would satisfy. The extant literature on why race fails as a biological category is already well established and has, as far as I am concerned, concluded and won the debate over whether the taxonomies and racial classificatory schemas are empirically tenable (Zack 2002). What survives in the public imaginary, however, are attributes that are taken to have moral salience which are applicable to persons designated by historical and biologically fabricated markers. Sociological studies on the formation of European American ethnic identities reveal a broad swath of traits that Europeans (some later designated as white) held about other groups believed to belong to different races. These traits ranging from dirty, productive, smart, God-fearing, clean, efficient, and lazy, to cognitively immature and irredeemably evil, were allocated among the various groups of raciated individuals with those assigned the most negative traits falling the lowest on the prestige index of the group rankings. To be black was to have, throughout the history of US racial classifications, the least prestigious identity (Waters 1990).

A morally salient factor about holding a racial identity is that one has to engage in affected ignorance or willed self-deception about oneself and about others. In the face of competing evidence, one holds certain views about oneself and about others that are causally linked to a form of racial subjectivism. The latter holds, among other things, that certain attributes one deems praiseworthy are laudable because one has them, and one has them because those attributes are causally primed by having the racial identity one has. The logical inverse of this form of reasoning is that if others have those attributes that are racially primed within themselves, they must have them incidentally, accidentally, or, more than likely, they do not have them at all or, at best, others have them imitatively. Whites who hold a strong racial identity and predicate white superiority on, say, advanced cognitive functioning that is treated as an irreducible primary because of its statistical consistency across a white population (especially when compared to the cognitive functioning of nonwhite populations) must engage in empirical obfuscation in order to maintain a psychologically consistent view of themselves over time. This self-cohesion depends on the willful distortion of the agency of others precisely because of imagined attributes the demoted group has which the superior group cannot logically have. The inverted reasoning of whites who hold a strong racial identity would seek to identify whites who lack advanced mental functioning as simply a failure on their part to exercise an innate potentiality within them, while blacks who display cognitive superiority are exceptional abberants who are merely aping the behavior of whites in whose image they have fashioned themselves. This is what, of course, is today called "white normativity" (Hill 2000).

But the moral ambitiousness of racial designators is not to be found in the attempts of its users to function like epistemological and conceptual wholesalers in the realm of locating moral agency within racial registers. No robust theoretical claims can be made about moral attributes if they are indexed to racial identities. The moral ambitiousness of those who utilize racial designators involves bypassing the claim of empirical untenability on the individual level, that is, that some members of the demoted race are in fact better or smarter than they are. That certain members of the alleged superior groups are cognitively inferior and certain members of the designated inferior group have cognitively superior members become irrelevant. The racially and morally ambitious practitioners disambiguate the individual from his own cognitive register and wed his overall moral efficacy and superior status to his *associative relationship* to the group. A moron in the alleged superior group is not only less of a moron but, speaking in terms of the aggregate, he is actually not a moron since his character is appraised against the highest denominator or normative features in his group. The essential defining characteristic of his group is predicated on superiority: genius, articulacy, cognitive superiority, productiveness, cleanliness, and efficiency. Inversely, the cognitively superior in the low-prestige group is always adjudged by the lowest common denominator element in his group, which is taken as the definitive feature that he and all members of his group intrinsically hold, in spite of individual exceptions such as himself. Nothing in human reality could explain why, for example, the English held steadfastly to the view that try as he might, a colonial subject, regardless of how well he mastered the Queen's language, how respectably he comported himself and impeccably he dressed and, above all, executed the most exquisite manners in the public sphere, could never become English. A colonial subject could never be an English man, and the same fact held for women.

Holding a racial identity voluntarily, it turns out, is problematic not just because of the false beliefs on which it is predicated. Those holding racial identities who exercise institutional power can and have caused great harm. There is no need to revisit that argument in this essay as it is pretty old hat. What makes holding a racial identity highly problematic is that it is a form of *biological collectivism*. This biological collectivism which allows individuals to be judged not by their characters, but by the codified character traits and actions of a collective of ancestors which approximates some vague undefinable ideal, trades on associative identification as a short cut for earning and arduously maintaining a moral identity as an individual. To be a biological collectivist in this case means that one rides on the prestige value of one's racial identity, an identity suffused with the moral attributes of everyone but oneself. Holding a racial identity in this sense means that one is morally lazy. Inversely, those who hold strong racial identities make others who are individuals into biological collectivists by judging them according to a racially subjective algorithm whose formulae are the actions and attitudes of others that are codified and given a racial denotation. This racial denotation becomes a metaphysical template that is the foundation of all racial stereotypes.

To exercise moral laziness regardless of whether one holds a view that one has duties to oneself is condemnable to the extent that such laziness implicates others, condemns them, and relegates them to oppressive modes of existence. One could argue that moral laziness that results in intermittent failures to cultivate the moral traits or virtues such as honesty, benevolence, a propensity for promise keeping and fairness, may not be condemnatory, simpliciter. Given, however, that most if not all moral traits and virtues are relational and do affect the lives of other people, it is difficult to imagine how moral laziness could ever not affect others negatively. Moral laziness that is the direct result of holding a racial identity that stems from a race consciousness that generates false beliefs about oneself and others is philosophically indefensible.

We are to understand that the absence of constraints and any other imaginable coercive acts against an individual's agency and bodily integrity commits her to cultivating the ethical dimensions of her character, because such an endeavor entails qualifying and equipping one to treat people with fairness and justice—in short, to treat one's fellow human-being ethically.

What makes holding a racial identity in the cultural or biological sense morally problematic is that one makes not just a short cut to achieving a moral character; rather, one engages in the appropriation of characterological traits of one's ancestors and relies on a specious form of chemical predestination and associative identification to cultivate a sense of self-esteem and moral self-worth. The moral untenability of holding a racial identity is brought into sharper relief if we go beyond the fact that it breeds a form of moral laziness because it disincentivizes one from creating an individually constructed moral identity by riding on the social prestige of one's ancestors and deriving self-esteem and moral status from associative affinity. This, as we have seen, arises simultaneously from psychologically and existentially attenuating the agency of those outside the sphere of the extoled group for the enhancement of one's racial prestige. Moral laziness is a direct corollary of the act of valorizing ascription over achievement.

RACIAL SUBJECTIVISM AND POLYLOGISM

Let us consider a deeper question of why holding a racial identity is ethically untenable. To do so, we will revisit the two concepts on which all racial identities are predicated: racial subjectivism and polylogism. All holders of racial identities are racial subjectivists and polylogists. These two character markers are so egregiously wrong and harmful—both to oneself and to others—that to adhere to the structures of thought that inform them is to engage in massive agential distortion. *Racial subjectivism* holds that an individual's inborn racial constitution determines his mental processes, his intellectual outlook, his feelings, his thought patterns, and his conclusions; *polylogism* is the view that each racial racial group has its own logic. Such conclusions are held to be valid only for the members of a given race, all of whom share the identical underlying constitution (Peikoff 1983). Nazi theorists claimed that knowledge and truth were peculiarities that originated in specific forms of consciousness and are aligned exclusively with the essence of their "father consciousness." What is presupposed here is an unbridgeable epistemological gulf that separates human beings of different races and which prevents peaceful conflict resolution. Nazi philosopher Carl Schmitt wrote: "An alien may be as critical as he wants to be . . . he may be intelligent in his endeavor, he may read books and write them, but he thinks and understands things differently because he belongs to a *different kind*, and he remains within the existential condition of his own kind in every decisive thought" (Peikoff 1983, 64).

Holding a racial identity is not only morally compromising, it is misanthropic because it introduces a gulf between the humanity of oneself and those outside of one's group on the basis of speciously formulated and arbitrary racial taxonomies that determine ascriptive racial identity. The adoption of a racial marker, the moral grammar of which is hinged to the denigration of outsiders and "necessary illusions" about the allocation of ethical attributes among persons of the world, is the voluntary adoption of an irrational form of discriminating among human beings. This is self-evident. What is not self-evident is that the misanthropy is the expression of an act that once executed becomes almost irreversible: recusing oneself from a significant segment of the human population for reasons that are morally irrelevant. Recusing oneself from the human project is in and of itself not necessarily immoral. Suicides do just this, as do hermits and recluses. And while a rational case can be made for suicide and living as a hermit, one is here hard pressed to see how said recusement can have an ethical dimension. The racial misanthrope who recuses himself from the human project establishes a new humanity, one that is idolatrous and narcissistic and fashioned in his own image replete with all the normative attributes he reserves from himself and his kind, attributes that others by virtue of their racially essentialized identities can never acquire. Peoplehood in this world is a brute axiom as invariable as the laws of nature. It is not an aspiration based on moral and political principles.

Those outside the pantheon of the recusive racial misanthrope's highly artificial world are also, in the strong sense, outside the domain of the ethical. Because race in the biological sense has already been disproved, a belief in race is tantamount to a belief in elves, fairies, and winged horses. A socially constructed belief in race still runs the risk of implicating one in psychologically investing in race, simpliciter (in and of itself). Whether socially constructed or biologically posited, racial attributes are almost always reified in the consciousness of those who invest in them and/or hold them. In this sense, they have a biological connotation in the minds of their practitioners and, because of this, holding a racial identity almost always permits some degree of psychosis.

There is, though, another sense in which it is believed that holding a racial identity can be ethical. When one holds a racial identity and uses that identity as a form of political advocacy rather than, say, a cultural identity that promotes a sense of racial particularism, then one can ethically hold the identity. Thinkers such as Alain Locke and Cornel West have advocated this notion. West goes further in arguing that blackness can be viewed as an ethical construct. West notes that blackness has no meaning outside of a system of race-conscious people and practices. Being black within the context of historical abuse and degradation means being minimally, subject to white supremacist abuse and being a member of a rich culture and community that has fought such abuse (West 1994).

West's attempts to classify "blackness" as a competitor term to the historical one that equated it with inferiority and a phalanx of negative attributes that stripped black people of dignity and agency is understandable. Blackness, however, once it is recused from its racist and racialized definition, one that falsely constructed it along the inferior axis of human agency is an empty set—a nonconcept. It is a nonconcept, because it cannot securely codify the necessary and sufficient characteristics that would apply to black individuals that would allow us to signify "blackness" in a way that would designate an unqualifiable attribute that would pertain to black people. When we think of terms such as "generosity," "bravery," "sarcasm," or "narcissism," we think in terms of fundamental attributes that give the terms their identities and which squarely denote the behaviors of those to whom the terms apply. It would be ludicrous to refer to a person who freely gives of her time and money to sundry causes as "miserly." The point is that blackness is conjoined to a person who exhibits a plethora of behavioral traits from hooliganism to sophistication and dignity. There are no fixed behavioral traits that we find among blacks that singularly apply to all black individuals. No leader of a disenfranchised group—be he Martin Luther King Jr., Mahatma Gandhi, or Nelson Mandela—has ever fought injustice from either a racial identity or by appealing to a core dimension of the racialized identity as a basis for advocacy. King, Mandela, and Gandhi all used universal moral vocabularies that circumvented the appeal to stand-point particularity. King appealed equally to Vietnam War veterans as he did to the poor of all races and social classes. His racial identity was incidental, an existential platform for advocacy, but not an ontological grounding for rights and social and political enfranchisement as used by a garden variety of black nationalists.

Because blackness is a nonconcept and cannot be conceptually distinguished from the behavior of the lowest common denominator of its adherents, any more than it can from its most ethically exalted, the term itself should be dropped from the social imaginary. It gives us an approximate understanding but refers to literally *no-thing* in reality. It is, in effect, a floating abstraction, that is, a concept that is bandied about with no specific referent to any tangible object in reality, under which is subsumed no specific units that tie the concept into a coherent and metaphysically perceivable existent. Those who use the term "blackness" to gauge the ethical status of those identified as black are left conceptually out of focus when the term is also used to describe ethically transgressive behaviors of individuals who apply the term to themselves. And it is this that proves the untenability of attempting to use racial terms in definitional senses. If race is an arbitrary and metaphysically illicit construct, then there can be no manner in which a subsidiary term such as, in this case, "blackness" can lead to anything but conceptual indistinctness and, a fortiori, cognitive confusion. Blackness is not an ethical identity. It is an empty set.

Cosmopolitan Identity

There is, however, a successor term that does the ethical work of advocacy for those disenfranchised by markers of race and class, sexual orientation, religious affiliation, and gender. Not only is the term a wholesaler in the realm of the moral work it does on behalf of representing seemingly disparate groups of people who are unjustly treated, it is also a viable replacer for racial identities. Unlike holders of racial identities, the *cosmopolitan* is both the possessor of a distinct self with a unique moral psychology and the holder of an identity suffused with real attributes.

Cosmopolitanism is not just a sentiment or a perspective as many thinkers have made it out to be. It is both a moral system and a theory of the self that can provide authentic answers to probing issues in the contemporary era. Cosmopolitanism in its weak form is a variant of multiculturalism, but in its strong form it becomes a moral and intellectual system to contend with. It debunks the shibboleths of group solidarity by demystifying the selective and arbitrary criteria on which group identity rests. It is highly individualistic in form, and its proponents argue that only individual persons—not cultures, or races, or ethnic groups— are the bearers of rights and the possessors of an inviolable status worthy of respect.

Cosmopolitanism as a philosophical movement with historical roots in the Cynic and Stoic philosophical traditions has championed the inviolable dignity of each individual and posited that each person (not groups) be a unit of ethical concern (Heater 1996). The core notion of cosmopolitanism is that one's identity is not determined solely nor primarily by any racial, national, or ethnic background (Hill 2005). A cosmopolitan is an individual who disavows all partisanship and parochial commitments of localities, city-states, and principalities. Diogenes and the ancient Cynics began the cosmopolitan tradition by forming the notion that an individual could have a primary identity apart from the one he or she inherited from the polis. In deemphasizing the value of class, status, national origin, and gender, the Cynics simultaneously placed great emphasis on the value of reason and moral purpose. Here is the revolutionary idea that the Cynics achieved which is a given in the Western concept of personality and its concomitant dependence on dignity: regardless of how much one is deprived of the concrete goods that are constitutive of social identity, one possesses a larger universal identity grounded in reason, moral purpose, and, above all, human dignity. Today, when contemporary cosmopolitans speak in terms of a universal human identity that they share with others, they are invoking concepts bequeathed to them by the ancient Cynics (Heater 1996).

The concept of world citizenship in the sense of belonging to all of humankind gained ascendancy in the Hellenistic era. It is among the core features of Stoic thought, which, along with its great rival Epicureanism, were reactions to the gradual disappearance of the small city-state in an age of empire. (One of the reasons, it goes without saying, for the current upsurge in interest in cosmopolitanism, is our own relation to empire.) As Philip of Macedonia and then his son Alexander the Great imposed an overarching monarchy on the Greeks and conquered new territories, not only did the *poleis* cease to be the sole seat of political authority for citizens, they were no longer insular safe havens in which local identities could be formed.

The *cosmopolis*, that vastly growing space beyond the insular polis, the place that heretofore had been the home of barbarians, was conceived of as a place where social and cultural distinctions were irrelevant compared to an essential sameness to all human beings who were bound together regardless of their backgrounds, by their subjection to natural law. Human beings may live in a multiplicity of ways, but there is a law that holds the variations in their actions and behaviors to a recognizably human model. The people in one village may live in an area populated with plants, some of which are poisonous and some of which are not; those of another may live off the meat of animals. In the first scenario someone has to learn how to detoxify plants and classify them and establish that as an art or science. In the second scenario, one has to establish procedures for effective hunting. In both cases, each individual must live by the evidence of his or her experience. That is what is to be expected since human beings are conceptual animals and this shared nature provides the basis for a universal humanity. So goes the reasoning of the Stoics (Heater 1996).

Today, a contemporary cosmopolitan would point out that in no culture would you find mothers arbitrarily offering up their young to strangers, that individuals in all cultures have capacities for responding to shame and loss of dignity, that ethical human beings in every culture historically have condemned incest and rape, and that such examples are just a few among several that are the shared core features that all human beings have and that override local particularity.

Cosmopolitanism stands in contrast to multiculturalism and pluralism. Pluralists defend the view that individual identity is to be configured within the parameters of a conceptually neat, ethnic, national, or racial paradigmatic prism. Pluralists are not separatists, but they do insist that the boundaries that make separate identities distinct (Italian, German, Native American, for example) are protected and kept in place. Group solidarity and group identity, then, are the important values upheld by those in the pluralist camp (Earle and Cvetkovich 1995).

Cosmopolitans, in keeping with the pro-individual stance first evinced by Diogenes, are of the view that human socialization takes place in the world where human intercourse takes place: in the multiple spaces that we inhabit and among the myriad human beings with whom we interact and exchange stories, experiences, values, and norms. Strong cosmopolitans repudiate the tendencies of cultural nationalists and racial ideologists to impute moral value to the morally neutral features like skin pigmentation, national origin, and ethnic background. Strong cosmopolitans argue that there is no one fundamental culture to which any one individual is biologically constituted, and they leave the question of identity entirely to the individual. That is, individuals ought to be able to cull their own identities based on the extent to which their experiences and their life roles have allowed them to experience themselves as the persons they take themselves to be, rather than the passive wearers of tribal labels assigned to them by their culture or by the society at large.

In keeping with its dignitarian stance, cosmopolitans are more egalitarian than those with racial identities who, however, benignly, still discriminate on the basis of constructed racial attributes. Cosmopolitans assume that all persons regardless of racial ascriptions have intrinsic equal moral worth, and they allocate equal moral attention to all persons who have equal standing in the domain of the ethical. All "races" and all persons belonging to those fabricated racial groups have equal standing. All individuals are treated as such—individuals—who, incidentally, belong to contrived racial groups. Because groups as such have no prima facie ontological standing within the cosmopolitan world schema, it is the inviolable individual worth of the individual that is extoled. As such, there can be, under the cosmopolitan morality, no search for social prestige and glory and psychological well-being via an appeal to racial membership in a community. Strong cosmopolitans would frown upon such a goal for the simple reason that it is a form of moral appropriation or theft. The moral and existential endowments and achievements of individual members of a racial group are the property and achievements of the individuals who have created them.

I hope that the case against the holders of racial identities, whether they be German Aryans, black or Hindu nationalists, or Native American tribal leaders who claim ancestral rights to the artworks of their tribal members, has been made. Riding on the prestige of the moral and existential endowments of a fellow racial tribesman is, as I have argued, morally lazy, a form of appropriation, and, I might add, indicative of a gross deficiency in self-esteem and self-respect. That is, no self-respecting person of any "race" will attempt to make himself feel better by riding on the largesse of a fellow ascriptive member. The moral cosmopolitan would simply feel inspired that someone from the human community has made it possible for her to aspire to greater heights by demonstrating that, say, human greatness and achievements are possible. The strength of the moral cosmopolitan here lies in the fact that no group or its members assumes a greater share in humanity than any other.

Cosmopolitanism racially and ethnically cleanses the individual of a false identity that is constructed, for reasons I have outlined, are psychologically untenable, and existentially and empirically false. The construction of race—the great ecological disaster of the modern world—has inflicted so many human casualties and moral harm in the world that whether one relies on a racial identity to feel a sense of belonging in the world or a misguided sense of false pride from holding such an identity becomes irrelevant. I submit that any ethically minded person who holds a racial identity ought to strategically give it up out of recognition that racial worlds are, inevitably, warring worlds.

Strong cosmopolitans—not the weak and multicultural variant—have as their goal the complete deracination of peoples of the world—in the psychological and moral sense of the word. For a full treatment of that topic, readers should refer to my book, *Beyond Blood Identities: Post Humanity in the 21st Century* (Hill 2009).

Suffice it to say that each of them suffers from the metaphysical concomitant of any variant of biological collectivism and its existential corollary, tribalism, which manifests itself in the following: an unspeakable inability to create a moral and independent identity of their own separate and apart from the codified record of their ancestors and current racial compatriots; a narcissistic need to see individuals who look like them reflected in the realm of values; and a chronic inability to stand on one's own without the buoyancy of "racial uplift." The holder of a racial identity is, therefore, when all is said and done, not so much immoral as he is mired in a form of psychic infantilism. He is unwilling or unable to matriculate outside the protective parental patronage of the tribe and, as such, remains cognitively in a state of arrested development—an unfortunate simulacrum of the original image of those who had constructed him as the racial archetype he spent his life rejecting; or, as in the case of a racial majority that constitutes itself as the normative standpoint of human aspiration, a bloated caricature without personal worth or value.

References

Earle, Timothy C., and George T. Cvetkovich. (1995). *Social Trust: Toward a Cosmopolitan Society*. West Port, CT: Praeger.

Heater, Derek. (1996). *World Citizenship and Government: Cosmopolitan Ideas in the History of Western Political Thought*. New York: St. Martin's Press.

Hill, Jason. (2000). *Becoming a Cosmopolitan: What It Means to be a Human Being in the New Millennium*. Lanham, MD: Rowman & Littlefield.

Hill, Jason. (2005). "Cosmopolitanism." In *The Edinburgh Dictionary of Continental Philosophy*, edited by John Protevi, 108–111. Edinburgh: Edinburgh University Press.

Hill, Jason. (2009). *Beyond Blood Identities: Post Humanity in the 21st Century*. Lanham, MD: Lexington Books.

Peikoff, Leonard. (1983). *The Ominous Parallels: The End of Freedom in America*. New York: Plume.

Waters, Mary C. (1990). *Ethnic Options: Choosing Identities in America*. Berkley: University of California Press.

West, Cornel. (1994). *Race Matters*. New York: Vintage Books.

Zack, Naomi. (2002). *Philosophy of Science and Race*. New York: Routledge Press.

CHAPTER 35

<hr>

EFFORTFUL AGON
Learning to Think and Feel Differently about Race

<hr>

JACQUELINE SCOTT

We are meritful;
     and are, before an end, perceptive.
We are hurt honey but we do retrieve.
We do not squirm, we do not squeal. We square off.
We blueprint
     not merely our survival but a flowering.
That's good. Because the Plight is serious in
     this field of electrified spikes and boulders.

We are Tilted;
but we are the Choosing People.
Ours is the Favorite Truth, we *are* Truth-tellers.
Truth-tellers are not always palatable.
There is a preference for candy bars.

Gwendolyn Brooks (1988)

PHILOSOPHY is often described as the "art of living," and because racism and racialized identities are very much a part of our lives here in the United States, philosophers need to take
them seriously (e.g., Hadot 1995; Nehamas 1998; Scott 2006). I am proposing ways that philosophy can and should inform the fight against racism and healthier racialized identities. I
will argue that approaching both through the lens of "effortful *agon*" will be fruitful. I have
argued elsewhere that we are at a crossroads in terms of racialized identities: no longer is race
seen as primarily biological, but it is also not clear that we can or should just jettison racialized identities altogether in order to solve the problem of racism (Scott 2006).

    In terms of race, some argue that racism is on the wane and will soon disappear. The evi-
dence for this claim is that a few people of color have attained positions of power/influence
and therefore racism is on the decline. I would contend that such an argument is spurious,
and that such a view tends to make racism less visible and therefore easier to ignore. At the

same time, whiteness as a racialized identity is often likened to an invisible identity. By this, philosophers like George Yancy and Linda Alcoff mean to say that whiteness is generally assumed to be the norm to such an extent that most whites do not *feel* that they have a racialized identity and assume that such an existential state should be the goal for all people (Alcoff 2006; Yancy 2012). We must continue to render the presence of these systems of oppression more visible. How might we use philosophy to help us formulate a healthier approach to racialized and gendered identities? First, I will clarify my own approach to "truth telling" in terms of racial matters. Second, I will utilize the arguments of Friedrich Nietzsche in arguing for my "tilted" truths about racialized identity formation for people of color and whites.

A Truth-Telling Agenda

I would like to discuss some hard "truths" about racialized identities that derive from my own experiences. In saying this, I am not using the word "truth" in the general way it is used in philosophy. Traditionally in philosophy, our goal has been to ascertain facts and arguments that are universally and unconditionally true (apply to all people and for all times). I am using truth in a different way here, and Gwendolyn Brooks captures my meaning quite well.

Gwendolyn Brooks wrote the poem excerpted in the epigraph to celebrate the inauguration of Spelman College's first black woman president in 1988. The poem describes how the "we" of the poem (I am assuming black women because Spelman is a historically black college for women) are working to formulate and execute our "agenda." She describes this agenda as aiming to "blueprint not merely our survival but a flowering" by seeing "the whole through our assaulted vision."

It is in this sense that I understand Brooks to be discussing "truth." This is not an objective, universal Truth whose goal is to serve as a foundation for all understanding/knowledge (here think of Descartes or Kant). Brooks's "truth" is an understanding of one's self and the world around one that is derived from one's subjective experiences ("our assaulted vision"), and if one's experiences are those of someone who has been marginalized in society (we are "Tilted," "we are hurt honey but we do retrieve," "the plight is serious in this field of electrified spikes and boulders"), then I understand her to be saying that this vision might have epistemological primacy because that marginalized standpoint (she labels it as the "tilted" perspective) aids us in gaining a deeper understanding of the problems of society. One is then to use the knowledge gained from this "tilted" perspective to help formulate an "agenda" that will aid one in flourishing, despite having to exist in our racist and sexist society.

In this sense, then, she claims that "we are Truth-tellers." I understand her to mean that the epistemological standpoint of black women grants us a particular, important, and incisive understanding of the interlocking systems of racism and sexism that will be beneficial to everyone within those systems—both those advantaged and disadvantaged by them (Mills 1998). The ultimate goal of this truth telling is not the discovery of universal truths, but instead to use this knowledge in "devis[ing] our next return/to sense and self and mending. And a daylight/out of the Tilt and Jangle of this hour." The aim then is an existential well-being that is derived from an understanding of the racist and sexist world in which we live and the well-being involves attempts to affirm oneself despite this "tilted" and "jangly" world in which we live. As I will argue, the goal is a Nietzschean, healthy life affirmation that emerges out of self-knowledge and mastery—and this is an ongoing project.

When Brooks writes, "Truth-tellers are not always palatable./There is a preference for candy bars," I understand her to be claiming that the "truths" told by us (black women, those who have been marginalized, as well as those who have insight into the experiences of those who have been marginalized) regarding how we diagnose the ills of our society (racism, sexism, classism, homophobia, etc.) are not "palatable." These truths are neither pleasant tasting nor acceptable (they are kind of like raw kale, a superfood, but not necessarily a food that one craves at midnight). A palatable truth told about racism is that we have elected a black president and therefore we live in a postracial society. As a society, we crave palatable truths just as we crave candy bars. They are tasty, they make us feel good, and they curb our hunger. But only in the short term. In large amounts, though, they are dangerous to our health, and they tend to conceal and exacerbate long-term harms for short-term pleasure.

In terms of racism (and other forms of oppressions), for the health of our nation and for our own individual health, we need to learn to retrain our palates and learn to appreciate and desire that which is less palatable. We need to learn to resist the temptation for that which only makes us feel good in the short term but causes long-term damage. We need to recognize when we are craving, seeking, and holding on to these types of "concealing truths" because we find other truths to be too difficult or daunting. Given this, I now want to tell some "truths" about race from my tilted standpoint in this profession and society. I want to offer a diagnosis of a particular problem regarding race and offer an alternative way of approaching the problem through the use of philosophy.

THE TILTED VIEW OF RACISM:
IT IS PERMANENT AND INCURABLE

How can we use philosophy as an aid in formulating a healthier approach to creating racialized identities? For many this might seem counterintuitive, given philosophy's historic (and to large extent contemporary) reluctance to see racial issues as being properly philosophical.

However, it is also noteworthy that the history of philosophy (and contemporary philosophy as well) has a small but critical mass of philosophers who have questioned this silence on race (as well as other marginalized identities) and have taken the discipline to task for its silence and refusal to acknowledge its philosophical import (Nietzsche 1967). Friedrich Nietzsche is one such philosopher, and I want to use his arguments to sketch out healthier approaches to "blueprint[ing] not merely survival but a flowering" of racialized identities. Nietzsche's prime criticism of philosophy is its overemphasis on "discovering" universal and unconditional Truth. He calls this the will to Truth, and his diagnosis of the philosophy and culture of his time is that this will to Truth has been the primary cause for the decline of philosophy and his culture. He argues that there are no universal and unconditional Truths to be discovered, and that our lives are inherently meaningless. Therefore, any "truth" that seems to help make life meaningful is created by us and will need to be re-created as we, and the circumstances of our lives, change (Scott 1998). Nietzsche's argument is that we create "truths" that help us to affirm life and then we create systems of values to guide us in implementing that meaningful life.

Nietzsche also argues that being born into a meaningless world plagues us—he calls it nihilism—and if untreated (life remains meaningless for us) it can lead to suicide. He likens his problem of meaninglessness to a congenital and chronic disease that he calls *décadence* (Scott 1998, 2014). We cannot "cure" ourselves of this meaninglessness, and all we can do is try to come up with treatments that aid us in contending with this disease. The main problem with the will to Truth of traditional philosophy is that it tries to deny the disease altogether or assumes that there is a cure for it—that we can successfully pretend that it does not exist or that we can find a way to put an end to it by "discovering" a universal and unconditional true meaning of life (Nietzsche 1966).

I have likened this chronic disease of decadence to racism in our society (Scott 2014). What if we assume that racism, like meaninglessness in life, is a congenital and permanent condition in our society? This is an offshoot of Derrick Bell's concept of racial realism (Bell 2005). What if we also assume that all of us are infected by racism? We would then assume that to varying degrees and in different ways, we are infected by racial bias. If we make these assumptions and we do not immediately try to "cure" ourselves of this "disease" of racism, and yet we do not want to maintain the status quo, then what?

Bell's point about racial realism is that many have been so intent on ending racism once and for all that they have fallen into despair when that goal has seemed to be elusive, and have given up altogether. Instead, Bell argues that the civil rights "cure" of making rational arguments against the injustices of racism and waiting for it to die out has stalled in improving the existential and material lives of most black folks. He argues that making arguments and marching against injustice, overall, have put whites and those privileged within these systems of oppression at the center of the argument, and they have not succeeded in disrupting the comfort that most of them enjoy in these systems (Bell 1992). In Nietzschean language, there does not seem to be a single cure that can put an end to systemic racism once and for all.

He calls on black folks to focus on empowering ourselves in these systems of racialized advantages and disadvantages (Bell 2005). Returning to Nietzsche's disease metaphor, we need to turn our focus from bringing about a cure to racism and instead try to fortify our bodies/immune systems and minds/psyches, so that we can better flourish despite this disease. Using Gwendolyn Brooks's language, such an approach will be more fruitful in helping us move beyond mere survival toward a "flowering" or "daylight out of the Tilt and jangle" of our experiences.

What sorts of (*Versuchen*) experiments (philosophical, sociological, psychological) should we engage in to bring out this type of racialized health? The goal here is less about ending racism, and more about finding a way to celebrate ourselves as individuals and communities and our power to struggle against seemingly impossible odds. For Bell, it is in this struggle that our lives become meaningful (Bell 2005). For Nietzsche, genuine philosophers are *Versucher* (experimenters, tempters, and attempters) who revel in creating a different, more life-affirming way of fashioning meaning in their own lives (as opposed to traditional philosophers, who aim to discover Truths for all people and all time) (Nietzsche 1974b; Nietzsche and Hollingdale 1996). For Nietzsche, this struggle against nihilism is like the ancient Greek concept of *agon* in that it is less about annihilistic warfare and more about struggle to achieve excellence for the combatants. In this way, Nietzsche argues that individuals and communities of individuals can create their own "truths" or values that make their lives meaningful in the face of their particular experiences of racism.

For Nietzsche, and I will argue that for those of us struggling against racism, one must first endeavor to understand one's strengths and weakness and utilize them as one attempts (*versucht*) to make one's life meaningful—to affirm one's life (Nietzsche 1996). Nietzsche's argument then is that health is not about the absence of disease, but instead it is the profound self-knowledge and mastery of one's strengths gained through the struggle against the disease of *décadence* (Nietzsche 1974b). Translating this to healthier racialized and gendered identities, we would then turn from trying to end all racism and instead aim to use our individual and communal strengths (Nietzsche uses the term *Kräft* to describe these creative powers) to affirm our lives (Nietzsche 1974a).

Furthermore, the goal of these agonistic *Versuchen* is not a type of color-blindness where we all racially move through the world with "effortless grace" (Yancy 2013). Most white people, and some people of color, can move through the world like this, and this is why they often view themselves as not having a racialized identity.

I take Yancy to be saying that one of the effects of racism in our society has been that some categories of people are allowed to create and enact their individual value systems in a way that comes from a "deep sense of freedom, connectedness, and reciprocity" (Yancy 2013, 239). These privileged folks feel as though there are few racialized external limitations on them as they endeavor to affirm their own lives. They do this as part of a majority culture, and their quest for affirmation has the appearance of being effortless and of being an expression of God's favor. One might understand this as being behind the liberal goal of achieving a color-blind society, but in my view, people of all races must forgo that state as a goal.

"Effortless grace" for some has come at the price of too much effort and too little grace for others who must circumscribe their own desires, instincts, and values so their efforts can aid the first group. We must instead first recognize that efforts as individuals and communities to affirm our lives, to engage in strong, healthy, and graceful *Versuche*, affect other people and require the aid of other people. To achieve this agonistic struggle for excellence across society, we must first see racism in a different way: it is less a sickness to be cured and more a congenital handicap that, if we accept it, might help us to find new ways of being in the world and emerge stronger.

An important aspect of this effortful *agon* is that we all need to learn to live with, and even search out, racialized discomfort (see, e.g., Medina 2012 and Sullivan 2006). If we accept racism as permanent, then we will need to learn to distinguish between the healthy pain of growth and the debilitating pain that saps one's strength. Most women and people of color already know how to do this. We have learned, overall, to distinguish fairly consistently when a racialized conversation, altercation, or encounter fosters vitality and when it saps vitality. Unlike many whites and men, we do not necessarily view any talk of race or racialized conflict or disagreements with "fear/dread/ignorance" (Yancy 2012). Many whites, because their racialized identities are invisible to them, want assurance, comfort, and unchanging stability, when it comes to race and gender. If it falls short of that, then it is a problem that must be solved or avoided. Their tendency is to act like amoebas who react negatively to an external stimulus and retreat. But they have the ability to engage in higher order reactions other than merely running away—and yet they do not. They try to eliminate the perceived source (which is generally only a symptom or a symbol) of the fear/discomfort. This happens at the theoretical level (when race or racism is denied or ignored in philosophy), and it can have tragic practical consequences (e.g., Trayvon Martin). In other words, these folks who go through the world with effortless grace in terms of race tend to shy away from having to make an effort in negotiating the racialized "field of electrified spikes and boulders" that seem, for them, to rear up from nowhere, even though these issues are pervasive.

Here is an example of this fear and avoidance of racialized discomfort. I gave a talk at a community college in Queens, New York. After my talk, which was directed toward people of color and how we might have healthier racialized identities in the face of the potential fact that racism is permanent, a philosophy professor made sure to ask one of the first questions (in a roomful of undergraduate philosophy majors of color) and asked how my talk would speak to or persuade someone like him who is white, well-meaning, and progressive. He asked what hope I had for him if racism is permanent. In his view, my talk lacked anything to help him because I had not directly spoken about whiteness and the role of whites. I just wanted to say, "It's not about you today." Instead, I explained that this talk was not directed at helping him work through his racial issues, that the civil rights approach and liberalism had tried to provide that help but "progress" has stalled, so I was not focusing on him and those like him. He was taken aback. He literally did not know how to respond.

Yancy calls this reaction a "white distancing strategy" (Medina 2012; Yancy 2012). As opposed to recognizing the fact he (and those like him) were not the focus of the talk, and to adopt a position of listening and learning about the "truths" of a different group of people, and do the work of figuring out how it might speak to him, he tried to reorient the discussion to him and his point of view and recenter the conversation on him. In doing this, he effectively distanced himself from my decentering of whiteness and the discomfort it caused him. He distanced himself from his own responsibility in creating, perpetuating, and/or remaining silent about the racism that was the cause for the effortful *agon* of people of color. He distanced himself from the opportunity to sit in this discomfort caused by my talk and requested that I offer him a "cure" or at least some relief from this discomfort by telling him how I might extend my talk to him.

In asking for me to act as his physician in helping him deal with the "disease" of racism, he missed a key point of my talk. Healthier racialized identities require:

1. the willingness to engage in *Versuche* about how to negotiate the racism and sexism in one's life;
2. the willingness and ability to ascertain self-knowledge of one's strengths and weaknesses;
3. the ability to utilize this self-knowledge to master these strengths and diminish the weaknesses (self-mastery); and
4. undertaking those actions that aid one in making one's life meaningful (life affirmation).

To engage more productively in these *Versuche*, one needs to be ready and willing to accept the hard truths of racism (how it affects everyone in society, one's complicity in it, etc.) and then to be willing to do the hard work of enacting real change. One need not do this alone, but he seemed unwilling to do any work at all, and instead asked me to do it for him. He wanted a candy bar.

He did not want to disrupt the comfort he had established in his racialized world, and he rejected the discomfort that I caused in decentering his experiences and in giving primacy to the particular racialized ways of being in the world of people of color. The discomfort and possible suffering he felt was not life denying, it did not endanger him physically, and in fact, if he had "tarried" with that discomfort and tried to digest those hard truths described in my talk, he might have experienced a beneficial workout of his racial "muscles" (Yancy 2013).

It was as if I showed him the course of a marathon. He had no idea how he could complete it, and so he asked me to drive him in a car to the finish line. He did not want to work to figure out whether he had the strengths necessary to complete the marathon, to figure out what weakness he had that might impede doing the necessary training (self-knowledge), to experiment (*versuchen*) with different types of training programs, and then start running to see if he could attain his goal. He just wanted me to do the work for him.

What might it look like to get whites and/or those privileged by the racially based systems of advantages and disadvantages to feel the full effects of their privileges (to render them visible) and to keep them from getting stuck in shame, resentment, and self-victimization (racism is bad and because I am accused of it, I feel guilt even if I didn't actively do anything and/or I did not intend to do anything)?

We need to come to see that engaging in an agonistic struggle with racism and forging healthier racialized and gendered identities as learning to work out our racial "muscles." We need to see the possibility of racialized discomfort as potentially being about growth, and not necessarily as a sign that something is wrong. It, therefore, requires courage. In this way, the approach is not that race is to be avoided, but it is also not something that can be engaged solely as an epistemological project that will result in objective and unconditional truths. Instead, we need to see these *Versuche* as ethical and existential projects about living well at the individual, group, and societal levels (Taylor 2014). In this way, uncertainty, discomfort, failures, and doubt are potential signs of "health, future, growth, power and life" (Nietzsche 1974b, 35). This should not be a hard sell in philosophy, given that many place Cartesian doubt as an important foundation and starting point for understanding philosophy and what it can do. The issue in part is that the ultimate goal of this Cartesian doubt is attaining objective certainty (and discounting anything that falls short of that goal of unconditional and universal Truth). But we in philosophy need to recognize the possible disjuncture between epistemologically certain Truth and existential health—particularly as it comes to gender and race.

Conclusion

In some sense, then, this brings me full circle. So the initial goal is *not* to solve racism and sexism, to eradicate it, but also not to just maintain the status quo. To figure out how to navigate this crossroads, we need a shift in thinking so that can then allow for a shift in feeling/embodying/racialized habits. Following Bell, I have recommended that we start with the premise that racism and sexism are permanent. Using Nietzsche and Bell, I recommend that we learn from the example of people who have used *Versuche* to create meaningful lives despite racism and sexism, not by fleeing or denying them, but by deepening their self-knowledge, mastering their strengths (*Kräfte*) and weaknesses, and deploying their strengths to affirm their lives. They recognize that this is an ongoing task that involves uncertainty, suffering, and failure. This is what I am calling "effortful *agon*," and it is a departure from the "effortless grace" that we generally hold up as the ideal for racial and gendered identities.

I have tried to establish an analogy between the type of unconditional and universal Truth that has been the traditional goal in philosophy and effortless racial grace. I have also argued that this philosophical approach has been hampered by philosophy's inability to speak to the possible flowering in the lives of women and/or people of color. Yet, in philosophy, we still tend to think that only epistemological truths that are unconditionally and universally True will yield a human flourishing of effortless grace in which race is either invisible or is only marginally a factor. Within this approach, the only racialized experiences that count are those on which we can have universal agreement. We reject those "truths" that are too subjective—that are "Tilted."

In philosophy in general, we devote a lot of time to clarifying our understanding of an issue or problem, as well as to asking the right questions. I am calling on philosophy to turn these formidable analytic skills to the enduring problems of intersecting oppressions and the tilted racialized identities they create, in a fashion that will yield healthier identities. Not only can we philosophers do it (as I hope I have shown), but we should do it.

References

Alcoff, Linda. (2006). *Visible Identities: Race, Gender, and the Self*. Oxford: Oxford University Press.

Bell, Derrick. (1992). *Faces at the Bottom of the Well*. New York: Basic Books.

Bell, Derrick. (2005). "Racial Realism." In *The Derrick Bell Reader*, edited by Richard Degado and Jean Stefancic, 73–77. New York: New York University Press.

Brooks, Gwendolyn. (1988). "Agenda." Unpublished poem presented at the Inauguration of President Johnnetta Cole, at Spelman College, Atlanta, GA.

Hadot, Pierre. (1995). *Philosophy as a Way of Life*. Oxford: Blackwell.

Medina, José. (2012). *The Epistemology of Resistance: Gender and Racial Oppression, Epistemic Injustice, and Resistant Imaginations*. Oxford: Oxford University Press.

Mills, Charles. (1998). *Blackness Visible: Essays on Philosophy and Race*. Ithaca, NY: Cornell University Press.

Nehamas, Alexander. (1998). *The Art of Living: Socratic Reflections from Plato to Foucault*. Berkeley: University of California Press.

Nietzsche, Friedrich. (1966). *Beyond Good and Evil*. Translated by Walter Kaufmann. New York: Vintage.

Nietzsche, Friedrich. (1967). *On the Genealogy of Morals*. Translated by Walter Kaufmann. New York: Random House.

Nietzsche, Friedrich. (1974a). "Attempt at a Self-Criticism." In *The Birth of Tragedy*, translated by Walter Kaufmann, 17–27. New York: Vintage Books.

Nietzsche, Friedrich. (1974b). *The Gay Science*. Translated by Walter Kaufmann. New York: Vintage.

Nietzsche, Friedrich, and Reginald John Hollingdale. (1996). *Nietzsche: Human, All Too Human: A Book for Free Spirits*. Cambridge: Cambridge University Press.

Scott, Jacqueline. (1998). "Nietzsche and Decadence: The Revaluation of Morality." *Continental Philosophy Review* 31: 59–78.

Scott, Jacqueline. (2006). "A Genealogy and Revaluation of Race." In *Critical Affinities: Nietzsche and African American Thought*, edited by A. Todd Franklin and Jacqueline Scott, 149–171. Albany: State University of New York Press.

Scott, Jacqueline. (2014). "Racial Nihilism as Racial Courage: The Potential for Healthier Racial Identities." *Graduate Faculty Philosophy Journal* 35 (1–2): 297–330.

Sullivan, Shannon. (2006). *Revealing Whiteness: The Unconscious Habits of Racial Privilege.* Bloomingon: Indiana University Press.

Taylor, Paul C. (2014). *Graduate Faculty Philosophy Journal* 35 (1–2): 331–351.

Yancy, George. (2012). *Look a White: Philosophical Essays on Whiteness.* Philadelphia: Temple University Press.

Yancy, George. (2013). "Trayvon Martin: When Effortless Grace is Sacrificed on the Altar of the Image." In *Pursuing Trayvon Martin: Historical Contexts and Contemporary Manifestations of Racial Dynamics*, edited by George Yancy and Janine Jones, 237–250. Lanham, MA: Lexington Books.

PART VIII

....

CONTEMPORARY SOCIAL ISSUES

Education, Health, Medicine, and Sports

....

THE history of political ideologies of race, the revision of posits of biological racial taxonomy in the sciences, differing approaches to race in philosophy, the complexity of racism, and a certain amount of expert disagreement and confusion regarding racial identities, altogether suggest that there would be ongoing, evident social problems regarding race. And, of course, there are. Racial identities, differences, relations, offenses, and injustices, recognition based on race, race in entertainment, racial representation in media, fashion associated with race—these are only a very few of the topics involving race that get public attention in the early twenty-first century.

When "race" is in the news, the public accepts it at face value. Everyone knows what it is, even though few could define it or would have the patience to endure scholarly treatments of it. Contemporary social discourse involving race may begin by accepting disparities as a normal part of ordinary life, but when solutions to specific problems are aired, discussion is apt to become controversial or contentious. Both the initial awareness and ensuing disagreement often occur without prior intellectual consideration of great depth. It is therefore sometimes appropriate to approach some examples without extensive prior theorizing.

The authors in this section are very much aware of how the subjects or contemporary problems they analyze are already broadly understood and discussed. Their starting point is common sense or public opinion. But that does not mean that what they have to say is a mere matter of "applied philosophy" or, in this case, applied philosophy of race. Rather, philosophical consideration of contemporary social issues pertaining to race yields insights that may inspire or revise more theoretically specialized attention.

From 2012 through 2015, mass and social media riveted public attention on a succession of police killings of unarmed young black men, which followed local practices of racial profiling (selecting and engaging suspects based on racial appearance). These incidents very rarely resulted in indictments or convictions of the officers responsible. It was never clarified during this time whether the onslaught of often-videotaped brutal police attacks was a new practice or a customary practice receiving new attention. The ethics and legality of police racial profiling have not been settled through the ubiquity and intensity of media coverage. Despite or because of its urgency, the subject of racial profiling requires philosophical analysis.

Annabelle Lever distinguishes between two academic approaches to racial profiling: the question of whether it is morally right to apply statistical group characteristics to individuals, and how the association of black people with crime is part of or reflects unjust racial hierarchies, or racial inequality and oppression. Philosophically, Lever is concerned with "whether the mere fact that a society has a racist past, whose consequences are still manifest in racial inequalities and injustices in the present, is *sufficient* to render all forms of racial profiling unjust." Specifically, her focus is on police action that relies on the race, ethnicity, or national origin of an individual, to intervene for crime prevention. She asks, "Is there is something about *racial generalizations* themselves that makes racial profiling an *unjustified* form of statistical discrimination? And her answer is that background racial injustice contributes to a disproportionate burden on black people who are racially profiled, so that even in the absence of police brutality, preemptive racial profiling is unjust.

In the United States, high black crime rates have been associated with lower educational achievement, as well as disadvantaged opportunities and resources. Lawrence Blum notes that education or learning has a long history in terms of race, because as soon as blacks and other nonwhite racial groups were identified as such, their intellectual inferiority to whites was taken for granted. Blum examines how different socioeconomic backgrounds and barriers to education have contributed to lower educational achievement among blacks, Latinos, and Native Americans, compared to American whites and Asians. He believes that the failure of legal integration to close the racial achievement gap is the result of prejudice on the part of teachers, as well as a scarcity of culturally relevant curricula materials for nonwhite children. As a plausible solution to these problems, Blum refers to recent studies showing that poor children do better in classes where middle-class children are also present. The rationale is that middle-class children already have habits and values that support success in the educational system. Integrated schools are not sufficient, because they are often divided into "tracks" that reproduce racial segregation. Blum also suggests that racial diversity in the K-12 classroom is fruitful preparation for civic engagement in a pluralistic society made up of citizens from diverse backgrounds.

Racial health disparities in major diseases, as well as in general well-being and longevity, have been in public awareness for some time. Laurie Shrage examines recent studies revealing a correlation between HIV/AIDS and other sexually transmitted diseases among African American women and high rates of incarceration among African American men. A plausible explanation is that HIV/AIDS is spread to the wider community by men who have sex with other men in prison but are otherwise heterosexual. However, these connections have not received much attention, because blacks are too readily stigmatized for unhealthy and immoral lifestyles, which makes it easy to blame them for their vulnerability to certain diseases. Shrage discusses research that blacks are in fact less likely to engage in illegal drug use or risky sexual behaviors than whites, but that their disproportionate incarceration for minor offenses increases their vulnerability to HIV/AIDS as inmates. She also observes that other areas for concern, further study, and reform, include high rates of rape and sexual coercion among prison populations, as well as the large segment of the inmate population suffering from untreated mental illness.

The next two essays in this section consider several underlying theoretical issues related to race and medicine and race and IQ tests. In "Race in the Biomedical Sciences," Michael Root begins with a distinction between the use of race to explain morbidity and mortality on a population level and the use of race to diagnose and treat individuals in clinical settings. Both epidemiological and pharmacological research find significant differences in disease rates and drug reactions, associated with race. Physicians often select treatment for individual patients by applying statistical variations on the level of racial populations, to them as individuals. And although self-reports of health are notoriously inaccurate, it is widely assumed that self-reports of race are accurate. The physicians use these self-reports to categorize patients racially. However, a number of factors may complicate the accuracy of self-reports of race: different criteria for how much black ancestry a person who is white can have; complexities of mixed race; lack of family information. Moreover, genes that determine drug response vary independently of race, and there is no guarantee that the criteria for race used by researchers are the same used by doctors in clinical settings. Also, responses to drugs may vary as much within races as between them. Root therefore concludes as follows:

> The question at the population level is not whether race should be used as a population variable in health research but which racial categories should be used and how members of a population should be assigned to them. The question at the individual level is whether race should matter at all, given the variation within each race in the response of patients to medical treatments.

Mark Alfano, Andrew R. A. Conway, and LaTasha Holden first take on the task of updating philosophers on "the state of the art in the scientific psychology of intelligence." They then explore several theoretical issues pertaining to the *measurement invariance* of intelligence tests, or the fact that blacks, Latinos, women, poor people, and other marginalized groups perform worse than average on a variety of intelligence tests. But Alfano et al. also consider the skepticism now surrounding measurement invariance, specifically in terms of *stereotype threat* or the correlation of decreased performance level with prior exposure of test takers to stereotypes about themselves. (Stereotype threat also applies to majority groups, so that, for example, white males do worse on math tests when reminded that Asians outperform whites.) The authors conclude with suggestions for countering the pernicious aspects of stereotype threat based on research that people's conceptions of intelligence influence how their own intelligence is expressed. They stress the importance of emphasizing that intelligence is not an essential or racially determined property, so that "inducing people to give up the idea that intelligence is an entity might shield them from academic underachievement." In a recent study, students at risk of dropping out of high school benefited from this kind of intervention, with higher grades and better performance in core courses.

Finally, it is obvious that race is a huge factor in contemporary sports and that sports are a vital, pervasive part of US life. At different times, specific sports have been dominated by distinct racial or ethnic groups as a means for socioeconomic advance in the United States. (Basketball, for instance, was invented by a Canadian physical education instructor for young white men in Massachusetts during the late nineteenth century and then spread through the YMCA and the US Army. Professional basketball was dominated by Jewish immigrants in the early twentieth century.) At present, it is still widely believed that athletics provides an opportunity for fair advancement, based on talent and discipline.

While John H. McClendon III in "'Race' to the Finish Line" does not doubt the importance of sport to African Americans, he argues through historical examples in basketball, baseball, football, golf, boxing, and horse racing that progress in sports requires the same dismantling of racism, as progress in any other area of US life. In reviewing the history of twentieth-century sports and race, McClendon shows how struggles for nonwhite opportunity and recognition in athletics have been parallel to such struggles in wider society. He writes, "Racism is not just an attitude or belief that there exist inferior and superior races. More important, it is behavior and institutions that lend material support to such attitudes and beliefs by the actual suppression of the supposed inferior group." McClendon concludes that part of what needs to change in athletics is the perceived requirement for white recognition of black excellence, in addition to whatever has been required and achieved for black excellence itself. The bottom line is that in sports, as in the rest of society, despite inspiring myths and ideals, there never has been a magical or effortless escape from racism.

FURTHER READING

Goodman, Sander L., ed. (2013). *Race in Contemporary Medicine.* New York: Routledge.
Gould, Stephen Jay. (2006). *The Mismeasure of Man.* New York: W.W. Norton.
Smith, Earl. (2013). *Race, Sport, and the American Dream.* Durham, NC: Carolina Academic Press.
Stevenson, Howard C. (2014). *Promoting Racial Literacy in Schools: Differences That Make a Difference.* New York: Teachers College Press.
Zack, Naomi. (2015). *White Privilege and Black Rights: The Injustice of US Police Racial Profiling and Homicide.* Lanham, MD: Rowman & Littlefield.

CHAPTER 36

RACIAL PROFILING AND THE POLITICAL PHILOSOPHY OF RACE

ANNABELLE LEVER

PHILOSOPHICAL reflection on racial profiling tends to take one of two forms. The first sees it as an example of statistical discrimination, raising the question of when, if ever, probabilistic generalizations about group behavior or characteristics can be used to judge particular individuals (Harcourt 2004; Risse and Zeckhauser 2004; Lippert-Rasmussen 2006, 2007, 2014; Risse 2007; Applbaum 2014; Hellman 2014). This approach treats racial profiling as one example among many others of a general problem in egalitarian political philosophy, occasioned by the fact that treating people as equals does not always require, or permit, us to treat them the same. The second form is concerned with how racial profiling illuminates the nature, justification, and reproduction of hierarchies of power and privilege based on skin color and morphology. Let's call this "the social construction approach." This form of reflection on racial profiling is therefore less about the justification for judging people based on the characteristics of the group to which they (appear to) belong, and more concerned with the specific ways in which the association of racialized minorities—and, in particular, black people—with crime, contributes to, and reflects, racial inequality, and oppression (Kennedy 1998; Lever 2005, 2007; Zack 2015). Both approaches to profiling have much to recommend them and, taken together, they form an essential component of the political philosophy of race. The statistical approach has the merits of linking racial profiling, as practice, to a body of *other* practices that generate and justify inequalities based on factors other than race, but it typically offers little by way of insight into the role of racial profiling itself in sustaining racial inequality and injustice. The racial construction approach, for obvious reasons, is rather better at the latter task, but its insights tend to come at the price of a broader understanding of the ways in which inequality is reproduced and justified, or of the ethical dilemmas raised by our competing claims to security. As we will see, insights from both approaches can be synthesized to clarify what, if anything, is wrong with racial profiling and what broader conclusions for equality and security follow from the study of profiling.

Preliminary Clarifications

Philosophical approaches to racial profiling tend to operate at some remove from actual police practice, and this is particularly true for the statistical determination approach to racial profiling. The reason is fairly straightforward: you do not need philosophical analysis to protest policy brutality and racism. Most philosophers suppose that racial profiling can only be justified if it is consistent with respect for the bodily integrity, the dignity, and the freedom and equality of racial majorities and minorities. They are therefore only interested philosophically in its justification (or lack thereof), on the assumption that it is a practice which is not intrinsically brutal, demeaning, humiliating, and of no particular use in combatting crime. However, even those philosophers working at a fairly high degree of abstraction, such as Mathias Risse and Richard Zeckhauser, Arthur Applbaum and Kasper Lippert-Rasmussen, are clearly aware of, and concerned by, racial injustice in our societies. They explicitly assume that racial profiling as currently practiced is not consistent with justice. What they want to know, however—and what they hope philosophical analysis will reveal—is whether the fact that existing practices of racial profiling are unjust means that *all* forms of racial profiling must be unjust. They are particularly interested in the question whether the mere fact that a society has a racist past, whose consequences are still manifest in racial inequalities and injustices in the present, is *sufficient* to render all forms of racial profiling unjust. Thus, even when the philosophical debate on profiling abstracts from police brutality and from the deliberate humiliation and mistreatment of minorities by the police, it assumes that we are interested in racial profiling within societies much like contemporary democracies, in which formal commitments to political equality coexist with very substantial constraints on the freedom and equality of people, as a result of laws that tolerated and sometimes mandated racial discrimination in the not-so-distant past.

"Racial profiling is a crime prevention and detection method, used by police officers, which takes racial identity into account to select and investigate suspects" (Zack 2015, 47), although police are generally not concerned with people's personal "identity," but rather with their "race" as conventionally defined. So let's define racial profiling as "any police-initiated action that relies on the race, ethnicity, or national origin and not just on the behavior of an individual" (Risse and Zeckhauser 2004, 136.) And let's concentrate on *preventive/preemptive profiling*, rather than *postcrime profiling*. The latter is concerned to narrow down the range of suspects necessary to identify the perpetrator of a known crime; the former is an effort to identify those who are about to commit a crime, such as drug or weapons smuggling, whether or not they have already engaged in illegal acts, such as buying an illegal weapon, in order to do so.

Preemptive racial profiling is controversial both because it is preemptive—no known illegal act has yet been committed—and because of the racial component in the decision to intervene. As no known crime has been committed, preemptive police tactics, such as "stop and search" or "stop and frisk," raise the natural concern that unless the acts to be prevented are limited in number and carefully described, police efforts to prevent crime will undermine the principle that people should be able to get on with their lives without explaining themselves to political authorities, if they are not evidently a threat to the rights and liberties of others. The racial dimension of racial profiling makes those concerns more acute, and it is therefore the twin factors of preemption plus race that lie behind much of the political and philosophical controversy concerning racial profiling.

To get to the heart of the philosophical controversy about racial profiling, let's follow Risse and Zeckhauser in limiting our discussion to cases that (a) involve the use of *behavior*, not just skin color and morphology, in the determination of suspicion; and that (b) include profiles of "whiteness" as well as "blackness," where whiteness is an appropriate element in the statistical profile of the person likely to commit a particular type of criminal act. (c) Let us also abstract from issues of police brutality and what relationship, if any, police brutality might have to the practice of profiling people as likely criminals—although, as Randall Kennedy, Naomi Zack, and I explain, there are good reasons to think that police brutality is endogenous to preventive profiling, and not merely a matter of a few bad cops, or an institutionally racist police culture (Kennedy 1998, 153; Lever 2005, 103–104; Zack 2015, 61). The reasons to make these abstractions for philosophical purposes are fairly clear: if race, however defined, is sufficient to justify police stopping and searching people, independent of what they are doing, it would have little probative value in preventing crime, as most people, whatever their skin color or morphology, do not commit crimes. More specifically, if racial profiling meant simply stopping black people, regardless of their behavior, it would be a case of racial discrimination pure and simple, and it would be seriously unjust. It would be seriously unjust even if police stops and searches involved no brutality, rudeness, or fear whatsoever, because being stopped and searched by the police is, in itself, an unpleasant experience that requires an instrumentally rational justification, and because racial discrimination by the police, whose job is to protect us, is an exceptionally grave injustice. Indeed, the fact that discrimination by the police, and by officers of the state more generally, is so morally serious makes it impossible to see how it could ever be justified for the police to stop people based on their visible racial characteristics alone.

The reasons why the term "racial profiling," at least for philosophical purposes, should be limited to cases where police use racial characteristics, *as well as* behavior, to determine who to stop therefore explains why it can be helpful to abstract from issues of police brutality and the obviously discriminatory use of police powers. As we have seen, even if police were polite, and even if we abstract from issues of brutality and fear, it would be unacceptable for the police to treat skin color alone as the basis for police stops and frisks. And this would be true, even if we did not live in societies with a history of racial discrimination and subordination, because the justification for police powers, in a democratic society, requires the police to protect the liberty, as well as the equality and bodily integrity, of all people, regardless of their skin color or morphology.

Let us take "race" to refer to social hierarchies of power and privilege, which group people according to their skin color and physical morphology (Haslanger 2012, 221–247). Although some arguments for racial profiling appear to assume that we can distinguish people into biological races with heritable characteristics of character and intelligence (Levin 1997/ 2005), arguments in favor of racial profiling need not depend on the acceptance of biologically based ideas of race. Indeed, arguments for and against racial profiling, politically and/ or philosophically, may reflect no agreed-upon view about the implications of skin color and morphology for individuals and group behavior, and they may not require any very clear concept of "race" (McPherson and Shelby 2004, 191).

GENERALIZATIONS, PREDICTIONS, AND POLICING

We navigate the social world using generalizations to guide us—generalizations about what is useful, desirable, realistic, and possible. Thus, philosophical objections to racial profiling cannot rest on the thought that it is a form of statistical discrimination, because we constantly have to discriminate between courses of action, people, material objects, and values based on generalizations about the particular properties that they are likely to have, and such behavior is generally morally unobjectionable. Objections to racial profiling, therefore, need to be developed against the background assumption that generalizations about other people are generally morally justified, in order to isolate what it is about *racial generalizations for police stops* that makes them unjustified.

As a first approach, we can note that police can hardly be required not to generalize from experience and from verified evidence when determining how to act. Otherwise the problem with racial profiling would be that it involves *generalizations* about behavior that indicate a readiness to commit a crime quite as much, or even more than, objections to the use of *racial* generalizations in preventive policing. We must therefore assume that *some* generalizations are allowed in police work in order to prevent crime. It therefore looks as though, even abstracting from police brutality and from discriminatory policing, there is something about *racial generalizations* themselves that makes racial profiling an *unjustified* form of statistical discrimination.

Obvious as it might seem that it is the character of racial generalizations that makes racial profiling morally problematic, what is wrong with racial generalizations is not self-evident. As Risse and Zeckhauser suggest, we generally feel very differently about the racial profiling of white, as opposed to black, people and this implies that it is not racial generalizations per se that make racial profiling unjust, but the fact that black people are disadvantaged compared to white people. Hence, according to Risse and Zeckhauser, if we do not object to the assumption that the profile of serial killers should include the description "white men," as long as we have reason to suppose that most serial killers are white men, but would object to the idea of using "black men" or "black teenagers" as part of an accurate criminal profile, our problems with racial profiling are not with racial generalizations in police work, but with the background injustice of our societies (Risse and Zeckhauser 2004, 148; Risse 2007, 14). We should therefore seek to remedy the latter—which, in any case we are bound in justice to do—*and* allow racial profiling if it can be carried out in ways that are fair, based on appropriate evidence of its utility, and clearly distinguishable in practice from a license to harass, brutalize, and intimidate racial minorities.

But this conclusion goes too fast: from the fact that *some* racial generalizations in police work are acceptable, it does not follow that racial generalizations are *generally* acceptable, even if they are accurate. It is not simply a matter, as Applbaum suggests, that we need to know the relative importance of the crimes to be prevented compared to the burdens that racial profiling generates (Applbaum 2014, 228). More fundamentally, there is the question of what racial generalizations we are concerned with, how they are arrived at, and what their use in police profiles will likely imply for people's civil rights, liberty, and dignity. To see this point, it helps to realize that serial killers are mercifully rare, and that while white serial killers are more common than nonwhite serial killers, very few people will fit the profile "white serial killer" (Bonn 2014a, 2014b). A license to use race generalizations in the effort to prevent serial killing is, therefore, a very constrained license to frisk or search people who, because of their race and behavior, look as though they may be about to commit a very serious crime. Indeed, as a serial killer will, by definition, commit several murders of the same type, the use of profiles in the case of serial killers generally presupposes the existence of at least one prior murder, and so what is being looked for is an actual killer who may strike again, rather than someone who is about to kill for the first time.

If these points are correct, it would be a mistake to generalize from the fact that we allow race to figure in the profile for serial killers, to our views about the use of race in other cases. For example, if white people were much more likely than other people to drive when drunk, would we allow police to use race in the profile for drunk drivers? Indeed, would we agree to the use of profiles, rather than other forms of detection and prevention, in the case of drunk driving? These are not easy questions to answer, but as long as we concern ourselves with the case where the driver is not obviously inebriated or unable to control his or her vehicle, the answer to both questions is probably "No," for reasons which are both moral and political.

A Hypothetical Case: Race and Drunk Driving

Drunken driving is dangerous, and it is implicated in much serious injury and death. But setting aside the question of what should count as the *legal evidence* of drunkenness (i.e., what quantity of alcohol in the blood should be deemed sufficient for the legal offense of drunk driving), there is the question of what would count as the *behavioral evidence* that might justify a policy stop, once we set aside those people who are driving dangerously and, therefore, are appropriate objects of police attention whether or not they are drunk. Should it be leaving a pub or bar in a car? That would seem a reasonable supposition, even if some people in pubs and bars do not drink alcohol, and some of those who do drink alcohol are careful to stay within the legal limit. Such a hypothetical stop strategy, even if instrumentally rational and better than the alternatives, would bias police searches away from those who drink in restaurants, private houses, hotels, and such. It would therefore leave much—perhaps most—drunk driving relatively unpoliced and undeterred. There might even be a type of class bias involved, insofar as pubs and bars are less socially exclusive and expensive than restaurants and hotels that serve alcohol. But imagine that, despite its limitations, police use of "race + leaving a pub or bar," as behavioral indicators of drunk driving, helped to improve the identification and arrest of those driving while drunk over the most likely alternatives, such as random or universal searches (i.e., barriers that lead everyone in the area to be searched for a defined amount of time). Would that be sufficient for us to agree with Risse and Zeckhauser that the use of racial generalizations is morally unproblematic in preventive policing?

Again, I think the answer must be "No." First, it is hard to believe that there would not be a great deal of protest about this hypothetical police tactic, because most white people are not used to being treated as incipient criminals, and people who drive over the alcohol limit, like people who drive over the speed limit, tend not to consider themselves as criminals or as menaces to the lives and limbs of others (Lever 2005, 102). We should expect, then, that there would be passionate and repeated demands for evidence of the rationality of this police tactic, and of the justification of using race as a component of a profile for drunk driving, given that alternative ways to prevent (if not to police) drunk driving exist, and that the policy is likely to criminalize people who, in all other respects, have led blameless lives. The dreadful consequences for the families of those unfortunates caught driving with a bit too much alcohol in their blood will be cited as evidence that the hypothetical policy is not as rational as it first seems, that it has hidden costs which are not adequately accounted for by focusing simply on "hit rates" for the identification and arrest of those driving over the legal alcohol limit. (For the application of these points to the profiling of black men, see Kennedy 1998, 151–155.) In short, it seems reasonable to suppose that there would be a great deal of political protest about such a policy, even by people who are normally quite sympathetic to the strenuous legal enforcement and prosecution of the law. Some of that protest might be hypocritical and reflect racist ideas that what is ok in the policing of disproportionately black offenses is unacceptable in the policing of majority-white ones. Still, there *is* clearly something morally important about such objections, which might apply beyond concerns with *racial* generalizations, to profiling for behavior that is *widespread*, even if it is, and ought to be, illegal.

People's failure to comply with the law need not reflect evil intent, or selfish indifference to the needs and claims of others. Instead, it may reflect behavior that is hard for people to control, such as precisely calibrating how much to drink or agreeing to take part in popular and generally pleasant social rituals with everyone else. Lawbreaking may also reflect behavior that is the outcome of momentary but overwhelming emotions—relief, anger, sadness, joy—or more long-term difficulties with depression, rage, loneliness, and the need to please or to fit in. These problems need not be especially personal—they may, in fact, reflect real social problems, and they may persist even when people are informed about the law, the reasons for it, and the way that it will be enforced. Our example, then, suggests that objections to racial profiling, in at least some real or hypothetical cases, likely reflect doubts about the wisdom, desirability, and/or morality of engaging in the use of preemptive stops for acts that are very widespread (such as drunk driving or the use of marijuana) and that may not best be approached through the *criminal* law, even if deserving of legal condemnation. In short, objections to policing based on racial generalizations may be motivated less by concerns with *race* specifically than with the use of preemptive police scrutiny of particular individuals as a way to get large, amorphous groups of people to desist from drugs or risky behavior or otherwise to behave as they ought (Reiman 2011).

But even people who are habitually concerned to ensure that civil rights are protected might object to the use of white skin as an indicator of drunk driving in my hypothetical example, even if accompanied by behavior suggestive of alcohol consumption, such as leaving a bar or pub. After all, who *is* actually stopped by police is likely to be pretty arbitrary, unless the police stop everyone coming out of a pub/bar—which would turn the type of stop involved into something much closer to a universal stop (albeit of those leaving bars, rather than entering cinemas or airports). Indeed, the larger the disparity between the potential population stopped and the number of actual stops, the more acute the concern that arbitrary, perhaps unconscious, factors are affecting police decisions about who to test for drunk driving—for example, people whose cars look old or damaged, or which appear to have lots of passengers, or a foreign license plate, or even a foreign-looking driver. Ex hypothesi, none of these factors are part of the profile for drunk driving, and so there is no justification for using them as a criterion for police investigation into drunk driving. Moreover, insofar as these often unconscious factors reflect prejudice, such as class prejudice, prejudice against aliens or immigrants, or particular ethnic or religious groups, there would be compelling *moral* objections to allowing such stops and searches to go ahead and to allow convictions based on such searches. In short, insofar as these race-based searches involve only a small fraction of those who might be stopped (as is usually the case), worries about the arbitrary character of those stops call into question the justification of what might, in other respects, be a useful form of policing.

These two seemingly contradictory worries—that too many are affected by profiling, and that too few are affected—are actually consistent and mutually reinforcing. The problem highlighted by the first worry is not that very many people *will be* stopped, but that a great many people are *threatened* with being stopped with no warning, as they go about doing the sorts of things that law-abiding people, as well as criminals, normally do. By contrast, the second worry is that unless the police *actually stop* a very large number of people from this large target population—which would, in effect, approach the use of a deliberate policy of universal searches of anyone coming out of a pub/bar—the best explanation of who in fact *is* stopped will almost certainly have nothing to do with the task of preventing drunk driving, or the profile of a drunk driver itself and may, unfortunately, reflect unexamined and unjustified prejudices peculiar to the particular officer, or common among the police more generally. Either way, it would seem the reasons to find racial profiling attractive (because it may be a rational and reasonably effective strategy for handling behavior that is widespread, but not easy to detect, deter, and punish) are themselves reasons for doubting that profiling is morally appropriate, or that it is the best way for the state to protect people's lives and limbs.

Finally, we could imagine that some civil-rights defenders might worry that the use of "white," in efforts to prevent drunk driving, trades on unjustified stereotypes, albeit unacknowledged, and that there is therefore a much closer connection than one might expect between the use of racial profiles and the tendency for prejudice against some, or all, white people.

Given how prevalent drunk driving probably is and, ex hypothesi, how serious are its harms, the fact that white people, in our hypothetical example, are significantly more likely to engage in it than other groups might make it reasonable for the police to infer that there is something about being white that makes one particularly prone to drunk driving. Precisely because statistical profiles are agnostic about causation, they leave the path open to the hypothesis that being white is causally related to drunk driving, rather than being merely a statistical indicator that may have no causal role at all (Applbaum 2014, 227–228). Unfortunately, the larger the group to be profiled, the more tempting causal claims about race and crime are likely to be; and the more tempting a specifically *essentialist* assumption about the intrinsic characteristics of, in this case, white people, related to criminal behavior. After all, if lots of white people are associated with drunk driving—and sufficiently more proportionately than other groups for race to be part of a predictive profile—it becomes much more difficult to imagine the factors that might make race an important correlate of drunk driving, without it being a causal factor. The larger the group delineated by the police profile, the more varied their social situation and personal characteristics are likely to be. It may therefore seem reasonable—if not self-evident—that whatever it is that explains why white people are predisposed to drunk driving, it must be something that all white people share. And that—or so it might seem—is simply their whiteness. Unfortunately, then, the practice of profiling may lead people to adopt essentialist ideas of race, even if they did not hold them before, as well as to attribute to these essential racial features a causative role in serious crime, which they might previously have assumed to be false.

The problem with racial profiles, then, is not simply that they have the quality of a self-fulfilling prophecy, because if the police stop sufficiently more black people than white people, they are likely to find more black people who are breaking the law than white people *even if* police stops of black people actually are less good at identifying crime than police stops of white people (Harcourt 2004, 121–125; Harris 2003, 223–225; Zack 2015, 48–51). Nor is the problem simply that disconfirming evidence for the special utility or desirability of the profile will be hard to establish, absent evidence of the total number of those driving while drunk—evidence that, by its nature, is impossible to establish (Applbaum 2014, 228). In addition, preemptive racial profiling seems particularly likely to reinforce racist beliefs about groups, by fostering misplaced claims about the causal importance of race in criminal behavior and by fostering a misplaced essentialism about race, be it biological or cultural. The antidote to such thinking, of course, is to remember that while most police profiles concern groups whose members are disproportionately likely to behave in ways that are criminal, *the vast majority of the members of that group are statistically unlikely to behave that way* (Sampson and Wilson 1995, 229; Holbert and Rose 2004, 126; Sampson, Morenoff, and Raudenbush 2005, 227–228; Zack 2015, 55). However, if the disproportion is sufficiently marked, and the behavior in question is sufficiently serious, racial profiles may look like a rational solution to the problem of fair and effective policing. And a focus on *the reasons* for profiling—a focus that is natural both for the police, who have to carry out the profiles, and for those who have to justify the policy publicly—may obscure the fact that most of those who fit a predictive police profile will not do anything wrong and, a forteriori, most people, whatever the racial group to which they belong, will not do so either.

We can conclude, then, that statistical profiles for policing purposes and, especially, profiles that use racial generalizations, are *intrinsically* problematic, even if we abstract from contemporary concerns with police brutality. The problems with profiling are moral and practical, and both types of problems will be especially acute where the factors that go into the profile are widely shared, such that very large numbers of innocent people are threatened by preventive police stops because they meet the criteria of the profile. These problems are moral, insofar as morally arbitrary factors, such as prejudice, are likely to explain which, of the many people who fit the statistical profile, policy actually stop. It may cement prejudice about the frequency, severity, and distribution of criminal behavior in society because profiling draws public attention *to* differential rates in the propensity to break the law, and *away from* evidence that most people do not engage in crime, whatever the ascriptive or voluntary groups to which they belong. Finally, statistical profiles may create prejudice, as we saw from the hypothetical case of the racial profiling of drunk drivers, by encouraging essentialist causal explanations of what is, at best, an accurate, though perhaps temporary or misleading, statistical correlation.

Each of these *moral* problems reflects *practical* problems intrinsic to the use of statistical generalizations in preventive policing. Because crime is rare, the overwhelming majority of the people who fit a police profile will never commit the particular crime for which the profile has been drawn up, and will be unlikely to engage in criminal activities at all. Predictive police stops on the basis of statistical profiles alone are therefore most unlikely to catch criminals, so their instrumental justification depends on their *relative virtues* compared to other ways of detecting and preventing crime, not on their *absolute* advantages. However, it is difficult to estimate those comparative advantages when the size of the criminal population is a matter of speculation, when prejudice and unequal legal resources may affect arrest rates, and when rates of legal convictions may also reflect legal and extralegal incentives to plead guilty even if one is innocent (Rakoff 2014; Gertner et al. 2015). Thus, it is difficult to show that preventive profiling is an effective police tool, or more effective than the alternatives, and these problems are particularly acute, because the best way to prevent crime may not be a matter of *policing* at all (Sampson, Morenoff, and Raudenbush 2005; Wolff 2011, especially p. 123).

We have seen, then, that statistical profiling is intrinsically problematic, *whether or not it concerns the profiling of disadvantaged racial minorities.* Indeed, part of the reason why racial profiling is inherently problematic is because the use of predictive profiles is already hard to justify even if we are not concerned with a particularly stigmatized and disadvantaged ascriptive minority. Once we consider the disadvantages inherent to the profiling of a disadvantaged racial minority, it is hard to see how predictive racial profiles could be justified on deontological grounds. Respect for our fellow citizens is inconsistent with the use of police tactics that will predictably exacerbate the disadvantages and injustices from which they already suffer, absent compelling evidence that those tactics are necessary to avert grave injustice to others. (Lever 2007; Reiman 2011). However, once we consider the effects of background injustice on the way we can describe and evaluate morally significant consequences, it becomes plain that racial profiling cannot be justified on consequentialist grounds either.

Background injustice can affect consequentialist moral judgments about a police policy in several ways. It might, for example, make us skeptical about why a particular policy has been chosen, the quality and quantity of the evidence used to support it, the adequacy of the alternatives that were considered, and the likelihood of it being implemented fairly (Sampson and Wilson 1995, 41–43). However, background injustice also means that it matters how the costs and benefits of a police policy are distributed, in order to avoid exacerbating unjust patterns of advantages inherited from the past. In the case of racial profiling, for example, there are good reasons to be skeptical of the assumption, found in Risse and Zeckhauser, and Applbaum and Lippert-Rasmussen that, were it not for racist policing and brutality, black people would generally be net gainers from accurate racial profiles, because black people form the overwhelming majority of the victims of black crime. Part of the reason to make such an assumption is to see what difference, if any, it would make to the justification of racial profiling. But these authors clearly suppose that the assumption is plausible (for example, Lippert-Rasmussen 2014, 286–287).

However, even if black people are the main victims of black criminals, it is hard to see how the *racial profiling* of black people would advantage black people. Given residential and occupational segregation, "black on black" crime likely occurs in neighborhoods and employments where most people are black, just as "white on white" crime likely occurs in neighborhoods and employments where most people are white. In short, although any racial or ethnic group will benefit from police success in catching or preventing attacks against them, it is doubtful that racial or ethnic profiles will be particularly useful in the process. Just as you are unlikely to distinguish one academic from another by looking for a middle-aged white man among the professors on most European or American campuses, so looking for a "young black male," in an area where young black males are common, is unlikely to help you deter crime. Rather, it seems that the main beneficiaries of the racial profiling of black people will be white people, because white people make up the majority of the population who will be safeguarded and will be able to benefit from any advantages that racial profiling brings without suffering the main burdens of racial profiling. On the other hand, young black men, and those who love and depend upon them, will bear the overwhelming share of the costs of racial profiling, whether or not they share in the benefits. This division of the costs and benefits of security cannot be justified as an ordinary part of policing, once we take background injustice into account, for that would be to compound the burdens on some of the most vulnerable groups in our societies and to exacerbate injustices that we have a duty to repair. The legacy of racism is not, in itself, sufficient to show that racial profiling is unjust. However, the legacy of racism affects the *weight* we can ascribe to the benefits and burdens of a police policy, depending on how these are distributed across social groups (Lever 2007). So while racial profiling might be justified in very exceptional circumstances, as long as special forms of approval, supervision, accountability, and compensation are in place, philosophical reflection shows that racial profiling is nearly always unjustified given its intrinsic properties and its likely consequences, even if we abstract from the shame and horror of police violence, brutality, and prejudice.

References

Applbaum, A. I. (2014). "Bayesian Inference and Contractualist Justification on Interstate 95." In *Contemporary Debates in Applied Ethics*, edited by Andrew I. Cohen and Christopher Heath Wellman, 2nd ed., 219–232. Chichester, UK: Wiley.

Bonn, Scott (2014a). "5 Myths About Serial Killers and Why They Persist." *Scientific American*, October. Accessed May 18, 2016. http://www.scientificamerican.com/article/5-myths-about-serial-killers-and-why-they-persist-excerpt/.

Bonn, Scott. (2014b). *Why We Love Serial Killers: The Curious Appeal of the World's Most Savage Murderers*. New York: Skyhorse Publishing, Inc.

Gertner, N. B., P. Shechtman, and J. S. Rakoff. (2015). "Why Innocent People Plead Guilty: An Exchange." *New York Review of Books*, January 8. Accessed May 18, 2016. http://www.nybooks.com/articles/archives/2015/jan/08/why-innocent-plead-guilty-exchange/.

Harcourt, B. (2004). "Rethinking Racial Profiling: A Critique of the Economics, Civil Liberties, and Constitutional Literature, and of Criminal Profiling More Generally." *University of Chicago Law Review* 71 (4): 1275–1381.

Harris, David A. (2003). *Profiles in Injustice: Why Racial Profiling Cannot Work*. New York: The New Press.

Haslanger, S. (2012). *Resisting Reality: Social Construction and Social Critique*. Oxford: Oxford University Press.

Hellman, D. (2014). "Racial Profiling and the Meaning of Racial Categories." In *Contempory Debates in Applied Ethics* edited by Andrew I. Cohen and Christopher Heath Wellman. 2nd ed., 232–245. Chichester, UK: Wiley.

Holbert, S., and L. Rose. (2004). *The Color of Guilt and Innocence: Racial Profiling and Police Practices in America*. San Ramon, CA: Page Marque Press.

Kennedy, R. (1998). *Race, Crime, and the Law*. New York: Vintage.

Lever, A. (2005). "Why Racial Profiling Is Hard to Justify: A Response to Risse and Zeckhauser." *Philosophy and Public Affairs* 33 (1): 94–110.

Lever, A. (2007). "What's Wrong with Racial Profiling? Another Look at the Problem." *Criminal Justice Ethics* 26 (1): 20–28.

Levin, Michael E. (1997/2005). *Why Race Matters: Race Differences and What They Mean. Human Evolution, Behavior, and Intelligence.* Westport, CT: Praeger Publishers/Greenwood Publishing Group.

Lippert-Rasmussen, K. (2006). "Racial Profiling Versus Community." *Journal of Applied Philosophy* 23 (2): 191–205.

Lippert-Rasmussen, K. (2007). "Nothing Personal: On Statistical Discrimination." *The Journal of Political Philosophy* 15 (4): 385–403.

Lippert-Rasmussen, K. (2014). *Born Free and Equal? A Philosophical Inquiry into the Nature of Discrimination.* New York: Oxford University Press.

McPherson, L. K., and T. Shelby. (2004). "Blackness and Blood: Interpreting African American Identity." *Philosophy and Public Affairs* 32 (2): 171–192.

Rakoff, J. S. (2014). "Why Innocent People Plead Guilty." *New York Review of Books*, November 20. Accessed May 18, 2016. http://www.nybooks.com/articles/archives/2014/nov/20/why-innocent-people-plead-guilty/.

Reiman, J. (2011). "Is Racial Profiling Just? Making Criminal Justice Policy in the Original Position." *Journal of Ethics* 15 (3): 3–19.

Risse, M. (2007). "Racial Profiling: A Reply to Two Critics." *Criminal Justice Ethics* 26 (1): 4–19.

Risse, M., and R. Zeckhauser. (2004). "Racial Profiling." *Philosophy and Public Affairs* 32 (2): 131–170.

Sampson, R. J., J. D. Morenoff, and S. Raudenbush. (2005). "Social Anatomy of Racial and Ethnic Disparities in Violence." *American Journal of Public Health* 95 (2): 224–232.

Sampson, R. J., and J. W. Wilson. (1995). "Toward a Theory of Race, Crime and Urban Inequality." In *Crime and Inequality*, edited by John Hagen and Ruth Peterson, 37–54. Palo Alto, CA: Stanford University Press.

Wolff, J. (2011). *Ethics and Public Policy: A Philosophical Inquiry.* London: Routledge.

Zack, N. (2015). *White Privilege and Black Rights: The Injustice of U.S. Police Racial Profiling and Homicide.* New York: Rowman and Littlefield.

CHAPTER 37

···

RACE AND K-12 EDUCATION

···

LAWRENCE BLUM

HISTORICALLY, race has had a close relationship with education. In the European and American ideas of race, so-designated racial groups were arranged on a hierarchy of presumed mental capacity. Groups at the bottom were provided with minimal or inadequate education, justified by the idea that they did not have the capacity to learn beyond a certain level. This rationale was not necessarily the actual reason the "lower orders" were denied education, and some of the real reason contradicted this official racial rationale. For example, during the slave era in the United States, in the 1830s many states passed laws that forbade slave owners from teaching slaves to read, and criminalized slaves themselves learning to read (Wallenstein 2007). This was done to prevent slaves from reading material that challenged slavery, such as David Walker's *Appeal to the Colored Races of the World* (1829/2000). Such laws obviously presumed that slaves were capable of learning; their purpose was to prevent them from doing so. Nevertheless, the official rationale for inferior education for slaves was their mental incapacity, and many whites believed this official rationale was true.

The idea that conventionally defined racial groups differ in intelligence has been largely discredited by contemporary science, and popular adherence to it has declined sharply. But it has by no means entirely disappeared in popular thought, and a more statistically based form has arisen in genetic science as well. In the United States, both forms are encouraged by a basic fact on the ground in education—often referred to as the "achievement gap"—that by almost every plausible measure, black, Native American, and Latino students do not do as well in school as white and Asian students (Gándara and Contreras 2009; Harris 2011, 4–8; Fischer and Stoddard 2013). This gap encourages the view that there is something educationally deficient about black, Latino, and Native American students. Racial achievement gaps can be explained by a range of factors, most of which concern black and Latino students' circumstances rather than their innate capacities—poorer health among disadvantaged racial minorities; less parental education, which disadvantages students in various different ways; lower parental socioeconomic status (SES), often leading to unstable home and living situations and moving from school to school; stress from not having decent and regular employment; teacher racial prejudice, ignorance and insensitivity; living in neighborhoods of concentrated disadvantage; and cultural factors relating to school engagement among minority youth.

This range of factors cannot be examined here, but it is important to recognize that the educational plight of racial groups is affected by factors not distinctly racial in character. Because blacks, Latinos, and Native Americans are disproportionately of lower SES status than are whites and Asians, disadvantaging factors related specifically to SES (e.g., stress regarding employment and income, comparatively less parental education) that are shared with particular whites and Asians, will contribute to explaining why the former groups generally do less well educationally as groups. Moreover, in addition to nonracial influences on the racial achievement gap in education, different histories and circumstances result in different educational barriers for distinct groups.

THE DIVERSITY OF THE RACIAL ACHIEVEMENT GAP

The No Child Left Behind legislation of 2001 (a reauthorization of the 1965 Elementary and Secondary Education Act) requires states to report test scores (mandated by the legislation) broken out by "major racial and ethnic groups," generally understood as whites, blacks, Asian/Pacific Islander, Native Americans, and Latinos/Hispanics.

Injustice and the White–Black and White–Native American Education Gap

Many view the white–black disparity as the most unjust among the disparities between whites and other groups, because its causes are understood to lie in a history of oppression that includes slavery, segregation, discrimination in housing and educational provision, and continuing failures to rectify those previous inequalities. The legacy of prior deprivation lives on in the present, where it joins contemporary forms of educational discrimination (see later) to produce disparate educational outcomes. The white–Native American disparity has a comparable normative standing. The immiseration of Native Americans and a history of attempts to use schools to suppress Native American culture render current disparity a legacy of historical mistreatment (Adams 1995; Mader 2014).

Immigration and the White–Latino Education Gap

White–Latino educational disparity shares some features with that of blacks and Native Americans, but it differs due to the conditions of immigration. Mexican Americans, comprising about 60 percent of Latinos, have a history of discrimination and segregation in education. The racial/pan-ethnic category "Latino" is often associated in non-Latinos minds with lower ability and laziness, and this stereotype often affects how teachers treat Latino students and what degree of learning they expect of them, similarly to how blacks are viewed (Gándara and Contreras 2009). Latino immigrants, especially Mexicans and Puerto Ricans, are relatively disadvantaged compared to the American population as a whole, with less education and fewer financial resources at the point of immigration (or of entry, in the case of Puerto Ricans, who are US citizens). However, although lower SES is educationally disadvantageous, possessing that characteristic at the point of entry may not be a matter of injustice.

(It may be a matter of injustice internationally, if lower SES is the result of US foreign policy.) Immigrants from Spanish-speaking as well as other non-English-speaking nations are also educationally disadvantaged by not knowing English as well as natives (including native Latinos), and it is not a matter of injustice if someone does not speak English. Still, the current language approach in US schools is largely responsible for making it a learning disadvantage. Spanish language students could fairly easily catch up to native students if English as a Second Language were taught properly, and it would indeed be advantaged by being bilingual) (Gándara and Contreras 2009).

Asian Americans

Asians as a racial group present yet a different set of issues. Historically in the United States Asians were regarded as racially inferior, like blacks but superior to them (Strum 2010). They were a target of educational segregation in the state of California, where they were most numerous. Asians were seen as alien and unassimilable, and their imposed perpetual foreignness was both a cause and product of their being prevented from naturalizing, until the lifting of racial restrictions on naturalization in 1952 (Haney-Lopez 1996; Takaki 1998). This sense of Asian foreignness has not entirely disappeared in American culture (Kim 1999).

Nevertheless, the large majority of current Asian Americans have arrived since racial restrictions were lifted in the 1965 Hart-Celler Immigration Act, and this group is distinctly advantaged in key respects compared to the other racial groups in the United States, including whites. Asians have higher incomes and a much stronger educational profile (Kao et al. 2013, 89). Educationally, Asians are not on the short end of an "achievement gap" as are blacks, Latinos, and Native Americans. Still, racial barriers in education persist, such as stereotyping as good students, so that teachers sometimes fail to recognize struggling Asian students and do not give these students appropriate attention (Lee 2009). The related stereotype as a "model minority" has the additional deleterious effect of harming relationships between Asian Americans and blacks and Latinos (Wu 2003). We should note that stereotyping of racialized groups is not always wholly racial in character and for Asians it is generally regarded as based on assumed cultural, rather than innate, characteristics.

Thus, race does not always carry the same normative valence across races in the context of educational racial disparities. The distinctive history of each racial group has influenced its educational attainment, the barriers it has faced as a group, and the degree and character of injustice involved in its educational situation (Ngai 2004).

SEGREGATION, DESEGREGATION, AND INEQUALITY

The Meanings of "Segregation"

The 1954 *Brown v. Board of Education* decision overturned the 1896 *Plessy v. Ferguson* ruling that permitted separate facilities for blacks and whites (railroad cars, in the *Plessy* case), as long as the facilities were equal. In several cases prior to *Brown*, plaintiffs had argued that particular educational facilities were not in fact equal, forcing provision of facilities that the defendant had not intended to provide. The *Brown* decision took the next step of declaring that segregated facilities were "inherently unequal" (*Brown* 495).

But the decision contained two important ambiguities. The Court seemed to cash out "inherently unequal" in terms of the psychological effect of state-mandated segregation on black school children, arguing that segregation would necessarily have deleterious effects on the children's psyches, independently of whether the actual educational facilities were equal or not. But if so, this would be a causal effect of segregation, not something "inherent" in it. So it is not clear what "inherently unequal" should be taken to mean.

The second ambiguity has haunted the issue of school integration ever since. In the decision, "segregation" is generally understood as state-mandated separation of racial groups into different schools, although at one point the Court recognizes that school racial separation could be produced by other social processes. The former meaning drove a ruling in *Mendez v. Westminster* (1947) involving Mexican American school segregation, that the California district in question was compelled to stop segregating Mexican American school children, partly on the grounds that state-mandated separation conveyed an expressive harm to them (Strum 2010, 136).

An example of a process leading to racial separation but not driven by state mandate is residential separation together with a neighborhood-based school assignment policy. Such *resultant* school racial separation is today frequently referred to as "segregation." Segregation in this sense is currently at a very high level in the United States, much higher than it was in the late 1980s (Frankenberg and Orfield 2012; Orfield et al. 2014).

The two meanings of "segregation" are quite different. The wrong of state-mandated separation stems substantially (though not solely) from the expressive harm of declaring blacks or Mexicans to be unfit to go to school with whites. It is a great harm to school children to attend separate schools which they recognize as expressing this message of their inferiority. But the same cannot be said for mere separation itself in the absence of any official message expressed by this arrangement. W. E. B. Du Bois recognized the importance of this distinction in a 1935 essay, "Does the Negro Need Separate Schools?" He said that blacks should seek schools that were equal to those of whites; whether they were racially separated was a secondary matter. Du Bois said that in most American segregated schools in the South, were blacks to be admitted, "the education that colored children would get in them would be worse than pitiable" (Du Bois 1935, 329), so that separate schools are necessary for these children. However, he also said that blacks often rejected separate schools because they themselves had internalized the message that "black was inferior," a message conveyed in countless ways in the system of Jim Crow segregation (and, in partly similar and partly different ways, in its Northern counterpart). Du Bois urged blacks to reject this message, and thus not to spurn all-black schools on the grounds that their demographic rendered them inferior (Du Bois 1935).

Schools that are one-race dominant but not a product of segregative processes that embody and express the message of inferiority may still be objectionable; but if so, this must be for different reasons than the expressive harm. In two cases in the late 1960s and early 1970s, the Supreme Court recognized that in practice the line between separation-expressive-of-inferiority and separation-not-expressive-of-inferiority was not always sharp. In these cases the Court saw that some separation was a *legacy* of inferiority-expressive processes without being *direct expressions* of those processes, and that the state could lend its imprimatur to segregative processes and meanings without directly generating them. In *Green v. County School Board of New Kent County* (1968), the Court stated that the effects of prior segregation in the present must be eliminated "root and branch," and in *Swann v. Charlotte-Mecklenburg Board of Education* (1971) the Court held that race-informed student assignment policies might be necessary to achieve a system free of the effects of prior state-mandated segregation.

Furthermore, school segregation is partly a by-product of residential de facto segregation, which cannot be regarded as free of the effects of state-sponsored discriminatory and stigmatizing processes (Anderson 2010, chapters 3 and 4). Despite its legal prohibition, widespread discrimination in lending and real estate practices has been documented throughout the country, supporting and maintaining residential segregation (Oliver and Shapiro 2006). Moreover, historically, federal housing policy was explicitly discriminatory against blacks, putting in place black disadvantage that remained once these policies were officially discontinued (since whites did not have to give up homes they secured under the discriminatory regime) (Katznelson 2006; Oliver and Shapiro 2006).

Thus, there are in reality three different possible meanings of "segregation"—(1) directly state-mandated separation, expressing the view of one racial group as inferior, (2) racial separation as a byproduct of neutral and nonobjectionable processes, and (3) racial separation that is partly an effect of prior segregative processes in the sense of (1), or of stigmatizing or discriminatory processes permitted, but not officially sanctioned, by the state. How much of today's school separation is segregation in sense (2) and how much sense (3) is an empirical matter. But most of it is likely to be of sense (3), as Elizabeth Anderson argues in her comprehensive review of the literature (Anderson 2010; see also Frankenberg and Orfield 2012).

Integration and Equality

The *Brown* Court's ruling assumed that bringing black and white children into the same schools and classrooms, and with the same teachers, would result in the two groups being provided with equivalent educations and thereby performing educationally at the same level. This has proven a mistaken assumption, for several different types of reason. First, teachers are susceptible to racial prejudice and stereotyping and thus do not necessarily treat all students the same by providing appropriate instruction and treatment suitable to each individual student. Since the teaching force has remained overwhelmingly white, even though only 50 percent of students are now non-Hispanic white (Maxwell 2014), the prejudice and stereotyping on the part of whites tends to mean that black, Latino, and Native American students are on average likely to receive inferior treatment in schools compared to white students. In addition, while it may be assumed that on the whole teachers of color are less prejudiced than white teachers toward students of color, teachers of color may be as prejudiced as white teachers toward members of racial groups other than their own, and indeed some hold education-distorting views even of students from their own racial group.

A second reason school integration does not always lead to equal education concerns curriculum and instructional approaches. It is plausible to think that black, Native American, and

Latino children from disadvantaged backgrounds learn better when the curriculum reflects something of their own histories, experiences, and heritages, and when teachers acknowledge these features of those students, and this is not always the case (Delpit 1995; Nieto and Bode 2011). A third reason school integration does not always lead to equal education is that students' background and family circumstances have an impact on in-school learning. This fact was officially recognized by the Coleman Report of 1966, commissioned by the federal government as part of the Civil Rights Act of 1964 and its attempt to provide equality of opportunity (Coleman 1966). And subsequent research has greatly expanded our understanding of the manifold ways that, as briefly mentioned earlier, out-of-school factors affect learning and school performance (Duncan and Murnane 2011; Carter and Welner 2013).

The Equality Argument for Classroom Integration and Detracking

In recent decades, a new argument for integration has emerged: All else being equal, working-class and poor students benefit from being in schools and classes dominated by, or at least with a strong norm-setting presence of, middle-class children. This claim, while based on class characteristics, has implications for race in that black, Latino, and Native American children are substantially more likely than whites to be disadvantaged in regard to those class characteristics. The claim depends on the idea that middle-class children bring stronger habits and norms promoting school success from their homes to school than do working-class students; sharing classes exposes the latter to the former, resulting in the working-class students picking up the superior norms from the middle-class students (Oakes 2005; Kahlenberg 2012).

The argument requires students from different groups to be in the same classes, not merely co-present in the same school. Often this does not happen because many multiracial schools "track" students into different levels of classes, basing placement strongly, though not exclusively, on prior performance (Oakes 2005). Although that criterion is neither explicitly race- nor class-based, in practice, and in line with the findings of the Coleman Report, racial minority students and lower income students start school behind middle-class students in crucial educational skills (Coleman 1966). So if placement in one grade is dependent on performance in the previous grade, there will be a vicious circle in which the disparities at any given level will be reproduced and generally intensified at the next level(s), as the students in the higher track classes are provided with richer curriculum and generally more qualified teachers. In addition white middle class parents are often more successful than black and Latino parents at advocating higher track placements for their children, holding previous performance constant (Oakes 2005). The integration argument here is that the process of "de-tracking" puts students of varying levels of prior performance into the same class and permits them to be taught in a way that shrinks that gap.

A great deal of research supports the link between classroom integration and reduction of race-based (and class-based) disparities, and shows how instructional and school organizational practices can be tailored to the detracked classroom (Oakes 2005; Kahlenberg 2012). The salutary effect on racial disparities is greater than that brought about by more recent currents in school reform, such as charter schools, high-stakes testing of students and teachers, and the proliferating of school operators (Orfield et al. 2014).

THE CIVIC ARGUMENT FOR INTEGRATION

However, there is a further, civic argument for racial plurality in classrooms and schools that is only barely mentioned in the integration-for-equality literature. That argument is that a primary function of schooling is to produce informed and engaged citizens, who have a sense of, and a commitment to, the common good and to ideals of equality, liberty, and democracy. As well, education should support an ability to analyze social and political issues and processes, in order to inform civic participation. This civic argument relates to racial and class plurality, because students are more likely to gain civic knowledge and to learn civic virtues if they are exposed to and are encouraged by their teachers and schools to engage with students of different backgrounds (Blum 2012, Conclusion).

Some civic knowledge and virtue can be imparted through curriculum directed at that end in monoracial classrooms and schools. And racial plurality in classes is by no means sufficient for imparting civic capability. Nevertheless, the desired civic result is much likelier when the civic curriculum is accompanied by racial plurality in the classroom, because students are more likely to engage with a curriculum if members of groups studied therein are present in the class.

A form of the "civic value of diversity" argument goes back to the origins of the "common school," the first American public schools, in the mid-1800s (Tyack 2004). It has been rearticulated by the Supreme Court in its affirmative action decisions governing higher education admissions, especially *Grutter v. Bollinger* (2003), although the Court provided only a partial view of the civic virtues involved, failing to adequately recognize the importance of students learning about the histories, heritages, and experiences of racial and ethnic groups other than their own (O'Connor opinion). (The Court focused primarily on learning not to stereotype groups.)

The civic argument construes the benefits of integration as accruing to all groups, to middle-class and white students as well as to working-class, poor, and racial minority students. By contrast, the equality argument posits benefits only to the latter groups, not to the advantaged group, whom, the literature claims, are not benefited, though they are not harmed, by detracking. Indeed, one of the unfortunate features of the equality argument for integration in the absence of a civic argument is that it seems to play into a contemporary version of Du Bois's worry mentioned earlier that a message is conveyed that disadvantaged students bring deficits to the educational context, deficits that can be remedied only by going to school with more advantaged students. This worry can be somewhat mitigated by making it clear that the deficits in question are not inherent in the groups in question but are a product of their circumstances and a history of discrimination.

The civic argument, by contrast, makes clear that all students are valuable educational resources for all other students, including advantaged ones, and that racial minority students have perspectives, insights, and ways of thinking from which white students, whose ignorance of and misleading notions about the racial history of the United States are well documented, can learn and benefit, as can minority students of other groups (Mills 1997; Doane and Bonilla-Silva 2003).

Cultural Explanations of Educational Inequality and Their Normative Import

A current of educational thought has recently shifted the explanation of educational disparities from discriminatory treatment, a legacy of racial subordination, and class-based disadvantages, to culture, which is understood as a set of values and norms generated within a given racial group and adhered to by its members. The most prominent of these attempts to explain the white–black educational disparity is that black students are beholden to a culture of low school achievement. They allegedly do not hold themselves to high standards of achievement partly because they associate doing well in school with "acting white."

Many commentators who subscribe to this culture view draw a normative conclusion from it regarding equality: If students' culture is the reason students do not do better, this is their own fault, and their failure to achieve at a level equal to whites is not a matter of injustice. Sometimes it is implied that it is not schools' responsibility to increase these students' achievement because if something is a matter of culture, nothing can be done about it by any external agent; the change can only come about through actions of the group themselves (Thernstrom and Thernstrom 2003). A somewhat similar but distinct argument is that schools' responsibility is only to provide equality of opportunity to students. If a student's culture hinders her from taking those opportunities, that is too bad, but the school has done what it is required to do.

The "oppositional culture" hypothesis has never had a strong research basis. It is more in the nature of an "urban myth" that garnered an enormous amount of public attention and penetrated the education world as well (Harris 2011). It also influenced politics, for President and then-Senator Obama mentioned in a much-noted speech before the Democratic National Convention in 2004 (Obama 2005) the idea that black students' conceptions of their racial identity led them to disengage from learning.

A 2011 review by Angel Harris of the literature on school achievement and attitudes toward school suggests that black families actually have a stronger belief in the value of education than white ones, that black students are as committed to school success as whites, and that they make as much of an effort to succeed as do white students, once class characteristics are controlled for (Harris 2011). The causes of black underperformance lie elsewhere, suggests Harris, in weaker skills and (partly in consequence) diminished teacher expectations of black students. Nevertheless, the more general idea of cultural explanations of school performance raises valuable normative and philosophical issues. We will discuss the oppositional culture idea as a specific example, but the discussion is applicable to cultural explanations more generally.

Deeper Explanations of Oppositional Culture

Cultural explanations can be superficial or deep. Because we are looking at the normative significance of explanations, we need to explore explanations at the appropriate normatively significant level, and this can be at a deeper rather than a superficial level. Two proposals have been made that accept the existence of oppositional culture (i.e., black students reject school success as something inconsistent with black identity) but provide a deeper explanation of this cultural formation, which impedes black students' educational success. The first is that of John Ogbu, the originator of the oppositional culture idea. Ogbu claims that black students are part of an "involuntary minority" group that has historically been denied equal opportunities. They have not seen gaining an education as paying off in access to jobs; rather, discrimination has placed a barrier to advancement, thereby cutting into the actual worldly value of education, and giving rise to the idea that educational striving is a "white thing." Ogbu says that this perception within the black community has not only been historically accurate but continues to be somewhat accurate; that is, blacks do not get the same return on education as do whites. (Harris confirms this view [2011, ch. 2].)

On Ogbu's view, but not the popular account, society is partly to blame for the black students' cultural attitudes. His explanation implies that society should stop discriminating against blacks in employment (and ensure that this development is well recognized by blacks), and perhaps make up for past discrimination through some sort of reparations program. Ogbu does not deny that there is an oppositional culture that harms black students. It would be better if they responded to a perception of blocked mobility by saying they are just going to do their best and hope that that improves their chances of employment. (This stance is essentially what Harris finds to be the case among the black community and black students [2011, ch. 4].) But his deeper explanation of why black youth have an oppositional culture has a different normative implication than the more superficial view that the values are simply generated from within the black student community, which seems to render blacks themselves wholly responsible for their failure to avail themselves of the educational opportunities out there (Lewis 2012).

Karolyn Tyson provides a second example of a deeper explanation of oppositional culture. Tyson finds an oppositional culture among blacks but almost solely in mixed, white-dominant schools. In such schools, more advanced courses almost always have disproportionately white (and Asian) students, and the nonadvanced, basic-level courses are disproportionately black (and Latino). Identifying school success with whiteness is thus a reasonable interpretation by black students of what they see going on in their school. It is not a correct interpretation according to Tyson's account, since (on her view) students are not placed in the different levels of classes based on their actual academic abilities, but on misapprehensions of those abilities and other practices not drawing on actual ability, such as white parents being more effective at advocating to get their children into higher track classes (Tyson 2011, 150–153).

Thus, on Tyson's view, black students in integrated schools tend to develop oppositional culture attitudes, because those schools practice tracking students by race (even if unintentionally). If the schools were untracked, or if black students were proportionally placed in all different levels of courses, they would not develop these cultural attitudes.

Tyson's argument is analogous to Ogbu's in identifying oppositional cultural attitudes and seeing them as the result of something deeper. In addition, both views place the blame or responsibility for the genesis of those cultural attitudes on something outside the students themselves, which can then be held responsible for the students coming to have those attitudes. For Ogbu, it is the society at large; for Tyson, it is the school and its specific practices. In both cases the deeper explanation places less blame on the black students themselves than does the popular cultural explanation.

Do Cultural Explanations Relieve Schools of Responsibility for Racial Disparities?

If an oppositional culture does exist and does explain a good part of the underperformance of black students, most proponents of the oppositional culture hypothesis take that to mean that the education system more generally, or the society, is relieved of its responsibility to do more to enhance the education of individual members of the group possessing the oppositional culture, since fault lies with the group itself.

This normative assumption has been challenged by Christopher Lewis (Lewis 2012). Lewis argues that from the perspective of an individual black student, the existence of an oppositional culture among his black peers would constitute an externally imposed cost to him of becoming a high-achieving student. According to the oppositional-culture idea, the individual black student risks being shunned by his peer and friendship groups if he is perceived to be aiming to achieve at high levels. This would be a serious cost to a secondary school student and would provide him with a rational reason to dampen his commitment to school success. It is analogous to other costs of high achievement, for example parental expectations for a student to take care of his younger siblings, also at a cost to his schoolwork.

In such situations it seems reasonable to expect the school to try to help the student achieve, as a matter of meeting challenges individual students present. The teachers could work with the student to supply countermotivation to the oppositional-culture motive not to achieve, while recognizing the student's legitimate fear of alienation from friends.

Lewis distinguishes such cases from those where the student himself buys into the oppositional culture norms, and rejects other students who aim for high achievement. Some might think that this latter case more definitively relieves the school of responsibility and that the student is to blame for self-defeating values he himself holds.

But even if the student himself holds oppositional values, his peers holding those values and applying them to him still constitutes a force detracting from his educational success—just as it does if he does not espouse those values. So again, the school seems to have some responsibility to mitigate or counter the force of those values. How it does so will differ from how teachers do so when the student himself does not hold oppositional values. It is easier to help someone counter the force of values he himself does not hold than ones he does. However, it is still possible to help the student. A teacher can try to help him see the short-sightedness of the oppositional values and can help him see how students can remain loyal to a race-based social group, even while taking courses with few members of that group in attendance (Carter 2007). To accomplish this, teachers, especially white teachers, will have to gain a more fine-grained understanding of the lives and situations of black students than they now generally do.

Also, a "you dug your grave, now lie in it" approach does not seem a responsible attitude for school personnel to take toward students who are not yet fully developed adults. Teachers who see students buying into unfortunate values have some responsibility as moral educators to teach them better values, of a piece with their responsibility to teach civic values. We do not, or should not, take value stances by students as simple givens that cannot be challenged.

To sum up: Conservatives and others take the alleged existence of an oppositional culture among black students to relieve schools and society of responsibility for that part of their failure to achieve that is caused by the oppositional culture. We have challenged that position on two grounds. First, a deeper explanation of the existence of an oppositional culture may show that society or the school has some responsibility for the educational gap caused by the oppositional culture, because they have responsibility for the oppositional culture itself. Second, independently of this point, schools have responsibility for individual students' achievement even where an oppositional culture exists within the student's peer group.

Even though research does not support the existence of oppositional culture among blacks to any greater extent than among whites (Harris 2011), these two arguments are broadly applicable to culturalist explanations of educational disparities that are used to relieve schools and society of responsibility for remedying racial disparities in education.

References

Adams, David Wallace. (1995). *Education for Extinction: American Indians and the Boarding School Experience, 1875–1928.* Lawrence, KS: University Press of Kansas.

Anderson, Elizabeth. (2010). *The Imperative of Integration.* Princeton, NJ: Princeton University Press.

Blum, Lawrence. (2012). *High Schools, Race, and America's Future: What Students Can Teach us About Morality, Diversity, and Community.* Cambridge, MA: Harvard Education Press.

Brown v. Board of Education of Topeka, 347 U.S. 483 (1954).

Carter, Prudence. (2007). *Keepin' It Real: School Success Beyond Black and White.* New York: Oxford University Press.

Carter, Prudence L., and Kevin Welner, eds. (2013). *Closing the Opportunity Gap: What America Must Do to Give Every Child an Even Chance.* New York: Oxford University Press.

Coleman, James, principal investigator. (1966). *Equality of Opportunity Study.* Washington, DC: US Department of Health, Welfare, and Education.

Delpit, Lisa. (1995). *Other People's Children: Cultural Conflict in the Classroom.* New York: The New Press.

Doane, Ashley W., and Eduardo Bonilla-Silva, eds. (2003). *White Out: The Continuing Significance of Racism.* New York: Routledge.

Du Bois, W. E. Burghardt. (July 1935). "Does the Negro Need Separate Schools? *The Journal of Negro Education* 4 (3): 328–335. http://links.jstor.org/sici?sici=0022-2984%28193507%294%3A3%3C328%3ADTNNSS%3E2.0.CO%3B2-K.

Duncan, Greg, and Richard Murnane, eds. (2011). *Whither Opportunity: Rising Inequality, Schools, and Children's Life Chances.* New York: Russell Sage Foundation.

Fischer, Stephanie, and Christiana Stoddard. (2013). "The Academic Achievement of American Indians." *Economics of Education Review* 36: 135–152.

Frankenberg, Erica, and Gary Orfield, eds. (2012). *The Resegregation of Suburban Schools: A Hidden Crisis in American Education.* Cambridge, MA: Harvard Education Press.

Gándara, Patricia, and Frances Contreras. (2009). *The Latino Education Crisis: The Consequence of Failed Social Policies.* Cambridge, MA: Harvard University Press.

Green v. County School Board of New Kent County, 391 U.S. 430 (1968).

Grutter V. Bollinger (02-241) 539 U.S. 306 (2003).

Haney-Lopez, Ian. (1996). *White By Law: The Legal Construction of Race.* New York: NYU Press.

Harris, Angel L. (2011). *Kids Don't Want to Fail: Oppositional Culture and the Black-White Achievement Gap*. Cambridge, MA: Harvard University Press.

Kahlenberg, Richard D., ed. (2012). *The Future of School Integration: Socioeconomic Diversity as an Education Reform Strategy*. New York: The Century Foundation Press.

Kao, Grace, Elizabeth Vaquera, and Kimberley Goyette. (2013). *Education and Immigration*. Malden, MA: Polity Press.

Katznelson, Ira. (2006). *When Affirmative Action Was White: An Untold History of Racial Inequality in 20th Century America*. New York: W.W. Norton.

Kim, Claire Jean. (1999). "The Racial Triangulation of Asian Americans." *Politics and Society* 27 (1): 105–138.

Lee, Stacey J. (2009). *Unraveling the "Model Minority" Stereotype: Listening to Asian American Youth*. 2nd ed. New York: Teachers College Press.

Lewis, Christopher. (2012). "Oppositional Culture and Educational Opportunity." *Theory and Research in Education* 10 (2): 131–154.

Mader, Jackie. (2014). "The State of American Indian and Alaska Native Education in California 2014." *Education Week*, Oct. 15., 5.

Maxwell, Lesli. (2014). "U.S. School Enrollment Hits Majority-Minority Milestone." *Education Week*, August 20. Accessed May 18, 2016. http://www.edweek.org/ew/articles/2014/08/20/01demographics.h34.html

Mendez v. Westminster School District of Orange County, 64 F. Supp. 544 (C.D. Cal. 1946).

Mills, Charles. (1997). *The Racial Contract*. Ithaca, NY: Cornell University Press.

Ngai, Mae M. (2004). *Impossible Subjects: Illegal Aliens and the Making of Modern America*. Princeton, NJ: Princeton University Press.

Nieto, Sonia, and Patty Bode. (2011). *Affirming Diversity: The Sociopolitical Context of Multicultural Education*. 6th ed. New York: Pearson.

Oakes, Jeannie. (2005). *Keeping Track: How Schools Structure Inequality*. 2nd ed. New Haven, CT: Yale University Press.

Obama, Barack. (2005). *The Audacity of Hope*. New York: Crown Publishers.

Ogbu, John. (1978). *Minority Education and Caste: The American System in Cross-cultural Perspective*. New York: Academic Press.

Oliver, Melvin, and Thomas Shapiro. (2006). *Black Wealth/White Wealth: A New Perspective on Racial Inequality*. 2nd ed. New York: Routledge.

Orfield, Gary, and Erica Frankenberg, and Associates, eds. (2013). *Educational Delusions: Why Choice Can Deepen Inequality and How to Make Schools Fair*. Berkeley: University of California Press.

Orfield, Gary, and Erica Frankenberg, Jongyeon Ee, and John Kuscera. (2014). *Brown at 60: Great Progress, a Long Retreat and an Uncertain Future*. Los Angeles: UCL Civil Rights Project.

Strum, Philippa. (2010). *Mendez v. Westminster: School Desegregation and Mexican-American Rights*. Lawrence: University Press of Kansas.

Swann v. Charlotte-Mecklenburg Board of Education, 402 U.S. 1 (1971).

Takaki, Ronald. (1998) *Strangers From a Different Shore*. Revised ed. Boston: Little, Brown, and Co.

Thernstrom, Abigail, and Stephan Thernstrom. (2003). *No Excuses: Closing the Racial Gap in Learning*. New York: Simon and Schuster.

Tyack, David. (2004). *Seeking Common Ground: Public Schools in a Diverse Society*. Cambridge, MA: Harvard University Press.

Tyson, Karolyn. (2011). *Integration Interrupted: Tracking, Black Students, and Acting White After Brown.* New York: Oxford University Press.

Walker, David. [1829] (2000). *Appeal to the Coloured Citizens of the World.* Edited by Peter P. Hinks. University Park: Pennsylvania State University Press.

Wallerstein, Peter. (2007). "Antiliteracy Laws." *Slavery in the US: A Social, Political, and Historical Encyclopedia,* edited by Junius P. Rodriguez, 172–173. Santa Barbara, CA: ABC-CLIO.

Wu, Frank. (2003). *Yellow: Race in America Beyond Black and White.* New York: Basic Books.

CHAPTER 38

RACE, HEALTH DISPARITIES, INCARCERATION, AND STRUCTURAL INEQUALITY

LAURIE SHRAGE

AFRICAN Americans suffer disproportionately high rates of incarceration and illness. Are these phenomena connected? New studies are showing that, with respect to some diseases, such as HIV/AIDS and posttraumatic stress disorder (PTSD), they are. The positive correlation between incarceration and serious lifelong illness raises urgent moral and legal questions. I will explore the correlation between incarceration and the spike in HIV/AIDS rates in African American communities, and the moral significance of recent public health and medical research on this. I then make some initial and general suggestions about what steps must be taken in order to address the dual crises of mass incarceration and the HIV/AIDS epidemic in black communities.

MASS INCARCERATION AND HEALTH DISPARITIES ACROSS RACIAL GROUPS

For over a decade now, HIV/AIDS has been a leading cause of death among young adult African American women (Centers for Disease Control and Prevention [CDC] 2015a). In 2007, Hillary Clinton drew public attention to this issue in a Democratic presidential candidates debate: "Let me just put this in perspective. If HIV/AIDS were the leading cause of death of white women between the ages of 25 and 34 years, there would be an outraged outcry in this country" (Clinton 2007). In 2010, African American women accounted for 64 percent of new HIV infections, while representing only 13 percent of the US female population. According to a Kaiser Family Foundation report:

> In 2010, the rate of new HIV infections for Black women was 20 times higher than the rate for white women (38.1 per 100,000, compared to 1.9); the rate for Latinas (8.0) was 4 times higher. Rates of women living with an HIV diagnosis follow a similar pattern.

> The likelihood of a woman being diagnosed with HIV in her lifetime is significantly higher for black women (1 in 32) and Latinas (1 in 106) than for white women (1 in 526).
> Black women accounted for the greatest share of deaths among women with HIV in 2010 (64%), followed by white women (18%) and Latinas (12%). (Kaiser Family Foundation 2014a)

Moreover, the report states:

> Heterosexual transmission accounts for a greater share of new HIV infections among black women and Latinas (87% and 86%, respectively) compared to white women (76%). (Kaiser Family Foundation 2014)

This statistic is perplexing because, among black men, gay males represent more than two-thirds of new cases of HIV. More specifically, the CDC reports that:

> In 2010, African American gay, bisexual, and other men who have sex with men . . . represented an estimated 72% (10,600) of new infections among all African American men. (CDC 2015b)

In the United States, HIV/AIDS spread first among the gay male population. Because gay men do not generally have sex with women, bisexual men are commonly blamed for the spike in HIV infections among women.

But why are HIV rates higher among African American women than other female groups? There do not appear to be higher rates of bisexuality among African Americans, and bisexuals, in general, are a tiny segment of the American population. This unexplained and disturbing high rate of infection among black women seems to have inspired the "down low" theory, which is that there is a large group of secretive bisexual men in the African American community who do not disclose their gay sexual activities to their female partners (Millett et al. 2005). Because this hypothesis posits a secretive group, it is hard to prove or disprove. However, the homophobic aspect of this theory might make us somewhat skeptical in that it blames a stigmatized sexual minority for spreading disease to the larger population, and it overlooks the role of heterosexual men in contributing to the spike in HIV rates among women (Cohen 1999).

Joe Biden's comments in the 2007 candidates' debate mentioned earlier (Clinton 2007) reflects the common but unsubstantiated hypothesis that black men are less likely to use condoms than other men. However, a 2010 scientific study shows that black men and women are more likely to use condoms than other groups (Reece et al. 2010; The Black AIDS Institute 2015). A more plausible theory that is now being investigated looks at the role of "men who have sex with men" (MSM) in prison, but who identify as heterosexual. HIV prevalence among incarcerated men is higher than among nonincarcerated men (The Center for HIV Law and Policy 2015), and black men have disproportionately high rates of incarceration. Moreover, prisons rarely provide inmates with condoms (Sylla, Harawa, and Resnick 2010), and there are significantly high rates of sexual assault, as well as coercive and consensual sex, among male inmates (Wooden and Parker 1982). MSM in prison or jail are not "bisexual," if sexual orientation is understood as a psychological disposition and social identity (Wooden and Parker 1982), and when they are released from prison they generally pursue only women as sex partners.

According to some public health researchers, people incarcerated in the United States are at greater risk for HIV/AIDS and other sexually transmitted illnesses (STIs) due to "the dynamics" of incarceration, that is, the conditions of prison life (Johnson and Raphael 2009).

These conditions include higher prevalence of HIV; lack of access to condoms; increased risk of sexual assault; and a higher incidence of depression, which is linked to higher rates of risky behaviors, such as unprotected sex, IV-drug use, tattooing without sterilized needles, and the failure to adhere to treatment when available (Blankenship et al. 2005; Johnson and Raphael 2009; Scheyett et al. 2010; Westergaard et al. 2013). According to Ernest Drucker,

> There is now growing evidence that mass incarceration is contributing to the continued high incidence of HIV in the United States. This relationship is particularly powerful for US racial minorities. While constituting 12 per cent of the US population, African Americans account for 45 per cent of all new AIDS diagnoses and are now estimated to have an incidence rate eight times that of white Americans. For African American women, the magnitude of these racial disparities is even more pronounced—their HIV rates are nearly 23 times the rate for white women. (Drucker 2015, 1454)

Because people tend to select sex partners from within their communities, higher rates of HIV among men with a history of incarceration raise the risk of infection for members of the communities in which they live (Blankenship et al. 2005; Johnson and Raphael 2009). Some studies focus on how the high rates of incarceration of black men have significantly altered sex ratios in black communities, and they suggest that this can affect the spread of HIV by reducing the negotiating position of black women in sexual relationships, and also by increasing the average number of sex partners of black men (Pouget et al. 2010).

Higher rates of all STIs, along with other physical and mental health problems acquired or exacerbated by those who spend time in prison, burden these communities' limited health resources. Illness and disability, in turn, can jeopardize one's chances for economic security and social support. This vicious cycle can account for much of the disparity in health outcomes between African Americans and other ethnic or racially defined groups. As Johnson and Raphael conclude,

> Given the sizable racial differentials in incarceration rates at the beginning of the AIDS epidemic and the increases in these differentials thereafter, our model estimates suggest that the lion's share of the racial differentials in AIDS infections rates for both men and women are attributable to racial differences in incarceration trends.
>
> While we have focused explicitly on the transmission of HIV/AIDS, both the theoretical story being told here and the empirical analysis can easily be extended to other communicable diseases that have high prevalence among prisoners. (Johnson and Raphael 2009, 286)

The media's recent focus on the many African American lives lost due to homicides committed by law enforcement officials has brought needed attention to systemic forms of racism within our criminal justice system. We also need to draw attention to less visible and immediate, but similarly devastating, threats to health and life faced by people and communities which interact at disproportionately high rates with the criminal justice system in the United States. Latino and immigrant communities similarly face disproportionately high rates of incarceration and HIV/AIDS prevalence, and the relationship between these factors is beginning to get more attention (Comfort et al. 2012; Capó 2013).

The War on Drugs and the increase in incarceration rates for nonviolent offenses (Blankenship et al. 2005; Alexander 2010), racial profiling by law enforcement, de facto racial discrimination throughout our criminal justice system, and higher crime rates in poor black communities in part due to inadequate protective policing that forces people "to take the law into their own hands" (Leovy 2015) all contribute to higher incarceration rates for African Americans. Both the experience of incarceration and the social stigma it carries take a huge toll on a person's physical and mental health. The recent suicide of Kalief Browder, a young man who spent three years in the Rikers Island Correctional Facility in New York City, because he was misidentified and wrongly accused by a witness of stealing a backpack when he was sixteen, is one of many tragic outcomes of our racially unjust society. Browder was repeatedly and brutally beaten by prison guards and inmates, and he spent approximately two years in solitary confinement while a teenager (Gonnerman 2014, 2015a). Essentially, he was physically and mentally tortured while in the custody of city officials and then left prison with debilitating mental health problems, probably due to his solitary confinement (Guenther 2012, 2013), which eventually ended with his suicide. How does this happen to a child and his family in the United States?

While there has been some public discussion of the spike in HIV/AIDS cases among African Americans, as well as mass incarceration and its disproportionate impact on blacks in the United States, these two topics are rarely discussed together. Public debates about the black/white disparity in HIV/AIDS rates in the United States typically focus on individual lifestyle factors, such as risky sex or drug use, which further stigmatizes African Americans who are then presumed to be leading unhealthy lifestyles. Such debates about the HIV epidemic overlook the structural and social factors that place black Americans and gay men at greater risk for HIV. For example, a Bureau of Justice Statistics survey shows that "LGBT prisoners were abused by other inmates at a rate more than ten times higher than straight prisoners" (Just Detention 2013). Men who are young or small, whether they are gay or not, are also more subject to sexual assault in a prison setting. In a jail or prison, victims are housed with their abusers and are often afraid or unable to report abuse, protect themselves from ongoing sexual abuse, obtain condoms to protect their heath, or access health care resources to get tested and treated. In communities with higher numbers of people who have passed through jails, prisons, and juvenile detention centers, there are predictably higher rates of illness.

Contrary to common stereotypes, researchers have not found any significant differences among racial groups in and outside prison in regard to drug use or risky sexual behaviors (Blankenship et al. 2005; CDC 2006; Alexander 2010, 7). According to Blankenship et al.:

> In general, African Americans report less risky drug use and sexual behaviors than their White counterparts. In terms of drug use, White adolescents are more likely to use illicit drugs than their African American counterparts . . . in a study of risk behaviors of female jail detainees, rates of reported needle sharing were much higher among non-Hispanic Whites than among either African American or Hispanic women. Examination of sexual risk reveals that, as a group, African Americans also do not appear to be engaging in riskier sexual behavior than their White counterparts. Though African American youth do report more sexual behavior earlier than White youth, consistent use of a reliable means of contraception has been more strongly associated with African American than White youth; reported condom use is higher among Blacks than among other racial and ethnic groups. (2005, 2)

The main differences between black and other communities in the United States are higher rates of incarceration, higher rates of poverty and unemployment, and racial segregation. Michelle Alexander claims that mass incarceration has perpetuated a racial caste system in the United States, which now has significantly higher percentages of its population in prison than any country, and incarcerates more of its racial and ethnic minorities than any other society, including China and Russia (Alexander 2010, 6–7). In discussing these factors, Drucker concludes:

> The adverse effects of incarceration on individual prisoners include the ongoing consequences of poor healthcare services in prisons; failure of prison security to provide a safe environment (the ensuing rape, violence, and gang activity that have become a routine part of prison life); serious and persistent mental health problems and inadequate mental healthcare in prisons. . . . All this is in addition to the immediate and longer-term psychological implications of trauma associated with overcrowding, poor prison conditions, and many severe disciplinary methods, including isolation and solitary confinement. (Drucker 2015, 1451)

Kalief Browder's short life puts a human face on the adverse effects of incarceration. The spike in HIV/AIDS rates in African American communities is another adverse effect. Placing moral blame on individuals for what is largely the result of misguided social policies and practices will do little to solve the health crises in black communities. We need to focus more on the structural factors responsible for health disparities, and less on individual risk factors (Blankenship et al. 2005).

What the foregoing discussion suggests is that an important part of addressing the HIV/ AIDS crisis in black communities is reducing incarceration rates overall, but especially among black Americans. Addressing racial biases in policing and judicial proceedings, reducing sentences for nonviolent offenders, and addressing poverty and unemployment are critical strategies for accomplishing this. Another important goal is to change the living conditions inside jails and prisons so that detainees have a reasonable measure of personal security, along with access to condoms, clean needles, testing, and treatment. Some states are beginning to do some of this (Lavender 2015) and have adopted essentially a harm reduction approach toward activities that are prohibited in prison. Of course, addressing the HIV/ AIDS epidemic involves improving sex education programs in schools and providing wider access to quality health care, but these measures alone are insufficient to address the structural factors that are contributing to racial disparities in health outcomes.

Another area for policy development and implementation is the problem of prison rape. Corrections officials need to take much more aggressive steps to prevent sexual assault and to stop coercive sexual practices in which vulnerable inmates exchange sexual services with other inmates for personal protection. Discussing this problem over a decade ago, Daniel Brooks states:

> The prevalence of rape in prison *is* fearsome. Line officers recently surveyed in one southern state estimated that one in five male prisoners were being coerced into sex; among higher-ranking officials, the estimate was one in eight. Prisoners themselves estimated one in three . . . Female prisoners are the victims of rape as well, though they are usually assaulted by male guards, not other inmates.
>
> Despite its prevalence, prison rape has generally been treated by courts and corrections officials as it has by novelists and filmmakers—as a problem without a solution. Prison rape is rarely prosecuted; like most crimes committed in prison, rapes aren't taken on by local district attorneys but left to corrections officials to handle. (Brook 2004, 3)

In "Why We Let Prison Rape Go On," Chandra Bozelko writes,

> According to the Bureau of Justice Statistics, around 80,000 women and men a year are sexually abused in American correctional facilities. That number is almost certainly subject to underreporting, through shame or a victim's fear of retaliation. (Bozelko 2015, A19)

When the victims of a crime are viewed as criminals or social outcasts, there is relatively little public sympathy for them. Another possible reason that nonconsensual sex among male inmates is often tolerated is that "rape" historically (and culturally and legally) has been defined as a crime that happens to women. Until 2013, the FBI and the "Uniform Crime Reports" definition of rape was the "carnal knowledge of a female forcibly and against her will" (Federal Bureau of Investigation 2013). This definition renders invisible male victims of rape, as well as coercive sex not involving physical force. In 2003, Congress passed the "Prison Rape Elimination Act" (National PREA Resource Center 2015), but many public commentators have questioned whether rates of sexual assault in US jails and prisons have decreased in the last decade (Beck et al. 2013).

Prisons have also neglected the mental health problems of their population, which are correlated with high-risk behaviors and nonadherence to treatment (Scheyett et al. 2010). A Human Rights Watch statement to a Senate Judiciary subcommittee summarizes the situation in regard to mental health needs and care in prisons:

> According to the Bureau of Justice Statistics, 56 percent of state prisoners and 45 percent of federal prisoners have symptoms or a recent history of mental health problems. Prisoners have rates of mental illness—including such serious disorders as schizophrenia, bipolar disorder, and major depression—that are two to four times higher than members of the general public.
>
> Unfortunately, prisons are ill-equipped to respond appropriately to the needs of prisoners with mental illness. Prison mental health services are all too frequently woefully deficient, crippled by understaffing, insufficient facilities, and limited programs. Many seriously ill prisoners receive little or no meaningful treatment. (Human Rights Watch 2009)

Public discussion of disease prevention rarely focuses on incarceration and its impact on human health. The full costs to our society of mass incarceration, and to black communities in particular, have not been balanced against its estimated benefits in reducing crime, and it may not even reduce crime (Clear 2007; Western and Pettit 2010). According to Todd Clear, when children grow up in destabilized families, without fathers and older siblings, they are more likely to enter a life of crime. In sum, the violence and moral crimes our society tolerates against black citizens in the name of allegedly reducing crime is shameful.

One of the huge challenges for those concerned about the human rights abuses caused by mass incarceration in the United States is public apathy when it comes to the well-being of people who are in or who have been through our prison system. The problems of people living in prisons, along with those living in black segregated communities, are often invisible to those who are socially more privileged. Consequently, if addressing the problem of black/white health disparities involves not just addressing the persistence of poverty and segregation but also the unfairness of our criminal justice system, then the goal of improving health outcomes in black communities will be significantly more difficult to reach. But the role incarceration plays in producing health disparities cannot be ignored (Hatzenbuehler et al. 2015).

MORAL AND LEGAL CONSIDERATIONS

Unjust detention and incarceration are morally problematic for many reasons, but especially because they violate our basic rights to liberty, equal treatment, and the pursuit of happiness.

But when we factor in the lifelong health problems that can result from the living conditions in our prisons and how these affect the ability to exercise any of our rights, detention—whether just or unjust—is morally problematic. The physically and mentally unhealthy living conditions, as well as vigilante violence, that inmates regularly face constitute *extrajudicial* punishments. Such punishments, which have not been approved by any judicial or legislative process, can sometimes amount to a death sentence, a rape, or a lifelong disability. When a particular community or ethnic group is subject to both legal and extrajudicial punishment at a higher rate, because of a criminal justice system that racially profiles this group, imposes "zero tolerance" sentencing (the "school to prison pipeline") for nonviolent drug offenses not imposed on other groups, which then makes a considerable percentage of this group ineligible to vote and serve on juries (Alexander 2010), this amounts to political and social persecution. The political and social persecution, and human rights violations, suffered by black Americans is similar to the persecution of minority ethnic and religious groups in countries often criticized by the United States, and it deserves the same level of international attention and intervention (US Department of State 2014).

Historians have well documented the legacy of slavery in the United States, and the ongoing denial of basic civil rights to black Americans is part of this legacy. The disproportionately high rates of incarceration among black men, and our dismal prison conditions, are also part of this legacy (Alexander 2010). Detention and incarceration in the United States not only deprive a person of liberty, but they often subject the detained to despicable forms of cruelty and humiliation, such as the excessively long periods of solitary confinement suffered by Kalief Browder, and the brutal treatment of Sandra Bland by an officer who stopped her for allegedly failing to use a signal when changing lanes. Bland died mysteriously while in detention a few days later (Giroux 2015). Similar to soldiers in a military zone, inmates suffer from severe anxiety, depression, and PTSD, which can have devastating effects for themselves and their families (Goff et al. 2007). Detainees (and soldiers) are not only targets for violence themselves but witness acts of violence against others, which can be highly disturbing, in part due to their helplessness to stop them. But unlike military personnel, inmates and former inmates receive little public respect, sympathy, and assistance. While the sources of PTSD in a military zone may be difficult to eliminate, we should be able to substantially eliminate them from our prisons.

Cruel and unusual punishment is not supposed to take place in the United States. The Eighth Amendment to the US Constitution explicitly prohibits the infliction of "cruel and unusual punishments" by agents of our government (Findlaw 2015; Legal Information Institute 2015a). Yet, when we knowingly subject detainees to high rates of violence and the extreme deprivation of basic needs, leading to lifelong health problems or death from suicide or an untreated STI, this is cruel and unusual punishment. When prison guards commit rape and unjustified beatings, or allow detainees to commit acts that can cause serious and lifelong injuries and premature death, this constitutes acting with "deliberate indifference" to an inmate's well-being and rights, which is the current rather high standard that plaintiffs must meet to prove that their Eighth Amendment right was violated (Human Rights Watch 2001). Currently, to meet this standard, sexual assault victims must show that prison officials knew that they were at a significantly high risk for rape or assault. This has been virtually impossible to prove, as a Human Rights Watch Report points out, because the requirement gives prison officials an incentive to remain ignorant about the problems and threats inmates face (Human Rights Watch 2001). However, according to David Ries, with the passage of the Prison Rape Elimination Act (PREA), which requires prisons to gather data about sexual abuse in prison,

Inmates should be able to use the data and recommendations that are a result of the new federal law to bring stronger claims against prison officials who fail in their duty to protect prisoners against sexual assault by other prisoners. (Ries 2005, 990)

Moreover, the PREA explicitly states that "The high incidence of sexual assault within prisons involves actual and potential violations of the United States Constitution" (particularly the Eighth Amendment), and that "Prison rape undermines the public health by contributing to the spread of these [HIV and other STIs] diseases, and often giving a potential death sentence to its victims" (Legal Information Institute 2015b). Although the legal "principle of less eligibility" requires that prisoners not enjoy a standard of living above the lowest classes of society, this does absolve correctional officials of the responsibility to protect the lives and health of those housed in our jails and prisons. Unlike the poor, these individuals have been deprived of their freedom and, along with it, much of their ability to protect themselves.

When faced with tragic and avoidable losses of human life, we tend to look for a cause that is as evil as the effect. But perhaps Hannah Arendt's "banality of evil" theory better fits the customary treatment of US prisoners and the repeated denial of civil rights to African Americans. The theory holds that one need not be a monster to perform acts that one knows will have horrible consequences. Ordinary people sometimes do evil things in the service of what they misguidedly hold to be higher ends (Berkowitz 2013). The large majority of police officers, prison guards and administrators, and judges (and some of them are men and women of color) whose decisions and acts result in disproportionately high rates of incarceration for African Americans and brutal prison conditions are probably not vicious and violent racists. Most of these people are ordinary civil servants who aim to do their jobs well and contribute to combatting crime, but who altogether are part of a social machine that commits evil. The ongoing denial of rights to blacks is not the result of a few bad eggs. When certain practices become routine, we tend not to scrutinize them for their moral qualities, but go along with and even participate in the degrading, injurious, and inhumane treatment of others. But sadly, as Owen Li notes in commenting on the cruel and violent treatment of detainees in our youth prison system, "evil is never banal to those impacted" (Li 2012). The effects of evil are horrible, even when the causes are merely thoughtless cooperation with a very bad system.

OVERCOMING PUBLIC APATHY TOWARD THE INCARCERATED

But if thoughtlessness is a part of the problem, then how can we make our fellow citizens more thoughtful about mass incarceration and its destructive consequences? Or, is mass thoughtlessness as inevitable as the massive injustices it produces? Is it as inevitable as some believe that pervasive racism is? I am not convinced that thoughtlessness and racism are inevitable. Some people hold that the sexual assault of women by men is inevitable, and that women should be taught to protect themselves. But recently, sexual assault survivors and activists have started holding men's behavior and attitudes responsible for sexual assault. Deeply entrenched misogyny, social approval of masculine aggressiveness, and general attitudes about male sexual entitlement lead to predatory sexual behaviors and society's response to them, not some unchangeable human nature. To stop sexual assault, men have to stop assaulting women (and other men). Amy Schumer's comedy sketch, in which a football coach announces such changed expectations to his shocked and outraged players and their families, humorously reflects this new and more widely endorsed approach to sexual assault (Schumer 2015). In the skit, the members of the team trot out the many misogynous rationales and ridiculous (but, sadly, often effective) strategies that rapists use to get away with their acts, and the coach simply says "no" to each one. We need a similar approach to the behavior of police and prison guards. To stop the abuse of black people and those in detention, police officers and prison guards have to stop violating their rights and permitting others to do the same. We should no longer tolerate such behaviors in those entrusted with keeping public order and protecting us. Police chiefs and prison wardens across the country need to convey this to all employees in our police departments and corrections systems. As in Schumer's skit, some may throw down their equipment and refuse to play, but most will not, and radically changed expectations from those in authority will shape their behavior.

Perhaps this is already happening but, if not, how can we make this happen? While videos of police arrests are putting some pressure on police departments to change their racially hostile practices, the public has little access to videos or other evidence of how adults and children are treated behind the walls of our prisons, such as the one *The New Yorker* magazine managed to get of Kalief Browder (Gonnerman 2015b). In this footage, we see Browder getting thrown to the floor by a guard, for no apparent reason, and then getting attacked and beaten by a group of inmates. Just as bystander-produced videos of police arrests are generating a national conversation about policing methods, we need much more bystander interaction with our prison population, beyond the families and friends of inmates, so that people working in this system can be held accountable. There are numerous philanthropic groups, such as religiously affiliated prison support groups, college student criminal justice organizations, and other community nonprofit agencies that are willing to provide basic services to inmates, such as job training and schooling, and legal assistance, but are regularly denied access. Some of these groups are willing to provide services at no or little cost to taxpayers. Sometimes for legitimate reasons, prisons are reluctant to let outsiders in, such as the inability to provide needed supervision and ensure the safety of visitors. But prisons often unnecessarily cut detainees off from support networks that would both help them through the various ordeals they face, as well as ensure some needed transparency about what goes on inside our jails and prisons.

The contribution of our prison system to the health crises that communities of color now face demands greater transparency in regard to prison conditions. The public has a right to know how prisons are exposing people to a variety of lifelong illnesses that they will ultimately bring back to their communities. We need to hold prisons accountable for reducing assaults, injuries, and infection rates, and increasing access to testing and treatment. Whether private or public, prison officials are not above the law, and they should be accountable to the public. A prison sentence should not turn into a death sentence or a lifetime disability due to neglect or the routinization of extrajudicial punishment and cruelty (Dolovich 2004). We can also reduce the injuries and deaths that result from our prison and jail conditions by reducing cases of unfair arrest and detention of people who pose no threat to others, as the tragedy of Sandra Bland underscores (Purdy 2015). We should never trivialize or treat casually the damage that interacting with our prison system can do to people's lives and health. The lives of people inside our prisons matter, and their health and well-being should not be sacrificed to promote public safety. Indeed, removing people from society and then returning them with debilitating mental and physical health conditions now appears to be contributing to the spread of infectious and costly illnesses, community devastation, family instability, and economic insecurity, and therefore crime.

Having a history of incarceration and having an STI are both stigmatizing conditions. Regardless of the circumstances in each case, some make the assumption that "people get what they deserve." But too often people and entire communities do not get what they deserve—good or bad. The spike in HIV/AIDS cases in African American communities results from structural and systemic injustices that increase a black person's chances of ending up in a US prison. The latter phenomenon alone represents a grave injustice, but when this situation is compounded by the fact that our prisons put detainees at higher than average risk for a lifelong illness or injury, while reducing their access to adequate care networks both within and outside of prison, the injustice is too serious for any decent person to ignore (Hatzenbuehler et al. 2015).

Although there is little evidence to support the "down low" theory about the HIV epidemic in African American communities, many people still default to explanations like this when presented with evidence of health disparities among different groups. Such speculation about individual lifestyle factors makes it difficult for public health officials and black community leaders to mobilize an effective response to this health crisis, because discussing the epidemic often invokes homophobia or self-blame and shame (Cohen 1999). By focusing on the contribution of mass incarceration to health disparities in the United States, along with the failure to bring down rates of sexual violence and coercion in our prisons, we can develop a more effective response.

According to a recent National Research Council Report:

> Inmates with HIV who remain incarcerated have lower viral loads and higher CD4 counts (i.e., their HIV is better controlled) than those who have been released and reincarcerated, meaning that those cycling repeatedly through the correctional system are not only less healthy but also more infectious. (National Research Council 2014, 222)

What this suggests is that some US citizens now have better access to testing and treatment for HIV while incarcerated than after they are released. Today, medicines for HIV infections can reduce a person's viral load to a level that can make the risk of transmission extremely low. If an infected person is unable to continue treatment once he is released from prison (due to unemployment, housing discrimination, depression and other mental illnesses, and so on), then his health will deteriorate and the risk to his intimate partners will increase. In sum, in order to genuinely get a handle on the HIV/AIDS epidemic in African American communities, testing and treatment programs for STIs need to be expanded both inside and outside of our prisons. In addition, we need to seriously rethink the misguided policies that have led to mass incarceration (Alexander 2010; Western and Pettit 2010), end racially biased practices in our law enforcement and criminal justice systems, significantly reduce sexual violence and coercion both inside and outside of prisons, and challenge vicious stereotypes about people living with HIV/AIDS and racialized groups. By focusing on these structural factors, we are more likely to improve both our health care and criminal justice systems.

REFERENCES

Alexander, Michelle. (2010). *The New Jim Crow: Mass Incarceration in the Age of Colorblindness.* New York: The New Press.

Beck, Allen J., Marcus Berzofsky, Rachel Caspar, and Christopher Krebs. (2013). "Sexual Victimization in Prisons and Jails Reported by Inmates 2011–12." *Bureau of Justice Statistics.* Accessed May 19, 2016. http://www.bjs.gov/index.cfm?ty=pbdetail&iid=4654.

Berkowitz, Roger. (2013). "Misreading 'Eichmann in Jerusalem'" *The New York Times*, July 7. Accessed May 19, 2016. http://opinionator.blogs.nytimes.com/2013/07/07/misreading-hannah-arendts-eichmann-in-jerusalem/.

The Black AIDS Institute. (2015). "Condom Use Higher among Blacks Than Other Groups but Not Enough to Beat HIV." Accessed May 19, 2016. https://www.blackaids.org/index.php?option=com_content&view=article&id=677:condom-use-higher-among-blacks-than-other-groups-but-not-enough-to-beat-HIV&catid=53:news-2010&Itemid=120.

Blankenship, Kim M., Amy B. Smoyer, Sarah J. Bray, and Kristin Mattocks. (2005). "Black-White Disparities in HIV/AIDS: The Role of Drug Policy and the Corrections System." *Journal of Health Care for the Poor and Underserved* 16 (4 Supplement B): 140–156. doi: 10.1353/hpu.2005.0110.

Bozelko, Chandra. (2015). "Why We Let Prison Rape Go On." *The New York Times*, April 17. Accessed May 19, 2016. http://www.nytimes.com/2015/04/18/opinion/why-we-let-prison-rape-go-on.html?.

Brook, Daniel. (2004). "The Problem of Prison Rape." *Legal Affairs.* Accessed May 19, 2016. http://www.legalaffairs.org/issues/March-April-2004/feature_brook_marapr04.msp.

Capó, Julio. (2013). "Why It's Time to Stop Stigmatizing Haitians for Having HIV." *Plus Magazine*, May 21. Accessed May 19, 2016. http://www.HIVplusmag.com/case-studies/world-news/2013/05/21/why-its-time-stop-stigmatizing-haitians-having-HIV.

The Center for HIV Law and Policy. (2015). "Prisons and Jails." Accessed May 19, 2016. http://www.HIVlawandpolicy.org/issues/prisons-and-jails.

Centers for Disease Control and Prevention. (2006). "HIV Transmission Among Male Inmates in a State Prison System—Georgia 1992–2005." *Morbidity and Mortality Weekly Report* 55 (15): 421–426.

Centers for Disease Control and Prevention. (2015a). "Leading Causes of Death in Females: Black Females by Age Group- United States, 2013." Accessed May 19, 2016. http://www.cdc.gov/women/lcod/.

Centers for Disease Control and Prevention. (2015b). "HIV Among African Americans." Accessed May 19, 2016. http://www.cdc.gov/HIV/group/racialethnic/africanamericans/index.html.

Clear, Todd R. (2007). *Imprisoning Communities: How Mass Incarceration Makes Disadvantaged Neighborhoods Worse.* New York: Oxford University Press.

Clinton, Hillary. "2007 Democratic Primary Debate at Howard University, sponsored by PBS: on Health Care." Accessed May 19, 2016. http://www.ontheissues.org/ArcHIVe/2007_Dems_Howard_U_Health_Care.htm.

Cohen, Cathy J. (1999). *The Boundaries of Blackness: AIDS and the Breakdown of Black Politics.* Chicago: University of Chicago Press.

Comfort, Megan, Carmen Albizu-García, Timoteo Rodriguez, and Carlos MolinaIII. (2012). "HIV RISK and Prevention for Latinos in Jails and Prisons." In *HIV Prevention with*

Latinos: Theory, Research, and Practice, edited by K. C. Organista. doi:10.1093/acprof:oso/
9780199764303.003.0012.

Dolovich, Sharon. (2004). "Legitimate Punishment in Liberal Democracy." *Buffalo Criminal Law Review* Spring. Accessed May 19, 2016. http://ssrn.com/abstract=503468.

Drucker, Ernest. (2015). "Prisons: From Punishment to Public Health." *Oxford Textbook of Global Public Health*, edited by Roger Detels, Martin Gulliford, Quarraisha Abdool Karim, and Chorh Chuan Tan, 1445–1460. Oxford: Oxford University Press.

Federal Bureau of Investigation. (2013). "Uniform Crime Reports: Crime in the United States 2013: Rape." Accessed May 19, 2016. https://www.fbi.gov/about-us/cjis/ucr/crime-in-the-u.s/2013/crime-in-the-u.s.-2013/violent-crime/rape.

Findlaw. (2015). "Cruel and Unusual Punishment." Accessed May 19, 2016. http://criminal.findlaw.com/criminal-rights/cruel-and-unusual-punishment.html.

Giroux, Henry. (2015). "America's New Brutalism: The Death of Sandra Bland." *Counter Punch*, July 24. Accessed May 19, 2016. http://www.counterpunch.org/2015/07/24/americas-new-brutalism-the-death-of-sandra-bland/.

Goff, A., E. Rose, S. Rose, and D. Purves. (2007). "Does PTSD Occur in Sentenced Prison Populations? A Systematic Literature Review." *Criminal Behavior and Mental Health* 17 (3): 152–162.

Gonnerman, Jennifer. (2014). "Before the Law." *The New Yorker*, October 6. Accessed May 19, 2016. http://www.newyorker.com/magazine/2014/10/06/before-the-law.

Gonnerman, Jennifer. (2015a). "Kalief Browder, 1993–2015." *The New Yorker*, June 7. Accessed May 19, 2016. http://www.newyorker.com/news/news-desk/kalief-browder-1993-2015.

Gonnerman, Jennifer. (2015b). "Exclusive Video: Violence Inside Rikers." *The New Yorker*, April 23. Accessed May 19, 2016. http://www.newyorker.com/news/news-desk/exclusive-video-violence-inside-rikers.

Guenther, Lisa. (2012). "The Living Death of Solitary Confinement." *The New York Times*, August 26. Accessed May 19, 2016. http://opinionator.blogs.nytimes.com/2012/08/26/the-living-death-of-solitary-confinement/.

Guenther, Lisa. (2013). *Solitary Confinement: Social Death and Its Afterlives* Minneapolis: University of Minnesota Press.

Hatzenbuehler, M. L., K. Keyes, A. Hamilton, M. Uddin, and S. Galea. (2015). "The Collateral Damage of Mass Incarceration: Risk of Psychiatric Morbidity among Nonincarcerated Residents of High-Incarceration Neighborhoods." *American Journal of Public Health* 105 (1): 138–143.

Human Rights Watch. (2001). "Deliberate Indifference: State Authorities' Response to Prisoner-on Prisoner Sexual Abuse." *No Escape: Male Rape in U.S. Prisons., Chapter VIII.* Accessed May 19, 2016. http://www.hrw.org/reports/2001/prison/report8.html.

Human Rights Watch. (2009). "Mental Illness, Human Rights, and US Prisons." Accessed May 19, 2016. https://www.hrw.org/news/2009/09/22/mental-illness-human-rights-and-us-prisons.

Johnson, Rucker C., and Steven Raphael. (2009). "The Effects of Male Incarceration Dynamics on Acquired Immune Deficiency Syndrome Infection Rates among African American Women and Men." *Journal of Law and Economics* 52 (2): 251–293.

Just Detention International. (2013). "The Basics about Sexual Abuse in U.S. Detention." Accessed May 19, 2016. http://www.justdetention.org/en/fact_sheets.aspx.

Kaiser Family Foundation. (2014a). "Women and HIV/AIDS in the United States." Accessed May 19, 2016. http://kff.org/HIVaids/fact-sheet/women-and-HIVaids-in-the-united-states/.

Kaiser Family Foundation. (2014b). "Black Americans and HIV/AIDS." Accessed April 25, 2014. http://kff.org/HIVaids/fact-sheet/black-americans-and-HIV-aids/.

Lavender, George. (2015). "California Prisons Aim to Keep Sex Between Inmates Safe, If Illegal." *NPR.* Accessed May 19, 2016. http://www.npr.org/2015/01/21/378678167/california-prisons-aim-to-keep-sex-between-inmates-safe-if-illegal.

Legal Information Institute. (2015a). "Eighth Amendment." Accessed May 19, 2016. https://www.law.cornell.edu/constitution/eighth_amendment.

Legal Information Institute. (2015b). "U.S. Code Title 42, Chapter 147 (Prison Rape Elimination), Section 15601." Accessed May 19, 2016. https://www.law.cornell.edu/uscode/text/42/15601.

Leovy, Jill. (2015). *Ghettoside: A True Story of Murder in America.* New York: Spiegel & Grau, Random House.

Li, Owen. (2012). "The Banality of Evil." *Ella Baker Center for Human Rights.* January 17, 2012. Accessed May 19, 2016. http://ellabakercenter.org/blog/2012/01/the-banality-of-evil.

Millett, Gregorio, David Malebranche, Byron Mason, and Pilgrim Spikes. (2005). "Focusing 'Down Low': Bisexual Black Men, HIV Risk and Heterosexual Transmission." *Journal of the National Medical Association* 97 (7 Supplement): 52S–59S.

National PREA Resource Center. (2015). "Prison Rape Elimination Act." Accessed May 19, 2016. http://www.prearesourcecenter.org/about/prison-rape-elimination-act-prea.

National Research Council. (2014). *The Growth of Incarceration in the United States: Exploring Causes and Consequences.* Edited by Committee on Causes and Consequences of High Rates of Incarceration, J. Travis, B. Western, and S. Redburn. Washington, DC: The National Academies Press.

Pouget, Enrique R., Trace S. Kershaw, Linda M. Niccolai, Jeannette R. Ickovics, and Kim M. Blankenship. (2010). "Associations of Sex Ratios and Male Incarceration Rates with Multiple Opposite-Sex Partners: Potential Social Determinants of HIV/STI Transmission." *Public Health Reports* 125 (Supplement 4): 70–80.

Purdy, Jedediah. (2015). "Sandra Bland, Citizen." *The Huffington Post,* July 26. Accessed May 19, 2016. http://www.huffingtonpost.com/jedediah-purdy/sandra-bland-citizen_b_7874568.html.

Reece, M., D. Herbenick, V. Schick, S. A. Snaders, B. Dodge, and J. D. Forenberry. "Condom Use Rates in a National Probability Sample of Males and Females Ages 14 to 94 in the United States." *Journal of Sexual Medicine* 7 (Supplement 5): 266–276

Ries, David. (2005). "Duty-to-Protect Claims by Inmates after the Prison Rape Elimination Act." *Brooklyn Journal of Law and Policy* 13: 915–990.

Scheyett, Anna, Sharon Parker, Carol Golin, Becky White, Carrie Pettus Davis, and David Wohl. (2010). "HIV-Infected Prison Inmates: Depression and Implications for Release Back to Communities." *AIDS and Behavior* 14 (2): 300–307.

Schumer, Amy. (2015). "Football Town Nights." *Inside Amy Schumer, Comedy Central.* Accessed May 19, 2016. https://www.youtube.com/watch?v=TM2RUVnTlvs.

Sylla, Mary, Nina Harawa, and Olga Ginstead Resnick. (2010). "The First Condom Machine in a US Jail: The Challenge of Harm Reduction in a Law and Order Environment." *American Journal of Public Health* 100 (6): 982–985. doi: 10.2105/AJPH.2009.172452.

US Department of State. (2014). "Annual Country Reports on Human Rights." Accessed May 19, 2016. http://www.state.gov/j/drl/rls/hrrpt/.

Westergaard, Ryan P., Anne C. Spaulding, and Timothy P. Flanigan. (2013). "HIV Among Persons Incarcerated in the US: A Review of Evolving Concepts in Testing, Treatment and Linkage to Community Care." *Current Opinion in Infectious Diseases* 26 (1): 10–16. doi:10.1097/QCO.0b013e32835c1ddo.

Western, Bruce, and Becky Pettit. (2010). "Incarceration & Social Inequality." *Dædalus*. Accessed May 19, 2016. https://www.amacad.org/content/publications/pubContent.aspx?d=808.

Wooden, Wayne S., and Jay Parker. (1982). *Men Behind Bars: Sexual Exploitation in Prison*. New York: Plenum Press.

CHAPTER 39

RACE IN THE BIOMEDICAL SCIENCES

MICHAEL ROOT

RACE is used as a category in the biomedical sciences at two levels: the population and individual. In population-level studies, race is used to describe or explain variations in morbidity and mortality; at the individual level, race is used in the clinic in the diagnosis and treatment of individual patients. Both uses are controversial and raise questions about the nature and importance of racial categories in science and everyday life. But one, the use of race in the clinic, is more controversial.

The use of race in the biomedical sciences at the population level is considered in the first five sections and at the individual level in the last three. The first two sections describe the history of racial categories and their use in population surveys in the United States and especially within epidemiology. The third section considers how individuals are assigned to today's official racial categories, the fourth the category of mixed race, and the fifth the relation between race and ancestry. The sixth section considers the use of race as a proxy and the seventh and eighth consider racial profiling in medicine.

RACIAL CATEGORIES

The term "race" first appeared in English in the sixteenth century and was used to pick out and group people based on their looks, customs, and (suspected) origin or ancestry. However, in the eighteenth and nineteenth centuries, "race" acquired a specifically biological meaning, and the groups picked out as different races came to be viewed as different subspecies or lineages of man (Banton 1977). The biological concept of race was accompanied by the belief that members of some races are superior in ability or virtue to members of others and was often invoked to justify the control of one group of people by another and, in particular, to defend the Atlantic slave trade and the colonization of Africa and Asia by the countries of Europe.

Biological conceptions of race persist and, though contested by social as well as biological scientists, continue to shape how race is understood or talked about. Ashley Montague argued in a number of popular books and articles (Montague 1980) that race is a social rather than biological category, and Franz Boas showed that the cross-cultural generalizations advanced by proponents of the biological conception of race were mistaken (Boas 1982). Richard Lewontin maintained, based on research in population genetics, that the genetic differences between blacks in the United States are as great as any between blacks and whites (Lewontin 1972). At the level of genes, Lewontin argued, blacks do not differ from whites any more than they differ from one another; race, in this respect, is not biological.

People in the United States have classified each other by race since the founding of the country but not always in the same way. The federal government has classified people in the United States by race since the first Census in 1790, but the racial groups into which people were placed changed from one decade to another. There were nine Census races in 1930 and five in 2000, and six of the nine races in 1930 were not races at all in the 2000 Census (Bennett 2000).

In 1930, ethnic Japanese and ethnic Koreans in the United States were members of different races. In 2000, they were members of the same. Many blacks in 2000 would have been mulattos had they lived in 1880. To the extent that race is a social rather than biological category, an individual's race can change with time and place even if his skin color and ancestry remain the same.

To classify members of a population by race, a member has to be assigned to one or more of a fixed number of racial categories. Most biomedical researchers, when classifying members of the US population by race, rely on the classification system and standards for the collection and presentation of data on race adopted by an agency of the federal government, the Office of Management and Budget ([OMB] 1997).

According to an OMB directive (Directive 15), there are five races, with five racial categories (black; white; American Indian or Alaskan Native; Asian; Native Hawaiian or Other Pacific Islander) into which members of the United States are to be classified or grouped whenever their race is counted or reported. These five categories provide a minimum standard for maintaining, collecting, and presenting data on race for federal reporting purposes and are used to code all health data collected by an agency of the US government.

Population studies of health risks in the United States rely on these government data and on the federal government's five racial categories in describing or explaining how the risk of mortality and morbidity in the population varies with race. These categories are also used to classify patients within a hospital or clinic; patients are routinely assigned an OMB race when they enter, and their assigned race becomes part of their medical record.

Most biomedical researchers follow the federal government and treat race and ethnicity as different categories. A member of the US population, according to the OMB, can be Hispanic and a member of any of five races, and a member of any OMB race can be Hispanic or belong to any of a variety of different ethnic groups. As a result, Hispanics in the United States can be either black or white, and the health risks of black and white Hispanics can be different.

POPULATION STUDIES

Using the five OMB categories in their studies of differences in health within the US population, epidemiologists routinely find that the rates of many diseases, including major infectious diseases, many cancers, diabetes, asthma, and stroke, are different between the races. In addition, they find that blacks in the United States are seven times as likely to die of tuberculosis as whites and three times as likely to die of HIV/AIDS. Black infants are twice as likely to die as white infants, and black adults are twice as likely as white adults to die of stroke, heart disease, and diabetes. All-cause mortality rates in the United States, research shows, are 50 percent higher for black than white women and 70 percent higher for black than white men. In short, with a few exceptions, people classified as "black" have a poorer health profile than those classified as "white" (Agency for Healthcare Research and Quality 2008). Given the differences between the OMB races in rates of morbidity and mortality, race, in the view of most biomedical researchers, is an important descriptive and analytic variable in population studies of health in the United States.

In epidemiology, race is used to describe or explain differences within a population in the risk of injury, illness, or death much as race is used in sociology to describe or explain differences in the risk of poverty, homelessness, or incarceration or the rates of graduation or unemployment. While epidemiology and sociology draw on data collected by federal, state, or local government, sociology uses race to describe or explain how members of the US population differ in social or economic status, and epidemiology uses race to describe or explain how they differ in measures of health.

Epidemiology is not the only biomedical science that uses race as a variable in population research; pharmacology does as well. Studies of drug disposition and sensitivity show differences between the OMB races in the metabolism of a number of different drugs. Blacks and whites, according to a variety of drug studies, differ in response to cardiovascular drugs, psychotropic and central nervous system drugs, morphine, and beta-blockers (Yasuda 2008). These differences are clinically significant for they recommend differences in treatment; if blacks respond to a given drug therapy differently than whites, then a physician, in choosing a therapy for a patient, might want to know the race of her patient and adjust the therapy accordingly.

Using race as a descriptive or analytic variable in population research is different from using race at the individual level in the clinic as a reason to treat one patient differently from another; nevertheless, the statistical generalizations that result from the population-level research are often employed in individual decision making and are a basis for what has come to be known as racial profiling in medicine.

ASSIGNING RACE

The current OMB standard for collecting and reporting data on race lists five categories but is silent on how members of the population should be assigned a race and how to decide whether a member is one race (e.g., black), rather than another (e.g., white). While the US Bureau of Census assigns members an OMB race based on the race they report themselves to be, the National Center for Health Statistics assigns them a race based on the race on their birth or death certificate. However, a member's self-reported race can be different from the race on his birth or death certificate. As a result, he can be assigned one race at birth, a different race as a young adult, and a different one again when he dies (Hahn 1992). When measuring errors in mortality statistics, researchers routinely treat a decedent's race on his death certificate as his "apparent" race and his race on an earlier population survey or birth certificate as his "actual" one, if the two are different. They assume that a member's race cannot change, but that his race can be misreported.

In the United States, self-reported race has become the most common way of assigning race ("the gold standard") to members of a population in biomedical research (Friedman 2000). Assigning a member the race he assigns himself is often the easiest or most respectful way to assign him to a racial category. By allowing each individual to be the arbiter of his or her own race, the researcher displays the subjective and social nature of our system of racial classification and gives individuals control over their own identity. Nevertheless, the easiest or most respectful way to identify someone's race might not give race as much descriptive or explanatory power as a less easy or respectful one.

Self-reports are used in biomedicine to assign members to a variety of categories, to demographic categories like race and ethnicity and to categories of health and illness as well. However, there is evidence that self-reports do not measure the true value of some variables, and that their value is different from the self-reported one. In the study of alcohol abuse, for example, alcohol consumption is routinely measured by self-reports. Individuals are counted as lifetime abstainers if they report themselves to be that on a survey of alcohol consumption. A recent examination of the accuracy of these reports compared the never-drinking responses of respondents in three surveys and found that only 46 percent of the respondents gave the same response in all three and that many members reported being moderate drinkers when their actual consumption was greater (Rehm 2008).

Epidemiologic studies of cancer routinely use self-reports to measure cancer history. Studies of the accuracy of the reports compare them with medical records and show that only 33–61 percent of documented cancers were reported in interviews or surveys and the overall rate of false-negative reporting is also very high (Desai et al. 2001). The self-reports of cancer and alcohol consumption are proxies, and their accuracy is measured by how well they match a clinical measure of the variable, and, as many studies show, they do not always match them very well at all.

Though many self-reports of health are unreliable or inaccurate, most biomedical researchers assume that self-reports of race are reliable and accurate. Why? Because, on their view, the different ways of assigning race to members of a population usually give the same result; most members are assigned the same race whether their race is assigned by self-reports, other reports, or race on a birth or death certificate. As a result, a member's race is taken to be a fact about him that can be picked out in a number of different ways but remains the same whichever way is used to assign him to a racial category.

However, a workshop at the National Academy of Sciences concluded that research is needed to compare the race members of the US population assign themselves and the race they are most likely to be assigned by others (Edmonston 1996). Studies conducted since suggest that self-reports and other reports of a member's race are sometimes different, and many foreign-born and Hispanic members of the population do not take themselves to be the race they are most often taken to be by others (Harris et al. 2002). Other studies show that the self- and other-reported race of mixed-race members of the population (the offspring of parents of different OMB races) are often different or that the race that many members of the population report themselves to be varies with how, when, and by whom they are asked their race (Waters 2000).

Many members of the population seem to have a variety of context-specific self-identities, but, despite their self-identities, if many are consistently identified as black by others, then a researcher who is interested in racial discrimination or how access to housing, education, mortgage lending, employment opportunities, or morbidity or mortality varies with race has a reason to take other reports rather than self-reports as the best measure of the person's race. Officials who decide social or health policy have a reason to take other reports as the best measure as well.

MIXED RACE

Some members of the US population report themselves to be mixed race, rather than one or more of the five OMB races, if "mixed" is one of the racial categories they are able to choose from. Between 1990 and 1997, many individuals and groups lobbied Congress and the OMB to alter the list of official races to include a stand-alone multiracial classification and include "mixed" as an option in the 2000 Census (Project Mixed Race 1997).

However, if "mixed" was an official option, on what basis should a member of the population be assigned to that category, on the basis of a self-report, the race of his parents, or the race others take him to be? Moreover, should a member be counted as mixed if one of his parents is mixed or only if his parents belong to two different OMB races?

"Mixed" is not a racial category in the US Census but neither is the category used in most studies of racial differences in health. In most studies of differences in infant mortality, for example, an infant's mother's race is usually taken to be his actual race, whatever the race of his father, and no infant is taken to be mixed race rather than one of the five OMB races (Kleinman and Kessel 1987).

Beginning in 1989 the race of infants in the United States was based on that of the mother in all natality statistics. Prior to 1989, an infant's race was based on a father's race as well, and an infant could be both black and white. If the 1989 practice were to be applied retrospectively to births in 1987, white births would increase by 1.7 percent and black births would decrease by 4.7 percent (Hahn and Stroup 1994). If "mixed" was a category in infant mortality studies, the rate of black infant death would decrease, but the amount of decrease would depend on how "mixed" was assigned to infants. Using his mother's race to predict an infant's risk of morbidity or mortality (the current practice) biases the estimate of black–white differences in risk if infants with parents of different races have different risks of morbidity or mortality than infants with same-race parents.

RACE AND ANCESTRY

Though humans differ from one another genetically, in the frequency of many genes or alleles (including medically relevant ones), the existing racial categories do not capture these differences very well. Geographic ancestry captures them better, since there is less genetic variation within groups identified by common ancestry than groups identified by race.

Between 20 and 30 percent of self-reported blacks and whites in the United States, according to some estimates, have mixed African and European ancestry (Parra et al. 1998). The median proportion of European ancestry among self-reported blacks is 18.5 percent, and the average proportion is 14 percent (Tishkoff and Bustamonte 2009). Proportions vary from region to region of the United States, and self-reported blacks in California have the highest proportion of European ancestry and in Georgia the lowest (Parra et al. 1998). However, in every region of the United States, many people who identify themselves as black have both African and European ancestors and many who identify as white do as well.

If a small percentage of African ancestry is enough to count as black, then many members of the US population who take themselves to be white are black since between 20 and 30 percent of self-reported whites in the United States are estimated to have between 2 and 20 percent African ancestry. While the apparent race of 20 to 30 percent of self-reported whites would be white, their actual race would be black if "black" were defined as more than 0 percent African ancestry. If 20 to 30 percent of self-reported whites are black, then the US Bureau of Census overcounted the number whites or blacks in the United States in 2000 by between 20 and 30 percent.

Though race is associated with ancestry, the relationship between ancestry and today's racial categories is loose since self- and other-reported OMB race vary independently of ancestry, and OMB race is most often assigned to members of the US population based on self- or other reports. While more and more Americans are of mixed ancestry, most are assigned to one of the five OMB races rather than counted as "mixed" when Census or other survey responses are combined or aggregated.

Biomedical researchers cannot capture something as complex as race with a single measure of race. Race has a number of different dimensions and one measure of race, one way of assigning members of a population to racial categories, can be a better measure of one dimension and a worse measure of another. As a result, at the population level, the way race is assigned to individuals, some researchers suggest, should be allowed to vary (rather than remain fixed) from one risk to another, and an individual taken to be one OMB race in relation to one risk and different race in relation to another (Root 2009). To allow the methods of assigning race to vary would follow a recommendation of the National Research Council that reports of race should rely on multiple methods of measurement rather than one, since no one measure can capture all the different ways races can affect the health of members of a population (National Research Council 2004).

RACE AS A PROXY

While epidemiologists often use race as a population variable in their studies of differences in morbidity and mortality, at the individual level, doctors often use race in the clinic as a proxy to predict how a patient will respond to a treatment. One variable X is used as a proxy for another Y when X is used in the place of Y to make a judgment or decision. Let Y be a variable that cannot be measured directly but is material to an interest I; let X be a variable that can be directly measured and, though not material to I, correlates with Y. X is a proxy for Y if used instead of Y in making a judgment or decision in order to further I.

Scores on college admission tests are used as a proxy for first-semester college grades when admissions officers choose between applicants based on the scores; race is used as a proxy for performance when employers practice what economists call "statistical discrimination" and use race to choose between applicants for a position, and race is used as a proxy in law enforcement when police officers base traffic stops on the race of motorists. To use race as a proxy, in any of these circumstances, is to engage in what has come to be called "racial profiling."

RACIAL PROFILING IN MEDICINE

When doctors use race as a proxy for a drug response or police officers for crime, they engage in racial profiling; how they treat a patient or motorist depends on the race they take him to be. The doctors' use of race, however, seems reasonable, whereas the police officers' use does not for, according to population-level studies, while drug response varies with race, crime does not. Arrests vary with race but since many criminals are not arrested and many of the arrested are not criminals, arrests are not markers of crime. Many doctors believe that racial profiling in medicine is reasonable and fair even if racial profiling in law enforcement is not; stopping a motorist based on this race is wrong, but, in their eyes, prescribing a drug to a patient based on his race is unobjectionable.

According to recent population-level studies of drugs for congestive heart failure, whites respond better to some drugs, such as angiotensin-converting-enzyme (ACE) inhibitors, than blacks do (Exner et al. 2001). Based on these studies, doctors use race as a proxy for a response to an ACE inhibitor when they target their white patients for the drug but not their black ones. Drug response is the material trait, whereas race is the proxy. Doctors do not know how an individual patient will respond to the drug, but they know or think they know a patient's race, and given the correlation between drug response and race, they predict that a white patient will respond well to an ACE inhibitor, whereas a black one will not.

However, for a doctor to use a patient's race to predict his response to a drug is problematic for at least three reasons. First, to select whites but not blacks for a drug treatment based on a population-level study ignores intraracial differences in response to the drug and adversely affects black patients for whom the "white" drug would be an effective treatment. Though the ACE study showed that whites and blacks as a group respond differently to the drug, it also showed that a significant number of blacks respond as well as whites do to the drug. Thus, treating all black patients the same, denying the drug to all of them, denies some blacks an effective treatment for congestive heart failure.

Second, targeting blacks assumes that race is the best predictor available, but the rate at which a drug is metabolized varies as a result of many factors, including environment and lifestyle. Most studies that show a racial difference in drug response do not control for differences between the black and white patients in socioeconomic status (SES) or other factors that are known to influence drug metabolism. As a result, the studies do not offer good evidence that the differences in response are due to race rather than to a third factor that varies with drug response and race. If differences in SES or lifestyle explain most of the variance between the black and white patients in response to a heart drug, it would be more reasonable for a doctor to use these as a proxy for the response than race.

Third, even if the difference between blacks and whites in drug response is due to a bio-logical (genetic) difference, there is no reason to treat race as an independent variable that causes or explains the difference, since the genes controlling drug response vary indepen-dently of race. Race, in this respect, is different from sex as a marker of biomedical difference. While there are no race genes or chromosomes, there are sex chromosomes and genes. As a result, a gene that controls drug metabolism or sensitivity might be located on a sex chromo-some and, if so, would vary with sex though independently of race, and sex would explain why male and female patients differ in their response to a drug.

There is no reason to believe that when doctors assign a race to their patients, their assign-ments match the assignments of race on which a study of drug response relies. Drug studies routinely rely on self-reported race; subjects are assigned the race that they assign themselves when asked. However, there is considerable evidence that self-identification is not robust and how individuals report their race varies with who is asking and the choices a person is given (Harris 2000). Individuals with mixed parents, for example, are likely to describe themselves as mixed race or multiracial if given the option but as a member of an OMB race if they are not. The subjects in most drug studies were not given a mixed-race option, and had they been, the results of the study would likely have been different.

Some doctors assign patients a race other than their self-reported one, and different doc-tors sometimes assign a different race to the same patient. A patient can be white to one doc-tor and black to another. As a result, the race a doctor assigns a patient might not be the race he would have been assigned had he been enrolled in the drug study.

When doctors use race as a proxy for a patient's response to a treatment, they employ a particular form of statistical inference and reason as follows: (1) a high percentage of blacks with this medical condition do not respond as well to treatment A as to treatment B; (2) this patient is black and has the condition; thus, (3) this patient is likely to respond better to B than A.

The inference is reasonable only if (1) and (2) include the best available evidence relevant to whether the patient will respond better to one treatment than the other. That is, (3) should be judged on an evidential base that includes the best available evidence, for the credence which it is rational to give a statement at a time is determined by the degree of confirmation that the statement possesses on the best evidence available at the time (Hempel 1965).

Most doctors consider age, environment, and lifestyle as well as race, if they consider race at all, when they choose a treatment for a patient. The question is how or whether a doctor should allow race to enter into the treatment decision. Ideally, a doctor would treat a patient as an individual rather than a representative of a group, but if the doctor treats him as a rep-resentative of any group at all, the group should not be identified by race if race masks a population-level variable that bears more directly on a treatment response.

Proxies are only useful when we lack direct access to a material trait. A college does not need to use test scores or high school rank to infer a student's college grades if it has access to the student's college transcript. Doctors, given advances in genetic technology, may soon have access to a patient's genetic transcript. Should she have his transcript, the doctor will not need to infer from his race whether he is disposed to respond better to one treatment rather than another.

However, even when the technology is available, doctors will have access to some but not all patients' genetic profiles, for patients will not have equal access to this technology any-more than they do to present-day health care. For patients who are not able to afford or who refuse the genetic tests, proxies will continue to have a use in diagnosis and treatment, but race should not be used as a proxy if other variables have more predictive power and, unlike race, do not require doctors to draw a color line or decide which of their patients are black and which are white.

DEFENSE OF PROFILING

Supporters of racial profiling in medicine often remind us that not many years ago we objected to drug research that tested the safety or efficacy of a drug, especially heart drugs, on white males and applied the findings to blacks and females. In response to these objections, doctors began to look for differences in drug response between the races and sexes and, finding differences, began to discriminate between their patients based on their sex or race. As a result, profiling, the supporters say, is an enlightened and salutary response to the doctors' past indifference to differences in response.

Sex, however, is a much better proxy than race for a response to a drug. A gene encoding a drug-metabolizing enzyme could vary with a gene on a sex chromosome, but there are no race genes or chromosomes for an enzyme-encoding gene to vary with. As a result, doctors have a better reason to study sex differences than racial differences in drug response and a better reason to use sex than race as a proxy for a response when deciding how best to treat an individual patient for a medical condition.

Should race ever be used in medicine as a proxy for a patient's response to a drug? I suggest we divide the question in two. First, we might ask how an individual doctor should view his patient's race and, second, how doctors as a group should view the race of their patients. Some black patients might be better off if their doctor selects one drug for them rather than another (e.g., a beta-blocker rather than an ACE inhibitor) because of their race, while, as a group, black patients might be worse off if doctors, as a group, base their choice of drugs on race. The practice of basing drugs on the race of patients could leave blacks less well off as a group, even if some individual black patients benefit from the practice given the variation within each racial group in response to a drug and the variation in how doctors assign a race to their patients. While individual doctors might be permitted to choose a drug for a patient based on his race, doctors as a group might adopt a policy of ignoring race when choosing drugs for patients. While the policy would recommend a race-blind choice of drugs, individual doctors would be permitted to make a race-conscious one.

CONCLUSION

To stratify health statistics by race is reasonable, as long as employment, housing, income, education, or health care is stratified by race; but to use race as a proxy for a response to a medical treatment is questionable because members of the same race often differ as much in their response to a medical treatment as members of different races do, and racial profiling in medicine, no less than in law enforcement and schooling, helps to sustain a harmful racial ideology. The question at the population level is not whether race should be used as a population variable in health research but which racial categories should be used and how members of a population should be assigned to them. The question at the individual level is whether race should matter at all, given the variation within each race in the response of patients to medical treatments.

REFERENCES

Banton, Michael. (1977). *The Idea of Race*. London: Tavistock Publications.

Bennett, Claudette. (2000). "Racial Categories Used in the Decennial Censuses, 1790 to Present." *Government Information Quarterly* 17: 161–180.

Boas, Franz. (1982). *Language and Culture*. Chicago: University of Chicago Press.

Desai, Mayur, Martha Livingston Bruce, R. A. Desai, and B. G. Druss. (2001). "Validity of Self-Reported Cancer History: A Comparison of Health Interview Data and Cancer Registry Records." *American Journal of Epidemiology* 153: 299–306.

Edmonston, Barry, Joshua Goldstein, and Juanita Tamayo, eds. (1996). *Spotlight on Heterogeneity: The Federal Standards for Racial and Ethnic Classification*. Washington, DC: National Academies Press.

Exner, Derek V., Daniel L. Dries, Michael J. Domanski, and Jay N. Cohn. (2001). "Lesser Response to Angiotensin-Converting-Enzyme Inhibitor Therapy in Black as Compared with White Patients with Left Ventricular Dysfunction." *New England Journal of Medicine* 344: 1351–1357.

Friedman, Daniel, Bruce Cohen, Abigail Averbach, and Jennifer Norton. (2000). "Race/Ethnicity and OMB Directive 15: Implication for State Public Health Practice." *American Journal of Public Health* 90: 1714–1719.

Hahn, R. A. (1992). "The State and Federal Health Statistics on Racial and Ethnic Groups." *Journal of the American Medical Association* 267: 268–271.

Hahn, Robert A., and Donna F. Stroup. (1994). "Race and Ethnicity in Public Health Surveillance: Criteria for the Scientific Use of Social Categories." *Public Health Reports* 109: 7–15.

Harris, David R. (2000). "Demography's Race Problem." Paper presented at the 2000 Meeting of the Population Association of America. Accessed May 19, 2016. http://www.nichd.nih.gov/cpr/dbs/sp/harris.htm.

Harris, David, R., and Jeremiah Joseph Sim. (2002). "Who is Multiracial? Assessing the Complexity of Lived Race." *American Sociological Review* 67: 614–627.

Hempel, Carl G. (1965). *Aspects of Scientific Explanation*. New York: The Free Press.

Kleinman, Joel C., and S. S. Kessel. (1987). "Racial Differences in Low Birth Weight: Trends and Risk Factors." *New England Journal of Medicine* 317: 749–753.

Lewontin, Richard. (1972). "The Apportionment of Human Diversity." In *Evolutionary Biology*, edited by T. Dobzhansky, M. K. Hecht, and W. C. Steere, 381–398. New York: Appleton-Century-Crofts.

Montague, Ashley. (1980). *The Concept of Race*. Westport, CT: Greenwood.

National Research Council. (2004). *Measuring Racial Discrimination. Panel on Methods for Assessing Discrimination*. Edited by Rebecca M. Blank, Marilyn Dabady, and Constance F. Crito. Committee on National Statistics, Division of Behavioral and Social Sciences and Education. Washington DC: The National Academies Press.

Office of Management and Budget. (1997). "Revisions of the Standards for the Classification of Federal Data on Race and Ethnicity." Accessed May 19, 2016. http://www.whitehouse.gov/omb/fedreg/1997standards.html.

Parra, E. J., A. Marcini, J. Akey, J. Martinson, M. A. Balzer, R. Cooper, T. Forrester, D. B. Allison, R. Deka, R. E. Ferrell, and M. D. Shriver. (2008). "Estimating African American Admixture Proportion by the Use of Population Specific Alleles." *American Journal of Human Genetics* 63: 1839–1851.

Project Race. (1997). "From the Executive Director." Accessed May 19, 2016. http://www.projectrace.com/hotnews/archive/hotnews-102997.php.

Rehm, Jurgen, H. Irving, Y. Ye, W. C. Kerr, J. Bond, and T. K. Greenfield. (2008). "Are Lifetimes Abstainers the Best Control Group in Alcohol Epidemiology? On the Stability and Validity of Reported Lifetime Abstention." *American Journal of Epidemiology* 168: 866–877.

Root, Michael. (2009). "Measurement Error in Racial and Ethnic Statistics." *Biology and Philosophy* 24: 375–385.

Tishkoff, S. A., F. A. Reed, F. R. Friedlaender, C. Ehret, A. Ranciaro, A. Froment, J. B. Hirbo, et al. (2009). "The Genetic Structure and History of African and African Americans." *Science* 324: 1035–1044.

US Preventive Services Task Force. "Agency for Healthcare Research and Quality." (2008). Screening for Colorectal Cancer: US Preventive Services Task Force Recommendation Statement. A HRQ Publication (2007): 08-05124.

Waters, Mary C. (2000). "Immigration, Intermarriage, and the Challenges of Measuring Racial/Ethnic Identities." *American Journal of Public Health* 90: 1735–1737.

Yasuda, S. U., L. Zhang, and S. M. Huang. (2008). "The Role of Ethnicity in Variability in Response to Drugs: Focus on Clinical Pharmacology Studies." *Clinical Pharmacology and Therapeutics* 84 (3): 417–423.

CHAPTER 40

INTELLIGENCE, RACE, AND PSYCHOLOGICAL TESTING

MARK ALFANO, LATASHA HOLDEN, AND ANDREW CONWAY

THE *Stanford Encyclopedia of Philosophy* has an entry for "Logic and Artificial Intelligence" (Thomason 2014) and "Virtue Epistemology" (Turri, Alfano, and Greco, 2016), but no entry for "Intelligence." Likewise, www.philpapers.org, the largest curated database of philosophical publications in the Anglophone world, has entries for "Philosophy of Artificial Intelligence," "Special Topics in Artificial Intelligence," "Philosophy of Artificial Intelligence, Miscellaneous," "The Nature of Artificial Intelligence," "Artificial Intelligence Methodology," "Extraterrestrial Life and Intelligence," and "Ethics of Artificial Intelligence," but nothing for "Intelligence," "Human Intelligence," or "Intelligence and Race." As of the writing of this chapter, there were just three entries in the category "Race and IQ": Alfano (2014), Block (1996), and Kaplan and Grønfeldt Winther (2014). A contribution on the philosophy of race and intelligence is long overdue.

That said, there is an immense amount we cannot address in this chapter. Among other things, we will discuss only superficially the ontology of race, the use of intelligence testing to justify oppression and the potential implications of this, and finally how one might mitigate the outcomes associated with racial group stigmatization in this context. This chapter has two main goals: to update philosophers on the state of the art in the scientific psychology of intelligence, and to explore more recent and relevant theoretical phenomena surrounding the measurement invariance of intelligence tests. First, we provide a brief history of the scientific psychology of intelligence. Next, we discuss the metaphysics of intelligence in light of scientific studies in psychology and neuroimaging. Finally, we turn to recent skeptical developments related to measurement invariance. These have largely focused on attributability: Where do the mechanisms and dispositions that explain people's performance on tests of intelligence inhere—in the agent, in the local testing environment, in the culture, or in the interactions among these? After explaining what measurement invariance is in the context of intelligence testing, we will discuss stereotype threat as evidence challenging measurement invariance views of intelligence. In conclusion, we will review recent psychological theories that provide ways for combatting the pernicious and stigmatizing effects of this phenomenon.

BRIEF HISTORY OF THE SCIENTIFIC
PSYCHOLOGY OF INTELLIGENCE

The notion that people differ in their mental abilities is as old as philosophy itself. In *De Anima*, for example, Aristotle spoke of the faculties of the soul, which include not only perception but also imagination. References to smart or clever people can be found throughout literature as well, perhaps most notably in the works of Shakespeare, who puts these words in the mouth of Richard III: "O, 'tis a parlous boy; / Bold, quick, ingenious, forward, capable / He is all the mother's, from top to toe." Already in the sixteenth century, Shakespeare expresses the idea that intelligence is a trait, and moreover that it is heritable.

The scientific construct of intelligence dates to the late nineteenth and early twentieth centuries. In hindsight, it may seem surprising that it took so long for people to develop measurements of intelligence, but in the West until the nineteenth century, rationality and reason were seen by most people as divine gifts from God, so it may have seemed pointless to measure mental ability. In addition, it was not until the middle of the nineteenth century that compulsory education laws were introduced in Europe. This led to practical societal problems such as of the assessment of learning, abilities, and disabilities. Indeed, it was this need for assessment that paved the way for modern intelligence testing.

Ironically, the first scientific intelligence test was constructed primarily to detect intellectual *dis*ability, not to measure and compare people of normal intelligence. In 1904, the French government called upon psychologist Alfred Binet to develop a scale that could be used to identify students who were struggling in school so that they could receive alternative or supplemental instruction. Binet, in collaboration with his student Theodore Simon, developed an array of tasks thought to be representative of typical children's abilities at various ages. They administered the tasks, now known as the Binet-Simon test, to a sample of fifty children: ten children in each of five age groups. The children in the sample were selected by their schoolteachers for being average, or representative, for their age group (Siegler 1992).

The test initially consisted of thirty tasks of increasing difficulty. The simplest tasks tested a child's ability to follow instructions. Slightly more difficult tasks required children to repeat simple sentences and to define basic vocabulary words. Among the hardest tasks were a digit span test, which required children to recall seven digits in correct serial order, and a rhyming task, which required children to generate rhyming words given a target word (Fancher 1985). Binet and Simon administered all the tasks to the sample of children, and the score derived from the test was thought to reflect the child's mental age. This initial standardization allowed educators to determine the extent to which a child was on par with his peers by subtracting the child's mental age from her chronological age. For example, a child with a mental age of 6 and a chronological age of 9 would receive a score of 3, indicating that he was mentally three years behind his average peer.

While Binet and Simon were primarily interested in identifying children with learning disabilities, their methodology was quickly adapted and extended. For example, at Stanford University in 1916, Lewis Terman published a revision of their test, which he termed the Stanford-Binet test. Terman expanded the battery of tasks and adopted the intelligence quotient (IQ) rather than Binet's difference score, an idea first proposed by German psychologist and philosopher William Stern. IQ is the ratio of a child's mental age to her chronological age, times 100. Thus, an average IQ is 100, and scores greater than 100 reflect higher IQ. Terman used IQ scores not only to identify children at the low end of the distribution, as Binet did, but also at the top of the distribution, as he began to study factors that lead to giftedness and genius.

While Terman and others can be credited with the first instances of group intelligence testing, the first large-scale testing was conducted with 1.7 million US soldiers during World War I. The US military, in consultation with psychologists such as Terman and Robert Yerkes, developed two tests, the Army Alpha and the Army Beta, to help categorize army recruits based on intelligence and aptitude for officer training. The Army Alpha was a text-based test that took an hour to administer. The Army Beta was a picture-based test designed for nonreaders, who made up approximately 25 percent of the recruits. The administration of intelligence tests for job placement in the military continues to this day; the modern test is known as the ASVAB (Armed Services Vocational Aptitude Battery). It was first administered in 1968 and currently consists of eight subtests: word knowledge, paragraph comprehension, mathematics knowledge, arithmetic reasoning, general science, mechanical comprehension, electronics information, and auto and shop information. The ASVAB is currently administered to over 1 million people per year.

American college admissions tests such as the SAT and ACT can also be considered intelligence tests. The history of their acronyms, however, speaks volumes. Initially, "SAT" stood for "Scholastic Aptitude Test." In 1990, the acronym was retained, but its meaning was changed to "Scholastic Assessment Test." Just three years later, subject-specific tests in writing, critical reading, languages, mathematics, and the sciences were introduced. These were called the SAT II battery, in which the "A" stood for "Achievement." The old SAT became the SAT I: Reasoning Test. Finally, in 1997, the College Board, which makes the SAT, declared that the capital letters in the test's name did not stand for anything (Applebome 1997). The ACT underwent a similar metamorphosis, standing initially for "American College Testing" but then, starting in 1996, for nothing at all.

Besides the ASVAB, SAT, and ACT, the most popular intelligence tests in use today are the WAIS (Wechsler Adult Intelligence Scale) and the WISC (Wechsler Intelligence Scale for Children), which were originally developed by psychologist David Wechsler. The WAIS and the WISC each consist of several subtests. The verbal subtests, such as vocabulary, comprehension, and general knowledge questions, are not unlike components of Binet's original test battery. However, the nonverbal subtests, which consist of matrix reasoning, working memory, and processing speed tests, differentiate the WAIS and WISC from most other tests. These components, which Wechsler referred to as Performance IQ, are linked to a psychological construct known as *fluid reasoning*, the capacity to solve novel problems. Importantly, fluid reasoning is largely independent from prior knowledge. Furthermore, it is strongly correlated with a range of complex cognitive behaviors, such as academic achievement, problem solving, and reading comprehension.

One natural criticism of intelligence tests that employ vocabulary and general knowledge questions is that they are liable to be parochial. Vocabulary in these tests tends to be from standard English (or any language in which they are administered), but as linguists are fond of pointing out, a language is just a dialect with an army and a navy. If this is right, then intelligence tests in which standard-language vocabulary predominates may systematically privilege test takers whose culture matches the contemporary power structure, while discriminating against test takers whose culture fails to match. Perhaps the most notorious example of this comes from an SAT analogy in which runner:marathon::oarsman:regatta.

It is not a leap to suspect that test takers who had participated in or observed a regatta would do better with this analogy than those who had not. To make a similar point, Robert Williams (1972) developed the Black Intelligence Test of Cultural Homogeneity (BITCH-100), a vocabulary test oriented toward the language and experience of urban blacks. This test included terms such as "alley apple" and "playing the dozens." Unsurprisingly, blacks tend to outperform whites on the BITCH-100 (Matarazzo and Wiens 1977).

It was in this milieu that so-called culture-free tests of intelligence rose to prominence. The promise of such tests is that they circumvent problematic items related to parochial vocabulary and supposedly general knowledge. The most straightforward way to do this is to avoid language altogether, as in Raven's Progressive Matrices (Raven 2003) and the Culture Fair Intelligence Test (Cattell 1949). Even these tests, however, may not be entirely culturally neutral (Aiken 1996). This is especially damning because allegedly neutral tests that obscure their own bias may be even more damaging than tests that wear their bias on their faces, as they constitute a form of what Jason Stanley calls "undermining propaganda," which "is presented as an embodiment of certain ideals, yet is of a kind that tends to erode those very ideals" (Stanley 2015, 53).

The Positive Manifold and the Metaphysics of Intelligence

At the same time that Binet was developing the first modern intelligence test, British psychologists were developing the statistical tools necessary to analyze the measures obtained from such tests. Sir Francis Galton, along with his student Karl Pearson, proposed the correlation coefficient, which is used to assess the degree to which two measurements are related, or covary. The Pearson product moment correlation coefficient, r, ranges from -1, which is a perfect negative correlation, to $+1$, which is a perfect positive correlation. Perhaps the best-replicated empirical result in the field of psychology is the *positive manifold*: the all-positive pattern of correlations that is observed when several intelligence tests, of varying format, are administered to a large sample of subjects. While the positive manifold may not seem surprising, it is important to note that, a priori, one may not have predicted such results from intelligence tests. One may have predicted instead that individuals who do well on one type of test, say vocabulary, may suffer on a different kind of test, such as mental rotation. This raises the questions: What accounts for the positive manifold? Why is it that any measure of any facet of intelligence correlates positively with any other measure of any other facet of intelligence?

One natural answer is that all measures of intelligence tap aspects of the same *general ability*. This is Spearman's (1904) solution to the positive manifold, according to which there is a single general factor, g, of intelligence. Spearman's model has been criticized for failing to account for the fact that some intelligence tests correlate more strongly with each other than others. For example, a verbal test of intelligence will typically correlate positively with both another verbal test of intelligence and a spatial test of intelligence, but more strongly with the former than the latter. Such patterns of clustering led Thurstone (1938) to argue for a model of intelligence that included seven primary mental abilities and no general factor. In the ensuing decades, it has become clear that both Spearman's model and Thurstone's models capture part of the truth, leading to the development of higher order and bifactor models. These models have a hierarchical structure in which a general factor explains the covariance of multiple domain-specific factors (Carroll 1993).

It is important to bear in mind that these factors, whatever their exact structure, are mathematical abstractions based on interindividual differences. While it is tempting to reify them as referring to concrete intraindividual properties or processes, one must proceed with caution when identifying the grounds of intelligence. Moving from a mathematical structure to a biological or psychological process should be construed as an abductive inference to the best explanation (Harman 1965), not a straightforward identification. This is not to say that identifying the neural or cognitive mechanisms that explain intelligence is impossible, just that it is fraught with uncertainty.

Spearman notoriously identified g with "general mental energy," a rather mysterious domain-general process. A more attractive alternative, first proposed by Godfrey Thompson in 1916, is that the positive manifold manifests itself because any battery of intelligence tests will sample processes in an overlapping manner, such that some processes will be required by a shared subset of tasks, while others will be unique to particular tasks. This idea was given a cognitive-developmental twist by van der Maas et al. (2006), who suggest that the positive manifold arises because independent cognitive processes engage in mutually beneficial interactions during cognitive development. Through a process of virtuous feedback loops, these processes eventually become correlated, resulting in the positive manifold. More recently, the idea of overlapping and mutually reinforcing processes has been corroborated by a wealth of studies in the cognitive psychology of working memory as well as the neuroimaging of executive processes and working memory. The latter studies show that regions of the brain are differentially activated by tasks that tap different facets of intelligence, with executive processes associated with both fluid intelligence and working memory capacity occurring more in the prefrontal cortex while other processes associated with crystalized intelligence occur farther back in the brain, for example, in the parietal cortex and cerebellum.

These results and the "process overlap model" that emerges from them are explored at greater length in Conway and Kovacs (2013, 2015). The basic upshot, however, should be clear: the best explanation of interindividual differences on intelligence tests and the positive manifold is that intelligent performance results from the interaction of multiple, partially overlapping processes that sometimes feed into one another both ontogenetically and synchronically. Hence, to describe someone as more or less intelligent is to say that the overlapping psychological and neurological processes that conspire to produce their behavior in the face of cognitive tasks tend to work together better or worse than the average person's in the context in which those tasks are administered.

RACE, INTELLIGENCE, AND THE MEASUREMENT INVARIANCE PROBLEM

For decades, some ethnic minorities, blacks, Latinos, especially, and other marginalized groups, including women and the poor, have performed worse than average on a variety of intelligence tests. How is this phenomenon to be understood? In a lengthy article, Arthur Jensen (1969) argued that developmental interventions such as Head Start failed to attenuate the race gap in IQ. While he did not go so far as to outright assert that group differences are genetic, he has been (often still is) read as supporting such a position. His controversial thesis provoked a deluge of responses and rebuttals. In fact, Jensen's provocation may be the single most cited article in the entire field of intelligence research. A couple of decades later, Richard Herrnstein and Charles Murray (1994) in *The Bell Curve: Race and Class Structure in American Life* revived a version of Jensen's argument. Since the publication of this book, there has been a contentious dialogue, based on experimental data, surrounding the topic of innate differences in intelligence. As opposed to the pseudo-scientific theories (e.g., *On The Natural Varieties of Mankind* by Blumenbach 1775/1969) proposed about race and the inherent characteristics of personality and intelligence during the eighteenth century, Herrnstein and Murray use empirical data to support their claims. The primary argument of *The Bell Curve* is that intelligence is a cognitive construct which is dispersed in a normal distribution or "bell curve" throughout the population. Moreover, they argue that differences in *average* intelligence between different ethnic groups is not explained by a small number of exceptionally high- or low-scoring members of different groups; instead, they show that the entire distribution of intelligence scores for ethnic minority groups (especially blacks and Latinos) is shifted down from the corresponding scores for whites. The authors claim that the difference in intelligence emerges from innate differences in ability based on the notion that intelligence is approximately 70 percent heritable and 30 percent emergent from environmental factors. Herrnstein and Murray therefore suggest that there is little that minority group members can do to overcome this difference, since most of it is genetically hardwired and cannot be altered or enhanced by environmental factors.

Still more recently, Nicholas Wade (2014) once again revived these arguments in *A Troublesome Inheritance*. Wade argues that "human behavior has a genetic basis that varies from one race to another" (184), with almost the entire contemporary human population comprising just three categorically distinct races: European, East Asian, and sub-Saharan African. He goes on to claim that "national disparities in wealth arise from differences in intelligence" (189) determined in large part by race. Wade singles out "the adaptation of Jews to capitalism" (214), which, he says, accounts for the high rate at which Jews win Nobel prizes. He also argues that the genetic predisposition to "nonviolence, literacy, thrift and patience" (160) among the English upper-class eventually propagated throughout the English population, which, he suggests, accounts for the Industrial Revolution and Britain's subsequent dominance as a world empire. Of course, if race itself is not genetic, then racial differences in intelligence are a fortiori not genetically grounded. We will not address that issue here; for a summary of the main views in the philosophy of race, see Mallon (2006).

While some might be tempted to make a facile Aristotelian assumption that there is some unified property or process of individual agents in which intelligence innately inheres (e.g., something essential about their DNA), persistent differences between groups in scores on intelligence tests admit of a variety of potential explanations. Furthermore, just as we should avoid reifying *g* (the general intelligence factor) as referring to a unified, concrete process or resource in the brain, so we should be wary of inferring that someone's race straightforwardly determines his intelligence through the expression of essential genetic properties.

Indeed, as we saw in the previous section, current scientific thinking on intelligence holds that it is not unified at all, but rather emerges from the interaction of multiple, partially overlapping processes that sometimes feed into one another both ontogenetically and synchronically. Furthermore, some of these processes are *domain-specific* (that is, relative to a structure or context of learning) which means that a test of intelligence that fails to account for test takers' different experiences of domain content is liable to produce biased results (recall the "regatta" analogy). Interference with any one of the overlapping processes is likely to interfere with related processes. And when it comes to domain-general processes (e.g., working memory capacity), aspects of the testing environment that interfere with their functioning are especially likely to interfere with others.

How, then, should we interpret the well-documented differences between racial and ethnic groups on intelligence tests? In the psychological literature, this is understood as a question of *measurement invariance*. A procedure exhibits measurement invariance across groups when it measures the same construct in them. In the ideal case, it also measures the target construct with the same degree of precision and accuracy across the groups. Moreover, in order for a test to be measurement invariant, there should be no systematic bias in test performance based on group membership—measurement invariance is violated if scores on some ability are not independent of group membership. In other words, measurement invariance holds if the distribution of manifest scores of variable Y based on latent ability η for group v is equal to the distribution of manifest scores on variable Y based on latent ability η. That is, scores are invariant based on group membership alone (see Wicherts et al. 2005; Wicherts and Dolan 2010). A simple example illustrates this concept: imagine a spectrographic test that is meant to determine, based on the light a tomato reflects, whether it is ripe. Such a test could not, without adjustment, be sensibly used for both Campari and Kumato tomatoes. It also could not sensibly be used for both Kumato tomatoes in a greenhouse lighted with incandescent bulbs and Kumato tomatoes in a greenhouse lighted with fluorescent bulbs.

In much the same way, researchers have raised concerns about the measurement invariance of intelligence tests. Perhaps intelligence tests measure intelligence in whites but some other, related construct in other test takers. This would not be that surprising in light of the fact that intelligence tests were first developed for use with white populations. Or perhaps intelligence tests do measure intelligence in all Anglophone populations but are more accurate or more precise with some groups than others. Once again, the history of these tests makes this a hypothesis worth considering. Bowden et al. (2011) showed that average scores on the WAIS are slightly higher in Canada than in the United States for representative populations; this could mean that Canadians are, on average, more intelligent than Americans, but it could also mean that the test does not tap the construct of intelligence with the same accuracy in both countries.

The same holds for differences between racial and ethnic groups within the United States and elsewhere. Do the mechanisms and dispositions that explain people's performance on tests of intelligence inhere in the agent, in the local testing environment, in the culture, or in the interactions among these? This question is unavoidably laden with moral, social, and political value judgments, but there is empirical evidence that at least points toward a broadly interactionist conclusion. We will briefly review some of this evidence here; for further philosophical discussion of how best to interpret group differences in intelligence tests, see Alfano (2014) and Alfano and Skorburg (2017).

STEREOTYPE THREAT AND MEASUREMENT INVARIANCE

Perhaps the best-known challenge to standard measurement invariance views of intelligence tests comes from the literature on *stereotype threat*, a phenomenon first investigated by Claude Steele and Joshua Aronson. They began with the idea that if you are worried that others will view your performance on a task as emblematic of your group, and your group is stigmatized as low performing or of low ability on that task, then you will experience a level of threat that people from another group might not. Such threat, in turn, is expected to lead to performance decrements. Thus, Steele and Aronson aimed to demonstrate that standard views of intelligence tests as measurements of ability were inherently flawed. Contrary to the notion that such tests measure innate ability, stereotype threat effects suggest a potential violation of measurement invariance in the form of a systematic measurement bias based on group membership. In particular, since there is a stereotype in the United States that blacks are poor students, blacks will experience a level of threat that white students do not experience on the same task. This experience, in turn, mediates performance: the more nervous you are about the inferences others might draw about you or your group based on your individual performance, the worse you are likely to do on the test. To demonstrate this, Steele and Aronson (1995) conducted an experiment with black and white undergraduates at Stanford University. Participants were randomly assigned to one of two groups. Only the first group was told that the test they were about to take was diagnostic of ability. Thus, their threat level was increased: if they performed poorly, it could reflect poorly both on them and their whole group. As predicted, black students in the first group underperformed their matched peers in the second group: merely being told that the test they were about to take was indicative of ability led to performance decrements. Based on such findings, social psychologists argue that, rather than an innate difference derived from genetics, environmental factors such as the stigma of belonging to an ethnic minority group might be responsible for much of the observed differences between groups on intelligence tests.

While the synchronic effects of stereotype threat are not fully understood (see Stricker and Ward 2004; Wei 2012; Ganley et al. 2013 for a review on the replicability and durability of the effect), one promising line of research suggests that stereotype threat interferes with working memory capacity. As we mentioned earlier, working memory capacity is highly associated with fluid g, a domain-general process involved in many of the overlapping processes that together constitute intelligence. For example, Schmader and Johns (2003) found that compared to controls, those under either racial or gender related stereotype threat showed significant decreases in their working memory capacity. Indeed, in this study, the effect of stereotype threat on standardized test performance on a math GRE was found to be fully mediated by decreased working memory capacity. In the same vein, Beilock and Carr (2005) have shown that in scenarios where situational pressure is induced, only individuals high in working-memory capacity "choke under pressure" on math problems that demand extensive use of working memory. Ironically, it seems that the most qualified test takers are the most susceptible to stereotype threat, in large part, because, in their case, working memory capacity resources are spent on worrying about the test and how their performance on it will be interpreted by others instead of devoting these resources to actual test performance. Likewise, Beilock and DeCaro (2007) showed that individuals high (but not low) in working memory capacity suffered performance decrements when trying to solve multistep math problems under pressure because they reverted to unreliable heuristics, but that they enjoyed improved performance under pressure when trying to solve math problems for which a heuristic was the optimal strategy. As a whole, these studies provide insight into what might be interfering with performance for some groups taking intelligence tests compared to others: it is likely that differences in group performance could be the result of measurement bias (a violation of measurement invariance) rather than the manifestation of innate differences in ability.

Stereotype threat may also influence scores on intelligence tests diachronically by interfering not only with the *performance* of acquired skills but also with *learning* itself. In a dramatic demonstration of this, Taylor and Walton (2011) showed that black students who were tested in a threatening condition performed worse than white students in the same condition. They also showed, however, that black students who studied in a threatening condition performed even worse than other black students who studied in a nonthreatening condition. As Taylor and Walton put it, this suggests that stereotype threat generates a kind of "double jeopardy," in which both knowledge acquisition and knowledge manifestation suffer interference. Recall that, according to contemporary theories of intelligence, independent cognitive processes often engage in mutually beneficial interactions during cognitive development. Instances of double jeopardy like those documented by Taylor and Walton (2011) are liable to derail such virtuous feedback loops during ontogenesis (i.e., individual development).

Results like these lead Wicherts et al. (2005, 705) to conclude that "bias due to stereotype threat on test performance of the minority groups is quite serious." Whereas measured intelligence explains as much as 30 percent of the variance in numerical ability among majority test takers, it explains only 0.1 percent of the variance in numerical ability among stigmatized minorities. As they put it, "due to stereotype threat, the Numerical Ability test has become completely worthless as a measure of intelligence in the minority group" (2005, 705). This is in large part because intelligence tests are especially ineffectual in pinpointing the intelligence of highly intelligent minorities, blunting their discriminatory power.

The preceding discussion may seem unremittingly gloomy. We are therefore eager to provide some balance by pointing to interventions that have been shown to buffer against stereotype threat both synchronically and diachronically. Why do white students (especially middle- and upper-class white men) tend to fare well even in high-stakes academic tests? One theory that has recently gained purchase is that their sense of belonging in the world of elite academics shields them against the nagging concerns that mediate stereotype threat in minority students. Because they tend to be certain that they are and will be judged academically capable regardless of how they perform on any particular test, they are better able to shrug off worries about how *this* test might reflect on them or their group. By contrast, stigmatized minority students often find themselves in the precarious situation in which every mistake is taken to redound not only to their own intellectual detriment but also to the detriment of everyone else who belongs to their group. Accordingly, decreasing students' sense of belonging in academia should make them more susceptible to stereotype threat, while increasing their sense of belonging should buffer against stereotype threat. Along these lines, Walton and Cohen (2007) showed that black (but not white) students earned higher college grades when they were given an intervention that mitigated doubts about their social belonging in college.

Beyond, but also conceptually related, to academic belongingness, self-affirmation and growth mindsets have been shown to buffer against stereotype threat and academic under-achievement, respectively. An example of the former is a field study by Cohen et al. (2006), who split students in a racially mixed high school in Massachusetts into self-affirmation and other-affirmation groups. A couple of weeks into the semester, the self-affirmation group identified something they valued, then wrote for fifteen minutes about why the valued it, while the other-affirmation group identified something they did not value, then wrote for fifteen minutes about why someone else might value it. Whereas white students' grade point averages did not differ across the two conditions, black students in the self-affirmation con-dition ended up with grade point averages roughly .3 greater on a 4.0 scale—basically the difference between a B+ and an A–. This corresponds to a 40 percent decrease in the racial achievement gap at that school.

The growth mindset literature is primarily associated with Stanford psychologist Carol Dweck. Her basic idea is that intentional states directed at other intentional states dynami-cally interact with their targets, whereas intentional states directed at other types of targets typically do not. Your beliefs about your own first-order cognitive dispositions shape how those dispositions are expressed. Your beliefs about the solubility of salt do not shape how that disposition is expressed. Salt dissolves in water whether you think so or not. As Dweck and her colleagues have shown, your ability to learn partly depends on how you conceive of that ability. Dweck distinguishes two ways of conceiving of intelligence: the *entity theory*, according to which intelligence is innate and fixed, and the *incremental theory*, according to which intelligence is acquired and susceptible to improvement with effort and practice (Dweck et al. 1995). Using this distinction, she has shown that adolescents who endorse the entity theory get lower grades in school and are less interested in schoolwork (Dweck 1999), and that different regions of the brain are activated for people who endorse the entity theory when responding to mistakes: they show increased activity in the anterior frontal P3, which is associated with social comparison, and decreased activity in regions associated with the formation of new memories (Mangels et al. 2006). Together, these results suggest that peo-ple's conceptions of intelligence influence how their own intelligence is expressed.

As we saw earlier, intelligence is often conceived of as an essential and racially determined property. It stands to reason, then, that inducing people to give up the idea that intelligence is an entity might shield them from academic underachievement. In a large-scale demon-stration of this idea, Paunesku et al. (2015) used both growth-mindset and sense-of-purpose interventions through online modules in the hopes of helping students persist in the face of academic challenges. Students at risk of dropping out of high school benefited from both interventions in terms of their grades and their performance in core courses. Although the interventions were least beneficial to students who were not at risk, this result strikes an encouraging note.

The current chapter aimed to survey the race and intelligence literature and update the reader on present models and interpretations from a philosophical and psychological per-spective. Taken together, these findings provide compelling evidence regarding theories surrounding race and intelligence. We observe that, contrary to previous theories, intel-ligent behavior emerges from an interaction of abilities across several task domains, not a single unitary factor, and differences in these abilities may not result primarily from genetic inheritance. Moreover, the psychological construct working memory capacity is an impor-tant domain general factor that is related to intelligence and is disrupted when people are put into situationally stressful or stigmatizing environments—a finding that has been observed across several aspects of social identity, including racial identity. In addition, we have reviewed empirical evidence suggesting that one's domain-specific skills are learned to a larger degree than what was once thought—providing support for the importance of environment. In sum, the current chapter highlights a more nuanced interpretation than before: intelligence cannot be summarized by just a unitary factor model or the tradeoffs between nature versus nurture and overcoming the so-called 70/30 arguments directed at explaining group and individual differences in ability. On the contrary, current psychological theory demonstrates both cognitive and social factors at work in the process of producing intelligent behavior. Moreover, as it pertains to race, there is evidence that changing the way stigmatized individuals think about themselves, their abilities, and by extension, their intelligence may mitigate stereotype threat effects and bolster academic achievement and performance.

References

Aiken, L. (1996). *Assessment of Intellectual Functioning.* 2nd edition. New York: Springer.

Alfano, M. (2014). "Stereotype Threat and Intellectual Virtue." In *Naturalizing Epistemic Virtue,* edited by O. Flanagan and A. Fairweather, 155–174. New York: Cambridge University Press.

Alfano, M., and A. Skorburg. (forthcoming, 2017). "The Embedded and Extended Character Hypotheses." In *Philosophy of the Social Mind,* edited by J. Kiverstein. New York: Routledge.

Applebome, P. (1997). "Insisting It's Nothing, Creator Says SAT, Not S.A.T." *The New York Times,* April 2. Accessed May 19, 2016. http://www.nytimes.com/1997/04/02/us/insisting-it-s-nothing-creator-says-sat-not-sat.html.

Beilock, Sian L., and Thomas H. Carr. (2005). "When High-Powered People Fail Working Memory and "Choking under Pressure" in Math." *Psychological Science* 16 (2): 101–105.

Beilock, S., and M. DeCaro. (2007). "From Poor Performance to Success under Stress: Working Memory, Strategy Selection, and Mathematical Problem Solving under Pressure." *Journal of Experimental Psychology: Learning, Memory, and Cognition* 33 (6): 983–998.

Block, N. (1996). "How Heritability Misleads about Race." *Boston Review* 20 (6): 30–35.

Blumenbach, J. [1775] (1969). *On the Natural Varieties of Mankind.* New York: Bergman.

Bowden, S., D. Saklofske, and L. Weiss. (2011). "Invariance of the Measurement Model Underlying the Wechsler Adult Intelligence Scale-IV in the United States and Canada." *Educational and Psychological Measurement* 71 (1): 186–199.

Carroll, J. (1993). *Human Cognitive Abilities: A Survey of Factor-Analytic Studies.* New York: Cambridge University Press.

Cattell, R. (1949). *Culture Free Intelligence Test, Scale 1, Handbook.* Champaign, IL: Institute for Personality and Ability Testing.

Cohen, G., J. Garcia, N. Apfel, and A. Master. (2006). "Reducing the Racial Achievement Gap: A Social-Psychological Intervention." *Science* 313: 1307–1310.

Conway, A., and K. Kovacs. (2013). "Individual Differences in Intelligence and Working Memory: A Review of Latent Variable Models." *Psychology of Learning and Motivation* 58: 233–270.

Conway, A., and K. Kovacs. (2015). "New and Emerging Models of Intelligence." *Wiley Interdisciplinary Reviews: Cognitive Science* 6 (5): 419–426.

Dweck, C. (1999). *Self-Theories: Their Role in Motivation, Personality, and Development.* Philadelphia: Taylor and Francis / Psychology Press.

Dweck, C., C. Chiu, and Y. Hong. (1995). "Implicit Theories and Their Role in Judgments and Reactions: A World from Two Perspectives." *Psychological Inquiry* 6 (4): 267–285.

Fancher, R. (1985). *The Intelligence Men: Makers of the IQ Controversy.* New York: Norton.

Ganley, C., L. Mingle, A. Ryan, K. Ryan, M. Vasilyeva, and M. Perry. (2013). "An Examination of Stereotype Threat Effects on Girls' Mathematics Performance." *Developmental Psychology* 49 (10): 1886–1897.

Harman, G. (1965). "The Inference to the Best Explanation." *Philosophical Review* 74 (1): 88–95.

Herrnstein, R., and C. Murray. (1994). *The Bell Curve: Intelligence and Class Structure in American Life.* New York: Simon & Schuster.

Jensen, A. (1969). "How Much Can We Boost IQ and Scholastic Achievement?" *Harvard Educational Review* 39: 1–123.

Kaplan, J. M., and R. Grønfeldt Winther. (2014). "Realism, Antirealism, and Conventionalism about Race." *Philosophy of Science* 81 (5): 1039–1052.

Mallon, R. (2006). "'Race': Normative, Not Metaphysical or Semantic." *Ethics* 116 (3): 525–551.

Mangels, J., B. Butterfield, J. Lamb, C. Good, and C. Dweck. (2006). "Why Do Beliefs about Intelligence Influence Learning Success? A Social Cognitive Neuroscience Model." *Social Cognition and Affective Neuroscience* 1 (2): 75–86.

Matarazzo, J., and A. Wiens. (1977). "Black Intelligence Test of Cultural Homogeneity and Wechsler Adult Intelligence Scale Scores of Black and White Police Applicants." *Journal of Applied Psychology* 62 (1): 57–63.

Paunesku, D., G. Walton, C. Romero, E. Smith, D. Yeager, and C. Dweck. (2015). "Mind-Set Interventions are a Scalable Treatment for Academic Underachievement." *Psychological Science* 26 (6): 784–793.

Raven, J. (2003). "Raven Progressive Matrices." In *Handbook of Nonverbal Assessment*, edited by R. S. McCallum, 223–237. New York: Springer.

Schmader, T., and M. Johns. (2003). "Converging Evidence That Stereotype Threat Reduces Working Memory Capacity." *Journal of Personality and Social Psychology* 85 (3): 440–452.

Siegler, R. (1992). "The Other Alfred Binet." *Developmental Psychology* 28 (2): 179–190.

Spearman, C. (1904). "General Intelligence, Objectively Determined and Measured." *American Journal of Psychology* 15: 201–293.

Stanley, J. (2015). *How Propaganda Works.* Princeton, NJ: Princeton University Press.

Steele, C. M., and J. Aronson. (1995). "Stereotype Threat and the Intellectual Test Performance of African-Americans." *Journal of Personality and Social Psychology* 69: 797–811.

Stricker, L., and W. Ward. (2004). "Stereotype Threat, Inquiring about Test Takers' Ethnicity and Gender, and Standardized Test Performance." *Journal of Applied Social Psychology* 34 (4): 665–693.

Taylor, V., and G. Walton. (2011). "Stereotype Threat Undermines Academic Learning." *Personality and Social Psychology Bulletin* 37 (8): 1055–1067.

Thomason, R. (2014). "Logic and Artificial Intelligence." *The Stanford Encyclopedia of Philosophy*. Edited by Edward N. Zalta. Accessed May 19, 2016. http://plato.stanford.edu/archives/win2014/entries/logic-ai/.

Thurstone, L. (1938). *Primary Mental Abilities.* Chicago: University of Chicago Press.

Turri, J., M. Alfano, and Greco. (2016). "Virtue Epistemology." *The Stanford Encyclopedia of Philosophy*. Edited by E. Zalta. Accessed August 29, 2016. http://plato.stanford.edu/archives/

fall2016/entries/epistemology-virtue/; http://plato.stanford.edu/entries/epistemology-virtue/.

Van der Maas, H., C. Dolan, R. Grasman, J. Wicherts, H. Huizenga, and M. Raijmakers. (2006). "A Dynamic Model of General Intelligence: The Positive Manifold of Intelligence by Mutualism." *Psychological Review* 113: 842–861.

Wade, N. (2014). *A Troublesome Inheritance*. New York: Penguin.

Walton, G., and G. Cohen. (2007). "A Question of Belonging: Race, Social Fit, and Achievement." *Journal of Personality and Social Psychology* 92 (1): 82–96.

Wei, T. (2012). "Sticks, Stones, Words, and Broken Bones: New Field and Lab Evidence on Stereotype Threat." *Educational Evaluation and Policy Analysis* 34 (4): 465–488.

Wicherts, J., C. Dolan, and D. Hessen. (2005). "Stereotype Threat and Group Differences in Test Performance: A Question of Measurement Invariance." *Journal of Personality and Social Psychology* 89 (5): 696–716.

Wicherts, J. M., and C. V. Dolan. (2010). "Measurement Invariance in Confirmatory Factor Analysis: An Illustration Using IQ Test Performance of Minorities." *Educational Measurement: Issues and Practice* 29: 39–47.

Williams, R. (September 1972). "The BITCH-100: A Culture-Specific Test." American Psychological Association Annual Convention, Honolulu, Hawaii.

CHAPTER 41

"RACE" TO THE FINISH LINE

African Americans, Sports, and the "Color-Line"

JOHN H. MCCLENDON III

> Racism is not just an attitude or belief that there exist inferior and superior races. More important, it is behavior and institutions that lend material support to such attitudes and beliefs by the actual suppression of the supposed inferior group.
>
> John H. McClendon III

ALTHOUGH the philosophy of race with respect to the African American experience has considerably grown and substantially developed in the past few decades as an academic enterprise, its relationship to philosophy of sports apparently remains of minimal concern. In tandem, the subfield of philosophy of sports has demonstrated marginal interest in African Americans, and this is especially true if we compare it with work in sociology, history, and political science among other areas in the social sciences addressing athletics (Edwards 1973; McClendon and Ferguson 2012). Yet sports is a pervasive and important part of US society, with extensive economic influence. Also, sports can yield ideals and hopes as one part of contemporary life that may not be tainted by racism. However, sports in the United States have not been free of antiblack racism. Du Bois's philosophy of history shows how the "color-line" must be understood as part of the history of sports and why racism needs to be dismantled for progress through and by means of sports.

THE IMPORTANCE OF SPORTS

Sports—in its multiple dimensions—has almost a ubiquitous presence in not only contemporary black popular culture but in the society at large. Even for non–sports followers, a number of African American athletes today have household name status. Many instantly recognize the names Serena and Venus, Tiger and LeBron, not to mention long-retired athletes such as Muhammad Ali, Mike Tyson, Michael Jordan, and Magic Johnson. The image of the black athlete looms large on the landscape of communications media and cultural outlets. Furthermore, a certain kind of sports ethos, intimately linked to African American sports figures, permeates mass and popular culture.

How does this importance of sports regarding black people have an impact on the meaning of race as a dynamic social category? If "race matters" in society, can sports tell us in what way? Is the notion of racial progress applicable with respect to the status of African Americans in contemporary sports? How would we measure and thus define the progress of the black race in sports? And if we grant there is such progress, what does this mean for other aspects of African American life? Does progress in sports signal advancement in other areas of social life?

In addition to the mega-millions invested into broadcasting sports events that are predominantly black, such as the National Basketball Association (NBA) as well as the NCAA March Madness and the NFL Super Bowl, we find that sports gear—with personalized named endorsements from black athletes—has become casual attire worn to a host of venues relating to African American cultural and social activities. The ever-popular "Jordans" is a reference to the various basketball shoes of the Nike brand for the Michael Jordan line. Indeed, the iconic representation of the hip-hop generation is infused with the cultural symbols associated with sports gear. Are these signs of black progress and advancement? Have sports provided African Americans more opportunities for greater public recognition than in other sectors of society?

Sports gear is a multi-billion-dollar business. With black athletes providing star power for the marketability of sporting goods as commodities, such goods are becoming increasingly fashionable and popular, especially among the youth and including whites, and other ethnic and racial groups, as well as African Americans. Thus, the influence of corporate capitalist interests such as Nike, Under Armor, and Adidas, among others, in the structural development of sports, both amateur and professional, is essential to our understanding of contemporary sports in all of its manifestations, that is, racial, economic, social, cultural, and political (Wetzel and Yaeger 2000).

Indeed, the racial aspect of sports cannot be removed from its political economic foundation in finance monopoly capitalism on a global scale. The production and exchange of gym shoes alone is an international commodity market involving poor people of color, including but by means limited to African Americans (Slack 2005). Investigative reporting has exposed that a considerable amount of athletic shoe production is often done in sweat shops with child labor at very low wages by people of color. As recently reported,

> Now workers making Nike's Converse shoes at a factory in Indonesia say they are being physically and mentally abused. Workers at the Sukabumi plant, about 60 miles from Jakarta, say supervisors frequently throw shoes at them, slap them in the face, kick them and call them dogs and pigs ... Indonesia is Nike's third-largest manufacturing base, after China and Vietnam, with 140,000 workers at 14 contract factories. Of those, 17,000 produce its Converse line at four factories. After years of criticism over its labor practices at factories abroad, Nike in 2005 became the first major apparel company to disclose the names and locations of hundreds of plants that produce its sneakers, clothes and other products. It admitted finding "abusive treatment," either physical or verbal, in many of the Nike plants. ("Nike Workers ..." 2011)

The racial dimension of capitalism finds expression in sports both on and off the field/court. From a domestic and global perspective, we find lively debates about how race and racism are vital factors in the day-to-day business of athletics. Such polemics in sports are ever expanding and continue from the airwaves and mass media to the various neighborhood establishments where black folk gather. For instance, when in 2014 it was made public that then owner of the LA Clippers, multibillionaire Donald Sterling, made racist comments about his alleged girlfriend's association with black players, the reaction reverberated not only within the NBA but also across the country, including the pages of news media such as *The Wall Street Journal*. Despite Sterling's ouster as owner of the Clippers, and his replacement by the former AOL Time Warner CEO Richard Parsons as general manager and who is black, the issue remains today in the headlines amid ongoing court cases. Additionally, the recent trading of key black players of the Philadelphia Eagles by Chip Kelley, its white head coach, has generated intense polemics about the racial (if not racist) intent of the trade. The view has been expressed that outspoken black players are not welcomed in Philly, despite the measure of their talents (Gains 2015).

THE UNLEVEL PLAYING FIELD: CONCEPTUAL AND EMPIRICAL PROBLEMS

The *symbolic link* between race/racism with athletics is also prevalent in the popular culture. Often we find that even in conversations addressing race and racism, sports metaphors come into play. We discover that a standard expression for equal opportunity is the phrase "a level playing field" or the idea of justice as "fair play" (Early 2011). Many at a pedestrian level think of sports as the leading model for principles of meritocracy. It is proposed that if merit is a core principle in sports, cannot sports stand as a beacon for the rest of society? This, of course, presupposes that the explicit rejection of attendant forms of racism is synonymous with fair play in sports. Thus, the question, Is sports an exception to the rule of racism? Or at least, Does sports provide a more progressive and forward-looking view on race and racism?

In 2013 MLB gained considerable favorable public attention with the cinematic release of 42, the remake of the 1950 *Jackie Robinson Story*. With estimated earnings of $27.3 million for its opening weekend, the film was the best showing ever of a Hollywood production focused on baseball. The number 42 was Robinson's jersey number in the MLB and every April 12th, players throughout the MLB wear the number in tribute to Robinson and the historic date of April 12, 1947, when Robinson became the first African American in the twentieth century to play in the Majors. It is also important to note that a few black players such as Bill White and Moses Fleetwood Walker played in the MLB in the nineteenth century, before African Americans were forced out of the professional game due to the imposition of Jim and Jane Crow (Zang 1995).

Recently, sports commentator Larry Schwartz expressed the viewpoint that eight years before Ms. Rosa Parks's heroic resistance in Montgomery, Alabama, Jackie Robinson broke through the color-line in baseball. This commentator aimed to establish that Robinson's admission into the ranks of Major League Baseball (MLB) was ultimately a ground-breaking moment within the civil rights movement and a formidable blow against the color-line.

Moreover, there is the presumption that MLB was more progressive minded on the question of race than other sectors of the society. But, from the standpoint of philosophy, the plausibility and veracity of such an assessment should be justified rather than accepted as axiomatic (Schwartz n.d.).

For now, what must be kept in mind is the underlying connection of sports history with the African American struggle and the adjoining relationship to the color-line. From a conceptual standpoint, this is essentially a matter of a racial view of the philosophy of history. Implicitly, what has sometimes been elaborated are presuppositions adjoined to the philosophy of history, wherein the MLB is a guiding light of progress in matters of race. Thus, Robinson's role as player in the MLB becomes synonymous with civil rights activism, and the MLB is viewed as a pioneering equal opportunity employer. ESPN commentator Larry Schwartz states,

> Baseball might only be a game, but in the area of black and white, it often is a leader. Robinson's debut for the Dodgers in 1947 came a year before President Harry Truman desegregated the military and seven years before the Supreme Court ruled desegregation in public schools was unconstitutional. (Schwartz n.d.)

This viewpoint about baseball ignores the fact that a civil rights struggle to end segregation in baseball, extending over a decade, preceded Robinson playing as a Brooklyn Dodger. In addition to African American sports writers such as Wendell Smith and Sam Lacey, among others on the Left, Paul Robeson, Ben Davis, and Lester Rodney (sports editor for the Communist Party's *Daily Worker*) were actively engaged in fighting MLB segregation. They fought against what was dubbed as "Outlawed by Baseball! The Crime of the Big Leagues!" (Silber 2003).

Moreover, professional football—the All American Football Conference and the National Football League—had two players each join their ranks in 1946. Hence, Bill Willis, Marion Motley, Kenny Washington, and Willie Strode preceded Robinson into professional sports during the era of segregation (Gelhar 2014). Moreover, the National Basketball League (NBL), a precursor to the NBA, had individual players on different teams. And most important, the NBL had the Dayton Rens, an all-black team (Rayl 1996; Abdul-Jabbar and Obstfeld 2007).

However, when the NBA formed—out of a merger between the NBL and the Basketball Athletic Association (BAA)—the decision was made to institute the color-line, as it had been previously done in the BAA. Thus, the NBA, which is today predominantly composed of black players, began as a lily-white organization. Hence, while football and baseball permitted individual black athletes into their leagues, the NBA decided not to allow any black participation within its ranks. How in these circumstances can we put forth the proposition of black advancement in basketball?

One of the beneficiaries of the new NBA arrangement was Abe Saperstein, the owner and coach of the Harlem Globetrotters. With black players having limited professional basketball options, Saperstein held a virtual monopoly on the hiring of African American talent. Saperstein, a paternalistic racist, was convinced that the employment of a playbook and running plays was too complicated for his black players. He also believed that a meaningful wage was not necessary because the material needs of African Americans were not as high as white ballplayers (Thomas 2002).

MEASURING THE COLOR-LINE IN SPORTS

In light of the foregoing, we must ask in what way, if any, does participation in the activity of sports portend to go beyond the landscape of the racial status quo? Is there a realm of values—if you will, an axiological dimension—that sports tend to nourish that will take us to alternative modes of envisioning social relations outside of the parameters of racism? Indeed, sports victories are indicators for the outcome of athletic games, which are generally measured according to the fastest time and the highest or longest jump or throw, as well as the most points scored in an athletic contest. Here, race is ostensibly removed from athletic competition. The formal rules of the game are viewed as nonpartisan, and thus equal measure in judgment becomes overriding. Given such measuring rods, prima facie, sports does provide a "level playing field," since athletic prowess is the key to victory.

However, what does it mean to win the "race," when racism becomes an integral factor in the athletic equation? When the finish line is also what W. E. B. Du Bois describes as the "color-line"? In 1935, the events leading up to when Joe Louis fought the Italian fighter Primo Carnera amplified the connection between race, racism, and sports, precisely because it was evident that Italy was planning to invade Ethiopia in that year. Especially in the African American community, Louis became a symbol of black resistance. Louis's defeat of Carnera thus had political implications. Dr. Rayford Logan predicted, "I am afraid that the defeat of Carnera by Louis will be interpreted as an additional insult to the Italian flag, which will promote Mussolini to start again the recent attempt by Italy to annihilate Abyssinia [Ethiopia]" (Ashe 1993, 13).

The historical experiences of black athletes bring to the fore the fact that slavery was the original color-line. Most black athletic competition during slavery was dictated by white slave masters, who pitted slave against slave. The black athlete often competed in sports as a means to bring profits to slaveholders. To the extent that black slaves garnered a modicum of social advancement, it was at an individualized level for prize winnings, and sometimes on rare occasions certain slaves achieved manumission for athletic performance (Ashe 1993; McClendon and Ferguson 2012).

Black males as slaves were sometime pitted against one another in fights where the winner would be granted freedom, or if not freedom at least certain privileges not afforded to other slaves. Tom Molineaux gained his freedom when he defeated another slave by the name of Black Abe, in Richmond, Virginia. Molineaux went on to England to fight professionally under the tutelage of African American trainer and boxer Bill Richmond (Wiggins and Miller 2002, 9–13).

The solitary African American woman to compete in antebellum boxing, Sylvia Du Bois, however, was pitted against white men to bring profits for her slave master. There was no pretense that her womanhood—femininity—was an encumbrance to engaging in combat with white men. As a slave, Du Bois was property to be utilized as her master saw fit and having a black woman in physical combat with white men—unlike black males, who were not pitted against white men, lest they win—was of no social consequence (Larison and Lobdell 1998). This was related to the idea that black women as "Amazons" had more in common with men in physical stature, a view recently expressed about tennis stars Serena and Venus Williams (Rankineau 2015).

Despite Du Bois's experiences, seldom were African American slaves allowed to compete against white opponents. The notable exception was horse racing. The black jockey is a curious development in both antebellum and postbellum periods of African American life. Horse racing, in the antebellum period as a spectator sport, was followed by rich and poor, African Americans and whites, as well as men and women. Black jockeys such as Abe Hawkins, Cato, Cornelius, Austin Curtis, "Monkey" Simon, and Charles Stewart gathered notoriety and in some instances money (if not freedom) for their riding skills. A slave named Jesse was at the White House and rode horses for Andrew Jackson. The stamp of the "peculiar institution" made race and racism inseparable from the character of antebellum horse racing, and it extended throughout society (Hotaling 1999, 3–4).

In the postbellum period, horse racing became a professional sport, at least from the first Kentucky Derby in 1875. Some ten thousand in attendance and the greater majority of the jockeys were African American. Black jockey Oliver Lewis won the race on that May 17 day and Ansel Williamson, the trainer of his winning horse, Aristides, was a former slave. Lewis and Williamson set the stage for other black jockeys such as Isaac Murphy, Willie Sims, Isaac Lewis, and Jimmy Winkfield, and fifteen of the (first) twenty-eight Kentucky Derby races were won by black jockeys. Yet, over the span of twenty years, black jockeys were persistently forced out of racing. As *Plessy vs. Ferguson* (1896) legally sanctioned the color-line across the country, big (monopoly) capitalist interests also invaded horse racing to push out the black jockey. One commentator notes:

> The money also made it tougher for the small owners and trainers to survive. In Kentucky, this weakened the Black jockeys' base, since the small stables traditionally schooled most of the African-American kids. In the good old capitalist tradition, a few giants pushed everyone else out of the way . . . . Given the setting, it is nothing short of astounding that the Black jockeys were able to perform so brilliantly in the early mid-1890s. From 1889 through 1892, Goodwin's official turf guide, which gave the records of the prominent riders, would list at least 10 to 15 African-Americans out of a total of thirty-seven to fifty-six jockeys. (Hotaling 1999, 285–286)

After slavery, there was segregation. In part, it is segregation that is the focus of Du Bois's iconic expression that the history of the twentieth century would be the history of the "color-line" (Du Bois 1999, 5, 17). And that is the context for how black achievement in the sports arena can be best understood. Moreover, for many in the African American community, black sports victories over white opponents constituted explicit (public) measures for all to see, in line with the overall move forward in the black struggle, that the presuppositions undergirding the color-line could be challenged.

In baseball, from the 1920s until Jackie Robinson's entry into MLB, the Negro League players defeated white MLB participants in exhibition games nearly 66 percent of the time (Holway 2001). Despite being excluded from the existing white professional basketball leagues, the Harlem Rens, who were black owned and coached by African American coach Robert Douglass, won the basketball world championship in 1939 (Abdul-Jabbar and Obstfeld 2007). This victory came in the wake of the heavyweight championship of Joe Louis in 1937 and Jesse Owens's domination of the Berlin 1936 Olympics with four gold medals. Such sports victories were cultural highlights during the bleak conditions of the Great Depression.

The social import of black sports achievements, respecting race relations and black progress, was not lost on some civil rights activists and African American scholars. As the editor of the NAACP *Crisis*, W. E. B. Du Bois maintained a column explicitly dedicated to African American sport accomplishments. And Du Bois was not alone in such efforts concerning African Americans in sports. A. Philip Randolph devoted the pages of his *The Messenger* to African Americans in sports and Carter G. Woodson's press, The Associated Publishers, published Edwin Henderson's historic book, *The Negro in Sports* (Henderson 1911, 1949). African American newspapers covered sporting events and athletic accomplishments. Prior to Jack Johnson's defense of his world heavyweight championship, the *Chicago Defender* declared (February 5, 1910) "The Future Welfare of His People Forms a Part of the Stake" (Ashe 1993).

Considered the pinnacle of sports championships, the world heavyweight championship belt was denied to black competitors until 1908. The son of former slaves, Jack Johnson won the world championship (1908) in Sydney, Australia, defeating Tommy Burns. White consternation over a black man as heavyweight champion provoked a movement to find a "white hope" to upend Johnson's reign. Jim Jeffries, who had earlier refused to fight black fighters, came out of retirement to contest Johnson. In the wake of Johnson's championship defense with former champion Jim Jefferies in 1910, race riots broke out throughout the country and several black people were injured and killed (Gilmore 1975). Why? As Du Bois so eloquently stated: "It comes down, then, after all, to this unforgivable blackness" (Wiggins and Patrick 2002, 81). Hence, when Jack Johnson was finally allowed to compete for the heavyweight championship of the world, his winning the title was only a pyrrhic victory with respect to the color-line. Twenty-two years would pass before another black person would have the opportunity to compete and gain the world title, when Joe Louis defeated James Braddock in 1937.

On an additional note, former MLB pioneer Moses Fleetwood Walker became so disgruntled with black life behind the color-line that in the same year Johnson became the first African American world heavyweight champion (1908), Walker wrote a booklet, *Our Home Colony: A Treatise on the Past, Present, and Future of the Negro in America*. Walker outlined how African Americans were treated like colonial subjects, and he called for black people to return to Africa (Zang 1995). It should not be lost on the reader that some contemporary intellectuals argue for a notion of domestic or internal colonialism as the explanation for black status under white racism today (Pinderhughes 2011).

The color-line in sports itself brings forth a number of challenging questions. Foremost is the question, How can we determine when the time has come to write the color-line's obituary? Did Jackie Robinson's entry into MLB mark the death knell of the color-line for African Americans? If so, why did it take over a decade—Pumpsie Green joined the Boston Red Sox in 1959—after Jackie's admission before every MLB team had at least one player? Furthermore, why are there fewer African Americans in MLB today than just two decades ago? Despite Tiger Woods extraordinary accomplishments, as well as the pioneering contributions of Pete Brown, Charlie Sifford, Lee Elder, and Calvin Peete, why do we have so few African Americans on the PGA tour? How is it that since the pioneering path of Althea Gibson that black women are virtually invisible in playing golf in the Ladies Professional Golf Association (LPGA) (Sinnette 1998)? How about the decline in the number of African American coaches in professional and collegiate football? With the steady increase of African American women as student-athletes in collegiate basketball and volleyball, how many black women coaches are in the ranks of those particular sports?

One could very well argue that in many respects the color-line is alive and well in the contemporary sports arena (Miller and Wiggins 2004). Thus, the scare quotes around race, in our title, signify the metaphorical locus of the nomenclature—race. This is because the race against racism is a cardinal feature of the material context for sports and the African American experience in the United States. Although racism in sports is not limited to the United States or the African American experience—indeed, the legacy of tennis great Arthur Ashe extends to the fight against South African racism, and Jim Thorpe's plight is a notable instance of the racism faced by Native Americans (Buford 2012).

Understanding Du Bois's "Color-Line": A Problem in the Philosophy of History

While typically philosophy of sports scholars address concerns about applied ethics, social and political philosophy, and even on occasion issues relating to epistemology, seldom do they address the problems associated with the philosophy of history and its racial dimension. I contend that given that Du Bois's concept of the color-line is framed within a historical context that it, in turn, offers to disclose a substantive meaning about the nature of black identity as a racial category.

Arguably, the concept of the color-line itself is part and parcel of a racial dimension of the philosophy of history. Du Bois understands the color-line as substantively historical in character. He is alerting us that the meaning of blackness is inseparable from the historical context of the color-line. Blackness as a racial category is no mere metaphysical/social construction. Consequently with this dialectical connection between race and history, we have both historical and philosophical questions to address. Foremost, how do we conceptualize the historic meaning of the color-line in sports?

With the color-line as the backdrop, the attendant philosophy of history has as its object of investigation the idea of black advancement or progress in history. It is understood that African American advancement or progress is to be measured according to how the color-line is confronted, resisted, and broken. Given this crucial theoretical nexus on our examination of racism and sports, we must be clear as to what is meant by philosophy of history. Philosophy of history in its method of inquiry, as a branch of philosophy, is primarily *conceptual* rather than *empirical*. The philosophy of history is, subsequently, a second-order inquiry into the very meaning of the subject matter of history itself.

Although historical research uncovers facts to ground its interpretations, philosophy of history has a different set of tasks. First, it critically evaluates historical presumptions, evaluations, and judgments. Second, philosophy of history also makes assumptions about the truth of specified interpretations for the expressed purpose of founding broader generalizations about historical events and processes. Third, philosophy of history is both speculative and practical. As speculative inquiry, it seeks to attain the grand sweep and scope of history; and in its practical aspect it makes suggestions as to what is to be done based on considerations about the meaning and lessons of history (McClendon and Ferguson 2012, 85–108).

THE JACKIE ROBINSON MYTH

On what basis can we presume that Jackie Robinson's entry into the MLB is commensurate with Rosa Parks and her stand that led to the Montgomery bus boycott? How do both of these events enter into the equation of black progress and advancement respecting the color-line? On the one hand, Robinson's admission was based on the strategy of "entry without confrontation with racism" in baseball. Dodger President Branch Rickey thought the *plan of action* was to take *no action* against the racist assaults and abuse that Robinson faced, not to mention Rickey's benign neglect of the structural character of racism in the MLB.

Ricky's viewpoint of methodological individualism (a theoretical assumption that structures reduce to individual actions) effectively neglected the institutional nature of the problem. Subsequently, moral suasion leading to white acceptance of Robinson—as an individual black person—was a strategy that took precedence over confronting the MLB and its institutionalized racism and adjoining power relations. The reality of the racist color-line in the MLB did not end with Robinson's admission. The myth that Robinson broke through the color-line obscures the historical record respecting race and sports.

As the empirical study by Brian L. Goff, Robert E. McCormick, and Robert D. Tollison demonstrates, whatever Ricky's intentions, he found it "advantageous to incorporate additional and potentially more productive inputs previously unavailable due to law, custom, or managerial discretion" because of the "profit opportunities offered by integration" (Goff et. al. 2002, 16). To overlook the profit motive as a central dynamic of racial integration further obscures the historical record respecting capitalism, racism and sports. It is worth noting that similar processes are at work in the decline of African American baseball players in relationship to the increase of Latino baseball players. Owners of baseball teams view Latino players as potentially more "productive inputs," who bring the possibility of more wins and realizing more profits.

On the other hand, Mrs. Parks not only personally confronted the very institution of segregated mass transportation but also in the wake of her actions a mass movement (boycott) emerged that was carried out at great sacrifice on the part of the Montgomery African American community. This mass strike for over one year, driven by the political will of Montgomery's black working class, actually demolished the color-line in Montgomery's public transportation. The focal point of their struggle was direct nonviolent confrontation with racist institutions of power. Organizationally the movement grew from the Montgomery Improvement Association (MIA) into the Southern Christian Leadership Conference (SCLC) headed by Ella "Ma" Baker and Martin Luther King Jr. (Ransby 2003).

However, nothing comparable emerged within the MLB to fight its own racism. Hence, we discover that when Jackie Robinson was inducted into the Baseball's Hall of Fame at Cooperstown, New York, he harshly criticized the MLB for its failure to hire at least one African American general manager. Robinson's criticism was an open admission that the color-line in baseball was alive and well (in 1962) some fifteen years after his entry as a player in 1947. It was not until 1975 that Frank Robinson became the first MLB black general manager, three years after the death of Jackie Robinson (Robinson 1975, 103–106, 108, 110).

What is overlooked by most commentators on professional baseball is that Rube Foster, the founder of the Negro National League, envisioned that dismantling institutionalized racism via the MLB would require the integration, not of solitary individuals, but rather of complete teams from the Negro leagues. In that manner, the balance of power would substantially change for inclusion and that would entail players, coaches, managers, owners, and other officials of the game. The Foster plan recognized that if the color-line was to be dismantled, then the power behind the institution had to be radically altered in real structural and institutional terms. Hence the opening epigraph, "Racism is not just an attitude or belief that there exist inferior and superior races. More important, it is behavior and institutions that lend material support to such attitudes and beliefs by the actual suppression of the supposed inferior group," is pivotal in our analysis of whether or not we can now write the obituary of the color-line.

Have African American achievements in sports effectively overturned institutionalized racism in athletics? In a penetrating article, "The Meaning of Serena Williams," Claudia Rankineau astutely observes, "There is a belief among some African-Americans that to defeat racism, they have to work harder, be smarter, be better. Only after they give 150% will white Americans recognize black excellence for what it is" (Rankineau 2015, MM39). At the foundation for such assumptions is the notion that white recognition is the anchor for black excellence. It is not enough to just win the race to demonstrate excellence; there is the additional burden of winning over white people to acknowledge this excellence.

However, if black excellence is contingent upon white acceptance, then how far have we come in dismantling the influence of white power? In determining the measure of black achievement or excellence, does institutionalized racism continue to rule over the formal grounds of the "race" game? Is not one of the key functions of the color-line the exercise of white power over black people? Lastly, is the black athlete powerless in changing the attitudes and beliefs of white racists if this is ultimately contingent upon white acceptance rather than black excellence? And, if white acceptance is the pivotal concept, then power does not rest in the hands of black people. It seems the Foster plan understood the material reality about the nature of the "race" to the finish line/color-line.

REFERENCES

Abdul-Jabbar, Kareem, and Raymond Obstfeld. (2007). *On the Shoulders of Giants.* New York: Simon & Schuster.

Ashe, Arthur R. (1993). *A Hard Road to Glory: Boxing, The African-American Athlete in Boxing.* New York: Amistad.

Buford, K. (2012). *Native American Son: The Life and Sporting Legend of Jim Thorpe.* Lincoln: University of Nebraska Press.

Du Bois, W. E. B. (1999). *The Souls of Black Folk: Authoritative Text, Contexts, Criticism.* Edited by Henry Louis Gates and T. H. Oliver. New York: W.W. Norton.

Early, Gerald. (2011). *A Level Playing Field: African American Athletes and the Republic of Sports.* Cambridge, MA: Harvard University Press.

Edwards, Harry. (1973). *Sociology of Sport.* Homewood, IL: Dorsey Press.

Gains, C. (2015). "Ex-Eagles Running Back LeSean McCoy accuses Chip Kelly of Getting Rid of 'All the Good Black Players.'" *Business Insider.* Accessed August 1, 2015. http://www.businessinsider.com/philadelphia-eagles-lesean-mccoy-chip-kelly-2015-5.

Gelhar, Alex. (2014). "'Forgotten Four' Artfully Depicts Pro Football Integration in 1946." *NFL. com.* Accessed August 14, 2015. http://www.nfl.com/news/story/0ap3000000392534/article/forgotten-four-artfully-depicts-pro-football-integration-in-1946.

Gilmore, A-T. (1975). *Bad Nigger!: The National Impact of Jack Johnson*. Port Washington, NY: Kennikat Press.

Goff, Brian L., Robert E. McCormick, and D. T. Robert. (2002). "Racial Integration as an Innovation: Empirical Evidence from Sports Leagues." *American Economic Review* 92 (1): 16–26.

Henderson, Edwin B. (1911). "The Colored College Athlete." *Crisis* (July): 115–118.

Henderson, Edwin B. (1949). *The Negro in Sports*. Washington, DC: Associated Publishers.

Holway, J. (2001). *The Complete Book of Baseball's Negro Leagues: The Other Half of Baseball History*. Fern Park, FL: Hastings House Publishers.

Hotaling, E. (1999). *The Great Black Jockeys: The Lives and Times of the Men Who Dominated America's First National Sport*. Rocklin, CA: Forum.

Larison, Cornelius Wilson, and Jared Lobdell. (1998). *Sylvia Du Bois: A Biografy of a Slave Who Whipt Her Mistres and Gand Her Freedom*. Oxford: Oxford University Press.

McClendon, John H., and Stephen C. Ferguson. (2012). *Beyond the White Shadow*. Dubuque, IA: Kendall Hunt.

Miller, Patrick B., and David K. Wiggins. (2004). *Sport and the Color Line*. New York: Routledge.

"Nike Workers 'Kicked, Slapped and Verbally Abused' at Factories Making Converse." (2011). *Daily Mail*, July 13. Accessed August 1, 2015. http://www.dailymail.co.uk/news/article-2014325/Nike-workers-kicked-slapped-verbally-abused-factories-making-Converse-line Indonesia.html#ixzz3k7z2MywJ.

Pinderhughes, Charles. (2011). "Toward a New Theory of Internal Colonialism." *Socialism and Democracy* 25 (1): 235–256.

Rankineau, Claudia. (2015). "The Meaning of Serena Williams: On Tennis and Black Excellence." *New York Times Magazine*. Accessed August 27, 2015. http://www.ny times.com/2015/08/30/magazine/the-meaning-of-serena-williams.HTML?.

Ransby, B. (2003). *Ella Baker and the Black Freedom Movement: A Radical Democratic Vision*. Chapel Hill: University of North Carolina Press.

Rayl, Susan J. (1996). *The New York Renaissance Professional Basketball Team, 1923–1950*. PhD dissertation, Pennsylvania State University.

Robinson, Louie. (1975). "Frank Robinson Makes Baseball History." *Ebony* 30 (6): 103–106, 108, 110, 113.

Schwartz, Larry. (n.d.). "Jackie Changed Face of Sports." *ESPN.com*. Accessed July 2, 2015. http://espn.go.com/sportscentury/features/00016431.html.

Silber, Irwin. (2003). *Press Box Red*. Philadelphia: Temple University Press.

Sinnette, Calvin. (1998). *Forbidden Fairways*. Chelsea, MI: Sleeping Bear Press.

Slack, Trevor. ed. (2005). *The Commercialisation of Sport*. New York: Routledge.

Thomas, Ron. (2002). *They Cleared the Lane*. Lincoln: University of Nebraska Press.

Wetzel, Dan, and Don Yaeger. (2000). *Sole Influence*. New York: Warner Books.

Wiggins, David G., and Patrick B. Miller. (2002). *The Unlevel Playing Field*. Urbana: University of Illinois Press.

Zang, David W. (1995). *Fleetwood Walker's Divided Heart*. Lincoln: University of Nebraska Press.

PART IX

....

PUBLIC POLICY, POLITICAL PHILOSOPHY, AND LAW

....

MOST philosophers of race would claim that public policy regarding US race relations has favored whites at the expense of nonwhites. Historically, such public policy has formed as the result of societal practice, for example, slavery and segregation, that was legitimized in local, state, and national law. The most striking example of racist law was the original US Constitution stipulation that slave populations would count as three-fifths for apportioning congressional representation and taxation (Article 1, Section 2, Paragraph 3). Racially unjust public policy and law have been corrected through constitutional amendments, for instance the Civil War Constitutional Amendments XIII, IV, and XV, or by the US Supreme Court, as in *Brown v. Board of Education*. These ultimate legal changes have in principle resulted in new public policies, including the illegality of racially segregated schools and residential neighborhoods. However, the temporal sequence of societal practice, public policy, highest legal decision, and then new public policy is hardly a structural cycle of progress, because there has not been reliable or constant progress in the history of US race relations. (Schools and residential neighborhood remain racially segregated.)

The contemporary conjunction of formal equality as a result of the 1960s civil rights and immigration reform legislation, with ongoing nonwhite disadvantages, is an insistent paradox. After Barack Obama took office as the first African American President of the United States, the number of white supremacist organizations increased almost tenfold and anti-immigration sentiment intensified. There have been unprecedented numbers of highly publicized homicides by police against unarmed young black men. Rates of nonwhite incarceration and residential segregation are at all-time highs, as are income and wealth disparities between white and nonwhite households. Many progressives believe that this situation is the result of "backlash" against previously achieved progress in race relations; others have described proactive conservative or reactionary obstacles to the extension and protection of civil rights for minorities, such as the War on Drugs. Political observers have also criticized early twenty-first century trends that diminish voting rights for the poor and elderly, with disproportionate effects on minorities, for instance in new state requirements for photo IDs at the polls. Also, speculation abounds about a growing lack of confidence in the good will of white political leaders toward black constituents, for example in the slow and inadequate federal response to mostly black victims of Hurricane Katrina, in 2005. Many nonwhites are described as having lost faith in the ability of present democratic processes to represent their economic interests. High rates of unemployment in poor black neighborhoods persist, in contrast to recovery from the Great Recession of 2007–2008, in other places and populations.

We should note that the legal and public policy disadvantages attending nonwhite race are neither limited to blacks within the United States nor to distinctively American forms of oppression on an international level. For instance, immigration policy has consistently favored people from Northern Europe, even after the Immigration and Nationality Act of 1965 opened US borders to new waves of entrants from Asia and South and Central America. Racial prejudice against undocumented immigrants from Mexico has accompanied resurgence of early twentieth-century populist and nativist ideology, along with the activist Minuteman Project, begun in 2004 and xenophobic conservative rhetoric during the 2016 presidential campaign. Decisive legislation pertaining to undocumented immigration is pending as of this writing.

Native American spokespersons and advocates have consistently stressed the importance of retaining or reclaiming some measure of internal sovereignty. Unlike African Americans and immigrants, they have been less concerned with sharing the goods of majority life than maintaining resources for their own self-sufficient traditional lifestyles. Few treaty provisions protecting Native American land rights have been honored by the US federal government, leading to the irony that some Indian tribes have been able to retain their traditional lands only through profits from running gambling casinos on reservations, in states where gambling is otherwise illegal. By contrast, on a global level, the nonwhite poor constitute cheap labor for multinational corporations or clients for development projects. These populations are also the most vulnerable to physical harm in natural disasters and dislocation due to civil wars, and territorial and political disputes between neighboring states.

African American pessimism regarding antiracism was discussed in Part VI, and confidence in social constructions of positive nonwhite identities was not robust throughout the essays of Part VII. The analyses of contemporary social issues involving racial disparities in Part VIII were not enthusiastically optimistic. Sober reassessments of the role of law in correcting racial injustice are undertaken by the authors in this part. It should of course be kept in mind that legal changes are subject to political and social climates that are difficult to predict, so that even extreme changes in federal law or court rulings may not be implemented in reality.

David Lyons's "Reparations for Slavery and Jim Crow" examines the historical effects of past oppression. Although slavery was abolished in 1865, racial subordination was maintained under Jim Crow, and those wrongs have caused lasting harms. Slavery and Jim Crow were total systems predicated on a persisting ideology of white supremacy. Lyons claims that governments, institutions, and corporations are morally accountable today, if they supported or profited from slavery or Jim Crow in the past. Contemporary reparations might include cash payments, but moral wrongs are not fully repaired by material compensation. Overall, reparations should enable those wronged to rebuild their lives, free of oppressive racism.

In "Race, Rectification, and Apology," Rodney Roberts calls attention to "rectificatory justice" as a subject of political philosophy, with specific focus on the rectification of the racial injustices perpetrated against Africans and people of African descent. Rectificatory justice sets unjust situations right, and apology is an important aspect of that undertaking, along with restoration, compensation, and punishment.

Roberts here examines the relationship between rectification and apology. He notes that "philosophers have often burdened the notion of apology with emotional requirements and the assumption that reconciliation is the proper aim of an apology." However, a clarification of rectificatory justice, including a conception of apology that is grounded in justice, suggests that emotional requirements, for example, sorrow and regret sincerely expressed, are not necessary. Moreover, reconciliation need not be the goal of the expression or performance of apology. According to Roberts, the just apology expresses respect:

> The *wrong* of injustice is the disrespect shown to another when that person's rights are violated. Acknowledging that what one has done is wrong entails an acknowledgment that the person affected by the act is undeserving of the treatment given. By apologizing the perpetrator reaffirms that the victim is a person and is therefore worthy of respect.

Roberts shows how according to these relevant measures, the apology to African Americans by the US Congress in 2009 failed as a legitimate apology.

Tina Botts provides an analysis of the US Supreme Court's idea of race, which can be inferred from its application of the Equal Protection Clause of the Fourteenth Amendment. (The Equal Protection Clause precludes biased treatment of individuals by government officials, but it is vague in that government officials usually have discretion in deciding how to fulfill their duties.) Botts claims that as equal protection law developed over the twentieth century, the Supreme Court's concept of race moved from sociocultural/sociohistorical aspects of race to biological ones. During the same time, the humanistic and scientific view of race moved in the opposite direction, as essentialist biological notions of race were replaced with analyses of race as social constructions. That is, the solely biological meaning of race seems to be in the background of the Court's rulings in recent affirmative action cases that there be no preferences for admissions or hires on the basis of race alone. If race is only biological, then it is not also historical. As a result, the ongoing effects of past discrimination cannot be taken into account in crafting contemporary policies, because to do that would favor nonwhites at the expense of whites. But formal equality has been taken to mean that unjust history is no longer relevant, implying that there is little remaining race-based injustice that needs to be corrected. Indeed, the court's reasoning has been that any "unnecessary" consideration of race becomes invidious or unfair, regardless of whether minority or majority races are considered. If Botts is correct about the Court's restricted view of race, according to that view, racial integration or diversity is no more than variety only and not very important, again, because formal equality is presumed to preclude discrimination.

Suppose, as the US Supreme Court seems to, that fairness and justice exist, given and guaranteed with the formal equality of the 1960s civil rights legislation. Suppose further that "race" refers only to differences in skin color, with historical injustice having no legacy. It could plausibly be concluded that race-related disparities in achievement are the result of individual choices, including perhaps, values that do not support achievement within minority cultures. This is the conservative view of disparities in well-being among racial groups at this time, and it is consistent with an attitude of blaming nonwhites themselves for whatever disadvantages they experience that might otherwise be attributed to structural or institutional, as well as individual prejudice and discrimination.

Progressives tend to have a more historically comprehensive social picture that seeks causes for disparities that are not the moral responsibility of individuals less well off. If disparities are the result of structural inequalities, then inequalities are unjust and solutions to them need to be sought on a structural level. Affirmative action policies in higher education were intended to accomplish that, because in the United States, education has been the single most important means for socioeconomic advancement. The reasoning in support of affirmative action was that if minority identities were affirmed in higher education admissions policies, not only would additional individuals given access to higher education be better off, but they would also become leaders and help other members of their groups. However, these cultural, as well as historical, arguments for affirmative action have been rejected by the US Supreme Court since the late 1970s. The result has been a weak support of diversity or a mix of different racial identities on college campuses, not so much to help minorities or otherwise correct injustice, but because racial variety in a college setting is of benefit to members of majority groups. White college graduates will be better able to perform their jobs in business, the professions, and the military, if they have had experience with nonwhites.

In "Affirmative Action for the Future" James Sterba begins by noting that the goal of *diversity affirmative action*, the most widely implemented form of affirmative action at present, is simply diversity that has its own benefits in educational and work contexts. However, even when universities have implemented measures to increase racial diversity, lawsuits by white students claiming "reverse discrimination" have been successful and curtailed those efforts. Sterba claims that, nevertheless, educational institutions are morally obligated to respond to discrimination in the wider society. But such a response need not require race-based diversity as a form of identity. Sterba advocates future programs that will bring students of any race to campus who have witnessed, as well as personally experienced, discrimination.

In "Ideal, Nonideal, and Empirical theories of Social Justice," I argue that ideals of justice may do little toward the correction of injustice in real life. The influence of John Rawls's *A Theory of Justice* has led some philosophers of race to focus on "nonideal theory" as a way to bring conditions in unjust societies closer to conditions of justice described by ideal theory. However, a more direct approach to injustice may be needed to address unfair public policy and existing conditions for minorities in racist societies. *Applicative justice* describes the applications of principles of justice that are now "good enough" for whites, to nonwhites (based on prior comparisons of how whites and nonwhites are treated).

FURTHER READING

Bell, Derek. (1987). *And We Are Not Saved: The Elusive Quest for Racial Justice*. New York: Basic Books.

Churchill, Ward. (1994). *Indians are US? Culture and Genocide in Native North America*. Monroe, ME: Common Courage.

Corlett, J. Angelo. (2003). *Race, Racism, and Reparations*. Ithaca, NY: Cornell University Press.

McCarthy, Thomas. (2009). *Race, Empire and the Idea of Human Development*. Cambridge: Cambridge University Press.

McGary, Howard, and Bill E. Lawson. (1992). *Between Slavery and Freedom*. Bloomington: Indiana University Press.

Pinckney, Darryl. (2014). *Blackballed: The Black Vote and US Democracy*. New York: New York Review of Books.

....

CHAPTER 42

REPARATIONS FOR SLAVERY AND JIM CROW

Its Assumptions and Implications

....

DAVID LYONS

I develop the case for reparations to African Americans today, based on wrongdoing that began with slavery. Critics of such claims remind us that slavery was abolished a century and a half ago; no one who was either a slave or a slave holder is alive today; and moral culpability cannot be inherited, from which they infer that the time for reparations is long past (Brophy 2006). Defenders of reparations reply that racial subordination did not end with the abolition of slavery but was maintained under Jim Crow; that the wrongs of those systems have caused deeply entrenched, lasting harms; and that state and federal governments, as well as some of today's corporations, universities, and individuals, are morally accountable because they helped establish or support slavery or Jim Crow or have profited from them (Coates 2014).

References to the harms that were caused by slavery and that were sustained or caused by Jim Crow may suggest that reparations could consist of cash payments to compensate for any persisting harms. Cash payments would seem an important component of reparations, but I will suggest that they would not suffice. On the one hand, moral wrongs are not reducible to material harms and cannot be fully repaired by material compensation. On the other hand, slavery and Jim Crow were not just a collection of wrongs, such as unpaid labor and poor housing. They were all-encompassing systems that prevented African Americans from developing their interests, their intellects, and indeed their lives as they were morally entitled to do. This subordination of African Americans was justified by a profoundly insulting ideology of white supremacy that has greatly affected American culture and has contaminated the attitudes of whites and blacks. A morally adequate program of reparations would enable the survivors of those systems to rebuild their lives, free of oppressive racism, as far as that is possible.

The argument proceeds as follows: The first section reviews the historical background. The second section discusses the moral considerations that underlie reparations claims. The third section suggests what reparations were due when slavery was abolished. The fourth section extends that reasoning by suggesting what reparations were called for when Jim Crow was officially abolished and what is called for today. The final section notes some wider implications of the moral considerations that are assumed by the reparations argument.

THE HISTORY

English colonists on mainland North America adopted slavery by the 1630s (Takaki 2008; Lyons 2013). Virginia and its neighboring colonies focused on the profitable business of raising tobacco and other cash crops for export. Indentured servants initially provided the labor, but the colonial elite soon decided to rely primarily on slaves, most of whom came, directly or indirectly, from Africa.

In the late eighteenth century or shortly thereafter, many of the newly independent states abolished slavery. At the same time, they ratified a Constitution that supported slavery (agreeing, for example, to return escaped slaves). Slave labor became the foundation of southern economic growth and prosperity, which in the antebellum period exceeded that of the North. Slave-grown cotton became America's leading export, its total value greater than all other exports taken together (Kolchin 1995, 95, 194).

By 1865, when slavery was abolished, America was the inhospitable home to 4 million slaves. Following emancipation, legal reforms enabled African Americans to vote, hold public office, and serve on juries, despite violent resistance by supporters of racial subordination. Federal troops routed terrorist organizations that sought to overthrow Reconstruction. But the government soon abandoned those efforts. In 1877, federal troops ceased enforcing Reconstruction laws. Federal courts subsequently weakened the new constitutional amendments and laws that sought to secure African Americans' legal rights (Foner 1989).

As the former slaves received no reparations for their enslavement (not even the "40 acres and a mule" that some were loaned during the Civil War; Foner 1989, 70–71), they lacked the wherewithal to realize the promises of emancipation. Most became sharecroppers for plantation owners whose fraudulent accounting kept them perpetually in debt. With force, fraud, and strength of numbers, white supremacists regained control of southern governments, which then revised their laws in order to exclude African Americans from the ballot box, public office, and jury service. Federal courts accepted the enactments so long as they were superficially race-neutral. The Supreme Court approved state-sponsored racial segregation, on the condition that separate facilities be equal, which was openly flouted.

Throughout the nation, inequality and oppression were imposed. African Americans could be killed or assaulted with impunity, as there was no owner to compensate for the loss and no chance of officials intervening. The ever-present threat of lynching was a crucial means of racial resubordination, especially in the 1890s, when thousands were lynched (Zangrando 1980). Pogroms destroyed black communities that appeared to prosper (Browne-Marshall 2013, 66–72). The result was an exceedingly cruel and degrading system that subjected African Americans to indignities, assaults, and oppressive social practices that openly expressed profoundly insulting white supremacist ideology. Many southern blacks who were able to escape the South migrated North or West, greatly enlarging black communities in cities across the United States (Wilkerson 2010). There they confronted systematic discrimination in housing, education, and employment, which led to the creation of black urban "ghettos" and deeply entrenched racial stratification (Martin and Yaquinto 2007).

The development of industrial unions and New Deal programs during the 1930s brought some benefits to black workers and their families. During World War II many Americans saw that Jim Crow resembled the racism of America's wartime foes, such as Nazi Germany, and civil rights campaigns received wider support. Those efforts were intensified as black veterans of the segregated armed forces returned home unwilling to accept second-class citizenship (Dittmer 1994, chap. 1). President Truman created a Committee on Civil Rights, which catalogued Jim Crow's inequities: African Americans had substantially less access to medical care than European Americans, much higher infant mortality, and lower life expectancy; inferior housing and schools; restricted access to jobs, skilled trades, and professions; much lower wages for comparable work, much higher unemployment rates, much longer periods of unemployment, and much lower family income. They were subjected to police brutality and to widespread bias in the legal system (President's Committee 1947).

During the postwar period, America competed with the Soviet Union around the world. Each sought military alliances with the newly independent, postcolonial nations of Asia and Africa, as well as their resources and markets. America's reputation among peoples of color and its global aspirations were threatened when images were broadcast abroad of peacefully demonstrating African Americans who sought to exercise their legal rights being met with official violence on US soil. In that context, the federal government denounced white supremacy. The Supreme Court ruled against state-sponsored racial segregation and Congress enacted significant civil rights legislation, which federal courts upheld and the executive branch enforced. African Americans were elected and appointed to public office in greater numbers, and opportunities increased in education and the workplace (Franklin and Moss 1994, 528).

But federal interest in reform was once again limited, in both scope and duration. As to scope: the reforms failed to address entrenched inequalities, such as the consequences of Jim Crow housing policies. For decades, government agencies, banks, and insurers had intensified the impact of segregation by making private homes more expensive and often unaffordable for African Americans. Black families' resulting lack of financial resources blocked upward mobility and left them without funds when they faced illness, unemployment, and other emergencies. De facto segregation was further intensified as government at all levels supported programs of "urban renewal," which reduced the stock of affordable housing, and constructed highways that facilitated "white flight" from urban centers to racially restrictive suburbs. Housing reforms were promised, but when the Fair Housing Act was enacted in 1968, it lacked enforcement provisions; and when they were added, in 1988, they were not funded. After federal courts ruled against racial segregation in public housing, funding for housing projects disappeared (Massey and Denton 1993; Oliver and Shapiro 2006).

By the 1980s, despite continuing widespread poverty, Congress began reducing antipoverty programs. Affordable housing programs were neglected. Government policies intensified unequal rates of arrest, conviction, and incarceration, which disrupted black families, reduced their housing options, and extinguished employment opportunities. The effects led some scholars to speak of a "new Jim Crow" (Alexander 2010). As if to confirm this interpretation of events, a number of states adopted voting restrictions that seem clearly aimed at excluding people with limited resources from the polls, including many African Americans. And, despite those developments, the Supreme Court weakened the Voting Rights Act (*Shelby County v. Holder* 570 US [2013]).

MORAL CONSIDERATIONS

The history recounted in the first section supports a moral argument for reparations (understood as compensation for wrongful injury, as distinct from compensation more generally, which repairs loss that is suffered for any reason, and from restitution, which relinquishes gains that were derived from wrongdoing, not necessarily that of the beneficiary). As both slavery and Jim Crow involved such practices as morally unwarranted imprisonment, coercion, and homicide, rape, torture, and mutilation, they clearly violated the moral requirement that we treat others with consideration and respect, including those with whom we have no established relationships and to whom we have made no binding commitments. The moral wrongs of slavery and Jim Crow involved economic, physical, and psychological harms, many of which have had profound, lasting effects on African Americans today, such as the wealth gap between black and white families, which stems from income differences combined with discriminatory housing policies.

Morality calls for the repair of such wrongs, within moral as well as practical limits. Individuals may be morally required to repair, or to help repair, the wrongs, for at least three different reasons: first, because they helped initiate or supported slavery or Jim Crow; second, because they failed to combat such practices when it was incumbent on them to do so; and third, because they profited from them. Regarding those in the first category, although no one who supported chattel slavery in America is alive today, some individuals are alive who supported Jim Crow or who have worked to maintain racial subordination. Perhaps more important, for present purposes, institutions, such as governments, universities, and for-profit corporations, which can last for generations, acquire moral responsibility for their acts and policies and their predictable consequences. Thus, President Clinton properly apologized on behalf of the US government in 1997 for the Tuskegee syphilis study of 1932–1972 (which misinformed poor blacks of their illness and denied them effective treatment when it became available; Washington 2006, chap. 7); and Congress did right in 1993 by apologizing to the people of Hawaii for the US government's part in the overthrow of the Hawaiian government a century earlier (US Public Law 103-150). Second, we are morally required not only to act justly and avoid supporting injustice but also to help combat systematic injustice, as the moral stakes require and circumstances allow. This suggests that many Americans were culpable for failing to help end or ameliorate slavery or Jim Crow when the stakes were sufficient to justify the risks involved. It would not have been unduly dangerous for many more Americans to have supported the antislavery movement than actually did so, and the same could be said even more emphatically of the civil rights movement that challenged Jim Crow. To this we may add that ignorance that is caused by the failure to pay adequate attention to systematic injustices of which one is vaguely aware and to which attention can be paid without much difficulty does not nullify one's culpability for failing to address such egregious social wrongs. Third, we can be morally required to relinquish wrongful gains—benefits that stem from wrongdoing that is not necessarily our own. For example, the otherwise blameless child of a slave owner whose inheritance stemmed partly from slave labor would have been morally required to relinquish the relevant portion of that legacy. And those who have benefitted from discrimination against African Americans may now be required to share the resulting advantages with those who have suffered the discrimination or its consequences.

Reparations are due those who suffer directly or indirectly from slavery or Jim Crow or the harms they have caused. But moral wrongs are not reducible to material harms. On the one hand, people can suffer harms when no one is at fault, when caused by accidents or natural events; on the other hand, repairing material harms, such as economic losses, cannot fully repair moral wrongs, such as rape, torture, the forcible division of families, unwarranted contempt, and the denial of dignity. At the very least, those who are culpable must also acknowledge and apologize for their wrongdoing. Furthermore, reparations for slavery and Jim Crow should maximize the autonomy of its beneficiaries, for example, by enabling them to decide how to use cash payments (Martin and Yaquinto 2007).

Two final points. First, given the egregious wrongs of slavery and Jim Crow and their legacy of deeply entrenched harms, it might seem that compensation and restitution under a morally adequate reparations program could impoverish many Americans. It should therefore be noted that what may properly be demanded of individuals is limited by considerations of humanity as well as justice. All persons must be treated with dignity and due consideration, so that no one, including wrongdoers, should be impoverished by the reparations programs. Second, someone who was or still is entitled to reparations, such as a former slave or an African American who has lived under Jim Crow or who has suffered its persisting harms, may be said to have (or to have had) a valid moral claim to compensation. As we have noted, however, the former slaves received no reparations following emancipation. Some defenders of reparations today may reason that, as the reparations that were morally required were not forthcoming, moral claims to reparations have been passed down, like property, from one generation to the next, until they are honored (Boxill 2016, sec. 8). On this view, such an inherited moral claim could soundly be asserted today, quite independently of any continuing harms. No such reasoning is assumed in the argument that follows. The idea that such moral credits can be passed from one generation to another seems no more plausible than the idea that moral culpability can be inherited by a descendant of a wrongdoer. In what follows, neither principle is assumed.

1865

What should a reparations program have been like when slavery was abolished? One approach would have been to provide the former slaves with funds equivalent to the cash value of the wrongs that were imposed by slavery. That would have enabled those who should have benefitted most directly to decide how best to do so.

The initial problem when contemplating this approach would be to determine the rates at which compensation should be paid. Consider a relatively simple example: compensation for unpaid labor under slavery. We might imagine that the amount owed to a former slave was the product of the duration of unpaid labor and the prevailing rate for the same sort of work among free workers at the time (plus interest, in view of the delay of the payment). But it is unclear what prevailing rate should be used, or even whether compensation at a prevailing rate would be fair. On the one hand, free black workers were paid less than whites for the same work; on the other hand, it is possible that the prevailing rates for white workers when slavery dominated the economic system were depressed by the prevalence of slave labor. These considerations suggest that compensation to the former slaves for their unpaid labor should be more generous than might initially seem appropriate.

A more serious problem is that such compensation should not be regarded as settling the moral account for unpaid labor under slavery. For an essential aspect of slave labor is that it is coerced without moral justification, and the wrong of unjustifiably coercing someone is independent of wrongfully withholding compensation from that person (because compensation can be wrongfully withheld for labor that is not coerced—a problem that is faced today by many workers). Furthermore, coercion has no standard cash equivalent.

The problem here is quite general: moral wrongs are not reducible to the material harms they involve, so the wrongs of slavery could not be repaired simply by compensating the former slaves for the material harms done. Furthermore, morality does not determine appropriate cash payments for any moral wrongs, including the wrongs of slavery, which range from wrongfully separating parents from their children to rape.

I do not mean to dismiss cash payments. In our society and many others, they are conventionally made to acknowledge wrongdoing. This suggests that a morally acceptable reparations program would have included substantial cash payments for all ex-slaves, and I shall assume that hereafter. But how might these be determined? By a fair process of negotiations in which the former slaves or their chosen representatives were among the principal participants.

So far we have looked at reparations for slavery as if it could consist in the piecemeal repair of a diverse collection of wrongs. But repairing the wrongs done by slavery in America could not be like returning an item that was stolen, repairing a piece of property that one has carelessly damaged, and so on, down the line of injuries. African Americans under slavery were denied the opportunity to develop their lives under the freedom and with the resources to which they were morally entitled as human beings. They accordingly had a valid moral claim to be enabled to rebuild their lives as far as that was possible. The claim would have held against American governments at all levels and many individuals who had supported slavery; many individuals, universities, and businesses who had profited from it; and all those who failed to help end slavery or ameliorate its wrongs when it was morally incumbent on them to take such action. The institutions and individuals who were thus morally liable were morally obligated to contribute to a reparations program that would have enabled the former slaves to rebuild their lives, as far as that was possible.

A morally adequate reparations program in 1865 would have included, first of all, the provision of services to address the former slaves' most urgent needs, such as aid to trauma victims, general medical care, adequate housing, provisions, and clothing. The reunion of families that were divided under slavery would have been facilitated, as well as the relocation of those who wished to rebuild their lives elsewhere. The former slaves would have been offered the literacy training they had been denied.

Extensive organization would have been needed to provide such services. Experience indicates that it would have been best if the former slaves (or, if necessary, their chosen representatives) implemented specific reparations programs, as they had already established their organizational and technical competence. During the Civil War, for example, escaped slaves had been allocated large plantations that had been abandoned by their owners. Without supervision by others, they made excellent use of the resources and created self-governing communities. What they had achieved was undone when President Johnson ordered that such lands be auctioned off or returned to their original owners (Foner 1989, 158–163).

In addition to addressing the ex-slaves' most urgent needs (which was required by ordinary considerations of justice), a morally adequate reparations program would have provided them with sufficient resources to rebuild their lives. One way of beginning to think about this is suggested by the 1865 proposal made by the Radical Republican congressional leader Thaddeus Stevens, that the federal government confiscate 400 million acres that were owned by the wealthiest 10 percent of southern landowners, to be used as follows: forty acres were to be allotted to each adult ex-slave, and the remaining land was to be sold in lots of up to five hundred acres, the proceeds to provide pensions for Civil War veterans, compensation to loyal unionists for property losses in the Civil War, and retirement of the national debt (Foner 1989, 235–237, 307–316).

Stevens's plan could have provided the core of a morally acceptable reparations program, though much more would have been required. Necessary additions would have included providing the former slaves who received land allotments with the materials and equipment that they would have needed to establish well-functioning farms, and insuring their access to credit, supplies, and markets, while those who wished to pursue other lines of work would have been provided with the necessary training and equipment. The importance of Stevens's plan is suggested by the fact that members of the African American community were pressing at the time for just such a distribution of land to the ex-slaves. It appears that most ex-slaves wished to secure their freedom and gain economic independence as free farmers in their homeland, which was the rural South. If Stevens's plan had been implemented with the necessary supplements, the ex-slaves' objective would have been realizable, for they had already established their capacity to work productively, with skill and foresight. Such a plan would have helped the ex-slaves realize another aspect of social freedom: land reform would have helped undermine the large landowners' autocratic control of the South. It would also have helped promote genuine democracy.

The actual history of Reconstruction tells us that a morally adequate reparations program would also have included whatever measures were needed to secure the former slaves against resubordination. This would have required that the federal government vigorously enforce their civil rights through an effective, systematic campaign, as extensive and as long-lasting as needed, against white supremacist ideology.

How could such a reparations program have been funded? First, individuals and institutions that engaged in or supported slavery were morally obligated to help repair the wrongs to which they had contributed. Second, some of the revenue from sale of the confiscated land might have been diverted to support the program. Third, general taxation might also have been needed. A fourth source of funding would have been restitution: the relinquishing of wrongful gains that had been received even by nonculpable parties. This would have been an important source, as slave labor had contributed very substantially to income and wealth that went to others throughout the nation. Thus, nonculpable persons could have been called upon to help pay for reparations through both restitution and general taxation.

Such a program would have resembled a forward-looking reconstruction of society. But it would have focused on what was owed to African Americans, including cash payments, partly for morally symbolic reasons. Its backward-looking character would be confirmed by the requirement that all culpable parties acknowledge and apologize to the former slaves for the wrongs of enslavement. It is quite possible that a morally adequate reparations program for slavery would have required a radical reconstruction not only of the South but of American society as a whole. That would have been a virtue, not a fault, of such a program.

1965/2015

Instead of reparations for slavery, African Americans experienced resubordination under Jim Crow. Slavery was abolished, but enslavement continued in various forms, such as debt peonage and convict leasing (Blackmon 2008). Lynching helped consolidate Jim Crow, and pogroms helped maintain racial subordination. The last major, directly relevant legal advance of recent years was the Voting Rights Act of 1965. That year will count, for present purposes, as the official end of Jim Crow, for it then lost significant support from the federal government (though many state governments in the Old South officially and practically opposed federal policy on civil rights; Webb 2005).

What reparations did morality require in 1965? Like slavery, Jim Crow was not a collection of diverse wrongful practices, but an all-encompassing system of subordination that embodied the doctrine of white supremacy. It is true that the black community had become large enough and separate enough in urban areas to enable some African Americans to create successful businesses, acquire an education, become professionals, and afford decent housing. But all functioned within the constraints and damaging insecurity of a system that was predicated upon black vulnerability and white impunity. A morally adequate reparations program for African Americans in 1965 would have dismantled the entire structure.

The 1947 report by the President's Committee catalogued many of Jim Crow's inequities, which had not substantially diminished by 1965. Those deficits resulted not from racial inferiority (as white supremacists maintained) but from the nation's failure to repair the wrongs of slavery and its resubordination of African Americans under Jim Crow. But a morally adequate reparations program would have done more than attack such deficits. Morally adequate reparations would have included crash programs to reduce infant and maternal mortality among African Americans, provide adequate medical care more generally, reduce the various forms of environmental pollution that typically plague black neighborhoods, and promote life expectancy. It would also have reviewed arrests, prosecutions, and sentencing in order to identify, correct, and compensate for inequities in the administration of the law, and it would have provided job training and productive jobs, on as large a scale as needed. (Much work could have been provided by, for example, repairing and expanding the nation's infrastructure, including public transportation, and constructing affordable housing.) A morally adequate reparations program would have attacked the wealth gap between black and white families that results from Jim Crow housing policies, by enabling black families to acquire the homes they would otherwise have secured. It would have provided safe and affordable child care and good public schools. It would have increased wage and salary levels so that parents would not need to work multiple shifts and could devote adequate time with children.

A morally adequate program would also have persuasively explained the moral need for reparations and undertaken a vigorous, long-term program to combat white supremacist ideology. It would have insured that culpable parties acknowledge and apologize for the wrongs of racial subordination and contribute to the cost of enabling African Americans to rebuild their lives. And it would have taken whatever measures might be necessary to insure that resubordination could not occur again.

How would the cost of such a program be covered? Partly by payments from parties found culpable, especially governments and private institutions; partly by restitution—the transfer of wrongful gains; and partly by general taxation. But some of the costs would be offset by increased family incomes, which would promote spending, sales, manufacturing, jobs in the private sector, and increased tax revenues.

It seems clear that a morally adequate reparations program in 1965, as in 1865, would have required substantial changes across American society. Very little of this was done (Morris

2014). As we have noted, the government never confronted the deeply entrenched legacy of slavery and Jim Crow, and its commitment to reform soon faded.

We should now consider the present. What morality requires today by way of reparations is not much different from what it required in 1965. As official measures now threaten the development of a "new Jim Crow," government must first of all reverse its course. So, for example, justice requires a rapid end to the mindless, costly, wasteful, self-defeating policies that result in mass incarceration of nonviolent offenders under mandatory sentencing laws. The following are called for: the use of alternatives to imprisonment; adequate public financing for projects to expedite the release of prisoners who are demonstrably innocent of the crimes for which they were convicted; the provision of jobs with futures for those who have served their time; and the repeal of rules that exclude ex-felons from public housing and the ballot box. Also required are multiple measures to address the needs of those at the very bottom; and for the re-establishment of voting rights reforms that have been nullified by restrictive state laws and the Supreme Court's decision in *Shelby County v. Holder* (Rutenberg 2015). To these items must be added those listed under reparations for 1965 that are not covered here.

Once again, many of these measures could be justified on general considerations of justice, without recourse to reparations. But a reparations program would focus on what was owed to African Americans, would include cash payments, and its backward-looking character would be confirmed by the requirement that all culpable parties be required to acknowledge and apologize to African Americans for supporting Jim Crow or failing to help combat its wrongful legacy.

EPILOGUE/WIDER IMPLICATIONS

It is time to acknowledge even wider applications of the moral considerations that I have discussed. While slavery subordinated African Americans almost exclusively, its white supremacist rationale deeply affected other segments of American society that are conventionally categorized as nonwhite. Insofar as my moral assumptions are sound, reparations on a very large scale can reasonably be claimed by Native Americans, Asian Americans, Latino Americans, and many immigrants who were seriously abused. There is neither room here nor the need to discuss all of these cases or to trace differences among them. It will suffice for present purposes to illustrate the general point with two examples.

During World War II, when Japan was one of America's principal foes, 120,000 Japanese Americans were ordered from their West Coast homes and sent as prisoners to distant, isolated, barren "relocation centers." These facilities functioned as concentration camps. Symptomatic of that was the orientation of guards and their weapons, which were directed inside, at the residents, so that some residents who wandered close to the fences were shot and killed (Irons 1989).

Elements of the internment program were challenged, separately and unsuccessfully, by Gordon Hirabayashi, Minoru Yasui, and Fred Korematsu. *Korematsu v. U.S.* (323 US 214 [1944]) was the last of the three to be decided by the Supreme Court. Writing for the Court, Justice Black accepted what he thought was the judgment of the military that internment was a necessary wartime security measure. In their dissents, Justices Murphy and Jackson each characterized the internment program as "racist."

In 1983, the Commission on Wartime Relocation and Internment of Civilians established that the internment policy had been implemented despite the fact that all American security agencies at the time had denied the need for any such measures and that their judgments and corresponding objections to internment by civilian officials had been suppressed by the government when it defended the internments in federal court (Korematsu v. U.S., 584 F.Supp. 1406 [1984]). These revelations led Congress and a somewhat reluctant president in 1988 to grant reparations of $20,000 apiece to living survivors of the camps or their heirs (Civil Liberties Act of 1988, 102 Stat. 904). Three points may be made about the case. First, as Justices Jackson and Murphy made clear, even the evidence that was available to the Court in 1944 indicated that the internment policy reflected official bias and pressure from white Americans who wanted to be rid of their Japanese American neighbors. Second, the reparations program that was implemented accounted for only a small fraction of the economic costs of internment: entire families were uprooted; internees lost their homes, careers, and property; some internees lost their health; and some lost their lives. Third, the program acknowledged only a fraction of the injuries that had been inflicted on Japanese Americans by long-standing discrimination, beginning with the federal law that denied US citizenship to Japanese (and many other) immigrants who officials classified as nonwhite. To that insult, states along the West Coast added the injury of alien land laws, which were upheld by federal courts, that prevented noncitizens from acquiring real property. A morally adequate reparations program for Japanese Americans would have repaired all of those injuries, as far as that was possible.

Now consider what reparations may reasonably be due Native Americans. The process of displacing, exterminating, and enslaving American Indians began before African Americans arrived in the New World. It continued throughout the next four centuries, and it has not yet ended. Almost all of American territory, including Hawaii, has been taken from Native Americans—illegally, by America's own legal standards. Indian land cessions were coercively or fraudulently imposed. Federal treaties that pledged permanent land rights and financial support have almost always been broken by the US government. Measures, such as poisoning wells and destroying food sources, have deliberately been taken to deprive Native Americans of subsistence (Stannard 1992). Royalty payments for resources extracted from tribal lands have rarely been paid. And the federal government continues to deface and dishonor sacred Native American sites. The wrongs inflicted upon American Indians have been so devastating, it is difficult to imagine what a morally adequate reparations program for them might be like (Dunbar-Ortiz 2014).

In the present political climate it is difficult to imagine even one major component of any morally adequate reparations program being undertaken. European Americans harbor greatly exaggerated conceptions of past reforms and as a result are generally blind to the deeply entrenched legacy of slavery, Jim Crow, and other systematic wrongdoing, such as the two examples mentioned. Mainstream politicians reinforce persisting racial stereotypes, exploit economic anxieties, and mislead the public about long-term costs and benefits of reform.

Without minimizing the case for reparations to African Americans today, it seems clear that the full implications of reparations reasoning would call for much more than reparations—an overhaul of American society to end racial stratification and create substantive conditions of equal opportunity for future generations. However daunting such an aim may seem, experience shows that, while the success of efforts to achieve reform is unpredictable and can depend on fortuitous circumstances, reform cannot be expected without persistent political struggle.

REFERENCES

Alexander, Michelle. (2010). *The New Jim Crow.* New York: New Press.

Blackmon, Douglas. (2008). *Slavery by Another Name.* New York: Doubleday.

Boxill, Bernard. (2016). "Black Reparations." *The Stanford Encyclopedia of Philosophy.* Edited by Edward N. Zalta. http://plato.stanford.edu/archives/sum2016/entries/black-reparations/.

Brophy, Alfred. (2006). *Reparations Pro and Con.* Oxford: Oxford University Press.

Browne-Marshall, Gloria. (2013). *Race, Law, and American Society.* New York: Routledge.

Coates, Ta-Nehisi. (2014). "The Case for Reparations." *Atlantic Monthly*, May 21, 2014: 1–62.

Dittmer, John. (1994). *Local People: The Struggle for Civil Rights in Mississippi.* Champaign: University of Illinois Press.

Dunbar-Ortiz, Roxanne. (2014). *An Indigenous People's History of the United States.* Boston: Beacon Press.

Foner, Eric. (1989). *Reconstruction 1863–1877.* New York: Harper & Row.

Franklin, John Hope, and Alfred A. Moss, Jr. (1994). *From Slavery to Freedom.* New York: McGraw-Hill.

Irons, Peter. (1989). *Justice Delayed.* Middletown, CT: Wesleyan University Press.

Kolchin, Peter. (1995). *American Slavery, 1619–1877.* New York: Hill and Wang.

Lyons, David. (2013). *Confronting Injustice.* Oxford: Oxford University Press.

Martin, Michael T., and Marilyn Yaquinto, eds. (2007). *Redress for Historical Injustices in the United States.* Durham, NC: Duke University Press.

Massey, Douglas, and Nancy Denton. (1993). *American Apartheid.* Cambridge, MA: Harvard University Press.

Morris, Monique W. (2014). *Black Stats.* New York: New Press.

Oliver, Melvin, and Thomas Shapiro. (2006). *Black Wealth/White Wealth.* New York: Routledge.

President's Committee on Civil Rights. (1947). *To Secure These Rights.* Washington, DC: US Government Printing Office.

Rutenberg, Jim. (2015). "A Dream Undone." *The New York Times*, August 2, MM30.

Stannard, David. (1992). *American Holocaust.* New York: Oxford University Press.

Takaki, Ronald. (2008). *A Different Mirror.* Boston: Little Brown.

Webb, Clive. (2005). *Massive Resistance.* New York: Oxford University Press.

Wilkerson, Isabel. (2010). *The Warmth of Other Suns.* New York: Random House.

Zangrando, Robert L. (1980). *The NAACP Crusade Against Lynching, 1909–1950.* Philadelphia: Temple University Press.

CHAPTER 43

....

RACE, RECTIFICATION, AND APOLOGY

....

RODNEY C. ROBERTS

THE black experience in what is now the United States of America has been one of perpetual racial injustice from the arrival of the first enslaved Africans in the early seventeenth century to the present day. Much of the global community acknowledged the importance of rectifying these injustices after the World Conference Against Racism, Racial Discrimination, Xenophobia and Related Intolerance held in Durban, South Africa in 2001. The conference report acknowledged that "slavery and the slave trade are a crime against humanity and . . . are among the major sources and manifestations of racism, racial discrimination, xenophobia and related intolerance, and that Africans and people of African descent, Asians and people of Asian descent and indigenous peoples were victims of these acts and continue to be victims of their consequences" (United Nations 2002, 11–12). The report "strongly reaffirm[ed] as a pressing requirement of justice that victims of human rights violations resulting from racism, racial discrimination, xenophobia and related intolerance . . . should be assured of having access to justice, including [*inter alia*] the right to seek just and adequate reparation" (United Nations 2002, 24).

Unfortunately, Western philosophy has historically had little concern for rectificatory justice generally, much less with the rectification of the racial injustices perpetrated against Africans and people of African descent in particular. Aristotle's account of rectificatory justice is generally taken to be Western philosophy's classic statement on the matter. On Aristotle's view, rectificatory justice is concerned with rectifying transactions where someone has been treated unfairly, and so unjustly, by another. When one has inflicted harm on another and has thereby profited, it is the aim of rectificatory justice to restore equality between the parties. For Aristotle, what is just in rectification is what is intermediate between loss and profit (Aristotle 1999, bk. V). However, very little discussion of matters concerning rectificatory justice occurred between Aristotle's time and the twentieth century. According to John Locke, for example, all "men" in the state of nature who have received damage as a result of having a right transgressed have, "besides the right of punishment common to him with other Men, a particular Right to seek *Reparation* from him that has done it" (Locke 1988, 273, bk. II chap. II). And on Immanuel Kant's view, "in the case of injustice done to others mere repentance is not enough: it must be followed by endeavor to remedy the injustice" (Kant 1963, 131). Most of the relevant literature began to emerge around the middle of the last century (e.g., Lamont 1941) with a noticeable increase in scholarship beginning in the 1960s (e.g., Ginsberg 1963 and Feinberg 1966), and into the 1970s (e.g., Nickel 1976 and MacCormick 1977–1978), the 1980s (e.g., Arnold 1980 and O'Neill 1987), and the 1990s (e.g., Wheeler 1997 and Askland 1998).

One particular area of concern in injustice theory is the relationship between rectification and apology. Although philosophers have often burdened the notion of apology with emotional requirements and the assumption that reconciliation is the proper aim of an apology, a clarification of rectificatory justice, including a conception of apology that is grounded in justice, shows that emotional requirements are unnecessary, that the assumption of reconciliation as the telos of apology is mistaken, and that the apology to African Americans by the US Congress in 2009 fails as a legitimate apology.

RECTIFICATORY JUSTICE AND APOLOGY

The aim of rectificatory justice is to rectify injustice by setting unjust situations right. When rights circumscribe the sphere of justice, the transgression of a right constitutes an injustice. To account for the rectification of these transgressions, a conception of rectificatory justice should include at least four essential elements: restoration, compensation, apology, and punishment. When an injustice occurs, those upon whom the injustice has been perpetrated oftentimes suffer a loss. Restoration, which calls for the return of precisely that which has been lost as a result of injustice, as in the case of stolen property, is required whenever possible. When restoration is not possible, compensation can address any losses that remain unaccounted for. Compensation is meant to counterbalance an unjust loss with something else that is equivalent in value to that loss. This requirement in justice for rectificatory compensation is often what is meant by "reparation(s)." Since providing compensation means providing something other than the exact thing that was lost, compensation is in this way distinguishable from restoration. Rectification also calls for an apology. Since restoration and compensation can only address unjust losses, an apology is needed in order to effect rectification because it is the apology that addresses the wrong of an injustice. What makes an injustice a wrong is the lack of respect shown to right-holders when their rights are violated. Hence, the righting of a wrong is accomplished by way of an apology—an acknowledgment of wrongdoing that includes the reaffirmation that those who suffered the injustice have moral standing. Punishment is part of a conception of rectificatory justice because, unlike restoration, compensation, and apology, which address what the victims of injustice are due, punishment addresses what may be due to the perpetrators of injustice. Although punishment has been a perennial concern in Western philosophy, when discussed in the context of justice, the concern has typically been with punishment as retribution, not as part of rectification (see Roberts 2002).

ARE EMOTIONAL REQUIREMENTS NECESSARY FOR A LEGITIMATE APOLOGY?

Many philosophers think that a necessary condition for a legitimate apology is that it be sincere and that sincerity requires emotions like sorrow or regret and a commitment to behavioral reform. On Kathleen Gill's view, for example, there are five necessary conditions for a legitimate apology, two of which are these sincerity conditions. Insofar as feelings are concerned, the person apologizing "must have an attitude of regret with respect to the offensive behavior and a feeling of remorse in response to the suffering of the victim." Insofar as behavioral reform is concerned, since the apologizer's behavior following the apology serves as a test of sincerity, the person receiving a sincere apology "is justified in believing that the offender will try to refrain from similar offenses in the future" (Gill 2002, 114). In what Nick Smith calls a categorical apology, conveying regret "in the sense that the offender wishes that the transgression could be undone," is "[m]ore important than its sympathy, sorrow, or guilt[.]" For Smith, apologizers explain that they regret their actions because the actions are morally wrong, because they wish they had done otherwise, and because they will never make the same mistake again (Smith 2005, 483). On Trudy Govier's view, when wrongdoers sincerely apologize, they cancel or "unsay" the message of moral worthlessness toward the victim caused by their wrongful acts. For Govier, when apologies are insincere, they just add moral insult to the already injured victim (Govier and Verwoerd 2002a, 70, 79; 2002b, 142; Govier 2006, 69). But is sincerity in the sense that there are emotions like sorrow and regret and a commitment to behavioral reform really necessary for an apology to be legitimate?

In sharpest contrast to those who think that legitimate apologies are necessarily sincere, Louis Kort thinks that insincere apologies are "full-fledged apologies nonetheless." He posits five conditions that are separately necessary and conjointly sufficient for an apology, one of which is the condition that individuals must express regret about the wrongful act. However, on Kort's view, the apologizer need not have any actual regret. Rather, they "can, and frequently do, apologize, and so express regret, with no genuine regret about whatever they are apologizing for" (Kort 2002, 107). His approach is also absent any requirement for behavioral reform. Richard Joyce also endorses the idea of insincere apology. Even though he thinks that sincerity in an apology is "usually a desirable feature," he does not think that the expression of regret in an apology needs to include actually having regret (Joyce 1999, 167). According to Joyce, "[s]incerity is not a necessary component of an apology" and he doubts that "we really require the formal apologizer to feel particular emotions" when offering an apology (Joyce 1999, 167, 166). For him, apologies do not necessarily include a commitment to behavioral reform. On this view, apologizers who have every intention of repeating the same wrongful act can still insincerely apologize for that act. However, in addition to being insincere, Joyce finds this sort of apology infelicitous and usually "malicious in the same way as falsely promising is usually a malicious action" (Joyce 1999, 166). Like Kort and Joyce, Glen Pettigrove thinks that an insincere apology does not fail to be an apology. However, like Joyce, he thinks that apologies without attitudinal states like regret and remorse are "morally deficient" and "infelicitous." Moreover, Pettigrove thinks that an apology "indicates one's intention to refrain from similar actions in the future." For him, an apology without this intention may have "so explicitly deviated from the implicit conditions of an apology that it would fall beyond the pale" (Pettigrove 2003, 323, 324). Although we would still have an apology without intending behavioral reform, like an apology without the appropriate attitudinal states, Pettigrove finds such apologies infelicitous.

Just Apology

The popularity of the two sincerity conditions may be explained by the extent to which theorists have conceived of apology within the context of the whole of morality. Smith, for example, takes his idea of "categorical apology" to be representative of "the *maximally mean-ingful* apology" (Smith 2005, 473). For Govier, the concern is with "full-fledged moral" apology (Govier and Verwoerd 2002a, 73). Justice, however, is not the whole of morality. Rather, it is only a particular segment of it (Hart 1994, 157; see also Mill 2001, 49). Hence, the content of apologies in response to injustice is prescribed first and foremost by justice, not by the whole of morality. When an apology is given following an injustice, it is not an apology all things considered that justice requires, that is, not in a general sense what might be called a *moral apology*. What is specifically required is a *just apology*.

Contrary to those who think that when rendering a legitimate apology one must *really* be sorry for that which he or she is apologizing, the just apology does not include as a necessary condition that those who apologize have certain feelings. Just apologies need only be sincere in the sense that the person uttering the words is making a true statement about the unjust act and making a commitment to providing or at least earnestly attempting compensation. Would it be better if the person apologizing was racked with guilt, shame, sorrow, and regret when uttering the words? Of course it would. Would this being the case make the apology a more substantive acknowledgment of the victim's moral worth than just making a statement? Perhaps. In any event, justice is not in the business of prescribing which feelings people ought to have and when they ought to have them. Rather, it is in the business of prescribing the way we ought to act toward one another. Justice is that sphere of morality which functions as the primary arbiter of social behavior. While we might agree with John Stuart Mill that the moral rules of justice "are the main element in determining the whole of the social feelings of mankind," this is far from thinking that *the rules of justice themselves* require that particular feelings be held (Mill 2001, 59). It may be that morality in a general sense calls for feeling regret or remorse when we have committed an injustice, but there is no ground for this requirement in the specifics of justice.

The idea of justice, or of an action being just, always includes some consonance with principles of moral right. When rights circumscribe the sphere of justice, acting rightly insofar as justice is concerned means respecting the rights of others. We demonstrate our understanding that all individuals are equally worthy of respect by respecting everyone's rights. Therefore, when we fail to show the proper respect due another, we treat that person unjustly. The *wrong* of injustice is the disrespect shown to another when that person's rights are violated. Acknowledging that what one has done is wrong entails an acknowledgment that the person affected by the act is undeserving of the treatment given. By apologizing the perpetrator reaffirms that the victim is a person and is therefore worthy of respect. The just apology includes a statement that expresses an acknowledgment by the actor, or the actor's representative, that the action was wrong. It is in this way that an apology addresses the wrong of an injustice. Consequently, an apology is due after an injustice whether or not the victim has sustained any unjust loss. However, this is not to deny the essential relationship between apology and compensation where the latter legitimizes the former. Since rectificatory justice requires that unjust losses be restored or compensated for, apologies purported to be given in cases where compensation is due but not provided (or at least earnestly attempted) are illegitimate. This is so because, in such cases, one's actions are (at best) inconsistent if one acknowledges the injustice perpetrated but fails to provide an equivalent in value for the losses sustained by the victim as a result of that injustice. Moreover, in cases where there is an unjust loss, it is in large part by way of fulfilling (or earnestly attempting to fulfill) the restorative or compensatory requirements of rectificatory justice that a perpetrator's apology is rendered sincere.

Since face-to-face speech is the most effective and the most personal way in which we communicate complex ideas to each other, just apologies ought to be given verbally and face-to-face by the perpetrator whenever possible, or by the perpetrator's representative when it is not. As Nicholas Tavuchis observes, verbal face-to-face communication is apology's "energizing medium." Without it, one misses the "sociological core of apology" (Tavuchis 1991, 23). Beyond one-on-one apologies where groups are involved, all members of the groups concerned should have a reasonable chance of hearing the apology. In state-rendered apologies for major injustice, for example, the number of relevant parties may run into the millions. In such cases the apology ought to be broadcast widely. The apology should also be widely published, both for the record and so that any relevant parties who did not hear the apology have a reasonable chance of reading it.

One advantage of the conception of the just apology is that it makes better sense of the idea of demanding an apology than do apologies in which particular feelings are required. If we think that the person apologizing must be "really sorry" for the injustice in order to render a legitimate apology, then it seems odd that we should ask, much less demand, that one be given. In such cases we would be demanding that people possess certain feelings. What justice requires from the perpetrator is to act justly in the wake of injustice, to endeavor to make things right—not to have particular feelings. To demand a just apology is to demand an acknowledgment of the perpetration of injustice and the taking of responsibility by the perpetrator (or the perpetrator's representative) for ensuring that compensation is provided for any unjust loss. "When we think that a person is bound in justice to do a thing, it is an ordinary form of language to say that he ought to be *compelled* to do it" (Mill 2001, 48, emphasis added). A demand is sometimes necessary because in our nonideal world people may need to be reminded that justice requires an apology following injustice. Like a mother who brings her child face-to-face with someone the child has wronged and commands, "Tell Mr. Jones you're sorry," adults may need to be reminded when an apology is due. This is part of developing what John Stuart Mill describes as the external sanction of "the hope of favor and the fear of displeasure from our fellow creatures" (Mill 2001, 28). Our moral faculty, while "susceptible of being brought by cultivation to a high degree of development," is sometimes too weak to prompt us to act justly on our own (Mill 2001, 31). As Aristotle reminds us, we are not born with prudence and wisdom; they arise in us and grow "mostly from teaching." That is why the possession of these virtues only comes with "experience and time" (Aristotle 1999, 18, 1103a15). It therefore makes sense to think that when an acknowledgment of wrongdoing is "expressed" in an apology, it will sometimes include more than having put the acknowledgment into words. It may also include a sense in which (pursuant to the Latin origin of "express") the acknowledgment is obtained in part by way of pressure; that the apology was pressed or squeezed out of a (reluctant) apologizer.

Another advantage of the conception of the just apology is that it makes better sense of the idea of a national or state-to-state apology than do apologies in which particular feelings are required. Here the concern has been that national or state-to-state apologies require entire groups to feel sorrow, remorse, or regret in order for the apology to be legitimate. On Joyce's view, for example, when a representative of a group expresses regret for some injustice, the sincerity of this expression "depends not on what *she* feels, but on what the group now feels and what the group intends" (Joyce 1999, 167). Since it seems likely that there will be many cases in which everyone in the apologizing group will not have the requisite feelings, an apology where one or more of those feelings is necessary means that national and state-to-state apologies will often be impossible. Not so with the just apology.

The just apology does not have as a necessary condition that it be sincere in the sense that by apologizing one commits oneself to not repeating a particular wrongful act. Kant suggests this point when he observes that "[a]nyone can be free, as long as I do not impair his freedom by my *external actions*, even though I am quite indifferent to his freedom or would like in my heart to infringe upon it" and thereby perpetrate an injustice (Kant 1991, 56). Wronging a person and then wanting to wrong that person again in the very same way may speak ill of my character, but it is not unjust (on apologizing for failures of character, see Pettigrove and Collins 2011). Although I acted unjustly toward you in the past, my present desire to do so again is not itself an injustice. It is therefore difficult to see how a commitment to refrain from the performance of a particular wrongdoing can follow from an acknowledgment of having perpetrated that wrongdoing. Smith, for example, thinks that apologies "promise to never repeat the offense because they denounce their transgression as morally wrong" (Smith 2005, 485). On his view, the promise of behavioral reform is entailed in the expression of regret and the declaration of the wrongness of the transgression (Smith 2005, 484, 483; cf: Waller 2007; Verdeja 2010). But why should we infer a *promise* not to repeat an act from the mere fact of having denounced the past performance of that act? There is no obvious reason why we should. Of course, even when we have not apologized, if X is an injustice for which an apology is due, then X is a rights violation that we already had a duty not to do in the first place. Hence, a fortiori, we ought not to do X again.

JUST APOLOGY AND RECONCILIATION

Some may object to the idea of a just apology because they endorse the popular view that apologies are best understood as aiming at reconciliation (see Joyce 1999, 164; Pettigrove 2003, 323; Zutlevics 2002, 72; Govier 2006, 69). This understanding is often found in public apologies. The 1993 US apology to Native Hawaiians, for example, "apologizes" to the Hawaiian people "on behalf of the people of the United States for the overthrow of the Kingdom of Hawaii . . . and the deprivation of the rights of Native Hawaiians to self-determination." It "acknowledge[s] the ramifications of the overthrow . . . in order to provide a proper foundation for reconciliation between the United States and the Native Hawaiian people" (US Congress 1993). However, the document does not express a commitment to compensate for the wrongful losses that arose from these injustices. In the reconciliation report drafted by the government seven years after the apology, the notion of reconciliation is seen as a way toward healing that "requires action to rectify the injustices and compensation for the harm" (US Department of the Interior 2000, i) (reconciliation hearings were held on several islands in 1999). However, no compensatory action was ever taken. As Haunani-Kay Trask rightly observes, the question "is one of national injury and national responsibility." When injustice has been done, "justice must be rendered before reconciliation can be considered" (Trask 2003, 45).

Reconciliatory apologies may not even be possible in many cases. Such apologies are often inapplicable to situations where an apology is otherwise warranted. Aiming at reconciliation assumes that the situation in question is conciliable, that relations between perpetrator and victim can in fact be made friendly. In those cases where it is not, reconciliation, and therefore the aim of apology, is impossible. Reconciliation also begs the question of a prior friendly relationship. Positing it as the telos of apology assumes that, like many cases of spousal reconciliation, the parties in question had some relationship in the past that should be again. Although "reconcile" and "conciliate" can be taken as synonymous, the former is literally *re* and *conciliare*—a bringing together or making friendly *again*. This idea does not apply when victim and perpetrator are strangers and neither has any desire to be friendly with the other. In short, the reconciliatory approach to apology misses the point. The aim of an apology following injustice ought to be first and foremost to further the rectification of that injustice, not to establish particular feelings or beliefs between perpetrators and victims.

THE APOLOGY BY THE US CONGRESS TO AFRICAN AMERICANS

Well over a century after the Thirteenth Amendment to the US Constitution ended the enslavement of African Americans, and more than a half century after the end of de jure racial segregation, a Congressional resolution purporting to apologize for slavery and Jim Crow segregation was passed by the US House of Representatives (US Congress 2008). The following year, in 2009, the US Senate, in a concurrent resolution with the House, "[a]pologiz[ed] for the enslavement and racial segregation of African-Americans" (US Congress, S. Con. Res. 2009) (The American government also passed a similarly inadequate apology resolution to Native Americans in 2009; buried inside a DOD appropriations bill, it purports to apologize for the "many instances of violence, maltreatment, and neglect" inflicted on them, US Department of Defense 2010, 3453–3454). The resolution recognizes that "African-Americans continue to suffer from the consequences of slavery and Jim Crow—long after both systems were formally abolished—through enormous damage and loss, both tangible and intangible, including the loss of human dignity and liberty" (US Congress, S. Con. Res. 2009).

The apology resolution's sponsor, Senator Harkin, rightly observed that collective injustices warrant collective apologies. According to Harkin, "[a] national apology by the representative body of the people is a necessary, collective response to a past collective injustice" (US Congress, Cong. Rec. 2009, S6762). Strangely, both Harkin, and the resolution's co-sponsor Senator Brownback, miss the point. The point is to provide a statement acknowledging the wrongs perpetrated against African Americans, made sincere by a commitment to fulfill (or at least earnestly attempt to fulfill) the restorative and compensatory requirements of rectification. Instead, Brownback thought that the injustice requiring a collective response was not the injustice of slavery and Jim Crow, but the injustice of not having apologized for slavery and Jim Crow in the past. According to Brownback, what the resolution does is to "right that wrong of not offering an apology previously" (US Congress, Cong. Rec. 2009, S6764). As for Harkin, he thought that the collective response required for the injustice of slavery and Jim Crow was not a collective apology and compensatory efforts in favor of African Americans, but that "truly the best way to address the lasting legacy of slavery and Jim Crow" is to "continue to work together to create better opportunities for all Americans"

(US Congress, Cong. Rec., 2009 S6763). Moreover, as the apology resolution itself states, "a formal apology for slavery and for its successor, Jim Crow" is important so that the people of the United States "can move forward and seek reconciliation, justice, and harmony for all people of the United States" (US Congress, S. Con. Res. 2009). So, although the resolution acknowledges that American slavery and its consequences were unjust, its aim is reconciliation, not rectification.

Just apologies rendered by a state ought to be given verbally by a representative and be both widely broadcast and widely published. Unfortunately, there is almost no sense in which the apology resolution was communicated to African Americans. In fact, there is barely a sense in which it was verbally delivered to the Senate. Although the resolution was read by the Senate's clerk, and was passed with unanimous consent, the Senate chamber was nearly empty when the resolution was being considered. Senator Harkin noted that a public apology ceremony would "bring home to all of us and to the American people the enormity of what we have done in terms of finally acknowledging the official role of the U.S. Government in promoting and sanctioning slavery and Jim Crow laws." However, the "fitting ceremony" that Harkin said was "being planned for sometime early in July [2009] that w[as to] take place in the main Rotunda of the Capitol to mark th[e] occasion" never took place (US Congress, Cong. Rec. 2009, S6767). Since it was merely read by the clerk as part of standard Senate procedure, the purported apology was not delivered in person and few Americans had a reasonable chance of hearing it. Indeed, relatively few Americans had a reasonable chance of even hearing that the resolution existed and that it had been passed. Save for a daytime broadcast of the Senate proceedings on the C-Span television network, news coverage of the resolution seems to have been almost nonexistent (as William Douglas observed, the resolution was "sponsored with little fanfare" [2009, A1; see also, Mayes 2008, 28, and Ransom 2009, 11]). As for publication of the resolution, while it is obviously part of the Congressional record, the government has not seen fit to publish it elsewhere.

Finally, the apology resolution makes no mention of compensation for the "enormous damage and loss, both tangible and intangible, including the loss of human dignity and liberty" arising from slavery and Jim Crow segregation. According to Brownback, the resolution "specifically does the apology but deals with nothing else." He says that a disclaimer is included in the resolution "to leave that issue aside" (US Congress, Cong. Rec. 2009, S6767). Senator Burris, a slave descendant and the only African American in the Senate during the 111th Congress, "want[ed] to go on record making sure that the disclaimer in no way would eliminate future actions that may be brought before [the Senate] that may deal with reparations" (US Congress, Cong. Rec. 2009, S6765). The disclaimer states: "Nothing in this resolution—(A) authorizes or supports any claim against the United States; or (B) serves as a settlement of any claim against the United States" (US Congress, S. Con. Res. 2009). While this does not directly foreclose the possibility of rectificatory compensation for African Americans, since the resolution begins by acknowledging the injustices done, then ends by denying that this acknowledgment can support a claim for the rectification of those injustices, the disclaimer effectively negates any acknowledgment of wrongdoing.

The 2009 US apology to African Americans for slavery and Jim Crow segregation effectively contains no acknowledgment of wrongdoing and makes no commitment to providing compensation for unjust loss. It was not communicated verbally and in person, nor was it widely broadcast or widely published. Consequently, the action taken by the United States fails as a legitimate apology.

REFERENCES

Aristotle. (1999). *Nicomachean Ethics*. 2d ed. Translated by Terence Irwin. Indianapolis: Hackett.

Arnold, C. (1980). "Corrective Justice." *Ethics* 90 (2): 180–190.

Askland, A. (1998). "A Justification of Compensation to the Descendants of Wronged Parties: An Intended Analogy." *Public Affairs Quarterly* 12 (4): 363–368.

Douglas, W. (2009). "U.S. Senate Oks Apology for Slavery." *Wichita Eagle*, June 19. https://rsecure.newspaperarchive.com/registrationtrialnewv10?gclid=CJWmor_PusoCFUiGf godMTgGSA.

Feinberg, J. (1966). "Duties, Rights, and Claims." *American Philosophical Quarterly* 3 (2): 137–144.

Gill, K. A. (2002). "The Moral Functions of an Apology." In *Injustice and Rectification*, edited by Rodney C. Roberts, 111–123. New York: Peter Lang.

Ginsberg, M. (1963). "The Concept of Justice." *Philosophy* 38 (144): 99–116.

Govier, T. (2006). *Taking Wrongs Seriously: Acknowledgement, Reconciliation, and the Politics of Sustainable Peace*. Amherst, MA: Humanity.

Govier, T., and W. Verwoerd. (2002a). "The Promise and Pitfalls of Apology." *Journal of Social Philosophy* 33 (1): 67–82.

Govier, T., and W. Verwoerd. (2002b). "Taking Wrongs Seriously: A Qualified Defence of Public Apologies." *Saskatchewan Law Review* 65: 139–162.

Hart, H. L. A. (1994). *The Concept of Law*. 2d ed. New York: Oxford University Press.

Joyce, R. (1999). "Apologizing." *Public Affairs Quarterly* 13 (2): 159–173.

Kant, I. (1963). *Lectures on Ethics*. Translated by Louis Infield. Indianapolis: Hackett.

Kant, I. (1991). *The Metaphysics of Morals*. Translated by Mary Gregor. Cambridge: Cambridge University Press.

Kort, L. F. (2002). "What Is an Apology?" In *Injustice and Rectification*, edited by Rodney C. Roberts, 105–110. New York: Peter Lang.

Lamont, W. D. (1941). "Justice: Distributive and Corrective." *Philosophy* 16 (61): 3–18.

Locke, J. (1988). *Two Treatises of Government*. Edited by Peter Laslett. Cambridge: Cambridge University Press.

MacCormick, D. N. (1977–1978). "The Obligation of Reparation." *Proceedings of the Aristotelian Society* 78: 175–193.

Mayes, E. E. (2008). "House's Slavery Apology Rebuked, Called a 'Stunt.'" *Chicago Defender*, August 6–12. http://newspaperarchive.com/us/illinois/chicago/?gclid=CNy8pavQusoCFQ FsfgodubkCbQ.

Mill, J. S. (2001). *Utilitarianism*. 2d ed. Edited by George Sher. Indianapolis: Hackett.

Nickel, J. W. (1976). "Justice in Compensation." *William and Mary Law Review* 18 (2): 379–388.

O'Neill, O. (1987). "Rights to Compensation." *Social Philosophy and Policy* 5 (1): 72–87.

Pettigrove, G. (2003). "Apology, Reparations, and the Question of Inherited Guilt." *Public Affairs Quarterly* 17 (4): 319–348.

Pettigrove, G., and J. Collins. (2011). "Apologizing for Who I Am." *Journal of Applied Philosophy* 28 (2): 137–150.

Ransom, L. (2009). "Senate Apologizes for Slavery; African Americans Say 'Ho-Hum.'" *Chicago Defender*, June 24–30. http://newspaperarchive.com/us/illinois/chicago/?gclid=CN y8pavQusoCFQFsfgodubkCbQ.

Roberts, R. C. (2002). "Justice and Rectification: A Taxonomy of Justice." In *Injustice and Rectification*, edited by Rodney C. Roberts, 7–28. New York: Peter Lang.

Smith, N. (2005). "The Categorical Apology." *Journal of Social Philosophy* 36 (4): 473–496.

Tavuchis, N. (1991). *Mea Culpa: A Sociology of Apology and Reconciliation.* Stanford, CA: Stanford University Press.

Trask, H. (2003). "Restitution as a Precondition of Reconciliation: Native Hawaiians and Indigenous Human Rights." In *Should America Pay?: Slavery and the Raging Debate on Reparations,* edited by Raymond A. Winbush, 32–45. New York: Amistad Press.

United Nations. (2002). *Report of the World Conference Against Racism, Racial Discrimination, Xenophobia and Related Intolerance, Durban, South Africa, August 31-September 8, 2001,* U.N. Doc. A/CONF. 189/12.

US Congress, S. J. Res. 19, 103rd Cong., 1st sess., 23 November 1993.

US Congress, H. Res. 194, 110th Cong. 2nd sess., 29 July 2008.

US Congress, S. Con. Res. 26, 111th Cong. 1st sess., 18 June 2009.

US Congress, 155 Cong. Rec., 18 June 2009.

US Department of Defense Appropriations Act, 2010, Public Law 111-118-Dec. 19, 2009, 123 Stat. 3409.

US Department of the Interior. (2000). *From Mauka to Makai: The River of Justice Must Flow Freely.* Report on the Reconciliation Process Between the Federal Government and Native Hawaiians. Washington, DC: US Government Printing Office.

Verdeja, E. (2010). "Official Apologies in the Aftermath of Political Violence." *Metaphilosophy* 41 (4): 563–581.

Waller, B. N. (2007). "Sincere Apology without Moral Responsibility." *Social Theory and Practice* 33 (3): 441–465.

Wheeler, S. C., III. (1997). "Reparations Reconstructed." *American Philosophical Quarterly* 34 (3): 301–318.

Zutlevics, T. L. (2002). "Reconciliation, Responsibility, and Apology." *Public Affairs Quarterly* 16 (1): 63–75.

CHAPTER 44

THE CONCEPT OF RACE AND EQUAL PROTECTION LAW

TINA FERNANDES BOTTS

OVER the course of the development of equal protection law, roughly from 1868 (the year the Fourteenth Amendment to the US Constitution, which contains the Equal Protection Clause, was ratified) to the present day, as the US Supreme Court's concept of race moves from being understood as a sociocultural/sociohistorical phenomenon to being understood as a purely biological phenomenon, there is a concomitant shift on the part of the Court from understanding racial discrimination as problematic because it reinforces the legacy and vestiges of American chattel slavery, to understanding racial discrimination as problematic per se. The Supreme Court's adoption, over time, of a purely biological concept of race is a curious state of affairs, given that academic thinking on the topic of race has taken the opposite turn during the same time period. That is, concurrent with the change in the Supreme Court's concept of race from sociocultural/sociohistorical to purely biological, the academic concept of race moves from being understood as purely biological to sociocultural/sociohistorical. Over the same period of time, whites begin to become successful at using the Equal Protection Clause to protect *them* from "racial discrimination." One explanation for this curious state of affairs is that the current utilization by white Americans of the Equal Protection Clause for protection against "racial discrimination" is among the most recent examples of the progressive divestiture of the rights of blacks for the benefit of whites, over time, in the United States since the end of the civil rights movement.

THE SUPREME COURT'S SWITCH FROM SOCIOCULTURAL/SOCIOHISTORICAL RACE TO BIOLOGICAL RACE

To say that, in the nineteenth century, the Supreme Court understood race primarily as a sociocultural/sociohistorical phenomenon is to use contemporary terminology to describe a way of thinking about race that views race as deeply ensconced and invested in the cultural identity, history, and even geography of a given era. That is, the significance of race (its telos, its Aristotelian "function") had more to do with considerations of social structure, social mores, in-group/out-group psychology and power dynamics than with phenotype, physiognomy, or physical characteristics (Aristotle, 1.7). To be a member of one race or another was a story about cultural belonging, and about the customs and laws of the country, including citizenship laws, federal naturalization laws, and Supreme Court decisions in which race was a factor. The nineteenth-century case law reveals that, for the Court at the time, blackness or whiteness as such, or per se, in the "philosophical void," as it were, did not exist. Instead, the Supreme Court correlated blackness and whiteness with geographical origins, traditions, and cultural narratives, that is, for example, with the sense of being "a people" in the DuBoisian sense (Du Bois 1897/2001). While it is true, however, that even in the nineteenth century, the Supreme Court, at times, associated human racial categories with, among other things, heritability or "ancestry," the case reports reveal that there was no sense on the part of the Supreme Court in the nineteenth century or even the early twentieth century that race was a purely biological phenomenon, or that race could be separated from culture, history, or geography, in the way that the Court talks about race today.

Over time, however, the Supreme Court's concept of race changed. What can be seen in the case reports of Supreme Court cases grappling with the concept of race from the mid-nineteenth century to the present, in direct opposition with the trajectory of academic thinking on the topic, is a switch from understanding race in a sociocultural/sociohistorical way, to understanding race in a purely biological way in the late twentieth and early twenty-first centuries. To develop an appreciation for how the Supreme Court came to adopt a purely biological concept of race, it is helpful to take a close look at the language the Court has used in pivotal cases over the years in which race was at issue.

Early Supreme Court cases correlated human racial blackness with slavery, not with biology. This is true of both cases decided before the enactment of the Fourteenth Amendment and cases decided just afterward. In the landmark *Dred Scott v. Sandford*, decided in 1857, eight years before the Civil War broke out and eleven years before the enactment of the Fourteenth Amendment, the plaintiff, Dred Scott is described as a "a free Negro of the African race" whose ancestors had been brought to the United States and sold as slaves (*Dred Scott* 1857, 393). The pivotal question in the case was whether Scott could avail himself of the court system. The Supreme Court held that he could not avail himself of the court system in virtue of the fact that he was not a citizen of the United States within the meaning of the US Constitution.

The Court delved into the text of the Constitution for references to support its position. There were only two clauses in the Constitution that referred to persons such as Scott, the Court said, and in neither case were such persons considered citizens. Not being a citizen, Scott could not avail himself of the "special rights and immunities" guaranteed to citizens by the Constitution, including availing oneself of the court system (*Dred Scott* 1857). By persons such as Scott, the Court explained that Scott's ancestors had never been intended to be citizens but only as property to be bought and sold. The Court wrote, "The question is simply this: Can a negro, whose ancestors were imported into this country, and sold as slaves, become a member of the political community formed and brought into existence by the Constitution of the United States, and as such become entitled to all the rights, and privileges, and immunities, guaranteed by that instrument to the citizen?" (*Dred Scott* 1857, 403). The Supreme Court's answer was no. In other words, Dred Scott was prohibited from filing suit in federal court, not because of his so-called biological race per se, but because according to the Constitution, his ancestors were not citizens, but slaves.

Just after the enactment of the Fourteenth Amendment, the Supreme Court's concept of race vis-à-vis former slaves was no different. In *The Slaughterhouse Cases* (1873), the Court wrote that since the Thirteenth Amendment was insufficient to protect "the colored race" from certain laws enacted in the southern states that imposed upon them "onerous disabilities and burdens and curtailing their rights in the pursuit of life, liberty, and property to such an extent that their freedom was of little value" (*The Slaughterhouse Cases* 1873, 70), the Fourteenth Amendment was passed through Congress to provide additional protection for "the unfortunate race" who had "suffered so much" (*The Slaughterhouse Cases* 1873). In *Slaughterhouse*, the facts of the case were that the Court denied white butchers the right to invoke the Equal Protection Clause of the Fourteenth Amendment to protect their interests. The Court's rationale was that whatever were the white butchers' complaints, they had not experienced the denial of their rights in the same way that "the colored race" had as a result of the Jim Crow laws enacted after the end of slavery. To be "colored," in other words, meant that one was a member of a group with a pressing need to be protected by federal law from the infringement of one's rights by state laws designed to reinforce the badges of slavery.

In a series of cases decided just after *The Slaughterhouse Cases*, the Court repeatedly associated being "colored" with having one's rights trampled on by invidious state laws in the aftermath of slavery. For example, in *Strauder v. West Virginia*, the Court referred to black people as "a race recently emancipated" (1880, 306); and in *The Civil Rights Cases* (1883), state laws were struck down that discriminated on the basis of any "previous condition of servitude" (*The Civil Rights Cases* 1883, 4).

The case of *Plessy v. Ferguson* (1896) brings into full focus the Court's understanding of race at the end of the nineteenth century. In that case, Homer Plessy was a person of "mixed descent" ("seven-eighths Caucasian and one-eighth African blood" (*Plessy v. Ferguson* 1896, 537) who possessed no obvious physical trait identified with the black race, i.e., ". . . the mixture of colored blood was not discernible in him" (*Plessy v. Ferguson* 1896, 537). Plessy had boarded a Louisiana train on the afternoon of June 7, 1892, for the purpose of taking a public stand against a Louisiana law mandating "equal but separate accommodations" for persons of "the white and colored races" on public conveyances. Upon boarding the train, no one stopped Plessy as he took his seat in first class, a section reserved exclusively for whites. It was only after Plessy voluntarily and openly declared that under Louisiana law he was a "colored" man, that the conductor directed him to the colored car (Fireside 2004, 1). Plessy was charged with, and soon convicted of, breaking the Louisiana law.

Plessy appealed his conviction up through the Supreme Court of Louisiana, who held (as had all of the lower courts) that the Louisiana law was constitutional. In his appeal, Plessy challenged the constitutionality of the law to the Supreme Court. Reportedly, Plessy argued that owing to being seven-eighths Caucasian, he was "entitled to every right, privilege and immunity secured to citizens of the United States of the white race" (*Plessy v. Ferguson* 1896, 541). The Court did not address Plessy's claims of being biologically white for all intents and purposes, but instead proceeded as if it were obvious that he was black, and therefore in clear violation of the law. This could be attributable to the so-called one drop rule, prevalent in Jim Crow laws of the time, but it is more likely attributable to the fact that the Court understood race as a sociocultural/sociohistorical phenomenon rather than a biological phenomenon. Plessy was black because that is the way he was understood by society, regardless of any talk of "blood." The most convincing proof that the *Plessy* Court was operating with a sociocultural/sociohistorical conception of race, however, is the fact that the Court was trying to uphold *social* distinctions and *social* segregation, through its decision to uphold the Lousiana law. To reinforce this point, and referring to the power of the train conductor, the Court wrote, "The power to assign to a particular coach obviously implies the power to determine to which race the passenger belongs, as well as the power to determine who, under the laws of the particular State, is to be deemed a white and who a colored person" (*Plessy v. Ferguson* 1896, 549). In other words, the determination of "to which race the passenger belongs" was linked, in the Court's mind, to the discretion of the conductor and the power of the State, not to anything more theoretically "objective" like biology.

In the early twentieth century, persons of various nonwhite races other than black began to bring cases before the Supreme Court claiming that they were white and were therefore entitled to certain rights. The outcomes of these cases turned on the racial status of the persons bringing the cases before the Court. An examination of the Supreme Court's reasoning process in these cases helps us get a clearer picture of how the Supreme Court thought about race at that time. In the following three cases, which are typical of the time, the Court explicitly grapples with whether race should be understood to be biological or sociocultural/sociohistorical.

The first of the three cases is *Ozawa v. United States* (1922). In *Ozawa*, a Japanese person wished to become a naturalized citizen. The Supreme Court held that Mr. Ozawa, having been born in Japan, did not qualify as a "free white person" under the federal naturalization laws, and therefore could not become a citizen of the United States (*Ozawa v. United States* 1922, 194–199). Having been born in Japan meant that Mr. Ozawa was problematically not "Caucasian," the Court explained, and therefore not white. Attempting to explain its reasoning process, the Court wrote, "[t]he intention [of the naturalization law] was to confer the privilege of citizenship upon that class of persons whom the [founding] fathers knew as white, and to deny it to those who could not be so classified" (*Ozawa v. United States* 1922, 195). In other words, Mr. Ozawa was not white because he was not Caucasian, and he was not Caucasian because the founding fathers would not have wanted people like to Mr. Ozawa to be citizens. There is no mention, on the part of the Court, of Mr. Ozawa's "biology," phenotype, or physical features.

One year later, however, the Court decided that being white no longer turned on being Caucasian. In *U.S. v. Bhagat Sing Thind* (1923), when denying the status of "free white person" (for purposes of the same federal naturalization law) to a gentleman who had been born in India, the Court indicated that whether Mr. Thind was "Caucasian" or not was irrelevant. Explaining why qualifying as Caucasian was not sufficient for qualifying as "white" in this particular case, the Court wrote,

> [The word "Caucasian"] is at best a conventional term, with an altogether fortuitous origin, which under scientific manipulation, has come to include far more than the unscientific mind suspects. According to Keane, for example . . . it includes not only the Hindu, but some of the Polynesians . . . , the Hamites of Africa, upon the ground of the Caucasic cast of their features, though in color they range from brown to black. We venture to think that the average well-informed white American would learn with some degree of astonishment that the race to which he belongs is made up of such heterogeneous elements. . . . The various authorities are in irreconcilable disagreement as to what constitutes a proper racial division (*U.S. v. Bhagat Sing Thind* 1923, 211).

Having established that race was not susceptible to conclusive scientific analysis, and that the "average white American" was really the best judge of who was "white," the Court turned to the intent of the framers of the naturalization law, and to "words of familiar speech" to support its understanding of who qualifies as "white." The Court writes, "The words of familiar speech, which were used by the original framers of the law, were intended to include only the type of man whom they knew as white" (*U.S. v. Bhagat Sing Thind* 1923, 213). The "white" group clearly includes, according to the Court, those "from the British Isles and Northwestern Europe" and those from Eastern, Southern, and Middle Europe and their descendants since these were the immigrants who "constituted the white population of the country" when the naturalization law was adopted (*U.S. v. Bhagat Sing Thind* 1923, 214). The test for whiteness, according to the Court, was whether the white people who drafted the naturalization laws would consider a given person white or not. The test for whiteness, as was the case in *Ozawa*, was the discretion of white people, not biology.

Together, *Ozawa* and *Thind* seem to indicate that in 1923, to be white (at least for naturalization purposes), according to the Supreme Court, meant to be Caucasian when the person wishing to be considered white was Japanese, but meant the ordinary understanding of the term "white," when the person wishing to be considered white was Indian.

The third case, *Korematsu v. United States* (1944), was different in two important respects from *Ozawa and Thind*. First, Korematsu was an American citizen of Japanese descent, instead of an immigrant, and second, rather than claiming that he should be considered white and therefore able to escape certain negative consequences for those deemed legally nonwhite, claimed his right to equal protection had been denied by a federal evacuation order, because of his race. Korematsu had been convicted in a federal court of remaining in San Leandro, California, contrary to an executive order directing that all persons of Japanese ancestry should be excluded from that area, and moved into internment camps, after May 9, 1942. He appealed the conviction all the way to the Supreme Court. The Supreme Court concluded that the executive evacuation order did not violate Korematsu's right to equal protection, because the country's right to protect itself in a time of war was more important than protecting Japanese Americans from racial discrimination.

On the topic of race, the *Korematsu* case was focused on persons of Japanese ancestry. In upholding the executive order, the Court stated that it was impossible to segregate loyal from disloyal Japanese Americans and cited information coming in from investigations that approximately five thousand American citizens of Japanese ancestry had refused to swear unqualified allegiance to the United States and to renounce allegiance to the Japanese emperor. On the topic of race, the Court repeatedly refers to "ancestry" and repeatedly states that the case is not about "racial prejudice" but about "military dangers": "Korematsu was not excluded from the Military Area because of hostility to him or his race. He was excluded because we are at war with the Japanese Empire.... [among other non-race-related reasons]." Justice Roberts's dissenting opinion in this case would have found an equal protection violation, pointing out that Korematsu was forbidden in the relevant area "solely because of his ancestry" (*Korematsu v. United States* 1944, 226).

The relevant issues in *Korematsu* for answering the question of what the Supreme Court's concept of race was in the first part of the twentieth century are as follows: (1) How, if at all, is the concept of race at work in *Korematsu* the same or different from the concept of race at work in *Ozawa* and *Thind*? (2) Is this concept more sociocultural/sociohistorical or biological? In all three cases, the relevant issue seems to be ancestry, that is, geographic origin. And the relevant test for who counts as what race seems to be the discretion of those either creating or implementing the laws, which is a subjective or social judgment, rather than an objective biological determination. As the twentieth century wore on, and into the twenty-first century, the Court began to think about race in more biological terms, and eventually in biological terms divorced from considerations of history or social context.

Substantially contributing to the trend of the Supreme Court's beginning to think about race in biological rather than sociocultural/sociohistorical terms was a line of reasoning regarding the concept of *immutability* that entered into the equal protection discussion through cases of discrimination against women. In *Frontiero v. Richardson* (1973), the Supreme Court concluded, in a plurality decision, that discrimination on the basis of sex (what we now call gender) was unconstitutional for the reason that "sex, like race and national origin [was] an immutable characteristic" (*Frontiero v. Richardson* 1973, 686) such that discrimination on the basis of sex (what we now call gender) "would seem to violate the basic concept of our system that legal burdens should bear some relationship to individual responsibility" (*Frontiero v. Richardson* 1973, 686).

This "immutable characteristic" language (which implicated that race was based in biology and this was the reason that racial discrimination was problematic), then moved from a case addressing discrimination against women (i.e., *Frontiero*) to cases addressing racial discrimination. It is important that at no point prior to *Frontiero* had the Court stated that the "immutable characteristic" of blackness (and certainly not the "immutable characteristic" of race) was a constitutionally impermissible basis upon which to legally discriminate against persons. However, beginning with *Regents of the University of California v. Bakke* (1978), the Court began to reason in these terms, that is, it began to use the concept of the immutability of race in its reasoning process. In subsequent cases, the Court continues to speak of race as if it were "immutable," see, for example, *Fullilove v. Klutznick* (1980), and eventually speaks as if the immutability and purely biological nature of race are obvious and not in need of justification or explanation.

THE ACADEMIC SWITCH FROM BIOLOGICAL RACE TO SOCIOCULTURAL/SOCIOHISTORICAL RACE

In direct contrast to the trajectory of Supreme Court thinking on the concept of race, the academic concept of race started out in the nineteenth century—at least in European thought—as an understanding of race as a biological phenomenon and then moved, particularly in the past seventy-five years or so, into an understanding of race as a purely sociocultural/sociohistorical phenomenon. It is widely accepted that leading theorists of race in the late eighteenth century, such as Immanuel Kant and Johann Friedrich Blumenbach, generated the concept of biologically based human races, relying on travelogues provided by travelers involved in missionary work, colonization, and the slave trade for their information (Bernasconi and Lott 2000). Based on these travelogues, Kant's "Of the Different Human Races," for example, is commonly understood as the first attempt to give a "scientific" definition of race, according to which there were four, biologically based human races: "white," "Negro," "Hun," and "Hindu" (Kant 2000, 11). Interestingly, under the Kantian schema, the distinction between "Negroes and whites" was "self evident" (Kant 2000, 12). The 1781 version of Blumenbach's "On the Natural Variety of Mankind" added a fifth biological race (although the term he used was not "race" but "variety"), so the list of races became "Causasian," "Ethiopian," "Mongolian," "Malay," and "American," each with an associated "colour" (Blumenbach 2000, 27).

Based on this eighteenth century, academic concept of race as biologically based, as time went on, what I will call the traditional folk concept of race developed, according to which race was also biological. This conception of race is very popular even today in the United States, according to which human racial categories are real, biologically based, pure, and exist in a hierarchy, with the white race at the top of the hierarchy and the black race at the bottom. A key feature of the traditional folk concept of race is that there are, at bottom, only two races: white and black. This unique feature of American racial consciousness is sometimes referred to as the "black–white binary" (Sundstrom 2008). The traditional folk concept of race, however, fell out of favor in the academic community starting in the mid-twentieth century and is still out of favor in academia today (see Montagu 1942; UNESCO 1951; Livingstone 1962; Lewontin 1972; Hubbard and Wald 1993; Graves 2001).

Within the discipline of philosophy, and over the past thirty-five years or so (particularly within the critical philosophy of race), in the aftermath of the general consensus in the scientific community since roughly the 1950s that biological race does not refer to anything in the world, several more viable concepts of race have developed. These are that (1) race is not real and there is no such thing as race; (2) race is real and is based in biology, but does not carry with it the concepts of racial purity or a hierarchy of the races; (3) race is real, but is a social kind rather than a biological kind, that is, race is socially constructed. Charles Mills calls these three philosophically viable concepts of race (1) eliminativism/error theory, (2) racial biologism, and (3) antieliminativist constructionism, respectively (Mills 2014, 89).

A bit of additional detail on these three metaphysical positions on the concept of race adds insight. Eliminativism is the view, generally, that since the word "race" has no referent, we should stop using it. Kwame Anthony Appiah and Naomi Zack were the early proponents of this view (Appiah 1992, 1995, 1996; Zack 1994). "Racial biologism," as Mills defines it, is the view that a biological concept of race can (and by implication, should) be retained that does not carry with it some of the less palatable aspects of traditional, biological race such as a hierarchy among the races (see, e.g., Spencer 2012); and "anti-eliminativist constructionism" is the view, generally, that race is a social kind rather than a natural kind (Mills 2014, 89). Further distinctions are sometimes made between strong and weak constructionism. In broad strokes, "strong" constructionism entails the belief that race has a metaphysical referent in the world (or multiple metaphysical referents), whereas "weak" constructionism does not entail this claim (see Atkins 2012, 57–71). In both cases, however, biologically based ontology is dropped. Although there is controversy within the discipline of philosophy over which of these three metaphysical positions is the most convincing, outside of philosophy, almost all academic disciplines accept the weak social constructionist account of race, according to which race is a purely sociocultural/sociohistorical (contingent, context-dependent) phenomenon.

A CHANGE IN UNDERSTANDING OF THE PROBLEM WITH RACIAL DISCRIMINATION

As the change in the Court's thinking about race takes place from sociocultural/sociohistorical to biological, the Equal Protection Clause moves, vis-à-vis racial discrimination, from being understood as a remedial measure to curb the vestiges of chattel slavery, to a device for protecting everyone, regardless of racial identification, from "racial discrimination." Thus, while the early Supreme Court cases interpreting the Fourteenth Amendment stressed the remedial purpose of the Equal Protection Clause in light of the problem of the continued subordination of blacks after the Civil War, as time went on, the cases began to back away from this remedial purpose of the clause, and simultaneously began to equate racial discrimination with differentiating on the basis of race at large. This can be understood as a kind of whitewashing of the Equal Protection Clause, in the sense that the historical purpose of the clause as a remedy available to descendants of slavery for very specific reasons was no longer discussed.

The Equal Protection Clause of the Fourteenth Amendment to the United States Constitution was placed into the Amendment as a remedial measure for the purpose of providing a means for black people to challenge state-enacted laws that either reinforced or perpetuated what the Supreme Court called the "badges of slavery" after the end of the Civil War. The Congressional debates that took place in 1866 during the 39th Congress bear this fact out. When Congressman Stevens introduced the Amendment in the House, he characterized its purpose as "the amelioration of the condition of the freedmen" (Cong. Globe, 39th Cong., 1st Sess. 2459, 1866). Additionally, proponents of the Fourteenth Amendment repeatedly emphasized that one of the Amendment's primary purposes was to place in the Constitution itself the principles of Section 1 of the Civil Rights Act of 1866. The purpose of this Act was to give citizens "without regard to race and color, without regard to any previous condition of slavery or involuntary servitude . . . full and equal benefit of all laws and proceedings for the security of person and property, as is enjoyed by white citizens" (Civil Rights Act of 1866). Proponents of the Fourteenth Amendment in the early Congressional debates repeatedly stated that the Fourteenth Amendment's primary purpose was to address the manifest unequal status of black people as a group. Therefore, the historical evidence shows that rather than being designed to address racial discrimination as such, "the [Congressional] debates reveal overriding concern with the status of one racial group [i.e., blacks]" (Baer 1983, 138).

The enactment of the Thirteenth, Fourteenth, and Fifteenth Amendments to the US Constitution, known collectively as the Civil War Amendments, mirrored the purpose of the Civil Rights Act of 1866. In December of 1865, the Thirteenth Amendment, which banned slavery everywhere in the United States, was ratified (Rawley 1989). Two and a half years later, in July 1868, the Fourteenth Amendment (containing the Equal Protection Clause) was ratified, and then about two years after that, in March of 1870, the Fifteenth Amendment, prohibiting discrimination in voting "on account of race, color, or previous condition of servitude," was ratified. Taken together, these Civil War Amendments suggest that the Equal Protection Clause was included in the Fourteenth Amendment to make clear that equal protection under the law for black Americans could and would be federally enforced. Accordingly, Justice Miller stated in the 1873 *Slaughterhouse Cases* that the Fourteenth Amendment had "one pervading purpose," that is, "the protection of the newly made freeman and citizen from the oppressions of those who had formerly exercised unlimited dominion over him" (*Slaughterhouse Cases* 1873, 71).

The *Korematsu* case represents a turning point. In addition to identifying Japanese Americans as a "racial group," the *Korematsu* case also held that all legal restrictions which curtail the civil rights of a "single racial group" were immediately suspect and should be subjected to "the most rigid scrutiny" (*Korematsu v. United States* 1944, 216). In other words, the *Korematsu* Court suggested that the Equal Protection Clause should be understood or interpreted to provide special protection for a "racial group" (whatever that concept might entail) when a given law negatively impacted the rights of that group qua group. With this case, the Court began to find legalized racial discrimination problematic in itself, rather than problematic when directed toward a specific "racial" group, specifically the descendants of slaves.

In the late twentieth century, the concept of immutability entered into the Supreme Court's understanding of the concept of race and began to affect how the Court understood racial discrimination. That is, the Court began to use the supposed immutability of race to support its position that all racial classifications were invidious, even those that disadvantaged whites, and all racial classifications were therefore in violation of the Equal Protection Clause. The Court's reasoning in *Regents of the University of California v. Bakke* (1978) is typical. Whiteness is just as immutable as blackness, the Court reasoned, such that a classification that disadvantages whites is no more constitutional than a classification which disadvantages blacks. Justice Rehnquist's dissent in *United Steelworkers v. Weber* (1979) is also typical of the time period: "The evil inherent in discrimination against Negroes is that it is based on an immutable characteristic. . . . The characteristic becomes no less immutable and irrelevant, *and discrimination based thereon becomes no less evil*, simply because the person excluded is a member of one race rather than another," he wrote (*United Steelworkers v. Weber* 1979, 255, emphasis added).

The recent cases of *Gratz v. Bollinger*, 539 U.S. 244 (2003) and *Grutter v. Bollinger*, 539 U.S. 306 (2003), collectively known as "the Michigan cases" solidified the Court's transition to understanding racial discrimination as problematic per se. The result is that equal protection law currently protects white Americans more often than black Americans from "racial discrimination," and it leaves black Americans largely unprotected by the Equal Protection Clause.

THE WAGES OF WHITE PRIVILEGE

The Supreme Court's contemporary understanding of the concept of race as a purely biological phenomenon is in direct contrast to contemporary academic thinking on the topic of race, which understands race as a sociocultural/sociohistorical phenomenon. Moreover, the Court's switch from a sociocultural/sociohistorical (or, in philosophical terms, a social constructionist) concept of race to a purely biological concept of race during the same period of time that the academic concept of race reverses itself in the opposite direction is a curious state of affairs, given that the result is that the Equal Protection Clause, vis-à-vis racial discrimination, has moved from a device to protect black Americans to a device that protects primarily white Americans. One explanation for this state of affairs is that the appropriation by white Americans of the usage of the Equal Protection Clause for protection against "racial discrimination" is part of the larger phenomenon of the divestiture of the rights of blacks for the benefits of whites over time since the end of the civil rights movement. Arguably, were the Court to follow academic wisdom and utilize a sociocultural/sociohistorical concept of race rather than a biological one, it would then have to confront that racial discrimination is not something that happens in a vacuum. It would have to confront that racial discrimination does not mean, as some scholars contend, behaving as if race were important when it is not. Instead, racial discrimination is something that occurs in a context in which the vestiges or "badges" of slavery are not a thing of the past, but are perpetuated through policies and laws that treat black people as less "equal" than whites. The Supreme Court's present reliance on a purely biological concept of race at virtually the same point in time as the biological concept of race is dropped from academic legitimacy is therefore both anomalous and disturbing.

REFERENCES

Appiah, K. A. (1992). *In My Father's House: Africa in the Philosophy of Culture.* New York: Oxford University Press.

Appiah, K. A. (1995). "The Uncompleted Argument: DuBois and the Illusion of Race." In *Overcoming Racism and Sexism,* edited by L. Bell and D. Blumenfeld, Lanham, MD: Rowman and Littlefield.

Appiah, K. A. (1996). "Race, Culture, Identity: Misunderstood Connections." In *Color Conscious,* edited by Anthony Appiah and Amy Gutmann. Princeton, NJ: Princeton University Press.

Aristotle and R. Crisp. (2014). *Nicomachean Ethics.* Cambridge and New York: Cambridge University Press.

Atkins, A. (2012). *The Philosophy of Race.* Durham, NC: Acumen Publishing.

Baer, J. A. (1983). *Equality Under the Constitution: Reclaiming the Fourteenth Amendment.* Ithaca, NY: Cornell University Press.

Bernasconi, R., and T. L. Lott, eds. (2000). *The Idea of Race.* Indianapolis: Hackett.

Blumenbach, J. F. (2000). "Of the Natural Variety of Mankind." in *The Idea of Race,* edited by Robert Bernasconi and Tommy L. Lott, 27–37. Indianapolis: Hackett.

(The) Civil Rights Cases, 109 U.S. 3 (1883).

Cong. Globe, 39th Cong., 1st Sess. 2459 (1866).

Dred Scott v. Sanford, 60 U.S. 393 (1857).

Du Bois, W. E. B. [1897] (2001). "The Conservation of Races." In *Race,* edited by Robert Bernasconi, 84–91. Malden, MA: Blackwell.

Fireside, H. (2004). *Separate and Unequal: Homer Plessy and the Supreme Court Decision that Legalized Racism.* New York: Carroll & Graf Publishers.

Fullilove v. Klutznick, 448 U.S. 448 (1980).

Gratz v. Bollinger, 539 U.S. 244 (2003).

Graves, J. L. (2001). *The Emperor's New Clothes: Biological Theories of Race at the Millennium.* New Brunswick, NJ: Rutgers University Press.

Grutter v. Bollinger, 539 U.S. 306 (2003).

Hubbard, R., and E. Wald. (1993). *Exploding the Gene Myth: How Genetic Formation is Produced and Manipulated by Scientists, Physicians, Employers, Insurance Companies, Educators, and Law Enforcers.* Boston: Beacon Press.

Kant, I. (2000). "Of the Different Human Races." In *The Idea of Race,* edited by Robert Bernasconi and Tommy L. Lott, 8–22. Indianapolis: Hackett.

Lewontin, R. C. (1972). "The Apportionment of Human Diversity." *Evolutionary Biology* 6: 381–398.

Livingstone, F. (1962). "On the Nonexistence of Human Races." *Current Anthropology* 3: 279–281.

Mills, C. W. (2014). "Notes from the Resistance: Some Comments on Sally Haslanger's *Resisting Reality.*" *Philosophical Studies* 171 (1) :85–97.

Montagu, M. F. A. (1942). *Man's Most Dangerous Myth: The Fallacy of Race.* New York: Columbia University Press.

Ozawa v. United States, 260 U.S. 178 (1922).

Plessy v. Ferguson, 163 U.S. 537 (1896).

Rawley, J. A. (1989). *Turning Points of the Civil War.* Lincoln: University of Nebraska Press.

Regents of the University of California v. Bakke, 483 U.S. 265 (1978).

Slaughterhouse Cases, The, 83 U.S. 36 (1873).

Spencer, Q. "What 'Biological Racial Realism' Should Mean." *Philosophical Studies* 159 (2): 181–204.

Strauder v. West Virginia, 100 U.S. 303 (1880).

Sundstrom, R. R. (2008). *The Browning of America and the Evasion of Social Justice* Albany: State University of New York Press.

UNESCO. (1951). *Race and Science: The Race Question in Modern Science.* New York: Columbia University Press.

United Steelworkers v. Weber, 443 U.S. 193 (1979).

U.S. v. Bhagat Sing Thind, 261 U.S. 204 (1923).

Zack, N. (1994). "Race and Philosophic Meaning." *APA Newsletter on Philosophy and the Black Experience* 94 (1): 14–20.

CHAPTER 45

AFFIRMATIVE ACTION FOR THE FUTURE

JAMES P. STERBA

THE most widely implemented form of affirmative action in the United States today is diversity affirmative action. Its goal is not to remedy discrimination, whether present or past. Rather, its goal is diversity, which in turn is justified in terms of either the educational benefits it provides or its ability to create a more effective workforce in such areas as policing and community relations. The legal roots of this form of affirmative action in the United States are most prominent in *Regents of the University of California v. Bakke* (1978).

THE BAKKE DECISION: THE BEGINNINGS OF AFFIRMATIVE ACTION IN THE UNITED STATES

In *Bakke*, a majority of the US Supreme Court found both the use of quotas in the affirmative action program of the Davis medical school and the school's goal of remedying the effects of societal discrimination to be in violation of the Civil Rights Act and the Equal Protection Clause of the Fourteenth Amendment of the US Constitution. However, a different majority (with only Justice Powell as the common member of both majorities) seemed to allow that taking race and ethnicity into account as a factor to achieve diversity does not violate the Equal Protection Clause of the Fourteenth Amendment.

The legal effect of the Bakke decision was to allow affirmative action programs in higher education, but to significantly limit the way that they could be practiced and justified. The Bakke Court also required *strict scrutiny* of any race-based affirmative action program in education. This meant that an affirmative action program in education was permitted only if it was narrowly tailored to meet a compelling government interest and here the interest was diversity. This constraint was taken to be required by the Equal Protection Clause of the Fourteenth Amendment.

However, the same US Congress that passed the Fourteenth Amendment in 1867 also passed race-conscious statutes providing schools and farmland to both free blacks and former slaves that do not appear to satisfy the constraints that the Bakke majority found implicit in the Fourteenth Amendment. So it is difficult to see how the constraints on the use of racial classifications imposed by the Bakke court could be grounded in the Fourteenth Amendment as that amendment was understood by those who enacted it. What we have here is a new understanding of the Fourteenth Amendment whereby it is no longer utilized to protect blacks from racial domination and discrimination by the white majority, but rather primarily to protect the white majority from governmental action that favors blacks and other minorities.

For almost twenty years, Powell's opinion in *Bakke*, supported by Justices Brennan, Marshall, Blackman, and White, was the rationale for the affirmative action used by most American colleges and universities. However, in 2003, the US Supreme Court again addressed the question of the use of affirmative action in *Grutter v. Bollinger* and *Gratz v. Bollinger*. Lee Bollinger was then president of the University of Michigan. *Grutter* addressed the University of Michigan Law School affirmative action policy and *Gratz* addressed the undergraduate admissions policy of the university. Both cases were brought by white plaintiffs who claimed they had been discriminated against in being denied admission on the grounds of race.

Without a doubt, the most important finding of the Court was that it was constitutionally permissible to use racial preferences to achieve the educational benefits of diversity. That, of course, had been the opinion of Justice Powell in *Bakke*. Even so, there had been considerable debate about whether Powell's opinion represented the holding of the Court in *Bakke*. In *Grutter*, Justice Sandra Day O'Connor, writing for the majority, cut short that discussion by simply adopting the opinion of Powell in *Bakke* as the opinion of the majority in *Grutter*. "Today, we hold that the Law School has a compelling interest in attaining a diverse student body." In doing this, the Court also deferred to "the Law School's educational judgment that such diversity is essential to its educational mission." The grounds for this deference is the First Amendment's protection of educational autonomy, which secures the right of a university "to select those students who will contribute to the 'robust exchange of ideas'" (quoting Powell). At the same time, the court was moved by evidence of the educational benefits of diversity provided by the University of Michigan Law School and by briefs of the amicus curiae (friends of the court):

> American businesses have made clear that the skills needed in today's increasingly global marketplace can only be developed through exposure to widely diverse people, cultures, ideas, and viewpoints.
>
> What is more, high-ranking retired officers and civilian leaders of the United States military assert that "[based on [their] decades of experience," a "highly qualified, racially diverse officer corps . . . is essential to the military's ability to fulfill its principle mission to provide national security."

While affirming the constitutional permissibility of using racial preferences to achieve the educational benefits of diversity, the Supreme Court in *Grutter* accepted the University of Michigan Law School's affirmative action admissions program at the same time that the court in *Gratz* rejected the undergraduate school's program. The difference between the two programs, according to the majority in *Grutter*, is that the undergraduate program operated in a too-mechanical, nonindividualized manner. The University of Michigan College of Literature, Science, and the Arts, facing the task of admitting 5,000 of 25,000 applicants, had chosen to automatically assign 20 points (out of 150 points) on the basis of race or ethnicity.

The court ruled that its requirement of strict scrutiny, which demands that any use of race or ethnicity in admissions be narrowly tailored to achieve the educational benefits of diversity, cannot be met unless each and every applicant's qualifications are individually considered. If race or ethnicity is to be a factor in admissions, the majority contended there needs to be "individualized consideration of each and every applicant." The law school, seeking to admit 350 students from 3,500 applicants, had used a more individualized admissions process that the Court did endorse.

What the law school in its pursuit of the benefits of diversity had done is judge that *racial diversity*, at least for our times, is a very important means for achieving that goal and that racial diversity required a "critical mass" of minority students (where a critical mass is the number of students sufficient to enable underrepresented minority students to contribute to class dialogue without feeling isolated). Nor is a critical mass a quota if it is fixed by the requirements of educational pedagogy and not to achieve a certain percentage of underrepresented minority students in the entering class.

Predictably, the Supreme Court's decision in *Grutter* met with a number of objections. Some denied that the educational benefits of diversity are an important enough state purpose to justify the use of racial preferences to achieve them. Others allowed that the educational benefits of diversity were an important enough state purpose to justify the use of racial preferences; they just contended that there are other means that are preferable, because they can achieve the same educational benefits of diversity in a race-neutral way. Still others maintained that diversity affirmative action is objectionable, because it harms those who receive it. Let us examine each of these objections in turn.

DIVERSITY IS NOT IMPORTANT ENOUGH

In their amicus curiae brief before the Supreme Court in the Michigan cases, the Michigan Association of Scholars maintained that "even where diversity in their classrooms is a genuine merit, it is simply not the case that their work, their teaching, their research, cannot go forward successfully in its absence." When making this claim, however, opponents of affirmative action must not be thinking about what happens in classrooms when racial issues are discussed, or analogously, what happens in classrooms when gender issues are discussed. Surely, the teachers among us who have led discussions on racial issues in our classrooms, both with and without minority students being present, know what a significant difference the presence of minorities normally makes in such contexts. And usually there is a similar loss when gender issues are discussed in the absence of women. So when opponents of affirmative action maintain that diversity is unnecessary for successful teaching, they must not be thinking about courses focused on racial (or gender) issues.

Nevertheless, without denying the educational benefits of diversity, it still might be argued that achieving those benefits does not constitute an important enough state purpose to justify the use of racial preferences to secure them. This would seem to be the position of Justice Thomas in his dissent in *Grutter*. Thomas argues that the only kind of state purpose that would be important enough to justify the use of racial preferences in a nonremedial context is national security or, more broadly, "measures the State must take to provide a bulwark against anarchy, or to prevent violence." In *Grutter*, however, no one, except Justice Scalia, joined Thomas in defending such an extreme limitation on the use of racial preferences.

The key question here is: Whose interpretation of the Equal Protection Clause of the Fourteenth Amendment should we accept? The majority, to support their interpretation of the amendment, could have appealed to the original intent of the Congress that formulated and passed the amendment (Schnapper 1985, 753–798). As noted earlier, the same Congress that formulated and passed the Fourteenth Amendment, also formulated and passed race-conscious statutes that provided schools and farmland to both free blacks and former slaves. In fact, this same Congress viewed its passing of the Fourteenth Amendment as a necessary means of supporting the legality of its race-conscious statutes. However, rather than appeal to the original intent of the Congress that formulated and passed the Fourteenth Amendment, the majority in *Grutter* relied upon an interpretation given to the Amendment by a number of Supreme Court cases in the last seventy years or so.

The history of this interpretation of the Fourteenth Amendment is usually traced to *Korematsu v. United States* (1944), although sometimes Justice Harlon Stone's note in *United States v. Caroline Products Co.* (1938) is cited as an earlier source. In *Korematsu*, Justice Hugo Black, while upholding the constitutionality of the interment of the Japanese Americans during World War II on grounds of national security, held that "all legal restrictions which curtail the civil rights of a single racial group are immediately suspect. That is not to say that all such restrictions are unconstitutional. It is to say that courts must subject them to the most rigid scrutiny." Using this interpretation of the Equal Protection Clause of the Fourteenth Amendment, the Supreme Court in a number of decisions prior to *Brown v. Board of Education of Topeka, Kansas* (1954) struck down state laws segregating blacks and whites but only on the grounds that the segregated facilities were not of equal quality.

In *Brown*, the Supreme Court went further, ruling that the legally required separation of the races cannot be equal, and demanding the desegregation of public schools on the grounds that the separation of blacks and whites is motivated by and reinforces attitudes of racial superiority. In so acting, the Court emphasized the invidious nature of this use of racial preferences. In *Regents of the University of California v. Bakke*, however, the Court faced a use of a racial preferences that appeared to be motivated, not by invidious intent, but rather by a desire to remedy past wrongs. As we have noted, in a fractured decision, a majority of Powell and the Brennan group held that race can be used as a factor in admissions decisions. But another majority of Powell and the Stevens group held that the appropriate standard for evaluating the use of racial preferences is *strict scrutiny*. According to this standard, there must be a compelling state interest (which in this case Powell took to be diversity), and the use of racial preferences in pursuit of that interest must be narrowly tailored.

It is Powell's approach in *Bakke* that was been endorsed in a number of subsequent Supreme Court decisions, right up to, and including, the *Grutter* decision. Thus, in *Grutter*, O'Connor writes:

> We have held that all racial classifications imposed by government must be analyzed by the reviewing court under strict scrutiny.

O'Connor also adds, quoting herself from *Adarand*, that strict scrutiny need not be "fatal in fact." And this is just where the disagreement between the majority in *Grutter* and Thomas and Scalia is joined. In *Adarand*, Thomas had claimed, with Scalia in agreement:

Government-sponsored racial discrimination based on benign prejudice is just as noxious as discrimination inspired by malicious prejudice.

In *Grutter*, Thomas reiterates basically the same claim, making it clear that his grounds for rejecting all racial preferences are the bad consequences that result from their use. This means that, in Thomas's view, it must be the case that the state of Michigan would be better off with a law school that is diverse, but not elite, than it would be with a law school which is both diverse and elite. Unfortunately, neither Thomas nor Scalia bothers to set out the required consequentialist argument to show that this is the case. And it is surely the failure of Thomas or Scalia to provide the necessary consequentialist argument, along with Michigan's Gurin Report and over one hundred amici curiae briefs attesting to the benefits of affirmative action, that persuaded O'Connor to join with the more liberal side of the Court in this case.

THERE ARE BETTER MEANS

It is easy to see that the claim that there are better means, typically race-neutral ones, is just another way of continuing the consequentialist evaluation required by the strict scrutiny standard. The Texas Top Ten Percent Plan and the Florida Top Twenty Percent Plan have been put forward by opponents of affirmative action as race-neutral ways of securing the educational benefits of diversity.

The Texas Top Ten Percent Plan and the Florida Top Twenty Percent Plan were successful in admitting minorities into their undergraduate institutions at levels that either match, or, in Florida's case, surpass, what they had accomplished with race-based affirmative action programs. This was not accomplished, however, without a substantial increase in scholarship aid for minorities in both states, and without, in the case of Texas, using smaller classes and a variety of remedial programs. Both plans also rely on at least de facto segregated high schools in their respective states to produce the diversity they have. If the high schools in both states were in fact more integrated, the plans would not be as effective as they are with respect to undergraduate enrollment.

Even so, the plans employed still had some serious drawbacks. First, the plans did nothing for law schools, medical schools, and other graduate and professional schools where ending affirmative action has been devastating. Those schools were only able to rebound after the *Grutter* decision. Second, the Texas Plan has a detrimental effect on the admission of minorities not in the top 10 percent. Third, such plans restrict universities from doing the individualized assessments that would be required to assemble a student body that is not just racially diversity, but diverse in other desirable ways as well. Fourth, an analysis of data from the Florida Plan showed that students at seventy-five of Florida's high schools could have carried a C+ average and still have ranked in the top 20 percent of their class. Fifth, such plans only work, if at all, for universities that admit primarily from a state-wide population. Only 11 percent of the applicants to the University of Texas at Austin are nonresidents, whereas many elite colleges and universities recruit students from a national and international pool, and so cannot apply this percent model to their selection of student bodies

There is, however, still another reason that may trump all the others as a reason for rejecting these so-called alternatives to a race-based affirmative action. It is that despite their claims to be race-neutral, these percentage-plan alternatives are really race-based themselves. They are means that are chosen explicitly because they are known to produce a desirable degree of racial diversity. In this regard, they are no different from the poll taxes that were used in the segregated South, which were purportedly race-neutral means, but were clearly designed to produce, in that case, an objectionable racial result—to keep blacks from voting. Accordingly, if we are going to end up using a race-based selection procedure to get the educational benefits of diversity, we might as well use one that most effectively produces that desired result, and that appears to be a selection procedure that explicitly employs race as a factor in admissions.

It is not surprising, therefore, that this is exactly what the University of Texas did once the Supreme Court's Grutter decision nullified the authority of the Hopwood decision over the university. Subsequently, the University of Texas has sought and received the authority to limit the number of students it must admit using the Top Ten Percent Plan to 75 percent of its incoming class. What this shows is that the practitioners of the most highly regarded alternative to affirmative action in the country, those very same people who were in the best position to assess its merits and limitations, chose to at least supplement the Top Ten Percent Plan when it was legally able to do so. That seems to me to be very strong evidence against the viability of the Texas Top Ten Percent Plan and the Florida's Top Twenty Percent Plan as alternatives to affirmative action.

It Harms Those Who Receive It

Thomas Sowell has claimed that affirmative action mismatches minorities with the colleges and professional schools they attend, such that a greater number of them perform unsatisfactorily than would otherwise be the case without affirmative action. To make this point, Sowell quotes at length from an article by Clyde Summers of Yale Law School:

> If Harvard or Yale, for example, admits minority students with test scores 100 to 150 points below that normally required for a nonminority student to get admitted, the total number of minority students able to get a legal education is not increased thereby. The minority students given such preference would meet the normal admissions standard at Illinois, Rutgers or Texas. Similarly, minority students given preference at Pennsylvania would meet normal standards at Pittsburgh, those given preference at Duke would meet normal standards at North Carolina, and those given preference at Vanderbilt would meet normal standards at Kentucky, Mississippi and West Virginia. Thus, each law school, by its preference admission, simply takes minority students away from other schools whose admissions standard are further down the scale. . . . In sum, the policy of preferential admission has a pervasive shifting effect, causing large numbers of minority students to attend law schools whose normal admissions standard they do not meet, instead of attending other law schools whose normal standards they do meet. (Sowell 2004, 145–146)

William Bowen and Derek Bok attempt to meet this mismatching-leading-to-greater-failure argument by pointing out that the schools in their study have high graduation rates for minorities (Bok and Boden 1998, 61, 259). Sowell counters by claiming that Bowen and Bok's sample of twenty-four private and four public elite schools is untypical and that there are other elite schools, particularly elite public universities where the SAT gap between white and minority students is generally greater, leading to lower graduation rates for minority students. But although there may be some elite schools where the SAT gap is greater, the gap does tend to be fairly constant over elite schools. In addition, if we look at the University of Michigan, an elite public school, when it used race-based affirmative action, we find that although there was a graduation gap for minorities, it is still a few percentage points higher than it is for whites graduating from all 305 large universities that participate in Division I–level NCAA athletics. This would seem to suggest that the causes of the lower graduation rate among underrepresented minorities have little to do with whether those minorities benefited from diversity affirmative action.

Richard Sander has subsequently attempted to support Sowell's view that minorities are being harmed by affirmative action, at least at US law schools. Sander provides a statistical argument that affirmative action mismatches black students at law schools by admitting them with lower LSAT scores and undergraduate grades that put them at an academic disadvantage, thereby resulting in their having lower grades and lower rates of graduating and passing the bar. Sander further argues that if affirmative action ended, blacks would cascade to lower ranked schools where they would perform dramatically better, causing a net increase of 8 percent in the number of new black lawyers, and a net increase of 22 percent in the number of blacks passing the bar on their first attempt (Sander 2004, 367).

Sander's original article went on to create so much controversy that the following year a special issue of the *Stanford Law Review* was published containing four critiques of it and a reply by Sander himself. In his original article, Sander had argued that without affirmative action blacks would cascade to lower ranked law schools, where they would get higher grades and have higher rates of graduation and bar passage. To determine how well cascading blacks would do at the lower ranked schools, Sander assumed that they would do as well as whites at those schools were doing with the similar LSAT scores and undergraduate grades, given that, according to Sander, LSAT scores and undergraduate grades are the only relevant criteria for predicting law school success. On this basis, Sander was able to claim that blacks who receive affirmative action to attend a higher ranked law school are "mismatched"—they would be better off if they had attended lower ranked schools.

However, when some of Sander's critics proposed determining how cascading blacks would do at the lower ranked schools by, more plausibly, assuming that they would do as well as blacks at those same schools were doing with similar LSAT scores and undergraduate grades, Sander's statistical argument began to collapse. Under this assessment, it turned out that cascading would not help blacks at all; they would do better if they remained at higher ranked schools as beneficiaries of affirmative action.

In his "Reply to Critics," Sander, attempting to salvage his argument, granted that he should have been comparing blacks to blacks to determine the benefits from cascading, but then claimed that blacks, whom he had wrongly expected to be better off from cascading, must have had "unobservable characteristics" that enabled them, even while experiencing the "disadvantages" of affirmative action, to outperform blacks who were at lower ranked schools where, given their LSAT scores and undergraduate grades, the cascading blacks seemed to belong (Sander 2005, 1963). Yet while there surely are other factors involved in law school admission other than just LSAT scores and undergraduate grades (the only factors that Sander had initially recognized), Sander's treatment of such factors now as "unobservable characteristics" and his appealing to them when, and only when, their absence would cast doubt on his argument against affirmative action, surely is too ad hoc an appeal to such factors to provide a defense of his view.

Sander also recognizes that without affirmative action at elite law schools, black enrollment would decline from around 8 percent to 1–2 percent. This is particularly significant, given that 40 percent of the lawyers at top law firms and 48 percent of black law professors come from the top ten law schools. On his website, Sander also estimates that without affirmative action, there would be zero, or nearly zero, blacks at Harvard Law School and Yale Law School. Again, this is particularly significant given that 25 percent of black law professors in the United States have graduated from just those two law schools. Thus, cascading would not help blacks presently attending such elite law schools from which, Sander grants, 95.3 percent graduate. So, for Sander, the benefits from blacks cascading only occur for those blacks attending less than elite schools. Yet exactly how these benefits would overcome the losses that would occur from such a drastic decline in blacks enrolled at elite law schools, Sander never makes clear.

In any case, Sander maintains in his "Reply" that the impact eliminating affirmative action would have on the production of black lawyers (the 8 percent increase he mentioned in his original Stanford article) is "really a side issue," and so no longer a central claim of his view. Now his central thesis is simply that the rate of first time (but not eventual) bar passage will be higher for black law graduates with cascading. Yet why should we be concerned with such a meager payoff? Isn't what really counts in this regard, not the rate of first-time bar passage, but rather the rate of eventual bar passage? And, with respect to that outcome, Sander's critics argue (and Sander himself implicitly concedes by focusing simply on the rate of first time passage) that ending affirmative action would have no impact at all. The real impact of ending affirmative action, Sander's critics contend, would be on the production of black lawyers. According to one estimate, there would be about a 21 percent drop. This, of course, contrasts with Sander's initial claim, now abandoned in "Reply," that ending affirmative action would produce an 8 percent increase of (nonelite) black lawyers. Nor does Sander directly critique the 21 percent drop claim made by some of his critics. Rather, he allows that these critics are "strongest when discussing the consequences of eliminating racial preferences on the production of black lawyers" (Sander 2005, 1996). So again, we need to ask exactly how blacks or black lawyers could be better off with a 21 percent drop in the production of black lawyers, and with a more than 75 percent drop in black lawyers graduating from elite law schools, especially in view of the positions that black graduates from just those elite schools have been acquiring on law school faculties and at top law firms? Sander never explains how this could be the case.

THE FUTURE OF AFFIRMATIVE ACTION

In 2013, the US Supreme Court in *Fisher v. University of Texas* held that lower courts were correct in finding that *Grutter* calls for deference to the University of Texas's experience and expertise about its educational mission, but incorrect in giving the University of Texas deference with respect to whether the means it chose to attain that diversity was narrowly tailored to its goal. On this point, the Supreme Court held that at all times the university has an obligation to demonstrate, and the judiciary an obligation to determine, that admissions processes "ensure that each applicant is evaluated as an individual and not in a way that makes an applicant's race or ethnicity the defining feature of his or her application." The Court also held that the judiciary had an obligation to determine that it was necessary for the university to use race to achieve the educational benefits of diversity, such that no workable race-neutral alternatives would produce those benefits. The Supreme Court then remanded the case back to the Fifth Circuit to correct its mistake.

Abigail Fisher, a white student, had applied to the University of Texas at Austin in 2008. In that year, applicants to the university were admitted in one of two ways. Under the first, the Top Ten Percent Law, a student in the top 10 percent of his or her high school graduating class is offered automatic admission to the university. Under the second, the Holistic Review, a student is admitted to the university based on the applicant's entire application, including but not limited to academic credentials, extracurricular activities, socioeconomic status, and race. Under this second holistic approach, no one factor is dispositive. Fisher did not graduate in the top 10 percent of her high school class and was also rejected under the university's Holistic Review. It was this second rejection, involving race, which the university claimed as a factor, to which Fisher objected.

On reconsideration, the Fifth Circuit Court reaffirmed its prior ruling. Having scrutinized the university's plan again, the Fifth Circuit concluded that the university's consideration of race was narrowly tailored to achieve the compelling goal of diversity and that race-neutral alternatives would not suffice. More specifically, the Fifth Circuit held that the Top Ten Percent Law left a gap in an admissions process that was seeking to create the multidimensional diversity that the Supreme Court had envisioned in *Grutter* and *Gratz*. By taking into account an applicant's entire application, Holistic Review compelled admission of diverse students who would otherwise not be admitted on class rank alone, under the Top Ten Percent Law. According to the court, the university's Holistic Review was narrowly tailored to achieve its compelling interest in attaining a multi- rather than a single-dimensional diversity, one that was based on class rank alone. On June 29, 2015, the Supreme Court announced that they would hear another challenge to the University of Texas's admissions policy. (The case will be heard in the Court's Fall 2015 session.)

One central question has repeatedly come up in the *Fisher v. University of Texas* court cases is this: What is the goal of the University of Texas's race-based affirmative action program, and when will we know that goal has been reached? Now we can try to answer this question quantitatively or nonquantitatively. Answers offered that appear quantitative are "meaningful numbers," "meaningful representation," and "a number that encourages underrepresented minority student to participate in the classroom and not feel isolated," "numbers such that underrepresented minority students do not feel isolated or like spokespersons for their race." A nonquantitative answer favored by the University of Texas is the goal of providing educational benefits that diversity is designed to bring about, such as wider perspectives, increased professionalism, and more civic engagement. Those who are opposed to the University's non–Top Ten Percent admissions program favor quantitative answers. This is because it presents a catch-22 problem for the university. Thus, if the university provides a definitive quantitative answer, say 25 percent, then it can be accused of employing a quota or engaging in racial balancing, both of which are constitutionally prohibited. But if the university does not provide a quantitative answer when a quantitative answer is deemed to be appropriate, then the university can be accused of failing to demonstrate how its program is narrowly tailored to meet a goal it has not adequately quantitatively specified. There is some likelihood that a majority of the Supreme Court either sees or wants to place the University of Texas in just such a catch-22 situation.

Nevertheless, there is still the possibility that the more qualitative answer by the University of Texas to the central question may yet win out. The University wants us to start by looking at the kind of diversity that the Top Ten Percent Law provides. It is a diversity that is based simply on attaining a high class rank in de facto racially segregated schools where the gaps in educational preparation and achievement are substantial. Clearly, Top Ten Percent students coming to the University of Texas from such schools will be anything but comparable in terms of their educational preparation and achievement, and their differences are even more likely to promote racial stereotypes than dissipate them. That is why the University of Texas wanted to pursue something other than the one-dimensional diversity provided by the Top Ten Percent Law and thereby have a way of admitting more non–Top Ten Percent minority students from academically better high schools who would have educational qualifications more comparable to Top Ten Percent Caucasian students coming from those same academically better schools.

The University of Texas has also implemented various non-race-based ways of increasing minority enrollment. It has created scholarship programs designed to increase yield among minority students, expanded its outreach to high schools in underrepresented areas of the state, and launched additional recruiting efforts at low-performing schools. In fact, the university claims that it has implemented every race-neutral effort that its detractors insist must be exhausted prior to adopting a race-conscious admission program. But these measures have generally increased simply the number of minorities who are now taking advantage of the Top Ten Percent Plan to come to the University of Texas. These additional programs have not enabled the university to get beyond the one-dimensional diversity provided by that Plan. That is the University's justification for using race as a factor of a factor in its non Top Ten Percent admission program.

Nevertheless, there may still be a non-race-based way of achieving that multidimensional diversity that the University of Texas wants. We need to begin with the realization that racial discrimination continues be a very serious problem in the United States, affecting many different aspects of our society. (The troubling arrest of Sandra Bland captured on video and her subsequent death while in lockup in Hempstead, Texas, which is just about 100 miles from the University of Texas's flagship campus in Austin is just one recent example [Montgomery 2015].) Accordingly, this non-race-based alternative goes on to affirm that it is of the utmost importance that we effectively address the problem of racial discrimination in our educational institutions. This is seen to require that we bring to those institutions, students, in particular, who can speak with authority about such racial discrimination. In the United States, this will typically involve admitting students from disadvantaged racial minorities who have themselves suffered such discrimination. But it can also, as the University of Michigan's and the University of Texas's undergraduate affirmative action programs allowed, admit Caucasian students who attended an inner-city high school in Detroit or San Antonio and are otherwise qualified.

Putting these two elements together, such a diversity affirmative action program would be designed to look for students who either have experienced racial discrimination themselves or who understand well, in some other way, how racism harms people in the United States, and thus are able to authoritatively and effectively speak about it in an educational context. This basis for selecting someone as a diversity affirmative action candidate can then be satisfied by Caucasian applicants who because of their disposition and experience can speak authoritatively and effectively about racial discrimination, and it can fail to be met by disadvantaged racial and ethnic minorities who because of their disposition and/or lack of experience cannot speak authoritatively and effectively about racial discrimination. This clearly seems to be a form of non-race-based diversity affirmative action that both proponents and opponents of the University of Texas's race-based affirmative action program could embrace. It could also eventually eliminate any need for the Top Ten Percent Plan, which is problematic, not just for the reason the University gives—the one-dimensional diversity it provides—but also because it is race-based in just the way poll taxes in the past are now regarded as race-based discrimination. Accordingly, this non-race-based alternative could be the future of affirmative action.

REFERENCES

Bakke v. Regents of the University of California, 438 U.S. 265(1978).

Bok, Derek, and William Bowen. (1998). *The Shape of the River*. Princeton, NJ: Princeton University Press.

Brief of Amicus Curiae, The Michigan Association of Scholars in Support of Petitioners. Accessed May 22, 2016. http://www.vpcomm.umich.edu/admissions/legal/gru_amicus/mas_both.pdf.

Brown v. Board of Education of Topeka, Kansas. (1954). https://www.law.cornell.edu/search/site/Brown%20%20v.%20Board%20of%20Education%20of%20Topeka%2C%20Kansas%20%281954%29%2C.

Fisher v. University of Texas, 570 U.S. (2013).

Fisher v. University of Texas No. 09-50822 (5th Cir. 2014).

Gratz v. Bollinger 539 U.S. (2003).

Grutter v. Bollinger, 539 U.S. (2003).

Korematsu v. United States. (1944). https://www.law.cornell.edu/supremecourt/text/323/214#writing-USSC_CR_0323_0214_ZS.

Montgomery, David. (2015). "Sandra Bland Was Threatened with a Taser, Police Video Shows." *The New York Times*, July 21. Accessed May 22, 2016. http://www.nytimes.com/2015/07/22/us/sandra-bland-was-combative-texas-arrest-report-says.html?_r=0.

Sander, Richard. (2004). "A Systematic Analysis of Affirmative Action in American Law School." *Stanford Law Review* 57: 367–483.

Sander, Richard. (2005). "A Reply to Critics." *Stanford Law Review* 57: 1963–2016.

Schnapper, Eric. (1985). "Affirmative Action and the Legislative History of the Fourteenth Amendment." *Virginia Law Review* 71: 753–798.

Sowell, Thomas. (2004). *Affirmative Action Around the World*. New Haven, CT: Yale University Press.

United States v. Caroline Products Co. (1938). https://www.law.cornell.edu/search/site/United%20%20%20States%20v.%20Caroline%20Products%20Co.%20%281938%29.

CHAPTER 46

IDEAL, NONIDEAL, AND EMPIRICAL THEORIES OF SOCIAL JUSTICE
The Need for Applicative Justice in Addressing Injustice

NAOMI ZACK

> Social information just dribbles in, bit by bit, and we simply get used to it. A single story about a person really hits home at once, but the grinding injustices of daily life are endured. It is easy to ignore them and we do.
>
> Judith Shklar, *The Faces of Injustice* (Shklar 1990, 110)

IDEAL theory about justice extends from Plato's *Republic* to John Rawls's *A Theory of Justice*, including many careers devoted to analyses and criticism about such texts in political philosophy. Rawls offers a picture of the basic institutional structures of a just society, on the premise that in order to correct injustice, we must first know what justice is. According to Rawls, while "partial compliance theory" studies the principles that govern how we are to deal with injustice, full compliance theory, or ideal theory, studies the institutional principles of justice in a stable society where citizens obey the law. Rawls began *A Theory of Justice* with the claim: "The reason for beginning with ideal theory is that it provides, I believe, the only basis for the systematic grasp of these more pressing problems" (Rawls 1971, 8).

Rawls's ideal theory is too abstract to correct injustice or provide justice for victims of injustice in reality, because it is based on a thought experiment and the assumption of a "well-ordered" society in which there already is compliance with law (Zack 2016, 1–64). What people care about in reality concerning justice is not what ideal justice is or would be, but how immediate injustice can be corrected. Injustice is always specific in concrete events that are recognizable as certain types, for example, theft, murder, or police racial profiling. Injustice can be corrected by punishing those responsible for it in specific cases and instituting social changes that prevent or reduce future occurrences of the same type.

Rawlsian *non*ideal theories of justice, constructed for societies where people do not comply with just laws, rely on ideal theory as a standard for just institutional structures. The main question driving nonideal theory is how to construct a model or picture of justice that will result in the future correction or avoidance of present injustices. John Simmons quotes John Rawls from *Law of Peoples*, on this matter.

> Nonideal theory asks how this long-term goal might be achieved, or worked toward, usually in gradual steps. It looks for courses of action that are morally permissible and politically possible as well as likely to be effective [LOP p. 89]. (Simmons 2010, 7)

However, injured or indignant parties may not care about the long-term goal of justice that could lead to balance or compensation for their situations. Not only are what P. F. Strawson (1962) called "reactive attitudes," such as moral indignation, blame, and a desire for deserved punishment, strong in their focus on injustice, but the best theory of justice in the world does not tell us what to do about the injustices we are faced with in the here and now, especially "the more pressing problems" of race-related injustices. Such questions cannot be answered with reference to ideal theory or some application of ideal or nonideal theory to their concrete situations, because the a priori nature of both of these does not provide a fit with specific contingencies—ideal and nonideal theories do not generate practical bridge principles. As theories, they posit ideal entities, but without the apparatus of scientific theories which provides connections to observable entities or events. (Moulines 1985). The correction of injustice or injustice theory requires a philosophical foundation for itself.

Models of justice have often been naïvely utopian throughout the history of philosophy, because they are based on an assumption of automatic total compliance, as though the right words or pictures by themselves have the power to transform reality, or as though agreement with those right words or pictures will automatically result in action that will automatically make the world instantiate those words or pictures. When they are not fantastically and ineffectively utopian in this way, such models have been used to justify the already-existing dominance of some groups over others. (A prime example is John Locke's *Second Treatise of Government*, written decades before 1688 Glorious Revolution, to express the interests of the new rising class of landed gentry, which were eventually fulfilled by a Protestant king on the throne and a strong representative parliament after that revolution [Laslett 1988].)

Models of justice have legitimately served to inspire law in modern societies with government constitutions and national and local law. But, sometimes, as in US founding documents, although universal and absolute justice is proclaimed, subsequent events make it clear that this language was intended to legitimize just treatment for members of selected groups only, that is, white male property owners, at first. As a result of just law and its selective application, over time, there comes to be justice for an expanding group, but still not everyone in society. However, what is written, together with descriptions of real justice for some, can be a powerful lever for obtaining justice for at least some of the excluded. To understand how that works, it is necessary to develop an approach to justice that begins with injustice, in real situations where there is already some degree of justice in a larger whole. The extension of existing practices of justice to members of new groups is *applicative justice*, a concept with substantial historical and intellectual precedent, although not by that name. In what follows, more will be said about the idea of applicative justice and then its history will be considered. Voting rights and housing rights are examples of candidates for applicative justice in our time. Finally, content in the form of narrative may be motivational for social change.

The Idea of Applicative Justice

Applicative justice is an approach to justice with the goal of making the unjust treatment of some comparable to those who already receive just treatment. Applicative justice takes a comparative approach, for example, comparing how young black males are treated by police officers in contemporary US society, to how young white males are treated (Jones 2013; Zack 2013, 2015). Applicative justice rests on a pragmatic approach to social ills, which includes the premise, based on Arthur Bentley's 1908 insights in *The Process of Government*, that government is much more than the apparatus of state and written laws and court decisions. Government is an extended, dynamic process, an ongoing contention among interest groups in society. This full-bodied, empirical and pragmatic view of government process entails, for example, that we consider as parts of the same political mix/phenomenon/raw material all of the foregoing: the Fourth and Fourteenth Amendments, the 1960s Civil Rights Legislation, doctrines of probable cause, the disproportionate incarceration of African Americans, racial profiling, and police homicide with impunity. Thus, Rawls's insistence that "the rights secured by justice are not subject to political bargaining or to the calculus of social interests" (Rawls 1971, 4), should be understood as "the rights secured by justice *should not be* subject to political bargaining or to the calculus of social interests." In reality, "the rights secured by justice" are constantly subject to political bargaining and the living calculus of social interests. One consequence of this empirical perspective is that moral outrage, critiques of white supremacy, or analyses of white privilege, along with other forms of blame, cannot be assumed to have the power to change anything, by themselves. By contrast, changing relationships between police officers and their local communities, or changing the rules of engagement when police stop or attempt to stop suspects, might on this view have some causal power (Ayres and Markovits 2014). It is important to realize that such changes in practice would not be specific applications of a theory of justice, but ways of changing social reality into a different political mix.

However, a better theory of justice, even a more racially egalitarian one and even a theory of applicative justice that was widely accepted, would still be no more than a change in what Bentley calls "political content." Any theory of justice or any set of just laws is compatible with widespread racially unequal and unjust practice. And the converse also holds. Unjust laws or laws with gaps for unjust practice are compatible with just practice. Thus, applicative justice is pragmatic in taking the whole political mix/phenomenon/raw material as its subject for a specific injustice. Unlike ideal or nonideal justice theory, the applicative justice approach brooks little faith that reality can be changed by a special conceptual space or mode of critical moral discourse that is undertaken apart from reality. Reality cannot be changed by normative pronouncements, by or on behalf of the oppressed, but only by shifts in existing interests of groups of real people. To base hopes for change on normative content alone may paralyze the means for taking action that could result in change, because such content proceeds as though matters of justice were only matters of argument. Those who have opposed social racial justice have understood this well enough, because instead of mainly arguing against new just law over the twentieth century, they have taken action to block progress.

RACE AND JUSTICE

Consideration of race and injustice together, within political philosophy, focuses on the need for specific groups to not be treated unjustly. For a group to be treated justly, a large number of its members need to be treated justly. But for a group to be treated unjustly, it is sufficient if a smaller number or lower proportion than required to meet the standard of just treatment be treated unjustly. One reason for this asymmetry is that just treatment is easily normalized within communities, whereas unjust treatment of only a few is disruptive and considered abnormal among other members of the group to which victims belong (although not necessarily by members of groups who are generally treated justly). The unjust treatment of a small number ripples from their friends and relations to other members of the same group, who realize that they are subject to similar unjust treatment from their membership in that group alone.

More broadly, if the group treated justly and the group treated unjustly belong to the same larger collective, such as whites and blacks in the United States, then the unjust treatment of even a very small number of that total collective of residents or citizens should be disruptive to the whole collective, given promulgated principles of "justice for all." But that does not always happen, at least not in ways that result in real change. Apathy and self-absorption of those not treated unjustly is part of the reason, although another significant part is that the group treated justly already knows that the national collective rhetoric of justice is intended to apply primarily to them. It is that kind of disparate treatment, which does not disrupt everyone, even though it should, which calls for a theory of applicative justice, on the abstract level where people call for justice.

But applicative justice is not only an abstract theory. Applicative justice requires comparisons of group treatment. If minorities are treated unjustly, a description of that injustice does not require an ideal or nonideal theory or model of justice, but simply a comparison with how the majority is treated. (The term "minorities" refers to those disadvantaged or oppressed, because sometimes minorities are greater in number than "majorities," e.g., blacks under apartheid in South Africa, American slaves in some Southern states, or black Americans in some twenty-first-century cities.) The principles and mechanics of justice that work well enough for most white Americans need to be applied to nonwhite Americans. For rhetorical purposes, it might be evocative to talk about black lives or black rights, but strictly speaking the subject is a racial framework that is color-blind in an important part of law—constitutional amendments and federal legislation—but not in reality. This gap between written law and social reality can be viewed as hypocrisy, racial bias, or white supremacy, only if one assumes that written law is an accurate description of, or blueprint for, social reality. But a perspective that takes in the whole process of government reveals that the gap and what is permissible within it, are parts of the same whole process. The contrast between blueprints and maps is important to consider. Political philosophers often proceed as though their writings about justice are blueprints, when they should instead begin by constructing maps.

Present politics or a political party in power may present obstacles and challenges to applicative justice in any specific case. Those who aim for applicative justice must struggle against such obstacles and challenges, as well as the ignorance, prejudice, and ill will of large parts of voting publics under democratic government, and in addition, media misrepresentations, business interests in a status quo, and lack of understanding of oppression by those who are treated unjustly. For example, the injustice in the disproportionately large number of African Americans in the US criminal justice system has been supported by law-and-order politics, the War on Drugs, belief in racial gender myths (e.g., the larger-than-life black rapist), explicit racism, media sensationalism of crime committed by black men, profits made by for-profit prison corporations, and embrace of self-destructive subcultures by some black men who become incarcerated. At the same time, as an efficient cause or precipitating factor, ongoing racial profiling by police helps feed the system with new suspects, about 90 percent of whom plead guilty in preference to the risks and costs of a trial (Kerby 2013; Rakoff et al. 2014). Intergenerational poverty, unemployment, and undereducation contain people within this system, and the high rates of nonwhites in the prison population are used as official justification for racial profiling (Zack 2015, chap 2).

Thus, the complexity of causes and background factors associated with the disproportionate number of African American male prison inmates can be understood through a number of approaches. The normative approach of applicative justice would be to address those causes or factors, distinctly and individually, through specific changes in concrete practice, as well as changes in law, as relevant.

THE HISTORY OF APPLICATIVE JUSTICE

The history of real-life applicative justice has not yet been reflected in the history of moral and political philosophy. However, the idea of applicative justice is only new under that name. As a political practice, it is as old as reactions to injustice. But reactions to injustice are by no means uniform. Judith Shklar noted that "political retaliation, which occurs when a personal sense of injustice resorts to public action in response to political injuries . . . is an exceptionally complicated notion because each instance is unique, depending on the historical situation of which it is a part" (Shklar 1990, 95). This historical complexity may be partly why the historical correction of injustice does not lend itself to clean, abstract constructions in political philosophy. Law in reality is made up of and refers to specific laws, court decisions, arrests, fines, and trials. One way to tell the history of applicative justice is by recounting corrections to discrete injustices that were first supported by law. Examples include the Emancipation Proclamation (1863), *Brown v. Board of Education* (1954), the Civil Rights Act of 1964, the Voting Rights Act of 1965, and the Immigration and Nationality Act of 1965. In each of these cases, justice that existed for racially and ethnically white people was extended to nonwhites.

With the exception of John Stuart Mill's *On the Subjection of Women* and *The Communist Manifesto* by Marx and Engels, it is difficult to find canonical texts in Western political philosophy that begin with conditions of injustice. Rousseau refers to that beginning ("Man is born free but he is everywhere in chains"), but his real interest culminates in a utopian republic (i.e., *The Social Contract*), complete with a common will, where some must be compelled to be free.

The utopian focus is changing in light of more deflationary analyses of government from writers such as Giorge Agamben (Agamben 2005) and Amartya Sen (although Sen, a student of Rawls, is an economist and not a political philosopher; Sen 2009), as well as many who write about racial injustice, injustice to women, poverty, disability, exploitation, militarization, and so forth. Strong voices in US philosophy have emerged within nonideal theory, such as Tommy Shelby (Shelby 2007) and Charles Mills (Mills 2009). Sally Haslanger's methodological project of approaching social injustice through the idea of unintended but determining "social meanings" is another example of starting from injustice (Haslanger 2014). There are also important intellectual antecedents in American history, when philosophical thought has worked as a survival tool for black Americans. Lucius Outlaw writes in the entry for "Africana Philosophy," in the *Stanford Encyclopedia of Philosophy*:

> The survival and endurance of conditions of racialized and gendered colonization, enslavement, and oppression not conditions of leisured freedom—*compelled* more than a few African and African-descended persons to philosophize. Almost daily, even on what seemed the most mundane of occasions, oppressed Black people were *compelled* to consider the most fundamental existential questions: . . . Die at one's own initiation? Or, capitulate to dehumanization? Or, struggle to find and sustain faith and hope for a better life, on earth as well as in the afterlife. (Outlaw 2010)

However, so far, few contemporary philosophical efforts are presented as standing on their own toward a theory of injustice, or injustice theory that is intellectually worthy of competing with theories of justice, on the ground of political philosophy. The projects mentioned tend to be presented as work within nonideal theory (Mills and Shelby), as analyses of culture (Haslanger), or as specific accounts of race-related struggle (Outlaw). Sen presents his capabilities approach, which is avowedly comparative, in contrast to what he calls Rawls's "transcendental institutionalism," as an alternative view of justice that goes directly to practical support of what real human beings can do. But Sen's address is to dire problems of poverty and human desperation, rather than contradictions between existing positive just law and unjust practice, or situations that proclaim justice for all but deliver justice only to some, which are present US concerns. Agamben's thought is radically focused on extreme practices of government as a "killing machine," where those who survive are reduced to bare life. While black ghetto life in early twenty-first-century America may resemble Agamben's subject, Agamben seems focused on opening up a possibility for revolution (through his interpretation of Walter Benjamin's notion of "pure violence" [Humphreys 2006]). But, few, if any, US critics think that violent revolution is either possible or likely to succeed. So we have to meliorate (Zack 2016, chapter 2).

In the most general and formal international context, the Preamble to the United Nations' 1948 Universal Declaration of Human Rights (UDHR), written by a group of scholars that included philosophers, is about injustice:

> Whereas disregard and contempt for human rights have resulted in barbarous acts which have outraged the conscience of mankind, and the advent of a world in which human beings shall enjoy freedom of speech and belief and freedom from fear and want has been proclaimed as the highest aspiration of the common people, Whereas it is essential, if man is not to be

compelled to have recourse, as a last resort, to rebellion against tyranny and oppression, that human rights should be protected by the rule of law. (United Nations 1948)

Nowhere in the UDHR do its authors define human rights, say where they come from, or put forth a positive, comprehensive, positive theory of justice. The urgency of the universal human rights proclaimed is vaguely referred to individual human dignity based on common membership in a human family: "Whereas recognition of the inherent dignity and of the equal and inalienable rights of all members of the human family is the foundation of freedom, justice and peace in the world." ' Readers of the UDHR are not told that human rights are absolute and that it is morally right to recognize them and politically right to protect them. Rather, the readers of the UDHR are warned that, because human rights are the "highest aspiration of the common people," "disregard and contempt" for them in an absence of protection by law will result in "rebellion against tyranny and oppression." In other words, human rights must be respected as a condition for peace. The argument in the UDHR is thus pragmatic and its subject is human rights as something that must be protected in order to have peace. The subtext is that human rights have been violated in the past and should not continue to be violated. Although the language of justice and injustice does not lead the discussion in this general preamble to specific rights, the focus of the entire document is on human rights that were unjustly violated during and just after World War II (and continue to be violated today). Recognizing the UDHR's origins in apprehension about the consequence of injustice is not the same thing as pretending that the declaration has been an *effective* statement of an ideal, or that it does much more than continue to inspire. Rather, we simply note that the purpose of the document is to address and prevent injustice. But, of course, no document can do that. Only human beings, in their concrete and habitual practices over time, have the power to correct injustice.

VOTING RIGHTS AND RESIDENTIAL SEGREGATION

The coexistence of just law, principled progressive rhetoric, and unjust practice is clearly evident in US race-related voting policies and residential segregation. In both the Voting Rights Act of 1965 and the 1968 Fair Housing Act, legal justice was announced, which has been circumvented by apparently legal unjust practices.

Many whose interests are at stake do not regularly vote, because of a general political cynicism or local experience that their votes do not affect their lives, or in some cases, new political barriers to voting. The Voting Rights Act of 1965 was meant to protect the rights of blacks to vote in southern states and localities where white officials had violated that right. The Act required federal judicial jurisdiction over "voting qualifications or prerequisites." The 113th Congress passed the Voting Rights Amendment Act of 2014, stating that it "Expands the types of violations triggering the authority of a court to retain such jurisdiction to include certain violations of the Act as well as violations of any federal voting rights law that prohibits discrimination on the basis of race, color, or membership in a language minority group." However, the 2014 Amendment Act also "Excludes from the list of violations triggering jurisdiction retention authority any voting qualification or prerequisite which results in a denial or abridgement of the right to vote that is based on the imposition of a requirement

that an individual provide a photo identification as a condition of receiving a ballot for voting in a federal, state, or local election" (113th Congress, 2013–2014). After the 2014 Voting
Rights Amendment Act, a number of state legislatures passed, or began the process of passing, voter photo identification requirements, and a debate is in process. Proponents of the
2014 Amendment Act claim that photo IDs prevent voter fraud. Opponents claim that the
risk of voter fraud has been exaggerated and that photo identification requirements make it
more difficult for some poor, nonwhite, and elderly citizens to vote—and that the requirements favor Republicans, because those voters without photo IDs are more likely to vote for
Democratic candidates (Charen 2014). No one can credibly say that nonwhite citizens do not
have a right to vote. But for some, that right is mediated by requirements that they may not
be easily able to meet; that is, their right to vote is obstructed.

Race-related unjust practices by federal government agencies and local government have
been more specific than the general pronouncements of the Fair Housing Act, as well as the
Voting Rights Act. The 1965 Fair Housing Act outlawed racial discrimination in housing, but
the exclusion of nonwhites from housing available to whites continued from earlier polices
that were in place higher up the property chain than direct discrimination at the point of
sale or rental. In a 2014 report for the Economic Policy Institute, Richard Rothstein provides an historical account of how government policy on state and local levels explicitly supported residential racial segregation, and how the fact of racial segregation restricted the
kind of housing that nonwhites could buy or rent. Rothstein's focus is on the race-related
housing history of Ferguson, Missouri, and nearby townships. But, insofar as he is referring
to national practices, instituted or approved by the federal government, and insofar as many
communities throughout the United States have racially segregated, substandard housing,
with substandard infrastructure and public services, Rothstein's report is a description of
national injustice. Rothstein writes that in spite of the Fair Housing Act, the following practices became commonplace:

> Many . . . explicitly segregationist governmental actions ended in the late 20th century but
> continue to determine today's racial segregation patterns. In St. Louis these governmental
> policies included zoning rules that classified white neighborhoods as residential and black
> neighborhoods as commercial or industrial; segregated public housing projects that replaced
> integrated low-income areas; federal subsidies for suburban development conditioned on
> African American exclusion; federal and local requirements for, and enforcement of, property
> deeds and neighborhood agreements that prohibited resale of white-owned property to, or
> occupancy by, African Americans; tax favoritism for private institutions that practiced segre-
> gation; municipal boundary lines designed to separate black neighborhoods from white ones
> and to deny necessary services to the former; real estate, insurance, and banking regulators
> who tolerated and sometimes required racial segregation; and urban renewal plans whose
> purpose was to shift black populations from central cities like St. Louis to inner-ring suburbs
> like Ferguson. (Rothstein 2014, 2)

Rothstein also notes that governmental actions supported a segregated labor market so that
most African Americans could not afford to move to into middle-class communities, and
when they did, unscrupulous real estate agents scared white owners into selling their property at below-market prices. The inability to accumulate intergenerational wealth through
home ownership creates a further dimension of the injustice of US segregated residential
housing (Rothstein 2014, 6).

One way to approach situations such as unfairly segregated housing would be through additional legal action that positively specified both how such progressive formal law (e.g., the Fair Housing Act, Hud.Gov. 2015) was required to be implemented and how violations would be penalized. It is naïve to assume that the only thing necessary for racial equality in housing is that sellers and landlords not discriminate, when the regulatory and sales apparatus of the housing industry is discriminatory. The net effect of that apparatus is that many African Americans, whose parents cannot subsidize a down payment for home ownership or three-months' rent in advance for first-time rentals, will not face racial discrimination if they try to buy or rent in a segregated black ghetto! General ignorance about the history of housing segregation, with government support on federal as well as local levels, indicates that there is much about the relationship between written law and societal reality that requires empirical research to support the discourse of injustice theory. At the very least, the ways that the freedoms legitimately inherent in private property rights have been abused by some to limit the freedoms of others should be considered as part of any theory of ownership.

A NOTE ON NARRATIVE

The overall task of US racial justice is replete with practical challenges to achieving justice for nonwhites, which is comparable to the justice secured by and for whites. This is an overwhelming practical task, composed of myriad practical challenges. Just law and principled ideals are unable to directly change reality, despite how inspiring they may be to individuals. This empirical truth supports some equanimity in approaching that practical task because it is a matter of getting things done in specific concrete situations, rather than the monumental battle against ossified malevolence that an emphasis on a monolithic system of racism might imply.

However, it is primarily cognitive political content that is separate from practice. Some social content, such as narrative, may have the power to motivate change. Narrative has the power to activate emotions, aspirations, and moral feelings that can motivate practical action, because stories are removed from cognitive political content and have the power to bypass it. Although narrative has no structured access to political action, it can serve as a background justification for political action that otherwise serves dominant interest groups whose leaders do not openly reveal their interests. Consider in this regard the death of Walter Scott.

Many local demonstrations and protests about police homicide of unarmed African Americans, under banners such as "Hands Up, Don't Shoot," "I Can't Breathe," "Black Lives Matter," and "No Justice, No Peace," were highly publicized by the mainstream media, as were successive police homicides after the death of Trayvon Martin in 2012. While sensationalistic, much of the mainstream media coverage provided close-up information about the injustice of these cases, reporting when victims were unarmed and when their behavior did not indicate aggression or criminality. The mainstream media also followed cases to grand juries or trials and gave detailed accounts of the lack of indictments or convictions of police officers responsible (Zack 2015). However, a widespread public consensus about injustice did not emerge, in the wake of these news reports, because there was much response by and for US police departments about the dangers of patrolling crime-ridden neighborhoods and the criminal appearance of police homicide victims (Giuliani and Tyson 2014; Yancy and Zack 2014). But the *New York Times* settled uncertainty for at least one such homicide of an unarmed black man, on April 6, 2015, by posting a video of Walter Scott, who was black, being shot in the back while fleeing a white police officer in South Carolina. The video also showed the officer hand-cuffing Scott, after he was inert. There were over four thousand comments accompanying that news story and video, with near-unanimous condemnation of the officer's evident actions, which according to the video, were not consistent with his original report. The officer was almost immediately charged with murder following the release of the video (Schmidt and Apuzo 2015). Here, there was a common narrative of events and shared judgment about injustice.

Except for cases like Walter Scott's, although there is more rhetorical reliance on narrative than is politically effective, American blacks and whites do not share a narrative about American race relations. Also, in most specific cases, even if there is video evidence, consensus is rare. This is a problem on both a general level and in specific cases, because the call for change comes mainly from blacks. Whites, who are resistant to change, as well as blame, have the political, social, and economic power to block change. Whites do not want to hear that the United States is a white supremacist society or that whites are privileged solely on the grounds of race. Blacks do not want to hear that the United States is a racially equal society and that their miseries are either their own fault or within their power to overcome on individual levels. Needed is a narrative that could move both sides into understanding a common need for change. Such a narrative would be an account of contemporary black/white relations that was clear and easy to understand, without detailed or specialized knowledge of history, social theory, or philosophy. For a while, during the end of his candidacy and the early days of his first administration, Barack Obama provided such a narrative—he celebrated the success of blacks, identified himself with them, and expressed gratitude to whites for allowing that to happen (Obama 2008). But many black people quickly realized that Obama's success was not the same thing as their success and many whites bitterly regretted what Obama's success symbolized. So we need a new narrative about the meaning of racial difference in the United States and what its future could and should look like.

References

113th Congress (2013–2014). "All Bill Information (Except Text) for H.R.3899—Voting Rights Amendment Act of 2014." Accessed May 22, 2016. https://www.congress.gov/bill/113th-congress/house-bill/3899/all-info.

Agamben, Giorgio. (2005). *The State of Exception*. Translated by Kevin Attell. Chicago: University of Chicago Press.

Ayres, Ian, and Daniel Markovits. (2014). "Ending Excessive Police Force Starts with New Rules of Engagement." *The Washington Post*, December 25. Accessed May 22, 2016. http://www.washingtonpost.com/opinions/ending-excessive-police-force-starts-with-new-rules-of-engagement/2014/12/25/7fa379c0-8a1e-11e4-a085-34e9b9f09a58_story.html.

Bentley, Arthur. (1908/2008). *The Process of Government: A Study of Social Pressures*. New Brunswick and London: Transaction Publishers.

Charen, Mona. (2014). "The Voter-ID Myth Crashes." *National Review*, October 28. Accessed May 22, 2016. http://www.nationalreview.com/article/391262/voter-id-myth-crashes-mona-charen.

Giuliani, Rudolph, and Michael Eric Dyson. (2014). "Giuliani and Dyson Argue over Violence in Black Communities." *Meet the Press*, November 24. Accessed May 22, 2016. http://www. nbcnews.com/storyline/michael-brown-shooting/giuliani-dyson-argue-over-violence-black-communities-n254431. (For a transcript see http://www.realclearpolitics.com/video/ 2014/11/23/fireworks_giuliani_vs_michael_eric_dyson_white_police_officers_wont_be_ there_if_you_werent_killing_each_other_70_of_the_time.html).

Haslanger, Sally. (2014). "Social Meaning and Philosophic Method." *Proceedings and Addresses of the American Philosophical Association* 88: 16–30.

Humphreys, Stephen. (2006). "Legalizing Lawlessness: On Giorgio Agamben's *State of Exception*." *European Journal of International Law* 17 (3): 677–687.

Jones, Janine. (2013). "Can We Imagine *This* Happening to a White Boy." In *Pursuing Trayvon Martin: Historical Contexts and Contemporary Manifestations of Racial Dynamics*, edited by George Yancy and Janine Jones, 141–154. Lanham, MD: Lexington Books.

Kerby, Sophia. (2013). "The Top 10 Most Startling Facts About People of Color and Criminal Justice in the United States: A Look at the Racial Disparities Inherent in Our Nation's Criminal-Justice System." *Center for American Progress*, March 13. Accessed May 22, 2016. http://www.americanprogress.org/issues/race/news/2012/03/13/11351/the-top-10-most-startling-facts-about-people-of-color-and-criminal-justice-in-the-united-states/.

Laslett, Peter. (1988). "Introduction." In *John Locke, Two Treatises of Government*, 3–136. New York: Cambridge University Press.

Mills, Charles W. (2009). "Rawls on Race/Race in Rawls." *The Southern Journal of Philosophy* 47: 160–185.

Moulines, C. Ulises. (1985). "Theoretical Terms and Bridge Principles: A Critique of Hempel's (Self-) Criticisms." *Epistemology, Methodology, and Philosophy of Science*. Essays in Honor of Carl G. Hempel on the Occasion of His 30th Birthday, January 8, 1985, edited by W. K. Essler, H. Putnam, and W. Stegmüller, 97–117. Netherlands: Springer. (Reprinted from *Erkenntnis*, 22 (1,2,3), January 8, 1985).

Obama, Barack. (2008). *Presidential Victory Speech*. Accessed May 22, 2016. http://www.huff-ingtonpost.com/2008/11/04/obama-victory-speech_n_141194.html Accessed M. 2015.

Outlaw, Lucius. (2010). "Africana Philosophy." In *The Stanford Encyclopedia of Philosophy*. Accessed May 22, 2016. http://plato.stanford.edu/entries/africana/.

Rakoff, J. S., H. Daumier, and A. C. Case. (2014). "Why Innocent People Plead Guilty." *The New York Review of Books*, 61: 6–18.

Rawls, John. (1971). *A Theory of Justice*. Cambridge, MA: Harvard University Press.

Rothstein, Richard. (2014). "The Making of Ferguson: Public Policies at the Root of Its Troubles." *Economic Policy Institute*, 1–41. http://www.epi.org/files/2014/making-of-ferguson-final.pdf.

Schmidt, Michael S., and Matt Apuzzo. (2015). "South Carolina Officer is Charged with Murder of Walter Scott." *The New York Times*, April 7. Accessed May 22, 2016. http://www.nytimes. com/2015/04/08/us/south-carolina-officer-is-charged-with-murder-in-black-mans-death. html.

Sen, Amartya. (2009). *The Idea of Justice*. Cambridge, MA: Harvard University Press.

Shelby, Tommie. (2007). "Justice, Deviance, and the Dark Ghetto." *Philosophy and Public Affairs* 35 (2): 126–160.

Shklar, Judith N. (1990). *The Faces of Injustice*. New Haven, CT: Yale University Press.

Simmons, A. J. (2010). "Ideal and Nonideal Theory." *Philosophy and Public Affairs* 38: 5–36.

Strawson, P. F. (1962). "Freedom and Resentment." *Proceedings of the British Academy* 48: 187–211.

United Nations. (1948). *Universal Declaration of Human Rights*. Accessed May 22, 2016. http://www.un.org/en/documents/udhr/index.shtml#ap.

US Department of Housing and Urban Development. (2015). "Fair Housing Laws and Presidential Executive Orders." Accessed May 22, 2016. http://portal.hud.gov/hudportal/HUD?src=/program_offices/fair_housing_equal_opp/FHLaws.

Yancy, George, and Naomi Zack. (2014). "What 'White Privilege' Really Means." *The New York Times*, November 6. Accessed May 22, 2016. http://opinionator.blogs.nytimes.com/2014/11/05/what-white-privilege-really-means/?smid=fb-nytimes&smtyp=cur&bicmp=AD&bicmlukp=WT.mc_id&bicmst=1409232722000&bicmet=1419773522000&_r=0

Zack, Naomi. (2013). "Racial Inequality and a Theory of Applicative Justice, Philosophy and the Black Experience." *The American Philosophical Association Newsletter* 13: 1.

Zack, Naomi. (2015). *White Privilege and Black Rights: The Injustice of US Police Racial Profiling and Homicide*. Lanham, MD: Rowman and Littlefield.

Zack, Naomi. (2016). *Applicative Justice: A Pragmatic Empirical Approach to Racial Injustice*. Lanham, MD: Rowman and Littlefield.

PART X

....

FEMINISM, GENDER, AND RACE

....

In surveying the subjects of philosophy of race and African American thought, it goes without saying that the human *subject* is blacks and other people of color. The subject is thus racial groups who have typically resided in certain places and occupied subordinate social positions, throughout the history of modern Western culture. Sometimes, as during slavery, families were broken up, and other times families were united by arrangements counter to mainstream white ideals, for instance with female heads of household or without legal marriage. But, overall, nonwhite peoples have been considered as integral historical human groups. By contrast, women or female human beings, as the primary subject of feminism or gender theory, are dispersed. Women are integral parts of all historical human groups, but unlike racial groups, they do not have distinct geographical locations, apart from other groups.

In the post–civil rights era liberatory part of the academy, there has been a pervasive focus on "women and people of color," because historically, the academy has been overpopulated and dominated by white men. But in real life and in human history, gender and race are not comparable categories. It is therefore not surprising that apart from progressive contexts and resistance to liberatory reform, it would be very strange to consider them in the same sentence or the same breadth. To speak of women is to refer to about half of all human beings. To speak of people of color refers to all nonwhites. Both are natural groups (albeit culturally constructed), but their conjunction does not refer to a natural group. The term "women and people of color" refers to people who may share experiences of oppression by white males— it is a political term. Still, for the sake of theorizing, in considering the history of ideas, and to some extent for designing practical political reform in the face of conservative or reactionary ideologies, we are stuck with this odd conceptual combination.

Nineteenth-century America was a century of both racial liberation through the abolitionist movement and Civil War, and feminist liberation through the suffragist movement. That black men received the right to vote in 1870, fifty years before women did in 1920, caused a lasting political split between advocates for race and gender. When both women's liberation (later known as "feminism") and black civil rights became cultural movements in the 1970s, the political rift had not been resolved. Feminism soon came to be criticized for its focus on the problems of white middle-class women, and black political groups were criticized for their more or less exclusively male leadership and general indifference to the subordinate status of women.

For identifying a subject of complex oppression, *intersectionality* is a sociological concept that admits of both quantitative study and metaphorical-modeling applications. The core idea is that many people experience multiple identities that result in oppression, for instance, nonwhite race and nonmale gender and disability, or, nonwhite race and poverty and same-sex preference. Awareness of intersectionality affords permission for flexibility in analysis. This does not tell us when racial differences are more important than gender or class differences or how to rank or prioritize different sites or identities of oppression. But the flexibility to consider issues of gender, alongside, or in contrast to, issues of racism and racial identity, is important for the development of historical awareness and understanding of contemporary culture, as well as abstract theorizing. Also, as the writers in this part demonstrate throughout, sometimes insults and injuries based on gender are relevant to those based on race, and other times insults and injuries based on race are relevant to those based on gender.

In "Ethnological Theories of Race/Sex in Nineteenth-Century Black Thought: Implications for the Race/Gender Debate of the Twenty-First Century," Tommy Curry examines the intellectual history of black ideas of race and gender during the era of nineteenth-century *enthology* or theories of race in society. While this area of thought would today be dismissed as pseudo-scientific or speculative along racist white supremacist themes, it retains interest both for how it was taken up by black writers and its lingering legacy in popular imagination. Curry notes that the presumed opposition between man and woman is a very recent phenomenon in the historical scope of gender. Black people were thought to be "ungendered" throughout modern history. Over the nineteenth century, many white ethnologists assumed that only the white race was gendered, because gender, especially femininity, was believed to be an effect of evolution toward civilization. By the same token, races themselves were gendered in the white racist imaginary and the black race was considered feminine, the "lady" of human races. Against this ideology, a number of black "racial uplift" writers endeavored to develop and support white ideals of patriarchy and femininity within black culture and society. This led to a black social movement and literature concerning manners, morals, hygiene, grooming, and domestic economy.

T. Denean Sharpley-Whiting in "Jefferson's Paradox, or a Very Brief History of Black Women's Sexuality, Hip-Hop, and American Culture," explores representations of black women's sexuality, from the political culture of eighteenth-century America to the public and popular culture of the twenty-first century. Hip-hop culture, especially gangsta rap music, is at the center of Sharpley-Whiteing's discussion, because its misogyny against black women both directly devalues black women and spreads stereotypes that cross over into white entertainment. At the same time, in popular representations, white women appropriate hairstyles and skin shades from black women, and black women strive to emulate white aesthetic standards. Sharpley-Whiting argues that the origins of such misogyny, disrespectful stereotypes, and aesthetic ambivalence are as much white as black. Thomas Jefferson's racial musings on blacks and black women, in his *Notes on the State of Virginia* (written and rewritten from 1781 to 1787), was a tortured aesthetic critique of black women that established a black misogynistic tradition. Jefferson drew political implications from what he assumed to be a natural white superiority that deprived black women of flowing hair and smooth skin, which, he said, made them aesthetically unappealing to white men. That judgment was, of course, hypocritically at odds with his own long-term sexual relationship with his wife's mixed-race half-sister. And just as Jefferson and his father-in-law benefitted economically and sexually from their slaveholder status and its sexist-racist rhetoric, the simultaneous devaluation and exploitation of black women endures today in US economic, social, and cultural life.

In "The Violent Weight of Whiteness: The Existential and Psychic Price Paid by Black Male Bodies," George Yancy begins with the question, "What is the lived experience of the black male body within the context of white America in the twenty-first century?" For an answer, he explores the existential and psychic dimensions of "black male bodies" as they negotiate their lives within the context of white hegemony, which truncates them according to a distorted and racist picture in the white imaginary. Yancy argues that within the context of this white imaginary, the black male body constitutes "a site of contamination." As such, within the white body politic, black male bodies are always targets of the state, regarded as "criminals," "monsters," or "thugs," before they even do anything. Yancy regards the idea of a postracial America as mythical.

In "Gender Theory in Philosophy of Race," I consider the theoretical crosscurrents implied by real-life intersections of race and gender and conceptual difficulties raised by the apparent privileging of black male problems and the black male subject. Both feminism and critical race theory are *critical theories*. A critical theory is sufficiently abstract to analyze and normatively assess a large area of human life that is a site of injustice. Critical theories have leading ideas and subjects—race and black men for critical race theory, gender and white women for feminism. The injustices experienced by women of color do not fit into either critical theory, and this raises the question of whether there is something unique about their identities and status. The answer lies in the ways that the biological products of women of color, especially the sexuality and children of African American women, have been both devalued and appropriated without compensation, as a form of plunder. I suggest that these experiences of black women support *critical plunder theory*, a new critical theory that would specifically address the oppression of women of color, as both nonwhite and female.

Finally, in the last essay for Part X and the volume, Cynthia Willett brings us back to concerns of everyday life in "The Sting of Shame: Ridicule, Rape, and Social Bonds." Willet begins with this question:

> What if a devastating dimension of violence and material damage cannot be understood apart from the cruelty of the joke or the sting of ridicule? What if a shaming insult constitutes the significant sting at the heart of much racial and sexual discrimination or assault?

Willett here seems to suggest that the greatest injury of racial injustice, the thing that "gets" and "gets to" most victims, is not physical or other material harm but disrespect, disregard, contempt, or a sense that who they are as human beings, or that they are human beings, just does not matter.

Willett considers how public ridicule (as expressed, for example, in anti-Islamic cartoons) works. Ridicule depends on its source having more power in a context or system than its target, so that the sense of superiority manifested by satire is a cruel source of pleasure. At the same time, in-group solidarity may be strengthened by drawing on awe, an appreciation for what is larger than the individual self. Here, there is sublimity in the idea of the group, which is imagined to be on the other side of the spectrum from the target of ridicule. Willet draws on Audre Lourde's reference to *eros* as a lifeforce that women of color need to reclaim from draining atmospheres of white, male, or white male mockery. The excess of pleasure experienced by perpetrators of crimes of shame is akin to rape. And yet it is also important to keep the value of the community connection in mind and look toward amelioration. Willett concludes: "The old adage about sticks and stones has something to teach us after all—not to endure stoically the insult, but to breathe in deeply before one reacts and think about how to counter the aggression and repair social bonds."

Further Reading

Allen, Paula Gunn. (1992). *The Sacred Hoop: Recovering the Feminine in Native American Traditions.* New York: Open Road.

Flexner, Eleanor, and Ellen Fitzpatrick. (1996). *Century of Struggle: The Woman's Rights Movement in the United States.* Cambridge, MA: Belknap Press.

hooks, bell. (1982). *Ain't I a Woman? Black Women and Feminism.* Boston: South End Press.

Spelman, Elizabeth. (1988). *Inessential Woman: Problems of Exclusion in Feminist Thought.* Boston: Beacon Press.

Zack, Naomi. (2005). *Inclusive Feminism: A Third Wave Theory of Women's Commonality.* Lanham, MD: Rowman and Littlefield.

Zinn, Maxine Baca, and Bonnie Thornton Dill, eds. (1993). *Women of Color in US Society.* Philadelphia: Temple University Press.

CHAPTER 47

ETHNOLOGICAL THEORIES OF RACE/SEX IN NINETEENTH-CENTURY BLACK THOUGHT

Implications for the Race/Gender Debate of the Twenty-First Century

TOMMY J. CURRY

Everywhere and always the Negro has been interested rather in expression than in action; interested in life itself rather than in its reconstruction or reformation. The Negro is, by natural disposition, neither an intellectual nor an idealist like the Jew, nor a brooding introspective like the East Indian, nor a pioneer and frontiersman like the Anglo-Saxon. He is primarily an artist, loving life for its own sake. His metier is expression rather than action. The Negro is, so to speak, the lady among the races.

Robert E. Park

Africa is woman; her races are feminine.

Jules Michelet

THOUGH unstated, history continues to assert itself as the justification for the significance that concepts like race, class, or gender have in our philosophical analyses. To say that gender or race functions historically in some particular way—that our category is historical—is to suggest that the idea has empirical substance, and in the case of categories like race, class, or gender a peculiar realness needing our immediate philosophical attention. Despite the reliance of Africana philosophers, as well as race and gender theorists, on history to legitimize the causal relationship between their asserted category or categories and the phenomena one aims to attend, there has been no historical analysis in Africana philosophy investigating the assertion that categories like race, class, and gender, as currently deployed, can in fact capture the reality of our present moment, much less the dynamics between and within groups over the past two centuries. It is common practice for black philosophers to simply assert that the ideas of nineteenth-century thinkers like W. E. B. DuBois, Martin R. Delany, or Anna Julia Cooper, who wrote about racism, manhood, womanhood, and labor, can be expressed within our configurations of race, class, and gender in the twenty-first century. When figures disagree, it is asserted that their differences of opinion are explained by their particular location as raced, classed, and gendered. DuBois or Douglass believe (x) because they are men or patriarchal, whereas Anna Julia Cooper believes (y) because she is a woman. In place of careful historical surveys of the eras from which these authors emerge, philosophers articulate history as a function of totalizing cognitive narratives—picking and choosing the examples they believe constitute proof that their renderings are in fact true. Specific cultural and popular understandings, as well as evidence of the scientific consensus of the times, are thought to be irrelevant to these philosophical analyses, despite being not only prevalent in the period black figures emerge from but also held by the figures themselves. Because philosophy lacks an empirical method to test its claims (be it archival, quantitative, etc.), only the outcome of the analysis is held in high regard. The actual ideas of race or sex held by these black thinkers are thought to be history, not philosophy, because the meanings these terms had in the nineteenth century simply do not resonate with the political projects deemed philosophical in the twenty-first century. Stated differently, historical accuracy, or the actually known and verifiable facts of the matter, are taken to be irrelevant to how philosophers theoretically situate the relationships between historic thinkers, or how the racial, economic, or sexed groups these figures are taken to represent are thought to relate to each other. Labeling an analysis "history" as opposed to "philosophy" is a commonly accepted disciplinary dictum, thought to legitimize all sorts of revisionism to text and time, in an effort to make the chosen thinker relevant to *our current* philosophical projects.

However, it is possible to articulate the difference between nineteenth-century ethnological understandings of race, class, and gender, and our contemporary deployments of these categories. In the nineteenth century, what we know as gender was believed to exist only among civilized races. It was this very division between what we now think of as the masculine and feminine that positioned the superior races' claim of evolutionarily developed sex roles over the androgynous character of savage races. Founded upon analogy, many contemporary ventures into the study of race and gender in Africana philosophy mistakenly assume that manhood and womanhood are synonymous with masculinity and femininity, and thereby imply the presence of a dominant or hegemonic masculinity structure and patriarchy in the black community. Under ethnological systems of thought, races were gendered as proof of their evolutionary development above other races. This meant that there were no shared categories of manhood or womanhood across racial groups. The white man was a member of a completely different species than that of a black man. Rather than simply being political designations or derision against the female sex, designating races as feminine or "ladies" indicated their racial temperament—what they were capable of thinking, or aspiring toward—their spiritual strivings.

The voluminous historical works in this area of study cannot be surveyed in one essay, but a relatively modest intervention can be introduced. I argue that ethnological understandings of race included the masculine and feminine as part of its meaning, thereby making gender an ethnological or racial designation. Under nineteenth-century ethnological thinking, races were gendered, rather than those bodies biologically designated as male or female by sex. The members of the racial group expressed either the masculine or feminine personality of that racial group, which meant that even in a dominant racial group like the white Anglo-Saxon, femininity is a masculine trait—something only possible in a patriarchal race. Historically, ethnology is associated with biological determinism and thought of as a science of white superiority. In point of actual fact, ethnology was not only adopted to some extent by all of the historical thinkers Africana philosophy concerns itself with in the nineteenth century, but it was the scientific justification used to explain "racial uplift" ideology as the evolutionary progress of savage races to the realm of civilization.

THE SCIENCE OF ETHNOLOGY: ITS ASSUMPTIONS AND STUDY

The origins of disciplines have always been subjects of contention. The origin and distinction between ethnology and anthropology are no different. The American Ethnological Society was founded in 1842, only months apart from the Ethnological Society of London. "Modern Ethnology," which had the benefit of Charles Darwin's *Origin of the Species* in 1859 and Adolf Bastian's *General Principles of Ethnology: Prolegomena to the Foundation of a Scientific Psychology on the Material of Folk Ideas* in 1884, focused on racial psychology and idealism. The approaches influenced by those sources concern us here, because it was in the combination of evolutionary thinking and idealism that the development of the races toward some ultimate end was introduced as the driving force behind civilization. Before the late 1800s, races were thought of as fixed biological groupings arranged by God hierarchically. By the 1890s, however, ethnology emerged as that specialized science dedicated to understanding the ends and origins of contact between the races; or what is gained and lost by such engagements.

A. H. Keane's *Ethnology: Fundamental Ethnical Problems; the Primary Ethnical Groups* regards ethnology as a specialized field of anthropology dedicated to understanding the "structural differences, which have to be gauged by comparative anatomical studies" (1909, 2). Emphasizing the niche of racial contact, Keane sees ethnology as "that branch of general anthropology which deals with the relations of the different varieties of mankind to each other . . . from both the physical and psychological sides" (Keane 1909, 2). In the nineteenth century, ethnology proceeded by "the comparative method, coordinating its facts with a view to determining such general questions as: the antiquity of man; monogenism or polygenism; the geographical centre or centres of evolution of dispersion; the number and essential characteristics of the fundamental human types; the absolute and relative value of racial criteria: miscegenation; the origin and evolution of articulate speech and its value as a test of race; the influence of the environment on the evolution of human varieties, on their pursuits, temperament, religious views, grades of culture; the evolution of the family, clan, tribe and nation" (Keane 1909, 2).

With the rise of anthropology, however, there was some concern that the term "ethnology" was too narrow. It was recognized at the close of the nineteenth century that anthropology itself was concerned with two aspects of mankind: the physical and the ethnical or social. As Juul Dieserud (1908) maintains in *The Scope and Content of the Science of Anthropology*,

"It would therefore surely seem that for purposes of classification we are at the present state of anthropology perfectly justified in adopting two main subdivisions of our science, viz., Physical anthropology or Somatology and Ethnical anthropology also called Psychical and Culture anthropology" (Dieserud 1908, 17). While Dieserud nonetheless believed that "Ethnology alone is too narrow" (1908, 17), he was aware of a need for a term able to capture the venture "as psycho socio-cultural science" (17). Anthropology and ethnography were concerned with the somatological classification of the races (Deniker 1904, 280–298), while ethnology (ethnological anthropology, ethnical science) focused on the racial character and the evolutionary temperaments of the races—their final evolutionary-teleological end. Rather than seeking to discover through evidence the actual character and aims of the specific races, ethnology sought to rationalize the supposed superiority of the white Anglo-Saxon race to all others. As J. S. Haller (1971) explains, "ethnology was the comparative and developmental study of social man and his culture. Concerning himself with the science of culture, the ethnologist enumerated the conditions and modes of existence of specific non-Western peoples, and only touched tangentially upon the contemporary problems of Western life" (Haller 1971, 710). The ethnologist was primarily interested in the nature and end of racial temperament (psychology). The ethnologist differed from the sociologist in that he did not study his own society, and used evolution as their foundation, making "liberal use of his studies of human thought and institutions in their embryological stage to suggest the same unilinear phylogeny for the advanced civilizations" (Haller 1971, 710). The German ethnological tradition launched by Bastian shared proximity to imperialism. As Haller remarks, "The ethnologist thus walked an unstable course between his science and his assumptions in the nineteenth century, offering suggestions in and out of his discipline, and generalizing about human behavior in its various aspects" (Haller 1971, 710).

Phylogeny involved more than simply charting the taxonomy of human groups emerging as the victors in the struggle for survival. For the ethnologist, evolution disclosed the intent of history, it revealed which groups should survive the struggle against nature, and it intimated the hierarchies established by nature between them. The personalities and racial characters of the surviving groups were then understood as proof of developmental differences marking the distance between those who are superior and those who are inferior—and it is these groups ordered by nature that the ethnologists studied under the designation of "races" (Grinder 1969). Moreover, ethnological science was not simply imposed by white scientists, but assimilated by nineteenth-century black intellectuals. It was the basis of the cultural assumptions used to articulate many of the positions contemporary scholars consider to be radical black political theory, as well as those like the protection of the home, which many of the same scholars would deem conservative.

THE INEQUALITY OF RACE AS THE DISTANCE FROM THE MASCULINE AND CLOSENESS TO THE FEMININE

Among race scholars in the United States, Arthur De Gobineau's *Inequality of the Human Races* remains a constant reminder and example of biological racism at the dawn of the twentieth century. However, what is often not commented upon in this text is the relation racial inequality has to the dominance of the male or female characteristics of the race. Gobineau believed that "every human activity, moral or intellectual, has its original source in one or other of these two currents, 'male' or 'female'; and only the races which have one of these elements in abundance (without, of course, being quite destitute of the other) can reach, in their social life, a satisfactory stage of culture, and so attain to civilization" (Gobineau 1915, 88). Civilization is founded upon the masculine or female principle operating to build a republic. Gobineau insists that "institutions . . . invented and molded by a race of men make the race what it is. They are effects, not causes" (40). Unlike our twenty-first-century theories of social constructionism, Gobineau holds that the creations of our society emanate from the inner personality and substance of races. "The male nations look principally for material well-being, the female nations are more taken up with the needs of the imagination" (89). The superiority of the German stock is birthed from the generational accumulation of blood from male races, while degenerate European races are accepting more feminine blood in their South. This is the foundation from which philosophy and poetry, language and literature grow. The mark of races' male and female principle is so remarkable that De Gobineau writes:

> If a degraded people, at the lowest rung of the racial ladder, with as little significance for the "male" as for the "female" progress of mankind, could possibly have invented a language of philosophic depth, of aesthetic beauty and flexibility, rich in characteristic forms and precise idioms, fitted alike to express the sublimities of religion, the graces of poetry, the accuracy of physical and political science—such a people would certainly possess an utterly useless talent, that of inventing and perfecting an instrument which their mental capacity would be too weak to turn to any account. (182)

The result of De Gobineau's racial divide between the Negro and the Anglo-Saxon is that black men and women could not share the "genders" established within the dominant race. The nineteenth-century ideas of race and gender (if such a term can even apply to black Americans) were the result of what were believed to be complete differences in evolutionary-species-kind between racial groups. Because of evolution, this meant that every race would have different gendered kinds within its group, despite its "level" of civilization. Nonwhite/savage/primitive groups were altogether denied the specific race-gender distinctions that whites had, because such distinctions were *specific to*, the exclusive mark of, the civilized white races. In this sense, there were no categories or universals that captured the shared historical experiences between these groups. Commenting on British racial taxonomies, Anne McClintock (1995) writes:

> Racial stigmata were systematically, if often contradictorily, drawn on to elaborate minute shadings of difference in which social hierarchies of race, class and gender overlapped each other in a three-dimensional graph of comparison. The rhetoric of *race* was used to invent distinctions between what we would now call classes. At the same time, the rhetoric of *gender* was used to make increasingly refined distinctions among the different races. The white race was figured as the male of the species and the black race as the female. Similarly, the rhetoric of *class* was used to inscribe minute and subtle distinctions between other races. The Zulu male was regarded as the "gentleman" of the black race, but was seen to display features typical of females of the white race. (McClintock 1995, 55–56)

According to McClintock's historical schema, nineteenth-century ethnologists categorized the Negro as the racial instantiation of white females. Franz I. Pruner-Bey argued, "the black man is to white man what woman is to man in general, a loving being and being of pleasure" (Hunt 1863, 39), while Carl Vogt remarked:

> The grown-up Negro partakes, as regards his intellectual faculties, of the nature of the female child, and the senile white. He manifests a propensity for pleasure, music, dancing, physical enjoyments, and conversation, while his inconstancy of impressions and of all the feelings are those of a child. (Dunn 1866, 25)

The Negro race was designated as female as a mark of its uncivilized lack of the masculine. In this sense, gender was a property of races that led to the divisions between sexes within the race—it did not imply the ideas of privilege and identity as it does today. Like other primitive races, the Negro was thought to be too savage, and degraded, to have evolved gender distinctions between the male and female sex. In an anthropological, but not political, sense, black men did not yet met the evolutionary register to be "men," and black women were not women in the sense that white women were. Blacks were anatomically sexed but held to strive toward gendered divisions as an indication of their ability to achieve racial uplift and attain civilization.

Racial Uplift as Evolutionary Doctrine

The nineteenth-century ethnological-anthropological perspective on race formed the condition that made racial uplift possible for black men and women, since racial manhood, just like lady-like womanhood, was accepted as necessary for evolutionary development and political progress. That is, the theory of gendered evolution was accepted by black and white thinkers alike and endorsed by some of our most well-known black women thinkers as the basis of racial uplift. Louise Newman explains:

> As the personal and political struggles of Anna Julia Cooper, Ida B. Wells, and Mary Church Terrell suggest, civilization, racial progress, and woman's protection within the home were interconnected in ways that made it impossible for black women to repudiate altogether the prevailing ideologies of the cult of domesticity and true womanhood. Like their white counterparts, black women reformers also used evolutionist discourses of civilization to justify their own social activism. They asserted their duty to "elevate" and "uplift" the masses of black women, upholding the values of domesticity, chastity, temperance, and piety that the white middle classes considered to be evidence of a civilized race. (Newman 1999, 9)

But, ironically, it is perhaps the quote Anna Julia Cooper is most well-known for which actually demonstrates Newman's point about the salience of evolutionary thought amongst black women reformers. In an 1886 essay entitled "Womanhood: A Vital Element in the Regeneration and Progress of a Race," Cooper wrote:

> The late Martin R. Delany, who was an unadulterated black man, used to say when honors of state fell upon him, that when he entered the council of kings the black race entered with him; meaning, I suppose, that there was no discounting his race identity and attributing his achievements to some admixture of Saxon blood. But our present record of eminent men, when placed beside the actual status of the race in America to-day, proves that no man can represent the race. Whatever the attainments of the individual may be, unless his home has

moved on *pari passu*, he can never be regarded as identical with or representative of the whole. Not by pointing to sun-bathed mountain tops do we prove that Phoebus warms the valleys. We must point to homes, average homes, homes of the rank and file of horny handed toiling men and women of the South (where the masses are) lighted and cheered by the good, the beautiful, and the true,—then and not till then will the whole plateau be lifted into the sunlight. Only the BLACK WOMAN can say "when and where I enter, in the quiet, undisputed dignity of my womanhood, without violence and without suing or special patronage, then and there the whole Negro race enters with me." (Cooper 1998, 63)

Today this quote is taken to assert that Anna Julia Cooper argues that black women, because of their identity as black and women, are the (*intersectional*) key to the race and racial progress. But what Cooper is actually saying is that the race can only advance on equal footing within the homes of the rank and file of the race. The masses must be lifted up. Because homes are reflective of the status held by the women of the race, women must be civilized to achieve true racial uplift. This is why Cooper insists that the average homes of working-class men and women must be advanced "pari passu" or on equal footing, with the most exceptional of the race. The motivation to develop gender division within the black middle class was not politics, but the application of ethnological science. Cooper believes that the civilization of America is superior to other world cultures because of the role the good woman has in sustaining the home (1998, 53–54). Unlike the races of the East, whose homes are impure, the power of American civilization is recognized by nations across the world as the natural product of "the homage Americans paid to women . . . the influence of an American woman in home is all-powerful" (E. C. 1880, 26), because it nurtures manhood.

In the nineteenth century, such distinctions between men and women, the status of the home, and the condition of a race's women indicated the evolutionary stage of the race. The fundamental nature of womanhood was to develop manhood in the race, not as an independent political trajectory from black patriarchy as individually maintained, but as a shared racial characteristic. "The race is just twenty-one years removed from the conception and experience of chattel, just at the age of ruddy manhood," remarks Cooper (1998, 61). To make the race *more masculine* or more civilized, mothers and the development of homes were fundamental. Anna Julia Cooper was clear on this point: "A stream cannot rise higher than its source. The atmosphere of homes is no rarer and purer and sweeter than are the mother in those homes. A race is but a total of families. The nation is the aggregate of its homes. As the whole is sum of all its parts, so the character of the parts will determine the characteristics of the whole. These are all axioms and so evident that it seems gratuitous to remark it" (1998, 63).

Cooper's view was not unique; it was the established evolutionary program of the time. In his 1883 essay "The Black Woman of the South: Her Neglects and Needs," Alexander Crummell calls for a domestic revolution to remedy the neglect of the black woman in the South. To advance the home, the black woman in the South must first be taught the science of domestic economics by Christian women of intelligence and piety, so they may learn "the ways and habits of thrift, economy, neatness, and order; to gather them into 'Mothers' Meetings' and sewing schools; and by both lectures and 'talks' guide these women and their daughters into the modes and habits of clean and orderly housekeeping" (Crummell 1891, 76). However, he went on:

If you want the civilization of a people to reach the very best elements of their being, and then, having reached them, there to abide, as an indigenous principle, you must imbue the womanhood of that people with all its elements and qualities. Any movement which passes by the female sex is an ephemeral thing. Without them, no true nationality, patriotism, religion, cultivation, family life, or true social status is a possibility. (79)

Crummell claims manhood may bring innovation to a people: "The male may bring, as an exotic, a foreign graft, say of a civilization, to a new people. But what then?" (1891, 79). For such traits to become permanently embedded within the race, womanhood, specifically her powers of regeneration, is needed.

Cooper models her understanding of racial development as dependent on the status of the woman on Crummell's "The Black Woman of the South." She acknowledges Crummell's previous work on black women in the South as that of a prophet or Moses (Cooper 1998, 60). When Cooper then says, "The position of woman in society determines the vital elements of its regeneration and progress" (1998, 59), her claim rings as true because it has been the acknowledged origin of America's rise in power and civilization for the better part of the nineteenth century.

Beyond Cooper and Crummell, this woman-centered view of black racial uplift was widely held among the black women social scientists of the late 1800s. In her keynote address to the 1897 woman's meeting of the Atlanta Sociological Laboratory, Ms. Lucy Laney held:

> Motherhood, honored by our blessed Master, is the crown of womanhood. This gives her not only interest in the home and society, but also authority. She should be interested in the welfare of her own and her neighbors' children. To woman has been committed the responsibility of making the laws of society, making environments for children. . . . The chief joy of home is mother. (Laney 1897, 57)

To build homes, the race needs men to protect the lady-like character of the black woman. As Anna Julia Cooper herself writes, black women "need men who can let their interest and gallantry extend outside the circle of their aesthetic appreciation; men who can be a father, a protector, a brother, a friend to every weak, struggling unshielded girl" (1998, 64). The black woman in the South needs chivalry, regardless of her station. It is the protection of her honor and sexuality from the various classes of white men, by black men that the "colored girl" of the South needs. Cooper observes that the black girls in the South are "often without a father . . . or stronger brother to espouse their cause and defend their honor with his life's blood" (1998, 61). As husband, as father, by name, Cooper calls for black men to take up their manhood to advance the cause of the race and womanhood. In calling for black men to protect, she is laying claim to a schema of racial advancement, the division of roles, and the protection of weaker women. She is calling for a gendered division of the sexes within the race.

Glenda Gilmore observes in *Gender and Jim Crow*:

> By admonishing men to fulfill their potentials, Cooper executed an end run around patriarchy. Ideal patriarchy should not limit women; it only did so when the man in question was stunted. In fact, men could take women's striving as a useful early warning sign to encourage them to exercise patriarchy more strenuously. If women were gaining in the race of life, men should run faster. (Gilmore 1996, 44)

Gilmore further claims that "Cooper never addressed the problem that her reasoning created—that is, if patriarchy ceases to limit women, is it still patriarchy?—by calling the hand of the patriarch" (1996, 44). However, if we look at Anna Julia Cooper's recommendation as an articulation of evolutionary doctrine rather than politics, we understand there is no tension between the manhood and womanhood of the race, because they necessitate and depend on each other.

The move from savagery into the register of the civilized was thought to bring with it obligations and white respect for black humanity. It was assumed that white society would be able to recognize civilization within the notable black classes, despite race. This assumption was the grounding for much of the activism of black intellectuals, journalists, and poets during the late 1800s. Michelle Mitchell claims in *Righteous Propagation: African American and the Politics of Racial Destiny after Reconstruction* that "Concerns for sexual purity, child rearing, habits of cleanliness and self-improvement enabled club women and race men to promote certain modes of behavior to instruct their brothers and sisters on how to attain a range of ideas" (2004, 84). For black Americans, who saw themselves as the Best men and women of the race, there was a demand that "class serve as a marker of manhood and womanhood" (Gilmore 1996, 75). Because class denoted intraracial divisions, those who had elevated— the upper class—took responsibility to improve the (uncivilized) rank and file. According to Kevin Gaines: "Because of their own embrace of Victorian manners and morals, middle-class black men and women worried constantly about poor black people's public activities" (1996, 75). Thus, instead of simply being a gendered or patriarchal assertion about the status of black people, racial uplift was a concerted effort between race men and women to create distinctions and specialized gender roles among the lower classes of black Americans. Given the missionary aspects of black manhood and womanhood, Kevin K. Gaines suggests in *Uplifting the Race: Black Leadership, Politics, and Culture in the Twentieth Century* that racial uplift actually describes "a black middle class ideology, rather than a black middle class" (1996, 14). Gaines writes:

> It was precisely as an argument for black humanity through evolutionary class differentiation that the black intelligentsia replicated the dehumanizing logic of racism . . . however problematic, the bourgeois cultural values that came to stand for intra-racial class differences—social purity, thrift, chastity, and the patriarchal family—affirmed their sense of status and entitlement to citizenship. (1996, 4)

For the contemporary scholar, Gaines's analysis means that the meanings and beliefs commonly attached to gender or black patriarchy/masculinity/femininity are in fact class ideologies and not the actual state of gender (which could only possibly possessed by black elites) among blacks in the nineteenth century.

CONCLUSION

Manliness and manhood were civilizational terms used by whites and blacks in the nineteenth century to describe both the solidified racial hierarchies of their day, and the malleable racial aspirations of the black men and women of tomorrow (Mitchell 2004, 58). Contemporary Africana philosophy remains unaffected by the mountainous work on race, gender, and sexuality undertaken outside of philosophy during the late 1800s and early 1900s, despite holding that racism, classism, and patriarchy are its primary intellectual (and interdisciplinary) concerns. Philosophy interprets gender ahistorically. Gender is intuited as distinct from the category of race, then "intersectionally" engaged to establish its prior historical relation in theory. That is, race and gender are thought to be different categories that are mapped onto specific bodies through identity in ways that simply do not make sense in the 1800s. To speak about race and gender in the nineteenth century is to usually focus on the black woman. This configuration, however, misses that in the nineteenth century, to speak of a black woman is to speak of a female-female, not a woman, just as to speak of a black man is to speak of a female-child-male. Intersectionality assumes a gender can be applied to bodies almost intuitively based on their sexual designation. This is a highly suspicious claim under nineteenth-century schemas.

Read historically, gender, like race, is a colonial category. It arises from white patriarchy to assign social roles to men and women within empires that are necessary to propagate white patriarchy. Colonialism was often justified as an effort to save the savage from themselves, from their brute males. As Louise Newman puts it, "For over a century, Westerners had presumed that primitive women were overworked, sexually abused, or otherwise badly treated by men of their cultures" (Newman 1999, 161). Similarly, Gail Bederman's offers the opinion that

> Savage (that is, nonwhite) races, had not yet evolved pronounced sexual differences—and, to some extent, this was precisely what made them savage. Savage men had never evolved the chivalrous instinct to protect their women and children but instead forced their women into exhausting drudgery, cultivating the fields, tending the fires, carrying heavy burdens. Overworked savage women had never evolved the refined delicacy of civilized women. (1995, 28)

Ethnological designations made the white-Anglo-Saxon the father and mother of the female and child races. It was the white race's duty to civilize the lower races. This burden utilized imperialism and colonization to spread civilization; while the white woman was the mother and teacher of the savage races, they were her children. Philosophers have a tendency to view slavery and colonization in heteronormative terms (Zack 1997), with sexual violence being directed toward the racialized female, but history has shown that conquest involved multiple erotics, making both white men and women the rapists of enslaved and colonized men and women (Foster 2011). Because the inferior races were deemed female and children, white men and women used their colonies to exorcise their sexual fetishes without contradiction or penalty.

Gender did not exist *within* the Negro race in the 1800s in ways that mirror its current usages. As such, many of our contemporary notions of feminism, race, and gender assume a distance between thinkers that did not historically exist. Middle-class black men and women both supported many if not most of the same ideas concerning gender, ideas inherited from white gender roles, and norms that marked the height of civilization. Acknowledging this distance between the reality of the past and our present terminology used to speak about the past is necessary. Although all of history is subject to interpretation, it is our resistance against anachronism and revisionism that increases the accuracy of our theorizations, allowing us to critically assess the categories, movements, and thinkers we make central to our conceptual projects. Considering ethnology's role in uplift ideology generates a new historiography that would not only address what is lacking in our present conceptual models but enables us to better understand what historical black thinkers were aiming toward and motivated by, in our interpretation of their texts.

REFERENCES

Bastian, Adolf. (1884). *General Principles of Ethnology: Prolegomena to the Foundation of a Scientific Psychology on the Material of Folk Ideas*. Berlin: D. Reimer.

Bederman, Gail. (1995). *Manliness and Civilization: A Cultural History of Gender and Race in the U.S., 1880–1917*. Chicago: University of Chicago Press.

Cooper, Anna Julia. (1998). "Womanhood." In *The Voice of Anna Julia Cooper*, edited by Charles Lemert and Esme Bhan, 53–71. Lanham, MD: Rowman and Littlefield.

Crummell, Alexander. (1891). "The Black Woman of the South: Her Neglects and Needs." In *Africa and America: Addresses and Discourses*, edited by Alexander Crummell, 59–82. Springfield, MA: Willey.

Deniker, Joseph. (1904). *The Races of Man: An Outline of Anthropology and Ethnology*. New York: Walter Scott.

Dieserud, Juul. (1908). *The Scope and Content of the Science of Anthropology*. Chicago: Open Court Press.

Dunn, Robert. (1866). "Civilisation and Cerebral Development: Some Observations on the Influence of Civilisation Upon." *Transactions of the Ethnological Society of London* 13–33.

F. C. (1880). "Woman's Influence." *Otago Witness*, May 22: 26.

Foster, Thomas. (2011). "The Sexual Abuse of Black Men during Slavery." *Journal of History and Sexuality* 20 (3): 445–464.

Gaines, Kevin. (1996). *Uplifting the Race: Black Leadership, Politics, and Culture in the 20th Century*. Chapel Hill: University of North Carolina Press.

Gilmore, Glenda. (1996). *Gender and Jim Crow: Women and the Politics of White Supremacy in North Carolina, 1896–1920*. Chapel Hill: University of North Carolina Press.

Gobineau, Arthur de. (1915). *The Inequality of the Human Races*. New York: G.P. Putnam's Sons.

Grinder, Robert E. (1969). "The Concept of Adolescence in the Genetic Psychology of G. Stanley Hall." *Child Development* 40 (2): 355–369.

Haller, John S., Jr. (1971). "Race and the Concept of Progress in Nineteenth Century American Ethnology." *American Anthropologist* 73: 710–724.

Hunt, James. (1863). *On the Negroes Place in Nature*. London: Trubner & Co.

Keane, A. H. (1909). *Ethnology: Fundamental Ethnical Problems; The Primary Ethnical Groups*. Cambridge: Cambridge University Press.

Laney, Lucy. (1897). "Address before the Woman's Meeting." In *Social and Physical Condition of Negroes in Cities*, edited by W.E.B. DuBois, 55–58. Atlanta: Atlanta University Press.

McClintock, Anne. (1995). *Imperial Leather: Race, Gender, and Sexuality in the Colonial Contest*. New York: Routledge.

Mitchell, Michelle. (2004). *Righteous Propagation: African Americans and the Politics of Racial Destiny after Reconstruction*. Chapel Hill: University of North Carolina Press.

Newman, Louise. (1999). *White Women's Rights: The Racial Origin of Feminism in the United States*. New York: Oxford University Press.

Zack, Naomi. (1997). "The American Sexualization of Race." In *Race/Sex: Their Sameness, Difference, and Interplay*, 145–155. New York: Routledge.

CHAPTER 48

JEFFERSON'S PARADOX, OR A VERY BRIEF HISTORY OF BLACK WOMEN'S SEXUALITY, HIP-HOP, AND AMERICAN CULTURE

T. DENEAN SHARPLEY-WHITING

HISTORICALLY and culturally, black women in the United States have been either dubiously represented in mainstream popular and political culture or erased. In black popular culture, particularly in the male-dominated culture of hip-hop and its music, which crossed over into the American mainstream and marked its rise as a global phenomenon in the 1990s, black women have had the dubious distinction of being both misrepresented and overrepresented. While debates about hip-hop's gender politics have raged since the 1970s, the 1990s onward mark a disquieting turn in the cultural politics of representation of black women. But no discussion of the present, or future, is complete without engaging history. Unpacking the racialized sexism and sexualized racism directed toward black women requires a backward look—to the eighteenth century, the nation's founding—in order to look forward into the twenty-first.

BLACK WOMEN'S SEXUALITY, HIP-HOP'S TEXTUALITY, OR BLACK RESPECTABILITY POLITICS AND AMERICA'S ANTIBLACK MISOGYNY

At least since the 1990s, with the commercialization of rap music alongside the emergence of gangsta rap, hip-hop culture has been a touchstone for congressional hearings and national conversations about retrograde images and ideas about women and sexuality (hooks 1981, 1992, 2003; Rose 1994, 2008; Kitwana 2003; Dyson 2004; Pough 2004; Hill Collins 2005, 2008; Sharpley-Whiting 2007). So when white radio personality Don Imus referred to the

Rutgers University's women's basketball team as "nappy-headed hos" on April 4, 2007, he further enlivened those debates (Chiachiere 2007).

Coverage of the Imus debacle was wall to wall on cable news networks (MSNBC, FOX, CNN) as well as on the blogs, Internet, radio, and in newspapers. Imus's rather bizarre attempt to blame hip-hop culture, more specifically black male hip-hop artists calling women bitches and hos, for his misstep gave the story legs. So much so that it was only the tragic shooting of thirty-two students and faculty at Virginia Tech University on April 16 by South Korean gunman and student Cho Seung-hui that provided Imus and hip-hop a brief reprieve from the hot seat (Hauser and O'Connor 2007).

Over the course of twelve days, black scholars, media personalities, cultural critics, and public intellectuals offered more sophisticated analyses about the degradation of women as an American cultural phenomenon and pushed back against cries of a double standard from the white mainstream. The latter double-standard argument offered on behalf of white males was effectively, "rappers say it, why can't we," which morphed, into lamentations about why whites cannot say "nigger" ("Across the Nation . . ." 2007). Those steeped in James Baldwin's school of thought on racism, race, and the invention of the "nigger" (Baldwin 1963) seemed to collectively shrug in tacit agreement: white Americans invented the word; the idea of the nigger is a critical cog in the wheel for constructing whiteness and white identity, and therefore some whites would lobby for a free pass to say the word publicly ("Don Imus and Hip-Hop" 2007).

Also ensnared in these debates about American culture and history, in general, and representations of black women, in particular, were notions of black respectability. Black respectability politics emerged earliest and most poignantly in slave narratives. Frederick Douglass's many iterations of his life as a slave describe his venerable Aunt Esther, who is repeatedly lashed to bleeding because she defiantly chooses romantic love with another slave rather than willingly submit to her master's tyrannical sexual coercion (Douglass 1845, 1855, 1892). Harriet Jacobs's *Incidents in the Life of a Slave Girl* (1861) grapples with the tensions between the cult of true womanhood and Victorian-era sexual politics and respectability and slave women's often-foiled attempts (herself included) to resist the unspeakably violent and gendered peculiarity of the institution. Jacobs too chooses a path of resistance in trying to escape her sexually predacious master and maintain her sense of self and dignity. She makes the distinction between giving oneself and submitting. That she also begins her narrative describing her mother as noble and womanly despite her being enslaved speaks profoundly to the desires on the part of captive blacks to complicate and snatch models of respectability from white's-only clutches (Jacobs 1861; Glymph 2008).

In freedom, blacks, whether newly emancipated or born free, poor or middle class, further attempted to codify behaviors of respectability (Hine 1989, 1999; Gray White 1995, 1999; Giddings 1996). Black women historians have noted that many black women adhered to Victorian ideology and strived to self-represent as scrupulously moral. From their experiences and the treatment they observed reserved for middle-class white women, they believed that such adherence would offer protections against sexual abuse and demonstrate their class status and blacks' suitability for citizenship and social equality (Davis 1983; Gray White 1985, 1999; Hine 1989, 1999; Higginbotham 1994; Hunter 1998; Harris Perry 2013). This is not to say that black women did not resist everyday practices of sexism as well as de jure sexism that attempted to restrict their access to full citizenship (Giddings 1996; Painter 1997); but living under Jim Crow required various strategies for uplift and survival that often included assimilation and adaptation. Black respectability politics were thus critically and crucially tied to the protection and social mobility of black women, as well as to the larger project of racial justice, opportunity, and respect for all black Americans (Hine 1989, 1999; Giddings 1996; Hunter 1998). Respectability, they believed, would bring about common decency on the part of white Americans.

In 1892, feminist Anna Julia Cooper wrote in *A Voice from the South*, "Only the Black Woman can say when and where I enter, in the quiet undisputed dignity of my womanhood, without violence and without suing or special patronage, then and there the whole Negro race enters with me" (Cooper 1892). By the 1920s–1930s, the era of jazz and the emergent Harlem Renaissance and New Negro movements, writer and editor Jessie Fauset chafed as both a writer and woman under that maxim, throttled against the "thou shall not" around which middle-class black women's lives as race representatives were organized and constrained. Fauset felt the "refined colored woman" was stretched to near breaking in trying to follow the scripts of respectable womanhood. And though she was as much an advocate as an adherent, the politics of respectability led to her trans-Atlantic rupture, a year-long stay in Paris where she worked on her bestselling novel, *Plum Bun*, a racy work of fiction that explored interracial and premarital sex and racial passing (Sims 1980; Sharpley-Whiting 2015).

Fauset was a highbrow woman (if ever there was one) and her experiences provide a window for exploring the push and pull of patriarchy (black and white) on black women's lives. These tensions were the seeds for twenty-first-century conflicts around respectability, sex, race, and gender (Pough 2004; Rose 2008; Thompson 2012; Harris Perry 2013; Henderson 2013). Hip-hop culture can represent, as did jazz and blues during Fauset's era, a free space for play, creativity, and self-expression (Davis 1999; Pough 2004; Henderson 2009, 2010, 2013). As part and parcel of hip-hop culture, black women participate and have participated in a range of roles in the culture as performers, purchasers, and dancers. Yet they are framed conventionally in ways that seem to short-circuit their access to complex representation in the very cultural spaces that they helped to nurture and create (Rose 1994; Dyson 2004, 2007; Sharpley-Whiting 2007). Thus, for some critics, hip-hop has become uniquely defined, with respect to black women, as a culture of *misogynoir*, or antiblack misogyny, a neologism coined by Moya Bailey, a queer black feminist scholar and co-organizer of the Spelman College protest against rapper Nelly's salacious 2003 "Tip Drill" video, where he swipes a credit card between a woman's buttocks (Bailey 2010).

HIP-HOP ON TRIAL: THE SELLING (OUT) OF BLACK WOMEN AND MUSIC

It is precisely this aspect of hip-hop culture and American culture in general that led to a 2007 congressional hearing by the Interstate Commerce Committee, chaired by Democratic Congressman Bobby Rush of Illinois, on the interstate trafficking of degrading images of women. The 2007 hearing was not the first of its kind.

Late civil rights activist C. Delores Tucker, who had essentially decried hip-hop culture as a "culture of disrespect" embodied in gangsta rap, spearheaded boycotts and stormed corporate board meetings throughout the 1990s. Tucker's brand of respectability politics with regard to hip-hop culture and rap music were summarily poo-pooed by the purveyors of the music and culture (corporate and artistic, male and female), hip-hop consumers, and cultural critics, as misguided and misplaced. Nonetheless, her political agitation led to congressional hearings in 1994 in the aftershock of the commercially successful gangsta rap juggernauts "The Chronic," "Strictly 4 My N.I.G.G.A.Z.," and "Doggystyle."

The second iteration of congressional hearings, originally scheduled for July 2007, was held on September 25. That day's assembly, from morning to late afternoon, included music executives from Universal and Warner; cultural critics and scholars Michael Eric Dyson and Andrew Rojecki; recording artists Master P and David Banner; Dr. E. Faye Williams, national chair for the National Congress of Black Women on behalf of the Women's Coalition on Dignity and Diversity; and Benjamin Chavis, president of the Hip-Hop Summit Action Network. A range of diverse opinions abounded from the expert witnesses on the subject of the "Business of Stereotypes and Degrading Images of Women" (Congressional Hearings 2007).

Some, such as Southern rapper David Banner, defended hip-hop and its artists by saying that "some women act like hos" (Congressional Hearings 2007). But, others, such as Benjamin Chavis, provided a more nuanced critique at the hearing. Chavis stated:

> Misogyny, disrespect of women, racial prejudice, violence, crime, drug abuse, greed for money, and explicit sexuality all are symptomatic of what has been historically rooted and embedded in the fabric of American society. There is an unfortunate tendency today to try to scapegoat or blame hip-hop for the contradictions of society. (Chavis, Congressional Hearings 2007)

Here, Chavis made a particularly astute observation about American culture, patriarchy, and capitalism. Still, in the hearing, white male executives and black male performers, in a sort of unambiguous concession to patriarchal privilege at black women's expense, predominantly filled the seats of those accused. Chavis's insights did not go far enough to explicitly take apart how hip-hop and the Imus kerfuffle—which were the catalysts for the hearings—impact sociocultural and political perceptions and representations of black women in America. It is not enough to be critical of structural gender biases and the hypersexualization of women, which cuts across race and class and is reiterated in the media. Left unexamined are black women's experiences locally (in their communities from which many artists claim to derive their representations of real life), nationally, and in the global marketplace of sexuality, desire, and representation.

Interestingly, in the lead up to "hip-hop on trial redux," the *New York Times* magazine ran the cover story, "The Music Man," by journalist Lynn Hirschberg on the bearish-looking music mogul Rick Rubin. Rubin had been handpicked to turn around the ailing Columbia Records. But before Rubin crossed over into more mainstream CEO territory, he founded Def Jam Records with Russell Simmons. Def Jam produced hip-hop acts such as LL Cool J, Kurtis Blow, and Run DMC, who collaborated with AeroSmith on the crossover hit "Walk This Way" (which effectively revived Aerosmith's waning music career). But what was most intriguing about the *New York Times* article is the naked revelation, widely accepted and understood now, but not then, that the music industry has lost its way because it is no longer concerned with "making music" but with "selling music" (Hirschberg 2007). And indeed this is true.

The selling of music, of lifestyles through music, and the marketing of images in music have become quite formulaic, and it is very much dependent on the sexualization of women across genres. In popular music, more specifically in hip-hop, the formula is heavily dependent upon the stereotyping of black masculinity and black women as sexual virtuosos—henpecking, unruly bitches in need of a smackdown—and pimped and played understudies in these masculinist narratives distributed in print culture, on celluloid, digitally, lyrically, and electronically. The formula, as others have argued, is indispensable to the mass-media engineered appeal of popular music (Dyson 2004, 2007; Hill Collins 2005; Hurt 2006; Sharpley-Whiting 2007; Rose 2008; Henderson 2013). This formula cultivates already existent tastes and desires as well as panders to them. There is a division of the labor in the commercial hip-hop industry; predominately white and male presidents and chief executive officers, marketing staff, videographers, and studio engineers oversee predominately black and male productions of beats and rhymes, who in turn act as taskmasters to a predominately black female backup chorus of dancers, video models, and hook singers. Such a division of labor results in black women's diminished social, political, and cultural capital in American pop culture, and it appears to have repercussions in mainstream socioeconomic and political culture.

THE ORIGINS OF A NARRATIVE, OR THE RACIAL-SEXUAL CONTRACT

Demeaning, degrading, appropriating, and objectifying black women would seem to be profitable American capitalist endeavors; and black women, as noted, no more morally herculean, but rather just as protean as others, paradoxically participate in such endeavors. Video dancers grind for a paycheck, just as Lil' Kim and Nicki Minaj squatted, open-legged for theirs. The saga of Rachel Dolezal, a transracial appropriator of nonpareil proportions, reads like a passing strange narrative: Blond white woman birthed by fundamentalist Christian white parents who also adopt transracially three black children, including one black girl named Esther; white woman becomes enamored with black culture and doffs white family and identity to enact her own version of "eating the other" (hooks 1992); she becomes a light-skinned black woman by donning curly-afroed wigs and tanning. Adopted sister Esther accuses older, white male sibling, Joshua Dolezal, of sexual abuse. White parents ignore accusations and send Esther off to a home for neglected children. Dolezal sides with Esther in legal proceedings against biological brother. Dolezal's parents out her as white and a fabulist to a news outlet. Media and blogosphere go wild with Rachel Dolezal interviews on Matt Lauer's "Today," MSNBC's "Melissa Harris-Perry" show, among others, and a *Vanity Fair* pictorial exclusive (Moyer 2015; Samuels 2015).

At the center of Rachel Dolezal's undoing is a real, live, and allegedly abused black female body. Among the chattering classes, Esther's familiar tale of interracial sexual abuse, white transracial adoption, parental neglect, and suspect white Christian missionary work is scuttled to parse Dolezal's unfathomable choice. That Dolezal voluntarily coopted a negated identity left heads scratching, though many agreed that she made for a much more attractive black woman than the pale, corn-silk-haired white woman that she was. Appropriation of black female aesthetics by white women is hotly debated terrain (Goff 2015; Wilson 2015). While black women themselves are whited out in American mainstream culture, their aesthetics and markers—hair, buttocks, color, speech patterns—their histories, and even their pain remain available for profitable appropriation and consumption.

Such gainful appropriation again brazenly rears its head without and within author Kathryn Stockett's 2009 bestselling novel *The Help*. The uncredited sourcebook for *The Help*, who eventually sued the writer, was Ablene Cooper, a longtime domestic worker in Stockett's brother's household (Donaldson James 2011); while the colorful and sorrowful stories of the black domestic workers in the novel catapult the listless, white protagonist, Skeeter, into a career as a writer in New York. Thinly drawn affable and sassy black women paper over the reality of rape of black women domestic workers in those same respectable white southern homes where they worked (McGuire 2010). The critically and commercially successful film *Crash* (2004) glosses over an upper-middle-class black woman character being framed as an uppity "ho" who is digitally raped by a white officer who then later rescues her from a car crash—thus "redeeming" the white male officer in an era of rampant unchecked police brutality against black women; Joyce Carol Oates rewrites the Tawana Brawley story in her 2015 novel *The Sacrifice* as a sympathetic but nonetheless "lying ass ho." In effect, a "we don't love them [black] hos" ethos permeates American culture packaged as Hollywood entertainment, literary high art, and daily interest new stories. The *misogynoir* aspects of hip-hop culture then are merely on a "connect-the-dots" historical continuum of black women's hypersexualization and objectification.

Although most Americans continue to single out hip-hop culture, primarily because of its brashness and overtly libidinous displays of maleness and masculinity tied to female subordination and subjection, the starting point on the American continuum emerged simultaneously with the nation's formation. As part of British North America, Middle Passage documents from sailors to slave cargo insurers provide clues to the cartography of black women's representation in the new nation that was separate and apart from its imperial mother country (Hahn 2005; Rediker 2007; Horne 2014).

In 1781, a mere five years after penning that hallowed document of a new nation, *The Declaration of Independence*, that prized freedom while sanctioning perpetual bondage, our founding father Thomas Jefferson set his sights on writing on his beloved state of Virginia. The text, *Notes on the State of Virginia*, is Thomas Jefferson's only monograph. He completed the work in 1781, but returned over the years to revise and add to the text until its first print run of two hundred by a Paris publisher in 1785; still dissatisfied with the volume, Jefferson corrected and revised again, searching out an English publisher, John Stockdale, for the volume's republication in 1787 (Wilson 2004). In between pages on flora and fauna and other philosophical musings in *Notes on the State of Virginia* (1787), Jefferson addressed the question of human equality and delivered a prophecy about race-based slavery in the United States.

He imagined that the new country called America would be eventually engulfed in a race war as blacks recalled all the injuries and injustices visited upon them by whites; and whites, unable to overcome their own prejudices and treat blacks equitably due to their natural superiority, would resist the various steps toward social equality. While Jefferson's white supremacy thesis is a threadbare justification for whites' systemic injustices and structural advantages, it nonetheless rings some true notes given the as-yet-unfinished project of American democracy. Perfecting the union remains wholly elusive because of white racism (Feagin 2009).

For Jefferson, this natural white superiority extends to the realms of aesthetics, beauty, and sexuality. Drawing from the more racialist thinking of the evolving fields of natural history, anthropology, evolutionary biology, and the "Great Chain of Being" thesis (Linnaes 1758; West 2002) where differences are fixed in nature, the first aesthetic difference that struck Jefferson was "that of colour" (264). At pains to explain this difference scientifically, Jefferson reaches for a vocabulary chocked full of words such as "recticular membrane," "scarf skin," "secretions," and "bile" (264).

As if anticipating Du Bois's discussion of the veil in the *Souls of Black Folks* (1903), Jefferson calls blackness an "immoveable veil" (264). The veil of blackness covers over emotions that can be readily seen in whites. Blushed and flushed shades of red and pink typically associated with whiteness and a range of emotions—embarrassment, anger, shyness, coquetry—are also indicative of superior emotional evolution and intelligence versus the brute and elemental crying, sighing, pleading, and howling that enslaved blacks typically expressed at Monticello. Despite Jefferson's best efforts to paint himself as a gentleman farmer, Monticello was a large-scale operation where overseers, his father-in-law, and Jefferson himself were complicit in whippings, sexual predation, and tearing enslaved families asunder to pay off debts and as punishment (Wiencek 2012).

Mid-disquisition on blacks, Jefferson paused to romanticize about the beauty of the "red" (264)—the Powhatan, the Chickamauga, the Rappahannock, among others—which offered them no protection against colonization, reneged-upon treaties, land grabs, and rape (although Jefferson engaged in nothing like Jacksonian-era mass genocide and Manifest Destiny–style expansionist politics). In following the prescriptions of the ancient Greeks for judgments of beauty as related to symmetry of face and form, Jefferson mentions whites' "flowing hair" (265) and blacks' preference for whites, before concluding that whites are in the main better endowed "in both mind and body" (270)—even though the predilections of Jefferson's father-in-law and Sally Hemings's father, John Wayles, and Jefferson himself would seem to contradict his theses on whites' aesthetic and sexual tastes and preferences (Gordon-Reed 1998, 2008; Wienciek 2012).

But Jefferson's totting up and casting blacks low does not end here. Of black women, he suggested that they were more "ardent" and preferred "uniformly" by the male "Oranootan" over females of "his own species" (265). There were no orangutans to be found in Albemare County, Virginia, to substantiate such an observation. This fact was of little consequence to Thomas Jefferson. Jefferson's obtuse philosophies on race and sex trumped reason in an age just as dubiously committed to reason and enlightenment.

A deeply complicated and conflicted man, Jefferson, as is widely acknowledged, had a prolonged, nonconsensual sexual relationship with the slave girl and his sister-in-law Sally Hemings, beginning when she was fourteen years old and he was forty-one. Jefferson owned his children and his wife's siblings, which included Sally Hemings. He did not free Hemings in his will, though the Hemings–Jefferson liaison produced seven children, between 1790 and 1808 (Gordon-Reed 1998, 2008; Wiencek 2012).

With *Notes on the State of Virginia*, our nation's third president sealed an odious social contract, a racial-sexual contract, within our national fabric regarding black women. And Jefferson's paradox has had an enduring legacy in the United States. Against this unequivocal founding doctrine, black women have been continuously struggling both in the courts of law and public opinion, in their own communities, and on America's airwaves and in its movie entertainment complexes.

TOWARD A NEW RACE-GENDER POLITICS

From slave narratives to postemancipation writings and films, down the historical line, black women have been steadfast in decrying attacks on their character and morality. When after the president of the Missouri Press Association wrote an open letter addressed to an Englishwoman attempting to cast aspersions on the credibility of antilynching crusader Ida B. Wells, he made plain that black women "had no sense of virtue" and "character" (Giddings 1996). In response, the black women's club movement organized in July 1895 to defend their name. And they haven't stopped since with the emergence of the antiviolence against women group, A Long Walk Home Foundation; the blogosphere's Crunk Feminist Collective; and the Why We Can't Wait campaign, which challenged President Obama's My Brother's Keeper initiative that excluded young black women and girls.

There is then a through line in the fabric of American society regarding the ills that hip-hop culture has come to represent; and more specifically, we see that through line with respect to black women in some of the earliest writings produced by a founding father. When Jefferson wrote *Notes on the State of Virginia*, he had been a slaveholder for seventeen years and "Master of the Mountain" of Monticello for eleven. His views were not unique but widely held (although not universally shared) (Storozynski 2009; Wiencek 2012). Such views informed an emergent nation and have set the course for black women ever since.

That hip-hop culture bears the brunt of criticism is tied to the sleight of hands of power in the game of *misogynoir* in which corporate financial interests, product and taste makers, and consumers fully participate. A vicious cycle is cleverly introduced where the industry blames consumer tastes, consumers blame artists, and artists point back to their record labels' bottom-line demands. At the very bottom though, the profits to be had at black women's expense are deemed more valuable than the costs of caricaturing their persons. The range of black women's successes and the diversity of their lives and career paths have been congealed into myriad stereotypes for mass consumption, lazy digestion, and recirculation.

That sexism and misogyny appear to be working overtime in America to box black women into these very narrow depictions are part and parcel of the Jeffersonian contract. Hip-hop culture is certainly waist deep in the muck of this race-gender chauvinism. Male feelings of displacement in a perceived topsy-turvy female-dominated world with increased competition from women and girls in every facet of American life (Wolf 1993; Mansfield 2006; Sandberg 2013) contribute to male-on-female-gender drive-bys. And black women's seeming resiliency, despite America's continuing race and gender biases, as well as their strengths, are flung back at them and condensed into clichés such as the late New York Senator Patrick Moynihan's "black matriarch" (1965), as emasculating superwomen—or better still *bitches* in need of checking, sexing, or some combination of the two.

Though America drinks to bursting from that Jeffersonian well, it is imperative that young women become more politically and socially conscious about the choices they make and the opportunities they take. For it has become abundantly clear that it is not so much that black women do not count. They obviously do in various insidious ways. The truth of the matter though is that they do not add up to much, certainly not more than the profits, in the billions, to be had at their expense.

REFERENCES

"Across the Nation with Bob Dunning." (2007). "Catholic Radio Station." *Sirius Radio, Sirius radio Catholic Channel*, 159, April 20, 2007. http://www.siriusxm.com/thecatholicchannel.

Bailey, M. (2010). "They Aren't Talking About Me." *Crunk Feminist Collective*. Accessed July 20 2015. https://www.youtube.com/watch?v=0ObxJeP87z8.

Baldwin, James. (1963). "Take This Hammer." Interview. KQED. Vimeo, https://vimeo.com/ 13175192.

Brooks Higginbotham, E. (1994). *Righteous Discontent: The Women's Movement in the Black Baptist Church, 1880–1920*. Cambridge, MA: Harvard University Press.

Chiachiere, R. (2007). "Imus Called Women's Basketball Team "Nappy Headed Hos." Accessed August 10, 2015. http://mediamatters.org/research/2007/04/04/imus-called-womens-basketball- team-nappy-headed/138497.

Clark Hine, D. (1989). "Rape and the Inner Lives of Black Women in the Middle West." *Signs: Journal of Woman and Culture in Society* 14 (4): 912–920.

Clark Hine, D., and K. Thompson. (1999). *A Shining Thread of Hope: The History of Black Women in America*. New York: Broadway Books.

Congressional Hearing. (2007, September 25). "From Imus to Industry: The Business of Stereotypes and Degrading Images." House Energy and Commerce Subcommittee on Commerce, Trade & Consumer Protection, Washington, DC. http://www.c-span.org/video/ ?201163-1/stereotypes-degrading-images.

Cooper, A. J. (1892). *A Voice from the South*. Xenia, OH: The Aldine Printing House.

Davis, A. (1983). *Women, Race, and Class*. New York: Vintage.

Davis, A. (1999). *Blues Legacies and Black Feminism: Gertrude "Ma" Rainey, Bessie Smith, and Billie Holiday*. New York: Vintage.

"Don Imus and Hip Hop." (2007). *MSNBC Live*, April 140, 1–2. *LATimes* http://articles.latimes.com/keyword/don-imus.

Donaldson James, S. (2011). "Black Maid Sues, Says "The Help" Is Humiliating." *ABC News*, February 22. Accessed August 10, 2015. http://abcnews.go.com/Health/lawsuit- black-maid-ablene-cooper-sues-author-kathryn/story?id=12968562.

Douglass, Frederick. (1845). *Narrative of the Life of Frederick Douglass: An American Slave, Written by Himself*. Boston, MA: Anti-Slavery Office.

Douglass, Frederick. (1855). *My Bondage and My Freedom*. New York: Miller, Orton & Mulligan.

Douglass, Frederick. (1892). *The Life and Times of Frederick Douglass, Written By Himself*. Boston: De Wolfe & Fiske.

Du Bois, W. E. B. (1903). *The Souls of Black Folk*. Chicago: A. C. McClurg.

Dyson, M. (2007). *Know What I Mean: Reflections on Hip Hop*. New York: Basic Books.

Dyson, M. (2004). *The Michael Eric Dyson Reader*. New York: Basic Books.

Feagin, J. (2009). *The White Racial Frame: Centuries of Racial Framing and Counter-Framing*. New York: Routledge.

Giddings, P. (1996). *When and Where I Enter: The Impact of Black Women on Sex and Race in America*. New York: William Morrow.

Glymph, T. (2008). *Out of the House Bondage: The Transformation of the Plantation Household*. Cambridge: Cambridge University Press.

Goff, K. (2015). "White Women Have Always Stolen Black Beauty." *The Daily Beast*, June 13. Accessed August 10, 2015. http://www.thedailybeast.com/articles/2015/06/13/why-are-people-suddenly-so-concerned-about-hijacking-black-culture.html.

Gray White, D. (1985). *Arn't I a Woman: Female Slaves in the Plantation South.* New York: W. W. Norton.

Gray White, D. (1999) *Too Heavy a Load: Black Women in Defense of Themselves, 1894–1994.* New York: W. W. Norton.

Gordon-Reed, A. (2008). *The Hemings of Monticello: An American Family.* New York: W. W. Norton.

Gordon-Reed, A. (1998). *Thomas Jefferson and Sally Hemings: An American Controversy.* Charlottesville: University of Virginia Press.

Hahn, S. (2005). *A Nation Under Our Feet: Black Political Struggles in the Rural South From Slavery to the Great Migration.* Cambridge, MA: Belknap Press.

Harris-Perry, M. (2013). *Sister Citizen: Shame, Stereotypes, and Black Women in America.* New Haven, CT: Yale University Press.

Hauser, C., and A. O'Connor. (2007). "Virginia Tech Shooting Leaves 33 Dead." *The New York Times*, April 16. Accessed August 10, 2015. http://www.nytimes.com/2007/04/16/us/16cnd-shooting.html?pagewanted=all&_r=0.

Henderson, C., ed. (2009). *American and the Black Body: Identity Politics in Print and Visual Culture.* Teaneck, NJ: Fairleigh Dickinson University Press.

Henderson, C., ed. (2010). *Imagining the Black Female Body: Reconciling Image in Print and Visual Culture.* New York: Palgrave.

Henderson, C. (2013). "It's All in the Name: Hip Hop, Sexuality, and Black Women's Identity in *Breakin' In: The Making of a Hip Hop Dancer.*" *Palimpsest: Journal of Women, Gender, and the Black International* 2 (1): 47–58.

Hill Collins, P. (2005). *Black Sexual Politics: African Americans, Racism, and the New Racism.* New York: Routledge.

Hill Collins, P. (2008). *Black Feminist Thought: Knowledge, Consciousness, and the Politics of Empowerment.* New York: Routledge.

Hirschberg, L. (2007). "The Music Man." *New York Times Magazine*, September 2: 26.

hooks, bell. (1981). *Ain't I a Woman: Black Women and Feminism.* Boston: South End Press.

hooks, bell. (1992). *Black Looks: Race and Representation.* Boston: South End Press.

hooks, bell. (2003). *We Real Cool: Black Men and Masculinity.* New York: Routledge.

Horne. G. (2014). *The Counter-Revolution of 1776: Slave Resistance and the Origins of the United States of America.* New York: New York University Press.

Hunter, T. (1998). *To 'Joy My Freedom: Southern Black Women's Lives and Labors after the Civil War.* Cambridge, MA: Harvard University Press.

Hurt, B. (2006). *Beyond Beats and Rhymes.* Arlington, VA: PBS Independent Lens.

Jacobs, H. (1861). *Incidents in the Life of a Slave Girl, Written by Herself.* Boston: Thayer & Eldridge.

James, J. (2002). *Shadowboxing: Representations of Black Feminist Politics.* New York: Palgrave.

Jefferson, T. (1787). *Notes on the State of Virginia.* London: Stockdale.

Kitwana, B. (2003). *The Hip-Hop Generation: Young Blacks and the Crisis in African-American Culture.* New York: Basic Books.

Linnaeus, C. (1758). *Systema Naturae.* Stockholm: Holmiae Impensis.

Mansfield, H. (2006). *On Manliness.* New Haven, CT: Yale University Press.

McGuire, D. (2011). *At the Dark End of the Street: Black Women, Rape, and Resistance—A New History of the Civil Rights Movement from Rosa Parks to the Rise of Black Power.* New York: Vintage.

Moyer, J. (2015). "Rachel Dolezal's Brother, Author Joshua Dolezal, Faces Trial for Alleged Sexual Abuse of a Black Child." *The Washington Post*, June 16. Accessed July 30, 2015. http://

www.washingtonpost.com/news/morning-mix/wp/2015/06/16/rachel-dolezals-brother-author-joshua-dolezal-faces-trial-for-alleged-sexual-abuse-of-a-black-child/.

Moynihan, P. (1965). *The Negro Family: The Case For National Action*. Washington, DC: Office of Policy Planning and Research, United States Department of Labor.

Painter, N. (1997). *Sojourner Truth: A Life, A Symbol*. New York: W. W. Norton.

Pough, G. (2004). *Check It While I Wreck It: Black Womanhood, Hip Hop Culture, and the Public Sphere*. Boston: Northeastern University Press.

Rediker, M. (2007). *The Slave Ship: A Human History*. New York: Penguin.

Rose, T. (1994). *Black Noise: Rap Music and Black Culture in Contemporary America*. Middletown, CT: Wesleyan University Press.

Rose, T. (2008). *Hip Hop Wars: What We Talk About When We Talk About Hip Hop—and Why It Matters*. New York: Basic Books.

Samuels, A. (2015). "Rachel Dolezal's True Lies." *Vanity Fair*, July 19. Accessed July 30, 2015. http://www.vanityfair.com/news/2015/07/rachel-dolezal-new-interview- pictures-exclusive.

Sandberg, S. (2013). *Lean In: Women, Work, and the Will to Lead*. New York: Knopf.

Sharpley-Whiting, T. (2007). *Pimps Up, Ho's Down: Hip Hop's Hold on Young Black Women*. New York: New York University Press.

Sharpley-Whiting, T. (2015). *Bricktop's Paris: African American in Paris Between the Two World Wars*. Albany: State University of New York Press.

Sims Janet L. (1980). "Jessie Redmon Fauset (1885–1961): A Selected Annotated Bibliography." *Black American Literature Forum* 14 (4): 147–152. *African American Review* (St. Louis University) Stable. http://www.jstor.org/stable/2904406.

Storozynski, Alex. (2009). *The Peasant Prince: And the Age of Revolution*. New York: Macmillan.

Thompson, L. (2012). *Beyond the Black Lady: Sexuality and the New African American Middle Class*. Urbana: University of Illinois Press.

West, C. (2002). *Prophecy Deliverance!* Louisville, KY: Westminster John Knox Press.

Wiencek, H. (2012). *Master of the Mountain: Thomas Jefferson and His Slaves*. New York: Farrar, Straus, and Giroux.

Wilson, Douglas L. (2004). "The Evolution of Jefferson's *Notes on the State of Virginia*." *Virginia Magazine of History and Biography* 112: 98–133.

Wilson, K. (2015). "Towards a Radical Re-appropriation: Gender, Development and Neoliberal Feminism. Development and Change." *Forum* 46 (4): 803–832.

Wolf, N. (1993). *Fire with Fire: The New Female Power and How It Will Change the Twenty-First Century*. New York: Random House.

CHAPTER 49

THE VIOLENT WEIGHT OF WHITENESS

The Existential and Psychic Price Paid by Black Male Bodies

GEORGE YANCY

A phenomenology of "being stopped" might take us in a different direction than one that begins with motility, with a body that "can do" by flowing into space.

Sara Ahmed

That invisibility to which I refer occurs because of a peculiar disposition of the eyes of those with whom I come in contact. A matter of the construction of their inner eyes, those eyes with which they look through their physical eyes upon reality.

Ralph Ellison

I am *fixed*.

Frantz Fanon

THERE are many daily manifestations of black *racialized* trauma that do not take the form of a racist spectacular event, where white people watch and are entertained in the thousands, where fingers point accusatorily and excitedly, where hate, curiosity, and bloodlust fills the eyes of those who have come to witness "white justice," where the lust for flayed black flesh eventually fills their nostrils, where hearts palpitate with excitement, where little white children learn how to take up the vision of manifest destiny, and where a racialized and perverse libidinal economy structures the entire scene. Yet, because of the historically routine enactment of such horrible scenes, their iterative performances can become transmuted into forms of banality, where publically witnessed castrations and torn and mutilated flesh are expected, where those gathered *to see* are well aware of what will happen, where the spectacular has a texture of normality, the everyday. Perhaps it is partly this textural transmutation that constitutes the greater sin, the greater offence against humanity.

There are many daily manifestations of black male *racialized* trauma that whites fail or refuse to see. Either way, the trauma experienced is no less painful. In 2015, I was invited to be a plenary speaker at a philosophical conference where the body is taken seriously as a topic of phenomenological engagement. Not being seduced by the Cartesian conceptualization of the subject as an ontologically distinct thinking thing (res cogitans), and the body as an ontologically distinct material thing (res extensa), where the subject is thought of as the proverbial ghost in the machine, the philosophers gathered at this conference, the majority of whom were white, understood, or so I thought, the deeper social ontological and political importance of embodiment and how we are embedded within various structures of oppression—patriarchal, racist, sexist, ableist. I felt a shared sense of being philosophically at home within a space in which I thought the participants shared my doxastic assumptions, and philosophical intuitions regarding the centrality of embodiment as an important site for doing (nonideal) theory, a space where we all tarried with the ways in which bodies actually suffer under sociohistorical and political realities that are oppressive and hegemonic.

Surrounded by "kindred spirits," I explored in my plenary talk various insights regarding the violence and pain of racialized corporeality as articulated by Frantz Fanon, who understood all too well, and painfully so, what it meant to be embodied and raced within an antiblack world. As a black man, and thereby deemed racially ersatz, violent, evil, hypersexual, immoral, and disposable, Fanon (1967) knew that "in the white world the man of color encounters difficulties in the development of his bodily schema" (110). Before I arrived at the conference, I assumed that the philosophers in attendance knew what it meant *not* to leave existence "by the wayside" (Fanon 1967, 110), *not* to engage in forms of ontology that were undergirded by ahistorical assumptions. Instead, it was a space where philosophers could come clean about how bodies suffer, how bodies undergo differential experiences of sexual and racial fragmentation, how they experience fixity through problematic discursive sociopolitical orders and logics predicated upon imaginaries and material arrangements that are oppressive. In short, it was a space where we would do, what I call, "high-stakes" philosophy, that is, philosophy that mattered on the ground and refused to flee the messiness of the real world.

So, I engaged the black body, more generally, and *my black body*, in particular, and explored the complex processes of black *Erlebnis*. I named and marked racism as I encountered it within everyday spaces of sociality. "Knowing" that philosophers at this conference were receptive to deeper levels of self-interrogation, I hammered home the importance of white people engaging in the practice of what I call being *unsutured*, that is, creating in their lives modes of epistemic, affective, embodied, and spatial vulnerability vis-à-vis black bodies and bodies of color. To be unsutured, or to strive to maintain the reality of unsuturing as a disposition, meant that white people would nurture, tarry with, the reality that they are not atomic and bounded, but always already precarious and porous, having been sutured by a history written by themselves and for themselves. As Baldwin (1985) writes, "In great pain and terror one begins to assess the history which has placed one where one is and formed one's point of view" (410). To be sutured meant to cover over, stitch over, as it were, the stench of racist mythopoetic assumptions about black bodies and bodies of color. Remaining sutured involves remaining "safe," closed off from any risk of crisis in one's white identity; it means that, as white, there are layers of epistemic, affective, and embodied closure that are yet to be plumbed. My plenary talk was a call to action and to challenge my white colleagues, no matter how philosophically nonideal the conceptual themes they engaged, that there was much more work to be done. I wanted to encourage them to step forward, *to act*, to move closer to the precipice of the deeper rabbit hole of white racism—both explicit and implicit. As James Baldwin (1962) writes, "To act is to be committed, and to be committed is to be in danger. In this case, the danger, in the minds of most white Americans, is the loss of their identity" (8). My aim was to raise important issues related to white embodiment and to telescope the implications of such embodiment as these relate to the issue of white racist complicity.

As expected, given the centrality of the concept of corporeality, my plenary talk struck a nerve. I could tell that the nerve struck was a sensitive one, especially as evidenced during the Q&A. I could feel the unease within the white audience, the feeling of being unnerved. I had effectively created a "dangerous" space at that conference, *at that moment*, as I spoke, a space where risk was being demanded, where white embodied existence was made to feel marked, visible, cornered. I wanted to make it difficult to flee in bad faith, to seek psychological or ethical shelter, to suture. I wanted those white philosophers to open their eyes even wider, *to see me*, to see black pain and suffering; to use that shared "familial" conceptual space (focus on embodiment) to engage in a form of invocation that would lead to a form of solicitation—etymologically, to trouble. After all, we shared in the messiness of nonideal theory, where "the body" was far too abstract. Didn't we?

Yet very few white philosophers, as evidenced in their actual papers, remained grounded in nonideal theory. For the most part, it was "the body" that became the lingua franca. As Adrienne Rich (1984) writes, "Perhaps we need a moratorium on saying 'the body.' For it's also possible to abstract 'the' body. When I write 'the body,' I see nothing in particular" (215). Yet is it not the *white* body that attempts to obfuscate its raced identity and to appear as nothing in particular? Rich continues, "To locate myself in my body means more than understanding what it has meant to me to have a vulva and clitoris and uterus and breasts. It means recognizing this white skin, the places it has taken me, the places it has not let me go" (215–216). What was to become apparent to me at that conference was the rigidity of whiteness, white embodiment, and how whiteness shaped and truncated the range of perceptual nuance. Whites failed to recognize or refused to know the psychic places where their whiteness had taken them or the psychic spaces it has not let me go. As a result, their white gazes *fixed* me, gazes that attempted to render my body invisible, and yet hypervisible. The violent weight of whiteness was all too present. The translation of nonideal theory into action seriously failed, which raises another question: What does it mean for white philosophers to become unnerved *during* a talk that challenges whiteness and white embodiment, apparently to valorize nonideal theory, only for them to become confident and settled back into their white modes of being, to live as if ideal theory is all that matters, *after* such a talk? Perhaps Richard Wright (1940) is correct where he notes, "We [those of us at the conference] shared a common tongue, but my language was a different language from theirs" (213). In retrospect, I wonder *what* they had heard, *who* they had heard. And yes, there wasn't anything *spectacular* about the process of being "sealed into that crushing objecthood" (Fanon 1967, 109); it was all too mundane and insidious. As I moved through that conference space, being one of only two black philosophers there, I felt *stopped*, truncated, and made into a solid type—"Look, the black!" It was not that I was stopped and frisked by New York's finest. Yet there was a feeling of loss or perhaps excessiveness; an excessive blackness. There was the sense of being profiled, placed under a racial typology that allowed for no nuance.

The day after I had given my plenary talk, the other black philosopher, one senior in age to me and who had written about the racist "epidermalization" of the black body schema when I was a young teenager, arrived at the conference. On the day that he arrived, I was tired and had decided to sleep late. So I *was not* at the conference when he arrived. Then again, was I?

He shared with me that several conference attendees approached him with no apparent hesitancy or ambiguity. "That was a *very* important talk that you gave yesterday," one white philosopher said to him. Another white philosopher said, "Wow, great talk!" "Inspiring," came from another. No less than seven congratulatory gestures were made. Had there been one, perhaps I might have brushed it off as an "honest" mistake. But seven times? This was more than a mistake; it was the manifestation of an all-too-familiar mode of being white—white habits of perception, white racist iterative processes of seeing black bodies through a fixed imago. My colleague, the black philosopher who had *not* given the talk, somehow "became" me. We were fungible qua black male philosophers and unrecognized in our distinct individualities, our embodied differential concretion. We were flattened out, seen as surface things, one-dimensional, indistinct and repeatable. We were excessive; one black identifiable mass: "Look, the black!" Fanon (1967) says, "A man was expected to behave like a man. I was expected to behave like a black man—or at least like a nigger" (114). The two of us became *one* black man; perhaps *any* black man; perhaps *any* nigger.

The whites failed to see *me*, and they failed to see *him*. Yet they did see something. The "something" that they saw seemed to be both relevant and yet irrelevant. What they saw was relevant because "*the* black male philosopher" had to be thanked; irrelevant because *any* black man (within that conference space) would have apparently been sufficient to thank. The other black male philosopher did not look like me. In fact, as stated, he was older, but also taller, heavier, and very gray. He told me that in response to each interpellation, he said, "Thanks, but I didn't give the talk." One can expect the look of surprise, but not necessarily the self-reflexive cognition that this was not a simple mistake, but the enactment of white privilege and power *not to see* and thereby racist. As Charles Mills (1997) points out, this also involves important *moral* implications as "whites will then act in racist ways while thinking of themselves as acting morally" (93). Then again, perhaps some of those whites thought that he had forgotten that he in fact had given the talk. After all, the white gaze knows what it sees and sees what it knows. There is a sense in which whites in that room, though having not all gotten together and intentionally agreed that he was me, reached a consensus, where presumably multiple perspectives converged and merged "into a single, unified perspective" (Medina 2013, 303). This was a space within which a certain social knowledge was produced or perhaps a species of ignorance maintained. That conference space became one governed by what M. Merleau-Ponty (1962) terms operative intentionality "or that which produces the natural and antepredicative unity of the [white] world and of [white] life, being apparent in [white] desires, [white] evaluations and in the landscape [whites'] see" (xviii). When the other black philosopher shared his experiences with me, I could feel the existential weight of being *any* black male. Being thanked for a talk that he had not given was just one register of the burden. He had to endure the process of dis-identifying himself from me, of being mistaken. In absentia, I endured the burden of being where I wasn't, of being "the black." Imagine the mantra, "A black man did it!" And then watch as whites engage in hysterics and fanatic insularity, where all black men begin to look alike ("criminals," "aggressors," "rapists") and thus needing to be stopped, and, indeed, in so many cases, stopped dead. Susan Smith, a white woman who in 1994 drowned her two children and blamed it on a black man, and Charles Stuart, a white man who in 1998 shot and killed his pregnant wife and blamed it on a black man, were not only guilty of murder, but guilty of invoking the white racist historical sedimentation of the white imago of the black male body as inherently and unconscionably violent and cruel, which is a form of death by racist semiosis, one that can and does easily translate into an actual killing of black men who "fit the description."

At the conference, I felt that peculiar responsibility that Fanon (1967) notes: "I was responsible at the same time for my body, for my race, for my ancestors. I subjected myself to an objective examination, I discovered my blackness, my ethnic characteristics; and I was battered down by tom-toms, cannibalism, intellectual deficiency, fetishism, racial defects, slave ships . . ." (112). I wanted to move lithe in that conference space, to move with effortless grace, but my individual embodiment's meaning had been confiscated and I was returned as racially *static*. "The movements, the attitudes, the glances of [those whites] fixed me [and him] there, in the sense in which a chemical solution is fixed by a dye" (Fanon 1967, 109). Within another context, I would have been lynched because some white woman said that a black man had accosted and raped her, though I was nowhere close to the alleged act. Lynching *any* black male body that "fit the description" would have been sufficient; indeed, within the context of North American white supremacy, any black body would have served the larger purpose of white nation building, of performing what it meant not to be black. Then again, a black woman would have no doubt first been brutally raped, or perhaps burned alive while pregnant and her unborn baby cut from her abdomen, only to have its little, fragile skull crushed beneath some white man's boot heel after it fell and hit the ground. This was the tragic ordeal of twenty-one-year-old Mary Turner in Lowndes, County, Georgia, in 1918 (http://www.maryturner.org/documents.htm). White nation building is putrid with black bodies at its base, many thousands literally dead and so many socially dead and dying. White nation building is not only about white forms of suturing white bodies, rendering them imaginatively bounded and invulnerable; it also has as one of its struts the practice of suturing black bodies through white gazes that flatten out blackness into an amorphous thing. This raises the issue of the fungible again. Critically engaging the space of visual culture, Alessandra Raengo (2013) raises questions about the "kind of visual culture, scopic regimes, logics of seeing, and archival structures" (130) that are needed to suture differences—in this case the differences between me and the other black philosopher. The visual field through which those whites exchanged the two of us as identical presupposes a range of epistemic and "disciplinary, formations that sustain this mapping of the visual field" (Raengo 2013, 130).

Within that white conference space, my embodied experience and the embodied experience of the other black philosopher became a "site of social stress" (Ahmed 2007, 161). Fanon (1967) reminds Jean-Paul Sartre that he "had forgotten that the Negro suffers in his body quite differently from the white man" (138). Being mistaken for someone else no less than seven times, within the same conference day and within minutes apart, is not simply stressful, but a species of annihilation, where the white visual mapping at the conference refused to see me, him. "To feel negated is to feel pressure upon your bodily surface; your body feels the pressure point, as a restriction in what it can do" (Ahmed 2007, 161). On this score, as individuals, we were not extended into space (153). Rather, we already occupied a certain place in space, fixed as the "same" body, a continuous black mass. We entered a white space, a site where we already had a place. "Whiteness is inherited through the very placement of things" (155). Being in that place as "the black male body" as such, white bodies at that conference did not feel stressed, had no need to be oriented toward their whiteness; they were able to "trail behind actions" (156). The other black philosopher's body did not trail behind, but faced itself as a problem; the one which had to summon the strength to say yet again: "Thanks, but I'm not the one." He was the one who had to enter into battle yet again with the black imago in the white imaginary. He was the one who had to suffer from being mistaken, that is, "fitting their description" so many times. Think here of the anxiety and vexation endured, the physiological impact. The white philosophers at the conference not only had the privilege of being "unraced," but they were able to move through space with ease, unstressed. Shannon Sullivan (2015) advances critical race theory and critical philosophy of race through theorizing the ways in which white power and domination are constitutive of white physiology, noting that "the relatively good health of many white Americans—lower incidence of hypertension, high blood pressure, and so on—can be considered a product of white privilege rather than a neutral or 'normal' physiological condition" (134). Hence, white physiology is itself deeply political.

Perhaps like Fanon (1967), my black colleague had made up his mind to laugh himself to tears, "but laughter had become impossible" (112). However, unlike twenty-two-year-old Guinean Amadou Diallo who in 1999 was said to "fit the description" of a wanted rapist, and who was killed upon taking out his wallet, indeed, shot at forty-one times and hit with nineteen bullets, my black colleague did come away with his life. We both knew that the battle had already begun; we both knew the white terrain all too well. There was nothing inaugural about this moment for him or for me. It involved the daily display of white refusal, the refusal to see us for who we were/are; the refusal to challenge their own white epistemic flaws and white productive ignorance, embodied scopic iterations, and affective intensities that misinform and exaggerate. When it comes to white bodies vis-à-vis black male bodies, there was the failure of epistemic responsibility (Medina 2013, 156) to know me, to know him. As black male bodies, we arrived at the conference *too early* vis-à-vis the black imago within the white imaginary, while, simultaneously, in terms of our actual embodied presence, having arrived already *too late*. Such encounters with white people are not experienced as benign, but as assaultive and traumatic to our sense of self.

White people stereotype us; they ontologically truncate and police us; and, they do violence to our sense of integrity. The state plays no small role in this. For example, in drug interdiction operations, which are federally funded, there is the oppressive discriminatory experience of driving while black (DWB). Michelle Alexander (2010) notes, "In New Jersey, the data showed that only 15 percent of all drivers on the New Jersey Turnpike were racial minorities, yet 42 percent of all stops and 73 percent of all arrests were of black motorists— despite the fact that blacks and whites violated traffic laws at almost exactly the same rate" (131). Walking while black (WWB) is no better. Naomi Zack (2015) notes, "There were 4.4 million stop and frisks in New York City from 2002–2012. Overall, 2.2 million blacks were stopped by police and 90 percent or close to 2 million were innocent. That is a lot of innocent people!" (57). *I would add, that is also a lot of traumatization and psychic scarring!* In both these cases, the discriminatory state apparatus is marked. In addition to the racially discriminatory state apparatus, Baldwin (1995) was correct where he said, regarding his white countrymen, those who differentially benefit from the state, "that they have destroyed and are destroying hundreds of thousands of [black] lives and do not know it and do not want to know it" (5). This form of ignorance is not nugatory. It has deadly and devastating consequences for black male bodies, those who are deemed *ontological* threats, as it were. Nor does this ignorance let whites off the proverbial hook as they are responsible, complicit in the embodied psychic wounds that they leave behind. The white bodies at the conference, for example, were able to playfully engage theory without the pain and suffering of entering into battle with their white selves (Baldwin 1985, 410). There was no need to know *otherwise*. From their perspective, there was nothing more to know. By stressing the places that her white embodiment has taken her and the places it has not let her go, Rich (1984) understands the heteronomous dynamics of whiteness and how whiteness operates according to logics that close off, occlude, conflate, suture, erase, distort, and create distances—epistemological, aesthetic, embodied, affective, political.

For many whites at that conference, "Abstractions [were] severed from the doings of living people [and], fed back [to them] as slogans" (Rich 1984, 210). However, as black men, that conference experience was indicative of a long history that has informed us that we must move with precision and embodied calculation in a world where we are deemed criminals, monsters, rapists, thugs, as ones always already on the precipice of being "up to no good." As Fanon (1967) notes, "The Negro is the symbol of sin. The archetype of the lowest values is represented by the Negro" (189). Given the racist sociohistorical facticity in terms of which black men have been thrown, there is a fundamentally racist, agonistic sociality that they are damned to experience. In this way, it might be argued that black men live their freedom in the mode of postponement. As they begin to aspire (etymologically, "to breathe"), move lithe into the world, and exercise black embodied motility, they find themselves threatened by the black imago in the white imaginary, a threat that can deliver literal death with all deliberate speed. As Fanon (1967) writes, "I shouted a greeting to the world and the world slashed away my joy" (114–115). To shout a greeting to the world, which can also function as a philosophical address, as when I delivered my paper, is to "reach out," to extend one's embodiment into the world. Yet my greeting was also "slashed away." Apparently, it was not even necessary *for me* to have delivered the paper or shouted the greeting. As white philosophers moved through that white conference space, there was an agreeable dialectic between their embodiment and the social integument through which they moved. Fanon speaks to this dialectic when he discusses reaching for his pack of cigarettes and where he implicitly knows where to reach for the matches. He describes this process as "a definitive structuring of the self and of the world—definitive because it creates a real dialectic between my body and the world" (111). For me and my black colleague, the "real dialectic" did not occur at the majority white conference; it was a problematic structuring that created an experience of stagnancy, of being stopped, occluded, where, within that white space, it became hard to breathe, to aspire. On this score, black male bodies move through space in the form of "I cannot" (Ahmed 2007, 161).

The cries of Eric Garner in Staten Island in 2014 constitute a clarion call of the suffering black male body in twenty-first century America: *I can't breathe. I can't breathe. I can't breathe. I can't breathe. I can't breathe. I can't breathe. I can't breathe. I can't breathe. I can't breathe. I can't breathe. I can't breathe.* As the white police officers encircled Garner's body, while Daniel Pantaleo engaged a chokehold (according to the medical examiner), and as other officers were on top of Garner, his head pressed to the cement, what did they see or hear? Eleven cries for help? No immediate medical assistance? What were the distorted assumptions, affective rigidities, and moral opacities that occluded the movement necessary for those white police officers to see/hear that Garner was in distress, struggling to breathe, to aspire? It has to do with, as Ellison says in the epigraph, the construction of their inner eyes. Toni Morrison (1970) locates the problem, which she sees as a *white problem*, "somewhere between retina and object, between vision and view" (48). The white gaze, though, is predicated upon various racist discursive sedimentations, white normative regulations, desires, institutional structures, and other (non-ocular-specific) embodied stylizations. In this way, the white gaze is not the beginning point, but reproduces a larger historical context, "reproducing of a [larger] historical situation" (Warren 2001, 454). Baldwin (1985) argues that whites "are impaled on their history like a butterfly on a pin and become incapable of seeing or changing themselves, or the world" (410). Baldwin writes about how he has seen in the eyes of white rookie cops a deep fear. He says that they "had to pretend to themselves that the black junkie, the black mother, the black father, the black child were of different human species than themselves" (Baldwin 1985, 413). Did the white police officers "see" a subhuman person, a large, ubiquitous, threatening black body that needed to be "put down," rendered devoid of breath? Or perhaps they saw the "threatening" agency of a black male who insisted, "It stops today!" (https://www.youtube.com/watch?v=JpGxagKOkv8). Those white police officers failed to grapple with themselves, their fantasies of black "bestiality," black "disgust," black "excessiveness"; they refused to face the pain and terror that is necessary for them to assess the force of history which has placed them where they are, and through which they have come to *misunderstand* the world, that is, the world as constituted by complex material, social, epistemic, and affective racist arrangements that too frequently lead to the destruction and denigration of black male bodies. As Baldwin says, they are impaled. They failed or refused to understand how whiteness (their whiteness) is structured by a racial Manichean valence that installs black male bodies as disposable, and that enables them to disavow (consciously or unconsciously) any racism on their part in the perpetuation of the actual disposal of said black male bodies.

Perhaps deep within the unconscious of white America, black male bodies are thought to be "*ineligible for personhood* (Cacho 2012, 6), though linked to a dialectic that automatically grants personhood to whites. Indeed, perhaps black subpersonhood, the *Untermensch*, is necessary for white identity, security, and power. As Mary E. Hobgood (2009) writes, "For whites to construct an identity outside the racist contract, we would need to give up our socially constructed white selves and embrace the rejected parts of our humanity that requires scapegoats" (54). Of course, Baldwin was keenly aware of this concept as early as 1963: "What you say about somebody else, anybody else, reveals you" (https://www.youtube.com/watch?v=LoL5fciA6AU). The construction of white identity as the *not-black* would help to explain the passivity or active contempt vis-à-vis Garner's cries for help, his suffering "monstrous" black body. Garner is no monster qua monster. Rather, the black body is forced into existing white material, discursive, and political power configurations that relationally mark and exclude the black body as fit for teratology. In this way, monsters are illicit vis-à-vis the licit, that is, the nonmonstrous white body. White police officer Daren Wilson, who shot and killed eighteen-year-old Michael Brown, described him as a "demon" (http://time.com/3605346/darren-wilson-michael-brown-demon/). Ben Stein even described Brown's black body as a "weapon." According to Stein, invoking images of teratology, Brown "wasn't unarmed. He was armed with his incredibly strong, scary self" (Blue 2014). It is not hard to imagine that these were some of the same racially apprehensive specters that those white police officers saw as they brutally tackled Garner to the ground. Garner became "the site at which that racist violence fears and beats the specter of its own rage" (Butler 1993, 20). In their refusal to act on Garner's behalf, to respond to his entreaty, the actions of the white police officers were loud and clear: "Your life doesn't matter!" Recall that it was on April 2, 2015, in Tulsa County, Oklahoma, that forty-four-year-old black male Eric Harris was shot in the back "by accident" by white male Robert Bates, a seventy-three-year-old reserve deputy.

While a police officer's knee is on his head, which, like Garner's, is pressed to the ground, Harris is heard screaming, "Oh, my God, I'm losing my breath!" Like Garner's cry, the illocutionary force of the expression was a plea, a species of supplication. That plea was met with a ruthless response: "Fuck your breath!" (http://thinkprogress.org/justice/2015/04/12/ 3646057/fuck-breath-officer-caught-video-mocking-unarmed-black-man-fatally-shot-police/). To hear Harris's screams, and the vitriol returned by the white police officer, only to know that he will later die from the gunshot wound on that same day, produces more than moral outrage; it leaves that potent and confusing sense of embodied powerlessness, emptiness, stress, fear, nausea.

If the cries—"I can't breathe"—of Eric Garner in Staten Island in 2014 constitute a clarion call of the suffering black male body in twenty-first-century America, then "Fuck your breath!" is the twenty-first-century response in 2015 and perhaps beyond. It is a response that installs black male bodies in the mode of waiting, a temporary delay in the inevitability of violent death by complex forms of white hatred, white occlusion, white suturing, white embodied habits, white material and state power, and a perverse economy of white desires. "Fuck your breath!" is the callous and haunting articulation of a form of contempt, in this case, for black male life. The materialization of this contempt has been witnessed over and over again as unarmed black males, what might be called the zone of the "state of exception" (http://www.borderlands.net.au/vol6no3_2007/ chowdhury_once.htm), have been and are being brutally killed by white police officers, those who have sworn to protect and serve. For example, in 2013, twenty-four-year-old Jonathan Ferrell, after crashing his car and seeking help, was shot ten times by a white police officer as he ran toward them, perhaps out of confusion. Even black male bodies that seek help are transmogrified into threats that must be stopped. In 2014, thirty-five-year-old Levar Jones pulled into a gas station and got out of his vehicle. He was approached by a white police officer. The officer told Jones to show him his license. As Jones reached back into his vehicle for his license, the police officer fired multiple shots, one bullet hitting Jones in the hip. On the one hand, "resist" arrest and one is sure to be killed. On the other hand, follow the orders given by white police officers and one may still be killed. Through the white imaginary, black male bodies pulling out wallets, seeking help, or following orders are still construed as transgressive, racialized furtive movements. Jones, after all, was compliant. The problem is that they are still shot, and in so many cases killed, because they are always already "storied" by white racist narrative scripts, by "adjectival signifiers" (Jackson 2006, 50) that militate against slippage.

In 2014, having a toy gun in his waistband, twelve-year-old Tamir Rice was shot and killed by a white police officer. The officer, within two seconds after exiting his vehicle, shot Rice. His fourteen-year-old sister, who ran to see about him, was thrown to the ground and handcuffed. Imagine not being able to hold your young brother as he has just been shot and will soon die. Like Garner, Rice was not given immediate first aid. Confused, shaking, and no doubt finding it hard to breathe, a black twelve-year-old boy's dreams and hopes were *stopped*, given only two seconds to convince two white police officers that he is twelve, simply a boy, and has a toy gun. Unfortunately, white supremacist history was against him. It was also in 2014 that twenty-two-year-old John Crowford was shot and killed by a white police officer as he walked around a Wal-Mart store carrying an air rifle, one actually sold at the store. Crowford, like Rice, was not dangerous, was not threatening anyone. Both were nonchalantly moving through space, minding their own business. Yet, as they moved through space, similar to the ways in which I moved (and my colleague moved) through the space at the conference, their bodies, too, failed to trail behind their actions. Being black males, our bodies are already subject to hypernoticeability. White gazes and white bodily forms of comportment solidify and fixate the black male body "into a fully exteriorized frontality" (Raengo 2013, 43). We were reduced to our black bodies, forced to encounter our bodies as objects. "To be black in 'the white world' is to turn back toward itself, to become an object, which means not only not being extended by the contours of the world, but being diminished as an effect of the bodily extensions of [white] others" (Ahmed 2007, 161). Hence, it is not simply about guns—toy or otherwise. Rather, black male bodies are dialectically linked to those white bodies that move through various spaces with ease, with a form of white immunity and the presumption of moral innocence. Remember, Michael Brown's black body *was* a "weapon." No innocence there. The a priori lack of innocence regarding black male bodies is apparently why in 2015, fifty-year-old Walter Scott had to be shot in the back. The white police officer, contrary to what video evidence revealed, said that Scott had taken his Taser and that he was "afraid" for his life. According to the logic of whiteness, which is structurally binary with normative binary implications, a fleeing black male body *is* still a violent body that must be killed. Also in 2015, forty-three-year-old Samuel DuBose was shot in the head (and instantly killed) after he attempted to drive his car away (to flee) from a white police officer who had stopped him. The white police officer said that he was being "dragged" and so had to shoot DuBose, an account "corroborated" by two other white officers on the scene. As in the case of Scott, the video evidence tells a different story, one that belies the one white officer's "official" white narrative, and the one supported by his fellow white officers. Through a white racist inflected narrative of intelligibility, Scott and DuBose were not killed because of being actual threats to the lives of the white officers; rather, they were killed by virtue, in these cases, of being black males, perceived as immoral and dastardly black bodies who were/are always already on the verge of either delivering a death blow to the white body politic or contaminating the "virgin sanctity of whiteness" (Butler 1993, 18).

REFERENCES

Ahmed, S. (2007). "A Phenomenology of Whiteness." *Feminist Theory* 8 (2): 149–168.

Alexander, M. (2010). *The New Jim Crow: Mass Incarceration in the Age of Colorblindness.* New York: The New Press.

Baldwin, James. (1985). *The Price of the Ticket: Collected Nonfiction, 1948–1958.* New York: St. Martin's Press.

Baldwin, James. [1962] (1995). *The Fire Next Time.* New York: The Modern Library.

Blue, Miranda. (2014). "Ben Stein: Michael Brown 'Wasn't Unarmed. He Was Armed With His Incredibly Strong, Scary Self'." *RightWing Watch*, 8/27/2014 12:14 pm. http://www.rightwingwatch.org/content/ben-stein-michael-brown-wasnt-unarmed-he-was-armed-his-incredibly-strong-scary-self.

Butler, J. (1993). "Endangered/Endangering: Schematic Racism and White Paranoia." In *Reading Rodney King: Reading Urban Uprising*, edited by Robert Gooding-Williams, 15–22. New York: Routledge.

Cacho, L. M. (2012). *Social Death: Racialized Rightlessness and the Criminalization of the Unprotected.* New York: New York University Press.

Fanon, F. (1967). *black Skin, White Masks.* Translated by Charles Lam Markmann. New York: Grove Press.

Hobgood, M. E. (2009). *Dismantling Privilege: An Ethics of Accountability*. Cleveland: The Pilgrim Press.

Jackson, R. L. (2006). *Scripting the black Masculine Body: Identity, Discourse, and Racial Politics in Popular Media*. New York: State University of New York Press.

Medina, J. (2013). *The Epistemology of Resistance: Gender and Racial Oppression, Epistemic Injustice, and Resistant Imaginations*. New York: Oxford University Press.

Merleau-Ponty, M. (1962). *Phenomenology of Perception*. Translated by Colin Smith. New York: Routledge.

Mills, C. (1997). *The Racial Contract*. Ithaca, NY: Cornel University Press.

Morrison, Toni. (1970). *The Bluest Eye*. New York: A Plume Book.

Raengo, A. (2013). *On the Sleeve of the Visual: Race as Face Value*. Dartmouth, NH: Dartmouth College Press.

Rich, A. (1984). "Notes Toward a Politics of Location." In *Blood, Bread, and Poetry: Selected Prose, 1979–1985*, 211–231. New York: Norton.

Sullivan, S. (2015). *The Physiology of Sexist and Racist Oppression*. New York: Oxford University Press.

Warren, John. (2001). "Performing Whiteness Differently: Rethinking the Abolistionist Project." *Educational Theory* 51 (4): 451–466.

Wright, Richard. (1940). *Eight Men: Short Stories*. New York: Harper Perennial.

Zack, Naomi. (2015). *White Privilege and black Rights: The Injustice of U.S. Police Racial Profiling and Homicide*. Lanham, MD: Rowman and Littlefield.

CHAPTER 50

GENDER THEORY IN PHILOSOPHY OF RACE

NAOMI ZACK

FEMINIST philosophy or gender theory, like philosophy of race or racial theory, is a new addition to philosophy, with subjects of analyses that include the history of philosophy, reclaimed authors, contemporary social injustice, the history of oppression, and identity. Gender theory is relevant to philosophy of race, and philosophy of race is relevant to gender theory. Both gender theory and philosophy of race address sites of injustice that involve large parts of the human population in ways that run counter to Enlightenment democratic ideals of equality, human dignity, and political representation. However, gender theorists (/feminist philosophers) and critical race theorists (/philosophers of race) have at best had a troubled meeting of the minds. The leading idea in gender theory, namely sexism, seems not to be compatible with racism as the leading idea in critical race theory. As theoretical subjects, women of color have been excluded in both types of theory, and it is therefore important that critical race theory and gender theory either begin to include them or else recognize a new critical theory that is able to generate conceptual understanding of the distinct existential problems of women of color, especially African American women.

Relevant theoretical intervention in critical race theory includes reexamination of patriarchal values and metaphysical ideas of the relation between race and gender; feminist philosophy has in recent decades included racial differences, racism, and concerns voiced by women of color (Zack 2005). The historical and theoretical background for the exclusion of nonwhite women continually inspires new possibilities for criticism and intervention. However, any intervention that leaves the leading methodological concept in each theory— sex or race—undisturbed is unlikely to accomplish inclusive goals. A proposal for a new critical theory that emerges from the material foundations of critical theory thereby becomes worthy of consideration and perhaps even somewhat urgent.

HISTORICAL AND THEORETICAL BACKGROUND

After the French Revolution, the nineteenth century held both the abolitionist movement against slavery and the movement for women's suffrage. But the leaders of each movement did not express solidarity with the other movement. Following the Civil War, when black male leaders sought voting rights to achieve equal citizenship rights, some educated suffragists thought that they were more deserving of the vote than freed black men. Black women were excluded from white women's political efforts and club networks but reacted by creating their own organizations. Black female activists and writers also protested lynching and sought to secure educational opportunities for black women, as well as correct racist stereotypes of sexual immorality and counter sexual assaults on black women by white men (Sterling 1997). But despite exceptional leadership and eloquence from thinkers and activists such as Ida B. Wells, Mary McLlyod Bethune, Sojourner Truth, Julia A. Cooper, Ella Baker, and Fannie Lou Hammer (Hine 2005), black women's issues were not at the forefront of nineteenth-century emancipatory efforts concerning race or gender. Even during the twentieth-century civil rights movement, black women did not have equal standing with black men within the leadership segments of political organizations (Brown 1992; Barnett 1993; Collier-Thomas and Franklin 2001).

Although African American men got the right to vote with ratification of the 1870 Fifteenth Amendment to the US Constitution, few were permitted to vote in states of the former confederacy until the Voting Rights Act of 1965—and some observers believe that obstructions to black voting persist to the present day (Von Drehle 2013). American women did not get the right to vote until the Nineteenth Amendment of 1920. Many feminists believe that date marked the end of the first wave of feminism, with a second wave beginning in the 1970s (Nicholson 1997), and a third or fourth wave that continues to address gender issues such as domestic violence, rape, income inequality, and unequal access to powerful institutional positions throughout society.

Still, there is now formal equality for women and men of all races and on that basis, the (white) US general public largely believes that present society is no longer plagued by injustices to racial minorities and women. But academic specialists in race and gender do not generally believe that equality has been achieved in either case, and they advance critical race theory and feminist theory to further analyze and understand substantial and widespread ongoing inequalities of material well-being and human dignity experienced by nonwhites and women. Both types of theorists have criticized mainstream philosophy for its neglect of gender and race. For example, there have been feminist critiques of John Rawls, the preeminent twentieth-century political philosopher, concerning with his initial assumption that the political subjects of his well-ordered society that could practice his ideals of justice were male heads of household (Abbey 2013), as well as criticism from philosophers of race that he virtually ignored the subject of race throughout his writing, even though he lived through intense crises in US race relations that his theory of justice could have addressed (Mills 2009).

THE EXCLUSION OF WOMEN IN CRITICAL RACE THEORY

Issues of existential exclusion also pertain to contemporary philosophy of race. Philosophy of race has also not robustly addressed issues of poverty and social class. This is understandable, because few poor people of color remain poor after they get their PhDs, and tenure-related jobs in philosophy enable entry into the socioeconomic class(es) of most others already in the academy. By contrast, most women of color do remain women after they become philosophers of race. Many of these more recent female philosophers experience a puzzling male dominance in the subfield, which is impervious to their existential realities.

Feminist philosophers have been more welcoming of philosophy of race than philosophers of race have welcomed feminism, but each of these critical theories privileges its own leading concept, seeking to reduce the other's leading concept to its own. Feminism has allowed for pluralism among its leading terms with the concept of *intersectionality* (the insight that individuals may experience multiple oppressions, based on their identities) (Crenshaw 1991). By contrast, critical race theory has not been analogously pluralistic. The critical race theory approach proceeds as though race and racial differences are more important for understanding social inequality and injustice, than either economic class or gender (Outlaw 1990). This methodological presumption is ironic, because critical theory in general originated in Marxist class-based analyses of society (Geuss 2001). Still, many philosophers of race point to statistics supporting the view that on every class level of society, compared to whites, nonwhites have less of the goods of life, such as infant survival, high-quality education, professional employment, health, accrued wealth, livable income, and civic and work honors (Thernstrom and Thernstrom 2009). And those critical race theorists assume that the residue of relative disadvantage is the result of institutional and hearts-and-minds racism.

The insistence on racism as a primary methodological concept in critical race theory entails that genderism, ableism, classism, oppression of nonmales, disability, and poverty cannot rise to the same theoretical prominence as methodological tools. If a black person claims to experience gender discrimination, poverty, or police persecution, as a primary problem, the response of many critical race theorists might begin and end with the fact that the person is black and thereby subject to antiblack racism as his or her greatest or over-riding oppression. In this sense, many male philosophers who work in philosophy of race are not unlike white male philosophers in the history of philosophy. They are not themselves significantly afflicted by problems other than those of their intellectual focus—racism—and they are not female, poor, disabled, or disadvantaged in other ways that have received liberatory scholarly attention. There may be no deliberate exclusion of women or poor people as the subjects of critical race theory, but neither is there evidence of a compelling need to include them. Notice, however, that this is not a case of demographic identity politics but the result of an implicit or explicit assumption that antiblack racism, pure and simple, is *the* primary problem of oppression (combined with the absence of direct personal experience that might indicate otherwise). The beginning and end point is that liberatory work on the poverty or gender of black people tends to be subsumed under antiracist work. Furthermore, much contemporary critical race theory work is accomplished by black male philosophers who arrived first in the field that they founded. Like many other human beings in positions of power and authority, it would be natural for them to pass on the yokes and mantles of their work to others who are similar to them. This is how paradigms work in all fields and subfields, and there is nothing extraordinary occurring here (Kuhn 2001).

Intersectionality has been a useful tool for theorists of race in the social sciences and literature. However, it has not so far become a widely used tool in philosophy of race, because it puts all forms of oppression on the same theoretical level (insofar as they come together in individuals) and philosophy of race posits racism as the main oppression. From the standpoint of women of color and feminist theorists in philosophy of race, this may make philosophy of race an unsatisfactory way to address their concerns, at this time. So far, no one working in philosophy of race has produced a plausible theory of gender capable of coexisting with, or dislodging, the hegemony of the normative concept of racism in critical race theory. How might that be done?

THEORETICAL INTERVENTIONS IN THE EXCLUSION OF WOMEN FROM CRITICAL RACE THEORY

To restate the problem: Critical race theorists proceed as though racism is the primary oppression, and these theorists abstractly consider the subject of racism, with the result that the subject of critical race theory almost always turns out to be male, not deliberately, but by default. (The subject is also middle class, by default, with an according neglect of poverty, but that is not the focus here.) Many women of color suffer on the grounds of their female gender, but that suffering does not rise to primary consideration in critical race theory. To say that they suffer distinctively because they are black, Hispanic, Asian, or Native American women does not fully comprehend their suffering *as women*. This means that critical race theory excludes the suffering of women of color, as women. Three candidates for theoretical intervention will be considered here: male patriarchy as a value; the metaphysics of critical race theory; and the material or economic foundation of critical theory. Each of these interventions would require a fundamental rethinking of the basic assumption of critical race theory, which is really *critical racist theory*. However, the examination of the economic foundations of critical theory will suggest a new critical theory: *critical plunder theory*.

Male Patriarchy as a Value

Either racism is a primary phenomenon or else it is an effect or expression of something more powerful in human motivation and society. Critical race theory implicitly treats racism as a primary phenomenon, just as gender theory or feminism traditionally treats sexism. But maybe critical race theorists are overlooking something here. One could suggest that critical race theorists, particularly critical race theorists of US black experience, reconsider who the primary agents of antiblack racism were and still are. These agents are not only white men, but given the real and intellectual history of racism in the United States, white women, also. However, the white women who are antiblack in reality, as well as those who have advanced feminism, have been subordinate to white men. Even when they themselves achieve equal power with men, the evidence is scant that they change the masculine values of that power or the structure of the power system they enter (Mann 2013). Many white women remain subordinate to white men in reality, whether they are aware of it or not, while white feminists deliberately seek to theorize resistance to the domination of white women by white men. If we add to this that both white men and white women are oppressive to blacks, the conjunction reduces to white male dominance, because the antiblack white women are subordinate to white men, just as the liberatory feminists are aware that they themselves are. On the grounds of a feminism without race, this is called "patriarchy." On the grounds of critical race theory, it could be understood as "white patriarchy."

Critical race theorists do not yet appear willing to criticize white patriarchy, perhaps because they have been and still are reluctant to criticize patriarchy. To criticize white patriarchy is to admit an intersection that could dislodge the primacy of white racism as a theoretical term. To criticize patriarchy introduces another term alongside racism, and it may introduce a value that black male critical race theorists are not prepared to criticize, because they aspire to or support patriarchy for black males, or they do not believe that patriarchy is a social construction, but rather a natural human tendency. The focus in black-male critical race theory has been on pernicious constructions, by whites, of black male gender or male blackness. Perhaps black male critical race theorists could pay more attention to dangerous constructions of white male gender or male whiteness. Perhaps it is necessary to reconsider how the patriarchal values of white patriarchy, and not just its racism, have been harmful to both women and men of color.

White patriarchy has harmed both males and females of color, because it is both a form of white male dominance over all females and a form of white male dominance over males of color. There are, in addition, many professional, economic, and raw power hierarchies among white males. Males of color and white women, as objects of domination, pose a threat to those who dominate them and so do other white males. However, for our purposes, it is important to glean from an examination of white male patriarchy evidence of motives and goals that extend beyond race into gender. There are important questions about theoretical aims here: Are black male critical race theorists, in resisting white male patriarchy, resisting the fact that white males are the dominant patriarchs, so that others could take their place or occupy parity with them as patriarchs? Or, are black male critical race theorists committed to resisting patriarchy, regardless of the race of patriarchs? In the first case, it should not be surprising that black women are left out, because the battle is between men who are dominant over women and other men. In the second case, black male critical race theorists would become feminists.

The Metaphysics of Critical Race Theory and Critical Race Pluralism

To speak of metaphysics here is to speak of a worldview, rather than how things literally are, in reality. Suppose that in our worldview there are things or substances and that these things or substances have attributes. The relation between thing and attribute is expressed in language by the relation between noun and adjective. The attribute/adjective qualifies or attributes something to the thing/noun, for example, red hat, round ball, frozen lake. The thing that the noun stands for is, in our minds, metaphysically more foundational or important than the quality that the adjective stands for. If we think of humankind as socially divided into races and also acknowledge that humankind is made up of male and female human beings, then studies of race and gender generate this question, concerning blacks: Are there black males and black females, or, are there male blacks and female blacks? That is, is gender or race the thing? For gender theorists, the primary metaphysical division is probably that between males/men and females/women (assuming no other genders), so it makes sense for them to speak of black men and black women, or white men and white women. But for critical race theorists, race seems to be the primary substantive. Therefore, conceptually, they are referring to male blacks and female blacks and male whites and female whites. Notice that the feminist metaphysical distinction divides humankind into males and females, whereas the critical race theorist metaphysics unites gender on the grounds of race. Is that the right metaphysics for critical race theory, in terms of concerns about women?

Lewis Gordon answers, or may have answered, Yes, in his brilliant 1997 essay, "Race, Sex and Matrices of Desire in an Antiblack World." Gordon there derived metaphysics or ontology from desire. In an antiblack world, the ultimate object of desire is white, and the ultimate object of rejection is black. Desire is erotic and evaluative, so that in an antiblack world, the *phallus* (symbol of male power) is white skin (Gordon 1997). On Gordon's model, race is the noun/thing, so that "the logic of gender in an antiblack world can be demonstrated to converge with the logic of race in ways that question the very meaning of sex" (1997, 129–130).

If race is more foundational than sex or gender, then patriarchy, including black patriarchy, cannot be justified in critical race theory, because patriarchy depends on strong gender divisions—only men can be the fathers who rule. Again, critical race theory seems to admit only one leading concept. Again, is it more important whether a person is male or female, after which she may be black or white? Or is it more important whether a person is black or white, so that his gender is an attribute? Gordon's analysis suggests that not only is it more important whether a person is black or white than male or female, but that being either black or white is so important that it generates sexual or gendered desires that override whether the black or white person is male or female. Gordon has here radically theorized racism in an antiblack world. What racism primarily results in, or is, is a racial desire: *It is best to be white, and it is worst to be black. Desire white and reject black! Whiteness is the desired desire, and blackness is the rejected existent* (Gordon 1997, 127–128).

Insofar as racism is the leading concept in critical race theory, desire may be as good an idea as any for explaining what racism is. That is, for Gordon, racism is racial desire. But recall that the titanic battle for black critical race theorists is a battle by black men, against white men, for the phallus, which is presently white skin. This battle is for whose skin color will be the phallus, that is, symbolize the power of powerful masculinity. On Gordon's analysis, white women are "coded" with the helplessness of their femaleness, which is black, given the white-skin color phallus; and black women occupy the lowest position of helplessness and passivity, so that they are doubly black, that is, black because they are female and black because they are racially black. Therefore, if the ruling concept in critical race theory is racism and racism is a desire for whiteness, then there really is no interesting, active place for black women, because they would be the least desired.

However, Gordon's analysis takes race as a leading concept to an extreme. As racism, race according to Gordon simply wipes out sex (gender). Most black critical race theorists, who are men, would not go that far in knowingly using racism as a leading concept, to erase the existence of black women, as women. Perhaps black patriarchal values would result in care and concern for black women. But whether black women, and/or other women of color, are avowedly feminist or womanist, or not, this is not a viable theoretical solution for putative black/nonwhite female or female black/nonwhite critical race theorists. Patriarchy does not allow for women's equality, because it is rule by men.

The only plausible gender intervention against a path that equates ultimate power with skin color in an historically contingent manner—white now/black later—would be to insist on a pluralism of leading concepts in critical race theory. This need not be a pluralism that occurs all the time or at the same times. Perhaps sometimes a subject calls for an analysis in terms of raced gender, and at other times, a subject calls for an analysis in terms of gendered race. That is, maybe ultimate power ought not to be aligned with either race or gender, exclusively, as a method for theoretical analysis. The critical race theorist would in principle agree on a methodological realignment away from race, but if the alignment of power and masculinity is also rejected, then critical race theory becomes gender theory, albeit raced gender theory. But it may be that neither "raced gender" nor "gendered race" gets things right metaphysically as we can, or should, imagine social reality. Perhaps, instead, both "raced gender" and "gendered race" are intellectual defenses to constructions and events in the history of Western thought that simply do not work for black women on a theoretical level. Perhaps a new name and concept are needed.

Economic or Material Foundations of Critical Race Theory

Critical theory is economic in its Marxist roots, which means that a contemporary relation of critical theory to critical race theory would at this time include capitalism. However, there are aspects of critical race theory, which while economic in the sense of pertaining to material exchange, do not directly refer either to capitalism in its present historical form of competitive material exchange with private end-consumers, or even to its precursors. Slavery, for instance, was part of agricultural business in a merchantile international economy (Conrad and Meyer 1958; Coclanis 2010). The US prison system, which disproportionately "drafts" inmates from black ghettos (Wacquant 2001), is capitalistic on the level of private contractors, but it is also part of the public sector in the paid work it provides for police officers, public prosecutors, prison guards, and administrators. The poor relatives of inmates who receive government welfare assistance and varied employees and shareholders in this system are end-consumers, but they do not directly buy the main products of the prison system (punishment), although they may buy its by-products (e.g., license plates made by prisoners).

Slavery, prison leasing, and sharecropping were all businesses in US history that depended on the exploitation of black people. The same can be said of the contemporary prison industry, insofar as a disproportionate number of African Americans in that system provide work for those who put them into the system and keep them there, as well as profits for corporations that physically construct prisons and then administer them. The primary goal of race-associated exploitation businesses is to make money. Toward that goal, barbarous practices against humanity have been developed, that is, enslavement, coerced labor, and racial profiling, which have been justified by myths and lies about the "race" of the nonwhites exploited. But although only some have been picked out as victims of such exploitative systems, it is arguable that the primary goal of the systems has been to pick out those people to oppress and abuse them in certain ways, as critical race/racist theory would seem to construe it. One could as well argue that the primary goal has been to make money, on the ground of classic Marxist critical theory.

The oppression of women of all races has been part of these exploitative US businesses associated with race and class. But there are gender differences on the grounds of race. White women have been exploited through their traditional family roles as wives and mothers, which benefit men with unpaid material convenience, sex, child bearing and rearing, and domestic labor (Barrett 1997; Hartmann 1997). This business of domestic economy was, and still is, usually a personal exchange, mediated by prescribed emotions, for example, love and duty, so that the women themselves have not been directly commodified or monetarized as women. Material, as well as biological goods, are prepared, processed, and produced in ways that do not look like a business at all. At the same time that ideas of modern home life developed, there were elaborate new constructions of white female gender, in a move from a one-sex to a two-sex imaginary. (The older Aristotelian system that posited women as inferior males was replaced with a system that recognized radical social and sexual differences [Laquer 1990].) That change resulted in ideas of white women as fragile, spiritual, virtuous, and without strong sexual desires. Women of color, especially black women, however, received a different gender construction, which remarkably resembled the older, supplanted gender construction of white women. Black women were construed as lustful, fertile, and with vices contradicting the virtues of white women (Zack 1997). But even this debased construction of black women, which endured during slavery and Jim Crow, was brought lower by the "Welfare Queen" and "Crack Whore" stereotypes of the 1980s (Alexander 2011; McCorkel 2013). The miscegenation of black women during slavery added the value of new lives to the capital base of slavery (National Humanities Center 2015), but the derogations of the 1980s were part of the ideological justification of the new criminal justice system that melded the black ghetto with prisons about half full of black men (Wacquant 2001; Alexander 2011).

There have been exchanges of money, to the benefit of white male owners, merchants, or workers, in which black women—and other women of color, although not to the same degree as black women, because of the history of slavery—have routinely been commodified in unique ways that are different from racism against black men or sexism against white women. Under slavery and as part of the ghetto industrial complex, both black female motherhood and sexuality have been treated as alienable commodities. (Thus, although women of all races, including white women, have been prostituted, prostitution is usually recognized as a distinct practice from both the traditional roles of white women and the sex and gender exploitation of black women.)

Critical Plunder Theory

Racism seeks to subdue or destroy black men. Sexism subordinates white women. But a third distinctive practice has been inflicted on black women. Their sexuality and children are implicitly valued, although both have been put to different uses than the uses by power elites of white women's sexuality and children. (The prostitution and human trafficking of white women would be exceptional, on this view.) Black women do not own or control or possess the biological results of being biological women, in the same ways that white women may take for granted. Under slavery, their children were commodities, and under "The New Jim Crow," their children are constructed as criminals (Alexander 2011). Black men have not uniformly been able to exercise patriarchal rights over black women, so as to own them in ways that would prevent the alienation to others of their sexuality and reproduction. As a result, white men and women seem to have been free to use, exchange, sell, exhibit, and abuse these biological capacities and products of black women, without compensation to black men, women, or children.

The phenomena of symbolic and real reproductive biological appropriation, as inflicted on black women, is not racism pure and simple and neither is it sexism in the same way as that is inflicted on white women. We have already seen how ideas of racism and sexism cannot be combined to understand the plight of black women, on the most abstract theoretical levels, as they are now understood. Needed here is a new idea that captures an undertheorized existential condition. I suggest that we view and call the oppressive experiences of black women, as women in a biological sense that is overlayed with social derogation, *plunder*. Feminist theorists of racism against black women, in the context of critical race/racist theory might now insist on a new discourse that both addresses their concrete experience and takes its place as a critical theory on the same level of abstraction as feminism, critical race theory, or critical theory (with its original Marxist connotations)—*critical plunder theory*.

Plunder usually occurs in two stages, first appropriation, and then repurposing. Both forms of violence require active and theoretical resistance. In addition, there have been and continue to be a plethora of creative, productive, and life-affirming positive activities. Black women, especially in the United States, have richly and brilliantly proceeded with such activities, in addition to their resistance of plunder. But it is important for intellectual recognition and respect, particularly in philosophy of race or critical race theory and feminist philosophy or feminist theory, that plunder be addressed on its own, on the most intellectually privileged and prestigious theoretical levels. (Other nonwhite groups and animals are also subject to plunder.)

References

Abbey, Ruth, ed. (2013). *Feminist Interpretations of John Rawls*. College Park: Penn State University Press.

Alexander, Michelle. (2011). *The New Jim Crow: Mass Incarceration in the Age of Colorblindness*. New York: The New Press.

Barnett, Bernice McNair. (1993). "Invisible Southern Black Women Leaders in the Civil Rights Movement: The Triple Constraints of Gender, Race, and Class." *Gender and Society* 7 (2): 162–182.

Barrett, Michelle. (1997). "Capitalism and Women's Liberation" In *The Second Wave: A Reader in Feminist Theory*, edited by Linda Nichols, 123–130. New York: Routledge.

Brown, Elaine. (1992). *A Taste of Power: A Black Woman's Story*. New York: Doubleday.

Coclanis, Peter. (2010). "The Economics of Slavery." *The Oxford Handbook of Slavery in the Americas*, edited by Robert L. Paquette and Mark M. Smith. New York: Oxford University Press. Accessed May 23, 2016. http://handsonhistory.k12albemarle.org/ModuleResources/Economics%20of%20Slavery.pdf.

Collier-Thomas, Betteye, and V. P. Franklin, eds. (2001). *Sisters in the Struggle: African American Women in the Civil Rights-Black Power Movement*. New York: New York University Press.

Conrad, Alfred H., and John R. Meyer. (1958). "The Economics of Slavery in the Ante Bellum South." *Journal of Political Economy* 66 (2): 95–130.

Crenshaw, Kimberle. (1991). "Mapping the Margins: Intersectionality, Identity Politics, and Violence against Women of Color." *Stanford Law Review* 43 (6): 1241–1299.

Geuss, Raymond. (2001). *The Idea of a Critical Theory: Habermas and the Frankfurt School.* Cambridge: Cambridge University Press.

Hartmann, Heidi. (1997). "The Unhappy Marriage of Marxism and Feminism: Toward a More Progressive Union." In *The Second Wave: A Reader in Feminist Theory*, edited by Linda Nicholson, 97–122. New York: Routledge.

Hine, Diane Clark, ed. (2005). *Black Women in America.* 3 vols. Malden, MA: Blackwell.

Kuhn, Thomas. (2001). *The Structure of Scientific Revolutions.* Accessed May 23, 2016. http://projektintegracija.pravo.hr/_download/repository/Kuhn_Structure_of_Scientific_Revolutions.pdf.

Laquer, Thomas. (1990). *Making Sex: Body and Gender from the Greeks to Freud,* Cambridge, MA: Harvard University Press.

Mann, Bonnie. (2013). *Sovereign Masculinity: Gender Lessons from the War on Terror,* New York: Oxford University Press.

McCorkel, Jill A. (2013). *Breaking Women: Gender, Race, and the New Politics of Imprisonment.* New York: New York University Press.

Mills, Charles. (2009). "Rawls on Race/Race in Rawls." *The Southern Journal of Philosophy* 47: 160–185.

National Humanities Center Resource Toolbox. (2015). "On Slaveholders' Sexual Abuse of Slaves: Selections from 19th- & 20th-century Slave Narratives." *The Making of African American Identity* 1: 1500–1865. Accessed May 23, 2016. http://nationalhumanitiescenter.org/pds/maai/enslavement/text6/masterslavesexualabuse.pdf.

Nicholson, Linda. (1997). *The Second Wave: A Reader in Feminist Theory.* New York: Routledge.

Outlaw, Lucius. (1990). "Toward a Critical Theory of Race: A need for Rethinking." In *The Anatomy of Racism*, edited by David Theo Goldberg, 58–82. Minneapolis: University of Minnesota Press.

Sterling, Dorothy, ed. (1997). *We are Your Sisters: Black Women in the Nineteenth Century.* New York: W. W. Norton.

Thernstrom, Stephan, and Abigail Thernstrom. (2009). *America in Black and White: One Nation, Indivisible.* New York: Simon and Schuster.

Von Drehle, David. (2013). "High Court Rolls Back the Voting Rights Act of 1965: Racially-Troubled Counties No Longer Need Federal OK to Change Local Election Laws." *Time,* June 25. Accessed May 23, 2016. http://swampland.time.com/2013/06/25/high-court-rolls-back-the-voting-rights-act-of-1965/.

Wacquant, Loïc. (2001). "Deadly Symbiosis: When Ghetto and Prison Meet and Mesh." *Punishment and Society* 3 (1): 95–133.

Zack, Naomi. (1997). "The American Sexualization of Race." In *RACE/SEX: Their Sameness, Difference and Interplay*, 135–156. New York: Routledge.

Zack, Naomi. (2005). *Inclusive Feminism: A Third Wave Theory of Women's Commonality.* Lanham, MD: Rowman and Littlefield.

CHAPTER 51

THE STING OF SHAME
Ridicule, Rape, and Social Bonds

CYNTHIA WILLETT

AT racial and gendered intersections of our social identities lie some of the most difficult emotions we may ever experience. Consider how those micro-aggressions that are part of the ordinary fray of life—the casual slur or the odd stare—can tear us apart emotionally. Mere mention of these occasionally humorous or "entertaining" barbs (entertaining to some) can at times seem petty and irrelevant to substantial ethical issues. Often it is not even clear if any real harm is meant. Yet the barest suggestion of an insult can drain us of joy, casting us down in shame or arousing indignant outrage. Of course, more often than not insults roll off our back as minor annoyances. However, when micro-acts of aggression, such as mild taunts or callous mockery, evoke patterns of long-term or structural abuse, the impact can be seriously harmful, even traumatic.

Racism and sexism characteristically take the shape of extensive patterns of symbolic violence such as verbal or visual insult as well as exploitation, physical violence, and other forms of substantial, material abuse. We think of physical acts of sexual or racial violence such as police brutality or sexual assault as more significant harms than racial ridicule and minstrelsy or the sexist humor found in a rape joke. Indeed, modern liberal Western societies typically classify only the former as punishable crimes. In the United States, the dominant culture's continued allegiance to individualism sanctions the insult, with or without humor, to a significant extent through free speech rights. Sticks and stones may break our bones, but names, as the children's nursery rhyme goes, will never hurt us.

But what if the sting of symbolic aggression—as seemingly minor as an insult dressed up in the pleasantries of a verbal or visual joke—in fact accounts in many instances for the more acute pain of the physical assault? To be sure, physical and material assaults against our selves and our property can injure bodily integrity and material well-being, puncturing that sense of self-ownership known as autonomy. But what if a devastating dimension of violence and material damage cannot be understood apart from the cruelty of the joke or the sting of ridicule? What if a shaming insult constitutes the significant sting at the heart of much racial and sexual discrimination or assault?

THE STING OF RIDICULE

Let's approach the significance of the sting of an assault by considering the politics of ridicule. Cartoonists in the Western world predictably risk setting off a firestorm of events when they mock Islamic religion and traditions as premodern, non-Western, and irrational. Few doubt the irritation that mockery can provoke among those targeted. Needling the other is the point of mockery. Yet the outrage in the Islamic community strikes many secular modernists as out of proportion to the harm inflicted by mockery. The ridicule of the prophet Mohammed in the French satiric magazine *Charlie Hebdo* in 2015 generated not only outrage in the Islamic community but killings of cartoonists. (Scott 2015). Representations of the event in Western mainstream media expressed shock over the murders and righteous defenses of free speech (Scott 2015). After respecting a period of mourning for the murdered cartoonists, we might consider again the liberties assumed in such acts of ridicule. What are the ethical and political implications of insults such as those harbored in verbal or visual jokes and ridicule, generally?

Ridicule, which may take the form of satire, in contrast with various other forms of humor, typically directs an insult toward a target. To the extent that the insult manifests wit, it may draw on ironies, double meanings, and humorous incongruities. Yet, while the humorist and audience may derive pleasure from ridicule's artistry, ridicule's pleasure is hardly innocent of power. Indeed, one might say ridicule's pleasure turns on power. Unlike other forms of humor, ridicule augments the ridiculer's own social location at the target's expense. A well-aimed taunt takes its target down a peg or two on the social ladder, while elevating the social status of the humorist. As philosophers from Plato to Hobbes have observed, ridicule generates pleasure through a sense of superiority (Morreall 2009). The ridiculer's wit may mask the act of aggression as sheer entertainment all the while increasing through the clever disguise his own pleasure at the expense of the target. Note that this pleasure is not the ordinary kind sought by the pleasure-seeking hedonist, who enjoys satisfying appetites or at least relieving stress through food, drugs, material consumption (such as shopping), or sex. This pleasure is the experience of power.

Not all forms of humor generate this power dynamic. Some laughter is enjoyed with others. The mutual teasing among close friends may trade on pretend superiority while the ultimate effect mocks any such claim by increasing intimacy. But sometimes laughter among friends entails laughing at others. This is the case in ridicule. The pleasure of intimacy pops up in ridicule but with a distinctly edgy power dynamic. When the ridicule of one social group, such as a racialized gendered group, targets another group as inferior, the social pleasures of a group bond combine with the pleasures of asserting superior group status. The intense affect of sharing a common enemy may compound the pleasure, by further strengthening the group bond. This compounding of affects renders ridicule's occasionally dangerous pleasures especially seductive.

Regardless of whether drawn from the wit of ridicule or the playful innocence of camaraderie, a heightened pleasure stems from a strong sense of belonging. We humans are generally a highly group-oriented species. Our modern, Western ideologies of individualism obscure the intensities of group dynamics. It is difficult to grasp the rich significance of the pleasure of camaraderie and the painful sting of assaults apart from those interpersonal and group connections that reach to the inner sanctum of our ownmost personal identity.

AWE AND RIDICULE

The strong desire for a symbolic sense of identity with something larger than oneself, through in-group ridiculing of out-groups, exposes dimensions of human nature too often neglected by modern moral perspectives based on rational individualism. Most modern moral thinkers, including liberal theorists, valorize the individual whose rational side does not allow her to get swept away by overwhelming desires. Yet at least since the time of the ancients, philosophers have pondered the profound ambiguities of an overpowering desire originating outside of what modernists term the self. Some of these philosophers, aiming to outmaneuver modernism's blindspots, invoke from Plato the untranslatable Greek term *eros*. Audre Lorde's 1978 essay "The Uses of the Erotic," after carefully distinguishing the ancient Greek term from its modern references to sex, explores eros as the "lifeforce" that gives women creative power and a strong sense of connection with others (Lorde 2007). More recently, psychological research into what we could identify as this lifeforce, or the mysteries of the erotic (in the Greek sense), have given special attention to the capacity to experiences of awe, wonder, and the sublime (Haidt 2012; Piff et al. 2015).

The sublime and ridiculous lie at opposing ends of a spectrum of psychological experience. The sublime heightens our experience, while the ridiculous diminishes it by putting us closer to what is lowly, disgusting, or shameful. Certainly both experiences carry individuals away in waves of laughter or felt mysteries exceeding the fragile boundaries of the self.

Psychological studies of our human capacity for awe are part of a larger shift in moral psychology. Psychologist Jonathan Haidt explains that throughout much of the twentieth century, psychologists (like many philosophers) thought that moral cognition and freedom require suspending emotions in order to rely upon reason alone (Haidt 2012). More recently, a number of psychologists and philosophers have rejected modern rationalism to study the constitutive role in the self of the social emotions. They argue that emotions play a more significant role than reason for understanding how communities are held together through cooperation and empathy. Drawing upon empirical data as well as philosophical speculation, Paul Piff, Dacher Keltner, and Jonathan Haidt argue that awe in particular, as the ultimate "collective emotion," has especially profound implications for humans as a highly evolved group-oriented species (Haidt 2012; Piff et al. 2015). Their theory proposes that our species' survival depends significantly on learning to suppress individual interests for the sake of cooperating within a larger group. A sense of belonging, more centrally than those capacities for self-direction and self-awareness that define autonomy, reflects that capacity to cooperate.

Awe as prompted by witnessing beauty in nature has been viewed by modern philosophers as relevant to aesthetics, but not to ethics. However, these psychologists have found evidence suggesting that the seemingly amoral force of awe can generate a strong sense of belonging to a group by devaluing the ego as relatively small and insignificant. Of course, many have assumed that this function of social binding occurs through religion, but religious interpretations overdetermine the meaning of awe-inspiring experiences. By breaking down the barriers of individualism, we become more sensitive to what post-Heideggerian philosophers term our "ecstatic self"—that is, to the ontological priority of our relatedness to others and to a sense of a lifeforce beyond the self.

This research corroborates that awe-inspiring circumstances can in fact prompt unexpected acts of altruism and sacrifice, supporting the profound ethical relevance of this collective emotion. The experiments themselves are simple. One experiment divides control and experimental groups according to how many awe-related events they experience on a regular basis. Then each participant was given ten lottery tickets that could win them a cash prize. The researchers instructed the participants that they could either keep the tickets or give them away. Those who reported that they felt more wonder and beauty in the world around them were more likely to be generous to strangers. The scientists conclude that awe augments social bonds, motivating acts of collaboration that enhance social group cohesion and communication (Piff et al. 2015).

Ridicule, as awe's underside, might be suspected of prompting sharply contrasting behavior, undermining group identity and cooperation. But the story turns out to be a bit more interesting. To be sure, some acts of ridicule target singular others for individual advantage. In these acts, the aggressor plays a zero-sum game, aiming to raise her own social position by lowering the target's. Ridicule can demonstrate a lack of generosity and undermine cooperation, functioning like awe's simple opposite. Ridicule, however, can also work to tighten the bonds of a group identity, positioning both aggressor and target in warring social groups. The group camaraderie, while hardly innocent, can generate joy in expanded social power.

Imagine the joy found in the secular Europeanist's mockery of the irrationality of Islam. The ridicule easily sweeps the individual out of the boundaries of a contained self and toward the nonrational joys of felt membership in what is experienced as a higher, and more rational (or rather "more rational"), social group. Indeed, in this instance of mockery, the ambiguities multiply. For while awe-inspiring experiences (including the aesthetic sublime with which they are associated) carry some sense of the infinite beyond, common laughter at what is rendered ridiculous elevates one not on the otherworldly plane of transcendental transport but instead along the antagonistically group-bound axis (or axes, as we shall see) of social hierarchy. Ridicule lifts one not beyond the struggle for group-based domination and social power but holds one fast within this struggle. The struggle aims to advance neither self-interest nor autonomy per se. In fact, the excesses of the struggle (think of war) can jeopardize the individual tout court for the sake of the nonrational politics of group power. That is, ridicule often enough is a group-based game of power.

Of course, for embodied social creatures, awe also has its own dangerous politics. Think of the racialized political campaigns of the German fascists or of other nationalists. They may employ the sublime to deadly effect. No doubt rationalists are right to be circumspect about any of these ecstatic emotions. And yet, as the unsuspecting potency of political ridicule well establishes, these ecstatic emotions are ineradicable forces in the social field. Rather than vainly attempting to quash our collective emotions through reason, we might consider how to enhance the kind of situations where they generate positive lifeforce.

In sum, the central contrast between awe and ridicule turns on distinguishing two sorts of vertical axes structuring human experience. On the one hand, an awe-inspiring experience correlates with the capacity to rise above (as it often turns out some social) differences. Beethoven's sublime choral finale at the end of the Nineth Symphony calls forth a joyous passion for universal brotherhood. On the other hand, humans strive to achieve individual and group status in society along a hierarchy of social positions. The distinction between the two vertical axes—the elevation of awe and of social hierarchy—sharpens the contrast between awe and ridicule, even as both may catch us up in obscure waves of collective emotion.

INTERSECTIONALITY

The pleasures and cruelties of ridicule lay bare like nothing else the social hierarchies of our species. Wit arms us in social battles by playing on often subtle if not invisible social differences. Much of our social identity, like the iceberg, lies below the surface of ordinary awareness. In various ways we may enjoy social entitlements, such as educational status, citizenship, race, or gender, and so forth, without thinking much about them. We may also suffer social liabilities without having the capacity to understand them. The art of ridicule exposes the boundaries of status differences. The slap in the face of the witty insult can reveal personal weaknesses we did not realize we had or desire to own up to. Or wit's sting may exploit through a pointed barb social vulnerabilities due to social location. In this case, these barbs may turn on stereotypes embedded in verbal or visual symbols.

The prevalence of ridiculing racial and gender stereotypes in politics and popular culture mocks any presumption that modern liberal societies have achieved a level "playing field." Stereotypes warp the social space in ways that vex individual awareness and self-direction (aka autonomy). These stereotypes reinforce social hierarchies and group conflicts through reasserting individuals into social locations. The Charlie cartoonists' caricatures of Muslims—whether aiming, as some claim, to undermine racism or to reinforce it—exemplify the complexity of the problem. Theorists of social location describe the vectors of the social field in terms of not just one, but of multiple, intersecting axes of power. These axes multiply the strands of the vertical axis of social domination discussed earlier. In liberal societies, individuals motivated by a strong sense of equality and fairness might act diligently to avoid say racism, and yet find themselves in the position of having displaced a dynamic of domination centrally onto an alternative axis.

As marked along lines of both race and gender, women of color can hardly afford to not be aware of the complexities of this dynamic. Kimberlé Crenshaw introduced the term "intersectionality" in her article "Demarginalizing the Intersection of Race and Sex" to call attention to how women of color experience oppression on the basis not only of their gender but also of their race, sexuality, ethnicity, and/or class location (Crenshaw 1989). She argued that black women often experience "double-discrimination—the combined effects of practices which discriminate on the basis of race, and on the basis of sex. And sometimes, they experience discrimination as Black women—not the sum of race and sex, but as Black women" (149). In 1991, she developed a theory of intersectionality in "Mapping the Margins" (Crenshaw 1991). There she distinguished three spheres of its operation: *Structural intersectionality* traces patterns of oppression that differentially impact the material well-being of black women (1245). *Political intersectionality* refers to the ways in which black women are marginalized in the political arena (1245). *Representational intersectionality* highlights how popular culture depicts black women (1245).

Crenshaw's analysis of the multiple axes of social identities in representational intersectionality is useful for teasing out both the ambiguity and the danger of the power dynamic lurking in images and symbols. Her 1991 article leads the way by disambiguating interlocking systems of racism and sexism in the controversial lyrics of rap group Two Live Crew (2LC). An intersectional analysis clarifies what can be troubling in seemingly well-considered views of white and black male commentators. George Will employed unreflective stereotypes of black men as violent sexual predators in his attack on the rap group's callous treatment of black women and rape. As Crenshaw observes, his view demonstrated how a single concern for protecting women from black men blinded him to the particular standpoint of black women in a power gird entangling sexism with racism. Black women as subjects with a unique perspective disappear entirely as his attack on 2LC's misogyny drifts to the case of a white woman who was raped by black men in Central Park (1291). Henry Louis Gates defends 2LC's music as an artistic expression rooted in black oral traditions employing humor to mock stereotypes and "show the ridiculousness of racism" (1292). Crenshaw cautions that an uncritical defense of African American culture similarly "marginalizes Black women and exposes them to violence in the service of anti-racism" (1295).

This interlocking analysis of racism and sexism draws attention to the multiple vectors of representational intersectionality and their impressive social force. The controversy over 2LC's lyrics takes for granted that ridicule can pack quite a punch on the social field. It also cautions us with regard to the ambiguities of a social force that turns on a capacity to both explode and exploit multiple stereotypes in different directions at once. Garry Trudeau, the creator of the satiric cartoon "Doonesbury," called Charlie Hebdo out for "punching downward," for targeting laughter at the vulnerable and powerless, in particular France's Muslims and immigrants (Trudeau 2015). But such judgments are hardly ever simple, and often risky. An intersectional analysis demonstrates how mockery may target a single dimension of oppression, racism, at the expense of those marked by gender and vice versa. Mockery plays in a complex field of multiple forces. Stereotypes serve as a seductive mask for domination, but who is dominating whom and where the correct allegiances should lie, are politically fraught questions. Are white men satirizing brown men who dominate their women and terrorize others, or are these white men using brown women to provoke brown men through ridicule and shame? The weapons of comedy point to a significant source of the social power of groups. In-group cooperation and solidarity can mask underneath their pleasing surfaces ulterior motives that are—perhaps less awe-inspiring than complicated, multilayered, and, more often that we think, ugly.

MOCKING IMAGES AND ATMOSPHERIC EFFECTS

Racialized and gendered representations turn on standard fair of the comic such as caricature, along with visual and verbal jokes. Caricatures draw from an endless reservoir of racial and gender stereotypes. Patricia Hill Collins has developed Crenshaw's intersectional analysis of representations by laying out stereotypes that black women in particular confront in popular culture (Hill Collins 1991). Stereotypes ranging from the sexually aggressive Jezebel to the sexless mammy exemplify what she explores as "controlling images." The controlling function takes on an extra twist through what Naomi Zack interprets as minstrelsy and we might term "mocking images" (Zack 2013). These ridiculing images function to enhance power over others by undermining their social status and warping relationships, possibilities of friendship, and mutual belonging.

Adding mockery's insult to the injury of control compounds the harm. Not only do outgroups suffer material and economic harm, one's sense of self waxes and wanes through its felt extension outward into a fabric of relations. How we are represented whether in the social media or through face-to-face gossip enhances or diminishes the very being of our person. The ridiculer taps into images to enhance one group's or individual's social status at the expense of another. This enhanced status is experienced as pleasure, but this pleasure is also social power. Social power may well be for social animals the most significant form of power and thus the most dangerous source of inequality. The social power of ridicule can drain vital energy from the targeted group in favor of the aggressor and his group. Our felt sense of being alive—that vital energy—grows and diminishes through changes in social status. This dynamic of power registers on social group status and thereby penetrates to the subconscious core of the self, where mocking images may fragment and restrict the range and capacity of our desire as expansive social creatures, or what Lorde theorizes as our eros.

Lorde's reference to the fundamental desire of life as eros advances beyond much of twentieth-century critical theory, where conceptions of the erotic core of the self were typically understood exclusively as sexual in origin. Lorde decisively reappropriates the term from psychoanalytic theories of sexual seduction toward a philosophy of emancipation. Lorde exhorted black women to reclaim the lifeforce siphoned off by oppressive social and cultural systems (Lorde 2007, 55). This energy or drive is not just sexual but does include sexuality. More originally eros is a creative, vital force of experiencing oneself as fully alive, contrasting sharply with melancholy and depression. A woman of color may experience the draining of this vital energy in white-dominated space prior to or apart from any particular encounter, testifying to a network of affect-laden vectors that color and charge social space (Willett 2004). For like music, however difficult to articulate, social space has a tone and a groove. As waves of energy, the affects propagated through social space can be contagious, spreading from person to person, signaling such experiences as friendship or alienation and shame (Willett and Willett 2014). As Teresa Brennan observes, one senses the impact of an atmosphere as soon as one walks into a room (Brennan 2004).

An atmosphere of laughter is hardly neutral. Consider the contrast between an inviting and an inhibitory social space. At the most primordial level of ridicule, prior to any particular joke, one can sense a mocking atmosphere. While a jovial atmosphere enhances a felt sense of being alive and belonging, a mocking atmosphere heightens group boundaries. Ridicule disturbs the atmosphere, draining us of erotic energy. As social creatures, the air we breathe harbors information-carrying vectors—what Lorde describes as "an electrical charge"—that can nourish our souls or drain them.

What Lorde describes as erotic energy—the vital feeling of being alive—resonates with the pivotal metaphor of the flesh as it appears in Hortense Spiller's 1987 essay, "Mama's Baby, Papa's Maybe" (Spillers 2003). In her study of the impact of slavery and its contemporary reverberations, Spillers distinguishes the objectified body from living flesh for what is at stake in "captive and liberated bodies" (206). Mutilation, torture, or violation, she explains, physically and psychically obliterates the person who experiences herself fully alive through her flesh. Damage to the flesh occurs through physical violence but also through symbols. "We might concede, at the very least, that sticks and stones might break our bones, but words will most certainly kill us," she cautions (209). Symbols possess the deadly power to strip the body of the vitality of flesh—its lifeforce. Through mocking representations, social groups or individuals may augment their power while deriving surplus pleasure through the act of domination itself. To be sure, racialized and gendered bodies serve material and physical needs of dominant elites. However, there is an excess of pleasure in the sheer act of domination. That excess, Nietzsche, that master of power's ruses mused, is akin to the plea-sure of rape (Nietzsche 1956).

RAPE, "SHAME CRIME," AND SOCIAL BONDS

For the target, the feeling of a degraded social status can be embodied in the deadening or dirtying of the flesh as numbness or shame. Of course, not every target of mockery feels drained or shamed. Some may rightly feel outrage. Rape as a crime of degradation and power exemplifies the complexities of these affective responses. Rape, as an assault on an individual's lifeforce, impacts levels of vital energy, status, and belonging. Because rape impacts the relational extension of person into social space, it induces changes in affective experience other than that contained in modern references to emotions owned by a subject (aka nonecstatic and/or noncollective ones).

A clue to the profound social resonances of violent sexual assault comes from the use of the term "shame" across various cultures to signify not primarily a subjective emotional response but an objective status harm (Ober 1989). This alternative meaning occurs in ancient Greece and survives in some non-Western cultures. Ancient Greeks viewed action-able offenses such as rape as "shame crimes," interpreting the harm as aimed not just at indi-viduals but at the fabric of communal relationships, and at individuals precisely through those relationships. A psychological emotion, which is where modernists locate shame, might accompany this harm. But the ancient meaning of shame points beyond this psychol-ogy to the structural nature of the harm and the collective character of the emotion. Rape harms the social status of the victim and those bound with her through their social location. In this respect rape is viewed as functioning in some respects like an insult.

In fact, insults too constitute what the ancient Greeks treated as shame crimes. Consider the various ways in which ridicule even today might inflict harm on a vulnerable target. Targeted groups might experience ridiculing racist or sexist stereotypes through a modern psychology of shame. However, here too, as in the case of sexual assault, the shaming function of mocking images can damage status and relationality apart from any psychological emotion of shame owned on the part of the conscious subject or, for that matter, any emotion or intention to do harm owned up to by the agent (Willett 2001). It is difficult for modern philosophical per-spectives to grasp the nature of the harm of these shame crimes. The harm of symbolic assault is not the primary concern of modernism's autonomous individual. For the rational individ-ual, sticks and stones, not names, do the real damage. The rational individual is detached from social manipulation and abuse, or at least aims to be. Yet mocking images warp social fields, distort relationships, and dampen the lifeforce that rebounds through these relationships. It impacts the pre- and postmodern individual—the soul of the person—through her erotic sociality. In short, the sting of abuse impacts all of us whether we own up to it or not.

The ancient Greeks had their own word for shame crimes, *hubris*, and they represented its dangers in their tragic theatre. Notoriously, moderns have misinterpreted hubris as an individual vice, and thus as a personality problem, translating this pivotal cause of tragedy as excessive pride or arrogance. The ancients viewed hubris as the crime of shaming others, that is, not as a character vice but as an act with an objective impact on the community, and in this sense more dangerous than a mere flaw of an individual's character. To be sure, shame crimes could have consequences on the autonomous self (or individual ego) that is identified by modernists as the center of the psyche. But the emotions of the modernist self cannot capture the implications of shame crimes on the ecstatic self caught up in the political climate and social mood of the *polis* (or community).

The ancients Greeks defined shame crimes as violations of status and social bonds. Their democratic values led them to see hubris as a crime of passion and power committed by the elite on the less powerful. Democratic Athens suffered from socioeconomic inequalities and countered injustice with discourses of equality. But in contrast with modern liberal theories of equality, they did not construct abstract theories of justice predicated on a level playing field. They acknowledged the reality of social hierarchies, portraying hubris as an abuse stemming from elites. Ethical norms and legal limits against excess counterbalanced the asymmetries, specifically aiming to control dominant groups.

From this perspective, insults and ridicule along with rape constitute shaming acts. They can puncture social relationships, with potentially tragic consequences. Recall how the humiliating treatment of the Germans after their surrender in World War I provoked a second World War. Yet despite the continued relevance in Europe and modern Western cultures, modern political and moral theories lack a theory of shame as more than a psychological emotion, and hence of the dangers of our relational status in a gendered and racially charged social space. Under the modern interpretation, acts of humiliation do not typically count as significant harms calling for legal prohibition and do not receive nearly the attention they deserve from the moral sphere. Sexual assaults such as rape constitute a crime against the bodily integrity of the person. Yet sexual assault leads not just to personal damage. Such an assault may register as damage to the sociality of the person—to his or her status and relationships. In this particular sense, an aspect of the harm of rape is similar to the harm of an insult. In either case, the shaming function of the act lowers the social status of the target, fracturing the capacity to relate to others. The aggressor's pleasure, whether through ridicule or rape, exceeds sexual or material benefits. The pleasure of domination punctures the flesh of our social relationships through which we thrive.

To the degree that the symbolic dimension defines a core harm of what would otherwise pass as a physical violation, we humans are more profoundly social creatures than we let on. The ill-considered freedom to insult another—perhaps under the cover of good fun—asserted as a right of autonomy, in this case, of free expression, inflicts a harm that frays the social fabric of our interwoven lives. Our individual identities grow surprisingly more like vines in an affective web of social bonds than as self-directed agents of private autonomy. These social affects account for the symbolic aspect of violation—even those defined as crimes against property or bodily integrity. Think of the sting felt by the target of physical assaults or theft. Even these kinds of assaults leave us feeling violated, if not insulted or shamed. We live through vectors of social space.

CONCLUDING THOUGHT ON SOCIAL BONDS

Attention to the symbolic dimension of assaults alters our understanding of harm but also our sense of an appropriate ethical or legal response. What is an appropriate response to an aggressive act that like the slap in the face bears through its very physicality the sting of the insult? A punitive, disciplining reaction against the aggressor does not tend to the web of relationships that bind both aggressor and victim. Punishing the rapist or racist risks further damaging the lifeforce, bent as it is on connectivity. The repair of social bonds fractured through assault would require something more nuanced. Contrary to the general thrust of our moral and legal systems, the victim as well as the aggressor would have to be poised to suspend at some point their adversarial stance—the one seeking retribution, the other evasion—sufficiently to redress the sting of the assault, its shame. The old adage about sticks and stones has something to teach us after all: not to endure stoically the insult, but to breathe in deeply before one reacts and think about how to counter the aggression and repair social bonds.

References

Brennan, Teresa. (2004). *The Transmission of Affect*. Ithaca, NY: Cornell University Press.

Crenshaw, Kimberle. (1989). "Demarginalizing the Intersection of Race and Sex: A Black Feminist Critique of Antidiscrimination Doctrine, Feminist Theory, and Antiracist Politics." *University of Chicago Legal Forum* 1989: 139–167.

Crenshaw, Kimberle. (1991). "Mapping the Margins: Intersectionality, Identity Politics, and Violence Against Women of Color." *Stanford Law Review* 43 (6): 1241–1299.

Haidt, Jonathan. (2012). *The Righteous Mind: Why Good People Are Divided by Politics and Religion*. New York: Vintage.

Hill Collins, Patricia. (1991). *Black Feminist Thought*. New York: Routledge.

Lorde, Audre. (1984). *Sister Outsider*. Freedom, CA: Crossing.

Lorde, Audre. (2007). "Uses of the Erotic: The Erotic as Power." In *Sister Outsider*, 53–59. Berkeley, CA: Crossing Press.

Morreall, J. (2009). *Comic Relief: A Comprehensive Philosophy of Humor*. Malden, MA: Wiley-Blackwell.

Nietzsche, Friedrich. (1956). *The Birth of Tragedy and The Genealogy of Morals*. Translated by Francis Golffing. New York: Anchor Books.

Ober, Josiah. (1989). *Mass and Elite in Democratic Athens*. Princeton, NJ: Princeton University Press.

Piff, Paul, Matthew Feinberg, Pia Dietze, Daniel M. Stancato, and Dacher Keltner. (2015). "Awe, the Small Self, and Prosocial Behavior." *Journal of Personality and Social Psychology* 108 (6): 883–899.

Scott, A. O. (2015). "In a World that Won't Laugh With You." *The New York Times*, June 7: 1 (L).

Spillers, Hortense J. (2003). "Mama's Baby, Papa's Maybe: An American Grammar Book." In *Black, White, and in Color: Essays on American Literature and Culture*, 203–229. Chicago: University of Chicago.

Trudeau, Garry. (2015). "The Abuse of Satire." *The Atlantic*, April. http://www.theatlantic.com/international/archive/2015/04/the-abuse-of-satire/390312/.

Willett, Cynthia. (2001). *The Soul of Justice: Social Bonds and Racial Hubris*. Ithaca, NY: Cornell University Press.

Willett, Cynthia. (2004). "The Social Element: A Phenomenology of Racialized Space and the Limits of Liberalism." In *Racism in Mind*, edited by Michael Levine and Tamas Pataki, 243–260. Ithaca, NY: Cornell University Press.

Willett, Cynthia, and Julie Willett. (2014). "'Going to Bed White and Waking up Arab': On Xenophobia, Affect Theories of Laughter, and the Social Contagion of the Comic Stage." *Critical Philosophy of Race* 2 (1): 84–105.

Zack, Naomi. (2013). "Black Female Crossover Comedy: Freedom, Liberty, and Minstrelsy." In *Philosophical Feminism and Popular Culture*, edited by Sharon Waugh and Joanne Crasnow, 37–50. Lanham, MD: Lexington Books.

INDEX

CPSIA information can be obtained
at www.ICGtesting.com
Printed in the USA
BVHW050733251118
533481BV00003B/3/P